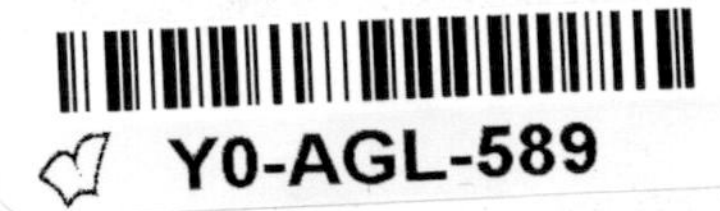

THE INSIDER'S GUIDE TO LAW FIRMS

Third Edition

EDITED BY FRANCIS WALSH AND SHEILA V. MALKANI

Mobius Press

THE INSIDER'S GUIDE TO LAW FIRMS (Third Edition)

Edited by Francis Walsh and Sheila V. Malkani

Cover Design by Nancy V. Rice

Readers with comments or questions should address them to: Mobius Press, P.O. Box 3339, Boulder, Colorado 80307.

ISBN 0-9637970-6-9

Contents

Preface

With the third edition of *The Insider's Guide to Law Firms*, Mobius Press hopes to continue to demystify the daunting task of identifying and getting hired at a law firm that best suits your needs. *The Insider's Guide to Law Firms* originated one night in September, 1992 when during my third year at Harvard Law School, I was going through the daily fall routine of law students nationwide trying to figure out what to do with their lives. After sifting through numerous firm brochures and other similar sources my exasperation was complete. "All these firms look alike," I burst out to fellow classmate, original co-editor, and now husband, Michael Walsh. "I'm sick of hearing about 'collegial' firm atmospheres."

Having each worked in several firms, Mike and I knew they differed dramatically. Moreover, every fall Harvard Law School buzzes as second- and third-year students informally exchange information about what law firms are really like. It is this information, we believe, that is most valuable to people who consider working in law firms. But, it requires persistence to sift through all the stories and luck to hear about the firm that appeals to you. We decided to collect all these anecdotes, impressions, and pieces of information from our peers not just at Harvard, but across the country, and organize them. Our idea was to provide law students and others with a single source of information on the nation's most well-known firms which was collected and disseminated by law students rather than the law firms themselves.

Before launching the project, we made a trip to New Haven to talk with the Editor-in-Chief of *The Insider's Guide to the Colleges*, a book which provides inside accounts of life at the major colleges across the country, and which is written by Yale undergraduates. Our detailed discussions about the Yale operation provided us with a game plan and convinced us that *The Insider's Guide to Law Firms* was feasible. Back up to Cambridge. Next, we surveyed law school campuses across the country to obtain a list of students who had worked at each of the major firms we wanted to profile. We put together an extensive questionnaire touching on issues which we, and our friends, believed to be most important to law students. These included, among others, questions about the work atmospheres, the firm cultures, hiring processes, practice areas, associate development programs, treatment of women and minorities, and other distinguishing features. By early October 1992, we were ready to begin interviewing for the first edition.

We began our cold-calling a little unsure of the reaction we would get. But, as we had hoped, most people were incredibly enthusiastic about the project and more than willing to chat our ears off about their firms. In some cases, we actually had to cut them off. While many were initially somewhat skeptical of divulging information, almost everyone we interviewed quickly became anxious to help when we explained that the purpose of the project was not to dig up dirt on law firms, but to describe them in a way that enables people to distinguish them.

The interviews were lengthy and detailed. On average, each interview took an hour. We interviewed between three to nine people from each firm, with more interviews conducted for "controversial" firms. We spoke with both law students and permanent associates, but conducted the majority of the interviews with students. We emphasize, however, that the profiles in *The Insider's Guide* are only meant to provide an anecdotal snapshot view of the firms. They do not represent a scientific study of the firms, nor do they necessarily reflect a representative survey. Much of the information included in each profile is impressionistic and anecdotal and represents the views of a few people. No one should disqualify a firm offhand after reading one of our profiles. Those who find something that does not appeal to them should seek a second and third opinion.

On the other hand, we believe that the profiles included in this guide are a valuable resource that will help students and others match their needs and personalities to the law firms covered in the book. Every firm has a distinct personality. Some are aggressive and fast-paced, others are more restrained and deliberate; some are highly structured and even bureaucratic, others are informal and sometimes disorganized; some emphasize social skills, others prefer quiet, hard-working personalities. We have heard countless stories of people who don't "fit in" at their firms. Given the limited information on the culture and character of the nation's firms, we believe this book is a good source with which to begin your search.

After writing the firm profiles, we sent the draft versions to most people we interviewed and asked them to verify the information included and to edit the profiles. The response was overwhelming. Person after person responded that we had captured the "feel" or the "essence" of his firm. Many wished the book had come out before they made their final decisions on firms. We received very few overall critical responses, but in those cases, we conducted additional interviews.

Then began the process of editing, gathering the other information included in the book, and checking the facts contained in each profile. In addition to having friends and family across the country help us edit, we contacted each firm profiled in the book to provide it an opportunity to verify the factual information we had gathered during our interviews.

For the third edition, Mike and I enlisted the research and editorial talents of the very capable Francis Walsh. The Mobius Press team identified and contacted junior associates at each firm profiled in the book, who reviewed and commented on the existing profiles of their firms. They also completed a questionnaire regarding recent developments at their firms. The profiles on each firm were revised based on the information provided by these associates. We then sent each firm a copy of the updated profile for comment. (In the few cases where we did not receive sufficient responses from associates to completely update the existing firm profile, we sent the profile directly to the firm for its review and comments.) Every firm, except Wolf, Block, Schorr & Solis-Cohen in Philadelphia, responded, providing us current information regarding practice areas, associate development programs, recruiting policies, and other areas covered in the profiles. The firm profiles were then revised to reflect the firm's input. In addition, the statistical information that appears at the top of each profile has been made current to 1997, except in the case of Wolf Block.

We have learned a lot about law firms during the course of this project, and hope that we have been able to convey the wealth of information we have gathered. We hope that this book will serve as a resource for our readers in their search for a firm that suits their needs. We wish you success in this sometimes long and difficult process. Good luck!

Sheila V. Malkani

Note on Statistics

Every law firm profile in this book begins with a statistical abstract. In most cases the figures are from 1997. When no figures were available, the symbol NA (*i.e.* not available) has been used. For the most up-to-date information, you should contact the law firms directly.

Address is the most up-to-date address of the profiled firm's office.

Telephone is the most up-to-date general telephone number of the profiled firm.

Hiring Attorney is the lawyer at the firm who is in charge of hiring law students. In some cases there is more than one lawyer sharing these duties.

Contact is the person to whom cover letters and résumés should be sent. This person is usually called the recruiting director or hiring coordinator.

Associate Salary is the annual salary that is paid to associates. We usually indicate in parentheses the year for which the figure applies. In most cases we provide first-year associate salary and in many cases we provide the salary increments for successive years.

Summer Salary is the weekly salary that is paid to summer associates at the firm. We usually indicate in parentheses the year for which the figure applies.

Average Hours includes the average number of hours that all associates at the firm worked annually (*i.e.* the total number of hours they were at the firm), the average number of hours they billed (*i.e.* charged to a client), and the minimum number of hours that the firm requires its associates to bill.

Family Benefits provides the number of paid and unpaid weeks of maternity and paternity leave provided by the firm. The abbreviation "cbc" means that leave is provided on a "case-by-case" basis. This section also lists other related benefits, such as on-site day care.

1996 Summer provides the number of students eligible for permanent associate offers in the summer of 1996 and the total number of students who received offers.

Partnership provides the percentage of the total entering associates in the listed years who were made partner. Note that this figure is taken over different years for different firms and that frequently no data is provided for certain years.

Pro Bono provides the percentage of the firm's total practice which is pro bono work.

Lawyers at the Firm provides the total number of attorneys at the firm. Note that this figure sometimes includes the total number of counsel or senior attorneys if they are designated as such at the firm. Thus, the sum of the total partners and total associates may, in some cases, be less than the figure provided for total lawyers at the firm.

Associates Per Partner is the total number of associates divided by the total number of partners. Note that in some rare cases the firm includes of cousel or senior attorneys in the total number of associates.

Total Partners is the total number of partners at the firm as of the date provided in the box. It also lists the total number and percentage of female partners (out of total partners) and the total number and percentage of partners who are members of minority groups. Our statistics include figures for African-American, Asian-American, Latino, and Native American attorneys. Where there is no listing, there are no partners in these groups at that firm. Some firms voluntarily provided us statistics of their openly gay partners, and we have listed this information.

Total Associates provides the same information for associates as in the total partner category (see above).

Practice Areas lists the major areas of practice at the firm as well as the number of lawyers working in that practice. Note that the total number of lawyers listed in the practice areas often does not add up to the total number of lawyers at the firm because many lawyers work in more than one practice area, the practice area list includes of counsel, and on occasion, small practices at the firm are not listed.

The Insider's Scoop on Getting the Offer

Each year, law students spend thousands of dollars on law school tuition, text books, horn books, and outlines. They spend most weekdays in classes, and much of their remaining time preparing for classes or exams. Many are driven in this intense classroom effort by the desire to land a good job after graduation. Frequently, however, students devote comparatively little time and effort to the recruitment process when a relatively small effort can yield far greater employment results than toiling away for hours to raise a torts grade from B+ to A-. During the course of interviewing over one thousand hiring partners, law firm associates, recruiting coordinators, and law students, we heard many stories about applicants who successfully employed innovative techniques to distinguish themselves from their classmates. Since many of these students did not have particularly outstanding law school records, their success in landing a job was frequently tied to the effort they invested in these techniques.

The first part of this introduction briefly describes the hiring process by which most law firms fill their summer and entering associate classes. Part one is intended primarily for first- or second-year law students who are experiencing law firm recruiting for the first time. The second part of the chapter summarizes the innovative techniques used by people we interviewed to identify and get hired at their top choice firms.

Overview of Law Firm Recruiting

Most major law firms rely primarily on their law student summer associate programs to meet their incoming associate needs. The summer associate program serves as a trial period for both firms and law students. It allows a firm to evaluate each candidate and to decide whether to extend an offer for a permanent position; at the same time, it provides law students the opportunity to learn about the firm and to decide whether they want to work there full-time. Most summer associates hired are second-year law students. Some firms also hire a smaller number of first-year students and third-year students who will begin judicial clerkships in the fall.

Except for students at the top law schools, it is uncommon for first-year students to land jobs at the country's top firms. Most on-campus recruiting targets second-years. One Ls often must use other means to contact the firms. A number of the "Insider's Tips" below outline techniques for successfully contacting and landing jobs at firms outside the on-campus recruiting system.

For most second-year law students and some first years, the best prospects of employment come through on-campus law firm recruiting. The largest law firms regularly conduct interviews at the top ten or twenty law school campuses and at nearby regional law schools. On-campus interviews provide a relatively inexpensive and effortless means to make initial contact with a number of law firms. Entering the process is usually as simple as putting your name on a law firm's interview list at your school's career center. The career center typically forwards résumés of interested students to the firms, which then return a list of candidates they will interview. At some prestige schools, firms interview almost everyone that applies. Most career centers post a schedule of available interview slots and the names of applicants who made the first cut. These applicants may then schedule their interviews on a first come, first served basis. Other schools assign students to interview slots.

Most firms use on-campus interviewing to screen the many candidates who apply and only call back a manageable number to their offices for more extensive discussions. Although this initial encounter is brief, many firms make tentative decisions to extend summer offers based on the information and impressions gathered at this time.

Unlike callback interviews which can vary considerably in form and content, on-campus meetings are usually conducted by a member of the firm's recruiting committee and have certain basic elements. Most on-campus interviews are conducted by one or two persons and last thirty minutes or less. The interviewer will usually have your résumé in front of her. Typically, many interview questions at this stage focus on aspects of your résumé or your interest in the firm. It is crucial that you be prepared to answer detailed questions about anything on your résumé, and it is a good idea to spend some time before your first set of interviews anticipating questions that might arise from your résumé. Many interviewers tire of asking the same questions about your law school or your most recent job and frequently move to more personal topics. As a result, students may find themselves talking about a hobby or a project they worked on years ago that they never expected to be explaining to a recruiter who is evaluating them on their responses. If you list hobbies or personal interests on your résumé, be ready to enthusiastically explain how you made your own canoe from a tree in your back yard, and how that experience motivated you to found your school's crew team.

Much of the conventional advice for any corporate-type job interview applies: dress neatly and, for the most part, conservatively; present a firm handshake and make good eye contact with your interviewer; and be friendly and polite. Most firms rely on the on-campus meeting to collect various materials for the hiring committee to review at a later date. It is generally a good idea to have a copy of your transcript, a writing sample (preferably legal writing), and a list of references prepared for each interview.

On-campus recruiters typically record their impressions of students in writing between interviews during the day and after they have completed all the interviews. Candidates that have made big mistakes usually are eliminated at this point. Students whose meetings went well get more detailed notes. The recruiter usually forwards these reviews as well as transcripts and writing samples to the firm's hiring committee for further review. Different firms weigh each aspect of the information packet differently and there is a good deal of subjectivity in the reviews. However, at this point in the process, most firms decide whether a particular candidate meets their threshold standards for employment. Students that are granted callback interviews in most cases have already "made the grade" with respect to their paper qualifications.

The number of interviewees that are called back depends on the emphasis the firm places on screening during the on-campus interview, and the school at which the interview takes place. Firms call back roughly one quarter to one third of the students at the very top law schools. At less well-known law schools, the major firms may only call back a few of the applicants interviewed.

Firms typically notify students of callback interviews by letter or phone call. Some firms respond within days after the campus meeting; others may take months. Along with notifying the student of a callback, firms will request the interviewee to contact a designated person at the firm, usually the recruitment coordinator, to schedule the interview, and to make any other necessary arrangements. In most cases, it is advantageous to visit the firm as quickly as possible. Summer positions are generally filled in a fashion similar to that of college rolling admissions. The first to interview have the best prospects of receiving offers. Where a firm has predetermined the number of available summer positions, as most do, interviewing after a substantial number of offers have been extended decreases your chances considerably.

In most cases where travel to the callback interview is required, the law firm or its travel agent will make the arrangements. Typically round trip transportation and accommodations at a nice hotel located near the firm are provided. Meal and other travel-related expenses are reimbursed by the firm. Interviewees must keep a record of their expenses (including receipts) which they submit to the firm for reimbursement.

When you visit the firm's office, the recruiting coordinator will, in most cases, be the first person you meet. The recruiting coordinator will typically chat briefly with you and provide you with a schedule of the names of attorneys you are to meet, their practice groups, and their status as partner or associate. The lawyers you encounter will probably represent a mix of seniority levels (including, in some cases, everyone from the managing partner to first-year associates) and practice areas. Some of the interviewing attorneys will be members of the recruiting committee, some will not. Often firms specifically arrange meetings with attorneys that practice in your expressed area of interest or that went to your law school. However, it is not unusual for attorneys to be called away on client business and for your schedule to change during the course of your visit.

While many variations exist, most callbacks involve meeting four to eight attorneys for approximately thirty minutes each. The vast majority of firms take the interviewee to lunch at a nice restaurant. A few take "prospectives" out for drinks or dinner. Usually, you will dine with at least one lawyer with whom you interviewed and a few others whom you haven't met. Attorneys often make an effort to make you feel comfortable and relaxed during the lunch, but it is important to keep in mind that the recruiting meal can be just as much a part of the hiring process as the interviews. At some firms, your dining companions complete evaluations of your conduct at lunch.

After the callback concludes, the firm's hiring committee will review the evaluation forms completed by your interviewers. The forms ask for assessments of interviewees in areas such as confidence, maturity, poise, ability to articulate oneself, and intelligence. Some forms require attorneys to rate interviewees numerically, others ask for written comments. The hiring committee considers the evaluation forms, transcripts, writing samples, and any other information gathered in making final hiring decisions. Most firms extend summer associate offers to at least half the callback interviewees. In many cases, however, firms intend to hire most of the students they call back, barring some disaster during the interview. Usually the hiring partner will call to extend an offer and will follow the call with a formal offer letter.

The law firm recruiting process can appear daunting. Some large firms interview well over a thousand law students on many campuses and receive thousands more unsolicited résumés. From these they select a few hundred hopefuls for firm interviews. In the end, only fifty or sixty from a pool of thousands end up employed at one of these firms. Many students we interviewed beat the odds and attained employment at their top choice firms by employing innovative techniques to get hired. Their insights into the hiring process are summarized below.

Insider's Tips on the Recruiting Process

Before the Interview

Insider's Tip # 1: Strategic targeting. You can't get a job unless a firm reviews your résumé. Many offices are overwhelmed by the sheer volume of résumés they receive through normal recruiting channels. In some cases, a good share of the cover letters and résumés sent to law firms are never reviewed. In others, they are read by an administrative person who may not understand the firm's particular hiring needs or be receptive to your special qualifications. Half the battle in securing a job is piercing the large firm recruiting bureaucracy and placing your résumé in the hands of a person who can appreciate your particular interests and qualifications and has authority to hire or interview you.

One of our contacts described how she landed multiple job offers with top New York law firms after her first year of law school by ensuring that her résumé got to the right person. After receiving numerous rejections from a mass mailing to law firms, she identified ten firms that were particularly suited to her interests and sent personalized cover letters and her résumé directly to the hiring partners via Federal Express. Most cover letters sent to hiring partners by ordinary mail never make it to their intended destinations. They are intercepted by a secretary and forwarded to the recruiting department. Partners at law firms almost always personally review anything that is "Federal Expressed" directly to them. Moreover, a letter that is FedEx'd carries an aura of importance and urgency that is missing from a letter sent by ordinary mail. A fax has a similar effect. This person followed the FedEx mailing immediately with calls to every partner she contacted; most set up special interviews for her. While her classmates were experiencing waves of rejections from law firm mass mailings, this person had secured a number of offers from top firms. Since this method is somewhat expensive and is intended to bypass the recruiting bureaucracy, this person did not recommend contacting recruitment coordinators this way.

Another one of our sources successfully employed strategic targeting despite her average law school record. This person had years of experience in the banking industry, but her extensive mailing campaign met with uniform rejection. Not ready to give up, our contact researched a number of firms that had noteworthy or expanding banking practices and sent personalized letters, that detailed her extensive experience in the industry, directly to the partners in charge of the banking groups. She also attached a portfolio of past banking-related work. This strategy worked. Our contact was hired directly by the banking partners at one of the prestigious firms profiled in this book, despite the fact that she probably would not have been granted an on-campus interview with this firm.

Another way to bypass recruiting bureaucracies is to communicate directly with any contacts you may have at the firm. We learned of one insider who relied on a series of contacts to land a summer job as a first-year student in a difficult legal market. He made a list of all acquaintances who worked for law firms in the city and wrote them personal letters describing his interest in the firm. While not everyone was able to offer a job, many notified the firm's recruiting department of his interest, giving him a further edge in the hiring process. If you don't have any law firm contacts, another useful technique is to target the firms that most interest you and to identify attorneys at those firms who are alumni of your law school. This information is available in *Martindale-Hubbell*, a comprehensive directory of the nation's attorneys available in virtually any law library and certain on-line databases. Write or call these alumni and send them a copy of your résumé. A personal edge always gives you an advantage in hiring.

The above stories illustrate that it is crucial, when targeting firms, to identify the attorneys that make hiring decisions, and to determine which firms have strong departments in your areas of interest and whether those practices are expanding. Research the firms, talk to any contacts that may be familiar with these firms, and use any other resources at your disposal to access information. Once you have gathered the necessary information, a strategic, focused employment effort yields considerably more success than mass mailings. Moreover, do not limit yourself to the normal fall and early winter recruiting seasons. Firms have unexpected and necessary hiring needs throughout the year, particularly in practice areas that are growing. These openings often offer the strategic job-seeker the best chances of employment.

INSIDER'S TIP # 2: PERSISTENCE PAYS. Although the yield from mass mailings is generally low, they are still worth the effort, particularly where strategic targeting is impossible. A mass mailing is the only way to make contact with a broad range of firms. As a general rule, the more effort you put into the process, the better your results will be. Therefore, it is best to cast your net wide and be prepared for hundreds of rejection letters. It is not uncommon for students to send out two hundred letters in their first year. Although the process is time consuming, there is no reason not to send out as many letters as you can. Computers have made mail merges increasingly simple and a few hundred letters can be sent out in a couple of days. Compare the cost of a mass mailing with your expenditures on commercial outlines before you decide a mailing is too expensive. Once you have sent letters, make follow up phone calls and write additional letters to firms with which you think you have better prospects. Persistence pays. One of our insiders sent a résumé to a major Washington, D.C. firm. After he received a rejection letter, he mailed that firm his résumé again, was offered a callback interview, and later was hired!

INSIDER'S TIP # 3: BE PROFESSIONAL. Your cover letter and résumé are often a firm's first introduction to you. It is crucial that you present yourself as professionally as possible. Spend some time picking out high quality paper and matching envelopes. Sending letters and résumés on regular copy paper appears cheap and unprofessional; it detracts from your overall presentation. All letters should be typed or printed and personally addressed to the designated contact at the firm. Envelope addresses should be typed or affixed with computer generated mailing labels. Although some students secure jobs without making this extra investment, it is best to exploit every edge you can. In addition, make sure your cover letters and résumé are well drafted and error-free. Law firms want to see that you will not make mistakes on important documents. One error on a résumé is enough to disqualify a candidate at many major firms. Ask your career services office, friends, and family to review your résumé. It never hurts to test on other people the summary of your achievements that you have developed for potential employers.

Interviewing Tips

INSIDER'S TIP # 4: TAKE FULL ADVANTAGE OF ON-CAMPUS INTERVIEWS. On-campus interviews offer the greatest prospects for getting hired at a major firm. Firms devote considerable resources to their on-campus recruiting programs and rely on them for most of their hiring needs. Most lawyers never again have such broad exposure to so many potential employers. Take full advantage of on-campus recruiting and sign up for as many interviews as you think you can handle. It is much more difficult to get a job after graduation.

INSIDER'S TIP # 5: FRIENDLY CONVERSATION IS THE KEY. The best law firm interviews are often friendly conversations. The ability to converse well is more important than any legal skills you can demonstrate in an interview. Many recruiters judge your intelligence and legal skills based on your grades and résumé. The interview identifies whether you would be a good representative of the firm. While it is difficult to generalize, older partners tend to be concerned that you appear professional, polite, and courteous. Junior associates, some of whom may not have significant input into the hiring decision, often care most about whether they would enjoy working with you. Many interview questions can be anticipated, and it is a good idea to think about your responses to these questions before the interview. Some frequently asked questions appear in the box on the next page.

Many law students mistakenly believe that they should impress an interviewer with their legal knowledge. Our conversations with hiring partners and attorney interviewers have led us to believe that this approach frequently backfires. One attorney recruiter described her negative reaction to a law student who, in response to her first question, launched into a fifteen minute explanation of his favorite law school class. He then responded to her second question about law school with a similar dissertation that lasted until the time allotted to the interview was up. Before he had completed his second monologue, the interviewer had already decided that he was not right for the firm. Keep in mind that attorneys do not expect students to display significant substantive legal knowledge. A candidate must simply display an ability to grasp legal concepts. This is not to say that you shouldn't answer direct questions about legal topics to the best of your ability, but answer the question briefly and to the point. Evince a sincere and earnest tone in your response. Few interviewers are impressed by a know-it-all. The most common interview advice we have heard from our sources is: be "friendly."

INSIDER'S TIP # 6: BE PREPARED TO ASK QUESTIONS ABOUT THE FIRM. One of the most common interview questions is, "What can I tell you about the firm?" Recruiters like to give students an opportunity to ask questions about the firm, particularly because it provides the recruiter a chance to sell the firm. Be ready for this inquiry by preparing a number of questions that you feel comfortable asking. Most recruiters expect that you will ask some questions—if you don't, you may appear uninterested. However, the interview is your opportunity to tell the firm about yourself, so it is generally not a good idea to spend too much time asking questions. If possible, try to ask questions that reflect your interests and personality.

Some Frequently Asked Questions

- (About a past employer) How did you like working for Judge Smith?
- (About your résumé) I see you were a member of your school's Ski Club, Black Law Students Association, Health Law Clinic, etc. How did you like that? What did you do there?
- What did you write your law review note, journal note, or seminar paper about?
- What areas of the law interest you, and why?
- Do you like law school; what was your favorite class? (Alumni often ask about a particular professor, class, or tradition at your school.)
- What hobbies or interests do you have outside the law?
- Why did you decide to go to law school?
- Why do you want to work at this particular law firm?
- Why do you want to work for a law firm?

Some Suggested Questions

- Ask about a particular practice area: Does the firm have an active environmental practice?
- Ask the interviewer about her practice: How does your practice tie in with the other attorneys in the Corporate Group?
- Do you ever have the opportunity to work with attorneys from the firm's other offices?
- How did you make the decision to come to this firm?
- Does the firm structure training programs for new associates or does it encourage you to learn on the job?
- Are new attorneys assigned to a group immediately upon joining the firm, or does the firm have a rotation system?
- Ask the interviewer to tell you about something she's currently working on.
- What type of assignments are new associates in the litigation, tax, etc., group given?
- What sets this firm apart from others in the city?

INSIDER'S TIP # 7: ONE STRIKE AND YOU'RE OUT. Most hiring committees meet regularly throughout the recruiting season to review applications of candidates and to extend summer associate offers. Many committees make their decisions by majority vote. Some, however, do not extend a summer associate offer unless the candidate is unanimously supported by the committee members. These consensus based hiring practices underscore the importance of making a good impression on everyone with whom you interview. Even if you had dynamite interviews with seven attorneys at the firm, annoying your eighth interviewer can ruin your chances of an offer. Some individuals react very strongly to certain opinions or ideas. Spend some time in each interview getting a feel for your questioner and what might potentially offend him. It is better to have generally positive interviews with everyone then to have a stellar performance with some while leaving others questioning whether they want to hire you.

INSIDER'S TIP # 8: NIGHTMARE INTERVIEWER. Although most law firm interviews are laid back, conversational, and generally avoid substantive legal topics, you should be prepared for the occasional nightmare interview in which some attorney decides to play Socrates with you as his pupil. One insider endured one such interview after his first semester of law school. After initial greetings, the interviewer excused himself to get a cup of coffee and told our contact to formulate, in the interim, a legal problem based on issues he had encountered in his first semester law classes and to analyze it for the remainder of the interview. While our insider was able to come up with a legal problem on the spot, the interrogator proceeded to dispute every point of his analysis and eventually forced him to give up.

Another contact was grilled extensively about an assignment he had completed in a prior legal job. The attorney asked the interviewee to describe in detail the issue involved, the method of research used, and the legal principle under which the issue was resolved.

Some firms have intimidating interview formats. A few hold interviews in conference rooms with five to 12 attorneys who fire questions at the interviewee; others are known for their deposition-type interviews. Some firms combine interviews with cocktail parties and extensive dinners, while others interview students casually in a lounge-type setting. Although it is impossible to anticipate and prepare for every type of interview in store for you, it is a good idea to learn about as many different kinds as possible. The profiles in *The Guide* discuss the interview formats of the firms that are reviewed. Fellow law students are also a valuable source of information regarding their experiences interviewing with a particular firm or recruiter. Keep in mind that although you should be prepared for the rare nightmare interview, they are not very common.

INSIDER'S TIP # 9: CONSISTENCY AND SINCERITY. As you move from interviewer to interviewer, it is important to be consistent regarding your interests and experiences. Do not feel obliged to tell the corporate partner who interviews you how much you love corporate law if you are genuinely interested in litigation. Interviewers compare notes and will not look favorably on inconsistent statements. It is also important to be frank about any previous negative work experiences. Many firms call previous employers whether or not you list them as a reference. Use the interview to cast a positive light on any past adverse experiences rather than attempting to hide them.

Post Interview Tips

INSIDER'S TIP # 10: THE THANK YOU LETTER. Some law students write thank you letters to the attorneys who interviewed them, others do not. While neglecting to follow an interview with a note probably will not hurt you, a well-executed letter can improve your chances of receiving an offer. An effective thank you letter specifically references conversations between the candidate and the interviewer and summarizes the applicant's interest in the firm. Form thank you letters are impersonal and won't do much to help your case.

The timing of a thank you letter can be critical. Many attorneys complete interviewee evaluations shortly after the meeting and that is their last contact with the hiring process. A thank you letter will generally be most effective if the attorney receives the note before she completes the evaluation form. One of our sources let us in on a special technique that landed her a job at her top choice firm in San Francisco, a firm where she considered her employment prospects to be a "long shot." Before heading to the airport for her flight home after her interview, she dropped by a local Kinko's where she drafted personalized letters to each person she had met. She returned to the firm that day and personally delivered the letters to the firm's reception desk, apparently making a big impression on the attorneys who received the letters only a few hours after the interview. After she received an offer to work at the firm, many of these attorneys personally called this enterprising student to congratulate her on the offer and to urge her to join the firm.

INSIDER'S TIP # 11: LONG TERM VIEW. Although the legal profession is fairly mobile, most attorneys spend a few years in their first job. Your first employer can have a major effect on your future, and it is a good idea to position yourself for the best outcome. In making career decisions, it is important to determine whether the practice group extending you an offer is growing or shrinking; whether the department is highly regarded in the legal community or just supporting more profitable areas of the firm; and whether the attorneys for whom you will work are well known in their field. Whether you like the size and culture of the firm are equally important. You can, to a large extent, control the circumstances under which you launch your legal career. It is well worth giving these factors serious consideration. Read *The Guide*, talk to friends and career counselors, and determine what type of firm and practice group fits your needs. You will save considerable time and agony if you make the right decision at the outset.

Atlanta

Law Firms Ranked By Associates Per Partner

1.	SMITH, GAMBRELL & RUSSELL	0.5
2.	SUTHERLAND, ASBILL & BRENNAN	0.7
3.	KILPATRICK STOCKTON	0.8
4.	POWELL, GOLDSTEIN, FRAZER & MURPHY	0.8
5.	ALSTON & BIRD	1.0
6.	TROUTMAN SANDERS	1.1
7.	KING & SPALDING	1.2
8.	LONG, ALDRIDGE & NORMAN	1.3

Law Firms Ranked by Percentage of Associates Who Make Partner
(over varying years)

1.	SMITH, GAMBRELL & RUSSELL	77
2.	KILPATRICK STOCKTON	23
3.	ALSTON & BIRD	NA
4.	KING & SPALDING	NA
5.	LONG, ALDRIDGE & NORMAN	NA
6.	POWELL, GOLDSTEIN, FRAZER & MURPHY	NA
7.	SUTHERLAND, ASBILL & BRENNAN	NA
8.	TROUTMAN SANDERS	NA

Law Firms Ranked by Percentage of Pro Bono Work

1.	SMITH, GAMBRELL & RUSSELL	8-10
2.	SUTHERLAND, ASBILL & BRENNAN	5
3.	KILPATRICK STOCKTON	4
4.	LONG, ALDRIDGE & NORMAN	2-4
5.	ALSTON & BIRD	NA
6.	KING & SPALDING	NA
7.	POWELL, GOLDSTEIN, FRAZER & MURPHY	NA
8.	TROUTMAN SANDERS	NA

Law Firms Ranked by Percentage of Female Partners

1.	KILPATRICK STOCKTON	18
2.	ALSTON & BIRD	14
3.	LONG, ALDRIDGE & NORMAN	14
4.	POWELL, GOLDSTEIN, FRAZER & MURPHY	14
5.	TROUTMAN SANDERS	13
6.	SUTHERLAND, ASBILL & BRENNAN	12
7.	KING & SPALDING	10
8.	SMITH, GAMBRELL & RUSSELL	7

Law Firms Ranked by Percentage of Female Associates

1.	SMITH, GAMBRELL & RUSSELL	53
2.	POWELL, GOLDSTEIN, FRAZER & MURPHY	50
3.	TROUTMAN SANDERS	47
4.	ALSTON & BIRD	45
5.	SUTHERLAND, ASBILL & BRENNAN	42
6.	KING & SPALDING	38
7.	LONG, ALDRIDGE & NORMAN	38
8.	KILPATRICK STOCKTON	29

Law Firms Ranked by Percentage of Minority Partners

1.	KILPATRICK STOCKTON	5
2.	LONG, ALDRIDGE & NORMAN	3
3.	POWELL, GOLDSTEIN, FRAZER & MURPHY	3
4.	SUTHERLAND, ASBILL & BRENNAN	3
5.	KING & SPALDING	2
6.	TROUTMAN SANDERS	2
7.	ALSTON & BIRD	1
8.	SMITH, GAMBRELL & RUSSELL	1

Law Firms Ranked By Percentage of Minority Associates

1.	POWELL, GOLDSTEIN, FRAZER & MURPHY	13
2.	SMITH, GAMBRELL & RUSSELL	13
3.	TROUTMAN SANDERS	13
4.	ALSTON & BIRD	11
5.	KING & SPALDING	9
6.	KILPATRICK STOCKTON	7
7.	SUTHERLAND, ASBILL & BRENNAN	4
8.	LONG, ALDRIDGE & NORMAN	3

Alston & Bird

Atlanta Washington

Address: One Atlantic Center, 1201 West Peachtree Street, Atlanta, GA 30309–3424
Telephone: (404) 881–7000
Hiring Attorney: Mark C. Rusche
Contact: Emily C. Shiels, Director of Recruiting; (404) 881–7014
Associate Salary: First year $67,000 (1996)
Summer Salary: $1000/week (1996)
Average Hours: 2341 worked; 1923 billed; 1800 budgeted
Family Benefits: Cafeteria plan for medical, vision, and dental; maternity leave; 401K plan; 4 weeks vacation; employee assistance program; prof. devel. allowance
1996 Summer: Class of 32 students; offers to 28
Partnership: NA
Pro Bono: NA

Alston & Bird in 1997
316 Lawyers at the Atlanta Office
1.0 Associate Per Partner

Total Partners 148		
Women	21	14%
All Minorities	2	1%
Afro-Am	2	1%

Total Associates 149		
Women	67	45%
All Minorities	16	11%
Afro-Am	13	9%
Latino	2	1%
Asian-Am	1	1%

Practice Areas	
Litigation*	54
Medical Products & Services*	28
Real Estate	26
Antitrust/Investigations	25
Capital Markets	21
Intellectual Property*	21
Labor (management)	20
Communications & Tech.*	18
Securities Litigation*	18
Corporate Healthcare*	17
Environmental*	16
Federal Income Tax*	16
International*	13
International Tax*	12
ERISA & Employee Benefits*	11
Healthcare-Regulatory*	11
Bankruptcy*	10
ERISA Litigation*	10
Finance*	9
Financial Services Litigation*	8
Public Finance*	8
Construction*	6
State & Local Tax*	7
Estate Planning & Fiduciary*	7
Utilities*	6
Financial Services*	2

*Attorneys split time with other practices.

jocular culture

Don't be misled by Alston & Bird's position as one of Atlanta's oldest, largest, and most prestigious law firms. It has a virtue uncommon in most firms of its caliber—a sense of humor. Though lawyers at this firm take their work seriously, they do not always take themselves seriously. Alston & Bird attorneys share a unique "camaraderie" and engage in "a lot of practical jokes and silliness." One disconcerted past summer associate had first-hand experience with the firm's penchant for pranks when he overslept and missed the bus to the firm outing. Alston & Bird, a firm in which "someone is always looking out for you," arranged for the summer associate to fly to the outing. That night at the semi-formal dinner, much to the delight of the whole firm and the embarrassment of the summer associate, a waiter served him a plate topped with a loudly ringing alarm clock.

upbeat atmosphere

Alston & Bird's work atmosphere is upbeat. "It's a Southern firm and it's generally pretty friendly," commented one contact. Nor is the firm overly hierarchical. There "definitely is a pecking order," said another. Nevertheless, associates who sit on the various management committees are taken seriously. Another observed that Alston & Bird is "not as leveraged as other firms, and partners are not as much an elite aristocracy." Partners are expected to work, not just supervise teams of associates and bring in business. Most of the partners are excellent teachers and enjoy working with associates, we were told. Like most Atlanta firms, attorneys dress fairly formally; women's "pantsuits are a pretty new idea," one contact informed us. The firm recently instituted a policy of casual dress on Fridays, however.

community involvement

Alston & Bird has been actively involved in the Atlanta community. Judge Conley Ingram, a former Justice on the Georgia Supreme Court, is still very active at the firm, and Sidney Smith, the former Chief Judge of the Northern District of Georgia is a retired partner. Other former attorneys with the firm now serve as judges. The former chairman of the Democratic party in Georgia is a partner at the firm, as is Oscar Persons, who is General Counsel to the Georgia Republican Party. Pierre Howard, Lieutenant Governor of the State of Georgia, is a firm partner in the utilities practice group. Attorneys are founders and board members of numerous non-profit entities, ranging from educational to arts-related organizations. The firm was actively involved in helping Atlanta prepare to host the 1996 Olympics. During the Olympics, the 46th floor was reconfigured into a hospitality area with almost around-the-clock dining and beverages available, as well as several large screen TVs for Olympic event viewings.

Pro bono work "is strongly encouraged" at Alston & Bird. Attorneys serve on the Board of the Atlanta Legal Aid Society, and many associates participate in its Saturday Morning Lawyer's Program. The firm separately records the time that attorneys spend on pro bono work and considers it in their evaluations. In honor of the firm's centennial celebration in 1993, lawyers and staff built two Habitat for Humanity houses and plans are underway to build another one soon.

practice areas

Alston & Bird's full-service practice is organized into roughly 25 practice groups. Alston's antitrust practice enjoys a "national reputation." It was involved in the antitrust suit filed against major airlines, and it also represents Borden, Inc. John Train is a well-known attorney in this field. The antitrust section has been hiring new associates to handle the heavy work volume, we were told.

The healthcare and medical malpractice group, which is also active, represents Grady Hospital, the largest public hospital in the country. This group is headed by Jud Graves and Bernard Taylor, both highly-regarded partners in their fields. Vaughan Curtis, well-known in the healthcare finance industry, is a partner in the corporate healthcare group. The firm's growing environmental practice is reportedly one of the "most well-known in the Southeast." The practice includes prominent environmental partners such as Jim Stokes, who heads the group, and Nill Toulme, who is Chairman of the Georgia Bar Association's Environmental Law Section. The labor (management side) practice is also noteworthy. Neal Batson, a nationally recognized attorney, is a bankruptcy partner at the firm. Alston's transactional practice includes a large banking group that regularly represents NationsBank and First Union. The firm's litigation section gained national prominence in its ongoing representation of DuPont in the Benlate fungicide products liability cases. This representation encountered difficulties in 1995 as a result of a court order accusing Alston & Bird defense lawyers of deceptive trial practices. This court order recently was "overturned and the matter remanded for reconsideration," according to a firm spokesperson.

associate development

Alston & Bird assigns entering associates to a particular practice group or department. Each assigns work differently, but most associates develop close working relationships with one or two partners. One contact pointed out that there is a real emphasis on teaching younger attorneys and giving them responsibility, though opportunities for responsibility depend considerably on individual initiative. Another person commented that an associate's work responsibilities are an "individual thing. The more you go after it, the more you get. I know people who are in court by their second year, and others are still writing memos." Alston & Bird offers a four-day orientation for entering associates and has formal training programs, including a seminar and workshop series in both corporate law and litigation. In addition, each department hosts regular working lunches. People we interviewed praised Alston's "excellent" feedback system. Both summer and junior associates are assigned partner mentors who critique their work "line by line." The "firm is known for taking very good care of associates," said one contact. Another commented that Alston provides "a lot of feedback and hand holding."

work hard party hard

Attorneys at Alston & Bird "enjoy a work hard, party hard lifestyle." During the day, "people talk in the halls, stop by offices, and go out to lunch." Several groups of associates are "close friends," and frequently go out after work. One person described the after-work social life as a "party hard, bar scene." Many of the firm's attorneys are also actively involved in sports. There is a "strong golf contingent" at the firm. Alston was home to famous golfer Bobby Jones. In addition, many attorneys work out at a gym across the street from the firm and play on the firm's softball team. Alston organizes a number of social events throughout the year, such as a Friday evening cocktail party, department retreats and parties, associate and partner retreats, and a Christmas party. The firm frequently distributes tickets to Braves games and cultural events in the city. "Being social is important" at Alston, commented one source. Another person noted that "there is an emphasis on getting people who 'fit in,'" further commenting that "Alston & Bird is a fairly homogeneous workplace."

social summer program

The summer program is also "really social" and very well-run. The summer coordinators plan long in advance for this "summer camp-like experience." One person noted appreciatively that the firm takes care of everything from setting up summer housing to sending students extensive questionnaires regarding their preferences on a variety of matters relevant to the summer program. Summer associates do "not have to do a lot of work," although the firm has begun to emphasize work more than it did in the past. One past summer associate commented, "We were out of the office at least one day a week." By six o'clock in the evening, summer associates were informed which bar the firm was "hitting" that night. It was a "real rah-rah" experience! However, a more recent contact informs us that the "rah-rah" aspect of the program has been toned down somewhat. "There is less emphasis on 'partying' and more on work and getting senior attorneys involved. It is no longer a rah-rah program, although still lots of fun."

sensitivity to diversity

While some women expressed concern about the atmosphere at Alston & Bird, one person commented that some female attorneys at the firm are the "most highly-regarded around" Atlanta. Karol Mason, who is a member of the Recreation Authority and an African-American partner, is well-known in Atlanta. Alston & Bird has sent two of its women lawyers to judgeships on the Georgia Supreme Court and the Federal District Court for Atlanta. One source noted that many of the female partners are "single or put their careers first." Though the firm's policy of maternity leave was a concern in the past, we were told that this and related issues are presently being aggressively addressed via the firm's active women's committee. Alston & Bird, we were informed, is "aggressively trying to recruit" minority law students. People noted, however, that the firm currently has very few minority partners. One person told us that the two African-American partners, Bernard Taylor and Karol Mason, "openly discuss" minority issues and that the firm has put a lot of time and effort into studying associate retention, women's issues and lifestyle issues in order to make it a better place to work. Alston & Bird participates in the Georgia Bar Association's Minority Clerkship Program under which it hires one minority first-year student from one of four major Georgia law schools every summer.

management

A litigation partner, Ben Johnson, took over as the firm's new managing partner in early 1997. He and the partners' committee set firm policy. Associates do not formally participate in governance of the firm. They are eligible for non-equity partnership after seven years at the firm and are considered for equity partnership one year later or on a case-by-case basis. People we interviewed reported that the firm is economically conservative and financially healthy. Alston recently leased two more floors in its main office building for occupation in May 1997. The firm's Washington, D.C. office has also expanded. Alston & Bird recently attracted attention in the city's law firm community for pioneering a "covenant" clause in its employment agreements with its staff. The clause requires that for two years after leaving the firm, employees not disclose attorney-client secrets or other confidential materials. Though bitterly resisted by a few associates, the agreement is now part of firm policy.

impressive offices

Alston & Bird's main offices are the "most impressive thing about the firm," praised one contact. The facilities and equipment are "new and nice." Attorneys receive individual offices, some of which have windows. They also receive personal computers networked to a system that includes electronic mail and computer research facilities. The "helpful" support staff is available nearly 24 hours. The firm has an attorney dining room and a break room for support staff. The offices are equipped with locker rooms for attorneys.

hiring tips

Alston & Bird hires "bright people" but also places "a high premium on personality." One person commented they are not overly concerned about grades. Another noted that the firm wants someone who is "assertive, but not aggressive, and someone who will get along with clients and with people." At the same time, Alston is less interested in "someone who looks like all other attorneys there...It is trying to be diverse and open." The firm hires most of its summer associates from a handful of the top national schools outside the South and many southern law schools such as Duke, Emory, Vanderbilt, the University of Georgia, the University of Virginia, and Wake Forest. Usually two attorneys conduct Alston & Bird's on-campus interviews. One insider advised that if you are not from Atlanta, emphasize that you are serious about working in the city, noting that the attorneys "complain a lot about people who only fly out for a weekend" to interview just for the free trip. The firm covers the expenses of applicants and their spouses for a trip to Atlanta for one day and night, during which time the applicant is interviewed by six attorneys and taken out to lunch and dinner by a few more.

Alston & Bird is a well-established Atlanta law firm with a sense of humor. It is also one of Atlanta's largest firms. One person noted that "if you are scared of big firms, you won't be happy here," because despite the friendly work environment, at times the firm can be almost all-consuming. "It's a very demanding work place. Your work, social life, and community work are all centered around the firm," said one source. Another person concurred that "the only major drawback at Alston & Bird is that at times the workload gets pretty heavy. Alston & Bird generally staffs, at least in transactional work, pretty thinly, which is bad for your work schedule, but great experience."

Some people complained that the firm is "too regional." Overall, however, people recommended the firm highly. People noted that the work atmosphere is "not stuffy;" "the people are likable; it's a friendly place;" "the firm may be regional, but it's not provincial;" and, "the facilities blew me away." If a southern firm with lots of prestige, a wide array of practice areas, and a challenging workload appeals to you, Alston & Bird may be your kind of place.

Kilpatrick Stockton

Atlanta Augusta Charlotte Raleigh Washington Winston-Salem
Brussels London

Address: 1100 Peachtree Street, Suite 2800, Atlanta, GA 30309–4530
Telephone: (404) 815–6500
Hiring Attorney: William H. Brewster
Contact: Kim S. Dechiara, Recruiting Manager; (404) 815–6301
Associate Salary: First year $67,000 (1997); subsequently, associate compensation is tied to performance
Summer Salary: $1000/week (1997)
Average Hours: 2000 worked; 1736 billed; NA required
Family Benefits: 90 days paid leave; short-term disability; 3 weeks paid parental leave for primary care-giver upon adoption of child
1996 Summer: Class of 14 students
Partnership: 23% of entering associates from 1982–1988 were made partner
Pro Bono: 4% of all work is pro bono

Kilpatrick Stockton in 1997
182 Lawyers at the Atlanta Office
0.8 Associates Per Partner

Total Partners 102		
Women	18	18%
All Minorities	5	5%
Afro-Am	5	5%
Latino	2	2%

Total Associates 75		
Women	22	29%
All Minorities	5	7%
Afro-Am	2	2%
Asian-Am	2	2%
Latino	1	1%

Practice Areas	
Business	47
Litigation	33
Intellectual Property	24
Labor, Employment, Immigration	20
Environmental	13
Tax	11
Financial Restructuring	9
Health Care	8
Real Estate	7
Employee/Benefits	6

One of the largest and most prestigious law firms in Atlanta, Kilpatrick Stockton is the only major Atlanta firm to have international offices in London and in Brussels. While Kilpatrick has many regional clients, it also represents a number of large corporations with international operations. The firm was known as Kilpatrick & Cody prior to its 1997 merger with North Carolina-based Petree Stockton. The merger considerably increased the size of the firm to 350 attorneys. It also extended its international practice, since many technology companies in North Carolina's Research Triangle Park are globally oriented. In line with the merger, Kilpatrick Stockton is expected to increase the size of its European team.

comfortable atmosphere

Kilpatrick's work atmosphere is "comfortable" and "not uptight or stuffy." Attorneys "work pretty hard," but are generally "sociable" and "friendly." People frequently stop by each other's offices to chat. One person noted that there are "many people you can go to who will answer questions. You are not left hanging." Partners also are "generally accessible," though there is little "social interaction" between them and associates. Though known as a firm where attorneys wear "pretty conservative dress," there is now a more casual wardrobe atmosphere, including firmwide casual Fridays. Although our contacts noted that the firm is slightly "more Republican than Democrat," they also claimed that the "firm respects any political involvement" of its attorneys and the firm has attorneys "who are powerful in organizations on both sides of the political spectrum."

broad practice

It is almost ironic that one of the men who established Kilpatrick also did some of Coca-Cola's earliest legal work, because now PepsiCo is one of the firm's major clients. With a full-service general civil law practice, Kilpatrick represents primarily corporate clients in matters ranging from litigation to tax. National clients include Delta Air Lines, Radio Shack, Lockheed, Union Camp, and Bell South. Litigation, the firm's largest practice area, includes a number of prominent litigators such as Matthew Patton. One person noted that "more is demanded" of litigation associates than of corporate associates. Under the leadership of the very respected Miles Alexander, Kilpatrick is known nationally for its intellectual property practice. The group consists of 47 attorneys devoted full time to intellectual property law. The firm also has a developing international corporate practice. It opened a Brussels office in 1992 and has had a London office for 12 years. Kilpatrick's environmental practice is also thriving. One person noted that the environmental attorneys "seem to get along particularly well." One co-chair of the department, Vance Hughes, is the former counsel to the Natural Resources Lands Division of the Justice Department. The other co-chair, Richard Horder, was formerly assistant counsel to Georgia Pacific. He is also, we were told, the "number one authority on adoption law in Georgia." A merger in 1994 with Knox and Zacks of Atlanta and Augusta created a "very well respected" health care department at the firm.

pro bono

As for pro bono, people commented that many junior Kilpatrick associates participate in the Atlanta Legal Aid Society's Saturday Morning Lawyers Program. Kilpatrick lawyers contribute both legal and nonlegal services to the community. Examples on the legal side include Kilpatrick's General Counsel representation of Hands on Atlanta, a non-profit organization that matches volunteers to community projects, the counseling provided to residents of a homeless shelter, environmental cases, and work with several children's organizations such as Georgians for Children. On the nonlegal side, Kilpatrick reportedly provides more volunteers for the Midtown Alliance Mentoring Program than any other firm or company. Its lawyers are active in civic, cultural and charitable causes from the American Cancer Society to Good Government Atlanta to the Ronald McDonald House. Although one contact noted that the firm is "not stringent about billables," Kilpatrick does credit pro bono hours as billable time for purposes of considering performance and bonuses.

unstructured professional development

Entering associates are assigned to a particular department when they join the firm. Attorneys distribute work to new associates "on a need basis"; there is no structured assignment system. Over time, associates develop working relationships with certain partners. "During slow times, it becomes necessary to solicit work," commented one insider. First-year litigation associates primarily handle research assignments, though they occasionally take depositions. Most associates do not play an active role in court until their third or fourth year at the firm. Corporate associates typically engage in a lot of document drafting and some negotiations after their first year at the firm. One person commented that "by the time you are a fourth- or fifth-year corporate associate, you are acting primarily on your own with direction from a partner."

Associates receive most of their training on-the-job. Kilpatrick partners, however, do make presentations on various legal skills, and the firm sends attorneys outside for advanced training in litigation skills. Partners are responsible for critiquing the work of the associates who work for them, but one contact told us that "we receive very little feedback." Another person noted that "sometimes the signals are not clear, but there is an effort to let people know if they are not on partnership track." The firm is supposed to evaluate its associates twice a year, but "in reality it occurs once a year," we were told. Summer associates are evaluated every two weeks.

lively social activities

While Kilpatrick attorneys work hard, they also know how to have a good time, giving Kilpatrick a lively, social atmosphere. During the day, attorneys "go out to lunch all the time." Many of them share season tickets to Braves games. The summer program is similarly social. The firm sponsors many social events but they are not "exhausting or high-pressure." In a recent year, these included an opening party for the entire firm to kick off the summer, picnics, department parties, and firmwide luncheons. The firm also organizes social events throughout the year. It hosts a weekly Friday cocktail party at the firm and distributes tickets to many events at Chastain, an open-air amphitheater. It also organizes separate associates and partners weekend retreats.

diversity

People commented that Kilpatrick has a "good attitude" toward women, noting that the firm has some influential female partners. These include Virginia Taylor, an intellectual property partner, and Susan Cahoon, a litigation partner. There are five minority partners at the firm.

management

Run by a managing partner and an executive committee, Kilpatrick's management solicits very little input from associates, according to people we interviewed. According to a firm spokesperson, the managing partner meets quarterly with associates, and associates are encouraged to submit matters that they would like to have on the agenda for discussion at the meeting. According to a firm insider, however, such meetings "rarely occur quarterly; they occur, rather, a maximum of three times a year." The firm is "financially conscious, but not penny pinching" and has been economically healthy in recent years. Its litigation practice is "a constant money maker," and the environmental practice has "expanded tremendously, as has its intellectual property practice." The international practice is expected to be enhanced even further as a result of the recent merger with Petree Stockton.

gorgeous offices

Located in midtown Atlanta, Kilpatrick's "gorgeous" offices are set with "marble hallways." All attorneys have individual offices that offer "pretty views of trees, hills, and forests" around Atlanta. An internal staircase connects each floor, and the office is equipped with a staff cafeteria that is open everyday. The lawyers' dining room serves catered food daily, with the exception of Wednesday. The library is "pretty big," and the research staff is "phenomenal." All computers are networked, and each has access to Westlaw and LEXIS.

personality interview

As for recruitment, Kilpatrick places a premium on "law review membership, moot court, grades, and work experiences" in making its hiring decisions. At the same time, however, it also seeks "someone who can add to the social side of the firm. They are not interested in people who are quiet, reserved, or withdrawn." One person commented that "they want smart people who are fun to work with." Most people selected by the firm for a callback interview are treated to dinner the night before, usually at an attorney's home. One person noted that the callback is a "straightforward...personality-type interview." The firm recruits heavily at Duke, Emory, Georgia State, the University of Georgia, the University of Virginia, and Vanderbilt. It also hires from a number of top national schools outside of the South.

People on balance recommended Kilpatrick as a good place to work, though there were some reservations. One person expressed some concern that individual attorneys "need to rustle up work" for themselves. Another commented that the firm "expects a lot from associates early," noting that some may view this as a drawback. We also heard criticisms of the "stingy benefits package" (which, however, appears to be true across Atlanta firms) and of salaries which are "not as high at midlevel and senior associate levels" as at comparable Atlanta firms. At the same time, others pointed out that Kilpatrick is one of only two or three firms in Atlanta that is truly full-service and "has all the practice groups." In addition, "you have a better chance of enjoying law here more than at other firms," said one contact. Another declared that at most Atlanta firms, "the practice is much more local and regional and lacks resources. Kilpatrick combines great people with national and international clients and offers tremendous career possibilities."

King & Spalding

Atlanta New York Washington, D.C.

Address: 191 Peachtree Street, Atlanta, GA 30303–1763
Telephone: (404) 572–4600
Hiring Attorney: W. Clay Gibson
Contact: Patty B. Blitch, Director of Recruiting; (404) 572–3395
Associate Salary: First year $67,000 (1997)
Summer Salary: $1100/week (1997)
Average Hours: 2465 worked; NA billed; NA required (1996)
Family Benefits: Family leave available; back-up childcare provider
1996 Summer: Class of 42 students; offers to 40
Partnership: 10 partners made in 1997 (Atlanta office)
Pro Bono: NA

King & Spalding in 1997
253 Lawyers at the Atlanta Office
1.2 Associates Per Partner

Total Partners 105		
Women	10	10%
All Minorities	2	2%
Afro-Am	1	1%
Latino	1	1%

Total Associates 127		
Women	49	38%
All Minorities	11	9%
Afro-Am	6	5%
Asian-Am	5	4%

Practice Areas	
Corporate	47
General Commercial Litigation	36
Product Liability	30
Intellectual Property & Technical	20
Real Estate	18
Labor, ERISA & Employment	17
Banking & Finance	12
General Special Matters	11
Toxic Tort	11
Bankruptcy & Commercial Litigation	10
Public Finance	10
Tax	10
Environmental	7
Contracting, Construction & Procure.	6
Trusts & Estates	6

serious culture

One of the oldest and largest firms in the South, King & Spalding is generally considered "the biggest game in town." Its profits per partner, at about $485,000, are the highest in Atlanta and rank among the top 100 firms in the nation. King & Spalding's "main asset that separates it from other firms in Atlanta is its client base and its unique work. It has a more national, very high-profile list of clients." Of all Atlanta firms, King & Spalding comes closest to a "corporate Wall Street practice in the Southeast."

King & Spalding has a "fairly serious atmosphere." It is "very intense for associates...there is a lot of pressure and stress to reach billables. It's a rat race toward partnership," according to one person. At the same time, however, it "is a fairly friendly place with an open door policy." One person commented that "compared to other firms, it may be more formal," but insisted that it is "not as stuffy or uptight as its reputation." King & Spalding is also reputed to be Republican, but people commented that "it's a big firm," reflecting a "broad diversity" in political opinions.

Brooks Brothers attire

Our contacts admitted, however, that King & Spalding is "fairly conservative" in dress. It is "a Brooks Brothers firm. People wear dark suits, white shirts, and bold power ties," said one source, commenting that his secretary seemed almost shocked when he wore a striped shirt to work. "She had never seen stripes there before." Attorneys sometimes dress down a little on Fridays and "wear gray slacks and a blue blazer."

Wall Street practice

One of Atlanta's oldest firms, King & Spalding "does just about everything" and has represented virtually every major corporation that operates in the city, including Coca-Cola, Exxon, and General Motors. The firm enjoys a close relationship with many of these clients. The former managing partner of the firm, for example, is now legal counsel for Coca-Cola. King & Spalding also represents large, international clients such as Honda.

King & Spalding is quite departmentalized, with a "fairly rigid separation between teams" of practice areas. Among the firm's interesting practice "niches" is a white-collar criminal defense practice group, known as the special matters group. Under the leadership of Griffin Bell, this group has handled a number of internal investigations for large corporations, such as Exxon after the Valdez oil spill, and for Dow Corning. Bell is a former Fifth Circuit Judge and served as Attorney General under President Carter. The special matters group also represented President Bush in the Iran-Contra matter. King & Spalding's environmental, toxic tort and intellectual property practice are growing rapidly. The firm also has a substantial products liability defense practice that represents General Motors and other automobile manufacturers.

King & Spalding offers a strong corporate practice and is increasing its international practice. To this end, it merged with the New York law firm Porter & Travers in 1992. This development encountered difficulties in 1996, however, when New York partner Gilbert Porter led a five lawyer departure to Chicago's McDermott, Will & Emery, reportedly because King & Spalding did not have the international presence to support a project finance practice. Former United States Senator Sam Nunn joined the firm in January of 1997 after serving 24 years in the U.S. Senate. "His national and international experience and reputation will be a tremendous asset for the firm" as King & Spalding continues to build upon and expand its national and international presence. The firm's tax and public finance practice is well-regarded. King & Spalding also served as general counsel to the Atlanta Committee for the Olympic Games, a task requiring significant pro bono work, estimated at $5 million. Former partner Charlie Battle was a senior official of the Olympic Committee. Two other King & Spalding partners, Horace Sibley and Charlie Shaffer, were also actively involved in preparations for the 1996 Olympics. King & Spalding includes many well-known partners among its ranks, such as George Busbee, former Governor of Georgia.

sponsors pro bono internship

King & Spalding has an active pro bono program. The firm encourages its summer associates to work for part of the summer in a public interest internship or another pro bono activity, during which time they are paid their full firm salary. In addition, King & Spalding is affiliated with numerous public interest organizations and makes pro bono matters easily available to attorneys. However, one person remarked that "associates receive no billable hours for their pro bono work. Performing pro bono work while meeting billable hour goals simply means more work for the associate."

King & Spalding hires entering associates into one of the firm's practice teams. Usually each team leader distributes work to the new associates, although some teams assign associates to work with particular partners and other associates informally receive work from all partners in the team. The opportunities for responsibility at King & Spalding depend on personal initiative and on the partners with whom the associate works. One person commented, "I know a fourth-year associate who is a really sharp guy. He did the opening and one cross-examination in a trial." Unless you are unusually talented, however, "you are a memo machine, a deposition taker, and a highly paid paralegal," claimed this person.

King & Spalding is a "very structured firm," offering an "extensive program of formal training." It provides an array of weekly seminars and other training and development presentations. The firm's training "runs like a clock. It is very impressive," commented one contact. Another, however, claimed that, at times, the training program lacks flexibility, commenting that the firm "concentrates on developing you the way they think you should be developed." Specialized training in particular practice areas varies greatly among teams. The firm formally reviews associates once a year. According to one person, the somewhat "impersonal" work atmosphere at King & Spalding makes many "associates a little nervous" regarding their performance. Summer associates also have a "pretty structured review program." They receive "written and oral evaluations from people they work for, from the practice team, and then from the central body." The summer program is reportedly "energetic" and "very well-organized."

social summer

King & Spalding's long work hours somewhat limit its attorneys' social lives. "Atlanta is a fun place, but I don't think the young associates see much of it," said one person. There is, however, quite a bit of "socializing" during the summer. Each summer associate is assigned both a partner and an associate advisor who make an effort to take their summer associate out to lunch and dinner. In addition, summer and permanent associates play on intramural sports teams, go to Braves games, attend events at Chastain park (an open-air amphitheater), take raft trips, play golf and visit bars. Summer associates also make a weekend trip to a resort area, such as Amelia Island Plantation near Jacksonville, Florida. Throughout the year, the firm organizes partner, associate, and practice area retreats. Practice teams occasionally have lunch together, sometimes in the firm dining room. The firm serves doughnuts every Friday morning.

diversity

Overall, King & Spalding provides a comfortable atmosphere for women. "I'd say they are completely neutral toward women except for a few older partners who are still stuck in the Southern tradition," said one contact. It was welcome news at King & Spalding when it received top billing in 1996 from the Harvard Women's Law Association report on firms congenial to women. This ranking contrasts with its earlier reputation. According to a story in *The American Lawyer,* King & Spalding held a swimsuit competition in the 1980s for summer associates, at which time a partner at the firm was quoted in the *Wall Street Journal* as saying about the associate who won the contest, "she has the body we'd like to see more of." The firm was also charged in the 1980s in a sex discrimination suit by Elizabeth Hishon, who was passed over for partner, a case that wound up in the U.S. Supreme Court. Regarding racial diversity, one source claimed that King & Spalding is a "WASPish firm." It has one African-American partner, Larry Thompson, a former U.S. Attorney of the Northern District of Georgia and the head of the special matters group.

King & Spalding is "run like a top" by a managing partner and management team. The heads of each team and numerous committees also assist in management. The partnership is organized in two tiers.

first-rate resources

King & Spalding's gorgeous office facilities offer first-rate resources. The firm is located in the top 10 stories of a 50-story office building completed in 1992. The "beautiful" offices boast "lots of marble and windows overlooking the city." The firm displays an extensive art collection of different styles, and oriental carpets dot the floors. The conference rooms have glass walls that one person marveled will "smoke out so you cannot see in" at the flick of a switch. The firm also has a "very nice" library. "I never leave the building to do any research," declared one source. A substantial library staff "makes research ridiculously easy." If you "write the cites of cases you need, they will send you copies." The support staff is "super-professional, efficient, and very numerous." The lawyers' dining room offers a buffet-style lunch catered by the Ritz Carlton, and is somewhat formal with "white cloths on the tables, except on Fridays, when clients are not invited and attorneys are encouraged to shed their coats." Attorneys can also order lunch at their desks through their computers, and the Ritz will deliver it to them. Every attorney has a personal computer linked to an up-to-date network system.

To land a summer position at King & Spalding, you "must have certain grades and have done well academically. Enrollment at a prestigious law school, law review, journal, or moot court experience helps. You must have exhibited leadership skills." The firm "likes go-getters, people with initiative who will make business for them," commented one source, who described the summer associates as "bright-eyed and bushy-tailed." King & Spalding's callback interview is a marathon-like experience. Students meet with about six to eight attorneys for twenty minutes each and are taken out to both lunch and dinner by the firm. People advised applicants to be friendly, positive, and enthusiastic in interviews. Be prepared for "challenging questions that make you jump some mental hoops," warned one insider, noting that an applicant was once asked to suggest reforms to the Professional Responsibility Code that would improve the public reputation of the legal profession. King & Spalding hires from law schools throughout the United States, with an emphasis on national schools such as Harvard, Yale, the University of Michigan and the University of Virginia. It also hires summer associates from a number of southern law schools, including Duke, Emory, the University of Georgia, Vanderbilt and Washington & Lee.

King & Spalding is one of Atlanta's top firms. It offers virtually unparalleled work and resources, but as with most large firms, there are some tradeoffs. One person noted that it is "big and impersonal." Others commented on the "long hours and stressful work." One person noted that "if you want to litigate and be in the courtroom from day one, it is not the place for you. You have to pay your dues and do research." Others, however, believe that associates enjoy "the challenge of the work and the high-profile cases." King & Spalding "gets the best and most interesting work in Atlanta" and offers "a solid financial foundation." One contact nicely summed up the situation, noting that King & Spalding has the best national reputation of all Atlanta firms, but "our hours are probably the highest" and you have "the lowest probability of making partner.

Long, Aldridge & Norman

Atlanta Washington
London Paris

Address: One Peachtree Center, Suite 5300, 303 Peachtree Street, Atlanta, GA 30308
Telephone: (404) 527–4000
Hiring Attorney: Mark S. Kaufman
Contact: Jennifer Queen, Manager, Attorney Recruitment; (404) 527–4139
Associate Salary: First year $67,000 (1997)
Summer Salary: $1000/week (1997)
Average Hours: 2200 worked; 1900 billed; no requirement; 1950 is utilized for budgeting
Family Benefits: 12 weeks paid maternity leave (12 unpaid)
1996 Summer: Class of 19 students; permanent offers to all 12 2Ls
Partnership: No prescribed time for consideration for admission; determination made on individual merit
Pro Bono: 2–4% of all work is pro bono

Long, Aldridge & Norman in 1997
131 Lawyers at the Atlanta Office
1.3 Associates Per Partner

Total Partners 58		
Women	8	14%
All Minorities	2	3%
Afro-Am	2	3%

Total Associates 73		
Women	28	38%
All Minorities	2	3%
Afro-Am	2	3%

Practice Areas	
Litigation	30
Mergers & Acquisitions	22
Corp. Securities/Public Fin.	17
Financial Restructuring	13
Real Estate	11
Energy (D.C.)	11
Tax & Emp. Ben. (incl. T&E)	11
Gov. & Reg. Industries	8
Healthcare	5
Environmental	3

Long, Aldridge & Norman is young, "fast-paced, high-energy," and dynamic. Founded in 1974, it has quickly emerged as one of Atlanta's top law firms. Much of Long Aldridge's growth has resulted from adding lateral partners. Though some sources believe that the firm "plans well financially," others remarked that in the recent past Long Aldridge "overgrew its client base," commenting that it is "highly-leveraged and can't fully utilize associates." This situation has improved more recently as the firm has reached the size and status it desired. It has instituted a program of growth from within and, according to a recent source, "associates are busy, yet not overworked."

team structure

Long Aldridge is organized in a number of teams that specialize in a particular area of law. Though in general the firm has a "younger atmosphere," each team varies. Most associates are "very friendly" with each other. Associates work closely with partners, and the firm is not especially hierarchical. One person noted, however, that the firm's management is concentrated in the hands of a few partners. Attorneys wear business attire, but the firm is "not like King & Spalding where you have to wear power suits." Women wear slacks to work and the firm recently instituted "casual Fridays." Attorneys at the firm represent a wide range of political views with a decided tilt, however, in the Democratic party direction, we were informed by one emphatic contact. Jack Watson, former Chief of Staff under President Carter, is a litigation partner at the firm. He heads the Washington office, which focuses on energy regulatory work. Corporate partner Gordon Giffin is a key advisor to President Clinton on political matters in the South and serves as a Presidential appointee to the Board of

Directors of the Overseas Private Investment Corporation. He is the head of the administrative and regulatory team at the firm. Buddy Darden, former U.S. Congressman, is also a partner with the firm. Other partners have supported Republican candidates and have run for office as Republicans. Matt Towery, who serves as "of counsel" to the firm, previously served in the Georgia House of Representatives for two terms. Towery is also Newt Gingrich's campaign chairman.

practice areas

Under the leadership of Long Aldridge chairman Clay Long, the firm has developed a highly respected corporate practice that is particularly well-known for corporate finance and mergers and acquisitions work. The firm also offers a busy administrative law and regulated industries team. Ed Sims heads the firm's burgeoning health care practice. Al Norman, whose principal areas of practice include public utility and communications law, attracted Atlanta Gaslight, a major client, to the firm. The work-outs and creditors' rights team is headed by name partner John Aldridge, who, along with two other lawyers in the firm, currently is living and working in Europe (for a year) restructuring portfolio investments for a major client. The firm is contemplating growth in that region of the world to add to the Atlanta and Washington practices. The firm's environmental practice is growing with the recent addition of two new partners, one of whom is from the State Attorney's office.

Long Aldridge's litigation practice is organized into four teams. The partners who head the teams meet regularly and share responsibility for running the litigation practice. One person commented that the general litigation team is "highly-leveraged" and that the partner-in-charge "controls everything." The banking and litigation team enjoys a solid reputation. The "two partners are the most incredible people—intense and brilliant, but good personally," one contact informed us. Long Aldridge recently formalized its sports and entertainment practice as a subset of the corporate team. The sports and entertainment practice represents both athletes, such as world heavyweight boxing champion Evander Holyfield, and business concerns, such as its representation of the Atlanta bid committee, which was awarded Super Bowl XXXIV.

strong pro bono

Long Aldridge has a well-organized pro bono practice under the leadership of Deborah Ebel. Ebel practiced with the Atlanta Legal Aid Society for 10 years and was formerly lead counsel in Atlanta for the Mariel Cuban litigation. She is immediate past President of the Board of Directors of the Atlanta Volunteer Lawyer's Foundation. Long Aldridge associates participate in the Saturday Morning Lawyer's Program organized by the Atlanta Legal Aid Society. Attorneys and paralegals at the firm, with the help of support staff, act as *guardians ad litem* in child custody cases.

associate development

Long Aldridge hires entering associates into a particular team. Junior associates as a rule appear to get significantly early responsibility. Our contention, in the prior edition of the *Insider's Guide,* that litigation associates "receive little responsibility in their early years" was spiritedly contested by the firm and several young litigation associates. One such associate observed that, "unlike many large law firms which tend to 'coddle' litigation associates during their first two years by merely assigning them research and writing projects, Long Aldridge Norman's litigation teams tend to engage in more of a 'trial by fire' approach. Litigation associates rarely do work for other associates, but rather work directly with partners." Another litigation associate, noting that "my experience may not be typical," remarked that "I have written more briefs and motions than I have research memos (no joke)." So, we stand corrected; mea culpa!

Junior corporate associates also receive significant opportunities for responsibility and one source commented that there is "great client contact and experience for young associates." Long Aldridge provides a combination of formal and on-the-job training with a strong emphasis on the latter. "You learn as you do," stated one contact. Entering associates participate in an orientation program when they join the firm, and attend evening seminars designed to address specific legal issues. In addition, each team provides its own specific training program for its associates, which often includes monthly meetings and retreats. The firm also maintains a Long, Aldridge & Norman Endowment Fund to sponsor learning opportunities for the firm's lawyers. In addition, an associates' committee, responsible for developing training programs and addressing associates issues, organizes a firmwide retreat. One person commented, however, that there is "very little feedback from the partners."

We heard some complaints about Long Aldridge's summer program. Summer associates usually rotate through two to four practice teams of their choice, with a designated attorney on each team. One person told us, "if you work in teams that are not hiring, you may not get hired." This can create a somewhat high-pressure and unnerving atmosphere during the summer. Another person pointed out, however, that summer associates can choose which practice teams they will rotate through, which provides them with somewhat more control over their offer prospects and another person remarked that "if you perform well and people like you, you will get a job offer." A representative for the firm pointed out to us that "over the last five years every summer associate who performed well and fit in with the firm has received a job offer. Hence, whether the teams through which the summer associate rotated had a place for the prospective lawyer, the firm made offers to every qualified applicant and assigned the new lawyer to a team that was hiring." Summer associates are supposed to receive feedback at the end of each rotation, but some contacts complained that feedback was spotty.

party summer

Long Aldridge associates work fairly long hours, but enjoy a "good mix of social life and work." The firm organizes many social events. The summer program begins with a weekend at Seaside in Florida for the summer associates and a group of partners and associates. One source commented, "We partied the whole weekend. You could really be yourself." Other summer events have included a trip to the zoo, a lobster boil, a country hoe-down, a golf outing, a white water rafting trip, and a bowling night. One person noted that spouses and children of attorneys attended some of these events. Long Aldridge also assigns each summer associate one or more mentors who help them meet attorneys at the firm and take them out to lunch with various partners. The firm organizes occasional happy hours and an annual Christmas party.

diversity

Long Aldridge has a "liberal" attitude "toward women balancing work and family," asserted one source. In another's opinion, however, "you have to do a good bit of business" before making a part-time work arrangement. The firm has few minority attorneys, but one contact commented that the one African-American partner at the firm is "a star." He handles a lot of corporate and licensing work for Evander Holyfield.

offices

In 1993, Long Aldridge moved into the top nine stories of a brand-new office building located in the heart of downtown Atlanta and built by the nationally renowned architect John Portman. Although the firm may have a premier location, one source complained that inside, the offices have a "cold, contemporary look." We were told that someone "messed up the office layout. There are a few offices on each floor that are long and narrow, like closets." Initially, these offices were given to new associates, but, perhaps in response to complaints, these spaces are presently used as paralegal offices and war rooms. Every attorney has an individual office with a new personal computer. Long Aldridge is equipped with a lounge area where it serves bagels and doughnuts on Monday mornings.

Long Aldridge hires law students with "top grades and law review." It also values people "with an entrepreneurial spirit" and looks to hire those "who can pick up the ball and run with it and can explore new avenues." Long Aldridge interviews are generally "conversational" and friendly. An applicant should "show that you are an open person" and that you "like law school but have a life outside law," advised some insiders. Also, you are urged to "be interested and prepared with good questions." The firm hires summer associates from some of the top national schools, including Columbia, Duke, Harvard, New York University, Penn, Stanford, Texas, the University of Michigan, the University of Virginia and Yale, and from many law schools in Georgia and the Carolinas.

recruits self-starters

Powell, Goldstein, Frazer & Murphy

Atlanta Washington

Address: 191 Peachtree Street, N.E., Sixteenth Floor, Atlanta, GA 30303
Telephone: (404) 572–6600
Hiring Attorney: Steve G. Schaffer
Contact: Paige Prater, Manager of Attorney Recruitment; (404) 572–6810
Associate Salary: First year $67,000 (1997)
Summer Salary: 1L $1000/week; 2L $1125 (1997)
Average Hours: NA worked; NA billed; 1850 billable required; 550 nonbillable required
Family Benefits: 12 weeks paid maternity leave (12 unpaid)
1996 Summer: Class of 18 students
Partnership: NA
Pro Bono: NA

Powell, Goldstein, Frazer & Murphy in 1997
150 Lawyers at the Atlanta Office
0.8 Associates Per Partner

Total Partners 76			Total Associates 62		
Women	11	14%	Women	31	50%
All Minorities	2	3%	All Minorities	8	13%
Afro-Am	2	3%	Afro-Am	8	13%

Practice Areas	
Litigation	65
Public Finance	33
Corporate	29
Financial Products	23
Antitrust/Commercial Litigation	16
Real Estate	15
Labor	14
Tax	13
Trusts & Estates	13
Environmental	12
Health	11
Intellectual Property	11
Government Contracts	9
Liability/Personal Injury	9
Corp. Technology	6
Securities	6
Bankruptcy	5
Banking	4

One of the few premier Atlanta firms with a national and international practice, Powell, Goldstein, Frazer & Murphy handles a lot of work that cannot be found in many other Atlanta firms. Its banking practice, for example, with its New York and Washington, D.C. flavor, is "atypical for Atlanta."

working but fun-filled atmosphere

Powell Goldstein is a high-powered, "structured" law firm; its "work atmosphere is professional but "not stuffy." While everyone is "very intelligent and hard-working," there is no "cut-throat" atmosphere as in some other firms of its size, according to one source. The "firm hires people who push themselves," said one contact, adding that "they all know they work hard, but they joke about it and laugh about it." Although "there is order" at Powell Goldstein, it is not overly hierarchical, we were told. "Even the managing partner is approachable." Though attorneys usually dress in business attire, the firm has designated approximately two days a month, plus every Friday from Memorial Day to Labor Day, as casual dress days. On these days jeans and sneakers are permitted, "within the bounds of good taste." Even on non-casual days, work wardrobes are fairly relaxed. Women often wear skirts and sweaters or blouses, pant suits, etc. Men wear sportcoats and ties rather than suits on occasion.

"It is fun to go to work" at Powell Goldstein because the associates know how to entertain themselves during the work day. "Turn off your E-mail, otherwise someone will take advantage of it to send around a funny message under your name," cautioned one contact. Attorneys at Powell Goldstein are an "eclectic" lot, "less homogeneous" than at other large firms, one insider told us. Another contact noted ruefully, however, that "our firm is so diverse and contains so many different personalities that sometimes it is difficult to get things done because everyone has a different opinion."

practice areas

Litigation, Powell Goldstein's largest department, is highly-regarded. Several of the firm's attorneys are listed as top rate trial lawyers. Powell Goldstein primarily handles a wide range of commercial litigation. It also offers a growing environmental practice. The firm's thriving banking department represents international clients, such as the Canadian bank Toronto Dominion. One person noted that attorneys in the "lending department constantly go to New York and D.C." Other large clients include Hayes Coca-Cola Enterprises and Hayes Microcomputer, although the firm suffered a slight financial blow when Hayes Microcomputer filed for Chapter 11 and U.S. Bankruptcy Court Judge Hugh Robinson effectively severed the firm from what for several years had been one of its largest clients. Partner Scott Hobby, who handled that account, left the firm along with five others, diminishing the ranks of the corporate technology group. Powell Goldstein also represents some high-profile individuals and entertainment groups such as the Black Crows, the firm's current client du jour. Powell Goldstein's real estate department is "growing and very busy," according to one source. The real estate department has been augmented recently by the addition of a number of "high powered lateral partners who brought large portfolios of clients with them and, as a result, work has increased throughout the firm," we were told.

pro bono

When it comes to Powell Goldstein's pro bono practice, there is "a lot of it going on." Powell Goldstein attorneys participate in the 1000 Lawyers for Justice program and Atlanta Legal Aid. A few have worked for six years on a death penalty case. The firm encourages pro bono "mostly in litigation to get young associates some courtroom experience," according to one source. Powell Goldstein has a somewhat low billable hour requirement (1850), which is combined with a non-billable hour requirement (550) which "encompasses civic and professional activities, pro bono work, legal education, recruiting, etc."

associate development

Powell Goldstein assigns entering associates to particular practice groups. Prospective associates may express their preference for a particular area, but one person told us that the firm doesn't confirm which department a new associate will enter until the summer before he joins the firm. The firm is, however, "good about letting you switch" between departments. Opportunities for responsibility depend considerably on individual initiative: "the more you prove yourself, the more responsibility you get."

Litigation associates initially handle mainly research and writing assignments, though they often independently manage pro bono cases. One contact reported "handling two magistrate court trials and arguing motions in Superior Court" during the first two years at the firm. Junior real estate associates frequently speak with clients on the telephone. Most associates, across practice areas, also play a "significant role in factual development, which often involves working closely with clients and their employees."

Powell Goldstein offers a "phenomenal" training program. One person works full-time managing the education of the attorneys. She organizes weekend conferences, a working lunch program, and a number of other training activities. The firm formally evaluates summer and permanent associates, but most attorneys are slow to provide informal day-to-day feedback unless you "screw up." We were told that concerned associates "have to ask" for feedback. One contact, however, contested this viewpoint, noting that "with semi-annual reviews, I think feed-back comes more often than in firms with only annual reviews. In addition, I feel that I receive significant feedback on a regular basis, particularly from those partners with whom I work most closely."

social
summer

Social life at Powell Goldstein can be "as active as you want it to be." Many attorneys go home after work, but many small groups of associates go out on Friday nights. Attorneys also play on the firm softball team and go out for pizza and beers. The summer program is very active, but the firm "doesn't try to pretend that it [the active summer social life] was year-round, which was refreshing," said one person. Summer events have included "shooting the hooch" (a raft ride down the Chattahoochee River), white water rafting, a dinner at a partner's home, Friday evening cocktail parties and a Braves game. In addition, there is the formal summer party for all attorneys and summer associates (and guests), which was held at the High Museum of Art this past summer, and the summer associate retreat at the Inn at Blackberry Farm in Tennessee. Regular associates, we were told, "all vie for an opportunity to attend the retreat because it's a weekend of good food, fine dining and tons of fun."

diversity

"Being a woman does not hinder you" at Powell Goldstein, one contact informed us. There are several well-respected female attorneys at all levels in the firm—associates, counsel, and partners. Maternity leave policy is very flexible: three months paid leave and up to three months additional unpaid leave. Upon returning, each attorney may negotiate her own part-time arrangement if desired. "One recent mom arranged to work for the firm as a contract attorney from her home. Her computer and phone are tied into the firm, so she is kept up-to-date on all the goings-on." As for racial minorities, we were told that Powell Goldstein has made a serious effort to recruit minorities and has attended a minority job fair at Georgia State.

management

The direct management of the firm has changed from one managing partner (Bob Harlin) to four. Three senior partners handle discrete areas of management, such as personnel or financial performance, and then individually report to Bob Harlin. "As a result, associates are kept more informed about the performance, progress, and direction of the firm than they have been in the past," according to one insider. Significant decisions regarding the direction and operations of the firm are made by the Board of Partners, a group of approximately ten partners from both the Atlanta and Washington, D.C. offices. There were rumors at the time this book went to press that Powell Goldstein's management was in the process of making a significant decision; according to some news reports the firm was considering a merger with McGuire, Woods, Battle & Booth, a firm based in Richmond, Virginia. Powell Goldstein's partnership is structured with ten different tiers. Lower-tier partners initially receive a salary and share in the firm's equity only as they move up through the tiers. Associate compensation is not incentive driven and is lockstep throughout the associate ranks.

modern offices

Powell Goldstein's "absolutely beautiful" offices are extremely modern and decorated in glass, bronze and marble. All attorneys receive individual offices and personal computers. The firm is presently upgrading its computer system. The new system is "expected to be top-of-the-line, with capabilities for in-house optical imaging, scanning and direct on-line access." First-year associates sometimes occupy interior offices. The firm's offices are equipped with a staff lounge, with an eating area and a big television, and an attorney lounge, which is like a "nice parlor." The support staff is "wonderful."

interview process

Powell Goldstein likes to hire high-energy, "type-A" people. The firm places a "strong emphasis on personality," said one contact. Summer associates generally have "character and are really alive, enthusiastic, and ambitious." We were informed that at least one interviewer is quite "a character;" you will never have a "standard interview" with him. If you are from out-of-town, you will have to convince the firm that you are seriously interested in working in Atlanta, cautioned one successful applicant. Another person observed, however, that "there is no sort of 'residency requirement' (in fact, a large percentage of the firm's attorneys are from outside Atlanta and Georgia), but the hiring committee looks for a sincere interest in what the city has to offer rather than just a sincere interest in getting a job." While Duke used to provide a sizable block of summer associates, more recently Vanderbilt, Virginia and Georgia have taken over as leading feeder schools, but summer associates are drawn from schools all over the country. Powell Goldstein regularly interviews on-campus in New York, Massachusetts, Georgia, Virginia, North Carolina, Washington D.C., Tennessee and Florida.

Powell Goldstein is a large, structured firm. Associates must learn to cope with the firm's bureaucracy and procedures, said one insider. At the same time, Powell Goldstein is "not stuffy or conservative. There are so many people who have great personalities." One person declared that "it's the best of both worlds. It is respected and has high-quality standards. Yet there is a sense that there is more to life than the firm. They want you to be well-rounded and involved in the community." Combine these assets with a "phenomenal" training program and "absolutely beautiful" offices, and Powell Goldstein makes a very attractive place to practice law.

Smith, Gambrell & Russell

Atlanta

Address: 1230 Peachtree Street, N.E., Suite 3100, Atlanta, GA 30309
Telephone: (404) 815-3500
Hiring Attorney: John C. Ethridge, Jr.
Contact: Sherri M. Knight, Hiring Coordinator; (404) 815-3523
Associate Salary: First year $67,000 (1997)
Summer Salary: $1000/week (1997)
Average Hours: 2178 worked; 1811 billed; 2000 required
Family Benefits: 6 weeks paid maternity leave (6 unpaid)
1996 Summer: Class of 10 students; offers to 7
Partnership: 77% of entering associates from 1985–1996 were made partner
Pro Bono: 8–10% of all work is pro bono

Smith, Gambrell & Russell in 1997
111 Lawyers at the Firm
0.5 Associates Per Partner

Total Partners 69		
Women	5	7%
All Minorities	1	1%
Afro-Am	1	1%

Total Associates 32		
Women	17	53%
All Minorities	4	13%
Afro-Am	2	6%
Asian-Am	2	6%

Practice Areas	
Corporate	33
Litigation	31
Tax	10
Real Estate	9
Bankruptcy	8
Securities	6
Intellectual Property	5
Financial Institutions	5
Environmental	4

Although in its current form Smith, Gambrell & Russell is the product of a mid-1980s merger between Gambrell & Russell and Smith, Cohen, Ringle, Kohler & Martin, the Smith side of the firm traces its roots back more than 100 years in Atlanta. One of the firm's founders, E. Smythe Gambrell, was very active in charitable and philanthropic activities and funded a building at Emory University. He was also "infamous" for his regimented style that shaped the firm's culture for years. Among other quirks, he "required people to wear hats to work everyday, and held partner-associate meetings at 7:30 A.M. every Saturday morning." The youngest associates were charged with stocking these meetings with coffee and doughnuts. One person told us that at one point, "Gambrell & Russell was the biggest sweatshop firm in Atlanta," but observed that the firm "is OK now" and has been since 1980. Another contact confirmed that the firm's historical reputation is largely quaint folklore now: "There are no Saturday meetings. In fact, the lights go off in the office at 1 p.m. on Saturday and they are off all day Sunday."

independent atmosphere

Historically, Smith Gambrell was fairly "formal" in terms of dress; most male attorneys wore dark suits and white shirts to work. Today, blue shirts are very much in evidence, women often wear slacks, and Friday is a casual dress day. Generally, "independence and informality" characterize the work atmosphere. "People are very much quartered off in their own areas," one person commented. "You are given portions of a large case, and then away you go until you come back with it. There is not much interaction between partners and associates." However, this isolation is not firmwide; one contact protested that "he works with partners every day; there is plenty of interaction." In any event, associates are friendly with each other and share "a lot of humor and jokes."

two Atlanta offices

Smith Gambrell occupies two offices, one in midtown Atlanta and the other in the Lenox Mall or Buckhead area, but the two offices will be consolidated into the midtown office in the fall of 1997. Each office has a slightly different work atmosphere, perhaps reflecting the difference in office layout. One person told us that the offices in the Lenox Mall facility are "right on the hall," making it easy for attorneys to mill about and chat. The midtown offices are located "off the hallway," and its attorneys interact less.

practice areas

A full-service law firm, Smith Gambrell handles general corporate and litigation work out of both offices. Some specialty practice areas, such as environmental, however, are located entirely in one or the other of the two offices. Constituting a significant portion of the firm's work, the litigation group is "doing well." It primarily handles a variety of commercial matters. In addition, the firm has recently been involved in quite a bit of construction litigation. The environmental and intellectual property practices are also growing.

corporate international

Smith Gambrell's corporate practice handles general corporate and securities work. It also has a growing franchise practice. In addition, the firm is developing an international corporate practice focusing on Western Europe. The firm has hired five lawyers who are German, Finnish, or Belgian nationals and who have been admitted to practice in Georgia. It also participates in a foreign lawyer exchange program and is affiliated with firms in England, Italy, and Canada. Smith Gambrell represents mostly corporations, large contractors, and wealthy individuals based in the Southeast, as well as some national clients such as AT&T. Smith Gambrell is general counsel to Trans World Airline, one of the firm's largest clients, and was general counsel to Eastern Airlines before it was bought by Texas Air.

strong pro bono

Smith Gambrell has a strong commitment to pro bono work. It is one of the few Atlanta firms to formally credit up to 50 pro bono hours toward the 2000 billable hour goal. "Mr. Russell places a big emphasis on pro bono," said one person. Mr. Gambrell founded the Atlanta Legal Aid Society, and many of the firm's associates participate in its Saturday Morning Lawyer's Program. In addition, one person noted that a number of associates handle two or three active pro bono cases at a time.

Smith Gambrell assigns entering associates to a particular practice group or "section," usually according to their preference. Partners in the group directly assign work to new associates. Summer associates rotate through the litigation, corporate, and real estate sections, and both offices. Unless they previously worked at the firm as a first-year student, "[they] do not get a choice" in the work assigned, with the workload typically allocated forty percent corporate, forty percent litigation, and twenty percent real estate. An associate or a partner in each department is responsible for assigning work to summer associates during their rotations.

rapid professional development

Smith Gambrell offers junior associates significant early responsibility, particularly in the litigation department. Many associates take depositions within 10 months of joining the firm, and frequently try a small case or a pro bono matter by the end of their first year. Most associate training occurs "on-the-job." Smith Gambrell is "very good" about ensuring that summer and permanent associates receive feedback on their work. The firm assigns two attorneys who independently evaluate each summer associate's work and, every four weeks, review any written comments made by assigning attorneys. The firm also formally evaluates permanent associates twice a year for the first two years, and once annually thereafter.

social life

Smith Gambrell has an extremely active and social summer program with numerous cocktail parties, softball games, a weekend at Hilton Head, and other events. The firm also organizes a partners' and an associates' retreat, an annual Firm Outing, and a Christmas Party.

diversity

Although Smith Gambrell currently employs fewer female and minority attorneys than some firms, people we interviewed said the firm actively recruits lawyers from these groups and "recent statistics support these observations," according to a firm spokesperson. Most believe that women and minorities are "treated equally and very professionally," but one source noted that, like most in Atlanta, "this is a white male firm." A number of "good old Southern boys" work at the firm, stated one contact, which was then flatly disputed by another. In addition, in offering only six weeks paid maternity leave, Smith Gambrell appears less committed to family issues than some other firms in the city.

beautiful offices

Smith Gambrell is run by a managing partner, elected for a one-year term, from the five member executive committee of partners elected annually. Economically successful, the firm's relatively new "beautiful" midtown offices are located in the Promenade

II building on Peachtree. Lined with wood paneling, the offices showcase a large chandelier in the reception area. The older Lenox Mall offices have a similar look. All attorneys have individual offices with windows. The support staff is very friendly and helpful, and couriers run books between the libraries of the two offices. The computer system, which "needed help" in the past, has been upgraded and includes state of the art computers and software including Internet access. The firm budgets and spends a significant amount of money each year to avoid falling behind in the computer area again, we were told.

unique interview

Smith Gambrell hires law students with a "wide range of personalities," "solid academic backgrounds," and "good writing and communications skills." People advised applicants to "be outgoing" when interviewing with the firm. "They are good-natured people who have a job to do...They are looking for nice people," said one successful applicant. Smith Gambrell has a unique callback interview, which is conducted on one of two predetermined weekends. It begins with a cocktail party on a Friday evening, at which "almost all the firm shows up" to meet the candidates. Following the party, each applicant is taken out to dinner by two partners or a partner and an associate. The interviews take place the following day. One applicant complained that because it is a weekend day, "you don't get a sense of the firm." Another noted, however, that "the attorneys are not bustling around with work. They are there for you."

Smith Gambrell has a "good, solid reputation," but it does not draw as many national clients as some other large firms in town. Still, the firm has "plenty of midsize and national clients, including GE, AT&T and TWA." Though it offers early responsibility, one critic believes that the firm "is not a dynamic place." Yet, a firm booster observed that "you can actually make partner here", which is a nice plus. This person also pointed out that at Smith Gambrell, "you are rewarded for doing well as a young associate; there is *no* step ladder compensation system." Finally, most of our contacts gave the firm's "open and warm" work atmosphere high reviews.

Sutherland, Asbill & Brennan

Atlanta Austin New York Washington, D.C.

Address: 999 Peachtree Street, N.E., Atlanta, GA 30309–3996
Telephone: (404) 853–8000
Hiring Attorney: William H. Bradley
Contact: (Ms.) Carter M. Hoyt, Director, Recruitment & Prof. Dev.; (404) 853–8763
Associate Salary: First year $67,000 (1996); salaries are lockstep for the first 2 years, then progress on a merit-based scale with a range of salaries per class
Summer Salary: $1000/week (1996)
Average Hours: 2400 worked; 1700 billed; NA required
Family Benefits: 12 weeks paid maternity leave (up to 12 unpaid); paternity covered under Family & Medical Leave Act
1996 Summer: Class of 13 students; offers to 12
Partnership: NA
Pro Bono: 5% of all work is pro bono.

Sutherland, Asbill & Brennan in 1997
128 Lawyers At the Atlanta Office
0.7 Associates Per Partner

Total Partners 68			Total Associates 50			Practice Areas	
Women	8	12%	Women	21	42%	Litigation	50
All Minorities	2	3%	All Minorities	2	4%	Tax	26
Afro-Am	2	3%	Afro-Am	2	4%	Corporate & Securities	21
						Real Estate	17
						Banking & Finance	14

Founded as a tax firm, Sutherland, Asbill & Brennan has grown to be a full-service law firm with over 250 lawyers practicing in Atlanta, New York, Austin and Washington, D.C. Ranked among the nation's top 100 firms, with profits per partner at about $335,000, it is the third-most profitable firm in Atlanta. A well-established law firm, Sutherland Asbill is proud of its history, to which it "turns for the identity of the firm, which has been greatly influenced by one of its founders, Judge Elbert Tuttle, who sat on the 11th Circuit Court of Appeals until his recent passing." The firm also continues to abide by the philosophy articulated by another founder, Bill Sutherland, who said: "We wanted to build a firm that was 'top flight' in every sense. Second-class work would never be tolerated in our firm. Every piece of work that left our offices was to be of the very highest quality, regardless of whether the firm earned money or not." This focus is very much in evidence at the firm today. One person commented that "there can be tremendous pressure to be perfect in producing work products;" another stated that "the partners have high expectations of associates."

intense atmosphere

Sutherland Asbill is a smoothly run and efficient firm. It does not, however, offer a "lot of structure" and is "not going to provide a ready-made family" for its attorneys. Sutherland Asbill attorneys are bound together solely by "sheer academic pride in their work." While most people appreciate the firm's individualistic and somewhat intense atmosphere, others can find the firm too demanding and unsupportive. Contacts we interviewed agreed that Sutherland Asbill attorneys can be "overworked and tired," but one explained that most thrive because "the firm really encourages people to excel. It's a very unique firm. It encourages people to be individuals. I felt a lot of freedom to do the work the way I wanted, provided that it was up to a certain caliber. Most people are strong, independent personalities. People who are unhappy generally are the ones who need more support." Some sources indicated that there are a few Sutherland attorneys who are "competitive" with each other, noting that on a personal level, many "don't know each other" very well outside of their own practice area group.

professional emphasis

The work atmosphere is somewhat "reserved" and "formal." Sutherland Asbill attorneys dress conservatively, reflecting the firm's "emphasis on professionalism." Fridays, are, however casual dress days at the firm. "On a personal level," however, "people at the firm respect each other very much," and "associates are very comfortable dealing with partners because the underlying respect takes the edge out of the...hierarchy."

nationally recognized tax practice

Sutherland Asbill's practice is organized into five large departments: corporate, banking and finance, real estate, tax and litigation. Sutherland has many wonderful clients, commented one person, but "they typically are not the 'marquee' clients that some Atlanta firms have." The firm's tax practice is "particularly noteworthy." One partner, N. Jerold Cohen, the former Chief Counsel to the Internal Revenue Service and the immediate past Chair of the tax section of the ABA, is known as one of the country's top tax lawyers. Randolph Thrower, a former Commissioner of the Internal Revenue, and Walter Hellerstein, reputedly the nation's leading authority on state and local tax, are other noteworthy partners in the tax practice at the firm. The firm's nationally reputed tax department attracts large clients. Cohen, for example, has handled tax litigation for McDonald's and provides advice to General Motors and Coca Cola. The department is involved in a wide range of tax matters including tax litigation, corporate planning, not-for-profit incorporations, and international tax. In 1993, Sutherland Asbill merged with a Wall Street firm, Boyle, Vogeler & Haimes, to establish a small New York office to solidify its entry into the area of international tax. One person remarked, however, that although the firm is retaining a small presence in New York, "it is not attempting to develop its practice there."

real estate corporate

Sutherland Asbill's real estate practice is "one of the stronger practices in Atlanta." The group has been particularly busy of late, representing large clients such as Mobil Properties and John Hancock. The litigation, corporate, and banking and finance departments attract regional and national clients, including Ford, for whom the company is the southeast regional counsel in dealer and general non-products litigation. These departments house many specialty areas including an intellectual property group that has represented the Miss Universe pageant in trademark matters; an education practice involved in representing school boards in desegregation cases and other matters; an environmental practice which handles numerous regulatory matters; and a noted alternative dispute resolution practice, led by senior partner Jim Groton. The corporate practice is developing a new focus on the technology company market, as well as in the merchant processing arena. The firm also has an Austin office that primarily represents energy and health care clients.

commitment to pro bono

Sutherland Asbill has a strong and well-organized pro bono practice. Junior litigation associates are encouraged to participate in the Saturday Morning Lawyer's Program organized by the Atlanta Legal Aid Society and in the 1000 Lawyers for Justice program organized by the Atlanta Bar Association to assist in representing indigent criminal defendants. Pro bono work is also done at the Legal Clinic for the Homeless, to assist in resolving day to day disputes of homeless persons. In addition, the firm encourages its attorneys to become involved in bar association activities. William Barwick, a partner at the firm, is the former President of the Atlanta Bar Association, and Charlie Lester served as President of the State Bar of Georgia Association in 1991 and 1992, and was formerly president of the Atlanta Legal Aid Society.

Sutherland Asbill assigns entering associates to particular areas according to the firm's needs and the associate's interest. The work assignment coordinators in every department distribute assignments to associates. However, partners often directly request associates to assist them on particular matters. An associate on the hiring committee coordinates summer associate assignments. Summer associates typically work on projects in their area of interest and also handle other assignments in a variety of practice areas.

professional development

Legal matters at Sutherland Asbill are "leanly staffed," and associates who display initiative and confidence get a lot of responsibility. One contact noted that Sutherland "gives associates tremendous responsibility from the beginning of their careers forward, accelerating the maturation process as well as the learning curve." Junior associates "are thrown into the water" and have to figure things out on their own and ask for help when they need it. First-year litigation associates initially handle research and writing assignments, but typically take depositions by the "three-quarter mark of their first year." Although a second-year associate may act as the lead attorney on a smaller case, most third and fourth-year associates typically sit second chair at trials. In the corporate area, most transactions are handled by a single associate working with the partner in charge. On very large deals, a senior associate may be "first chair" and a junior associate may back him or her.

extensive training

Sutherland Asbill offers an extensive training program designed to meet the continuing legal education requirements of the State Bar of Georgia. Associates receive numerous hours of formal training in their first three years at the firm, including seminars in various substantive areas of the law and workshops in specific legal skills. One person commented that, today, "the training program is no longer so formal, although many in-house CLE courses are offered." The firm also hires an Emory Law School professor as a writing consultant during the summer months to confidentially review and critique summer associate work product. People reported that feedback at the firm is "generally good"; most partners are "willing to give you feedback if you ask for it." The firm formally evaluates first-year associates every six months. The "associate review begins with a lengthy self-appraisal that is then compared with partner ratings," reported one source. Another noted that, because Sutherland Asbill is a firm of "perfectionists, the feedback can be critical. It is very demanding and can be discouraging."

long hours

Though Sutherland Asbill does not have a formal billable hour requirement, people we interviewed believed that the informal target is closer to 2000 hours per year. The firm seems very "concerned about productivity and billables." One person commented that "long hours are not unusual, but partners aren't watching you come and go—but you're expected to handle a heavy load and handle it well," adding that "a significant number of attorneys work after 6 P.M., and most people work late regularly." Another person remarked that "because of the lean staffing, it is not uncommon to find yourself completely tied up and spending long and stressful hours at work for long stretches of time."

mature social life

Social life at Sutherland Asbill occupies the "middle ground between very social firms and those where you do your work and leave." The firm has a "more mature social life since many of the attorneys are married," explained one source, adding that it is "more limited for younger people or summer associates." Several junior associates are somewhat facetiously attempting to redevelop the now dormant Single Associate Support Group, which "goes out spontaneously in the evening." The firm formally organizes summer social events, including bowling, baseball games, cocktail parties, dinners, and barbecues. One critic complained, however, that the "social activities were too planned. There were few spontaneous lunches." The firm does not reimburse summer associate meals that are not a part of the planned program, even if a summer associate is invited out by an associate or partner. One morning every week is designated "Lawyer's Coffee", at which time attorneys gather for coffee, doughnuts, and socializing.

diversity

Sutherland Asbill is "responsive to women's issues." The firm offers detailed information regarding its sexual harassment policy, which sets out procedures for complaints. One person commented that "since this is not the kind of firm that goes out and parties, you don't get the feeling that kind of thing [sexual harassment] happens much." The firm also recently implemented a part-time work policy utilized by several female associates with young children, "although the response to the policy has been mixed," commented one person. Sutherland Asbill employs few minority attorneys, but one source commented that the firm gives the "same amount of respect and work" regardless of racial background or gender.

management

Sutherland Asbill does not have a head office. A firmwide executive committee runs the firm, and each office has a managing partner. The firm is, however, striving for more centralized management, with Jim Henderson of the Atlanta office as the new managing partner of the entire firm. Sutherland Asbill is more aggressive about developing business than it has been in the past, said one contact, who nevertheless noted that the firm plans to grow in its traditionally "slow and controlled" manner. Another contact pointed out that the focus in 1996 has been on "a detailed marketing survey designed to help the firm adapt to changing conditions in the legal market."

elegant offices

Sutherland Asbill has a "strong reputation in the Atlanta community and is happy with where it is. It is not into the fighting game and is a very self-confident firm." Unlike other Atlanta firms, Sutherland Asbill is "not into being at the top of the tallest building and is not in the most prestigious building." Nevertheless, the firm's offices were ranked the best large law firm offices by the *ABA Journal* law office design competition. The offices are "one of the real assets of the firm," concurred one source. They were described as "beautiful and elegant offices with a lot of dark wood; wooden floors in the reception and hallways; and a lot of windows...and very modern and bright." The firm is proud of its unusual modern art collection that includes some "three dimensional pieces." All associates have equal-sized individual offices with windows. A personal computer sits in every office, all of which are networked and have electronic mail and internet capability. Also, most, if not all, attorneys have printers at their desks. The support staff was described as "wonderful." The firm has a large "break room" for attorneys and staff that is outfitted with lunch tables and vending machines. The library is fairly large and well-equipped with private carrels and small rooms with telephones. The location of the firm, in midtown, is convenient but "slightly isolated," noted one person.

very high recruiting standards

Sutherland Asbill is a "very academic firm that seeks people who will produce very good work." The firm "looks for intellectual ability. Grades and law review are extremely important," revealed one source. Most attorneys at the firm are members of the Order of the Coif, Phi Beta Kappa, or have received other academic honors. The majority were editors or members of a law review, and many have served as judicial clerks. In addition, the firm "wants people who are mature and can work well independently." It values "people with strong personalities who don't need the firm to give them personality." One insider advised that Sutherland Asbill is also looking for people "who are willing to commit to the firm for the duration. The firm looks to hire people who will be there 20 years later." Finally, the firm hires "people who don't mind putting in the hours." Applicants who interview with the firm are advised to "concentrate on what is unique about them, or what they like to do." Callback interviews are usually conducted over a full day, and the firm, as a rule, treats students to dinner the night before. Sutherland Asbill traditionally draws heavily from Emory, Harvard, Duke, Yale, Tennessee, Michigan, Georgia, Georgetown, and Stanford to fill its summer class.

Sutherland Asbill is not the place for everyone. It is an intense and hard-working law firm whose attorneys are reserved and place a high premium on excellence. While some view the individualistic work atmosphere as competitive, others see it as liberating. One person commented that "the pressure most noticeable to junior associates is the pressure for perfection. Also, because responsibility is given generously early on, it can be frustrating to feel 'in the dark' about the tasks at hand." Pay is competitive in the early years but "may not keep pace for mid and senior level associates," according to one contact. A spokesperson for the firm informed us that, as a result of a recent adjustment of associate compensation, "the resulting compensation levels, I believe, make us fully competitive with other large firms in the Atlanta market." Sutherland Asbill has a top-notch reputation both in Atlanta and the nation and is an excellent choice for someone who is seeking the unique "freedom to do what he or she does best."

Troutman Sanders

Atlanta Washington, D.C.

Address: 600 Peachtree Street, N.E. NationsBank Plaza, Suite 5200, Atlanta, GA 30308
Telephone: (404) 885–3000
Hiring Attorney: DeWitt R. Rogers
Contact: Jodie R. Kapral, Recruiting Administrator; (404) 885–3000
Associate Salary: First year $67,000 (1997); merit increases
Summer Salary: $1000/week (1997)
Average Hours: 2103 worked; 1800 billed; NA required
Family Benefits: NA
1996 Summer: Class of 27 students
Partnership: 7.5 year track; all equity partners
Pro Bono: NA

Troutman Sanders in 1997
213 Lawyers at the Atlanta Office
1.1 Associates Per Partner

Total Partners 95			Total Associates 105			Practice Areas	
Women	12	13%	Women	49	47%	Corporate	75
All Minorities	2	2%	All Minorities	14	13%	Public Law	68
Afro-Am	2	2%	Afro-Am	7	7%	Litigation	55
			Asian-Am	5	5%	Real Estate	15
			Latino	2	2%		

centralized management

Tracing its roots back to 1897, Troutman Sanders is one of Atlanta's oldest and largest law firms. Formerly Troutman, Sanders, Lockerman & Ashmore, it grew significantly in the 1980s, merging with a series of smaller firms. Troutman Sanders is organized into practice groups and the work atmosphere in each group varies depending on the personality and working style of the group leader. In general, partners are approachable, and the firm is not overly hierarchical. In fact, in a favorite tradition, summer associates "put on a skit that makes fun of all the partners" at the firm's annual beach outing. The management of Troutman Sander's is in the hands of the firm's executive committee and its compensation committee. Most day-to-day decisions are made by the managing partner, Bob Webb. Also still influential in the firm's decision making is former managing partner and former Georgia Governor, Carl Sanders. One contact told us that Sanders "basically has an entire floor in the building to himself." Another contact informed us that the present management set-up represents a transition "from just Sanders running the show to Sanders plus five or six others running the show."

independent culture

Troutman Sanders offers a comfortable work atmosphere. Its lawyers "are nice, outgoing, and friendly. There is not a lot of competition and they help each other," said one source. Another commented that the associates "are for the most part great people and good friends. When I was a first year, people were incredibly helpful, showing me how to do things." For Atlanta, the firm is pretty laid-back and fairly informal. Attorneys can be themselves and women feel comfortable wearing dresses or pants, instead of suits, to work. The lawyers are "really independent," according to one contact, who explained that Troutman Sanders is a "large firm with a smaller firm atmosphere. Each section governs a lot of its own affairs. People feel a little more in control of their destinies." Traditionally, Troutman Sanders associates "have had a good attitude about their work." Concluded one source, "I think they have a very good balance between work and priorities in life generally. They take work seriously, but not themselves seriously enough to sacrifice themselves for work." However, another contact disagreed and pointed out that, with the recent growth of the firm, "attorneys are working longer hours and there has been an increasing emphasis on billable hours." This person claimed that "finding a week to go on vacation will be tough, although most people do take a week vacation every year. Plus, on my floor, if you leave before 7:00 p.m., people will notice."

practice

Troutman Sanders is a full-service law firm, representing both national and international clients. Troutman Sanders reportedly has "more true international legal work than any other major law firm in Atlanta." During the past five years, the firm has handled transactions in Australia, Pakistan, Indonesia, China, Argentina and other places. The firm, we were told, is scheduled to open an office in Hong Kong in early 1997. Troutman Sanders' work is organized in four practice sections: corporate, litigation, public law, and real estate. The litigation practice is closely tied to the public law practice which represents a number of public utilities. The public law practice includes interdisciplinary practice groups such as environmental and communications. The firm handles a substantial amount of utility litigation and regulatory work for Georgia Power Company, one of its largest clients.

represents Cable News Network

Troutman Sanders' corporate practice represents a broad range of clients, from large corporations such as AT&T to individual start-up companies. It represented Ted Turner when he began his career as an entrepreneur and, today, handles most of the Cable News Network's (CNN) corporate, communications, and other legal needs. The corporate finance team also does a lot of work for Turner. This group can "be very intense when a bond issue is being put together," said one observer. The corporate practice also represents the Southern Company, a public holding company for five power companies in the South, handling its energy projects and joint ventures all over the world. The firm's real estate team, according to a firm spokesperson, "is, and has been, one of the largest and busiest in the city." Overall, people commented that Troutman Sanders has been "very, very busy," The firm expects some of its burgeoning practice areas, such as environmental, to continue growing. In addition, with the Southern Company engaging in an increasing number of foreign ventures, the firm "sees itself as becoming more global," according to one source. Lastly, the firm's recently established Washington D.C. office, which handles transportation, utilities and legislative work, has been growing.

Although Troutman Sanders encourages attorneys to become involved in pro bono work and participates in the Saturday Morning Lawyer's Program, organized by the Atlanta Legal Aid Society, one contact remarked that other firms in the city are more well-known for their pro bono work. The firm does, however, allow 40 hours of pro bono work to count for billable hours.

significant responsibility

Troutman Sanders assigns entering associates to a practice section of their choice. Each group distributes assignments fairly informally. Partners directly request associates to work for them, and associates ask particular partners for work. Because the firm represents an array of smaller clients, associates often receive responsibility early. Junior litigation associates usually work on smaller projects, such as landlord-tenant disputes, foreclosures, or other matters involving court hearings. By their second year, they frequently take depositions. Troutman Sanders trains associates both on-the-job and through formal presentations made by partners. The partners also provide good feedback on summer and permanent associate work product. Most people enjoy "a good dialog with the attorney they work with on a regular basis."

summer program

Troutman Sanders' summer program includes a number of events, such as dinners at restaurants and partners' homes, Braves games (representing Turner is key for this), an associates party, and a weekend trip to a nearby beach resort, such as Hilton Head. The firm also organizes an associate retreat and a Christmas party every year.

diversity

Although Troutman Sanders has made an effort to recruit female and minority attorneys, one contact commented that its efforts have not been as strong as the efforts of some other large Atlanta firms. Another commented that "we have a lot of women here, but not very many minority attorneys." The firm has two African-American partners, one of whom is very influential in Atlanta city politics. Several female partners "take leading roles in the firm." They are "visible and considered important," remarked one source. Although the firm does not list its policy on maternity leave, it is "willing to accommodate," according to one observer, and several women associates with small children are currently working part-time.

Troutman Sanders' "gorgeous" and "plush" offices are very modern. The "beautiful" library is designed to resemble the Supreme Court's library. All attorneys receive individual offices with windows. One critic complained, however, that the windows in summer associate's offices are virtually "teeny little slits" because of pillars on the outside of the building. Attorneys also receive personal computers that are on a network system and the firm's computer system is presently being significantly upgraded. Troutman Sanders building includes a cafeteria that is open to all occupants and a parking lot located underneath the building. The firm pays for membership to the health club that is also in the building, as well as parking for all associates.

hiring tips

"Grades are not the sole determining factor" in landing a summer position at Troutman Sanders, although a firm spokesperson pointed out to us that Troutman Sanders "has been second to none in recruiting students who are at the very top of the market." The firm looks to hire "a competent, intelligent person who is willing to work hard." Troutman Sanders wants people who "don't take themselves too seriously," noted one contact, commenting that the firm's attorneys are a "very warm group of people" who "want people who are happy with themselves." This is not a firm that "wants someone who really wants to be a gunner," one person commented.

People advised applicants to "relax and enjoy" the interview. At some schools, the firm invites all students interviewing on campus to a cocktail party that evening where, according to one person, the attorneys "observe how people do in that context." Those who are invited to interview for a full day at the firm are usually taken out to dinner the night before. Some people are treated to fancy restaurants, while others have enjoyed more casual dinners at an attorney's home. People advised applicants "to be themselves because that is absolutely what the firm wants." The firm recruits heavily at Emory, Harvard, Vanderbilt, Georgetown, and the Universities of Florida, Georgia, North Carolina and Virginia.

Because Troutman Sanders' associates are assigned to a particular section, they have a "pretty narrowly focused range of work." One source noted that the firm primarily has a "utility oriented practice." However, Troutman Sanders has "a lot of capacity to grow" and represents a number of interesting clients, such as CNN. It also does, for Atlanta, a significant amount of international work. Perhaps most importantly, people stressed that Troutman Sanders attorneys "are wonderful people." One insider declared, "If I had to pick any group of people in the city with whom to work, I'd pick them." Finally, one firm enthusiast urged law students to "know what they're getting into when they sign up for a big firm career or they won't be happy. If you're going to do it, however, this is the place to come."

Baltimore

Law Firms Ranked By Associates Per Partner

1.	WEINBERG AND GREEN	0.4
2.	WHITEFORD, TAYLOR & PRESTON	0.7
3.	MILES & STOCKBRIDGE	0.8
4.	SEMMES, BOWEN & SEMMES	0.9
5.	VENABLE, BAETJER AND HOWARD	1.0
6.	PIPER & MARBURY	1.2

Law Firms Ranked by Percentage of Associates Who Make Partner
(over varying years)

1.	PIPER & MARBURY	46
2.	WEINBERG AND GREEN	43
3.	SEMMES, BOWEN & SEMMES	42
4.	MILES & STOCKBRIDGE	NA
5.	VENABLE, BAETJER AND HOWARD	NA
6.	WHITEFORD, TAYLOR & PRESTON	NA

Law Firms Ranked by Percentage of Pro Bono Work

1.	WHITEFORD, TAYLOR & PRESTON	8-10
2.	SEMMES, BOWEN & SEMMES	5-10
3.	PIPER & MARBURY	3
4.	WEINBERG AND GREEN	3
5.	MILES & STOCKBRIDGE	NA
6.	VENABLE, BAETJER AND HOWARD	NA

Law Firms Ranked by Percentage of Female Partners

1.	SEMMES, BOWEN & SEMMES	19
2.	WEINBERG AND GREEN	17
3.	WHITEFORD, TAYLOR & PRESTON	14
4.	PIPER & MARBURY	13
5.	VENABLE, BAETJER AND HOWARD	13
6.	MILES & STOCKBRIDGE	11

Law Firms Ranked by Percentage of Female Associates

1.	WHITEFORD, TAYLOR & PRESTON	53
2.	PIPER & MARBURY	45
3.	VENABLE, BAETJER AND HOWARD	45
4.	WEINBERG AND GREEN	40
5.	MILES & STOCKBRIDGE	36
6.	SEMMES, BOWEN & SEMMES	32

Law Firms Ranked by Percentage of Minority Partners

1.	PIPER & MARBURY	6
2.	WEINBERG AND GREEN	5
3.	WHITEFORD, TAYLOR & PRESTON	4
4.	MILES & STOCKBRIDGE	2
5.	VENABLE, BAETJER AND HOWARD	1
6.	SEMMES, BOWEN & SEMMES	0

Law Firms Ranked By Percentage of Minority Associates

1.	VENABLE, BAETJER AND HOWARD	16
2.	PIPER & MARBURY	12
3.	WHITEFORD, TAYLOR & PRESTON	8
4.	WEINBERG AND GREEN	7
5.	MILES & STOCKBRIDGE	4
6.	SEMMES, BOWEN & SEMMES	0

Miles & Stockbridge

Baltimore Cambridge Columbia Easton Frederick McLean Rockville Towson Washington

Address: 10 Light Street, Baltimore, MD 21202
Telephone: (410) 727-6464
Hiring Attorney: Cynthia C. Allner
Contact: Valerie R. Smith, Recruitment Director; (410) 385-3563
Associate Salary: First year $60,000 (1997)
Summer Salary: $925/week (1997)
Average Hours: NA worked; NA billed; NA required
Family Benefits: Maternity leave/disability
1996 Summer: Class of 8 2L students; offers to 6; 6 1L's participated in the summer program
Partnership: NA
Pro Bono: NA

Miles & Stockbridge in 1997
170 Lawyers at the Baltimore Office
0.8 Associates Per Partner

Total Partners 96			Total Associates 74			Practice Areas	
Women	10	11%	Women	27	36%	Litigation	82
All Minorities	3	2%	All Minorities	3	4%	Business	60
Afro-Am	1	1%	Afro-Am	3	4%	Banking/Real Estate	23
Asian-Am	1	1%				Government Relations	2
Latino	1	1%					

Miles & Stockbridge is one of the oldest and most prestigious Baltimore firms. With nine offices in Maryland and Washington, D.C., Miles is ideally situated to be a regional powerhouse. The firm has grown exponentially since the mid-1970s, increasing in size from 30 lawyers in 1975 to almost 200 lawyers firmwide. Managing partner, Jim Eylie, was recently appointed to the Court of Special Appeals. Joseph Welty, formerly of the Frederick office, is now the President of the firm and is in charge of day-to-day operations of the firm. The Fairfax and Washington, D.C. offices have recently been consolidated and relocated to Tysons Corner in Mclean, Virginia. The firm now maintains a small office of only a few lawyers in downtown Washington.

sports fraternity culture

Miles & Stockbridge prides itself on its "friendly" work atmosphere. Those we interviewed reported a strong camaraderie and "a great social life" among lawyers at the firm. The people were described as "normal people," who still value life outside of work. Miles is a "more livable firm," one contact reported. "Work is not the end-all to these people. Their social lives include everyone they work with." Another commented that "people go out and party together. They go to baseball games and drink." This is especially true of a "group of the younger attorneys" at the firm. Miles' summer softball team is a central focus of the firm's social life for some people. This sports focus is said to be great for those who fit into the firm culture. Some people, however, described the firm as "clubby" and "fraternity-like." One source claimed that, particularly in the litigation practice, "some of the women said they felt left out of the goings-on. Many of the men in that department socialized together and played on the softball team."

practice areas

Miles & Stockbridge is divided into three major departments: litigation, business and commercial, and real estate. The litigation group was described as "very outgoing," "tight knit," with "a large clique of good old boys in the department." Another person observed that litigation is now broken into three areas and that, more recently, an "us vs them" mentality has developed between these groups. The "bread and butter" of the practice is insurance, medical malpractice, and commercial litigation. The firm does very little appellate litigation work. The business group was described as "mostly male," but "less rowdy and spirited" than the litigation group. It handles a broad range of transactions for clients such as Black & Decker, Lockheed Martin, and a number of investment and commercial banks, including Nations Bank. Although Miles does not have a highly developed pro bono practice, a number of the business attorneys have established a pro bono program to help entrepreneurs start small businesses. Miles, however, does "not have an organized way for summer associates to do pro bono work," complained one observer.

improved summer program

Although many aspects of the summer program were described as somewhat disorganized in the past, the program is now more structured, and the firm "tries to expose summer associates to *real* work and practice situations," we were told. Typically, students work half the summer in litigation and half in the other two areas. They receive assignments directly from the lawyers, and their work is monitored by a group of associates. The firm extends permanent associate offers for a specific department. Junior associates usually do a variety of work within a department before specializing in a particular area.

unstructured atmosphere

Miles is not the kind of firm that will "coddle" you, one contact stated. "It's not a place for the faint of heart. You have to be secure and bold...You will be thrown right into the thick of things. It's good for those who want to get started practicing law right away." Miles attorneys get a lot of responsibility early. "The firm doesn't staff many people on its cases...Some were getting exposure right away. There were second-year associates who were trying administrative cases on their own," said one person. Another observed that some second-year attorneys had conducted their own jury trials. Miles, however, is "not big on formal training programs"; most training at the firm happens on-the-job. Feedback is also informal and unstructured: "If you want feedback, you can get it, but otherwise, no news is good news." The evaluation process has, however, become more "formalized" of late, we were told. Also, Miles is now placing "more of a focus on hours and 'collections'—money brought into the firm on your billings." This makes bonuses more difficult to obtain in the early years since they are based on dollars collected and not hours billed.

old-school

Miles is "definitely a male-dominated firm," claimed one insider. It is reputed to be "old-school," according to another. With respect to women, the firm is not "as totally committed to affirmative action as other places are these days." One person observed that "for whatever reasons, many younger women end up leaving the firm." In the litigation department, "some women made remarks about crude jokes that were going around," reported one source. Another noted that although, at times, the firm lacked sensitivity to women's concerns, "they are trying to change this but don't quite seem to know how!" One person commented that the atmosphere for women is "changing." An "influential" woman partner now heads the hiring committee, and several women recently have been made partner. One source informed us that "Miles has been experimenting with part-time work for women who have children," but qualified the statement by observing, "I'm not sure how successful it has been." Another person remarked that the firm is "still not really progressive on women's issues, such as part-time, maternity leave, etc., although they appear to be more open-minded."

diversity

Miles is also "not an overwhelmingly diverse firm." It is primarily a "WASP firm" and "not a real ethnic place," claimed one contact who could not think of "any significant minority players at the partnership level." Miles talks about the need for more minorities, but it is "hard to tell whether it is more than lip service," according to one source. People did note, however, that recent summer classes have included an increasing number of minority law students.

Miles' offices are located right next to Baltimore's biggest tourist attraction, the Inner Harbor. The offices are decorated in "Colonial Maryland," and the interior design is said to be "functional but not beautiful." The firm is currently being renovated, one floor at a time. Every associate has a private office at the firm. The biggest complaint concerns the firm's computers, which one reviewer characterized as a bunch of "old clunkers." This situation is now changing, however. Presently, we were told, "all computers are being upgraded; some departments are currently networked, with plans for the entire firm to be networked in the future." Also, summer associates are now each provided with their own computer.

blunt interview questions

Miles is among the three most competitive Baltimore firms at which to land a summer associate position. The firm draws its summer class from a diverse range of schools, but principally from the top 10 national and local law schools. Miles does not recruit on many law school campuses and is very open to hiring students who contact the firm independently, said one person. The firm looks for "no-nonsense workers who are not prima donnas. It places a big premium on people being able to get along with each other," reported another.

Callback interviews usually involve meeting with two or three different pairs of attorneys. It is not uncommon for Miles' interviewers to ask "blunt and direct" questions in the interviews. For example, one successful applicant was specifically asked about a number of her grades and certain substantive legal issues covered in law school classes. Another person, who had an advertising background, was asked to answer a question from the perspective of a "hot shot ad man." Some interview questions can be unnerving, but don't let it "rattle" you, advised one person.

Piper & Marbury

Baltimore Easton New York Philadelphia Washington

Address:	36 South Charles Street, Baltimore, MD 21201
Telephone:	(410) 539–2530
Hiring Attorney:	Sheila Mosmiller Vidmar
Contact:	Ms. Dusti Johnston, Recruitment Coordinator; (410) 576–1943
Associate Salary:	First year $67,000 (1997)
Summer Salary:	$1000/week (1997)
Average Hours:	2053 worked; 1619 billed; NA required
Family Benefits:	12 weeks paid maternity leave; 12 weeks paid paternity leave
1996 Summer:	Class of 12 students; offers to 9
Partnership:	46% of entering associates from 1979–1983 were made partner
Pro Bono:	3% of all work is pro bono

Piper & Marbury in 1997
160 Lawyers at the Baltimore Office
1.2 Associates Per Partner

Total Partners 68		
Women	9	13%
All Minorities	4	6%
Afro-Am	4	6%

Total Associates 83		
Women	37	45%
All Minorities	10	12%
Afro-Am	6	7%
Asian-Am	3	4%
Latino	1	1%

Practice Areas	
Litigation	38
Corporate, Securities & Tax	36
Public Finance & Admin.	16
Real Estate	16
Labor & Employment	13
Creditors' Rights & Bankruptcy	10
Trusts & Estates	8
Employment/Benefits	8
Environmental	7

Piper & Marbury's history stretches back to the American Revolution. The firm bears the name of a relative of William Marbury, plaintiff in the historical and famous constitutional law case *Marbury v. Madison.* Piper has continued to gain prestige over the years. While many large Baltimore firms are regional powers, Piper has sought to establish itself as a national law firm. The firm has a large office in Washington, D.C. and has established a strong presence in Philadelphia and New York, making it the closest thing to a national law firm that Baltimore has to offer. Although Piper has expanded rapidly in recent years, our sources said that the firm is known for its conservative management. The firm has planned its moves carefully over the years to avoid becoming overextended. One contact informed us that "Piper's growth emphasis is likely to remain on growing its New York and D.C. offices," which have expanded significantly in the past few years. Piper was recently cited by the *National Law Journal* as "one of two firms located outside New York city "most used" by corporate counsel around the country per a national survey on the topic," according to a firm insider.

litigation

Piper's practice expanded considerably in recent years when Frank Bernstein, a prominent Baltimore law firm, dissolved and 10 of its senior "rainmaking" partners joined Piper. Litigation is the firm's largest and most well-known practice area. This group is the "life of the party" at the firm, exclaimed one insider. The department handles a broad range of matters, such as products liability, securities, and commercial litigation, and is well known for its antitrust litigation practice. The department has an excellent technical support team and recently installed a "very modern...litigation management support division that takes up three-fourths of one floor."

corporate

The corporate department offers a "good mix between securities and more traditional corporate work," said one contact. Piper partners enjoy close ties with Alex Brown, USF&G, Baltimore Gas & Electric, and Allied Lyons. The trusts and estates department is small, but a "heavy hitter." The Johns Hopkins Hospital trust is one prominent client. Stan Klinefelter, who is the head of this department, is reputedly a particularly nice attorney with whom to work. Piper's bankruptcy practice is "booming," and its attorneys work very hard. The bankruptcy group is known as somewhat "cutthroat," and its work atmosphere is affected by some personality conflicts, according to one person. The tax department "combines a few older partners and some young rising stars." It was described as "quieter" and less cohesive than other departments at the firm.

The pro bono practice at Piper is managed by a pro bono committee. Piper lawyers work primarily with the Maryland Volunteer Lawyers Association in conjunction with the University of Maryland Law School. The firm offers each summer associate an opportunity to work on at least one pro bono project.

Beautiful People social life

Everyone we interviewed described Piper as a friendly and social firm, though they reported that it is not particularly "chatty" during work hours. The firm is fairly social in the morning and after work, but during the day, people work hard, said one person. At times, the social life takes on a "fraternity" flavor, commented several of our sources. One person claimed that the social atmosphere tends to be dominated by the "Beautiful People" or the "Pretty People"—"the Anne Taylor or Brooks Brothers types." This person explained that "these people all knew each other in high school. Many grew up in Baltimore and...get on the same committees at the firm...They live life in the fast lane for Baltimore. Some people can find it intimidating if they are not from the Baltimore clique." Many Piper associates attended college together, and one person remarked, "There is a lot of 'who did you room with in college?' If you are in the middle of it, it's wonderful; if not, it's intimidating." According to another person, Piper social life "tends to be like the undergraduate fraternity-type of activities: beer–in–one–hand–with–khaki–pants–on kind of gathering."

training

Though hard-working, Piper is not intense and high-pressured. It provides a fairly supportive and structured work environment. The firm sponsors a full range of formal training, especially in the litigation department. Litigation associates participate in mock depositions, oral arguments, and trials. "You get as much courtroom experience as you can expect during the first year at a big firm, and Piper is very good about providing mock training sessions," said one person. A few first-year associates try their own cases, and most associates begin to manage cases by their fourth year at the firm.

organized summer program

The summer program is also "well-coordinated." Each summer associate is assigned to both a partner and associate mentor and rotates through different departments at the firm. One lawyer in each department is responsible for overseeing summer associate assignments. This system eliminates most coordination problems and usually protects summer associates from being overworked. One summer, after a number of the summer associates received poor mid-term evaluations for their writing skills, the firm hired a writing tutor. Most summer associates work directly with senior associates and occasionally with partners. The summer social life is also well-organized and revolves around softball games, summer outings, and informal get-togethers.

good place for women

When it comes to women, Piper "has a reputation for being conservative, but they don't like this reputation, and they are trying to be as progressive as possible, but not radical," said one person. Everyone we interviewed said Piper is a good place for women to work. A number of women are members of the hiring committee, and Sheila Vidmar is the firm's hiring attorney. The firm is flexible with family leave arrangements and is "very good about cracking down" on inappropriate comments, commented one contact.

Piper's offices are located on Charles Street, right outside Baltimore's Inner Harbor area. The firm has a very good lease, and its overhead is comparatively low for a "prime piece of real estate," noted one observer. The office decor is "gorgeous," and the second floor displays an art collection worth more than two million dollars. Every associate has an individual office with a computer. As evidenced by the litigation management system, Piper emphasizes "cutting-edge" technology. The computer system is fully networked and modern. Piper's in-house cafeteria includes refrigerators stocked with free sodas and juices.

hiring tips

The firm's recruitment practices reflect what one person described as a deadlock on the hiring committee. Though many senior partners attended Harvard or Yale law schools and would like to recruit heavily at these schools, many younger attorneys came from local schools and would like to see more students hired from their alma maters. In recent years, the summer classes have been composed of two-thirds law students from the University of Baltimore and the University of Maryland, and one-third from other law schools around the country.

panel callback interview

Piper's callback interview is unique. Students are interviewed by a small panel of the firm's attorneys. The panel interview was described as "pretty friendly—they want to draw you out to see how well you can articulate yourself. They ask you about your classes and which ones you like best. They ask you why you want to work in Baltimore, and what you can contribute to the city. They ask you what your college experience was like, and whether you were active in your community. They want well-rounded attorneys." After the panel interview, applicants typically meet with two or three attorneys individually for additional interviews.

Piper & Marbury is a firm steeped in history and tradition that brings the first-year law student's introductory constitutional law course to life. This forward-looking firm also seeks to keep abreast of modern trends in business and technology and offers a strong national practice in Baltimore. Although there is more emphasis on the bottom line today at Piper than in the past and "perhaps less institutional loyalty these days than at other, smaller firms because of this," it is still the case that "the firm's 'culture' (*i.e.* hardworking, yet friendly, sociable, and non-cuthroat generally) is a lure to both clients and lawyers at other local firms who would love to come here," according to one firm enthusiast. If this appeals to you, plus being a stone's throw from the fabled Camden Yards Stadium, home of the Baltimore Orioles, then perhaps Piper & Marbury is your firm.

Semmes, Bowen & Semmes

Baltimore Hagerstown Salisbury Towson Washington Wilmington

Address: 250 West Pratt Street, Baltimore, MD 21201
Telephone: (410) 539–5040
Hiring Attorney: Steve McCloskey
Contact: Andrea Bremer, Professional Personnel Coordinator; (410) 576–4803
Associate Salary: First year $51,000 (1997)
Summer Salary: $950/week (1997)
Average Hours: NA worked; NA billed; 1850 required
Family Benefits: 6–8 weeks paid maternity leave (8 unpaid)
1996 Summer: Class of 3 students; offers to 1
Partnership: 42% of entering associates from 1978–1983 were made partner
Pro Bono: 5–10% of all work is pro bono

Semmes, Bowen & Semmes in 1997
80 Lawyers at the Baltimore Office
0.9 Associate Per Partner

Total Partners 36			Total Associates 44			Practice Areas	
Women	7	19%	Women	14	32%	Litigation	31
All Minorities	0	0%	All Minorities	0	0%	Worker's Comp. & Emp. Liab	27
						Corporate	9
						Labor/Employment	6
						Real Estate/Health Care	4
						Insurance & Regulatory	3
						Maritime & Commerce	3
						Prof. Malpractice	3
						Semmes Public Affairs	3
						Tax/Estates & Trusts	3
						Transportation	3
						Environmental	2
						Family Law	2
						International	1

economic upheaval

The 1990s have not been kind to Semmes, Bowen & Semmes. The firm experienced a major upheaval in 1992 when most of its labor department, one of its highly profitable practice groups, left the firm, taking with it much of its business. More recently Semmes went through a significant downsizing, "when a number of attorneys left or were separated from the firm, and the firm cut back its administrative staff." Semmes presently employs approximately 80 attorneys, down considerably from 135 attorneys in 1994. Although starting salaries "have been increased to $51,000," this figure is still lower than the salary of $52,000 that the firm used to pay first-year associates prior to its economic difficulties. The firm has, however, recently opened offices in Hagerstown and Salisbury, Maryland, and Wilmington, Delaware, and the partners have restructured their relationship "by merging the former individual professional corporations into one firmwide professional corporation."

practice areas

Semmes has "rebuilt its labor practice, adding two principals and several associates within the past two years." In addition, the firm does litigation, environmental, corporate, and bankruptcy work, and is known for its insurance defense work and its worker compensation practice. The firm's legislative practice has grown, and there is a developing intellectual property practice with expertise in both litigation and planning.

Semmes is developing an international practice with an emphasis on the Pacific Rim and Europe. It has also worked on the North American Free Trade Agreement. A number of the firm's lawyers have contacts in Asian countries and the firm has hosted foreign interns for years. Though Semmes has a pro bono practice, it is not formally structured. Some people commented, however, that pro bono work is highly encouraged.

little formal training

The work environment at Semmes is flexible and unstructured. The firm is not as rigidly departmentalized as some other law firms. Although Semmes hires new associates into specific departments, to some degree it "allows its associates to mold their practice to fit their needs." Lawyers often work in multiple areas. Summer associates choose their assignments from a pool of projects and work in the areas in which they express interest.

Semmes is not known for its training programs. Summer associates receive little formal training, although they are assigned two mentors at the firm. The firm offers permanent associates a limited number of formal programs, but most training occurs "on-the-job." People noted that opportunities for responsibility can come early to those with initiative. For example, a number of litigators took depositions within their first year and appeared in court in their second and third years, but one source claimed that most of the work involves "writing memos and doing research for the first few years." People also commented that the firm is fairly straightforward in informing associates about their partnership prospects.

view of Camden Yards

Semmes' offices set the tone for the firm's somewhat more relaxed work environment. The office location would be a baseball fan's dream if the view into Camden Yards were not blocked by the scoreboard. Some fortunate attorneys can see three-fourths of the field from their offices. The office also has a balcony on the 19th floor from which one can view the city and the Chesapeake Bay.

conservative dress code

Though Semmes associates do not face much billable hour pressure, the work atmosphere is said to be "businesslike" and the dress code conservative. Most men wear dark blue and gray suits with white shirts. However, the firm has declared every other Friday to be "casual day." Semmes is not known for a singles' social scene, said one person. A number of young, single attorneys work at the firm, but it is not one of the more social firms in the city. Semmes has also cut back on some summer program activities in recent years and does not offer a wine and dine summer experience. Its summer program is presently quite small; in 1996, there were three summer associates, and only one received a permanent associate offer. It has a softball team and a basketball team which "won the lawyer's basketball league for each of the past two years," and sponsors a big crab feast and a big picnic each summer.

women minorities

Semmes received mixed reviews regarding its atmosphere for women. On the one hand, our contacts indicated that a number of women exercise influence at the firm, including prominent lobbyist Maxine Adler. On the other hand, however, one source described many partners as "good old-boys," and another said the firm is not very progressive with respect to its parental leave policies. Not many minority attorneys work at Semmes.

hiring tips

Semmes hires students from a broad range of schools but focuses on local and regional schools. Callback interviews at Semmes usually involve meeting four to five attorneys at the firm and going to lunch. Occasionally the firm conducts full-day interviews in which candidates meet about 10 attorneys. One person advised applicants to emphasize anything in their backgrounds that is interesting and different. "Emphasize the amount of energy you have and ask a lot of questions," one successful applicant advised. "Stress an interest in more than one department and in the city. They really want people who are dedicated to the city and who are willing to set down roots there."

Although in many ways Semmes resembles many of the large, established Baltimore law firms, people we interviewed said that it stands apart in providing a more relaxed and unpretentious atmosphere in which to work. Although it fell on hard times in the early 1990s, Semmes continues to offer flexible practice opportunities.

Venable, Baetjer and Howard

Baltimore McLean Rockville Towson Washington

Address: 1800 Mercantile Bank & Trust Building, 2 Hopkins Plaza, Baltimore, MD 21201
Telephone: (410) 244–7400
Hiring Attorney: C.G. Capute
Contact: Grace Cunningham, Director of Legal Recruitment; (410) 244–7653
Associate Salary: First year $60,000–$70,000; second $61,000–$71,000 (1997)
Summer Salary: $1000/week (1997)
Average Hours: 2000+ worked; 1750 billed; 2200 (combined) required
Family Benefits: Medical, vision, dental
1996 Summer: Class of 20 students; offers to 15
Partnership: NA
Pro Bono: NA

Venable, Baetjer and Howard in 1997
262 Lawyers at the Baltimore Office
1.0 Associate Per Equity Partner

Total Partners 141		
Women	19	13%
All Minorities	2	1%
Afro-Am	2	1%

Total Associates 88		
Women	40	45%
All Minorities	14	16%
Afro-Am	9	10%
Asian Am	4	5%
Latino	1	1%

Practice Areas	
Litigation	85
Business	55
Environmental	18
Intellectual Property	18
Labor	18
Regulatory & Legislative	18
Real Estate	17
Government Contracts	13
Employee Benefits	7
Health Care	7
Creditor's Rights	6
International	4
Public Finance	3

A regional powerhouse, Venable, Baetjer and Howard is ideally poised to service the Washington, D.C.-Baltimore corridor, which one person described as "the fourth-largest city in the country." Venable has the largest D.C. office (about 85 attorneys) of any Baltimore firm. It also has Maryland offices in Towson and Rockville, as well as an office in McLean, Virginia. Because it is "the only firm that has this type of presence...Venable will be a major player" in the region, asserted one contact.

formal atmosphere

Even among the city's most established firms, Venable is known as a "conservative" firm with a somewhat "formal" work atmosphere. Walking into the firm reminded one person of entering a "library." Venable exudes a "very professional feeling." Its attorneys are not particularly outgoing; they are "formal when you first meet them, but after you get to know them they are friendly," said one source. Another contact assured us that the apparent formality at the firm "should not be taken to mean that the firm is somehow stuffy or humorless. Quite to the contrary, I have found the atmosphere at Venable to be friendly and supportive." Venable's conservative atmosphere has, moreover, been tempered somewhat in recent years with the infusion of younger partners into leadership positions, we were told.

practice areas

Venable is "very departmentalized and there is not much interaction among the departments or among the different offices," reported one person. However, a new focus on cross-sectional practice groups, such as gaming and education, has created more of a "legal community" atmosphere at the firm. The firm prides itself on the diversity of its practice, described as a mix of "white-collar, blue-collar, high-tech, and government." Formally, its practice is divided into three areas: litigation/labor, business, and government. Litigation spans the "whole gamut" of matters, including appellate and bankruptcy litigation. The firm also represents a number of pharmaceutical companies and is "nationally known" for its products liability litigation. George Johnson, head of the litigation group, is well known in the labor and employment field. The litigation group is "very hard-working, tough, and competitive," said one person. The business group, however, was described as "happier and more pleasant than the litigation group." The business group houses the firm's corporate tax practice, which is one of the largest in the city and does a lot of work with financial institutions. In the 1980s, Venable had to pay a fine related to its representation of a savings and loan institution.

community involvement

Venable is known for its high-profile government connections and Baltimore community involvement. Though most of the firm's government work is handled in the D.C. office, many of the Baltimore lawyers maintain extensive contacts in politics, the government, and the judiciary. Partner Benjamin Civiletti served as Attorney General in the Carter Administration and is one of the firm's major rainmakers. He works in both the D.C. and Baltimore offices. Prominent partner Bill Quarles was nominated to the federal bench under President Bush and is now a judge on the Baltimore City Circuit Court. John P. Sarbanes, son of Senator Sarbanes, also practices at the firm, as does Elizabeth Hughes, the daughter of former Maryland Governor Hughes. The firm has an active pro bono practice. Venable attorneys are involved in numerous community organizations such as Paul's Place, a local soup kitchen. The firm has formed a partnership with Black Charities and Morgan State University to promote economic development.

training

Venable offers a series of formal training programs for its permanent associates. The firm also recently instituted a Preceptor program in which "every entry level associate is assigned to a partner or senior associate who is responsible for that associate's training for the first two years at the firm," according to a firm spokesperson. As part of the program, the billable hours expected from new associates is 1700; 300 hours are expected to be spent in training programs or under the tutelage of one's preceptor. Our contacts noted that the smaller branch offices offer much greater responsibility than the Baltimore office. Some complained that junior associates in the Baltimore office do a lot of grunt work, and that most associates do not get to court until their third or fourth years. Others praised the firm for the opportunities for early responsibility, with one new litigation associate informing us that "I have already taken depositions on my own and traveled to Tokyo and Hong Kong to assist in conducting interviews." Business associates tend to receive more responsibility earlier, perhaps because, as one insider observed, the work is "shorter-paced and quicker." People also criticized the summer associate work assignments. "Much of what you do is not particularly substantive. There is a lot of Blue Booking and editing textbooks," complained one contact, who warned that junior associates "do this stuff, too."

disorganized summer program

Although most aspects of Venable are highly structured, people we interviewed complained that the summer program is unstructured and disorganized. While formally the summer program is coordinated by partner John Roberts, and summer assignments are to be allocated among summer associates by program coordinators, we received some complaints about the actual workings of the system. One past summer associate commented that "no formal orientation program exists for summer associates, and they do not rotate through departments. All summer projects are compiled in a central assignment book, and summer associates are individually responsible for obtaining work." Another added "before I arrived, no one told me how assignments were handed out. They are assigned on an *ad hoc* basis, and the firm does not make any effort to accommodate what you want to do." Though some liked the flexibility of the summer program, others found the assignment system somewhat overwhelming. You must "hit the ground running," cautioned one person. Venable does, however, provide a structured feedback system for summer associates. Every attorney for whom a summer associate works writes a detailed two-page memo evaluating the summer associate's work. Summer associates receive midsummer and final evaluations.

Because Venable's atmosphere appears formal to the newcomer, it is hard for summer associates to become socially integrated into the firm. "The Baltimore office is not a place where you walk in as a summer associate and people say, 'hi.' It's very formal," commented one source. Another observed that the "D.C. office is much different. It's friendly and the associates go out to bars together" after work. Although Venable is not a party firm, it provides one of Baltimore's more "lavish" summer programs, according to people we interviewed. Summer activities include parties, shows, baseball games, and crab feasts.

office decor

Venable's office facilities, which are located in an approximately 25-year-old building four blocks from the Inner Harbor, also contribute to the firm's formal atmosphere and "conservative" feel. The offices are decorated in navy blue, browns, and greens. The computer system at the firm was recently upgraded and was described as "excellent." Moreover, Venable was one of the first large firms to have its own Web page, which has won "several awards for both form and content." The firm also has available remote dial-in capability for working at home or on the road and offers "multimedia laptops and multimedia presentation rooms."

Venable is governed by a chairman, Benjamin Civiletti, a managing partner, James Shea, a board of 12 partners, and the partnership. An associates committee, called the legal personnel committee, is "responsible for all non-partner legal stuff." One source claimed that the management is fairly open about financial issues but another expressed "frustration and confusion" regarding the firm's compensation system and associate evaluation process. Although all partners for whom an associate worked during the preceding six months are polled about the associate's performance, the associate receives only a synthesis of this information and is not permitted to actually read the evaluations. This sometimes creates a "situation where the associate is surprised by an evaluation and cannot determine the source of the comments or specifically address performance problems."

committed to advancement of women

With respect to its treatment of women, Venable is "as good as any firm in Baltimore." A number of prominent women work at the firm, including Constance Baker, who is prominent in the health care practice, Elizabeth Hughes, who is well known in the business field, Ariel Vannier in tax, Elizabeth Honeywell in products liability litigation and Jana Carey in labor and employment. In 1996, Venable received the President's Award from the National Association of Woman Lawyers in recognition of their commitment to advancing women within the firm, as well as Network 2000's first "Business 2000 Award" for its commitment to the advancement of women in leadership positions. One person assured us that Venable is "very liberal on parental leave" issues and is one of the "best firms in the city" for lawyers with young children. Terri Turner, a prominent minority attorney at the firm, became in 1995 the firm's first African-American woman partner and was later appointed to the firm's Board of Directors.

hiring tips

Venable hires people who are committed to Baltimore. If you are not from Baltimore, it is important to "know something about the town," one insider explained. "Baltimore is a secondary law market, but a major city. Many of the people who do the hiring are worried that the people they hire will later jump to D.C. They want to make sure new associates will stay in Baltimore and stay with Venable." Though the firm hires a large number of students from local schools, it also hires students from law schools across the country, including Columbia, Duke, Georgetown, Harvard, Penn, Stanford, University of Texas, University of Chicago and the University of Virginia. The interview with Venable is somewhat more rigorous than those at other firms. Most interviews, both on-campus and at the firm, are conducted by pairs of attorneys. At the on-campus interview, attorneys will "go through your résumé line-by-line and ask specific questions about your interests." At the callback, the firm makes an effort to have students interviewed by attorneys from the same law school, college, or city.

Venable's summer program is somewhat disorganized, and many of the attorneys can be socially reserved. Permanent associates are assigned to specific departments and enjoy formal training programs and close friendships with their immediate colleagues. Venable's increased emphasis on technology positions the firm well for the new legal technological market. If you are seeking a firm which has fashioned a comfortable niche as a major player in the Washington, D.C.-Baltimore corridor, Venable may be your choice.

Weinberg & Green

Baltimore

Address: 100 South Charles Street, Baltimore, MD 21201
Telephone: (410) 332–8600
Hiring Attorney: Dana N. Pescosolido
Contact: Jeanne V. Porter, Recruitment Coordinator; (410) 332–8723
Associate Salary: NA
Summer Salary: $1000/week (1997)
Average Hours: 1880 worked; 1700 billed; 1700 required
Family Benefits: Disability; flexible spending account program–dependent care/medical care
1996 Summer: Class of 4 students; offers to 1
Partnership: 43% of entering associates from 1979–1984 were made partner
Pro Bono: 3% of all work is pro bono

Weinberg and Green in 1997
60 Lawyers at the Firm
0.4 Associates Per Partner

Total Partners 42		
Women	7	17%
All Minorities	2	5%
Afro-Am	1	3%
Native Am	1	3%

Total Associates 15		
Women	6	40%
All Minorities	1	7%

Practice Areas	
Litigation	24
Corporate Securities	14
Wills & Estates	8
Banking & Commercial Law	4
Real Estate	4
Labor	3
Tax	2
Employee Benefits	1

Over the past several years, Weinberg experienced significant economic hardship, which led to "several rounds of downsizing." In fact, the firm has contracted by almost fifty percent from 116 lawyers in 1994 to 60 lawyers in 1997. Not surprisingly, this reduction lowered morale at the firm. Even over the past year, Weinberg "downsized quite a bit," one source informed us. Another reported that "although the Baltimore market as a whole has been somewhat unstable over the past several years, I believe that Weinberg has experienced generally greater instability over that time."

open atmosphere

Despite the economic hardship, Weinberg & Green offers a culture and atmosphere unique among the large Baltimore firms. With one of its founders being a prominent Jewish lawyer, Weinberg has been influenced by a nontraditional history. The firm is receptive to hiring lawyers with varied ethnic and religious backgrounds. Weinberg lawyers are "really an open-minded group of people," one insider informed us.

Weinberg is more casual and informal than other large Baltimore firms. "Men don't wear white shirts and red ties, and women do not wear suits to make themselves look like men," said one associate. If you want the IBM atmosphere, go somewhere else." Another contact informed us that "the Weinberg attitude is to get the work done, while being comfortable and having fun doing it." Weinberg is also "a firm where people feel very strongly about their convictions," reported one source. "Those who voice their thoughts" are happiest at Weinberg, agreed another. "It's not a firm for wimps."

practice areas

Unlike some of the more established Baltimore firms, Weinberg does not have a large institutional client base. The firm made its name by representing smaller clients. One contact criticized the firm for its "relatively small, insular client base." Weinberg offers a prominent, broad-based litigation practice spanning a wide variety of areas, including patent, securities, personal injury, medical malpractice, employment, banking, commercial, corporate, and labor litigation. This practice includes some highly-regarded lawyers including Ted Sherbow, one of the firm's top-notch trial lawyers, who has been listed in the *Best Trial Lawyers of America* and was described as a "preeminent First Amendment litigator." Former Judge Al Figinski is the firm's foremost appellate litigator and reputedly can "set the courtroom on fire." Charles Monk, the firm's managing partner, was the lead counsel for the California Executive Life insolvency matter. The firm is said to have a national reputation in insurance and securities litigation. The litigation department, we were told, is "informal" and "lots of fun." Because the firm handles so many small cases, junior associates sometimes get the opportunity to go to court in their first or second years. However, one contact cautioned that "if you are a litigator in search of hours in the courtroom, you will be disappointed here. There is time in court, but it is not prevalent." Weinberg often permits litigation associates to independently handle Maryland District Court cases, but higher court appeals must be supervised by a partner, said one person.

The corporate department is headed by the well-known Harry Shapiro. This department is more "uptight" and "straightforward" than the litigation department and has lately been very busy. According to one insider, "today at Weinberg, the corporate department is the 'place to work.'" The benefits department has a "bad reputation" among associates and has had difficulty retaining them, one source informed us. The banking group has "diminished dramatically" of late (from 20 attorneys in 1994 to four lawyers this year), we were told. Recently, the firm has added partners and senior associates in selected growth areas such as bankruptcy, securities litigation, labor, and has a well-known health care group led by attorney Stephen Sfekas.

Weinberg has a well-organized pro bono practice and a billable hour system that encourages attorneys to do pro bono work. First- and second-year attorneys are required to bill 1800 regular hours per year, plus 100 Management By Objective

(MBO) hours that cover hours billed to pro bono work, community service, and business development. All other attorneys, from third-year associates to partners, are required to bill 1700 hours plus 200 MBO hours. The firm takes contributing to the community "very seriously," observed one source. The firm maintains close ties to organizations such as the Maryland Volunteer Service and the Maryland Lawyers Campaign Against Hunger. In addition to being the lead firm initiating the Lawyers Campaign for the College Bound, Weinberg began its own annual statewide student community service essay scholarship program in 1993 to assist eight high school seniors with college expenses.

training Weinberg has a formal training program for litigators to hone their skills in opening and closing statements and direct- and cross-examination. The firm also provides a formal training program in business development skills. Additionally, the firm sponsors educational classes for young associates in the transactional practices. At Weinberg, those who take the initiative learn the most, said one person, noting that an individual "can slide by and not get training."

salary Weinberg associates work reasonable hours. Lawyers in the litigation group work about five weekend days per month, one source informed us. The corporate and real estate lawyers come to work about two weekend days per month, and the trust and estates lawyers rarely come in on the weekends. Some of our contacts claimed that the salaries for mid- and senior-level associates at Weinberg lag behind those of associates at some other large Baltimore firms. The firm has, however, recently "restructured associate salaries to make them competitive with the top-third of firms in Baltimore," reported one insider.

summer events Weinberg does not offer a "lavish" summer program. Most summer activities are laid-back and informal, such as baseball games, movies, and barbecues. The highlight of the summer is the McCormick Cup, the annual softball series where summer and permanent associates team up against the partners. Although the associates easily win every year, the challenge, one person chuckled, is to delicately throw the second game in the three game series without the partners catching on, so they stay happy and buy the after-game drinks. The firm also throws a cocktail party on the first Friday of each month throughout the year, at which time summer associates can meet the firm's attorneys in a relaxed atmosphere.

diversity Recent summer associate and associate classes have had balanced numbers of women and men and minorities. Weinberg is "very good about allowing people to take family leave. In better economic times, the firm is excellent," one female associate reported. A few years ago, Weinberg appointed partner Harriet Cooperman to head their labor and employment practices. She was reportedly the first female department chair among all the major Baltimore firms.

unusual offices Designed in the early 1980s, Weinberg's offices are unusual. The lights in the office automatically go on and off when you enter and leave a room. The firm also has a few internal offices, which according to one person, are like a "bubble" or a "fishbowl" because they have dark glass windows that prevent the occupant from seeing out, but permit passersby to easily view in. It is not "invasive, but it's not exactly pleasant," said one person. The offices, which had previously spread over four floors, were recently consolidated to two floors so as to "reduce the amount of space we lease in a way that more favorably compares with the smaller number of attorneys at the firm," reported one person. The floors are connected by a spiral staircase and there is a footbridge that connects to the Inner Harbor. The research librarian, Allyn Simon, is "outstanding" and is a "real lifesaver as far as finding material in and out of the library."

Be prepared for a slightly unusual interview process at Weinberg. "Sandwiched" (no pun intended, the source in question assured us) between a series of morning and afternoon interviews is a "lunch" held in the firm's offices, during which time members of the hiring committee drop in randomly to "sit around and schmooze." One associate on the recruitment committee said that the firm assumes that 99 percent of the people it chooses to interview are "top-notch legal students" and that most of the interview selection process is designed to assess whether a particular individual would fit in well with the firm culture. After each interview, the attorneys write evaluations of each student, assessing their professionalism, intellectual ability, and personal impact. Weinberg primarily hires students from Baltimore-area law schools who are in the top 10 to 15 percent of their law school classes.

unique interview format

Weinberg is unusual for a prestigious Baltimore firm. It has smaller clients and offers more responsibility than other firms of similar caliber. This firm also provides a more progressive, casual, and open work atmosphere, and is more committed to public interest work than other large Baltimore firms. Additionally, according to one source, "ethics *never* take a back seat to the bottom line" at Weinberg, a firm at which there is "a heightened awareness of the attorney's responsibility to abide by the letter of the Rules of Professional Conduct."

Whiteford, Taylor & Preston

Baltimore Alexandria Columbia Towson Washington

Address: Seven St. Paul Street, Baltimore, MD 21202–1626
Telephone: (410) 347–8700
Hiring Attorney: Warren N. Weaver, Jonathan Z. May
Contact: Susan Bolyard, Recruitment Administrator; (410) 347–8706
Associate Salary: First year $55,000 (1997); Judicial Clerkship $57,000
Summer Salary: $900/week
Average Hours: 1700 worked; 1615 billed; 1800 required
Family Benefits: Maternity leave
1996 Summer: Class of 5 students; offers to 2
Partnership: NA
Pro Bono: 8–10% of all work is pro bono

Whiteford, Taylor & Preston in 1997
119 Lawyers at the Baltimore Office
0.7 Associates Per Partner

Total Partners 70		
Women	10	14%
All Minorities	3	4%
Afro-Am	3	4%

Total Associates 49		
Women	26	53%
All Minorities	4	8%
Afro-Am	3	6%
Latino	1	2%

Practice Areas	
Banking	na
Bankruptcy	na
Commercial/Bus. Litigation	na
Commercial/Surety/Constr.	na
Community Association	na
Corporate Securities	na
Environmental	na
Estates & Trusts	na
General Litigation	na
Government Affairs	na
Health Care	na
Medical Malpractice	na
Product Liability	na
Real Estate	na
Tax	na

Although it has grown rapidly over the years, Whiteford, Taylor & Preston has maintained a friendly and informal atmosphere. One Whiteford associate commented that many Baltimore firms are "stuck-up, and others think they are God's gift to law." By contrast, Whiteford is "laid-back and is one of the fun places to work." Everyone we interviewed described Whiteford as a chatty, social, and casual firm. "Loud ties" and "double breasted" suits are acceptable. Women actually "dare to wear pants" to work, said one person. Fridays are casual dress days at the firm.

top-notch litigation

Founded in 1933 as an insurance defense firm, Whiteford is now reputedly one of two or three top litigation firms in the city. Dick and Bill Whiteford, sons of the firm's founder, are two of Whiteford's more prominent litigators. "Bill is probably one of the best malpractice defense lawyers in the state, and Dick is a very well-regarded business litigator," raved one person. The litigation practice is organized in a number of subgroups. The insurance defense group is among Baltimore's best and is said to be one of the most "laid-back at the firm." The products liability group is strong and makes Whiteford "one of the main defense firms involved in asbestos litigation." The commercial litigation group, headed by name partner Wilbur "Woody" Preston, is well-known for its antitrust, securities, and environmental work. Preston, also the chairperson of the firm, was asked to serve on a federal commission examining failed savings and loan institutions. The commercial litigation group has represented the Marriott Corporation in disputes with creditors and bondholders. The commercial litigators form an "extremely bright and hard-working group of people." One source called them "straight, narrow, and uptight." Whiteford also handles medical malpractice, surety, construction, transportation, and bankruptcy litigation.

significant experience

One associate claimed that Whiteford "is better than any other big firm in town as far as getting into court." It is not unusual for associates in general litigation to appear in court within their first year. The commercial litigation group, however, tends to handle much larger cases than the other litigation groups, and its associates often do not go to court until their third or fourth years.

business practice

In addition to the litigation practice, Whiteford has a large business department that is organized in corporate securities, banking, real estate, estates and trusts, community associations, bankruptcy, health care, and tax groups. The corporate securities practice principally involves counseling and some transactional work, noted several contacts. This group represents many small and medium-sized clients and offers associates early responsibility, they said. Whiteford recently opened an office in Columbia, in Howard County, to take advantage of the sizeable growth in high-tech firms in that area.

pro bono

Whiteford is also known for its pro bono practice, which has been recognized for its excellence by the local and federal courts. Whiteford is connected to eight major organizations in Baltimore, including the Maryland Volunteer Lawyer Service and the House of Ruth. The firm provides a variety of services in areas including, among others, domestic violence, disability law, and children's law.

summer assignments

Whiteford hires new associates into specific departments. Most people get their top choice, but there are no assurances. A summer coordinator assigns projects to summer associates. People commented that Whiteford is good at providing summer associates with projects in their areas of interest. The firm also allows summer associates to rotate through its D.C. and Towson offices. One insider observed that the Towson office is "very relaxed and fun. You get all the benefits of a small and big firm and none of the drawbacks. It was a very good experience."

training

Whiteford does not provide extensive formal training, but it does offer a few in-house training and continuing legal education programs. The firm has a formal feedback system. Each summer associate receives an evaluation for each project completed. The evaluation covers approximately fifteen different topics, including ability to handle crisis situations, writing and research ability, timeliness, thoroughness, and conscientiousness. Summer associates receive mid- and end-of-summer reviews. Permanent associates receive semi-annual evaluations.

Whiteford is not a sweatshop, and its associates do not face severe billable hour pressure. The minimum billable hour target of around 1800 is, however, more rigorously enforced than in the past and serves as a "benchmark for bonuses," one person informed us. Another commented that the firm has placed increasing emphasis on entrepreneurial skills in its partnership evaluations: "the focus is moving toward how entrepreneurial you are and what kind of business you develop. Some have been made partners in the past who were not go-getters. This isn't as true anymore. They are getting to the point where those people who aren't going to make it are informed very early in the game." Another contact informed us that associates are both "encouraged and supported in marketing efforts" to assist in their entrepreneurial work.

diversity

Whiteford provides a "very good" atmosphere for women, and they are "involved in all stages of the firm's operation." One person noted that the hiring committee is almost evenly divided between women and men. People also praised Whiteford's commitment to racial diversity. The firm's three African-American partners work in the products liability subgroup. One of these partners is the co-chair of the hiring committee.

management

Unlike many large Baltimore firms, Whiteford has not been besieged by associate layoffs, though it has cut back on social events. The firm is run by a three partner management committee, a 15 partner executive committee, and 15 subcommittees composed of both partners and associates. In addition, the "real associates committee," originally established by the associates to protest the partners formation of an associates committee comprised entirely of partners, has input into firm management.

Whiteford's offices were described as modern and tastefully decorated in "muted colors." The firm has recently completed installing a state-of-the-art computer system. All secretaries and paralegals at all of Whiteford's offices are linked to networked work stations.

unique interviews

Whiteford primarily hires its summer associates from the top 10 percent of their classes at the Universities of Baltimore and Maryland. It also draws upon law schools such as Georgetown, George Washington, Emory, the University of Virginia and William & Mary. Whiteford places a premium on hiring people from Baltimore. Those who are not from the area will probably be asked questions about their reasons for wanting to work in Baltimore. Whiteford has a unique interview system. Rather than having a scheduled set of interviews in individual attorneys' offices, applicants interview in the same room, where they meet five to 10 attorneys who drop in over the course of an hour and a half. One insider noted that most of the attorneys asked interview questions from a prepared list, such as "What are your favorite subjects in law school?" and "Why do you want to work at Whiteford?"

The people we interviewed said that one of the best reasons to choose Whiteford over other large Baltimore firms is the early responsibility that it offers. Others commented on the "friendly atmosphere at the firm." People also praised the firm's litigation and pro bono practices. There were complaints, however, about compensation. One person observed that, at Whiteford, you get "less pay, but the same hour requirements, as at comparably sized firms." Still, the overall tenor of comments on the firm was very positive. Motivated students with an interest in or connections to Baltimore will find Whiteford a good firm to be at.

Boston

Law Firms Ranked By Associates Per Partner

1.	BROWN, RUDNICK, FREED & GESMER	0.5
2.	PEABODY & ARNOLD	0.6
3.	SHERBURNE, POWERS & NEEDHAM	0.6
4.	GOULSTON & STORRS	0.8
5.	HILL & BARLOW	0.8
6.	SULLIVAN & WORCESTER	0.8
7.	BURNS & LEVINSON	0.9
8.	FISH & RICHARDSON	1.1
9.	NUTTER, MCCLENNEN & FISH	1.1
10.	FOLEY, HOAG & ELIOT	1.2
11.	HALE AND DORR	1.2
12.	MINTZ, LEVIN, COHN, FERRIS, GLOVSKY AND POPEO	1.2
13.	PALMER & DODGE	1.2
14.	BINGHAM, DANA & GOULD	1.3
15.	CHOATE, HALL & STEWART	1.3
16.	ROPES & GRAY	1.3
17.	GOODWIN, PROCTER & HOAR	1.7
18.	TESTA, HURWITZ & THIBEAULT	2.6

Law Firms Ranked by Percentage of Associates Who Make Partner
(over varying years)

1.	SHERBURNE, POWERS & NEEDHAM	90
2.	BROWN, RUDNICK, FREED & GESMER	42
3.	SULLIVAN & WORCESTER	31
4.	MINTZ, LEVIN, COHN, FERRIS, GLOVSKY AND POPEO	29
5.	GOODWIN, PROCTER & HOAR	28
6.	NUTTER, MCCLENNEN & FISH	27
7.	ROPES & GRAY	26
8.	CHOATE, HALL & STEWART	24
9.	TESTA, HURWITZ & THIBEAULT	20
10.	PALMER & DODGE	18
11.	BINGHAM, DANA & GOULD	17
12.	HALE AND DORR	14
13.	PEABODY & ARNOLD	9
14.	BURNS & LEVINSON	NA
15.	FISH & RICHARDSON	NA
16.	FOLEY, HOAG & ELIOT	NA
17.	GOULSTON & STORRS	NA
18.	HILL & BARLOW	NA

Law Firms Ranked by Percentage of Pro Bono Work

1.	GOULSTON & STORRS	8
2.	CHOATE, HALL & STEWART	5-7
3.	FOLEY, HOAG & ELIOT	5
4.	NUTTER, MCCLENNEN & FISH	5
5.	SHERBURNE, POWERS & NEEDHAM	5
6.	HILL & BARLOW	4.5
7.	BINGHAM, DANA & GOULD	4-5
8.	ROPES & GRAY	4
9.	PALMER & DODGE	3-5
10.	SULLIVAN & WORCESTER	3
11.	HALE AND DORR	2.7
12.	BROWN, RUDNICK, FREED & GESMER	2-3
13.	GOODWIN, PROCTER & HOAR	2
14.	MINTZ, LEVIN, COHN, FERRIS, GLOVSKY AND POPEO	2
15.	TESTA, HURWITZ & THIBEAULT	1.6
16.	BURNS & LEVINSON	NA
17.	FISH & RICHARDSON	NA
18.	PEABODY & ARNOLD	NA

Law Firms Ranked by Percentage of Female Partners

1.	SULLIVAN & WORCESTER	21
2.	GOULSTON & STORRS	19
3.	FOLEY, HOAG & ELIOT	18
4.	HILL & BARLOW	18
5.	MINTZ, LEVIN, COHN, FERRIS, GLOVSKY AND POPEO	18
6.	NUTTER, MCCLENNEN & FISH	18
7.	PEABODY & ARNOLD	17
8.	CHOATE, HALL & STEWART	16
9.	GOODWIN, PROCTER & HOAR	16
10.	SHERBURNE, POWERS & NEEDHAM	16
11.	BROWN, RUDNICK, FREED & GESMER	15
12.	ROPES & GRAY	15
13.	HALE AND DORR	13
14.	PALMER & DODGE	13
15.	TESTA, HURWITZ & THIBEAULT	13
16.	BINGHAM, DANA & GOULD	11
17.	BURNS & LEVINSON	11
18.	FISH & RICHARDSON	8

Law Firms Ranked by Percentage of Female Associates

1.	PALMER & DODGE	54
2.	GOULSTON & STORRS	50
3.	SHERBURNE, POWERS & NEEDHAM	48
4.	BURNS & LEVINSON	47
5.	NUTTER, MCCLENNEN & FISH	47
6.	TESTA, HURWITZ & THIBEAULT	47
7.	MINTZ, LEVIN, COHN, FERRIS, GLOVSKY AND POPEO	45
8.	BINGHAM, DANA & GOULD	43
9.	GOODWIN, PROCTER & HOAR	41
10.	HILL & BARLOW	41
11.	BROWN, RUDNICK, FREED & GESMER	40
12.	CHOATE, HALL & STEWART	40
13.	ROPES & GRAY	40
14.	FOLEY, HOAG & ELIOT	37
15.	FISH & RICHARDSON	35
16.	PEABODY & ARNOLD	35
17.	HALE AND DORR	34
18.	SULLIVAN & WORCESTER	34

Law Firms Ranked by Percentage of Minority Partners

1.	PEABODY & ARNOLD	5
2.	FISH & RICHARDSON	4
3.	FOLEY, HOAG & ELIOT	4
4.	GOODWIN, PROCTER & HOAR	4
5.	BURNS & LEVINSON	3
6.	CHOATE, HALL & STEWART	3
7.	HALE AND DORR	3
8.	PALMER & DODGE	3
9.	BROWN, RUDNICK, FREED & GESMER	2
10.	HILL & BARLOW	2
11.	ROPES & GRAY	2
12.	SULLIVAN & WORCESTER	2
13.	TESTA, HURWITZ & THIBEAULT	2
14.	BINGHAM, DANA & GOULD	1
15.	GOULSTON & STORRS	1
16.	MINTZ, LEVIN, COHN, FERRIS, GLOVSKY AND POPEO	1
17.	NUTTER, MCCLENNEN & FISH	0
18.	SHERBURNE, POWERS & NEEDHAM	0

Law Firms Ranked By Percentage of Minority Associates

1.	BROWN, RUDNICK, FREED & GESMER	13
2.	FISH & RICHARDSON	12
3.	FOLEY, HOAG & ELIOT	10
4.	MINTZ, LEVIN, COHN, FERRIS, GLOVSKY AND POPEO	10
5.	PEABODY & ARNOLD	10
6.	ROPES & GRAY	10
7.	GOODWIN, PROCTER & HOAR	9
8.	GOULSTON & STORRS	9
9.	BINGHAM, DANA & GOULD	8
10.	HILL & BARLOW	7
11.	NUTTER, MCCLENNEN & FISH	7
12.	BURNS & LEVINSON	6
13.	HALE AND DORR	6
14.	SULLIVAN & WORCESTER	6
15.	PALMER & DODGE	5
16.	SHERBURNE, POWERS & NEEDHAM	4
17.	TESTA, HURWITZ & THIBEAULT	4
18.	CHOATE, HALL & STEWART	3

Bingham, Dana & Gould

Boston Hartford Washington
London

Address: 150 Federal Street, Boston, MA 02110
Telephone: (617) 951–8000
Hiring Attorney: Sula R. Fiszman
Contact: Maris L. Abbene, Director of Recruitment; (617) 951–8556
Associate Salary: First year $79,000 (1997)
Summer Salary: $1500/week (1997)
Average Hours: 1973 worked; 1944 billed; NA required.
Family Benefits: Emergency childcare center on site; maternity and paternity leave; dependent care and medical care assistance plans
1996 Summer: Class of 25 2L students; offers to 25
Partnership: 17% of entering associates from 1980–1988 were made partner
Pro Bono: 4–5% of all work is pro bono

Bingham, Dana & Gould (firmwide) in 1997
247 Lawyers at the Firm
1.3 Associates Per Partner

Total Partners 95		
Women	10	11%
All Minorities	1	1%
Latino	1	1%

Total Associates 127		
Women	55	43%
All Minorities	10	8%
Afro-Am	2	2%
Asian-Am	6	5%
Latino	2	2%

Practice Areas	
Litigation	61
High Tech/Entrepreneurial	32
Banking/Bankruptcy	26
Real Estate/Project Finance	25
M&A/Specialized Finance	21
Investment Management	15
Tax	11
Probate	9

Bingham, Dana & Gould is one of Boston's top law firms, boasting such high-profile clients as the Boston Red Sox, the New England Patriots, the Bank of Boston and the *Boston Globe.* The firm celebrated its centennial in 1991. Bingham has a "very old-line tradition which carries over into the firm culture, but not more so than the other long established Boston firms," stated one source. Bingham tends to be more low-key than its competitors, and a number of people found it to be more "honest" and straightforward. One source remarked, "It's a place where people work hard, but have less of an attitude and less arrogance than at some of the other well-known firms in Boston. This is a plus in the way associates are treated by partners and, in general, in the way the firm operates. There is less a sense that we are the best and the greatest in the world. Bingham combines excellent lawyers with a more down-to-earth attitude."

hard working atmosphere

The firm's solid reputation comes from the high quality of its lawyers and from its work ethic: "They are very honest about the fact that they work hard and expect people to work hard." The resulting environment is "businesslike," according to one person. Another observed that "it is quite common for attorneys to informally walk into each others' offices (both partners and associates) to bounce ideas off each other and share tips and techniques learned in one situation that might be helpful in another."

practice areas

Bingham began as an admiralty law firm, but its practice has expanded considerably over the years. The two largest departments are business and litigation. Jack Curtin, the former president of the American Bar Association, is a major litigation partner and rainmaker. Like all firm departments, the litigation group is divided into "teams."

People commended Bingham's First Amendment team as being one of the best in the city if not the country; among its high-profile clients is the *Boston Globe*. Although it is very difficult to get hired by this team, one person commented that "if you are aggressive, you can do it." Bingham also has a strong white-collar crime practice. In addition, Steve Hansen, a former branch chief of the Securities and Exchange Commission (SEC), is a prominent securities litigator. The business department, led by partner Justin Morreale, includes a strong banking and financial institutions practice, which represents a number of large institutional clients (such as Bank of Boston), and has an extensive investment company practice (representing companies such as Citibank, N.A.'s proprietary mutual funds—The Landmark Funds). Bingham's venture capital and emerging company practice is one of the fastest-growing and the largest at the firm. With its London office established in 1973, Bingham has a significant international corporate practice for a New England firm, we were told. Bingham is also expanding its work in Latin America and elsewhere.

The firm's pro bono practice is headed by Neal Rosen and Marijane Benner Browne. Bingham sponsors a broad variety of pro bono projects and pro bono hours are credited as billable hours. In addition, the firm pays full salary for two people each year to do six-month rotations at Greater Boston Legal Services and for 12 attorneys each year to spend one month at the Plymouth County District Attorney's office.

structured environment

Bingham is a highly structured and "well-run" law firm. Beginning associates are hired specifically into one of the major departments. Those who enter the business area are not immediately assigned to one of the five business "teams," but instead are part of a "pool," giving them the opportunity to experience a variety of work. Associates are assigned to a team after their second year. Summer associates generally rotate through two of the firm's departments and gain exposure to a number of practice teams. Typically, students split their time between business and litigation, but they also may select smaller practice areas. Everyone agreed that the summer program is well-run: "All the attorneys who worked on the summer program were good people and were very receptive to students' concerns. They went out of their way to make it pleasant." The program is not lavish, however: "There were lunches twice a week and every now and then a dinner and a cocktail hour. There were a number of get-togethers at different people's houses. The social activities did not seem excessive. It was the right amount."

extensive training

With a full range of formal training programs, Bingham is committed to the development of its associates. The opportunities for associate responsibility are somewhat limited in litigation but not so in business, "where significant responsibility and client contact are available from the start," observed one source. A second contact observed that "most cases are handled by partners and associates working side by side." Also, junior associates can assume nearly full responsibility for pro bono cases. Bingham has an extensive formal evaluation system. Summer associates receive mid- and end-of-summer reviews, and associates are reviewed annually (except first years, who are reviewed every six months). Most summer associates thought the feedback was good. One commented that Bingham "was very up front about their expectations and what they thought the outcome would be. If you performed in a certain way, you could expect an offer." Another person observed that "Bingham expects to be able to offer a permanent position to everyone in the summer associate program."

management

Bingham has a fairly young, entrepreneurial managing committee, led by the dynamic managing partner Jay Zimmerman. The firm's increased focus on marketing and a strong economy has led to a significant increase in work and hiring. Additionally, Bingham recently acquired a substantial portion of a Hartford firm, following an earlier acquisition of a portion of a D.C. firm. Amidst all this growth, one source observed that Bingham is "not over-expanding its practice even though the economy has picked up." Another person remarked that the partners "care about the associates, their workload and their career development." One of the few complaints we heard concerned the firm's benefits package which does not include 401(K) matching and offers only an expensive family insurance plan.

diversity

The female partners at Bingham have met in the past to discuss the difficulties and challenges facing women in the legal profession. One woman remarked that it was "refreshing to hear people acknowledge that the legal profession has a male culture and that there are difficulties with that. Bingham was very up front about the fact that there are problems, and it was refreshing that people were thinking about it. I give them high marks for doing this." One source pointed out that some women partners work part-time and another noted that there are women in influential and high-profile positions. The firm provides on-site emergency day care. People had positive views about Bingham's treatment of racial minorities. The firm "made a real effort to try to get people of color into the summer program," stated one source.

Bingham's offices were described as comfortable, but not "plush or fancy." The firm has plans to refurbish the offices, including the addition of a cafeteria, another floor and more conference rooms. All attorneys have window offices, which vary in size "depending upon how important you are." Bingham reportedly has "one of the biggest private libraries in Boston." The firm has a Windows-based computer system, with networked access to a number of CD-ROM libraries, desktop Westlaw and LEXIS, e-mail, and remote access to word processing.

hiring tips

Bingham hires its summer associates from a broad range of schools. Most applicants are from New England or attend Boston law schools, but there are a number from Ivy League and other well-known eastern law schools, such as New York University. Although Bingham is among the most competitive Boston firms, one successful applicant suggested that candidates from top law schools need not be academic standouts to get offers. Interviews at Bingham are relaxed. Callback interviews, which usually involve meeting four attorneys, were described as "pleasant chats." One source reported that "they are just trying to see if you would fit in and whether you have a personality." Bingham doesn't "look for one mold of person," remarked another insider. Instead, it seeks "all different types with different backgrounds."

Brown, Rudnick, Freed & Gesmer

Boston Hartford Providence

Address: One Financial Center, Boston, MA 02111
Telephone: (617) 856-8200
Hiring Attorney: William R. Baldiga
Contact: Martha Mueller, Human Resources Director; (617) 856-8337
Associate Salary: First year $76,000 (1997); second $80,000; third $85,000; fourth $90,000; fifth $95,000; sixth $100,000; seventh $100,000; 7+years $100,000
Summer Salary: $1403/week (1997)
Average Hours: 2100+ worked; 2010 billed; 2000 required
Family Benefits: 8 weeks paid maternity leave; unpaid family leave up to 12 weeks; emergency day care; dependent medical insurance (90% funded)
1996 Summer: Class of 8 students; offers to 7
Partnership: 42% of entering associates from 1978–1989 were made partner
Pro Bono: 2-3% of all work is pro bono

Brown, Rudnick, Freed & Gesmer in 1997
85 Lawyers at the Boston Office
0.5 Associates Per Partner

Total Partners 55			Total Associates 30			Practice Areas	
Women	8	15%	Women	12	40%	Corporate	26
All Minorities	1	2%	All Minorities	4	13%	Litigation	21
Afro-Am	1	2%	Afro-Am	2	7%	Real Estate	20
			Asian Am	2	7%	Banking & Finance	13
						Health Care	4
						Sports Law	1

Brown, Rudnick, Freed & Gesmer was founded in the 1940s by four Jewish men who set out "to form a firm that was different from the typical WASP firm." For many years, Brown Rudnick was known as a "Jewish firm," although it is now considerably more "diverse." The firm's history continues to shape its culture and, in particular, its management. Compared with other Boston firms, Brown Rudnick is known for its inclusiveness and openness. There is a "low level of hierarchy" at Brown Rudnick, and there are bi-weekly departmental meetings and regular partner-associate luncheon meetings where a wide variety of issues are discussed. "They let it all hang out, and there is a commitment to having everyone involved in decisions. It's very democratic," reported one person. A second contact observed that there are "very open relationships among the partners and associates can speak their minds."

practice areas

Brown Rudnick historically has been best known for its real estate practice. Joel Reck, 1996 President of the Boston Bar Association and head of the department, was described as "fascinating and funny;" the entire group has "a great sense of humor." Recently, however, bankruptcy, creditors' rights and banking have been "the fastest growing" areas at the firm, and the firm's litigation and business practices also have become more prominent. The litigation department, which represents the Commonwealth of Massachusetts in seeking to recover medicaid expenses from the tobacco industry, has grown considerably. The business department handles a broad range of work, including structured finance, securitization, and Securities and Exchange Commission work. Brown Rudnick has also developed a major health care practice over the past several years, and has more recently added a sports law practice. In addition, the firm's Hartford and Providence offices have expanded of late. Brown Rudnick's pro bono efforts are "loosely" coordinated by a pro bono committee that issues a newsletter. Although some attorneys are very "committed" to pro bono work, we received mixed opinions on how much of its resources the firm devotes to pro bono.

modern management

Brown and Rudnick is "run like a business from the financial point of view." One person opined that Brown Rudnick is "very well managed. They're very conscious of the economic issues that face the profession, and they recognize that the days of the good old-boy law firms have passed by." Another contact praised the significant "time and effort devoted to business planning" at the firm, which includes "training in marketing, etc. for both associates and partners." With a self-proclaimed "conservative" management philosophy, Brown Rudnick has avoided the financial problems that have plagued some of the more expansion-minded Boston firms. Most people thought that the firm has focused more on the "bottom line" in recent years, with one contact complaining that the "firm places too much emphasis on achieving at least 2,000 billable hours per year."

family atmosphere

To date, however, the no-nonsense approach apparently has not affected Brown Rudnick's working environment. By Boston standards, the firm is not particularly intense; it has a cordial atmosphere and "people care about their lives outside of work." One contact observed that "there are many young attorneys who are starting families and have young children. A few female partners and associates work reduced hour schedules to spend more time with their kids. Moreover, the firm does not emphasize formal get-togethers. Most summer activities, such as softball games and golf outings, are casual. Recent summer classes have participated in "Outward Bound" programs.

associate development

Brown Rudnick provides an in-house training program consisting of weekly seminars taught by outside consultants, as well as by experienced lawyers and paralegals at the firm. In addition, the firm has an associate-mentor program. All summer and first through fourth year associates are assigned mentors who are responsible for their professional development. Although mentors technically supervise summer workloads, one person suggested that "in reality, you can get projects through anyone." Another person remarked that "the partners go out of their way to help young associates. They are committed to the mentor program." Brown Rudnick associates frequently have early opportunities for responsibility. As might be expected, most summer and first-year associates "write a lot of memos and do a lot of research," but most associates take on their own matters by their third or fourth years, and some do so as early as their second year. Discerning an atmosphere of "respect" among Brown Rudnick attorneys, one insider noted that even summer associates can make a significant contribution to a matter. The firm has a two-tiered, seven-year partnership track, with both equity and salaried partners. "People understand what the track for partner is like and what you have to do," claimed one source. "There is a general sense that if you do good work at the firm, it will be fair to you."

diversity

There are eight female partners in the firm. Barbara Lenk, a former litigation partner and member of the firm's policy committee, left the firm in 1993 to become a Superior Court Judge and now sits on the Appeals Court. One woman commented that there are some "extremely supportive women; I felt like the women there take an interest in the other women at the firm." There are a number of women on the hiring committee. Most agreed that Brown has a "strong commitment to diversity;" recently the firm hired laterally an African-American male partner into the corporate department.

Brown Rudnick's offices have a "new," "light and airy" look. Each attorney has an individual office with a window. The offices are located directly across from South Station, near Chinatown.

hiring tips

Brown Rudnick is "extremely concerned with personalities" in its hiring. One source observed that "there is an academic cutoff, but they look for people in terms of compatibility." Another emphasized that "they want a certain attitude—interesting, nice, self-confident, but not aggressive." Although there are a number of "law review" attorneys at Brown Rudnick, such credentials are not at a "premium." One contact suggested that the firm "looks for someone with a little more individuality. There are a number of older, second-career people, and people with interesting and varied backgrounds. They go beyond grades and look for something on your résumé that you don't find on other résumés." Callback interviews, which are "less rigid" by Boston standards, usually involve meeting three to four attorneys, who generally are not much "interested in law school stuff." Unlike many firms, Brown Rudnick often does not take its applicants to lunch; candidates "don't get food until they get hired." People with whom we talked said the firm generally has extended a high percentage of offers. Brown Rudnick hires mainly from Harvard, Boston College, and Boston

University, but also recruits at Columbia, Georgetown, Michigan, Northeastern, NYU, Penn, Suffolk, Northwestern, Chicago, and Yale.

Burns & Levinson

Boston Hingham Wellesley

Address: 125 Summer Street, Boston, MA 02110–1624
Telephone: (617) 345–3000
Hiring Attorney: Raymond E. Baxter
Contact: Christine Mead, Employee Relations Manager; (617) 345–3812
Associate Salary: First year $50,000–$52,000; second $55,000–$60,000; third $60,000–$62,000
Summer Salary: NA
Average Hours: NA
Family Benefits: 8 weeks paid maternity leave (8 unpaid); dependent care and medical care assistance plans
1996 Summer: NA
Partnership: NA
Pro Bono: NA

Burns & Levinson in 1997
110 Lawyers at the Boston Office
0.9 Associates Per Partner

Total Partners 54		
Women	6	11%
All Minorities	2	3%
Asian Am	1	2%
Latino	1	2%

Total Associates 47		
Women	22	47%
All Minorities	3	6%
Asian-Am	3	6%

Practice Areas	
Litigation	45
Business Litigation	19
Intellectual Property	12
Corporate	10
Family/Matrimonial	7
Entertainment	6
Real Estate	6
Trusts & Estates	6
Finance/Bankruptcy	5
Environmental	4
Tax	4
Government Relations	1

Founded in the 1960s, Burns & Levinson is not "an old-line Boston firm" and displays "more of a street-fighter culture that promotes aggressive behavior," we were told. Associates are "expected to work long, hard hours, and the firm does not encourage socializing," said one associate, who noted that "the associates were not so bad, but the partners were humorless." Some departments expect associates to work from 7:00 a.m. to 7:00 p.m. Others informed us that the firm offers "high billables and low pay" compared to other similar Boston firms.

practice areas

Until recently, Burns & Levinson offered one of Boston's strongest litigation practices. In the spring of 1993, one of the firm's biggest litigation rainmakers, Larry Cetrulo, and a number of other litigation partners and associates left the firm. The departures were accompanied by a decrease in business. More recently, in an effort to hold its own, the firm has focused on "acquiring smaller practices," including the absorption of "what was left at Cuddy, Bixby & Lynch." Although litigation has been the firm's forte, Burns & Levinson's practice includes a number of other areas, most notably intellectual property, which was recently bolstered by the addition of the "nationally known patent litigator," D. Dennis Allegretti. Name partner Larry Levinson is a distinguished corporate lawyer.

minimal training

The firm is organized into different sections that have "little interaction" with one another, we were told. Starting associates have "no" choice in their practice area assignments, according to our contacts. The firm disputes this, maintaining that "the entire recruitment process is conducted on a departmental basis." People also complained that Burns & Levinson offers only "minimal" training to its associates. New associates receive a "crash training course," but for the most part they are "thrown into the firm and given assignments," remarked one insider. The firm also offers fairly limited responsibility, and most junior associates do "research and document work," stated one source.

summer program

The earlier edition of *The Insider's Guide* criticized Burns & Levinson's summer program for a number of shortcomings, including lack of professionalism and inattentiveness to summer associates. Current contacts have informed us that the firm no longer has a summer program.

diversity

Burns & Levinson received fairly favorable reviews regarding its atmosphere for women. "There are influential women at the firm," we were told. A number of women at the firm have been pregnant and the firm "seemed to make arrangements," remarked one source. However, no African-Americans work at the firm. Burns & Levinson partners "don't discriminate," but according to one person, they are not particularly "cosmopolitan."

management

Burns & Levinson is run by a management committee composed of a "handful of powerful partners." It has not been immune to the recent economic downturn in Boston, but unlike many other firms, it chose to address its problems by cutting costs rather than laying off associates. In the last few years, associate salaries have been cut. Permanent associate salaries start at $52,000.

Burns & Levinson's office facilities are "spacious" and "nice," with a "slightly contemporary" decor. Each associate has a private office with a "state-of-the-art" computer. The library staff received particularly high reviews, although one person noted that the library resources are somewhat limited.

hiring practices

Burns & Levinson seeks "people who are ready to do a lot of work and put in lots of hours," one insider informed us. A number of sources informed us that, because of its "high turnover rate," the firm does not "have partnership in mind" and hires people whom they can "get a lot out of over a few years time." Callback interviews at Burns & Levinson are "not too hectic," but "some of the partners ask you tough questions that make you think on your feet." Candidates should "not be meek" in their interviews, advised one successful applicant. The firm respects aggressive people who have personal initiative. It sometimes calls applicants back for multiple interviews before making a hiring decision. "They are really [careful] about offers. They want to make sure that many of the attorneys have met you," said one person who was called back to the firm five times and met two or three people on each occasion. Even though the firm has a very extensive hiring process, one person pointed out that "they never feed you" at an interview.

Choate, Hall & Stewart

Boston Manchester

Address: Exchange Place, 53 State Street, Boston, MA 02109
Telephone: (617) 248-5000
Hiring Attorney: Sarah Chapin Columbia
Contact: Lianne Marshall, Director of Recruiting; (617) 248-5000
Associate Salary: First year $76,000 (1997); second $80,000; third $87,000 plus bonus; fourth $95,000 to $100,000
Summer Salary: $1450/week (1997)
Average Hours: 1950 worked; 1850 billed; NA required.
Family Benefits: 10–14 weeks paid maternity leave (4–24 unpaid); 2–6 weeks paid paternity leave (4–24 unpaid); childcare options provided
1996 Summer: Class of 18 students; offers to 17
Partnership: 24% of entering associates from 1979–1987 were made partner
Pro Bono: 5–7% of all work is pro bono

Choate, Hall & Stewart in 1997
165 Lawyers at the Firm
1.3 Associates Per Partner

Total Partners 69		
Women	11	16%
All Minorities	2	3%
Afro-Am	1	1%
Latino	1	1%

Total Associates 89		
Women	36	40%
All Minorities	3	3%
Afro-Am	1	1%
Asian-Am	1	1%
Latino	1	1%

Practice Areas	
Litigation	64
Corporate	40
Tax/Estate Trusts	18
Labor Management	17
Health	15
Real Estate	13
Bankruptcy	8
Patents	7
Environmental Land Use	4
International	2

strong camaraderie

One of Boston's oldest and most prestigious top-tier law firms, Choate, Hall & Stewart is distinguished by the strong "camaraderie" that its associates, particularly the men, share. A fraternity-like atmosphere pervades the firm, said several people. People feel free to poke irreverent fun at each other in Choate Hall's friendly environment. In an annual tradition at the country club outing, new associates perform a skit satirizing the partners. One person remarked that "associates do enjoy socializing together and there is a camaraderie among associates, particularly those who enjoy golf, tennis and other clubby sports," while another source observed that in recent years the firm is not as "fraternity-like as it may have been in the past."

practice areas

Choate Hall is organized around five major departments: business, litigation, real estate, health care, and tax/fiduciary. Litigation is the largest department. Although the practice encompasses a wide range of areas, it mostly handles large, complex cases. Choate Hall also offers a busy corporate practice, which the firm has developed extensively in recent years. Choate Hall's health care practice "is one of the most substantial in the city," asserted one person. The firm's fiduciary department is also especially well-regarded. The firm manages and provides investment counseling to a number of high-volume trusts. Marion Fremont-Smith is well-known in this area. Choate Hall also boasts a "nationally known" charitable foundations practice that represents, among others, the Boston Museum of Fine Arts. Choate Hall's real estate practice is now growing and looking to expand in the future and its bankruptcy practice is also doing well. The bankruptcy practice is reputed to be a particularly "aggressive" and male-dominated group, asserted one insider. You can get "sucked up" in the work in this "rough and tumble practice," agreed another. Choate Hall's labor and employment practice has "grown a lot over the last few years" and has now stabilized, "although it remains popular among incoming associates." One partner, Weld Henshaw, has a small family law practice. The firm also houses a small political consulting group, known as the "Choate Group." Though most Choate Hall attorneys are "supportive" of the firm's pro bono practice "if an associate takes the initiative," there is no "real concerted effort" to develop it, commented one source.

summer program

Summer associates are assigned an advisor who is responsible for assigning projects and supervising the summer associate's work. All advisors attend weekly Monday meetings at which projects are distributed. Each advisor "looks out for" assignments for his or her summer associate. Once the projects are assigned, the summer associate is responsible for approaching the attorney in charge of the matter and completing the assignment. People commented that the advisors did a good job of getting them the type of work in which they were interested and noted that the projects were "real assignments for real clients."

Starting associates may join a particular group or work in two of the firm's departments during their first year at the firm, or longer in some cases. Most rotate through either the litigation or the corporate department, and one smaller department, reported one person. Each department offers junior associates varying responsibilities. Because many litigation cases are large and complex, associates begin with a lot of research and memo writing. In the patent group and some other smaller groups, however, junior associates often have "responsibility for clients right off the bat." One firm enthusiast remarked that, at Choate Hall, "young associates receive numerous opportunities to take on challenging, sophisticated assignments and responsibility."

inadequate training

Choate Hall's assignment and training systems for permanent associates are not presently operating optimally, we were informed. "The assignment system is very haphazard and results in uneven distribution of work" and "the training programs have been inadequate of late and certainly are not on a par with other large firms." Choate Hall is aware of the deficiencies and is taking steps to improve matters. One contact told us that "this past summer the firm implemented a structured partner-associate mentor program to facilitate individualized attention to associates' professional development and training."

committee management

Given its affinity for structure, Choate Hall has "committees for everything," said one person. The committees handle most of the firm's administrative business, while "the Firm Committee makes all the important decisions," reported one source. Many of the firm's routine business decisions, however, are made by a non-lawyer business manager with an MBA degree. A special associates committee provides a formal avenue for communicating associate concerns to the partners, "although members of the committee are *not* chosen by associates."

Choate Hall selected two young attorneys, John Nadas and William Gelnaw, in early 1996 to become the firm's managing partners. This will, according to one insider, "make it easier for the management to stay in tune with current associate issues and developments as a whole." Included in this set of issues is the matter of becoming a partner at the firm. One person informed us that "there were no new partners made this past year, which caused some problems with associate morale, particularly since the associates who were up for partner were very well-liked and well-respected by their fellow associates." Another critical item brought to our attention was compensation: "we received a pay raise but it was not comparable to pay raises received by several of the larger firms." Finally, the "haphazard" training programs and assignment distribution system described above "is one of the biggest complaints of associates." Choate Hall appears to be addressing these concerns, we were were told.

diversity

Choate Hall is "supportive" of the women who work at the firm, commented some individuals. Others noted, however, that some women may feel uncomfortable in the "clubby" and "fraternity" atmosphere at the firm. In the earlier edition of the *Insider's Guide*, we reported that there was a widespread feeling that the firm was "not all that progressive" with respect to parental leave issues. A firm spokesperson informed us recently that Choate Hall has "made changes in its policies within the last two years and they are competitive with others in the city." Moreover, an insider told us that "I recently returned from a six month maternity leave and the firm has been very accommodating of my needs. In particular, I have elected to return to work on a part-time schedule and the firm and the individual lawyers with whom I work have been very flexible in working with me to make my part-time schedule successful." Few racial minorities work at the firm, but Choate Hall is trying hard to change its WASP image. Nevertheless, it has a hard time attracting minorities to the firm, our contacts noted.

offices and staff

Choate Hall's office facilities are "nice," but not "lavish." The decor is "simple and modern," said one source. The firm has a big library, which however is "presently being reduced somewhat to accommodate additional associate offices," and a number of auxiliary libraries conveniently located near the practice groups that use them. The library staff received good reviews. The firm cafeteria, called the "Firm Bite," serves great muffins in the morning, reported one person. We heard a number of complaints regarding various aspects of the office facilities and administrative management. Although each attorney has a private office, some past summer associates have been doubled or tripled up in one office. In addition, we were told that the firm maintains a "tight reign" on its secretarial and paralegal staff. Attorneys must request special permission to obtain overtime help, and these requests are reportedly not always approved. Moreover, "secretary's time is closely monitored; it is even hard to take your secretary out to lunch with your group because they have to rush back," complained one person. Another person noted that the "computer systems are antiquated and the upgrade process is extremely slow."

hiring tips

Choate Hall hires its summer associates from law schools across the country. In the past three summers more than half the summer associates have come from schools outside Boston, including Stanford and Boalt Hall. Choate attorneys "take the interviews very seriously" and "pick very carefully" based on personality, commented another insider. Another insider remarked, however, that "grades have become more important in recent years because of a change in the hiring partner; however, her term is up and the new partner has not been chosen."

Choate Hall offers a wide variety of attractive practice areas. Moreover, it recently opened a new office in Manchester, New Hampshire, led by Jeffrey Howard, the outgoing attorney general of New Hampshire. The New Hampshire office will primarily serve clients with corporate, regulatory compliance and litigation needs. Stephen Merrill, the former New Hampshire governor, is scheduled to join the firm shortly as Of Counsel. Merrill "will maintain offices in both New Hampshire and Boston as well as devoting a portion of his time to representing firm clients in Washington,D.C." If working for one of Boston's oldest and most prestigious firms, with a new outpost in New Hampshire, appeals to you, then Choate Hall may be your destiny.

Fish & Richardson

Boston Houston La Jolla Menlo Park Minneapolis New York Washington

Address: 225 Franklin Street, Boston, MA 02110–2804
Telephone: (617) 542–5070
Hiring Attorney: Jodi L. Sutton
Contact: Jill E. McDonald, Recruiting Coordinator; (713) 629-5070
Associate Salary: First year $86,000 (1997)
Summer Salary: $1450/week (1997)
Average Hours: NA worked; NA billed; 2000 required
Family Benefits: Health insurance; life insurance and AD&D; profit sharing 401(K); four weeks vacation; dental insurance; long-term disability; medical and parental leave
1996 Summer: Class of 5 students; offers to 5
Partnership: NA
Pro Bono: NA

Fish & Richardson in 1997
51 Lawyers at the Boston Office
1.1 Associates Per Partner

Total Partners 24			Total Associates 26			Practice Areas
Women	2	8%	Women	9	35%	Intellectual Property 100%
All Minorities	1	4%	All Minorities	3	12%	
Asian-Am	1	4%	Asian-Am	2	8%	
			Latino	1	4%	

premier patent firm

One of the nation's oldest firms specializing in patent law, Fish & Richardson is perhaps the premier patent firm in Boston. Founded in the 1800s in Boston as Fish, Richardson & Neave, Fish & Neave, the New York office, split off in 1965. Fish & Richardson now has spread nationwide with offices in New York, Washington, D.C., Houston, Minneapolis, La Jolla, and Silicon Valley. About 90 percent of its practice involves patent law, including "one of the biggest biotech practices in the Boston area." Bob Hillman and Jack Williams are two of the most well-known patent lawyers in Boston. In addition, the D.C. office features Rene Tegtmeyer (a former Assistant Commissioner of the Patent and Trademark Office). The firm also has a small and "isolated" trademark department and occasionally handles copyright issues. More than half the patent practice entails prosecution work—the writing and filing of patent applications. The remainder concerns "fairly large, high-stakes patent litigation involving lots of document production." One person noted that patent cases are rivaled only by some securities cases in the sheer number of documents involved. In recent years, Fish has made a concerted effort to increase the size of its litigation practice and has hired laterally in this area. The firm does very little pro bono work.

attorneys are individualists

The work atmosphere at Fish & Richardson was described as "individualistic." There is "not a lot of teamwork," explained one insider. "I think it's the nature of intellectual property work. There is a lot of technical material, and the young people are technical experts and experts on individualism." This attitude is further reflected in the distribution of work: new associates are not assigned to particular departments, and junior associates largely solicit work from partners and senior associates, although there is a central allocation system available if needed. Some found this system "cumbersome," but others valued the resulting freedom to develop their own type of practice. Fish & Richardson recently instituted a program of group leaders whose functions include the monitoring of associates' work flow; this system may bring greater order to the firm's work assignment procedures than heretofore has existed. The volume of work at the firm "is very high. People are very busy. They are not forced to crank out hours, but there are lots of deadlines, and the pressure is to meet the deadlines created by clients with special needs." Fish & Richardson recently increased its billable hour requirement from 1900 to 2000 hours. This number is, however, a "realistic" goal, in contrast to other firms where the billable hours targets are merely "nominal," according to one insider.

minimal social life

The autonomous environment at Fish & Richardson does not make it an unfriendly place; everyone agreed that the firm has a comfortable work atmosphere. The firm recently instituted "Casual Day" each Friday to enhance this feeling, and the firm has a monthly social event. However, Fish is not a great place for social life: "Many of the attorneys at the firm are older. The average age is high because of the amount of education you need to get hired at the firm (many of the attorneys have advanced degrees in the sciences). The firm sponsors some official events, but there is very little social interaction outside of work."

training

Fish & Richardson expects its young associates to take on responsibility early. Client contact frequently occurs "right off the bat," and most young associates are "heavily involved quickly." One summer associate explained that Fish "encourages you to go out and get your own clients. They don't expect to be checking your work, and they don't tolerate sloppy work." A second person remarked: "They will check your work for about six months and then cut you loose." Another pointed out that there are considerably more opportunities for responsibility in the prosecution practice than in litigation. On the prosecution side, most associates gain responsibility for their "own" clients in their first two or three years. By contrast, it can take many years to be first chair in a litigation case because most of the litigation work is for "really huge clients." While the firm offers weekly tutorials to train members of the patent prosecution and litigation departments, our contacts felt that Fish provides very little formal associate training, and noted that most instruction depends on individual relationships with particular partners. According to a firm spokesperson, "the firm hired a director of training in February of 1997 to help institute more formal training programs. The firm is currently revamping the entire process."

low-key management

Fish & Richardson's managing partner reports to a low-key, eight partner management committee, membership in which is essentially voluntary. Many partners, however, exhibit genuine apathy: "no one wants to be on the management committee. Many are just not interested in it." Everyone agreed that management is very open about decisions. One source noticed that "there was a period of time when the firm went around to all the associates to collect their opinions," but the firm "gave up on it because it was too much of a hassle." Not surprisingly, management is strongly committed to having the latest in workplace technology. One person characterized Fish as a "pretty slick-run operation. There are lots of computers and networks and other funky stuff...They are on the cutting edge of office technology."

salary

Associate compensation starts at $86,000 and is heavily "performance-based" after the first year. "Some legal assistants going to law school make more than first-year attorneys at other firms," according to one insider. A firm spokesperson added that these persons were Technology Specialists with advanced degrees or Ph.D's, often attending law school at night.

little diversity

There are relatively few female and minority attorneys at Fish & Richardson. People surmised that although there is no apparent hostility toward women or minorities, the firm has not gone out of its way to promote diversity. There is only one Latino and no African-Americans. One source remarked that Fish is "more diverse than most intellectual property firms," but it is still "very white and male and WASP. It's a reflection of people who have a combination of technical and law degrees. There is a tremendous financial investment in getting those degrees."

Fish & Richardson's offices are "nicer than those at the average Boston firm" and have been written up in the real estate section of the *Boston Globe*. The offices are laid out very "intelligently," with a winding marble staircase connecting the first and second floors. There are conference rooms with hardwood floors and "nice dark wood" furniture. All associates have their own offices with windows. As noted above, the offices are equipped with the "full complement of existing technology." The firm is connected among its offices and with some of its clients by electronic mail and video conferencing.

technical background

Fish & Richardson hires students who are specifically qualified to work at a patent law firm. "Without a technical background, you can forget being hired," concluded one insider, although a firm spokesperson claimed that technical training is not a hiring prerequisite, particularly with the increase in number of litigation attorneys. The most common interview question is "why did you leave engineering school for law school?" Fish hires mainly from the top law schools; in addition, many of its lawyers attended either Harvard, MIT, or local technical schools for their undergraduate training. Another person contended that to be hired by Fish, a candidate either had to attend a "brand name school, or have very high grades" and had to have a great interview. The on-campus interview is "standard," stated one. "They just want to make sure that you don't have two heads." The callback interview involves meeting four to six people (a mixture of partners and associates) for fifteen to thirty minutes each. Overall, the interviews were described as "informative" and conversational, without any "pressure tactics" or "quizzes." One person who has conducted interviews for the firm noted that Fish emphasizes writing ability and that each new associate has "to go through a baptism over writing skills. It is really tested there." The firm requires candidates to supply a writing sample, transcripts, LSAT scores, and school ranking.

Foley, Hoag & Eliot

Boston Washington

Address:	One Post Office Square, Boston, MA 02109
Telephone:	(617) 832–1000
Hiring Attorney:	Carol Hempfling Pratt, Chair, Hiring Committee
Contact:	Dina M. Wreede, Director of Legal Recruiting; (617) 832-7060
Associate Salary:	First year minimum of $76,000 (1997)
Summer Salary:	A minimum of $1450/week (1997)
Average Hours:	2101 worked; 1885 billed (including pro bono); no minimum required
Family Benefits:	12 weeks paid maternity leave; 4 weeks paid paternity leave; childcare flexible spending account; emergency day care center
1996 Summer:	Class of 18 students; offers to 10 of 11 eligible
Partnership:	NA
Pro Bono:	Over 5% of all work is pro bono

Foley, Hoag & Eliot in 1997
174 Lawyers at the Boston Office
1.2 Associates Per Partner

Total Partners 79		
Women	14	18%
All Minorities	3	4%
Afro-Am	3	4%

Total Associates 92		
Women	34	37%
All Minorities	9	10%
Afro-Am	3	3%
Asian-Am	5	5%
Latino	1	1%

Practice Areas	
Litigation	53
Business	53
Environmental	14
Intellectual Property	11
Labor/Employment	11
Administrative	9
Real Estate	8
Tax	8
Trusts & Estates	6

academic atmosphere

Foley, Hoag & Eliot is a top Boston law firm with an "academic" and "tolerant" atmosphere. A number of prominent professors began their careers there, and one person noticed that there always are a couple of professors making "guest appearances at the firm." Foley is home to more "law review types" than most of its Boston counterparts, and many go there with the idea of teaching in mind. The firm's culture is respectful of differences among its attorneys. One source indicated that some Foley attorneys have a reputation for being "eccentric," and another noted that there were more "beards" there than at any other firm at which she had worked. The "bookish" nature of the attorneys affects the work atmosphere; the firm is extremely concerned about the quality of its work and pays particular attention to writing skills.

strong public interest

Another distinctive feature of Foley's culture is its ardent commitment to public interest work. The firm established itself as a powerful civil rights advocate through its pro bono work on one of the major Boston school desegregation cases. Since then, Foley has maintained an unusually strong dedication to public interest work. For example, partner Toni Wolfman helped two associates initiate a battered women's advocacy project to help women obtain restraining orders; in addition, the firm serves as counsel to Planned Parenthood of Massachusetts, and there "is lots of pro bono work stemming from this." One partner specializes in education law and brings in a number of related projects, such as advising colleges on minimizing the incidence of acquaintance rape and dealing with the associated liabilities. Pro bono hours are fully credited toward billable hours. Moreover, the firm has established the Foley, Hoag & Eliot Foundation, using the funds it won in the aforementioned desegregation case to sponsor projects that promote racial harmony throughout the community. One person remarked that at Foley, "you hear about pro bono work all the time and are encouraged to do it." Foley was "one of a very few Boston firms" to sign on to the ABA's pro bono challenge in which the firm committed itself to devoting at least 5% of annual billable hours to public interest matters.

government ties

The firm's public interest work has been accompanied by strong ties to government and, in many cases, Democratic politics. Foley is one of the few firms in Boston with a well-developed government relations practice. Paul Tsongas, a partner at the firm until his death in 1997, was very active in this practice. Foley's government relations practice continues to grow under the leadership of Gloria Larson, former Massachusetts Secretary of Economic Affairs; Dennis Kanin, Senator Tsongas' former Chief of Staff; and Doug McGarrah, former Chief Counsel for the Central Artery/Tunnel project. Jim Brown, a partner, is also well known in Boston politics. In addition, one of the firm's partners, Alan Baron, a former prosecutor, was recently appointed by U.S. Senator John Glenn to act as Chief Counsel for Investigations to the Governmental Affairs

Committee, and "he will direct the Democratic side's investigation of political fund-raising and spending," we were told.

business, litigation practices

Foley's practice is broad and includes a number of interesting and noteworthy areas, and high-profile cases. The firm is organized into two major practice areas: the "business" practice, which includes corporate, real estate, taxation, and trusts and estates; and the "disputes" practice, which includes administrative, labor, and litigation. Foley's business department continues to expand in terms of personnel and volume. The department has completed a large number of initial public offerings in the past year and was ranked 15th in the country by the SEC for the first half of 1996 as issuers' counsel. The corporate department is reportedly one of the firm's largest and fastest growing. Its work has included domestic and international joint ventures, initial public offerings and mergers and acquisitions. Foley recently represented Powersoft Corporation in its acquisition by Sybase, the largest software deal in the U.S. at the time. Litigation is considered a "feisty" practice area, with Michael Keating being one of the best-known litigators. The business crimes practice (headed by Gary Crossen and Nick Theodorou, both former Assistant U.S. Attorneys), along with intellectual property litigation and accounting malpractice, continue to be the fastest growing areas in the firm's litigation department.

labor, IP, environment

Foley also has a "strong" management-side labor practice, featuring David Ellis. Phil Burling does "interesting" work in administrative and university law. Headed by Laurie Burt, who has handled a number of "national cases," the environmental practice is "the largest in New England," we were told. The department recently represented the state authority charged with the cleanup of Boston Harbor, the nation's largest waste-water treatment project. Foley's intellectual property practice has expanded greatly; the firm now has eight lawyers who are licensed to practice before the U.S. Patent & Trademark Office. The practice does patent prosecution work in the areas of biotechnology and electrical engineering as well as infringement and misappropriation matters for pharmaceutical companies. One insider said, "for law students interested in labor, environmental or intellectual property practice, FHE is the place to be." Foley also has a strong health care practice, and the firm is part of an international law network that works on international issues.

training

Even though Foley is one of Boston's larger firms, it has "tried to resist specialization more than other firms have." One insider remarked, however, that "the trend is unavoidably to specialization—a switch in the firm culture may be underway." New associates may join either the disputes or the business practice areas and can rotate to the other practice area after one year before finally choosing an area of specialization. Foley provides a full range of training programs, which are considered more "informal" and "relaxed" than those of other large Boston firms.

As part of the firm's emphasis on writing skills, past summer associates have been offered training on writing legal briefs. The summer program also includes workshops on corporate drafting skills, depositions, alternative dispute resolution, and professional responsibility. One person explained, however, that there is "more learning through work" than "systematic" training. Some praised the laid-back system, but others complained that attorneys "have to push to get formal feedback, particularly in the business department." Each summer associate is assigned a mentor who supervises the student's work. Some mentors spend "hours" going over summer associate memos, whereas others provide only minimal feedback. Although some junior associates assume a good deal of responsibility, most of their work involves researching and writing memos. Actually, one contact informed us, junior associates no longer write "memos" but rather write "discovery and court papers," since "clients don't like to be billed for memos much anymore."

minimal social life

Foley is not known for its "raging social life." Most associates are married and do not see each other after work. People described the firm as "friendly" and "relaxed," but one person commented that socializing in the office "was not a pervasive thing. You get the sense that people are there to do their work" and then get home to their families. The summer program is not as "lavish" as those of some other large Boston firms. The firm organizes events such as dinners and theater outings about every two weeks, and the softball team is popular. One insider declared that one of the dinners she attended was actually "painful" because it involved "people who don't socialize a lot together having to sit together and socialize. It is a very different atmosphere" from that of other Boston firms. Similarly, as part of Foley's down-to-work attitude, the associates tend to finish their work and go home earlier; there is no pressure to "outstay" other attorneys. People also advised that there is not much billable hour pressure, as Foley stresses "quality over quantity" in its work. This may be changing, however. One source informed us that "Foley seems to be becoming somewhat more 'bottom line' oriented. While 'quality of life' remains better than at other top firms, this isn't as openly cited by firm management as in the past."

conservative management

Foley is managed by a rotating executive committee of five members, who serve four-year staggered terms. All partners are "privy to management information, and a significant amount of information, including that on firm finances, is shared with associates," according to one contact. The management prides itself on a conservative growth strategy, which enabled the firm to avoid the excesses of the 1980s and has produced financial stability over the years. One source explained that Foley "never got sucked into the big consumption and spending mode. They are solid." One person informed us that at Foley one settles for "lower pay and somewhat less high-profile work than at the top three or four firms in the city," but that Foley is not a "sweatshop in comparison with Ropes, Hale, etc." At Foley, "high quality work is still emphasized over mere billables."

supportive of diversity

Foley has a number of high-profile female partners, including the aforementioned Toni Wolfman and Sandra Shapiro, well-respected in real estate and former President of the Women's Bar Association of Massachusetts. Sandy Lynch, a prominent litigator at the firm was recently appointed by President Clinton to the First Circuit Court of Appeals; she is the first woman ever appointed to that court. One person observed that "there is at least one woman on each of the major committees," and women partners head two of the firm's seven departments (Deborah Breznay and Stephanie Cantor). Laurie Burt currently serves on the firm's Executive Committee. Moreover, many female attorneys work part-time while they raise their children. Although there are not many minorities at the firm, the atmosphere is "supportive," and, according to one source, "the number of minority associates seems to be growing." Charles Beard is a high-profile African-American partner. The firm has "several openly gay lawyers, with whom no one seems uncomfortable."

renovated offices

Since the last edition of the *Insider's Guide*, the firm has added two office floors to its space, and the offices have undergone a complete renovation. The decor now features marble conference room tables, glass and marble walls in the reception area and custom lobby carpets based on Frank Lloyd Wright designs. A large, multipurpose conference center is in constant use. The firm has also updated its computer facilities significantly. Lawyers and other employees now have desktop access via a newly installed Windows 95-based computer network to on-line legal research databases, the internet, electronic mail and desktop faxing. The library facilities are "adequate" but somewhat limited in resources.

hiring tips

In keeping with its academic reputation, Foley generally hires law students with academic inclinations. Writing experience (law review or other journals) and other academic interests are a big plus. "Several summer associates had masters degrees in areas totally unrelated to law, such as anthropology, engineering, and French," one insider reported. "People were very academic. They also get people who do things that are different. Some of the people are really bookish and some have a broad variety of interests." Another pointed out that "Foley is much more receptive than other firms to people who have public interest backgrounds or who are thinking about going into government or teaching and aren't sure about working in a big firm...As a result of its reputation, it tends to attract interesting people." Foley draws many of its students from Boston College, Boston University, Columbia, Harvard, New York University, University of Chicago, and Yale; it also hires occasionally form Northeastern. Foley requests writing samples from applicants, and one insider stated that Foley "doesn't let you know about summer associate offers for a few extra days because the firm takes time to examine the writing samples carefully." On occasion, the firm has asked an applicant to submit an additional writing sample if it felt the original did not adequately reflect the candidate's abilities. Callback interviews involve four to five half-hour sessions and a lunch with several attorneys. People warned that some interviewers may ask unusual questions or push students to defend a particular viewpoint. One person considered the interviews at Foley to be more "thoughtful" than those at other firms.

Goodwin, Procter & Hoar

Boston Washington

Address: Exchange Place, Boston, MA 02109
Telephone: (617) 570–1000
Hiring Attorney: Lawrence R. Cahill
Contact: Maureen A. Shea, Director of Legal Personnel; (617) 570–1288
Associate Salary: First year $79,000 (1997); second $87,000
Summer Salary: $1500/week (1997)
Average Hours: 2175 worked; 1905 billed; NA required
Family Benefits: 12 weeks paid maternity leave; 4 weeks paid paternity leave; dependent care plan; emergency childcare; elder care resource and referral plan; employee assistance plan
1996 Summer: Class of 42 students; offers to 42
Partnership: 28% of entering associates from 1979–1988 were made partner
Pro Bono: 2% of all work is pro bono

Goodwin, Procter & Hoar in 1997
318 Lawyers at the Boston Office
1.7 Associates Per Partner

Total Partners 119		
Women	19	16%
All Minorities	5	4%
Afro-Am	2	2%
Asian-Am	3	3%

Total Associates 203		
Women	84	41%
All Minorities	18	9%
Afro-Am	8	4%
Asian-Am	9	4%
Latino	1	1%

Practice Areas	
Corporate	141
Litigation	78
Real Estate	43
Labor	16
Environmental	12
Trusts & Estates	11
Tax	10
ERISA	7

While many attorneys at Goodwin, Procter & Hoar grudgingly acknowledge that Ropes & Gray is Boston's most prestigious firm, they stand firm in the belief that Goodwin, along with Hale & Dorr, ranks "a close second." One contact, however, took exception to this characterization, insisting that while "Ropes & Gray has a *longer-established* prestige, I don't think that their practice, or their attorneys, are any better or more sophisticated than Goodwin's or Hale & Dorr's." Goodwin is, moreover, now the largest firm in Boston, having just this last year overtaken its competitors.

strong ties to Boston

Founded in 1912, Goodwin, Procter & Hoar is an older Boston law firm intimately connected with its history. The son of one of the firm's founders, partner Sam Hoar, only recently retired from the firm. Goodwin's longstanding and "strong commitment to the City of Boston" sets it apart from many other firms in the city. This commitment extends far beyond the provision of pro bono legal services. Most notably, Goodwin partners have established the SEED (Support for Early Educational Development) program, a $1 million permanent endowment fund for which it received a Presidential Citation from the White House Office of Private Sector Initiatives. The income from SEED is used to fund innovative educational programs in the Boston public school system. Goodwin also permits two attorneys each year to elect to work for up to six months with the Middlesex County District Attorney's Office while earning their regular firm salary.

pro bono

Under the leadership of managing partner Jeff Dando, Goodwin encourages its attorneys to be active in the community, both as lawyers and as citizens. Many Goodwin attorneys are involved in the City Year youth service program and in a variety of other city organizations and services. Many also have tried their hand at politics and have connections to the government and the judiciary. Massachusetts State Attorney General Scott Harshbarger is a former Goodwin associate. Jim Rehnquist, son of Supreme Court Chief Justice Rehnquist, has been elected a partner at the firm and is expected to return to the firm after serving at the U.S. Attorney's office in Boston. Brackett Denniston, former chief of staff to Governor Weld, was a partner at Goodwin.

practice areas

Goodwin's corporate, litigation, real estate, and environmental practices each rank among the top three in Boston, claimed one source. Although the "booming" corporate practice "drives" the firm, other practices are equally active, including capital markets, banking, and private equity. The corporate department primarily represents large institutional clients, but also houses a venture capital practice that represents many entrepreneurial start-up companies and "buy out" funds. The diverse mix of clients offers associates varied work and responsibilities. The litigation department, housing well-known litigator, Marshall Simonds, is similarly attractive to entering associates particularly because the firm's public interest rotation program provides unusually early responsibility. Goodwin's real estate practice is also thriving. It represents a number of developers and, like other departments, has a mix of small and large clients. Gil Menna, a corporate/real estate securities partner, has the largest REIT (real estate investment trust) practice in the country, according to *The American Lawyer*, we were told. Commenting on the nature of the work pursued at Goodwin, one insider observed that "our practice tends to be more transactionally-oriented than client-oriented," which in part explains why Goodwin has developed "some of the very sophisticated practices" it is known for.

summer associates

"Bright," "curious," and "self-starter" summer associates are most successful at Goodwin, we were told. They must pursue the projects that interest them from the central pool of assignments made available to all summer associates. Goodwin guarantees that associates will be assigned their top choice department; an associate, moreover, is not required to work in only one practice area, but rather may elect to split his time between several practice areas.

excellent training

Goodwin received high reviews for its commitment to professional development. The firm offers one of Boston's best formal training programs, asserted one contact. It provides numerous in-house formal training sessions in each major department. The litigators compete in mock trials and also receive a full range of formal, specific skills training. Goodwin also received high marks for its informal training: "partners in the individual departments really take a lot of time and care" in training the junior associates; you get "more responsibility at Goodwin than you would think," considering that it is such a large firm.

hierarchy

Although Goodwin partners have adopted an "open-door policy," one person commented that "partner interaction with associates isn't as free as it could be." Another noted, however, that it is "better than at other firms in the Boston area." Partners may have their own "pyramid of power," but "partners and associates socialize together," commented one insider, who elaborated: "I am told by associates at Ropes and at Choate that Goodwin associates have a much friendlier relationship with partners than at their shops." Associates, however, tend to be "left a little in the dark about...policy decisions...You have to take a lot of things on good faith and hope a lot of things turn out well," one insider told us. Goodwin associates recently had their first associates' retreat, from which a number of changes resulted, principally relating to salary increases and compensation structure. Still unclear, however, is the "path to partnership." One contact explained that "with a few exceptions, people making it to partnership are top billers, so associates assume that is the main way to make it." This is a prospect which reportedly does not thrill all.

conservative expansion

A financially successful firm, Goodwin is proud of its philosophy of "contained, but not over-expanded growth" and has remained "very mobile in terms of taking on new clients and bringing in new business without paying tons of lawyers for sitting around." Goodwin also has made a concerted effort to strengthen its smaller practice areas and to become a full-service firm. The firm's 10-attorney Washington, D.C. office, for example, does regulatory work as well as supporting the firm's other practices. Goodwin attorneys are also actively developing new practices, such as a practice focused on the Pacific Rim.

diversity

Despite being an old-line Boston firm, Goodwin is "absolutely a good place for women" to work, declared one person. Many women work at the firm, particularly among the associate ranks. Goodwin offers a generous family leave program to both men and women with "no stigma." Moreover, the firm provides an on-site emergency childcare center that is available to all its employees. Goodwin will accommodate part-time attorneys; "there are even part-time partners at Goodwin," one contact reported. Goodwin has "one of the highest proportions of minority attorneys in New England," according to one insider, and the firm is continuing its effort to promote diversity.

Goodwin's offices are conveniently located downtown at Exchange Place. The office facilities are equipped with all the modern conveniences. "Everything you need is right there. The firm is really big on this. They want to make sure everyone is happy with the facilities, from the senior partner to the receptionist," asserted one person. Goodwin has replaced its outmoded WANG computers with a "state-of-the-art" PC system that runs WordPerfect, Excel, Netscape and "a number of other productivity and information applications."

hiring tips Goodwin seeks to hire attorneys who display a "positive attitude." The firm "has a reputation for being a friendly, more sociable, laid-back place, and they are looking for someone" who can fit this mold, said one contact. They also want "someone they can trust," another added. Goodwin hires its summer associates from all across the country. Goodwin's callback interviews are "low-key" and do not involve "tough questions." The interview is "more an opportunity for you to find out more about the firm," said one successful applicant. If you make it to the callback stage, "there is a presumption in your favor" that you will be hired, commented another. "They just want to make sure they can work with you."

One of Boston's most prestigious firms, Goodwin is also progressive with respect to women's issues and permits a balance between work and family. One firm enthusiast observed that "although we work hard, there's a collaborative feel, and a sense of humor that I don't see at other firms I work with. I think that there's more of a recognition at Goodwin that there's more to life than moving deals along." A second contact observed that "the people at Goodwin are exceptional. A combination of smart and interesting people; different from what you would expect at an old school, white shoe Boston firm. There is a sense of pride in the work we do—an ingrained sense of competitiveness to be better than other firms in the quality of work." With an extensive history of involvement in Boston, Goodwin is also an excellent place to go if you want to work in a firm and help out in the community at the same time.

Goulston & Storrs

Boston

Address: 400 Atlantic Avenue, Boston, MA 02110–3333
Telephone: (617) 482–1776
Hiring Attorney: Steven R. Astrove
Contact: Nancy Needle, Recruitment Director; (617) 574-6447
Associate Salary: First year $76,000 plus bar review course and application fees (1997)
Summer Salary: $1450/week (1997)
Average Hours: 1900 worked; 1850 billed; none required.
Family Benefits: Maternity leave; paternity leave; same sex domestic partner health insurance
1996 Summer: Class of 8 students; offers to 7
Partnership: NA
Pro Bono: 8% of all work is pro bono

Goulston & Storrs in 1997
128 Lawyers at the Firm
0.8 Associates Per Partner

Total Partners 70		
Women	13	19%
All Minorities	1	1%
Afro-Am	1	1%

Total Associates 58		
Women	29	50%
All Minorities	5	9%
Afro-Am	4	7%
Latino	1	2%

Practice Areas	
Real Estate	56
Corporate	28
Finance	28
Business	25
Securities	25
Litigation	21
Environmental	18
Healthcare	12
Tax	10
Bankruptcy	9
Trusts & Estates	9

Established before the turn of the century by a group of determined Jewish lawyers who refused to succumb to the "difficulty of getting the old-line Boston business," Goulston & Storrs rose to prominence as one of Boston's top real estate firms. Traditionally a firm of Jewish lawyers and clients, Goulston & Storrs is considerably more diverse today, but continues to be known as a "predominantly Jewish" firm.

family-oriented

Goulston's family-oriented culture and its strong support for family-related work arrangements distinguishes it from other large Boston firms. The firm is said to take an "enlightened view of women" in the workplace. "The vast majority of attorneys at the firm are married and have children," reported one person, who also noted that the firm is "supportive of anyone having problems balancing a family and working." Many of the firm's female attorneys have children and work part-time. Even the firm's social life revolves around "family get-togethers," which unfortunately can "put those who don't have an immediate family at somewhat of a disadvantage in becoming part of the firm," warned one contact. Goulston does not force its attorneys to choose the firm over a normal life. "You don't stay late unless absolutely necessary," said one source. Another contact remarked that "Goulston attorneys do not stay in the office because of any visibility requirement imposed by the firm, but they often work long hours because of the needs of the clients of the firm."

Goulston is not the best place for young, single attorneys who are looking for an active social life, people we interviewed commented. Though it sponsors some dinners and cocktail parties, the firm does not offer a lavish summer program. Most people we interviewed agreed, however, that during the day, "the atmosphere is very friendly—not chatty—but very friendly." The firm regularly schedules attorney lunches, and attorneys get together once a week for a "social" hour. Goulston's office is outfitted with an outdoor deck which is well-used around mealtime during the summer.

strong real estate

Despite Goulston's expansion into other areas, real estate remains its "bread and butter" practice. Jordan Krasnow, one of Boston's most well known real estate attorneys, is prominent in this practice. The real estate group handles a broad variety of matters, including acquisitions, leasings, government sponsored housing projects, commercial developments, and malls and shopping center developments. Goulston was involved in a "majority of the regional mall developments in the past 10 to fifteen years," claimed one observer, and has become increasingly dominant in the office building market as well. The practice involves representation of real estate investment trusts (REITs) active nationally in the office, retail, and residential markets. The firm is also involved internationally, including the development of manufacturing and shopping center facilities overseas, particularly in Latin America.

practice areas

During the real estate slowdown of the early 1990s, Goulston successfully warded off the ill-effects of the recession by expanding its bankruptcy and litigation practices, and by developing new practice areas. Goulston's corporate practice has also grown significantly. Its client base is independent of the real estate clients. By contrast, much of the firm's litigation work arises from the real estate clients. However, the litigation practice is expanding beyond its traditional base and covers a range of commercial and personal disputes. Rudy Pierce, a former judge, is a prominent litigator and African-American partner at the firm. Goulston now offers a growing private and public environmental practice which, like litigation, is closely integrated with the real estate practice. Goulston hired former State Senator Patricia McGovern to, among other things, expand its existing health care practice, which has experienced significant growth of late. The health care practice is under the leadership of Alan Goldberg, the founding president of the Massachusetts Health Lawyers Association. The firm also has developed expertise in infrastructure financing issues, led by Doug Husid, former Chief of Staff of the Massachusetts Executive Office of Transportation and Construction, and Peter Corbett, former Associate Commissioner of the Metropolitan District Commission. Husid played a central role in guiding the Central Artery project.

strong pro bono

Goulston & Storrs traces its pro bono practice to its high-profile defense of Sacco and Vanzetti during the Red Scare era in Boston. The firm is as strongly committed to pro bono today. Led by David Abromowitz, the practice affords many attorneys the opportunity to represent a diverse range of pro bono clients. Rudy Pierce is active with the Boston School Board. A number of the real estate attorneys are involved in community development work, and one partner has worked substantially with federally funded urban community development corporations. Goulston has recently been involved in the founding and organization of STRIVE/Boston Employment Service, Inc., a job training and placement service for economically disadvantaged young adults in Boston. Members of the firm currently serve as directors and officers of the corporation. The firm fully credits pro bono hours.

flexible work environment

Having grown rapidly to become a large law firm, Goulston has begun to add structure to its traditionally flexible work environment. The firm hires entering associates for a particular department. Goulston, not known for highly structured training programs in the past, has reportedly made progress in this area. Goulston has instituted a formal associate training program which "includes regular seminars covering the basics in all practice areas and general lawyering skills," reported one contact.

informal management

Despite its growth and increasing structure, Goulston's management continues to operate relatively informally and is open and receptive to associate ideas. The executive committee holds monthly meetings to administer the firm's business, after which it meets with associates to discuss any decisions it made and to solicit their input. The firm also provides attorneys "incentives to cooperate and share work" through the partnership compensation system, which rewards the attorneys for bringing in business as well as for working for other firm clients.

partnership prospects

Unfortunately, Goulston's growth may have affected its traditionally "good track record" of making partners. One person we interviewed noted that "at this time there is an inverted triangle in terms of ratio of partners to associates" and expressed concern about the limited number of future partners that the firm can make. The firm has discussed lengthening the partnership track from six or seven years to eight or nine years. "This is a big issue" among associates, commented one person. We were told, however, that the firm continues to have a seven-year partnership track, with one tier of partners.

diversity

Goulston & Storrs has encouraged a culture of inclusiveness, said some people. There are presently five African-American lawyers at the firm, one of whom, partner Rudy Pierce, is a member of the executive committee and is influential at the firm. He is also open and "accessible" to summer associates, one insider remarked. According to another insider, "the firm is dedicated to increasing diversity and is an active participant in the initiatives of the Boston Law Firm Group. Goulston is working with diversity consultants to sensitize and educate the entire firm on issues regarding diversity."

office facilities

Goulston's offices are located in a renovated brick warehouse, "right on the waterfront." The firm displays art from local galleries in its offices against a background of exposed wooden beams and brick walls. Most of the firm's private offices have windows. Goulston has updated its outmoded computer system to a firmwide network of Windows-based PC's. The system has "firmwide e-mail, fax, and dial-in capabilities. The network also provides access to outside on-line services."

Many Goulston lawyers are graduates of either Harvard's college or its law school. In general, Goulston tends to hire "mature" candidates who have had previous work experience. Many past summer associates had worked for several years before entering law school. One person commented that Goulston "looks for people who can hit the ground running." Callback interviews involve meeting with about four attorneys and going to lunch with a few more. Candidates who are invited to the firm for a callback are presumed to be academically qualified to work at Goulston, and the major purpose of the interview is to assess whether the applicant "fits in" with the firm culture. Attorneys ask very few "substantive legal questions" in the interviews, our contacts told us. The firm will schedule interviews with attorneys who work in the candidate's area of interest, if any has been expressed. Those who express an interest in or have some background in real estate are at an advantage in getting hired, one insider noted. **hiring tips**

Goulston is one of few large Boston law firms with a strong family orientation. It is an excellent firm for "mature" law students, but it is "not a good firm for someone looking for a cadre of young people to go out and have a good time with after work," cautioned one person.

Hale and Dorr

Boston Washington
London (joint venture with Brobeck, Phleger & Harrison)

Address: 60 State Street, Boston, MA 02109
Telephone: (617) 526–6000
Hiring Attorney: Susan W. Murley
Contact: Evelyn M. Scoville, Director of Legal Personnel; (617) 526–6590
Associate Salary: First year $80,000 plus $2,000 graduating bonus (1997)
Summer Salary: $1420/week (1996)
Average Hours: 2190 worked; 1968 billed; no minimum
Family Benefits: Parental and medical leaves—three months paid, up to 12 months LOA; in-house emergency day care; long term disability; life, dental and health insurance; same sex domestic partner coverage available for health and dental plans; four weeks vacation; 401(K); bar association dues
1996 Summer: Class of 33 students; offers to 32
Partnership: 14% of entering associates from 1979–1988 were made partner
Pro Bono: 2.7% of all work is pro bono

Hale and Dorr in 1997
250 Lawyers at the Boston Office
1.2 Associates Per Partner

Total Partners 105		
Women	14	13%
All Minorities	3	3%
Afro-Am	2	2%
Asian-Am	1	1%

Total Associates 131		
Women	44	34%
All Minorities	8	6%
Afro-Am	4	3%
Asian-Am	3	2%
Latino	1	1%

Practice Areas	
Corporate/Employment/Ben.	98
Litigation	75
Real Estate	25
Intellectual Property	11
Labor & Employment	11
Bankruptcy & Commercial	9
Trusts & Estates	9
Tax	8
Environmental	4

Widely acknowledged as one of Boston's two most well-known and prestigious firms, Hale and Dorr is distinguished by its "work hard" culture. Hale and Dorr is a "sweatshop," commented one source. The firm is presently very busy, and its billable hours have increased significantly since our last edition. A number of our contacts pointed out that it is not unusual, especially in the corporate practice, to bill 2400 hours annually. One contact remarked that "despite the high relative pay, compensation is not enough in light of the insane hours worked." Another insider noted that "management has made a sincere effort to discourage the notion that billing over 2200 hours a year is an appropriate target for associates." The firm is, however, making "great efforts to hire laterally, which hopefully will ease some of the workload pressures on associates," according to one insider.

spirited and social summer

Hale and Dorr is known to have a modest social calendar throughout the year but a spirited set of social events during the summer months. The summer associates program had "lavish events every week," recalled one contact. "We all had specially made shirts with our names stitched on the front." There had been a "fraternity" atmosphere in the summer program, but this has waned in recent years, we were told. For the remainder of the year, "the firm has cocktails for attorneys every Friday (an event referred to as 'CAMS,' the Chowder and Marching Society), and everyone goes and chats and hangs out." The firm also sponsors a fall outing for all attorneys and a holiday party for attorneys, staff, and guests. One insider exclaimed that the "holiday season is booked with fun events."

practice areas

Hale and Dorr offers one of Boston's broadest ranging practices. The litigation department, one of the strongest in the city, was built by many prominent litigators, including James St. Clair, former Special Counsel to President Nixon, and Jerry Facher, who has taught at Harvard Law School for many years. The department primarily handles large, complex defense cases, but some smaller subgroups provide an interesting variety. Bob Keefe is prominent in the firm's criminal defense practice, which includes white-collar criminal litigation and government compliance work. Jeff Rudman is renowned as a securities litigator, Bill Lee has a strong reputation in patent infringement litigation, and senior partner Joan Lukey has been honored for her work in employment litigation, we were told.

Hale and Dorr's corporate practice is also among the city's best. The firm boasts a particularly strong initial public offering (IPO) practice, which one person claimed is the best in the region. Mark Borden and David Redlick play leading roles in the firm's IPO work. Borden, co-chair of the corporate department, was named this past year by *The American Lawyer* as one of the country's top 45 lawyers under the age of 45. Steve Singer has established a significant biotech corporate practice, and Paul Brountas, recently named in the the *National Law Journal* as one of the 100 most influential lawyers in the country, initiated the firm's highly regarded "emerging company" practice some years ago. In 1990, the firm co-founded with Brobeck, Phleger & Harrison the independent law firm Brobeck Hale and Dorr International, located in London, to serve the firm's clients on a worldwide basis. Among other matters, the international corporate group has handled the legal work for a number of joint ventures in Russia, the Pacific Rim, and Europe.

pro bono and public service

Hale and Dorr's pro bono practice handles a broad variety of matters, and the firm is a signatory to the ABA's Pro Bono Challenge. Associates are "encouraged to take in pro bono work and all of the firm's resources are made available to them." One insider informed us that "pro bono is huge in the litigation department and is an important aspect of the firm's personality." A formal pro bono committee oversees the practice, and pro bono hours count toward billable hours. The practice provides each summer associate the opportunity to try an administrative hearing involving issues such as unemployment compensation or welfare benefits. The firm provides assistance to the

Hale and Dorr Legal Services Center of Harvard Law School, a clinical teaching facility that "has assisted more than 20,000 low-income persons over the last 20 years," according to a firm spokesperson. Hale and Dorr attorneys also maintain political connections with both parties. Massachusetts Governor William Weld is a former partner of the firm, and the aforementioned Paul Brountas was the national chair for the Dukakis presidential campaign. The U.S. Attorney for Massachusetts, Donald Stern, is a former Hale and Dorr partner, and former Assistant U.S. Attorney, Karen Green, recently returned to the firm as a senior partner.

strong formal training

Hale and Dorr provides extensive formal training. Partner Brenda Fingold works full-time developing training programs for associates and partners. The firm provides a wide range of formal training programs and each major department offers regular training seminars in substantive areas of the law. One contact informed us, however, that due to recent heavy workloads, "training programs have been fewer and less well attended." Another contact told us that "while the corporate department training programs did slip last year due to the number of transactions and offerings being worked on, it is now back on track and is as good if not better than any in the city." One insider remarked that "the litigation department basically shuts down a couple of days each year so that associates and partners can participate in day-long training programs. Preparation and participation time are billable." Summer associates may participate in weekly formal training programs, including sessions on depositions, presentations, negotiations, and client and ethical dilemmas.

lean staffing, better experience

Junior associate responsibilities vary considerably depending on the department. In litigation, one person said you "could be doing document production forever," but the smaller departments are more likely to offer greater responsibility. Another person informed us that "in recent years, partners have concentrated on providing associates with 'quality' work—not just volume. As the firm is busier than it has ever been, and understaffed, associates are getting considerable experience, early and often." This person added that "numerous first-, second-, and third-year associates have primary responsibility for cases with oversight by a senior partner. Cases at Hale and Dorr are staffed leanly." We were also told that Hale and Dorr's expertise in the "emerging company" practice provides associates opportunities for "regular client contact and significant responsibility."

We heard a number of complaints regarding case load management by the firm. One contact remarked that partners need to be "routinely reminded to honestly estimate the time that will be involved for a junior associate to complete projects. I have frequently been told that a project would take a 'few hours' and have instead worked through a weekend to complete the project." Another insider remarked that "the purported case manager never seems to remember the case you *have* and tries to give you *more*; you pretty much have to scream before you get any help." Not all expressed these sentiments, however. One contact praised the corporate work load committee, stating that "I am asked if I am interested in the work and whether I am in a position to take it on."

feedback

The feedback at Hale and Dorr can be "spotty," claimed some we spoke with. Permanent associates are reviewed twice a year, and the review process (at least for new associates from the first through fourth year) was described as "thorough," according to one contact. Associates, however, are not well informed regarding their partnership prospects, asserted some people. "A majority of the people are floating in terms of knowing where they are in the firm," commented one source. Another person remarked that "the firm has made it *very* clear that it is being *very* selective about elevation (to senior partnership), yet it fails to explain the decision process...You'd do better to count on winning the lottery than making senior partner." Others, however, pointed out that formal evaluations are "very explicit" with respect to partnership chances.

With respect to the summer program, summer associates receive formal mid- and end-of-summer reviews. Hale and Dorr considers both work performance and an individual's ability to fit into the firm's culture when deciding whether to extend offers for full-time employment to summer associates, one source told us. One insider remarked that "in Hale and Dorr's summer program, an offer is yours to lose...Last summer only one person out of over 30 did not receive an offer."

management Hale and Dorr is organized as a tiered partnership. It is run by a 14 person executive committee on which sit managing partner and real estate attorney John Hamilton, an assistant managing partner, and a nonlawyer executive director. The remaining members are elected on a rotating basis. The firm experienced difficult economic times in the early 1990s, and laid off a number of associates at that time. The financial condition of the firm is greatly improved today. The partners reportedly made more in 1996 than ever before, and one contact informed us that "in the past four years, Hale and Dorr has increased associate pay twice and has implemented bonus programs."

diversity Hale and Dorr received mixed reviews regarding its work atmosphere for women. A "good number" of female attorneys at the firm form a "tight-knit group and have lunch together regularly," claimed one source. Another commented that "an amazing group of very strong women" work at the firm. Women associates and partners are invited to spend a day together on Thompson Island in an outward bound type program, we were told. On the other hand, even though Hale and Dorr has an emergency, on-site day care center that is open to everyone at the firm, people said that it is not the best firm for attorneys with children. The firm is "oriented toward the bottom line," and "economic pressures" make it difficult to take the time away from work to have children, said one observer. Hale and Dorr has a relatively small number of female associates compared with other Boston firms, but "women comprise 57% of our 1997 summer associate class and 56% of our 1997 incoming associates class," a firm spokesperson informed us. Few minority attorneys work at Hale and Dorr, but the firm " is an active member of the Boston Law Firm Group, a consortium of Boston law firms whose mission is to address the problem of minority recruitment and retention." One African-American partner and prominent litigator, Harry Daniels, is reportedly very "accessible" to summer associates.

office facilities Hale and Dorr renovated its office facilities in the early 1990s and has a long-term lease at its current location. More recently, the firm added an additional floor to the existing ten to provide space for additional attorneys, a litigation technology center, and extra conference rooms. The firm has a cafeteria and a fitness center operated by Fitcorp. As an accommodation to associates who have to work late, Hale and Door now provides free dinner to all attorneys and staff at 7:00 P.M. in the firm's cafeteria. The secretarial support system got mixed reviews. We were told that "secretaries still cater to the senior partners to the detriment of associates. Many associates have to request night help and stay all hours of the night just to get their work done." Many, however, praised the secretarial support staff, including one insider who remarked, "my secretary is the Charles Atlas of the secretarial set." Yet another person informed us that "the firm adopted WordPerfect, and the conversion has been a nightmare, with the system failing at odd times."

hiring tips Hale and Dorr is one of the more competitive firms at which to get hired in Boston. "Due to its excellent success in the corporate department and litigation department, the firm is very choosy," reported one contact. To land a summer associate position at Hale and Dorr, you have to attend a top school, and be on law review or have great grades, declared one insider. People emphasized that Hale and Dorr hires people who will mesh well with its culture. The firm is looking for "smart, articulate, and well-rounded law students and lawyers who seem committed to Boston," we were told. "A lot has to do with personality and how they perceive you," said one person. Callback interviews involve meeting about four attorneys and going to lunch.

Hale and Dorr continues to share its rank as Boston's top firm with Ropes & Gray. This prestigious firm is an excellent place to launch a career. Hale and Dorr is not a firm where people stay for long, however. Its rate of partnership is among the lowest in the city. So, if for a few years you want to be a high-energy lawyer who works extremely hard while receiving top-notch training, this may be the firm for you. As one insider put it, "I believe that the firm is an excellent place to practice law, whether your long-term ambitions are to remain in a big-firm environment or to eventually move on to something else."

Hill & Barlow

Boston

Address: One International Place, Boston, MA 02110
Telephone: (617) 428-3000
Hiring Attorney: Joseph D. Steinfield
Contact: Elaine Carmichael, Director of Personnel; (617) 428-3000
Associate Salary: First year $76,000 (1997)
Summer Salary: $1400/week (1997)
Average Hours: 1813 worked; 1718 billed; 1800 required
Family Benefits: Birth and childcare leave; emergency day care
1996 Summer: Class of 19 students, offers to 17
Partnership: NA
Pro Bono: 4.5% of all work is pro bono

Hill & Barlow in 1997
99 Lawyers at the Firm
0.8 Associates Per Partner

Total Partners 51		
Women	9	18%
All Minorities	1	2%
Asian-Am	1	2%

Total Associates 41		
Women	17	41%
All Minorities	3	7%
Afro-Am	1	2%
Asian-Am	1	2%
Latino	1	2%

Practice Areas	
Litigation	35
Corporate	30
Real Estate	20
Labor & Employment	15
Commercial/Bankruptcy	11
Trusts & Estates	9
Environmental	8
Tax	6

pro bono commitment

Hill & Barlow is distinguished by its historically strong public interest commitment, which can be traced back to the firm's controversial handling of the Sacco and Vanzetti appeal during the Red Scare in Boston in the 1920s. Though it lost many of its largest clients because it chose to handle this famous case, Hill & Barlow is "proud" that it remained resolute in its beliefs. These convictions are still significant at the firm. All pro bono hours are credited toward billable hours, and today pro bono work averages about five percent of the work done at the firm. Hill & Barlow does "more pro bono work than almost anyone else in the city," declared one source. Although there is no formal pro bono department at Hill & Barlow, many "partners and associates...have an inclination toward public interest," explained another. Partner David Hoffman, formerly a staff attorney for the American Civil Liberties Union, handles numerous civil rights cases. In addition, Hill & Barlow's lawyers have been actively involved in school finance issues, domestic violence cases, death penalty appeals, and institutional reform cases, among others.

political connections

Hill & Barlow also has a long history of close connections to politics. Three Massachusetts Governors—Weld, Dukakis, and Peabody—are former Hill & Barlow partners. The firm's two African American partners, Reginald Lindsay and Deval Patrick, left in 1994 to become, respectively, a Massachusetts Federal District Judge and Assistant Attorney General for Civil Rights. Recently, partner Nonnie Burnes became a State Superior Court judge. Many of the firm's lawyers are active in political campaigns. Interest in politics and political involvement provides an excellent vehicle to get to know many Hill & Barlow attorneys, one source informed us.

litigation

Hill & Barlow is well known for its litigation department, which constitutes about one third of the firm's practice. The department represents a mix of large corporate clients and individuals. A number of Hill & Barlow litigators are prominent in the city. Gael Mahony and Dick Renehan are two of Boston's top-ranked trial lawyers. Gael Mahony chaired the Governor's commission that was established to evaluate the Massachusetts Department of Social Services and he is a former president of the American College of Trial Lawyers. Dick Renehan served as president of the Boston Bar Association and has represented a number of law firms in legal malpractice defense cases. The highly-regarded Joe Steinfield heads the firm's excellent First Amendment practice.

corporate

Hill & Barlow's corporate practice is the fastest growing within the firm, now roughly equal in size to litigation. The department represents numerous public, private and professional clients. Areas of particular strength include general corporate, securities, mergers and acquisitions, corporate finance, and construction law. The department has grown recently both internally and by lateral hires, including high-profile partners with large client portfolios. The firm's real estate practice is one of the best in the city, and is growing in both numbers and business. Hill & Barlow also offers an expanding environmental practice and a well-established trusts and estates practice.

flexible structure

Hill & Barlow is a large firm, but it is relatively unstructured. New associates remain unassigned for their first year at the firm, after which time they may join one of the firm's departments. The firm usually allows attorneys to select their departmental assignments and even has supported a number of attorneys in developing new practice areas for the firm. The corporate and real estate departments have been the fastest growing in recent years; last year, of the seven newly assigned associates, three joined corporate and three joined real estate.

significant experience

"The biggest selling point at the firm" is the early responsibility that it offers junior associates. First-year associates have responsibility for "big pieces of cases" or transactions. Most cases are leanly staffed; usually a partner and one or two associates work closely together. Overall, Hill & Barlow does not emphasize formal training. The firm does, however, strongly encourage training through the many outside seminars available in Boston, for which purpose a liberal budget is available. "You are pretty much thrown into the work and left to figure it out on the way," said one person. There is also "no training for summer associates...They give you assignments and you have to figure them out or ask for help," we were told.

The summer program, like the permanent associate development program, is fairly unstructured. Work is distributed through a single coordinator. For some, the lack of structure provided flexibility to obtain the type of work they wanted. Others, however, complained about a "lack of clear organization." The firm has now placed the chair of the hiring committee in charge of summer associate work assignments to address this problem.

outdoor social events

Hill & Barlow's summer program is not a formal wine and dine experience. The program emphasizes "outdoorsy events." Summer associates have climbed a mountain, spent time at a house on a lake, and "went to a house without electricity on the bay." It was "great if you like the outdoors, but it wasn't the ballet," commented one person. Recently, the firm has added a few cultural activities to the summer program, including an evening at the theatre. Overall, Hill & Barlow is not a hopping place for young, single people. The lawyers are "not a big late night crowd," said one person. Most attorneys go home between six and seven p.m. "Many young people are married. It's a family oriented firm." Another contact remarked that "Hill and Barlow truly respects a person's life outside the firm. Few partners will 'order' you to work nights or weekends." This person further commented that "both the type and quantity of work you do is very largely within your control. The billable hour target (including pro bono) is 1800."

family orientation

In fact, one source told us that Hill & Barlow has "implemented policies to encourage families," such as the provision of emergency day care and generous maternity leave. A "substantial" number of women work at Hill & Barlow, and they have held a number of get-togethers throughout past summers. Some women exert significant influence at the firm. Winifred Li, former head of the trusts and estates practice, is a member of the management committee and Miriam Sheehan chairs the tax department. A number of women are members of the hiring committee. Litigation, however, is more "male-focused" than the other practice areas at the firm and may be less desirable for women, said one woman, who commented that "there is a sense that you have to be tougher to be in the litigation group."

diversity

With a growing number of gay and lesbian attorneys among its ranks, Hill & Barlow is known as a progressive law firm that "treats people with respect." Hill & Barlow was among the first Boston firms to adopt spouse equivalent benefits for gay attorneys. In addition, there are "good role models for minorities" at the firm. One contact remarked that Hill & Barlow is "arguably the most friendly firm in Boston towards female, gay, and minority attorneys."

open management

Hill & Barlow's management is open and accessible. The firm is bound by what one person labeled a "modern partnership agreement"; approximately 80% of compensation is calculated by set formulas so that each partner has significant "control" over his own practice, "subject to meeting the firm's expectations that all partners will carry their fair share of the workload," we were told. All of the firm's partners have access to its financial books and to specific information about individual member compensation. Associates have occasional meetings with the firm's management committee to discuss issues of concern, and are given substantial access to financial information regarding the firm.

office facilities

Located at One International Place, Hill & Barlow's offices are close to both Downtown Crossing and South Station. The offices are decorated with "modern art." The firm has a recently expanded dining room, where catered lunches are served once a week, and a rooftop deck with tables. A health club is located in the office building, and the firm subsidizes memberships for all associates. Each associate has a private office, but past summer associates have had to share offices. There is not much difference in size between partner and associate offices.

hiring tips Hill & Barlow hires people who "can take responsibility early," said one person. The firm places a premium on previous work experience and hires many people who are in their "second career." The firm hires from a very broad range of schools. The 1996 summer and new associate classes came from more than ten different law schools. Callback interviews involve meeting four or five attorneys at the firm for about a half hour each. Most interviews involve discussions about a student's background and experiences in college and law school.

With its flexible work environment, open management, and progressive attitude toward female, gay and minority attorneys, Hill & Barlow offers its associates an "unpressured" environment. Hill & Barlow has a strong pro bono commitment and maintains extensive political connections. Further, this firm provides the prestige and starting salary of a large law firm. In later years, however, you are likely "to earn somewhat less than a lawyer in a 200 or 300 attorney firm, but you're also working significantly less (1800 vs. 2500 billable hours)," stated one insider. For those students interested in a firm that combines significant government or public interest work with a challenging mainstream practice, Hill & Barlow may be just the place.

Mintz, Levin, Cohn, Ferris, Glovsky and Popeo

Boston Washington

Address: One Financial Center, Boston, MA 02111
Telephone: (617) 542–6000
Hiring Attorney: Rosemary Allen, Chair, Hiring Committee
Contact: Letha A. Hemingway, Manager of Attorney Recruitment and Training; (617) 348–1793
Associate Salary: First year $79,000 (1997)
Summer Salary: $1520/week (1997)
Average Hours: 2068 worked; 1902 billed (including pro bono); 1875 target
Family Benefits: 8 weeks paid parental leave (4 unpaid); extended leave permissible; emergency day care on-site
1996 Summer: Class of 10 students; offers to 10
Partnership: 29% of entering associates from 1981–1988 were made partner
Pro Bono: 2% of all work is pro bono

Mintz, Levin, Cohn, Ferris, Glovsky and Popeo in 1997
184 Lawyers at the Boston Office
1.2 Associates Per Partner

Total Partners 84		
Women	15	18%
All Minorities	1	1%
Afro-Am	1	1%

Total Associates 100		
Women	45	45%
All Minorities	10	10%
Afro-Am	5	5%
Asian-Am	3	3%
Latino	2	2%

Practice Areas	
Litigation (Labor & Employ.)	60
Business	59
Real Estate	16
Health/Government	15
Employment Labor & Benefits	11
Commercial	7
Environmental	8
Tax	4
Trusts & Estates/ERISA	4

"In 1850 Chicago was a village, and by 1875 it was a huge city. This is Mintz Levin," commented one observer. A firm of 70 lawyers just a decade ago, Mintz Levin has grown explosively to become one of Boston's largest law firms. The growth of this aggressive and dynamic firm has stabilized over the past five years, and Mintz

Levin has acquired additional office space to absorb its earlier dramatic increases. The offices were renovated in 1995–96, and the library was expanded at the same time. The library affords a "beautiful view of Boston Harbor," we were told.

energetic culture

Not surprisingly, Mintz Levin is hard-working and high-energy. There is a very "upbeat" feel to the firm, said one insider. Its go-getter lawyers are chatty, energetic, and entrepreneurial. People communicate well and the environment fosters openness; it is not a place for shy people. The lawyers tend to express themselves in hyperbole: things aren't "good," they are "fabulous," and everything is "extreme." One source said, "There are a lot of jokers there. It's a place where you have to be able to give and take a joke. It's very vocal and very friendly, and many people try to make it a fun place to be."

ethnic culture

Mintz Levin is distinguished from other large Boston firms by its ethnicity and political connections. Founded at the beginning of the Great Depression by Jewish lawyers, Mintz Levin "views itself as an outsider firm because it was hiring Jews and Catholics when others didn't," said one contact. Mintz Levin "is very ethnic. If you are ethnic and that is important to you, it's the best environment in Boston. It's a tolerant place. You can be yourself there," raved another. The number of minority attorneys at the firm has increased in recent years. Darin Smith, an African-American attorney, and Christina Hernandez-Malaby, an Hispanic attorney, are members of the firm's hiring committee.

Democratic firm

Mintz Levin is reputedly a Democratic political insider firm and many of its lawyers are well-connected to city and state politics and government. The firm has defended a number of high-profile politicians such as Nick Mavroules, Vinnie Piro, and John Silber. Name partner, Bob Popeo, is said to have connections with "everyone" and is very active in politics and political campaigns. Frank Bellotti, former Massachusetts Attorney General, is a partner at the firm. Fran Meaney, who "was big with Dukakis," is the firm's former managing partner. Although Mintz Levin is known as a "liberal" firm, it is not uncomfortable for most conservatives. "It's an open place with lots of political discussion. You can always find a heated argument going on," said one commentator.

top public finance practice

Mintz Levin offers one of the city's top public finance practices, which regularly taps into the firm's extensive political connections. For years, Mintz Levin almost exclusively counseled the State of Massachusetts on bond issues. Although the department no longer enjoys a lockhold in this area, it continues to remain one of Boston's premier municipal bond practices. Mintz Levin represents a large number of state and municipal entities. The firm regularly works on issues for the Massachusetts Turnpike Authority, the Massachusetts Bay Transportation Authority, the state's housing finance agency, and the state's student loan agencies.

corporate

Mintz Levin also offers a large corporate practice, which houses "hot" biotech, venture capital, and information technology practices. The corporate practice has recently become a "larger and more lucrative practice group within the firm," reported one insider. An increasing volume of the firm's corporate work is for public companies, and the firm regularly handles IPOs for both issuers and underwriters. In addition, a growing component of the practice is international.

dynamic litigation

In the 1960s, Mintz Levin was primarily a corporate boutique firm. The firm got more than it bargained for, however, when it added Bob Popeo to bolster its litigation practice. Now the firm's largest practice, litigation is the "tail wagging the dog," said one insider. Much of the department's enormous growth over the last 20 years is attributable to Popeo, who is described as the "father" and "spiritual guru and decision-maker at the firm." Mintz Levin's most prominent litigator, "he is an enormous positive force and a phenomenal business generator," noted one source. The bulk of the litigation practice is business litigation, which includes substantial work in the areas of construction, securities, and product liability, among others.

pro bono

Although Mintz Levin has a formal pro bono practice coordinated by a 10-lawyer pro bono committee, it is characteristically fairly unstructured. As in other aspects of Mintz Levin's practice, the firm is very supportive of individual innovative efforts, and encourages interested employees to assist shelters, advocacy groups, and other organizations on firm time. Mintz Levin is very active in battered women's advocacy issues and was an original sponsor of the Jane Doe project. In recent years, domestic violence has been a top priority for the pro bono committee, we were told. The firm has worked on political asylum cases through the citywide PAIR Project, and it also provides services to homeless men and women through The Lawyers Clearing House on Affordable Housing, and the Homelessness Clinic at the Pine Street Inn. Hours worked on pro bono projects are credited in the same manner as client billable hours, we were told.

associate development

Mintz Levin attempts to assign entering associates to their top choice departments, but it's somewhat of a "black box process," said one person. After one year at the firm, associates may elect to rotate into another department. Everyone we interviewed praised the firm's commitment to associate development. Most first-year associates work closely with senior associates and partners and receive good training and feedback from both. In addition, Mintz Levin provides a "strong in-house, ongoing education program," reported one person. It also provides detailed feedback for summer associates. One person noted that almost everyone she had contact with completed extensive evaluation forms. Because even the staff completes evaluations of the summer associates, "it's important to impress the staff as well as the attorneys," one insider advised prospective summer associates. The firm conducts mid- and end-of-summer reviews at which time it goes over "an enormous sheaf of papers" that evaluate summer associate performance. Mintz Levin's open atmosphere also results in frank feedback for permanent associates. Most associates are well-informed about their partnership prospects. Mintz Levin has a two-tier partnership with equity and salaried partners. One insider informed us that in recent years, "partnership prospects for young associates are slim, as the firm has grown so rapidly and added so many partners. Frankly, there isn't much room. And crossing the line from salaried partner to equity partner gets more difficult each year."

frank management

Mintz Levin's management exhibits a "refreshing openness," said one person. The firm allows its associates to review certain financial information during a day-long retreat each year. The firm holds regular associate/partner meetings and does not closely guard information about the firm and its decisions. The meetings are frequently "controversial" with frank, "unedited" remarks, reported our contacts. Mintz Levin named a new managing partner, Irwin Heller, in late 1996, "charged with trimming the fat, increasing profits per partner, raising the profile of the firm—basically enhancing the bottom line," reported another contact, who additionally observed that "there is real concern within the firm about what will happen here in five or six years when Bob Popeo decides to retire. He is such a pillar. If I were a prospective summer associate, that is the question I would want answered."

summer program

The firm "pulls out all stops for its summer program," said one source. The program includes "ball games, symphony trips, dinners, miniature golf outings, sporting events, etc." It hosts a beer and wine get-together at the office every Friday. It's a "fun place to be in terms of social activities," said one person. The summer associates also participate in two community service activities each summer—one arranged by the firm for its attorneys and summer associates and one arranged by the Association of Boston Legal Recruitment Administrators for all Boston summer associates. Summer associates are also encouraged to leave work by 5 P.M. each day and are not subjected to the rigors of associate life. Associates typically work until 7 P.M. and come to the office on two weekend days per month. "If you're willing to stay until 10:00 P.M. every night, then you could avoid weekends altogether," stated one person. The litigation group has the "classic, I–have–no–life syndrome," said another, who noted that when the group is busy, it is not uncommon for associates to work until 2 A.M. Associate compensation has been a sore subject in recent years, we were told. "The firm has lagged behind other leading firms in the city as far as associate pay is concerned, a fact that has been widely noted and discussed among associates," reported one contact. A firm spokesperson informed us that, as of April 1, 1997, the firm revised its compensation system, "both base and bonus components, in order to remain competitive in salaries with the largest firms in the city and to reward our top performers."

enlightened lawyers

"For women," Mintz Levin "is an astonishingly nice place." Hiring partner Rosemary Allen is said to be a very successful lawyer at the firm. One woman we interviewed stated that Mintz Levin includes "the most enlightened group of male lawyers I have ever worked with." The firm is progressive on family issues, said several people, and has emergency day care for its employees. Mintz also reportedly does well in offering paternity and maternity leaves. The firm is, however, "struggling to adjust to the demands of part-time work, with so many female attorneys," we were informed.

recruits entrepreneurs

With its success, Mintz Levin has become one of Boston's more competitive firms at which to get a summer associate offer. The firm hires its summer associates from a broad range of law schools, drawing heavily from the top 10 national and Boston-area law schools. One person claimed that Mintz Levin hires a number of students from Northeastern Law School, many of whom work at the firm during the school year. Mintz Levin places special emphasis on hiring people with entrepreneurial qualities. It has overlooked more academically qualified candidates for those who have demonstrated personal initiative or entrepreneurial skills, asserted one insider. Mintz Levin also hires a number of older students with interesting backgrounds or people in their second careers. The firm is more "willing to take chances" in its hiring than other Boston firms, commented one person.

In recent years Mintz Levin has come to rely more heavily on lateral hiring, both among associates and partners. There are fewer and fewer "home grown" Mintz Levin lawyers who started out at the firm as summer associates and worked their way up. "As a result, there is a noticeably different feel to the place: more impersonal, more corporate, less friendly. With increasing demands on attorneys to bill and to produce, with a larger firm housed on five separate (but contiguous) floors, and with more and more laterals among the attorneys it has become less of what Mintz Levin used to be and more of what it never wanted to be," according to one insider. In addition, we were told that turnover among lawyers has increased (a point the firm disputes), several important partners have left in the past year or so, and "associate morale has suffered as compensation has lagged behind other firms and partnership prospects have grown bleak."

Nutter, McClennen & Fish

Boston Hyannis

Address: One International Place, Boston, MA 02110–2699
Telephone: (617) 439–2000
Hiring Attorney: Lisa C. Wood; Summer Hiring Committee: James E. Dawson (Chair) Peter R. Brown, Timothy M. Smith
Contact: Amy L. Johnson, Legal Hiring Coordinator; (617) 439–2351
Associate Salary: First year $76,000 (1997)
Summer Salary: $1462/week (1997)
Average Hours: NA worked; NA billed; 1800–2000 required.
Family Benefits: Pregnancy and child rearing leave; family leave; dependent care assistance plan, childcare referral service
1996 Summer: Class of 10 students; offers to 10
Partnership: 27% of entering associates from 1976–1987 were made partner
Pro Bono: 5% of all work is pro bono

Nutter, McClennen & Fish in 1997
113 Lawyers at the Boston Office
1.1 Associates Per Partner

Total Partners 51		
Women	9	18%
All Minorities	0	0%

Total Associates 55		
Women	26	47%
All Minorities	4	7%
Afro-Am	2	4%
Asian-Am	2	4%

Practice Areas	
Business	36
Litigation	31
Real Estate & Finance	14
Trusts & Estates	13
Labor	8
Environmental	6
Intellectual Property	7
Hyannis	5
Tax	5

a solid firm proud of its history

Founded in 1879, Nutter, McClennen & Fish is one of Boston's older firms. "The firm takes great pride in its history," said one source. Former Supreme Court Justice Louis D. Brandeis is a co-founder of the firm, and an office wing is named after him. Nutter provides a lunchtime lecture on its history to summer associates. Though it is a top-tier Boston law firm, Nutter is not "driven to keep its name at the top of the list," noted one insider. "You get the sense that they are happy with who they are—a solid firm. The lack of hype eases things for people there."

Nutter experienced some tough economic times during the recession of the early 1990s, partly because it had over-expanded in the 1980s. At that time, it "envisioned itself as a global rather than a regional law firm," said one source, and it unnecessarily rented expensive offices at One International Place. More recently, the firm has made a strong comeback, we were told. It has recently signed a new five year lease at One International Place at "very favorable terms," and there is a "real excitement about the financial future," reported one insider.

litigation

Nutter's litigation department handles a broad range of litigation matters and primarily represents large business interests. The litigation department is run by a three-member "steering committee," unlike other departments which have individual heads. The committee is composed of Neil Motenko (Chair), Ned Leibensperger, and Dan Gleason—all well-known and well-respected trial lawyers "who have brought a lot of energy to the job." Partner Bob Ullmann, formerly Senior Litigation Counsel in the U.S. Attorney's office, has a growing white-collar crime practice. Nutter also offers an environmental group that was established as a "spin off of the litigation practice in the

1980s." Partners Mary Ryan and Robert Fishman are well-regarded for their aggressive efforts to market the firm's environmental practice.

business

The business department, headed by Steve Andress, is now the largest department in the firm. These partners are among the firm's most "accessible" to associates, we were told. The business department has an intellectual property group consisting of about a half a dozen intellectual property lawyers. The group plans to hire more attorneys, we were told. The business department has handled some international work in Europe and Asia. Nutter is a member of the "Tech Law Group," an international network of six U.S. and five European law firms "serving the legal needs of business, institutions, and individuals involved in technology."

real estate

The real estate practice has recovered nicely from the slowdown of the early 1990s. Its leader, Gary Zanercik "is aggressive and runs a tight ship. He is very energetic and driven," stated one person, who gave this department "a plus for its leadership in finding ways to keep business going and responding creatively."

trusts and estates

The trusts and estates lawyers form a "tight group" and enjoy "a good working relationship," reported one source. The practice is assisted by an affiliated Nutter Investment Advisors, which manages trust accounts. Nutter's management-side labor lawyers handle some interesting alternative dispute resolution work.

Nutter does not have a formal pro bono committee, but rather a pro-bono partner, Andy McElaney, who serves on many non-profit committees in the city. Many partners are active in the community, including Michael Bohnen, who is the past president of the Combined Jewish Philanthropies. Nutter also supports a number of community organizations and donates conference room space for their meetings. Many associates do projects for the "Volunteer Lawyers Project," a Boston-based clearinghouse for individual cases, and "receive billable credit for these cases, which are usually small enough that you can handle them on your own," reported one contact. The aforementioned Mary Ryan, is President Elect of the Boston Bar Association.

improved training

Nutter, McClennen & Fish offers a "friendly" and informal work environment. It places most new associates in their top-choice departments and permits them to pursue their professional interests. Nutter has, moreover, improved its formal training programs of late, we were told. "Each department has a program—for example, litigation just finished a four-session deposition seminar series (run by partners), and is having a deposition workshop to practice techniques, and a two-hour mock trial," reported one insider. The firm also conducts monthly training for associates, junior partners, and paralegals on such topics as "effective time management" and "sexual harassment in the workplace." In addition, Boston Bar Association and MCLE courses are available to supplement in-house training.

Most cases are leanly staffed which "means early responsibility and learning directly from experienced partners—the biggest plus about Nutter," reported one contact. A number of second-year associates represent "a handful of their own clients," pronounced another contact. "By the second or third year people are in control of the cases they work on." People also praised the feedback given to summer and permanent associates. Attorneys complete written evaluations of each project submitted by summer associates. Nutter attorneys then meet with summer associates at mid- and end-of-summer to review their written evaluations.

management

Highly respected tax partner Mike Mooney serves as Nutter's managing partner. He is "completely dedicated to the firm and actively tries to maintain an open relationship with attorneys," one commentator stated. People are "happy with him and trust him."

Nevertheless, "the management at Nutter has meetings with associates only quarterly. The partners own the business and run the show, and they don't seem very open about sharing information," complained one source. A firm spokesperson pointed out that, in addition to the quarterly meetings with Mike Mooney, associates and junior partners also have monthly meetings with senior partners on the firm's legal personnel committee.

diversity

Nutter is "not a close-minded place that is locked into traditions," said one contact. Though Nutter has "lots of men in charge," a significant number of women work at the firm and are making "inroads...into the partnership." Currently, nine of the firm's 51 partners and five of the firm's nine junior partners are women. Described as a "role model," Mary Ryan heavily influences the environmental department. The corporate department, by contrast, is characterized by a more "masculine environment," said one person. Though an "eclectic" group, Nutter attorneys do not include many minority attorneys. Nutter is, however, making "inroads in minority hiring (the present first-year class has two African-Americans), although unfortunately progress is slow throughout Boston," one contact informed us. Nutter is a member of "The Boston Law Firm Group," a coalition of the largest Boston firms formed in 1986 "for the purpose of consolidating resources toward a joint commitment of achieving a higher representation of blacks and other minorities in the ranks of practicing attorneys within the major law firms in the city."

Nutter's offices are located near South Station and "right on the harbor." The library received high praise: one person noted that it is "well-kept and staffed," and another exclaimed that the "library staff *must* be one of the tops in the city." Every attorney has a private office that is decorated in "light colors and light wood." The firm's computers are on a Local Area Network and run Windows. "The computer system has the usual perks—in litigation a bunch of CD ROM databases, Westlaw, and LEXIS," attested one contact.

hiring tips

For summer hires, Nutter has a "Summer Hiring Committee," composed of three partners. Nutter hires most summer associates from the top 10 national and Boston-area schools. The firm draws heavily on Boston College and Harvard. Almost all the summer associates who do not attend top schools are members of a law review or Moot Court, one insider noted. At the callback, candidates usually interview with a member of the Summer Hiring Committee, one or two senior partners, and one or two senior associates. They then go out to lunch with two junior associates. Most callback interviews are conversational. No one we interviewed was asked substantive legal questions. According to one insider, the partners make the hiring decisions, and they are mainly "looking to see if you fit" into the firm culture.

Nutter is a well-established and carefully managed law firm. Nutter's overall pluses include a "friendly, informal atmosphere with a lot of contact with partners on a professional level, allowing associates to learn first hand from top-notch attorneys," remarked one contact. Moreover, according to this person, associates at Nutter "probably bill a little less than the average 'big firm' associate in the city." The downside is that associate salaries, "while attractive to first-year hires, do not increase nearly as rapidly as at other big firms in the city. New associates looking exclusively for the big bucks may find Nutter frustrating." That said, if you are seeking early responsibility in litigation or business, a more relaxed work environment in other areas, and are attracted by the flexibility of Nutter's professional development opportunities, it may be the place for you.

Palmer & Dodge

Boston

Address: One Beacon Street, Boston, MA 02108
Telephone: (617) 573–0100
Hiring Attorney: Scott P. Lewis
Contact: Katy von Mehren, Director of Associate Recruitment; (617) 573–0172
Associate Salary: First year $73,000 (1996)
Summer Salary: NA
Average Hours: 2124 worked; 1852 billed; 1800 required
Family Benefits: Parental leave; emergency day care; medical, life and disability; 401(K); employee assistance program; dependent care plan; subsidized membership in health club
1996 Summer: Class of 15 students; offers to 12
Partnership: 18% of entering associates from 1979–1985 were made partner
Pro Bono: 3–5% of all work is pro bono

Palmer & Dodge in 1997
167 Lawyers at the Firm
1.2 Associates Per Partner

Total Partners 71		
Women	9	13%
All Minorities	2	3%
Afro-Am	1	1%
Latino	1	1%

Total Associates 84		
Women	45	54%
All Minorities	4	5%
Afro-Am	1	1%
Asian-Am	1	1%
Latino	2	2%

Practice Areas	
Corporate	64
Litigation	41
Public Finance	18
Probate/Trusts	14
Real Estate	11
Labor (management)	7

Palmer & Dodge is "one of the friendliest" firms in Boston, said one person. It offers a low-key environment without excessive billable hour pressure. It is a chatty firm, and its lawyers form a tight-knit group. Most Palmer & Dodge lawyers are married and enjoy "lives outside of the firm," and very few lawyers "leave Palmer & Dodge for other large law firms," we were told. Palmer is, however, changing. It is losing some of its laid-back life-style-allure and becoming a busier place. "Associates are working *very* hard and maintaining a life outside the firm is difficult," reported one insider.

lack of structure

Although Palmer & Dodge is now one of Boston's larger firms, its lawyers have resisted developing many of the large firm institutional structures necessary to organize its growth. In many ways, Palmer & Dodge continues to function like a medium-sized firm with a relatively informal and flexible work atmosphere. Some people praised the opportunities and flexibility provided by the firm, but others complained that it lacks organizational structure. A firm spokesperson pointed out, however, that Palmer & Dodge has focused a great deal of management effort on the organization of practice groups and on business growth.

improved summer program

In the earlier edition of *The Insider's Guide*, we reported that many complaints had been voiced regarding Palmer & Dodge's summer program. Things appear to have changed for the better. The distribution of assignments is managed by a team of three members of the Hiring Committee, who seek to provide "summer associates with opportunities to work on projects that they choose, but also to ensure that they have exposure to the broad range of work" that the firm does, we were told. Last year, Palmer & Dodge introduced a "paired partner" program for summer associates interested in the firm's transaction practice. Summer associates were given an opportunity to "spend about half of their summer working with two transactional partners on whatever deals they were handling at that time," thus allowing the summer associates to "get a good handle on an otherwise elusive, but critical aspect of every business law firm." Palmer & Dodge has also made efforts to improve the frequency and quality of feedback to summer associates. The entire portfolio of work completed by each summer associate is "reviewed and evaluated (at least twice each summer) by a partner who is a member of the Hiring Committee," a firm spokesperson reported. A firm insider informed us that feedback tends to vary in quality with the particular partner or senior associate that the summer associate is working for.

considerable associate development

Permanent associates are hired into a particular department from which they receive all their assignments. The firm offers a number of formal training programs such as a trial advocacy workshop and a negotiation skills seminar. Programs in technical lawyering skills as well as ethics and marketing are also offered by the firm. Palmer & Dodge also encourages participation in outside training programs. The firm devotes considerable resources to associate development. One lawyer devotes all of her time to training and development, and she is overseen by a professional development committee that is made up of both partners and associates.

practice areas

Palmer & Dodge has major departments—litigation, business law, public finance, real estate, probate (private client), and labor—as well as a number of cross-departmental groups that offer unusual and interesting practices for a large law firm. Palmer & Dodge offers perhaps the only large law firm entertainment and publishing practice in the city. John Taylor Williams, who was voted best-dressed by *Boston Magazine* and answers to "Ike," co-chairs the group which represents major publishing, film and television clients. Mark Fischer, a leading entertainment lawyer, has recently joined the firm as partner. This practice is affiliated with a literary agency for writers, which recently represented O.J. Simpson in connection with a book deal.

litigation

Palmer & Dodge is a "great firm to go to for litigation," said one source. It has represented the Massachusetts Institute of Technology (MIT) in a prominent antitrust case. The department also handles products liability, construction, and insurance litigation. In addition, it houses an interesting First Amendment practice. The litigation attorneys are "the most dynamic and personable people in the firm and...work extremely hard," claimed one contact.

growing corporate

The business department is the largest department in the firm and represents a number of large institutional clients such as banks, insurance carriers, and universities. One contact informed us that "the business department has added so many laterals lately that when I walk down the hall, I am never sure of the identity of the person passing me." The commercial lending group is said to be quite busy and has added new associates from both the summer program and laterally. The hottest group at the firm is a growing and successful technology practice encompassing both high-tech and biotech matters. This group has recently increased its size substantially with the addition of several intellectual property attorneys. The firm is also said to be developing an international joint venture practice.

public law practice

Palmer & Dodge is home to a highly-regarded public law department that handles a variety of bond offerings and public finance projects at the city and state level. People noted that the public finance group is noticeably partner heavy. It has recently hired lateral attorneys but has difficulty retaining associates, we were told.

labor and real estate

Palmer & Dodge's labor department is small but strong. It can be difficult, however, for summer associates to get assignments in this group, our contacts informed us. They also noted that the department has not hired many new associates recently. Palmer & Dodge also offers a real estate practice that is small but very busy, despite the slow real estate market. The real estate attorneys are said to be "cohesive."

pro bono

People praised Palmer & Dodge's pro bono practice, which is headed by a litigation partner. All hours billed to pro bono count toward billable hours, and associates are encouraged to pursue pro bono cases. Several associates participate in the Bar Advocate Program, providing criminal defense representation to indigent clients in Boston's Municipal Court. Others have spent considerable time representing detained Mariel Cubans in obtaining parole. The firm's lawyers also engage in a variety of other pro bono projects, from representing battered women to handling zoning issues for halfway houses.

diversity

Palmer & Dodge provides a good atmosphere for women, according to people we interviewed. It has established a gender issues committee, and there is "a lot of talk about gender issues" at the firm, noted one source. Palmer & Dodge is also "very open to women working part-time," and there has "never been any question that women who left to raise children could come back to the firm," one person told us. The litigation department provides a better environment for women than the corporate department, we were told. A number of prominent women work at the firm, including Judith Malone, who is influential in the labor department, Laurie Gill and Tamara Wolfson, who are highly regarded in the litigation department, Maureen Manning in the business department, and Ruth-Ellen Fitch, an African-American and a former hiring partner at the firm. Though very few minority attorneys work at Palmer & Dodge, the firm is aware of the need for greater diversity, and Fitch is committed to increasing the number of minority attorneys at the firm.

conservative management

Palmer & Dodge is managed conservatively by a five partner executive board that includes the "well-liked" managing partner, Ron Kessel. The firm did not over-extend itself in the 1980s and remained financially stable through the recession of the early 1990s. Several people however, were critical of the firm's compensation system. Although the firm implemented an associate bonus system that reportedly raised associate pay to levels comparable to other large Boston firms, regardless of seniority, one insider informed us that "associates are largely dissatisfied with the bonus program and have complained to the Executive Committee about its many faults." Another contact told us that "there is more than a little resentment among associates about the current (salary) situation. After an associate's third year, his or her salary is frozen at $83,000—with a mystery bonus at the end of the year. As the individual's seniority increases, the 'bonus' makes up a greater and greater portion of his or her salary. Therefore, it isn't a bonus at all."

office facilities

Palmer & Dodge has an "awesome" cafeteria that serves breakfast, lunch, and great "health food" at subsidized prices, we were told. After 7 P.M. the cafeteria leftovers are stored in an accessible refrigerator, providing an abundance of snacks for those who work late. Palmer & Dodge's offices are located at One Beacon Street in the middle "of three huge areas that will never be developed, so there never will be huge sky scrapers around the building," asserted one person. The facilities are "not plush, but are clean and professional." Every attorney has a private office with an IBM computer that can access both Westlaw and LEXIS and a host of CD-ROM products. People especially praised the library and its staff. A Fitcorp gym is located in the building, and the firm subsidizes half of the membership cost for any of its employees.

hiring tips

Although a large number of Palmer & Dodge partners attended Harvard Law School, the firm now hires law students from a wide range of top schools. Almost all the students that the firm hires from local schools are in the top quarter of their law school classes. However, the firm places surprisingly little emphasis on law review membership, we were told. The firm considers personality at least as much as grades when it makes hiring decisions, claimed one insider, who also said that Palmer &

Dodge places a premium on hiring people with interesting backgrounds. Interviews at the firm are informal and "a good time." One person commented that "everyone knew I was coming for the interview, and they had constructive questions to ask me." Much of the interview involves asking attorneys questions about the firm, said another person. This person advised candidates to come to the callback prepared with a number of questions.

Palmer & Dodge is a firm that offers "significant responsibility very early," has lean staffing on most assignments, and provides a "strong sense of camaraderie" among associates. The firm has been very busy of late, and hence hiring, both of recent graduates and laterals, is on the increase. The partners are "generally not abusive. They expect associates to work hard and do quality work but they treat us with respect and as professionals and recognize that we have a life outside of work," commented one insider. Another person praised the partners for being "approachable" and "very appreciative of our efforts." Overall, the reviews we received of associate life at Palmer & Dodge were quite favorable, aptly summed up by one contact's observation that, "all in all, I wouldn't want to work anywhere else. The atmosphere is intense, but extremely collegial. Isn't that the most you can expect from a big firm?" The one sustained criticism that came to our attention concerned compensation, which is less than at some other comparable firms in the city, and relatedly the benefits package, which could be "beefed up." For example, there is no dental coverage, we were told. This aside, if you have good teeth and are looking for a firm with social cohesion and exciting practice areas, Palmer and Dodge should get a look.

Peabody & Arnold

Boston Portland Providence

Address: 50 Rowes Wharf, Boston, MA 02110
Telephone: (617) 951–2100
Hiring Attorney: John P. Connelly
Contact: Aimee E. Maescher, Recruitment Coordinator/Marketing Support Specialist; (617) 261–5133
Associate Salary: First year $74,000 (1997)
Summer Salary: $1423/week (1997)
Average Hours: 1864 worked; 1749 billed; NA required
Family Benefits: 12 weeks paid maternity leave; part-time available until child's first birthday
1996 Summer: Class of 3 students; offers to 3
Partnership: 9% of entering associates from 1980–1986 were made partner
Pro Bono: NA

Peabody & Arnold in 1997
109 Lawyers at the Boston Office
0.6 Associates Per Partner

Total Partners 64			Total Associates 40			Practice Areas	
Women	11	17%	Women	14	35%	Litigation	52
All Minorities	3	5%	All Minorities	4	10%	Business	44
Afro-Am	1	2%	Afro-Am	2	5%	Trusts & Estates	13
Asian-Am	2	3%	Asian-Am	2	5%		

Founded by a Harvard Law School graduate and an English barrister who came to the U.S. to practice law, Peabody & Arnold is one of Boston's oldest and most prominent law firms. It has grown tremendously in recent years but strives to maintain a small firm atmosphere, although the expansion has occasioned "severe growing pains for attorneys and staff," according to one insider. Despite its established history, Peabody has come to be known as one of the more progressive firms in Boston. Peabody is a firm where there is "very little, if any competition to kill yourself by working long billable days. Most associates lead active lives outside the firm and are out of the office by 6:00 or 6:30 P.M."

open management

Peabody & Arnold has an open and receptive management. Its managing partner, Joe Hinkley, is "an amazingly nice guy and *very* intelligent," said one person. He "spends a lot of his time—he says all of his time—walking around talking to lawyers and listening to people." An associates committee meets regularly to discuss issues of importance and serves as a formal channel to the firm's management committee. "However, the layered structure of the firm's management often results in the dilution of the committee's issues before they reach the highest level," we were told. Some of Peabody's management is handled by nonlawyers. The "personnel director, the head of the library, the person in charge of the facilities, and the head computer manager make many of the management decisions at their levels," reported one source.

practice areas

The litigation and business law departments are the "bread and butter" of Peabody's practice. The litigation department has experienced quite a bit of change in the last three years. During this period, two practice groups left the firm and a group of attorneys from the now defunct firm of Parker, Coulter, Daley & White joined Peabody. The recently incorporated litigators from Parker practice in insurance defense, products liability, employment, and general liability. The group also includes an outstanding practice in directors and officers liability coverage. Peabody is "most well-known" for its insurance and surety defense work and has been very busy with work related to the Federal Deposit Insurance Corporation (FDIC). A top trusts and estates boutique firm in its early days, Peabody & Arnold maintains a strong trusts and estates department which serves as trustee for a number of large family trusts, some of which have been managed by the firm since its inception. This practice also houses a group of nonlawyers, including a number of certified public accountants, trust management personnel, and an investment banker.

The firm's business law group consists of corporate, banking, finance, and real estate attorneys. Although in the past much of Peabody's corporate practice involved providing services to the firm's litigation clients, this is not as true today. Peabody's real estate and banking and finance practices have been busy with loan workouts as well as new loans. One contact informed us that "the firm has placed an emphasis on expanding its business and corporate practice, but progress has been slow and several midlevel corporate associates have left the firm."

Peabody has a pro bono practice, but most pro bono involvement is left to individual initiative. Former managing partner John Brooks helped found the Greater Boston Legal Services Board, and this organization sends the firm a number of pro bono cases. The firm's pro bono program is coordinated by two equity partners. Pro bono activities are not counted as billable hours, we were informed.

early litigation experience

Peabody prides itself on providing early responsibility. One insider noted that the "biggest advantage for litigators at Peabody is the early and frequent in-court time. Many partners believe in a fair amount of hands-off, autonomous practice for the associates." Another contact further praised: "I have daily client contact and the partners trust my judgement and ability to handle myself with clients. They don't handle the 'major' calls themselves. When I can't handle a meeting alone, I am often brought along because it would be worthwhile training." Most associate training occurs informally and on-the-job; the formal training and mentoring arrangements were both criticized as being inadequate. Similarly, "there is not a whole lot of guidance" in the summer associate program, remarked one source. Past summer associates have been assigned a mentor whom they could "go to for help," but most "only get feedback if they ask for it." Summer associates also complained that they never received a mid-summer review and that, in most cases, the end-of-summer review was a mere formality. According to a firm spokesperson, the firm has subsequently improved its feedback system, by providing students with substantive mid-summer and end-of-summer reviews, but our contacts reported otherwise.

balanced lifestyle

Peabody encourages its attorneys to lead a "balanced lifestyle," and most of its lawyers are "family oriented." People commented that the firm is "not a good place for social life" for young, single attorneys. The summer program is not a wine and dine experience, though the firm arranges a wide variety of social events, many of which are family oriented. From time to time the firm hosts a "wind down" cocktail party, which used to be held at the Boston Harbor Hotel but more recently is held at the firm. One contact lamented the lack of "any firmwide [social] event during the year which is off the firm's grounds," to which spouses and significant others are invited.

lower salary

Peabody's laid-back work environment does not come without some sacrifice. Peabody associates are paid less than some of their counterparts at other large, prestigious Boston firms. Although the starting salary of $74,000 is on par with most big firms, the salary curve is "smoother" than at other big firms. At Peabody, there is "not a big divergence between first- and fourth-year salaries," remarked one source. Another source commented that Peabody's "salary scale pales in comparison with firms of comparable size, and associates generally earn $10,000 to $15,000 less than their contemporaries elsewhere." Peabody partners also make less than their counterparts at some of the top firms. The average Peabody partner makes between two and three hundred thousand dollars a year, reported one person. Peabody has "no million dollar partners," nor does it greatly distinguish compensation among the partners, which reflects the firm's egalitarian culture.

partnership

With a low associate turnover rate, Peabody & Arnold prides itself on making a high percentage of partners (but see above statistics). One person noted, however, that most Peabody partners are young, and expressed concern about "where that leaves me seven or eight years down the road when these partners are all in their 50s and 60s." Another person observed that "the number of partners has grown to outnumber associates at a ratio of nearly 2 to 1." A third contact remarked that "there is certainly associate concern about this, but the steering committee has responded that they don't see it as a problem (there is enough room for all able-bodied, qualified associates)."

liberal firm

Peabody has a comfortable environment for women. A number of women exercise influence at the firm. Molly Sherden and Suanne St. Charles have served as hiring partners, and a woman partner has served, and another is presently serving, on the firm's steering committee. Deborah Griffin is a prominent litigator. Peabody is also progressive on family issues and recently adopted a paternity leave policy which, however, "remains unchartered waters for male attorneys," we were told. Described as "liberal," Peabody is also very receptive to hiring gay attorneys, praised one insider. The firm is home to an openly gay partner who handles a lot of work for some of the "major gay activist organizations" and is very active in gay political associations in Boston.

waterfront offices

Peabody occupies some of Boston's nicest offices. The firm is located right on the waterfront at 50 Rowes Wharf, which is "the premier newer development in Boston," according to one contact. The "office space in the building juts out in little wings over the water. Peabody occupies the top floor and a portion of the floor below. There is a big triumphal arch that opens onto the water, and at the top of the arch is a dome around which the library is built, looking down on the arch. It's gorgeous. The offices have a deck with umbrella tables." When the Tall Ships come into Boston they sit right outside the firm's windows. Peabody's offices are illuminated with halogen lamps and decorated with a "mix of English antiques and Early American and modern art." The two-color walls are fashioned in light wood with dark stripes. The conference rooms are either chrome and glass or wood and leather. "They may be the most beautiful offices in the city," claimed one source. Another source, however, remarked that the firm presently is experiencing "limited space" for its growing number of attorneys. The firm has lunch for attorneys and staff delivered daily which is available in the pantry for anyone who wishes to eat in the firm cafeteria or on the deck. Cost for the meals is deducted monthly from payroll. The information we received on secretarial staffing and the firm's computer system indicated that improvement would be welcomed in both areas.

breakfast interview

Some of Peabody's callback interviews begin with breakfast at the Boston Harbor Hotel. After breakfast, applicants return to the firm for interviews with three attorneys. Candidates may elect, instead, to skip the breakfast and to interview at the firm throughout the day with lunch in between. Interviews with each attorney typically last twenty minutes to a half hour, and usually involve "conversations about law school" or anything interesting in your background. Peabody attorneys assume that you can do the work if you are invited to interview at the firm. The primary purpose of the interview is to assess your personality, and whether you are "someone they would like to work with," said one successful applicant. The firm wants to hire someone with a pleasant personality, agreed another. In the past, Peabody has reportedly rejected people at the top of their law school classes because the attorneys felt they would not fit in well with the firm culture. One person claimed that about a quarter of the students that the firm hires are from Harvard, a quarter are from Boston College, and a quarter are from Boston University. Others come from "a variety of other distinguished law schools—Cornell, Notre Dame, Duke, etc."

Peabody is an open and inclusive law firm. It offers a pleasant work atmosphere and beautiful offices. It is not known as a "high pressure" firm. If you find this attractive, and are not deterred by its lower salaries, Peabody may be the place for you.

Ropes & Gray

Boston Providence Washington

Address: One International Place, Boston, MA 02110-2624
Telephone: (617) 951–7000
Hiring Attorney: Kenneth W. Erickson
Contact: Phyllis A. Spiro, Administrative Assistant; (617) 951–7000
Associate Salary: First year $79,000 (1997)
Summer Salary: $1515/week (1997)
Average Hours: 2275 worked; 1925 billed; no minimum required.
Family Benefits: 13 weeks paid maternity leave (13 unpaid unpaid); 2 weeks paid paternity leave (13 unpaid); 4 weeks paid family care leave (9 unpaid); emergency day care center on site; dependent care assistance plan; multiple reduced time options
1996 Summer: Class of 52 students; offers to 52
Partnership: 26% of entering associates from 1980–1987 were made partner
Pro Bono: 4% of all work is pro bono

Ropes & Gray in 1997
305 Lawyers at the Boston Office
1.3 Associates Per Partner

Total Partners 129		
Women	19	15%
All Minorities	3	2%
Afro-Am	2	2%
Asian-Am	1	1%

Total Associates 169		
Women	68	40%
All Minorities	16	10%
Afro-Am	4	2%
Asian-Am	11	7%
Latino	1	1%

Practice Areas	
Corporate	121
Litigation	77
Tax	22
Health	21
Estates & Probates	16
Real Estate	14
Employment/Benefits	12
Labor & Employment	12
Creditors' Rights	6
Municipal	4

Ropes & Gray is well-recognized as the "pre-eminent" Boston firm, said one person. Like a number of prestigious law firms, Ropes has been tagged as a stuffy and formal firm. Ropes is acutely aware of and self-conscious about this image. Though most people we interviewed said the firm does not fully deserve this label, it is supported by vestiges of truth. One person termed Ropes "reserved," noting that "people are not loud" at the firm; "there is a palpable air of respect here." In fact, the lawyers "are sort of academic. There are a fair number of the firm's attorneys who can be seen lost in thought and wandering around the firm's offices." Another person claimed that Ropes "has a reputation for being more formal," adding that "certainly etiquette is observed and followed at the firm." "Casual day" has not yet arrived at Ropes, but you can see a "good number of female associates wearing pantsuits" and "lawyers do call each other by their first name," we were informed. Insisting that the firm is not as formal as its image might suggest, one person recounted a prank in which some summer associates were summoned to an emergency client meeting at which, they were informed, they would have to take notes all afternoon. When they showed up, the "emergency" turned out to be a trip to the Mass Bay Brewery, a lively Boston bar (which also happens to be a firm client).

management

Ropes & Gray is "solid as a rock" financially. The firm is managed by a small, nine to 10 member "Policy Committee," whose role and responsibilities are "not widely or well-known even by the partners, but they make all the decisions," according to one insider. A firm spokesperson observed, however, that the firm is "managed on a consensus basis by a Policy Committee that functions like the administration at a university; lawyers throughout the firm make decisions about hiring, work assignments, training, practice development, and associate evaluation." Yet, Ropes & Gray received its lowest score (and tied for lowest in the city) on *The American Lawyer's* Midlevel Associates Survey in 1996 on "management openness." The firm, perhaps aware of shortcomings in this area, appears to be making improvements. One insider informed us that, of late, "there has been a movement by the Policy Committee to be more open and inclusive." The firm's top-notch legal reputation has continued to generate new business over the years. Ropes has done a "great job of establishing multigenerational loyalty" with its clients.

top-notch corporate

Ropes is known for having one of the best, if not *the* best, corporate practices in Boston. The firm "has the best corporate clients in New England (and beyond), and this generates the good work at Ropes," one source observed. Ropes recently represented Gillette (one of its oldest clients) in its acquisition of Duracell for about $7.8 billion—"the largest merger in New England history," we were told. The corporate practice at Ropes is now "exceptionally busy" which "makes for a rewarding experience" for associates, according to one insider. It also has its downside, however. A second contact informed us that "the high volume of corporate work means long hours and tight schedules." This is especially the case at present since "unfortunately, it seems a lot of midlevel corporate associates decided to leave during the past year." Another insider observed, more generally, that "there seems to be a significant amount of turnover among associates," adding that "the firm has redoubled its efforts to keep associates in the fold." Unlike many other Boston firms, Ropes has an international presence in Europe and Russia, and has clients "all over the world (France, Israel, etc.)." Truman Casner, who heads Ropes & Gray, is one of the firm's most prominent corporate attorneys.

other practice areas

In terms of attorneys, the litigation department has grown much less rapidly than the corporate department since our last edition, and one person observed that "corporate is the engine that drives the firm." Some people have expressed concern regarding the firm's litigation practice. One person remarked that "it has always been less strong than corporate and people in that department feel less secure about their future prospects at the firm." Another contact informed us that "last winter approximately six associates in litigation were told that they were not 'on track.' The firm says this was not without warning and it is kinder than stringing people along, but some associates call it a layoff plain and simple." A firm representative instructed us that "this rate of departure was not different from prior years" and that "litigation associates advance to partnership at rates equal to those in other areas of the firm."

The firm's trust and estates and tax practices are "small in the firm, but big...compared to similar practices in other firms." Ropes has one of the best trusts and estates practice in the country, asserted one contact. The tax practice encompasses a wide range of work, from corporate to estate planning and benefits. Ropes offers a "terrific" health care practice, praised as the "best in the country" by one insider; it has been very popular among summer associates. The health care practice represents almost all of the hospitals in Boston, and recently scored a "huge coup" in landing Stanford University. The firm has established an office of one attorney (who rotates out of the Boston office) in Palo Alto to handle this account. The health care practice, we were told, is "booming; in fact, it's too busy!" In addition, a number of Ropes attorneys enjoy special connections to politics. Partner Eldie Acheson was Hillary Clinton's roommate at Wellesley and is now the Assistant Attorney General for Policy Development. Corporate partner Peter Erichsen now serves in the White House as Associate Counsel to the President.

pro bono

The pro bono practice at Ropes is said to be "average to strong." While pro bono work is "encouraged," lawyers have to take personal initiative to do it. A pro bono committee oversees the practice, and partner Richard Ward manages much of it. Pro bono hours count fully toward billable hours. One contact informed us that "there has been some confusion over this matter amongst the associates but the firm insists it's true." Attorneys work on death penalty cases, criminal appeals, and represent battered women. The firm also "quietly" represents the homeless in Atlanta in their suit against the city. Numerous summer associates in 1996 were able to work substantial hours on this project.

professional development

Despite the firm's reputation for formality, people we interviewed said that Ropes is loosely structured. Starting associates may work in different departments for approximately two years before joining a particular department. "There is no formal edict from above," one insider noted; "in fact, the firm strongly encourages its new associates to explore and experiment in a number of different areas, even within a particular department, in order to gain a strong base of fundamental skills." Another contact pointed out, however, that "perhaps because the firm is so busy lately, it can be difficult to extricate yourself from one department to switch to another." Summer associates have considerable latitude in choosing the projects on which they work, we were told.

training

Ropes & Gray provides a considerable amount of formal training. Ted Finnegan runs a trial advocacy program that people claimed is better than most trial advocacy programs offered at top law schools. Ropes also offers many training seminars in substantive areas and permits two associates each year (usually third- to fifth-year litigation associates) to work in the Middlesex County District Attorney's office at full salary for six months. Ropes provides "one of the best training programs around. It's very thought out and organized," raved one source. Feedback is reportedly very good at Ropes & Gray.

In addition to the excellent training, we were told that responsibility generally comes earlier at Ropes than at many other large Boston firms. Most associates "have significant contact and responsibility after one or two years which allows for a learning curve which is steep, challenging, and rewarding," observed one contact. Another person commented that "corporate associates get a lot of client contact almost from day one." On the other hand, we were told that "if you want to be a trial lawyer, this is not the place to get experience in court. They'll teach you excellent research and writing skills, and Ted Finnegan runs a great workshop but forget about running to the courtroom on a regular basis." A firm spokesperson took exception to this observation, noting that many litigation associates "were first chair in trials, arbitrations, and dispositive motions during 1996."

cooperative atmosphere

The work atmosphere at Ropes was described as very "supportive" and "helpful." One contact remarked that, at Ropes, "there is a cooperative spirit. I don't feel in competition with my colleagues and I never hesitate to ask someone, even a senior partner, a small question. Everyone is incredibly helpful." Attorneys at Ropes are very "serious about their work" and demand the highest "work quality." Ropes is not a "chatty" firm. Most lawyers work hard during the day, and the firm's annual hours worked (2,275) are among the highest of the Boston firms we surveyed. Our contacts said there is not much billable hour pressure on junior associates, but noted that pressure grows more intense as associates approach partnership. One person noted, however, that "it is remarkable how little pressure (none) there is to bring in clients. There is a respectful atmosphere here," and another person observed that "people do not make unreasonable demands on your time and are flexible."

understated social life

Most Ropes attorneys "are married and have families. They go home after work. Ropes is not a good 'party with your associates' firm," although one contact informed us that "my class has a great core of partyers." The firm offers "fewer sponsored social activities than other firms" and exerts "less pressure to attend firm functions," commented one source. "It's not the kind of place where they take the summer associates out and get them plastered. It's kind of an understated place...Throughout the year they have a couple of events, but to a lesser extent than other firms," said another. Ropes sponsors a regular, firmwide, in-house attorneys' lunch, but one person described these lunches as events where "an associate gets up and talks about a case he is working on and feels like he has to give all the facts of the case to prove to the partners that he has a mastery of it." They can be "boring" affairs.

diversity

At the time of our last edition, Ropes & Gray had a low percentage of female associates and partners relative to the other Boston firms we surveyed. Since then, the firm's numbers have improved slightly; the 1996 summer associate class and the 1997 entering class are both 42% female. One contact informed us that "the female partners are really making an effort to reach out to associates. They have organized discussion groups to talk about issues like mentoring." Prominent female partners at the firm include the aforementioned Eldie Acheson and Mary Weber, a corporate attorney. One person noted that many smaller departments, such as real estate, tax, and health care, are areas in which women have "done well." People also described Ropes as a "very white" firm, but noted that the firm is "very conscious of this and is trying to improve it." One insider made the observation: "True, this place is no Benetton ad but it is trying and moving forward. We will not, however, sacrifice excellence for a number on a firm bio sheet."

office facilities

Ropes & Gray moved into the top 10 floors of One International Place in the early 1990s, and everything at the firm offices exudes "newness." The firm recently acquired an additional floor to accommodate its burgeoning corporate practice. The office building itself was described as a "monument to the 1980s" with the "1980s super-gaudy look." The lobby is "two and a half stories high, all done in marble." Ropes' offices have "terrific views" of the harbor on both sides. Every attorney has a private office and a personal computer that can access LEXIS, Westlaw, and the Internet. In addition, "there is a great home-to-office hookup free of charge." An extremely "knowledgeable librarian" oversees the good-sized library.

academic emphasis in hiring

Grades are important in getting hired at Ropes. Ropes hires "very smart, accomplished people—many law review types," mainly from the top 10 national and local schools. "Everyone who got callbacks" from a local school "did exceptionally well" in law school. Ropes looks for "very bright people—someone who is sharp and has a certain quickness." They don't go for "glitz and bull. They are pretty down-to-earth people." Because the firm is trying to alter its homogeneous image, one successful applicant advised, "Try to accentuate what is different about yourself. This is to your advantage...If something is unusual about you, talk it up, and make it apparent." Another source noted that Ropes prides itself on the "low-key selling approach—they don't bash other firms in Boston." One person informed us that "the firm so understates itself that it's barely a whisper. The attitude is, if you haven't the sense to come here, we don't want you."

Ropes & Gray is well-known for its high offer rates to summer associates. "They feel that people accept the summer position with the expectation that they will get an offer, and it is unfair not to be able to extend an offer," one person explained. The firm batted a perfect one thousand this past summer, making offers to all 52 summer associates.

Ropes & Gray is an "old-style firm"; it is non-competitive and "people are fairly well-mannered and reserved in the way they behave toward one another. To the extent you like that, you will be O.K.," said one person. It is also the most prestigious firm in the city and offers the best corporate practice in Boston. One especially enthusiastic insider instructed us that "although one or two firms may do more than Ropes in a very particular area, no other firm has the depth of work and talented attorneys that Ropes does across so many different fields, especially in the corporate area." This person made the additional observation that "some people leave Ropes for smaller firms in order to work fewer hours, but most realize that by doing so they sacrifice the opportunity to practice at the cutting edge of law."

Sherburne, Powers & Needham

Boston

Address: One Beacon Street, Boston, MA 02108
Telephone: (617) 523–2700
Hiring Attorney: Paul M. James
Contact: Norma S. Hanson, Recruitment Coordinator; (617) 573–5865
Associate Salary: First year $67,000 (1997); second $68,000; third $70,000; fourth $72,500; fifth $75,000; sixth $77,500; seventh $80,500
Summer Salary: $1250/week (1997)
Average Hours: 2289 worked; 1821 billed; 1800 required
Family Benefits: Parental leave, employee assistance program, cafeteria plan for day care
1996 Summer: Class of 4 students; offers to 4
Partnership: 90% of entering associates were made partner (over all the years for which information is available)
Pro Bono: Approximately 5% of all work is pro bono

Sherburne, Powers & Needham in 1997
66 Lawyers at the Firm
0.6 Associates Per Partner

Total Partners 38		
Women	6	16%
All Minorities	0	0%

Total Associates 23		
Women	11	48%
All Minorities	1	4%
Afro Am	1	4%

Practice Areas	
Litigation	27
Business/Corporate	21
Trusts & Estates	13
Securities/Syndication	10
Real Estate	7
Tax	7
Construction	6
Environmental	3

significant opportunity

Sherburne, Powers & Needham offers junior associates unusually early responsibility and unique exposure to a broad variety of areas. Unlike many larger Boston firms, Sherburne is not divided into rigid departments, and no "formal structure" limits junior associates to one particular area. Neither junior associates nor summer associates specialize; they are expected, we were told, to be flexible enough to handle anything that comes through the door. "You tell the firm what you are interested in, and they feed you these assignments to the extent that they are available, but they give you others as well," explained one contact. "They want you to work in a large number of areas and to be exposed to many different things." Sherburne encourages new associates not to choose an area of specialization until they have been with the firm for at least a year, but they are encouraged to join one or two of the firm's practice groups, which include construction, education, employment, syndication, and intellectual property, among others. Another person remarked that "after you have been with the firm for awhile, usually a year or more, you tend to gravitate towards a department and gradually concentrate in a couple of areas while still working with a broad enough variety of cases to keep things interesting." Sherburne entrusts most associates with responsibility shortly after their arrival at the firm. One person remarked that "cases are staffed quite leanly, usually one shareholder and one associate." "You don't have to wait until you're a shareholder to entertain clients. There is a special fund set up that associates can use to entertain clients," raved another person. One summer associate proudly pointed out that she was given the opportunity to try a pro bono bench trial.

tight-knit atmosphere

The atmosphere at the firm is "warm" and friendly. The lawyers at Sherburne are a close and tight-knit group of people. Many of the attorneys "go out together for lunch on a regular basis, associates and shareholders alike." One commentator remarked that it is essential to "get along with everyone at the firm, given that one can't hide here like one might at a large firm. Some people have idiosyncrasies...but most of the lawyers have their closest friends at the firm." Another person commented that "terrific friendships are created and maintained here—it's an incredibly supportive atmosphere."

practice areas

Sherburne's practice is broad-ranging for a firm of its size. Litigation is the firm's largest practice area. Sherburne is particularly known for its expertise in construction and intellectual property litigation. The firm also handles a fair amount of bankruptcy and employment litigation. Sherburne has an environmental litigation practice that draws on lawyers in the litigation, land use, and real estate practices. The business and corporate practice is well-known for its syndication subgroup, led by William Machen and Jim McDermott, that handles issues pertaining to tax credits for low income housing developments. In addition, Sherburne offers a general corporate practice that also does some venture capital and international work. Sherburne is a charter member of Globalaw, a network of international law firms. Although some firms are downsizing their trusts and estates practices, Sherburne "is still growing in this area." The firm also has a flourishing trademark infringement practice and represents both Reebok and Champion, as well as other major brand names (Adidas, Nike, Polo, Tommy Hilfiger).

Although Sherburne's pro bono practice was described as "minimal" and "unorganized," we were told that the firm "strongly encourages the independent pro bono work of its attorneys." Currently, however, pro bono hours do not count toward billable hours. Many of the firm's lawyers are involved in Boston's City Year youth service program, and many others handle pro bono matters "for charities or interests of their choice."

haphazard training

Sherburne's lack of structure influences its training and feedback. One source complained that training is "pretty haphazard." Another noted that "there is not much official formal training. They have some continuing legal education and videotapes, so you can go and look back at them, but the bulk of the training is on-the-job." The litigation department provides a more formalized training program which also includes a mock trial. The feedback is more structured for summer than for permanent associates. Summer associates receive a midterm evaluation, which one person described as a mere "formality," and a final review of all the evaluation sheets completed by the attorneys for whom they worked throughout the summer. Permanent and summer associates are assigned to a mentor; most of their feedback depends on their individual relationships with their mentors and the other attorneys for whom they work, but "the firm strongly encourages feedback," according to a firm spokesperson.

family oriented social life

Sherburne is "not the place to cultivate single social ties." "Many more attorneys at the firm are married than single...It's really a family oriented firm. Most people go home after work." The social life at the firm also tends to be family oriented. The firm sponsors a "family softball outing" and a number of other family get-togethers. Other summer events have included a trip to the Boston Pops, a concert, a Broadway play, a reggae picnic at Castle Hill Beach, and a country club outing. The firm has also organized a miniature golf outing and sponsored a dinner "at a local popular steak house which is also a client of the firm."

Consistent with its family orientation, Sherburne offers its associates the prospect of having a life outside the firm. The 1800 billable hour requirement is on the low side for Boston, and the management does not dwell on the numbers. One associate remarked that "there was someone who just made shareholder who indicated that he never reached the 1800 hour goal in any of the seven years that it took him to make shareholder." Sherburne is proud of its "very low" turnover rate. One associate commented that "most people don't leave unless they change geographic locations or get an incredibly attractive offer." The shareholder membership track is typically eight years, and "if an attorney has pulled his weight and in all other respects is proven satisfactory, there is a high likelihood he will be made a shareholder. This is in contrast to some of the firms with entering classes of twenty, who make only a few partners out of the group." The five attorneys who started at the firm together eight years ago "were all invited to join the membership of shareholders," exulted one insider.

management

The firm is managed by a seven member Board of Directors that includes President C. Thomas Swaim. Swaim was described as "an exceptional person. He has the general consensus of the firm that he is the guy to head it." The management is said to be open with associates regarding firm business; a special associates committee serves as a liaison to the shareholders. Economically, the firm has been healthy, with each year since 1989 being better than the last, claimed one associate. Sherburne has grown at a slow, steady rate of about two to five attorneys a year. It avoided much of the chaotic growth and overreaching of the 1980s. The firm has experienced a healthy growth spurt in the 1990s, adding a number of lateral attorneys at both the associate and the shareholder levels.

diversity

Sherburne's shareholder membership includes six women. One was made a shareholder while she was working part-time, and she continues to work part-time, which is "significant," one insider pointed out. Currently there are no women on the management committee, but there are four women on the hiring committee. Sherburne presently employs one African-American attorney. One associate remarked that "it's a goal of the firm to attract minorities, but there is a big complication. Because Sherburne is a smaller firm and has to compete with the top Boston firms for talent, sometimes it is tough to compete with bigger firms for minorities."

office facilities

Sherburne's offices are at a "very desirable" location, easily accessible to Beacon Hill as well as the financial district and court buildings. Every attorney has a private office. First-year associates and summer associates generally have an office with a window. Sherburne's office building houses a dining facility and Fitcorp health club.

hiring tips

In making hiring decisions, Sherburne values "high academic achievement." The firm recruits at many top schools, with Boston College, Boston University, Georgetown, Harvard, Virginia, and Chicago figuring prominently. The callback interviews at Sherburne are somewhat unusual. A pair of attorneys conducts each interview. At the end of the day, it is not unusual for an applicant to have interviewed with 10 to 12 attorneys at the firm. "For its size and number of hires, it invests a disproportionate amount of time and resources in the hiring process," remarked one source. Because the firm offers significant early responsibility, it seeks people who can handle clients immediately. The firm is "looking for people who won't worry about someone looking over their shoulder. They want self-starters," advised one successful applicant.

Sherburne, Powers & Needham is a small, close firm where associates come to stay. One person pointed out that "the size of the firm is key—big enough to handle big cases and small and personal enough to represent individuals as well. As a result, there's a great variety of work." Though Sherburne attorneys earn less than lawyers at the bigger Boston firms, and the firm occasionally misses "some big clients who simply go to the biggest firms such as Hale and Dorr and Ropes & Gray because of the name recognition," the people with whom we spoke said that associates don't seem to mind these minor handicaps. The associates thrive in an individualistic atmosphere that affords them the chance to take control of their projects and become permanent members of the firm.

People praised the firm for the early responsibility it provides ("young associates are asked to take first-hand responsibility and get quite a bit of in-court experience") and for the absence of face-time ("you do the work that needs to get done and you go home; no one looks over your shoulder to see how many hours you're here"). Another attractive feature of work at Sherburne is the "realistic emphasis on client development." One contact observed that, although "the need to develop business can be a source of some stress by the time you're in the fifth or sixth year out of school, the fact is that it's something all lawyers need to do. Sherburne encourages and supports it at all levels. As a result, when you're further along in your career and client development is more important, it's not completely new, alien, and frightening." If you're aching for early responsibility and client development opportunities, in a setting that emphasizes broad exposure in the law alongside supportive colleagues, Sherburne, Powers & Needham is worth a close look.

Sullivan & Worcester

Boston New York Washington

Address: One Post Office Square, Boston, MA 02109
Telephone: (617) 338–2800
Hiring Attorney: William J. Curry
Contact: Janet M. Brussard, Legal Recruitment Administrator; (617) 338–2806
Associate Salary: First year $74,000 (1997)
Summer Salary: $1425/week (1997)
Average Hours: 1913 worked; 1731 billed; NA required
Family Benefits: Maternity/parental leave; dependent care assistance plan; backup day care
1996 Summer: Class of 9 students; offers to 7
Partnership: 31% of entering associates from 1978–1984 were made partner
Pro Bono: 3% of all work is pro bono

Sullivan & Worcester in 1997
118 Lawyers at the Boston Office
0.8 Associates Per Partner

Total Partners 57			Total Associates 47			Practice Areas	
Women	12	21%	Women	16	34%	Corporate	55
All Minorities	1	2%	All Minorities	3	6%	Litigation	16
Asian-Am	1	2%	Afro-Am	1	2%	Tax	15
			Asian-Am	1	2%	Real Estate	14
			Latino	1	2%	Trusts & Estates	10
						Bankruptcy	8

Founded in 1941, Sullivan & Worcester used to be described as a firm "with a lot of emphasis on traditional ideas of what a firm is like" and "on doing things the old way." However, we were informed that such a description does not capture the firm's essence today. Sullivan is presently not "very formal or structured; there is a lot of freedom to do your own thing," reported one contact. Another insider observed that Sullivan "does not impose a restrictive culture on its associates; there is not a lot of protocol and associates have a lot of freedom."

corporate practice

The atmosphere at Sullivan & Worcester varies considerably in its three major departments—corporate, litigation, and tax. The tax and corporate practices make up the "bread and butter of the firm." The corporate work is varied, but consists mostly of mergers and acquisitions, public and private securities offerings, bank lending, new ventures, and mutual fund work. The *American Lawyer* ranked the firm among the top law firms in the nation in the category of most mutual fund and REIT new issues in 1995 and in the category of most money raised for REITs in 1996. The department boasts Alex Notopoulos, a former editor of the *Harvard Law Review* and one of the firm's best-known corporate lawyers. Sullivan represents a number of foreign banks in Europe. Although most of its international work is done in the New York office, some of it "spills over to Boston."

premier tax practice

The tax department "is pretty straight and narrow, and most of the people have advanced law degrees." Although tax is not the largest practice at the firm, people commented that it may be Sullivan's most prominent area, and one claimed that it is one of Boston's premier practices. Though most of the work involves corporate tax, Sullivan also handles a lot of innovative start-up company and business planning work. In addition, many of the tax attorneys do work for non-profit organizations.

litigation practice

The litigation department contrasts with other practice areas at the firm. It has a strong female presence. "Other departments are run by Anglo males, but in litigation the most powerful partner is Laura Steinberg...Of the male partners in litigation, several are Jewish and one is Indian. It is much more diverse and younger than other departments." Steinberg, described as a "dynamo" and a "wonder woman" type, is influential in the litigation department's success. Most of the firm's litigation work has "sprung out of the corporate clients." Except for some recent high-profile cases and the high level of activity of the employment law group, the litigation department as a whole "generally has a less demanding life style than the corporate department," reported one insider. This has enabled litigation associates to have more flexible work schedules, including part-time arrangements.

Sullivan's real estate department is presently in transition, after its head left to join a client. One source claimed that because of "personality conflicts," the real estate department can be "unpleasant to work in." A firm spokesperson informed us, however, that "a popular young partner recently has been selected to head the real estate department," which should ease any tensions.

Sullivan recently expanded its high-tech/new ventures group to include two new partners and two full-time patent lawyers. The firm appears to be looking to grow in this area and to expand its existing ties with the MIT Business Enterprise Forum and other start-up hot beds. At the same time, three influential partners (two from the corporate department and the aforementioned head of the real estate) recently left Sullivan to join major clients of the firm. "Although their departure caused some fear among the associates, the net effect of it seems to be a strengthening of ties with these big clients," reported one insider.

Many Sullivan partners enjoy close ties to politicians and business leaders. Christopher Weld, a cousin of Massachusetts Governor William Weld, and Paul Kirk, former Chairperson of the Democratic Party, are counsel at Sullivan. Two Sullivan attorneys are members of the influential Cabot families.

pro bono

Described as "*ad hoc*," Sullivan's pro bono practice is not formally organized. Nevertheless, individual lawyers devote substantial time to pro bono matters, including the Family Law Project for Battered Women and the Federated Dorchester Neighborhood Houses. Pro bono hours count toward billable hours at Sullivan, and the firm has been involved with everything from "environmental to civil rights causes." The firm traditionally has done a lot of work for Associated Catholic Charities.

unstructured atmosphere

Sullivan & Worcester provides a very unstructured work atmosphere. Starting associates are not assigned to any particular department, but rather are "encouraged to float around for a year, with the firm taking into account what they want to do. A lot of people come into the firm saying they want to do this or that. If you are smart enough, they will accommodate you," advised one source. The firm is ideal for someone with a lot of personal initiative, noted others. "It's a great place for people who are ready to start practicing, and who...have a good bit of motivation and self-confidence to get right in there and play an important role in the firm early on." With regard to feedback, Sullivan is "self-motivationally oriented." One insider asserted that "if you ask an individual attorney for feedback you can get some, but in general it's not given without initiative."

Sullivan pays for continuing legal education programs, but it does not provide an extensive set of formal training programs. "The best training is working directly with the attorneys," remarked one source, noting that there is plenty of hands-on training at Sullivan for "motivated" individuals. Even summer associates have client contact throughout the summer. People emphasized, however, that "you can just do research for a whole year if you are not motivated."

summer program

The summer program is run by two partners. Assignments come from all areas of the firm. The tone of the program is "generally laid-back," we were told, because "there is a presumption that the firm will hire its summer associates and the social calendar is usually fun." In the past, summer associates have attended baseball games, theater, cocktail parties at partners' homes, and enjoyed a "great summer outing to the Cape."

lawyers are individualists

Many Sullivan attorneys are married and spend their free time with their families. "Although attorneys work hard, there is life outside the office," observed one contact. Sullivan is the "type of place where most people have their own interests and their own lifestyle. They go to work and then go home. They keep their social life and work life separate," said another source. They are also "pretty independent. There is not a big feeling of firm culture...It's not a particularly social environment in that people are not there to make their best friends," agreed another. Not surprisingly, the firm does not "sponsor a lot of social life."

changing of the guard

Sullivan & Worcester is managed conservatively and deliberately did not grow massively in the 1980s. It "claims that it has no long-term debt," and that "it has been doing better in terms of gross receipts every year," reported one person. The firm is managed by a committee of partners that was described in the past as "a little too autocratic as far as how decisions are made. Decisions came down from out of the blue and no one knows how they are arrived at." Similarly, the associates committee was described as having "limited input power and no decision-making authority." However, recently Sullivan appointed a new managing partner and a new executive director, and the reviews on this new management team were positive. One contact reported that "from an associate's point of view, this changing of the guard is beneficial because the new management team seems more active and more attuned to running the firm from an associate's/practitioner's perspective than their predecessors." A second contact observed that "there has been an effort to get more input from associates. The new managing partner and executive director are making the firm more structured and organized."

atmosphere for women

The atmosphere for women varies considerably by practice group. Headed by Steinberg, the litigation department provides a particularly comfortable atmosphere for women, whereas other departments are more male-dominated. One contact noted that "part-time associates, such as parents, have a tough time doing the balancing act. While there is a part-time policy, I am not sure how highly respected it is." Sullivan "is not the type of place where sexual harassment is tolerated," stated one source. There are "many old-line boys at the firm, but they are into behaving in classy ways." There are relatively few minority attorneys at Sullivan, which is a real "sore spot" for the partnership, we were told.

two dollar lunches

Sullivan occupies four floors in One Post Office Space Square, and each attorney has a private office. The office facilities are decorated with a "nautical theme" with "ships everywhere." The hardwood floors are dotted with oriental rugs. Everyone commented on the nice cafeteria, which is a "great convenience," according to one insider. The firm has its own cook who makes "special meals every day" at very low prices. You can have a complete lunch for about two dollars, raved one person. The firm has an IBM computer system, and Internet and e-mail capabilities; in the words of one insider, "the firm tries to be computer literate."

hiring practices

Sullivan hires most of its students from Boston College, Boston University, Harvard, and other nationally recognized schools. Sullivan prefers "people with a good attitude who are motivated and interested in getting involved quickly in the real practice of law." There is "not a big emphasis on grades or being on the law review," one source assured us. "You can be in the middle of your class from a top-tier school or at the top of your class from a lower-tier school." Students usually interview with four or five attorneys at the firm for about twenty minutes to half an hour. Most interviews are laid-back and conversational and often involve discussions about personal interests.

Sullivan is a firm of motivated individualists who thrive on its unstructured professional development opportunities. "As an associate, there is a lot of flexibility in the work available, and associates have the opportunity to choose their paths," praised one contact. The firm gives associates a high level of responsibility early on. "Staffing is lean, and there are not layers of midlevel associates between you and the partner or client," observed another insider. Some people are not well suited to Sullivan's "take responsibility" approach; "they wait on the sidelines where they can be overlooked or underutilized," according to one contact. If, however, you are a self-starter looking for a place where you can immediately begin to practice the law that interests you, and you enjoy reasonable work hours, Sullivan & Worcester may well be the place for you.

Testa, Hurwitz & Thibeault

Boston

Address: High Street Tower, 125 High Street, Boston, MA 02110
Telephone: (617) 248–7000
Hiring Attorney: Jin-Kyung (Kay) Kim
Contact: Judith A. St. John, Recruitment Administrator; (617) 248–7401
Associate Salary: First year $79,000 (1997); second $88,000; third $100,000.
Summer Salary: NA
Average Hours: 2124 worked; 1814 billed; 1800 required
Family Benefits: Family medical; parental leave; 13 weeks paid maternity leave (13 unpaid); emergency day care benefit
1996 Summer: Class of 30 students; offers to 29
Partnership: 20% of entering associates from 1983–1988 were made partner
Pro Bono: 1.6% of all work is pro bono

Testa, Hurwitz & Thibeault in 1997
196 Lawyers at the Firm
2.6 Associates Per Partner

Total Partners 53		
Women	7	13%
All Minorities	1	2%
Asian-Am	1	2%

Total Associates 138		
Women	65	47%
All Minorities	6	4%
Afro-Am	1	1%
Asian-Am	4	3%
Latino	1	1%

Practice Areas	
Corporate	109
Litigation	31
Patent	25
Labor	13
Tax	9
Technology Specialists	5
Real Estate	4
Environmental	2
Probate	2
Bankruptcy	1

Testa, Hurwitz & Thibeault is one of Boston's youngest and fastest-growing big firms. This "new kid on the block" offers an "intense," "no-nonsense" practice. Founded as a venture capital and high technology boutique firm in 1973 by Dick Testa, Testa Hurwitz began as a "spin off" from the now defunct Gaston & Snow and, over the years, developed a "national reputation" in the venture capital field. Though initially committed to remaining small and focused on its corporate practice, the firm has grown rapidly in both size and scope. One person commented that "there are clients coming through the doors all the time with more and more work."

workaholic atmosphere

Along with the firm's rapid growth and success, Testa has gained a reputation as a "workaholic-type place." One insider reported that "the people there now are always working about one and a half times what they should." Another person commented, however, that "as a factual matter this is not true. Testa's billables are in the middle of Boston's top firms. The perception that people work so hard at Testa can probably be explained by the tremendous responsibility that Testa gives its associates—resulting in a more intense experience." Associate salary increases in "lockstep" in order to avoid associate competition for plum clients and annual bonuses. Reportedly, "the lack of competition among associates tends to create a more cooperative environment."

live and breathe law

The intense atmosphere of the firm is at least partly due to the enthusiasm Testa attorneys have for their work. The attorneys "are definitely into the type of work they do and enjoy talking about technical aspects of the work." Many Testa associates, particularly in the corporate practice, "live and breathe" the law. These people "genuinely get excited about 10(b)(5)," according to one insider. "Many of the attorneys have a nerdy side to them, but they are very nice people."

flexible for women

Though Testa is hard-working and intense, its "parental leave policy is generous, and people are happy with it." Several men, as well as women, have recently taken advantage of the program. One source commented that "there is a lot of leeway for women who want to have a family." One woman, who made partner while on maternity leave, came back to the firm and worked part-time. Overall, the firm was described as "progressive" regarding female attorneys. A number of powerful women are members of the corporate department, including Leslie Davis, Robin Painter, and Karen Copenhaver. Though not as many women work in the smaller litigation department, people commented that it is "coming along." The firm has not, however, been able to attract as many minority candidates; there are currently seven minority attorneys at the firm, including one African-American. It's not for lack of effort, however, according to one member of the firm who reports that "Testa does seem to try to attract minority candidates." This person described Testa's approach to this challenge as a "refreshing change for me."

As might be surmised, Testa is not one of the more "social" firms in Boston. Although the firm sets the stage by planning a few events, attorneys frequently choose family over the firm social life once they have finished working. In past summers, Testa has organized a picnic, baseball games, bowling, and some other similar events, but we were told that the firm is not known for a vibrant social atmosphere. "Going out is not in these people's genes," said one person. Recently, however, "a strong group of singles who do socialize together after work" has developed at the firm.

renowned venture capital group

Although Testa's practice has expanded considerably, the firm's forte remains its venture capital/high technology practice. Dick Testa is known nationally in the high technology field. He "calls the shots" and, in many ways, the firm reflects his character. He was described as "down-to-earth," a "nice guy," and a "brilliant attorney." Our contacts noted that the high technology practice can be particularly dynamic and exciting. Clients come in "with just an idea on the back of a napkin and in twenty years they have a major corporation." Testa represents these companies as start-ups and maintains a long-term relationship, handling many other matters as well. Corporate, copyright, trademark, and patent issues that arise for emerging companies, are handled by the patent/intellectual property group and the business practice group (especially the licensing area) at the firm.

Some of the work in Testa's other practice areas is generated by the venture capital practice. Two of the most noteworthy of these practice areas are litigation and corporate, about which one insider declared: "Litigation has grown exponentially. Corporate is always looking for more people. No matter how many they hire, they still need more." Testa plans to continue its expansion to become a "full-service firm." The firm has groups practicing tax and ERISA, labor and employment, real estate, trusts and estates, bankruptcy and creditor's rights, and environmental law.

pro bono

Testa's pro bono practice is not highly-structured, and most pro bono work is "individually based," according to one source. Two partners oversee the pro bono practice and a committee screens projects. Pro bono hours count toward billable hours. A number of the attorneys are involved in the Lawyers' Committee for Civil Rights Under Law, Volunteer Lawyers for the Arts, and the representation of indigent individuals in various civil matters..

flexible associate development

Testa provides significant flexibility in associate career development. Summer associates who receive permanent offers at Testa are given a choice among specific offers in a number of different departments. There is no formal rotation system. Starting associates at Testa can expect early responsibility. Associates on the corporate side usually "take on their own clients within a year, although there is always a senior associate or partner involved for supervision." In litigation, responsibility comes "a little slower. You usually don't get responsibility for a big case until they put you through the rickets. Once you show you are capable, by the third or fourth year you can have significant responsibility for a case." Testa provides "a good opportunity for someone who feels he does not need a name like Ropes behind him. It's a place where people are valued for who they are. It is different from a place like Ropes where you are asked to toe the line and keep in place within a hierarchy. If you show you can do it at Testa, you will be given the reins and told to go for it," summarized one contact.

Most of the training at Testa happens on-the-job, but the firm also offers a variety of formal and informal training programs. The firm provides frequent in-house training on legal issues associated with start-up corporations and other matters. The litigation department holds frequent meetings and provides formal deposition training programs for all departments which engage in litigation. Testa recently hired Elaine Ohlson from the Massachusetts CLE as the new director of its professional development program. This program arranges for weekly in-house seminars given by partners and senior associates to almost all groups at the firm. One contact remarked that "I'm not aware of any firm in Boston with training as extensive and comprehensive as Testa's."

plain offices

Testa places greater emphasis on meeting client needs than on slick appearances and does not provide a "polished firm atmosphere." The firm deliberately avoids spending a significant amount on office decorations and furniture (although associates are granted a stipend to decorate their own offices). Testa moved into new offices in September, 1995. Our earlier edition described Testa as the "worst dressed firm in Boston," to which one commentator remarked: "this is bizarre. Lawyers dress like lawyers dress." Things have apparently taken a sartorial turn for the better: "Testa attorneys' dress has improved markedly in the past two years. Some are quite fashionable dressers," reported another insider.

Although Testa's offices are far from lavish, all summer and permanent associates have private offices, most with a window. Due to Testa's expansive growth, some summer associates have to share offices. LEXIS and Westlaw are available at each attorney's desk.

hires self-starters

In hiring attorneys, Testa looks for "individuals rather than Academic All-Americans." One person commented that Testa "really looks for self-starters and people who want to take lots of responsibility early on." Getting hired at Testa is not as academically competitive as it is at some of the other big name Boston firms, although of late "the selection process has become more selective regarding grades." One insider noted that most students hired from Boston College and Boston University are in the top 20 percent of their classes. Another noted that many successful applicants "have done something interesting before law school. The firm hired many older people who had done different things."

Interviews at the firm typically involve meeting between four and six attorneys for 30 minutes each. One insider "found the interview to be friendly and open. No punches were pulled and there were no trick questions." Another advised that you will set yourself apart and enjoy an advantage in getting hired if you are interested in something other than the venture capital practice, which is the most popular area among students. Nevertheless, this source stressed that the hiring decisions really depend on whether the firm has openings for someone in a particular area.

Testa, Hurwitz & Thibeault is growing dramatically; it now numbers just under 200 lawyers, a sizeable increase from just a few years ago. Testa has a unique base of clients that have products and services "that are on the cutting-edge." Its patent and intellectual property group has grown to such an extent that this group, "if it were to become its own separate law firm, would be the largest patent law firm in Boston." Because of the nature of its clients, Testa attorneys "often act as more than just legal counsel to its clients. Sometimes our clients ask us for business advice, especially if the clients are start-ups." But, if you go to Testa, be ready for "frenetic, fast-paced work, all of the time."

Because the firm has witnessed tremendous growth in recent years, Testa is changing from a friendly, medium-sized firm into a large firm where it is impossible to know everyone. Testa is experiencing some growing pains. One insider reported that "the complaint I hear the most is that associate hours worked can be erratic and vary greatly, but the attorneys here are trying to resist having Testa become another faceless and uncaring large firm." If you like to work hard and do not require the frills of a big firm, Testa's robust venture capital practice and ambitious atmosphere may be for you. One firm enthusiast optimistically remarked to us, "I think that Testa, more than almost any other firm, is poised for the future."

Chicago

Law Firms Ranked by Associates Per Partner

1.	SACHNOFF & WEAVER	0.4
2.	HOPKINS & SUTTER	0.5
3.	MCDERMOTT, WILL & EMERY	0.5
4.	ROSS & HARDIES	0.6
5.	RUDNICK & WOLFE	0.6
6.	CHAPMAN AND CUTLER	0.7
7.	JENNER & BLOCK	0.8
8.	SIDLEY & AUSTIN	0.8
9.	SONNENSCHEIN NATH & ROSENTHAL	0.8
10.	BAKER & MCKENZIE	0.9
11.	KATTEN MUCHIN & ZAVIS	0.9
12.	KECK, MAHIN & CATE	0.9
13.	GARDNER, CARTON & DOUGLAS	1.0
14.	HOLLEB & COFF	1.0
15.	LORD, BISSELL & BROOK	1.2
16.	MAYER, BROWN & PLATT	1.2
17.	KIRKLAND & ELLIS	1.3
18.	JONES, DAY, REAVIS & POGUE	1.5
19.	WINSTON & STRAWN	1.6

Law Firms Ranked by Percentage of Associates Who Make Partner (over varying years)

1.	JENNER & BLOCK	91
2.	HOPKINS & SUTTER	90
3.	SACHNOFF & WEAVER, LTD.	64
4.	GARDNER, CARTON & DOUGLAS	60
5.	BAKER & MCKENZIE	30
6.	CHAPMAN AND CUTLER	30
7.	KECK, MAHIN & CATE	28
8.	SIDLEY & AUSTIN	26
9.	KATTEN MUCHIN & ZAVIS	25
10.	SONNENSCHEIN NATH & ROSENTHAL	25
11.	HOLLEB & COFF	NA
12.	JONES, DAY, REAVIS & POGUE	NA
13.	KIRKLAND & ELLIS	NA
14.	LORD, BISSELL & BROOK	NA
15.	MAYER, BROWN & PLATT	NA
16.	MCDERMOTT, WILL & EMERY	NA
17.	ROSS & HARDIES	NA
18.	RUDNICK & WOLFE	NA
19.	WINSTON & STRAWN	NA

Law Firms Ranked by Percentage of Pro Bono Work

1.	JENNER & BLOCK	5
2.	GARDNER, CARTON & DOUGLAS	4-7
3.	HOLLEB & COFF	4
4.	SONNENSCHEIN NATH & ROSENTHAL	4
5.	HOPKINS & SUTTER	3
6.	KIRKLAND & ELLIS	3
7.	SACHNOFF & WEAVER	3
8.	SIDLEY & AUSTIN	3
9.	ROSS & HARDIES	2
10.	WINSTON & STRAWN	2
11.	CHAPMAN AND CUTLER	1-3
12.	KATTEN MUCHIN & ZAVIS	1-3
13.	MCDERMOTT, WILL & EMERY	1-3
14.	BAKER & MCKENZIE	NA
15.	JONES, DAY, REAVIS & POGUE	NA
16.	KECK, MAHIN & CATE	NA
17.	LORD, BISSELL & BROOK	NA
18.	MAYER, BROWN & PLATT	NA
19.	RUDNICK & WOLFE	NA

Law Firms Ranked by Percentage of Female Partners

1.	MCDERMOTT, WILL & EMERY	24
2.	JONES, DAY, REAVIS & POGUE	21
3.	KATTEN MUCHIN & ZAVIS	20
4.	SONNENSCHEIN NATH & ROSENTHAL	19
5.	ROSS & HARDIES	18
6.	GARDNER, CARTON & DOUGLAS	17
7.	HOPKINS & SUTTER	17
8.	MAYER, BROWN & PLATT	17
9.	LORD, BISSELL & BROOK	16
10.	KIRKLAND & ELLIS	14
11.	SIDLEY & AUSTIN	14
12.	RUDNICK & WOLFE	13
13.	WINSTON & STRAWN	13
14.	KECK, MAHIN & CATE	12
15.	SACHNOFF & WEAVER, LTD.	12
16.	CHAPMAN AND CUTLER	10
17.	BAKER & MCKENZIE	9
18.	HOLLEB & COFF	8
19.	JENNER & BLOCK	NA

Law Firms Ranked by Percentage of Female Associates

1.	KECK, MAHIN & CATE	58
2.	SACHNOFF & WEAVER	57
3.	MCDERMOTT, WILL & EMERY	56
4.	SONNENSCHEIN NATH & ROSENTHAL	53
5.	HOPKINS & SUTTER	51
6.	RUDNICK & WOLFE	51
7.	CHAPMAN AND CUTLER	49
8.	ROSS & HARDIES	48
9.	GARDNER, CARTON & DOUGLAS	44
10.	LORD, BISSELL & BROOK	41
11.	HOLLEB & COFF	39
12.	JONES, DAY, REAVIS & POGUE	39
13.	KATTEN MUCHIN & ZAVIS	39
14.	SIDLEY & AUSTIN	37
15.	KIRKLAND & ELLIS	34
16.	WINSTON & STRAWN	34
17.	BAKER & MCKENZIE	33
18.	MAYER, BROWN & PLATT	31
19.	JENNER & BLOCK	NA

Law Firms Ranked by Percentage of Minority Partners

1.	BAKER & MCKENZIE	11
2.	WINSTON & STRAWN	5
3.	GARDNER, CARTON & DOUGLAS	3
4.	HOLLEB & COFF	3
5.	RUDNICK & WOLFE	3
6.	CHAPMAN AND CUTLER	2
7.	HOPKINS & SUTTER	2
8.	KATTEN MUCHIN & ZAVIS	2
9.	MCDERMOTT, WILL & EMERY	2
10.	SACHNOFF & WEAVER	2
11.	SONNENSCHEIN NATH & ROSENTHAL	2
12.	KIRKLAND & ELLIS	1
13.	LORD, BISSELL & BROOK	1
14.	MAYER, BROWN & PLATT	1
15.	SIDLEY & AUSTIN	1
16.	JONES, DAY, REAVIS & POGUE	0
17.	ROSS & HARDIES	0
18.	JENNER & BLOCK	NA
19.	KECK, MAHIN & CATE	NA

Law Firms Ranked By Percentage of Minority Associates

1.	BAKER & MCKENZIE	16
2.	SACHNOFF & WEAVER	14
3.	SIDLEY & AUSTIN	14
4.	HOLLEB & COFF	13
5.	WINSTON & STRAWN	13
6.	RUDNICK & WOLFE	11
7.	KATTEN MUCHIN & ZAVIS	10
8.	CHAPMAN AND CUTLER	9
9.	MAYER, BROWN & PLATT	9
10.	SONNENSCHEIN NATH & ROSENTHAL	9
11.	GARDNER, CARTON & DOUGLAS	8
12.	JONES, DAY, REAVIS & POGUE	7
13.	KIRKLAND & ELLIS	6
14.	ROSS & HARDIES	6
15.	HOPKINS & SUTTER	5
16.	LORD, BISSELL & BROOK	5
17.	MCDERMOTT, WILL & EMERY	4
18.	JENNER & BLOCK	NA
19.	KECK, MAHIN & CATE	NA

Baker & McKenzie

Chicago Dallas Los Angeles Miami New York Palo Alto San Diego San Francisco Washington
34 Foreign Locations

Address: One Prudential Plaza #3500, 130 East Randolph Drive, Chicago, IL 60601
Telephone: (312) 861–8000
Hiring Attorney: James M. O'Brien
Contact: Eleonora Nikol, Recruitment Coordinator; (312) 861–2924
Associate Salary: First year $75,000; second $80,000; third $86,000; fourth $88,000; fifth $90,000; sixth $92,000; seventh $94,000; eighth $96,000 (1997)
Summer Salary: $1450/week (1996)
Average Hours: 1780–2330 worked; 1780–2330 billed; 1780–2330 required
Family Benefits: 12 weeks paid maternity; 12 weeks paid paternity after minimum of 1 year's service
1996 Summer: Class of 17 students; offers to 12
Partnership: 30% of entering associates from 1951–1996 were made partner
Pro Bono: Attorneys are credited with up to 100 hours of pro bono time

Baker & McKenzie in 1997
161 Lawyers at the Chicago Office
0.9 Associates Per Partner

Total Partners 86		
Women	8	9%
All Minorities	9	11%
Asian-Am	4	5%
Latino	5	6%

Total Associates 75		
Women	25	33%
All Minorities	12	16%
Afro-Am	1	1%
Asian-Am	3	4%
Latino	8	11%

Practice Areas	
International	37
Litigation	30
Tax	24
Corporate & Securities	18
Banking/Fin./Major Projects	14
Comp. & Employ. Law	14
IP/Information Technology.	13
Sp. Remedies/Bankruptcy/RE	11

world's largest international firm

Baker & McKenzie is a truly multi-national firm. With approximately 50 offices in 34 countries, the firm employs a total of more than 1800 lawyers, the majority of whom are nationals of countries other than the United States. Affectionately referred to as "McFirm" because it has expanded rapidly with offices around the globe, Baker & McKenzie displayed an uncanny vision of "the growing internationalization of world business" long before most other U.S. law firms. The Chicago office, which is at the helm of this behemoth firm, offers an unparalleled international legal practice in Chicago.

departments are separate

Though Baker & McKenzie's various offices work together and marshal worldwide resources for the benefit of their large corporate clients, each office has a distinct work atmosphere and structure. This compartmentalization once extended even into the Chicago office, where the litigation department, for example, was virtually "a firm within a firm" and made hiring and compensation decisions independently. The firm has recently restructured into eleven practice groups with more overlap among groups than previously existed among the departments. However, each group still evaluates its own hiring needs and separately extends offers for summer and full-time employment.

autonomous litigation department

The litigation group is located on two separate floors in the firm's offices. Its attorneys form a cohesive group, and most have limited social interaction with lawyers in other departments. The litigation group's work atmosphere is less informal and relaxed today than in the past due to the recent firm restructuring. Even so, lawyers interact easily with each other. Though business attire is required, one person told us that "you will see an occasional bright colored dress or suit, and it certainly isn't frowned on." In the office, men rarely wear their jackets and often loosen their ties.

The litigation group has a well-established insurance defense practice that represents insured parties in numerous products liability and professional malpractice suits. This subpractice group has "come under close scrutiny in recent years," according to one contact, who added that "a majority of its clients will no longer be represented by the firm in 1997." A correlated downsizing in partners and associates is likely to follow, we were told. The litigation group also houses an employment practice group that handles commercial and equal employment litigation. In conjunction with the corporate and securities, and foreign trade groups, the litigation group handles securities litigation and some international litigation matters. One litigation partner works exclusively on white-collar criminal matters.

early litigation opportunities

New litigation associates are hired into one or more subgroups within litigation. With a "strong motion call practice," as well as numerous deposition intensive matters, the litigation group offers early opportunities for responsibility to its junior associates. Motion call and deposition duty rosters are frequently circulated among junior associates, who are expected to volunteer for these assignments. The more substantive motions are handled by the senior attorneys. Smaller products liability and employment discrimination cases, however, "go immediately to younger associates." One person we interviewed commented that the huge amount of responsibility was the "best and worst part of B&M," noting that the work environment has been referred to "as sink or swim by some people," but that "everyone seems to swim there."

litigation training

The litigation group organizes training sessions for associates every other week which cover every aspect of litigation and trial skills. One recent contact reported, however, that Baker & McKenzie is not as much a "teaching firm" as it was known to be in the past: "an overemphasis on profitability and the 'bottom line' has decreased Baker and McKenzie's commitment to training." The litigation group does not engage in "a lot of hand-holding," and day-to-day feedback is minimal. However, for the proactive associates, it is still the case that "it is always easy to ask other attorneys questions, and they take a lot of interest in seeing us develop."

litigation Boat Party and more

The litigation group does not have "a lot of organized social life," but its attorneys "like to have a good time." Though many of the attorneys are "married and settled," on Fridays after work they often drop in for a drink at the Chicago Bar & Grill which is on the ground floor of the building. In past summers, the litigation group has organized a barbecue at a partner's home and provided summer associates with tickets to both Cubs and Sox games. Perhaps the highlight of the year is the Boat Party held in honor of the litigation administrative staff every summer. The party begins at the Navy Pier at noon with lunch and drinks at a bar. We were told that "all the secretaries are there at 12:01 P.M. Those who aren't afraid of getting seasick go out for a boat ride, then return to the dock to continue festivities. Following that, those who want, go to Brehan's, a local pub." In addition, the firm has annual traditions such as a firm dinner or "prom," held during the summer, and the firm Christmas party, which is reportedly "wild and fun." Baker & McKenzie also participates in a summer softball league, and attorneys from all the departments enjoy playing in and attending the games.

Although morale has slipped in recent years, one person noted that "everyone likes each other and likes to socialize together. This is a very fun group with a lot of joking around." People "smile and stop and talk to each other. It's very friendly." One person commented that "very seldom did people slave away at night." There is a "real sense that you have a life outside the law." People work few weekends unless a case is about to go to trial.

transactional departments are quieter

Corporate associates are expected to work harder than the litigation associates. Those in the foreign trade group work even later hours, but the tax associates work fewer hours than corporate associates. Nevertheless, the work atmosphere in these practice groups, according to the people we interviewed, is more relaxed than "you would expect from a big firm." Unlike litigation, the transactional attorneys are not "overly friendly" with each other. The tax group is a "little subdued," said one contact, noting that its attorneys generally dress conservatively. Some transactional attorneys go out after work, but overall the social life seems "pretty limited in corporate," said several of those we interviewed. "Most people go their own way." The tax associates frequently socialize together on Friday evenings.

international transactional practice

The work in the transactional groups is more internationally oriented than that in the litigation department. These groups typically represent large U.S. corporations with foreign operations and foreign multinationals with U.S. operations. One person told us that Baker & McKenzie has advised almost every Fortune 100 company. The firm has a full-service tax department that is involved in matters ranging from litigation to tax planning. Approximately two-thirds of its work involves international tax issues. The tax work is less driven by the corporate work than at other large firms, we were told. Baker & McKenzie's international business legal work was described as "uniquely fantastic," particularly because "a lot of foreign nationals" work in the Chicago office. The firm has a very strong Latin America and Southeast Asia practice and has developed a strong practice in former Soviet bloc countries. It already has offices in Moscow, Kiev, St. Petersburg, Warsaw, Budapest, and Prague.

New corporate associates work closely with one partner to whom they are assigned when they begin work at the firm. Though the firm expects them to develop working relationships with other partners, most associates typically work closely with just a few partners. Junior corporate associates generally do "a lot of library work" and quite a bit of traveling. Foreign trade associates are strongly encouraged to rotate through one of the firm's overseas offices. Baker & McKenzie has been praised for its hands-on training for corporate associates. Each year at its annual regional meetings, groups of fourth to eighth year associates participate in an elaborate transaction based on one of the firm's recent deals. At the end of the one day program, associates review the different aspects of the exercise and learn how to handle various issues that arise. Most associate training for newer associates occurs "on-the-job," though the transactional departments have weekly meetings and encourage attorneys to attend outside seminars. Tax associates are encouraged to enroll in L.L.M. courses. Feedback is spotty for associates, but "if you ask for it, you get it," reported one contact.

pro bono

Baker & McKenzie has a strong pro bono commitment. It credits up to 100 hours of pro bono time toward the billable hour requirement and its attorneys staff both the Chicago Volunteer Legal Services Foundation and the Howard Area Community Center for Hispanic Speaking People one day each month. Summer associates work on at least one pro bono project during their stay with the firm. The firm also sponsors the Public Interest Law Initiative Fellowship under which, during the summer prior to entering the firm, associates may elect to work half time in a public interest organization in the city, while earning the regular firm salary.

response to NBLSA ban

Because of its international focus and large number of foreign lawyers, both in the overseas and the U.S. offices, Baker & McKenzie is an internationally diverse firm. In addition, the firm has recently made concerted efforts to increase the racial diversity of its American attorneys. Since 1989, the firm has provided financial assistance to minority law students in excess of $700,000. Baker & McKenzie has also made an effort to recruit minority applicants and to provide sensitivity training to its attorneys who interview minority student applicants. These efforts were instituted in 1989-90 in response to an interviewing ban imposed on the firm by the National Black Law Students Association (NBLSA). The ban resulted from complaints regarding an inappropriate interview question posed by a litigation partner to an African-American female applicant. NBLSA lifted the interviewing ban on the firm in March 1990, and the firm has since actively recruited at minority law student job fairs across the country. However, very few minorities (other than foreign nationals) are employed in the Chicago office, which results in part, according to one contact, from "a small number of candidates" available. The firm details its efforts and provides useful information regarding its offer and acceptance ratios in its *Annual Reports* on its Equal Employment Opportunity Program/Enhanced Minority Recruitment, which can be obtained from the EEOP coordinator in the Chicago Office. We didn't hear any negative comments about the atmosphere for women at the firm. However, the firm has received much negative press for its handling of sexual harassment issues and was recently ordered to pay $3.5 million in a sexual harassment verdict against former partner Martin Greenstein in a suit involving Rena Weeks, a secretary who worked in the firm's Palo Alto office in 1991.

worldwide management

Baker & McKenzie's worldwide operations are "run out of Chicago." The firm has a two-tier partnership in Chicago wherein attorneys can become partners of the Chicago office before becoming partners of Baker & McKenzie worldwide. The worldwide partners meet each year in a different city of the world to make the firm's major decisions. Each partner has one vote. One person commented that this meeting is "like a U.N." gathering complete with translators. Associates are involved in some aspects of management. Although they typically have little input in large issues affecting the firm, they did participate significantly in the remodeling of the Chicago office facilities, which some described as "terrible." As for the future, Baker & McKenzie will continue to increase its worldwide presence. The litigation group is working to further diversify its practice and to attract more complex litigation. The firm's employment practice group is growing.

departmental recruiting

Baker & McKenzie hires law students from both the top national law schools and heavily from Chicago-area law schools. Different practice groups employ different hiring criteria. The litigation group seeks "confident, articulate" individuals "who will handle themselves in stressful situations." It also wants "people who can work together as a team," as demonstrated by an athletic or musical background, or some other extra-curricular activities. People advised litigation applicants to go into the interview "with a sense of humor and not take yourself too seriously." Interviewees are also urged to "show a more human side." The group wants to know: "Can you meet with a client, and can you litigate?" Applicants to the transactional groups are advised to emphasize previous work experience. Foreign trade applicants must be fluent in a foreign language. The tax group, we were told, prefers people who are "good with numbers," or who have accounting backgrounds. In all of these practice groups, it helps to express a specific, focused interest in a particular area, rather than a general interest in international law. Some practice groups do not extend offers for permanent employment to first-year students until the summer after their second year of law school. However, the tax group has made permanent position offers after first-year summers.

Baker & McKenzie offers a "unique international practice" in its transactional groups and early opportunities for responsibility in the litigation practice. The biggest drawback of the firm, according to the people we interviewed, is its compartmentalization which, in the past, prevented even summer associates from rotating between groups. Recently, Baker & McKenzie has addressed this situation by "encouraging associates to work concurrently in two practice groups," according to a firm spokesperson. For someone who has identified a specific area of interest in which they want to focus and is interested in the unique practice offered by the firm, Baker & McKenzie is an excellent choice.

Chapman and Cutler

Chicago Phoenix Salt Lake City

Address: 111 West Monroe Street, Chicago, IL 60603–4080
Telephone: (312) 845–3000
Hiring Attorney: Edward V. Sommer
Contact: Tina Young, Legal Recruiting Coordinator; (312) 845–3805
Associate Salary: First year $73,000 (1997); annual increments in early years of $3,000–$5,000; annual increments in later years of $8,000–$12,000
Summer Salary: $1300/week (1997)
Average Hours: 2000 worked; 1750 billed; NA required
Family Benefits: 12 weeks paid maternity leave (cbc unpaid); flexible spending accounts for health and dependent day care expenses.
1996 Summer: Class of 15 students; offers to all 11 2Ls
Partnership: 30% of entering associates from 1978–1984 were made partner
Pro Bono: 1–3% of all work is pro bono

Chapman and Cutler in 1997
169 Lawyers at the Chicago Office
0.7 Associates Per Partner

Total Partners 97		
Women	10	10%
All Minorities	2	2%
Afro-Am	1	1%
Latino	1	1%

Total Associates 69		
Women	34	49%
All Minorities	6	9%
Afro-Am	1	1%
Asian-Am	5	7%

Practice Areas	
Corporate & Securities	35
Corporate Finance	30
Banking	24
Municipal	20
Special Litigation	16
Real Estate	9
Tax	9
General Litigation	8
Health & Education	6
Trusts & Estates	6
Private Activity Bonds	2
Public Utilities	2
Environmental	1

recent negative press

Chapman and Cutler, a prominent financial legal services law firm with a reputation for "quality, conservative legal work," has experienced problems in recent years. The firm has downsized considerably since our last edition. The number of attorneys at the Chicago office is now 169, down from 236 in 1994. The firm fired 17 associates in March 1995, and a number of partners and associates have defected, including Daniel Bird and Dave Galainena, well-known attorneys in the area of structured financing. In addition, in 1995 and 1996, the firm received negative press regarding the billing practices of former partner, Maureen Fairchild. Most recently, the *Chicago Daily Law Bulletin* reported that Fairchild pleaded not guilty on November 15, 1996 to a 23-count federal indictment charging she defrauded Chapman and some of its clients out of $900,000 through concocted legal billings and expenses. Another partner, Jim Spiotto, has been the subject of a *Wall Street Journal* article critical of his billing practices. The article said Spiotto had billed over 6,000 hours in 1993. Not surprisingly, associate morale has also been problematic although it "has been steadily improving from its all time low in 1995 when 17 associates were fired," we were informed by one contact, who further observed that the "partners are very anxious to keep people and make them happy." Regarding the low morale point, another person concurred that "there does not currently seem to be any lingering effects;" but, a final contact noted that "in the last year we've had a lot of people leave which is always a little disheartening."

practice areas

In terms of practice areas, Chapman & Cutler offers a pre-eminent state and municipal finance department that has counseled government agencies and authorities nationwide and has handled financings of airports, hospitals, housing, and university facilities, and other infrastructure projects. The firm now also handles public offerings of corporate securities, typically in the role of counsel to the issuer or the underwriter, and has developed a thriving securities department. This department has represented large Wall Street investment banks that are attracted by the firm's sophisticated "New York practice with Chicago rates," reported one source. Chapman also has a strong and well-established banking practice and is general counsel to Harris Trust, one of Chicago's largest banks.

The nationally recognized bankruptcy, workout and special litigation department is one of the largest of its kind and one of the busiest at the firm. Under the leadership of Jim Spiotto, this department handles all aspects of litigation arising from insolvencies, restructurings, and other related matters. It is particularly well-known for its expertise in representing bondholders, indenture trustees, and institutional investors. One contact described the department as "very hierarchical," with only "one person in charge." It also has a reputation for being "really tense and workaholic," claimed another. The firm also offers a corporate finance department, which handles all types of financing transactions, and houses a particularly strong aircraft finance group.

Chapman has a committee to promote and coordinate pro bono activities. People agreed that quite a few attorneys in the small, general litigation department handle pro bono matters. One source noted that a "large part of the firm is composed of finance people who don't get into it as much," whereas a second person remarked that "several high-ranking partners do a lot of 'non-litigation' pro bono projects."

professional development

Chapman assigns new associates to a specific department, usually consistent with their preferences, and to a particular partner who monitors the associate's workload. The departments have different work distribution systems. In the banking department, first- to third-year associates are "really bench players." In other words, they work with almost all the partners from time to time and are "called upon for various deals and play various roles." Eventually the midlevel associates fall naturally into a pattern of working for one or two partners, but "in many cases even eighth-year associates retain the 'bench players' status." The corporate finance department assigns teams to work on particular projects, whereas the more informal state and municipal finance department puts associates to work on a variety of projects as needed. Most junior associates handle research assignments and progress to drafting documents. One person noted that associates in the special litigation department are frequently entrusted with greater responsibility than those in other areas.

summer program

Summer associates are organized in three groups that are supervised by two Summer Associate Program Coordinators and Assignment Coordinators who distribute work according to the interest of the summer associates. In the past, the groups rotated though the major practice areas at the firm for three weeks each, and the firm is currently evaluating the merits of each work distribution system. Some critics complained about the type of work assigned to summer associates. "I got some work that was ridiculous," asserted one contact. Another stated that the firm assigns "a lot of 'make work'" in the summer. Each associate advisor is responsible for obtaining feedback for the summer associates from the assigning attorneys. While some people believe the feedback is "really good," one source complained that it is "not helpful" or "constructively critical."

feedback

We heard similar mixed views regarding the feedback provided to permanent associates. The day-to-day feedback is "fairly good," claimed one person. A second person commented that "I work with several partners. I would say feedback is generally adequate but mostly informal 'good job' type of feedback." Another remarked, however, that "associates don't really learn much from" the formal annual reviews. This person conceded, though, that the "firm will tell you if you do something wrong."

businesslike environment

Overall, the work atmosphere at Chapman is "relaxed" and "informal," but somewhat hierarchical. Each department has "some really influential partners," explained one contact. In general, most attorneys are "down-to-earth" and "much more concerned about their families" than one would expect for large firm attorneys. A number of the attorneys "run kids' softball leagues," noted one contact. Though Chapman attorneys are "very friendly people" and most departments are "cordial," they are also "very businesslike," commented one person, noting that there is "not much hanging out" during the work day. In banking, however, "there is a tremendous amount of camaraderie. There is always someone to chat with," observed one contact, who further noted that "we even have daily breaks akin to a coffee break."

social life

After work one source told us that a "group of young gentlemen" in the corporate finance department hang out together "almost like a fraternity." Another person commented that "people get together a lot" for softball, followed by dinner and trips to bars. In the summer of 1996, the firm activities included baseball game outings, a lakefront boat cruise, a theatre outing to "Chicago," and a dinner at the Civic Opera House.

homogenous firm

Chapman and Cutler is making an effort to increase the number of women and minorities at the firm, but one person commented that the firm has had difficulty retaining them. At least in the banking department, "a lot of partners are men," one contact revealed. Another agreed that this department is shaped by "an old-boy network." However, a "couple of powerful women" work at the firm, stated one source.

revamped management

Chapman revamped its management structure in 1995, replacing its old five member management committee with a nine member policy committee headed by securities partner, John Dixon. This change occurred amid the downsizing and drop in firm revenues experienced at that time. One of the issues that the new management team has had to address pertains to the firm's partner compensation system, which had been lock-step and seniority-based and which reportedly caused some grousing among younger partners.

offices

Chapman's offices are located in the Harris Trust Bank building. Each associate is assigned a private office, but many are internal offices. Attorneys and summer associates receive their own networked Macintosh computers. People praised the support staff and office services, with one person calling our attention to the "firm's great support, from both staff and other lawyers." The offices were described as well-maintained, with quality furniture and art work collected by an art acquisition committee. One discordant voice, noted however that "physically, the firm's building and layout leaves something to be desired, although the firm has interior specialists analyzing the firm's layout and they will hopefully make changes." The firm has a remodeled library that is well-stocked. One critic complained, however, that the most frequently used books, reporters, and codes are on movable shelves, which can make these materials difficult to use.

hiring practices

Chapman and Cutler hires law students from a wide variety of schools including Harvard, Columbia, Georgetown, and many midwestern schools. Applicants are advised that though the firm wants people "who will do quality work," it doesn't hire "a lot of gung ho, ultra-serious people." Some contacts noted, however, that many past summer associates had journal experience. Chapman interviewers ask mostly casual questions, according to one insider, and are more interested in learning about the kind of person you are than about your academic interests.

Chapman and Cutler is a much smaller firm than it has been in the recent past but it continues to do high-quality work in finance and bankruptcy. This is not a firm, however, for people who are not sure what they want to do because associates work almost exclusively for one or two partners, and only sometimes for several. The firm provides a good atmosphere and good people with whom to work. In the words of one contact, "I think the advantage of this firm is that it does quality work in a relatively informal atmosphere where partners realize that both they and associates have lives outside of the office that are important. It is a place to do high-level work without excessive pressure."

Gardner, Carton & Douglas

Chicago Washington

Address: 321 N. Clark Street, Suite 3400, Chicago, IL 60610–4795
Telephone: (312) 644–3000
Hiring Attorney: Wendy Freyer
Contact: Joanne DeSanctis, Legal Recruitment Administrator; (312) 245–8529
Associate Salary: First year $73,000 (1997)
Summer Salary: $1350/week (1996)
Average Hours: 2152 worked; 1880 billed; 1900 required
Family Benefits: maternity leave; family leave
1996 Summer: Class of 11 2L students; offers to 11
Partnership: 60% of entering associates from 1979–1989 were made partner
Pro Bono: 4–7% of all work is pro bono

Gardner, Carton & Douglas in 1997
202 Lawyers at the Chicago Office
1.0 Associate Per Partner

Total Partners 98		
Women	17	17%
All Minorities	3	3%
Afro-Am	2	2%
Latino	1	1%

Total Associates 96		
Women	42	44%
All Minorities	8	8%
Afro-Am	3	3%
Asian-Am	2	2%
Latino	3	3%

Practice Areas	
Corporate/International	55
Litigation	46
Employment/Benefits	18
Health	16
Intellectual Property	15
Environmental	11
Labor	9
Trusts & Estates	9
Tax	5
Creditors' Rights	4
Real Estate	4

In the past 25 years, Gardner, Carton & Douglas has grown from a firm of under 50 attorneys to over 200 attorneys in its Chicago and Washington, D.C. offices. Gardner offers a "friendly" environment where "people work well together." At "some firms, you are rewarded for being a jerk. That gets no respect at Gardner," declared one source, noting that "there is no benefit to treating people badly, and they don't want people that are that way." Another person commented that the firm has a "nice atmosphere, generally good people, and many (though by no means all) have a reasonable life style." Gardner also allows "wide latitude for being different," and a "variety of attitudes" are represented at the firm. Finally, the firm "treats people with respect" and is a "humane" place to work.

prominent corporate practice

A full-service law firm, Gardner is most well-known for its corporate and health care work. One source asserted that Gardner has "one of the top 10 corporate practices in Chicago." The firm handles a traditional array of corporate matters including general corporate advising, mergers and acquisitions (M&A), and securities law issues ranging from venture capital financing to public offerings and private placements. It also has been involved in significant international matters involving Germany, Europe, the Pacific Rim, India, South Africa, and Latin America.

health care environmental

Under the leadership of Ed Bryant, Gardner also has a nationally recognized health practice. This department has counseled hospitals and not-for-profit health institutions nationwide in general corporate matters, bond issues, M&A, and antitrust. This practice is "one of the five best in the country," declared one contact. Gardner is also well-known for its environmental department, which is one of the largest and reportedly "one of the best in the Midwest." The department was under the leadership of Richard Kissell, former chairman of the Illinois EPA. He recently stepped down to chair the firm's management committee; Susan Franzetti now heads the group.

Gardner has not traditionally been known for its litigation practice, and one person commented that unless you are interested in health or environmental related litigation, it is a "bad choice for litigation." The litigation department recently went through a period of turbulence, with the departure of seven associates in a two month period. In 1995 the litigation department underwent a major change in philosophy which coincided with a change in department leadership. Mike Hayes, the former Illinois Deputy Attorney General, and present chair of the litigation department, was instrumental in merging the firm's public law practice into the litigation department. The litigation department now emphasizes high profile public interest litigation while maintaining its more traditional commercial litigation practice. The firm recently represented the Democratic Party National Convention Committee in litigation challenging the demonstration policies at the 1996 Democratic Convention. Gardner also offers a strong intellectual property department, headed by Pam Walter, which has been growing rapidly and becoming more prominent every year.

pro bono

Gardner has designated an attorney to coordinate its pro bono program and will automatically credit up to 50 pro bono hours toward its billable requirement of 1900 hours. One person noted that Gardner permits attorneys to donate more time to a particular pro bono project on a case-by-case basis. Gardner attorneys staff a Chicago Volunteer Legal Services Clinic on a regular basis. The firm signals its commitment to pro bono work by designating a pro bono attorney of the year award annually.

summer associate program

Summer associates' work is thoroughly reviewed halfway through the summer in written evaluations, where suggestions for improvement, if necessary, are made. Candidates are again reviewed at the end of the summer. Over the past four summers, Gardner has extended permanent offers to over ninety percent of its summer associates, with classes ranging from 15-20 per summer.

on-the-job training

Gardner does not make permanent offers to summer associates by department. New associates are asked for their department preferences, and are initially assigned to a practice area shortly before they begin work. "Every effort is made to take the new associate's practice area preferences into account, although this depends on the needs of the firm and its clients at the time," according to a firm spokesperson. As with most firms, junior associates spend a significant amount of time exploring the library, but we were told that at times they are also entrusted with "substantive work." Each department is responsible for training its associates. Most departments meet regularly, and some organize training seminars and workshops. The bulk of associate training, however, occurs "on-the-job."

social life

Perhaps because Gardner is a "respectful place" with a "commitment to valuing people's lives," many attorneys "have social lives away from the firm." The attorneys "get along with one another" and, during the work day, "hang out in each other's offices." Younger associates frequently "go out for beers and shows" after work. The firm organizes a number of events, such as the well-attended attorney lunches held every Thursday and the annual Holiday party. Summer events include numerous informal cocktail parties, softball games, a summer picnic, and a formal party.

diversity efforts

The treatment of women at Gardner is "excellent compared to that at other Chicago firms", observed one contact. A number of female attorneys are in positions of influence, such as the head of the intellectual property department, the head of the environmental department and two senior-level women in the labor department. The Professional Evaluation Committee and the Recruitment Committee are also chaired by women, and there is a woman on the management committee. The firm has an active Women's Committee that meets regularly. This committee sponsors an annual Women's Business Development Cocktail Party and a summer event for female summer associates. In addition, one person commented that the firm has "been paying attention to issues" involving maternity leave and part-time arrangements. Gardner has adopted a "very good sexual harassment policy" that was drafted by Kathleen Mulligan, a partner at the firm and former supervisory trial attorney with responsibility for complex classification cases at the Equal Employment Opportunity Commission (EEOC). The firm, according to people we interviewed, is making a "fairly active effort to recruit and retain minorities." The firm requires all attorneys to attend diversity training workshops.

Gardner is governed by a managing partner and a six partner management committee. The firm continues to build its litigation and labor and employment rights practices and to increase its international corporate work. It also expects the intellectual property department to continue growing.

elegant offices

The firm's office facilities are "fairly elegant," with a lot of "wood and dark colors." One person described them as having a "wealthy individual's living room look." All attorneys are assigned private offices, though first-year associates have internal offices. Each attorney has a personal computer, with e-mail, LEXIS and Westlaw access. The firm is equipped with a cafeteria, and people use a health club located in an adjacent building.

hiring tips

Gardner hires law students who "will get along well with the people in the firm." It wants "reasonably personable people" and is "not a place for quiet, asocial people." The summer class usually consists of students with "really diverse beliefs" and "people with character." One insider advised students not to "come across as uptight or self-important" in the interviews. Gardner hires most of its summer associates from national schools such as Cornell, Harvard, Michigan, Northwestern, and the University of Chicago, and a few from a variety of other local Chicago and midwest schools.

For someone who is interested in a corporate or health care practice, Gardner is an excellent choice. People criticized the office facilities, particularly the offices on the south side of the building, which "get pretty hot" in the afternoon sun. A second source of complaint we heard from a number of people concerned pay. One person remarked that "the money might not be as good as at some other larger firms in the mid to senior level associate range." A second person commented on the "smaller bonuses and fewer rewards for associates who bring in work." A firm spokesperson informed us that "the firm made an across the board market adjustment to all associate salaries in November 1996," in an effort to address these matters. Gardner, however, is a "good, fun place to practice law" and does "good quality work." It also has an extremely good reputation. One insider declared that "if you are going to practice law, you might as well practice it in a place that is fun, and Gardner is such a place.

Holleb & Coff

Chicago

Address: 55 East Monroe Street, Suite 4100, Chicago, IL 60603
Telephone: (312) 807–4600
Hiring Attorney: Susan K. Marr
Contact: Dawn M. Marlin, Recruiting Coordinator; (312) 807–4600 (ext. 2649)
Associate Salary: First year $70,000 (1997)
Summer Salary: $1350/week (1997)
Average Hours: 2131 worked; 1832 billed; 1950 required
Family Benefits: cbc maternity; cbc paternity
1996 Summer: Class of 9 students; offers to 9
Partnership: NA
Pro Bono: 4% of all work is pro bono

Holleb & Coff in 1997
130 Lawyers at the Firm
1.0 Associate Per Partner

Total Partners 64		
Women	5	8%
All Minorities	2	3%
Afro Am	2	3%

Total Associates 62		
Women	24	39%
All Minorities	8	13%
Afro-Am	1	2%
Asian-Am	3	5%
Latino	4	6%

Practice Areas	
Litigation	26%
Corporate	22%
Bankruptcy	10%
Real Estate	9%
Health	8%
Tax	7%
Environmental	5%
Intellectual Property	5%
Labor/Employment	5%
Probate	5%

Holleb & Coff is one of the most "humane" of the large and prominent Chicago firms. Its attorneys "are really nice," and it is not a "big, power hungry place." Though "work is a priority," everyone "has a life" and is not "expected to give all to the firm," we were told. In fact, most Holleb attorneys are "family oriented" and "strong relationships of trust, cooperation and friendship between partners and associates" are common at the firm. This successful firm has reportedly become a refuge for associates seeking a more laid-back lifestyle because it provides a "reasonable balance between working and outside lives."

egalitarian culture

Holleb is also distinguished by its unusual emphasis on "fairness." Unlike many other firms where senior partners are typically rewarded with spacious corner offices, Holleb & Coff's corner offices serve as general use conference rooms, and little disparity exists in the size of attorneys' offices. Moreover, the secretarial staff is treated with respect and invited to virtually all social events. Furthermore, associates are given unusual opportunities to voice their concerns, and unlike most Chicago firms, Holleb & Coff only has one tier of partnership. One contact pointed out to us that of late the firm may be "becoming a bit less fair. It used to be that if you worked hard and were talented, you'd make partner. This is not true anymore."

practice areas

Holleb & Coff offers a full-service legal practice that represents large and medium-sized corporations and some individuals. Although we were told that all its practice areas are growing at a steady pace, the firm recently asked four partners to resign, something which "hadn't happened in a long time," according to one contact. As one of its largest clients, BTR, Inc. (formerly known as British Tire and Rubber) brings some international work to the firm. The bankruptcy and environmental departments have experienced especially strong growth in recent years, though this may now be "tapering off somewhat" we were told. The firm has a very well-reputed and thriving litigation department that handles a range of commercial litigation matters. The litigation practice was recently divided into several subgroups, including healthcare and employment/labor. Of course, a general litigation department still exists. Martin Redish, whose civil procedure textbook is well-known to many law students, teaches at Northwestern and is counsel at the firm. The corporate department advises many corporations, financial institutions, and banks. Employment/labor and healthcare are also growing very fast and are very busy, and the firm has recently created a new intellectual property and technology department.

pro bono

Holleb & Coff enjoys a high profile in the Chicago community. Founding partner Marshall Holleb is "very philanthropic" and has been involved in numerous civic activities, from low-income housing initiatives to restoring one of the city's historic theaters. With the Museum of Contemporary Art as one of its clients, Holleb & Coff is also "into art." As a result of these activities, the firm has many opportunities to receive tickets to exhibitions at the museum and to shows in the historic theater. All employees, including support staff, receive these tickets on a first-come, first-served basis. Though pro bono work is encouraged at the firm, and litigators at the firm handle a wide range of pro bono matters, we were told that Holleb does not have a particularly organized system for distributing pro bono assignments. Pro bono matters come in through various partners and departments.

professional development

Holleb & Coff usually assigns entering associates to the department of their choice. The department coordinator distributes work to the associates, or partners and senior attorneys may directly request associates to work for them. In addition, associates may request work from particular partners. Junior associates are entrusted with an "unbelievable amount of responsibility," said one contact, a sentiment confirmed by all we interviewed, noting that they handle projects that "fifth-years are not doing at other firms." While junior associates handle their share of research and document-drafting assignments, it is not uncommon for first-year associates to take depositions and appear in court on all types of matters. Second-year associates have both taken and defended depositions and cross-examined witnesses in significant trials.

Each department is responsible for training its associates and has fashioned its own program for the development of important associate skills. The firm also organizes informal monthly seminars in which partners make presentations. People agreed, however, that most of the training at Holleb & Coff happens "on-the-job." Associates receive straightforward formal evaluations twice a year. For the formal evaluations, the partners complete detailed forms on each associate who has worked for them and then meet as a group to discuss the associate's performance.

unstructured fun social life

Holleb is a "fun place" to work and a "very social firm." Attorneys "get along quite well." One person commented that "a closed door is a peculiarity...people poke their heads into each others' offices." Social life at the firm is "very unstructured, and people follow their natural impulses." Attorneys often celebrate their colleagues' birthdays with doughnuts and cake in one of the firm's coffee rooms. The organized social life revolves around family life. In addition, the associates organize a few Friday night parties a year which include dancing, drinking, lazer-tag and "no kids," according to one informant. A summer picnic outing is held each year and activities for the day include swimming in the pond, going on tractor rides, and eating ice cream from a Good Humor ice cream truck. Other summer events include going to Sox and Cubs games and maybe a pre-season Bears football contest.

family issues

The number of female attorneys at Holleb has increased significantly in recent years. The firm has a published parental leave policy which "involves up to three months paid leave and up to an additional three months unpaid leave to all lawyers depending upon how long they have been employed at our firm," reported a firm spokesperson. In addition, decisions related to specific part-time and work-at-home arrangements for attorneys who "request flexibility beyond what is provided for in the parental leave policy" are decided "case by case." One contact claimed, however, that "no one ever knows what they may be able to arrange," and further, that "you take a big pay cut and go off-track" at such times.

The management of Holleb is "fairly centralized." Most of the firm's day-to-day decisions are made by its managing partner, who chairs a nine member executive committee. Associates hold frequent meetings to discuss their concerns. Most feel free to express their views. They have "as much influence as one would expect," one person told us.

offices

Holleb's offices occupy three floors. Every associate and partner has a private office with a window. All the offices are about the same size and offer views either of Lake Michigan or the city. The firm recently installed a brand-new computer network system. Usually two attorneys are assigned to one secretary. The library is adequate and improvements are presently underway to both expand the library and to create room for a high-technology conference center at the firm. The firm is also equipped with three kitchens that have vending machines and free refreshments.

hires for the long haul

Holleb usually hires a small summer class and, unlike many other firms, has generally avoided problems of over hiring. It places a premium on hiring people with strong Chicago ties who will likely stay at the firm for the long haul. Personality also plays a big role in the hiring decisions. Holleb hires "energetic, enthusiastic, nice people." The callback interviews are informal. Holleb hires students from national law schools such as Harvard, the University of Chicago, the University of Michigan, and Yale, as well as from local Chicago schools. In 1996, the firm made offers for permanent employment to all nine summer associates. It has a remarkably high acceptance rate from its summer classes.

Holleb & Coff is growing rapidly but is small relative to other prominent Chicago law firms. In addition, many aspects of its practice are "less high-profile and not as sexy as those at the big firms." Accordingly, one contact observed, "the pay is less" and, when you get a bonus, it tends to be "less than what you could get elsewhere." Moreover, Holleb doesn't "have a lot of national recognition because we have only a Chicago office," according to one contact. Nevertheless, associates are very satisfied at Holleb & Coff. One person noted that you "can't do much better if you are working in a firm." Holleb is an "easygoing place" and the people are friendly. "There is respect for your life outside work which you probably won't find elsewhere," commented another person. Associates "like the way they are treated," and it is "easy to build relationships with partners." Associates get "substantive work from the beginning," and though there is "a lot of on-the-job pressure," the hours are reasonable, as are the "expectations placed on how hard you work." Someone who is "interested in life outside the law" and wants a "good shot at partnership" should consider Holleb & Coff, although, as pointed out earlier, making partner today is less certain than in the past.

Hopkins & Sutter

Chicago Detroit Washington

Address: Three First National Plaza, Chicago, IL 60602
Telephone: (312) 558–6600
Hiring Attorney: R. Lee Christie and Van E. Holkeboer
Contact: Jamie L. Bailey, Recruiting Coordinator; (312) 558–6519
Associate Salary: First year $73,000 (1997)
Summer Salary: $1400/week (1997)
Average Hours: 2240 worked; 1902 billed; 1900 required
Family Benefits: 12 weeks paid maternity leave; short and long-term disability; family and medical leave
1996 Summer: Class of 15 students; offers to 12
Partnership: 90% of entering associates from the classes of 1978–1986 were made partner
Pro Bono: 3% of all work is pro bono

Hopkins & Sutter in 1997
133 Lawyers at the Chicago Office
0.5 Associates Per Partner

Total Partners 88			Total Associates 43			Practice Areas	
Women	15	17%	Women	22	51%	Litigation/Regulatory Services	44
All Minorities	2	2%	All Minorities	2	5%	Tax-Related Services	34
Afro-Am	1	1%	Afro-Am	1	2%	Corporate Transactions	16
Asian-Am	1	1%	Latino	1	2%	Financial Services	14
						Real Estate Services	13
						Public Law & Finance	10

Hopkins & Sutter "partners made a firm commitment to make it a pleasant place to work." New associates are warmly welcomed during their first few hours at the firm by fellow attorneys who drop by to introduce themselves. The firm makes a "real conscious effort not to have too much hierarchy," and attorneys "maintain an open-door policy," said insiders we spoke with. Partners try to "work with" associates rather than "have associates working for them" and "take an interest in associates' lives." Through a "training partner" in each practice group, the firm even makes an effort to ensure that associates "are not overworked." One person told us that "I expected a sort of driven element to the people at the firm...and that there would be times when their lives would not be their own. That was not what I found. I heard it was a nicer place to work, and I found this to be true...their lives are not run by the firm." Another person informed us that "it really is possible to know the names of everyone (staff included) who works here, which makes a huge difference in the atmosphere. It is an extremely comfortable place to work."

practice areas

Founded in 1921 as a pre-eminent tax boutique firm, Hopkins & Sutter is now a full-service law firm. Its tax department, once described as "the most elite group in the firm," has downsized substantially of late with the departure of a significant number of tax partners from the firm. Hopkins & Sutter has represented the Resolution Trust Corporation (RTC) and the Federal Deposit Insurance Corporation (FDIC) since 1965, and rose to national prominence in the 1980s as counsel for these institutions in their savings and loan prosecutions. As one of the top billing firms in this area, and with this practice constituting a significant portion of the firm's work, Hopkins & Sutter suffered a blow in 1991 when the federal government limited the amount that any one firm could "bill" on savings and loan litigation and related matters. This has led to a considerable downsizing of the firm's D.C. office in recent years. The litigation department handles a wide range of commercial matters, including tax, bankruptcy, and other business litigation for small and medium-sized companies. The litigation department has recently been reorganized, and renamed the litigation and regulatory services, in recognition of the large contributions by the "public utilities" group under Paul Hanzlik's supervision. Hopkins also has a well-established banking practice. One insider told us that the firm broke Mayer, Brown & Platt's "stranglehold" in the area of international banking and now enjoys a "substantial base of foreign bank clients."

The tax and corporate departments represent clients ranging from Fortune 500 companies to individuals. In addition to providing general corporate legal services, Hopkins has a number of interesting specialty practice groups. The firm's public finance practice is reportedly doing well. Hopkins also houses an airport finance group which, under the leadership of Lynn Goldschmidt, has worked on the financings of both the Denver and Chicago airports. The firm also has a "solid bankruptcy department," whose attorneys are frequently appointed to become bankruptcy trustees. Hopkins & Sutter recently opened an office in Detroit to provide services to a major railroad client, Canadian National Railway, which had eliminated its in-house legal department. This office currently has six to eight attorneys. At the same time, the Dallas office has been closed after the partners in the Dallas corporate/transactional section left the firm.

pro bono

Hopkins does not treat pro bono hours the same as billable hours, but it does offer a year-end $3000 bonus to the associate who "best exemplifies the firm's commitment to pro bono." The firm does a lot of work with the American Civil Liberties Union, and one of its partners, Mike Ficaro, a former Cook County attorney, handles a number of criminal pro bono cases. The firm also encourages transactional attorneys to perform pro bono service, and many attorneys serve as counsel to community groups and local tax-exempt organizations.

unstructured environment

Hopkins & Sutter is informal and not highly departmentalized. New associates are hired into a particular department but are permitted to work in more than one area. The firm encourages a "lot of mixing between practice groups to draw on people's specialties," and attorneys in different areas often work together. The "training partners" in each practice area supervise the training of junior associates. Associates may receive their work from the training partner or directly from other partners or senior associates. One contact informed us that "work is not always evenly distributed. Some 'training partners' do not take an active role in seeing the work distributed equitably." Summer associates choose assignments from an assignment book maintained by an assignment attorney. People commented that although each practice group organizes a series of training seminars and workshops, much of the training is "on-the-job."

Hopkins is "diligent" about providing summer associates with helpful mid-summer and end-of-the-summer reviews. It also formally reviews permanent associates twice a year.

early opportunities

Associate responsibility at Hopkins is, according to one contact, "absolutely amazing. Part of that comes from its size—you can't overstaff a matter if you don't have that many lawyers. But it also reflects the way the partners think of associates—as colleagues. A partner will involve an associate in a matter that he or she is working on, and expect the associate to do everything that he or she is capable of doing on that matter, regardless of years of experience." According to another source, "lean staffing on cases/deals means associates work directly with partners and are given responsibility early in their careers." Bankruptcy and public finance associates are entrusted with significant early responsibility. In addition to other assignments, junior corporate associates rotate on "blue sky duty," which involves monitoring changes in the "blue sky" law of all fifty states, and junior litigation associates rotate on "docket duty," which involves attending routine status and motion calls. One person informed us that litigation associates are expected to be able to take depositions, write briefs, and sometimes cross-examine witnesses by the end of their second year.

moderate social life

Hopkins & Sutter is a friendly firm during the day, but there is "no expectation to socialize outside work." People are supportive of each other and are constantly "in and out of each others' offices." A "kidding" and "light" atmosphere pervades the firm. Most associates feel comfortable in Hopkins' work environment, and although in general there is relatively little turnover at the firm, this has changed somewhat of late. One person told us that there "has been a fair amount of turnover recently. The firm is very 'dynamic' right now, with people leaving and new people arriving." People go out to lunch together, work out together at a nearby health club, and sometimes "hang out after work for drinks, food, or plays." Many attorneys, however, are married and have children, or have "outside lives." The firm sponsors a number of activities during the summer, including trips to sporting events and restaurants, and a golf outing.

committed to diversity

When questioned about diversity at Hopkins, one source stated that there is room for "a lot of individuality" at the firm. The firm is committed to increasing the number of its female and minority lawyers. The 1997 summer program included nine second years, of whom six were women and three were minority attorneys. Hopkins has a "fair number of female equity and income partners who are women's women and a lot of strong female associates. There is a real camaraderie," praised one admirer. Another pointed out that there are a number of female "rainmakers" in the aviation department. The firm is "very encouraging of maternity leave," said one insider, noting that women have become partners after taking time off to have children. Hopkins has been flexible in permitting part-time work schedules. The firm received generally favorable reviews regarding its commitment to racial diversity. Hopkins now has two minority attorneys, neither of whom is an equity partner.

new management

The management structure has undergone major changes in recent years. The Executive Committee consists of seven members, and meets quarterly; it is charged with broad managerial oversight. The more detail-oriented management is handled by the newly created six-member Operations Committee.

office upgrade underway

Located in the downtown Chicago Loop, Hopkins & Sutter is an easy commute. First-year associates receive "internal" offices without windows, second-years progress to "twin windows," and third-years graduate to "big windows." A computer is provided for every attorney and major upgrades, in both hardware and software, are currently underway. One contact informed us that "technologically, Hopkins is behind other big firms in at least one respect: we do not yet have access to outside e-mail at our desks. Although it may seem like merely a convenience, many clients prefer to communicate via e-mail, or wish to transmit documents between offices electronically." This person further informed us that Hopkins is in the process of making outside e-mail available to all attorneys at their desks, a task that ought to be accomplished by year's end. Three attorneys are assigned to each secretary. The support staff is very good. One person commented that the library could stand some expansion. Every floor is equipped with a kitchen with vending machines. The physical facility itself, we were told, is in need of significant upgrading. "Carpeting needs to be replaced. A paint job would go a long way. Also, the art collection is hideous." One contact informed us, however, that "the firm is starting renovations to its offices, aimed at improving conference facilities and the general aesthetics of the office."

friendly interviews

In hiring decisions, Hopkins places a "premium on friendly people" and "values someone who values other people." Hopkins looks "above all, for people who are going to get along in the firm," and "someone you won't mind spending long hours with." Applicants were advised to "be genuine" in their interviews. You "don't have to tap dance as much as for other places," one contact assured us. The interviews at Hopkins are conversational. One past successful applicant reported that interviewers were "far more interested in what I did outside law school and in my interests." Hopkins hires law students from the top national law schools and regional midwest law schools.

Hopkins does not enjoy the national reputation of some of Chicago's largest law firms, but it is a "fairly large firm—big enough to attract good-sized deals and good-sized litigation." It is also "less pressured." One significant drawback, according to some at the firm, is that the firm is top-heavy with partners. "Senior income partners are concerned about whether there is 'room' for them to become equity partners," asserted one insider. On the other hand, a second contact informed us that "Hopkins hires with the expectation that everyone in the class will make partner, rather than hiring 40 new associates because half of them will leave in the first two years:" Hopkins is for someone who wants sophisticated large firm legal work but prefers to "avoid big firm practice." The firm offers a "great mix of prestige...without the factory, boiler-room atmosphere." It is "a very livable place to be a lawyer" and is "very encouraging for women who want to have families." The people at Hopkins are "excellent," and the firm is "not cheap," assured one insider, declaring that you "can make quite a bit of money working at Hopkins." Another insider praised the firm's "generous bonuses," which in 1996 ranged from $7,000 to $22,000.

Finally, one upbeat contact put a positive spin on the negative "buzz" associated with Hopkins Sutter as a result of the early 1990s curtailment of FDIC business and related matters, noting that "Hopkins has been gradually shrinking for several years due to the end of the FDIC/FSLIC boom years, the weeding out of unproductive partners, and the departure of some partners dissatisfied about changes in the retirement system. In the law firm rumor mill, "negative growth" is always seen as negative, but in Hopkins' case, the new, smaller version of the firm is younger, busier, and much more lucrative than the old, bigger version. In Hopkins' case, smaller is better." Another contact informed us, however, that the "firm is currently in a state of flux, with a fair amount of turnover recently, which leads to low morale."

Jenner & Block

Chicago Lake Forest Washington

Address: One IBM Plaza, Chicago, IL 60611
Telephone: (312) 222–9350
Hiring Attorney: Gregory S. Gallopoulos
Contact: Gretchen L. Haas, Manager of Legal Recruiting; (312) 222–9350
Associate Salary: First year $73,000 (1996)
Summer Salary: $1400/week (1997)
Average Hours: NA worked; 1879 billed; 1900 required.
Family Benefits: 9 weeks paid maternity leave
1996 Summer: Class of 63 students
Partnership: 91% of entering associates from 1988–1996 were made partner
Pro Bono: 5.4% of work is pro bono

Jenner & Block in 1997
294 Lawyers at the Chicago Office
0.8 Associates Per Partner

Total Partners 160		
Women	NA	NA
All Minorities	NA	NA

Total Associates 133		
Women	NA	NA%
All Minorities	NA	NA%

Practice Areas	
Litigation	184
Corporate/Securities	27
Environmental	19
Commercial/Bankruptcy	15
Tax	12
Intellectual Property	10
Real Estate	10
Labor/Employment	9
Estate Planning	3
Government/Health	3

With a nationally acclaimed litigation and trial practice, Jenner & Block has been involved in many widely-publicized trials, investigations, and United States Supreme Court cases. Jenner & Block is increasingly becoming "known for its Supreme Court practice, particularly because of Bruce Ennis, a partner in the D.C. office." Barry Levenstam, a partner in Chicago, also argued before the Supreme Court recently, as have Don Verrilli and Paul Smith. "Bruce, Don and Paul were all mentioned as members of the Supreme Court's "Inner Circle" in a March 1997 *National Law Journal* article," we were told.

long hours

The firm provides high-quality legal services and "demands a high level of work and long hours" of its attorneys. Jenner & Block attorneys are hard-working. One source commented that they "are aggressive" on behalf of their clients "but not to each other." They "generally like each other and like the work they are doing," but the firm "can be stressful" at times. One person complained that there is "unwritten/unspoken pressure to put in "face-time;" there is "too much emphasis put on hours worked."

down-to-earth culture

In addition to the long hours, Jenner's "informal culture" shapes its work atmosphere. Attorneys enjoy playing practical jokes on each other, with the level of levity varying by work group. They have been known to circulate fake executive committee memos throughout the firm. Jenner does not emphasize dress as much as some other firms. One person commented that the firm is "unconcerned about how people dress," noting that many people dress casually on days when they are not going to court or meeting with clients. This is a "hard-working, roll–up–your–sleeves–and–get–down–to–work" kind of place and "not a white shoe firm" at all.

Jenner is "not oppressively hierarchical" and has an "open-door policy." Even the chairman of the firm has candy dishes in his office to provide an incentive for people to accept his standing invitation to drop by. The firm serves dinner at 6:30 P.M. Monday through Thursday for attorneys who are working late. Jenner is tolerant of differing views. For instance, attorneys openly display loyalties for rival politicians. Openly gay attorneys often bring their partners to firm social events.

primarily litigation

A little more than half of the Jenner attorneys work in the firm's renowned general litigation practice, which represents a wide variety of clients, from large corporations like General Dynamics, Tenneco, MCI, Hitachi and Comdisco, to small Chicago restaurants. One of Jenner's most well-known cases was its successful antitrust action against AT&T on behalf of MCI.

cluster system

The litigation practice is organized in five "clusters" of varying size and character. One person explained that the cluster system is "a conscious administrative device intended to break down the size of the litigation department into more manageable chunks," thereby increasing associate satisfaction. Each cluster is headed by a "rainmaking partner," and in theory, each is a general litigation group. In practice, however, some have niches in particular areas. The Valukas Cluster, headed by Anton Valukas, former U.S. Attorney for the Northern District of Illinois, handles white-collar criminal work. One person told us that "the Valukas cluster is less formal than most others." Partner William Van Hoere in this cluster is known for his black jeans and two-tone cowboy boots. The Chabraja Cluster, by contrast, is more formal and focuses primarily on litigation matters involving General Dynamics. The Solovy Cluster, headed by firm Chairman Jerold Solovy, has a general litigation practice, although Solovy has particular expertise in securities litigation. The other two clusters are under the leadership of Chet Kamin, the lead trial lawyer in MCI's antitrust battles against AT&T, and Ted Tetzlaff, the former chairman of the litigation section of the American Bar Association. Other well-known litigators at the firm include Judge Phillip Tone, formerly a judge on the Seventh Circuit who has written several books on alternative dispute resolution. New litigation associates are assigned to a specific cluster.

developing corporate

A little less than half of Jenner & Block attorneys work in one of the firm's rapidly expanding transactions practice groups. These groups are: corporate and securities, tax, commercial and bankruptcy, environmental, labor and employment, real estate, intellectual property, government contracts, healthcare and trade associations, and estate planning. The corporate group has advised General Dynamics, Tenneco and other companies in numerous substantial and sophisticated transactions. It has also recently represented issuers of securities as well as a number of publicly-held and private companies in acquisition and disposition transactions. To boost its growing corporate practice, the firm instituted a comprehensive in-house training program covering such subjects as buying and selling businesses, representing venture capital funds, and initial public offerings of securities. However, one insider, comparing the relative strengths of the corporate and litigation practices, cautioned that those interested in transactional work would be "taking a bet if they went to the firm for corporate."

committed to pro bono

Jenner & Block "hands down has the best pro bono work in the city," declared one contact. Firm patriarch Bert Jenner had a strong commitment to pro bono work, and the firm has continued the tradition. Throughout its history, the firm has handled many noteworthy cases including the landmark death penalty case of *Witherspoon v. Illinois*, decided in 1968, and, more recently, the "Baby Richard" adoption case. The litigation section of the American Bar Association recently awarded Jenner & Block the John Minor Wisdom Award for dedication to public service and pro bono representation. Also, the firm received the ABA Pro Bono Publico Award in 1995 in recognition of its outstanding pro bono record. The firm employs a full-time pro bono coordinator who manages day-to-day operations of the pro bono program. Jenner's billing requirements give associates a strong incentive to engage in pro bono work. The firm imposes a 350 hours "non-billable" requirement on attorneys, in addition to its 1900 billable hours requirement. Most young attorneys meet this requirement with considerable pro bono work, although administrative and bar activities are credited toward this requirement as well. The firm regularly updates its extensive list of available pro bono matters from which associates may choose projects. Jenner & Block is regularly appointed by the Seventh Circuit to represent indigent clients on appeal. Most of these cases are assigned to young associates.

professional development

Jenner & Block provides associates with formal training seminars and workshops on a range of basic legal and trial skills. Some litigation clusters also have monthly meetings to discuss active client matters and sponsor individual and specialized training sessions. The opportunities for responsibility vary by department. The corporate department is leanly staffed and extremely busy, so young corporate associates receive a "lot of responsibility." This is also true in the fast growing labor and employment department. One contact noted that "the bankruptcy associates get responsibility very early in comparison with their colleagues in other departments." This person advised that the department "may be a good alternative for people who want to get into court frequently and early in their careers, and those who want to combine litigation with corporate practice." Many first-year litigation associates handle research and document production work for paying clients and "use pro bono...to get practical experience." Opportunities for associates to handle depositions and to appear in court on behalf of paying clients varies among clusters and is in part determined by the luck of the draw. One person noted that because the Valukas and Kamin Clusters are small, they offer earlier responsibility. Another person complained, however, that in general there are "few opportunities (outside of pro bono work) to participate in trials or depositions (i.e. actually questioning witnesses) for young to mid-level associates" because the "cases are deeply staffed."

excellent summer program

Run by a pair of young partners, Natalia Delgado and Tom O'Neill most recently, Jenner's "summer program is excellent." A team, generally composed of one male and one female associate, acts as group leaders for every six to eight summer associates. The group leaders are responsible for distributing assignments and monitoring work load. Summer associates receive "very good" formal feedback from their group leaders. Jenner & Block also assigns each summer associate a "reader" -- an attorney assigned to read all of the summer associate's written work product and give constructive feedback throughout the course of the summer. In addition, the firm sponsors a writing program and a mock trial program for all summer associates.

active social life

Jenner is a friendly and social firm. Its attorneys form close friendships, and Jenner hosts a wide range of social activities. Jenner organizes a Fourth of July cruise on Lake Michigan for the summer associates. The firm also sponsors a well-attended cocktail party every Friday. One person commented that attorneys attend these "for fun, not elbow-rubbing." Another popular summer event is the tour of the county jail and criminal court complex at "26th and California," where the firm does many of its pro bono criminal trials.

gender and minority issues

Jenner is concerned about the low number of female and minority attorneys at the firm and openly discusses some of the problems that must be addressed. Partner Joan Hall, the first woman chair of the ABA Litigation Section, regularly holds lunches for women at the firm. Jenner also has made presentations to past summer classes during their two-day retreat about the firm's maternity leave policy and about the challenges of being a lawyer and raising a family. The firm "really tries to accommodate" an attorney's requests for part-time work schedules, praised one admirer. Another commented that Jenner is a "place where women can have kids" and do, although this will be done at the expense of family time if she is an associate, observed a third person. Jenner is also a firm, we were told, where any instance of sexual harassment "would be dealt with swiftly." Jenner has "a real commitment to minority recruitment and retention," although it has "not been remarkably successful in improving minority recruitment." The firm has a minority committee that is "very receptive to suggestions."

management

Jenner & Block is governed by an executive committee that consists of the cluster leaders, most heads of the other groups, and the CEO who is in charge of day-to-day business management. The executive committee oversees the day-to-day administration of the firm and brings major decisions to a full partnership vote. Associates may voice their concerns through an associates committee. In the future, the firm plans to maintain its excellent litigation practice and to continue to build its transactional practice groups.

offices

Built by Mies van de Rohe, an internationally acclaimed architect, Jenner & Block's office building was, nevertheless, described by one person as "a black-box building." The offices themselves, however, which have been recently re-modeled, "afford spectacular ceiling to floor views of the city's waterfront and architecture," according to one enthusiast. All associates are assigned private offices, most of which are separated from the internal corridor by a glass partition "covered with dirty curtains," criticized one contact. Each attorney is also assigned a computer and printer. The firm does not have a cafeteria, but caters in dinner four nights a week. "A lot of people stay, and it's a social time," we were told.

hires by GPA

As for recruitment, Jenner & Block is "a grades firm." It prefers law students from the top schools to have at least a B+ grade point average. The firm also seeks people with "interesting experiences" and "people who show they will do things...and do not require babying." Our sources advised applicants to emphasize the "kind of person you are" in the interview. The firm wants to hear about your interests. It generally appreciates "honest questions" that reflect those things about which you are concerned. Jenner also wants people "who will get along with others," but there is "no particular type." Jenner's "feeder schools" are Chicago, Harvard, Michigan, and Northwestern. Jenner also hires from a wide range of other top schools.

Jenner & Block is a big firm that requires its associates to work hard. Though Jenner pays a high salary, there is a "high turnover in the first few years." If you are interested in litigation, and are attracted to a prestigious and high-profile practice, it would be hard to do better than Jenner & Block. Jenner has the "best litigation practice in the city," one insider exclaimed. The firm provides a "remarkable work atmosphere," "phenomenal work" that is extremely diverse, top-notch training, and a "fantastic" pro bono program. Its partners are described as "down to earth, approachable, and fun to work with," but you will experience a "very demanding work load in terms of the time commitment required of associates."

Jones, Day, Reavis & Pogue

Chicago Atlanta Cleveland Columbus Dallas Irvine Los Angeles New York Pittsburgh Washington
Brussels Frankfurt Geneva Hong Kong London New Delhi Paris Riyadh Taipei Tokyo

Address: 77 West Wacker, Chicago, IL 60601–1692
Telephone: (312) 782–3939
Hiring Attorney: Lee Ann Russo
Contact: Pamela Nelson, Recruiting Administrator; (312) 269–4163
Associate Salary: First year $74,000 plus stipend (1997)
Summer Salary: $1220.93/week (1997)
Average Hours: 2100 worked; 1900 billed; NA required
Family Benefits: Family & maternity leave (generally 6-8 weeks paid disability and 4 weeks paid family leave, plus 12 weeks unpaid leave)
1996 Summer: Class of 15 students
Partnership: NA
Pro Bono: NA

Jones, Day, Reavis & Pogue in 1997
119 Lawyers at the Chicago Office
1.5 Associates Per Partner

Total Partners 42		
Women	9	21%
All Minorities	0	0%

Total Associates 62		
Women	24	39%
All Minorities	4	7%
Afro-Am	1	2%
Asian Am	3	5%

Practice Areas	
Litigation	44
Business Practice	40
New Associates Group	18
Government Regulation	11
Tax	6

With 20 offices in 11 countries, Jones, Day, Reavis & Pogue is the second largest law firm in the world. It is also a highly structured firm with centralized management. Unlike the branch offices of many other firms, all Jones Day offices operate as parts of a single cohesive entity under the leadership of the managing partner who currently resides in Cleveland. A "partner-in-charge" of each Jones Day office is responsible for the day-to-day management of the office and usually sets the tone of the office's work atmosphere. The Chicago office is very friendly, which may be due in part to the laid back nature of Bill Ritchie, the Chicago partner-in-charge. Ritchie and the practice group heads form the office's informal management committee. At times, there is some of the bureaucracy of a large firm but it mostly occurs behind the scenes, although one critic complained that associates face a lot of "bureaucratic bull" at the firm. The Chicago office is the "second busiest Jones Day office after New York;" yet its pace is described as quite "relaxed" for a large law firm.

young office

The Chicago office was established in 1987. It is a "young office," with many young partners. In contrast to the Jones Day reputation, we were told that the Chicago office is "not uptight or stuffy." Though men wear generally "conservative" suits to work, women have "more latitude" and wear "stylish clothing, including pantsuits." The Chicago office is not overly hierarchical. Attorneys leave their office doors open. Consequently, "you don't feel inhibited talking to anyone." However, one source admitted that "on a casual level, there is not much interaction between partners and associates."

practice areas

Jones Day's practice is organized around four groups: the business practice (which includes corporate, property, and finance), government regulation, litigation, and tax. Each group includes specialty sections such as labor (litigation) and antitrust (government regulation). Department heads coordinate the work of each group, recommend associate salaries, and organize retreats for all associates in the group. The litigation group represents a number of national Jones Day Fortune 500 clients and local Chicago-area companies in a range of business-related litigation. The litigation group also has an active environmental practice, which has been strengthened by the return of Vicki O'Meara, who served as head of the environmental section of the Attorney General's office under President Bush. The white-collar criminal litigation practice, headed by Dan Reidy, a former First Assistant United States Attorney, is also thriving. The office also has a strong practice in trademark, copyright, and patent infringement laws. The labor practice is doing extremely well under the leadership of Dennis Homerin, a well-known labor lawyer and former negotiator for the Tribune Company (owner of the Chicago Cubs).

The bankruptcy practice headed by David Kurtz, is "one of the most respected in Chicago and generates a ton of business." The firm also has a well-regarded energy practice and represents a number of utility companies in the Illinois and Wisconsin areas and elsewhere in the Midwest. The corporate practice handles a variety of matters from general advising to securities issues. This department also houses a growing health care sub-group which has expanded considerably with the recent addition of four partners from Chapman & Cutler. The real estate department, headed by Jim Hagy, offers opportunities to travel to Spain, France, and England, as several real estate clients have engaged in a number of transactions in these countries. Most pro bono work at Jones Day is left "up to the individual."

New Associates Group (NAG)

Entering Jones Day associates are assigned to the New Associates Group (NAG) for their first 12 to 18 months with the firm. The NAG program is designed to develop associate skills in a broad range of areas. One assigning partner distributes work from all areas and oversees the development of the associates. The firm also makes an effort to provide an associate with a high proportion of assignments in his particular area of interest. Once an associate is assigned to a practice area, he receives assignments from the assignment coordinator in that group and often directly from the partners in that group as well.

long hours responsibility

According to people we interviewed, the Chicago office is busy and growing; junior associates receive more responsibility in Chicago than in other Jones Day offices. With this responsibility, however, "comes a lot of hours. Chicago associates work crazy hours and it is not uncommon for young associates to bill 2500 hours," according to one insider. A firm spokesperson pointed out, however, that the average hours for associates is closer to 1900. First- and second-year associates typically handle research assignments and document drafting. Litigation associates also usually take depositions, prepare witnesses, argue minor motions, and attend status hearings. The firm receives a high volume of small cases from certain clients which litigation associates, beginning in their second-year, have the opportunity to handle from start to finish. They begin cross-examinations in their third year, and occasionally appear in court for trials and hearings after their third or fourth year at the firm. Junior corporate associates assist with due diligence and negotiations and draft all kinds of agreements, including loan documents, M&A documents, and purchase and sale agreements. Occasionally, junior corporate associates handle small matters on their own.

training

Within the NAG structure, Jones Day offers an extensive and well-organized training program for associates. Each year, entering associates receive firmwide orientation training in Cleveland. The Chicago office is equipped with a litigation center that has a moot courtroom where, as part of trial advocacy training, associates are videotaped and critiqued by other attorneys. The business practice department makes presentations once a month, at which transactions recently handled by the firm are analyzed and discussed. Other departments also have regular meetings which all NAG associates are encouraged to attend.

social life

As for social life, Jones Day associates "tend to go out" to restaurants, bars, and clubs after work. "Catch 35", an upscale restaurant and bar located next to the office, is a popular spot, as is "The Boss." Associates also enjoy participating on the firm's basketball and softball teams and golfing together. The firm organizes a "crazy" social life for summer associates. Activities have included Cubs games, golfing, boating, a bowling night, firm dinners and lunches, dinners at partners' houses, and trips to Ravinia and Second City. The firm also sponsors a Christmas party and a Jones Day Ball (jokingly referred to as the "Prom").

offices with gym

Jones Day has "beautiful" and "very roomy" offices. The five floors are connected by an internal staircase. Perhaps the nicest feature is "the little gym" located in the office and equipped with stairmasters, exercise bikes, Nautilus machines, a treadmill and showers. The firm also has a lawyer's lounge where lunch is served and another lunch room for all employees. All attorneys are assigned private offices with windows and a Hewlett-Packard computer on their desks. All Jones Day offices are linked together by E-mail and now have Internet E-mail access. The support staff is "fantastic," with "top-notch secretaries" and "24-hour word-processing" facilities.

academic emphasis in hiring

Jones Day emphasizes academic excellence in its hiring decisions. Most of the students it hires are in the top 10 percent of their class. It also hires students from prestige campuses who have a B+ grade point average or higher, according to one insider. Jones Day weighs writing ability and moot court experience heavily and is "attracted to people with judicial clerkships." As for interviewing, one person commented that Jones Day interviewers are more interested in learning about the kind of person you are and your interests than about your academic achievements.

We heard many positive things about the firm from our contacts. One person remarked that Jones Day is "above the fray; it does not have the infighting and political battles" that exist elsewhere. Another commented that the "Chicago office is young and pretty hip. I feel part of an institution that is here to stay." The training is excellent, both at the "Academy" (the four day gathering in Cleveland of all NAGS) and in the Chicago office, including a very effective writing seminar taught by an outside consultant. Moreover, your chances for partnership are good. "Jones Day is like your grandfather. They'll take care of you" is how one person described it. Another contact remarked that, because of the firm's growth, "I feel an enormous degree of job security. There is more than enough work to go around." And you will work hard. According to one person we spoke with, "you are expected to work a ton of hours and are not rewarded monetarily for billing over the 2000 hour minimum." But, this person added, although "you might get some complaints about salaries, that's not really accurate. While Jones Day doesn't throw money around like Kirkland and others, you definitely make as much as associates do" at comparable law firms.

Jones Day is a huge and highly structured international law firm, and its new Chicago office is starting to become as well-recognized as some offices in other cities. Jones Day's Chicago office is growing and offers its associates the resources of a huge firm, as well as exposure to national and international legal work while retaining the work atmosphere of a medium-sized firm. One person remarked that "although, contrary to expectations, I am not jet-setting around the globe, resources from all of our offices are available. For example, I recently had an informative conversation with a partner in the Paris office (with a wonderful accent!) regarding provisions of an agreement between a U.S. client of the firm and a French company." Jones Day Chicago, with prestige and an international reach, as well as the feel of a medium-size firm, makes an attractive destination for those wishing to practice their craft in the "Windy City."

Katten Muchin & Zavis

Chicago Irvine Los Angeles New York Washington

Address: 525 West Monroe Street, Suite 1600, Chicago, IL 60661
Telephone: (312) 902–5200
Hiring Attorney: David J. Bryant and Jeffery Larry (co-hiring partners)
Contact: Kelley Lynch, Director of Legal Recruiting; (312) 902–5526
Associate Salary: First year $73,000 (1997)
Summer Salary: $1404/week (1997)
Average Hours: 2000 worked; NA billed; 1980 required
Family Benefits: 12 weeks paid maternity leave (12 unpaid);
1996 Summer: Class of 27 students; offers to 26
Partnership: 25% of entering associates from 1985–1989 were made partner
Pro Bono: 1–3% of all work is pro bono

Katten Muchin & Zavis in 1997
303 Lawyers at the Chicago Office
0.9 Associates Per Partner

Total Partners 149		
Women	30	20%
All Minorities	3	2%
Afro-Am	2	1%
Asian Am	1	1%

Total Associates 140		
Women	54	39%
All Minorities	14	10%
Afro-Am	4	3%
Asian Am	6	4%
Latino	4	3%

Practice Areas	
Corporate	82
Litigation	73
Real Estate	37
Finance	31
Healthcare	16
Public Finance	12
Tax	12
Estate Planning	10
Labor	9
Environmental	6
International	6
Employee/Benefits	5
Real Estate Tax	3

salesman-like aggressive culture

Founded as a 24-attorney firm in 1974, the "younger, aggressive management" of Katten, Muchin & Zavis built the firm to ten times that size in fewer than 20 years. Mel Katten, Allan Muchin, and Michael Zavis continue to be a strong presence at the firm and, not surprisingly, greatly influence the firm culture. It has "a salesman-like culture," we were told, where it helps to "sell yourself and toot your own horn." Katten Muchin attorneys tend to be "aggressive and confident." One source admitted that the firm "can be uncomfortable if you are not that type of person," but assured us that people who do very good work and are confident in themselves, even if not aggressive, will do well at the firm.

chummy lawyers

An "extraordinarily young firm," Katten Muchin has "no old-line senior partners" and is definitely "not a mahogany wood place." It is an informal firm with an "aura of friendliness." The work atmosphere was praised as "almost chummy" and "casual." Katten Muchin is a "roll–up–your–sleeves" kind of place where men can sport "wild ties" and women can dress in "bright colors" and pantsuits. Almost everyone dresses casually on Fridays. All lawyers address one another by first name and an open door policy is readily visible. Though the firm has the usual partner-associate structure, it is not socially hierarchical. Partners and associates socialize together, and though the older partners may seem "a little more distant, they will go out with you if you seek them out," asserted one contact.

high-stress atmosphere

Nevertheless, there is "no question at Katten Muchin that it is a business. The bottom line is open and frank; they let you know it up front." Consequently, the firm can be an "intense" place. One insider acknowledged that "working in such an environment places a certain stress" on the attorneys. Katten Muchin gives new associates a lot of responsibility and expects them to be accountable for their work. The firm philosophy is that responsibility and client contact enable its associates to be better lawyers and develop their own practice much more rapidly than at firms where deals and cases are staffed with numerous attorneys. Katten attorneys form close relationships with their clients and many have left the firm to pursue in-house counsel opportunities. The firm is also "very serious about people clocking the hours." It expects attorneys to reach 2000 billable hours per year and awards associates bonuses for hours, billable and non-billable, in excess of requirements. Explanations are requested of attorneys who fail to reach the 2000 hours.

practice areas

Founded by tax attorneys, Katten Muchin is particularly well-regarded for its transactional practice. The firm originally represented smaller, entrepreneurial clients, but today it has "a nice mix" of small, midsize, and large clients. Katten Muchin's corporate practice is reportedly "one of the best in the city" and provides the full range of corporate services to many well-known entities, including the Chicago Bulls and the White Sox. Katten attorneys, Gerald Penner and George Pitt, put together owner Jerry Reinsdorf's deals to build the new Comiskey Park and the United Center. The firm recently organized a seminar, attended by sports franchise and government officials from around the country, on how to finance a new stadium. Our contacts noted that the department is "male-dominated" but has gained female attorneys over the years. Katten Muchin also has the largest health care practice in the Midwest, and one of the largest in the nation. This department represents hospitals, institutions, and other entities in the health care field and handles everything from tax and corporate work to bioethical issues.

Katten Muchin is also known for its real estate practice, which is headed by Marcia Sullivan and Nina Matis. This department has a diversified and national practice and has grown in recent years. Katten Muchin continues to have a noteworthy tax practice. One partner, Harvey Silets, has ranked among one of the top tax litigators in the country. Formerly an assistant U.S. attorney in Chicago who also served for two years as the chief tax attorney, he splits his work between criminal and civil cases. His clients include doctors, lawyers, accountants, and the union that represents IRS employees.

Katten Muchin's litigation department, now considered to be "one of the top departments in the city," handles a wide array of matters and has significant practices in complex commercial litigation, white-collar criminal, antitrust, commodities and securities, product liability and intellectual property. This department has been particularly busy recently, with prominent class action cases as well as representation of the vast estate of the late tobacco heiress, Doris Duke. Katten Muchin is also focusing on increasing its national and international presence. It has a large customs and international trade practice in its Chicago office.

full-time pro bono partner

Katten Muchin's pro bono practice was "not stressed greatly in the past, but is changing." One attorney now works full-time coordinating the practice and assists attorneys in obtaining pro bono assignments. This person was recently elected to partnership and the firm received several awards in 1996 for its pro bono work, including the National Public Service Award from the ABA. The firm credits up to 100 pro bono hours toward its billable hour requirement and has, in the past, credited more than 100 hours on a case-by-case basis.

significant opportunities

Katten Muchin hires entering associates for a particular department, but does not immediately "pigeon-hole" new associates into a specific area within the department. We were told, however, that "the level of interaction between groups is limited." Each department distributes its work to new associates differently. The litigation department has separate assigning attorneys for the junior, mid, and upper-level associates. In the corporate department, a three attorney assignment committee allocates work to associates in their early years, but as they develop working relationships within the department, individual partners will often assign them work directly.

Overall, Katten Muchin is "not a place where you are locked away in the library," but each department entrusts young associates with varying degrees of responsibility. In litigation, for example, junior associates often appear in court on routine matters, and enjoy significant day-to-day responsibility in dealing with clients, drafting pleadings and arguing substantive motions. Most associates take depositions in their early years, and a lucky first- or second-year associate may second-chair a trial. Similarly, the corporate department, because it staffs deals "very leanly," offers considerable responsibility to young associates. First- and second-year associates reportedly have "tons of client contact" and significant drafting responsibility, but only a small role in negotiations.

full-time training lawyer

Katten Muchin has assigned one lawyer on a full-time basis to organize and implement a firmwide training program of seminars and lunches on a variety of topics. This person also arranges the introductory training for summer and new associates. In addition, each department separately provides specialized training programs. The litigation department, for example, offers periodic workshops and seminars on a number of topics and has a trial skills program during the summer. The department also sends fourth-year associates to the National Institute of Trial Advocacy training workshop. Similarly, the corporate department holds monthly training meetings and also offers specialized seminars to first- and second-year associates.

serious evaluation process

Katten Muchin formally reviews associates at the six-month mark and at the end of the year. While the six-month review is reportedly somewhat cursory, the end-of-the-year review partially determines an associate's salary and is taken more seriously. The review committee obtains written evaluations of an associate's work from all the attorneys for whom the associate has worked. Members of the committee also personally discuss the associate's work with each of these attorneys. The committee then summarizes the evaluations and gives each associate a copy of the evaluation summary. Beginning with second-year associates, Katten Muchin pays a base salary set according to the associate's class year and a merit bonus based on the evaluation grade. After the second year, even an associate's base salary is set according to the formal review grade. One person indicated that third year associates earn $81,000 plus a bonus, ranging from $9,000 to $19,000.

Thursday Therapy

Social life varies by department. The litigation department is known for being particularly gregarious. The litigators organize a few full-day department outings every year, such as golf and skeet-shooting outings, trips to the racetrack, and others. Every Friday, about a dozen litigators congregate for a happy hour at a restaurant located on the ground floor of the office building. Other departments are less social. Certain firm activities also facilitate social life. There is, for example, an annual day-long retreat for attorneys in the summer. For some time, Katten Muchin has also organized afternoon hors d'oeuvres and cocktail parties every couple of weeks which are called Thursday Therapy. This is a time for attorneys and staff to socialize together. In addition, Katten Muchin has a very "social" dining room that serves lunch everyday to attorneys for only four dollars a meal. It offers, we were told, an excellent Caesar's salad and particularly good breads and cookies. Lunch is free on Saturdays.

lacks minorities

With its senior management in the past being primarily Jewish, Katten Muchin was known as a Jewish firm, but our contacts reported that the executive committee, management and attorneys at all levels are more diverse than the image suggests. Nevertheless, Katten Muchin employs very few minority attorneys. Also, the firm's D.C. office was recently sued by an African American, Lawrence Mungin, for failure to properly advance his path towards partnership.

KMZ Women's Forum

Everyone we interviewed, however, said that Katten Muchin provides "in general, a comfortable working environment for women." One person noted that the aforementioned Nina Matis is the "heaviest-hitting female in the firm." She is an equity real estate partner and also a member of the executive committee. She and a few other influential female partners have established the KMZ Women's Forum, a vehicle for the firm's female attorneys to support each other and discuss their concerns. The Forum is open to women at other law firms and businesses and meets regularly for a variety of roundtable and panel discussions. The litigation department is 50% female and, according to one contact, "Katten is a pretty good place to be a woman litigator."

Two female litigation partners were recently promoted to capital partnership and three female litigation attorneys played a significant role in putting together the 1996 National Conference for Women Litigators held in Chicago. One contact told us that the "Katten 'big boys' supported, encouraged, and were proud of Katten's role in developing the conference." This person added that "Katten's litigation women are tough, aggressive, smart and fun. No place for wallflowers." Katten Muchin has a sexual harassment policy in place and has made it mandatory for all employees of the firm to attend an office seminar on sexual harassment. One person commented that the firm has a clear structure to ease the reporting of anonymous sexual harassment complaints and is responsive to them. In addition, management has created a "diversity" program with the help of outside consultants. All firm employees are required to attend a half-day diversity workshop. Further, ongoing efforts to facilitate diversity have continued through the advent of several committees focusing on a variety of diversity-related topics and solutions.

management

Katten Muchin has a two-tier partnership comprised of income and equity partners. Michael Zavis, Allan Muchin, and Vince Sergi, the firm's managing partners, run the firm on a day-to-day basis. They are also members of the executive committee, which handles major firm decisions. Other governing bodies include the 28 partner Board of Directors and the committee heads of each department. Associates recently have had more input on major firm decisions than in the past, and the firm has an associates committee that provides a formal avenue for them to express their concerns to the partnership. In addition, associates in each department meet on a regular basis to discuss issues specific to their departments. Yet, one contact reported that personality and individual partner's whims "sometimes have undue effect on the management of the firm. Pitched battles occur between partners, leaving blood and scars and everyone catching their breath." The firm is economically healthy and has had record billings and profitability in the past three years.

modern offices

Katten Muchin's offices "are nice, but not outrageously ornate." They produce an "airy atmosphere with grey carpets and...modern art everywhere." Every attorney has a private office, a window, an oak or pine desk, and a personal computer. The computers are all linked by electronic mail and have access to LEXIS, Westlaw, numerous firm databases and the Internet. The support staff is "fabulous," and the library is "terrific." In addition to the dining room, every floor has a kiosk where staff and attorneys can get free Starbucks coffee, tea, milk, sodas, bread, and bagels.

hiring tips

Katten Muchin hires people "who are somewhat aggressive...and are confident in themselves." The firm also seeks "competency of a high level," but it doesn't necessarily hire "eggheads." The "people who are hired are individuals who have a range of interests, show ability to do excellent substantive work, and have the personalities to work with clients," attested one insider. The firm hires law students from top national schools, as well as from midwest and Chicago-area law schools. Callback interviews are typically conducted over the course of a half-day and involve meeting five to six attorneys of different departments and levels of seniority. The interviews are normally friendly and chatty.

Katten Muchin is an aggressive, bottom line oriented firm. "No one holds your hand and leads you through" Katten Muchin, one insider warned. Another remarked that "it may not be the easiest place for first-year lawyers." You have to be "proactive" to benefit from the advantages available. Further, you occasionally have the "feeling of being a 'number,' due to the sheer size of the firm." Obviously, this is not the place for everyone. However, for those who prefer "a frank and open atmosphere," Katten Muchin is hard to beat, particularly because it also offers significant responsibility and "truly excellent work." Though Katten Muchin demands hard work, it provides an informal environment and a terrific group of cooperative, non-competitive attorneys with whom to work.

Keck, Mahin & Cate

Chicago New York Washington

Address: 77 West Wacker Drive, Suite 4100, Chicago, IL 60601–1693
Telephone: (312) 634–7700
Hiring Attorney: By Committee
Contact: Joy A. Carlson, Manager of Marketing and Legal Recruiting; (312) 634–5504
Associate Salary: First year $73,000 (1997); thereafter salary increases are based on merit
Summer Salary: $1250/week (1997)
Average Hours: NA billed; NA required; 2000 required.
Family Benefits: Medical, disability, and life insurance plans
1996 Summer: Class of 11 students; offers to 9
Partnership: 28% of entering associates from the classes of 1979, 1980, 1981, 1982, 1983, 1985, and 1986 were made partner
Pro Bono: NA

Keck, Mahin & Cate in 1997
95 Lawyers at the Chicago Office
0.9 Associates Per Partner

Total Partners 34			Total Associates 31			Practice Areas	
Women	4	12%	Women	18	58%	Litigation	33
All Minorities	NA	NA%	All Minorities	NA	NA%	Corporate	22
						Intellectual Property	18
						Labor	12
						Real Estate	6
						Tax	4

dramatic contraction

Keck, Mahin & Cate completed its first one hundred years of legal practice amidst a storm of negative press. Founded in 1886 as a tax boutique firm, Keck, Mahin & Cate grew explosively in the 1980s into a large full-service firm. In 1991, it had as many as 350 lawyers in nine offices. However, in 1994, the firm's profits per partner sank to $250,000 from its high of $280,000 in 1992; and by the beginning of 1996, the firm had closed or sold six of its nine offices (in Houston, Los Angeles, Oak Brook, Peoria, San Francisco, and Schaumberg), and laid-off, released, or otherwise lost a significant number of partners and associates. This year the Chicago office numbers only 95 attorneys, down from 184 in 1994, and occupies only four and a half floors of the ten floors that it leased in 1993 in a then brand new Chicago office building. To make matters worse, the *Chicago Daily Law Bulletin* reported in August 1995 that the firm had to fend off more than one lawsuit (in Texas, Lake County, and Iowa) involving issues ranging from legal malpractice to fraud and civil conspiracy. "Consequently, the atmosphere at the firm has changed dramatically...The glory days of the 'big kick' are no more," according to one insider.

practice areas

Today, Keck's practice is organized around six service groups: corporate, employment, intellectual property, litigation, tax, and real estate, of which the first four are now reportedly the firm's main practice areas. Most of the firm's clients are medium and large corporate clients (Keck has a policy of not representing individual clients). The litigation group, the largest at the firm, handles a broad range of commercial and securities litigation. The employment law group is highly regarded in the city. The "core intellectual property group left the firm last year," we were told by one insider who nevertheless stated, "but there is still lots of IP work here and Keck is hiring intellectual property associates." Keck "encourages," we were told, but does not "overly emphasize" pro bono work.

individual initiative necessary

Keck assigns entering associates, consistent with their expressed interest, to a particular service group when they join the firm. Associates may move into another group within six months to a year. They also may work in both "primary" and "secondary" service groups. New associates usually receive their assignments from the partners in their group, but may also approach other people who are working on matters of interest to them. Because much of the firm's work distribution system depends on individual initiative, associates "occasionally slip through the cracks and end up short on hours," claimed one insider. Junior associates are initially assigned research and writing work, but depending on their ability, the client involved, and "whether they can get in under the wing of a senior associate or a partner," they may be entrusted with greater responsibility. People commented that the litigation group is more likely to offer early responsibility to junior associates than the corporate groups. One upbeat contact remarked that although "the upheaval of the last year...has been portrayed as quite negative in the press, it does have its bonuses...associates get responsibility early and will be rewarded for being proactive. There is also a sense of obligation to those who have held out over the last year on the part of the firm."

In general, Keck demands high "quality work," but does not overly emphasize billing hours. Despite the recent downsizing, one contact reported that "billables are still only 1900 and hours kept are reasonable." Though first-year associates often work late on big projects, most senior associates only work late when it is "absolutely needed." According to one person, the employment law group has a reputation for being "hard and critical." One person claimed that there are more office politics in this group than others at the firm.

training feedback

Each service group is responsible for training its associates. All groups meet regularly to discuss active client matters and new developments in the law. While some groups provide formal training programs, people commented that most training occurs "on-the-job." Associates are formally evaluated twice a year and, according to one person, "don't hear…much" on an informal basis. The general rule of thumb at Keck is that "no news is good news." Keck's summer program exposes summer associates to a variety of practice areas and provides excellent feedback, we were told.

social life

Keck is a "very vocal place" and remains relatively social, according to one contact. Another observed that, "all in all, Keck remains a rather humane place to practice law. Firm outings still continue and there is strong associate camaraderie," particularly within each practice area. The firm organizes a number of social events in the summer, including a billiards party and a Cubs rooftop party. The firm also organizes an annual holiday party.

diversity

Keck is fairly politically diverse, with active clusters of attorneys supporting both political parties. As for other diversity, one contact praised "Keck…for doing well with minority hiring and recruitment." The firm's recent summer classes have been fairly diverse with respect to both women and minorities. The firm has slightly more female associates than male associates.

management

Keck is governed by a managing group of seven partners. A chief executive officer, a chief operating officer, and a number of committees handle the day-to-day operations of the firm. Keck no longer has income partners and has switched to a one-tier partnership of equity partners. According to one insider, the recent upheavals at Keck have "left the firm somewhat bewildered at times and there are unresolved issues facing the firm. Some wonder if there is a 'Keck backlash' in the legal community. A push is underway to revamp the associate compensation, but salaries for two-to-six year [associates] are currently under market. The partners appear to be committed to resolving this, however." A firm spokesperson informed us that "the compensation committee has recently revamped the associate compensation with increases to market range."

offices

Keck moved into ten floors of a brand new building in Chicago in 1993, but as mentioned above has since contracted its space considerably. The office facilities are "very comfortable and efficient, but not lavish." All attorneys are assigned individual offices with windows, and all have computers with Internet access. The computer system is currently being upgraded, but presently uses Word Perfect. The support staff is "really good" and includes a word-processing pool available to any attorney. The firm is equipped with a "gorgeous" mahogany library with a "north view of the city," and a lunchroom with vending machines.

personality interviews

Keck hires people with "good grades" and "writing skills," but also stresses personality. The firm prefers "personable, very social, and outgoing" people. Keck is also "searching for diversity" and doesn't "want people who fit a mold." People we interviewed counseled applicants that the most important aspect of the interview with Keck is "to click with the interviewer" and to display "social skills." Interviewees were also advised to "talk about what makes you interesting or different." Keck typically hires law students from the top 20 law schools and from midwest and Illinois regional schools. One contact instructed us that, despite its recent downsizing, Keck "still has lots of work and associates are in high demand. Keck provides a good opportunity for the right person willing to take a chance." That seems like wise advise for a firm in the midst of a serious transition.

Kirkland & Ellis

Chicago Los Angeles New York Washington

Address: 200 East Randolph Drive, Chicago, IL 60601
Telephone: (312) 861–2000
Hiring Attorney: Helen E. Witt
Contact: Nancy Berry, Attorney Recruiting Manager; (312) 861–3230
Associate Salary: First year $73,000 plus an average bonus of $5,000 (1997); fifth $100,000 plus an average bonus of $32,000
Summer Salary: $1400/week (1997)
Average Hours: 2200 worked; 2000 billed; NA required
Family Benefits: 4–6 months paid maternity leave; dependent care assistance plan; emergency well child care; employee assistance plan; nursing mother's room
1996 Summer: Class of 42 students; offers to 41
Partnership: NA
Pro Bono: 3% of all work is pro bono

Kirkland & Ellis in 1997
323 Lawyers at the Chicago Office
1.3 Associates Per Partner

Total Partners 139		
Women	20	14%
All Minorities	1	1%
Afro-Am	1	1%

Total Associates 178		
Women	60	34%
All Minorities	11	6%
Afro-Am	6	3%
Asian-Am	3	2%
Latino	2	1%

Practice Areas	
Litigation	132
Corporate	103
Intellectual Property	34
Tax	14
Environmental	13
Employee/Benefits	9
Bankruptcy	7
Real Estate	7
Estate Planning & Probate	6

With profits per partner well above its nearest Chicago competitor, Kirkland & Ellis not only can compete with the top New York law firms, but also offers a New York-style practice for attorneys who want to live and work in Chicago. One contact pointed out, however, that "even though we are in Chicago we still have to travel to New York a lot and that can be overwhelming." This travel burden applies with particular force to "some corporate attorneys," according to a firm spokesperson.

bottom line emphasis

Kirkland & Ellis is run like a business. It is a "service oriented" firm whose primary goal is for the "client to be happy." Kirkland attorneys set "very high standards" of excellence and are "very hard-working." The firm is a "very results and performance oriented place. If you are contributing to the bottom line, you don't have to put up with a lot of formalism." Perhaps the most important dividing lines at Kirkland are those that separate the "good, better, and best" attorneys. One person confirmed that "if you are doing good work, the partner doesn't care if you are a first-year associate or a younger partner." People are "open to listening to ideas in the work context," without much protocol. Kirkland treats its associates professionally, and "face time" and appearances are less important. In fact, the offices are designed so that passersby cannot see if the occupant is at work. This allows "serious" attorneys the privacy to do their work well, but also reduces social interaction. Kirkland is "not a real social firm," asserted one contact. Another contact remarked that "Kirkland attorneys do not have time to 'shoot the breeze' at the office if they want to go home at a decent hour."

free market assignment system

Kirkland & Ellis is proud of its "free market system" of associate work assignments. With no formal system, associates are responsible for obtaining their own work, and partners simply call them for help on particular matters. Under this "entrepreneurial" theory, "if you do good work, you will be able to pick and choose" your assignments. Kirkland thus operates on the principle that, in a true "meritocracy, the cream will rise to the top." In addition, the "free market" provides a "way for associates to bargain for more responsibility." One person explained that when a partner calls, the "associate can say, 'I'm kind of busy,' and the partner will say, 'I'll let you do a deposition if you take this assignment.'" Another person commented that "associates are absolutely free to tell partners that they can't or don't want to work on a particular case or transaction." Associates must be "aggressive about what kind of work they want," noted one contact. It is certainly not a place for those who need coddling: "if you want help, you really have to solicit it." However, "if you ask for help, they are very good about it." Of necessity, Kirkland attorneys are "individualistic" and interested in "pursuing their own practices." The firm reportedly is "full of people who are very confident, sometimes bordering on arrogant."

practice areas

Kirkland & Ellis is a full-service law firm, generally representing more industrial concerns than banks and utility companies. The firm enjoys a close relationship with General Motors, one of its largest clients, perhaps because partner Elmer Johnson formerly was general counsel of GM. Amoco is another large client, and the firm's offices are located in the Amoco Building in downtown Chicago. The transactional and litigation parts of the firm are "very demarcated," and associates in these two areas tend not to cross over the line (this does not apply to summer associates however). Even the firm's social events are often segregated in this manner, with either "corporate parties" or "litigation parties."

Litigation, the "backbone of the firm," takes more cases to trial than other firms, according to one person we interviewed. The litigation department handles a full range of commercial litigation for major companies, including GM, Amoco, and Motorola, and has a relatively active antitrust practice. David Bernick, a well-known toxic tort litigator, handles breast implant matters for Dow Corning.

The firm has a full-service corporate practice with a particularly strong venture capital group that is under the leadership of Jack Levin, one of the three most powerful partners at the firm. Levin, former assistant to the Solicitor General for tax matters, was described as "a laser beam and a *summa* Harvard Law School graduate." Another person noted that he is one of the "premier venture capital lawyers in the country and a brilliant tax lawyer." Kirkland primarily represents venture capital funds, most of which are not Chicago-area clients, but sometimes represents the start-up companies themselves. Many other transactional partners are well-known, including tax lawyer Howard Krane. The tax group handles some international tax planning for clients with overseas operations, but Kirkland does not have an extensive international presence. The firm also has a large intellectual property department and a growing bankruptcy practice.

Some attorneys at Kirkland & Ellis are significantly involved in pro bono work, and the firm is a sponsor of the Public Interest Law Initiative. People suggested, however, that pro bono is "totally up to the attorneys" and "not institutionally promoted by the firm," which "views itself as a business institution."

thin staffing

Kirkland "leanly" staffs its matters, and a "great deal is expected of associates." Associates are "really given what they can handle" and typically take depositions and may sit second chair at trials by the end of their first year. Young litigators "are assigned to a certain aspect of a case and then become the go-to person for that case." Second-year corporate associates conduct client meetings and act as "point man on the deal."

evaluation ratings

Kirkland's litigation department sponsors an impressive training program taught by senior partners, some of whom are faculty members of the National Institute for Trial Advocacy (NITA). Sessions are held in the firm's own mock courtroom. Most practice groups meet regularly to discuss their work and new developments in the law. Much of the training is, however, "on-the-job." Kirkland has a unique evaluation system. Partners complete written evaluations of associates annually, and the firm then gives each associate an overall rating that lets an associate know how he is performing in relation to the rest of his class; associates learn of their standing during the formal annual reviews. Associate base salaries are the same for the first year, but then diverge based on their evaluation rating. All bonuses are merit-based. One person commented that associates "really like" knowing their rating because it lets them know whether they "are on the partnership track." This person noted that there is "competition with attorneys who are opposing counsel, but not among themselves." Kirkland has a two-tier partnership structure, with both income and equity partners. Summer associates also receive detailed formal mid- and end-of-summer reviews.

Morale generally is high at Kirkland & Ellis because associates receive "good work, responsibility, and compensation." One person explained that the associates "all enjoy the law and like working hard. They have a tremendous work ethic. The people like to excel. There is a real drive there." There are, however, some office-wide disparities on this score. One contact told us that "over half the associates in the corporate group started their legal career somewhere else and the culture of the group is changing. Associates are now saying, 'why should I work 2800 hours, when the litigators and support groups don't and they get paid the same as me?'" A spokesperson for the firm pointed out that, in fact, "corporate hours are not significantly higher than litigation hours."

limited social interaction

Socializing at Kirkland is hampered by the office design, which "makes it impossible to tell if someone is in without knocking on the door and peering in." More fundamentally, social life is dampened by the long work hours. One person recalled that the associates are "conscious of hours," and that they do "talk about billables and say, 'I billed 240 hours last month.'" There are small groups, however, particularly among young, single associates, who go out after work. The social ambiance varies by department. For example, the tax group has a stronger "work environment," although a group of attorneys routinely eat lunch together. The corporate and litigation departments are considered a little more social. Corporate associates play golf together and share season tickets to sporting events. Kirkland's summer program includes a wide variety of social events. Summer associates play on the firm softball team, which is "fun because the team is miserable, and though the firm is competitive professionally, they don't care about losing every game," declared one source. People go out for pizza and beer after the games. There also is a summer golf outing.

primarily white male law firm

Kirkland & Ellis is a "very WASP" and predominantly male firm. One person explained that because the firm views itself as a business, for a long time it "didn't see the political ramifications of not pursuing women and minorities." This person amplified that, although there is no "firmwide attitude of sexism or anti-minority-ism," the firm is predominantly "white male" and there inevitably must be "unrealized biases when interviewing, such as whom they have more in common with." Another contact qualified this observation, remarking that "the perceived attitude of anti-minorityism is most likely a result of the predominance of white males. It is not the result of the attitudes of those white males." One person recalled that some "female associates didn't view the firm as friendly to women because it is an aggressive, overly confident place with an overtly male attitude that turns women off." People generally agreed that women did not take much maternity leave. One person surmised that the firm's general attitude seems to be: "We pay you a lot of money, you figure out your personal life." Another contact spiritedly took exception to the general tone of much of the above commentary, noting that "I do not believe this is accurate and the general feeling of the firm is that it is inaccurate." Kirkland has a written sexual harassment policy, and a female attorney makes a presentation on the subject to summer associates.

Kirkland & Ellis is governed by a committee of 16 equity partners. Kirkland has done very well financially for the past few years and it continues to be the "most profitable firm in the city with the best paid lawyers."

state-of-the-art offices

Kirkland's well-equipped and efficient offices are located in the Amoco Building, just a few blocks from Lake Michigan. Associates all have private offices with windows and state-of-the-art telephones. All attorneys have laptop computers. The Amoco Building has a cafeteria for building employees, as well as a top-floor dining club. Kirkland's library and support staff are excellent.

hard-driving interview

Kirkland & Ellis hires law students with "high academic credentials and other indicators of law school success, such as moot court or a law journal." One person stressed that the firm certainly would look "no lower than the top quarter of the class." Work experience also can be an important consideration. The firm seeks "self-starters and people who can handle the firm's system, somebody who will thrive in that system, and people who will seek out interesting work." People advised applicants to be confident, animated, and enthusiastic about the law. One past successful applicant recalled that the interview at Kirkland is "more hard-driving than others. You have to put a foot in to get a word in edgewise." The firm typically hires law students from the top 10 national law schools and many midwestern and Chicago-area law schools.

Kirkland & Ellis is a "tough" place to work, and does not provide a "supportive" environment. One person commented that "our free-market system and review system both distinguish our firm and give it advantages in recruiting." But this system can be tough on associates. Another insider remarked that "associates are expected to step in on the first day and fit in without getting much guidance on the firm's culture and procedures." The firm, we were told, implemented a mentor program in 1994 that assigns a partner to each incoming new associate or lateral. According to one source, "associates who are doing well are very happy, but those who are struggling are not happy" because there is a feeling that the firm is "more willing to cut people loose." Kirkland does provide some of the "best work in Chicago," along with "outstanding training." For those seeking "a lot of responsibility, it is the best place to do that."

Lord, Bissell & Brook

Chicago Atlanta Los Angeles New York

Address: 115 South LaSalle Street, Chicago, IL 60603
Telephone: (312) 443–0700
Hiring Attorney: Mark R. Goodman
Contact: Kerry Jahnsen, Recruiting Coordinator; (312) 443–0455
Associate Salary: First year $73,000 (1997)
Summer Salary: $1350/week (1997)
Average Hours: NA worked; NA billed; 1900 required
Family Benefits: 12 weeks paid maternity leave (cbc unpaid); cbc unpaid paternity
1996 Summer: Class of 26 students; offers to 21
Partnership: NA
Pro Bono: NA

Lord, Bissell & Brook in 1997
242 Lawyers at the Chicago Office
1.2 Associates Per Partner

Total Partners 102		
Women	16	16%
All Minorities	2	1%
Afro-Am	1	1%
Asian Am	1	1%

Total Associates 125		
Women	51	41%
All Minorities	6	5%
Afro-Am	4	3%
Asian-Am	1	1%
Latino	1	1%

Practice Areas	
Business Litigation	39
Medical Litigation	35
Finance	19
Product Liability	15
Tax	10
Real Estate	8
Appellate	4

Lord, Bissell & Brook is internationally recognized for its expertise in counseling insurance companies. Since the firm's inception, Lloyds of London has been one of its major clients. Aside from being "one of the most low-key" of Chicago's largest law firms, Lord Bissell is also unique in the type of lawyers it attracts. "Unlike the other top 10 firms," one source informed us, Lord Bissell does not get people "who are after the glory. They are nuts and bolts lawyers and are happy at that. They want normalcy to their lives." Although associates work hard, they work late only "if they have to."

traditional law firm

Even in today's fiercely competitive legal market, Lord Bissell has remained a very traditional law firm. Lord Bissell has the good fortune of having Lloyds of London as an important client, which generates steady work for the firm. It has consciously maintained an old-fashioned firm culture where its lawyers have time to pursue interests outside the law. There is a real "sense among associates that they would prefer to keep billable hours where they are now rather than get a raise," attested one contact. Lord Bissell is a relaxed and "informal" place, with a "very open door policy."

insurance oriented practice

Though much of its corporate and litigation work is tied to Lloyds of London and other insurance companies such as Old Republic, Lord Bissell is a full-service law firm. There is "not much overlap" among the departments. One person commented that the firm's departments are run fairly "autonomously." Litigation is the firm's strongest practice. Lord Bissell represents insurance companies in a wide variety of tort litigation, including products liability, medical malpractice, officers' and directors' liability, and other professional liability cases. One person commented that, because the firm represents insurance companies rather than defendants, Lord Bissell attorneys avoid "the grunt work of litigation" but get the benefit of working on "very interesting cases." The firm also represents car companies such as General Motors and pharmaceutical companies such as G.D. Searle in products liability cases. Tom Burke, a well-known partner in the products liability department, counsels General Motors. Lord Bissell also provides corporate counseling to its insurance clients, and other corporations. The firm's corporate and finance practice includes representation of a number of noted Chicago area public companies and entrepreneurial privately held companies. The firm has a unique bankruptcy department that represents committees of equity shareholders. The firm has been involved in the bankruptcy of Wang Laboratories and the $2 billion reorganization of the El Paso Electric Company. Lord Bissell also provides legal services in tax and real estate development and financing.

pro bono options

Lord Bissell also offers a variety of pro bono options. It credits pro bono hours toward the 1900 hour minimum billable requirement, but one insider warned that, as with most businesses, you "have to be careful about that." A number of attorneys work, once a month, through the Chicago Volunteer Legal Services, at a legal clinic that is run out of a South Side Chicago community church. The firm's other major pro bono initiatives involve obtaining orders of protection for battered women and facilitating adoptions for poor families who want to adopt a neglected child relative. The firm also pays entering associates their regular salary while working half-time with the Public Interest Law Initiative in Chicago during the summer prior to beginning work with the firm.

assignment system

Entering associates are hired directly into a department and are assigned to a single partner who gives them work and monitors their assignments. There is not much overlap between departments which are fairly autonomous. Most associates obtain work by developing close working relationships with partners and senior associates in their department who work with their assigned partner. One source claimed that this system has the "potential for freezing out" associates who lack personal initiative. Another contact remarked that the firm is "very specialized from the outset. There is no opportunity to explore different areas of the law before specializing."

early trial experience

At Lord Bissell, "if you are destined to be a star, they will let you be a star," asserted one contact. Opportunities for responsibility vary by department, however. Associates in medical malpractice and products liability are entrusted with significant responsibility. These associates often find themselves taking depositions immediately. Other litigation groups typically handle larger cases where associates work on teams and at least initially will have fewer opportunities to handle court appearances on their own. Lord Bissell associates are in court far more often than associates at other large Chicago firms, even more, one insider claimed, than associates at Pope, Cahill & Devine, a Chicago law firm well-known for offering early trial experience.

training feedback

Although Lord Bissell provides some formal training programs, particularly litigation oriented workshops, most associate training happens "on-the-job." The firm does, however, provide annual "detailed, objective associate evaluations that it takes seriously." Each year a partner goes over evaluations with associates very carefully and discusses their future prospects at the firm with them. Summer associate evaluations are not treated lightly. Attorneys must complete written evaluations of all assignments done for them by summer associates. In addition, summer associates' partner mentors and associate buddies review their work.

genuine social life

Social life at Lord Bissell is minimal, "but very genuine." There is "not a lot of rah-rah firm unity. People are just friendly," praised one admirer. The firm is "a very chatty place" during the day. Associates often go out to lunch together and sometimes go out after work. They also participate on the firm's softball team. The firm organizes a golf outing and a holiday party every year and a firm prom every two years, which is held at a local hotel. The firm hosts monthly cocktail parties on Friday evenings. The realistic summer program, however, does not include "much wining and dining," and summer associates are "expected to do real work."

diversity

Lord Bissell is "not blue-blood at all," one source informed us. Although the firm was sued some years ago for gender discrimination, people we interviewed stated that women are "well-respected at the firm." Lord Bissell's female partners are "very dynamic," asserted one admirer. Women, or men, can request a part-time schedule but almost no one in fact works one. The firm has only a small number of minority attorneys.

conservative management

Lord Bissell is governed by its single-tier partnership. Major decisions are made by the full partnership. Day-to-day matters are handled by a five partner executive committee, a chief operating officer in charge of financial matters, and a chief executive officer responsible for general planning, and chairs of the firm's numerous committees. The management is fiscally conservative and has not invested heavily in the firm's physical resources. One person commented that Lord Bissell has "one of the lowest per capita overheads in Chicago."

Conveniently located in the Chicago Loop, Lord Bissell's offices are "not bad, but nothing to write home about." All attorneys are assigned private offices. Everyone has a personal computer, and the firm is taking steps to make its computer systems more state of the art. The support staff is "great," and the library, with a "very helpful" library staff, is "very good." The firm does not have a cafeteria; employees take advantage of the cafeteria of the Harris Bank, located in the same office building.

hiring practices

Lord Bissell seeks people who are "good team players." The firm generally hires summer associates from a number of Chicago area and midwest law schools as well as other top national law schools. Our contacts advised applicants who are not from the Chicago area to stress their connections to the city. Callback interviews are generally conversational. The interviewers are mainly trying to assess whether "they like you" as a person, reported one contact.

Lord Bissell has a good reputation and a stable practice. It is a traditional and "decentralized" law firm. Associates must, to some extent, "fend for themselves." On the other hand, Lord Bissell is one of the few large law firms with a "very humane practice" and "good morale." Attorneys at the firm probably on the whole lead more balanced lives than do attorneys at other large firms. The firm offers a big firm litigation practice and, according to one person, will reward you if you decide to work very hard. On the other hand, there is "a very long partnership track, now typically 10 years."

Mayer, Brown & Platt

Chicago Houston Los Angeles New York Washington
Berlin Brussels London Mexico City Tashkent

Address: 190 South LaSalle Street, Chicago, IL 60603–3441
Telephone: (312) 782-0600
Hiring Attorney: Michele L. Odorizzi
Contact: Kelly B. Koster, Recruiting Coordinator; (312) 701–7002
Associate Salary: First year $73,000 (1997)
Summer Salary: $1350/week (1997)
Average Hours: 2143 worked; 2017 billed; 2000 required
Family Benefits: 12 weeks paid maternity leave (cbc unpaid); part time policy for childcare
1996 Summer: Class of 42 students
Partnership: NA
Pro Bono: NA

Mayer, Brown & Platt in 1997
411 Lawyers at the Chicago Office
1.2 Associates Per Partner

Total Partners 170		
Women	28	17%
All Minorities	2	1%
Afro-Am	1	1%
Latino	1	1%

Total Associates 202		
Women	62	31%
All Minorities	17	9%
Afro-Am	5	2%
Asian-Am	7	3%
Latino	5	2%

Practice Areas	
Litigation	131
Business/Corporate/Finance	121
Tax	49
Real Estate	30
Labor	17
Environmental	15
Bankruptcy & Reorganization	13
Employee Benefits	13
Government Relations	13
Intellectual Property	10
Wealth Management	8

impersonal atmosphere

One of Chicago's largest and most prestigious law firms, Mayer, Brown & Platt is known for being hard-driving and hard-working. The attorneys "are not unfriendly," one person remarked, but they "are there to work." Mayer Brown attorneys have a "reputation as being eggheads," another commented. Perhaps because Mayer Brown is such a large firm, the attorneys "don't know everyone." They have been known to "meet each other for the first time at summer associate events after four years" with the firm. Though there are groups of friends and "people hanging out in friends' offices," Mayer does not exhibit "a real team feeling," said one contact. Another person remarked that the firm has "no real institutional soul; it is getting more and more like a Kirkland which was not what many of us expected when we came in." There are "a lot of silent elevator rides," concurred another. In a wave of cost-cutting in the early 1990s, Mayer Brown "cut a lot of things necessary to keep up morale," we were told. It "axed" the monthly practice group social "get-togethers" and the firmwide golf outing. More recently we were told that "many partners took 10-25% pay cuts because of losses from our foreign offices" and there is talk that "10-20 partners will be fired." A firm spokesperson pointed out to us, however, that "there was no large layoff and 1996 was an extremely good year for the firm." Though Mayer Brown continues to sponsor a wine and cheese party held every other month on a Friday afternoon, one person told us that many of the attorneys "are too busy to attend."

luxurious offices

Mayer Brown goes out of its way, however, to provide a luxurious working environment. It provides free doughnuts, pastries, bagels, and coffee every morning in the firm's lunchroom. In addition, the firm's office facilities are some of the most beautiful among Chicago law firms. The firm's office building, erected in 1986 and built of pink granite topped by six copper gables, revives Chicago's 19th century classicist architecture. The building's 45-foot bronze-framed entryways open from the street into a three-story foyer replete with gold leaf and marble. The firm's offices, decorated in deep green and oak, are enhanced by beautiful arched doorways. Designed to resemble an old English library, Mayer Brown's library occupies the top floor of the building and rises two stories from the floor to arched gables, from which elegant chandeliers hang. Oak tables and beautiful rugs fill the central length of the room, lined on either side by arched openings to the stacks of volumes. A picture window framed by an oak arch occupies one end of the library and offers a bird's-eye view of the Chicago Loop. All associates are assigned a private office equipped with a state-of-the-art computer network system. Attorneys are supported by a staff that is, one person told us, "absolutely insane in how good they are and will give you anything you want in 24 hours."

free-market distribution of work

Though Mayer Brown is "fairly bureaucratic," it is not highly structured. The firm relies on a "free market" system of work distribution. Associates are expected to obtain their own work assignments primarily by approaching partners who work in areas of interest to them. There are no formal departments at Mayer Brown, only practice groups. This flexible, almost "free-form" system of practice groups allows associates to practice in a variety of areas.

practice areas

Continental Illinois Bank, now part of Bank of America, had traditionally been one of the firm's most important clients. For many years, the firm was even located in the Continental office building. When the bank suffered financial difficulties in the 1980s, however, Mayer Brown not only diversified its practice considerably, but also absorbed many of Continental's in-house attorneys. It now provides a wide range of legal services to its "mostly institutional clients" and continues to have a nationally recognized banking practice.

Although neck and neck for many years with litigation, Mayer Brown's business practice has emerged as one of the largest practice groups at the firm. In the last two years, Mayer Brown has been involved in more public offerings of securities than any other Chicago-based firm and was ranked among the top ten U.S. law firms in the number of stock offerings, initial public offerings and high-yield debt offerings handled for issuers. In addition, the firm's securitization practice is highly regarded.

About a third of the firm's lawyers are litigators and the firm is particularly well-known for its appellate practice. Two of the firm's lawyers, Stephen Shapiro and Robert Stern, have written a leading treatise on the Supreme Court. Mayer Brown also handles a broad range of commercial litigation matters, some of which have been argued before the United States Supreme Court. One of the firm's former partners, Susan Sher, is now Chief Legal Counsel for the city of Chicago. Mayer Brown has done pro bono work for the city of Chicago in the past. Mayer Brown also has a thriving environmental practice group headed by nationally known environmental attorneys. Recently, the firm hired ten intellectual property lawyers, several of whom came over from Keck, Mahin & Cate.

Many other current and former Mayer Brown attorneys have close ties to city and state government, and the firm has a strong government relations practice group. Ty Fahner, former Illinois State Attorney General under former Republican Governor Jim Thompson, is a partner at the firm, as is Rich Williamson, a Republican candidate in the 1992 U.S. Senate race. Reflecting the firm's diversity, Democratic Senator Carol Moseley-Braun was a summer associate at the firm, and Chicago Mayor Richard Daley's brother, William Daley, was a partner at the firm before joining the Clinton administration. Former Cook County Circuit Court Judge Roger Kiley recently rejoined the firm after serving as Chief of Staff for Mayor Daley.

Mayer Brown also has an excellent tax practice with a "strong niche in international tax litigation involving transfer pricing issues." The firm "claims to be one of the top three firms in the country" in this area, one person pointed out. Mayer Brown has small offices in London, Brussels and Tashkent. It is also affiliated with Mexican and German law firms.

mini-legal aid clinic

Mayer Brown is "pretty open-minded regarding whom you do pro bono work for," one person remarked. The firm has a pro bono committee that oversees the practice and makes projects available to attorneys who express an interest. The firm runs a mini legal aid clinic. Mayer Brown also pays the full first-year salary to those entering associates who elect to work half-time with a public interest organization in the city for ten weeks during the summer prior to joining the firm. Pro bono hours are credited toward the firm's annual 2000 billable hour requirement.

opportunities and training

Associate responsibilities vary depending on the group into which they are hired. First- and second-year litigation associates typically handle research and document production assignments. You might take "a deposition if you're lucky," one person commented. Junior associates in the tax litigation, labor, and intellectual property groups, however, are likely to become "more involved," one person said. As for training, most happens "on-the-job." The firm, however, does offer in-house training sessions and a trial advocacy training program for third- and fourth-year associates run by the National Institute of Trial Advocacy (NITA).

female managing partner

Founded over 100 years ago by a Jewish (Mayer), a Protestant (Brown), and a Catholic (Platt) lawyer, Mayer, Brown & Platt is proud that it was, for quite some time, "known as the only Jewish-Catholic-Protestant firm in Chicago." In addition, it was the first major law firm in the country to name a woman, Debora de Hoyos, as its firmwide managing partner. The firm recently announced a new part-time policy which allows male and female lawyers to work on a part time basis for purposes of child care.

Mayer Brown is governed by a 10 partner policy and planning committee, some of whose members are elected by the partnership; other members are appointed. A number of other committees address specific issues of management, but the firm has little further structure. Mayer Brown will probably focus on international markets for future expansion, those we interviewed commented. The international tax litigation is expanding, as is the intellectual property group.

hires law review types

As for recruitment, Mayer Brown attorneys are a "very brainy group" and law school grades are an important consideration in the firm's hiring decisions. The firm is less concerned with "social skills or personality," claimed one person. People advised applicants to emphasize their "commitment to Chicago" in the interview, but one person believed that the "decision on offers is primarily made before the interview." The firm primarily draws from the top 15 national law schools, the top 10 regional schools, and the top five Chicago schools. Generally, a significant proportion of the summer associates are members of the law reviews at their law schools.

Mayer Brown is not the place for someone looking for a "fun" and a social work environment. It is for hard-working people who do not need a firm "committed to their emotional well-being." It is a place for people who can cope with a "loose organizational structure" and who want to work in a large, stable law firm where the "quality of lawyering is exceptional." One person described the lack of structure and guidance as creating a "sink or swim" environment which is "good for swimmers but not so for people used to lifejackets." Mayer Brown provides "challenging legal work" and is a "good place to pay your dues," commented one person. But the chances of partnership are "dismal," said one person. Indeed, the firm has made no litigation associate partner in the 1995-1996 years, resulting in the departure of several mid-level associates since "there's no pot of gold at the end of the rainbow anymore," added that person. A firm spokesperson informed us that "in 1997, the firm elected 19 new partners, three of them in the litigation area." In any case, one person told us that, as a Mayer Brown associate, you "can dictate your own future" career path.

McDermott, Will & Emery

Chicago Boston Los Angeles Miami New York Newport Beach Washington
Moscow St. Petersburg Vilnius

Address: 227 West Monroe Street, Chicago, IL 60606
Telephone: (312) 372–2000
Hiring Attorney: Michael L. Boykins and Byron L. Gregory
Contact: Karen K. Mortell, Recruiting Coordinator; (312) 984–7784
Associate Salary: First year $73,000 (1997)
Summer Salary: 1350/week (1996)
Average Hours: NA worked; NA billed; NA required
Family Benefits: 12 weeks paid maternity leave (cbc unpaid)
1996 Summer: Class of 22 students; offers to 22
Partnership: NA
Pro Bono: 1–3% of all work is pro bono

McDermott, Will & Emery in 1997
260 Lawyers at the Chicago Office
0.5 Associates Per Partner

Total Partners 176		
Women	43	24%
All Minorities	4	2%
Afro-Am	4	2%

Total Associates 79		
Women	44	56%
All Minorities	3	4%
Afro-Am	1	1%
Latino	2	3%

Practice Areas	
Litigation	98
Corporate/Real Estate	50
Tax	40
Estate Planning	31
Employee Benefits	25
Health	16

changing firm culture

Traditionally one of Chicago's largest law firms, McDermott, Will & Emery has become increasingly high-profile in the last 10 years. It went through a "period of transition" in the early 1990s which included the absorption of a large number of attorneys from the Washington-based boutique Lee, Toomey & Kent and more recently from Willian Brinks in D.C. The firm's culture may be changing, as billable hours and cost-cutting have become more important. Unlike many other firms, however, McDermott was quite attentive to its associates concerns during that transition period. Managing partner Larry Gerber "was very candid about the finances of the firm" and about his goal to increase billable hours in his meetings with associates at that time.

McDermott is "a big place," and "each department has a very distinctive feel to it." Generally speaking, "everyone there likes working at McDermott." There is a "lot of camaraderie between associates." McDermott is "not a competitive" place, and associates "always help each other out on projects that are new to them." The firm is considered somewhat hierarchical, but it is "not a big, steep pyramid," and associates are "pretty comfortable approaching partners," including the managing partner.

litigation

The litigation department, chaired by Charles Work, is the largest at the firm. This department consists of many varied practices, ranging from products liability law to large-scale Superfund and trademark litigation. McDermott's litigators have "a more flamboyant" reputation than other departments at the firm, and "good-natured yelling" is not unheard of. There is a "lot of movement within litigation" as entering associates sample its many different practice areas. The department distributes work informally, and associates gradually develop working relationships with partners. One person observed that "your initiative puts you into groups. I don't mind that. I can choose to work with whom I want." First-year associates can go to court, take depositions after attending a two-day training session, and handle smaller cases with minimal guidance. Although the litigation department offers an in-house trial practice program which culminates in a mock trial, we were nevertheless told that it operates under more of a "sink or swim" philosophy than the firm's other departments, with one contact noting that "you can go as far as you want or get nowhere at all. It's up to you."

tax

McDermott's tax department is large and nationally recognized, with one firm enthusiast challenging, "is there a bigger/better one in the country?" Alan Olson leads this group. The tax practice encompasses a number of specialties, including tax planning, state/local dispute resolution, and international taxation. The international tax practice is rapidly expanding and increasingly involving the firm's corporate lawyers as well. McDermott now has offices in Vilnius, Lithuania and in St. Petersburg and Moscow, Russia.

corporate

Headed by Stanley Meadows, McDermott's corporate department "has come into bloom." It is informally organized around groups with expertise in mergers and acquisitions, workouts, securities, and corporate finance. The real estate group and the bankruptcy practice are both located in the corporate department. We were told that the majority of corporate partners are generalists, with the exception of a group of former Mayer, Brown & Platt attorneys who compose the corporate finance group. Corporate attorneys handle general corporate and securities work and represent a wide range of corporate clients. Young associates can take on "more responsibility on less complex deals," particularly because there are relatively few senior associates. First and second-year associates typically do drafting work and also participate in client meetings and conference calls. As in litigation, corporate associates are "very much on their own" in obtaining work. They are exposed to all areas of the corporate practice. One person considered the process to be "haphazard, which I like. You can control it more. I feel comfortable saying 'no' most of the time." Associates typically establish working relationships with a few attorneys, with whom they do most of their work. The corporate department holds training sessions for young associates and distributes a much appreciated set of "corporate forms." The corporate department may be a "little more formal than the rest of the firm."

health care
estate planning

Health care is another of the firm's transactional departments. Founded by managing partner Larry Gerber, it is one of the leading practices of its kind in the country and represents perhaps more hospitals than any other law firm. It also represents virtually every other type of player in the health care field, including physicians groups, pharmaceutical manufacturers, and HMOs. The firm also has strong employee benefits and trusts and estates departments, both of which "assume they have to teach you a lot" and, accordingly, invest heavily in associate training. The estate planning department, in particular, headed by W. Timothy Bartz, is reportedly one of the strongest in the nation. The department conducts several meetings per month on various topics and partners encourage the career development of the associates.

pro bono

Although the firm was not known for its pro-bono work in the past, that is now changing. The firm recently pledged to meet the American Bar Association's challenge to donate to pro bono an amount of time equalling three percent of the firm's total billable hours. McDermott works with, among others, the ACLU, the Chicago Council of Lawyers, and the Lawyers' Committee for Civil Rights and has established its own legal aid clinic on the West side. It also represents not-for-profits and indigent individuals in civil and criminal matters. In 1997, the firm established an annual pro bono award process recognizing all attorneys who billed the three percent minimum, and providing special recognition to those who far exceeded that minimum commitment.

responsive management

As a result of management's attentiveness to associate concerns during the earlier transition period, morale reportedly is good at McDermott. One positive change relates to associate evaluations: the firm gives associates "written comments" biannually regarding their performance (which, however, are anonymous.). This procedure reportedly has "made a lot of difference" to associates. Day-to-day feedback varies by partner, with one person commenting that "more partners are responsive than not." Summer associates receive oral comments at their formal reviews which are held three times during the summer. One person described the informal feedback, however, as "cursory." In the past several years, McDermott has put into place a firmwide, early training program for first-year associates, that is tailored to lateral hires as well. Despite the new emphasis on billable hours, year-end associate bonuses still are based primarily on the quality of work. McDermott's associates reportedly average about 1950 billable hours, but according to one source, "hours simply aren't an issue. If you do your job, you'll get 1800–2000, which is fine." Moreover, this person added, "first year hours don't matter in reviews." Another person remarked that, although hours are long, there is no "face time."

limited social activities

Although associates can make friends at McDermott, one person noted that "you get busy." Another remarked that "the firm is not your life" and many attorneys go home to their families after work. A third person commented that McDermott does not "serve dinner or have a gym for a reason: no one wants them." The firm fields teams in some sports leagues, and many attorneys play basketball and baseball. However, the firm-sponsored social life "is not really strong." One person noted that "some lawyers hadn't met each other before," but McDermott apparently is "working on that."

sensitive to women

McDermott received high marks for its treatment of women, and people noted that the firm would like to increase its representation of minority attorneys. One person praised McDermott for having "probably one of the better attitudes I've come across in a law firm" with respect to women. The firm "has some flexibility" in permitting maternity leaves, but part-time work arrangements may slow (but not stop) advancement to partner and "heavily impact compensation."

management

McDermott is governed by a management committee of 21 capital partners. An executive committee of five partners handles day-to-day matters. Other committees address specific firm issues. Larry Gerber, the managing partner, reportedly wields a great deal of influence. Under his leadership, the firm has been "run tightly" with a view to the bottom line.

gorgeous offices

Several years ago, McDermott moved into the top 16 floors of the AT&T Tower. These beautiful offices offer gorgeous views of Lake Michigan, the Chicago River, and the city. Each attorney and paralegal is assigned a private office with a view. Each office has a networked computer (with WordPerfect, LEXIS, Westlaw, Internet accessible E-mail, and other programs specific to departmental needs). The library is excellent, and the head librarian ("a God!", according to one contact), a lawyer, teaches at a Chicago-area law school. The firm has its own cafeteria, and there are two restaurants and a Starbucks in the building. Two or three attorneys are assigned to each secretary, additional 24-hour word processing is available, and the support staff reportedly is very good.

hiring practices

McDermott hires "people who appear articulate and in control and self-assured." But "don't be cocky," one person warned. Candidates "need to be personable and have judgment and know what to say and what not to say." "Personality and self-confidence are key," according to one person. The firm reportedly asks itself, "Could we see you representing our name and firm?" People advised applicants that McDermott "likes people who look good in terms of dress." People also suggested that the "more interested you seem in their firm and a particular area, the easier the interview will go." One person added, "ask any questions you want. They want to hear the questions that challenge them." On balance, "be polite and upbeat." McDermott also "likes you to be as individualistic as you want." The firm hires law students from a wide range of national, midwestern and Chicago-area schools. According to one person, the firm is less concerned with the grades of law students at top 15 schools, as long as a flexible "sliding-scale" threshold is met. Another person noted that grades "count far less than at most firms. The true key is hitting it off with your initial interviewer because that person has impact in call-back schedules and whether offers are given."

McDermott has weathered the uncertain times of the early 1990s, and it continues to be a very pleasant place to work, offering the prestige and work of a large firm in a slightly less "driven" atmosphere. Those who can take the initiative to develop their own working relationships generally are "comfortable" at the firm and are "overall happy about being there." The bottom-line focus over the past several years "has been tremendously successful." The firm has been very profitable in recent years, and yet, according to one contact, "people are now tiring of the firm's 'nickle and diming' *(i.e.* orange juice was eliminated from the bi-weekly 'donut day' and the mailroom was outsourced, costing long-time employees their job unless they agreed to work for Pitney-Bowes for $9/hour.)" Moreover, while the culture at the firm is still open, friendly, and non-hierarchical, no one has made "capital partner without significant business in recent years. The income partner tier seems to have become a tragic dead end for lots of good lawyers." A firm spokesperson informed us that "numerous examples exist of recent promotions of income partners who do not have significant business. However, business generation has become a more important factor." Further, McDermott has pursued big name lateral hires in recent years, including Mike Pope (formerly of Pope & John, Ltd.), Neil Hartigan (former Illinois Attorney General) and, most importantly, the entire Willian Brinks Washington office. While this has led to considerable growth, it has also in the view of some "fragmented the firm culture" to some extent to have so many laterals, all of whom are big names, with big business. This makes it more difficult, according to one observer, to "slide through as a good lawyer loyal to the firm with a relationship with key partners." Yet, overall we sensed a very positive, upbeat attitude at the firm during this profitable, expansive period, with one contact remarking, "there is no place I'd rather be a partner."

Ross & Hardies

Chicago New York Somerset Washington

Address: 150 North Michigan Avenue, Suite 2500, Chicago, IL 60601
Telephone: (312) 558–1000
Hiring Attorney: Donald C. Pasulka
Contact: Chach Chico-Romo, Recruiting Coordinator; (312) 750–3539
Associate Salary: First year $70,000 (1997); second $72,500; third $75,000; fourth $79,800; fifth $84,000; sixth $89,250; seventh $92,400; eighth $101,325
Summer Salary: $1,250/week (1997)
Average Hours: 1960 worked; 1830 billed; 1950 required
Family Benefits: 12 weeks maternity leave; 401(K); dependent care, flexible spending care
1996 Summer: Class of 13 students; offers to 10
Partnership: NA
Pro Bono: 2% of all work is pro bono

Ross & Hardies in 1997
134 Lawyers at the Chicago Office
0.6 Associates Per Partner

Total Partners 77		
Women	14	18%
All Minorities	0	0%

Total Associates 50		
Women	24	48%
All Minorities	3	6%
Afro-Am	2	4%
Asian-Am	1	2%

Practice Areas	
Litigation	51
Corporate/M&A/Securities	22
Employment/Labor	21
Healthcare	11
Bankruptcy/Lender Liability	9
Environmental	9
Real Estate	4
Tax	4
Trusts & Estates	4
Antitrust	2
International Trade	2

friendly environment

Ross & Hardies is a large Chicago law firm with a full-service practice, but it is like a collection of "small, client-centered groups," we were told. This is especially true of the litigation department. Because the partners leading each group greatly influence its work atmosphere, "there is a great deal of variance in people's experiences" depending on their group assignment and the partner for whom they work, stated one contact. The attorneys in some groups have "bonded well," whereas relationships in other groups are more professional. Overall, however, Ross & Hardies provides an "amiable environment." The "associates are comfortable with each other and with partners;" there is a "lot of camaraderie among both lawyers and staff." Attorneys keep their office doors open and often "hang out around secretarial pods." They "joke around in the halls" in a friendly manner, we were told. Ross & Hardies is not "a stuffy place," reported one source. The dress code is relatively informal, with women wearing long skirts, sweaters, and boots. One partner works everyday in Dockers jeans, a button down shirt, and an inexpensive tie. Ross & Hardies also provides a balanced lifestyle and permits associates to work reasonable hours. When asked to comment on the positives of the firm, one person responded, "life style, life style, life style; both associates and partners work reasonable hours (8:30 to 6:00 or so)."

rigid group organization

Perhaps because of its rigid group organization, Ross & Hardies offers "little overall governance," sometimes making it a bewildering place for summer and entering associates, we were told. Entering associates are typically asked to join two groups, rather than rotate through a number of groups. Summer associates who plan to join the firm permanently are urged to try to "have as broad an experience as possible," since entering associates "sometimes have difficulty obtaining the practice area of their choice." Moreover, because some "inter-group tensions" exist, a permanent associate who wishes to switch groups must, we were told, "be politically astute."

practice areas

Ross & Hardies is "mostly considered a litigation firm," but it handles a broad range of matters for corporate clients of all sizes and some individuals. Formerly Ross, Hardies, O'Keefe, Babcock & Parson, the firm was reorganized in the 1980s and made significant additions of attorneys in the labor, environment, and commercial litigation practice areas in the first half of the 1990s. In addition, the firm brought in a group of bankruptcy lawyers, and bankruptcy is now a strong practice area of the firm. The bankruptcy group consists of an "eclectic" mix of people who work well together and "respect individuals," stated one source. The firm's litigation groups handle the traditional array of commercial litigation, boasting a particularly strong products liability practice. Ross & Hardies has a substantial employment and labor outfit that occasionally represents Pepsi on a nationwide basis. The environmental section, which handles litigation and compliance matters, and the health care group have expanded in recent years. Ross & Hardies also has a busy employee benefits and ERISA practice. There are many other groups at the firm perhaps because, one person explained, the "small group mentality lends itself to develop new areas."

group specific professional development

Not surprisingly, Ross & Hardies offers junior associates varying degrees of responsibility. Associates in the environmental groups are offered "as much responsibility as you are willing to accept," declared one contact. Health care associates often receive a "fair amount of responsibility," becoming immersed "right in the fray immediately," we were informed. Employment and labor offers junior associates less responsibility than other practice groups, according to one observer. Ross & Hardies does little formal in-house training of its associates. The partners formally evaluate the associates who work for them each year. Summer associates receive formal reviews during and at the end of the summer, but day-to-day feedback is reportedly sparse.

social life

Most attorneys are "family-oriented" and there is not a great deal of firmwide social life at Ross and Hardies. Attorneys in some practice sections, however, go out drinking, as do the people who play on the firm's sports teams. Many groups, however, "see the firm as a work environment and not a social environment," said one contact. The summer program, however, is a very social experience, perhaps because the several attorneys heavily involved in the program "like to party." Many summer activities revolve around drinking: "We went to Sox games and drank; Jazz bars and drank; an Annual Cocktail Party at a Yacht Club and drank," according to one source. Summer associates also had dinner at the hiring partner's home, and attended an outing at a country club that culminated in a dinner and dance. The summer program is "sort of like being in a frat," said one source, commenting that "it's not very comfortable if you don't like drinking pitchers until you can't stand." But other contacts disagreed, commenting, "I don't drink, period. I never felt *any* pressure," and, "I am not a drinker. I hate beer, and I enjoyed and felt very comfortable at social events."

tolerant but not PC

Ross & Hardies is "accommodating" and open to individual differences, both personal and religious. Three men at the firm wear earrings, noted one observer. Ross & Hardies actively recruits minority law students, with some success to date. When it comes to the firm's attitude toward women, however, we heard mixed reviews. "They're working on it," said one source. Women seem comfortable taking maternity leave, observed another. On the other hand, some of the firm's senior partners have been known in the past to use gender insensitive language. This included one partner who referred to female associates who worked for him as "Cupcake" and "Sweetheart." This situation is now history. One contact informed us that, although this attorney is still at the firm, she has "never heard these nicknames used" and believes "the partner no longer uses nicknames." A firm spokesperson pointed out to us that women at Ross & Hardies currently make up 18% of the partners, and there is a woman partner on the Executive Committee of the firm.

management

Ross & Hardies is governed by a seven partner executive committee whose members are elected every year for two-year staggered terms. Associates have little input in management and are usually informed of executive committee decisions after the fact, according to one source. Ross & Hardies is economically stable and is experiencing growth in the corporate, litigation, and healthcare groups. There have, however, been some budgetary cutbacks in recent years which have affected staff and income partners and have "led to some staff defections." Moreover, making partner has become "more dependent on bringing in clients." Indeed, according to one source, the present lack of institutional clients is putting "pressure on young attorneys to build a practice and to find clients."

office facilities

Ross & Hardies offers comfortable offices. Each attorney is assigned a private office, many of which have views of Lake Michigan. The firm recently installed a personal computer network system and provided all attorneys with a personal computer. Usually, two to three associates are assigned to one secretary. People praised the support staff, and the word-processing department is good. The firm has a well-stocked, excellent library.

hiring practices

Ross & Hardies hires law students who are "smart" and have "good writing skills." The firm hires from many of the top 15 national law schools and from midwest law schools and prefers those students with "initiative" to cope with the firm's decentralized organizational structure. Ross & Hardies also considers the applicant's "ability to interact with others." Summer associates generally are "gregarious, outgoing, and fun-loving people," one contact informed us. Applicants are advised to "come across as very outgoing and confident" in the interviews and to emphasize "outside interests" and "involvement in law school activities." "A couple of people conduct pressure interviews and will grill you," warned one successful applicant who advised candidates to "stand up for yourselves." Because Ross & Hardies is a firm that tends not to spend money on "luxuries and fringes, interviewees are not taken to lunch," according to one source.

Because of its group structure, Ross & Hardies is not a firm for people who would like to work with a variety of partners in a number of areas. Ross & Hardies is a large firm with large-firm resources that "tries to retain the benefits of a small firm practice" and that "allows and encourages individuality," reported one contact. Yet, this person observed that there is increasing "pressure to bill hours" while the salary remains "stagnant and is below average for a large Chicago firm." Ross & Hardies is, however, a firm which allows its attorneys to lead a balanced lifestyle and where there is stability of personnel with "relatively little turnover among attorneys." The firm's work is interesting and associates with initiative can receive quite a bit of responsibility.

Rudnick & Wolfe

Chicago Tampa Washington

Address: 203 North LaSalle Street, Suite 1800, Chicago, IL 60601
Telephone: (312) 368–4000
Hiring Attorney: Sandra Y. Kellman/Fredric A. Cohen
Contact: Marguerite E. Strubing, Recruitment Administrator; (312) 368–8928
Associate Salary: First year $73,000 (1997); fourth year less than $100,000; merit bonuses may be given
Summer Salary: $1400/week (1997)
Average Hours: 2000 worked; 1800 billed; 1900 required
Family Benefits: 3 months paid maternity
1996 Summer: Class of 14; offers to 13
Partnership: NA
Pro Bono: NA

Rudnick & Wolfe in 1997
205 Lawyers at the Chicago Office
0.6 Associates Per Partner

Total Partners 120		
Women	15	13%
All Minorities	4	3%
Afro-Am	2	2%
Asian-Am	2	2%

Total Associates 75		
Women	38	51%
All Minorities	8	11%
Afro-Am	6	8%
Asian-Am	1	1%
Latino	1	1%

Practice Areas	
Real Estate	75
Corporate	56
Litigation	55
Environmental & Land Use	29
Franchising	24
Health Care	21
Bankruptcy	15
Trademarks & Patents	12
Labor	7
Probate, Trusts & Estates	2

Founded as a real estate boutique, Rudnick & Wolfe is a relatively young and highly successful law firm. In the past 10 years, it has tripled in size. The firm has diversified its practice in recent years, but continues to be known in Chicago for its premier real estate practice.

Rudnick & Wolfe attorneys know how to enjoy themselves. They work reasonable hours and pursue outside interests. The work atmosphere is "very relaxed and friendly." Though people take their work seriously, they also know how to "goof around with each other." They "wander the halls," drop in to visit friends who usually leave their office doors invitingly open, and engage in a lot of "talking and joking." Younger attorneys at this firm are fun-loving and "very sports-oriented." Although Rudnick was described in the past as a "very young male" firm, "like a fraternity, albeit a nice fraternity," that situation is reportedly changing. Approximately fifty percent of the associates are now women.

casual homey atmosphere

Rudnick & Wolfe is "not a pretentious place." Attorneys address one another by first name. They drop their jackets the minute they walk in the door, and wear creative work attire including plaids, light greens, crazy ties, and loafers. Fridays are casual days at the firm. One contact reported that Rudnick & Wolfe offers an "extremely casual, homey atmosphere." Another labeled it "a family atmosphere." In fact, many partners have children and are "family oriented." Moreover, Rudnick is not particularly hierarchical, although one source commented that "people know how important people are"—the "import of people is defined by office size." But, the firm's partners are easily accessible and have been known to socialize with associates. One person commented that a number of the young partners "go out with associates after work."

real estate

Many of Rudnick & Wolfe's practice areas developed to meet the legal needs of the firm's real estate clients. As the firm became successful, it began to hire partners laterally to build a solid and diverse practice. At present, the firm is divided into real estate, litigation, and corporate departments, which in turn are subdivided into practice groups. The real estate department, which constitutes a great deal of the firm's work, is Rudnick's strongest area and has a national reputation. It has been involved in a number of large real estate deals and has represented a wide variety of clients, including large developers and big institutions such as banks, insurance companies, and pension funds. This department has "great depth" and the capacity to tackle virtually any type of real estate matter, from property development to commercial lending.

franchising

Rudnick also has a nationally renowned and unique franchising practice. Recently Rudnick's D.C. office merged with Brownstein & Zeidman, making it one of the largest franchise practices in the country. The firm represents a number of well-known national chains such as Dominos Pizza, Pizzeria Uno's, Blockbuster, and Alpha Graphics. Under the leadership of Lou Rudnick, the "franchise guru," the franchise practice handles both corporate and litigation matters for these clients. One person noted that the partners in this department are "very nice" and that "a lot of women" work in the department.

litigation

Rudnick's litigation practice handles a wide variety of commercial matters. Under the leadership of Stephen Schwab and Robert Hall, the firm has a booming insurance litigation practice. The litigation department was strengthened by the additions of Stanley Adleman, an experienced franchise, commercial, and antitrust litigator, and by Judge Seymour Simon, former Justice of the Illinois Supreme Court. The latter is supposedly fun to work with and is so "energetic" that most people "can't keep up with him." Recently four partners (litigation-franchise oriented) left the firm and started their own boutique. According to one source, "this has improved morale in the litigation department."

corporate

Rudnick's corporate attorneys advise many of the firm's real estate and franchise clients, as well as other publicly and privately held companies. One person described the corporate practice as a "younger, entrepreneurial practice with a lot of business counseling as opposed to straight lawyering." The bankruptcy practice, under the leadership of David Missner, has grown and the addition of several new hires in intellectual property law has doubled the firm's capacity in that practice area. Rudnick provides legal services in labor law and ERISA and is also attempting to develop an international practice.

sports and entertainment

With the addition of Peter Bynoe, an African-American partner who is a former owner of the Denver Nuggets and facilitator of the establishment of the new Comiskey Stadium, the firm is developing a sports and entertainment practice. In particular, Rudnick has participated in several transactions involving new athletic stadiums across the country. Eventually, the firm intends to expand this area to include representation of pro-athletes. Rudnick & Wolfe's health care practice group has also dramatically expanded. The practice group is divided into litigation, chaired by Miles Zaremski, and transactional, chaired by Deborah Gersh. This group represents a variety of health care providers and managed care entities, and is one of the fastest growing and busiest groups at the firm.

pro bono

Rudnick encourages its attorneys to handle pro bono work and expects all attorneys to work a minimum of 30 hours per year on pro bono matters. Pro bono hours are not billable but they do count towards the 1900 total hours required. The firm's daily memo usually announces available pro bono matters. Rudnick is regular counsel to the Greater Chicago Food Depository, a food bank, and provides legal services to indigent individuals.

Sally McDonald, a litigation associate, is chair of the Chicago Bar Association's Young Lawyers section and several other associates chair various practice sessions for the CBA. Other associates, such as Karen Harris, are board members of the Black Women's Lawyers Association and the Committee on Minorities in Large Law Firms.

opportunities training feedback

Entering associates are hired into particular departments, which are themselves subdivided into "trade" oriented practice groups. Each practice area offers varying levels of responsibility. First-year litigators typically find themselves doing quite a bit of "grunt work," although they will get, from time to time, smaller cases to handle themselves. In addition, according to one source, there is "lots of court practice and less research after the first year." The firm also offers an in-depth training program, including numerous in-house workshops, seminars, and regular practice group lunches. The firm assigns to each summer associate two readers, who critique each summer associate's work. Assigning attorneys and summer coordinators provide additional feedback. Associates are formally reviewed once a year. They also work very closely with partners; according to one contact, "matters are frequently staffed such that young associates work directly with partners and clients, thereby giving the associates greater experience and training."

social life

Rudnick organizes a wide range of social events for attorneys. Every Friday morning, three attorneys on each floor are responsible for organizing and providing breakfast for its attorneys. "People hang out and chat" on these occasions. Occasionally, Fridays end with the time-honored tradition of "porch parties," when many attorneys go downstairs to a local bar for drinks. The firm also sponsors a number of summer events including parties at partners' homes and a "wild" summer weekend for summer associates.

attention to women's concerns

Rudnick & Wolfe has made conscious efforts to recruit women and address life-style issues. The firm has an expanded flex-time program and an innovative independent counsel program. One of the firm's female partners, Portia Morrison, is the head of the real estate department. Another female partner, Deborah Gersh, is co-chair of the Health Care department and Sandra Kellman is the hiring partner. Every couple of months, Rudnick informally organizes an "all-women's meeting at which concerns of women" are discussed. In addition, the firm provides sexual harassment training.

management

Real estate partner Lee Miller is in charge of the firm and reports to a policy committee. Miller is "very young, in his early 40s, and very liberal and democratic-thinking," praised one admirer. With a real estate focused practice, Rudnick was heavily impacted by the downturn in the economy in the early 1990s. In 1992, it asked approximately 10 partners to leave the firm. However, a firm representative told us that the firm responded well to that downturn, adjusted its business direction toward representation of a significant number of institutional clients, and has enjoyed successful years from 1993 on.

modern offices

Rudnick's offices occupy the 15th through 19th floors of a "beautiful," modern office building. A large atrium begins in the center of the building on the 15th floor and rises to a skylight in the roof of the building. The walls around the atrium are made of glass, admitting light into the offices. The firm assigns private offices to all attorneys, though for their first two or three years at the firm attorneys receive interior offices that can be "small and claustrophobic." Rudnick also provides each attorney with a personal computer that is on a network system. One person commented that the firm is not as "technologically advanced as it should be," but that Rudnick is "now in the process of converting to pentium computers and Windows 95." People we interviewed gave the support staff positive reviews and commented that the library staff is extremely helpful. The firm is equipped with vending machines and a lunchroom.

hiring tips

Rudnick hires law students who "will fit in" with the firm's culture. One person commented that the firm is "not looking for book-smart, library-loving people," adding that "this is not a place for true academics." Like its clients, according to this person, the attorneys are "entrepreneurial and business oriented." People advised applicants to "emphasize social skills and common sense" in their interviews with the firm. Some people provided specific advice regarding interviews with particular attorneys who conduct many of the firm's interviews. One insider advised that, "if you interview with Leroy Inskeep, talk about football." Another revealed that you "might be asked viewpoint-based questions" on current events. Rudnick usually hires law students from the top national law schools and the top midwest and Chicago law schools.

Rudnick is a firm for people who are fun-loving and who place a premium on a balanced lifestyle. Although the firm does not, according to one source, "pay as well as some other big firms and bonuses tend to be smaller," Rudnick does high-quality work, the work atmosphere is "really fun," and the attorneys are a "good bunch to work hard with."

Sachnoff & Weaver

Chicago

Address: 30 South Wacker Drive, 29th Floor, Chicago, IL 60606
Telephone: (312) 207–1000
Hiring Attorney: Marshall Seeder, Chairperson, Hiring Committee
Contact: Nikki Silvio, Recruiting Coordinator; (312) 207–6445
Associate Salary: First year $72,000 (1997)
Summer Salary: $1,385/week (1997)
Average Hours: 1900 worked; 1800 billed; 1900 required
Family Benefits: 10 weeks paid maternity leave (24 unpaid); 4 weeks paid paternity leave (24 unpaid)
1996 Summer: Class of 2 students; offers to 1
Partnership: 64% of entering associates from 1980–1985 were made partner
Pro Bono: 3% of all work is pro bono

Sachnoff & Weaver in 1997
90 Lawyers at the Firm
0.4 Associates Per Partner

Total Partners 60			Total Associates 21			Practice Areas	
Women	7	12%	Women	12	57%	Litigation	33
All Minorities	1	2%	All Minorities	3	14%	Business	30
Afro-Am	1	2%	Afro-Am	1	5%	Trusts & Estates	10
			Asian-Am	1	5%	Finance	9
			Latino	1	5%	Real Estate	8

Chicago's alternative law firm

Sachnoff & Weaver is a "very liberal, alternative place to work in Chicago." The "most progressive of the large Chicago firms," Sachnoff attracts an "eclectic" group of people. One person commented that "they're still in the '60s," and many issues are the "subject of great political controversy." There even has been a controversy about the firm's "dreaded cookie room," which is home to "three enormous jars of cookies" that are filled several times a day. The controversy? Some groups at the firm wanted fruit instead. Reflecting its characteristic sensitivity, Sachnoff experimented with fruit in the cookie room, but the fruit "went too fast and cost too much, so they went back to cookies," reported one source.

changing firm culture

Sachnoff is an extremely responsive place. Founded in the 1960s as "a small liberal firm" with an informal "but intense" work atmosphere, Sachnoff has grown, "especially on the corporate and business side." Sachnoff attorneys have experienced a "changing firm culture, much to their chagrin." Traditionally, attorneys wore jeans to work, but kept a suit on hand for client meetings. With the addition of a number of lateral partners who possibly "brought with them conservative, traditional firm values," half the attorneys, including almost all associates, now dress casually at work, whereas the "other half wear suits." However, as one person noted, these "little differences are healthy tensions and are discussed." Differing ideas of Sachnoff's future have given rise to an "introspective process at the firm." Sachnoff is a "surprisingly wide-open place," even in terms of "communication between associates and partners."

high level of associate involvement

Although perhaps not as much as in the past, Sachnoff continues to be a democratic firm with considerable associate involvement. One person observed that Sachnoff attorneys do "not hesitate to complain." Associates meet monthly to discuss their concerns. According to one person, "they call in partners for the last 15 minutes and beat them up," verbally, of course. Another person termed this session as "basically a firing line" where associates voice their complaints and ask questions. Dialogue is a key feature of the firm's culture. Attorneys frequently discuss whether the firm really offers an "alternative approach to practicing" law or just misrepresents that it does. We were told that different people reach different conclusions, but on balance most believe that "even if the firm is under economic pressure, it is better than other firms in the city." We were told that there have been "big fights over a bonus system" proposed by the partners. Associates "wanted to be treated exactly the same because they didn't want to wreck the congenial atmosphere and create pressure to bill more hours." The associates recently lost this battle. The Board of Directors decided to enact a minimal bonus plan—to which many associates remain opposed. Finally, associate requests for better training resulted in a more active SWAT program: Sachnoff & Weaver Associate Training. One person observed "they're nothing if not responsive." This person added that the lawyers are "very hyper about their reputation. They wish the place were the way it used to be and try to overcompensate for it." This generally is a firm where partners "give associates what they want." Another contact remarked that the firm is run, if not totally democratic, as a "benevolent despotism."

practice areas

Originally known for its plaintiff class action work, Sachnoff's practice has become increasingly diverse over the years with the addition of several new groups. The lawyers are organized into five departments: litigation, business, real estate, financial services, and estate planning and probate. The litigation department handles a standard array of commercial matters. Some of its largest cases arose from the savings and loan crisis and actions brought by the Federal Deposit Insurance Company and the Resolution Trust Corporation. The firm also has handled defense of numerous derivative and class actions and increasingly handles defendants' work. Well-known name partner Lowell Sachnoff attracts much of the firm's litigation work. Other prominent litigation partners include Sarah Wolff and Marshal Seeder who represented Sears and Allstate in a big litigation win over Coopers & Lybrand arising out of the Phar-Mor collapse. Steven Miller, featured in a January 1994 Vanity Fair story as Chicago's "master of unsolved crimes" for his work in reopening old cases and winning convictions based on extensive detective work, recently joined the firm.

Sachnoff is well-known for its emerging company practice. The firm represents underwriters, venture capital funds, private financiers, and entrepreneurs and handles technology licensing and other intellectual property matters. One person ventured that "they like to think of themselves as the Wilson Sonsini of the Midwest." Bill Weaver, with his interest in high technology, brings in much of the corporate work. Sachnoff's bankruptcy group, which joined the firm four or five years ago, has been very profitable. The trusts and estates practice is strong and growing, as is the securities practice with the recent addition of several lateral hires in this area.

cause politics and pro bono

Sachnoff subscribes to the concept of "the liberal lawyer," and many of its attorneys are politically active in the Democratic party. A few attorneys were "actively involved in Carol Moseley-Braun's and Dick Durbin's senatorial campaigns." There is some political balance at the firm, however. Sachnoff partner Bill O'Connor is former chief counsel to former Republican governor, Jim Thompson, and a well known figure in

Republican circles. Sachnoff strongly encourages pro bono work, and the firm reportedly has a "very solid reputation in the pro bono community. It is disproportionately well-represented for a firm its size." One person noted that "Lowell Sachnoff is locally well-known and highly regarded in the public interest community." Another person rated Sachnoff a "good place to go" for people with "cause politics." The firm is well-connected with the Lawyer's Committee for Civil Rights, the ACLU, various aspects of the women's movement, and many other public interest organizations. Sachnoff allows each attorney to "bank" 50 hours of pro bono service, which time may be credited toward billable hour requirements. If some attorneys do not spend the suggested 50 hours, other attorneys can dip into the bank for more creditable pro bono hours "until the bank runs dry." A pro bono committee approves requests for billable hour credit for pro bono work, keeps an eye on the "bank," and encourages non-litigators to become involved in pro bono. The firm has also pledged to meet the American Bar Association's challenge to donate to pro bono an amount of time equal to three percent of its total billable hours. The firm already does roughly the amount of pro bono work that is suggested by the ABA. However, there are increasing concerns over the "lack of partner involvement in pro bono and the attempt by the pro bono committee to control hours," according to one source.

professional development and SWAT

Entering associates are hired into a particular department. The firm tries to accommodate requests to change departments. We were told that associates "have to be aggressive about getting assignments from partners." Each department distributes assignments differently, but one person told us that, overall, work is allocated relatively informally.

Young associates at Sachnoff are generally entrusted with a high degree of responsibility. One person informed us that "people who prove themselves get swamped." Associates typically acquire more responsibility than their counterparts at larger law firms, and second-year associates often appear in court on smaller cases. Many associates also handle pro bono cases independently. Because associates "complained" about the lack of training at Sachnoff, the firm established the aforementioned SWAT program, which includes many clinics, workshops, and monthly department lunches with speakers. The feedback for associates at Sachnoff generally is good, particularly if associates ask for critiques. This is an open firm, and the semi-annual associates reviews are straightforward. Summer associates receive both written and oral feedback.

high morale

Sachnoff attorneys have "consciously...traded dollars for lifestyle." We were told that attorney compensation is slightly lower than at larger Chicago law firms, but one person maintained that Sachnoff attorneys prefer to have "a good life and time for family rather than make millions of dollars." A firm spokesperson informed us that "1996 was a banner year for Sachnoff that resulted in substantial bonuses for its partners and salary increases across the board for associates." Sachnoff attorneys "are not grinds." They "don't live for the office and they are happier" because of it. One person noted tongue-in-cheek that the firm will "say this to you once a week: 'We've never lost an associate to another law firm.'" Sachnoff associates historically have left either to join the government or to do public interest work.

diverse social life

Sachnoff is an "informal" and "relaxed" place. Its attorneys enjoy working with one another and often go out after work, and, according to one person, sometimes during working hours as well. Many enjoy going out to "drinks after work on Friday afternoons." One person added that "there is no pressure to see people socially," however. Sachnoff attorneys have diverse outside interests ranging from theater, music, politics, and art to "general offbeat life in Chicago." The summer program is active, especially over the noon hour. The firm encourages each attorney to take every summer associate out to lunch, and Sachnoff attorneys are quite "diligent about" being good hosts. Summer events have included baseball games, a boat trip, and a day at a partner's home in the country. One person noted that the "summer associate stuff is downplayed and informal. You don't need to impress anyone." The firm also organizes a monthly wine and cheese gathering for the associates, monthly lawyer lunches either with speakers or an open discussion of noteworthy legal developments, and an annual holiday party. The cookie room, with its constant supply of cookies and coffee, is a favorite spot, as is the Coke machine, where one can buy perhaps the only 25 cent sodas in Chicago.

progressive policies

Sachnoff is progressive with respect to women. There are more women than men associates and there are seven women at the partner level. One person noted that the firm is "pretty liberal" regarding maternity leave and part-time work arrangements. Sachnoff adopted a "Freedom from Sexual Harassment Policy," has a committee of the same name, and has conducted formal training on sexual harassment. One person observed that the firm has "a strong contingent of very vocal women partners." Sachnoff also is trying to recruit more minority attorneys.

management

Sachnoff is governed by an executive committee, which often appoints other committees to address specific issues of management. The firm continues to operate in a democratic fashion, and associates are well-informed about major firm decisions. One person, however, was appalled at how "poorly managed" the firm was. Because of its earlier economic troubles, Sachnoff had to make the "traumatic" decision to let five to six people go in 1993. With the addition of new practice groups, however, Sachnoff currently appears to be economically sound and, as indicated above, 1996 was a very good economic year. The firm is building its real estate, litigation and estate planning practices.

Sachnoff has well-equipped offices. Each attorney is assigned an individual office with a computer. The entire computer system was recently updated to a Windows based network. The support staff and the library are good, and the lunchroom is a social area of the firm.

selective hiring

Because Sachnoff is a unique and comparatively small firm, summer positions are quite competitive. Sachnoff hires not only law students with top academic credentials and writing ability, but also people with "interesting...and different backgrounds." The summer class generally includes many "progressively oriented people." Past summer associates have worked for Planned Parenthood, the ACLU, and public interest law firms, among others. One person discerned that the firm is concerned about the frequent loss of its associates to public interest careers and may be "looking for stability" more so than in the past. Another person disputed this interpretation, stating that "the firm has debated whether it should change the criteria for the people it hires, but there has not been an official change." In any event, Sachnoff attorneys "don't want stiff, formal behavior." One person counseled that, within reason, "the more badly behaved you are, the better" the interview will be. In general, applicants are advised to "emphasize your personality." The interviewer is likely to be interested in "where you see yourself in the legal profession in the future" and "whatever you are interested in life." The firm generally draws from prestigious national and midwestern schools such as Chicago, Harvard, Michigan, and Northwestern.

It is easy to compare Sachnoff attorneys to the liberal lawyers of the 1960s, but one person suggested that "lawyers at Sachnoff & Weaver, I think, are actually very '90s in terms of their political concerns, etc." Sachnoff is, without question, an "alternative firm" that offers an open and informal work environment, interesting people, a commitment to pro bono work, and a balanced lifestyle. For someone seeking "the prototype of the alternative to the typical stuffed-shirt type firm," Sachnoff may be the place. A few years ago the summer associates created sweat shirts that captures what the firm is all about. The sweat shirts read: "Sachnoff & Weaver, a Different Kind of Sweat Shop"

Sidley & Austin

Chicago Dallas Los Angeles New York Washington
London Singapore Tokyo

Address: One First National Plaza, Chicago, IL 60603
Telephone: (312) 853–7000
Hiring Attorney: NA
Contact: Claudia M. Kreditor, Recruiting Coordinator; (312) 853–7714
Associate Salary: First year $73,000 (1997); lockstep increments for first two years; thereafter salary is determined case-by-case based on performance
Summer Salary: $1400/week (1997)
Average Hours: NA worked; 1882 billed; NA required
Family Benefits: 12 weeks paid maternity leave (32 unpaid); emergency childcare; 0 weeks paid paternity leave (32 unpaid)
1996 Summer: Class of 45 students, offers to 44
Partnership: 26% of entering associates from 1977–1988 were made partner
Pro Bono: 3% of all work is pro bono

Sidley & Austin in 1997
406 Lawyers at the Chicago Office
0.8 Associates Per Partner

Total Partners 226		
Women	32	14%
All Minorities	3	1%
Afro-Am	2	1%
Asian Am	1	1%

Total Associates 180		
Women	68	37%
All Minorities	26	14%
Afro-Am	10	6%
Asian-Am	15	8%
Native Am	1	1%

Practice Areas	
Litigation	108
Corporate & Securities	71
Banking	28
Intellectual Property	27
Regulated Industries	25
Commodities	20
Real Estate	19
Environmental	18
Labor (management)	15
Tax	15
Employment/Benefits	14
Trusts & Estates	14
Bankruptcy	11
Legislative & Zoning	11
Health Care	10

With over 600 lawyers in four domestic and three foreign offices, Sidley & Austin is one of Chicago's largest and most profitable law firms. Having recently celebrated its 125th anniversary, it is also one of the city's most well-established law firms. Sidley was ranked the "Best All-Around Firm" in a survey of the general counsels of 1,000 leading U.S. companies that was conducted by the *American Lawyer* magazine.

structured and bureaucratic

Like many "large institutions," Sidley is highly structured and departmentalized. One person commented that it can be "pretty bureaucratic." The firm has a "monolithic aura to it, especially at first," but is, we were told, "working hard to counteract" this image. Through its practice group system, Sidley helps its attorneys "carve out a niche," making the enormous firm "less daunting." One contact informed us that Sidley's "group structure is the key. You have all the resources of a 600 person firm, but you only have to work for 20 to 30 of them. You pick your own group, so you can select the 'culture' you want to join. It's like a university, with various academic departments. Some people are happy in Economics; some in English. At Sidley you have that same choice of styles. Plus, you do not have to work for anyone else at the firm (or at least it is more difficult for them to put the press on you). So ahead of time you can maneuver yourself away from the partner you really don't like, etc.."

professional atmosphere

Although not stodgy or formal, Sidley offers an "intense" and "professional" work atmosphere. Its attorneys "work a significant number of hours," and this client-oriented firm "expects you to do a certain amount of work of a certain quality." Nevertheless, for a large firm, "Sidley & Austin has a reputation for humane hours." One person noted that "they don't work you to death." Another person remarked that "like any other large corporate law firm, Sidley will work you to the bone if you let it. Unlike some others, Sidley does not appear to punish those who resist the pressure to bill 2600 hours so long as they do their fair share." It should be noted that the average billable hours at the firm are slightly under 1900 hours. Sidley is not hierarchical in the sense that attorneys are "divided along rigid lines," but its management and steering committees "make all the decisions."

practice areas

In 1972, Sidley grew dramatically through a merger with Leibman, Williams, Bennett, Baird & Minow, becoming the largest Chicago firm with the largest branch office in Washington, D.C. Shortly thereafter, the firm's involvement in the widely-publicized break-up of AT&T catapulted it to national recognition. The firm continues to maintain a close relationship with the telephone company. Today, Sidley's other clients include large corporations and institutions such as the Tribune Company, Commonwealth Edison, Citicorp, First National Bank, the Chicago Cubs (owned by the Tribune), KPMG Peat Marwick and General Electric. The firm serves its clients in a wide variety of areas of the law. Sidley's Chicago practice comprises about 50% litigation and administrative proceedings, 40% transactions, and 10% counseling and other work. The litigation practice consists of several groups including, among others, the complex and emergency litigation group, the products liability group, and the environmental group. The firm's environmental group is the largest in Chicago and "does everything," according to one person. The litigation department also handles a significant amount of appellate litigation.

unique legislative practice

Sidley has a strong government affairs practice, headed by Doug Donenfeld. The firm has strong ties to city and state politics in both parties. Sam Skinner, former Secretary of Transportation and Chief of Staff under President Bush, was a partner at Sidley and is now president of Commonwealth Edison. The governmental affairs practice is "a smallish group and may be hard to get into," cautioned one insider.

corporate

With perhaps the "best corporate practice...in the city," Sidley's banking and commercial transactions and corporate and securities practice groups have handled large securitization transactions, and mergers and acquisitions involving billions of dollars. Sidley also has a strong bankruptcy group, and its real estate group has been involved in a number of large transactions over the past years. The firm's intellectual property practice has grown dramatically with the addition of "several highly regarded partners in Chicago and the merger with a very solid Dallas IP firm," where Sidley has recently opened an office.

pro bono commitment

In the last few years, Sidley has received several awards for its pro bono work from various bar associations and public interest organizations. Pro bono work is readily available to associates who are interested. Tom Morsch, the attorney in charge of the practice, periodically circulates memos listing available matters. The firm reportedly has over 100 active pro bono matters at any given time. The firm provides a one year fellowship for an attorney to work in a Chicago-area public interest group and supports the Public Interest Law Initiative (PILI) fellowship, recipients of which work with a public interest organization half-time for five weeks before the bar exam and five weeks full-time after the bar, while earning the full Sidley salary.

slow associate development

Sidley typically hires entering associates into one of the two or three groups in which they express an interest, though some rotation is allowed. It is reportedly not difficult to change groups, with one contact remarking that "I have a number of friends who have done it, without incident. The firm wants you to be happy and goes out of its way to make accommodations to ensure this." The head of the practice group and other partners in the group assign work to the associates.

Associate responsibility varies by the group and the nature of its practice. According to one insider, corporate associates get "the most responsibility of anyone at the firm with direct client demands rushing in as soon as the first or second year." The environmental, complex litigation and labor practices also provide significant early responsibility, whereas "antitrust [associates] take longer to get the same level of responsibility and client contact." Young associates typically start at the "bottom of the ladder." The firm "brings you along slowly" and "exposes you to a lot but with little say." First-year litigation work usually involves research assignments. Second-year associates often take depositions and appear in court for motion calls. Junior associates in intellectual property are typically responsible for obtaining trademarks or patents for clients.

extensive formal training

Sidley provides intensive formal training. The firm provides a two and a half day firmwide orientation program for entering associates, and many of the practice groups provide group-specific orientations and skills training. In either their first or second year with the firm, Sidley associates may participate in the 22 week litigation skills program, which culminates in a full-scale mock trial. The corporate associates attend Sidley's Corporate College for training in corporate and securities matters. The real estate group and the intellectual property and marketing group conduct six-week orientation programs, covering discrete topics at one or two meetings per week. Other groups show videotape presentations and meet regularly to discuss work and new developments in the law. The firm formally reviews associates twice a year. Summer associates receive formal training in litigation, negotiation, drafting of documents and briefs, and research. Summer associates are assigned an associate advisor who oversees their development at the firm. The members of the summer program committee act as coordinators, provide feedback, and assist summer associates in obtaining assignments in areas of their interest. Sidley was praised for its feedback. The "partners are quick to sit you down and explain what they did and didn't like."

social life

Although Sidley attorneys are "cordial" with one another, the firm's atmosphere can be somewhat large and impersonal. The social life of Sidley associates varies greatly from group to group. Some, such as complex litigation, are more sociable and frequently go out after work. Other groups of attorneys go out to different ethnic restaurants once a month, play on the firm's various sports teams, and attend Cubs games together. The firm organizes a number of social events during the summer, including lunches, a boat cruise and a golf and tennis outing.

diversity

Sidley is attempting to increase the number of female and minority attorneys at the firm. A couple of female partners—DeVerille Huston, who brings in a lot of business in the banking group, and Virginia Aronson, a real estate partner and a member of the firm's executive committee—are quite influential. The firm permits part-time work arrangements and has received an award from the Part-time Lawyers Association of Chicago.

management

Sidley is governed by a seven partner management committee, which makes all major decisions. People we interviewed agreed that, though there is an associates committee, the associates are not heavily involved in important firm decisions. Because the firm has downsized through both "natural attrition" and by reducing the size of its summer class, it has not had any significant layoffs. Sidley is economically stable and continues to maintain its position as one of Chicago's most profitable firms. People we interviewed expected that the environmental and intellectual property groups, in particular, will continue growing.

state-of-the-art offices

Sidley's offices are located in a tall granite, box-like office building that is referred to as the "monolith." The offices are very "nice" and "not too ostentatious." They are "functional" and "client-oriented." One person explained that the firm spends its money on providing clients with state-of-the-art services rather than "extravagant" offices. The firm assigns all associates to a private office and personal computer. The up-to-date computers have E-mail features, can access LEXIS, Westlaw, and Counsel Connect, and run WordPerfect and time and billing programs. The computers even have a special fax feature that allows the terminal user to receive faxes directly. The firm is also in the process of developing a graphical user interface that will permit the user to run all the firm's software by a mouse and click system. Sidley also has 60 laptop computers available for use by its attorneys. The support staff is good, and the library is well-stocked. The conference rooms are "very nice," with "gorgeous marble tables," and the firm has video-conferencing capabilities. The firm has lunchrooms on almost every floor and offers a "Salads on the Go" service, whereby someone "comes around everyday with carts of soups, salads, and sandwiches." It also provides free hot chocolate and coffee, and sodas for 50 cents.

hiring tips

Sidley hires students with strong academic backgrounds who "will fit in and work as part of a team." It looks for people who are "self-motivated" and do "not require a lot of supervision." While Sidley hires only the top students from local Chicago law schools, many of those it draws from prestige campuses are not academic standouts. In recent years, Sidley has made offers for full-time employment to around 90% of its summer classes. During the call-back interview, Sidley arranges, to the extent possible, for applicants to be interviewed by lawyers who have similar backgrounds to them. Past successful applicants noted that many lawyers asked similar questions. One insider revealed that "everyone asked me 'Why I wanted to go to law school?' and 'Why I wanted to be a lawyer?'" Another advised applicants to "emphasize your ability to work well with other people. Your character is as important to them as showing you're smart."

Sidley & Austin's "size can be daunting." One source explained that "you walk down the hall and there are people you don't know." Another commented, "It's big. There is a certain amount of bureaucracy and a certain amount of impersonality." On the upside, Sidley offers "big firm resources and a variety of work." Sidley is a "well-known firm with a great reputation. You have high lateral mobility, and headhunters are always calling." One firm enthusiast instructed us that "Sidley's client base ensures that young attorneys have pretty interesting work in a generally humane environment. While both the quality of work and environment are available at other firms in the city, I am not aware of any other firm that combines the two," while a second contact informed us that "I wouldn't work anywhere else in Chicago but at Sidley. I wish they would expand casual days, and open a firm-wide cafeteria, but that's about it. If what you want to do is practice law each day with other lawyers, this is the place to be."

Sonnenschein Nath & Rosenthal

Chicago *Kansas City* Los Angeles New York San Francisco St. Louis Washington
London

Address: 8000 Sears Tower, Chicago, IL 60606
Telephone: (312) 876–8000
Hiring Attorney: David A. Lapins
Contact: Linda J Krecek, Manager of Legal Recruiting; (312) 876–8930
Associate Salary: First year $73,000 (1997)
Summer Salary: $1400/week (1997)
Average Hours: 1950 worked; NA billed; NA required
Family Benefits: 17 weeks maternity leave; 5 weeks paternity leave; payment of dependent care expenses possible on a pre-tax basis; emergency day care reimbursement
1996 Summer: Class of 20 students
Partnership: 25% of entering associates from 1980–1989 were made partner
Pro Bono: 4% of all work is pro bono (see below for more)

Sonnenschein Nath & Rosenthal in 1997
203 Lawyers at the Chicago Office
0.8 Associates Per Partner

Total Partners 111		
Women	21	19%
All Minorities	2	2%
Afro-Am	1	1%
Asian Am	1	1%

Total Associates 89		
Women	47	53%
All Minorities	8	9%
Afro-Am	2	2%
Asian-Am	3	3%
Latino	3	3%

Practice Areas	
Litigation	60
Real Estate	30
Corporate	33
Bankruptcy	10
Antitrust	8
Employee Benefits	8
Intellectual Property	8
Labor	8
Environmental	6
Healthcare	6
Insurance	6
Tax	6
Trusts & Estates	6
White-Collar Crime	4
Constitutional	2
Land Use/Zoning	2

Known for its large and pre-eminent real estate practice, Sonnenschein went through "some downsizing" in the early 1990s but has enjoyed strong financial years recently. It remains one of Chicago's largest and most prestigious law firms. Sonnenschein has a "strong work ethic" but is "not a sweatshop." Sonnenschein attorneys "can have a life outside the firm." One person described its lawyers as a "funny mix" of "quirky people," from the "nerds from high school to socially adapted people." Another person remarked that there is "great diversity and many outside interests" among the people at the firm. The firm tends not to attract people who "call a lot of attention to themselves," preferring instead "team players" who "quietly do their work." Sonnenschein is for people "who don't mind working hard and don't want or need a lot of glory," asserted one insider. It is a place where you "keep your nose to the grindstone" and can avoid "flashy litigators."

respectful culture

Sonnenschein is "pretty laid-back...for a law firm" and its attorneys have been known to wear "funkier" clothes to work. Every Friday is casual dress day. Sonnenschein is, however, also fairly hierarchical. While one source felt that associates are "kept in the dark" regarding many policy decisions involving, for example, salary increases and bonus ranges, the chairman and managing partner of the Policy and Planning Committee meet with associates regularly to share financial information, discuss current issues and future plans, get input from associates, and respond to questions. Sonnenschein insists on a "general respect for people" and "frowns upon yelling at secretaries." Attorneys generally "treat their secretaries and the mail room staff like they are human," according to one person we spoke with; another person, however, remarked that "some partners are notoriously disrespectful" toward staff.

practice areas

Sonnenschein's full-service practice, which covers everything from corporate work and real estate to trusts and estates, represents a number of large corporate clients, including Sears, Allstate, McDonald's (general counsel and trademark work), and IBM (local counsel on some matters). Last year, Sonnenshein was involved in a record number of public offerings. The firm served as counsel to Goldman, Sachs & Company, Merrill Lynch & Company, and George K. Baum & Company in one of the largest initial public offerings of the year—the $552 million initial public offering of CompuServe Corporation common stock.

The firm offers a strong litigation practice, its largest department, that handles a wide range of commercial matters. The group continues to represent McDonnell Douglas in the largest claim ever filed for contract termination, arising out of the U.S. Government's decision to terminate a multi billion-dollar contract to build the stealth A-12 tactical fighter aircraft for the Navy. The firm has handled significant insurance matters on behalf of Allstate Insurance, and Prudential is a "huge litigation client" now. Novelist Scott Turow, author of *One L*, *Burden of Proof*, *Presumed Innocent*, and *The Laws of Our Fathers*, is a partner at the firm and has brought fame to its white-collar defense practice. Edwin Rothschild, recently deceased, was involved in the Skokie case involving the right of neo-Nazis to march through the town of Skokie, Illinois, a predominantly Jewish town. The firm also was successful in a case involving Hewitt Associates before the U.S. Supreme Court and represented the author and publisher of *The Promised Land* in a First Amendment case. Sonnenschein also has developing labor and employment, environmental, products liability, and health care practices.

pro bono

Sonnenschein received mixed reviews for its pro bono commitment. A committee of four partners makes such work available. Many Sonnenschein attorneys have carved out niches in particular areas of public interest work. Scott Turow, for example, handles a number of criminal appeals, and Lorie Chaiten and Alan Gilbert focus on "the right to choose." In addition, a number of attorneys are involved in the ACLU and the Anti-Defamation League. In 1996, Sonnenshein received the Library Bell Award for outstanding community service, and, in recognition of its long-standing commitment to the poor and minorities, the firm received the Illinois State Bar Association's John C. McAndrews Pro Bono Award. The firm sponsors some beginning associates in a 10-week public interest fellowship. Although the firm states that hours worked on pro bono matters are taken into account in evaluation and bonus determinations, one source told us that "that's not how it is;" rather, associates are "penalized at bonus time for not having enough hours billed to paying clients." Another person remarked that with increased pressure to bill, "the pro bono commitment isn't what it used to be." Further, this person noted that Sonnenschein failed to meet its commitment to pro bono as a signatory of the ABA agreement (by .4%, noted a firm spokesperson.).

professional development

Entering associates may join a particular department or "float" among practice areas for an unspecified amount of time until they decide upon a particular area. New associates usually receive their initial assignments through an assigning coordinator, but quickly seek assignments informally. One person believed that, at Sonnenschein, the "squeakiest wheel gets the grease and you have to be aggressive about asking for work you want." Associates in their third year at the firm are typically entrusted with a "tremendous amount of responsibility," declared one insider. Junior litigators, however, mostly explore the library. They may, however, get court experience by working on loan, for up to three months, at a nearby public defender's office, in a recently pioneered program. The firm offers formal training programs for associates, including seminars, mock negotiations, mock trials, and routine department lunches at which attorneys deliver presentations on new developments in the law. Summer associates also receive formal training. Each summer, they come to Chicago from all the firm's offices for a mock trial program where partners, associates and paralegals participate as judges, witnesses and mentors in a half-day bench trial. Using a partner and associate-buddy system, Sonnenschein provides most summer associates with adequate feedback. One critic complained, however, that permanent associate feedback "gets backlogged," and another said that as an associate you "generally don't know what kind of curve you are on."

limited social life

Although Sonnenschein provides a "more working than social environment," the associates are "friendly enough" with each other in the office. The firm subsidizes lunch for lawyers who get together each day during the week. A free lunch is available for all who are in the office on Saturday. The younger single associates "pal around together," but a number of attorneys are married and go home after work. The firm organizes some social events, such as monthly cocktail parties during the summer recruiting season, and has pastries delivered to all attorneys and staff on the last Friday of every month, known as "pastry days." The firm also sponsors a number of events and "little *ad hoc* things" during the summer program. One of the highlights is a basketball game between summer and permanent associates. In addition, a number of partners take small groups of summer associates for rides in their boats, or invite them out to dinner. The firm also holds a holiday dinner party for all lawyers, the highlight of which is a "roasting" of senior partners.

committed to diversity

Sonnenschein was described to us as a "moderate" to "heavily Jewish, liberal" firm that is committed to promoting diversity among its ranks. One person told us that the firm "wants very badly to get minorities" and is "willing to talk about" ways to attract more minority attorneys to the firm. Another labeled the current dearth of minority attorneys at the firm a "chicken and egg problem." The firm is "not the most comfortable place for minorities, probably because there are so few" at Sonnenschein now, explained this person. Another person remarked that, although the firm wants minorities, particularly in light of its loss of two minority partners and one minority associate this past year, "the pool is greatly limited. Minorities definitely must be in the top of their class at top law schools like Chicago, Yale, Harvard, etc." This person observed further that the firm "does nothing to retain the minorities it has. Other firms offer much more supportive and nurturing environments."

Women attorneys are well represented at the firm. Marian Jacobson heads the legal development committee. Linda Harris is firmwide head of the corporate department. Another partner, Susan Benton-Powers, is well-known in Chicago for her work on sexual harassment cases. Although Sonnenschein was highly ranked in terms of women on a recent national survey, one contact noted that such a ranking "depends on whom you ask. Litigation is definitely a 'good old boy's' network where women must struggle for recognition and to get good work." The firm has a written work place harassment policy. One admirer praised Sonnenschein for putting a lot of "thought and real effort" into making the firm a better place for people with families. The firm has an extensive maternity/paternity leave policy, an individualized and flexible approach to part-time work arrangements, and offers emergency day care reimbursement. Moreover, part-time associates have been elevated to partner.

management

Though Sonnenschein is technically governed by committees, one person claimed that in effect, "three or four people run the firm." Although recently offices outside Chicago are gaining power and placing people on policy and planning committees, Chicago "tries to maintain control." The two most influential committees are the policy and planning committee and the legal development committee. Sonnenschein's managing partner reportedly "wields a great deal of power and influence." There is also an associates committee that, one insider told us, "gets to...moan" but doesn't significantly influence the management. Unlike many firms, Sonnenschein did not lay off attorneys in response to the early 1990s recession. However, associate salary raises were not as large as they had been in the past, and one person noted that "partnership decisions have become tighter and tighter." In 1992, only one of the eight associates evaluated was promoted to partnership. The firm also went from an up-or-out system of partnership consideration at seven years to extending partnership consideration to a window of seven to nine years. In 1993, the firm considered 19 associates and promoted 10 to partnership. The 10 successful associates included six of the remaining seven associates who were deferred in the previous year. In 1994, the firm promoted 12 associates to partner, five of whom were women and one of whom was African American. Nine associates made partner in 1996; two associates were deferred despite "banner years," according to one contact.

minimalist offices

Sonnenschein's offices are located in the Sears Tower. People noted that it can be a "pain in the neck to get around" inside the building. The building has three sets of elevator banks operating on different floors, making it cumbersome to get from the street level to the top of the building. The offices offer "beautiful views" but people complained that they are "minimalist and very '70s looking" on the inside. The firm has, however, completed a major renovation of these offices, which includes the creation of a conference center, a mock court room, and a two story library. Sonnenschein retains the services of the curator of the Art Institute of Chicago and has amassed an interesting art collection representing an "eclectic mix of African art, Asian art, and traditional stuff," observed one contact. "It's worth looking at," commented one insider; but another described it as "tacky." The firm assigns private offices to all associates. It has an updated and fully-networked IBM computer system. The firm's library is well-stocked. Attorneys can purchase food from an outside caterer in the lunchroom. The firm also provides a lawyer's lunch in a conference room at subsidized prices. The support staff was described as a "mixed bag" with some "real characters."

hiring tips

Sonnenschein hires attorneys who know how to be team players, but can also show initiative and can survive "on their own," because, according to one source, the firm does little "to further your career and make sure that you're developing legal skills." One insider noted that the firm has hired people who are "unafraid to speak their minds" and are "very opinionated." People advised those who interview at the firm to emphasize their willingness to work hard. One advised interviewees to "dress low-key." Another commented, "be yourself, be natural, be funny. Show your willingness to be a team player. They don't want egos."According to one contact, Sonnenschein "really wants to be a top player in the Chicago market and is placing a new emphasis on attracting stars—top students from top schools." Another person advised that if you interview at Sonnenschein, "you'd better be in the top of your class at a top school. Otherwise, don't bother. Law review helps too."

Sonnenschein weathered the economic downturn of the late 1980s well and has had good economic years recently. Still, we heard complaints about salary and related matters. One person commented that the base salary is "notably lower" than at comparable firms and since "no one gets even close to the top of the bonus range, the gap is even wider." Another person commented that the bonuses were "insulting," adding that the firm is "cheap, cheap, cheap" and that they need to realize that "this is no longer the warm fuzzy place they think it is, at least not for associates." The firm informed us that it increased associate salaries in 1996 and is presently reviewing its overall compensation structure. We were also told that morale is low and that there is increased pressure to bill and get clients. Concern was also expressed about partnership decisions. Sonnenschein has now started using the of-counsel position for associates who will not be made partner but who are allowed to stay at the firm. One person asserted that "communication lines are not functioning properly" and that they "seriously need to do damage control about what associates say about the place." On the other hand, we were told that associates "are very supportive of one another" and that, due to associate attrition, there is "very good experience to be had even by low level associates." A firm spokesperson pointed out to us that Sonnenschein ranked in the top third of Chicago firms in the 1996 mid-level associates survey, well ahead of the city and national averages.

Winston & Strawn

Chicago New York Washington
Geneva Paris

Address: 35 West Wacker Drive, Chicago, IL 60601
Telephone: (312) 558–5600
Hiring Attorney: Paul H. Hensel
Contact: Paulette R. Kuttig, Recruitment Administrator; (312) 558–5742
Associate Salary: First year $73,000 (1997)
Summer Salary: $1,350/week (1997)
Average Hours: 2000 worked; 2000 billed; NA required
Family Benefits: Paid maternity leave; paid paternity leave
1996 Summer: Class of 36 students
Partnership: NA
Pro Bono: 2% of all work is pro bono

Winston & Strawn in 1997
324 Lawyers at the Chicago Office
1.6 Associates Per Partner

Total Partners 124		
Women	16	13%
All Minorities	6	5%
Afro-Am	2	2%
Asian Am	1	1%
Latino	2	2%
Native-Am	1	1%

Total Associates 196		
Women	66	34%
All Minorities	26	13%
Afro-Am	10	5%
Asian-Am	7	4%
Latino	9	5%

Practice Areas	
Litigation	136
Corporate	95
Labor	24
Real Estate	18
Tax	17
Environmental	14
Intellectual Property	6
Trusts & Estates	5
ERISA	4
Healthcare	3
Legislative	2

One of Chicago's oldest and most prestigious law firms, Winston & Strawn is an excellent choice for someone interested in high-profile legal matters or politics, particularly Republican political activities. Former Republican Governor of Illinois James Thompson is chairman of the firm. Dan Webb, who served as special prosecutor against Admiral Poindexter in the Iran-Contra litigation and questioned President Ronald Reagan, is also a partner. Webb, we were told, is a "magnet for the most high profile litigation in the country." Winston & Strawn attorneys "pride themselves on doing good work and consider themselves the best firm in Chicago." Thompson appears poised to expand the firm's international capabilities, and has overseen the recent openings of offices in Switzerland and Paris.

old-boy atmosphere

Winston lawyers are friendly, "very professional and businesslike." Described as a "very formal, WASP, white-shoe kind of place," Winston is a fairly conservative firm in terms of dress and is reputed to be an "old-boy place," we were told. Fridays are, however, unofficial casual dress days year round and women attorneys regularly wear pantsuits. The firm is also quite hierarchical. It has a two-tier partnership and is "governed by a committee of rainmakers." The firm dining room, jokingly referred to as Chez Paul in honor of the partner whose brainchild it is, is open only to lawyers. At lunch, waiters dressed in black ties and white jackets wait on the dining lawyers. The "attorney only" rule is strictly observed. The dining room is not open to spouses or clients.

practice areas

Winston is a full-service law firm with practice groups ranging from corporate and litigation to government and health care. The firm represents, among others, large corporations, utilities, and hospitals, such as Kemper, Anheuser Busch (an intellectual property client), Commonwealth Edison, and Illinois Power. It has recently been hired as national counsel by Phillip Morris and Monsanto. Winston has a strong and "very broad" corporate practice with specialty groups in areas such as airplane leasebacks and bond issues for health care facilities. Winston's government practice group lobbies both in Springfield, Illinois and in Washington, D.C. One person commented that this is a "good firm to go to for involvement in city or state politics. It is very in touch with that." This person added that the government group "prefers people with a background in government." Sam Skinner's son is a partner in this department, but does mostly litigation work. The firm has a well-regarded and growing litigation department, as well as a number of other practice areas, including labor, environmental, tax, intellectual property, and ERISA.

pro bono

Winston makes pro bono work readily available. It regularly circulates a memo listing opportunities for attorneys. One person told us that "most young litigation associates get courtroom experience in pro bono matters." The firm recently won an award for its commitment to pro bono, though the "joke in the firm is that they bought it," said one contact. Pro bono hours count toward billable hours.

professional development

The firm hires entering associates into a particular department, usually their top choice. Partners in the department directly assign work to the new associates, who usually develop close working relationships with the partners. We were told that junior associates must do "some grunt work" but get more responsibility if they do good work. Most junior associate assignments involve research and writing memos. Winston offers some formal training programs and workshops, such as NITA deposition and trial training, but much of the training happens on-the-job. Each practice group also meets regularly to discuss new developments in the law.

formal evaluations

The firm has a comprehensive formal evaluation system for associates. Once a year, partners complete a "detailed and elaborate" six-page evaluation form grading each associate who worked for them on a range of topics including initiative, management, and ability to work with others. During the first three years, associates are graded pass/fail. After the third year, each associate receives a letter grade, from an "A" to a "D." The associate's compensation is then adjusted to reflect the evaluation grade. Bonuses are based on the firm's performance and the associate's billable hours.

unpleasant events

Winston & Strawn suffered a number of unpleasant events in the early 1990s. While under the leadership of former managing partner Gary Fairchild, the firm became increasingly bottom-line. In the fall of 1991, it laid off about 25 associates firmwide without any warning, and in the spring of 1992, fired 20 partners. People agreed that the layoffs were handled poorly. As a result, associates were "very conscious of the hours they billed." To make matters worse, in the spring of 1994 the firm announced that it had requested Fairchild's resignation after an internal investigation led it to believe that he may have stolen hundreds of thousand of dollars from the firm. The matter was turned over to the state bar's disciplinary committee, state prosecutors, and the U.S. attorney. The *Chicago Daily Law Bulletin* subsequently reported that Fairchild pleaded guilty in December 1994 to mail fraud and income tax charges. He was sentenced to 24 months in prison and three years of supervised release that will include 750 hours of community service. Winston & Strawn's situation is considerably improved today. The firm is now "very busy" and, reports one source, "I know of no associates who are concerned that their hours are too low." Winston recently hired about 30 lateral associates. Attorneys, particularly in litigation, have more than enough work these days.

limited social life

Although many Winston attorneys form close friendships at the firm, in general, they "do their work and go home." The firm organizes some social activities, but does not provide an extensive social calendar. Every other Friday morning, the firm provides bagels to each floor. During the summer, Winston hosts Friday evening "wine and cheese" parties in a conference room, which are well-attended by the summer committee members. The firm also organizes a Fourth of July boat cruise and has a regular supply of tickets to White Sox games, for which they have a skybox, and Cubs games.

diversity

We were told that Winston is "working on increasing the number of women and minorities" at the firm. In one insider's opinion, however, the firm lacks sensitivity to women's concerns at times. This person claimed that "women who are successful at Winston & Strawn are those who are willing to give up their femininity." The firm also has few minority attorneys. The recent addition of a sizeable number of lateral associates has, however, added diversity to the firm.

management

According to people we interviewed, associates are not well-informed regarding the management of the firm. The firm is governed by a "pretty centralized" management committee consisting of the most powerful partners. People commented that although Winston "made some tough decisions" to release some attorneys, the firm is now doing well economically and envisions itself expanding into a national law firm in the future. It has opened offices in New York and Washington, D.C.

gorgeous offices

Winston & Strawn has one of Chicago's most beautiful offices. It occupies the top floors of a brand-new 48-story office building that is all "marble, glass, and artwork." The firm's reception area, located in the top two stories of the building, has 30-foot high ceilings and an entire wall of glass that offers "an amazing view of the lake and city." It is elegantly decorated with "oriental rugs and marble...and reeks of money," according to one observer. The firm's dining room, the aforementioned Chez Paul, is also beautiful, and looks "like a restaurant." The firm assigns each attorney to a good-sized individual office with windows. It has a modern computer system and every lawyer receives a personal computer. The library and support staff are excellent.

hiring practices

Winston hires "bright, driven, and intelligent" people. When hiring first-year law students, the firm carefully considers their grades. One person advised students interviewing with the firm "not to be arrogant" and to "keep up on the Chicago Bulls and show an interest in Chicago." Winston draws upon a broad range of law schools in its hiring, from the top national law schools to local Chicago law schools.

Although the firm has become a more friendly place since Gary Fairchild's departure, there is a "lot of inner office friction," we were told, between the many new lateral partners and the long-time partners who feel that they are not compensated as fairly as the new laterals. Still, Winston remains one of Chicago's most prestigious law firms. It provides "interesting work" and excellent training with attorneys who "do good work." According to one person, they are "nice people" who, though they "work a lot of hours, enjoy the atmosphere" at the firm.

Dallas

Law Firms Ranked By Associates Per Partner

1.	GARDERE & WYNNE	0.5
2.	THOMPSON & KNIGHT	0.6
3.	STRASBURGER & PRICE	0.7
4.	HUGHES & LUCE	1.0
5.	WINSTEAD, SECHREST & MINICK	1.0
6.	AKIN, GUMP, STRAUSS, HAUER & FELD	1.4

Law Firms Ranked by Percentage of Associates Who Make Partner
(over varying years)

1.	AKIN, GUMP, STRAUSS, HAUER & FELD	86
2.	GARDERE & WYNNE	65
3.	STRASBURGER & PRICE	63
4.	HUGHES & LUCE	56
5.	WINSTEAD, SECHREST & MINICK	30
6.	THOMPSON & KNIGHT	NA

Law Firms Ranked by Percentage of Pro Bono Work

1.	GARDERE & WYNNE	2
2.	HUGHES & LUCE	1-5
3.	STRASBURGER & PRICE	1-3
4.	AKIN, GUMP, STRAUSS, HAUER & FELD	1
5.	WINSTEAD, SECHREST & MINICK	0.5
6.	THOMPSON & KNIGHT	NA

Law Firms Ranked by Percentage of Female Partners

1.	THOMPSON & KNIGHT	23
2.	AKIN, GUMP, STRAUSS, HAUER & FELD	21
3.	GARDERE & WYNNE	15
4.	WINSTEAD, SECHREST & MINICK	15
5.	STRASBURGER & PRICE	12
6.	HUGHES & LUCE	10

Law Firms Ranked by Percentage of Female Associates

1.	GARDERE & WYNNE	50
2.	STRASBURGER & PRICE	43
3.	THOMPSON & KNIGHT	41
4.	AKIN, GUMP, STRAUSS, HAUER & FELD	37
5.	HUGHES & LUCE	33
6.	WINSTEAD, SECHREST & MINICK	29

Law Firms Ranked by Percentage of Minority Partners

1.	GARDERE & WYNNE	3
2.	HUGHES & LUCE	3
3.	STRASBURGER & PRICE	2
4.	THOMPSON & KNIGHT	1
5.	WINSTEAD, SECHREST & MINICK	1
6.	AKIN, GUMP, STRAUSS, HAUER & FELD	0

Law Firms Ranked By Percentage of Minority Associates

1.	GARDERE & WYNNE	15
2.	HUGHES & LUCE	15
3.	THOMPSON & KNIGHT	9
4.	WINSTEAD, SECHREST & MINICK	7
5.	STRASBURGER & PRICE	3
6.	AKIN, GUMP, STRAUSS, HAUER & FELD	0

Akin, Gump, Strauss, Hauer & Feld

Dallas Austin Houston New York Philadelphia San Antonio Washington
Brussels Moscow

Address: 1700 Pacific Avenue, Suite 4100, Dallas, TX 75201–4618
Telephone: (214) 969–2800
Hiring Attorney: Daniel J. Micciche
Contact: Judy Dillon, Recruiting Administrator; (214) 969–2874
Associate Salary: First year $76,200 package (1997)
Summer Salary: $1000/week 1Ls; $1150/week 2Ls (1997)
Average Hours: 2150 worked; 1900 billed; 2000 target
Family Benefits: Medical and childcare flexible spending accounts; employee assistance; medical and dental insurance; 13 weeks paid maternity leave
1996 Summer: Class of 36 students; offers to 24 2Ls and 9 1Ls
Partnership: 86% of entering associates from 1979–1984 were made partner
Pro Bono: Approximately 1% of all work is pro bono

Akin, Gump, Strauss, Hauer & Feld in 1997
125 Lawyers at the Dallas Office
1.4 Associates Per Partner

Total Partners 48		
Women	10	21%
All Minorities	0	0%

Total Associates 65		
Women	24	37%
All Minorities	0	0%

Practice Areas	
Corporate	41
Litigation	35
Labor	14
Real Estate	9
Tax	8
Environmental	5
Intellectual Property	5
Bankruptcy	2
Public Law & Policy	1

flexible culture

Akin Gump is an unpretentious, fun, and fairly liberal place to work. Though formerly known as a firm with a "fraternity-like" atmosphere and a "jock culture," the athletic tempo at Akin Gump appears to have considerably slowed down of late. We have been informed that the firm "can't even field a softball team in the DAYL League" nowadays. But the firm still retains its "laid-back" culture. Akin Gump does not have a rigid structure. Some people praised the office for being "casual," "chummy," and "fun," though others criticized it for being "chaotic." Both attorneys and support staff operate on a flexible schedule. "When you have trials or big deals, you work 15-hour days, but if not, you are not expected to be hanging around the office to put in hours. They don't take attendance." People like to take off Thursdays and play golf, revealed one contact.

practice areas

The firm's laid-back attitude and casual style extends to its broad commercial practice. The firm is organized around sections, each of which has an expertise in a particular practice area, but there is no "top-down, client driven hierarchy," explained one source. "It is more like, the partners bring in their own clients and everyone works with whom they want." Dallas office attorneys are hired for a department "so they know what floor and side of the building to put you on, but they are flexible when you get there. Everyone does what is needed—everyone does due diligence, then everyone does discovery."

This firm is not anchored to one big client, which, according to some people we interviewed, helped during the economic downturn in the early 1990s. Both the corporate department and the litigation department have rebounded nicely from slow periods at the beginning of the decade and are doing brisk business today. The litigation practice includes both defense-side securities litigation for large corporations and plaintiff-side tort litigation on behalf of smaller businesses. The environmental practice handles planning and defense matters. It also has a venture capital practice, which represents companies from their inception onward. In recent years the Dallas office has added an intellectual property practice and a labor and employment practice through lateral acquisitions. The firm does a lot of international corporate work through its Dallas, Washington, D.C., and foreign offices. The firm represented LuKOil, a Russian oil company, in the first transaction in which a Russian company raised funds in Western capital markets. Cases and transactions are regularly staffed on a multi-office basis. Just recently, the firm announced the opening of a London office to concentrate on global capital markets. The firm also plans to open a Los Angeles office in late 1997. Attorneys at Akin Gump do substantial pro bono work, mainly for free legal clinics, indigent criminal defendants, charitable organizations, and small non-profit organizations. The firm gives associates credit for pro bono hours and has received many pro bono awards, including the "Superior Service Award" from the Dallas Bar Association in 1996.

"Lawyer's College"

The formal training program at Akin Gump in the litigation and labor areas has improved considerably over the past several years. The firm runs its own in-house continuing legal education courses, referred to as "Lawyer College," which are mandatory for litigation and labor associates during their first three years. The firm also encourages continuing legal education and attendance at seminars and institutes outside the office. Each associate is reimbursed for up to 20 luncheon seminars per year (chosen by the associate) at the Dallas Bar Association. Still, the firm puts great stress on early responsibility and learning-by-doing. One contact quipped, "on the day you get your certification from the bar, that afternoon you will be in front of a judge."

structured feedback

In contrast to its flexible work approach, the firm has a very structured associate evaluation process. One person reported that there is a rigid annual feedback policy for associates which he termed the "How You Stand on the Road to Partnership" mandatory review process. The process requires each partner and senior associate for whom the associate has worked to complete a detailed evaluation of the associate's work. The evaluation forms are six pages long and are designed to "elicit constructive criticism, rather than to simply grade an associate's performance in given areas." The process, moreover, is completely open. "Each associate will not only meet with his or her section head to discuss performance, but the associate will also receive copies of every completed evaluation form." Summer associates, on the other hand, had mixed feelings about the adequacy of their reviews, which often seemed perfunctory.

political leanings

The lawyers at Akin Gump span the political spectrum, but they are "more liberal than not." Akin Gump is a liberal firm for Dallas, in a "Texas-tempered, conservative way," explained one observer. A few attorneys hold fundraisers for political candidates or take a year off to work on campaigns. Vernon Jordan, a close personal friend of President Clinton, is a partner in the firm's D.C. office, and Robert Strauss, former Chairman of the Democratic National Committee and former Ambassador to Russia, is a name partner at the firm. Tom Foley, retired Speaker of the House, is a member of the firm. On the other hand, the firm includes many Republicans such as Don Alexander, former Commissioner of the Internal Revenue Service, as well as Jim Cicconi and Frank Donatelli, who formerly worked for President Bush. Mike Madigan, formerly of Akin Gump's D.C. office, recently left the firm to become Chief Counsel to Republican Senator Fred Thompson's committee investigating campaign financing.

fun social life

People report that Akin Gump offers a fun social life. The associates, many of whom are single, go out together a lot after work. The labor and employment section, on the other hand, is "very family oriented and understanding of the needs of lawyers with children." One associate left Akin Gump to buy a bar in Dallas with some other associates as his silent partners. There are always long lines there, but Akin Gump attorneys reportedly always get in first.

diversity

Akin Gump is said to be a good place for women. It is reportedly one of a small number of Dallas firms where about twenty percent of the partners are women. "This is completely an equal opportunity firm," declared one contact. "Some of the real top people are women." Partner Diana Dutton heads the environmental department and is a member of the executive committee, and partner Mary O'Connor is reputed to be one of the best litigators in the city of Dallas. Laura Franze, head of the labor and employment section, has received recognition as "one of the best employment lawyers in the country." Four female associates work part-time schedules. However, not all women may feel comfortable at Akin Gump. There was a sharp decline in the number of women associates at the firm over the 1993–1994 period. One person complained that the firm could be "rude" and "not the most PC type of place" for women. The firm is having a tough time recruiting minority attorneys, say some people we interviewed. However, 30% of the firm's 1997 entering class are minorities, we were told. People did say that the firm is "very accommodating" of people with disabilities, including people confined to wheelchairs and those with vision problems.

firmwide management

Until recently, Akin Gump was a loose conglomeration of offices in different cities: Dallas, Houston, San Antonio, Austin, Philadelphia, New York, Washington D.C, Brussels, London, and Moscow, with main anchors in Dallas and D.C. Each office was distinct and run separately as an individual profit center, but the firm has now tightened the relationship among its offices. An elected firmwide management committee makes decisions for the entire firm, such as setting associate bonuses and designing a compensation program for partners. Each office also has its own operating committee made up of partners, and there are a host of other mixed associate-partner committees such as the recruiting committee and the associates committee.

out-of-date offices

Akin Gump's facilities in Dallas are not especially attractive. "The decor is out-of-date: a flat gray with silver metallic stair railings and light fixtures" is how one person described it. A firm spokesperson informed us that "the firm distributes profits to the lawyers rather than hanging them on the wall." The firm does not have a gym or a cafeteria, but it caters in coffee, fruit juice, and soft drinks. All lawyers have their own offices with windows. Lawyers have computers in their offices with E-mail, Westlaw and LEXIS, though summer associates must receive permission to use LEXIS and Westlaw.

salary

Akin Gump's compensation is competitive. The Dallas office uses a lockstep formula to determine the base compensation of its associates, then pays them bonuses determined by the management committee. A predetermined bonus is paid at the end of the year and is based on hours. Then, if you bill 2100 hours or more, you're eligible for a "special" merit bonus.

hiring practices

Several people said that the firm looks to hire students from top law schools or those from lesser known law schools at the top of their classes. The Dallas office takes a lot of people straight out of law school, reported one former summer associate. The firm hires predominantly from the University of Texas and SMU, with other summer associates from schools such as Harvard, Duke, Columbia, NYU, Michigan, Boalt, and Virginia. The firm does not "give offers to nerds who are smart," said one insider, stressing the importance of personality to the offer. Several six-week clerkship positions are reserved for first-year law students, to whom the firm does not give offers of permanent employment at the end of the summer, but who may be invited back for a second clerkship based on performance. Returning second-year students are only required to spend three weeks with the firm.

One person praised Judy Dillon, the director of the summer program, for organizing a fun summer program. The summer program is informal, rather than formal. "Lots of things come up at the last minute" over the E-mail. Summer program events in recent years have included a Jamaican party, a Casino night, a picnic for all Dallas office employees, clerks and their families, happy hours, movie nights, and dinners at attorneys' homes.

People stressed that in interviewing with Akin Gump, interaction with other attorneys matters. Some remembered their interviews as "laid-back" and "pleasant." While the firm includes a very high proportion of attorneys who grew up in other parts of the country, one person stressed that interviewees should "be ready to talk about how much you love Texas."

Akin Gump is a "world-wide firm" which provides its attorneys the opportunity to "access resources and expertise across the world." It has a number of high-profile political figures in its employ and its compensation is "among the highest in the city." On the other hand, its billable hours requirement of 2000 is high and "the firm expects even more hours on non-billable projects." Its computer system, offices, and office furniture are "out-of-date" (so out-of-date that a firm spokesperson tartly told us that they are "anticipating future retro-trends!") But the firm provides early opportunities and responsibility in a "relaxed, friendly culture," prompting one firm enthusiast to observe that "as big firms go, it's one of the *best.*"

Gardere & Wynne

Dallas Houston Tulsa
Mexico City

Address: 1601 Elm Street, Suite 3000, Dallas, TX 75201
Telephone: (214) 999–3000
Hiring Attorney: Deborah Ryan
Contact: Tammy Tremont, Director of Recruiting; (214) 999-4177
Associate Salary: First year $66,000 (1997)
Summer Salary: $1200/week (1997)
Average Hours: 2060 worked; 1860 billed; no policy regarding required hours
Family Benefits: Paid maternity leave/paternity leave
1996 Summer: Class of 15 students; offers to 14
Partnership: 65% of entering associates from 1979–1982 were made partner
Pro Bono: 2% of all work is pro bono

Gardere & Wynne in 1997
172 Lawyers at the Dallas Office
0.5 Associates Per Partner

Total Partners 102			Total Associates 54			Practice Areas	
Women	15	15%	Women	27	50%	Trial	76
All Minorities	3	3%	All Minorities	8	15%	Corporate	23
Afro-Am	2	2%	Afro-Am	5	9%	Labor	15
Latino	1	1%	Asian-Am	1	2%	Business Law	13
			Latino	1	2%	Intellectual Property	13
			Native Am	1	2%	Tax	11
						Bankruptcy	7
						Employee Benefits	7
						Real Estate	7
						Banking	5
						Energy	2
						Computer Law	1

Created in 1969 from a merger of two full-service firms, Gardere has grown rapidly, to a point where the firm now numbers over 250 attorneys in all its offices. Recently, Gardere & Wynne merged with Sewell & Riggs in Houston. The Houston office now has the name Gardere, Wynne, Sewell & Riggs; the merger has reportedly been "very successful" and represents an important addition to the firm, which is now the fifth largest firm in Texas.

practice areas

Litigation is the largest area at Gardere & Wynne. It is divided into general civil and trial litigation, and specialized litigation sections. The specialized litigation section is organized around three groups: environmental, intellectual property, and labor. The environmental group coordinates the activities of the attorneys practicing environmental litigation in the Tulsa, Houston, and Dallas offices. These "highly respected lawyers" represent a growing practice area in the firm. The firm also has sections in general corporate and specialized business law, both of which include a number of groups. People praised the firm's corporate, environmental, tax, and real estate practices. The real estate practice group is, according to our sources, a fairly "relaxed" department in which to work. The labor group, on the other hand, reportedly "works all the time...be prepared to stay late—they work more hours, are understaffed, and have a lot of work." Ron Gaswirth, the head of the labor section, is well-known in Dallas. The firm's clients are mainly regional corporations from Texas and the Southwest. The firm is trying to develop an international practice through its Mexico City office.

Attorneys at Gardere & Wynne do pro bono work for legal clinics and community housing boards and take on death penalty appeals. In a number of recent years, the firm has received special recognition from the Private Bar Involvement Project of Legal Services in North Texas, as well as from the Dallas Bar Association. Also, one of the firm's partners, Ron Kirk, recently began a four-year term as Mayor of Dallas.

Associates are hired for a particular department. Gardere & Wynne offers a mock trial training program for its litigation associates. When questioned about day-to-day feedback, one critic complained that "you have to seek it out." This sentiment is not universally shared; others assured us that their feedback was adequate.

friendly atmosphere

Gardere & Wynne is not a sweatshop. One contact told us that there is "not much pressure to bill" hours. Another reported that attorneys work hard when they have a big project such as a trial, but on normal days they work from nine to five and the place clears out by six. The dress code is casual—what one person described as "anything goes." Men do not wear jackets in the halls. All attorneys address one another by first name, and there are few closed office doors. The attorneys are said to be "friendly" and "chatty."

Gardere is "a very social firm" full of "lots of normal and fun people." The attorneys, including the partners, are young. Groups of friends will socialize together after work. There are "lots of happy hours," noted one contact.

diversity

Some women exercise considerable influence at the firm, we were told. Real estate partner Debbie Ryan is the present hiring partner. One person reported that some female partners take the initiative during the summer to introduce themselves to the female summer associates and to stay in touch with them via lunches and other activities. Past summers have included a few "girls nights out" with the clerks at female associates' or partners' houses. The firm has no formal committees to deal with sexual or racial harassment issues, but it does have a Cultural Diversity Committee.

lacks cohesiveness

One person described Gardere & Wynne as an "eat–what–you–kill culture." A firm spokesperson told us that partner compensation is based on a number of factors, including fees generated as well as work for the firm, the community, and the bar association. Those we interviewed believed that the firm has an unusual compensation system by which partners earn profits from the business they bring in minus their share of the overhead costs. According to one person we interviewed, this structure "does not foster cohesiveness." Another person said that there is pressure to bring in new clients, even among partners; the firm does, however, provide each associate with a business development expense account to assist in this task. It was also brought to our attention that there is no 401K contribution by the firm for attorneys.

Gardere has seven floors of office space which are said to be well-decorated. All attorneys have computers in their offices, with access to Westlaw and LEXIS. There are also computers in the library available for use. The secretaries and other members of the office staff were described as "helpful."

summer program

Gardere & Wynne's summer program is less structured than some. There were "a lot of informal summer events organized impromptu, such as plans to meet at a bar and then go kicker dancing," recalled one person. The firm also organizes a number of informal dinners at partners' homes. The main event of a recent summer program was a trip to the new ballpark in Arlington to see a Rangers game. The firm chartered three buses and rented a suite that accommodated 150 people.

hiring tips

When it comes to hiring decisions, Gardere & Wynne is "a well-respected firm, but is not grade-snobby like some of the other Texas firms," said one person. "Grades are important, but can be overcome with energy and personality," said another. You have to click personally, stressed several people we interviewed. "Be a normal person, don't be an egghead," one source counseled. "Try to act like you have a personality." The firm hires mainly from Duke, the University of Michigan, the University of Virginia, and the University of Texas, but it "will go all over to hire." It takes a fair number of clerks from local Texas law schools, such as Baylor, SMU, and St. Mary's.

Hughes & Luce

Dallas Austin Houston

Address: 1700 Main Street, Suite 2800, Dallas, TX 75201
Telephone: (214) 939–5500
Hiring Attorney: Greg Taylor
Contact: Carra W. Garza, Recruiting Administrator; (214) 939–5517
Associate Salary: First year $73,000 (includes $61,000 base, $4,000 year end bonus, $6,000 summer stipend, $1,000 acceptance bonus, and paid parking of $1,000 per annum) (1997)
Summer Salary: $1150/week 2L/3L's; $1050/week 1L (1997)
Average Hours: 2100 worked; 1830 billed; none required
Family Benefits: 12 weeks paid maternity leave (12 unpaid); cbc weeks paid paternity (cbc unpaid)
1996 Summer: Class of 23 students; offers to 21
Partnership: 56% of entering associates from 1981–1989 were made partner
Pro Bono: 1–5% of all work is pro bono

Hughes & Luce in 1997
119 Lawyers at the Dallas Office
1.0 Associate Per Partner

Total Partners 59			Total Associates 60			Practice Areas	
Women	6	10%	Women	20	33%	Litigation	38
All Minorities	2	3%	All Minorities	9	15%	Financial Services	19
Afro-Am	1	1%	Afro-Am	3	5%	Corporate	18
Asian-Am	1	1%	Asian-Am	4	6%	Tax	14
			Latino	2	3%	Real Estate	13
						General Business	8
						Bankruptcy	5
						Labor	2
						General Assignment	2

Hughes & Luce may be best known as the firm that billionaire and former presidential candidate H. Ross Perot hand-picked in 1975 to do his legal work. The firm was founded by Tom Luce in Dallas in 1973 and now also has small offices in Houston and Austin. EDS, formerly owned by Perot, is a major client of the firm, and several Hughes & Luce alumni now work at that company. "EDS made Hughes & Luce," remarked one person. The firm also represents Perot Systems, the data processing company founded by Perot after he left EDS, the Perot Group, which is primarily a real estate group, and Ross Perot personally. Hughes & Luce's work for the Perot family has now entered a second-generation as Ross Perot, Jr. has begun to make a name for himself. The firm recently represented Perot, Jr. in his purchase of the Dallas Mavericks NBA basketball franchise and now handles the legal matters for the Mavericks.

practice areas

While Perot and EDS keep the firm busy, Hughes & Luce does many other kinds of work as well. Corporate finance and complex commercial litigation are two of the firm's standout areas. The firm reportedly has the largest tax group in Dallas, and name partner Vester Hughes is a nationally known tax practitioner. Hughes & Luce also enjoys a 20 year headstart in its technology practice for clients such as EDS, Perot Systems, Affiliated Computer Systems, and others. "This has allowed us to develop an Internet practice with C-Net and other providers," according to one insider. In addition, the firm recently hired a top venture capital/corporate group in Austin away from another firm to increase its expertise in this area. Hughes & Luce has established intersectional practice groups in such areas as energy law, property, intellectual property, international law, environmental law, and estate planning. It serves mainly a Texas clientele and has many small to medium-sized Texas companies and a variety of lenders as clients. A firm spokesperson pointed out that "while many of the firm's clients have headquarters in Texas, their legal needs are global in nature and we represent them around the world. In 1996, more than half of the firm's transactional work concerned clients and matters outside of Texas." Hughes & Luce represents technology companies, sporting goods companies, and companies in the music business, such as Vari-Lite, a company that does the lights for concerts and Broadway shows.

active pro bono

Hughes & Luce has an active pro bono practice which includes a strong commitment to public service in areas such as education. The firm represents many school boards and universities in education-related legal matters. The firm also helps sponsor a Thursday night legal clinic in East Dallas, accepts cases from the clinic, and represents those clients on an ongoing basis. One person noted that there are always flyers going around the office to advertise pro bono opportunities.

informal structure

Attorneys are not hired for a particular department. Upon joining the firm, a new associate may join one of the nine major practice sections or the general assignment section, which allows them to explore different areas. The firm, however, does place emphasis on focusing on an area of practice within a year or two. People praised the firm's informal structure, though its success seems to vary by department. One person observed that the "informal structure of the firm occasionally baffles first- and second-year associates who need to find a niche or a mentor." Another person reported that "there are some good young partners who take people under their wing, such as some partners in the corporate, general business, and tax sections." Litigation, however, is "looser." This single large department is not divided up, so associates work for many partners. To ensure a good experience in the litigation department, "you need to find a base," said one contact.

The attorneys are reported to be nice, friendly, and supportive. People are not stuffy or formal, said one person. Male attorneys do not wear their jackets in the halls, and women attorneys sport some "trendy" outfits that are "dressy but less formal" than average.

long work hours

Associates at Hughes & Luce tend to work harder than associates at many other Dallas firms. Associates routinely worked nine or ten hours per day and some weekends. "The firm expects a lot from the associates," revealed one contact. "It looks for the type of person who wants to put in a lot for personal satisfaction." Some note the loyalty that many associates have to the firm. But others complain that this attitude places pressure on young associates.

Despite this reported pressure, Hughes & Luce attorneys socialize easily with one another, both through firm sponsored events such as the annual golf tournament and through informal after-hours gatherings. There are a lot of single people who go out together after work, said one person. Another person remarked that "people at Hughes & Luce realize they are all bright and accomplished, so very few of the attorneys have chips on their shoulders." This person further observed that, whereas some Texas firm's are "sorority and fraternity bastions," Hughes & Luce is not as "looks" oriented as some of the other firms in Dallas.

diversity

The firm is actively trying to recruit women and minority attorneys to the firm, and has diversified its summer class in recent years. The firm actively recruits minorities at the University of Texas and through the Dallas Consortium for Minority Hiring. The firm offers the standard paid maternity leave to women, and several women work part-time. "They try to work with you to fix a schedule," said one woman. We were told that the financial services group, which has experienced high turnover of late and where the "Texas good ole boy" attitude prevails, has had a hard time keeping its female attorneys.

merit-based salaries

Associates are spurred to work hard by the existence of merit-based raises and the chance to make partner in seven to eight years. Five attorneys were made partners in the Dallas office and one in the Houston office at the end of 1995. After their first year, associates receive a base salary plus a bonus that is determined by merit, the hours worked by the associate, and an intangible component described by the firm as: "an associate's overall contribution to the firm." As regards compensation overall, one person reported that Hughes & Luce "is not on the cutting edge. It reacts to market conditions (and sometimes slowly)."

dynamic management

Hughes & Luce has been described as a "young firm with few really old partners." Management is dynamic and open; the newly-elected managing partner is only 45 years old. The firm is managed by partners, but associates have informal input into management decisions. Associates are also members of a number of committees including those addressing associate hiring, the summer program, business development, and technology issues.

award winning library design

Like the working environment at Hughes & Luce, the offices are "less formal than those of a lot of other big Dallas firms." The firm gives each associate a small allowance to "decorate their office in the manner in which they choose." The lobby of the building is "a monument to the '80s," according to one person, and the library is described as "beautiful—designed with arched windows and two floors open." The library has received an award from the *American Bar Journal* for its architectural design. The aesthetic appeal of the library is a good thing, said associates, because some of them spend a lot of time there. Each associate has a private office with a window. Hughes & Luce recently installed a Pentium computer Windows-based network system which has built-in fax and modem capability. Attorneys share secretaries (as do summer associates).

selective hiring

Hughes & Luce has a Texas flavor, but it hires its summer clerks from schools all over the country, including Harvard, Yale, Chicago, Duke, and Columbia. Law review and grades do not hurt when it comes to landing a summer job, caution some former summer associates, who stressed the competitive nature of the hiring process. Almost all of the summer associates have received offers of permanent employment in recent years.

Attorneys at Hughes & Luce work hard, but they are rewarded with good pay, young and receptive management, friendly co-workers, a flexible assignment system, and good pro bono opportunities. One person reported that "associates are quickly pushed to the forefront—which is good, but it means our hours are some of the highest in our salary range." Hughes & Luce is well respected in the Dallas legal community. It is "well diversified, not a WASP firm." It is not a Texas "good ole boy" firm (with the noted exception of the financial services section.) Nonetheless, one should have an interest in Texas to work at this firm, which is limited to Texas offices and a mainly Texas-based clientele. "Hughes & Luce is *the* Texas firm," concluded one person, with another person adding the observation that "Hughes & Luce has the Texas charm without the Texas bias."

Strasburger & Price

Dallas Austin Houston

Address: 901 Main Street, Suite 4300, Dallas, TX 75202
Telephone: (214) 651–4300
Hiring Attorney: David N. Kitner
Contact: Denise B. Thompson, Manager of Professional Recruiting; (214) 651–4502
Associate Salary: First year $60,000 (1996) plus graduation bonus of $6000, year end bonus of $2000, and moving expenses up to $2500
Summer Salary: $1100/week (1996)
Average Hours: 1986 worked; 1760 billed; 1800 goal
Family Benefits: 8.5 weeks paid maternity leave (cbc unpaid); cbc weeks paid paternity leave (cbc unpaid)
1996 Summer: Class of 20 2L students; offers to 18
Partnership: 63% of entering associates from 1979–1985 were made partner
Pro Bono: 1–3% of all work is pro bono

Strasburger & Price in 1997
196 Lawyers at the Dallas Office
0.7 Associates Per Partner

Total Partners 109		
Women	13	12%
All Minorities	2	2%
Afro-Am	1	1%
Latino	1	1%

Total Associates 75		
Women	32	43%
All Minorities	2	3%
Afro-Am	1	1%
Latino	1	1%

Practice Areas	
Commercial/Envir. Litigation	39
Gen Lit./Labor/Appellate	39
Bus./Real Estate/Creditors Rts.	25
Product Liability	21
Health	15
Intellectual Property	8
Tax/Estates/ERISA	8
International	6

Founded in 1939, Strasburger & Price has grown to be one of the largest firms in Dallas. It has an "old-line...conservative, professional image" on the outside, our sources say, "but on the inside, people are extremely friendly and helpful...People are very, very great." One contact remarked that "they have who you think would be at a Texas firm. Everyone is a good ol' person—really nice, ethical, caring, and giving."

primarily litigation practice

The firm practice is organized around eight divisions, each of which has a number of practice groups. Litigation is the mainstay of Strasburger & Price. The four litigation divisions—general litigation, business litigation, products litigation, and health law—employ over 75 percent of the attorneys at the firm. The practice is "litigation, period," declared one source. "If you don't want to go into litigation, don't go there." Strasburger represents many automobile manufacturers, including General Motors, Nissan, and Mitsubishi. Other representative clients include Columbia/HCA, Compu Com, Dell Computer Corporation, and the Southland Corporation. Medical malpractice is booming, including extensive breast implant litigation. The environmental, labor and employment, and intellectual property practices are growing. The firm also has a creditors' rights division, much of whose work arises through the litigation practice. The corporate and banking divisions function independently, but there is also a lot of cross-marketing with the litigation areas.

pro bono

Attorneys at the firm do some pro bono work for the South Dallas Legal Clinic, North Texas Legal Services, and various religious and community groups. Some Strasburger attorneys have volunteered in Helping Hand, a charitable group, doing non-legal community work such as helping to rehabilitate homes for indigent people.

Litigation training at Strasburger is extensive, highly praised and, according to one firm enthusiast, "the best in the Southwest." The firm offers new associates a one-year trial advocacy course run by more experienced attorneys that meets each week for lectures and culminates in a long mock trial. Each first-year associate is paired with another first-year associate for the trial. There is also a one-year training for the corporate practice, with one-day seminars each week on specific corporate law topics.

extensive training

Strasburger is a "structured, conservative, Republican firm," according to one person. Firm dress, described as somewhat "stuffy" in our earlier editions, has apparently lightened up in recent years. "With all the new female attorneys that start every year, the women's business attire is much more progressive," one insider instructed us. "Women wear pants all the time and rarely do men wear jackets in the halls!" Further, Fridays are casual dress days at the firm.

work atmosphere

The firm expects a lot from its associates, but it "does not expect you to kill yourself," revealed one source. "They don't really want you to bill over 200 hours per month because you will get worn out," said another. People show up each day "to work, not to bill." People do not work nights or weekends unless they have things to do, asserted one contact. One insider informed us that "your billing is really driven by the docket. If you have something heating up, you will tend to work more. If things are too hectic, the firm is good about realizing that help is needed; maybe they will hire a lateral or more new associates."

This focus on reasonable hours may be connected to the firm's emphasis on family. "People are family oriented and respect free time," said one person. "They know you have a family and a life and not just work," explained another. Many partners and associates at this firm are married. "If you are not married when you get there, you will soon be," joked one source. The attorneys at Strasburger are friends and socialize together with their families. Attorneys and family members attend baseball games together on weekends. Partners bring their spouses and children to parties.

family emphasis

The firm is making an effort to recruit women and minorities. "Women are the fastest progressing attorneys at the firm," said one person who noted that a number of women have made partner in recent years, some of whom have been mothers who took maternity leaves without being taken off the partnership track. Strasburger is willing "to work with women who need alternative working arrangements, such as two or three days a week or reduced billable hour requirements." The firm has successfully recruited two African-Americans to start this year, which "should significantly help our recruiting efforts" in the future, according to one person we spoke with.

promoting women

Strasburger occupies office space in the NationsBank Building, a "nice building with good access to health clubs and parking." The firm does not pay parking expenses, but does offer a corporate rate at a nearby health club. Some people liked the firm's decor: "dark cherry wood. Nice and expensive." There are outer and inner hallways so that people who walk around the firm cannot see the attorneys' offices, described one person. One person called the formal reception areas, decorated in burgundy and dark green, "beautiful." Most associates at Strasburger get their own offices with windows, though a few associates must wait a few months before getting window offices. All attorneys who request them have computers at their desks. One insightful contact pointedly observed for us that "the only attorneys without computers are those old-line partners who wouldn't even know how to turn them on!" All computers are hooked up to a network, and attorneys have access to the Internet.

beautiful reception areas

The firm is managed by the "standard hierarchy...a few gray-haired men at the top," described one contact. Efforts are being made, however, to "diversify this by adding

management

partner positions to the management committee that are younger." The firm is conservative fiscally and did not have to resort to any layoffs during the economic slowdown in the early 1990s. In fact, in 1990 the firm expanded by opening an Austin office, which now employs 25 attorneys, and in 1993 the firm opened a 6-attorney office in Houston, which has since expanded to a thriving 12-attorney practice. Salaries are "normal to low end" to start, one person told us, but the firm offers other advantages such as lighter hours and high annual increases. From their third year on, Strasburger associates earn five to ten per cent raises each year, depending on their hours and their work evaluations, as well as merit based bonuses in December. However, "benefits are somewhat less than at comparable Dallas firms." One person informed us that "the pay is definitely sub-par. You don't work at Strasburger to get rich; you work here because it's great work and it has good people. The firm is so fiscally conservative that even the partners make sub-par relative to other Dallas firms, but there is no debt and no partnership buy-in. That conservative stance is what makes the firm so stable and able to withstand even down times."

hiring practices

Former summer associates described the interviewing process at Strasburger as "laid-back. They talk to you like a person." Strasburger reportedly looks for people in the top third or quarter of their classes "who are normal and well-rounded." Strasburger recruits its clerks from Baylor, SMU, the University of Texas, Texas Tech, Vanderbilt, Duke, Michigan, Harvard, Virginia, and Georgetown, among other schools.

Attorneys go to Strasburger & Price for its "outstanding" people, interesting litigation, and family centered environment. Strasburger provides "great work with national clients without the sweatshop atmosphere." Also, the firm wants to keep its associates "because that is where they get their partners. The firm does not really believe in laterals—they like everyone to be 'homegrown' and try to make an environment where people stay for their careers." If you want to work at "the best litigation house in town" in a friendly and supportive environment, Strasburger & Price may be the place for you.

Thompson & Knight

Dallas Austin Fort Worth Houston
Monterrey, Mexico

Address: 1700 Pacific Avenue, Suite 3300 Dallas, TX 75201
Telephone: (214) 969–1700
Hiring Attorney: Dennis J. Grindinger, Chairperson, Hiring Committee
Contact: Laura V. Richardson, Director of Recruiting, and Associate Development; (214) 969–1379
Associate Salary: NA
Summer Salary: $1150/week (1997)
Average Hours: 2133 worked; 1875 billed; 1800 required
Family Benefits: Group life, health, disability, and accidental death insurance; family leave; moving expenses; bar association dues, and bar exam and review course fees
1996 Summer: Class of 38 students; offers to 35
Partnership: NA
Pro Bono: NA

Thompson & Knight in 1997
232 Lawyers at the Dallas Office
0.6 Associates Per Partner

Total Partners 132		
Women	30	23%
All Minorities	1	1%
Latino	1	1%

Total Associates 74		
Women	30	41%
All Minorities	7	9%
Afro-Am	1	1%
Asian-Am	3	4%
Latino	3	4%

Practice Areas	
Litigation/Intellectual Property	90
Corporate	47
Tax	30
Real Estate	23
Labor/Employment	14
Banking	9
Environmental	8
Bankruptcy	8
Oil & Gas	4

Founded in 1887 by William Thompson and R. E. L. Knight, Thompson & Knight is one of the largest and oldest firms in Dallas. Although Thompson & Knight is big and well-established, it exhibits many characteristics usually associated with a smaller firm: manageable hours, a regional focus, and a friendly and relaxed working environment. People who have worked at Thompson & Knight praise the firm for its internal cohesion, and the respect that the attorneys afford each other.

practice areas

The firm enjoys national prominence for its development of oil and gas investment vehicles. The business practice of the corporate and tax departments is organized around institutional investors as well as oil and gas industry clients. The tax department litigates often on behalf of oil and gas industry clients before various courts, including the United States Tax Court. Thompson & Knight's corporate attorneys are involved in all aspects of capital formation, and are actively involved in mergers and acquisitions. The corporate department has also developed specialized expertise in the franchising, healthcare, and intellectual property industries. Thompson & Knight's litigation practice embraces both commercial business litigation and personal injury and property damage. The personal injury and property damage attorneys handle a variety of malpractice, products liability, and toxic torts matters. While more often seen as defense counsel, the firm's litigation practice also includes representation of various claimants. This is especially true with the firm's growing intellectual property practice. The firm also enjoys a large real estate department and an administrative and public law practice.

A commitment to pro bono service is a long standing practice of the firm. Lawyers are encouraged to devote time to pro bono efforts either through individual efforts, the Dallas Housing Crisis Center or the North Texas Legal Services, which is a central clearinghouse run by Dallas-area law firms in conjunction with the Dallas Bar Association. An internal pro bono chairman administers the pro bono program.

Thompson & Knight offers general assistance to its clients through a segmented approach. One shareholder (the firm does not refer to its senior members as partners) serves as the primary contact for each client and coordinates the services for that client across sections. Attorneys from one area work with attorneys from other practice areas to fully serve a client. For example, attorneys from the oil and gas, tax, bankruptcy, and public law sections may work together to serve an oil developer.

relatively flexible organization

Attorneys are hired to work in a specific practice area and are expected to specialize in that area. While associates work within one section and do not rotate through practice areas at the firm, most have flexibility within their sections to work on available matters that interest them. In most sections, the shareholders send their assignments into a centralized pool for their section so that associates can choose the cases that interest them rather than always working with the same attorney. The firm has made associate training a priority and has developed an extensive training program. Workshops on such topics as presentation skills, developing a focused practice, Seven Habits of Highly Successful People, negotiation skills and an emphasis on mentoring from shareholders are some of the areas addressed.

social life

People at the firm treat each other with respect, and that extends to support staff as well as to attorneys. "People are family oriented and respect free time...It is important to them to do family and social events," said one person. Attorneys get to know their colleagues' spouses or significant others. Many attorneys, however, are single and they socialize together at bars or restaurants after work. One person complained that the firm is divided by department when it comes to social relations, though it was noted that this may be inevitable for a big firm.

wine and dine summer

The firm has a large summer program with many activities and "outrageous summer bashes." A wide cross section of attorneys from various practice groups host weekend parties, which give the summer associates a chance to meet all the attorneys in the firm, not just those in the sections in which they are working during the summer. There is also an emphasis on small dinner parties or other outings during the week to allow the summer clerks to get to know each other and the firm's attorneys. Summer associates are taken out to lunch and dinner frequently. Thompson & Knight's summer program is, according to a past clerk, "a tremendous wining and dining experience."

The firm is actively trying to hire more minorities and is a member of the Dallas Consortium for Minority Hiring which promotes minority interests. Half the 1996 summer associates were women and eight were minorities.

office facilities

Every associate at Thompson & Knight gets a private office with a window and a personal computer that directly accesses Westlaw and LEXIS. Some people praised the decor of the firm—beige carpet and brass accents—as "pretty," "light," and "airy." There is no gym or cafeteria in the building, but there is an eating area with vending machines in the firm. The firm provides attorneys with parking facilities. Attorneys share secretaries. One new associate reported that the firm is generous and accommodating in paying moving expenses.

hiring practices

Thompson & Knight recruits from both Texas and out-of-state schools. People from Texas are said to have better chances of being hired; the firm, however, is reportedly willing to take on people with few Texas ties who show an interest in the firm. The 1996 class of 33 clerks included students from Georgetown, the University of Texas, Duke, Vanderbilt, and Northwestern. One former summer associate described the interview as "laid-back...They tried to talk to you rather than asking cheeseball recruiting office questions."

The century-old Thompson & Knight has grown from a small practice into one of the largest firms in Dallas. Thompson & Knight offers associates the benefits of a large firm, including the chance to choose from among a wide variety of practice areas and to specialize in their chosen areas with back-up from attorneys in other areas. Thompson & Knight also features some personal touches less typical of a large firm. The litigation department, for example, holds coffee and doughnut breakfasts every Wednesday, which associates look forward to and attend regularly, one person reported. Several people we interviewed reported that associate job satisfaction was genuine. Associates seem pleased with the reasonable hours, flexible assignment system, and sense of family and mutual respect that drive this firm.

Winstead Sechrest & Minick

Dallas Austin Houston
Mexico City

Address:	5400 Renaissance Tower, 1201 Elm Street, Dallas, TX 75270
Telephone:	(214) 745–5400
Hiring Attorney:	J. Richard White, Esq.
Contact:	Dominique L. Anderson, Recruitment Administrator; (214) 745–5306
Associate Salary:	First year $62,700 (1997); second $66,500; third $73,100; fourth $80,000; fifth $83,000; sixth $90,000; seventh $92,000; eighth $99,000
Summer Salary:	$1150/week (1997)
Average Hours:	2100 worked; 1920 billed; NA required
Family Benefits:	12 weeks maternity leave; 8 weeks paternity leave; employee assistance program
1996 Summer:	Class of 17 students; offers to 15
Partnership:	30% of entering associates from 1981-1987 were made partner
Pro Bono:	0.5% of all work is pro bono

Winstead Sechrest & Minick in 1997
138 Lawyers at the Dallas Office
1.0 Associate Per Partner

Total Partners 68			Total Associates 70			Practice Areas	
Women	10	15%	Women	20	29%	Litigation	33
All Minorities	1	1%	All Minorities	5	7%	Real Estate	26
Native-Am	1	1%	Afro-Am	5	7%	Corporate/Securities	25
						Bankruptcy	13
						Financial Institutions	10
						Labor	9
						Aviation/Products Liability	6
						Intellectual Property	6
						Environmental/Energy	5
						Insurance Coverage	5
						Public Law/Zoning/Land Use	4
						Taxation	4
						Govt. Contracts	4
						ERISA/Employee Benefits	3
						Estate Planning	2
						Construction/Surety	2

Winstead Sechrest & Minick is a young firm, founded in 1973. Winstead "is informal and democratic. Everyone works with everyone else." The attorneys are described as "friendly." There is much laughing in the halls, and the firm has an open-door policy. Associates, partners, and support staff at this firm interact on a first name basis. Some "lady partners" wear "gregarious colors," and men do not wear their jackets in the hall. Fridays are casual dress days. The firm is conservative politically and reportedly "highly Republican," although Winstead attorneys are well connected in both the Democrat and Republican parties.

practice areas

Litigation, mainly commercial, occupies 20 to 25 percent of the attorneys at Winstead. The REIT and real estate practices are hot, active areas for the firm. Winstead's corporate and intellectual property practices are expanding rapidly, while the bankruptcy and financial institutions practices remain constant. The public law section is "an amalgam of international work in Mexico, lobbying in Austin, municipal work in Dallas, and land use planning, zoning, and eminent domain questions." This department also handles highway transportation matters.

The firm's clients are mostly midsized regional corporations and financial institutions. The firm is mainly "Texas-centric," but with the passage of NAFTA and the establishment of a Mexico City office, its Mexico-related work has increased significantly.

pro bono commitment to a school

Winstead has a pro bono committee which brings in pro bono matters for the firm's attorneys to work on. Ten years ago the firm adopted an elementary school in a predominantly Latino part of Dallas and built an outdoor patio area and a jungle gym at the school. Winstead employees are also involved in numerous school activities, from tutoring and playing basketball games against the faculty to participating in Law Days. The firm also provides a Christmas gift for every student (approximately 500) at the school.

CLE program

Associates are hired to work in a particular department. New associates start by attending a three-day lawyers college to learn "the basic things you never learned in law school." A professional development program (a two-year course of training featuring instruction in ethics and substantive topics tailored to the attorney's specific practice area) has recently been implemented at the firm. The CLE program is headed by a senior attorney whose primary responsibility at Winstead is this program. Associates are "watched real closely" and receive feedback and constructive criticism on their performance. Every associate has a "shareholder" who is a supervising attorney, as well as a mentor. Twice every year, the attorneys in each section sit down with their associates to provide comprehensive feedback. The junior associates are reported to work very hard. The firm is a meritocracy, said one person. "You get ahead with good work." A past summer clerk remembered that "I worked late every night, and there were always people there at night and every weekend."

social life

When they are not working, the associates attend parties, happy hours, and sporting events together. A highlight of the social year is the annual firmwide retreat, for attorneys and their spouses or dates, at which the firm also conducts a business meeting. Many associates have married in the past few years, according to one person, so that there are very few single attorneys currently working at the firm.

diversity

Women occupy positions of influence at Winstead. Two of Winstead's prominent sections (real estate and corporate/securities) are headed by female shareholders. In one past summer, eight women attorneys in the litigation section were pregnant. "Most people were positive about this, though when the managing partner found out that the eighth woman in the same section was pregnant, he blew up," chuckled one source. Most women at the firm take the paid maternity leave offered by the firm, though "some women…come back to work right after having their babies." There is a more significant presence of women than of minorities at the firm, according to one person we interviewed. The firm has made significant progress in recruiting minority associates through the Texas/Tulane minority clerkship program, the Dallas Consortium for Minority Hiring, and intensive on-campus interviewing at national law schools. Summer associate classes for the last five years have had significant numbers of minority students, we were told.

management

People reported that Winstead is very stable financially and is carefully managed. The firm boasts that it does not pay its salaries with debt, stated one person. Partners do not guarantee any debt (including lease obligations) or pledge any collateral to banks. The firm's shareholders are willing to share the rewards of success. In 1996, during a record year, the firm provided unscheduled bonuses to associates and support staff on two occasions, in addition to their regular year-end bonuses.

beautiful offices

People praised Winstead's "awesome" facilities, which include a well-designed office space that has a high open atrium with a built-in aquarium, a gym complete with state-of-the-art fitness equipment, lockers and showers, a dining room with vending machines, and a library atop the Renaissance Tower. People complimented the firm's "beautiful common areas" decorated with "beautiful art." The firm has completed updating its computer system, and will implement new software in 1997. All attorneys have computers at their desks connected to the firm's network system, and attorneys can dial into the system from outside the office. Each attorney shares a secretary, and there is a computer word processing center as well.

organized summer program

Summer associates reported that the summer program is "extremely organized," with daily lunches planned days in advance. The firm planned activities every weekend for the summer associates, including parties at partners' houses and at clubs, and various other outings. The attorneys at the firm are reported to be "extremely friendly to the summer associates." Each summer associate is assigned a partner PLA—a personal liaison attorney—to serve as a mentor and assist in assimilation to the firm. Some people complained, however, that summer associates do not receive adequate feedback.

personality hiring

To land a job at Winstead, "you must put out a good work product and have a great personality," said one person. The firm recruits roughly half and half from Texas and national law schools. During the office visit, the firm is extremely open with students, and encourages them to ask questions concerning financial stability, compensation structure, firm governance, associate development and workload, and firm culture. "Go in with a happy, rambunctious style and confidence to get a foot in the door," counseled one person. If you do choose to summer at the firm, "Make sure you get enough work. Take it upon yourself to get feedback," advised another.

Overall, the attractive aspects of work at Winstead outweigh the few negatives. The firm celebrated its 25th year in excellent economic condition, and is expanding some practice areas such as aviation/products liability law and labor and employment. Moreover, the firm provides significant responsibility to its attorneys via a "downstreaming of work" to lower-level associates. But, along with the responsibility comes an emphasis on "an extremely heavy workload." One contact observed that Winstead stresses "business development and an attorney's ability to bring in business. If you cannot do this, you may be at a disadvantage." Finally, the firm is managed extremely democratically, which one person pointed out can be "a fault—significant changes can take a great deal of time." Overall however, people generally had more positive than negative things to say about Winstead. If a young, dynamic firm still developing a national reputation appeals to you, this may be just the firm for you.

Houston

Law Firms Ranked By Associates Per Partner

1.	ANDREWS & KURTH	0.7
2.	FULBRIGHT & JAWORSKI	1.0
3.	LIDDELL, SAPP, ZIVLEY, HILL & LABOON	1.0
4.	VINSON & ELKINS	1.0
5.	BRACEWELL & PATTERSON	1.3
6.	MAYOR, DAY, CALDWELL & KEETON	1.3
7.	BAKER & BOTTS	1.4

Law Firms Ranked by Percentage of Associates Who Make Partner (over varying years)

1.	ANDREWS & KURTH	70
2.	LIDDELL, SAPP, ZIVLEY, HILL & LABOON	67
3.	FULBRIGHT & JAWORSKI	36
4.	BRACEWELL & PATTERSON	33
5.	MAYOR, DAY, CALDWELL & KEETON	33
6.	BAKER & BOTTS	31
7.	VINSON & ELKINS	NA

Law Firms Ranked by Percentage of Pro Bono Work

1.	BAKER & BOTTS	4-6
2.	FULBRIGHT & JAWORSKI	1-3
3.	LIDDELL, SAPP, ZIVLEY, HILL & LABOON	1-3
4.	ANDREWS & KURTH	1-2
5.	BRACEWELL & PATTERSON	NA
6.	MAYOR, DAY, CALDWELL & KEETON	NA
7.	VINSON & ELKINS	NA

Law Firms Ranked by Percentage of Female Partners

1.	BRACEWELL & PATTERSON	18
2.	MAYOR, DAY, CALDWELL & KEETON	17
3.	VINSON & ELKINS	17
4.	ANDREWS & KURTH	15
5.	LIDDELL, SAPP, ZIVLEY, HILL & LABOON	15
6.	FULBRIGHT & JAWORSKI	12
7.	BAKER & BOTTS	10

Law Firms Ranked by Percentage of Female Associates

1.	BAKER & BOTTS	47
2.	MAYOR, DAY, CALDWELL & KEETON	39
3.	ANDREWS & KURTH	35
4.	LIDDELL, SAPP, ZIVLEY, HILL & LABOON	35
5.	BRACEWELL & PATTERSON	34
6.	FULBRIGHT & JAWORSKI	33
7.	VINSON & ELKINS	33

Law Firms Ranked by Percentage of Minority Partners

1.	BRACEWELL & PATTERSON	6
2.	ANDREWS & KURTH	5
3.	BAKER & BOTTS	2
4.	LIDDELL, SAPP, ZIVLEY, HILL & LABOON	2
5.	MAYOR, DAY, CALDWELL & KEETON	2
6.	VINSON & ELKINS	2
7.	FULBRIGHT & JAWORSKI	1

Law Firms Ranked By Percentage of Minority Associates

1.	ANDREWS & KURTH	14
2.	MAYOR, DAY, CALDWELL & KEETON	13
3.	VINSON & ELKINS	12
4.	LIDDELL, SAPP, ZIVLEY, HILL & LABOON	10
5.	BAKER & BOTTS	9
6.	BRACEWELL & PATTERSON	8
7.	FULBRIGHT & JAWORSKI	5

Andrews & Kurth

Houston Dallas Los Angeles New York Washington The Woodlands London

Address: 4200 Texas Commerce Tower, 600 Travis, Houston, TX 77002
Telephone: (713) 220–4200
Hiring Attorney: Steven R. Biegel and James Donnell
Contact: Jennifer Daniels, Recruiting Coordinator; (713) 220–4378
Associate Salary: First year $75,000 (1997)
Summer Salary: $1150/week plus parking (1997)
Average Hours: 2097 worked; 1861 billed; no minimum required
Family Benefits: maternity/paternity leave
1996 Summer: Class of 18 students; offers to 18
Partnership: 70% of entering associates from 1981–1987 were made partner
Pro Bono: 1–2% of all work is pro bono

Andrews & Kurth in 1997
145 Lawyers at the Houston Office
0.7 Associates Per Partner

Total Partners 75			Total Associates 49			Practice Areas	
Women	11	15%	Women	17	35%	Litigation/Labor/Environment	55
All Minorities	4	5%	All Minorities	7	14%	Bankruptcy/Corporate/Finance	50
Afro-Am	1	1%	Asian-Am	2	4%	Real Estate/Energy	19
Latino	2	3%	Latino	5	10%	Tax/Estate/ERISA	17
Native-Am	1	1%					

With its principal office in Houston, Andrews & Kurth retains prestige as a high-powered firm while exhibiting "family-like" hospitality. Founded in 1902, Andrews & Kurth still follows the work ethic that "good people acquire interesting work if they are willing to strive for it," one source commented. The close-knit relationship between partners and associates enables newcomers to receive "hands-on training" early in their careers with the chance to excel.

practice areas

Andrews & Kurth has well-known practices in the areas of real estate, bankruptcy, corporate finance, tax, and oil and gas acquisitions. On a national level, the firm represents "mostly private corporations, from the largest to smallest," noted one person. The real estate department, which consists of 35 lawyers firmwide and is reportedly one of the largest in the country, worked on the Patriot American Hotel REIT last year. The corporate finance department is "swamped with work," and staffs its projects "leanly but not at the expense of quality of work product and services." It contains a number of young partners described as "excellent." The bankruptcy department has represented large companies, including Continental Airlines and the Bank of New England. Hugh Ray is a premier attorney in the bankruptcy department. The oil and gas section served as special counsel in the privatization of the Argentine energy industry.

The firm is in the process of rebuilding its reputation at the courthouse. One person complained that the litigation department "does not get enough recognition." The firm is recognized as one of the nation's leading energy litigation firms, especially in the field of natural gas pipeline contract litigation.

Other practice areas of the firm are said to be expanding. The environmental section is well-established in the Washington office and is branching off into the Houston office. The firm is currently counseling clients engaged in superfund matters in several states, and maintains an active caseload involving compliance with hazardous waste, clean air, clean water, and occupational safety and health laws.

Pro bono work recently has been "given more weight" at the firm since Andrews & Kurth committed itself to meeting the ABA's suggested pro bono guidelines, but the firm is still far short of the 5% ABA target figure. The responsibility for taking on pro bono work is left in the hands of each individual associate. "You do it if you're interested; you don't if you're not interested," commented one source.

team system

While there are few formal rules at Andrews & Kurth, the firm has an established "team framework" for assigning work. Junior and senior associates are assigned to teams led by partners who exert the most influence. "The senior partner approach keeps people busy," said one person. Another complained that within this framework, associates "tend not to get the most interesting work." Instead, most associates are expected to gain responsibility as a "logical consequence" of their efforts. Some associates, however, "can move up" and secure responsibility early in their careers. One source told us of having an opportunity to "sell a shopping center for a large insurance company in my first year—by myself." Litigation is an area where young associates have an opportunity to excel, we were told. "It's not uncommon for young associates to begin conducting depositions the first month they are at the firm. One second year already has been to trial seven times by himself."

training

The team framework ensures that junior associates "get real hands-on training," said one person. "From the very first day, they work closely with partners." Another person noted that the training program should be more formalized because the current system allows some associates to "slip through the cracks." The firm does provide a formal in-house associate development and training program. All new litigators also attend a formal trial advocacy program at the University of Houston, where they are videotaped in mock trials.

Even associate social life is structured around "the team framework." Attorneys on a team often get together for dinner or drinks after work. There are many young attorneys at the firm, noted one person. Sports are popular among attorneys; golf stands out as the firm favorite. Annual events include a firm picnic and the annual holiday party. Andrews & Kurth does its best to woo summer associates, with the firm's social life peaking during the summer recruiting months.

conservative atmosphere

Junior associates are "treated fairly well" at Andrews & Kurth. Among the reasons new associates chose the firm, many cited "the quality of the people." "It is a good place to work," one associate commented. "Lawyers are not stuffy like at other firms." Most people described the firm's attorneys as "homogeneous" and "pretty conservative." Attorneys dress formally, but khaki pants and a jacket and tie will suffice for male associates on Fridays, noted one person.

Andrews & Kurth is "not a cutthroat place." One insider described the firm as being "humane" and a place where attorneys "are not treated like machines." While associates may "compete for good and interesting work, you don't see associates cutting each other out," noted one person. There are "no real requirements" regarding minimum billable hours. Associates work overtime, including a few nights and weekends. "People felt you should increase your hours each year," said one source.

diversity

The firm is working to recruit more minorities, according to one person, who noted that the firm now has seven minority associates, up from three just a few years ago. One person commented that the firm is "not a very comfortable place for women." However, another said the firm has "as many female associates and partners on a pro rata basis as any of the other big firms in the city." The firm is also said to be generous in terms of maternity leave. Andrews & Kurth offers three months paid leave, with extra leave available if pregnancy-related complications arise.

management

The firm is run by a management committee composed of partners. Though the firm experienced a slowdown during the early 1990s economic downturn, that is not the case today. Andrews & Kurth is very busy and has recently hired a number of laterals. The international practice has been rapidly expanding, especially in Latin America, and the firm recently gave two raises to its attorneys to make salaries competitive with other firms in the city.

hiring tips

The firm primarily hires attorneys from Texas. Andrews' recruiting tends to favor graduates from the University of Texas and the University of Houston. The firm also hires from Baylor, Harvard, the University of Virginia, and Vanderbilt; it welcomes résumés from applicants who attend schools at which Andrews does not conduct on campus interviews. "Grades are less important than at other firms, but still count," one person noted. "Being on law review is a plus, but we don't just want a bright geek," said another. Another advised prospective summer associates to appear "well-rounded."

The prevailing attitude among associates at this firm is that people enjoy working at Andrews & Kurth. "We are all friends as well as co-workers. We are a very people-oriented firm." Our contacts praised the quality of both the work experience and the mentors. For the aspiring associate, Andrews & Kurth brings a "family-like atmosphere" to a high-powered work environment. Humanity, teamwork, and hard work are hallmarks of this firm. One contact summed up nicely, "I wouldn't work for any other major law firm in the city."

Baker & Botts

Houston Austin Dallas New York Washington
Moscow

Address: 910 Louisiana Street, One Shell Plaza, Houston, TX 77002
Telephone: (713) 229–1234
Hiring Attorney: James Edward Maloney
Contact: Joan C. Schwartz, Director of Attorney Employment; (713) 229–1809
Associate Salary: First year $75,000 (package) (1997)
Summer Salary: $1150/week plus parking (1997)
Average Hours: 2100 worked; 1902 billed; no minimum required
Family Benefits: Three months paid leave for the birth, adoption, and initial care of child
1996 Summer: Class of 38 students; offers to 36
Partnership: 31% of entering associates from 1971–1985 were made partner
Pro Bono: 4–6% of all work is pro bono

Baker & Botts in 1997
212 Lawyers at the Houston Office
1.4 Associates Per Partner

Total Partners 89		
Women	9	10%
All Minorities	2	2%
Afro-Am	2	2%

Total Associates 123		
Women	58	47%
All Minorities	11	9%
Afro-Am	3	2%
Asian-Am	3	2%
Latino	5	4%

Practice Areas	
Litigation	104
Corporate	55
Tax, Bus. & Estate Planning	29
Finance	13
Energy	6
Unassigned	5

One of the oldest and most prestigious firms in Texas, Baker & Botts was founded in 1855 in Houston by James Baker, great grandfather of James Baker III

(Secretary of State under Presidents Reagan and Bush), who joined the firm in recent years. The firm has been described as fairly "formal" and "conservative," with a Republican bent, but this description has become less appropriate in recent years.

somewhat impersonal

Although it remains one of the largest firms in Houston, Baker & Botts has considerably downsized its Houston office in recent years from 262 lawyers in 1994 to 212 lawyers in 1997. Several people we interviewed commented that the size and stature of Baker & Botts can make the firm somewhat impersonal, although this perception differs among practice groups. "Once I went out to get food in the middle of the day and a partner I knew didn't even recognize me," reported one source. Overall, however, the firm has a formal, but friendly atmosphere. The attorneys are "chatty" and keep their doors open, but are somewhat reserved. The partners are said to be "unpretentious." Attorneys dress "formally" and "conservatively." Male attorneys usually wear white shirts, although seersucker suits have been sighted in the summer. Female attorneys generally wear suits with skirts, although more recently dressy pantsuits are frequently worn as well.

practice areas

Baker & Botts has a well-rounded general practice that includes litigation, corporate, bankruptcy, tax, real estate, energy, and environmental departments, said several people we interviewed. "Choose this firm because the litigation department is less specialized and departmentalized than either Vinson & Elkins or Fulbright & Jaworski," said one person. Litigation is the largest department at the firm and is well-regarded. Baker & Botts played a large role in the massive Texaco-Pennzoil case and has represented major airlines in an antitrust litigation. The firm is best-known for its transactional work. Its numerous corporate clients include energy companies, banks, and other "institutional clients." Historically, the corporate department has handled a fair amount of international work, and the firm has had a strong international intellectual property practice. However, one contact informed us that "this will probably be reduced due to the move of several international attorneys to a new Houston branch of Baker & McKenzie." We were also told that the corporate department has suffered "a combination of increased work load and a significant attrition of associates, creating more (and sometimes unreasonable) demands on corporate associates and frustrating partners trying to staff new deals. As a result, morale is low in the corporate department."

Baker & Botts "does not actively discourage" its attorneys from doing pro bono work. A partner coordinates all pro bono matters, but according to one contact, "pro bono hours are only superficially recognized. Billable hours, regardless of the amount of time spent on pro bono matters, is what counts for associates at evaluations."

generalist philosophy

New associates are not hired for a particular department. They can choose a department upon joining the firm, or they may enter the firm's General Assignment Program and sample several practice areas simultaneously. The General Assignment Program—for both lawyers and summer associates—allows lawyers the "flexibility to tailor their own practice," we were told. Summer associates also receive work through the general assignment program. Each summer associate is assigned one partner and two associates to act as mentors and to monitor the associate's progress and work. One person described this mentor program as "fantastic." People praised Baker & Botts' training program, which includes lectures and practice group meetings. In addition, young trial lawyers receive "excellent training" through a ten day program run by the National Institute of Trial Advocacy (NITA). "The training is good because of the firm's structure," said one person, highlighting the firm's generalist philosophy. Baker & Botts' feedback received mixed reviews and was described by one person as "inconsistent," and by another person as "poor." One source stated that "smart first-year associates get lots of responsibility."

Baker & Botts attorneys work hard, but the firm is "not a sweatshop," said several people we interviewed. One person remarked that "40 to 50 hours is the norm for the most hardworking, and some associates consistently do less than this." Several people commented that the hours at this firm are "not insane, so people have lives." On the other hand, one insider noted that the firm has "zero emphasis on promoting (or permitting) a balanced life style."

sports-oriented social life

With respect to social matters, an associate's life generally includes a spouse. Baker & Botts is "a marrying firm," we were told. Due in part to the firm's marriage culture, Baker & Botts' associates tend to be "quieter" than their peers at other large Houston firms. Much of the social life at Baker & Botts revolves around sports, although the firm does have several well-attended happy hours throughout the year. The firm hosts an annual golf tournament. Softball is also popular. It is conventional wisdom in the Houston legal community that Baker & Botts attorneys are tennis players, Vinson & Elkins attorneys are golfers, and Fulbright & Jaworski attorneys are hunters, noted one person. Baker & Botts hosts many social events in the summer, such as dinners, concerts, theater, and parties on weeknights and weekends. Most people with whom we spoke praised Baker & Botts' "fantastic summer program." "If you want a fun summer experience with a good law firm where you can be well-fed—go there" said one summer associate.

diversity

Baker & Botts was perceived as an ethnically homogenous firm by the people we interviewed, though one person wondered if it was any different on diversity issues from the other big Houston firms. One person described the firm as "not racist, but a Texas blue-blood firm." They are "fairly white, but don't discriminate," that person explained. Baker & Botts is "one of the only big firms in town that has black partners," noted another person. Moreover, Baker & Botts has a number of Jewish partners, and the firm has "three openly gay attorneys." In general, however, the firm has a "reputation as being stuffy and old-boy" and received mixed reviews for its sensitivity to women's concerns. The male attorneys reportedly have a "gentlemanly" attitude. They open doors and hold elevators for the female attorneys. There are several prominent female partners in litigation and in the corporate department. The firm offers paid maternity leave, and attorneys can work part-time. One contact informed us that the firm "recently adopted a formal part-time work policy for associates, but the terms of the policy show a clear intent to discourage part-time work arrangements."

hierarchical

Baker & Botts is "pretty hierarchical," commented one person. The firm has offices in Houston, Austin, Dallas, Washington, D.C., New York, and Moscow. Each office is managed by a partner-in-charge who reports to the firmwide managing partner and executive committee. The Houston office is governed by committees composed mostly of partners. "Associates don't have much say," noted one person, but a second person observed that "associates are included in some firm committees, such as the hiring committee."

office facilities

Baker & Botts occupies what one person described as a "1960s type building with 1970s decor." The firm is decorated with "unusual blonde wood. People either love it or hate it," said one contact who was less than enthusiastic. Another person, however, described the office space as "stunning." Each summer and permanent associate in the Houston office receives a private office with two windows and a personal computer. The firm has "a great [computer] network, allowing searches of all system documents from all offices; access to the network from home terminals; LEXIS, Westlaw, and

Internet access; and a computerized phone system." The firm also pays for attorneys' parking.

downsizing

The economic downturn in the early 1990s affected Baker & Botts, leading to a sizeable number of departures of associates during that period. Most recently, the economic picture has improved considerably, although as noted above the firm has continued to downsize. The firm is reportedly very busy at present, and Baker & Botts increased the 1997 first-year associates package to $75,000, in addition to raising the salaries of all associates. The earlier edition of *The Insider's Guide* reported that Baker & Botts had been "tightening up" and making fewer permanent offers to its summer associates than in the past. The recent offer rates have, however, been quite good, although the size of present summer classes is smaller now than in the past. In 1996, the firm made offers to 36 of its 38 2L summer associates.

academic emphasis in hiring

Baker & Botts has "less of a native Texan atmosphere" than some other Texas firms, said one person. The firm recruits students from all areas of the country, though most attorneys have some connection to Texas. Baker & Botts is, according to one person, "one of the brainiest firms in town." Another insider remarked that "grades are of paramount importance in hiring." The firm is "crazy for fancy-named people" and tries "to be highbrow." It reportedly looks at people in the top quarter of their class at the University of Texas, the top ten percent of their class at the University of Houston, and the top half of their classes at national law schools such as Columbia, Harvard, Stanford, the University of Chicago, the University of Virginia, and Yale.

Though the old perception that Baker & Botts is somewhat "impersonal" and "kind of stodgy" persists, the firm offers associates good work, good pay, and "a good lifestyle." On the other hand, there is continuing concern regarding associate attrition, with one insider commenting that "most are well aware that they are easily replaceable." However, the quality of the work at the firm (large, complex transactions and trials) and the abilities of the firm's attorneys ("you work with lawyers who are smart and technically excellent") are a magnet for many young attorneys wishing to practice in Houston. One person advised, "If you want the biggest deals, and only the biggest deals, and you want to work at the knee of a senior partner for training—choose Baker & Botts."

Bracewell & Patterson

Houston Austin Dallas Washington
London Almaty

Address: South Tower Pennzoil Place, 711 Louisiana, Suite 2900, Houston, TX 77002–2781
Telephone: (713) 223–2900
Hiring Attorney: Craig L. Stahl
Contact: Alice Ann Telle, Manager of Attorney Employment; (713) 221–1296
Associate Salary: First year $75,000 total package (1997)
Summer Salary: $1150/week plus paid parking (1997)
Average Hours: NA worked; NA billed; 1800 budget
Family Benefits: Health, dental, life, long-term disability and ADI; maternity/paternity leave; sabbatical; vacation; 401(K) Plan; flexible benefits plan; worker's compensation
1996 Summer: Class of 33; offers to 30
Partnership: 33% of entering associates from 1980–1983 were made partner
Pro Bono: NA

Bracewell & Patterson in 1997
160 Lawyers at the Houston Office
1.3 Associates Per Partner

Total Partners 71			Total Associates 89			Practice Areas	
Women	13	18%	Women	30	34%	Trial	59
All Minorities	4	6%	All Minorities	7	8%	Corporate & Sec.	26
Afro-Am	1	1%	Afro-Am	4	4%	Real Estate, Energy & Finance	26
Latino	3	4%	Asian-Am	1	1%	School Law	16
			Latino	2	2%	Labor	12
						Tax	5
						Wills & Estates	5
						Environmental	4
						Financial Services	4
						Appellate	3

Bracewell & Patterson is a politically but not a personally conservative firm, according to people we interviewed. At the same time, the firm is fiscally conservative, managed carefully by what one source described as "the old guard." Many attorneys are members of the Republican Party, and the atmosphere at Bracewell is lively, friendly, and tolerant. Bracewell's former hiring partner, Pat Oxford, served as the general counsel to the Republican party during the Republican Convention in Houston in 1992. The firm has, however, some outstanding Democratic party activists as well, including Carrin Patman, a former congressional candidate.

Sports Day

Sports are an important focus at Bracewell. Each spring the firm gives all attorneys the day off to attend Sports Day, a day-long organized sports retreat. In addition, every year the attorneys and summer associates play broomball on ice. Several partners have season tickets to the Rockets, and there are lots of Astros tickets floating around the firm. Available tickets are announced on the electronic bulletin board or e-mail.

tough corporate practice

Bracewell is divided into two main practice groups: corporate and litigation. The litigation practice includes the general litigation, labor litigation, and school law sections. Commercial litigation makes up the bulk of the practice, said several people we interviewed. The well-known school law section, headed by the firm's managing partner, represents school districts throughout Texas. The corporate practice includes general corporate, real estate, finance, tax, trusts and estates, banking law, oil and gas law, and regulatory work. This practice represents many big and small industries and oil and chemical-related businesses. The corporate section is by far the hardest working. The partners are reportedly difficult to work with and the section has lost a number of associates recently. The most open-minded group at the firm is the relatively newly formed real estate, energy and finance group. The partners in this practice are generally regarded as low-key and as having a good rapport with their associates. Bracewell has expanded its London office to five lawyers and plans to continue this expansion, especially in connection with the firm's opening an office in Almaty, Kazakhstan in the summer of 1997.

training

Associates are hired for a department and usually work for a single partner in that department; in the labor section, associates work for a "pool" of partners. There is little formal training at Bracewell, although the firm has increased its attention to this area in recent years, we were told. The corporate group probably has the most training of any of the sections; it meets monthly to discuss current issues and the associates also meet monthly. Bracewell sends young litigation associates for trial training at the University of Houston. This program culminates in actual mock trials conducted in the state courts before real judges on Saturdays in the fall. Generally, however, training is "hands-on." Feedback depends on the partner to whom an associate is assigned.

Like training, pro bono work at Bracewell is "individually motivated, but encouraged," according to one person. Associates' ability to do pro bono "depends on your partner," reported one person. Partner Marcy Kurtz coordinates the pro bono program at Bracewell and offers cases for which attorneys may volunteer. The firm does pro bono work for civic, charitable, and religious organizations as well as for indigent clients. "A lot of people do pro bono, but it is not stressed," asserted one insider.

informal Bracewell is reported to be more informal and friendly than some of the more established Houston firms. The people we interviewed described Bracewell as "livable" and "relaxed." This firm is "not a closed-door mausoleum," explained one person. Bracewell's associates seem happy, "more than at other firms I know," said one person. Bracewell is generally a young firm. Most associates are in their twenties. A good number of the associates are married, but the married associates go out together with their spouses. Group dinners are a popular recreational activity at the firm. The firm hosts one formal dance each year for its attorneys.

diversity Bracewell is said to provide a decent environment for women. The firm "should do better, but is going in the right direction," said one person. Bracewell has a high number of female partners relative to other firms in the area, though we were told that "of the three women up for partner recently, two were passed up." As for racial diversity, Bracewell is "coming around slowly but surely," said one person. The firm is recruiting minorities heavily and doing well in the lower classes. There are currently four African-American associates and several Latino attorneys at the firm.

Bracewell was founded by and is still managed to some degree by what one person termed the "old guard." Two of the firm's three founders are still alive (the two Bracewells). Despite the continuing presence of the "old crew," the partnership is very democratic, according to one source. Bracewell has no managing or executive committee with voting power. Instead, all of the partners "vote on everything" that is significant. There are also a number of other committees that administer specific matters. One insider informed us that this democratic process appears to work, although the firm may be getting too big to continue this democratic management system. One person criticized the firm, moreover, for not being sufficiently forthcoming with the associates: "There is a definite feeling with the partners that the associates should be on a need-to-know basis only and the associates are given information or mis/disinformation about a number of firm-related topics." We were also told that the firm has a "senior partner" designation, but "who is or is not a 'senior partner' is not disclosed to associates," reported one insider. A firm spokesperson informed us that "the managing partner meets with all associates after each of the general meetings of the partners to inform the associates of and discuss the partners' actions. Each associate is paired with a liaison partner from another practice area for the purpose of sharing firm information and having a non-supervisory partner with whom the associate may address issues confidentially."

growth by laterals Bracewell's partners have been conservative and did not over expand the firm in the mid 1980s. The firm has, however, hired many laterals recently and is expected to increase by 50 attorneys in the next year or two. Although almost everyone at the firm knows everyone else's name, the increasing number of laterals has made this more difficult of late. In response, the firm has recently begun to make an effort to integrate the laterals in a more organized fashion. The relatively modest size of Bracewell has allowed it thus far to have a "family-like atmosphere, but how long this can last with the firm's recent growth is questionable," noted one contact.

ticky-tack penny pinching

Bracewell is "not very progressive in fringe benefits," complained one contact. Another insider chastised the firm for its "ticky-tack penny pinching (*e.g.* no 401K matching)" which has "caused some fallout" among associates. Bracewell associates are compensated with a salary plus a bonus. The firm recently instituted merit bonuses for fifth-year associates and up. We were told, however, that "despite partnership assertions to the contrary, the popular belief is that the sole purpose of the merit bonus is to compensate for the salary differential between Bracewell upper-level associates and other upper-level associates around town." Bracewell has also recently changed its partnership track to a two-tier system. After seven years, an associate is eligible to become a non-profit participating partner. Then, sometime within two years after becoming a first-tier partner, one is eligible to become a full partner. The structure is still a little unclear, however, reported one contact. In February of this year, "all new partners were non-participatory."

office facilities

Each attorney at the firm has a private office with a window and a personal computer. There are "windows everywhere," said one person who nonetheless complained about the "ugly orange carpet"—which, we were told, is "probably here to stay, given the number of UT partners who bleed 'burnt orange'." Bracewell is expanding its office space and expects to move its growing real estate, energy and finance group to a soon–to–be–built–out floor which was previously used for storage and a mock courtroom. The computer system is "equal to, if not better, than the norm around town." Associates can access LEXIS, Netscape, and CD-ROM libraries from their computers in their offices, and the firm is in the process of implementing desktop faxing. One insider praised the new computer apparatus as "cool." The library was described as "beautiful" by one insider and "hideous" by a second, and the librarians are "incredibly helpful."

hiring tips

Bracewell hires many clerks from the top of their classes at Texas schools. The University of Texas has the largest contingent, with other clerks coming from the University of Houston, Baylor, and, to a lesser extent, Duke, Vanderbilt, Tulane, SMU, Harvard, and the University of Virginia.

In hiring, the firm looks for personality and friendliness as well as high grades which results, according to one contact, in the "happier, more productive attorneys" found at the firm. There are "few boring nerd types" at this firm. Show them that "you will be effective interpersonally," advised one veteran of the process. Once the firm decides to extend a student an offer, it reportedly works hard to lure that person to the firm. After one person got his offer, he received 21 letters urging him to accept.

People chose Bracewell because it employs the "nicest people in the world." There is good work but no arrogance to be found at this firm, applauded one person who chose Bracewell because it does "high-quality legal work in an atmosphere that is less prestige-hungry and pushy" than some larger firms. Another person remarked that Bracewell is the "only firm in town that combines small firm friendliness with major firm presence and prestige."

Fulbright & Jaworski

Houston Austin Dallas Los Angeles New York San Antonio Washington
Hong Kong London

Address: 1301 McKinney Street, Suite 5100, Houston, TX 77010–3095
Telephone: (713) 651–5151
Hiring Attorney: Tom Godbold
Contact: (Ms.) Leslie Stiver, Recruiting Coordinator; (713) 651–5518
Associate Salary: First year $75,000 package (1997)
Summer Salary: $1150/week (1997)
Average Hours: 1900–2100 worked; 1850–1950 billed; NA required
Family Benefits: Twelve weeks paid maternity leave (cbc unpaid)
1996 Summer: Class of 32 students; offers to 25
Partnership: 36% of entering associates from 1984–1987 were made partner
Pro Bono: 1–3% of all work is pro bono

Fulbright & Jaworski in 1997
262 Lawyers at the Houston Office
1.0 Associate Per Partner

Total Partners 132		
Women	17	12%
All Minorities	1	1%
Latino	1	1%

Total Associates 130		
Women	43	33%
All Minorities	7	5%
Afro-Am	4	3%
Asian-Am	2	1%
Latino	1	3%

Practice Areas	
Litigation	97
Corporate/Banking/Business	37
Tax/T&E/Emp. Benefits	34
Health/Administration	18
Energy & Environmental	17
Real Estate/Oil & Gas	17
Labor & Employment Law	13
Admiralty	10
Intellectual Property	8
Public Law	7
Family Law	4

Fulbright & Jaworski is deliberately "Texas." Even in a state of patriots, Fulbright's deeply felt patriotism for its state is immediately apparent. The firm's offices are liberally dotted with "Texas memorabilia" of all kinds. One contact joked that some of its attorneys go "kicker dancing" or engage in other traditional Texas entertainment after work. Sociability is not the only thing occupying attorneys' time at Fulbright, however; the firm, reportedly, "has been the top revenue producing law firm in the State of Texas for many years."

Hard work and "billing hours are a...very big deal." Most associates are "at the firm on Saturday," said one contact, noting that those "who didn't work on weekends...got teased by other lawyers." The work atmosphere during the day is "very professional." Men wear conservative suits and women "don't wear dresses." They "mainly dress in suits." The political atmosphere is also fairly conservative.

exhausting social life

Influenced by the Texas culture, social life is also important at Fulbright. The firm sponsors a full range of elaborate social events throughout the year, peaking during the summer when the non-work activities become almost exhausting. "You have to be willing to spend 24 hours a day, six days a week" to attend all the firm's social events, commented one participant, adding that by the end of the summer program, "you don't want to have a nice meal again for six months." One literalist contact, unappreciative of the hyperbole of the foregoing comment, instructed us that "if one were to try to attend all of the [summer] social events, it would indeed be taxing. However,...nobody expects the summer associates to attend every social function. The reason that there are so many social functions is to accommodate the diverse interests of the summer associates." Fulbright treats summer associates to lunch almost every day and frequently to dinner as well. There is an annual formal dance and retreat that is commonly located in a resort in nearby Galveston or the Woodlands.

practice areas

Fulbright is most well-known for its litigation practice, which is organized into 10 to 12 teams and which, despite its recent drop in size, employs over a third of the firm's attorneys. The litigation group decreased in size from 113 lawyers in 1994 to 97 attorneys this year. The practice consists of a broad range of general civil litigation matters. About half the litigation teams are known as being very "aggressive," reported one source. The firm's excellent antitrust group is also reportedly "aggressive." Its attorneys "work all the time," said one source, explaining that "winning and working hard are very important to them. They bill tons of hours." The firm's trusts and estates group, which reportedly houses a "huge Baptist contingent," is "very stable," according to one contact. The "very stressful" tax group is home to partners who are "tough task masters," said one source, noting that there has been a significant defection of associates from this group. With foreign offices in Hong Kong and London and a close relationship with firms in Mexico and Zurich, Fulbright handles some international work but does not have an organized international department. As with most Texas firms, Fulbright's pro bono practice does not constitute a large percentage of the firm's work. One person noted, however, that partner Jim Sales, former chairman of the State Bar of Texas, strongly encourages pro bono work. Another person informed us that the firm has received "several awards for its participation in the Houston Volunteer Lawyers Association, which assists low income clients on civil matters."

summer rotation

Summer associates rotate through different practices for two to three weeks each. They are assigned an associate and a partner supervisor as well as a "social buddy," referred to as a "sponsor" at the firm. Because the firm hires associates into particular sections, it is very important to work with a group "that needs someone at the end of the summer," stressed one contact. This person related that one summer, six or seven summer associates worked in the labor section, which at the close of the summer did not need any new associates. Before working at Fulbright for the summer, it is important to talk to as many people at the firm as possible to learn which groups are growing and hiring, advised this source. Once it assigns a new associate to an area, Fulbright prefers that the attorney continue to work in that area. However, if the associate finds that the area is not where he or she wants to practice, Fulbright will attempt to move the associate to their area of choice if that practice area can accommodate the associate.

extensive formal training

Fulbright is proud of its extensive formal training programs. Entering litigation associates participate in a series of formal training programs, many of which are conducted in the firm's impressive in-house courtroom. The series, which begins with limited deposition exercises, continues with discovery and trial demonstrations by attorneys and the judiciary, and then culminates in a full mock trial conducted by first-year associates. The programs involve extensive critiques of each individual's performance by the firm's attorneys. The corporate sections receive "similar training through seminars and lectures." Day-to-day feedback on associate work product largely depends on the partners in the practice or team to which the associate is assigned. Summer associates receive regular formal feedback. At the end of each rotation through a practice, some of the attorneys discuss and critique the work product submitted during that rotation.

Each practice offers considerably varying responsibilities. Some associates in the insurance defense and tort litigation departments handle cases within their first year at the firm, reported one contact. By contrast, the commercial litigation, environmental, and antitrust teams primarily handle large, high-stakes, and complex cases, sometimes relegating associates to "document production for years," said one source.

diversity Fulbright's atmosphere for female attorneys received mixed reviews. A number of female partners work at the firm, including Carmody Baker, a star on the products liability team. In a past summer, a number of attorneys arranged a special female summer associate dinner to discuss women's issues with some of the firm's female attorneys. While the planned and structured social events provide a comfortable atmosphere for women and men, much of the firm's informal social life is "male-oriented," said one woman interviewee. The firm's "emphasis on billing hours and on performance" also makes the firm "not sympathetic to people taking care of children," commented this woman, noting that "you have to make your mark before you have a family." A firm spokesperson informed us, however, that the aforementioned Carmody Baker "had a family before she was made partner at the firm. In fact, she was made partner while pregnant with her second child." Fulbright's commitment to women's issues is "average," summarized one contact, stating that "they still have problems in this area, but not huge problems." Few racial minorities work at Fulbright.

management from beyond Fulbright is so large that "you don't really realize that there are people managing the place. It's more like working for IBM," one contact told us. The firm is run by a management committee headed by managing partner, Gus Blackshear, who was described as "open" and "very nice and personable." Notwithstanding Blackshear's leadership, we were told that currently the firm is not very "open and receptive to associates." For example, the firm reorganized its litigation sections by "thrusting people around" to work with new people without entertaining much associate input. Associates felt that "it was a decision from beyond," commented one source.

Decorated in dark wood with marble floors, Fulbright's offices are some of the most beautiful offices in Houston. The firm occupies 13 floors, with a library on almost every one. The support and library staff are "excellent." The firm is in the process of switching to Windows NT-based Pentium pro computers with CD-ROMs for each lawyer. Further, every attorney has access to the Internet from their computer.

hiring tips As one of Houston's most prestigious firms, it is very competitive to land a summer associate job at Fulbright & Jaworski. The initial hiring decisions screen candidates out based on grades, work experience, and the law school attended, according to one successful applicant, who claimed that students from the University of Texas need to be in the top quarter of their class, and those from South Texas need to be in the top 10 percent of their class. The firm also seeks to hire "someone willing to work very hard...someone who is hungry and ambitious, yet gets along well with other people," commented another source. Fulbright interviews at over 25 law schools and job fairs nationwide, according to a firm spokesperson.

Fulbright's callback interviews are low-pressure, usually involving individual meetings with six to 12 of the firm's attorneys, who ask very little about law school or law-related matters, according to one contact. Rather, they want to learn something about you as a person. Most "cut out the bull and try to talk you into coming to the place," said another, noting that in most interviews, at least one person will close the door and say, "I looked over your résumé, and you're the type of person we want here. What can I tell you about the firm to get you to come here?"

When asking our sources if there are any drawbacks to working at Fulbright & Jaworski, one enthusiastic contact replied: "The major drawback that I see is that Fulbright's extensive training program and ability to give young associates experience is so well recognized in the city that many firms in the city attempt to steal away our young associates. However, it's not bad to be wanted."

Liddell, Sapp, Zivley, Hill & LaBoon

Houston Austin Dallas

Address: 3400 Texas Commerce Tower, 600 Travis, Houston, TX 77002
Telephone: (713) 226–1200
Hiring Attorney: Marcus A. Watts
Contact: Lesley Keller, Director of Recruiting; (713) 226–1246
Associate Salary: First year $76,000 (package) (1997)
Summer Salary: $1175/week plus paid parking (1997)
Average Hours: NA
Family Benefits: 12 weeks paid maternity leave
1996 Summer: Class of 44 students; offers to 37 (all 3 offices)
Partnership: 67% of entering associates from 1982–1988 were made partner
Pro bono: 1–3% of all work is pro bono

Liddell, Sapp, Zivley, Hill & LaBoon (firmwide) in 1997
163 Lawyers at the Firm
1.0 Associate Per Partner

Total Partners 79		
Women	12	15%
All Minorities	2	2%
Afro-Am	1	1%
Latino	1	1%

Total Associates 81		
Women	28	35%
All Minorities	8	10%
Afro-Am	2	2%
Asian-Am	1	1%
Latino	4	5%
Native Am	1	1%

Practice Areas (Houston)	
Litigation	53
Corporate	31
Banking & Real Estate	22
Admiralty	14
Tax/T&E/Emp. Ben	14
Intellectual Property	6
Labor & Employment	5
Energy	4
Environmental	4

Liddell Sapp is best known as a well-respected Texas banking firm, although its corporate and litigation practices have gained "significant local and statewide recognition" over the past decade. Both the people and the practice at this firm have a distinct Texas flavor. This "real Texas firm" is Houston's second oldest, and its attorneys are "a friendly Texas bunch," reported one insider. Liddell Sapp was founded in 1916 as a small commercial practice. The firm celebrated its 80th anniversary with much fanfare this past year. According to one person, Mr. Liddell, after living through the Depression, decided that it was wise to be cautious and to keep the firm small. Mr. Sapp, who believed the firm needed to expand to meet the growing needs of its clients, got his way in the 1960s after Mr. Liddell died. The firm prospered and grew into the large, three office firm that it is today, with particularly significant growth occurring in the past few years.

banking and corporate

Banking and corporate are reported to be among the strongest departments at the firm. Commercial litigation is another standout area that "is making lots of money and has big clients," said one person. Many of the firm's clients are banks in Texas or the Southwest. Texas Commerce Bank, the biggest bank in Houston, "is a mainstay" and the main client of the firm; the firm's offices are located in the Texas Commerce Tower building. The firm does corporate work for a number of publicly-traded companies, and First Amendment litigation and counseling for the *Houston Chronicle* and a number of television stations. Medical malpractice defense work "is catching on," said one person. Another speculated that the firm will take on more tort litigation in the future. The firm recently added an intellectual property section, and has a growing labor law practice.

Pro bono work has not been strongly emphasized at Liddell Sapp, and according to one contact "could be emphasized more." However, the firm has represented the Salvation Army, the Houston Symphony, the Open Door Mission, the Lighthouse for the Blind, and other agencies on a pro bono basis. Although there is not much talk about pro bono work at the firm, some partners spend significant time representing the firm's pro bono clients. The firm takes on pro bono cases through the local bar association, and some attorneys do volunteer civic work and are involved in politics.

flexible work arrangement

Associates are not hired for particular sections and have significant flexibility to work in more than one area to determine the type of work they enjoy the most. One contact informed us that "the fact that the firm does not hire by section is one of the main reasons I came to work here. The firm...has 'practice areas' of which you can be a primary or secondary member. I am a primary member of one group and a secondary member of two others." Additionally, this contact elaborated, "associates are not assigned to work with a particular partner." Instead, "you have the opportunity to work with partners who seem interesting or have a practice you find particularly interesting. I have worked with every partner in my primary practice area, though I have now settled in with the two or three whose practice and personality fit well with my goals and personality." The training and experience that associates receive are said to vary with the individual partners. Feedback is also contingent on the particular partners for whom an associate works, and is generally not satisfactory. "They tried, but were not always efficient," observed one person. Another person commented that "structured feedback" was hard to come by, while still a third contact characterized feedback as "sporadic."

We received mixed views on the organizational structure at Liddell Sapp, with some people maintaining that the firm is hierarchical, with clear distinctions between partners and associates, and others claiming the opposite. The key here appears to be the practice group one is located in. Political opinions at the firm "vary from very liberal to very conservative," we were told. The firm is somewhat "formal," according to one person. The lawyers dress fairly conservatively. The men do not wear their jackets in the halls and only put them on when they leave the office, said one source. "Women frequently wear pants, especially since the arrival of the new class (7 out of 12 of whom are women)," reported one insider.

hard work required

The associates at Liddell Sapp "work hard to get ahead," with "the partners carrying more than their fair share of the load," reported one insider. Working on the weekends is said to be common, though not likely more so than at other large firms in the city. One person commented that "billable hours for associates are not overly emphasized," while another noted that "the key thing to note is that nobody here is keeping track of who is here on weekends. You don't have to come in on weekends 'to be seen' by the partners." The people we interviewed told us that most associates at the firm seem happy, though one person said that associates' happiness often "depends on the partner they are working with."

friendly culture

"Friendly" was the word most used to describe Liddell Sapp. People praised the "really nice people," the "extremely friendly work environment" and the open door policy at the firm. The firm hosts some structured social events such as the annual Christmas party, but most of the social interaction among associates is informal. Associates often play sports together. Tennis and golf are the favorites of Liddell Sapp attorneys, said one person. Another noted that "playing golf and hunting" are popular among attorneys at this firm. One person pointed out that there is a "strong emphasis on family at the firm; most attorneys are married and that positively impacts the culture."

diversity

Liddell Sapp received good marks for diversity. There are a number of female and two minority partners and two African-American associates at the firm. Additionally, the entering 1997 associate class includes two African-American women. One person told us that a lot of women at the firm have recently had children. Two or three women currently work part-time as staff attorneys. The firm is reportedly extremely accommodating of people with physical disabilities, and is generally wheelchair-accessible.

management

Liddell Sapp is reportedly "well-managed" and boasts "a solid group of rainmakers." There have been no layoffs at the firm. There is little opportunity for associate input, however, said another person. Associates are paid a salary plus a bonus determined by the partners based on their hours billed and their work product, we were told. Compensation is said to be on the high end for Houston. We heard some complaints that the firm does not pay for parking, something "most other large firms in the city do."

Liddell Sapp occupies six floors in the Texas Commerce Tower, which, according to one person, is a nice building in which to work. The firm's offices are decorated with "traditional dark wood." One person praised the firm's library. Associates at Liddell Sapp all get their own offices with windows. Each attorney has a portable laptop computer. The firm is reportedly short on staff: "triple secretarial assignments are common and we do not have a word processing pool," reported one contact.

recruitment

Although Liddell Sapp cut back its recruiting program somewhat in the recession-marked early 1990s, it has more recently expanded its program. In the summers of 1995 and 1996, "the firm hired a combined 55 second-year summer associates and extended offers to over 90% of them," one insider informed us. The firm's 1997 summer class numbers around 50. According to one contact, "the recruiting goes all out wining and dining. At a minimum, clerks have lunch with two to three attorneys every week. There are many planned events with small groups of clerks and attorneys."

hiring tips

When it comes to landing a job at this firm, people told us that grades are important but personality counts as well. Where you went to school is important, said one person. "Ivy League is good," said another. The firm also looks for non-Ivy Leaguers from the tops of their classes, according to one successful applicant. One person reported that many attorneys at the firm graduated from the University of Texas or the University of Houston law schools. Interest in the region is a factor in hiring. In interviewing, "be into Texas," counseled one person. "Be smart and confident," a former summer associate advised. Past summer hires remembered their interviewers as "nice." Once the firm decides that it wants you, it will work hard to get you. The firm is said to have persistent and "very aggressive" recruiting tactics. One person with offers from all of the major firms in Houston reported that various associates from Liddell Sapp sent her between 30 and 40 Christmas cards when she was deciding where to go. "It made me feel uncomfortable," she said.

Liddell Sapp pays its associates well to work hard with nice people in a friendly medium-sized atmosphere. The firm's banking, corporate, and litigation practices, and its friendly attitude are what make this firm stand out. All practice areas are "extremely busy," and hiring and partnership decisions at the firm are based "very much on individual merit, not on reading specified numbers, thus removing competition among peers to a large extent." Our contacts praised the flexibility at the firm ("you are given time to find your niche"), as well as the early opportunities for client contact ("we are encouraged to know the clients and are more than just ghost writers for the partners"). If you like friendly colleagues, early opportunities for responsibility, Texas, or any combination of the above, then you should give Liddell Sapp a long look—and if you do, you may receive some extra Christmas cards this Yuletide season.

Mayor, Day, Caldwell & Keeton

Houston Austin

Address: 700 Louisiana, Suite 1900, Houston, TX 77002
Telephone: (713) 225–7000
Hiring Attorney: Thomas A. Hagemann
Contact: Gail Gerber, Recruiting Coordinator; (713) 225–7024
Associate Salary: First-year $76,000/year (including bonuses) (1997)
Summer Salary: $1150/week (1997)
Average Hours: 2000 worked; 1900 billed; NA required
Family Benefits: Maternity leave; paternity leave if primary caregiver; cafeteria plan; insurance; savings plan
1996 Summer: Class of 29; offers to 24
Partnership: 33% of entering associates from 1984–1985 were made partner
Pro Bono: NA

Mayor, Day, Caldwell & Keeton in 1997
101 Lawyers at the Houston Office
1.3 Associates Per Partner

Total Partners 41		
Women	7	17%
All Minorities	1	2%
Asian-Am	1	2%

Total Associates 54		
Women	21	39%
All Minorities	7	13%
Afro-Am	2	4%
Latino	5	9%

Practice Areas	
Litigation	35
Corporate	19
Public Law/Public Finance	13
Energy/Environmental	11
Real Estate	8
Tax/Trusts & Estates	5
Employee Benefits	4

Mayor, Day, Caldwell & Keeton employs some of the happiest and brightest attorneys in Houston. Though it is difficult to get a job at this selective and "very intellectual firm," there is not much competition among associates once they are hired. One source remarked that "almost everyone is willing to help out those in need. Young associates have plenty of resources here." The attorneys at Mayor Day are said to have "really impressive résumés." At the same time, one source described the attorneys at Mayor Day as "a group of down-to-earth people. It is kind of amazing how friendly everyone is and how well people get along." After leaving this firm, said another, "you will have made the most sincere friends—not just for recruiting purposes—people you would want to keep in touch with. That is the most important thing there."

tolerant and diverse

Mayor Day is frequently described as "laid-back" and "tolerant." This medium-sized firm is "not hierarchical." Attorneys at the firm come from "diverse" backgrounds and are "easy to get along with." Mayor Day is "one of the few firms where I felt I could be myself and not have to alter my personality," said one person.

loose practice structure

While Mayor Day has formally organized departments, its practice is loosely structured and often attorneys' practices span across departmental lines. The firm occupies three floors of office space, one of which houses the litigation section and some smaller sections; another contains the transactional and public law sections. These floors and the practice areas "remain somewhat distinct."

practice areas

People we interviewed praised Mayor Day's litigation practice as "outstanding." The firm handles both commercial and tort litigation, including products liability, medical malpractice, and toxic tort cases. One person described the public law section, which advises city and county governments on eminent domain questions, bond issues, and other matters, as "one of the greatest public law practices in the country." The Houston Metropolitan Transit Authority is a significant client of this section, which also represents a consortium of energy users. The smaller corporate practice also received praise. One person referred to the firm's corporate practice as its "competitive advantage." The litigation, public law, and corporate sections are said to be expanding. The firm does a small amount of work involving Mexico. Mayor Day represents medium- and large-sized corporations, including many Texas-based clients. Texas Children's Hospital, Lyondell Petrochemical, W. R. Grace, and Battle Mountain Gold Company are a few of the firm's clients. The firm also is a member of DuPont's primary law firm network.

The firm "somewhat encourages" pro bono, said one person, but there is "not much coordination" of available pro bono matters. "You do it on your own." Attorneys can bring their own projects to the firm. Several lawyers recently worked on a death penalty appeal, and others have worked for arts groups and various political groups. Pro bono hours are "counted just as other billable hours at the end of the year (for purposes of bonus/reviews, etc.)."

minimal formal training

There is little formal training at Mayor Day. Attorneys are hired for a particular practice, but have flexibility in deciding where to work. While relatively infrequent, they can transfer among practice areas, and some work in two areas at once while they decide what work they want to do, explained one person. The litigation group participates in the National Institute of Trial Advocacy (NITA) trial practice program, but most training at this firm is "hands-on." There is a lot of contact with partners, said one person. Another person commented that "because associates tend to work directly with partners, associates get a lot of responsibility, exposure, and client contact very early on." They "toss you in the water" but will be there if you have questions. It is not unusual for a second- or third-year litigation attorney to handle a small litigation case on her own, said one person we interviewed.

Mayor Day stresses high-quality work, and attorneys at the firm work hard. Attorneys work some Saturdays and some evenings. There is a "direct connection between the hours you work and partnership," said one person; another exclaimed, however, that this was "not true this year!" A third contact pointed out to us that "there is not a significant focus on simply *billing* hours. There is little or no encouragement to put in face time."

relaxed office atmosphere

Everyone we interviewed praised Mayor Day's "friendly" and "relaxed" atmosphere. They noted the good relations between the office staff and the attorneys. People described the attorneys as "chatty," and reported that both partners and associates are friendly outside the office. "Partners are very active in the social life of the firm," said one person. Another person commented that the partners "get crazy" at firm formals. The firm hosts an annual party at Christmas, as well as a black tie anniversary party and a formal dance during the summer. Mayor Day has a relaxed attitude toward attorney attire. Women wear dresses and pant suits as well as more traditional suits. Male attorneys sport "a lot of bright, non-conservative ties."

more liberal than other firms

The attorneys at Mayor Day span the political spectrum. The four name partners, all of whom are still at the firm, hold different political views. The firm is "not real left wing, but more liberal than any other firm in Houston," commented one person. Another person remarked that Mayor Day is "more liberal politically and socially and not as stuffy as more traditional firms." Attorneys are active in both the Democratic and Republican parties as campaigners and fundraisers.

diversity

Mayor Day was praised for its diversity and tolerance. "People there tend to be sensitive to those issues," remarked one observer. The firm is reputedly a good place for women, who represent almost 20% of the firm's partners. One person called Mayor Day "one of the best firms in Houston for gay or lesbian attorneys" because of its tolerant attitude. Mayor Day employs a significant number of minority attorneys, and a firm spokesperson noted that more than 25% of the 1997 summer class are minority students.

open management

Mayor Day was formed in 1982 when a group of partners and associates left Butler & Binion because they wanted to build a "top notch mid-sized" firm. The management has attempted to grow the firm at a controlled pace while "they strive for high-quality work and a good client list." The firm is managed by partners, but due to its small size, "anyone who has something to say will be heard." There have been no layoffs at the firm, which is said to be "one of the fastest-growing firms in town." The firm has grown by more than a third in the past five years.

In addition to a base salary that is determined by the number of years they have been with the firm, associates receive a bonus after their first year, determined by the hours they work and the quality of their work. The salary increases by $3,000 to $8,000 each year, not including bonuses, and there have been "bigger raises the past two years—across the board," one insider informed us. The firm allows associates who do not make partner to "stick around for a while" and helps them to find alternate jobs. The firm "brags about its placement rates" in this endeavor.

office facilities

Mayor Day is located in the NationsBank Center, a "spectacular, cathedral-like building" designed by Philip Johnson. One person described the "modern" office as "spacious, not particularly fancy or outrageous, but tasteful." The name partners are big art connoisseurs, said another person, so the office boasts "some really fine contemporary art." All associates get their own offices with windows and computers. One person reported that the equipment is in good shape.

summer program

Former summer associates praised Mayor Day's summer program, which includes a firm sponsored weekend affair to Lake Travis in Austin. The firm charters a houseboat and everyone goes fishing and swimming, recalled one person. From time to time, the firm hosts a big party, such as dinner with the mayor of Houston or a black-tie party. There are also frequent informal happy hours at bars, concerts, and dances, plus four to five lunches and two dinners per week paid for by the firm. Each summer associate is given a social mentor (an associate) and is assigned to at least one partner for obtaining assignments. One person stated that there was "a lot of partner contact" in the summer program.

Ivy League orientation in hiring

Mayor Day has selective hiring criteria. The firm recruits on campus primarily at eight schools: Columbia, Harvard, Michigan, Chicago, the University of Houston, the University of Texas, the University of Virginia, and Yale. Although Mayor Day "will accept résumés from everywhere and will interview any qualified candidate," people told us that Mayor Day has a "real Ivy League inclination in its hiring" and a "strong preference for Harvard, Yale, and Texas people," who are said to constitute a large number at the firm. Mayor Day has become more grade-conscious recently and has an "intellectual emphasis in recruiting," but the firm "also wants people with personality. They are looking for an interesting person—one who can work with others." The firm "will take someone with above-average grades at an Ivy school with a pleasant enough personality, or someone on law review from a Texas school with a personality plus," claimed one successful applicant.

Once someone is hired into the summer program, she has a strong chance of receiving an offer of permanent employment. Summer associates will "get a job unless they mess up—like innocent until proven guilty," remarked one insider. However, another contact cautioned that "summer associates are expected to work responsibly and to produce quality work. Work product is an important factor in the review process of summer associates."

Mayor Day is said to be "one of those rare places where you can do big firm work in a medium-sized firm." One insider told us that "Mayor Day has great opportunities workwise, yet still remains relatively small (or has that feel). I think Mayor Day is the best firm in Houston. It's a good place to learn and the people are extremely bright and friendly. For the most part, partners are genuinely interested in ensuring that associates are happy, and are getting the experience necessary to develop their careers." Another contact praised Mayor Day as "the perfect combination of a top-notch law firm and a large support staff with a small firm atmosphere—everybody knows one another. There are no real boundaries between partners and associates. The partners' doors are always open. It's an open and fun environment." If you have the credentials to get hired and want to work with supportive and friendly people, this "anti-elitist," laid-back, "intellectual but not at all snobby" firm may be just the place for you.

Vinson & Elkins

Houston Austin Dallas Washington
London Moscow Singapore

Address: 1001 Fannin, 2300 First City Tower, Houston, Texas 77002-6760
Telephone: (713) 758–2222
Hiring Attorney: T. Mark Kelly
Contact: Patty Calabrese, Director of Attorney Employment; (713) 758-4544
Associate Salary: First year $70,500 (1996)
Summer Salary: $1,150/week (1997)
Average Hours: 1977 worked; 1942 billed; NA required
1996 Summer: Class of 64 students; offers to 56
Partnership: NA
Pro bono: NA

Vinson & Elkins in 1997
330 Lawyers at the Houston Office
1.0 Associate Per Partner

Total Partners 169		
Women	28	17%
All Minorities	3	2%
Afro-Am	1	1%
Latino	2	1%

Total Associates 161		
Women	53	33%
All Minorities	20	12%
Afro-Am	6	4%
Asian-Am	2	1%
Latino	12	7%

Practice Areas	
Litigation	131
Business and International.	51
Tax ERISA	34
Corporate	27
Public Finance	19
Health	14
Labor & Employment	15
Intellectual Property	14
Administrative/Environmental	12
Energy	12

Vinson & Elkins (V&E) is among the oldest, largest, and most prestigious firms in Houston, but its atmosphere is anything but old and stuffy. The firm takes an "entrepreneurial approach towards young lawyers," offering them great training and a variety of work. Moreover, V&E is a "firm that likes to party."

bouyant social life

Stories abound at V&E about "sex scandals in the 1980s. The firm once had a reputation for being the most fast and loose in Houston," said one person, relaying what is alleged to be "common knowledge at the firm." The famous *L.A. Law* scene in which Arnie Becker and Roxanne fell through the floor into a partner's office while locked in a romantic interlude is rumored to have been based on an event at V&E. In the actual scenario, the unlucky couple got "stuck between floors," claimed one source. Legend holds that a number of years ago, some partners and associates threw a nonfirm bachelor party to which they invited a female stripper. One summer associate reportedly was offended, and the firm was "embarrassed" by the incident. The firm has "calmed down" since the 1980s, but maintains its buoyant social atmosphere, reported another contact.

variety of work

Attorneys at V&E work as hard as they party and have great variety in their assignments. Everyone we interviewed praised V&E's "diversity of clients." The firm is employed by both big businesses and small clients in a wide range of areas. Lawyers are hired for a particular practice section, but can transfer among departments and can "pick and choose" their work within that department, said one source. Associates can choose to work on a small client's case and get a lot of responsibility early, often as the first- or second-in-charge of these cases, or they can choose to take a less prominent role on bigger matters, stated one contact.

practice areas

For years, "V&E's foothold in the Houston economy was oil and gas law and litigation," but it is now "a huge firm that has everything." The litigation department is said to be "outstanding" and very busy. The business litigation section is "high-powered" and "booming." The tort litigation section handles medical malpractice defense and insurance defense cases. The firm represents many hospitals and doctors. The general litigation section is the largest section at the firm, said one source, who also claimed it lacks "cohesiveness." One person we interviewed warned against working in this section because it is "unwieldy." The appellate attorneys are "haggard and overworked," but seem secure in their jobs, said one contact. Antitrust litigation is strong, reported another. V&E recently has begun taking on more contingency and high-profile commercial litigation cases. The employment litigation section is also busy and contains several nationally recognized partners.

V&E boasts a number of strong business sections and represents a large number of banks. The firm's public law section was touted by one source as one of the best public law practices in the country. V&E has foreign offices in Moscow, Singapore, and London. The management is working to develop a Latin American practice in Mexico and South America, and is becoming more involved in the Far East.

pro bono

V&E also allows its attorneys to work on the "full spectrum of pro bono, unless it conflicts with the clients," reported one contact. The firm has recently implemented a policy under which pro bono hours are treated as billed hours for associate evaluation purposes. The pro bono committee is run principally by partner Scott Atlas, who reportedly does a significant amount of pro bono work. During his first four years at the firm, Atlas devoted approximately one-third of his time to working on a death penalty appeal, and he still made partner in seven years. Pro bono is not limited to litigation matters. V&E attorneys help organizations establish tax-exempt status, structure deals to build school playgrounds, and create green space in poor neighborhoods. Tax partner Glen Rosenbaum has done the tax work for the Wortham Opera House. The firm's lawyers also have built two homes for Habitat for Humanity.

V&E offers top-notch formal training for its associates, especially those in the litigation department. The firm built its own "amazing multi-million dollar training facility" in the office. This 100-seat courtroom features adjacent conference rooms, a jury deliberation room, and a hi-tech video projection system. Associates and summer associates participate in an in-house NITA program in this courtroom, with partners serving as the judges and critiquing the performers. V&E offers a formal Business Lawyer Training Program for transactional work. Included in the program are courses in negotiation, drafting, and accounting. The firm chooses "impressive" speakers to address its attorneys. One person told us, however, that "the associates do not enjoy all the training that much. Some saw it more as a chore than as a privilege because it was during work hours and interfered with work."

extensive formal training

One person described V&E as "a Texas firm." It was founded by Texas Judge Elkins and employs many people from Texas. There is "still some old-boy Texas network feeling" at this firm, said one contact. V&E is "a predominantly conservative firm, but is more open than other big Houston firms," reported another. Attorneys at V&E span the political spectrum. There are "a lot of vocal Democrats," including friends of former Governor Ann Richards, reported one person. While one insider reported that the "old guard—the people really in power—are conservative," the managing partner, various section heads, and management committee members are reportedly liberal Democrats. The political affiliations of the attorneys tend to differ by department. Litigation is said to be predominantly Democratic, while corporate is more Republican.

Texas firm

Attorneys work hard at V&E, sometimes well over 2000 hours a year, according to our contacts. One contact informed us, however, that hours worked vary substantially by section: "new associates in labor and employment start out with 1600–1800 hours their first couple of years. There's a lot more emphasis on training and learning the substantive law in this area *(e.g.* by writing speeches and papers)." There is some competition among associates, we were told. The partners work as hard or harder than associates, according to one person. Another person observed that "there's a really good relationship between partners and associates; partners care about how associates are developing professionally."

hard-working

Despite the long hours, most associates seem to enjoy working at V&E, reported those we interviewed. People described the firm as having a "relaxed mood," though attorneys wear formal attire to work. "White shirts" are a common sight at the firm. Attorneys can dress less formally on Fridays, but still wear suits on these days.

When they are not working, the attorneys at V&E take time to party. They are described as "friendly" and "fun." This is "a very social firm," said one person. "Many friendships extend outside the office," said another. There has been some intra-firm dating among associates, and there is no formal rule against internal firm marriages. An attorney's "social life depends on the department," reported one insider. Litigation has more single attorneys who go out after work, for example, while tax attorneys "get along but don't socialize" frequently. Every year, the firm sponsors a huge bash called "The Prom" at various locations in Houston and invites "everyone who has ever worked at V&E," even those who are no longer with the firm. The firm hosts other annual parties as well and has rented out Astro World for the firm picnic. Most attorneys play sports, especially golf and softball.

social culture

This social environment is not just for men. "Women party hard, too," said one woman. The firm is reportedly a good place for women. Several women with children currently work part-time. Vinson & Elkins has a formal policy allowing such arrangements. There "seem to be a lot of women who leave and come back," noted one

women

contact. One female partner in litigation, who had three children while working at the firm, took maternity leave and made partner in one extra year. Most female litigation partners had no children before they made partner. The firm has in place a policy declaring that sexual harassment will not be tolerated, as well as a mechanism providing for recourse if such behavior surfaces.

diversity

V&E is "one of the best firms in Houston for gay attorneys," said one person. V&E received lower marks for racial diversity from the people we interviewed. There are "not as many minority associates as I'd expect for its size, especially at partnership level," said one person, noting that the "big power is almost exclusively white and male." The firm, however, implemented a program to actively recruit minorities, another contact pointed out, and had made some progress in this area in recent years.

management

V&E is managed by an executive committee elected by the partnership and led by a managing partner. Business has been very solid of late; this past year was reported to be the best in the firm's history. Most sections of the firm are busy, and the "firm has had to loosen up its former informal policy on not hiring laterals so it has the personnel to handle the increased business," we were told.

"Associates serve on several committees that report to the managing committee, but I don't know how much real influence they have," said one person. Associates receive salary plus bonus and reportedly "stand a decent chance" of making partner, although the firm does not make its partnership numbers available to us. Associates are considered for partnership after eight years. Associates who stay for eight years and do not make partner can stay at the firm for one more year, after which they will be reconsidered for partnership. Those who do not make partner at that time may be offered an "of counsel" position at the firm.

offices

V&E occupies 14 floors of office space. Texas-related photos and paintings of "boots and cactuses" adorn the walls. Every attorney gets her own office with a window and her own computer with full access to LEXIS and Westlaw. Summer associates also get their own offices and laptop computers. The helpful library staff reportedly will pull and copy cases for attorneys upon request. There is no gym or cafeteria on the premises, but the firm pays for partner memberships to the Houston Center Club, a local health club. The firm also pays for attorneys to use its building's parking garage.

extravagant summer

The firm has scaled back its recruiting program, say associates, though the program is still extravagant. "When they told us they cut back on the summer program, I didn't know what they did before," remarked one former summer associate. V&E is the "best recruiter in Houston and the nation," said another. "The summer program is a blast...It was the most fun I've ever had." People praised the firm's "outlandish parties," including a formal Casino Night at the Houston Museum of Fine Arts and a country and western party at the Houston Polo Club. Stories of summer fun are legend. In a recent summer, we were told, "several associates and recruits decided they weren't ready to end the evening when the bars closed at 2 a.m. So they rented the band from a local R & B club for $500. and held a spontaneous 'dance 'til dawn' party at the home of two young associates. The expenses were reimbursed by the recruiting office without any questions." Summer associates were taken to lunch every day in the summer and went out drinking or to dinners, parties, or softball games four or five nights per week. Although there were planned dinners, most were informal and arranged by the associates "who consider the recruiting season part of their compensation." On the weekends, various partners hosted dinners in their homes. There were Astros tickets available whenever summer associates wanted them. Clerks could use the tickets without an attorney present and could bring their friends. In earlier editions we reported that, since there were so many social events during the summer period, Mondays and Tuesdays were designated clerk's nights off so the clerks would not "feel overwhelmed with social events." A recent contact informed us that this is "not true anymore. There are dinners going on every night." The educational aspects of the program are equally extravagant. In the past the firm has taken summer associates on a limousine tour of Houston and hired the Dean of the Richmond Law School to give a two- or three-day negotiations seminar, for which the firm flew the D.C. summer associates to Houston.

Each summer associate is assigned to one sponsor who plans social events and makes sure the clerks meet people. One sponsor in each section oversees work assignments. "The recruiting office is in tune with who you are and matches you so you don't have to hang out with jerks," stated one contact. Another added, however, that there was "not much partner contact" in the program. In the last couple of years, the offers of permanent employment to summer associates has been in the 90% range; in 1996, offers were made to 56 of the 64 summer associates.

hiring tips

To get a summer job with Vinson & Elkins, grades are "of paramount importance." If you have "top grades, you're in. If not, you're not." But, one contact pointed out, "once you make it into the summer program, personality and work product are most important" to your future success at the firm. The firm hires mainly from the University of Texas, Harvard, the University of Houston, Virginia, Yale, and Columbia. It also occasionally hires graduates from Brigham Young University, the University of Tennessee, and the "top two graduates from South Texas," said one person. Most of the clerks from the "non-top 10" schools were on law review, noted one successful applicant. The majority of the summer clerks come from the University of Texas, and there is a "hierarchy" in the firm based on where you go to school, one person told us. "The power in the firm is the UT network." It is "harder to get an offer from the less prestigious schools," one noted. Personality is also important in hiring, said several people we interviewed.

Vinson & Elkins puts a lot of effort into everything it does, and its attorneys respond with equal vigor. The firm is experiencing good economic times, although overall the firm has slimmed down by about 45 attorneys since our last edition. The Dallas office is growing significantly. "If you're independent and business oriented, you would prefer V&E for its wide range of choice." V&E allows its associates to work on a range of cases and to learn both formally and informally in a lively social environment. "For a big law firm, it is very open and relaxed socially, and at the same time you work on very important clients—big cases and transactions. It's exciting work," said one person. Another commented that "for a large, old firm, Vinson & Elkins is extremely diverse and accepting. It's just a great place to work." When asked if there were any obvious negatives in being employed at V&E, this person remarked that "the elevators are slow."

Los Angeles

Law Firms Ranked By Associates Per Partner

1.	MANATT, PHELPS, PHILLIPS & KANTOR	0.6
2.	GREENBERG, GLUSKER, FIELDS, CLAMAN & MACHTINGER	0.8
3.	JEFFER, MANGELS, BUTLER & MARMARO	0.8
4.	MITCHELL, SILBERBERG & KNUPP	0.8
5.	MUNGER, TOLLES & OLSON	0.8
6.	IRELL & MANELLA	0.9
7.	MORGAN, LEWIS & BOCKIUS	1.0
8.	SHEPPARD, MULLIN, RICHTER & HAMPTON	1.0
9.	GIBSON, DUNN & CRUTCHER	1.2
10.	SIDLEY & AUSTIN	1.3
11.	LATHAM & WATKINS	1.4
12.	MORRISON & FOERSTER	1.4
13.	BROBECK, PHLEGER & HARRISON	1.5
14.	PAUL, HASTINGS, JANOFSKY & WALKER	1.5
15.	O'MELVENY & MYERS	1.6
16.	SKADDEN, ARPS, SLATE, MEAGHER & FLOM	2.7

Law Firms Ranked by Percentage of Associates Who Make Partner (over varying years)

1.	MITCHELL, SILBERBERG & KNUPP	46
2.	MORGAN, LEWIS & BOCKIUS	43
3.	LATHAM & WATKINS	36
4.	MORRISON & FOERSTER	31
5.	MUNGER, TOLLES & OLSON	29
6.	BROBECK, PHLEGER & HARRISON	28
7.	SHEPPARD, MULLIN, RICHTER & HAMPTON	25
8.	GREENBERG, GLUSKER, FIELDS, CLAMAN & MACHTINGER	24
9.	PAUL, HASTINGS, JANOFSKY & WALKER	21
10.	O'MELVENY & MYERS	17
11.	GIBSON, DUNN & CRUTCHER	NA
12.	IRELL & MANELLA	NA
13.	JEFFER, MANGELS, BUTLER & MARMARO	NA
14.	MANATT, PHELPS, PHILLIPS & KANTOR	NA
15.	SIDLEY & AUSTIN	NA
16.	SKADDEN, ARPS, SLATE, MEAGHER & FLOM	NA

Law Firms Ranked by Pro Bono Work as a Percentage of Total Work

1.	SKADDEN, ARPS, SLATE, MEAGHER & FLOM	5
2.	O'MELVENY & MYERS	4-7
3.	MORRISON & FOERSTER	4
4.	GIBSON, DUNN & CRUTCHER	3
5.	PAUL, HASTINGS, JANOFSKY & WALKER	3
6.	MUNGER, TOLLES & OLSON	2-5
7.	MORGAN, LEWIS & BOCKIUS	2
8.	IRELL & MANELLA	1-5
9.	GREENBERG, GLUSKER, FIELDS, CLAMAN & MACHTINGER	1-3
10.	MANATT, PHELPS, PHILLIPS & KANTOR	1-3
11.	SIDLEY & AUSTIN	1-3
12.	SHEPPARD, MULLIN, RICHTER & HAMPTON	1
13.	BROBECK, PHLEGER & HARRISON	NA
14.	JEFFER, MANGELS, BUTLER & MARMARO	NA
15.	LATHAM & WATKINS	NA
16.	MITCHELL, SILBERBERG & KNUPP	NA

Law Firms Ranked by Percentage of Female Partners

1.	JEFFER, MANGELS, BUTLER & MARMARO	42
2.	MORRISON & FOERSTER	27
3.	PAUL, HASTINGS, JANOFSKY & WALKER	22
4.	LATHAM & WATKINS	21
5.	MANATT, PHELPS, PHILLIPS & KANTOR	19
6.	MORGAN, LEWIS & BOCKIUS	17
7.	SIDLEY & AUSTIN	17
8.	GREENBERG, GLUSKER, FIELDS, CLAMAN & MACHTINGER	16
9.	BROBECK, PHLEGER & HARRISON	15
10.	GIBSON, DUNN & CRUTCHER	15
11.	MUNGER, TOLLES & OLSON	15
12.	IRELL & MANELLA	13
13.	MITCHELL, SILBERBERG & KNUPP	12
14.	O'MELVENY & MYERS	11
15.	SHEPPARD, MULLIN, RICHTER & HAMPTON	10
16.	SKADDEN, ARPS, SLATE, MEAGHER & FLOM	7

Law Firms Ranked by Percentage of Female Associates

1.	MANATT, PHELPS, PHILLIPS & KANTOR	48
2.	PAUL, HASTINGS, JANOFSKY & WALKER	46
3.	SIDLEY & AUSTIN	46
4.	GREENBERG, GLUSKER, FIELDS, CLAMAN & MACHTINGER	44
5.	GIBSON, DUNN & CRUTCHER	43
6.	MORRISON & FOERSTER	39
7.	MITCHELL, SILBERBERG & KNUPP	38

8.	SKADDEN, ARPS, SLATE, MEAGHER & FLOM	38
9.	LATHAM & WATKINS	37
10.	MORGAN, LEWIS & BOCKIUS	35
11.	SHEPPARD, MULLIN, RICHTER & HAMPTON	35
12.	JEFFER, MANGELS, BUTLER & MARMARO	33
13.	O'MELVENY & MYERS	32
14.	MUNGER, TOLLES & OLSON	31
15.	IRELL & MANELLA	28
16.	BROBECK, PHLEGER & HARRISON	21

Law Firms Ranked by Percentage of Minority Partners

1.	IRELL & MANELLA	10
2.	SKADDEN, ARPS, SLATE, MEAGHER & FLOM	10
3.	MUNGER, TOLLES & OLSON	8
4.	PAUL, HASTINGS, JANOFSKY & WALKER	8
5.	JEFFER, MANGELS, BUTLER & MARMARO	6
6.	LATHAM & WATKINS	6
7.	MANATT, PHELPS, PHILLIPS & KANTOR	5
8.	O'MELVENY & MYERS	5
9.	BROBECK, PHLEGER & HARRISON	4
10.	SHEPPARD, MULLIN, RICHTER & HAMPTON	4
11.	MITCHELL, SILBERBERG & KNUPP	3
12.	MORGAN, LEWIS & BOCKIUS	3
13.	GIBSON, DUNN & CRUTCHER	2
14.	SIDLEY & AUSTIN	2
15.	GREENBERG, GLUSKER, FIELDS, CLAMAN & MACHTINGER	0
16.	MORRISON & FOERSTER	0

Law Firms Ranked By Percentage of Minority Associates

1.	MORGAN, LEWIS & BOCKIUS	24
2.	MORRISON & FOERSTER	24
3.	GIBSON, DUNN & CRUTCHER	23
4.	MITCHELL, SILBERBERG & KNUPP	23
5.	LATHAM & WATKINS	22
6.	BROBECK, PHLEGER & HARRISON	21
7.	GREENBERG, GLUSKER, FIELDS, CLAMAN & MACHTINGER	21
8.	O'MELVENY & MYERS	19
9.	PAUL, HASTINGS, JANOFSKY & WALKER	19
10.	MUNGER, TOLLES & OLSON	18
11.	SHEPPARD, MULLIN, RICHTER & HAMPTON	17
12.	SIDLEY & AUSTIN	17
13.	JEFFER, MANGELS, BUTLER & MARMARO	14
14.	SKADDEN, ARPS, SLATE, MEAGHER & FLOM	14
15.	IRELL & MANELLA	13
16.	MANATT, PHELPS, PHILLIPS & KANTOR	10

Brobeck, Phleger & Harrison

Los Angeles Austin Denver New York Orange County Palo Alto San Diego San Francisco

Address: 550 South Hope Street, Los Angeles, CA 90071–2604 (www.brobeck.com)
Telephone: (213) 489–4060
Hiring Attorney: David M. Halbreich
Contact: Ellen M. Zuckerman, Recruiting Administrator; (213) 745–3562
Associate Salary: First year $77,000 (1997); second $80,000; third $84,000; fourth $88,000; fifth $95,000; sixth $103,000; seventh $108,000 (salaries under review at time of printing)
Summer Salary: $1300/week (1997)
Average Hours: 1911 worked; 1876 billed; NA required
Family Benefits: Maternity and family leave; life, medical, dental and vision insurance; long and short term disability; dependent care assistance
1996 Summer: NA
Partnership: 28% of entering associates from 1978–1984 were made partner
Pro Bono: NA

Brobeck, Phleger & Harrison in 1997
69 Lawyers at the Los Angeles Office
1.5 Associates Per Partner

Total Partners 26			Total Associates 38			Practice Areas	
Women	4	15%	Women	8	21%	Litigation	39
All Minorities	1	4%	All Minorities	8	21%	Business & Tech	10
Afro-Am	1	4%	Afro-Am	3	8%	Fin Sec. & Insolvency	10
			Asian-Am	3	8%	Real Estate	5
			Latino	1	3%	Tax	5
			Native Am	1	3%		

San Francisco-based Brobeck, Phleger & Harrison is one of California's largest and most profitable law firms. The Los Angeles office of this full-service law firm has a "serious" atmosphere. Its attorneys "are closed up in their offices" and "really don't know each other," said one contact, describing the work atmosphere as "cold and aloof." One source claimed that the attorneys are "not really friendly with each other." Another person we interviewed disagreed, however, observing that people take "time out to help each other." This person added that Brobeck provides "fairly open access to partners."

politics

Tom Bradley joined Brobeck in 1993 after serving as Mayor of Los Angeles for over a decade. The Los Angeles office, however, does not have a strong reputation for being either politically liberal or conservative. In one person's opinion, the firm exhibits a "more conservative bent." In matters of dress, however, the firm follows a "business casual" dress code Monday through Friday.

litigation groups

Brobeck's L.A. office was established in 1976 with only four attorneys and now numbers almost 70. This dramatic growth was driven largely by the litigation practice, which is loosely organized into groups according to the types of clients and practice area. One group, headed by George Link, primarily represents banking institutions. The environmental group is led by Ken Waggoner, a member of the firm's policy committee. He represents Chevron, one of the firm's largest environmental clients. Two people we interviewed claimed that the environmental group is a difficult place for women to work. Another group primarily handles securities and intellectual property litigation. It is, according to one insider, "known for being discovery-oriented and having really long cases." The litigation department also does some banking litigation and a "tremendous amount" of asbestos and product liability litigation. Partner John Larson, a premier high-tech lawyer and a well-known attorney in Silicon Valley, is a "big rainmaker" for the firm.

corporate practice

Brobeck also has a corporate department which is growing rapidly and is organized in two groups: financial services and business and technology. The former handles banking and bankruptcy matters and the latter works closely with the firm's high-tech groups in Palo Alto, Newport Beach, San Diego, Austin and New York. The business and technology practice, despite the recent loss of highly regarded Joshua Green, is "dynamic and growing" through its representation of a number of "hot" computer software, Internet, and biotechnology companies.

pro bono

The office's pro bono program received mixed reviews. One person told us that Brobeck "really encourages" pro bono work, but others claimed that it is "not a big thing" at the firm. Like many Los Angeles firms, Brobeck was actively involved in the Rebuild L.A. program, and logged over $1 million in counseling time to the effort.

choice of work

Upon joining the firm, Brobeck associates choose a particular practice group and receive their assignments from attorneys in the group. They are, however, free to work in other groups. People warned that associates who do not settle in one particular group tend to get the worst work. One source advised that "floating" is the "last thing you would want to do." Junior associates typically receive research and writing assignments, plus an occasional deposition or court motion. An associate's responsibility increases as she progresses at the firm and develops working relationships with more senior attorneys. Summer associates choose their assignments from a notebook of listings. As the summer progresses, summer associates develop working relationships with lawyers and may seek their assignments directly from those attorneys.

training and feedback

Brobeck runs a five-day firmwide trial advocacy training program at a retreat each summer for summer and permanent associates. In the L.A. office, each department meets regularly over lunch. The business and technology group, headed by Joe Stubbs, sponsors a two-week corporate and securities training program for first year associates each fall, and an ongoing series of seminars on various topics which are open to all associates. This group also holds biweekly meetings and training sessions every other Friday morning. Associates receive formal annual evaluations, and summer associates receive evaluations midway through and sometimes at the end of the summer.

minimal social life

When it comes to associate happiness, "some are and some aren't," reported one person. "There are hard hours and some unpleasant assignments." Nor is Brobeck an overly social firm. One person described the social life as "pretty non-existent." There is, however, a group of male attorneys who go out for drinks after work and enjoy golfing together, defended another. And the business and technology group sponsors surprise parties to celebrate associates' birthdays, weddings and births of children. As for firm sponsored social life, several critics complained that the firm is "cheap." Brobeck does, however, provide bagels and muffins or doughnuts every Friday morning to kick off the weekend, and it organizes some other events such as the annual firm outing and a boccie ball tournament (an Italian bowling game).

diversity

Brobeck employs few female attorneys, though this situation is improving of late. People commented that it is hard for women to balance raising children and working at the firm. Some attorneys work part-time, but the firm makes these arrangements on a case-by-case basis. Brobeck has, however, adopted a written family care leave policy and the firm recently elevated a female associate to partner after having a baby and taking off three months for maternity leave.

management

Firmwide, Brobeck is managed by a five partner policy committee chaired by the managing partner, Steve Snyder. The members of the committee are elected by the partnership for a two-year term, with successive terms permitted. Subject to the ultimate authority of the partners, the policy committee handles policy and planning matters, and makes recommendations to the whole partnership on allocating the firm's profits among partners. Other committees address specific issues of management. Associates may be members of the hiring committee.

The Los Angeles branch has its own managing partner, Thomas Burke, who runs the office. People we interviewed claimed that this office has been successful economically and plans to maintain a "conservative level of growth." The offices are brand new and "beautiful," with a lot of "blonde wood and big windows." All attorneys have private offices and computers. One critic complained that the library does not have enough work areas. People agreed that the support staff is "very good." However, the ratio of lawyers to support staff is 3:1 and there is "not enough document-processing support in off-hours," according to one contact, who added that "associates are expected to make up for this by typing and copying themselves."

emphasis on credentials

In hiring, Brobeck places a premium on "people with the most impressive résumés," said one past successful applicant. Another believed that academic qualifications take "precedence over other human qualities." The firm does "not want prima donnas," explained one contact. "They want someone who is going to show up, work their tail off, and not have an opinion about it." The people we interviewed advised applicants to display "energy and enthusiasm" in the interview. "Emphasize more of your work-related accomplishments as opposed to personal things," another insider advised, adding "keep it professional. Don't get too familiar."

People pointed to Brobeck's work atmosphere as one of its biggest drawbacks. One person commented that "practice skills are emphasized—socializing is not." Another noted that a "certain amount of competitiveness exists among people in the firm. There is a little less camaraderie than expected, and less of a team feeling." Another person, however, defended the firm, observing that Brobeck is "committed to people's development as lawyers and has good business and work." Also, we were told that the firm has an interesting high-tech client base which "allows younger lawyers to develop their own clients" prior to entry into partnership. Associates are encouraged to "speak and write articles - not just grind out hours - the firm is *very* marketing-oriented." One contact summarized the firm's virtues by observing that "it's a premier law firm in Los Angeles and it's steady."

Gibson, Dunn & Crutcher

Los Angeles Century City Dallas Denver Irvine New York San Diego San Francisco Washington, D.C.
Hong Kong London Paris Riyadh

Address: 333 South Grand Avenue, Los Angeles, CA 90071-3197
Telephone: (213) 229–7000
Hiring Attorney: E. Michael Greaney
Contact: Leslie Ripley, Recruiting Manager; (213) 229–7273
Associate Salary: First year $83,000 (1997)
Summer Salary: $1300/week (1996)
Average Hours: NA worked; 1967 billed; NA required
Family Benefits: Disability leave as needed
1996 Summer: Class of 26 students; offers to 20
Partnership: NA
Pro Bono: 3% of all work is pro bono

Gibson, Dunn & Crutcher in 1997
203 Lawyers at the Los Angeles Office
1.2 Associates Per Partner

Total Partners 92			Total Associates 111			Practice Areas	
Women	14	15%	Women	48	43%	Litigation	84
All Minorities	2	2%	All Minorities	25	23%	Unassigned	52
Afro-Am	1	1%	Afro-Am	4	4%	Corporate	41
Latino	1	1%	Asian-Am	18	16%	Labor	20
			Latino	3	3%	Tax	15
						Real Estate	11

As one of the most prestigious Los Angeles law firms, Gibson, Dunn & Crutcher has a more extensive and far-flung network of offices than any other Southern California firm. Unlike some firms, Gibson Dunn's many branches work closely with each other. The firm often permits its attorneys to transfer between its offices, providing them with many interesting career alternatives.

freewheeling atmosphere

For a behemoth firm, Gibson Dunn is unusually unstructured and provides very little guidance in professional development, or according to the firm, provides "ultimate flexibility to its associates regarding what they do and whom they work with." In fact, it is said that the firm borders on being "anarchic and chaotic." Gibson Dunn does not assign associates to any particular department or mentor during their first two years at the firm, nor does it provide formal channels through which work is distributed. There is, however, a work coordinator who assigns a limited number of projects, but "only in the event that an associate (rarely) is unable to obtain work that interests him or her." But, by and large, associates must obtain their work through "personal interaction" with the firm's partners. This freewheeling arrangement can be extremely rewarding to some, but traumatic for others. One insider explained that "through the chaotic distribution of assignments you develop strong working relationships with some of the lawyers; you have more individual control and you are not locked into working with a single lawyer. It's either great or terrible depending on your relationship with the lawyers. The disadvantage of the system is that it is more stressful. It's up to you to talk to people and get your assignments." Another person remarked that there is no reason for the system "to be terrible. The strength of the system is the opportunity and means it affords to choose your own working relationship."

high turnover

Although Gibson Dunn offers more formal training programs than many other large firms, most associate training occurs "on-the-job." One person elaborated: "You get thrown in and get training by picking the right people to work with and not being shy about walking into their office for help." Like many big and prestigious firms, Gibson Dunn offers interesting opportunities and expects a lot from its associates, but does not generally offer much early responsibility. Associates principally handle research assignments in their first few years. This does, however, vary across the firm, with one person commenting that "I have been given large responsibility for cases and have accumulated much experience relative to friends at other firms." Another contact observed that "I have found the responsibility daunting at times but always a challenge." A firm spokesperson pointed out to us that "the vast majority of associates within 'the first few years' have taken and defended multiple depositions, argued motions, negotiated deals, and a large number have even second-chaired trials and arbitrations." Many people view Gibson Dunn, with its prestige and resources, as an excellent place to begin their careers, but do not expect to stay very long. People noted the "high turnover" at the firm.

summer

Summer associates barely experience the reality of a Gibson Dunn associate's life. One insider claimed that a summer associate must only display the ability to produce good work with a few assignments and can then "cruise" for the remainder of the summer. Another contact cautioned, however, that "summer associates who 'cruise' do so at their own peril. There is a strong emphasis on quality work." And, more recently, the firm has reportedly expressed a "commitment to implementing a more rigorous 'vetting' process" for summer associates. Though summer associates are as likely to get an assignment while they are "in the lunchroom or the library" as they are from the firm's central assignment book, most are managed carefully by a summer coordinator who "protects" them from getting too much work, and who, in any event, approves all summer associate assignments.

extravagant program

The summer social life does not typify a permanent associate's experience. Summer associates are "treated like absolute royalty." The highlight of the summer program is the "summer academy," when the firm flies the summer associates from all its domestic offices to L.A. for "three days of bonding, drinking, eating, and California activities." One source went so far as to say that the summer program "almost provides too many fun events" and added that at the end of the summer, "I was happy to eat dinner by myself. I don't think I paid for a lunch the whole summer." By contrast, during the remainder of the year, Gibson Dunn was said to be a "family oriented" place where people are into doing their own thing. One person commented, "It's a comfortable place because people aren't in your business all the time." The firm "is not a clubby place, and it is not a place where you have to go drinking on Friday night." Another person remarked, "I have numerous close friends whom I party with often, without being obliged to do so."

commercial litigation

Gibson Dunn is recognized as having a solid practice in a broad range of areas, and it is hard to say that any one area has brought it more prominence than any other. Nevertheless, one person stated that Gibson Dunn is known as a "big time commercial litigation firm." Litigation is by far Gibson Dunn's largest department and commercial work is the core of the department. The commercial litigators, according to one person, are "very cool and very driven. They put in lots of hours. They are very intense and concerned with work quality."

premier media practice

Gibson Dunn handles some of the best media and First Amendment litigation in L.A.. In connection with these matters, it represents corporations such as the *Los Angeles Times*, the *Wall Street Journal*, *Time*, and Disney, and individuals such as Maury Povitch. However, the First Amendment group represents a small part of the firm's overall practice, and, according to one insider, to break into the group you "have to dedicate yourself to doing it, and you have to push yourself into it." Among the prominent litigators are Bob Cooper, one of the "major trial lawyers in L.A.," and Bob Warren, "one of the premier media attorneys in the country."

corporate tax and trusts

The corporate department, less busy than litigation in the past, has heated up more recently and is currently "swamped," we were informed by one insider. Indeed, the corporate department has been so busy of late that young associates are reportedly "doing the work of senior associates and junior partners." It boasts such prominent lawyers as Ron Beard and Aulana Peters, former commissioner of the Securities and Exchange Commission (SEC). One contact described the department as a group of "terrific people. Everyone was willing to help, and they all took their roles as mentors and teachers very seriously." Gibson Dunn has developed a small company and entrepreneur practice that is thriving. The tax department is almost "entirely male, very small, and top heavy. The tax lawyers are also very protective of people who want to work for them." Although one source said that some of the tax lawyers are the "easiest people at the firm with whom to work," the tax department is reputed to be a "boys club and a closed society of tax snobs." The trusts department was described as a group with a "comfortable" work atmosphere, comprised mostly of "avuncular" men.

pro bono

Pro bono hours count toward billable hours at Gibson, Dunn & Crutcher, and constitute about three percent of the total work done by the firm. Many of its lawyers have been involved in high-profile pro bono work in recent years, including advocating on behalf of Latin American refugees. In one recent summer, the firm sent a group of associates to Nicaragua to help investigate human rights issues. Gibson Dunn also participated in the Rebuild L.A. effort.

conservative atmosphere

Although Gibson Dunn has traditionally been categorized as a "WASP" and Republican firm, one insider claimed that it "doesn't feel that way at all." Another person noted that there has been recent "significant Democratic growth—former U.S. Congressman Mel Levine is a partner." Gibson Dunn's downtown office was described as conservative, both in atmosphere and in dress, whereas the lawyers "wear more double breasted suits and dress more chic in the Century City office", which is perhaps a reflection of the growing entertainment practice developing there. One observer asserted that many present associates have liberal leanings and stated that most of the firm's white shoe image belongs to past generations. Nonetheless, the firm's offices, designed in dark wood with a "traditional lawyerly" look, continue to exude a white shoe atmosphere, referred to, however, by one insider as "ugly."

minority retention

Gibson Dunn employs very few African-American attorneys and has a hard time retaining those that have joined the firm. "Gibson Dunn needs to do a better job of recognizing the problem and discussing it openly," one source commented. "They need to comprehend the position that blacks are in; they don't have anyone to talk to about these issues...Until they get the 'critical mass' there and build up a support system, it will not change." Another person remarked that "there are real efforts underway but it is a continuing problem." Presently, 2.5% of the firm's Los Angeles attorneys are African-American. The current minority percentage of associates is 23%.

women's issues

Although some prominent Gibson Dunn women such as Aulana Peters, who is also an African-American, serve as role models, we heard some concerns regarding the firm's commitment to women's issues in the workplace. One source complained that the firm "oversold" its maternity leave policy and gave women the impression that billable hours would not be a big consideration in partnership decisions. This, however, has turned out not to be the case. The reality has led to some frustration and disgruntlement. Gibson Dunn is "still working on this and is trying to accommodate women's issues," but one insider noted that "when push comes to shove, it has often come down to hours." Another contact observed that, in recent years, "extremely gifted female attorneys have been passed over for partnership in favor of their less well-regarded male peers." A firm spokesperson informed us that "a number of women who were out on pregnancy disability have made partner, and women who have consistently averaged less than 2000 hours have make partner."

candid management

Though Gibson Dunn is one of the country's largest firms, it is surprisingly open about its financial and management decisions. One source commented that it's "certainly a candid management. They disclose certain financial aspects of the firm fully—even to summer associates. It's very open for you to find out what's going on." Gibson Dunn was not immune from the economic hard times of the early 1990s, but one contact observed that the firm carries no long-term debt and is well-positioned for the future. The firm has recently given "substantial salary increases" and has restructured its partnership compensation and composition.

Concerning its hiring decisions, Gibson Dunn places a premium on academic excellence. It relies more heavily than some other large law firms on traditional measures of academic performance such as grade point averages and law review membership. The firm recruits most of its summer class from top national and local California law schools. Most of the students hired from local schools are in the top 10 percent of their classes, and most coming from the top 10 schools have above average grades at their schools. One source noted, however, that they don't hire the "whiz kids," but rather people who are "down-to-earth and hard-working with a good head on their shoulders." Another contact remarked that "personality and ability to survive in our work system are crucial." The firm hires many summer associates who have worked in other careers or have interesting backgrounds and did not go straight from college to law school. Gibson Dunn usually conducts the callback office interview over a full day and on occasion divides the applicant's interviews among the three Southern California offices.

premium on academic excellence

Gibson Dunn is remarkably unstructured for a firm of its size. The prestige and resources of the firm can't be beat in L.A.; the firm name "counts a lot," according to one insider. We heard complaints, however, that the somewhat limited opportunities for responsibility result in high turnover at the firm. Many go to Gibson Dunn to launch their careers but find that its long work hours and, at times, tedious work make opportunities elsewhere more attractive. On a more upbeat note, we have heard that recent pay raises and revisions to the bonus system have buoyed associate spirits.

Greenberg, Glusker, Fields, Claman & Machtinger

Los Angeles

Address: 1900 Avenue of the Stars, #2100, Los Angeles, CA 90067
Telephone: (310) 553–3610
Hiring Attorney: Glenn A. Dryfoos
Contact: Patricia G. Patrick, Recruiting Coordinator; (310) 553–3610
Associate Salary: First year $80,000 (1997); second $82,524; third $92,233; fourth $106,796; fifth $121,359
Summer Salary: $1300/week (1996)
Average Hours: 1933 worked; 1676 billed; 1825 required
Family Benefits: Maternity/Paternity leave
1996 Summer: Class of 6 students; offers to 5
Partnership: 24% of entering associates from 1980–1986 were made partner
Pro Bono: 1–3% of all work is pro bono

Greenberg, Glusker, Fields, Claman & Machtinger in 1997
88 Lawyers at the Firm
0.8 Associates Per Partner

Total Partners 56			Total Associates 32			Practice Areas	
Women	9	16%	Women	14	44%	Litigation	40
All Minorities	0	0%	All Minorities	7	21%	Real Estate	13
			Afro-Am	4	12%	Entertainment	11
			Asian-Am	2	1%	Bankruptcy	7
			Latino	1	1%	Probate	7
						Business	4
						Labor	3
						Tax	3
						Environmental	1

As one of the country's premier entertainment firms, Greenberg Glusker is not a typical large law firm. One source called it the "least stuffy firm I have ever been in." At Greenberg Glusker, "people can get away with whatever they want to wear." A few attorneys even come to work in jeans or a "black shirt and a pair of trousers." Though most wear suits, they have the top button of their shirts undone. The work atmosphere is informal, interactive, and chatty. "People yell at each other across the hall, they play games, such as Fantasy Players, in the firm, and place bets amongst themselves," said one contact.

social life

The sociability only increases at the end of the work day. Greenberg Glusker attorneys "go out after work with each other a lot more than lawyers at other firms." Many are sports and music enthusiasts, and others form a distinct "party crowd." The quality of life for associates is "very good," according to one contact. The relatively low billable hours target is 1825 and "there is no unspoken rule that associates must bill more than that amount in order to be viewed favorably."

practice areas

Greenberg Glusker has historically been known as a real estate and business firm with an entrepreneurial oriented practice. Today, however, the entertainment department and its clients account for about one third of the firm's business. Bert Fields, a nationally recognized entertainment lawyer, is a pillar of the department, which represents Tom Cruise, Oliver Stone, Warren Beatty, Dustin Hoffman, and Twentieth Century Fox, among others. Fields, the author of two novels published under the pseudonym D. Kincaid, has been profiled in Vanity Fair magazine. People cautioned, however, that Greenberg Glusker only hires about one new associate each year to work in entertainment. Joining this group can be "very competitive."

Although much of the firm's work, particularly litigation, arises from entertainment clients, other departments also have independent client bases and practices. Litigation, the firm's largest department, was described as social, "tight-knit," "fast-paced," and "hard-working." Harvey Friedman is a well-known litigator. The corporate department is headed by Jill Cosman. Paula Peters, a senior securities lawyer, was one of the first women to be hired by the firm, and one of the first women in L.A. to become a partner in a major law firm. Greenberg Glusker's corporate department is small and represents primarily entrepreneurial clients. The firm's real estate department is a top developer-oriented practice. One source claimed that it is somewhat cliquish and "male dominated." Name partner Phil Glusker (now semi-retired) and Stephen Claman are top real estate attorneys. Greenberg Glusker's trusts and estates lawyers are very highly regarded and tend to "keep to themselves." Though it has a pro bono practice, the firm doesn't "emphasize it, and it is not one of its strong selling points." Nevertheless, in a high-profile pro bono matter, the firm represented a man who provided assistance to Reginald Denny, when the latter was pulled from his truck and beaten during the L.A. riots.

associate development

Though it is an informal firm, Greenberg Glusker is fairly structured. It requires summer associates to rotate through the firm's major departments for approximately three weeks each and hires permanent associates into one particular department. One source complained, however, that the firm often does not inform entering associates which department they will work in until after they have taken the bar exam. New associates at Greenberg have unusually good opportunities for responsibility and client contact. Most litigation associates have substantial client contact and conduct depositions within their first year, and people noted that it is very common for first-year associates to appear in court.

management

Greenberg is economically stable. It did not have a big boom in the 1980s, and hence it did not face a subsequent collapse. Unlike some other large L.A. firms, Greenberg Glusker did not fire large numbers of attorneys, but some people commented that the management tends to be "hush-hush" about layoffs. Recently, associate salaries were raised and associates may now participate in the firm's 401K plan.

diversity

Founded as Hill, Jones & Attias in 1948 in West L.A., the firm changed names when Arthur Greenberg, Philip Glusker and Irving Hill (now a United States District Judge) began to practice together in 1959. Greenberg Glusker has long been known as a firm that values diversity. "It's a great firm for women," one insider exclaimed. Greenberg Glusker's parental leave policy is "really good—if you want a leave they will accommodate you." The firm recently became one of the first major law firms in Los Angeles to offer health insurance benefits to domestic partners. People similarly praised Greenberg Glusker's commitment to racial diversity. The recruiting coordinator, Patricia Patrick, is an African-American and is "very attuned" to issues facing minority attorneys. The firm has hired five minority attorneys since 1993.

renovated offices

Greenberg Glusker occupies floors 19 to 22 of an "old Century City office building" (opened in 1968 or 1969). The firm's offices were recently remodeled and are now sleek and elegant without being too trendy or stuffy. The new offices have two internal stairwells and a huge, well-stocked library. Every attorney has a private office with a personal computer and a stunning view of the Los Angeles area (L.A. smog permitting). Each day the firm provides a free catered lunch, free snacks, and soft drinks to all its attorneys and paralegals. The free lunch provides a real incentive for attorneys to hang out at the firm and talk about work during the lunch hour, noted one insider. In addition, Greenberg provides full dental and medical benefits for summer associates. "Save up your cavities for the summer," one observer advised.

hiring tips

As for recruitment, Greenberg Glusker is "not looking for some little dweeb who will be a slave," remarked one insider. "They are looking for people with other lives," who are "independent and unique." Although many students are attracted to the firm's entertainment practice, one source cautioned students interviewing with the firm not to "overplay the entertainment thing. Mention that you have some interest in it, but that you are not sure. The safest and best thing to say is that you might want to litigate—this is the fastest-growing and biggest area that always needs to fill its ranks." Greenberg Glusker hires most summer associates from California schools and draws heavily from Boalt, the Universities of California at Davis and Los Angeles, and the University of Southern California. Greenberg Glusker has "high standards" in terms of grades. All summer associates who attended the local schools were in the top third of their classes. The on-campus interview is usually conducted by two attorneys and is "cordial and chatty." Callback interviews for students interviewing from out of town are conducted over the course of a full day at the firm and typically involve meeting as many as 12 people and include both lunch and dinner. Callbacks for students from local schools are conducted over a half day.

As for interview advice, one insider noted that "the firm considers itself unique and if you can understand why it does and appreciate that, then you are better off right off the bat." Another advised students not to try to impress the attorneys too much. Although Greenberg is very interested in people with a commitment to L.A., it does hire people who have had no previous connection to the city.

Irell & Manella

Los Angeles Newport Beach

Address: 1800 Avenue of the Stars, Suite 900, Los Angeles, CA 90067
Telephone: (310) 277–1010
Hiring Attorney: Henry Shields, Jr.
Contact: Gary W. Maxwell, Administrative Director; (310) 277–1010
Associate Salary: First year $80,000 plus year end bonus of $3,000 (1997); second $83,000 plus bonus of $7,000; third $86,000 plus bonus of $17,000; fourth $88,000 plus profit sharing; fifth $90,000 plus profit sharing; sixth $100,000 plus profit sharing
Summer Salary: $1300/week (1997)
Average Hours: 2282 worked; 1873 billed; NA required
Family Benefits: 12 weeks maternity leave; 1 month paternity leave
1996 Summer: Class of 36 students; offers to 34
Partnership: NA
Pro Bono: 1–5% of all work is pro bono

Irell & Manella in 1997
160 Lawyers at the Los Angeles Office
0.9 Associate Per Partner

Total Partners 79		
Women	10	13%
All Minorities	8	10%
Afro-Am	4	5%
Asian-Am	3	4%
Latino	1	1%

Total Associates 72		
Women	20	28%
All Minorities	9	13%
Afro-Am	4	5%
Asian-Am	6	8%
Latino	1	1%

Practice Areas	
Litigation	66
Corporate	34
Intellectual Property	25
Real Estate	19
Tax	12
Entertainment	9
Environmental	9
Bankruptcy	8
White-Collar Crime	8
Labor	6
Insurance	5
Personal Financial Planning	5

Founded as a tax boutique firm by Larry Irell and Art Manella, two of the most distinguished tax lawyers in Los Angeles, Irell & Manella has grown dramatically to become one of L.A.'s best full-service law firms. Irell's growth continues to be driven by its intensity, a characteristic that the firm makes no effort to conceal.

high-energy high turnover

The intensity is palpable at this thriving, high-energy firm. One person commented that "as soon as you get there, you get the sense that the firm is intense. Everyone is very smart and anal. There is a lot of pressure to perform and even to do things like check the 'Blue Booking' [*i.e.*, verify the correct citation form]." Irell demands long, hard hours, and associates often work on weekdays until 9 or 10 P.M. and on weekends. Irell generously rewards associates who can cope with its intensity. Those who satisfy the firm's high standards can learn a lot and receive excellent mentoring. They also begin sharing in the firm's profits after their third year and are eligible for partnership after just six years, giving the firm one of the shortest partnership tracks in Los Angeles. New associates are hired directly into a work group, and gain responsibility quickly. However, not everyone can take the firm's intensity for the long haul. Irell has a high turnover rate, perhaps because "many associates at the firm feel stressed out or overworked." Associates who do stick around benefit from what the firm described as very favorable rules of partnership consideration; vote is by the entire partnership, not by committee, and only if a candidate is voted against by 20 percent of the partners is partnership denied. Irell presently has a nearly "one-to-one partner/associate ratio."

eclectic atmosphere

Though "everyone works very hard," Irell "at the same time is a younger firm with a strong sense of camaraderie" and provides a surprisingly informal work atmosphere. One person commented that Irell offers all the prestige of other major and established L.A. firms without the "extra layer of bull." Irell attorneys dress relatively casually. Although some people are "stylish" in their dress, men often arrive at work without ties, and women frequently wear pants with a sweater. In addition, Irell & Manella never developed an old-boy, white shoe atmosphere and has been regarded as a firm that encourages diversity. One person remarked, "Irell is a collection of very eclectic people. It's one of the things they like about themselves. Anyone can fit in because they are all so different. There is no uniform mentality or firm culture." Another person remarked, negatively, that the firm has "some idiosyncratic partners."

learning by immersion

Irell is a firm for entrepreneurs. People considering the firm are advised, "If you are not a self-starter, you could easily get lost at the firm." The firm has few formal structures to provide training and feedback, and no one, we were told, will "coddle" you. Each new associates is, however, given a senior associate ombudsman, and "most of the firm's groups have formalized partner/associate mentoring programs," according to a firm representative. Overall, however, associates are encouraged by the firm to "pursue the type of work in which they are most interested." One person commented that the firm believes in learning by immersion and offers junior associates substantial responsibility and client contact as early as their first and second years at the firm. "If you don't think you're up to that," one source remarked, "you wouldn't want to be at the firm." Irell makes few concessions to summer associates, who are also provided very little formal training or feedback. They are, however, assigned in groups of four to six to an associate summer coordinator who is charged with assigning them work according to individual preferences.

active social life

Irell's summer program social calendar is well-organized and packed with events. The highlight of the summer is a four-day trip to Mammoth where summer associates can mountain bike, play volleyball, hike, and engage in other fun summer activities. In addition, "Irell will show you the L.A. that you see in the magazines." The firm is "very into hitting the hot restaurants in town. Summer associates get taken to places like Spago, Ivy, Citris—all the hot restaurants that get written up." Throughout the summer, the partners also host both "extravagantly catered" dinners and more intimate gatherings at their homes. Summer associates also go horseback riding and Malibu grand prix racing. One person commented, "if you don't learn to say no, you will be overwhelmed." Irell attorneys continue to socialize throughout the year. For example, attorneys participate in and attend the games of the firm-sponsored softball and basketball teams. People commented that the firm has "lots of young single people who like to go out at night and socialize."

premier tax practice

Although Irell & Manella's tax department now constitutes a fairly small fraction of the firm's total practice, the firm continues to be regarded as "one of the best places to go to practice tax." Irell handles a broad range of tax issues, from corporate to international. In addition to Larry Irell and Art Manella, Larry Stone is one of the firm's most prominent tax attorneys at the firm; now retired, he is of-counsel. He is well-known for having drafted significant portions of Subpart F of the Internal Revenue Code, which sets forth rules pertaining to the taxation of certain U.S. income earned abroad. Other prominent Irell tax attorneys include Joel Rabinowitz, a former UCLA professor of international tax, Milton Hyman (currently head of the department), and Elliot Freier, well-known authorities in bankruptcy tax. The tax department is predominantly male and was described as "very friendly" and "less domineering" than some other departments. "I have never seen a department that works as a group as much as they do," one insider remarked. "They sit together and discuss problems all the time and have a good mentorship system."

aggressive litigation department

In contrast, the lawyers in the litigation department, the firm's largest practice area, were described as "aggressive and intense." Though the firm handles a broad variety of large commercial litigation cases, one source claimed that Irell & Manella is more known for representing smaller, entrepreneurial clients. The firm's intellectual property practice has been growing rapidly. Several authorities in the field, including David Nimmer, the current editor of *Nimmer on Copyright*, a position he took over from his father, and Richard Bernacchi, an authority on "computer law," have helped build the firm's client base of entrepreneurs. Irell's intellectual property litigation practice is led by highly-regarded partner Morgan Chu who recently, along with Kenneth Heitz, began serving as managing partner of the firm.

growing multimedia high-tech practice

The firm has a fast-growing practice in multimedia and high-technology spearheaded by young partners Bob Steinberg (intellectual property), Lois Scali (entertainment), and Ted Guth (corporate). Clients include Packard Bell, Times Mirror, House of Blues, and Disney. In particular, we were informed that the multimedia transactional practice is "booming". Irell represents many new start-up companies, such as software developers and website designers, and is "one of the few firms doing contracts for the Internet." A new client of the firm is Affymetrix, the inventor of the "gene chip" used in the human genome project.

Irell & Manella has a pro-bono practice, but it is not highly formalized. Presently the firm does considerable pro bono work for Steven Spielberg's Starbright Foundation which brings interactive media to children confined to hospitals.

diversity

Irell & Manella is a diverse place and is regarded as a firm that has hired people who were historically excluded from other large firms. The firm has four African-American partners, including Henry Shields, who formerly served on the Executive Committee. Additionally, Irell & Manella has three Asian-American partners, including the aforementioned Morgan Chu, who is "the first, or one of the very first, Asian-Americans to serve as the managing partner of a major law firm," according to a firm spokesperson.

mixed reviews for women

The work atmosphere for women received mixed reviews. The firm has women in key positions on the management and executive committees, and two women serve as coheads of their work groups. The management committtee includes Andrea Greene, a litigation partner who is a co-editor of *The Woman Advocate*, published by the ABA, and a frequent lecturer on the subject. On the other hand, we were told that the firm has had a difficult time retaining women. Irell is aware of this problem and has established a committee on gender to address the issue. It also interviewed women at the firm to determine their satisfaction with the firm and the possible causes for the high turnover among women. The firm has a part-time work policy targeted at attorneys with small children and, according to one person, Irell is "incredibly flexible and accommodating to individual needs and interests." There are three female partners and at least two female associates working part-time, and "one of the two women elected to the partnership last year never worked on a full-time basis as an associate, and does not do so as a partner," we were told. However, according to one contact, there are presently "no female full-time associates with children," since the "24 hours a day, seven days a week commitment" makes this combination especially difficult.

offices under renovation

"It is widely recognized that Irell has some of the worst office space in the city," one insider informed us. The firm currently has a "fabulous, dirt-cheap lease" for offices in an old Century City building. Because the firm has been slowly renovating the facilities, a task expected to be completed in mid-1997, the floors vary in attractiveness. The fifth floor is "all wood and marble with green carpeting," and the sixth floor offers a traditional dark wood decor. However, the seventh through the ninth floors were described as "horrendous" and "claustrophobic." The downtown office was, however, described as "very nice." Notwithstanding the aesthetic drawbacks, the firm provides everyone with an individual office and a personal computer. The support services are "excellent" and operate around the clock. The firm also has one large conference room, in which aerobics classes are conducted every Tuesday and Thursday.

hiring tips

"The intensity and intellectual aspects of the firm carry over into the hiring process." The firm frankly discusses with applicants the high expectations of Irell attorneys. Consequently, some find the interview process "intimidating." Irell carefully considers grades in its hiring decisions and, of the students it hires from the local law schools, most are in the top 10 percent of their classes. However, it does not rely exclusively on grades. The firm seeks a combination of "someone who is smart and independent and a self-starter."

The on-campus interview was described as "very conversational." The interviewer usually asks a lot of questions about your résumé and previous work experience. The call-back interview is conducted over a full day and usually involves going out to lunch and dinner with members of the firm. One person commented that "unlike other firms, in the Irell interview you will have a lot of opportunities to talk about yourself and what is important to you." This person advised that "you really know your résumé and what your strengths are and what you would like to talk about." Another person commented that, in the interview, they are just looking to see that "you are not a weakling type of a person."

Overall,we heard many positive comments from our contacts. Irell was praised for its "collegial atmosphere and good discussion of issues within groups"; for its "early on" responsibility and "lean staffing" on most jobs; for its lack of "rigid hierarchy" and lines between departments; for its "alternative" working arrangements (part-time work, working at home, telecommuting from other cities, etc.); for its "substantive, interesting work" and "access to partners and clients." But, as expected, it was widely observed that the pressures on associates are significant and that the "very fast pace" entails a "higher level of stress and requires more commitment to the job" than many other law firms. A firm spokesperson remarked that "Irell and Manella is, like other major firms, a hard-working firm, but we understand that both work and outside interests and family are very important. This understanding is reflected in our liberal policies on part-time work, our sabbatical program, and in our avoidance of monthy 'quotas' or 'goals' for associates."

If you enjoy a fast-paced, high-energy atmosphere and can deal with the intensity and pressure of Irell, it may be the firm for you. A less traditional, but no less prestigious, firm than many of the other more established operations in L.A., Irell offers an open and interactive environment and top flight tax and corporate practices that set it apart from many of the city's more well-known outfits.

Jeffer, Mangels, Butler & Marmaro

Los Angeles San Francisco

Address: 2121 Avenue of the Stars, 10th Floor, Los Angeles, CA 90067
Telephone: (310) 203–8080
Hiring Attorney: Neil C. Erickson
Contact: Leslie S. Drago, Recruiting Coordinator; (310) 201–3573
Associate Salary: First year $72,500 (1997)
Summer Salary: $1300/week (1997)
Average Hours: NA worked; NA billed; NA required
Family Benefits: After 2 years of employment, attorneys receive 1 paid week leave for every full year worked over 2, up to a maximum of 5 paid weeks
1996 Summer: Class of 5; offers to 5
Partnership: NA
Pro Bono: NA

Jeffer, Mangels, Butler & Marmaro in 1997
95 Lawyers at the Los Angeles Office
0.8 Associates Per Partner

Total Partners 53			Total Associates 42			Practice Areas	
Women	22	42%	Women	14	33%	Litigation	27
All Minorities	3	6%	All Minorities	6	14%	Corporate	24
Latino	3	6%	Asian-Am	2	5%	Real Estate	12
			Latino	4	10%	Tax	12
						Bankruptcy	7
						Labor (management)	7
						Intellectual Property	5
						Health	2
						Entertainment	2

Jeffer, Mangels, Butler & Marmaro is young, fast-growing, and rapidly emerging as a top ranked Los Angeles law firm. Though it has been enormously successful, Jeffer Mangels is distinguished by a work atmosphere that, on its surface, is perhaps less formal than many of the larger Los Angeles firms. Jeffer Mangels lawyers, we were told, "dress well and drive fancy cars and socialize more than lawyers at most firms. They wear nicely colored items and everyone is into working out. The people at Jeffer Mangels are physically attractive." The firm's associates, especially in the corporate department, are close-knit and very friendly. One person reported that "they all hang out together and party and play together. They go out after work all the time...All these people are smiling and happy. People who don't go out aren't excluded. It's just that a lot of people make the decision to have a social life." Another person commented on the firm's "casual atmosphere," noting that people are friendly, though "not everyone hangs out on weekends together—but most get along."

hip yet intense

Underlying the laid-back image, however, is a strong current of intensity. Jeffer Mangels lawyers were described as "entrepreneurial" and "aggressive." One insider acknowledged that "the firm portrays itself as being very hip," and its lawyers "portray themselves as relaxed and Century City-like," but observed that "they work as hard as anyone in L.A." Another noted that "Jeffers is not a place where appearance matters; if you get your work done, no one cares (or notices) that you arrive at 9:45 A.M. and aren't there on weekends." What counts is quality of work; "associates aren't slaves, but good work is expected."

Bruce Jeffer driving force

Jeffer Mangels, we were informed, "is Bruce Jeffer's firm." The firm is essentially "a one-horse show in terms of management" and derives much of its character and prestige from Bruce Jeffer. While Jeffer is the managing partner, decisions about the the firm are actually made by a management committee that meets weekly. Jeffer was described as "a big guy at six-foot-four who was drafted for the NFL" after being a lineman for UCLA. He "can be abrasive" and intimidating to many. Though this impressive man is "really outgoing" and friendly, he is "at the same time very much into running the firm as a business—very into the bottom line. He doesn't put up with any messing around." As the hard-driving force behind much of this success, Jeffer reportedly makes a "ton" of money. Partner and higher level associates' compensation is reportedly largely merit-based and bonus-heavy. One contact informed us that those who do "exceptional work are handsomely rewarded; others have been dissatisfied. Everyone is very secretive about their bonuses" and every year associates "push to restructure the salary system." Another contact remarked that the partners are "tightwads when it comes to money."

intense corporate practice

Much of Jeffer Mangels' work is generated by its corporate clients. Co-head Jim Butler leads the firm's interdisciplinary hotel industry group, which represents a number of clients involved with hotels and resorts "throughout the world." The corporate lawyers were described as very "aggressive" and "intense, but a fun group of people." They include "three or four women and the rest are men."

litigation practice

The litigation department, led by rainmaker Bob Mangels, is the firm's largest, and includes a number of important women. The department is extremely hard-working, but "it is also very friendly" and, like corporate, is also "aggressive." One person told us that the litigators "really go out and get clients. They don't do any characteristic work. They are scrappy and will take what they can get." More recently, however, litigation has built up a solid institutional client base. Though most of the department's work involves commercial matters, it also represents a number of entertainment clients and has litigated movie rights and First Amendment cases. The group represented the Eagles and Bryan Adams in recent entertainment litigation cases; Paramount Studies has also been a firm client. Additionally, the firm has been involved in some "high-profile" political work. Other highly-regarded Jeffer Mangels litigators include Marc Marmaro, a name partner of the firm, and Jeffrey Riffer, who heads the First Amendment practice.

unique tax group

Jeffer Mangels' unique tax department handles a range of corporate and partnership matters including tax planning. The department also does tax and estate planning for individuals such as basketball and baseball players and other entertainers One source described the department as "fun and athletic" and "mostly men." One person called it a "boys–will–be–boys department" and noted that "there has been a history of sexist jokes among them, and some at the firm have complained."

One person cautioned that the entertainment department is small and has not grown much in recent years. The group hires very few attorneys directly out of law school, preferring instead to hire laterally from within the entertainment industry.

Jeffer Mangels has a pro bono practice that receives most of its cases from Public Counsel in Los Angeles. Although the firm's stated goal is for each attorney to bill 35 hours to pro bono each year, most pro bono work is left up to individual initiative.

summer program

Partly because Jeffer has grown so rapidly, it has not developed highly structured summer and training programs. The firm's recruitment director and summer associate coordinator distribute work assignments to the summer associates and attempt to provide projects that are consistent with the students' interests. The firm requires each attorney who gives out a summer associate assignment to go over the completed assignment with the summer associate and make suggestions for improvement. The organized summer social events include dinners at partners' houses, but Jeffer Mangels is not known for a lavish summer program.

early client contact

Permanent associates also receive little formal training, but Jeffer Mangels more than compensates for this by providing extensive on-the-job training. Because the firm staffs cases thinly and has many small clients, most junior associates work directly with partners and have client contact early. "You will run your own trial there before you can believe it, and you will be seriously involved in all the cases," asserted one source. "It's not the kind of place where you will be writing memos and worrying about case cites."

diversity

A woman's experience at Jeffer Mangels varies somewhat by department. Litigation, which is home to many women and "a significant number of women partners with power," is "great for women" and provides an "excellent" atmosphere for women. The corporate, tax, and real estate departments, by contrast, are predominantly male. Whereas one source claimed that "there is a lot of male joking and women who are sensitive would find it offensive," another said "the guys in tax and real estate do the buddy-buddy thing. A lot of them play basketball, and not a lot of women play basketball, but I would never characterize this as sexist." One has to be able, however, "to take (and give back) sarcasm." When questioned about racial diversity, people responded that overall Jeffer Mangels is a "pretty white firm." Nevertheless, two Latina partners, Luzanne Fernandez and Marta Fernandez (no relation), head the labor department.

Nakotomi Plaza offices

Jeffer Mangels' offices are located in the "showcase building in Century City," the site of the filming of the movie *Die Hard*. People we interviewed referred to the locale as "Nakotomi Plaza," which is the name used for the building in the movie. The offices are decorated sparsely and in light colors. Every attorney has a private office with a personal computer that is outfitted with a color monitor.

hiring

A graduate of Harvard Law School, Jeffer reportedly favors hiring law students and attorneys who attended his alma mater. However, Jeffer is not a member of the hiring committee, and the firm also draws summer associates from the top 10 national and some local law schools. Most students whom the firm hires from the local schools are in the top ten to 15 percent of their classes, and the firm is "very conscious" of grades and school name. At the same time, Jeffer Mangels seeks a particular type of personality. The firm "expects you to be able to schmooze freely." One person emphasized that, consistent with the firm's culture, Jeffer Mangels lawyers look for an "entrepreneurial spirit." Another contact remarked that the firm is "not a place for the timid; responsibility starts on day one—you are thrown into the water to see if you can swim."

interviews

A Jeffer Mangels interview is typically very "friendly." One person commented that "they didn't make you talk about the firm or the work they do. Nor do they impress you about any important matter. They just talked about what the atmosphere is like and what the people are like." Students usually meet with about four attorneys for half-hour interviews. One insider advised that "they are looking primarily for litigators, so you are better off if you are interested in that," while another contact pointed out, on the contrary, that the firm's needs change yearly and that litigation is not privileged.

Jeffer Mangels evinces an interesting confluence of cultures. On the one hand, the firm's casual and laid-back atmosphere reflects its entertainment practice and clientele; on the other, many of the lawyers have an intense and entrepreneurial drive, which is embodied by the firm's leader and former football player, Bruce Jeffer. The firm also offers an active social life and a good network of young people.

Latham & Watkins

Los Angeles Chicago New Jersey New York Orange County San Diego San Francisco Washington
Hong Kong London Moscow Tokyo

Address: 633 West Fifth Street, Suite 4000, Los Angeles, CA 90071–2007
Telephone: (213) 485–1234
Hiring Attorney: Michael J. Caroll
Contact: Kathy Yaffe, Recruiting Coordinator; (213) 485-1234
Associate Salary: First-year $78,000 (1996); second $83,000; third $92,000; fourth $95,000 (plus 15 profit sharing units); fifth $101,000 (plus 20 units); sixth $108,000 (plus 25 units); seventh $115,000 (plus 30 units)
Summer Salary: $1300/week (1996)
Average Hours: NA worked; 2100 billed; 1900 required
Family Benefits: Paid maternity leave; paternity leave on a case-by-case basis; part-time work available for family care
1996 Summer: Class of 28 students; offers to 28
Partnership: 36% of entering associates from 1972–1989 were made partner
Pro Bono: NA

Latham & Watkins in 1997
210 Lawyers at the Los Angeles Office
1.4 Associates Per Partner

Total Partners 84			Total Associates 120			Practice Areas	
Women	18	21%	Women	44	37%	Unassigned	79
All Minorities	5	6%	All Minorities	26	22%	Litigation	45
Afro-Am	1	1%	Afro-Am	3	3%	Corporate	39
Latino	3	4%	Asian-Am	18	15%	Finance/Real Estate	22
			Latino	4	3%	Environmental	16
			Native Am	1	1%	Tax	9

Latham & Watkins is, along with O'Melveny & Meyers and Gibson, Dunn & Crutcher, one of the three most prestigious firms in Los Angeles. A relative newcomer to this trio, Latham & Watkins has grown into one of the largest and most established Los Angeles law firms. The Latham name counts; according to one contact, "it will not be hard to find employment post-Latham. Headhunters call every day."

participatory culture

Latham & Watkins is the "participator firm" of Los Angeles. At this team-oriented firm, we were told by one person that "people tend to approach problems in mass as opposed to individually" and by another person that "if you have a question, you just send an e-mail to other attorneys in your practice area." Latham attorneys participate without restraint in all facets of the firm, from its open and democratic management to its exuberant social life. For example, about half the members of the firm's partner selection committee are associates who have a hand in its decisions to promote associates to partnership. One source noted that "everyone participates in the firm's management" through regular meetings at which associates air their concerns and grievances to the managing partner. Summer associates who attended these meetings marveled at the frankness of these discussions, in which associates freely expressed their opinions without much fear of reprisal from partners. One critic claimed, however, that the firm is democratic and open "almost to a fault." Another person commented, positively, that "we get information on the firm's performance annually, including bonuses given (without names attached) and profits and revenues. It makes me feel like a part of the firm rather than just an associate working for the partners."

second family

To be a true Latham "participator" is a "full-time job," even for summer associates. In the summer, the firm and individual attorneys organize "events five or six nights a week and are constantly doing things," one contact remarked. "You have to get fired up in the morning with caffeine because you will be at the firm until 10 or 11 at night on a regular basis. Latham becomes your second family. You have barbecues and hang out together." Another person commented that attorneys are "encouraged to organize their own events to better get to know the summer associates but by no means are the summer associates expected to be at all the events all the time."

boot camp

Perhaps because Latham associates play so hard together and form an extremely cohesive group, the firm has a reputation for being "fraternity-like." Though one person told us that the reputation is overblown, others noted that Latham attorneys are typically "good looking" and many dress in "expensive suits" and "wear flashy ties." Still another person informed us that "the vast majority of people here are married and not everyone spends all their time with other Latham people." Every year Latham organizes the much anticipated "boot camp" for first-year associates. It is affectionately so called because, as one source joked, "you drink until you boot." Another person remarked, more seriously, that "it's like Army boot camp - you learn what you need to survive." All the first-year associates at Latham's domestic offices meet in San Diego for three days of socializing and business meetings. In addition, the firm sponsors another firmwide boot camp for fourth-year associates.

changing culture

People we interviewed claimed, however, that the firm's "clubby atmosphere" manifests itself less now than in the past, partially because of present "business realities" and partially because the firm moved into new offices that are less conducive to social interaction. During the day, Latham is a hard-working place with a businesslike atmosphere. The firm's compensation system, under which attorneys are paid extra bonuses for the hours that they work over and above the "suggested" target, leads to a very "competitive environment." Associates are essentially paid a salary, which starts at $78,000 for first-year associates, plus a year-end bonus for some. A typical 1996 first-year associate bonus (given at the end of the first complete work year), we were told, was $11,500, but could be as much as $30,000 or none at all. Second-year bonuses could be as high as $37,000, and third year bonuses as high as $65,000. Partner compensation is based upon the number of equity units that they hold in the firm, which are currently valued at around $950. We were told that first-year partners typically are allocated around 300 units ($285,000), and third-year partners are typically allocated about 400 units ($380,000). The firm limits all partners to 900 units ($855,000). Profits per partner are reportedly over $750,000 and several partners make over $1 million annually. The firm recently implemented an income partnership position for partners who "don't have what it takes" to make equity partner, but who the firm does not want to lose. According to one person we spoke with, this will make it "now harder than ever to make equity partner."

top-notch corporate

Founded in 1934 by Dana Latham and Paul Watkins as an "elite" tax and labor firm, Latham & Watkins now offers one of the broadest practices in Los Angeles. During the mergers and acquisitions boom of the 1980s, Latham was most well-known for its top-notch corporate department, which handled a good share of Drexel Burnham Lambert's bond work. Though the department slowed down considerably in the early 1990s, it has rebounded entirely over the past few years and is considered one of the top practices in the city. The department does more "cutting-edge deals that you read about in the newspapers" than any other L.A. firm, claimed one participator. Randall Bassett, one of the firm's major corporate rainmakers, represents the well-known takeover firm Kohlberg, Kravits & Roberts (KKR). Another major rainmaker, the highly regarded

Edward Sonnenshein, has built an extensive client base in the hotel and gaming industry. The corporate department was described as "very heavily male and white male-oriented." One source observed that the corporate lawyers "are a close-knit bunch at the firm and tend to be pretty formal."

With the resurgence of corporate deals, the Finance and Real Estate Department has had banner years of late. Young associates in this department are able to take on a lot of responsibility quickly because "so many associates left the department in the early 1990s when work was slow."

litigation

Litigation is the firm's largest practice area and is one of the firm's most productive departments. It houses a broad range of areas from commercial to constitutional litigation. The highly regarded litigation partner, Robert Dell, recently assumed the position of managing partner at the firm. The litigators, we were told, "tend to work very hard, but they go out a lot and are a fun department." Latham's environmental department is among the firm's fastest growing practice areas and includes one of the firm's most prominent women, B.J. Kirwan. One source commented that the department reflects her character: "It's really informal and very cooperative. People always call each other up on the phone and help out on different projects." Latham's pro bono practice is headed by an attorney. The firm is heavily involved in the Rebuild L.A. effort (partner Barry Sanders was the co-chair of the committee) and is affiliated with the Public Counsel's Office.

international practice

In recent years, Latham has worked hard to develop its international practice, which is headed by Harrison Wellford. Its well-established London office reportedly "is doing really well," and the firm recently founded law shops in Moscow, Tokyo and Hong Kong.

loose assignment system

Despite its democratic structures and emphasis on teamwork, Latham's work assignment system is loosely structured, quite individualistic, and according to one observer, favors those who are good at developing "personal contacts." The firm does not assign entering associates to a particular department for their first two years. Each new associate is responsible for obtaining work through the central "book system." Thus, much of a junior associate's experience at Latham depends on an individual's initiative. Many people praised this unstructured arrangement because it permits "you the freedom to choose the path you want to take; and, if you do a good job on assignments, people can request you. You get a reputation as someone who is good." Summer associates need not display as much initiative because all their projects are collected in a central book and are distributed by the summer coordinator. However, in order to obtain the assignments that they want they must express their individual preferences.

training

Latham & Watkins provides a "full array" of formal training, but it "is not mandated," and it was reported that "most people don't do it." Perhaps associates' biggest complaint about Latham is that it does not provide enough interesting work and responsibility. As with many big L.A. firms, junior associates at Latham spend most of their early years researching legal issues in the library. There is, however, variation here. One insider told us that "most young associates in the Finance and Real Estate Department get a lot of responsibility quickly and first years in litigation have taken depositions and argued motions in court." Another source noted, moreover, that the firm's pro bono practice offers opportunities for significant responsibility.

diversity

Latham never acquired the establishment WASP image projected by some other prestigious Los Angeles firms. One person reported that some large L.A. firms are much more "blue-blood and stuffy than Latham. This is what I really liked about the firm." At the same time, however, Latham is not the most diverse firm in the city, nor is it the most progressive with respect to female and minority attorney issues. One person commented that some women "may have problems with some of the partners, but most people wouldn't have any problem at all. They are not rude or crass." Another person commented, however, that the firm's atmosphere for women "is still not great and there have been problems this year."

office facilities

Latham's offices are located "just under the smog" in the tallest building in L.A., said one contact. The building is new and the office decor is "very gray and monochrome" according to one person, and "pleasant—gray and light wood," according to another. Throughout the office, the firm displays a collection of black and white prints by famous photographers. Latham gives every attorney an individual office with a window and a personal computer that can access Westlaw, LEXIS, and the Internet. The firm has its own dining facilities where many attorneys eat lunch regularly. It's "very social," and "you can sit down with different partners and chat with them over lunch." The firm does not have a private gym but has worked out a "good deal" for associates with the nearby YMCA.

interview tips

Not surprisingly, Latham recruits people with "social skills and the ability to schmooze." However, the firm is "not just looking for complete glad-handers, but for people who have a good mix of academics and a good personality." Latham traditionally hires from a broad range of top national law schools and the local California schools.

Latham conducts full-day callback interviews that include lunch and dinner and often last until 10 or 11 P.M. Because Latham carefully considers personality in making its hiring decisions, a fact stressed to us by several people we spoke with, the firm places great emphasis on getting to know its candidates well, in both formal and informal settings. "You can't hide" when interviewing at Latham, one successful applicant commented. Throughout the day, the interviewers asks questions such as, "What do you see yourself doing as a lawyer?" and, "What do you see yourself doing in five years?" One strategically-placed insider informed us that, though "we are given no guidelines at all as to what to ask a recruit, people here do focus on personalities." In addition, "the firm brings in your outside interests to assess whether you will fit in with the firm's personality," another insider noted. "You have to have personality. The firm is not big on having people locked away."

If you're team-spirited and think you would fit in well with Latham's cohesive culture, the firm offers a very attractive experience. Latham is "far more social than other firms in L.A.; it's easy to make friends. The partners are actually nice and pleasant to work with. The biggest advantage is the people!", according to one enthusiast. Latham's lawyers are tight-knit and enjoy unique opportunities to "participate" in all aspects of the firm, including its governance. Latham's prestige is on par with any other top L.A. firm, with its high compensation adding extra allure.

Manatt, Phelps & Phillips

Los Angeles Nashville Washington
Mexico City

Address: 11355 West Olympic Boulevard, Los Angeles, CA 90064
Telephone: (310) 312–4000
Hiring Attorney: Ronald B. Turovsky
Contact: Jennifer Malis, Recruiting Coordinator; (310) 312–4187
Associate Salary: Three groups: Tier one \$85,000 base, no bonus; Tier two \$95,000 base, \$0–\$25,000 bonus; Tier three \$115,000 base, \$0–\$50,000 bonus (1997)
Summer Salary: NA
Average Hours: 1913 billed; NA required; NA required
Family Benefits: 12 weeks maternity/paternity leave; flex plan to reimburse day care
1996 Summer: Class of 6; offers to 4
Partnership: NA
Pro Bono: 1–3% of all work is pro bono

Manatt, Phelps & Phillips in 1997
168 Lawyers at the Los Angeles Office
0.6 Associates Per Partner

Total Partners 108		
Women	21	19%
All Minorities	5	5%
Afro-Am	2	2%
Asian-Am	2	2%
Latino	1	1%

Total Associates 60		
Women	29	48%
All Minorities	6	10%
Afro-Am	4	7%
Asian-Am	1	2%
Latino	1	2%

Practice Areas	
Gen. Business Litigation	43
Financial Services	16
Corporate Securities	14
Music	14
Health Care	10
Labor/Employment	10
Government	9
Intellectual Property	8
International Trade	7
Legislative	7
Tax/Trusts & Estates	7
Motion Picture/TV	6
Real Estate	6
Creditors Rights	5
Entertainment Litigation	5
General Counsel	1

"Eclectic" is the word that most people applied to Manatt, Phelps & Phillips. Manatt Phelps lawyers are not, we were told, cookie cutter, big firm lawyers. The firm offers a unique mix of practice areas, including music and motion picture/TV law, and election and government law, which draws lawyers with unusual backgrounds from all walks of life. For example, John F. Kennedy Jr. spent a summer at Manatt Phelps as an aspiring motion picture/TV lawyer. One partner "once tried stand-up comedy, but certainly kept her day job." Another partner made a cameo appearance on Seinfeld. Other Manatt Phelps associates reportedly write screenplays, which is actually not that unusual since, according to a firm insider, "perhaps everyone in L.A. writes screenplays."

Democractic firm

Widely regarded as a premier Democratic firm, Manatt Phelps is also home to a number of political insiders. For instance, Charles Manatt formerly chaired the Democratic National Committee and was President Clinton's national campaign chairperson. Mickey Kantor, former Secretary of Commerce, was a name partner at the firm. Many Manatt Phelp's lawyers left the firm to become part of the Clinton administration. Like the partners, many Manatt Phelps associates evince liberal leanings. One insider recommended the firm as "the best place to be" if you are interested in politics, observing that Manatt Phelps is "much more hands-on involved in local and national politics than O'Melveny & Myers, and it is a much smaller and easier place at which to do well."

colorful atmosphere

Manatt Phelps provides a colorful and informal work atmosphere. Many entertainment lawyers wear jeans in the office and work unusual hours. One person summarized: "It's a less traditional firm. The people are very fun and eccentric, and even if you don't want to do election law or music law, it is fun to have these people around. It provides a fun flavor to have people in jeans, or music and motion picture clients around the office."

refocused management

The earlier edition of *The Insider's Guide to Law Firms* observed that Manatt Phelps was "not exactly managed like a 'tight-run ship.'" We also noted that the firm experienced some tough economic times in the early 1990s (actually "in the 1980s," according to a firm insider). These conditions have apparently righted themselves more recently. Under the present managing partner Gordon Bava, the firm is managed with greater attention to the bottom line and the firm is reportedly very profitable nowadays. The firm recently announced a "significant pay raise" as well as a new "associate compensation structure," together with a bonus structure that "makes no sense" according to one insider. "No one can figure it out. So it is hard to gauge how you can achieve the highest compensation level," this exasperated contact explained. A firm spokesperson, on the other hand, defended the new compensation system as "a smarter and fairer system than the ones other firms use; it emphasizes a variety of unique factors, including leadership and contributions to the firm."

strong corporate banking practice

Founded as a banking boutique firm by Chuck Manatt and Tom Phelps, who both left O'Melveny & Myers in the 1960s to establish the firm, Manatt Phelps has grown rapidly and covers a broad range of practices. Today, the firm is organized around various industry-based practice groups. Although the election and entertainment practices enjoy a high profile, the corporate banking practice traditionally has generated much of the firm's business. Tom Phelps "is a big name in banking," but one contact advised that, though the firm is well-known in the banking world, "if you want to do cutting-edge mergers and acquisitions work, I wouldn't recommend the firm." More recently, however, we have been told that the firm has been listed "in national rankings as among the most active in mergers and acquisitions work involving financial institutions." The banking department was described as "a little more stiff" than Manatt Phelps' other groups, but as "much less traditional and stiff than the banking and corporate practices at other firms."

litigation

Litigation, Manatt Phelps' largest department, has extended a significant number of offers to incoming associates in recent years. A large portion of the litigation department's work involves breach of contract issues and labor litigation. Although in the past the department handled "a much wider variety of smaller cases than you find at most of the national big firms," the litigation practice today reportedly handles "primarily large, highly sophisticated litigation matters."

motion picture/TV

The entertainment practice houses a music group and a motion picture/TV group. One source claimed that Manatt Phelps "does the most music work of any firm in L.A., outside of the boutique firms." Partners Lee Phillips and Jay Cooper, premier music attorneys, enjoy strong reputations throughout the entertainment industry. Manatt's Nashville office has a strong practice in music law for country stars. Overall, the lawyers in the music group were described as top-notch, "hard-working, motivated, bright, and social people." The music attorneys typically arrive at work between 9 and 10 A.M. and are reportedly "always there." By contrast, the motion picture/TV group is smaller, "older," and according to one person, slower than other areas at the firm. Neither the music nor the motion picture/TV practices hires very many new attorneys; however, it is slightly easier to be hired into the music group.

other practice areas

Manatt Phelps' government/administrative practice handles litigation, lobbying, and government regulation issues. "If you are a liberal Democrat or a moderate, it would be a fun place to work," one contact observed, but cautioned that "if you are a Republican or a conservative, you might feel alienated." However, another contact pointed out that "this would not be the case in the firm's Washington D.C. office which is considerably more conservative than the L.A. office. Jack Buechner, of the Washington D.C. office, was the former Republican deputy whip in the House of Representatives." Another warned that this is not one of the faster-growing areas at the firm, and it has only been hiring about one new associate each year. On the other hand, the firm's health law practice, which does a lot of regulatory work for hospitals, is "one of the most lucrative practices at the firm." Its success has been driven primarily by Sherwin Memel who headed one of the biggest health care firms in L.A. before he joined Manatt Phelps.

pro bono

Although Manatt does not engage in an overwhelming amount of pro bono work, its lawyers have high-profile connections to public interest organizations. Mickey Kantor was a member of the Christopher Commission, which launched the Rebuild L.A. effort in which a number of Manatt Phelps attorneys participated. Moreover, Steve Nissen, who now runs Public Counsel in L.A., once worked at Manatt Phelps. Consequently, the firm handles many pro bono matters for that organization, as well as for another similar organization, Bet Tzedek.

lack of formal training

Manatt Phelps is organized to benefit the self-starter. It assigns "no one to hold your hand." One person elaborated: "If you ask, you generally will get help…but no one will cater to your every whim." Manatt Phelps provides little formal training and virtually no institutionalized feedback to permanent associates. A recent contact informed us that though this situation is true, the firm is now "dedicating itself to institutionalized training." In particular, the firm runs a program referred to as the "Manatt Institute," which provides "hands-on seminars covering all aspects of the practice." The firm compensates for the relative lack of training and feedback by offering junior associates early and significant responsibility. It is not uncommon for first-year associates to appear in court. One contact pointed out that, as attractive as the opportunities for early responsibility at the firm are, the downside is that a "high degree of responsibility means you have plenty of rope to hang yourself with."

summer program

Manatt Phelps' summer program offers a little more structure and support. It is run by attorneys affectionately referred to as the "Summer Czars." The Czars are responsible for distributing assignments and monitoring feedback. Summer associates praised the Czars for successfully providing them with projects in their areas of interest and for ensuring that they received feedback. Each attorney for whom a summer associate works completes a form evaluating the summer associate and the work product. These evaluations provide the basis for the summer associate's mid- and end-of-summer reviews.

sports enthusiasts

Manatt Phelps is "good for social life." Its attorneys are "very fun people" and "include lots of different personalities." During the day, Manatt Phelps is a "real chatty firm" and many people "go out a lot after work." Although Manatt Phelps does not host a lavish summer program, it organizes many well-attended events, including regular Thursday afternoon cocktail parties and dinners at partners' houses. Many Manatt Phelps attorneys are sports enthusiasts and enjoy exercising in the gym located in the firm's office building, at which, incidentally, Bruce Springsteen has been known to work out. Basketball and tennis courts are also available adjacent to the office building. Bob Platt, one of the firm's partners, is general counsel to the NBA Los Angeles Clippers.

great for women

Manatt Phelps' female partners reportedly "have a lot of power" at the firm. Maria Hummer heads the land use practice, Lisa Specht is the chair of the administrative law section, and Donna Goldstein, a labor partner, is currently a member of the management committee. One person observed that many women are approaching partnership and predicted that the firm will have even better numbers in the near future. The firm is already, one source claimed, "totally flexible with respect to maternity leave." As a result of a "baby boom" a few years ago, two women worked half-time, one woman returned from maternity leave and four months later became pregnant again, and three women returned from maternity leave. The firm reportedly was very accommodating with respect to these arrangements, although some partnership decisions have been delayed. One insider noted that a music attorney who works three-fourths time is nevertheless "worshiped" at the firm.

openly gay

Unlike some of the more established L.A. firms, Manatt Phelps is not dominated by an "old-boys network." It is "more a microcosm of the real world than most law firms," remarked one contributor, adding that the lawyers "are tolerant of people's interests outside of the firm." This person also noted that there are "a lot of openly gay and bisexual people in the office." Manatt Phelps currently employs a small number of minority attorneys and is reportedly committed to increasing the diversity of its lawyers.

Manatt Phelps offices are in a "great location" in West L.A. Some of our contacts politely described the office decor as "not very traditional looking," whereas others frankly labeled it "ugly," or even "very ugly." A firm spokesperson naturally disputed these judgements, invoking the axiom "de gustibus non disputandum." The overriding theme, we were told, is "black and chrome and red plastic...the early 1980s tacky stuff." Every attorney is provided with his own computer.

hiring tips

Manatt Phelps lawyers "fancy themselves as a bit eccentric," and the firm tends to hire people "who will be aggressive and independent about getting work." One successful applicant believed that the firm looks for "initiative" when hiring people. Another advised, "It helps if you show some spark in the interview. They don't like people who are really typical attorneys—the button-down types...They like someone who will be more eclectic and has a good sense of humor." Most Manatt Phelps attorneys graduated from California law schools, although a number attended New York University or other top 10 national law schools. The firm is "not particularly grade-conscious—this is not the breaker for them," according to one contact. However, a second source was very forceful in instructing us that this policy is no longer operative. It is "not true anymore *at all.* The criteria has been increased and Manatt Phelps only interviews the top of the class." Callback interviews are "relaxed" and casual. In addition to the traditional interviews, there are opportunities for prospective candidates to "learn about the firm from the various partners, the director of client services, and the recruitment coordinator." These opportunities are part of an innovative recruitment program at the firm: a pair of "interview days" during which recruits are "escorted through a series of informational meetings (including a candid discussion session with associates), as well as lunch, interview sessions, and a reception at the close of the day."

If you are into Democratic politics or entertainment, then Manatt Phelps is hard to beat. It provides an open and tolerant atmosphere in which individuals can be themselves. Its offices are on the West side of Los Angeles which, for many, is a "nicer place to work than downtown." Manatt Phelps has more recently made new efforts to "increase the diversity of its clientele" and to hire "top-flight laterals" from other firms. It affords its associates a high degree of responsibility and client contact. One contact informed us that the firm "expects you to build your practice *and* bill 1950, so finding a balance can be tough," but this person added, "this is probably much better than other firms," where such possibilities do not exist.

Mitchell, Silberberg & Knupp

Los Angeles

Address: 11377 W. Olympic Blvd., Los Angeles, CA 90064
Telephone: (310) 312–2000
Hiring Attorney: David A. Steinberg
Contact: Laurel R. Travers/Stacy L. Zolke, Recruitment Administrators; (310) 312–3203
Associate Salary: First year $80,000 (1997); second $81,000; third $86,000; fourth $97,000; fifth $103,000; sixth $114,000; seventh $126,000; eighth $126,000
Summer Salary: $1300/week (1996)
Average Hours: NA worked; NA billed; NA required
Family Benefits: 12 weeks paid maternity leave (4 unpaid); cbc paternity leave
1996 Summer: Class of 5 students; offers to 3
Partnership: 46% of entering associates from 1979–1985 were made partner
Pro Bono: NA (but see below)

Mitchell, Silberberg & Knupp in 1997
116 Lawyers at the Firm
0.8 Associates Per Partner

Total Partners 58		
Women	7	12%
All Minorities	2	3%
Afro-Am	1	2%
Asian-Am	1	2%

Total Associates 47		
Women	18	38%
All Minorities	11	23%
Afro-Am	5	11%
Asian-Am	5	11%
Latino	1	2%

Practice Areas	
Litigation	47
Labor (management)	20
Corporate/Real Estate	18
MPTV	11
Tax/Probate	11
Music	7
Immigration	2

With its relaxed atmosphere and well-known entertainment practice, Mitchell, Silberberg & Knupp is "definitely a West L.A. firm" and is more casual than those located downtown. Attorneys address one another by their first names, and there is said to be "no real class difference" between partners and associates. The lawyers dress relatively informally; Friday is casual dress day. Mitchell Silberberg is also an open firm. It makes information about its financial situation and partner "draws" available to associates, explained one contact. The firm is also tolerant of differences among attorneys. One source found "it to be very open politically to people in both parties." The firm recently received national notoriety with litigation partner Dan Petrocelli's victory in the civil wrongful death action against O.J. Simpson in which the firm represented Ron Goldman's father, Fred Goldman.

independent atmosphere

Mitchell Silberberg attorneys work "fairly long hours," but one contact asserted that the "associates are friendly and approachable." Mitchell Silberberg, however, is "not a very cohesive firm" and evinces a "very independent atmosphere." As a result, "each department is very separate and like its own little firm," revealed one source, adding that "people don't really know people in other departments." A firm spokesperson pointed out that there is some "dependence between such departments as litigation and labor, and corporate and tax. Moreover, matters are frequently staffed on an inter-departmental basis."

motion picture/TV

Mitchell Silberberg is a full-service law firm. It is widely known for negotiating contracts and providing other legal services to distributors, banks, corporations, and talent representatives. The firm is most highly regarded, however, for its motion picture and T.V.

and music departments. The motion picture and music practices are reputedly the most relaxed and "freewheeling," because, according to one contact, "of the way their clients are." "Politics is very important" in the entertainment department, observed one source. It is not an easy group to join. We have been told that the department is no longer hiring summer associates for full time employment; the department is now only hiring laterals. Moreover, the department has reportedly undergone some changes of late, with the departure of a small group that had only recently joined the firm. The restructuring appears to have been accomplished with only minimal disturbance to the rest of the firm.

litigation

Litigation is the firm's largest practice area. It has handled extensive copyright and entertainment litigation, including the Milli Vanilli lip-syncing matter. Intellectual property, co-chaired by a new partner to the firm, Steve Shapiro, has recently developed as a practice area in the litigation department. The department also handles a range of commercial, tax, and white-collar criminal litigation. Ed Medvene is a well-known white-collar criminal defense litigator. Partner Arthur Groman represented Howard Hughes.

other practice areas

Mitchell Silberberg is "fairly well-known for labor," which is on the way to becoming the firm's "strongest" department, according to one contact. The labor group is "very close-knit." The firm offers a strong tax and estate planning practice group, which includes Allan Biblin, well-known for his expertise in this area. The corporate practice, which handles the financing of entertainment deals, has been slow in the past. Some of the firm's work has an international flavor, such as its film financing and multinational distribution agreement negotiations.

pro bono

Mitchell Silberberg attorneys devote a minimum of 35 to 40 hours per year to pro bono work. The firm credits any time spent on pro bono work toward the minimum billable hour goal of 1850 hours per year. Mitchell Silberberg is affiliated with many public interest organizations, and summer associates are required to work at least one day for Public Counsel.

work assignments

Summer associates receive their assignments from a general pool and may also elect to rotate through one or two departments for one or two week periods each. One attorney is responsible for gathering and distributing work assignments to summer associates, though sometimes lawyers directly approach summer associates with work. The firm extends offers of full-time employment to summer associates by department. These offers are based on the summer associate's overall performance and work for that department, the number of openings available, the department's interest in the summer associate, and the summer associate's interest in working in that department. The firm formally evaluates summer associates three times during the summer.

significant opportunity

Entering associates join a particular department and "there doesn't seem to be a lot of room for changing areas or mixing your work," according to one contact. Attorneys in each department monitor the workload of new associates and distribute assignments. New litigation associates are usually assigned to six or seven teams of attorneys handling different cases. They handle primarily research and writing assignments, although there are exceptions. Some first years "take and defend depositions regularly and do a lot of motion work," and recently a "first year litigation associate took a case to trial on his own—and won!", we were informed by one firm enthusiast. Others that we spoke with commented that there is "tremendous responsibility given to young associates who are willing to accept it" and that the firm attempts to provide associates "with a quality, diverse work load." Associates are advised to develop working relationships with particular attorneys. Noting that "a spirit of cooperation is very important" at the firm, one source cautioned that "word circulates quickly" about an uncooperative associate.

Mitchell Silberberg handles cases of many sizes and quickly offers junior associates responsibility on small cases. According to one contact, corporate associates are pulled in on deals quickly. The firm is a certified MCLE provider and accordingly offers formal training programs. New associates in the litigation and labor employment law departments participate in a formal training program "consisting of a dozen or so training sessions, for which they also receive continuing legal education credit required by the state bar." We were told, however, that most training occurs on-the-job. Each department meets regularly to discuss its work and new developments in the law. Those we interviewed commented that informal feedback is generally better in corporate and tax than in the litigation department.

social life

Social life at Mitchell Silberberg is "very informal," "relaxed and friendly" but for most lawyers "relationships don't go beyond working hours," said one contact. Another concurred that "people are well-balanced enough that they don't need the firm to provide" their social life. Mitchell Silberberg occupies one tower of a two-tower office building, which is pleasantly outfitted with a health club and tennis courts. The westside location of the firm is "nice," according to several people we contacted. Most attorneys limit their social interaction to the work day when they often play tennis or work out in the gym together. The firm organizes weekly Friday evening happy hours for its attorneys which, once a month, are open to the entire firm. Mitchell Silberberg also hosts a variety of events throughout the year, such as all-employee firm picnics, evenings at Disneyland (family members invited), and attorney dinner/dances. Each department also has an annual retreat.

diversity

Mitchell Silberberg was founded as a predominantly Jewish firm at a time when Jews were not widely hired by the established Los Angeles firms. The firm is "clearly committed to recruiting women," one contact told us. A "number of women are partners or up-and-coming stars." Litigation partner Lucia Loyoca recently completed three years as the firm's hiring partner. Other influential women include Deborah Koeffler, a labor partner, and Danna Cook, an African-American partner in the music group. One contact informed us that the labor department is a "great place for women," with a 2:1 ratio of women to men associates in the group, and "sensitive" leadership on the part of Deborah Koeffler. The firm is quite accommodating on family issues, said one source, noting that some women have nursed their babies in the office. When asked about sexual harassment, one person responded that the lawyers are "all very nervous about and afraid of it." This is perhaps due to the firm's "very strong policy prohibiting any type of harassment." The firm has had past experience with harassment issues, one person asserted.

Mitchell Silberberg experienced some economic difficulty in past years and laid off some of its associates in 1991. Although most people we interviewed believed that the firm is past its hard times, some noted that the corporate and real estate practice groups continue to be "problematic." In response to the changing economy, the firm has focused on running itself more like a business, and, according to a firm spokesperson, Mitchell Silberberg "experienced one of the most profitable years in its history in 1996." Further, the firm has restructured and reorganized its attorneys into practice groups targeting those areas of law that are of primary interest to its client base. The firm has also hired laterally to boost areas where the firm had not previously been involved. A few years back, it created a managing partner position to centralize some of the decision making authority, although overall, the firm continues to be run very democratically, with each partner having one vote on major firm decisions.

associates in the dark

Although associates have generally been well-informed regarding the financial condition of the firm, people commented that they were kept in the dark with respect to some of the firm's past financial hardships. Moreover, there is continuing concern about compensation, which one person noted "doesn't seem to be as favorable" as at other firms. This person also pointed out that "other firms give a first year bonus—plus a pay incentive upon passing the bar—Mitchell doesn't and this affects morale of first year associates." Another person informed us that the firm has "no 401K" plan. Not all news was grim, however, on the monetary front. A third person indicated that this past year "associates got raises."

Hollywierd support staff

Mitchell Silberberg shares its office building with another prominent L.A. firm, Manatt Phelps. In addition to the gym, and tennis and basketball courts, the building offers secured free parking. Each attorney has a private office and computer, described by one person as "rotten [and] outdated." Two attorneys share a secretary. One source labeled the support staff as "Hollyweird," commenting, "I have seen more cooperative xerox departments." Another person remarked that "a good secretary, even a competent floater, is a rare thing" at Mitchell Silberberg.

In addition to requiring good grades and perhaps membership on a law review, Mitchell Silberberg hires law students who have "outside interests, independence, and a self-assertive attitude." One insider stated that you must have the "ability to take the ball and run with it." The firm also expects associates to "socialize to an extent and looks for congeniality and self-assuredness." One observer believed that generally younger attorneys seek "competent people with charisma," and older partners "look very much to grades or law review."

interview tips

The interview process begins with an on-campus screening interview, usually conducted by two attorneys. At local schools, those students in which the firm is interested are invited for a second on-campus interview the following week. In past years, the firm has extended offers at the end of the second interview. Insiders advised that students interviewing with the firm not emphasize an interest in entertainment work. Many of the firm's attorneys believe that "people who want to practice entertainment law don't want to be attorneys, and instead want glamour," explained one source. The firm hires law students from the top 15 national law schools and Los Angeles-area schools.

Mitchell, Silberberg & Knupp offers an attractive array of practice areas, including a very well-reputed entertainment department. It also provides an informal and comfortable working environment and is a great place for women to work. One admirer declared that, though attorneys work hard, Mitchell Silberberg exhibits "far greater concern for the family unit and family life" than many other large firms.

Morgan, Lewis & Bockius

Los Angeles Harrisburg Miami New York Philadelphia Pittsburgh Princeton New York Washington Brussels Frankfurt Jakarta London Singapore Tokyo

Address: 801 South Grand Avenue, Suite 2200, Los Angeles, CA 90017–4615 (new address as of fall 1997: 300 South Grand Avenue, Los Angeles, CA 90071)
Telephone: (213) 612–2500
Hiring Attorney: Ann E. Stone
Contact: Cheryl C. Yoshitake, Recruiting Coordinator; (213) 612–2600
Associate Salary: First year $80,000; salary increases by approximately $10,000 per year for the first five years, after which increases depend heavily on merit; eligibility for merit-based bonus begins to accrue at third year
Summer Salary: $1450/week (1997)
Average Hours: 2279 worked; 1974 billed; 1925 required
Family Benefits: Maternity leave; back-up childcare and (EASE) family counseling program
1996 Summer: Class of 11 students; offers to 10
Partnership: 43% of entering associates from the classes of 1979, 1981, and 1982 were made partner
Pro Bono: 2% of all work is pro bono

Morgan, Lewis & Bockius in 1997
75 Lawyers at the Los Angeles Office
1.0 Associate Per Partner

Total Partners 35			Total Associates 34			Practice Areas	
Women	6	17%	Women	12	35%	Litigation	31
All Minorities	1	3%	All Minorities	8	24%	Business Finance	20
Latino	1	3%	Afro Am	3	9%	Labor (management)	16
			Asian-Am	4	12%	Tax	3
			Latino	1	3%	Government Regulation	3
						Trusts & Estates	2

The Los Angeles office of Philadelphia-based Morgan, Lewis & Bockius was founded in 1976 and is not as well-known as some of the firm's other older and more established offices. The nationally-recognized Morgan, Lewis & Bockius operates ten offices worldwide and is one of largest and most prestigious law firms in the country. The Los Angeles office has slimmed down considerably since our last edition, decreasing from a 101 attorney office to a 75 attorney office.

Philadelphia influence

The Philadelphia influence is immediately apparent upon entering the Los Angeles office, which, in contrast to the modern, light, and airy decor characteristic of L.A.-based firms, is decorated with dark wood fixtures. People described the office as exuding an "old-fashioned" and "stuffy" feel, reminiscent of "east coast" law firms. However, we were told that there is "much excitement" at the firm "surrounding the Los Angeles office's impending move to the One California Plaza Office Building, located next door to the Museum of Contemporary Art in the Bunker Hill area of downtown," which will reportedly catapult Morgan Lewis into the ranks of the "lighter and airier" Los Angeles law firms. The Morgan Lewis attorneys cement the "conservative" air of the firm with their restrained dress code. Men primarily wear dark navy to dark gray suits, although the women's dress style is more diverse. However, despite their dress and the firm's reputedly conservative management style, we were told that a majority of Morgan Lewis' young associates and partners evince liberal leanings.

practice areas

Firmwide, Morgan Lewis is widely regarded as one of the country's foremost labor firms. The L.A. office also offers a substantial labor practice that continues to grow and develop. One person described the labor department as both "very fun-loving" and hard-working and commented that though "there are lots of jokesters in that group, they are swamped with work and work longer hours than other departments."

The litigation practice is also "very exciting and diverse," we were told. Associates do not find themselves holed up in the library with no appearances in court. Rather, "associates are quickly given opportunities to draft whole motions, make appearances in court, and take and defend depositions."

The business and finance section, which is considerably smaller today than three years ago, represents a broad array of large corporations, including many members of the Fortune 500 list. The office's business and finance group handles primarily securities, mergers and acquisitions, licensing, project finance, commercial finance and real estate matters. Pro bono is "a commitment of the firm," we were told, and associates get billable hours credit for it. The firm gets most of its cases from Public Counsel, but much pro bono work is left up to individual initiative.

departmental assignments

Morgan Lewis hires entering associates for specific departments based on its needs and the associates' preferences. Though it is difficult to change a departmental assignment, "unofficially it is known that you can ask to be moved and the firm will accommodate you," particularly if you have real problems in the department. Morgan Lewis has not offered much formal training in the past, but it has now become more of a priority, we were told. According to one insider, "all associates get 50 'training hours' to 'play with'." Much of the training still occurs on-the-job in an "individualized" manner and depends on the responsible partner's commitment to teaching.

excellent summer feedback

The feedback in the summer program is excellent. The assigning attorney and one member of the summer committee review each assignment submitted by a summer associate. Each attorney completes extensive evaluation forms that include numerical ratings in different categories. Although one page of the evaluation is kept confidential, summer associates have access to the evaluations at all times throughout the summer.

tame social life

One source interpreted the apparent lack of firm sponsored social life throughout the year as an indication that the firm is "pretty tight with its money." Morgan Lewis certainly "doesn't throw money around," but it does organize an office retreat every October for all lawyers, paralegals, and administrators, and does host a few formal social events during the year. The firm also sponsors a "weekly soiree among the lawyers, staff and other employees of the firm, with a changing variety of food and drink, tailored to the time of year and holidays," reported one contact. Although a lavish social program is clearly not a firm priority, people reported that the spontaneous social life at the firm was fairly active and fun. Morgan Lewis employs many young associates who form a core group that likes to go out and have a good time. It is definitely not a "party" firm, however.

diversity efforts

Firmwide, Morgan Lewis has "traditionally been an old-boy's place," but this image is changing, one insider informed us. The L.A. office employs six female partners. Business and finance partners, Anne Stone and Kathy Johnson, both play a major role in the hiring process, and are "committed to increasing the number of female partners," we were told.

hiring tips

Morgan Lewis places great emphasis on hiring "team players" and seeks people who are down-to-earth and not "stuffy" or "conceited." The firm draws most of its summer class from the top 20 national law schools, but it also hires law students who attend local California schools. The Morgan Lewis interview process consists of an on-campus screening interview followed by a callback interview at the firm's offices where five or six attorneys interview the applicant. One person advised applicants that because the firm's fastest growing practice areas are business and finance, litigation, and labor, it is more likely to hire summer associates who express an interest in these practice areas.

The firm's major offices have a local office management committee "with substantial autonomy, but many macro-level decisions are made at the firmwide management level," a firm spokesperson informed us. For example, decisions such as those involving promotion to partnership are made on a firmwide basis. As a result, one source asserted, it is important to network throughout the firm to advance. Others had even harsher views regarding partnership prospects at Morgan Lewis. One contact observed that "partnership opportunities are not clearly defined or manifestly available. The firm appears to be adopting, as are other large national firms, a 'New York' style, in that associates are given much training and practice opportunities, but not much hope of making partnership from the associate track." A second contact observed, simply that "partnership here is only a distant possibility."

Morrison & Foerster

Los Angeles Denver New York Orange County Palo Alto Sacramento San Francisco Walnut Creek Washington, D.C. Brussels London Hong Kong Tokyo

Address: 555 West Fifth Street, Suite 2200, Los Angeles, CA 90013–1024
Telephone: (213) 892–5200
Hiring Attorney: Janie F. Schulman
Contact: Jannette M. Lyon, Recruiting Coordinator; (213) 892–5403
Associate Salary: First year $80,000 (1996)
Summer Salary: $1300/week (1996)
Average Hours: NA worked; NA billed; 1850 required
Family Benefits: 12 weeks paid maternity leave; family care leave
1996 Summer: Class of 17 students; offers to 14
Partnership: 31% of entering associates from 1979–1985 were made partner
Pro Bono: 4% of all work (firmwide) is pro bono

Morrison & Foerster in 1997
98 Lawyers at the Los Angeles Office
1.4 Associates Per Partner

Total Partners 37		
Women	10	27%
All Minorities	0	0%

Total Associates 51		
Women	20	39%
All Minorities	12	24%
Afro-Am	3	6%
Asian-Am	7	14%
Latino	2	4%

Practice Areas	
Corporate	NA
Real Estate	NA
Tax	NA
Litigation	NA
Labor	NA
Land Use/Environmental	NA
Financial Transactions	NA
Project Finance	NA

In the past 25 years, Morrison & Foerster, affectionately known as MoFo, has grown to be one of the country's largest and most prestigious mega firms. Although MoFo's L.A. office is technically a "branch" office of the San Francisco headquarters, people commented that it is hardly controlled by the San Francisco management. The two offices interact more as equals than as a home office and its branch. The Los Angeles office is an equal participant in management decisions and, unlike at many other branch offices, its associates are not at a disadvantage with respect to promotion to partnership.

informal atmosphere

Morrison & Foerster was described as a "friendly" and "informal" firm with a lot of chatting in the halls. Certain firm traditions, like bad tie day and ugliest plaid day, are hallmarks of the firm's casual atmosphere. The dress is more laid-back than some L.A. firms. Though attorneys do not wear jeans to work (except on "casual" Fridays), as do those at some entertainment firms, women feel comfortable wearing pants and dresses, and there is no "strict dress code" for men.

liberal leanings

Reputedly one of the nation's most progressive firms, MoFo exhibits a very "liberal bent" and, more than other places, professes its commitment to increasing the racial and cultural diversity of its attorneys and to pro bono work. One source claimed that Morrison & Foerster is widely regarded as a first-rate place for women and minority attorneys to work. Another remarked that the firm has "fantastic programs available for working parents." One of the firm's hiring partners, Janie Schulman, is one of many "heavy hitter" women at the firm. One African-American student we interviewed for another firm reported that, in general, African-American law students and attorneys believe that Morrison & Foerster and O'Melveny & Myers offer them the most open-minded and comfortable work environments in Los Angeles. Morrison & Foerster is also very receptive to attorneys who pursue alternative lifestyles and provides a tolerant atmosphere for its gay attorneys. One attorney underscored this for us, observing that "I can sign my partner on for my benefits and *all* performance evaluations are based on quality of work." Perhaps because of this atmosphere, the firm was the only law firm picked for inclusion in the list of *The 100 Best Companies to Work for in America.*

politically correct firm

Morrison & Foerster's democratic management style reflects its open culture. The firm's associates, unlike their colleagues at most other large firms, participate in a number of important management decisions. They also regularly evaluate the firm's partners, and these evaluations can affect partner compensation. Moreover, the firm regularly holds "roundtable meetings" where partners and associates discuss firm policies and other issues. One source believed, however, that the frank airing of attorney concerns can sometimes be distracting: "There is a lot of controversy at Morrison. People argue about policies such as what kind of diversity policy the firm should have, and how much weight should be given to certain things. There is more controversy because people talk more about it. It can be tiresome if you just want to work there, and not get involved in the politically correct rhetoric. It's a PC firm, and this can be a drawback." Not everyone agrees with this assessment; a second contact professed to be "not aware of any such conflict."

practice areas

Originally established to service a major banking client, the L.A. office has grown to around 100 lawyers, most of whom are members of either the litigation or the business departments. The business department, described as slightly more formal than the litigation department, was slow in the early 90s but has picked up considerably of late, particularly in the area of corporate finance. Managing partner Michael J. Connell is one of the firm's most prominent business attorneys. The department is actively developing a Pacific Rim practice, particularly in Tokyo and Hong Kong, which mainly handles issues arising from foreign investment in the United States. Morrison & Foerster's many offices regularly work together on these matters. The business department also houses a financial institutions group which was described as "high-powered, very busy, and high strung." Morrison & Foerster's litigation department covers a broad range of areas and represents many of the firm's Pacific Rim clients. One person noted that this pleasant department is "not a screaming litigation department. There aren't a bunch of yellers there." The office's fast growing practice areas include labor, intellectual property and litigation.

strong pro bono practice

People we interviewed raved about MoFo's strong commitment to pro bono work. Morrison & Foerster partners and associates, we were told, choose to accept a lower salary than their counterparts at some other prestigious L.A. firms so that they may maintain a more balanced lifestyle and donate a significant amount of time to public interest work. One person observed that "the minimum billable hours of 1850 (with a bonus available for those who bill 1950) and the actual billable hours per attorney are fairly low" compared to other firms of Mo Fo's size and prestige. However, this person noted that firm management is presently becoming "increasingly concerned about Mo Fo's traditionally lower than average profitability—rather than simply accepting it as a natural result of lower hours and a humane working environment." It is rumored that each partner would make "several thousand more per year if it were not farmed back into pro bono work," claimed one source. Pro bono hours count toward billable hours and bonuses, and the firm provides an encouraging and supportive atmosphere for pro bono work. The firm handles a broad range of pro bono matters and was involved in the Rebuild L.A. project.

flexible transfers

Morrison & Foerster hires associates to work in specific departments. Though the firm attempts to match individual preferences with its needs, it offers no guarantee that an entering associate will be placed in his or her top choice department. The firm is, however, very accommodating of attorneys who want to transfer among its many offices. One source related that occasionally a student worked at one office as a summer associate, but ended up accepting an offer from another office. Unlike associates, summer associates have the opportunity to experience a variety of the firm's practice areas. The summer coordinators assign projects to the summer class according, to the extent possible, to each person's particular interests.

limited opportunity

Because MoFo primarily represents the nation's largest corporations, it offers junior associates less responsibility than many firms with smaller clients. Many MoFo litigation assignments in the early years involve researching and writing memos. There are exceptions, however. We were informed of associates who, in their first year, did a "lot of written discovery, written motions and depositions." The business department reportedly offers its junior associates more responsibility and greater opportunities for client contact. The firm, moreover, provides substantial formal training to both summer associates and associates.

office facilities

Morrison & Foerster associates get along well together, and many socialize after work. During the day, however, the firm is slightly more formal, perhaps because its spacious offices offer reduced opportunities for social interaction. The offices have a very "modern black leather and shiny chrome look in the lobby areas." There is "a lot of whiteness all over," and "interesting" and "funky" sculptures are displayed throughout the office. Some people find the office "really nice," but others claim it looks like a "modern airport lounge." Every associate has a private office and a computer, which is linked into a PC network.

hiring tips

In recent years, Morrison & Foerster has hired diverse summer classes. One of the most diverse summer classes in recent years, 1992, included "only a couple of white men...who were not gay," claimed one insider. Another person observed that this was true in 1996 as well; there were "17 summer associates and only two straight white men." Morrison & Foerster places less emphasis on grades than on "how you react to the person" interviewing you. Students typically meet with about six or seven attorneys for 20 minutes to a half hour in their callback interviews. The firm draws most of its summer class from the California schools but also hires students who attend the top national schools.

MoFo is a "PC" firm. It provides an open atmosphere in which women and minorities feel comfortable. It is distinguished by having a particularly strong public interest commitment and by the opportunities that it provides for associates to participate in its governance.

Munger, Tolles & Olson

Los Angeles San Francisco

Address: 355 South Grand Avenue, 35th Floor, Los Angeles, CA 90071
Telephone: (213) 683–9100
Hiring Attorney: William D. Temko and Bart H. Williams, Co-Chairs, Recruiting Committee
Contact: Linda Cherry, Recruiting Coordinator; (213) 683–9208
Associate Salary: First year $80,000 (1997); second $85,000; third $90,000 plus bonus; fourth $95,000 plus bonus; fifth $100,000 plus bonus; sixth $100,000 plus bonus; seventh $100,000 plus bonus
Summer Salary: $1300/week (1997)
Average Hours: 1997 worked; 1997 billed; NA required
Family Benefits: 12 weeks paid maternity leave (4 unpaid); 4 weeks paid paternity leave (12 unpaid)
1996 Summer: NA
Partnership: 29% of entering associates from 1984–1990 were made partner
Pro Bono: 2–5% of all work is pro bono

Munger, Tolles & Olson in 1997
113 Lawyers at the Los Angeles Office
0.8 Associates Per Partner

Total Partners 62			Total Associates 51			Practice Areas	
Women	9	15%	Women	16	31%	Litigation	72
All Minorities	5	8%	All Minorities	9	18%	Corporate	17
Afro-Am	1	2%	Afro-Am	4	8%	Environmental	7
Asian-Am	2	3%	Asian-Am	2	4%	Real Estate	6
Latino	2	3%	Latino	3	6%	Tax	5
						Labor (management)	4
						Bankruptcy	2

Founded in 1962, Munger, Tolles & Olson has experienced dynamic growth and is now perched among the upper ranks of L.A.'s largest and most renowned firms. Widely considered a top-notch firm by law students, Munger reportedly hires only the most highly-qualified applicants, such as former members of a law review or prestigious judicial clerks. The firm's ability to attract the top legal minds emerging from law schools nationwide is, one person told us, the secret to its success.

democratic governance

It is no surprise that Munger is such an attractive choice for law students. The firm offers a unique combination of a truly participatory governance structure, a short partnership track, excellent on-the-job training, and broad exposure to a highly successful litigation practice. Munger is managed in an open and decentralized fashion with its "management" committee primarily playing a role of "facilitating consensus-building," a firm spokesperson informed us. The firm decides virtually every management issue, with some important exceptions such as associate compensation questions, by a vote of the entire firm. These decisions are all the more meaningful because Munger's management freely discloses information about the firm and its finances. All Munger associates, including summer associates, are "provided full details on the firm's finances" and have access to the firm's "balance sheet." Consequently, associates are fully informed participants in the decision-making process.

Munger's hiring practices highlight the firm's participatory nature. At the end of each summer, the firm compiles a book containing evaluations of all the summer associates' work product for the review of all its attorneys. The whole firm then votes to extend or withhold offers of full-time employment to the summer associates. Although everyone we interviewed praised Munger's democratic and open governance, one questioned the viability of this somewhat unwieldy system as the firm continues to grow.

early partnership opportunity

Munger's short partnership track and early opportunities for responsibility serve as a magnet for the brightest applicants. Munger considers its associates for partnership after four or five years, a shorter period than most major firms. Some Munger attorneys have even made partner in three years. In addition, because Munger partners outnumber the associates, the firm offers associates the opportunity to work closely with the partners. Although the firm does not heavily emphasize formal training, we were told that the partners provide excellent on-the-job training and feedback and dispense significant responsibility early. Associates are able to "choose their work, they can say no" but this requires "sufficient self-confidence to seek out experiences you want," we were told by one contact. It is not uncommon for first- and second-year litigation associates to argue motions in court, and most enjoy substantial client contact very shortly after joining the firm. One source claimed that "no one feels stuck in the library" at Munger, perhaps because the firm handles "a fair number of smaller cases...that can be done by associates." The same is true in the corporate department. One insider described a junior corporate attorney who "had full responsibility for drafting agreements ancillary to a major deal." Munger also allows starting associates the freedom to work in one area of interest to them, or to work in a number of practice areas.

intense atmosphere

Not surprisingly, Munger's work atmosphere is very "intense" and "can be stressful," but its attorney turnover rate is reportedly low. Munger lawyers, we were told, are genuinely interested in their work and work long hours, often well into the night. One person noted that Munger is "not a place to find a social life." Attorneys have lives away from the office and therefore tend to focus on their work while at the office. Many Munger attorneys have families and "want to leave and go home and get on to other things" at the end of the day.

Munger's summer program reflects the fact that it is "not a party firm." Although the firm hosts "sherry sips" on Friday afternoons and lunches year-round, the program does not include an "overwhelming" number of social events. Summer associates are invited to "in-home dinners, baseball games, concerts, and outings to local attractions." Munger does, however, provide summer associates a free membership at the YMCA located immediately across from its office building.

practice areas

Founded as a securities litigation, corporate, and tax firm, Munger, Tolles & Olson has grown in the last 10 years to cover a broad range of areas. It is perhaps best known for its excellent securities litigation practice. One insider described the securities litigation lawyers as "very intelligent" and "top-notch lawyers" and noted that the "young associates work their tails off." In addition to securities, the firm handles a variety of litigation and transactional matters and is not highly departmentalized. We were told that "people work on various things and partners have their own clients, but they work together. There is a lot of interaction among attorneys at the firm." Name partner Ron Olson is a driving force behind the litigation group and was described to us as a major rainmaker and one of the country's top litigators. Other well-known Munger partners include Bob Adler, who is a highly regarded transactional attorney, and Dick Volpert, who is a highly-regarded real estate attorney. This roster of distinguished partners could easily be greatly enlarged but that, according to one insider, would be "un-Munger." "We're a team and each element is necessary. Any list is too short."

pro bono Munger "pays more than lip service to allowing associates and summer associates to do pro bono work." Hours billed to pro bono matters count toward billable hours and the firm has a "very liberal pro bono policy." One of the firm's prominent partners, John Spiegel, served as deputy counsel for the Christopher Commission, and a number of Munger attorneys have been involved in the effort to rebuild L.A. Vilma Martinez, a prominent Latina partner, is the former head of the Mexican-American Legal Defense and Education Fund and is active in the community. The firm is also affiliated with the MacLaren Children's Center for abused or abandoned children. Munger was recently recognized by both the ABA and the State Bar of California for its "exceptional contribution in pro bono matters," we were told.

diversity Although Munger employs many more men than women, the firm reportedly provides a "comfortable" atmosphere for women and offers, according to one source, a "liberal" parental leave policy. The firm tries to offer "flexibility" to both new parents and other attorneys requesting part-time schedules. Recently, for example, one of the associates had a child and was able to return part-time with an hourly salary and a schedule limited to three days a week. Several prominent women, including labor law partner Vilma Martinez, corporate law partner Ruth Fisher, and "well-respected" partner Lucy Eisenberg serve as role models at the firm. Munger does very well with respect to minority employment, posting some of the best numbers in the city. In 1997, the minority attorneys at the firm included one African-American partner, Bart Williams, who rejoined the firm after time at the U.S. Attorney's office, and a number of other minority attorneys as shown in the statistics section above. The firm also has several openly gay attorneys who bring their partners to firm events.

offices Munger's offices are located in the IBM tower of the Wells Fargo Complex in downtown L.A. The "modern-looking" offices are decorated in "light wood" and exude an "open and airy" feel. Every associate is assigned a private office with a computer. Consistent with Munger's democratic and fair-minded culture, all of the firm's private offices are one of two sizes: large for partners and most associates, and small for first- and second-year associates. The firm has also eliminated all corner offices, which usually emphasize the hierarchy of office assignments, by locating its conference rooms in the corners of each floor.

hiring tips Munger hires law students who represent the "cream of the crop." The firm carefully examines applicants' academic records. It also emphasizes law review or judicial clerkship experience. Munger primarily hires students from the top 15 national law schools. The firm conducts a callback interview over a half day, during which the candidate meets individually with six or seven attorneys. Interviews for full-time hires are conducted over the course of a full day. Most interview questions pertain to college and law school experiences. One contact said that if you are on law review, they will often ask you about your role. Some members of the hiring committee are reportedly very concerned about "social commitment," and one particular attorney is known to ask about an individual's commitment to community involvement.

Munger's unstructured and open atmosphere makes it unique among L.A.'s top-ranked firms. However, it is very difficult to land a summer position at this law shop. Only the best students across the country have a chance to experience the many features that make Munger, Tolles & Olson such an attractive place.

O'Melveny & Myers

Los Angeles/Century City Los Angeles New York Newark Newport Beach San Francisco Washington
Hong Kong London Shanghai Tokyo

Address: Los Angeles: 400 South Hope Street, Los Angeles, CA 90071–2899
Century City: 1999 Avenue of the Stars, Suite 700, Los Angeles, CA 90067
Telephone: LA: (213) 669–6000
CC: (310) 553–6700
Hiring Attorney: LA: David D. Watts
CC: David I. Weil
Contact: LA: Cheryl Newton, Recruiting Manager; (213) 669–6046
CC: Luly Del Pozo, Recruiting Coordinator; (310) 246–6821
Associate Salary: First year $83,000 (1997); second $90,000; third $101,000; fourth $115,000; fifth $135,000; sixth $160,000; seventh $170,000; eighth $177,000
Summer Salary: $1300/week (1997)
Average Hours: NA worked; 1889 billed; NA required (both offices)
Family Benefits: 12 weeks paid maternity leave; disability leave (cbc unpaid)
1996 Summer: LA: Class of 49 students; offers to 45
CC: Class of 14 students; offers to 12
Partnership: LA: 17% of entering associates from 1978–1987 were made partner
CC: 21% of entering associates from 1978–1987 were made partner
Pro Bono: 4–7% of all work is pro bono

O'Melveny & Myers in 1997
216 Lawyers at the Los Angeles Office
1.6 Associates Per Partner

Total Partners 76			Total Associates 140			Practice Areas	
Women	8	11%	Women	45	32%	Litigation	78
All Minorities	4	5%	All Minorities	27	19%	Corporate	60
Afro-Am	2	3%	Afro-Am	5	4%	Labor & Employment	28
Asian-Am	2	3%	Asian-Am	12	9%	Real Estate	22
			Latino	10	7%	Tax	16

51 Lawyers at the Century City Office
1.1 Associates Per Partner

Total Partners 24			Total Associates 27			Practice Areas	
Women	2	8%	Women	8	30%	Corporate	13
All Minorities	1	4%	All Minorities	3	11%	Entertainment	13
Asian-Am	1	4%	Asian-Am	3	11%	Litigation	10
						Real Estate	8
						Tax	7

A member of L.A.'s trio of most prestigious firms, O'Melveny & Myers is the city's "establishment liberal" firm. Founded in 1885, it is one of the nation's oldest firms and has long been known as one of the most high-profile firms in the Democratic community. Many O'Melveny attorneys enjoy close ties with the Democratic party, including Warren Christopher, who recently returned to the firm as a senior partner after serving as President Clinton's Secretary of State. Other O'Melveny partners are involved in the California Democratic party running campaigns—one of the campaigns for mayor was run by a former O'Melveny partner, and the mayor himself is a former O'Melveny associate. In addition, O'Melveny is widely-recognized in L.A. for its commitment to pro bono work. We were told that "almost everyone is involved in the local scene." Many O'Melveny lawyers worked on the Christopher Commission. The firm enjoys this reputation and is, one source told us, "very proud of" and "talks a lot about" its illustrious history and long tradition of public service that lives on through a number of its attorneys whose "fathers and grandfathers worked at the firm."

Wall Street atmosphere

Described as "Wall Street California," O'Melveny's work atmosphere in both the Century City and downtown Los Angeles offices signals that "the primary focus is on work." Though the Century City office was described as somewhat casual, people applied the words "white shoe" and "stodgy" to the main downtown office. O'Melveny attorneys typically dress "conservatively" in navy blue and gray suits, and according to one contact, the downtown lawyers wear "darker colors" that match the office furniture. Though O'Melveny is not a "party firm," its attorneys get along well and are friendly in the office. In the downtown office, they socialize and eat together in the firm's dining facility (for lawyers and senior staff only), complete with white linen tablecloths. One person noted, however, that there is not much interaction between partners and associates in the dining room.

practice areas

O'Melveny's largest and most prominent departments are litigation and corporate. The litigation department handles many high-profile matters. It was lead counsel for Exxon in the litigation arising from the Valdez oil spill. The department houses some of the firm's "heavy hitters," such as Pat Lynch, who has worked on many high-profile antitrust and intellectual property matters over the years; Cheryl Mason, who is prominent in both antitrust and regulatory matters pertaining to utility companies as well as in insurance and environmental litigation; Bill Vaughn, who is the former head of the litigation department (currently headed by Henry Thumann); and Chuck Bender, who is the chairperson of the management committee. Kim Wardlaw, former President of the Women Lawyers of L.A., recently left the department to become a federal judge in the central district of California. The litigation department was described as "fairly formal," though one person pointed out to us that one of its most prominent members (the aforementioned Pat Lynch) "rarely wears a suit to the office, frequently plays basketball with junior associates, and drives around South Pasadena in an old, multicolored, VW van." The department is organized into red, blue, and yellow teams, though, in practice, matters are staffed with little regard for color group affiliations. The teams were established because it was thought that the "department had grown too large to have useful bi-weekly meetings involving the entire department."

corporate

O'Melveny's corporate department experienced a transition period a few years ago, during which time the department was divided into ten focus groups. The corporate department boasts many well-known lawyers, including Doug Kranwinkle, who formerly was prominent in the corporate department at Munger, Tolles & Olson, and Gil Ray, who, according to one insider, is the "West Coast version of Ron Brown—very tapped into everything politically."

real estate labor

O'Melveny's real estate department represents banks and lenders and, unlike the real estate departments of other firms, "has a lot of work...Even in distressed times there were lots of negotiations." The real estate lawyers were described as "very close-knit." The firm also has a labor department that primarily represents large corporations and school boards and engages in "preventive" work, such as seminars on sexual harassment, to make clients more "aware." Like the real estate lawyers, the labor lawyers were described as "very close-knit and chummy," but they were also said to be "very hardworking." One insider remarked that the labor lawyers "have a contest...for who can go the longest without taking a vacation." Although one contact described the labor lawyers as "relaxed," another claimed they are the "we–take–no–prisoners types."

Century City

The firm's Century City office, located approximately ten miles west of downtown Los Angeles, now employs 51 attorneys and is the focal point for the firm's representation of clients based in West Los Angeles and for the firm's entertainment industry practice. The firm's presence on the west side of Los Angeles dates back to 1938, when an office was opened in the CBS Building in Hollywood to serve a growing number of entertainment clients. Today the office enjoys a diverse practice in the areas of corporate law, banking, finance and securities law, litigation, real estate law, taxation, family law, and entertainment law.

international practice

Though O'Melveny does not have a formal international department (there is an interdepartmental global practice group), it was one of the first American law firms to establish a Tokyo office and now offers a developing international practice involving the Pacific Rim. It is one of a "very few firms with an office in Shanghai," according to a firm contact. It also has a rapidly growing Latin American practice, for which it needs lawyers with a Latin American background.

rotation system

Although O'Melveny's departments are rigidly separated, starting associates may, instead of joining a particular department, elect to participate in six-month rotations in two different departments. But one insider asserted that in order to advance one's career, it is best to specialize as soon as possible. Unless one specializes in one of the firm's smaller departments, O'Melveny does not offer junior associates significant responsibility or individual on-the-job training. According to one contact, it's a "hit and miss" affair. The firm "doesn't make a concerted effort to ensure that junior associates get significant responsibility or individual on-the-job training. It's more a function of the type of matter you're assigned and the partner you work with." Perhaps because its practice centers around "heavy-duty clients," junior associates receive little client contact. Most first- and second-year associates are assigned research or similar projects. One narrator recounted meeting a "pale-faced associate" who, after his second month at the firm, was assigned to document production for thirteen straight months. Another source explained, "It's a very big place and it's easy to get lost there. If you want close attention, it's not the place to go. You have to be a real fighter and have to be able to take care of yourself. No one will do it for you. But if you are this type, no one will stand in your way." We were told, however, that O'Melveny is good about recognizing the particular expertise or previous work experience of an attorney. In addition, the firm provides a wide range of formal training for both summer and full-time associates.

salary and partnership

Like its departmental organization, O'Melveny's compensation system is fairly structured. In general, O'Melveny's highest-paid partner is limited to a salary that is no more than three times the compensation of the lowest-paid partner. Associate compensation has recently been restructured into a system in which associates are paid a base salary and also receive a year-end bonus. Though the firm retains some discretion on the size of the bonus, the compensation for fourth year associates is $115,000, for fifth years is $135,000, for sixth years is $160,000, and seventh years is $170,000.

Partly because of past tougher economic times, the firm has extended its partnership track beyond seven years and has promoted fewer associates than usual to partnership within seven years. In 1989, the firm created the "special counsel" position for those not promoted to partnership after seven years. This position primarily serves as a way station for those who are still being considered for partnership. Special counsel may be reconsidered after a year or two. Although it delayed some partnership decisions and reduced the size of its entering associate classes in the early 1990s, O'Melveny avoided the large-scale economic layoffs that were common among L.A. firms at that time.

summer program

Summer associates are given the same type of assignments that first-year associates receive, we were told, and they "are judged by roughly the same standards." Summer associates work hard, though much of the "pressure" is self-imposed. In recent years, the offer rate "has hovered around 95%." Overall, O'Melveny's summer program is not lavish. The firm hosts well-attended weekly cocktail parties on Fridays, and organizes a four-day hiking trip in the Sierra Mountains. The trip is the highlight of the program, but is hardly rugged. One source remarked that "though they say you are roughing it, you had a...shower, and mules carrying your equipment, and porters put up your tent." Overall, the summer program is a "soft sell," not a high pressure recruiting process. Unlike some firms where summer associates are almost forced to socialize with firm members on a daily basis, summer associates at O'Melveny are "able to maintain an independent social life if they choose," according to one contact.

excellent for women and minorities

O'Melveny is widely considered as providing one of the most accommodating and open-minded work environments for female and minority attorneys in L.A. Partner Christine Olson and two prominent African-American partners, Cheryl Mason and Gil Ray, influence the firm's hiring and other decisions and serve as important role models. In addition, O'Melveny has established a special committee to recruit minority law students and to address other minority issues.

O'Melveny has an ownership interest in the downtown building that it occupies. The firm's offices are located across the street from the IBM and Wells Fargo Tower, near all the "hot spots" in town. The office is decorated in "darker woods," with a variety of art, including a number of original Ansel Adams prints. It is also outfitted with a small gym, but most attorneys prefer to use the nearby downtown YMCA. The firm provides every associate a private office with a window and a personal computer connected to a laser printer.

hiring tips

Like most firms, O'Melveny hired an "obscene" number of people in the 1980s, but it is now hiring fewer students. Having become more "elitist" in its hiring criteria, O'Melveny primarily draws on the top national law schools. The firm increasingly emphasizes grades and traditional indicators of academic excellence, such as law review membership. Most students that the firm hires from law schools outside of the top 10 rank at the top of their classes. The firm also places a high premium on hiring students with "unusual talents, such as multilingual or business backgrounds" and they tend to be "type-B personalities, low-key, pleasant and able to get along with others." Typically, two O'Melveny attorneys conduct each on-campus interview. They often take out for lunch or dinner those whom they consider their "top prospects" at the law schools they are visiting. The callback interview is "low-key" and not high-pressured.

One source told us, "if you say you are an O'Melveny lawyer, you get an instant badge of respect in L.A." O'Melveny is a great choice for those who want to work in one of L.A.'s most prestigious firms on high-profile matters in a somewhat more formal environment. O'Melveny is also recognized as one of the top firms for women and minorities, and it offers great connections to the Democratic party. The major complaints we heard were that "partnership prospects are fairly dim in general" and, that the firm does not make as much effort as it could to "integrate associates into the business development side of the practice."

Paul, Hastings, Janofsky & Walker

Los Angeles Atlanta New York Orange County San Francisco Stamford Washington West L.A.
London Tokyo

Address: 555 South Flower Street, Suite 2300, Los Angeles, CA 90071
Telephone: (213) 683–6000
Hiring Attorney: Leigh P. Ryan
Contact: Joy McCarthy, Director of Attorney Programs; (213) 683–6000
Associate Salary: First year $75,000 (1997) (increased to $79,000 effective February 1 after starting in the Fall); second $79,000; third $85,000; fourth $90,000; fifth $98,000; sixth year $111,000; seventh $125,000
Summer Salary: $1300/week (1997)
Average Hours: NA worked; NA billed; 1900 required
Family Benefits: Maternity and paternity leave; employee assistance program
1996 Summer: Class of 25 students; offers to 22
Partnership: 21% of entering associates from 1979–1984 were made partner
Pro Bono: 3% of all work is pro bono

Paul, Hastings, Janofsky & Walker in 1997
171 Lawyers at the Los Angeles Office
1.5 Associates Per Partner

Total Partners 60			Total Associates 91			Practice Areas	
Women	13	22%	Women	42	46%	Labor (management)	47
All Minorities	5	8%	All Minorities	17	19%	Real Estate	44
Afro-Am	1	2%	Afro-Am	3	3%	Business	37
Asian-Am	4	7%	Asian-Am	11	12%	Litigation	35
			Latino	3	3%	Tax	7

Established in 1951, Paul, Hastings, Janofsky & Walker is one of the fastest-growing firms in Los Angeles. It rose to prominence as a premier labor and employment law firm and has now emerged as a top-tier Los Angeles law firm. Unlike many large L.A. firms, Paul Hastings' founding partners still practice at the firm and strive to retain the fellowship and intimacy they shared when the firm was smaller.

conservative atmosphere

Paul Hastings was described as "friendly" and "chatty" and as exhibiting a "conservative" air. The firm's offices are equipped with a beautiful attorney dining room in which "a group of regulars, from first-year associates to partners, often hang out and talk." Many share politically conservative views. The West L.A. office is reportedly more casual and laid-back than the downtown office.

team system

As part of an effort to reduce the inevitable impersonality of a big firm and to maintain the supportive environment of a small firm, Paul Hastings is organized in many small "teams" of two to 10 lawyers who rotate periodically. The team system is designed to vest senior members of the firm with an interest in the progress and development of the firm's younger members and to provide an efficient system for assigning work. A typical team includes one or two partners, three or four higher-level associates, and one or two midlevel associates; each team's "lead partner" distributes work directly to all of the associates. One person praised the team system for providing junior associates "the opportunity to watch the styles of people above and a resource to bounce ideas off of."

training

Unfortunately, though the team system alleviates some of the drawbacks of large firm life, it highlights one of the disadvantages. Because Paul Hastings has a relatively high associate to partner ratio, it is not uncommon for junior associates to work under senior associates rather than working closely with partners. To compensate for this, and to execute its commitment to professional development, Paul Hastings has designated a full-time professional development director to structure and oversee formal training programs. In addition, each of the firm's practice areas also conducts specialized training programs. Although the firm considers its training program to be among the best in the country, some people complained that it can be overwhelming. One source remarked that "the associates grumble about it...because they do not get credit for the hours they spend participating in the programs." A firm spokesperson pointed out, however, that these hours are considered when the firm evaluates associates.

premier labor and employment

Though Paul Hastings offers a full-service practice, it is widely regarded to be a premier management-side labor and employment law firm. The labor and employment department was described as a "highlight" of the firm. More than half the practice involves employment law matters such as wrongful termination and discrimination issues. This practice, one person told us, enjoys a "national reputation" and includes some of the most respected and well-known lawyers in the field. Paul Grossman, the head of the department, is "nationally renowned" and has published a "definitive book" on employment law. Paul Cane is also well-known in the field.

The work atmosphere in the labor and employment practice is supportive and welcoming. One person reported that, like the litigation department, it offers "stellar" training and trial advocacy programs. Comprised of "a great bunch of people—friendly and encouraging," it is also "strongly represented by females and minorities" who serve as excellent role models. People described employment lawyer Nancy Abell as a "superwoman" and noted that Barbra Davis is nationally renowned in the field. One source cautioned that two employment partners are known as "barkers," but noted that they are easy to avoid.

real estate

Paul Hasting's real estate practice is one the firm's "busiest departments," having doubled in size since our earlier edition. The practice handles "a lot of restructuring and bankruptcy work and also a lot of development, both land use and more traditional work." The real estate attorneys were described as "high-caliber," "really sharp, and sophisticated."

other practice areas

Paul Hasting's litigation and business practice areas are not as well-known or strong as the employment practice. The litigation department is considerably smaller than it was just a few years ago. The firm's international business work, however, has been developing rapidly. Paul Hastings enjoys a vibrant practice in the Pacific Rim and has targeted its Latin American practice for future growth. Paul Hastings also has an "intense" and "hard working" tax practice, headed by Nancy Iredale. The tax practice handles both commercial and estate planning issues. Paul Hasting's pro bono practice is not its strong suit. Pro bono hours do, however, count toward billable hours.

summer program

Paul Hastings attempts to provide summer associates with a realistic permanent associate experience. For most of the summer, students receive assignments from a general pool, but they also spend two weeks in one or two of the firm's practice teams. Summer associates have the opportunity to experience some of the firm's formal training, and in one summer, participated in a deposition training workshop, which one person described as "intimidating." The summer social program is informal and laid-back, which reflects the permanent associates' spontaneous and informal social life. A cadre of young permanent associates socialize together outside the firm. During the summer, a number of the West L.A. office lawyers occasionally stop working at around 5 P.M. and play volleyball at a nearby beach.

women

As mentioned earlier, a number of women hold positions of leadership at Paul Hastings, particularly in the employment law and tax departments. The firm has also adopted accommodating part-time work policies that permit attorneys to elect to work three to four days a week at a percentage of their full salary. In addition, any incidents of sexual harassment in the workplace are addressed expeditiously. For example, one contact reported that in one such instance, the firm immediately warned the offending attorney that he would be fired if he did not promptly change his behavior.

minorities

In addition to its success in recruiting and retaining women, Paul Hastings employs a number of racial minorities. One source pointed out that a number of the associates are alumni of Howard University, and the firm has successfully recruited African-American students from that law school. Others noted, however, that Paul Hastings has had a very difficult time retaining minorities, and one person remarked that at times, the firm does not display sensitivity in its treatment of minority attorneys.

Paul Hastings' offices are "open and airy with lighter colors." All attorneys have private offices with a computer. There is a gym in the building, and the downtown YMCA is located nearby. The firm's dining room, serves all-you-can-eat meals for around $7.00. Summer associates may eat for free, and one person warned that they have "great desserts there—don't go there looking to lose weight."

hiring tips

Paul Hastings hires most of its summer class from local California and top 10 national schools. The summer associates who attend the local schools primarily rank in the top 10 percent of their classes, although the firm makes exceptions, especially for individuals with interesting previous work experiences. Many prominent Paul Hastings partners are alumni of the University of Southern California and UCLA, and the firm has had a "long history" of hiring from these institutions. In addition, our sources indicated that the firm has recently recruited heavily at Duke and the University of Michigan.

Paul Hastings' callback interviews involve meeting with six to seven attorneys for about half an hour each, typically followed by a meal. Most students interview with attorneys in the department in which they express an interest. The firm values "hard-working people with intellect," one source indicated, noting that in recent years, the firm has hired "smarter classes." Another commented that the firm "places great emphasis on determination to succeed and on having integrity." One contact remarked that the key to a successful interview "is to learn about the firm before you go there. Learn about the history of the firm and understand that the employment department is really impressive and that the attorneys in it have very impressive backgrounds. If you go into the interview conveying that you recognize that right off the bat, they will appreciate you." Another insider said that it is a firm that appreciates people being "up front" and advised applicants to "ask tough questions."

Paul Hastings has struggled to maintain the intimacy of a smaller firm as it has grown dynamically over the last few decades. Its "team" concept has helped reduce some of the impersonality of the large firm. The firm offers excellent formal training and one of the top employment practices in the country.

Sheppard, Mullin, Richter & Hampton

Los Angeles Orange County San Diego San Francisco

Address: 333 South Hope Street, 48th Floor, Los Angeles, CA 90071
Telephone: (213) 620–1780
Hiring Attorney: Jon W. Newby
Contact: Sally C. Bucklin, Recruiting Administrator; (213) 617–4101
Associate Salary: First year $80,000–$86,000 (1997); second $81,000–$95,000; third $85,000–$109,000; fourth $98,000–$128,000; fifth $106,000–$141,000; sixth $118,000–$161,000; seventh $122,000–170,000; eighth $122,000–$174,000
Summer Salary: $1300/week (1997)
Average Hours: 2314 worked; 2044 billed; 1900 required
Family Benefits: 12 weeks paid maternity disability (12 unpaid)
1996 Summer: Class of 14 students; offers to 14
Partnership: 25% of entering associates from 1978–1987 were made partner (firmwide)
Pro Bono: 1% of all work is pro bono

Sheppard, Mullin, Richter & Hampton in 1997
141 Lawyers at the Los Angeles Office
1.0 Associate Per Partner

Total Partners 69		
Women	7	10%
All Minorities	3	4%
Afro-Am	1	1%
Asian-Am	1	1%
Latino	1	1%

Total Associates 71		
Women	25	35%
All Minorities	12	17%
Afro-Am	4	6%
Asian-Am	6	8%
Latino	2	3%

Practice Areas	
Litigation (Incl. • areas below)	62
Corporate	21
Labor & Employment	21
Banking/Bankruptcy	20
Aerospace•	12
Intellectual Property•	12
Real Estate	11
Construction•	8
Antitrust•	7
Environmental•	7
Tax & Estate Planning	6
White-Collar Crime•	6

work atmosphere

Founded in 1927, Sheppard Mullin has a "reputation on the street of being an old white men's firm." Sheppard Mullin has always been a deliberate law firm, but things are moving a little faster now. One person told us that Sheppard Mullin "used to be a conservative, Republican, large L.A. firm, but the old guard is moving out and others are changing the direction of the firm." The firm is taking "a more expansionist route," with a new marked emphasis on becoming more aggressive in client development and by streamlining costs.

Sheppard Mullin may seem "initially businesslike," but it is a "very friendly place." People leave their doors open, and you "can pop in and talk to anyone." These are "very nice people," and according to one source, there are "not a lot of jerks." Sheppard Mullin lawyers still "genuinely care about your staying with the firm and becoming a good attorney," praised one contact. Two name partners remain active in recruiting. Name partner Gordon Hampton was considered a "father figure at the firm" prior to his passing away this past year. Sheppard Mullin is "more formal" than the West L.A. firms. Male attorneys wear conservative suits and, according to one person, "usually wear their jacket when they go out." Women can wear pantsuits of any color they choose, but "tasteful dressing is important," reported one contact. The firm now has casual dress on Fridays.

litigation practice

Litigation is the largest department at the firm. The litigation department handles a traditional array of commercial matters and is well-known for its excellent antitrust litigation practice led by Don Hibner. The department also represents a number of defense industry companies in government contracts and "Qui Tam" (whistle blower) litigation. It boasts substantial environmental, white collar, construction, securities and financial institutions practices as well.

unique banking and finance practice

Sheppard Mullin offers an excellent and unique banking and finance department. Attorneys in this group combine traditional banking transactional work with litigation matters. The department also houses an active bankruptcy practice. Sheppard Mullin worked extensively with Security Pacific before it merged with Bank of America; the firm now handles many matters for Bank of America. It also represents Wells Fargo and a number of Japanese banks.

other practice areas

The firm's corporate department represents Northrop-Grumman, one of its largest clients. Joe Coyne, a litigation partner who cemented the firm's relationship with Northrop-Grumman, has been "written up in L.A. magazines for being a rainmaker," noted one person. The firm also has an expanding intellectual property practice, bolstered recently by the addition of two partners and three associates from a small intellectual property firm with patent prosecution expertise, that represents clients in matters ranging from patent and trademark litigation to false advertising. Finally, Sheppard Mullin has very active practices in real estate and labor & employment. In 1996, a "good number" of Musick, Peeler's labor and employment group (including Richard Simmons) came over to Sheppard Mullin, forming now the "top labor group in the area," according to one source.

pro bono

Sheppard Mullin credits pro bono hours toward the firm's 1900 hour billable requirement. The firm encourages summer associates to work one day with Public Counsel in order to provide legal services to the indigents in Los Angeles. It also has permitted some attorneys to work virtually full-time on certain pro bono cases such as death penalty appeals.

departmental assignments

Sheppard Mullin requests entering associates to rank their preferred areas of practice before joining the firm and usually assigns them to their first-choice departments. The firm assigns new associates to partners who serve as mentors and monitor their workloads. Associates often work for a variety of partners in their practice area, in addition to their assigned partner. Sheppard Mullin makes an effort to accommodate summer associates' interests as well. Starting this summer, each student will rotate through four practice areas and be assigned to specific partners during each rotation.

opportunity

People we interviewed said that Sheppard Mullin associates receive "as much or more responsibility than peers" at other large Los Angeles firms. Banking associates appear in court for hearings or motions "within a few weeks of entrance to the bar." One person noted that "you can bury yourself in litigation, but can avoid it, if you take initiative." First-year associates are occasionally assigned "their own little cases" to handle. People told us that the labor and corporate associates "can take on as much responsibility as they want to."

training

Sheppard Mullin offers an extensive formal training program, including a number of continuing legal education seminars and workshops, and a series of firmwide luncheons where attorneys report on the work of each department. These, we were told, contribute to the cohesive atmosphere of the firm. In addition, one person commented that the firm provides "pretty exceptional on-the-job training." Another person remarked that "I spend a great deal of time working closely with partners. I am given a great deal of autonomy, and I have a pleasant environment to work in, *i.e.* I am not treated harshly for mistakes." Sheppard Mullin evaluates first-year associates semi-annually, and other associates annually. It also strives to provide good feedback to each summer associate. The hiring partner discusses written work evaluations with the summer associates at mid-summer.

active social life Sheppard Mullin is a "very good place for someone who is young and single." One insider remarked that "if you care to socialize with people from work, the opportunity is there and the associates do become good friends." People lunch together, and attorneys at the firm go out after work. The firm organizes a few social events throughout the year but, we were told, "no black tie kind of things and few dinner parties." The informal events include an annual summer trip to Big Bear Lake and a Holiday Party. Every couple of months, usually on the occasion of someone's leaving or joining the firm, attorneys get together for a happy hour at the Kachina restaurant. In addition, each department goes on retreats at various locations.

diversity Sheppard Mullin has been an "old-time, downtown firm for a very long time" and has "a WASP tradition," we were told, although one person remarked that "I have many friends of varying ethnic and religious backgrounds at the firm." The firm established a diversity committee a couple of years ago, which meets regularly to develop programs to attract minority attorneys to the firm. According to one contact, Sheppard Mullin "does a great job of hiring minority associates, but it has serious problems retaining them." Sheppard Mullin reportedly provides "a positive atmosphere" for women. Women are members of the firm's compensation, diversity and recruiting committees, although no woman has yet served on the executive committee. In recent years, several women have been promoted to partnership, some of whom have taken maternity leave shortly before or after the promotion. One contact pointed out that, in general, "women have a difficult time remaining in the profession in large firms when they decide to have families, but perhaps things are changing with the idea of senior attorneys or the possibility of non-equity partners."

management Sheppard Mullin is run by a seven partner executive committee, whose members are elected for three-year staggered terms. Some critics complained that associates have little input into the firm's management. Associates are, however, members of a number of committees, and are encouraged to talk to their partner mentors. The associates issues committee serves as a formal liaison to the partnership. Sheppard Mullin is financially stable and plans to continue its conservative growth. For the past several years, "each year has been an improvement with respect to profits," reported one source. Sheppard Mullin raised beginning associate salaries in 1996 to $80,000 plus a bonus up to $6,000, "which is among the highest in Los Angeles."

Sheppard Mullin's offices are presently being remodeled. The firm's art work is unique. Founding partner Gordon Hampton's contemporary art collection, which includes works by Andy Warhol and Jackson Pollock, is displayed throughout the firm. Every attorney has a large individual office with big windows and a personal computer. The 24-hour support staff was described as "really good." One admirer labeled the librarian "omnipotent."

hiring tips People advised applicants who interview with the firm to "emphasize having a life." One commented that it helps to know which practice areas you are interested in. The younger Sheppard Mullin interviewers are generally "thinking about whether you would be good to go out drinking with on Friday night," revealed one contact. Another strategically placed insider informed us that "when I interview I look for motivated, bright people with friendly personalities. It's important to be outgoing and have a pleasant personality in order to get along with others and facilitate efficiency."

Sidley & Austin

Los Angeles Chicago Dallas New York Washington, D.C.
London Singapore Tokyo

Address: 555 West Fifth Street, Suite 4000, Los Angeles, CA 90013-1010
Telephone: (213) 896-6000
Hiring Attorney: Richard J. Grad
Contact: Susan M. McGrady, Recruiting Coordinator; (213) 896-6855
Associate Salary: First year $74,000 (1997), increases to $78,000 effective upon passing the bar; year end bonus of approx. $5000; bar review course and bar exam fees paid; $8,500 stipend for use while studying for the bar
Summer Salary: $1400/week (1997)
Average Hours: NA worked; 1950 billed; none required
Family Benefits: 12 weeks paid maternity leave; health, life, OB insurance; health insurance for same-sex domestic partners; disability 6-12 weeks paid; flexible spending accounts
1996 Summer: Class of 16 students, offers to 16
Partnership: NA
Pro Bono: 1–3% of all work is pro bono

Sidley & Austin in 1997
99 Lawyers at the Los Angeles Office
1.3 Associates Per Partner

Total Partners 41		
Women	7	17%
All Minorities	1	2%
Afro-Am	1	2%

Total Associates 54		
Women	25	46%
All Minorities	9	17%
Afro-Am	2	4%
Asian-Am	5	9%
Latino	2	4%

Practice Areas	
Litigation	45
Corporate & Banking	15
Real Estate	15
Bankruptcy	11
Environmental	8
Tax	5

Founded in 1980, the Los Angeles office of Chicago-based Sidley & Austin grew out of Shutan & Trost, a pre-eminent bankruptcy boutique firm in Los Angeles. The office maintains a separate client base and is relatively independent of the home office. Although it benefits from belonging to a firm that employs over 725 lawyers worldwide, Sidley's L.A. office is actively striving to become one of the top Los Angeles firms in its own right.

conservative and formal

Though the firm evinces a perceptible hierarchy, Sidley is a "friendly" place. People told us that almost all partners are "approachable." One contact said, "I never felt like people were disparaging me because I was on the bottom of the totem pole." Although former Republican California Governor George Deukmejian is at the firm, Sidley is balanced politically. Sidley has individuals across the political spectrum. Lawyers in the firm dress conservatively. You won't find Sidley's lawyers frequently coming to work in casual clothes as is the practice at some of L.A.'s hipper firms. The firm has, however recently instituted a "casual Friday" policy during the summer months and is considering expanding the policy throughout the year.

practice areas

Sidley has six work groups: litigation, corporate, real estate, bankruptcy, environmental, and taxation. The firm is most well-known in Los Angeles for its strong bankruptcy practice, which one person called "the pride of the firm." Bankruptcy partner Sally Neely enjoys a national reputation and has taught at Harvard Law School. She has been elected to the prestigious National Bankruptcy Conference. Litigation, the office's largest area, handles a variety of complex commercial litigation matters, including appellate, high technology, intellectual property, professional liability, health care, products liability and real estate matters. The L.A. office is currently involved in a major defamation suit brought by a high profile Watergate figure, major litigation connected to the Orange County bankruptcy, and one of the largest class action lawsuits ever brought against an accounting firm in California. Two lateral partners recently joined the litigation group with substantial First Amendment/media expertise, raising Sidley & Austin's practice in this area into the "top tier in L.A."

Sidley's corporate department represents primarily national and west coast clients such as AT&T and film distributors. In addition, corporate partner and former Governor George Deukmejian and other prominent partners are major "rainmakers." The department handles a variety of matters, including mergers and acquisitions, initial public offerings, restructurings, and, more recently, securitization and project financing. The group is small but increasing in both size and stature and reportedly has handled "some of the largest corporate deals on the West Coast in recent years."

pro bono

Sidley has adopted the Los Angeles County Bar Association Pro Bono Policy, which encourages firms to commit a minimum of 35 hours per lawyer per year to pro bono work. It has also pledged to meet the American Bar Association pro bono challenge to contribute time to pro bono equal to three percent of its total billable hours. The firm gives billable hour credit for time spent on pro bono, as well as for associate training. The former President of the California Bar Association, Charles Vogel, was a partner at the firm until he was appointed to the California Court of Appeals in 1993. Summer associates invariably work on pro bono matters, and each year the entire summer class participates in the Public Counsel's project to assist the homeless.

departmental assignments

Sidley assigns entering associates to one of its six work groups based on associates' expressed preferences and the firm's needs. Each department distributes work differently: the litigation department assigns work through a central committee of young partners, and the real estate department runs more informally. Sidley is a "place where associates would be comfortable turning down work," said one contact. Summer associates obtain their work assignments from the summer committee chairperson. They are expected to carry two on-going projects at all times.

opportunity

Opportunities for responsibility at Sidley are good, especially for "self-starters." Junior litigators, in particular, appear to be challenged quite early. "Many take depositions in their first year of practice, and almost all associates get significant court and deposition experience by the end of their second year," according to one person we spoke with. Another person told us that opportunities to handle matters other than research "arise as quickly as an individual associate demonstrates the ability to handle more responsibility (assuming such assignments become available on a given case)."

training

Sidley organizes L.A. office and firmwide formal orientation training programs for new associates. Each work group is responsible for training its associates. According to the people we interviewed, each group provides a lot of in-house continuing legal education courses. In addition, each department hosts regular meetings, often over lunch, to discuss work. The firm's informal feedback is "uneven," but the (twice yearly) reviews "ensure that associates always know where they stand." Summer associates, moreover, get significant feedback throughout the summer. Each summer associate is assigned a partner "reviewer" who is responsible for critiquing all written work. The assigning attorneys also provide feedback.

social life

Although Sidley attorneys work hard, during the day "people stop to chat and keep their doors open." We were told that there exists at the firm a group of young, mostly single associates who socialize after work. However, most are "family oriented," and do not typically fraternize after work. The firm organizes a number of social events during the summer including a formal party, a beach party, various partner dinners and the firm retreat. There are "very relaxed" Friday evening cocktail parties. The firm also hosts an annual Christmas Party.

women

Sidley places great emphasis on recruiting and retaining women. In recent years, roughly half of summer and incoming associates have been women. One woman commented that the firm is much "better than I could have expected. They are making a conscious effort to make it a better place for women." People also commented that several female associates have children, and a few work part-time. One person observed that "one associate made partner recently—with her class—despite having had two children and taking two extended maternity leaves." "Women at the firm are very supportive of each other and talk about balancing family" and work, praised another. Another contact reported that "partners are very understanding about conflicting duties." Each summer, the firm organizes a dinner for Sidley's female attorneys and summer associates.

minorities

The firm is committed to minority recruiting. In June 1994, the firm added partner Johnny Griggs, an African-American, to its litigation department. In the last two years, six of the 22 incoming associates have been minorities. One insider commented, "I have been pleased to see Sidley's efforts result in more diverse summer and first-year classes every year" and pointed out that Sidley attends minority law students job fairs and co-sponsors the annual minority summer associate reception. Sidley's increased efforts to recruit minorities has resulted in an increase "to more than 10% minority attorneys in the L.A. office."

management

Three partners in the L.A. office sit on Sidley's firmwide executive committee and form the office's management. Other committees address specific management issues. An associates committee exists to facilitate communication between associates and partners on issues of importance to associates, including associate compensation, we were told. Approximately half the members of the firm's recruiting committee are associates.

office facilities

Sidley plans to grow slowly and "really wants to establish the L.A. office as one of the top firms in Los Angeles." The firm consolidated its Century City office into its downtown location. It "believes that to be a real player in the legal market, you need to be downtown," said one person. The L.A. office is a state-of-the-art facility. Every attorney has an individual office and computer, and the litigators have access to numerous document management data bases. The support staff was described as "very good."

substantive interview

Sidley & Austin places a premium on grades in its hiring. It usually hires summer associates from the top 10 law schools in the top 30 percent of their classes. The firm is "very traditional" and takes note of journal experience and judicial clerkships but hires all kinds of people from the "very outgoing" to the "studious type." People advised an applicant to "be a person in the interview." Another said that when interviewing, you should "feel free to talk about issues that concern you. They appreciate people with convictions." Applicants are warned, however, to "be prepared to talk about some project that you have done; and what the issues were. They ask substantive questions."

Sidley & Austin has tremendous resources, large clients, and a friendly work atmosphere. People noted that it is "pretty supportive" and "open to concerns of its associates." One person commented that, at Sidley, "associates are treated as human beings and not just fungible billing units," and went on to add that the firm has "few, if any, classic 'jerks' (e.g. screamers)." We were also told that the firm provides excellent work and a stable client base of a large firm "but we practice in a friendly, smaller firm atmosphere with 100 lawyers in the L.A. office." It is an excellent place "to start a career," said one person; another noted that in the past eighteen months, six associates in L.A.

have made partner, including three women. Yet another person summed up well the positives at Sidley & Austin by commenting that "while many of my classmates have either changed jobs or are unhappy where they are, I feel fortunate to be in a place that keeps me challenged and happy."

Skadden, Arps, Slate, Meagher & Flom

Los Angeles Boston Chicago Houston New York Newark San Francisco Washington Wilmington
Beijing Brussels Frankfurt Hong Kong Jakarta London Moscow Paris Singapore Sydney Tokyo Toronto Vienna

Address: 300 South Grand Avenue, Suite 3400, Los Angeles, CA 90071–3144
Telephone: (213) 687–5000
Hiring Attorney: Harriet S. Posner and Michael A. Woronoff
Contact: Carolyn A. Spain, Legal Hiring Assistant; (213) 687–5101
Associate Salary: First year $91,000 (1997)
Summer Salary: $1500/week for 2Ls and post-3Ls; $1300/week for 1Ls (1997)
Average Hours: NA worked; NA billed; NA required
Family Benefits: 4 weeks paid maternity leave; 4 weeks paid paternity leave
1996 Summer: Class of 17 students; offers to 16
Partnership: NA
Pro Bono: 5% of all work is pro bono

Skadden, Arps, Slate, Meagher & Flom in 1997
106 Lawyers at the Los Angeles Office
2.7 Associates Per Partner

Total Partners 29			Total Associates 77			Practice Areas	
Women	2	7%	Women	29	38%	Litigation	37
All Minorities	3	10%	All Minorities	11	14%	Corporate	46
Latino	3	10%	Afro-Am	8	10%	Tax & ERISA	13
			Asian-Am	3	4%	Real Estate	10

Skadden, Arps, Slate, Meagher & Flom is one of the country's largest and most profitable firms. Building on its expertise in complex mergers and acquisitions, Skadden has grown explosively since the 1970s to over one thousand lawyers practicing in 22 offices worldwide, including over one hundred attorneys in Los Angeles. This firm attracts and handles extremely high-profile, large, complex, and cutting-edge legal matters. Skadden is relatively centralized. "A lot of policy comes out of the New York office," said one person. For example, despite the less formal standards for legal attire in L.A., Skadden's attorneys wear suits and ties in the office, except on Fridays when all Skadden offices dress casually. The Los Angeles offices' legal work is, however, completely generated in Los Angeles, and the office reportedly has an "amazing number of 'rainmakers.'"

intense atmosphere

Skadden attorneys work hard and the work atmosphere is "pretty high-pressure." They are at the "high end of working hard for the Los Angeles market," said one person. The work day generally begins anywhere from 8:30 to 10:30 A.M. and continues "until the work is done." Many of the firm's matters, particularly in the corporate department, are "deal-oriented" and come in "peaks and valleys." One insider exaggerated that "you can work 15 days straight and then get off 10 days. Weekends are not important. It is a seven-day work week." Another observed that "people come in 7 A.M. to midnight when busy." The "work is high-geared," said one contact, with "not a whole lot of chitchat" in the office. The firm does not have a minimum billable requirement and does not publish the average hours its attorneys work. One source estimated that the average is over 2000 hours, while another insider informed us that "rumor has it that the average hours billed per attorney in the L.A. office is higher than any of the other Skadden domestic offices." Ever helpful, "Skadden is very good about making it easier on attorneys to do their work," one source observed. "You can take work home, and the firm will send a messenger out to pick it up." Support staff is available 24 hours a day. Attorneys often work through lunch, and Skadden permits them to bill their catered meals to the firm.

hierarchical

Skadden is hierarchical. The hierarchy is "driven by the nature of the work they do," according to one person, who explained that "the deals are so complex and large that young lawyers cannot take on most tasks. It is hierarchical in the downward flow of work." One person also observed that most of the firm's important "decisions are made solely by partners, and associates are kept in the dark," although the firm has reportedly "gotten better in recent years." Skadden is, for example, "very secretive about compensation...No one knows how partners are compensated." Although Skadden has changed its practice of paying all associates in a particular class the same salary as their New York counterparts, one insider reported that the firm "pays at the top of the scale in each local market." Another contact informed us, however, that New York, not Los Angeles, "makes the salary decisions" and, moreover, "it seems that some members of the same class at the same office are compensated differently."

bottom-line orientation

"Skadden is run like a business," said one person. "They are in it for the bottom line." This insider continued, "We are a business first and a law firm second...We are here to do a job and get it done and to stay on top of the field no matter what it takes." Associates are, however, "very friendly" with each other and are "friends outside the office." Attorneys interact informally, and the firm does not feel "stuffy," said one source.

top-notch practice

Skadden's practice is "unique and cutting-edge." The firm has, according to one person we interviewed and a recent *California Law* article, the "strongest corporate practice in Los Angeles." It represents Fortune 500 and other large and medium-sized international and West Coast-based corporations, investment banks, and financial institutions in corporate transactions, restructurings, and securities and finance matters. The firm also has a large real estate practice which has been involved in major local, national and international real estate developments. Built to replace the explosive mergers and acquisitions practice of the 1980s, the litigation department handles an array of commercial matters. It has handled a number of high-profile cases. Litigation partner Frank Rothman's defense of the National Football League in its free agency litigation received daily press coverage. According to one source, the department has begun to do a "lot of litigation for entertainment corporations." Lastly, the office also has active labor, employee benefits, tax and environmental departments and recently added lateral partners in banking and bankruptcy.

pro bono

Skadden has an organized commitment to pro bono work. A firmwide committee and an of counsel lawyer coordinate the firm's commitment to pro bono. The L.A. office has won numerous pro bono awards. Corporate associates incorporate non-profit corporations and offer them legal advice. Litigation attorneys do Legal Services work and some high-impact litigation. Many of the attorneys serve as directors or officers of various public interest organizations in Los Angeles. Skadden has also established the Skadden Fellowship, which funds 25 Public Interest fellows every year.

departmental assignments

Entering associates join a particular department. Assignment partners in the corporate and litigation departments distribute assignments to new associates and monitor their workloads. By the end of their first year at the firm, associates usually develop working relationships with more senior attorneys and obtain work informally. People we interviewed stressed that associates feel free to turn down work if they are busy.

training

We heard disagreement regarding the extent of hands-on responsibility that the firm offers junior associates, but everyone concurred that the firm "definitely trusts your judgment" even as a new associate. Both transactional work and litigation are "generally staffed leanly," we were told. Skadden is "precise about what is expected" from its associates. The firm provides a structured series of orientations and training programs. Summer associates participate in deposition, writing, research, and corporate seminars. One source revealed that the firm distributes, among other training materials, "two binders summarizing securities regulations." Every other Tuesday, either the corporate or the litigation department organizes a lunch time educational seminar. The firm also sends associates for one week of training to New York.

Day-to-day feedback is hard to get at Skadden. One person explained that "partners and associates are so busy that it is difficult to take the time to sit down and go over work with you." The firm formally evaluates associates twice annually. It also formally reviews summer associates twice during the summer. The summer program has a unique mechanism devoted to ensuring that summer associates receive feedback. The firm has established a committee, whose members are generally also members of the summer committee, which reviews the work of summer associates on a constant basis and provides constant feedback. This committee also evaluates summer associates for permanent offers of employment. The LA office "generally makes offers to substantially all of the 2Ls in its summer class," according to one insider. In 1996, Skadden made offers to 16 of its 17 summer associates.

minimal social life

Every Thursday, the firm hosts a catered attorney lunch in its lunchroom. This is both a social and an administrative meeting. In general, there is "not a lot of time for" social life at Skadden, but the firm "really takes care of summer associates." If a summer associate wishes to do so, he or she can keep busy "five nights a week" with informal happy hours, dinners, plays, the Hollywood Bowl, and other events.

male-dominated office

Skadden strives to recruit women, but the L.A. office has a reputation for being somewhat "male dominated." One person told us that the firm's "attitude is not as good as it should be." People disagreed on how accommodating the firm is on family issues. Skadden has adopted the Family Leave Policy allowing attorneys up to 12 weeks unpaid leave. One person commented, however, that "my perception is that they are probably not as inclined toward leaves. Work comes first." On the other hand, another source claimed that the firm is "very accommodating," pointing out that an attorney took three weeks off when his wife had a baby. Skadden employs relatively few minority attorneys, but one contact informed us that "the firm's recruitment of women and minorities has improved greatly over the past several years."

NY-centric management

The Los Angeles office is governed by a managing partner, in addition to a number of other committees which address specific issues. People commented that the managing partner has made a "real effort" to talk to associates "openly about salary and policies behind decisions." With much of the firm's authority centralized in its home office, however, one source commented that there is "a lot of guess work by associates. The Los Angeles partners will keep you as informed as they can, but a lot comes out of New York." Another source noted that it is "difficult" for the Los Angeles office to "influence certain policies." Members of the firmwide executive committee include five partners from the New York office, three partners from the Los Angeles office, and some partners from other offices.

Skadden's offices may not be the best in Los Angeles, but they provide some nice perks. The office is equipped with a gym open to all attorneys that is staffed by a fitness trainer. It boasts men's and women's lockers (really "general use cabinets," according to one astute observer), Universal weight machines, free weights, an ab-roller, treadmills, exercise bikes, and stairmasters. The firm also has an in-house caterer. The firm's support services are "great." Every attorney has an individual office with a window and a personal computer, connected to the firmwide network. Skadden is presently upgrading both its hardware and software.

recruits dedicated workers

In hiring, Skadden "wants people who aren't afraid of work." One source declared that the firm "wants someone dedicated and interested enough to put in long hours." People advised applicants who interview with the firm to emphasize their interest in its "highly specialized" practice. One recommended that you "show that you know what you are getting into. Talk to someone who has worked there." Another warned that the firm will "push you a little on why you are interested in corporate finance and corporate deals. They are wary of people who want quick bucks. That is where the turnover is." Skadden also seeks people "who can work well with others." There are "not a lot of attitudes floating around" the firm, asserted one person. Skadden usually hires law students who are near the top of their classes or are members of a law review. It allows a little more leeway with students from the top law schools. The firm hires most of its summer associates from the top 15 national law schools. Law students are drawn heavily from Boalt, Georgetown, Harvard, Stanford, and the University of California at Los Angeles. The firm also recruits at the University of Southern California, Loyola, and Hastings.

Skadden's work is said to be its biggest attraction. It "still has the biggest, highest-profile and best corporate work" in the city, commented one insider. Another person remarked that, at Skadden, you have "New York-type high profile corporate work in LA" and you have Skadden's resources worldwide (*i.e.* you can messenger a document out of the New York office or use the Delaware office for incorporating). Another contact also extolled the virtues of the work: "it is not the same as at other firms. It is exclusively Skadden. It is unique and cutting-edge." The firm handles "the big cases that you read about in the paper. It adds excitement to the work and a certain appeal." Skadden's work also provides a unique opportunity to "learn a lot." One insider old us that "much is expected of associates right away—it's great for learning but very stressful in the beginning." The firm, moreover, is presently "very busy" and "doing lots of hiring." In fact, Skadden recently opened a new floor to house additional attorneys.

People admit, however, that working at Skadden "is a high demand job. If you are into it, you stay for a while. Otherwise you leave. There is a fairly high degree of burnout." One insider informed us that there is "little freedom to decide your own schedule. Your friends get used to your predictions on being somewhere else and to the refrain: seventy percent chance I'll make dinner tonight, etc." It is also difficult to become a partner at Skadden, and many midlevel associates leave. The LA office, however, elevated three associates to partner this past year, we were told. To succeed, "you do need to make a pretty strong lifestyle choice. There are a lot of rewards in doing that, but also a lot of drawbacks. You are there for them...on an on-call basis. They expect you to take off on a Friday night for a corporate deal and drop everything." But, one firm enthusiast informed us, "if you love this kind of work, it's worth it."

New York

Law Firms Ranked By Associates Per Partner

1.	ANDERSON KILL & OLICK	0
2.	WACHTELL, LIPTON, ROSEN & KATZ	1.0
3.	WHITMAN BREED ABBOTT & MORGAN	1.0
4.	COUDERT BROTHERS	1.1
5.	HAIGHT, GARDNER, POOR & HAVENS	1.1
6.	WINSTON & STRAWN	1.2
7.	HUGHES HUBBARD & REED	1.3
8.	KELLEY DRYE & WARREN	1.3
9.	LEBOEUF, LAMB, LEIBY & MACRAE	1.3
10.	DONOVAN LEISURE NEWTON & IRVINE	1.4
11.	STROOCK & STROOCK & LAVAN	1.4
12.	KAYE, SCHOLER, FIERMAN, HAYS & HANDLER	1.5
13.	ROSENMAN & COLIN	1.5
14.	BAKER & MCKENZIE	1.6
15.	WINTHROP, STIMSON, PUTNAM & ROBERTS	1.6
16.	JONES, DAY, REAVIS & POGUE	1.7
17.	MILBANK, TWEED, HADLEY & MCCLOY	1.7
18.	PROSKAUER ROSE	1.7
19.	CHADBOURNE & PARKE	1.8
20.	PATTERSON, BELKNAP, WEBB & TYLER	1.8
21.	PENNIE & EDMONDS	1.8
22.	CAHILL GORDON & REINDEL	2.0
23.	MORGAN, LEWIS & BOCKIUS	2.0
24.	WEIL, GOTSHAL & MANGES	2.0
25.	BROWN & WOOD	2.1
26.	DEWEY BALLANTINE	2.1
27.	PAUL, WEISS, RIFKIND, WHARTON & GARRISON	2.3
28.	WHITE & CASE	2.4
29.	WILLKIE FARR & GALLAGHER	2.4
30.	KENYON & KENYON	2.5
31.	SULLIVAN & CROMWELL	2.5
32.	DAVIS POLK & WARDWELL	2.6
33.	ROGERS & WELLS	2.6
34.	DEBEVOISE & PLIMPTON	2.7
35.	FRIED, FRANK, HARRIS, SHRIVER & JACOBSON	2.7
36.	SCHULTE ROTH & ZABEL	2.8
37.	SIMPSON THACHER & BARTLETT	2.8
38.	FISH & NEAVE	2.9
39.	SHEARMAN & STERLING	2.9
40.	CLEARY, GOTTLIEB, STEEN & HAMILTON	3.
41.	SKADDEN, ARPS, SLATE, MEAGHER & FLOM	3.1
42.	CRAVATH, SWAINE & MOORE	3.9

Law Firms Ranked by Percentage of Associates Who Make Partner
(over varying years)

1.	ANDERSON KILL & OLICK	100
2.	WACHTELL, LIPTON, ROSEN & KATZ	41
3.	WEIL, GOTSHAL & MANGES	26
4.	SULLIVAN & CROMWELL	19
5.	MILBANK, TWEED, HADLEY & MCCLOY	18
6.	BROWN & WOOD	17
7.	ROGERS & WELLS	17
8.	WILLKIE FARR & GALLAGHER	17
9.	FRIED, FRANK, HARRIS, SHRIVER & JACOBSON	16
10.	LEBOEUF, LAMB, LEIBY & MACRAE	16
11.	FISH & NEAVE	15-20
12.	CLEARY, GOTTLIEB, STEEN & HAMILTON	15
13.	KENYON & KENYON	15
14.	ROSENMAN & COLIN	15
15.	SCHULTE ROTH & ZABEL	14
16.	SHEARMAN & STERLING	14
17.	CHADBOURNE & PARKE	13
18.	COUDERT BROTHERS	12
19.	DONOVAN LEISURE NEWTON & IRVINE	12
20.	WHITE & CASE	12
21.	WINTHROP, STIMSON, PUTNAM & ROBERTS	11
22.	KELLEY DRYE & WARREN	10
23.	SKADDEN, ARPS, SLATE, MEAGHER & FLOM	10
24.	STROOCK & STROOCK & LAVAN	10
25.	CAHILL GORDON & REINDEL	9
26.	DEWEY BALLANTINE	9
27.	DAVIS POLK & WARDWELL	8
28.	HUGHES HUBBARD & REED	8
29.	KAYE, SCHOLER, FIERMAN, HAYS & HANDLER	7
30.	CRAVATH, SWAINE & MOORE	6
31.	PAUL, WEISS, RIFKIND, WHARTON & GARRISON	5
32.	BAKER & MCKENZIE	NA
33.	DEBEVOISE & PLIMPTON	NA
34.	HAIGHT, GARDNER, POOR & HAVENS	NA
35.	JONES, DAY, REAVIS & POGUE	NA
36.	MORGAN, LEWIS & BOCKIUS	NA
37.	PATTERSON, BELKNAP, WEBB & TYLER	NA
38.	PENNIE & EDMONDS	NA
39.	PROSKAUER ROSE	NA
40.	SIMPSON THACHER & BARTLETT	NA
41.	WHITMAN BREED ABBOTT & MORGAN	NA
42.	WINSTON & STRAWN	NA

Law Firms Ranked by Percentage of Pro Bono Work

1.	WINTHROP, STIMSON, PUTNAM & ROBERTS	7
2.	DEBEVOISE & PLIMPTON	6
3.	FISH & NEAVE	5-10
4.	PAUL, WEISS, RIFKIND, WHARTON & GARRISON	5
5.	SKADDEN, ARPS, SLATE, MEAGHER & FLOM	5
6.	STROOCK & STROOCK & LAVAN	5
7.	CLEARY, GOTTLIEB, STEEN & HAMILTON	4
8.	HUGHES HUBBARD & REED	3.3
9.	FRIED, FRANK, HARRIS, SHRIVER & JACOBSON	3-5
10.	CRAVATH, SWAINE & MOORE	3
11.	DAVIS POLK & WARDWELL	3
12.	DONOVAN LEISURE NEWTON & IRVINE	3
13.	HAIGHT, GARDNER, POOR & HAVENS	3
14.	KENYON & KENYON	3
15.	LEBOEUF, LAMB, LEIBY & MACRAE	3
16.	MILBANK, TWEED, HADLEY & MCCLOY	3
17.	SCHULTE ROTH & ZABEL	3
18.	SIMPSON THACHER & BARTLETT	3
19.	SULLIVAN & CROMWELL	3
20.	WHITE & CASE	3
21.	WILLKIE FARR & GALLAGHER	3
22.	KAYE, SCHOLER, FIERMAN, HAYS & HANDLER	2
23.	PROSKAUER ROSE	2
24.	SHEARMAN & STERLING	2
25.	WEIL, GOTSHAL & MANGES	2
26.	WINSTON & STRAWN	2
27.	CHADBOURNE & PARKE	1.6
28.	COUDERT BROTHERS	1-3
29.	PENNIE & EDMONDS	1-3
30.	ROGERS & WELLS	1-3
31.	ROSENMAN & COLIN	1-3
32.	WACHTELL, LIPTON, ROSEN & KATZ	1-3
33.	ANDERSON KILL & OLICK	1
34.	KELLEY DRYE & WARREN	1
35.	MORGAN, LEWIS & BOCKIUS	1
36.	WHITMAN BREED ABBOTT & MORGAN	1
37.	BAKER & MCKENZIE	NA
38.	BROWN & WOOD	NA
39.	CAHILL GORDON & REINDEL	NA
40.	DEWEY BALLANTINE	NA
41.	JONES, DAY, REAVIS & POGUE	NA
42.	PATTERSON, BELKNAP, WEBB & TYLER	NA

Law Firms Ranked by Percentage of Female Partners

1.	ANDERSON KILL & OLICK	35
2.	HUGHES HUBBARD & REED	25
3.	JONES, DAY, REAVIS & POGUE	18
4.	SKADDEN, ARPS, SLATE, MEAGHER & FLOM	18
5.	DAVIS POLK & WARDWELL	17
6.	PATTERSON, BELKNAP, WEBB & TYLER	17
7.	FRIED, FRANK, HARRIS, SHRIVER & JACOBSON	16
8.	WINSTON & STRAWN	16
9.	KAYE, SCHOLER, FIERMAN, HAYS & HANDLER	15
10.	WEIL, GOTSHAL & MANGES	15
11.	WINTHROP, STIMSON, PUTNAM & ROBERTS	15
12.	SHEARMAN & STERLING	14
13.	CHADBOURNE & PARKE	13
14.	FISH & NEAVE	13
15.	KELLEY DRYE & WARREN	13
16.	ROSENMAN & COLIN	13
17.	DEWEY BALLANTINE	12
18.	SCHULTE ROTH & ZABEL	12
19.	STROOCK & STROOCK & LAVAN	12
20.	WHITE & CASE	12
21.	BROWN & WOOD	11
22.	DONOVAN LEISURE NEWTON & IRVINE	11
23.	HAIGHT, GARDNER, POOR & HAVENS	11
24.	LEBOEUF, LAMB, LEIBY & MACRAE	11
25.	WACHTELL, LIPTON, ROSEN & KATZ	11
26.	CLEARY, GOTTLIEB, STEEN & HAMILTON	10
27.	PAUL, WEISS, RIFKIND, WHARTON & GARRISON	10
28.	PENNIE & EDMONDS	10
29.	ROGERS & WELLS	10
30.	COUDERT BROTHERS	9
31.	CRAVATH, SWAINE & MOORE	9
32.	DEBEVOISE & PLIMPTON	9
33.	PROSKAUER ROSE	9
34.	MILBANK, TWEED, HADLEY & MCCLOY	8
35.	MORGAN, LEWIS & BOCKIUS	8
36.	SULLIVAN & CROMWELL	8
37.	WILLKIE FARR & GALLAGHER	8
38.	BAKER & MCKENZIE	7
39.	CAHILL GORDON & REINDEL	7
40.	SIMPSON THACHER & BARTLETT	7
41.	WHITMAN BREED ABBOTT & MORGAN	7
42.	KENYON & KENYON	3

Law Firms Ranked by Percentage of Female Associates

1.	JONES, DAY, REAVIS & POGUE	52
2.	WINSTON & STRAWN	52
3.	HUGHES HUBBARD & REED	49
4.	STROOCK & STROOCK & LAVAN	48
5.	DAVIS POLK & WARDWELL	46
6.	PATTERSON, BELKNAP, WEBB & TYLER	46
7.	DEWEY BALLANTINE	45
8.	HAIGHT, GARDNER, POOR & HAVENS	45
9.	COUDERT BROTHERS	44
10.	LEBOEUF, LAMB, LEIBY & MACRAE	44
11.	DEBEVOISE & PLIMPTON	43
12.	DONOVAN LEISURE NEWTON & IRVINE	43
13.	CHADBOURNE & PARKE	42
14.	MORGAN, LEWIS & BOCKIUS	42
15.	WHITMAN BREED ABBOTT & MORGAN	42
16.	CLEARY, GOTTLIEB, STEEN & HAMILTON	41
17.	PAUL, WEISS, RIFKIND, WHARTON & GARRISON	41
18.	PROSKAUER ROSE	41
19.	SHEARMAN & STERLING	41
20.	FRIED, FRANK, HARRIS, SHRIVER & JACOBSON	39
21.	KAYE, SCHOLER, FIERMAN, HAYS & HANDLER	39
22.	WINTHROP, STIMSON, PUTNAM & ROBERTS	39
23.	BROWN & WOOD	38
24.	KELLEY DRYE & WARREN	38
25.	ROSENMAN & COLIN	38
26.	SCHULTE ROTH & ZABEL	38
27.	SKADDEN, ARPS, SLATE, MEAGHER & FLOM	38
28.	WILLKIE FARR & GALLAGHER	38
29.	ROGERS & WELLS	37
30.	WEIL, GOTSHAL & MANGES	37
31.	PENNIE & EDMONDS	36
32.	MILBANK, TWEED, HADLEY & MCCLOY	35
33.	SIMPSON THACHER & BARTLETT	35
34.	WHITE & CASE	34
35.	CAHILL GORDON & REINDEL	33
36.	WACHTELL, LIPTON, ROSEN & KATZ	31
37.	FISH & NEAVE	28
38.	CRAVATH, SWAINE & MOORE	27
39.	SULLIVAN & CROMWELL	26
40.	BAKER & MCKENZIE	22
41.	KENYON & KENYON	22
42.	ANDERSON KILL & OLICK	NA

Law Firms Ranked by Percentage of Minority Partners

1.	ANDERSON KILL & OLICK	9
2.	KELLEY DRYE & WARREN	7
3.	CLEARY, GOTTLIEB, STEEN & HAMILTON	6
4.	HAIGHT, GARDNER, POOR & HAVENS	6
5.	DAVIS POLK & WARDWELL	5
6.	WILLKIE FARR & GALLAGHER	5
7.	BROWN & WOOD	4
8.	HUGHES HUBBARD & REED	4
9.	MORGAN, LEWIS & BOCKIUS	4
10.	PAUL, WEISS, RIFKIND, WHARTON & GARRISON	4
11.	SHEARMAN & STERLING	4
12.	SULLIVAN & CROMWELL	4
13.	WHITE & CASE	4
14.	DEBEVOISE & PLIMPTON	3
15.	JONES, DAY, REAVIS & POGUE	3
16.	KENYON & KENYON	3
17.	SKADDEN, ARPS, SLATE, MEAGHER & FLOM	3
18.	WACHTELL, LIPTON, ROSEN & KATZ	3
19.	WEIL, GOTSHAL & MANGES	3
20.	COUDERT BROTHERS	2
21.	LEBOEUF, LAMB, LEIBY & MACRAE	2
22.	MILBANK, TWEED, HADLEY & MCCLOY	2
23.	PROSKAUER ROSE	2
24.	ROSENMAN & COLIN	2
25.	SIMPSON THACHER & BARTLETT	2
26.	WINSTON & STRAWN	2
27.	WINTHROP, STIMSON, PUTNAM & ROBERTS	2
28.	CHADBOURNE & PARKE	1
29.	CRAVATH, SWAINE & MOORE	1
30.	DEWEY BALLANTINE	1
31.	FRIED, FRANK, HARRIS, SHRIVER & JACOBSON	1
32.	KAYE, SCHOLER, FIERMAN, HAYS & HANDLER	1
33.	ROGERS & WELLS	1
34.	WHITMAN BREED ABBOTT & MORGAN	1
35.	BAKER & MCKENZIE	0
36.	CAHILL GORDON & REINDEL	0
37.	DONOVAN LEISURE NEWTON & IRVINE	0
38.	FISH & NEAVE	0
39.	PATTERSON, BELKNAP, WEBB & TYLER	0
40.	PENNIE & EDMONDS	0
41.	SCHULTE ROTH & ZABEL	0
42.	STROOCK & STROOCK & LAVAN	0

Law Firms Ranked By Percentage of Minority Associates

1.	DAVIS POLK & WARDWELL	34
2.	CLEARY, GOTTLIEB, STEEN & HAMILTON	26
3.	WINTHROP, STIMSON, PUTNAM & ROBERTS	25
4.	PAUL, WEISS, RIFKIND, WHARTON & GARRISON	22
5.	HAIGHT, GARDNER, POOR & HAVENS	20
6.	DEWEY BALLANTINE	18
7.	SIMPSON THACHER & BARTLETT	18
8.	FISH & NEAVE	17
9.	LEBOEUF, LAMB, LEIBY & MACRAE	17
10.	BROWN & WOOD	16
11.	ROGERS & WELLS	16
12.	COUDERT BROTHERS	15
13.	KAYE, SCHOLER, FIERMAN, HAYS & HANDLER	15
14.	CHADBOURNE & PARKE	14
15.	HUGHES HUBBARD & REED	14
16.	PROSKAUER ROSE	14
17.	WEIL, GOTSHAL & MANGES	14
18.	WHITE & CASE	14
19.	WILLKIE FARR & GALLAGHER	14
20.	BAKER & MCKENZIE	13
21.	MILBANK, TWEED, HADLEY & MCCLOY	13
22.	PENNIE & EDMONDS	13
23.	SHEARMAN & STERLING	13
24.	SKADDEN, ARPS, SLATE, MEAGHER & FLOM	13
25.	SULLIVAN & CROMWELL	13
26.	WACHTELL, LIPTON, ROSEN & KATZ	13
27.	CAHILL GORDON & REINDEL	12
28.	DEBEVOISE & PLIMPTON	12
29.	FRIED, FRANK, HARRIS, SHRIVER & JACOBSON	12
30.	KELLEY DRYE & WARREN	12
31.	SCHULTE ROTH & ZABEL	10
32.	STROOCK & STROOCK & LAVAN	10
33.	WINSTON & STRAWN	10
34.	PATTERSON, BELKNAP, WEBB & TYLER	9
35.	MORGAN, LEWIS & BOCKIUS	8
36.	WHITMAN BREED ABBOTT & MORGAN	8
37.	CRAVATH, SWAINE & MOORE	7
38.	KENYON & KENYON	7
39.	DONOVAN LEISURE NEWTON & IRVINE	6
40.	JONES, DAY, REAVIS & POGUE	6
41.	ROSENMAN & COLIN	5
42.	ANDERSON KILL & OLICK	NA

Anderson Kill & Olick

New York Newark Philadelphia Phoenix Tucson San Francisco Washington

Address: 1251 Avenue of the Americas, New York, NY 10020
Telephone: (212) 278-1000
Hiring Attorney: Gabriella Jordan/Steven Cooper, Co-Chairpersons, Hiring Committee
Contact: Karyn Siskind, Recruiting Coordinator; (212) 278–1716
Associate Salary: First year $85,000 (1996); second $92,500; third $100,000; fourth $107,500; fifth $110,000; base salary is also supplemented with a percentage of the firm's profits
Summer Salary: $1635/week (1997)
Average Hours: 1800–2100 worked; 2000 billed; NA required
Family Benefits: 12 weeks paid maternity leave (12 unpaid)
1996 Summer: Class of 16 students; offers to 14
Partnership: 100% of entering associates from 1982–1988 were made partner
Pro Bono: 1% of all work is pro bono (but see below)

Anderson Kill & Olick in 1997
123 Lawyers at the New York Office
0 Associates Per Partner

Total Partners 123		
Women	43	35%
All Minorities	11	9%
Afro-Am	2	2%
Asian-Am	5	4%
Latino	3	2%
Other	1	1%

Total Associates 0	
Women	NA
All Minorities	NA

Practice Areas (by %)	
Litigation	60
Bankruptcy	10
Corporate	12
Intellectual Property	5
Real Estate	5
Criminal	3
Labor	3
Trusts & Estates	2

partner associate distinction eliminated

Founded in 1969, Anderson Kill & Olick is perhaps the most unorthodox law firm we surveyed. Anderson is organized as a professional corporation and has virtually eliminated the distinction between partners and associates. Anderson technically has no associates. Every attorney holds equity in the firm, and each lawyer's salary is a combination of a guaranteed base salary and an additional draw of the firm's profits. First-year lawyers earn a guaranteed salary of $85,000 with a very small percentage of their total compensation being drawn from the firm's profits. As lawyers gain in seniority their guaranteed salary becomes a smaller proportion of their total salary, and their draw of the firm's profits constitutes a larger percentage of their total compensation. The most senior attorneys' share of the firm's profits may constitute up to 80 percent of their total salary.

democratic management under siege

Anderson's unusual organizational structure alleviates some of the competition and hierarchy found in traditional law firms. For example, young lawyers have less reason to compete with each other because they are not vying for a limited number of partnership positions. Further, every lawyer participates in management and has one vote in major firm decisions. There are, however, indications that Anderson's unique experiment in democratic law firm governance may be under siege. Over the last few years, the firm lost a significant number of important attorneys, for a variety of reasons, and has gone from over 200 lawyers in the early 1990s to its present size of 153 attorneys. Former name partner David Oshinsky recently left the firm and took with him a large number of attorneys; consequently, the D.C. office, from which Oshinsky operated, is presently only a shell of its former self. In 1996, about 70 lawyers, including senior partner John Gross and almost two-dozen seasoned New York-based litigators, left the firm. Moreover, there are now questions regarding what the firm will look like in the future. The firm has always relied heavily on the democratic vision and the rainmaking talents of founder Gene Anderson, who is nearing 70, and who has been quoted as saying, "I don't know what's going to happen [to the firm] if something happens to me."

Anderson used to be managed entirely by a number of task-specific committees, none of which was supreme. Although these committees no longer fully manage the firm, they continue to exist and represent a broad cross-section of the firm's attorneys. Most lawyers serve on at least one committee. The committees develop proposals in their area of expertise for the entire firm to consider. For example, the firm's Executive Committee proposes the salaries, bonuses, and profit percentages for all Anderson's members; the entire firm then votes to accept, modify, or reject the plan. As Anderson grew in the 1980s, it found its democratic style of governance to be somewhat cumbersome. To "streamline" day-to-day management, the firm voted in the early 1990s to establish a three member Executive Committee and an 18 member board of directors. Board members are elected by the entire firm. These two committees, unlike the other Anderson committees, can make certain administrative decisions without a firmwide vote. Anderson initially had some difficulty adjusting to the new management regime, but people reported that the firm's day-to-day administration is running more smoothly and cost-effectively with the Executive Committee in charge.

still more democratic than most

Despite the recent rumblings, Anderson maintains much of its open and democratic management style. For example, the firm continues to provide detailed financial and management information to all members on a daily basis. Along with this information, the firm also announces the time and place of all committee meetings, which are open to any Anderson lawyer, except for meetings of the Executive Committee and the board of directors, the minutes of which are available to all members. People we interviewed believe that Anderson's innovative organizational system still works well. One person remarked that "everyone is a partner, so as a junior attorney you feel empowered." Most did comment, however, that although every Anderson attorney theoretically has only one vote, inevitably the rainmakers carry a lot of weight.

practice areas

Anderson is best-known for its excellent insurance and general litigation practices. Founding partner Gene Anderson and other lawyers at the firm won the first court judgment that required an insurance company to cover the expense of an environmental "clean-up." The firm usually represents corporations in claims against insurance companies, and a number of asbestos companies are firm clients. It also handles a variety of other commercial litigation matters for both corporations and individuals. Anderson also has smaller real estate and bankruptcy departments. The corporate practice has "grown tremendously in terms of business," according to one insider. The firm has, we were told, rebuilt its intellectual property practice after some attorney departures a few years ago. Anderson also encourages young lawyers to handle pro bono matters, particularly because such cases can provide valuable courtroom experience. Attorneys become engaged in pro bono projects ranging from asylum law to tenant advocacy.

cooperative environment

In many respects, Anderson provides "big firm resources in a small firm atmosphere," remarked one person. The work environment is cooperative, "very laid-back, polite, and friendly." One contact remarked that the friendly atmosphere insures that there is no "us" versus "them" feeling between junior and senior attorneys. An attorney can arrive at work in jeans and change into a suit at the office. On days with no client meetings, midlevel lawyers sometimes dress in khakis or shorts and polo-shirts.

"People get along well," observed one person. Attorneys frequently drop in each others' offices, and one person warned that you never know what you might see—attorneys keep a supply of Pez dispensers, Groucho Marx masks, and other toys on their desks. Because of the lack of hierarchy, young lawyers feel comfortable approaching more senior lawyers with questions and comments, or just to chat.

Anderson attorneys also are ideologically diverse. The firm has been home to Republicans, such as Mayor of New York City and former U.S. Attorney Rudolph Giuliani. Other senior partners, however, are staunch Democrats. Former New York Chief Bankruptcy Judge Roy Babbitt is of counsel, and John Doyle, a former Assistant U.S. Attorney, is a partner at the firm.

opportunities

Because Anderson is leanly staffed, it usually offers junior lawyers as much responsibility as they can handle. Third-year lawyers typically manage smaller cases, formulate interrogatories, take depositions, and appear in court by themselves or run a transaction. Anderson does not, however, emphasize training and feedback, although a firm spokesperson informed us that, recently "Anderson has substantially revamped its training program for junior attorneys, which now emphasizes practical litigation skills, such as deposition training and oral advocacy." As with everything else at the firm, "you have to go get it," one person emphasized. As a result of this "hands-on" experience, Anderson attorneys work fairly hard, and most junior lawyers probably bill more than the 1900 hour annual requirement.

social life for jocks and geeks

Anderson attorneys get to know each other well and often socialize after work. The lawyers have diverse backgrounds and interests—one person commented that the firm hires people from "jocks to geeks"—and their social proclivities range from "pub crawling" to visiting museums. Some attorneys attend the theater, while others play golf on weekends.

women

Certain women at Anderson reportedly believe that they lack influence because they are not well-connected to the most important senior partner. However, one of the two hiring partners is a woman, and in recent years, a woman has been one of Anderson's top billers. The firm reportedly is flexible about maternity and paternity leave arrangements and family emergencies.

challenging interviews

Not surprisingly, Anderson seeks to hire interesting people from diverse backgrounds. One person advised that applicants should not be afraid to voice their opinions on social and political issues. The firm prefers people who can argue persuasively for their own views, provided that they also have the maturity to acknowledge alternative positions. The on-campus interviews with Anderson's are intense and challenging. The previous hiring partner's favorite questions have been "Why should I hire you?" and "Why shouldn't I hire you?" Candidates should not prepare "canned" answers to these questions, advised one person, because honesty is highly valued: "the firm places a premium on honesty since its whole ideal of the law depends on honesty. The interview is designed to force students to demonstrate grace and not arrogance."

a firm worth investigating

Overall, people we interviewed considered Anderson lawyers to be quite content by New York standards. Although compensation at Anderson reportedly lags behind that of other New York firms, one contact observed, "I make less money than at other large firms, but it is a tradeoff. I feel I have more responsibility, control, and input in my work and in the firm's management." This person noted, additionally, that with the "open access to information, I always know what is going on financially and otherwise at the firm. This is empowering. Most of my friends at other firms have no information and thus are merely workers. I am part of the firm and its inner workings." Anderson's unique milieu undoubtedly accounts for the high level of attorney satisfaction. "Maybe it is the best of compromises; maybe it is the worst. But it is worth investigating" this very special work environment, advised one insider.

Baker & McKenzie

New York Chicago Dallas Miami Monterrey Palo Alto San Diego San Francisco Washington
46 Foreign Locations

Address: 805 Third Avenue, New York, NY 10022
Telephone: (212) 751–5700
Hiring Attorney: Robert L. Dumont
Contact: Christine M. Snyder, Recruitment & Professional Development Coordinator; (212) 751–5700
Associate Salary: First year $85,000 (1997)
Summer Salary: $1600/week (1996)
Average Hours: NA worked; NA billed; 2100 required
Family Benefits: Medical, dental, and life insurance; profit sharing and 401(K) plan; employee assistance program; business travel accident insurance; flexible spending accounts; long term disability; reimbursement of bar association fees; moving expense reimbursement; paid vacation
1996 Summer: Class of 9 students; offers to 9
Partnership NA
Pro Bono: NA

Baker & McKenzie in 1997
75 Lawyers at the New York Office
1.6 Associates Per Partner

Total Partners 29			Total Associates 46			Practice Areas	
Women	2	7%	Women	10	22%	Corporate	36
All Minorities	0	0%	All Minorities	6	13%	Litigation	19
			Afro-Am	1	2%	Tax	14
			Asian-Am	2	4%	Intellectual Property	4
			Latino	3	7%	Real Estate	2

world's largest international law firm

With 55 offices in 34 countries around the world, Baker & McKenzie is a premier international law firm. It is currently most heavily involved in Latin America, Eastern Europe, and Asia (particularly the Pacific Rim). With large litigation, tax, and corporate departments, the New York office actively participates in the firm's international practice. Most matters that the firm handles have an "international aspect," declared one contact. The firm offers its attorneys frequent opportunities to travel to all corners of the globe. Under an associate training program, certain eligible associates who have been with the firm for two years, may transfer for a period of between six months and two years to another Baker & McKenzie office. They must, however, then return to their original office. New York office associates have worked in Australia, Beijing, Hong Kong, Madrid, Vietnam, San Diego, and Washington, D.C. Moreover, in the past, summer associates have traveled overseas in connection with their assignments. In addition, each year the 20 summer associates accepted to the firm's International Clerkship program split their summer between a domestic and foreign Baker & McKenzie office.

Baker's litigation department primarily represents international clients and includes an active commercial arbitration practice. Many well-known international litigators and commercial arbitrators are partners at the firm, including Arthur Rovine, former assistant legal advisor to the State Department and former United States representative at the U.S.-Iran Claims Tribunal; Bob Davidson, well-known for his arbitration experience; and Lawrence Newman, Chairman of the United States Iranian Claimants Committee who has published numerous articles on international litigation. Baker & McKenzie's growing bankruptcy practice is also housed within the litigation department. One insider warned that "the litigation department can be rough to work in. The partners are demanding, the hours can be excessive, and pulling all-nighters before a brief is due is common." On the other hand, "litigation is very interesting at Baker & McKenzie. You do work that you will not do at other firms."

international litigation

Baker & McKenzie's tax department, reportedly considered to be one of the best in the country, handles a wide range of matters and boasts strong tax litigation and tax planning practices. Tax expert Michael Saltzman, formerly Assistant U.S. Attorney in the Southern District of New York and chief of its tax unit, and author of "the preeminent hornbook on IRS practice and procedure," is one of the firm's prominent tax partners. Robert Dumont and Brett Gold head up the tax department's burgeoning planning practice.

tax

The corporate department encompasses a number of practice groups, including insurance, securities, and corporate finance. The firm has a specialty in "captive insurance" work, which is managed by Gerald Hayes and James Cameron. The securities practice is divided into international transactions, headed by Malcolm Ross, and domestic transactions, headed by Howard Berkower. The securities group also has a growing mutual funds practice. The corporate finance group consists of lawyers working on traditional banking and financing transactions as well as international joint ventures and M&A work with a special emphasis on transactions in the Pacific Rim. The firm also has small, but burgeoning intellectual property practices. Its real estate group has dwindled from an 11 attorney group in 1994 to just a pair of attorneys today.

corporate

Though the firm officially encourages pro bono work, one source stated that he "was not struck by the amount of pro bono work done." Another observed that "if you wanted to do pro bono and had a good relationship with a partner, you would be okay." In addition to engaging in international pro bono work for the Hebrew Immigrant Aid Society, Baker & McKenzie also has provided legal services to, among others, the Midori Foundation, the Cirio Foundation, and New York Lawyers for the Public Interest. Every summer, a representative from the Urban Justice Center makes a presentation to the summer class regarding pro bono opportunities. In addition, the New York office supports fundraisers for The Legal Aid Society, The Urban Justice Center, and the Lawyers Committee for Human Rights.

limited pro bono

The work atmosphere in the New York office is "friendly and casual." One person commented that "it is incredibly easy to walk into anyone's office to chat. There is a real camaraderie, particularly among associates." Although associates are friendly and accessible, "partners are more reserved and harder to get to know." Everyone we interviewed agreed that the firm is "not stuffy." Associates are "low-key and down-to-earth." People do not dress particularly conservatively, and men regularly shed their jackets while at work. In addition, the firm has casual dress days on Friday year-round.

work atmosphere

Baker & McKenzie assigns entering associates to practice groups according to their stated preferences and the firm's needs. Most new associates work directly for the partners and the more senior associates in their practice group. "The level of responsibility you get depends on your relationship with the partner but, generally, initiative helps, and you get what you can handle," explained one source. Another noted that it

professional development

is not uncommon for first- and second- year corporate associates to find themselves "putting together joint ventures and reorganizations, doing due diligence and drafting documents, and having client contact." Junior litigation associates tend to research and draft motions and conduct some depositions.

Baker & McKenzie's professional development training program has become "less of a priority in recent years," reported one insider. Another contact reported, however, that "associates are given opportunities to attend outside seminars, and to ensure training programs are frequent and regularly scheduled." In addition, each department arranges its own monthly practice group meeting to discuss new developments in the law. The program for summer associates is "excellent and extensive." Summer associates attend a full-day legal writing workshop conducted by Harvard Law school professor Stephen Stark at the firm's offices. People commented that feedback at the firm could have been better, but "you get it if you ask for it." The summer program has recently been restructured, we were told, so that "feedback must be given to a summer associate by the assigning attorney."

active social life

Though Baker & McKenzie's lawyers work hard, their active social lives offer "a lot of opportunity to go out." Different groups at the firm go out for drinks, and lawyers will organize parties to celebrate significant events. According to one person, "birthdays are a big deal," and "people enjoy the frequent firm wine and cheese parties." There are also "firm breakfasts," held about once every other month. The firm also organizes a much enjoyed weekend to welcome all incoming associates in the United States and Canadian offices.

international diversity

An internationally diverse firm, Baker & McKenzie reportedly includes "a cross-section of ethnicities and cultures, even among its partners firmwide." This is not the case in its New York office, however, which has no minority and few women partners. "The firm is trying to do something about its reputation that it is not the best place for women," said one source. However, the Chicago office has received negative press for its handling of sexual harassment complaints brought against one of its former partners, who is now being sued for his alleged actions. In recent years, the firm has made "continuing" efforts to recruit women and minority applicants. It is also very interested in "recruiting people with the ability to communicate in South American and Asian languages." Several years ago, a former attorney filed a claim against the New York office alleging that he was dismissed because he displayed the symptoms of HIV. That claim has been settled. The movie *Philadelphia* is apparently loosely based on this incident.

management

Baker & McKenzie is organized as a worldwide partnership, with its headquarters located in Chicago. Every office has autonomous decision-making power with respect to summer associate and associate hiring decisions; however, the partners have delegated certain authority to an executive committee to make strategic decisions for the firm on a global basis. Although the New York office has an associates committee that meets with the managing partner on a regular basis, some felt that associates do not have much input into the firm's management.

functional offices

Baker & McKenzie's offices were described as "functional" and "mediocre." According to one source, "it is not the greatest office building, but the firm has a very good deal on the lease and plans to stay there." Baker & McKenzie occupies three floors, two of which are contiguous with each other. Partners enjoy corner offices; first- and second-year associates share offices. Each floor is equipped with a kitchen and snack machines. Some people complained that the library is too small. All Baker & McKenzie offices are connected by E-Mail. The firm has updated its computer system to a local area network using WordPerfect for Windows, but one insider reported that the computer network facilities "are not as advanced as they should/could be." Baker & McKenzie recently hired a new head librarian, and has arranged to put the firm library on the Internet "for quick and easy listings."

international orientation in hiring

Not surprisingly, Baker & McKenzie seeks lawyers "with an international background and outlook, who speak more than one language, have travel experiences, or have lived in another country." The firm frequently hires summer associates who were born outside the United States. People also commented that academic achievement is important to the firm. One person believed that students coming from prestige campuses "must have at least a B grade point average and some journal experience" to get hired at the firm. The firm hires its summer associates from schools such as Cardozo, Columbia, Duke, Fordham, Georgetown, Harvard, New York University, and Yale. According to another, Baker "looks beyond grades...they want people who can take initiative and do not have to be told what to do." People we interviewed advised prospective applicants to emphasize any international background and to portray themselves as an "aggressive, self-assured personality who can handle responsibility." You should be "rarin' to go." Baker & McKenzie's on-campus interviews are conducted by a pair of attorneys, but they are "not out of the ordinary."

Overall, Baker & McKenzie received positive reviews. Some people complained that the firm's attorneys could provide better feedback. Another complained that there is not much interaction between partners and associates, and that "junior and midlevel associates are not informed of some decisions made by management in a timely and systematic manner." Others believe that the firm's corporate and tax associates are more satisfied than its litigation associates. On the other hand, one source declared Baker & McKenzie to be the "best place to work in terms of work and people." The people are "nice and accessible," and the firm is a manageable size. The firm is "more entrepreneurial than other firms of similar size." Finally, with the largest international network of any law firm in the country, Baker & McKenzie is a good place to do top-quality international work, and offers "inexhaustive resources" with "the possibility for client contact early on."

Brown & Wood

New York Los Angeles San Francisco Washington
Beijing London Tokyo Hong Kong

Address: One World Trade Center, New York, NY 10048–0557
Telephone: (212) 839–5300
Hiring Attorney: Howard G. Godwin, Jr.
Contact: Maureen McGovern, Recruiting Coordinator; (212) 839–5406
Associate Salary: First year $86,000 (1997)
Summer Salary: $1625/week (1997)
Average Hours: 2100 worked; 1900 billed; NA required
Family Benefits: Maternity leave
1996 Summer: Class of 21 students; offers to 20
Partnership: 17% of entering associates from 1980–1985 were made partner
Pro Bono: NA

Brown & Wood in 1997
242 Lawyers at the New York Office
2.1 Associates Per Partner

Total Partners 77			Total Associates 165			Practice Areas	
Women	9	11%	Women	63	38%	Corporate/Securities	65
All Minorities	3	4%	All Minorities	28	16%	Securitization	44
Asian-Am	2	3%	Afro-Am	10	6%	Pooled Investment Ent.	32
Latino	1	1%	Asian-Am	12	7%	Litigation	30
			Latino	6	3%	Secured Lending/Proj. Finance	19
						Tax	19
						Real Estate	16
						Public Finance	11
						Private Clients	6

an old-world culture

If you yearn for the traditional law firms of yesteryear that maintained longstanding relationships with their clients and served them with unswerving commitment, Brown & Wood may be the place for you. Brown & Wood "is a white shoe firm with an old-world and conservative approach to the law. It is not an entrepreneurial firm in the Skadden sense," explained one contact. With close ties to the University of Virginia, Brown & Wood offers the additional charms of a gentlemanly Southern work atmosphere in fast-paced New York. One person commented that the old-world culture creates a "sense that people care about the firm and want to produce good lawyers." Brown & Wood attorneys are polite and supportive of each other in work-related and social matters. They respect one another, enjoy an easy camaraderie, and are interested in the lives and families of their colleagues. They usually leave their office doors open—an invitation to drop in—and are often found joking with one another and eating together in the cafeteria. Suit jackets are "never worn at the office unless meeting with clients," and the firm encourages casual dress on Fridays during the summer months.

cutting-edge finance law

Brown & Wood is best known for its corporate and securities and structured finance practice, which is organized into a variety of specialties. The structured finance practice group, the most "hard-core" department at the firm, was described as "pretty harsh for lower-level associates. It is detail-oriented and dull. There is an enormous amount of paperwork," according to one insider. The general corporate practice specializes in underwriting deals, country funds, privatizations, and structured finance for banks and export corporations doing business in Latin America. All groups enjoy a close relationship with Merrill Lynch, one of the firm's most important clients. The firm is well-known in the city for developing cutting-edge financial instruments. Brown & Wood also represents other large investment banks and financial intermediaries such as Morgan Stanley, Bear Stearns, Goldman Sachs, Lehman Brothers, Japan-based Nomura Securities, Paine Webber, Smith Barney, Chase and Citicorp.

other practice areas

In addition to its extensive Latin America work, Brown & Wood has a growing international practice. The firm has small but growing offices in London, Hong Kong, Beijing and Tokyo, all of which have active securities practices. The firm's Hong Kong office primarily works with Merrill Lynch's office, and the firm is issuer's counsel to the People's Republic of China. The firm's strong real estate department specializes in real estate investment trust (REIT) representation. Brown & Wood's securities litigation practice is well-known for its defense of major brokerage firms against challenges to the procedures and practices in the retail brokerage industry. As for pro bono work, the firm places summer associates at New York Lawyers for the Public Interest for one week of the summer. The firm's lawyers do a little pro bono work as well, and according to one insider the firm is "offering associates more opportunities for this."

training

Brown & Wood's philosophy is that associates "learn by doing." One person told us that "partners and senior associates will spend the time to bring you up to speed. They will give you a broad overview on a topic and are good at briefing you." The firm gives associates as much responsibility as they can handle. A third or fourth-year associate may even independently handle almost an entire deal involving complex financial products. Fourth- and fifth-year litigation associates frequently have responsibility for whole cases. Because cases are leanly staffed, associates are often directly responsible to the client. It is quite common for a first-year associate to travel to other cities to meet with clients on relatively small matters. The firm supplements its on-the-job training with formal training seminars on each of the firm's major practice areas and with firm meetings to discuss new legal developments. It also, at times, invites outside speakers to make presentations to its attorneys. In past summers, the chief counsel of Merrill Lynch and a representative from the Securities and Exchange Commission (SEC) have spoken to the associates.

golf
tennis
bars

Brown & Wood attorneys enjoy spending time together and have active social lives. They regularly play golf together and often go out to bars after work. Attorneys usually cap off summer softball games with dinner and drinks at New York's Pete's Tavern where, in the upstairs private room, they often subject summer associates to some good-natured ribbing. Even partners at the firm are accessible and periodically invite summer associates to play tennis or golf at their country clubs.

homogenous firm

Brown & Wood's New York office, we were told, is predominantly white and male, with the few female partners at the firm having little influence. Nevertheless, everyone we interviewed said that the firm handles sexual harassment issues appropriately. A partner who was notorious for offensive remarks and who had been warned repeatedly is no longer with the firm. Moreover, all firm personnel, including partners, associates, and support staff "undergo mandatory sexual harassment training." Brown & Wood is understanding of family emergencies, and lawyers often bring children into the office for the day if they have day care problems or doctor's appointments.

successful careful management

People praised Brown & Wood's cautious and well-reasoned management style. The firm is presently undergoing some significant change. It recently hired a management consulting group and, as a result of its report, has restructured the "corporate teams a bit, trying to diversify its practice a bit more (*e.g.* by increasing litigation to offset downturns in corporate work)." Consequently, the firm is "looking to bring in new practice groups and has already hired an employment lawyer and a tax litigator." The firm is fiscally conservative. It "does not give associates ridiculous advances. It also bills clients on time and collects fees efficiently," praised one admirer. One critic complained, however, that on the issue of salary versus hours required, "the firm is getting worse. They are trying to squeeze more out of fewer associates and yet are not paying competitive salaries. While first years may be on a par salary-wise, the discrepancies grow larger as you get more senior." Morale has, however, been high as Brown & Wood has grown rapidly in recent years and has been promoting associates to partnership at a steady pace. Brown & Wood's motto is "always be in search of a specialty." In recent years, the firm's success has tracked that of investment banks. Its practice areas evolve as financial markets and products change. As mentioned above, Brown & Wood now also views litigation as a potential growth area.

receptive management

The firm's management is receptive to what it considers appropriate associates' concerns, as evidenced by the recent formation of an associates committee comprised of an elected representative from each class and designed to interact directly with the firm's managing partner. Also, the firm changed the venue of the firm outing in response to associate concerns that the outing was traditionally held at a particularly exclusive country club. One observer stated, however, that though the firm responded to this concern, "it tried to downplay the issue rather than send around a memo discussing it. The tendency is to push such issues under the rug, even while responding."

computer upgrade scheduled

Brown & Wood's offices are located in the World Trade Center. The firm occupies all of floors 57, 58 and 59, as well as a portion of floor 56. Associates share offices until their third or fourth year. People are happy with the library and observed that the New York Law Institute, with its extensive library, is only a block away. The phone system has recently been upgraded, and all attorneys have speaker phones. The firm supplies everyone with a computer. The system, according to one insider, is "horrible" but the firm is "supposedly getting a new Windows/Lotus Notes system by the end of 1997."

hiring practices

Brown & Wood recruits heavily from the University of Virginia, where students with a grade point average of 3.1 or higher have a good chance of being hired at the firm, said one insider. The firm also hires from a wide range of other schools including Berkeley, Columbia, Fordham, Harvard, Michigan, New York University, Stanford, and Vanderbilt. Brown & Wood seeks hard-working people with interests outside the law. People recommended that students interviewing with the firm be very polite and emphasize their interest in business. An applicant should also display enthusiasm and an ability to do whatever tasks, including "grind work," that are required in connection with a transaction.

Brown & Wood is a stable place to work. The work is steady, if sometimes tedious and repetitious. The firm has a premier securities and corporate finance practice with a low-key profile. The firm has good people, declared one person, asserting, "I trusted them. It is not the kind of place where someone will stab you in the back to get ahead. It is a very human place." Another, who warned of the danger of getting pigeonholed into a narrow specialty like Investment Company Act law, nevertheless believed that "it is a good place to work if you are a normal person." Others elaborated upon this theme, pointing out that, whereas litigation (though "suffering from a severe lack of leadership and poor management skills") affords a variety of experiences, the corporate practice is "very specialized. You are placed in one group whereas other firms allow associates to work on a variety of different corporate transactions. It's a trade off—here, you become an expert in your field much more quickly and can therefore work more independently. I guess if you know what you want to do, this is a good place to be."

Cahill Gordon & Reindel

New York Washington
Paris

Address: 80 Pine Street, New York, NY 10005
Telephone: (212) 701–3000
Hiring Attorney: W. Leslie Duffy
Contact: Joyce Hilly, Hiring Coordinator; (212) 701–3901
Associate Salary: First year $88,000 (1997)
Summer Salary: $1600/week (1997)
Average Hours: NA worked; NA billed; none required
Family Benefits: 12 weeks paid maternity leave
1996 Summer: Class of 33 students; offers to 33
Partnership: 9% of entering associates from 1978–1984 were made partner
Pro Bono: NA

Cahill Gordon & Reindel in 1997
192 Lawyers at the New York Office
2 Associates Per Partner

Total Partners 62			Total Associates 130			Practice Areas	
Women	4	7%	Women	43	33%	Corporate	NA
All Minorities	0	0%	All Minorities	15	12%	Securities	NA
			Afro-Am	3	2%	Litigation	NA
			Asian-Am	10	8%	Tax	NA
			Latino	2	2%	Antitrust	NA
						Trusts & Estates	NA
						Environmental	NA
						Real Estate	NA

top profits per partner

With its highly successful mergers and acquisitions practice, Cahill, Gordon & Reindel received much attention from the press when the M&A boom of the 1980s went bust. The firm lost two major clients, EF Hutton and Drexel, at that time and shrunk from its height of about 285 lawyers to around 200 today. These clients have, however, been replaced by major corporate clients, particularly investment banks, such as Merrill Lynch, DLJ, Bankers Trust, and J.P Morgan. Cahill remains today a highly successful firm with profits per partner consistently among the highest in the country and well in excess of one million dollars.

cutting-edge corporate

Cahill has traditionally been well-regarded for its cutting-edge corporate department, which handles significant securities and investment bank matters, and which is currently "thriving." Cahill is also proud of its First Amendment litigation practice which is under the leadership of Floyd Abrams, who argues frequently before the U.S. Supreme Court. Cahill boasts major media clients such as CBS, NBC, CNN, Time-Warner, the *New York Times*, the *Wall Street Journal*, the *Washington Post* and Court TV. The firm also has an environmental litigation practice. Though Cahill does not have an international practice group, many of its corporate deals involve international issues, and its attorneys frequently travel both within the U.S. and abroad. One person commented that there are always "20 to 30 attorneys out of town."

active pro bono

Cahill attorneys are actively involved in pro bono matters. One contact told us, "One of the associates I knew came to Cahill because he could do more pro bono here than at his previous firm." The litigation department handles more pro bono work than other groups in the firm. The firm encourages summer associates to work for one week in one of three different public interest agencies in the city while earning regular firm salary. The firm credits all pro bono work toward billable hours.

survival of the fittest

In many ways, Cahill is structured to promote individualism and entrepreneurialism. Unlike many other firms which compensate partners by seniority, Cahill's profit allocation system is a non-lockstep system that takes into account contributions over recent years. One contact labeled Cahill "a survival-of-the-fittest partnership." Cahill functions more like a collection of smaller autonomous firms centered around certain powerful partners than as a traditional law firm partnership, which we were told provides very little incentive to invest in the firm's communal resources. According to one source, "partners care more about profits than about firm needs. They take the money and split it up." The firm's offices, for example, are located in an older office building, and the firm has only recently updated its antiquated word-processing system. However, the new computer system received "front page coverage in the *Wall Street Journal* for its modernity," reported one contact. The offices themselves leave a lot to be desired: "rugs are tattered and worn, the furniture is outmoded and the wall paper is peeling." Similarly, other support elements and amenities received critical reviews. We were told that the "food services was eliminated years ago," and the "support staff is quite poor. Attorneys do much of their own support work." In addition, three associates share one secretary, and summer associates have not had secretaries in the past, although we have been informed that secretarial support will be provided starting this summer.

personal initiative rewarded

The work atmosphere for associates at Cahill is very unstructured, informal, and "nonpretentious." One contact observed that Cahill is "very much a law firm of first generation lawyers, working-class and not snobby or elitist. It's the ultimate meritocracy. You are not rated on where you're from or where you went to school, but the quality of your work." Much of an associate's development and success depends on personal initiative. With no assignment coordinators, associates must build relationships with partners and solicit their work. One insider informed us that "in recent years, a few notably disagreeable partners have made life difficult for those who decline to work with them even if such declinations were due to overwork." More generally, however, this arrangement permits "junior associates not only to work with the associates and partners they wish to, but also to choose the type of assignment they wish to work on." Aggressive associates flourish in this atmosphere. They value the opportunities and freedom to work with the partners they like and to control their own work load. They are also entrusted with more responsibility, the opportunities for which can vary widely. Junior associates perform a wide range of tasks including researching and writing memos, going to the printers, and writing client letters. Corporate associates are particularly busy. It is "not at all unusual" for a first-year associate to go alone on his first trip to do due diligence, we were told. One contact informed us that "second year corporate associates frequently function as the senior associate on deals and go to drafting sessions on their own. This results from the lack of mid-level associates to run deals. It offers tremendous opportunity to obtain experience quickly, but can be overwhelming at times." A second contact told us that "in the corporate department, junior associates often travel by themselves and have a lot of client contact."

formal training: a joke

On-the-job training can vary widely for associates, and feedback is often hard to come by, although one contact observed that "questions are never looked down upon and all one has to do is ask." Formal training at Cahill, we were told, "has become a joke. The firm sends around memos at the beginning of the week to tell associates about Friday's upcoming training session and inevitably on Friday we receive an e-mail indicating the training has been cancelled."

The pressures created by the individualistic atmosphere at Cahill induce long, hard work hours and allow for little social life. Though the firm does not emphasize billable hours "at all," one source revealed that "first-year associates spend most of their waking hours working." Another source pointed out that "it is not unusual to see midlevel and senior associates in corporate work late at night and on weekends." The freewheeling atmosphere, however, often results in considerable differences in workloads, and according to one contact, attorneys' hours can vary anywhere from 1800 to 2800 a year.

efforts to increase diversity

Though at the time it was founded Cahill was known, in contrast to many of the "white shoe firms" at the time, as a tolerant and open firm which actively hired Catholics and Jews, it is, one person told us, "shockingly white male" in composition today. The firm is reportedly making an effort to recruit more women. "A lot of women are on the hiring committee," we were told. The firm has also made an effort to recruit minority law students, though it has not been very successful in recruiting or retaining minorities. Cahill has recently been successful in increasing significantly its number of Asian American associates. One contact informed us that "being religious, I have found Cahill to be very accommodating and tolerant."

complaints about salary

The firm is managed by a four partner executive committee. Associates reportedly have very little say in management decisions and even less chance of becoming partners. People commented that Cahill's management has become more bottom line oriented over recent years. In this connection, we heard complaints about Cahill's compensation system. One contact pointed out that "the firm failed to increase base salaries as had been rumored." Also, we were told that although the firm "paid a special bonus last summer because the firm had such a successful year, it was paid at a time when the firm was losing quite a few midlevel associates, leading people to believe it was more of a bribe than a bonus." In addition, criticisms were levelled at the fact that "the firm doesn't pro rate the bonus if you leave in the middle of the year, making it difficult to make lateral moves. Also the firm does not pay bonuses until three months after the end of the year."

recruits self-starters

Cahill, Gordon & Reindel hires "self-starters." One person noted that "you will do well at Cahill if you know how to look for your own work and make yourself well-known." Many Cahill associates are older and more experienced, we were told. "The firm hires interesting people like jazz musicians. There are a lot more personalities at Cahill than at other firms. The people are individuals." One person noted that the firm places a premium on writing ability. Cahill also seeks applicants with people skills, and does not look favorably upon people who come across as being arrogant. The hiring partner has been known to call former Cahill summer associates at certain law schools to inquire specifically about applicants from that school. Cahill hires students from the top national law schools, New York-area schools, and other law schools such as Villanova. Past successful applicants recommended that people interviewing with Cahill emphasize that they can work without much supervision.

Cahill, Gordon & Reindel can provide a remarkable experience for aggressive young associates. With hard work, these associates can get quality work and high levels of responsibility early in their careers. This is not a place for associates who want work automatically assigned to them, extensive feedback, and a high chance of making partner. Though becoming a partner is "more difficult at Cahill than at other firms," this past year saw three associates enter the partners ranks, among whom was the firm's first female corporate partner. The associates are "incredibly bright and generally have great personalities (you would become friends with them even outside of a work setting)," enthused one contact. The firm is "laid-back, less pretentious than other firms," and "the responsibility junior associates get is unmatched in New York City," praised another source. Cahill is a place for independent and self-reliant people, who are seeking a prestigious and high-paying law firm with high-profile work from which to launch their legal careers.

Chadbourne & Parke

New York Los Angeles Washington
Hong Kong New Delhi London Moscow Singapore

Address: 30 Rockefeller Plaza, New York, NY 10112
Telephone: (212) 408–5100
Hiring Attorney: Nancy W. Pierce, Chair, Recruiting Committee
Contact: Bernadette L. Miles, Director of Legal Recruitment; (212) 408–5338
Associate Salary: First year $89,000 base (1997); second $94,000 base plus potential merit bonus $10,000; third $108,000 plus pmb $14,000; fourth $127,000 plus pmb $18,000; fifth $145,000 plus pmb $25,000; sixth $160,000 plus pmb $25,000; seventh $165,000 plus pmb $30,000; eighth $170,000 plus pmb $30,000
Summer Salary: $1700/week (1997)
Average Hours: 2212 worked; 1919 billed; NA required
Family Benefits: Paid maternity and paternity leave, medical insurance, same sex domestic partner benefits, flexible spending account for medical and child care, emergency day care program, Employee Assistance Program (addendum to medical insurance)
1996 Summer: Class of 16 2L students; offers to 15
Partnership: 13% of entering associates from 1977–1987 were made partner
Pro Bono: 1.6% of all work is pro bono

Chadbourne & Parke in 1997
233 Lawyers at the New York Office
1.8 Associates Per Partner

Total Partners 72		
Women	9	13%
All Minorities	1	1%
Latino	1	1%

Total Associates 135		
Women	57	42%
All Minorities	19	14%
Afro-Am	4	3%
Asian-Am	10	7%
Latino	5	4%

Practice Areas	
Corporate/Corporate Finance	82
Litigation	66
Tax	21
Project Finance	16
Insurance/Reinsurance	12
Real Estate	9
Trusts & Estates	9
Employment	8
Intellectual Property	8
Bankruptcy	2

fast-growing international practice

Although not traditionally known as an "international" law firm, Chadbourne & Parke has rapidly developed a strong international practice. Chadbourne represents European and American banks, multinational corporations, international agencies and national governments. As one of the first law firms to establish a Russian presence, Chadbourne & Parke leads this legal market. The firm's Moscow office is a unique two-way joint office between Chadbourne and the Russian Union of Advocates. In 1996, Chadbourne represented the first Russian company to be listed on the N.Y.S.E. The practice is headed by William Holland, a highly-regarded authority on Western companies doing business with the former Soviet Union and author of *Moscow Twilight*, a quasi spy novel about post-modern Russia, as well as by Gene Sullivan and Robert Langer, resident partner in Moscow. Summer associates have also had interesting opportunities for involvement in this practice. One previous summer clerk worked for four weeks in the Moscow office, and a second is scheduled to do the same in 1997. Chadbourne has opened offices in London and Hong Kong in recent years and maintains a representative office in New Delhi, which provides administrative support to the firm's lawyers. It also opened an office in Singapore in 1997 and has affiliations with law firms in Tokyo, Kazakhstan, and Belarus. Chadbourne's international practice is further enhanced by partner, David Tillinghast, one of the foremost international tax experts in the country.

departmental practices

Chadbourne & Parke has recently grown rapidly, often acquiring entire practice groups from other firms. While this growth pattern has allowed the firm to draw the top lawyers in certain fields, it has also compartmentalized the firm into many different "power" centers, according to a contact. It is "hard to pin down a unifying firm culture," agreed another.

Chadbourne's corporate department, traditionally its strongest area, shrank during the general slowdown in corporate work in the early 1990s, but is picking up again. Much of the slack in this area was picked up by the addition of a leading corporate finance group headed by Dennis Friedman, and by the firm's premier project finance practice, headed by Rigdon Boykin, which primarily represents both developers and lenders internationally, in connection with power projects and other major infrastructural projects. These entrepreneurial practice groups aggressively develop business and are responsible for much of the firm's successful internationalization. Chadbourne's litigation practice is flourishing. It includes a very successful "product liability" litigation group, which primarily represents tobacco company Brown and Williamson.

Chadbourne was recently honored by Volunteers of Legal Service for exceeding the VOLS pro bono goal. The firm enhances its formal pro bono practice with interesting summer pro bono opportunities. Summer associates may work for a public interest organization for two weeks at full salary or may do pro bono work at the firm.

partying associates

Chadbourne offers a more "friendly and familiar" atmosphere than other large law firms. Associates work long hours and spend a lot of time together. "Whenever I hung around the firm there were always a lot of people there, especially the first-years," recalled one past summer associate, stating, "They would gab so much in the day that they would stay late to finish their work. They were all good friends who spend much of the day talking and not getting things done. One night I was there at 11 P.M. and there was a whole big group of them there eating pizza and talking. They would just hang out there." Chadbourne & Parke is a "good place for social life." Associates are always ready to take the summer associates out on the town, reported one interviewee. "It's a big drinking crowd," commented another. "The associates, especially the younger ones, go out every Friday for drinks and sometimes during the week," noted a third. Chadbourne sponsors a range of fun-filled events for summer associates. The firm also hosts monthly cocktail parties throughout the year.

flexible career development

Chadbourne's summer program permits summer associates to experience a broad range of practice areas and to meet a number of the firm's attorneys. Several partners are responsible for collecting and distributing work assignments to summer associates. Entering associates may join a specific department, provided there is a need in that area or they may remain "unassigned" for a year and work with many departments. Chadbourne is very flexible in associate career development: "The firm is really loyal to its people and it tries to accommodate you when you make a request. If you do a good job, it will really care about you," praised one source. Chadbourne is particularly flexible in allowing people to transfer between its offices.

mentor program

Chadbourne provides a number of formal training programs, such as corporate and litigation seminars, although it is not regarded as providing some of the better formal training in the city. Nor is it "particularly notable in the amount of responsibility" it gives young associates, commented one person. Most junior litigation and corporate associates handle "mundane" drafting and research assignments. They deal with "a lot of paper," complained one source. A mentor program was recently introduced at the firm to provide more direction to young associates. Every new associate has two mentors—of junior and senior level (one of whom is typically not from the practice area of the associate). The mentor program complements a newly instituted "extensive orientation program," which includes a one day orientation seminar in New York for all new associates from all offices.

few women and minorities

Although Chadbourne has few female or minority partners, the firm is very meritocratic and treats everyone with "respect", reported an interviewee. A number of well-respected women work at the firm. "People take maternity leave all the time. One female partner had two sons and took a lot of time off. It was quite manageable and the firm was good to her. The firm is very understanding," noted one contact. The current hiring partner is Nancy W. Pierce. Although there are few minorities at Chadbourne, one person noted that the firm is ethnically and religiously diverse.

fabulous new offices

Chadbourne & Parke is managed by a committee whose membership rotates, as well as a non-lawyer business manager at the firm. Associates are represented on both the professional staff and recruiting committees. The firm recently conducted a survey of all lawyers covering matters from work satisfaction to diversity issues and is working to address the issues raised by responses to the survey. In terms of economic success, one person commented that Chadbourne falls "in the middle of the pack" of large New York firms. It is "stable and solid" and will remain a top firm, but it is not in the very top tier. Chadbourne & Parke has experienced an "impressive growth rate." The firm relocated to larger space within their current office building in 1996 to relieve the pressures of overcrowding that were common in the early 1990s. One contact described the new accommodations as "fabulous." Along with the improved office accommodations, the firm's cafeteria has reportedly also upgraded "dramatically," and there exists a separate "smoking room" on the 31st floor for members of the smokers fraternity.

social interviews

Chadbourne & Parke hires "home-grown New York types," according to one source. It is not in the upper tier of New York firms and is less competitive than some of New York's most elite firms. In recent years, the firm has hired a large number of its summer associates from Columbia, Fordham, Georgetown, Harvard, and New York University. Like many firms, Chadbourne emphasizes academic achievement in its hiring, but more than others, it looks for "social people," according to one contact. Chadbourne's callback interviews usually involve meeting with four or five attorneys for a half an hour each and a lunch with a junior associate, although many last much longer, commented one successful applicant, noting that her callback interview was conducted over a six-and-a-half-hour period. Interviews are "friendly" and "comfortable."

Chadbourne & Parke is a firm where the work hours are said to be "tolerant" and which is "somewhat" understanding and considerate of associates' needs. It offers a supportive work environment together with "a lot of big-growth areas," especially in the booming mergers and acquisitions practice. Some concern was expressed that Chadbourne may be beginning to develop an "eat what you kill" mentality and that the prospects for partnership are "unclear for most associates." There was nothing but praise, however, for the international aspects of the firm's work, associated as it is with "lots of visiting attorneys, international deals, summer trips abroad, etc." If exotic experiences are your cup of tea, you should give Chadbourne & Parke a close look.

Cleary, Gottlieb, Steen & Hamilton

New York Washington
Brussels Frankfurt Hong Kong London Paris Tokyo

Address: One Liberty Plaza, New York, NY 10006
Telephone: (212) 225–2000
Hiring Attorney: Robert P. Davis, Chairman
Contact: Norma F. Cirincione, Director of Legal Personnel; (212) 225–3150
Associate Salary: First year $87,000 (1997); second $108,000; third $126,000; fourth $147,000; fifth $172,000; sixth $185,000; seventh $195,000; eighth $203,000; the firm contributes annually an additional 3% of each associate's salary into a deferred savings plan
Summer Salary: $1673/week (1997)
Average Hours: NA worked; NA billed; NA required
Family Benefits: 13 weeks maternity leave; 4 weeks paternity leave; emergency childcare; eldercare; health, life, disability insurance; flexible spending accounts; domestic partner benefits; employee assistance program
1996 Summer: Class of 56 students; offers to 56
Partnership: 15% of entering associates from 1983–1988 were made partner
Pro Bono: 4% of all work is pro bono

Cleary, Gottlieb, Steen & Hamilton in 1997
276 Lawyers at the New York Office
3.0 Associates Per Partner

Total Partners 71		
Women	7	10%
All Minorities	4	6%
Asian-Am	2	3%
Latino	2	3%

Total Associates 201		
Women	83	41%
All Minorities	53	26%
Afro-Am	21	10%
Asian-Am	17	8%
Latino	15	7%

Practice Areas	
Banking	NA
Corporate	NA
Finance	NA
Employment/Benefits	NA
International	NA
Litigation	NA
Mergers & Acquisitions	NA
Tax	NA
Real Estate	NA
Trusts & Estates	NA
Bankruptcy	NA

the happiest associates in New York

One of the nation's pre-eminent international corporate law firms, Cleary, Gottlieb, Steen & Hamilton has a reputation for having some of the happiest associates in New York. The firm is distinguished by its unique combination of an unstructured and noncompetitive work atmosphere, interesting clients, numerous opportunities for international travel, and some of the highest associate salaries in New York.

cooperative atmosphere

Cleary was founded in 1946 by seven lawyers including George Cleary, Leo Gottlieb, Mel Steen, and Fowler Hamilton, all of whom were near the top of their law school classes respectively at Harvard, Yale, the University of Minnesota, and Oxford. Formerly lawyers at Root, Clark, Buckner & Ballantine, they renounced their positions at that firm when it established a partner compensation system based on hours billed and clients generated. Firmly believing that lawyers should cooperate rather than compete within their own firm, they set up a system that compensates both associates and partners according to seniority. Also committed to a partnership based on a democratic and participatory style of governance, they sought to encourage the free exchange of information among partners. All partners are involved in important firm decisions, and like other financial information, each partner's share of the firm's income is known to all partners. The founders' imprint continues to distinguish Cleary today. One person quipped that Cleary "patterns itself after Yale Law School." The firm's attorneys "consider themselves a family," declared one insider. Another protested mildly: "friends yes, but family, no. This is still a law firm, and still a business devoted to work and making a profit."

polite restrained individualists

Cleary combines a cooperative work atmosphere with a respect for the individual. Those we interviewed described Cleary as "friendly," "relaxed," and polite with "little hierarchy." This is not to deny that a definite "pecking order" exists at the firm. As one contact pointed out to us, "when it comes to the work, it is always clear that the senior attorneys—and especially partners—call all the shots." Senior lawyers are "very willing to take the time to explain something and listen to questions," said one contact. Cleary insists on courteous behavior toward all, although one insider observed that "a few partners are known for being terrible to their secretaries." Cleary is not as "colorful, loud, or gossipy as some other New York firms. It is more distant, restrained, and white shoe," we were told. But Cleary lawyers feel free to express their individuality in their dress. "The firm doesn't care how you look," one source remarked. "They just want perfect work." Another commented that women wear "bright colors, funky outfits, and jewelry." One partner sports a ponytail and others wear cowboy boots. But, "men are required to wear suits and ties," observed one contact, wanting to keep matters in perspective.

the Cleary lawyer

Cleary's vision of the ideal attorney—the "Cleary Lawyer"—is an individual, an intellectual, and a generalist. Committed to an interdisciplinary philosophy of law, Cleary has no departments, only loose practice groups. In general, it permits new lawyers to work in a number of the firm's practice groups, which include structured finance, bankruptcy, international, tax, trusts and estates, mergers and acquisitions, and litigation.

pre-eminent international practice

With offices in New York, Washington D.C., Paris, Brussels, Frankfurt, London, Tokyo, and Hong Kong, Cleary is most well-known for its highly developed international corporate law practice. The firm represents corporations and lenders in joint ventures, corporate finance, and general corporate matters. It has also represented foreign governments, including Kuwait, in various matters. The international work frequently takes attorneys to foreign countries. Permanent associates who have worked at the firm for two years may elect to be placed for two or three years in a foreign office. When the foreign offices are busy, "associates have been asked to do their overseas work earlier in their careers, or to go to overseas offices for several weeks or months." Associates intent on making partner are well-advised to do a stint in a foreign office, believed one insider. In 1997, 21 summer associates will spend a portion of their summers in the Paris, Brussels, London, Hong Kong or Frankfurt offices.

other practice areas

Cleary reputedly houses the top "securities law experts in the city," one commentator disclosed. The firm also has a substantial insurance regulatory law practice and "the best tax practice in the city," claimed another source, who also cautioned that the tax lawyers are "very smart, but quirky, and hard to work with." Cleary's litigation practice focuses on bankruptcy, securities litigation, products liability, white-collar crime, and corporate contracts. Partner Larry Friedman does intellectual property litigation.

highly-rated pro bono

Cleary is committed to pro bono activities and regularly distributes a listing of available pro bono matters to all attorneys. The firm handles many cases for the New York Legal Action Center for the Homeless. Cleary also sponsors a program in which six associates each year staff two different public interest organizations (each for four-month periods) while earning full salary. Summer associates may also work for two weeks with a non-profit organization while remaining on Cleary's payroll. In addition, many summer associate events are linked to public interest events in the city.

opportunities training

Cleary expects high-quality work from its attorneys. "You can show up for work as a first-year associate and immediately be sent to a foreign country to do a negotiation," claimed one observer. "You have to be independent and confident." Cleary attorneys meet with clients, negotiate deals, and draft documents early in their careers. While associate responsibilities provide extensive on-the-job training, people we interviewed claimed that formal training and feedback are limited.

Cleary attorneys work hard because they are committed to providing quality legal services. The firm "treats you like an adult and as part of a team," stated one source. Cleary has no stated minimum billable requirement, and "a lot of people didn't even know how much they billed," one contact informed us. Another contact told us that "in the last several months, many midlevel litigation associates have left the firm. This seems to reflect normal, albeit coincidentally highly-concentrated turnover, rather than an exodus prompted by a common cause. The numerous departures will make life very busy for those litigators who remain."

social life

Younger attorneys at the firm frequently socialize with each other after work and go out in big groups to restaurants and bars downtown, on the West Side, or in Soho. Some attorneys at the firm date each other, and there have been a few intra-firm marriages. Despite the social life, however, Cleary is a very individualistic firm and "people generally mind their own business and do not interfere in other people's lives," remarked one spectator.

liberal Ivy League

The political atmosphere at Cleary is "liberal Ivy League within the confines of a law firm." Cleary makes a conscious effort to be welcoming to women. Female partners at the firm often hold special meetings with female summer associates to discuss their concerns regarding women in law firm careers. Everyone we interviewed praised the firm's open attitude toward maternity leave. People "are encouraged to have a life outside of the firm," one insider informed us. Another voiced some concern, however, that Cleary almost expects its attorneys to work a few years in an overseas office, a commitment that is often more difficult for women to make, according to this person. The firm is, reportedly, very flexible in permitting attorneys to take time off to pursue other interests; one woman took a one year sabbatical to join a Buddhist monastery.

Cleary is "ethnic in comparison to a lot of other WASP firms," said one of several people who praised the diversity of Cleary lawyers. Every year Cleary hires foreign lawyers with advanced degrees in law from U.S. law schools to spend six to nine months with the firm. They provide a multi-cultural atmosphere at the firm. In addition, the firm has responded to past criticism regarding the number of minority attorneys at the firm by actively recruiting and retaining minorities. Minorities at the firm seem "well-integrated," reported one insider. The firm also employs a number of openly gay and lesbian attorneys who have formed "an informal lunch group that meets three or four times a year." Cleary recently extended domestic partnership benefits to same-sex couples, but it was pointed out to us that "this benefit does *not* extend to unmarried heterosexual couples. The logic is that gay people cannot currently get married whereas heterosexual people can."

Cleary is said to be a well-managed firm. There is speculation that the firm plans to expand its intellectual property and Soviet practice areas, and it already has a "presence" in Moscow. Numerous committees guide the firm's day-to-day management. A wine committee composed of two to three partners, for example, carefully selects the wine for all firm events.

office facilities

Cleary is located at One Liberty Plaza, in offices described as "light and airy." The firm displays "a great modern art collection" in its offices; all the pieces are suggested by the firm's professional paid consultant and reviewed by the firm's art committee. Every attorney has a private office with windows. The firm is technologically advanced, and all offices are connected by E-mail. The support staff was described as wonderful and available 24 hours a day. Cleary hires developmentally challenged personnel for positions such as inter-office mail messengers.

academic bias in hiring

Cleary is very selective in its hiring. The résumés of Cleary attorneys are compiled in a book by the firm, many of which reflect "amazing undergraduate records, two years of public interest experience, lots of publications and a lot of higher degrees," listed one awed source. The firm has a "strong academic bias," and most summer associates have high grades and journal experience. "You have to have good grades to get a callback interview," one contact asserted. "At Harvard, that probably means over a B+ average," this person continued. The firm recruits heavily from Columbia, Harvard, NYU, and Yale, but draws on a wide range of schools including Stanford, Boston University, Cardozo, Northwestern, the University of Chicago, the University of Michigan, and the University of Pennsylvania. As difficult as it is to land a job at Cleary, it is reportedly even more difficult to make partner at the firm. One contact informed us that it is "almost impossible to make partner here. People can work 'round the clock for eight years, only to get the boot in the end."

hires offbeat applicants

In addition to strong academic records, Cleary seeks "interesting people with outside interests," said one successful applicant. The firm likes people with offbeat interests and is less attracted to mainstream people. Candidates with foreign interests and foreign language skills also fare well at Cleary. One person advised interviewees at Cleary to "be yourself because you really can be." People at Cleary "are honest and will respond honestly," agreed another. "You don't have to tell them you love corporate law because they accept that it is just a job," remarked another.

For someone interested in international corporate work, Cleary is an outstanding choice. Because it hires "highly intellectual people, everybody has confidence in everybody, and it is not very competitive," observed one person. "This is a great place to work in a relaxed, friendly environment," praised another. Cleary is "the best law firm to be at in New York City," raved another.

Coudert Brothers

New York Denver Los Angeles San Francisco San Jose Washington

Bangkok Beijing Berlin Brussels Hanoi Ho Chi Minh City Hong Kong Jakarta London Moscow Paris St. Petersburg Singapore Sydney Tokyo

Address: 1114 Avenue of the Americas, New York, NY 10036–7794
Telephone: (212) 626–4400
Hiring Attorney: James C. Colihan/Thomas J. Rice, Co-Chairpersons
Contact: K. Page Higgins, Recruiting Coordinator; (212) 626–4635
Associate Salary: First year $85,000 (1997)
Summer Salary: $1600/week (1997)
Average Hours: NA worked; NA billed; 2000 suggested
Family Benefits: 12 weeks paid maternity leave
1996 Summer: Class of 14 students; offers to 14
Partnership: 12% of entering associates from 1981–1988 were made partner
Pro Bono: 1–3% of all work is pro bono

Coudert Brothers in 1997
122 Lawyers at the New York Office
1.1 Associates Per Partner

Total Partners 57			Total Associates 62			Practice Areas	
Women	5	9%	Women	27	44%	Corporate	50
All Minorities	1	2%	All Minorities	9	15%	Litigation	25
Asian-Am	1	2%	Afro-Am	1	2%	Project Finance/Int. Corp. Fin.	15
			Asian-Am	7	11%	Tax	14
			Latino	1	2%	Customs	7
						Employee Benefits	4
						Real Estate	3
						Trusts & Estates	3
						Bankruptcy	1

a maverick law firm

The sons of a 19th century French revolutionary who plotted the overthrow of the King of France, the Coudert brothers founded one of the first truly trans-Atlantic law firms. These unconventional brothers continued their family's radical proclivities through the legal profession. As Catholics, the Coudert brothers made their mark on the New York legal scene by building one of the first large, nonexclusively WASP firms in the city. Even today, one person told us, Coudert associates "feel like they are the mavericks of large New York firms. They feel like they are having fun. They are very satisfied with Coudert."

pre-eminent international practice

From its inception as a small firm with connections to France, Coudert Brothers has grown to become New York's pre-eminent international law firm. In recent years, however, it has experienced some downsizing. With 15 offices outside the United States, Coudert has more foreign offices than most American law firms and a broader international network than almost any New York firm. Its international practice has historically focused on Continental Europe, but in the early 1970s the firm expanded to Asia, and its Asia offices are reportedly thriving. With respect to the downsizing, Coudert has experienced a "number of departures—both en masse and individually—over recent years, and there was a great deal of concern over the viability of the firm," reported one insider. More recently, however, the firm has obtained a number of new groups, and "people are content with the stability of the firm and are no longer worried about job security." According to one contact, "Coudert seems to have made a substantial commitment to developing a large network of corporate finance partners around the globe," and the firm has also grown "substantially" in the high-tech intellectual property area, especially in its California offices.

Coudert's main departments include litigation, corporate, tax, and finance. The firm also has small customs, bankruptcy, employment benefits, real estate, and trusts and estates departments. The litigation department, whose numbers have declined significantly since our last edition (from 45 lawyers in 1994 to 25 this year), handles mainly commercial litigation and international arbitrations. This department grew in the past with the addition of a group of antitrust litigators from Lord, Day & Lord. In recent years the decline of antitrust has forced the litigation department to choose whether it wants to be a service department for corporate clients or whether it wants to develop an independent client base, we were told. The department at present "seems to encourage both" and continues to develop expertise in everything from securities to First Amendment litigation.

The corporate department engages in general corporate counseling and provides advice in a number of specific areas, including securities and leasing. The department is organized into a number of practice groups that focus on different geographic areas of the world. The Russian and French practice groups are particularly strong. Other practice groups specialize in the European Community, Germany, Indonesia, Korea, Japan, Italy, and Singapore. There have been reports in the past of factions within the corporate department, in particular between the Asian and European groups, and of the difficulties this presented for associates in securing sustainable work assignments, but a firm spokesperson informed us that these conflicts "have been resolved."

The tax department has a strong international tax practice, which handles setting up offshore funds, international mergers and acquisitions, international corporate finance, and many transfer pricing matters. Coudert's tax practice offers unique challenges as every transaction involves a significant international component. In July of 1996, Coudert added eight project finance/corporate finance partners from Whitman Breed, including two tax partners. The firm now has a large and very active project finance and international corporate finance practice.

foreign travel opportunities

"Whenever anyone wants to go overseas, they go to Coudert," said one person. The firm's international matters require its attorneys to travel frequently. In addition, the firm encourages its associates to work for a few years in one of Coudert's foreign offices. Summer associates may rotate for three weeks through one of the offices abroad if consistent with the firm's needs. Past summer associates have worked in the firm's offices in Australia, Hong Kong, Moscow, Brussels, and Singapore.

unstructured environment

Coudert Brothers provides a very unstructured working environment for associates. Some people value the freedom which the firm provides. "You can talk a partner into letting you do what you think you can do," said one satisfied contact. Another contact remarked that "the firm is very responsive in trying to get associates the type of work they request. The only requirement is that the associate is persistent." Others noted, however, that the lack of structure increases the importance of office politics. "You have to get to know a partner or an associate to get work, and the relationships you develop become very important in terms of the work you get," we were told. One source noted, "the experience and work you get at Coudert is really the luck of the draw. Some people get on cases which allow them excellent experience quickly while others get on large cases which last forever and which do not have much potential for development." While most associate training occurs on-the-job, some departments, such as litigation and tax, organize lunch meetings at which they "discuss cases and bounce around ideas." The feedback that associates receive depends on both their own initiative and the responsiveness of the partner for whom they work. Associates receive formal midyear and annual reviews.

minimal social life

Coudert's offices are "subdued and quiet, not frantic. Doors are open, and people do stop to chat." But, the firm "isn't as social as other large firms," said one person. "People interact professionally. They are not overly friendly or critical. They quietly get things done." Another person remarked, more positively, that "associates are generally supportive of each other rather than competitive. People are appreciated for their strong points. While this may be more true in litigation than corporate, the associates are a close group." After-work socializing is said to be minimal. In response, the firm "has added an informal weekday cocktail hour on Fridays," reported one insider. One critic complained that the "associates didn't really reach out to summer associates," while another expressed surprise at this observation, commenting that this "probably depends a great deal on the department" where you are located. People agreed that partners at the firm are accessible and that the firm is not overly hierarchical. The dress code is flexible. Women wear pants, and men do not always wear a complete suit to work.

working on minority hiring

Coudert Brothers has "a European Continental culture if anything...There are a lot of anglophiles and europhiles," according to one contact, who noted that "some partners like to throw in French phrases every once in a while when speaking." Another contact noted that "the typical Coudert partner is significantly more 'quirky' or eccentric than partners at other large New York law firms." One person asserted that the firm's partnership is fairly diverse, noting that it includes people from all over the world. Another person, however, described the firm as "WASPy." People also pointed out that the firm's partnership is predominantly male and that few senior associates are American minority lawyers. There are, however, a sizeable number of Asian-American associates at the firm. Although we heard complaints that the firm does not actively recruit minorities, it does now recruit at Howard and attends the Northeast Black Law Students Association Job Fair.

associate anxiety regarding management

There appears to be some anxiety among Coudert associates regarding the management of the firm (particularly in light of the recent downsizing). The firm gave bonuses this past year for the first time in several years. The bonuses were generally (though not universally) well-received by the associates, we were told. There is continuing anxiety among some associates regarding the "loose style" at the firm which "really requires an associate to figure out what he wants and go after it. This loose style is not comforting to those who want more definite promises about their future." This anxiety is compounded by the weak partnership prospects at Coudert, which according to one contact, "look practically non-existent, at least in the New York office." Another contact remarked that "most new partners in New York have been laterals."

Coudert is managed by a five partner executive committee, the membership of which rotates on a regular basis. Partnership recommendations are made by the inter-office policy committee (affectionately known as "Interpol"), which consists of representatives from nearly all the branch offices. The entire partnership votes on these recommendations. Coudert is looking to its Moscow and Beijing office for potential growth. The firm "got in there early before the break-up of the Soviet Union," remarked one person. Coudert has opened offices in Vietnam. As for office facilities, Coudert moved into "gorgeous" offices in the Grace Building in 1991. Associates do not share offices and "those lucky enough to be on the south side of the building have a stunning view of the Statue of Liberty, the World Trade Center, and the Empire State Building."

foreign language interviews

Coudert Brothers looks to hire people with an international background and foreign language skills. It helps to "show interest either through background or through a course of study of a particular country or an area," advised one person. Applicants were advised to "emphasize that you are eager to learn about the law and other cultures. Do not appear parochial." One person advised applicants to read the newspapers and be prepared to discuss current events. Another warned that if you claim any language skills on your résumé, "they will interview you in that language." In 1996, the firm made offers for permanent employment to all 14 of its summer associates. The firm hires its summer class from a number of law schools, including Columbia, Harvard, New York University, Virginia, Georgetown, Boalt, Stanford, Fordham, Penn, and Pace.

Cravath, Swaine & Moore

New York
London Hong Kong

Address: Worldwide Plaza, 825 Eighth Avenue, New York, NY 10019–7475
Telephone: (212) 474–1000
Hiring Attorney: Timothy G. Massad/Peter T. Barbur
Contact: Therese B. Garrett, Recruiting Manager; (212) 474–3217
Associate Salary: First year $85,000 (1997); includes arrival bonus; an additional bonus of $6,000 is paid to associates in December following the completion of their first year
Summer Salary: $1525/week (1997) (plus rent subsidy; includes advance)
Average Hours: NA worked; NA billed; NA required
Family Benefits: Health insurance for associates, spouses (incl. same-sex domestic partners), and children; dental and life insurance; 16 weeks paid maternity leave (cbc unpaid); 4 weeks paid paternity leave (cbc unpaid); on-site emergency childcare center
1996 Summer: Class of 70 students; offers to 70
Partnership: 6% of entering associates from 1983–1989 were made partner
Pro Bono: 3% of all work is pro bono

Cravath, Swaine & Moore in 1997
326 Lawyers at the New York Office
3.9 Associates Per Partner

Total Partners 67			Total Associates 259			Practice Areas	
Women	6	9%	Women	70	27%	Corporate	180
All Minorities	1	1%	All Minorities	18	7%	Litigation	115
Afro-Am	1	1%	Afro-Am	3	1%	Tax	21
			Asian-Am	11	4%	Trusts & Estates	10
			Latino	4	2%		

name exposure connections

Cravath, Swaine & Moore "attracts lawyers committed to practicing law at its highest level and provides access to unlimited resources," commented one person we interviewed. Another observed that the firm also provides associates with "name, exposure, and connections." Cravath attracts large clients that bring to it some of the most cutting-edge legal work in the country. Associates routinely read about the matters on which they work in the *Wall Street Journal* and the *New York Times*. Cravath has a strong reputation for providing associates with good training and significant exposure to high-profile cases and transactions. To some, Cravath may well be the most attractive firm in New York because of the array of career options available to associates once they have worked at the firm. One contact remarked that "we have a very gung ho attitude, thinking we can and will work miracles. It can be exciting," while another observed that "for those planning to leave, Cravath maximizes options—head hunters call several times a day."

the Cravath System

The firm is proud of the "Cravath System," its unique method of assigning work. Under this system, an entering associate declares a preference for one of the firm's four departments and is assigned to work with a small group of partners in that department for approximately one year to eighteen months. At the end of this period, the associate is rotated to another group of partners. This rotation assures that the associate gets a general understanding of a practice area and prevents undue specialization. The Cravath System significantly shapes an associate's experience at the firm. Work assignments come from one channel: the partners in the group. Associates have less control than at other firms over the kind of work assignments they receive because the partner mentors exclusively determine the type and amount of work associates receive. One insider praised Cravath's rotation system, commenting that under it, associates cannot really compete with each other (since the only way to succeed is to satisfy the partners for whom you work); partners can't play favorites (since partners can only use associates assigned to them); and specialization is not allowed (since rotation forces associates to learn a variety of practice areas). On the other hand, a second contact observed that a major drawback of the rotation system is that "an associate may end up rotated to a partner with whom he may not get along. For example, there is one partner known to be quite short-tempered who has been rumored to call associates 'idiots,' give them no work to do and then ask them why they haven't found a new job. Rotation is always risky..." A third contact noted, however, that there are "escape hatches" if an associate doesn't get along with a partner: "the associate can drift and work for another partner in the group; the associate can be 'loaned out' to an entirely different group to work on one or more deals or cases; [or] the associate can have a short rotation and move on early."

challenging high-profile work

Cravath is well-known for its litigation and corporate practices. "Cravath's vibrant practice is constantly on the front pages of the law journals," declared one contact. Another remarked that Cravath has the "best litigation work out there. Most involves coming up with creative approaches to resolve difficult problems facing our clients," while a third person exclaimed that Cravath is "doing all the best, biggest, high-profile M&A deals in the country." Tom Barr, former head of the firm's litigation practice, is famous for his victory in the IBM antitrust litigation, and the firm is counsel to Time-Warner in various noteworthy litigations. Cravath's corporate department has been involved in several recent high-profile deals, including Boeing's acquisition of McDonnell-Douglas and the Dean Witter-Morgan Stanley merger. Cravath also served as lead outside counsel to CBS, Inc. in its $5.4 billion buyout by Westinghouse Electric Corp. and to Capital Cities/ABC, Inc. in its $19 billion purchase by Walt Disney Co. Cravath is counsel on many international deals, but does not have a specific international practice group. The firm has offices, however, in London and Hong Kong, and more than 30% of Cravath's largest clients are foreign corporations.

While it occasionally handles smaller individual cases, like the other practice areas, the pro bono practice specializes in large, high-profile, impact litigation cases. It represented the minority members of the Birmingham Fire Department and has represented large institutions such as Covenant House, the Oneida Indian Nation (for whom the firm also does non pro bono work), and the City of New York. As with paying clients, Cravath spares no expense in producing only quality work. In general, however, those interviewed believe that associates must make their own time to do pro bono work.

this isn't so bad after all

The work atmosphere at Cravath is fast-paced, high-energy, exciting, and professional. "While the atmosphere is ultra-professional, it is not harsh. The firm is simply bottom line oriented and not particularly emotional," explained one insider. Cravath associates work long hours. One contact observed that "although many law firms in the city require long hours similar to those routinely worked at Cravath, it is probably true that at Cravath more attorneys routinely work very long hours than at other firms in the city." The last edition of the *Insider's Guide* reported that it was "rumored that the firm has champagne parties for associates who bill 100 hours in one week." One insider set us straight on this matter: "If that's true, then I've missed a number of parties. I have been treated to dinner or lunch with partners after particularly gruelling deals. This tactic is very wise from the partners' view. Just as you're getting to be fed up with the hours, they take you someplace nice so that you think—gee, this isn't so bad after all."

One source believed that the firm's secret formula for producing hard-working associates is that "the firm tries to keep you hungry for recognition. That is why it gets so much work from its associates." Another contact remarked that the "firm seems purposefully to recruit insecure overachievers who then spend all their time vying for attention from partners or senior associates." A third person observed that "the firm hires dedicated and talented associates and then challenges them to improve continually. No one 'rests on their laurels' here." Others commented that Cravath is a professional firm and that people work hard because the work has to be done. For example, when discussing the amount of work-related travel, one contact declared, "you never know what you will be called on to do. You are a Cravath attorney and are expected to get the job done." Some contacts drew our attention to the "work hard, play hard" environment at the firm, which may be explained by the fact that the "attorneys have a somewhat macho self-image in that they are go-getters. There are more leaders than followers at the firm." Another contact remarked that while on the whole people at Cravath are rather reserved and you never see people yelling, "there's definitely a frat-boy contingency that goes to Hogs 'n' Heifers and such. They come in late the next day. I don't think people take those associates too seriously."

opportunity training feedback

We received mixed reviews on the amount of responsibility junior associates get at Cravath. "It is common to be the only associate on a deal," explained one insider. In litigation, according to another, "associates get a great deal of responsibility on written work. They are deposing witnesses within two years and are arguing in court by their sixth year." On the other hand, one contact remarked that junior associates get "relatively little experience. Clients come to Cravath expecting to pay a lot of money and they expect the partners to argue even trivial motions and take depositions. My friends at other New York firms have much more experience." Another contact observed that "often the antitrust cases we handle require massive amounts of documents and require associates to devote much of their time to document review." While the firm has good training, in the view of many it is weak on feedback and "praise is scant." One insider commented that, at Cravath, "there is a general lack of feedback, especially positive reinforcement for good work. Associates who lack self-confidence, or who require coddling, often find Cravath difficult and impersonal," while another contact remarked that at Cravath "'praise is scant' only because doing well is expected. It is silly to create an environment of 'go-getters' and then pat them on the back."

a true partnership

Associates at Cravath reportedly do not know much about the firm management. For associates "much is a black box in terms of partners," said one person. Another contact asserted that associates are unconcerned about their lack of involvement in firm management: "Associates understand the 'work hard, play hard' concept and do not whine...Cravath, after all, belongs to its partners." Apparently, the firm has no committees, and the managing partner executes administrative decisions. According to one person, "the firm is a true partnership...Each partner has one vote, and all have the same say...Partnership compensation is lockstep according to seniority."

Because it is very difficult to become a partner at Cravath (Cravath ranked last in partnership prospects among all New York firms who reported this information to us in our 1994 edition), most associates view their stint with the firm as a stepping stone in their careers. Despite the firm's prestige, long work hours, and high profits per partner—with profits per partner well over $1,000,000, Cravath routinely ranks among the top five firms in the nation—associates at Cravath are not paid more than their counterparts at other large New York firms and are reportedly somewhat disgruntled as a result. One contact reported "feeling that we are working harder than most other associates for less or equal pay," while a second contact instructed us that, at Cravath, "associates receive lower clerkship bonuses and get a maximum of only one year credit for clerking (even if they clerked for two years)." Associates, however, do receive fringe benefits, such as a subsidized membership to a nearby health club and access to a "tremendous cafeteria where one can order anything one wants" at subsidized prices. Our contacts informed us that the support services at the firm are excellent, "24 hours a day, 365 days a year." "Everything is done in-house...the firm allows absolutely no excuse for not doing the best possible job," declared one source. Another person commented that "the firm has excellent resources available and really tries to provide the support necessary to make our long hours as bearable as possible."

"women are workhorses"

There are, relative to other comparable New York firms, few female associates or partners at Cravath. The firm appointed two women partners in 1996, and there are now six women partners at the firm. One person remarked that "it is unclear whether this is a result of sexism or because it is institutionally difficult for this high-pressure firm to make allowances." Another insider informed us that "the firm tries hard to attract and retain women, without, I think, much success (at least in keeping them)...The crunch for women associates doesn't hit until they get to be midlevel. At that point, it begins to become apparent who the "favored sons" are, and they get taken to dinners, shows, golf outings, etc. The women don't....For women associates, there is little overt mentoring like what the men receive." This contact observed, additionally that "we women joke around among each other that we are the true workhorses around here. Male associates have been known to shirk responsibility for low-profile, document intensive work that has been assigned to other, often women, associates."

hiring practices

The people with whom we spoke emphasized that Cravath hires high-powered and aggressive people. The firm recruits from law schools all over the country, but a majority of its summer associates are students from Columbia, NYU, Harvard, and Yale. While grades are important in hiring decisions, the firm considers other factors. Summer associate offers have been extended to students who did not have straight As and were not at the top of their class. One person explained that "lawyers at the firm are talented, bright, interesting, and have highly developed attributes outside the law." Another contact, somewhat tongue-in-cheek, described the associates less flatteringly as "the largest group of young neurotics since the Children's Crusade," while a third person informed us that "the attorneys are highly individualistic—some quite eccentric, and the eccentricities are tolerated at all levels...The one attribute the lawyers have in common is that they devote themselves to work." Previous summer associates have had backgrounds in teaching, public interest, business, and Russian studies. Others have been playwrights and artists, although one insider cautioned that "this is far more the exception rather than the rule. Cravath has a full stable of white, upper middle class male associates who have gone straight from college to law school to Cravath." One person advised people interviewing with Cravath to "demonstrate anything imaginative or creative about themselves. One must mark oneself as unique and show some spark. One should talk about anything that one puts one's heart into. Show some passion, then Cravath thinks that it can harness it." Another person commented that the firm is looking for people who are focused about what they want in a legal practice and want to be challenged, while yet another contact informed us that Cravath "looks for recruits that have talent and 'grit' so that they can fit into the Cravath 'system'." The day-long callback at Cravath foreshadows the challenging nature of its practice. Interviewees meet with about four partners and five associates. In keeping with its fast-paced and straightforward culture, the firm often extends a job offer at the end of that day.

Cravath, Swaine & Moore offers associates a high-powered and intense legal experience. Cravath associates must thrive on challenge and be able to survive on little praise. The firm offers its associates the opportunity to work on important, cutting-edge, and news-breaking matters, but it demands that associates fully commit to practicing law and make Cravath the principal focus of their lives, "especially if one aspires to become a partner," observed one insider. Another contact observed that "Cravath is not the place for everyone, but for those who wish to grow and learn quickly by being thrown into the fire, it is *the* place." If you are aggressive, don't mind being thrown in over your head, don't require a supportive environment, are excited by the work, and are willing to devote a few years of your life to the firm, Cravath, Swaine & Moore may be the place for you.

Davis Polk & Wardwell

New York Washington
Frankfurt Hong Kong London Paris Tokyo

Address: 450 Lexington Avenue, New York, NY 10017
Telephone: (212) 450–4000
Hiring Attorney: William L. Rosoff
Contact: Bonnie Hurry, Legal Staff & Recruiting Administrator; (212) 450–4143
Associate Salary: First year $85,000 (1997)
Summer Salary: $1675/week (1997)
Average Hours: NA worked; NA billed; NA required
Family Benefits: 12 weeks paid maternity leave (cbc unpaid); 1 week paid paternity leave (cbc unpaid); emergency childcare program
1996 Summer: Class of 81 students; offers to 81
Partnership: 8% of entering associates from 1979–1985 were made partner
Pro Bono: 3% of all work is pro bono

Davis Polk & Wardwell in 1997
415 Lawyers at the New York Office
2.6 Associates Per Partner

Total Partners 109			Total Associates 282			Practice Areas	
Women	19	17%	Women	129	46%	Corporate	261
All Minorities	5	5%	All Minorities	96	34%	Litigation	108
Asian-Am	4	4%	Afro-Am	24	9%	Tax	32
Latino	1	1%	Asian-Am	63	22%	Trusts & Estates	9
			Latino	9	3%	Unassigned	5

polite civilized culture

Not only does Davis, Polk & Wardwell rank among the top five firms in the nation in profits per partner, it is also an "extremely polite and civil" place to work. The atmosphere at the firm was described as "pretty informal" by one contact; another person remarked that it is "pleasant, civilized, and increasingly imbued with a sense of humor." The firm cares a lot about how people treat each other. You have to be pleasant to everyone, including the staff. The "partners even ask you to work late nicely." The lawyers at Davis Polk are "committed to take the high road and still win, which sets a nice example of professionalism for young attorneys," praised one insider.

The work atmosphere at Davis Polk is "hard-working and serious, yet relaxed...There is no outrageous behavior. It is less high-energy and more laid-back. The hallways are quiet." The firm is fairly hierarchical. "There is a definite pecking order: senior partners, partners, senior associates, junior associates, etc.," described one contact. "Partners are treated as important," concurred another. Davis Polk attorneys dress fairly formally and stylishly. One person commented that women's attire ranged from "funky suits to the flower-child look."

practice areas

Davis Polk's pre-eminent corporate practice represents a number of financial institutions and large corporations, including important clients such as J.P. Morgan Bank, and Morgan Stanley. The corporate department has expanded considerably since our last edition, adding some 75 attorneys in the interim. The firm's Washington, D.C. office specializes in banking; its corporate attorneys primarily handle banking and related regulatory matters. However, because the firm's corporate practice is so large, the New York office handles the bulk of such work. The litigation department engages primarily in commercial matters ranging from representing public accounting firms to handling antitrust matters. It also includes a noteworthy white-collar litigation practice guided by former U.S. Attorney of the Southern District of New York Bob Fiske, "a star in the litigation department." Other prominent litigators include Jimmy Benkard and Gary Lynch, a well-known securities litigator. With offices in London, Paris, Frankfurt, Tokyo, and Hong Kong, Davis Polk has a thriving international practice, which offers its attorneys plenty of opportunity for travel. The Hong Kong office was described as "extremely busy." The firm also has a burgeoning Latin American practice.

Davis Polk encourages its attorneys to become involved in pro bono matters. The firm has a pro bono coordinator who circulates e-mail memos listing available pro bono matters to attorneys on a regular basis. He also "helps junior associates pair up with people who have experience in what they are interested in." Associates also have the option of finding pro bono work on their own, subject to approval by partners. Davis Polk does not have a billable hour requirement, but "if a person's time is disproportionately low compared to his colleagues, he will be asked to take on more work." Pro bono hours do "count in the assessment of how busy an associate is," reported one contact.

training feedback

Davis Polk provides "a fair number of training activities for junior associates in different departments." Each department organizes monthly breakfast or lunch meetings to provide "updates on new or hot matters in the department." The firm also pays for litigation associates to take the National Institute for Trial Advocacy (NITA) trial training program. One person commented that "litigation seems to have a shortage of senior associates, so younger attorneys have an opportunity to work with partners." Another person remarked, however, that "not all mid-level associates are taking depositions or arguing motions in court. Getting a good experience is hit or miss, unless you actively seek it. Those who try to get that type of work are usually successful, however." The corporate department has a rotation system in which each junior associate does two one-year rotations in either M&A, securities or banking with an option in most cases to do a third rotation. Junior associates are "placed in pods" during these rotations and work primarily with the three partners in their pod, we were told. The rotation system "encourages a broad knowledge, rather than specialization." Feedback for associates is informal and varies by partner. The firm formally reviews associates annually.

party social life

Davis Polk associates work fairly long hours. Associates typically work from 9:30 A.M. to 8 P.M., at which time "you can get a car home." Everyone we interviewed agreed that "junior-level people have to be flexible about working late." One person commented that "you don't plan weekends, unless you work in trusts and estates, which is a nine to seven job five days a week." Notwithstanding the long work hours, a large group of young, single Davis Polk associates "party together." This, in turn, has led to "a number of romances and marriages" within the firm. This situation may be encouraged by the fact that Davis Polk has "more good-looking associates than any other firm in the city," boasted one insider. A "number of attorneys play tennis together" at tennis courts at a nearby health club. The firm organizes a number of cocktail parties and other social events. The social life differs in the Washington, D.C. office. The D.C. office is more "family oriented" and organizes social events such as barbecues and picnics, whereas the New York office's social activities are "more country-clubby and upper-crust," said one contact.

liberal Ivy League

Davis Polk is ideologically diverse and offers "a liberal, Ivy League atmosphere." Davis Polk is a "pretty PC firm. It tries to create an atmosphere that looks down on bigoted, sexist or racist remarks." Davis Polk has very large groups of both women and minorities at the firm. In particular, one third of the associates are minorities, a number likely to be the highest in the city. Davis Polk is "very willing to install computers or fax machines in attorneys' homes, and women with kids did that a lot," we were told. However, though the firm permits part-time arrangements, "work must come first," cautioned one insider.

Davis Polk is financially stable. The firm "is taking a generally conservative approach to the future and is not booming as in the '80s," said one contact, although the firm has grown considerably over the past few years. Davis Polk has become more proactive in generating business and "is aggressively seeking business in Latin America and Spain for its corporate practice." Davis Polk's governing committee is "not wildly open about decisions," according to one person. It does, however, "value the associates' quality of life. Vacations are encouraged," we were told. The new managing partner, Frank Morison, is a true "man of the people," proclaimed one contact.

offices

Davis Polk provides first-rate office facilities. In 1992, the firm moved into a building "that was built with Davis Polk in mind." Office space at the firm is, however, somewhat tight; junior associates share offices, sometimes with summer associates. People described the computer and other support services as "phenomenal." The firm also operates a "huge cafeteria," offering "excellent," reasonably priced food to all employees of the firm, including the staff.

academic orientation in hiring

As for recruitment, Davis Polk seeks students with "high-level credentials," such as "high GPAs or law review or teaching experiences." A significant number of the summer associates are drawn from Harvard or Yale. Others are hired from a wide range of law schools. The firm is "pretty loyal to New York law schools," one insider declared. Davis Polk does not stop at credentials, however. It also "looks for people who are personable." As a general rule, the firm only hires summer associates that it believes can become permanent associates. Usually, all summer associates receive offers for permanent employment; all 81 summer associates in 1996 received offers. The interviews were described as "outrageously normal." Most people advised prospective applicants to "come across as personable and articulate."

One person advised, "don't go to Davis Polk expecting to make partner. They care about you, but they want to get their worth out of you." Another commented, "obviously there are lifestyle sacrifices, but in comparison to other New York law firms," Davis Polk associates "are pretty happy." If you are looking for a large, New York law firm, Davis Polk is an extremely attractive choice. Its associates are some of the most highly compensated and well-treated in New York.

Debevoise & Plimpton

New York Washington
Budapest Hong Kong London Paris

Address: 875 Third Avenue, New York, NY 10022
Telephone: (212) 909–6000
Hiring Attorney: John S. Kiernan
Contact: Ethel F. Leichti, Manager of Associate Recruitment; (212) 909–6657
Associate Salary: First year $86,000 (1996); second $103,000; third $121,000; fourth $143,00; fifth $170,000; sixth $185,000; seventh $195,000
Summer Salary: $1600/week (1996)
Average Hours: NA worked; 2000 billed; NA required
Family Benefits: 12+ weeks paid maternity leave (cbc unpaid); 2 weeks paid paternity leave (cbc unpaid); emergency in-home child and elder care; childcare flexible spending account
1996 Summer: Class of 52 students; offers to 52
Partnership: NA
Pro Bono: 6% of all work is pro bono

Debevoise & Plimpton in 1997
312 Lawyers at the New York Office
2.7 Associates Per Partner

Total Partners 80		
Women	7	9%
All Minorities	2	3%
Asian-Am	1	1%
Latino	1	1%

Total Associates 214		
Women	93	43%
All Minorities	26	12%
Afro-Am	8	4%
Asian-Am	15	7%
Latino	3	1%

Practice Areas	
Corporate	159
Litigation	111
Tax	35
Trusts & Estates	7

Debevoise & Plimpton attorneys have interesting backgrounds and a wide range of interests, giving the firm a colorful history. Eli Whitney Debevoise, a founder of the firm, is a descendant of Eli Whitney, inventor of the cotton gin. Francis Plimpton, also a founder, is the father of the popular humorist George Plimpton. Many present Debevoise attorneys continue to make the firm an interesting and unusual place. Louis Begley, corporate partner and chairman of the firm's international group, also writes novels such as *Wartime Lies*, which has won him book awards all over the world. Debevoise & Plimpton, according to one person, comprises "a lot of people who don't necessarily want to be lawyers. They really have other interests."

progressive atmosphere

The work atmosphere at Debevoise is "easygoing, casual, and relaxed." That is, quipped one insider, "in the context of New York law firms and not in any absolute sense." Debevoise "is rather progressive for a New York corporate law firm," declared one source. The firm is not overly hierarchical and generally "partners are happy to talk with associates." There have been problems of late at the firm, however, in connection with "associates' views not being solicited or considered, even for decisions that effect associates,"according to one contact. Another source informed us that "there is sometimes a lack of communication between partners and associates, but this has been acknowledged and the firm is working to improve the situation." In general, people told us that Debevoise is "a very humane place to work" and "associates are treated with a great deal of respect." Debevoise attorneys "perceive themselves as laid-back lawyers, concerned with the fine craft of lawyering." Although in the opinion of one source Debevoise attorneys "seem sort of snooty and high brow," perhaps they are better described as "intellectual." Another contact qualified this observation, noting that at least "on the corporate side, no one sits around pontificating; the emphasis is on efficiency and the most practical way to meet the client's needs."

primarily corporate practice

The assorted interests of Debevoise attorneys have given rise to a varied and constantly changing practice that has withstood the trend of specialization to which other large New York firms have succumbed. Traditionally a corporate law firm, corporate and tax matters now constitute approximately 60 percent of the firm's work. The firm has a significant international corporate practice with offices in Paris, London, Budapest, and Hong Kong. The firm also has a few attorneys in Prague, Moscow and Tokyo. Debevoise represents many private foreign investors in securities offerings and the privatization of industrial undertakings. It has also been involved in Latin American joint ventures and project finance deals. The firm represents Mitsui, a large Japanese trading house, and is involved in similar legal work in other regions in Asia. Roswell Perkins, who is a former president of the American Law Institute, counsels corporations that invest in Russia.

Debevoise's unique domestic corporate practice is also highly regarded. It represents well-known clients such as Phelps Dodge, Avon, Chrysler, and American Airlines, one of the firm's largest clients. The firm also represents Bankers Trust and was recently instrumental in settling the *P&G v. Bankers Trust* derivatives case. Mergers and acquisitions partner Franci Blassberg represents Clayton, Dubilier & Rice, a large takeover firm. Debevoise also represents Kelso & Company, another preeminent leveraged buyout firm. In 1992, Debevoise represented Equitable Insurance in a demutualization transaction, which in the words of one person was "the firm's proudest moment...It was the largest deal in history," and the firm continues to do "lots" of demutualization work.

litigation

The litigation department is the firm's most rapidly expanding. It has a flourishing accountant's liability practice and represented, in a significant capacity, an accounting firm involved in the BCCI scandal. The firm handles a broad spectrum of high-profile cases involving white-collar crime (including the recent Daiwa Bank case), product liability, SEC investigations, international arbitration, bankruptcy, insurance sales practice suits and sophisticated commercial litigation. The international arbitration practice is spearheaded by David Rivkin. James Goodale, former general counsel to The New York Times when *Times v. Sullivan* was argued before the Supreme Court, has a small First Amendment practice at the firm. The firm also has an intellectual property practice, headed by Bruce Keller, counsel to the International Trademark Association, which has experienced great growth in recent years, and includes such clients as American Express, the National Football League, the New York Times, CompuServe, and J.P. Morgan.

active pro bono

Debevoise & Plimpton takes pro bono seriously and "attracts people who put public interest high on their list" of priorities. The firm provides pro bono services in matters ranging from prisoners' rights and death penalty cases to asylum law. It circulates regular memos providing a list of available pro bono opportunities. Summer associates may elect to work with a public interest organization for one or two weeks while continuing to be paid by Debevoise. Pro bono hours count toward billable hours.

flexible organization

Debevoise values the generalist lawyer and is organized in a "very flexible" fashion. In particular, summer associates may elect to try both corporate and litigation work. The firm encourages all incoming associates to elect to work in one of the firm's major practice areas—corporate, litigation, tax, or trusts and estates. Incoming associates who do not select a particular practice area, or who express an interest in more than one area, may request projects from more than one department. Most associates elect a department by the end of their first year, we were told.

Though the firm does have staffing partners to assign work, "aggressive people never use that system," declared one source. Another contact contested this view, noting that "the 'aggressive thing' does not go over all that well here. But, you do stop using staffers when you develop relationships with certain partners." Associates routinely ask partners directly for work assignments, as do summer associates. Associates "can turn down requests" to work on additional matters if their work load is too heavy. Debevoise has developed a "formalized advisor system for associates, up to their fourth year," we were told. First- and second-year associate assignments typically involve doing research, drafting documents, and working directly with clients on smaller projects. By their third year, most associates have day-to-day responsibility on smaller matters. "One complaint is that litigators do not get much stand-up experience (depositions and trials) until they're fairly senior," reported one contact. The firm provides "lots of formal training for corporate associates (including a one week session in the fall);" otherwise formal training at the firm involves "sessions on topics such as taking depositions, workouts, copyright, Article 9, etc." Practice groups meet regularly for breakfast or lunch meetings. Associates are formally reviewed twice annually "during their first years; thereafter reviews are yearly." The associate evaluation committee collects from the partners and senior associates their detailed written evaluations of each associate who has worked for them. Each associate then receives an oral review from the partner of her choice. All associates, additionally, perform annual "upward" reviews of partners, and junior associates do likewise with respect to senior associates.

social life

Social life at Debevoise is "moderate." One contact said that "people get along well, but don't hang out a lot. They have their own lives." Though after-work socializing is minimal, the firm sponsors some well-appreciated social events. Debevoise organizes a "Tea" in the library twice a month, at which beer, wine, and hors d'oeuvres are served. The firm provides "first-rate" food at all events, complimented one admirer. The firm also encourages its attorneys to take summer associates out to lunch.

diversity

People we interviewed labeled Debevoise & Plimpton a "Democratic" firm, even though several of its litigators have been considered for Republican judicial nominations. Although historically Debevoise & Plimpton has been known as a white shoe, WASP firm, it has actively recruited minority attorneys, and its associate ranks are quite diverse. Although there are only a few female partners, some of them are particularly influential. The firm's most senior female partner, Barbara Robinson, recently served as the first woman president of the New York City Bar Association. Deborah Stiles was recently the firm's hiring partner and is head of Debevoise's actively supported part-time program for attorneys who are parents. Currently 21 women associates and three women partners work on a part-time basis. The firm also has a formal sexual harassment policy, a parental leave policy, and other policies addressing women's concerns.

Debevoise actively creates a supportive environment. Partners are paid according to lock step increments to promote more collegiality and teamwork and to reduce competition among attorneys. Moreover, unlike many major New York firms, Debevoise partners reduced their 1992 salaries to avoid laying off associates at that time. The office facilities "are not as glitzy as those at some other New York firms," but "the library is well-known for its tremendous views." The firm is particularly interested in expanding its practice into Eastern Europe, Latin America, and Asia, and it has a growing intellectual property department.

hiring practices

As for recruitment, the firm sends "non-conventional people to campus who don't like the party line," attested one past successful applicant. Though Debevoise does not require students to submit their transcripts for the on-campus interview, grades have traditionally been an important factor during the callback interviews, at which time most attorneys have the student's transcript and résumé "in front of them." The firm believes that good lawyering is a mix of talents that includes not only "smarts" and writing skills, but also the ability to relate to clients as human beings. People advised interviewees to talk about their interests outside the law. Somewhat facetiously, one insider advised that "it is probably better to talk about your interest in ancient Chinese literature than in the law." Another cautioned that during the callback, partners will ask you legal questions if you exhibit or claim knowledge about a particular area of the law. The firm usually hires students from the top national law schools and local New York schools.

Dewey Ballantine

New York Los Angeles Washington
Budapest Hong Kong London Prague Warsaw

Address: 1301 Avenue of the Americas, New York, NY 10019
Telephone: (212) 259–8000
Hiring Attorney: Mr. Junaid H. Chida
Contact: William H. Davis, Legal Recruitment Coordinator; (212) 259–7328
Associate Salary: First year $86,000 (1997); second $96,000 plus potential bonus $7,500; third $110,000 ppb $11,000; fourth $127,000 ppb $16,000; fifth $141,500 ppb $28,500; sixth $158,500 ppb $26,500; seventh $168,500 ppb $26,500; eighth $172,500 ppb $22,500; ninth $175,000 ppb $20,000; tenth $175,000 ppb $20,000
Summer Salary: $1550/week (1997)
Average Hours: 2350 worked; 2000 billed; NA required
Family Benefits: NA
1996 Summer: Class of 42 students; offers to 40
Partnership: 9% of entering associates from 1980–1986 were made partner
Pro Bono: NA

Dewey Ballantine in 1997
287 Lawyers at the New York Office
2.1 Associates Per Partner

Total Partners 84		
Women	10	12%
All Minorities	1	1%
Asian-Am	1	1%

Total Associates 179		
Women	81	45%
All Minorities	32	18%
Afro-Am	11	6%
Asian-Am	12	7%
Latino	9	5%

Practice Areas	
Corporate	132
Litigation	77
Tax	22
Real Estate	21
Bankruptcy	11
Environmental	7
Trusts & Estates	7

Dewey Ballantine has a rich and colorful history. Many of the firm's former partners are well-known today for their outstanding accomplishments. Among other things, they have made a significant mark on the New York corporate law firm community. Former Dewey attorneys (some were attorneys when the firm was Root, Clark, Buckner & Ballantine) established several of New York's most prominent law firms, including Cleary Gottlieb and Skadden Arps. In addition, Supreme Court Justice John Harlan was a partner at the firm, and name partner Thomas Dewey unsuccessfully ran for the U.S. presidency against Harry Truman. Although Dewey was a prominent political figure, he is more fondly remembered at the firm for the following (probably apocryphal) story that lawyers at the firm enjoy telling new associates:

Dewey, wearing his ever-present top hat, was riding in an elevator at work with one of his younger partners. He solicitously inquired of his bare-headed partner, "What does a man without a top hat do nowadays?" The younger man replied, "He goes to the White House." He was fired.

relaxed informal atmosphere

Fortunately, life at Dewey Ballantine is not quite as draconian these days as it was then, though it continues to "keep up its great traditions," according to one insider. Though the firm is not overly hierarchical there is a clear "distinction between partners and associates," said one source. People generally wear "fairly conservative suits to work," and women rarely wear pantsuits. Younger associates are generally treated "pretty well." Dewey Ballantine offers a relaxed and fairly informal work atmosphere. The people are "friendly" and there is a good sense of camaraderie at the firm. One contact reported that the "best thing about Dewey is the people—the partners and associates and staff. Dewey is an easy place to spend long hours if you have to."

practice areas

Dewey Ballantine's corporate and transactional practice constitutes approximately one-half of the firm's business. The firm's clients include large corporations and financial institutions such as First Boston, Smith Barney, Citibank, and Walt Disney, as well as "many insurance companies" (corporate insurance work is a *strong* practice at the firm, we were told). The firm's cutting-edge leveraged leasing practice "keeps its attorneys very busy," reported one insider. A large number of the leveraged leasing clients are domestic and international transportation enterprises. The firm also has a well-regarded tax practice. Though Dewey does not have an extensive international practice, it has offices in Budapest, Prague, Warsaw, London, and Hong Kong. Additionally, Dewey represents some Japanese clients and was involved in Mitsubishi's purchase of the Rockefeller Center from Columbia University. Dewey's diverse litigation department is well-known for its strong antitrust practice. The litigation department brought over eight partners from White & Case (along with their clients, including Ciba-Geigy) in 1995 and is "currently extremely busy."

Dewey views its pro bono practice as an excellent vehicle for junior litigation associates to obtain trial experience. According to one contact, however, "pro bono is not as encouraged as it should be." Summer associates may elect to work for one week at such public interest organizations as Bronx Legal Services and the Housing Courts of each borough. The firm pays them their full firm salary during this time.

work assignments

Dewey Ballantine hires incoming associates for a particular department. For the most part, it places them according to their preferences. Each associate is assigned to work with a team of partners ranging in size from one to five partners. People complained that most junior associate assignments involve "grunt work that has nothing to do with legal work." Junior litigators "are often required to spend months reviewing documents." Most junior corporate associates are responsible for the back-up paperwork, such as document distribution and keeping track of faxes. Some associates, however, get more responsibility. "It depends on your partner," asserted one source.

inadequate training

While Dewey offers continuing legal education programs, "associate training takes a back seat to work," according to one source. Another contact observed that Dewey's training programs have been "perennially lame, but a new program is about to start." Most training occurs on-the-job and involves "watching more experienced lawyers at work." One insider noted, however, that the "high turnover and lack of midlevel and senior associates to teach young people" means it is difficult for young associates to receive proper tutelage. Some departments such as the tax department have regular lunch training meetings. Associates are formally reviewed twice a year. The most concrete indicator of an associate's performance is the amount and type of work that the partner assigns to the associate. One person observed, "If you get more work, you're doing good work."

Morale at the firm "varies according to the group you are working with," we were told. Most associates view the firm "as a steppingstone in their careers and do not plan to stay for more than two or three years." They "get the experience and leave," we were told, since the "chance for partnership is low."

Wranglers

Social life at Dewey Ballantine is "pretty restrained in general. It's friendly, but not nosy." A number of attorneys are married, and there is not "much fraternizing after work." There are several groups of young associates, however, who "hang out and go to bars together," we were told. The firm "Wranglers," held every summer and fall, provide an opportunity for friendly rowdiness. At these dinners, incoming summer and permanent associates introduce themselves to the firm, traditionally at the behest of a master of ceremonies who subjects them to some good-natured "wrangling" or "gentle hazing." The firm also has an annual "fall dance," held at The Plaza, a "very elegant, very classy" affair, to which spouses and significant others are invited. The event consists of dinner, dancing, songs, and skits, providing "the only opportunity for associates to challenge authority," reported one insider. The summer program is "low-key" and designed to relax summer associates, according to one insider. Summer events included a theater outing, dinner parties at partners' homes, a Yankee game, and a tour of Soho art galleries. The atmosphere is "down-to-earth," praised one admirer. "You never feel like people are watching your etiquette skills." Unlike many other New York firms, Dewey Ballantine does not have a country club outing.

management diversity

Dewey Ballantine is governed by a management committee of partners that is "very diverse in terms of age, ethnicity etc." and that, according to one contact, "contains many Catholics." People commented that there are few minority attorneys in the upper ranks of the firm, but there is a very strong contingent of minority attorneys at the associate level. The women at Dewey "are treated the same as anyone else, very respectfully." Approximately half the new partners chosen recently have been women, we were told.

Dewey Ballantine remains tight-lipped regarding management decisions, and "associates only find out about things after the fact," according to one person. Dewey has been "more profitable in the last several years than ever before" and has expanded its office space. The offices have "a beautifully classy, old-world, elegant look" and are decorated in hardwood and marble floors with a brass, spiral staircase. Only first-year associates share offices. The firm is currently "extremely" busy and has recently hired many laterals. One person commented that the D.C. office, which has handled a lot of antidumping cases for the steel industry, is "a jewel for the firm."

hiring practices

As for recruitment, Dewey Ballantine emphasizes people skills and personality more than most firms. It likes "nice people who are compatible, not the arrogant go-getter, high-achiever type." People advised prospective interviewees to "be relaxed, self-assured, and confident in the interview, but not cocky." Dewey hires from a broad range of schools, including Columbia, Georgetown, Harvard, New York University, Rutgers, State University of New York at Albany, Tulane, the University of Virginia, and Duke.

Dewey received little criticism from the people we interviewed. One contact drew our attention to the fact that beginning associates will want to avoid "getting stuck in one group" for too long a period. Another expressed concern that the firm does not give incoming associates "a right of first refusal" in the practice group assignment. Most people, however, praised Dewey for its pleasant work atmosphere and commented that the excellent "people there make the difference." One insider summarized matters well in observing that "if you are self-loathing enough to become an associate at a big firm in New York, this is as good a place as you will find."

Donovan Leisure Newton & Irvine

New York Los Angeles Palm Beach
Paris

Address: 30 Rockefeller Plaza, New York, NY 10112
Telephone: (212) 632–3000
Hiring Attorney: Peter A. Bicks, Esq.
Contact: Dawanna L. Carmichael, Legal Hiring Coordinator; (212) 632–3147
Associate Salary: First year $87,000 (1997)
Summer Salary: $1670/week for 2Ls and 3Ls; $1620 for 1Ls (1997)
Average Hours: 2267 worked; 1876 billed; none required
Family Benefits: 12 weeks paid maternity leave; paternity leave (cbc)
1996 Summer: Class of 17 students; offers to 17
Partnership: 12% of entering associates from 1983–1987 were made partner
Pro Bono: 3% of all work is pro bono

Donovan Leisure Newton & Irvine in 1997
93 Lawyers at the New York Office
1.4 Associates Per Partner

Total Partners 35		
Women	4	11%
All Minorities	0	0%

Total Associates 49		
Women	21	43%
All Minorities	3	6%
Afro-Am	1	2%
Asian-Am	1	2%
Latino	1	2%

Practice Areas	
Litigation	53
Corporate	22
Real Estate	6
Trusts & Estates	6
Tax	4
International Trade	2

Donovan Leisure Newton & Irvine prides itself on being a "friendly and humane firm." Donovan Leisure partners are accessible; it is not unusual for them to stop by an associate's office to say hello. Although the firm handles a number of newsworthy matters, Donovan Leisure is not a "sweatshop" and "there is life after the law firm." One insider informed us that "on average, I work one or two all-nighters per year, one day per weekend each month and leave before 8 P.M. on most nights, *i.e.* I have a life." The associates work hard together and share "a certain closeness" and "a real spirit." One source summarized, "It's a nice, friendly place that is...content with its lifestyle;" another remarked that "I know the name of every single person in the firm which numbers some 200 individuals. It's a nice environment."

litigation focus

Founded over 60 years ago by General "Wild Bill" Donovan, one of the most decorated soldiers in World War I and a respected national figure of his time, Donovan Leisure has a proud history. Traditionally a pre-eminent antitrust litigation firm, Donovan Leisure is now a full service firm with, however, a special focus on litigation. The litigation practice covers virtually all areas of commercial law. The firm recently won a $138 million jury verdict, reportedly the second highest in 1995, arising from a commercial dispute, on a counter claim for Talley Industries, Inc. The firm also serves as Special Litigation Counsel to Maxwell Corporation and MacMillan, Inc. in connection with the collapse of the late Robert Maxwell's business empire. Donovan Leisure represents as well several of the nation's foremost research-based pharmaceutical, medical device and chemical companies in product liability and tort actions.

growing corporate

Donovan Leisure's corporate practice numbers among its clients the Alleghany Corporation, Orion Capital, Penn Traffic and Sharp, and is developing a reputation for expertise in project finance, IPOs, and venture capital. Although litigation and corporate are the largest practice areas at the firm, Donovan Leisure also has small tax, trade regulation, real estate, bankruptcy, and trusts and estates practices, and a few partners work exclusively on international trade matters. Most of Donovan Leisure's work involves representing well-known public corporations, but it also represents other entities and individuals. As for pro bono, Donovan Leisure is affiliated with MFY Legal Services, which runs a neighborhood legal clinic in Manhattan. The firm also regularly informs attorneys of other available pro bono matters.

professional development

Donovan Leisure assigns entering associates to a particular department. One partner in each department is responsible for assigning work to the associates. Young associates "get a lot of responsibility," according to one person we interviewed, perhaps because most "matters are staffed by one partner, a high-level associate, and a first-year associate." Another praised the firm for the variety of work provided: "an associate is not put into a box or taught just one type of transaction." Most first-year associate assignments involve legal or factual research, writing memos, or drafting or responding to pleadings and discovery. Once admitted to the bar, "it is not uncommon for an associate to attend or conduct depositions or to argue motions in court," we were told. Though the bulk of associate training occurs on-the-job, the firm conducts formal litigation and corporate training sessions. Because the associates "work closely with partners," they often receive a lot of informal feedback. People noted that the firm is pretty good about informing associates if their work does not meet its standards. The firm also formally evaluates associates twice a year.

softball tea ladies

Donovan Leisure attorneys strike a "good balance" between work and social activities. Many associates at the firm form strong friendships and are "supportive of each other." Attorneys often socialize together after work. The firm's social traditions reflect Donovan Leisure's commitment to improving the quality of life for its attorneys. The daily afternoon lull is broken by the "tea ladies," who each afternoon bring tea, cookies, and whatever fruits are in season to every attorney's office. "It's a really nice part of the day. You hear them coming down the hall and you run back to your office so that you can ask for a 'malomar,' a chocolate-covered marshmallow cookie," said one source. The firm has softball, basketball and volleyball teams. Another firm tradition is the annual Firm Dinner at which first-year associates perform a musical roast of the firm's partners written by more senior associates. Last year the theme was "'Sunset Boulevard,' except it was the head of the firm who was found dead on the main conference room table. Batman and Robin solved the crime. It was hilarious," reported one insider.

increasing diversity

Although Donovan Leisure used to have a "reputation for being a conservative Roman Catholic firm," we were told that is "not true anymore." While Ed Cox, Richard Nixon's son-in-law, is a partner at the firm and an active Republican, other partners are active Democrats. Mayor Rudolph Giuliani appointed former partner Paul Crotty as Corporation Counsel for the City of New York. Donovan Leisure is working to increase the diversity of its lawyers and consciously recruits minority law students. People agreed that "women are treated very well" at Donovan Leisure. According to one person, female associates "get some of the best assignments." Although Donovan has few minority associates, nearly 25 percent of this year's summer class are minority law students, we were told.

Donovan Leisure is governed by an executive committee. Because most associates have close relationships with partners, they are fairly well-informed about important firm decisions. One contact pointed out that "Donovan Leisure does not do enough marketing at the partner and senior associate level to bring in more business. Most people are satisfied that we have plenty of work; but while we pay our first and second years the market rate, Donovan quickly falls behind in the market for legal services and we lose good people. I believe the two are interrelated." A firm spokesperson pointed out, however, that "Donovan Leisure has a very low attrition rate." After signing a new lease in Rockefeller Center and taking on another floor, the firm recently completed a major renovation that included upgrading its computer system. The circular staircase which joins all three floors is "spectacular." Every Donovan Leisure associate has a private office with a window and a computer.

recruits based on grades and personality

Donovan Leisure's commitment to a pleasant work atmosphere and quality legal services underlies many hiring decisions. Although the firm recruits the best people from the top national and New York law schools, it also wants people who are "good co-workers and team players." It is "not looking for cutthroat people," declared one insider. Consistent with this philosophy, Donovan Leisure interviews are friendly and informal. One person recommended that interviewees stress that "they know what they are looking for and explain why Donovan is a logical fit for them." Many past summer associates have worked on journals or have been involved in moot court competitions.

If you are not looking for a New York sweatshop, Donovan Leisure is hard to beat. The firm is held in high regard. "The atmosphere is great," the lawyers are "talented and competent," associates get "good experience and training early," and it allows you to "have a life." One insider summarized matters nicely, observing that "I think Donovan is the best law firm in the city for its mix of quality work, formal training, and talented lawyers."

Fish & Neave

New York Palo Alto

Address:	1251 Avenue of the Americas, New York, NY 10020
Telephone:	(212) 596–9000
Hiring Attorney:	Richard M. Barnes and William J. McCabe
Contact:	Deirdre M. Rogan, Director of Legal Personnel; (212) 596–9118
Associate Salary:	First year $88,000 (1997); second $106,000; third $129,000; fourth $149,000; fifth $165,000; sixth $181,000; seventh $197,000; salary figures include base salary and typical bonus
Summer Salary:	$1665/week (1997)
Average Hours:	NA worked; NA billed; no requirement.
Family Benefits:	12 weeks paid maternity leave (12 unpaid)
1996 Summer:	Class of 13 students; offers to 13
Partnership:	15–20% (estimate) of entering associates from 1985–1988 were made partner
Pro Bono:	5–10% of all work is pro bono

Fish & Neave (firmwide) in 1997
147 Lawyers at the Firm
2.9 Associates Per Partner

Total Partners 38			Total Associates 109			Practice Areas	
Women	5	13%	Women	31	28%	Litigation	NA
All Minorities	0	0%	All Minorities	18	17%	Patents	NA
			Afro-Am	5	5%	Trademarks	NA
			Asian-Am	10	9%	Trade Secrets	NA
			Latino	3	3%	Copyrights	NA
						Licensing	NA

prestigious patent practice

"They think they are Number One in intellectual property in the country," declared one source, noting that "perfection is their motto for everything that goes out the door." Founded in the 1870s, Fish & Neave is one of the nation's premier patent firms. It has, throughout its history, represented some of the most distinguished innovators of their time. Among its illustrious clients were Alexander Graham Bell, the Wright Brothers, Thomas Edison, and Henry Ford. More recently, Fish & Neave attained further prominence for successfully representing Polaroid in a suit against Kodak for infringement of an instant camera and accompanying film patents. The lead partner on the matter, Herb Schwartz, secured a damage award of one billion dollars for Polaroid, one of the largest civil awards in history. Another well-known Fish & Neave partner, David Plant, was described to us as the "ADR king in intellectual property." More recently, Fish & Neave has suffered some setbacks: it lost longtime client DuPont; in an unprecedented move two partners left the firm; and the firm laid off a sizable number of associates in 1994 and 1995, which negatively affected firm morale. A firm spokesperson informed us, however, that "after a slowdown in business in 1994, the firm has bounced back and is growing rapidly."

Fish & Neave's practice focuses primarily on patent law, trademarks, and trade secrets. It also handles some computer copyright work. Fish & Neave is most known for its large, complex patent litigation work, which constitutes approximately 85 percent of its practice. A second part of the practice involves patent prosecution (the writing and filing of patent applications). Most of the firm's clients are Fortune 500 companies, including Ford Motor Company, Motorola, AT&T, General Electric, Nestle, Compaq, Exxon, and Gillette. The firm also represents some smaller, entrepreneurial high-growth companies such as Cyrix and biotech companies such as Biogen. Among the recent high-profile cases that Fish & Neave has been involved in is the firm's successful defense of Motorola against a preliminary injunction brought by the NBA. The firm is also representing Digital Equipment Corp. in an action against Intel.

As many of the firm's clients have "foreign sister patents," Fish & Neave's practice also has an international dimension. It handles international patent litigation matters, and it is developing both a European biotechnology and a Japanese client base. The firm also has an international trademark prosecution practice. It handles trademark infringement, unfair competition, and copyright litigation for clients such as Coca-Cola, Compaq, and Nestle.

Fish & Neave "has been trying to encourage pro bono work lately," one contact informed us. The firm recently stepped up its commitment to pro bono and "set up a few programs from which associates may choose." Summer associates have the opportunity to work for one week with a public interest organization while earning their regular firm salary.

opportunities

Fish & Neave assigns entering associates to a matter on which they work until it is resolved. Typically, they work for at least six to nine months on a single litigation matter. "However, the associate is generally kept on the matter until it is resolved, which can take two to three years," according to one insider. Once the matter closes, an associate can obtain more work from one of the firm's assigning attorneys. Alternatively, if "you have developed a reputation for good work, it comes to you because people know you do good work," attested one source.

Associates may also work on more than one matter at a time. Fish & Neave's "cases are staffed pretty heavily, and there is not much responsibility" for younger associates, although "as with most firms, this depends on the partner in charge and the associate's ability," remarked one contact. Most of the work involves "high stakes litigation, generally, in the tens or hundreds of millions of dollars. Clients want partners doing the work," explained one contact. "Generally, you don't try a case until you are a senior partner. Junior partners may examine less important witnesses." First- and second-year associate assignments usually involve researching issues, writing memos, drafting briefs and motions, and a lot of document production. By their second or third year, associates begin to take depositions and formulate interrogatories. A fourth-year associate might examine a witness in a trial. However, client contact can come early at Fish & Neave; one contact remarked that, "as a first year, I attended meetings with clients and presented research and discussed strategy."

training feedback

Fish & Neave provides a limited number of in-house training workshops—a writing seminar for first-year associates, deposition training for second-year associates, and a trial advocacy program for midlevel and senior associates. The firm also encourages associates to attend outside training and continuing legal education programs, including those provided by the National Institute of Trial Advocacy and the Practicing Law Institute. In general, the firm's training efforts were described as "inadequate and inconsistent" by those we spoke with. Although the informal feedback at the firm is fairly "spotty," the attorneys don't "mince words in the formal reviews. It's a pretty straightforward place." Associates know where they stand in the firm by "how sought out they are" by more senior attorneys, reported one insider. Another observed that "if you are not sought after, you may want to find employment elsewhere."

intense atmosphere

Fish & Neave is somewhat hierarchical and formal, but almost all partners are accessible for discussing work-related matters. The almost constant feeling that "there is work to be done" underlies the firm's intense work atmosphere. "You always see people rushing by you at seven or eight miles per hour in the halls or central areas," asserted one contact. Fish & Neave is not a leisurely place. The "attorneys work long hours." Because patent litigation trials can last for several weeks or more, the work hours can sometimes be grueling. For example, "during the Polaroid litigation, attorneys were away from their families for nine to 10 months," reported one person. Not surprisingly, there is quite a bit of turnover among associates, who now sometimes transfer to the intellectual property departments of other major New York firms, rather than becoming in-house counsel to the firm's clients as was the case in the past. In recent years, there has been "a lot of attrition and a huge influx of laterals," according to one insider, who added that "there are so many new faces, it can be difficult to tell if someone is a new associate, an expert, or opposing counsel." The high turnover among associates, the "long hours" at the firm, and other factors led to Fish & Neave's earning the lowest ranking among New York firm's on *The American Lawyer's* midlevel associates survey in the fall of 1996, prompting that magazine to quip that "Bitch & Leave" might better serve as the firm's name these days. A firm spokesperson instructed us, however, that "the firm believes that there has been a recent turn-around. It has made an increased effort to improve firm morale and provide more timely feedback. Its hiring of new attorneys also has helped reduce the workload of its associates."

work hard play hard

Fish & Neave is a "work hard, play hard" firm and offers a varied social life. "A core group of swashbuckling litigators who are like the 'good old-boys' from Texas," enjoy taking summer associates out drinking until two or three in the morning. Attorneys also invite summer associates out to various New York City cultural and sporting events. Associates also manage to "do a lot of things together" and often "hang out at one or two bars near the office building on Friday evenings." In addition, attorneys enjoy playing on the firm's softball, volleyball, and basketball teams, and frequently go out after games for burgers and beers. The firm also sponsors or participates in a number of well-attended social events, such as the Christmas party, a firm ball, and the Judge's Dinner for patent lawyers in New York.

diversity

Traditionally a predominantly male law firm, Fish & Neave "is kind of like a fraternity. They are socially the good old boys," stated one source. Another contact observed that "over the past few years, this image has been changing. There is a small group of males that does spend much time together; however, they are not the majority." Although the firm has made recent efforts to increase the number of its female associates, this effort has been hindered because the technical fields have tended to attract more men than women, said one contact. Another noted, however, that a few female Fish & Neave partners "command respect," citing Pat Martone who played a significant role in the Polaroid case. Though Fish & Neave has a maternity leave policy, there is frequently a "logistical barrier" to taking time off because many assignments are "multi-year projects, and losing someone for three months can affect the work," explained one person. Although there are no minority partners at the firm, minorities (especially Asian-Americans) are well represented in the associate ranks. People commented that the firm appears to be making an effort to recruit minority law students for its summer program.

A six member management committee handles the day-to-day administration of the firm, and makes recommendations on the major issues to the partnership for a full vote. The firm, according to one person, makes "conservative management decisions." The firm is reportedly financially healthy—"more so than ever before," according to one insider, who added that "there is no shortage of work." Fish & Neave's offices are located in the Exxon building of the Rockefeller Plaza. The firm provides "first-rate" support facilities; the support staff was described as "excellent." One person marveled that "the library cite-checks everything for you."

hires those with technical aptitude

Fish & Neave hires law students with a technical aptitude and interest in technology. Although most associates hold advanced degrees in biochemistry, engineering, or other sciences, it is not necessary to have such qualifications to get hired. The firm also seeks strong litigators, which according to one person, means they want "friendly outgoing people with communication skills." Fish & Neave "will not compromise the quality of its work" and is, therefore, "looking for perfectionists." The firm hires "people who will bust themselves and who will make it through eight years; people who are loyal to the firm." Fish & Neave hires first-year law students if they have high grades in an undergraduate science degree. It hires most of its summer associates from the top national law schools and New York-area law schools. The firm also has a Patent Agent Trainee program under which it hires people out of post-graduate schools in the sciences. These trainees work eight hours per day at the firm and also attend a New York-area law school part-time at the firm's expense.

Fish & Neave relies on its callback interviews to "get a sense of the chemistry" between the firm and the interviewee. The firm "looks for people whom partners and associates will want to work with," remarked one insider. No one we interviewed reported being asked any technical or substantive questions. People recommended that applicants emphasize their interest in science and technology, but one insider noted that the firm is "looking for fun people, not just engineering geeks."

Fish & Neave is not very supportive of its junior associates. People complained that because there are so few midlevel associates at the firm, there is very little "knowledge transfer to younger associates." Moreover, Fish & Neave has to fight off the stigma associated with its abysmal showing on the 1996 *American Lawyer's* survey. If you are looking for early responsibility, shorter hours than average, and a broad intellectual property practice that covers more than patent litigation, Fish & Neave may not be the place for you. On the other hand, if you are looking for a firm that handles some of the most high-profile patent litigation matters, and provides an energetic, environment, Fish & Neave is a good choice.

Fried, Frank, Harris, Shriver & Jacobson

New York Los Angeles Washington
London Paris

Address: One New York Plaza, New York, NY 10004
Telephone: (212) 859–8000
Hiring Attorney: Howard B. Adler, Gary P. Cooperstein, Peter L. Simmons; Recruitment Chairmen
Contact: Director of Recruitment; (212) 859–8540
Associate Salary: First year $89,000 (1997); second $102,000; third $121,000; fourth $145,000; fifth $170,000; sixth $185,000; seventh $195,000; eighth $200,000; salary figures include bonus amounts
Summer Salary: $1600/week (1997)
Average Hours: NA worked; NA billed; NA required; average work day from 9-10 A.M. to 8-9 P.M.
Family Benefits: Hospital and major medical; life insurance; accidental death insurance; disability insurance; 3 months paid maternity leave; paid paternity leave; dental insurance; disability partner benefits; 401K plan; emergency child care
1996 Summer: Class of 45 students; offers to 43
Partnership: 16% of entering associates from 1981–1988 were made partner
Pro Bono: 3–5% of all work is pro bono

Fried, Frank, Harris, Shriver & Jacobson in 1997
305 Lawyers at the New York Office
2.7 Associates Per Partner

Total Partners 82		
Women	13	16%
All Minorities	1	1%
Latino	1	1%

Total Associates 233		
Women	90	39%
All Minorities	28	12%
Afro-Am	5	2%
Asian-Am	11	5%
Latino	12	5%

Practice Areas	
Corporate	110
Litigation	81
Tax	22
Real Estate	19
Bankruptcy	18
Employee Ben. & Compen.	13
Environmental	12
White Collar Crime	11
Intellectual Property	10
Trusts & Estates	9

freewheeling atmosphere

"Everything is a crisis" at Fried, Frank, Harris, Shriver & Jacobson. One contact informed us that "Fried Frank gives recruits this report (i.e. *The Insider's Guide* report), and this line is well known by Fried Frank associates. The firm seems to be proud of this, and it is 100% accurate." Perhaps this is because clients turn to the firm as a last resort to solve specific problems that their regular counsel could not handle, explained one insider. This produces a hectic, hard-working, and high-energy work atmosphere. Fried Frank attorneys work long hours, but the firm is "very freewheeling and not at all stuffy. There is no pretense. You don't have to behave as if you are at work." One enthusiastic contact informed us that this lack of stuffiness applies to dress as well: the firm has "casual day every Friday year round, and it really makes a difference." Fried Frank is also "a very spirited place. People are not afraid to voice their opinions." In one person's judgment, "you will like the firm better if you are aggressive," but another maintained that the firm is "composed of both aggressive and non-aggressive people, and both types of people fit into the firm very well because both find compatriots." Another contact warned that "the stress is constant—you are on call 24 hours a day, 365 days a year." Moreover, this person pointed out that "the 'colorful' personalities and the need for an aggressive attitude to succeed at Fried Frank can drive people away."

high-profile corporate

Fried Frank is well-known for its top-notch corporate practice. The firm rose to prominence partly because of its involvement in some of the most high-profile mergers and acquisitions during the 1980s, a development described in the book *Inside Track*. The corporate department is also well-regarded for its securities and initial public offerings practices. Representative clients have included large corporations (Merrill Lynch, 3M, L.A. Gear, Reader's Digest, Bear Stearns, Merck, Lloyds of London) and motion picture companies (Tri-Star Pictures). The firm, already a regular outside counsel to Goldman Sachs, is now also one of Salomon Brothers' three main outside counsels as a result of Warren Buffett's naming former firm chairman Robert Mundheim as Salomon Brothers' General Counsel. Among the luminaries in the corporate department is Arthur Fleischer, Jr., co-author of the leading treatise on mergers and acquisitions. Harvey Pitt, former General Counsel of the Securities and Exchange Commission (SEC) and one of the nation's leading securities lawyers, practices out of the firm's D.C. office. Another major player is Steve Fraidin, regular counsel to the leverage buyout firm of Forstmann Little and a lecturer at Yale Law School. Like Pitt and Fraidin, many of the firm's lawyers serve as law school professors or lecturers at such schools as Columbia, Georgetown, Hofstra, New York University, and Yale.

litigation

The litigation department handles the traditional array of securities, antitrust, intellectual property, and other specialties, along with work in the area of white-collar civil and criminal defense, led by several former prosecutors, including the past heads of the Securities Fraud Unit and the Appeals Unit of the U.S. Attorney's office. The criminal defense work is "primarily corporate, as opposed to individual white-collar defendants," according to one source who added that "more than one associate has come here expecting a lot of white-collar work and has been disappointed." High stakes litigation involving Lloyds of London and Merrill Lynch are "the largest cases in the litigation department." One contact reports that Greg Joseph is "*the* standout in the litigation department." He was recently listed as one of the top ten litigators in the country by *The New York Law Journal*, and is reportedly "great to work with." Former partner Jed Rakoff, one of New York's best known criminal defense lawyers, recently left the firm when he was appointed as a federal district judge.

The firm's environmental group boasts Richard Schwartz, former Chief of the Environmental Protection Unit at the U.S. Attorney's Office. The firm also has a small

environment bankruptcy real estate

but busy bankruptcy department, led by Brad Scheler, and including Alan Resnick, a professor at Hofstra Law School. One person stated that the bankruptcy group "is not as strong as that at Weil Gotshal, but it is very strong." Another growing practice, the real estate group, regularly represents such clients as Tishman-Speyer and World Financial Properties.

tax

Fried Frank also has an especially strong tax department. One tax partner, Dick Loengard Jr., once served as the Special Assistant for International Tax Affairs at the U.S. Treasury Department, and another is a former math professor at Harvard University. The Washington office boasts Martin Ginsburg, a law professor at Georgetown Law School and husband of Ruth Bader Ginsburg, the U.S. Supreme Court Justice. Ross Perot endowed the Ginsburg Chair at Georgetown Law School after Ginsburg solved some of Perot's tax problems. Although Fried Frank is not known for its international practice, it has London and Paris offices. The firm also has focused on developing a strong practice in Latin America.

public service

We got mixed reviews on Fried Frank's pro bono practice. One person noted that "you have to want to do it." Another commented that "if you are working on a pro bono project that the firm thinks is important, you can count it in your billable hours." A third person, on the other hand, lauded the firm's "devotion" to pro bono, maintaining that it "stands out among New York law firms." This person added, "I have been asked to do pro bono work. I didn't have to go out looking for it." Partners serve on the boards of the NAACP Legal Defense and Educational Fund and the Mexican American Legal Defense and Educational Fund, and one partner formerly served as President of the Legal Aid Society. In addition, many of this "extremely Democratic" firm's partners have held high-level positions in the federal government, including Chairman of the Nuclear Regulatory Commission (Marc Rowden), General Counsel of the Federal Home Loan Bank Board (Tom Vartanian), General Counsel of the Peace Corps (William Josephson), and Head of the U.S. Delegation at the SALT negotiations (Max Kampelman). Name partner Sargent Shriver, President Kennedy's brother-in-law, served as U.S. Ambassador to France and Director of the Peace Corps. William Howard Taft IV, great-grandson of President Taft, served as Deputy Secretary of Defense (1984-1989) and U.S. Ambassador to NATO (1989-1992), and David Birenbaum served as U.S. Ambassador to the United Nations for U.N. Management and Reform.

Fried Frank consciously adopts a team approach to solving client problems. The attorneys "work well together...nobody holds back." One person, however, noted that "people work very hard and it's very competitive." Incoming associates may complete two six-month rotations in the departments of their choice before choosing one to join. One contact pointed out to us that "associates choose preferences, but the firm honors only some, depending on departmental needs. Several associates did not get the rotations they chose last year." With no fixed practice teams or working groups within departments, young associates are required to work on a wide variety of projects, which can be an advantage since you can get "good all-around experience" in this fashion, stated one source.

professional development

First-year associate work usually involves a lot of library research. Second-year and more senior associates are frequently immersed in as much responsibility as they can handle. The firm "takes formal training seriously;" on the job training, on the other hand, is "spotty." It sponsors a number of formal training programs, including negotiation workshops, mock trial and mock deposition sessions, and other seminars on specific substantive areas of the law. Each department also holds weekly or monthly meetings to discuss active client matters. Fried Frank formally reviews the work and progress of first-year associates twice annually. Once they specialize, associates are reviewed once a year. Informal feedback varies depending on the partner, but one person commented that at least in the tax department, partners place "a big emphasis on explaining things to you so that the work gets done." Another person remarked that "attention to explaining things to young associates ranges from thorough to non-existent."

Fried Frank associates often feel "overworked." Consequently, their after-work social life is limited. One contact noted that it is "hard to make plans because you could be called in to work at any time." Nevertheless, Fried Frank attorneys form close friendships with one another, and some groups of first- and second-year associates go out after work. Fried Frank attorneys look forward to the Friday evening firm cocktail parties, after which some attorneys may go out to dinner. One person remarked, however, that "although Fried Frank claims to have an 'open door' policy, in fact most doors remain closed through the day. The principal effect of this is that it discourages casual conversation in halls, which detracts from the sense of familiarity."

liberal colorful place

Composed of a group of "nonconformist" lawyers, Fried Frank is "a pretty liberal place" where you can be yourself. In fact, one attorney "has a big picture of Al Sharpton for Senator on his wall, and another has a basketball hoop in his office." Many of these colorful lawyers pursue diverse interests outside the law, ranging from art collecting to teaching. Although Fried Frank has traditionally been viewed as a "predominantly Jewish" firm, one source asserted that its "outreach is becoming less Jewish." With 13 female partners in New York, Fried Frank "really is great for women," praised one admirer. Two female partners are members of the hiring committee. Also, the "firm is good about giving maternity leave and is glad to have you back." Part-time work arrangements may be made on a case-by-case basis.

bottom line management

Fried Frank's management includes two co-chairmen and a steering committee. An executive director runs the firm on a day-to-day basis. The firm has an associates committee that includes both partner and associate members; many associates also informally discuss important issues with the partners with whom they work, we were told. Fried Frank is "pretty bottom line oriented." Consequently "it is hard to take vacations because it's never really a good time, but you just haggle for it," explained one source. Another person remarked that "you have to plan ahead, be aggressive and stand up for yourself to take time off, but if you do you can get close to or all of your four weeks." Although it was hurt by the demise of the M&A boom in the early 1990s, Fried Frank's business today is "great;" the firm is very busy. It has diversified into white-collar crime and environmental practice areas, and the bankruptcy and real estate departments are growing. Intellectual property is another growth area. The firm is also looking to its Latin American practice, described as "hot," for future growth.

beautiful modern offices

Fried Frank's office facilities, located in downtown Manhattan, offer great views of the rivers surrounding Manhattan and the Statue of Liberty. The downtown location is not an unmixed blessing. One contact cautioned: "forget about living in Westchester or Connecticut. People feel differently about this, but many of us consider it a significant drawback....People should seriously consider whether they want the extra commuting time." In any event, this "beautiful" and roomy facility is adorned by a large modern art collection. Each attorney has an individual office, though not all offices have windows. In general, two or three attorneys share one secretary (summer associates share a secretary with two associates). The staff was described as "fabulous," "outstanding," and "very knowledgeable; the firm ensures staff is always available to assist." The 24-hour-a-day secretarial and para-legal support is very helpful and professional. The firm uses a sophisticated Wide Area Network computer system, and has a strong Internet presence.

seeks unusual applicants

Fried Frank hires its summer associates from the top national law schools and local New York schools. (If you're from a prestige campus, we were told that a B+ average is usually good enough to be seriously considered for an offer.) While the firm emphasizes high academic achievement, one person stated that "you have to have something unusual on your résumé to get a callback." Bungee jumping or skydiving helps, but so does being an opera singer or enjoying math problems. Summer associates are usually "very bright, hard-working, confident, and assertive. It also helps to be creative." When questioned about permanent associate offers, one person stated that "it's harder to get an offer if you are from a local school; though if you are from Yale, you will definitely get an offer because Yalies stick together." But no generalization is sacrosanct; another contact gleefully informed us that "I know Yalies who didn't get offers!"

Fried Frank callback interviews are friendly and informal. The firm makes an effort to set students up with interviewers with whom they "will click." One person advised that Fried Frank "likes feisty people. Don't be afraid to have a personality. People are prized for their differences and eccentricities."

Fried Frank is a fast-paced law firm that can at times be stressful. This colorful law firm attracts high-energy people with varied interests and backgrounds. Despite its exciting work and friendly atmosphere, Fried Frank appears to have a high turnover rate. One person speculated that the "high attrition may be because many associates in their third and fourth year are told they won't make partner." Nevertheless, this firm is an excellent launching pad for a high-powered legal career. In the words of one ex-Fried Franker, "my search for a new position was painless—Fried Frank is very highly regarded and people are eager to hire Fried Frank-trained associates."

Haight, Gardner, Poor & Havens

New York Houston San Francisco Washington

Address:	195 Broadway, New York, NY 10007
Telephone:	(212) 341-7000
Hiring Attorney:	Richard A. Crowley, Chairperson, Legal Staff Committee
Contact:	Elise H. Rippe, Recruitment Coordinator; (212) 341-7041
Associate Salary:	First year $81,000 (1997)
Summer Salary:	$1550/week (1997); includes $2000 start-up bonus
Average Hours:	2069 worked; 1808 billed; 1900 target
Family Benefits:	12 weeks paid leave for primary caretaker
1996 Summer:	Class of 5 students; offers to 5
Partnership:	NA
Pro Bono:	3% of all work is pro bono

Haight, Gardner, Poor & Havens (firmwide) in 1997
75 Lawyers at the Firm
1.1 Associates Per Partner

Total Partners 35			Total Associates 40			Practice Areas	
Women	4	11%	Women	18	45%	Maritime	NA
All Minorities	2	6%	All Minorities	8	20%	Finance	NA
Asian-Am	1	3%	Afro-Am	1	3%	Aviation	NA
Latino	1	3%	Asian-Am	6	15%	Corporate	NA
			Latino	1	3%	Litigation	NA
						Bankruptcy & Workouts	NA
						Tax	NA
						Environmental	NA
						Labor & Employment	NA
						International	NA
						Real Estate	NA
						Regulatory	NA
						Securities	NA
						Computer Law	NA

maritime specialty

Traditionally a maritime law firm, Haight, Gardner, Poor & Havens has evolved into a full-service law firm with special expertise in matters involving the domestic and international transportation industry. The corporate practice group is headed by John Pritchard, who also heads the aircraft finance section. Much of the work in the firm's corporate finance practice involves structuring the financed purchases of ships, airplanes and railcars. The firm also handles the gamut of litigation. Haight's litigators have been involved in precedent-setting cases arising out of aviation and maritime casualties, product liability matters, coverages and other insurance related cases. The firm has defended clients in mass disaster litigation arising out of, for example, fires as well as major land, sea, and air accidents. A current case is the representation of TWA in connection with the TWA 800 crash off Long Island. Among the firm's prominent maritime partners are Brian Salter, who leads the firm's Rapid Response Team and is chair of the firm's management committee, and Chester Hooper, who is the former President of the MLA. Randal Craft is a prominent aviation attorney at the firm. Haight Gardner's insolvency group has handled the legal work involved in many of the major aviation bankruptcies of recent years, including those of Eastern, Pan American, Midway, Continental, America West, and TWA, and has represented lenders in many of the major shipping workouts of the past three decades. Haight Gardner also has expanded some of the non-traditional practice areas for the firm, such as environmental, employment, tax and computer/information technology.

Though Haight Gardner does not have a specific international practice group, almost all its corporate and transactional work, and a substantial portion of its litigation, is transnational in nature. Many of the firm's attorneys travel frequently. Haight Gardner is well known for its 47 year old international trainee program and hosts interns from law firms all over the world.

Pro bono work is not Haight Gardner's strong suit. The firm "facially encourages it, but it comes out of your own time," according to one source. Another observed that "pro bono is available; it is neither encouraged nor discouraged." Yet another noted that "some pro bono occurs, but not a ton." The firm gives 50 hours billable credit per year to associates handling pro bono matters. A firm spokesperson told us that the firm has recently revamped its pro bono program and all attorneys are encouraged to participate, but a recent contact informed us that there has been "no tangible change."

generally friendly environment

The earlier edition of *The Insider's Guide* reported that Haight Gardner's "partners are not young," and the firm is somewhat hierarchical. After recent retirements, however, only three partners are over the age of 55, we were told. However, one contact observed that the firm's "young partnership seems to have closed the doors on the chances of senior associates to become partner." Haight Gardner is a "moderately friendly" place. The "associates are generally nice. They are decent and helpful." As a rule "people respect each other and work well together." One contact noted, "this is not the kind of place where people yell at each other."

opportunities training feedback

The firm offers young associates "significant responsibilities at an early stage of your career." First- and second-year litigation associates typically research legal issues, write memos, draft briefs, take depositions, and formulate interrogatories. Although most first- and second-year corporate associate work involves document review, those associates who prove themselves, we were told, are given more responsibility. Most of the firm's training occurs "on-the-job," and according to one source "the more senior associates are very willing to provide training." Both the corporate and litigation practice groups organize regular breakfast and lunch meetings at which a partner or an outside speaker makes a presentation on an aspect of the practice. In 1994, the firm sponsored a ten week trial advocacy program which was conducted by a well-known law school professor. The firm annually reviews an associate's performance (first-years are reviewed twice). Associates who actively seek informal daily feedback are usually able to get it.

separate work and social life

Although Haight Gardner does not demand long work hours by New York standards, (1900–2000 billable hours, plus approved non-billables), most of its attorneys do not do "much more than work together." One person claimed that "there is no great sense of community" at the firm. A small group of associates goes out after work once a week, but most attorneys "have lives outside of the firm" and keep their work and social lives separate. There is little organized "firm activity," noted one person. The firm has an annual holiday party, summer outing, and fall cocktail party for its legal staff.

diversity efforts

A fairly homogeneous firm, Haight Gardner was described as "more WASP than anything else." One person stated that the lack of diversity is "not the firm's fault, but more a reflection of the field of maritime and admiralty law." The firm is consciously trying to "change." Haight Gardner's three person Executive Committee includes a Cuban-American and a female Asian-American. The firm is a signatory of the NYC Bar Association's Statement of Goals for Increasing Minority Representation and Retention. Minority law students join the summer program through the firm's participation in the Texas/Tulane Minority Clerkship Program, but to date "none have accepted permanent offers," we were told. Haight Gardner has adopted policies to make the firm a more comfortable place for parents and women. It permits any associate who is the primary caretaker of a newborn child to take a paid three-month leave of absence. It also has an extensive sexual harassment policy that provides detailed procedures for handling any such situation. The 1997 summer associate class reportedly will be all female.

businesslike management

Managed by a five partner management committee (Executive Committee and Firm Arrangements Committee), Haight Gardner is economically healthy. There have, however, been some recent lay-offs "primarily for 'cause,' but of a type that would probably be overlooked in better days. The environment is now more competitive." The firm has adopted, moreover, a more businesslike approach to management, which has included, among other things, hiring an in-house marketing coordinator, using an agency to both market the firm's services and to handle its public relations, as well as maintaining an associate marketing program which includes a budget for midlevel and senior associates to market and develop new business. The firm's traditional transportation practice has remained strong; its bankruptcy practice and other non-traditional areas such as employment and computer/information technology are growing, and its "aviation litigation is a big growth area."

We did, however, hear a number of complaints and misgivings from our contacts. The firm has recently undergone a "significant restructuring," with a new Executive Committee in charge and a greater emphasis on billable hours. Additionally, one source pointed out that "associate pay increases reduce considerably after the third year." Another contact remarked that "salaries don't keep pace with other similar sized firms, though this is true of partners and support staff also." It was also pointed out to us that, since "most clients are non-U.S. companies, it is very difficult to get an in-house position upon leaving the firm." There is significant unease about making partner at Haight Gardner. The firm recently created a two-tiered partnership, providing for the possibility that an associate be a non-equity partner for three years before becoming eligible for equity status. One contact remarked that "associates become concerned at about the three to five year point with where their careers are going. Is there a reasonable opportunity to become partner here? If not, where do I need to go?" This person pointed out that "opportunities for partnership will be rare (there has been no partnership *vote* in three years)." Another contact observed that "the partnership track is ill-defined; it appears to be at a ten-year plus level these days." Further, "no partners were made this year. This was poorly handled by the partnership, which did nothing to explain the reasoning and circumstances to other associates. This had a poor effect on morale." In short, "management is out of touch and non-communicative" and, further, "a disparity in work ethic among partners and associates is tolerated." Another person remarked that the "partners are a very contentious lot—they can't agree on anything themselves."

cramped offices

The office facilities at Haight Gardner are somewhat crowded; first- and second-year associates must share offices. All the offices of the firm are computer networked, and the firm is currently implementing access to Internet e-mail. All attorneys who want them are provided with their own state-of-the-art computers. People commented that the firm emphasizes traditional methods of legal research more than using electronic data bases. The firm is equipped with a small lunchroom and a somewhat cramped library. One contact reported that the support staff "complained a lot."

hiring practices

Haight Gardner recruits people with "good grades" who are "fairly personable," "motivated and intelligent." People with a specific background in maritime and admiralty law are at an advantage in getting hired, although this appears to be less true today than in the past. The firm hires law students from a wide range of schools, including Boston College, Columbia, Fordham, Hofstra, New York University, St. John's University, the University of Michigan, and Georgetown.

Hughes Hubbard & Reed

New York Los Angeles Miami Washington
Berlin Paris

Address: One Battery Park Plaza, New York, NY 10004
Telephone: (212) 837–6000
Hiring Attorney: George A. Tsougarakis/Daniel H. Weiner
Contact: Joann M. Byrne, Director of Legal Employment; (212) 837–6486
Associate Salary: First year $86,000 (1997)
Summer Salary: $1650/week (1997)
Average Hours: 2100 worked; 1750 billed; NA required
Family Benefits: 12 weeks paid maternity leave (cbc unpaid); cbc weeks paid paternity leave (cbc unpaid)
1996 Summer: Class of 24 students; offers to 24
Partnership: 8% of entering associates from 1979–1985 were made partner
Pro Bono: 3.3% of all work is pro bono

Hughes Hubbard & Reed in 1997
151 Lawyers at the New York Office
1.3 Associates Per Partner

Total Partners 53		
Women	13	25%
All Minorities	2	4%
Asian-Am	1	2%
Latino	1	2%

Total Associates 71		
Women	35	49%
All Minorities	10	14%
Afro-Am	4	6%
Asian-Am	5	7%
Latino	1	1%

Practice Areas	
Corporate	na
Litigation	na
Tax	na
Trusts & Estates	na
Employee Benefits	na
Corp. Reorganization	na
Pacific Basin	na
Intellectual Property	na
Environmental	na
Products Liability	na

Unlike most New York firms, Hughes Hubbard & Reed is "not incredibly fast-paced or competitive," declared one source; another source claimed it is not "a latter-day sweatshop." The firm "encourages congeniality and does it better than most firms." Although Hughes Hubbard has a "white shoe" reputation, "people are not reserved and are generally friendly," asserted one contact. Office doors are usually open, and there is "a lot of interaction between partners and associates, both on work-related matters and socially." Associates feel "comfortable approaching partners," and "everyone, including the staff, is treated with respect." The firm is also informal. People address each other by first name, and frequently change into casual clothes during after-work hours. Hughes Hubbard is "tolerant of differences in attorneys' appearances, such as long hair and earrings for men—while not common, there are a few men with such."

practice areas

Founded by Charles Evans Hughes, former Chief Justice of the United States Supreme Court, Hughes Hubbard has an illustrious history. It grew out of a firm founded by Walter Carter in 1903, which firm also gave rise to such other prestigious New York law outfits as Cravath, Cadwalder, Breed Abbott, LeBoeuf, and Donovan Leisure. As for practice, Hughes Hubbard represents a wide variety of corporations and financial institutions in litigation, corporate, and tax matters, as well as individuals in trusts and estates, tax, and immigration matters. The litigation department has represented ITT Hartford in breast implant and blood products litigations; Broadcast Music, Inc. (BMI) in a lawsuit against HBO, the cable company; Bob Marley's estate in a RICO action; Coopers & Lybrand in securities fraud and employment litigation; and a major foreign bank in multiple class actions involving consumer lending activities in the U.S. Hughes Hubbard also has an expanding bankruptcy department, which represented Continental Airlines in a reorganization, and currently represents the Japanese department store chain Isetan in its high-profile bankruptcy dispute with Barneys. The firm's intellectual property and products liability practices are also growing. Recently, the environmental practice has grown "substantially" due to the addition of environmental attorneys from the former firm of Mudge Rose.

The firm's thriving corporate department has six practice areas: banking and financial services, corporate reorganization, insurance, mergers and acquisitions, real estate, and securities. Well-known corporate clients include Merck, Knight-Ridder, and Viacom. Hughes Hubbard also represents government entities such as the Federal Deposit Insurance Corporation (FDIC). The firm also has a significant international corporate practice. Its Paris office has done franchising work on behalf of corporations such as McDonald's. The banking practice represents Sanwa Bank, the fourth largest Japanese bank. The small Pacific Basin practice is general counsel for Nikon and represents a significant number of other Japanese clients. The firm's small trusts and estates, immigration, and tax departments service the needs of the large corporate clients represented by the larger departments, as well as their own clients. Associates in these practice groups enjoy extensive direct client contact and very close working relationships with and training from senior associates and partners.

pro bono commitment

With a "substantial commitment to pro bono work," Hughes Hubbard has pledged 30 hours per lawyer per year in pro bono legal services to Volunteer Legal Services. In addition, the firm receives pro bono referrals on a regular basis from the Legal Aid Society, the Beth Israel AIDS Clinic, Lambda Legal Defense (lesbian and gay rights), Lawyers Alliance, the Lawyers Committee for Human Rights Refugee Project, Volunteer Lawyers for the Arts, and New York Lawyers for the Public Interest. Many Hughes Hubbard attorneys regularly help staff Beth Israel every other Thursday. The firm sends memos to all attorneys listing pro bono matters available. Hughes Hubbard considers the hours attorneys have billed to pro bono in making bonus calculations. "Additionally, associates receive some of their most valuable training in pro bono work, for which they assume primary responsibility while being assigned more senior associates to oversee their work. The pro bono assignments also give associates a chance to practice another area of law," according to one of our contacts.

work assignments

Most attorneys are hired permanently for a particular department, but some are permitted to rotate through two departments in their first years. Associate responsibility is "merit-based" at Hughes Hubbard. Junior litigators usually handle research and writing, and often take depositions while corporate associates engage in due diligence and "going to the printers." Some associates, however, occasionally receive greater responsibility. Recently, one second-year banking associate handled a matter almost independently for a small foreign bank.

training feedback

Hughes Hubbard has a "mentor oriented" training program, and associates work closely with partners. Most associate training occurs on-the-job. The corporate and litigation departments, however, "hold weekly one-hour training sessions for one to three months, to help with useful, every day practical skills, documents, etc." The litigation department also organizes a "pretty intensive" trial advocacy training program, taught by Peter Murray, a visiting Harvard Law School professor. Associates are trained, videotaped, and critiqued over a one-week period. Summer associates receive a one-day training session. Each department also holds monthly meetings to discuss client matters. These meetings often include presentations on legal issues by partners or guest speakers. Informal feedback is generally good. "Because of the size of the firm...you develop a rapport" with the people with whom you work, explained one person.

balanced lifestyle

Associates "feel fortunate to be at Hughes Hubbard," one source commented. "For a large Wall Street firm, it has a very nice feel to it. It allows for a livable lifestyle. People work hard, but are not crazy. You are not watched and are encouraged to get the work done and get out. Even the partners have lives outside the firm that they are committed to." One person cautioned, however, that "there are periods when people will have late nights, etc." Like other aspects of the firm, social life at Hughes Hubbard is balanced. Attorneys "have good relationships outside work and go out together." Some attorneys rent and share summer homes in the Hamptons. One person remarked, "my best friends are here. People socialize a lot together. It is fun!"

efforts to increase diversity

Hughes Hubbard has made an effort to recruit female and minority law students. The firm has established a Diversity Committee, comprised of partners and associates, to enhance minority recruiting and retention. A high proportion of the attorneys in the Pacific Basin practice are of Asian origin. The firm participates in the Texas-Tulane Minority Clerkship Program and the northeast minority job fair. It also sponsors minority recruiting events. Hughes Hubbard is sensitive to women's concerns as well, and recently won special recognition from the National Organization for Women for having among the highest number of women partners at any New York City law firm. It is reportedly "pretty flexible about family leave" and other non-related part-time arrangements. One attorney worked part-time while attending a film school in New York, and one second-year litigator took a one year leave of absence to work as a judicial clerk. A third attorney works "modified hours (9:30 to 5:30)."

increasingly businesslike

Hughes Hubbard is run by a managing partner and a 13 partner executive committee. The managing partner is "extremely open to suggestions and proposals" of the associates, praised one admirer. One critic complained, however, that "the firm is regressing from its traditional policy of congeniality and is developing a more down-to-earth business attitude." "The lifestyle is not as good as it used to be," this person continued, but the firm is "making record profits." The Hughes Hubbard partnership track can be long. The two attorneys who were made partners in the summer of 1992 were tenth-year associates. In 1993, three associates respectively in their seventh, eighth, and ninth years at the firm were made partner. Though Hughes Hubbard has not had any layoffs in recent years, one person commented that turnover is high, estimating that 20 to 25 people leave the firm each year. A firm spokesperson informed us that Hughes Hubbard recently expanded the size of its incoming class from 15 to 20.

Hughes Hubbard's office is located in downtown Manhattan. They have the "greatest view of the harbor and the Statue of Liberty," one person said. The offices are "beautifully decorated" with "marble entryways," a lot of "dark wood," and "big windows." First- and second-year associates share offices, all of which have windows. All attorneys have computers in their offices, and can receive and send e-mail through the Internet. One critic complained that the "secretaries are monopolized by the partners." The firm cafeteria was described as "a social part of the firm."

hiring stresses cooperation

Hughes Hubbard hires "outgoing, personable, friendly people" who are also "highly competent." Because a friendly and cooperative work environment is important to the firm, Hughes Hubbard hires "people they want to work with." The firm hosts an on-campus reception at some schools to meet the students as a group. Students were advised to "talk about outside interests" in the interviews. "Be yourself and express enthusiasm and energy," counseled a successful applicant. The firm generally hires from the top national law schools, as well as from a number of east coast and New York regional and local schools.

If you are looking for consistently high-profile work, Hughes Hubbard is probably not for you. As one person with whom we spoke observed, "It is not Cravath, and doesn't want to be." A representative for Hughes Hubbard observed, however, that the "firm has recently done high-profile work for ITT Hartford, Isetan, Chrysler, Viacom, Knight Ridder, and others." Hughes Hubbard & Reed is a firm that serves its clients well, does excellent work, and allows attorneys to enjoy their lives and their work. Several people remarked that the pay scale does not rise through the years of advancement as dramatically as it does at other New York law firms. "We start at comparable salaries but don't get the same raises as the largest firms" is how one person described it. But, said another, "we also don't work as hard." Hughes Hubbard is a firm for people seeking a more balanced lifestyle.

Jones, Day, Reavis & Pogue

New York Atlanta Chicago Cleveland Columbus Dallas Irvine Los Angeles Pittsburgh Washington
Brussels Frankfurt Geneva Hong Kong London New Delhi Paris Riyadh Taipei Tokyo

Address: 599 Lexington Avenue, New York, NY 10022
Telephone: (212) 326–3939
Hiring Attorney: Dan A. Kusnetz
Contact: Anne Beier, Recruiting Administrator; (212) 326–3949
Associate Salary: First year $86,000 (1997); includes base salary plus stipend
Summer Salary: $1600/week (1996)
Average Hours: 2100 worked; 1900 billed; NA required
Family Benefits: Family and maternity leave (generally 6-8 weeks paid disability and 4 weeks paid family leave, plus 12 weeks unpaid leave)
1996 Summer: Class of 17 students; offers to 16
Partnership: NA
Pro Bono: NA

Jones, Day, Reavis & Pogue in 1997
111 Lawyers at the New York Office
1.7 Associates Per Partner

Total Partners 40			Total Associates 66			Practice Areas	
Women	7	18%	Women	34	52%	Corporate	55
All Minorities	1	3%	All Minorities	4	6%	Litigation/Constr./Environ.	37
Afro-Am	1	3%	Asian-Am	3	5%	Real Estate	17
			Latino	1	2%	Transactional/Bankruptcy	13
						Securities	11
						Tax	6
						Intellectual Property	5
						Government Regulation	3

centralized mega firm

With 20 offices in eleven countries, Jones, Day, Reavis & Pogue is one of the largest law firms in the world. Organized as one big firm rather than as a collection of autonomous offices, Jones Day is highly structured. For the most part, firm policies are standard for all offices, and a state-of-the-art computer system links the entire network of Jones Day offices. The managing partner, Patrick McCartan, who is based in the home office in Cleveland, makes all major firm decisions after consulting with the partnership and the advisory committee.

midwest culture

The New York Jones Day office, the product of a merger with Surrey & Morse, opened its doors in 1986. It has grown by leaps and bounds. Although most of its early growth resulted from lateral hiring, the office has, more recently, focused on generating home-grown associates through its summer program. One person commented that only now is the office "starting to develop personality. It becomes more conservative as it becomes more Jones Day." The work atmosphere in the New York office "has a midwest flavor." It is "relatively relaxed and not really New York." The firm is not "high-pressure, uptight, or cutthroat." The "partners are humane," and the firm "recognizes that people have outside lives." Though people work hard, "they do not overdo it."

Jones Day "treats people very professionally," expecting its attorneys to dress professionally in suits. Women generally do not wear pantsuits. One person commented that the firm is more "reserved," perhaps because it does not have "a lot of uptight New Yorkers," adding that "the people are nice, but not necessarily warm." The office is not "a stuffy place," however. One person stated that it has a "small, close-knit, family atmosphere." Though Jones Day worldwide is very hierarchical, partners in the New York office are accessible to associates for work related matters, and everyone addresses them by first name.

practice areas

Jones Day firmwide organizes its work around four main practice groups: a business practice group consisting of corporate and real estate, government regulation, litigation, and tax. Each group includes a number of specialized sections. The New York office has developed a strong bankruptcy practice under the leadership of partner Marc Kirschner. It also has a highly-specialized real estate practice that represents, among others, parties involved in construction deals. In addition, the New York office has a strong intellectual property practice. The New York office serves as the center of Jones Day's firmwide mergers and acquisitions, lending and structural finance, and international commercial law practices. The firm's litigation practice handles the traditional array of commercial matters. Charles Carberry, former Chief of the Securities & Commodities Unit in the U.S. Attorney's office in the Southern District of New York, who prosecuted some of the big insider trading cases of the late 1980s involving Ivan Boesky and company, joined the firm in 1991 and heads the litigation practice. Many former assistant U.S. attorneys are members of the litigation group. Jones Day coordinates the activities of its international offices out of New York. Consequently, in addition to the clients developed in New York, the office represents many of the firmwide large multinational corporate clients, including many Fortune 500 companies.

Pro bono, we were told, "is not actively encouraged" in the New York office. One person observed that those interested in doing pro bono work must take a "a proactive approach" and seek out matters on their own, although the firm usually has a number of pro bono matters available from which associates may choose. Another contact remarked that "while the office welcomes the exposure (of pro bono work), it expects you to do the work on your own time."

NAG for new associates

New associates are placed for their first year with the firm in the New Associates Group (NAG), an associate development system designed to provide them with broad-based legal training. As part of this program, new associates are encouraged to handle work in all practice groups. Once associates join a particular practice, an assigning partner in each department distributes work and oversees associate development in that area. Most first- and second-year associate assignments involve research, writing memos, and drafting briefs. Junior associates usually do not take depositions or draft interrogatories, though one person said that "if you take the initiative, you will get more work." Another person observed that "as a young litigator, I have had significant experience managing my own cases, taking depositions, and making in-court arguments." Most associate training occurs "on-the-job," although two partners have been formally entrusted with developing formal training programs for associates. Each practice group holds regular breakfast or lunch meetings where the attorneys discuss new developments in the law.

minimal social life

Although Jones Day is not one of the more social firms, many of its attorneys develop friendships and often "pop into each other's offices." There is "no forced pressure to socialize outside the office. The firm realizes that people have family lives," remarked one source. A large number of attorneys, including younger associates, are married, and "people tend to go home after work." The firm does, however, sponsor a few social events. Entering associates from all the offices spend a weekend in Cleveland meeting each other, and once a year, each practice group has a firmwide retreat at a resort of its choice. New York office social events include the Cookie Hour held every Thursday at 4:30 P.M. in a conference room serving tea, coffee and cookies, variously described by our contacts as "amazing" or "lousy." Summer events have included a dinner and dance at the Boathouse in Central Park, weekly lunches, and bimonthly dinners.

Known nationwide as a "pretty WASP" and conservative firm, Jones Day New York is more diverse. One contact pointed out that there is "a high percentage of Jewish attorneys" in the New York office. There are few minorities in the office. Reportedly, women "are treated well" at the firm, and the female partners are held in high regard. There are approximately equal numbers of female and male associates in the New York office. But as with most firms, people noted that it may be hard to both raise a family and to make partner.

salary below market

The managing partner of the New York office, who is appointed by the firmwide management partner, handles the day-to-day operations of the office. We heard some complaints that Jones Day compensation is slightly lower than that at other prominent New York firms. However, first-year associate compensation which begins at $86,000 is comparable to other New York firms. After the second year, an associate's base compensation and bonus are both based on merit.

offices

Jones Day offices are "very nice, well-kept, new, and modern." Each associate has a private office with a window. The firm outfits each office with a computer, "a big brown mahogany bookshelf, and an attached desk." The computer is "amazing," and the support staff is "great." Two or three attorneys are assigned to a single secretary.

academic emphasis in hiring

Jones Day hires students with "very strong academic records." One person commented that the firm is "competing with Sullivan, Simpson Thacher, and Davis Polk" for associates and claimed that students coming from national schools need at least a B+ or A- grade point average to get hired. According to another, however, the firm "will take someone who doesn't have great grades, but who has done a lot of great activities" outside law school. Jones Day seeks "hard-working, bright people who are able to work with other people." The firm, one person told us, has "more team players than individual stars." Jones Day hires students from the top national law schools, some midwestern law schools, and New York-area law schools.

Jones Day associates are very happy with "the small firm atmosphere, the nice people, the quality work, and their own office." If you prefer a less pressured environment than most large New York law firms offer, but are attracted by the practice and resources of a large, international law firm and would like to dabble in a number of practice areas before specializing, Jones Day New York is worth considering.

Kaye, Scholer, Fierman, Hays & Handler

New York Los Angeles Washington
Beijing Hong Kong

Address: 425 Park Avenue, New York, NY 10022
Telephone: (212) 836–8000
Hiring Attorney: Andrew MacDonald, Renee Ring
Contact: Virginia L. Quinn, Legal Recruiting Administrator; (212) 836–8897
Associate Salary: First year $87,000 (1997)
Summer Salary: $1600/week (1997)
Average Hours: NA worked; NA billed; NA required
Family Benefits: 12 weeks paid maternity leave (12 unpaid); 12 weeks unpaid paternity leave; medical and childcare flexible spending accounts; emergency childcare
1996 Summer: Class of 35 students; offers to 35
Partnership: 7% of entering associates from 1978–1984 were made partner
Pro Bono: 2% of all work is pro bono

Kaye, Scholer, Fierman, Hays & Handler in 1997
259 Lawyers at the New York Office
1.5 Associates Per Partner

Total Partners 87		
Women	13	15%
All Minorities	1	1%
Asian-Am	1	1%

Total Associates 132		
Women	51	39%
All Minorities	20	15%
Afro-Am	6	5%
Asian-Am	7	5%
Latino	7	5%

Practice Areas	
Litigation	100
Corporate	69
Bankruptcy	26
Real Estate	17
Tax	10
Labor (management)	12
Trusts & Estates	9
Latin Am/Emerging Markets	6

practice areas

Kaye Scholer is a full-service law firm with offices in Washington, D.C., Los Angeles, Beijing, and Hong Kong, as well as New York. Predominantly a litigation firm, Kaye Scholer traditionally has been well-known for its strong antitrust practice. In addition, Kaye Scholer has an active bankruptcy practice resulting from its acquisition of Levin & Weintraub, a bankruptcy boutique. The firm also provides legal services in corporate and finance, intellectual property, international, labor and employment, real estate, and tax law. Kaye Scholer's clients are primarily midsized to large corporations and institutions. The firm represents a number of the nation's biggest banks including Chase Manhattan, in addition to Pfizer, Novartis, PepsiCo, Texaco, Estee Lauder, and others. Judge Fuld, who sat on the New York Court of Appeals, is now a prominent Kaye Scholer partner.

In order to encourage pro bono participation, at least one partner or counsel and associate from each of Kaye Scholer's departments is a member of the firm's pro bono committee. We were told that each department is involved in some pro bono work, all of which counts toward billable hours. Attorneys at the firm have accepted referrals from the Legal Aid Society, New York Lawyers for the Public Interest, Center for Battered Women Legal Services, Lawyers Alliance for New York, Lawyers Committee for Human Rights, Volunteer Lawyers for the Arts, and the Pro Bono Offices of the State and Federal Courts. One person commented that most of the work involves representing indigent individuals; another person told us that "pro bono work is encouraged."

professional development

Entering associates are hired to work in a particular department and receive work from an assigning partner. Not unexpectedly, first-year associates handle "the grunt work," but Kaye Scholer is a "meritocracy," such that "the more they like your work, the more responsibility you get." Consequently, some fifth-year associates have never taken a deposition, and some second-year associates have taken many. Because the firm represents many small clients, junior associates have better opportunities for responsibility than those at many other large New York firms. One person observed, however, that in litigation "cases are often staffed 'top-heavy,' making opportunities to progress and learn and get more experience difficult at times."

own moot court facility

As for training, each department at Kaye Scholer has developed a structured training program designed to provide associates with certain skills during their first few years at the firm. Kaye Scholer also offers continuing legal education (CLE) programs in which both partners and outside speakers make presentations. The firm also has developed a three to four-day trial advocacy training program with the assistance of the National Institute of Trial Advocacy (NITA), which program is conducted in the firm's own moot court facilities. Kaye Scholer formally evaluates associates (twice a year for their first two years and once annually thereafter), during which time they have a formal opportunity to comment on the partners for whom they have worked.

Kaye Scholer is neither a "back-stabbing, competitive firm," nor is it "macho in terms of billing." On average, attorneys work one weekend of every month. In the past, first-year associates were assigned to be "on call" for two weekends of their first year, but this policy has now been changed. Kaye Scholer has a very nice cafeteria which is "'pretty crowded' between 11 A.M. and 2 P.M. It is a very social area of the firm." The cafeteria, which has a wonderful selection of foods at very reasonable prices, was recently written up in the *New York Times* as "one of the best corporate cafeterias in the city."

low-key social life

The social life at Kaye Scholer is low-key. A number of attorneys are close friends, and there are groups of people who go out after work, some "almost every night." The firm sponsors a well-attended happy hour every Friday evening, after which attorneys frequently go out together. Each department organizes a party. Many of the firm's male attorneys are actively involved in its football, basketball, and softball teams. One contact pointed out to us, however, that the departments are segregated and, consequently, "if you weren't a summer associate here, you have to make some effort to know people in other departments. Accordingly, while Kaye Scholer has one of the highest percentages of female partners (among major New York law firms), it doesn't feel that way working in litigation, the largest department in the firm, where there are only two women partners."

friendly accepting culture

Kaye Scholer is a friendly, relaxed, and informal place. One source enthused that at Kaye Scholer "people actually take vacations." Associates work closely with partners and address one another by first name. Attorneys are "approachable and welcome questions." They are very "willing to help...and explain things to you." Dress is as informal as it can be in a New York law firm. Men shed their jackets upon arriving at work, and women can get away with "wearing blouses, skirts, and platform shoes." One person told us that women "can wear pants," and added, "I didn't wear stockings when I wore skirts." The firm has "dress down Fridays" from April through Labor Day. Kaye Scholer willingly accommodates the religious practices of its attorneys. One person commented that the firm is "very accepting of Orthodox Jews" and the fact that they "cannot work on Friday afternoons or Saturdays." Kosher food is always available at firm functions and can be ordered at the firm's cafeteria. Another contact also observed, pointedly, that there is a "a Christian associate who is always permitted to attend church on Sunday mornings, choir rehearsals on Tuesday nights, and any other church functions which may arise during the week because the partners for whom the associate works are respectful and recognize the associate's dedication to her religion."

comfortable for women

In general, people reported that the firm's atmosphere is "comfortable" for women. There are a number of "supportive women mentors," particularly in the corporate department. Many of that department's female partners have children, and younger women "feel comfortable taking maternity leave." The firm's parental leave policy, available to both men and women, does not extend the time of partnership consideration, we were told. Under the leadership of a female corporate partner, the firm recently adopted part-time and flex-time work policies. The firm also provides an off-site emergency child care facility that is available to all attorneys and support staff. While the firm employs few minority attorneys, it is actively recruiting. Kaye Scholer does not belong to nor does it schedule events at private clubs, the admissions policies of which have the effect of limiting or excluding women or minority members.

management issues

Kaye Scholer was the subject of much press attention in 1992 when it was sued by the Office of Thrift Supervision for its involvement in the Lincoln Savings & Loan Scandal and was forced to agree to a settlement of $41 million. The firm made a number of adjustments in its management to address the dramatic events of that year. The partners conducted regular formal meetings at which associates were informed about the firm's financial health. The firm also now has an associates committee through which associates voice their concerns. One person commented to us that there is "dialogue between associates and partners about the concerns of the associates." Another person observed that "more information is passed on informally" than formally. This informality, though, occasionally has its drawbacks: "when the firm is too informal, it can sometimes be annoying, because there can be delays in receiving reviews or important notices" is how one contact described the situation to us. Kaye Scholer is managed by an executive committee elected by the other partners for a limited term. A number of other committees, such as associate training, business development, legal personnel (which addresses performance), pro bono, professional ethics, and recruiting address specific issues and have associates as committee members.

crowded offices

The Kaye Scholer offices are somewhat crowded. Some first-year associates share offices, and sometimes second-year associates are assigned interior offices without windows. Each department in the firm has its own library. The firm has a new computer system with Wordperfect 6.1. The system is better than the old one but "many young associates complain that it crashes too much." A firm spokesperson, however, informed us that this is "no longer" the case. The support staff was described as "discontented" because "they feel like they have too much work." The firm assigns three attorneys to a single secretary.

hiring tips

Kaye Scholer seeks "bright" students who can "do good work" and usually hires law students from the top national and New York-area law schools. In addition, however, interviewers "look for people they can hang out with, and people who will fit in with the firm." Interviewers react positively to applicants who "have interests outside of work." Interviewees were advised to "really relax...and make believe that you are hanging out with friends. Don't try to impress them with things on your résumé." Another advised, "be forthright and straightforward...they don't like slick people." Nor do they like "obnoxiously arrogant know-it-alls," a strategically-placed contact informed us.

Kelley Drye & Warren

New York Chicago Los Angeles Miami Parsippany Stamford Washington
Brussels Hong Kong

Address: 101 Park Avenue, New York, NY 10178
Telephone: (212) 808–7800
Hiring Attorney: James J. Kirk
Contact: Libby Yoskowitz, Legal Personnel Manager; (212) 808–7516
Associate Salary: First year $87,000 (1997); second $92,000; third $100,000; fourth $111,000; fifth $123,000; sixth $130,000; seventh $140,000
Summer Salary: $1673/week (1997)
Average Hours: NA worked; 1971 billed; 2000 required
Family Benefits: 12 weeks paid maternity leave
1996 Summer: Class of 19 students; offers to 18
Partnership: 10% of entering associates from 1977–1986 were made partner
Pro Bono: 1% of all work is pro bono

Kelley Drye & Warren in 1997
158 Lawyers at the New York Office
1.3 Associates Per Partner

Total Partners 69			Total Associates 89			Practice Areas	
Women	9	13%	Women	34	38%	Litigation	61
All Minorities	5	7%	All Minorities	11	12%	Corporate	46
Asian-Am	4	6%	Afro-Am	1	1%	Real Estate	10
Latino	1	1%	Asian-Am	8	9%	Labor	12
			Latino	2	2%	Private Clients	9
						Tax	7
						Employee Benefits	6
						Bankruptcy	5
						General	2

Founded in 1836, Kelley Drye & Warren is a prestigious and highly-regarded full-service law firm. Unlike many well-established large law firms, however, Kelley Drye is "not a stuffy place." Because attorneys leave their office doors open, it is easy to drop in for a visit. The dress code is fairly relaxed, with casual Fridays during the summer, and attorneys address one another by first name. Partners are "generally incredibly friendly and respectful of associates," and the firm is "not cutthroat or competitive."

practice areas

Kelley Drye & Warren represents an impressive range of domestic and international corporations and financial institutions, including Bacardi Corporation, Pitney Bowes, Cigna, Chase Manhattan Bank, Matsushita Corporation, Equitable Life, Reader's Digest, New York Hospital, Union Carbide, and Sumitomo Bank. The strong litigation practice has handled many high-profile matters, including the representation of Union Carbide, one of the firm's largest clients, in the lawsuit arising from the company's industrial accident in Bhopal, India. The bankruptcy department has a strong reputation and was involved in the widely-publicized Revco D.S., Inc. and Interco bankruptcy cases. Other departments include corporate, which has declined in size since our last edition, employee benefits, labor, personal services, real estate, and tax. With offices in Brussels and Hong Kong, and affiliated offices in Tokyo and New Delhi, the firm also has a significant international practice. This practice has been reorganized into subgroups, each of which handles a particular geographical region. One such group, which grew out of the Union Carbide case and which comprises a number of Indian attorneys, focuses on matters involving India.

Kelley Drye places a "big stress on ethics and public service." Summer associates may elect to work with the Juvenile Rights Division of the Legal Aid Society during the summer. Kelley Drye attorneys are additionally involved in a wide range of community activities.

professional development

Entering associates remain "unassigned" to a department through January of their first year so that they may explore different areas of the firm's practice before committing to a particular department. During this time, they receive assignments from a central assignment coordinator. Summer associates also receive a variety of assignments from a central coordinator. Associate training and opportunities for responsibility vary by department. Junior litigation associate assignments typically involve researching and writing memos, and occasionally taking depositions or drafting interrogatories. In the third year, an associate "may start arguing motions," and in the fifth year some associates take an active, independent role in trial. On the other hand, first-year bankruptcy associates get "a lot of responsibility" and often appear in bankruptcy court. Junior corporate associates usually work on research and drafting assignments. Most associate training occurs on-the-job, though some departments hold regular meetings to discuss, among other things, active client matters. The corporate department recently reinstituted weekly training sessions covering a wide range of topics. Each department also makes presentations for the entire firm regarding new developments in the law.

playful atmosphere

Kelley Drye & Warren is a friendly firm, one that is not as impersonal as some other large New York firms. As an associate, "you are not a number" at this firm, and after some time, "your department becomes your family unit," praised one contact. There is "team spirit," we were told, in approaching a deal or researching issues. Associates often form close friendships, and a few married couples met at Kelley Drye. The firm sponsors a number of fun and "playful" social events. One summer event is a sailboat ride through the New York Harbor. Kelley Drye also sponsors a well-attended monthly cocktail party in its main lobby.

tolerant and diverse firm

Kelley Drye & Warren is an open and diverse firm. It is home to lawyers with unique international backgrounds, interesting "first" careers, or who are just plain characters. The firm "is willing to take a chance on someone with a different background...who would be an asset to the firm in the long run," praised one admirer. Past summer classes, for example, included law students in their second career, and students from foreign countries. Many interns from foreign law firms spend time at Kelley Drye. "The firm also is accommodating about maternity leave and permits some part-time work arrangements." In addition, its strong sexual harassment policy and procedures for reporting such incidents are made clear to all new associates.

We heard few complaints about the firm. However, according to one person, the firm's office "is the most negative thing about Kelley." Associates share "minute" offices until their fourth year. The firm's computers have E-mail, spreadsheet, and word processing software, and are on a network that includes all the domestic offices. Attorneys with home computers can log into the network instead of coming into the office, if otherwise not needed there. This is especially convenient for weekend and late night work.

hires those with unusual backgrounds

In its hiring decisions, Kelley Drye is particularly attracted to people with past work experiences or unusual backgrounds. Past summer classes have included students from Brooklyn, Columbia, Fordham, Georgetown, New York University, Rutgers, and the University of Virginia. People strongly recommended prospective applicants to "be themselves" during interviews with the firm. One person observed that frequently the attorneys end interviews by asking you if there is something about yourself that you would like to tell them.

Kelley Drye & Warren may not pay as well as some of New York's largest law firms. Its associates, however, enjoy working at the firm. One person commented that associates "like the work, are well-paid, and are working for a good firm." Kelley Drye & Warren is an excellent choice for someone seeking a friendly, diverse, and open work environment.

Kenyon & Kenyon

New York San Jose Washington
Frankfurt

Address: One Broadway, New York, NY 10004
Telephone: (212) 425–7200
Hiring Attorney: NA
Contact: Kathleen Lynn, Recruitment Administrator; (212) 425–7200
Associate Salary: First year $86,000 (1997)
Summer Salary: $1600/week (1997)
Average Hours: 2100 worked; 2000 billed; 1800 required
Family Benefits: 6 weeks paid maternity leave (12 unpaid)
1996 Summer: Class of 17 students; offers to 17
Partnership: 15% of entering associates from 1978–1984 were made partner
Pro Bono: 3% of all work is pro bono

Kenyon & Kenyon in 1997
120 Lawyers at the New York Office
2.5 Associates Per Partner

Total Partners 34			Total Associates 86			Practice Areas	
Women	1	3%	Women	19	22%	Intellectual Property	100%
All Minorities	1	3%	All Minorities	6	7%		
Asian-Am	1	3%	Afro-Am	3	3%		
			Asian-Am	3	3%		

intellectual property specialty

Kenyon & Kenyon offers one of the most diverse intellectual property practices in New York and is "well-known throughout the world." Founded over 100 years ago, it is a "very old and respected law firm." Its practice is loosely organized around three areas: patents, copyrights, and trademarks. The highly-regarded patent practice constitutes approximately 70 percent of the firm's work, and is allocated between litigation and patent prosecution. Kenyon's patent litigation practice involves large, complex cases, often with more than $10 million at stake. The firm defended Kodak when it was sued by Polaroid for infringement of its instant camera patent. It was also involved in Toyota's suit against Mead Data Central, which centered around the use of the names "LEXIS" and "Lexus." The patent prosecution practice obtains patent protection for inventors, ranging from large multinational corporations to individuals. The firm's clients are primarily large electronics, computer, chemical, pharmaceutical, automotive and manufacturing companies. The firm also handles registering and protecting trademarks and copyrights, as well as other intellectual property issues, such as trade secrets, licensing, and entertainment law. The firm added a new intellectual property group focusing on issues relating to the Internet.

Though the bulk of Kenyon's work involves U.S. domestic laws, the firm also coordinates patent registrations worldwide and has established working relationships with law firms throughout the world. A significant portion of Kenyon's clients are based in foreign countries, and the patent litigators frequently travel both within the U.S. and overseas.

Even though Kenyon & Kenyon has a pro bono practice that is connected to the Volunteer Lawyers for the Arts and the Columbia Arts Program, "not many associates do pro bono" work. It is "very difficult to do pro bono work in the field of patents," explained one contact. Hours billed to pro bono are not formally credited toward billable hours, but are taken into account.

formal culture

Kenyon & Kenyon is "a little bit formal" and very "stratified." The firm "will follow the letterhead in strict order" when allocating offices, illustrated one source. For most associates, Kenyon & Kenyon "is a low-stress law firm." Even "a high percentage of partners expect not to be there after 7 P.M. or on the weekends." According to one source, "it is not like a regular New York law firm that expects you to devote your whole life to the firm."

free market distribution of work

Kenyon's "capitalist market oriented system" for distributing work greatly influences an associate's work experience. Associates are not assigned to any particular department and, in their initial years, must be prepared to handle all aspects of the firm's practice. However, with time, they gradually specialize, usually building relationships with certain partners with whom they work most closely. One contact praised the firm's "lack of formal structure" which "gives associates more opportunity to seek out work that interests them."

opportunities

Those associates who develop close working relationships with partners receive more responsibility. "The entrepreneurial type" thrives in this atmosphere, said one contact, noting that less assertive people may "fall through the cracks" at the firm. There are some partners who "won't give work to first- and second-years until they have proven themselves," we were told. In general, the patent prosecution practice offers more responsibility earlier than the litigation practice. In patent prosecution, young associates often meet with inventors and have nearly full responsibility for drafting patent applications, although under the supervision of a more senior attorney. As this work is often highly technical, almost all associates in this area have science or engineering backgrounds. Because patent litigation lawsuits are large and complex, most junior associate assignments in this area involve researching, overseeing document production, and writing memos. A firm spokesperson noted, however, that a number of "first- and second-year associates take depositions." The "partners keep the best work," complained one critic. Another contact, on the other hand, enthused that "Kenyon associates get to work closely with the partners, some of whom are among the top people in the field. Associates here are considered part of the team, and not merely as fungible hired help."

minimal training and feedback

Kenyon allows associates the time to study for and to take the Patent Bar examination, and it pays for them to take a Patent Bar preparation course. Formal training, however, is "minimal after the first year." The firm doesn't "really understand the concept of continuing legal education," in one person's opinion. Another person remarked that "formal training is nonexistent. Junior associates learn how to prosecute patent applications by working closely with more senior attorneys, but litigators have to train themselves." This person noted, additionally, that "associates are not trained (or encouraged) to bring in work and develop their own client bases." Though it provides each attorney a $1000 allowance for outside seminars, the firm does not credit the hours spent at such seminars toward the billable hour requirement. The firm does, however, organize regular, voluntary firmwide meetings where lawyers in a practice area discuss the new legal developments in their area. Though associates are reviewed formally once a year, they receive "minimal and trivial feedback," according to one contact, who believes that the best indicator of performance is that the partners will just "stop giving you work" if you are not performing well.

Aside from an annual firm dinner, Kenyon & Kenyon does not sponsor many firm social activities. Small groups of attorneys form strong friendships, however, and younger attorneys go to lunch together and occasionally go out after work. During the summer, the firm sponsors cocktail parties for summer associates and the usual array of summer events.

diversity committee

Traditionally a predominantly white male firm, Kenyon & Kenyon has made an effort to recruit and retain more minorities and women in recent years. People claimed, however, that the firm has had particular difficulties because there is only a very limited pool of women and minority lawyers who also have engineering and science degrees. The firm has a committee of three male partners, three female associates, and two male associates which addresses issues of discrimination and other matters at the firm. Although this committee has discussed some issues pertinent to the retention of women and minorities, it has focused more on what one person labeled "a communication problem between partners and associates." The firm is fairly supportive of family concerns. Though it does not provide emergency day care, attorneys feel free to bring their children to work if the need arises, and on occasion the firm opens up one of its conference rooms for attorneys' children.

management

Kenyon & Kenyon is economically healthy, has grown significantly in recent years, and "has been extremely busy for the last three years," reported one insider. Despite the firm's growth over a number of years, Kenyon is "just starting to deal with" its changing management requirements—it recently hired an in-house marketing director. Currently, a management committee of high-level partners makes major decisions, while a number of other committees address specific issues. Traditionally, associates have not been very involved in managing the firm. "Partners will not share information with associates and will not involve associates in most committees," complained one critic. Recently, however, the firm has allowed associates to join a few of the marketing sub-committees, and the partners "meet occasionally with associate class representatives." The partners have also delegated much of the day-to-day management of the firm to non-lawyer administrators.

Kenyon & Kenyon is located in a historic building in downtown Manhattan, which is owned by the firm. The office windows, which can be opened, provide beautiful views of the Statue of Liberty. A terrace that wraps around the 11th floor of the building offers a view of Battery Park and is used for firm cocktail parties. First-year associates share offices that have windows. Second- and third-year associates are assigned private offices. The firm has a computer system and a highly-specialized library. It also has a cafeteria, which was recently renovated and enlarged, that offers catered food. The firm also has offices in Washington, D.C. and Frankfurt, Germany, as well as a recently opened office in San Jose, California.

hiring tips

Kenyon & Kenyon hires people who "will work hard, are intelligent, and have a technical background," though the last requirement is not absolutely necessary. The firm generally hires students from the top national, New York regional, and some southern law schools. People advised applicants to emphasize their interest in the intellectual property field and to be active participants in the interview. Kenyon & Kenyon "wants to find out who you are."

People criticized Kenyon & Kenyon's administrative and managerial structure. On some level, the firm lacks "synergy," said one critic, explaining that, despite its many talented lawyers, Kenyon consists of a "number of individual rainmakers who don't pool resources. It is a very old-style firm, a bunch of partners with their clients who find associates to help them." Despite this criticism, Kenyon & Kenyon has a great deal to offer someone who is interested in intellectual property. It provides better experience than the intellectual property departments at most general law firms. It attracts better cases because it is a specialist in the field and is home to some of the best patent lawyers in the country. In general, associates find the work interesting, receive good experience, are well-paid, and have a manageable work load. Unlike other intellectual property firms, Kenyon permits its associates to do copyright and trademark work in addition to patent law and to determine their own mix of work. Finally, the firm has a strong presence in intellectual property issues that arise in the electrical engineering and chemical fields.

LeBoeuf, Lamb, Greene & MacRae

New York Albany Denver Harrisburg Hartford Jacksonville LA Newark Pittsburgh Portland Salt Lake City San Francisco Washington
Almaty Brussels London Moscow

Address: 125 West 55th Street, New York, NY 10019
Telephone: (212) 424–8000
Hiring Attorney: John M. Aerni
Contact: Yiba C. Ng, Director of Legal Personnel; (212) 424–8882
Associate Salary: First year $85,000 (1997); second $98,000; third $110,000; fourth $125,000; fifth $140,000; sixth $150,000; seventh $160,000; eighth $170,000 (year-end bonus eligibility)
Summer Salary: $1635/week (1997)
Average Hours: 2200 worked; 2000 billed; NA required
Family Benefits: 12 weeks paid leave for primary parental caregiver (12 unpaid)
1996 Summer: Class of 22 students; offers to 22
Partnership: 16% of entering associates from 1981–1987 were made partner
Pro Bono: 3% of all work is pro bono

LeBoeuf, Lamb, Greene & MacRae in 1997
226 Lawyers at the New York Office
1.3 Associates Per Partner

Total Partners 82			Total Associates 109			Practice Areas	
Women	9	11%	Women	48	44%	Corporate	67
All Minorities	2	2%	All Minorities	19	17%	Litigation	37
Afro-Am	1	1%	Afro-Am	6	6%	Insurance	28
Asian-Am	1	1%	Asian-Am	10	9%	Tax	21
			Latino	3	3%	Unassigned	16
						Bankruptcy	14
						Real Estate	15
						Energy	13
						Trusts & Estates	9
						Insurance/Health	4
						ERISA	2

Formerly LeBoeuf, Lamb, Leiby & MacRae, the firm changed its name in 1994 to LeBoeuf, Lamb, Greene & MacRae. The firm is a comfortable place, where partners are approachable, and individual offices are usually kept open as an invitation for visitors. The firm is "less structured," and associates are "more in control of their work" than at other firms. One person remarked that there is "no master-serf mentality" at the firm. LeBoeuf is "not quite as cut throat" and does not require the "crazy hours" of other large New York firms, although this has changed somewhat of late. In today's competitive economy, LeBoeuf's reputation as a "lifestyle" firm is "still sort of true" but less so than in the past, we were told.

regulated industries practice

LeBoeuf, Lamb, Greene & MacRae was founded by Randall LeBoeuf, who began the practice of law in 1920, and served as Assistant Attorney General for New York on water power matters from 1925 to 1927. Today, LeBoeuf offers a cutting-edge regulated industries practice. The firm is particularly well-known for the wide variety of legal services it provides to insurance, energy, and utility companies. On the corporate side, the firm has handled some unusual mergers and acquisitions work, and has been actively involved in the wave of high-profile utilities mergers accompanying deregulation. Corporate/utilities partner Douglas Hawes is considered to be the "foremost expert on utilities mergers and acquisitions in the country." LeBoeuf represented the Public Service Company of Colorado in the acquisition of an electric cooperative. In 1996, LeBoeuf attorneys were involved in nine electric utility mergers, one of which represented the largest transaction of its kind to date, Duke Power Company and Pan Energy Corp. In another major deal, a LeBoeuf team served as counsel to Enron Corporation, in its $2.1 billion merger with the Portland General Corporation. LeBoeuf was also involved in the first demutualization of an insurance company, representing Axa in its acquisition of Equitable Life Insurance. The firm represents Lloyd's of London as its U.S. general counsel and was instrumental in settling the Names' litigation. LeBoeuf handles some unique insurance insolvency matters. Recently, the firm represented Nationwide Financial Services, Inc. in three public offerings closings, totaling almost $1 billion. The firm represents members of other regulated industries, including banking, financial services, telecommunications, transportation, and health care, providing legal services in areas such as corporate, litigation, bankruptcy, tax, real estate, and trusts and estates. Former ITT general counsel, Howard Aibel, is well known arbitration specialist at the firm. Aibel is chairman of the executive committee of the American Arbitration Association.

The firm achieved notoriety for a unique agreement that the litigation department made with one of its major clients—the Aluminum Company of America (ALCOA). The firm has agreed to handle all of the Pittsburgh-based ALCOA's outstanding litigation for a flat fee. The company is said to have over 500 outstanding litigation matters. A similar arrangement was more recently worked out with the Duquesne Light Co.

LeBoeuf offers a developing international practice focused on Europe and Eastern Europe. The firm has offices in Brussels and Moscow, and recently established an office in Almaty, Khazakstan. LeBoeuf has a strong presence in London even apart from its Lloyd's business, being one of a small number of U.S. law firms whose London practice includes a phalanx of English solicitors. In this capacity, it represents large multinationals in aerospace, high-tech, banking, manufacturing, and natural resources matters.

pro bono rotation

People we interviewed praised LeBoeuf's commitment to pro bono work. The firm credits pro bono hours toward the billable hour requirement. The practice is supervised by partners John Aerni and Cynthia Shoss. The firm staffs a full-time position at Brooklyn Legal Services, through which associates at the firm may rotate for four month periods. Summer associates who work at least 10 weeks of the summer at LeBoeuf may also be placed, at their election, in a two-week pro bono internship.

assignments training feedback

Because the work atmosphere at LeBoeuf is "unstructured," an associate has "to be aggressive to get work." New associates remain "unassigned" to a particular department for their first year at the firm and are encouraged to work in a range of areas before specializing. They may select a department at the end of their first year. First-year associates may seek assignments from an assignment coordinator in the early part of the year, but are eventually expected to obtain work independently. It doesn't hurt to "bang on doors." First-year litigation associates typically research, write memos, and draft motions and briefs. Third- and fourth-year associates regularly take and defend depositions among other things. Junior associate courtroom experience is, for the most part, limited to pro bono matters. First-year corporate associates usually handle document distributions and do a lot of proofreading on the larger deals and perform due diligence investigations. Associates who demonstrate capability to take on greater responsibility, however, are entrusted with such. The firm offers a mandatory formal training program for the initial six months of the first year, which includes training seminars provided by each department. The training program is "very general in nature and is structured as introductions to or overviews of departmental practices," one contact said. Another person observed that the "training program needs revamping and greater partnership commitment, although the firm has made more of an effort recently." LeBoeuf formally reviews associates twice a year.

lower salary

Hours vary depending upon which department you happen to be in, we were told. "The corporate average might be 2250; litigation average might be 1850. Monthly hours are also erratic, potentially varying from 125 to 275, at the trough and the peak." Associate compensation increases in lockstep increments. It begins at $85,000, which is about average for large New York firms, but we were told by some contacts that the annual increases are slightly smaller than those at other large firms. The second year base salary is $98,000. A firm spokesperson noted that LeBoeuf rewards associates whose "time commitment and performance are considered exceptional" with a year-end bonus that raises their yearly salary to higher levels. The bonus system has two levels: at 2000 hours, there is a mandatory 5% bonus; at 2250 hours, attorneys qualify for a second bonus of up to an additional 15%, or higher in some cases, of their base salary, depending on the quantity and quality of work. "Also, unlike some firms, associates are eligible for the second bonus level in the first year," one insider instructed us.

Many LeBoeuf associates form friendships with each other, particularly within their class and their departments. Young associates often go out after work for dinner or drinks. The "softball team is big," perhaps because it has been a winning team in the law firm league. A number of the associates attend the games and go out afterward. Many attorneys, however, have families and outside interests. They tend to work efficiently during the day so that they can leave work at a reasonable time.

sensitive to women's issues

From its inception, LeBoeuf has been very receptive to hiring and promoting female attorneys. Randall LeBoeuf, the founder of the firm, reportedly convinced his secretary, Sheila Marshall, to attend night law school. She was an insurance partner at the firm until her recent retirement. Partner Molly Boast chairs the litigation practice and is the second female member of the firm's 14 partner administrative committee. The other female member of this committee, Cecilia (Sue) Kemper, leads the firm's life and health insurance practice. LeBoeuf consciously strives to provide a comfortable atmosphere for women. "Nonetheless, female associates still feel there is great room for improvement," one person told us. In past summers, female partners have invited female summer associates to dinners where they discussed issues involved in balancing work and family. LeBoeuf has formal maternity and paternity leave policies and permits attorneys to work part-time. Primary care providers may take a three month paid leave of absence, and secondary care providers may take two weeks paid leave. Male attorneys reportedly feel "no qualms about taking paternity leave." However, one person claimed that some women in the corporate department have not felt comfortable taking maternity leave. The firm has a successful history of hiring minority law students.

LeBoeuf is governed by its administrative committee, which includes members of the firm's other offices, as well as a number of other committees that address specific management issues. Associates play an advisory role as members of some committees, but would prefer to be better informed on high-level management decisions, we were told. LeBoeuf is said to be fiscally conservative and economically stable. In the summer of 1992, the firm moved into new offices. First- and some second-year associates share offices, and every attorney has a personal computer with Windows and Wordperfect, access to LEXIS, and LAN access to a number of CD-ROM research tools which are relevant to the associate's practice. The office also has its own cafeteria.

recruits for maturity

As for recruitment, LeBoeuf is as interested in students' backgrounds as their grades and does not hire only those in the top 10 percent of their class. The firm "is receptive to people who have worked a few years between college and law school," according to one insider. Prior to entering law school, a few past summer associates had worked as paralegals or in the insurance industry. Overall, LeBoeuf seeks students who are "smart, dedicated, mature, interesting, and pleasant." People advised those interviewing with the firm to "emphasize your ability to be a human being. Be a person. They want to know what it would be like to work late with you." It never hurts to mention your ability to do good work, but "don't be neurotic," counseled one. The firm usually hires law students from the top national law schools and "law review types" from local New York schools.

One person commented that "at some level, LeBoeuf's clients are traditional and boring. Much of the work touches on insurance, even in the noninsurance departments." For some people, this can be a drawback. On the other hand, much of the cutting-edge work that the firm does, such as the demutualization of mutual insurance companies, changes the insurance industry. LeBoeuf has had major involvement recently in securitizations, derivative products and the wave of utility mergers. "The firm's clientele is increasingly diverse and less insurance-focused" than in the past, one contact pointed out to us. Associates at the firm have "more of their own life," and they are "more in control of the work." One person noted that LeBoeuf does not emphasize "success through sacrificing your life." LeBoeuf, Lamb, Greene & MacRae is an excellent choice for someone more interested in a balanced life than the excessive prestige and sacrifice offered by some other large New York law firms.

Milbank, Tweed, Hadley & McCloy

New York Los Angeles Washington
Hong Kong London Moscow Singapore Tokyo

Address:	One Chase Manhattan Plaza, New York, NY 10005
Telephone:	(212) 530–5000
Hiring Attorney:	Arnold Peinado/Theodore Burke
Contact:	Joanne DeZego, Recruiting Coordinator; (212) 530–5966
Associate Salary:	First year \$87,000 (1997); second \$103,000; third \$121,000; fourth \$143,000; fifth \$170,000; sixth \$185,000; seventh \$195,000
Summer Salary:	\$1673/week (1997)
Average Hours:	NA worked; NA billed; NA required.
Family Benefits:	Domestic partner benefits; 26 weeks S/T disability, male/female eligible; 4 weeks paid family leave (8 unpaid); emergency childcare; same sex benefits; dependent care program; employee assistance program
1996 Summer:	Class of 45 students; offers to 44
Partnership:	18% of entering associates from 1981–1984 were made partner
Pro Bono:	3% of all work is pro bono

Milbank, Tweed, Hadley & McCloy in 1997
229 Lawyers at the New York Office
1.7 Associates Per Partner

Total Partners 86			Total Associates 143			Practice Areas	
Women	7	8%	Women	50	35%	Corporate	140
All Minorities	2	2%	All Minorities	18	13%	Litigation	30
Asian-Am	1	1%	Afro-Am	3	2%	Bankruptcy	15
Latino	1	1%	Asian-Am	8	6%	Tax	15
			Latino	7	5%	Trusts & Estates	13
						Emerging Practices	11
						General	5

A pre-eminent Wall Street financial services firm, Milbank, Tweed, Hadley & McCloy doubled in size during the mergers and acquisitions (M&A) boom in the 1980s, only to have to downsize somewhat in the early 1990s when the boom went bust. More recently, Milbank has "significantly increased its hiring as business across the firm has rapidly grown," we were told. In the interim, Milbank reorganized its practice around certain areas, rather than around certain senior partners, and recently elected a new chairperson and executive committee who were described as "much younger and more progressive."

formal atmosphere

Although the work atmosphere at Milbank varies considerably by department, much of the firm's environment is informed by a fairly formal hierarchy. For example, in some departments people make clear distinctions between the partners, the senior associates, and the junior associates and, rather than dropping by each other's offices, attorneys may call each other to make appointments. Though attorneys dress in normal business attire, most do not wear their jackets all day. Women may wear pantsuits to work. Fridays are casual dress days. Milbank is not one of the more social firms in New York. Aside from small groups of friends, attorneys don't go out much after work. During the summer, each department organizes an event for summer associates.

primarily bank and finance

Primarily a financial services firm, historically Milbank's anchor client has been Chase Manhattan Bank. Today, the new Chase remains one of the firm's principal clients after the Chase/Chemical merger, and Milbank's offices are located in the Chase Manhattan building in downtown Manhattan. Although outsiders had expressed concern about the effect of the merger on Milbank, 1996 (the first year after the merger) was reportedly "the best year in Milbank's history." The firm also represents a variety of other national banks such as Citibank and J.P. Morgan, all of the major investment banks, numerous international banks, and large institutional investors. In addition, Milbank houses one of the foremost project finance practice groups in the country. The practice is a global one, with a particular focus on emerging markets. The firm's strong capital markets practice group is also very international, with a significant amount of work in Latin America and Asia. The general corporate/mergers and acquisitions group has become very busy in recent years. The firm also provides bank regulatory, institutional finance, real estate, and intellectual property and technology services to its clients. The firm's transportation finance group has over the last several years completed numerous industry leading "deals of the year," we were told.

bankruptcy litigation

Milbank has a strong bankruptcy practice that is independent of its corporate practice. This practice represents primarily creditors, but also represents some debtors. The litigation department is small in comparison to the corporate and financial services departments, but is broad and handles matters arising from mergers and acquisitions and large commercial transactions. William Webster, the former director of the CIA, joined Milbank's Washington, D.C. office in 1991 to help spearhead the firm's worldwide litigation practice. Since the arrival of Jeffrey Barist in 1996, the litigation practice has doubled in size.

tax
T&E

The large tax department provides a full spectrum of tax services, including counseling for domestic and international corporate transactions, individual planning, and litigation. Milbank also has a well-known trusts and estates department that has both a strong century-old relationship with the Rockefeller family and a long list of famous clients.

Milbank's international practice primarily involves its corporate, investment banking, and bank and institutional finance work. One of the first American firms to open a Tokyo office, Milbank has a strong Asian practice. The Asian practice further benefits from the firm's offices in Hong Kong and Singapore, as well as its affiliation with an Indonesian law firm. The firm also has a very active Latin American practice. Finally, the firm's London office is quite active in several areas of international project finance.

full-time pro bono partner

Milbank received positive reviews for its commitment to pro bono work. Partner Joe Genova coordinates the firm's pro bono activities on a full-time basis. Incidentally, he was very active in Judge Wapner's initiative to make pro bono mandatory for lawyers. Genova maintains a list of pro bono matters available for attorneys. Milbank offers every first-year associate the opportunity to do a three-month rotation with a public interest organization. Time spent on firm approved pro bono matters is given billable credit.

opportunities

New associates are usually assigned to the department of their preference. The firm reportedly looks, however, for associates with the flexibility to practice in more than one area. Associates in the busier departments, such as banking and institutional investment, capital markets, and project finance, usually get as much responsibility as they can handle. Many first-year associates are responsible for "small chunks of deals, document production, minute books, etc." In slower departments, on the other hand, "people are greedy about hoarding work," and junior associates tend not to get much responsibility. A firm spokesperson informed us that "within the past couple of years, this has not been an issue as all departments have been very busy." Associate workloads vary considerably from department to department; in 1996, associates averaged 2050 hours. Milbank has recently hired a "significant" number of lateral associates and partners, and the firm paid associates an additional bonus in 1996 because of the substantial firm profits for the year.

structured training

Milbank is committed to training and professional development. Its two-year "structured and intensive" training program for new associates is "very advanced and comprehensive." However, "on-the-job training is less available." The firm regularly invites professors and other professionals to teach courses in fields of interest to the attorneys. Associate performance is formally reviewed once a year. A summer associate who is not performing up to par will be notified by the mid-summer review.

progressive diversity committee

Although Milbank is reputedly a "white shoe" firm, it was described as "progressive" and "inclusive" of women and minorities. It has established a committee charged with diversifying the firm and, in recent summers, has sponsored a number of panel discussions on minority issues. Milbank is also trying to increase the number of senior associate women. The firm has a parental leave policy and has implemented same-sex health benefits. Firm policy requires that all written work use gender-neutral language.

Milbank is managed by a plethora of committees, although most major management decisions are made by an executive committee of three senior partners who are elected by the partnership. The firm also has a strategic planning committee that is charged with planning for and overseeing the firm's future development. The quality of life committee, developed to respond to associate concerns and better disseminate information, has become a number of smaller groups that work on specific projects, such as drafting the same sex benefits policy. Despite the increased involvement of associates in these aspects of the firm's management, one person claimed that associates still "feel totally in the dark." A firm spokesperson indicated that the firm is "actively undertaking several initiatives to improve communication across the firm." The firm has an "up-or-out" partnership track of eight to nine years.

committee management

Milbank's office facilities are spacious, with beautiful views of the harbor, the Statue of Liberty, and midtown Manhattan, but the downtown location is considered by some to be "inconvenient." The firm has expanded its space in a new mid-town location to better serve its mid-town clients. First-year associates share offices, and all attorneys, including summer associates, have their own computers. Laptops are readily available. The support staff was described as "professional." The firm has its own cafeteria.

Milbank hires law students who "have done well academically," and "who will fit in with the firm." One person noted that the ability to speak another language, particularly Spanish or an Asian language, is an asset. People advised applicants to emphasize in the interview why Milbank "is a good fit for you." One person advised applicants to emphasize "any commitment to foreign work, business experience, or languages." The firm hires students from the top third of their class from national law schools. It also hires top students from New York regional schools.

hiring tips

Morgan, Lewis & Bockius

New York Harrisburg Los Angeles Miami Philadelphia Princeton San Diego Washington
Brussels Frankfurt Jakarta London Singapore Tokyo

Address: 101 Park Avenue, New York, NY 10178
Telephone: (212) 309–6000
Hiring Attorney: Ian Shrank, Chair, Recruiting Committee
Contact: Brenda W. Ollman, Recruiting Administrator; (212) 309–6344
Associate Salary: First year $85,000 (1996)
Summer Salary: $1625/week (1996)
Average Hours: 2258 worked; 2043 billed; NA required
Family Benefits: Maternity leave
1996 Summer: Class of 27 students; offers to 26
Partnership: NA
Pro Bono: 1% of all work is pro bono

Morgan, Lewis & Bockius in 1997
226 Lawyers at the New York Office
2.0 Associates Per Partner

Total Partners 71		
Women	6	8%
All Minorities	3	4%
Asian-Am	1	1%
Latino	2	3%

Total Associates 145		
Women	62	42%
All Minorities	12	8%
Afro-Am	4	3%
Asian-Am	5	3%
Latino	3	2%

Practice Areas	
Business & Finance	101
Litigation	58
Labor (management)	18
International	15
Tax	12
Environmental	7
Personal Law	6
Real Estate	6

Morgan, Lewis & Bockius is one of the biggest law firms in the country. It has large offices in five major cities of the United States and six offices in Europe and the Far East. The New York office of Morgan Lewis has grown dramatically in recent years. The offices in New York, Philadelphia, and Washington each have over 200 lawyers. The firm prides itself on being a true "national" law firm and distinguishes itself from many New York-based firms by emphasizing its integrated, multi-office approach to complex problems.

humane work atmosphere

The work atmosphere at Morgan Lewis is distinct from that at most large New York firms. As one person pointed out, "They don't have the same attitude as Sullivan & Cromwell or Cleary." Everybody is treated as an "equal, regardless of their year." Morgan Lewis was described to us as "less high-pressured" and "humane." Its associates enjoy a pleasant work atmosphere, reasonable work hours for New York, and a balanced lifestyle.

practice areas

Morgan Lewis represents a wide variety of mostly large and medium-sized financial institutions and corporate clients, including Hitachi and Oppenheimer Co., Inc. The firm's business and finance department is organized around seven areas: mergers and acquisitions, securities, tax, equipment leasing and project finance, securitization, real estate, and bankruptcy. The firm has a strong leveraged leasing group that works on a variety of matters, including aircraft, real estate, and manufacturing facilities. Morgan Lewis also handles a number of corporate transactions that involve international issues and represents many Japanese, Latin American and European entities.

The litigation department covers a broad range of business and financial litigation. The department has a particularly active securities litigation practice, including for example a major role in the Orange County litigation, under the leadership of John Peloso, former Chief Trial Counsel for the New York office of the Securities and Exchange Commission (SEC). Peloso also has a regular column in the *New York Law Journal*. A number of other former SEC attorneys work at the firm, a few of whom are mentioned in *Den of Thieves*. One person noted that this practice provides associates with "great experience." Another growing practice area is intellectual property, where the litigators work closely with trademark, copyright and patent experts in the Washington, D.C. office.

nationally renowned labor group

The firm's nationally-renowned management-side labor and employment department is involved in all aspects of employment, labor, and employee relationships, including collective bargaining, development of employee policies, and all types of related litigation. This practice handles matters involving new areas of the law such as disability and harassment issues. The firm has a growing environmental department that provides both counseling and litigation services. The firm also has small real estate, and personal law (trusts and estates) departments. The pro bono practice was described as "faltering," but the firm "is working on it." The firm regularly circulates memos to all attorneys listing available pro bono matters. Pro bono hours are counted as billable hours.

opportunities

Associates receive "as much responsibility as they can handle." First- and second-year litigation assignments generally involve research, writing memos, and drafting briefs. In addition, junior litigation associates have attended court proceedings and are often included in strategy sessions and client meetings. Second-year associates regularly assist in taking depositions; third and fourth year associates often take depositions themselves. First- and second-year corporate associates frequently take charge of incorporations and closings. They also draft documents. Third- and fourth-year corporate associates are routinely involved in negotiations.

structured training

Morgan Lewis offers a structured training program. In addition to firmwide and office-wide training programs, each department organizes monthly training breakfasts to discuss specific areas of relevant law. Many litigation training sessions involve video presentations made by partners and associates. Written materials such as litigation tactics guidebooks and corporate forms are also made readily available. In addition, Morgan Lewis' informal atmosphere allows most associates to feel very comfortable discussing their projects with senior attorneys. Associates are formally reviewed every six months, and as part of this process "each associate's personal development goals are discussed."

social life

Morgan Lewis is a social firm. Most of its attorneys genuinely enjoy working together and are "very supportive" of each other. They usually keep their office doors open, and "you are always welcome to walk into anyone's office." The litigation attorneys are particularly "tight and get along well." The firm organizes well-attended cocktail parties on the last Thursday of every month.

lack of diversity

One of the few criticisms we received about Morgan Lewis concerned its lack of racial diversity. However, the firm is actively attempting to recruit more diverse summer classes. As for women, the firm has a number of influential female partners. Four of the 15 litigation partners are women, and the labor and corporate sections each has a woman partner.

management

Although governed as part of one large firm, Morgan Lewis New York has an independent client base and functions with relative autonomy. The New York office is managed conservatively by a five member managing committee and a managing partner. The office has laterally hired a number of attorneys in recent years and has grown significantly. Over the past decade, the firm has more than doubled in size, due in part to the addition of approximately 60 lawyers from the now defunct Lord, Day & Lord, Barrett Smith in 1994 and the more recent addition of six partners and several associates from Coudert Brothers. These expansions have caused "some growing pains" in accommodating the new arrivals in connection with office space and firm procedures. However, according to one source, "the upside is that it is exciting being part of a growing firm in the process of development." The firm's particularly high-growth areas are mergers and acquisitions, securities litigation and environmental, and it is always open to developing new departments.

functional elegant offices

Located at 101 Park Avenue near Grand Central Station in midtown Manhattan, Morgan Lewis offers beautiful views of the East and the Hudson Rivers. The light and airy offices contribute to the firm's pleasant work atmosphere. They were described as "functional" and "elegant" but "understated." First- and second-year associates share offices, but each has a personal computer networked to others by E-mail. The recycling bins strategically placed throughout the firm are evidence of the firm's environmental conscience. Associates particularly appreciate the phone system that identifies in-house callers by name, allowing them to avoid unwanted calls. Each floor is equipped with a kitchen area and coffee stations. People commented that the library is somewhat limited in resources but noted that books may be obtained from other law firms in New York. The support services were described as "great," although it is recommended that word-processing and copy center services be reserved in advance if needed after 9 P.M.

hiring practices

Morgan, Lewis & Bockius hires "outgoing, talkative, and friendly people with good academic backgrounds." The firm looks for "people that fit in." It "wants you to feel comfortable" and "wants people who like the firm and the atmosphere." People advised students interviewing with Morgan Lewis not to "put on an act." It is "a very honest place," explained one contact. You should "emphasize that you are a real person with a real personality." Another advised, "stress what is important to you." The firm usually hires students from the top national law schools and a number of New York and other east coast law schools.

Morgan Lewis is a well-established corporate law firm. At the same time, it is a humane firm that expects associates to bill about 50 hours per week. The firm does not permit attorneys to bank more than five days of their vacation time without approval from their section manager, and strongly encourages them to take the four weeks vacation to which they are entitled each year. Morgan Lewis lawyers enjoy working at the firm, particularly the labor attorneys who "really love what they are doing," declared one source. Morgan Lewis attracts people who want a balanced lifestyle and are unconcerned that the firm "doesn't lead the field" in compensation in New York; it should be noted, however, that the recent significant increase in compensation has brought Morgan Lewis into line with other major New York firms. Overall, Morgan Lewis offers a pleasant work atmosphere and cares about its attorneys.

Patterson, Belknap, Webb & Tyler

New York
Moscow

Address: 1133 Avenue of the Americas, New York, NY 10036
Telephone: (212) 336-2000
Hiring Attorney: Thomas W. Pippert
Contact: Robin L. Klum, Director of Professional Development; (212) 336-2733
Associate Salary: First year $85,000 (1997); the firm also pays for bar exam/course, provides salary advances and moving allowance, and pays for membership in two bar associations.
Summer Salary: $1643/week (1997)
Average Hours: 2000 worked; 1850 billed; no requirement.
Family Benefits: Disability (includes maternity); 6 weeks paid childcare leave for qualified men and women (0–26 unpaid); dependent care reimbursement; domestic partner benefits; employee assistance program
1996 Summer: Class of 8 2L students; offers to 8
Partnership: NA
Pro Bono: NA

Patterson, Belknap, Webb & Tyler in 1997
150 Lawyers at the Firm
1.8 Associates Per Partner

Total Partners 41		
Women	7	17%
All Minorities	0	0%

Total Associates 77		
Women	36	46%
All Minorities	7	9%
Afro-Am	6	8%
Latino	1	1%

Practice Areas	
Litigation	75
Corporate	34
Intellectual Property	25
International	24
Trusts & Estates	12
Exempt Organizations	12
Emp. Ben. & Executive Comp.	7
Products Liability	7
Tax	7
Real Estate	5
Bankruptcy/Creditor's Rights	4
Environmental	3

ties to local government

Patterson, Belknap, Webb & Tyler attracts "a lot of people who are refugees from other well-known 'sweatshop' firms in New York." Although there have been some recent changes, overall Patterson is a friendly firm with a "laid-back culture" where "people enjoy working." Some of its "kind of funky" young attorneys live in New York's East Village and Soho. They appreciate Patterson as a place where they can balance work with an outside life. The pay scale at Patterson is "somewhat lower" than at other large firms in the city and "the gap increases the more senior you become," but the hours worked are "moderate" by New York standards (1850 billable, 2000 total). Lastly, because Patterson is well-connected to the New York City community and government, attorneys often work on interesting local matters and have opportunities to become involved in government service.

In contrast to many of New York's stodgier firms, Patterson encourages its associates to become involved in the firm's management and governance. They even have had an opportunity to review partner performance anonymously. Though many major decisions are made by a seven person management committee, associates participate in the decisions which most directly affect them through the associates committee. One contact termed this description of active associate involvement "a stretch;" this person volunteered that "associates have the opportunity to comment upon decisions "after they have been made" Also, this person pointed out that "the associates committee was recently resurrected after a period of dormancy," which may signal greater associate activity in the future.

unusual practice

Patterson's litigation department houses a number of interesting subgroups which distinguish it from other New York firms. The firm is particularly noteworthy for its false advertising practice. Patterson has been involved in a number of trials in this area and has represented large corporations such as Johnson & Johnson, Pfizer Inc., Ciba-Geigy, Coca-Cola, Abbott Laboratories, Hertz Corporation, and the Rhone-Poulenc Rorer Group. The active intellectual property litigation practice has handled litigation concerning trademarks, copyrights, and patents for large corporations and well-known entertainers and composers. The litigation department also houses a strong media practice group which represents a number of television and cable TV stations, radio stations, and publishers. Past cases have included First Amendment issues, libel and slander, invasion of privacy, and enforcement of broadcast rights. The firm represents Capital Cities/ABC, Inc. and was involved in *Warner Wolf v. ABC*, a landmark employment contract case in the media field. Every year the firm organizes a trip for summer associates to watch the taping of World News Tonight and to meet Peter Jennings. The firm also represents Bill Cosby. Patterson provides other litigation services in product liability, antitrust, ERISA and benefits, securities, and other criminal litigation.

exempt organizations

The smaller corporate department is renowned for its exempt organizations practice group. Also known as the not-for-profit group, it is one of the largest practices of its kind in New York. The firm represents more than one hundred public charities, private foundations, and charitable trusts for whom it provides a full range of corporate, tax, and general counseling services. Its wide range of clients include the Rockefeller Foundation, the New York Wildlife Conservation Society, the FBI Agents Association, and the American University of Beirut. Patterson also has one of New York's most highly regarded trusts and estates departments, which represents several high profile and wealthy individuals and families. The corporate department also offers the full array of corporate legal services for a variety of large corporate clients, including Time, Inc., AT&T, and the Discovery Channel.

This firm has built a thriving practice in Russia and the rest of the CIS and now has a Moscow office. Patterson served as principal counsel to Dr. Andrei Sakharov before he passed away and is currently counsel to the Andrei Sakharov Foundation. It also represents the Central Asian Republic of Kyrgyzstan. The firm has been involved in a number of other projects in the region, ranging from work on legal reforms to organizing humanitarian relief shipments to Armenia, Azerbaijan, Russia, Georgia and South Ossetia. The firm has also provided legal services to U.S. clients who wish to do business in that part of the world.

pro bono rotation

Patterson heavily encourages associate involvement in pro bono and community projects. Partner Lisa Cleary has "organized the firm's pro bono activities and encourages partner and associate involvement." The firm has close ties to the New York Corporation Counsel's office and permits senior associates to rotate through the office for a few months at a time. Junior associates may also work at the Corporation Counsel' office for a two week stint, usually taking depositions. Summer associates are welcomed and encouraged to participate in the firm's extensive pro bono program. Patterson has an ongoing project carried out in cooperation with St. Luke's Hospital "to provide wills, health care proxies and standby guardianship documents for indigent AIDS patients." Patterson is also a leading provider to government authorities of pro bono public investigation services. Some of the firm's attorneys conducted an investigation into human rights abuses in El Salvador at the request of the State Department. The firm has also conducted several investigations at the request of the Mayor of New York and other city officials. Counsel Harold R. Tyler, Jr. oversees many of the public investigations performed by the firm. Tyler is a former United States District Judge and Deputy Attorney General of the United States.

Because Patterson has close ties to the government, many who leave the firm go on to work at the U.S. Attorney's office, the Mayor's office or other government offices. Former partners of the firm include the Mayor of New York City, the Secretary of the Army, the District Attorney for New York County and two United States District Judges for the Southern District of New York. Current partners and counsel of the firm have served as Undersecretary of State and General Counsel to the Department of Defense. President Clinton's chief speech writer is a former Patterson lawyer.

flexible work assignments

The work atmosphere at Patterson is informal and friendly, and attorneys "work well together." Patterson is proud of its "generally well deserved" reputation as a cordial workplace and works hard to maintain this atmosphere. Summer associates and first-years are assigned an associate and partner mentor who oversees their progress and answers any questions they have. New associates are generally assigned to one, or in some cases two, practice areas. Associates may solicit their assignments directly from partners or obtain them from an assignment coordinator.

Associates usually work directly with partners and receive as much responsibility "as they can handle." Young associates are "a lot more than paper-pushers," asserted one source. First-year litigation associates engage primarily in research and writing; second- and third-year associates regularly take depositions but occasionally handle small cases themselves. Sixth-year associates are actively involved in court trials. Associates outside of litigation are "often in contact with clients from their first year, and by the time the attorney is a mid-level, he or she will probably be dealing with certain clients on a regular basis and reporting back to the partner on the status of the matter," according to one contact. Feedback and training at Patterson leave something to be desired. According to one source, "many Patterson attorneys are not great about giving regular, day-to-day training and feedback. The firm has been criticized for this before and, unfortunately, its response has been to institute in-house training seminars which are often scheduled on Saturdays. The partners are enthusiastic about these, but many associates find them to be of questionable value." Associates are reviewed every six months for their first two years at the firm and every year thereafter.

Scotch Parties

Patterson associates enjoy an active social life. A medium-sized firm by New York standards, its attorneys "genuinely enjoy hanging out with each other," and often form long lasting friendships. "Many Patterson associates feel that their fellow associates are the best thing about the firm," reported one person. Younger associates, in particular, often go out after work for dinner and drinks. Patterson organizes a number of fun and informal social events, especially during the summer months. It is not uncommon, we were told, "to be sitting in your office on a Friday afternoon and hear bagpipes blasting over the PA system." Everyone knows that this signals another "Scotch Party," where attorneys congregate in one of the conference rooms for a buffet of Scottish food and "tons of scotch" for tasting. Arriving or departing attorneys are often feted at a "tea"—"a firmwide cocktail party at which are served plenty of finger food, wine and beer but, curiously, no tea."

part-time schedules difficult

Patterson is a diverse firm. Its attorneys are actively involved in both Democratic and Republican politics and events. It has few minority associates, but is making a strong effort to recruit more. Patterson generally received high reviews regarding its treatment of women in the workplace. Female partner Antonia Grumbach is the firm's former managing partner and highly-respected head of the exempt organizations practice group. In addition, Patterson is a "family oriented firm." Its attorneys "accommodate each others' families" and some women attorneys work part-time, but the story here is not wholly encouraging. One insider informed us that "while there are still a handful of part-time lawyers, it should be noted that it is very difficult for litigators to get or maintain part-time status, either because their request is denied or because the attorney doesn't get support from the people she works for. Non-litigators do better, but sometimes run into the problem of trying to manage a full work load on a part-time schedule for part-time pay." Patterson has a very generous childcare leave policy, and "generally speaking, people take full advantage of it and are not penalized for doing so." One insider judged that "overall, women at Patterson are not as satisfied as they used to be, although it is still a better place than most."

new plush offices

Patterson recently relocated from the Rockefeller Center to offices at 43rd Street and the Avenue of the Americas. The new facilities, designed by architecture giant Gensler and Associates, were described by our contacts as "plush," "very nice," and "nicely furnished." The cafeteria is "not bad," although it closes at 4 P.M. One insider surmised that "this may partly be to encourage us not to work all night." First year associates have to share office space. The support staff is "pretty good," though attorneys have to reserve support staff time after 5 P.M, and junior attorneys who share a secretary with a partner may have a hard time getting their work done. The firm's computers are on Word Perfect 6.1 for Windows. The firm has E-mail on the Internet, "but the only access to the Web is in the library." The library staff was described as "excellent."

non-elitist recruiting

Patterson hires "smart people who write well, but it is also concerned with personality." In fact, the firm regularly "turns down law review editors who are too intense and too cranky," revealed one source. It prefers "outgoing and social people" with interesting backgrounds. A number of past summer associates had been in other careers before going to law school. Some had been accountants, others worked on Capitol Hill, and one worked in a radio station. "Outside interests" are just as important to hiring decisions as interest in the law, according to one person. Patterson is "not elitist" and recruits from a broad range of east coast law schools including Brooklyn, Fordham, SUNY at Albany, and other New York schools, in addition to the top national schools.

As at many firms around the city, the early 1990s saw an increasing focus at Patterson on the bottom line and hours worked. "The nature of the firm has changed somewhat as a new generation of partners has come in—some lateral, some not—whose main pursuit is profit," according to one insider. This person additionally observed that "the firm has begun to hire a new breed of associates who are more work horses than Patterson people have typically been in the past. Economically, all this has paid off in that the firm is in great financial shape. In terms of the firm's culture, it has taken its toll in that Patterson is not as nice a place to be as it once was. That being said, I still believe it is a better place than the majority of big firms around the city, and there are plenty of 'old-line' partners and associates around who struggle to keep the faith with the firm's reputation."

Paul, Weiss, Rifkind, Wharton & Garrison

New York Washington
Beijing Hong Kong Paris Tokyo

Address: 1285 Avenue of the Americas, New York, NY 10019–6064
Telephone: (212) 373–3000
Hiring Attorney: Jay Cohen
Contact: Mindy J. Peck, Legal Recruitment Coordinator; (212) 373–2481
Associate Salary: First year $86,000 (1996) plus $2000 bonus; second $98,000 plus $5000; third $113,000 plus $10,000; fourth $132,000 plus $13,000; fifth $153,000 plus $17,000; sixth $165,000 plus $20,000; seventh $172,00 plus $23,000; eighth $178,000 plus $25,000
Summer Salary: $1650/week (1997)
Average Hours: 2025 worked (1996); 1875 billed (1996); NA required
Family Benefits: Health (including domestic partner); life; maternity and paternity leave; emergency childcare program; health care flexible spending account; relocation expenses
1996 Summer: Class of 59 students; offers to 59
Partnership: 5% of entering associates from 1984–1987 were made partner
Pro Bono: 5% of all work is pro bono

Paul, Weiss, Rifkind, Wharton & Garrison in 1997
295 Lawyers at the New York Office
2.3 Associates Per Partner

Total Partners 84		
Women	8	10%
All Minorities	3	4%
Afro-Am	1	1%
Latino	2	2%

Total Associates 194		
Women	80	41%
All Minorities	43	22%
Afro-Am	16	8%
Asian-Am	25	13%
Latino	2	1%

Practice Areas	
Litigation	111
Corporate	109
Tax	26
Real Estate	18
Bankruptcy	14
Trusts, Estates & Wills	9
Entertainment	5
Environmental	3

Founded as a place where people of different religions and ethnicities could work together, Paul Weiss was one of the first New York firms to hire non-WASP lawyers. Paul Weiss is also a self-described liberal Democratic law firm. Attorneys joke that only two of its partners are Republicans, although the addition of former Republican Senator Warren Rudman has bolstered their ranks. Paul Weiss has many ties to national Democratic politics, subscribes to diverse hiring practices, and is strongly committed to pro bono work. Its attorneys are characterized by their "high credentials," the fact that they "genuinely enjoy the law," and their drive to work extremely long hours. One contact pointed out, however, that "oftentimes, the more overtly cynical of the partners seem to go out of their way to remind associates that the bottom line is hours and money. That message all too frequently drowns out the 'genuinely enjoy the law' attitude."

intense hierarchical atmosphere

Paul Weiss is a "very busy place." Though one occasionally hears an attorney "bark orders," overall the firm is "very friendly and supportive." There is, however, considerable pressure to work long hours if "you want to move up through the firm hierarchy." One person noted that "the more you are over 2000 hours, the more likely you are to catch the eye of partners. The high billers (people who bill about 2500 hours) are renowned" at the firm. With a hierarchical atmosphere, the "partner-associate distinction is very evident" at Paul Weiss. Because "partners are extremely busy, you only bother them if you have something important" to talk about. On the other hand, associates interact comfortably with partners for whom they work regularly. Attorneys address each other by first names and usually take off their jackets in the office.

top-notch litigation practice

Paul Weiss has perhaps the most prestigious general litigation practice and some of the most well-known litigators in the nation. Arthur Liman is a luminary of the department and is famous for his appointment as Senate Special Counsel in the Iran-Contra investigation. He is also well-known for his role as chief counsel to Michael Milken. Lewis Kaplan, a pre-eminent commercial litigation lawyer, has recently been appointed to a seat on the U.S. District Court for the Southern District of New York. Another litigator, Jay Topkis, now of counsel at the firm, has argued a number of cases before the U.S. Supreme Court, including many involving death penalty issues. Colleen McMahon was appointed Acting Justice, New York Supreme Court, Bronx County (criminal division). The litigation department, which has slimmed down since our last edition, continues to represent a wide range of large enterprises, governments, and wealthy individuals. A team headed by Martin London handles the Sumitomo litigation worldwide; this client reported losses of $2.6 billion in connection with unauthorized copper trades.

corporate

The corporate department, traditionally overshadowed by the litigation department, is now roughly the same size as the litigation group. It is home to "some screamers," warned one source, noting that some partners have been known to yell at the associates. The department handles a significant amount of international work. Paul Weiss has a 12 attorney office in Paris and a smaller four attorney office in Tokyo. It has also established a two lawyer office in Beijing, and a six lawyer office in Hong Kong. The firm has growing practices in bankruptcy, banking, and environmental law, and a smaller but longstanding entertainment department.

commitment to pro bono

Paul Weiss has a serious commitment to pro bono. It is "very important to their self-image as a big, liberal firm," noted one observer. The firm has handled a number of death penalty cases, as well as many other high-profile public interest litigations. Pro bono work is treated like "real work," and some attorneys spend 20 to 30 percent of their time on pro bono matters. One contact observed that the firm's "commitment to pro bono work is genuine, with numerous partners setting the example by handling pro bono matters or encouraging and supporting matters handled by associates."

In addition to its pro bono work, Paul Weiss has long been known for its commitment to public service. Corporate partner Matthew Nimetz, who served as counselor to the State Department under former President Carter, was appointed by President Clinton to serve as a mediator between the former Yugoslav Republic of Macedonia and Greece. Corporate partner Theodore Sorenson served as Special Counsel to President Kennedy. More recently, the firm's Lesley Friedman received the Outstanding Young Lawyer of 1997 award from the New York State Bar Association. This award is given annually to the young lawyer, in practice for less than 10 years, who has the most "distinguished record of commitment to the finest tradition of the Bar through public service and professional activities," a firm spokesperson informed us.

training opportunities feedback

Paul Weiss provides a full range of continuing legal education and other training seminars. New associates attend a retreat held soon after their arrival in the fall, as well as a lecture and lunch series. The on-the-job training and opportunities for responsibility are generally good. In particular, the litigation department is now "slightly understaffed, so there is an increasing work load and more opportunities to take on greater responsibility early on," reported one insider. Junior corporate associates are likewise entrusted with quite a bit of responsibility, we were told. One criticism we heard in these matters was that "associates are fairly consistently overworked and underappreciated, and that not enough effort is made by the firm to encourage, and provide time for, associates concentrating on their own professional development." Paul Weiss formally reviews new associates two times a year, but some people claimed the reviews are "perfunctory." Reviews after the first year are performed annually.

The "work hard, stay late" ethic minimizes the social life of Paul Weiss lawyers. Most people go home at the end of a long day. However, because associates work long hours together, they often form close friendships. The firm organizes a Friday cocktail party which is usually attended by 20 to 40 attorneys.

diversity

Paul Weiss "prides itself" on the diversity in its history, and it has a good showing of women and minorities in its associate ranks, "but it has not had much luck in promoting women and minorities to partners," one person commented. The firm has one African-American counsel, Leon Higginbotham, formerly the Chief Judge of the Third Circuit Court of Appeals. The firm freely discusses with associates its concern about the low number of female partners. Its maternity leave policy offers 12 weeks of paid leave, and the firm offers emergency day care facilities at no individual cost to all personnel.

management

Paul Weiss is governed under a committee system with all partners having an equal vote. A 10 partner "Committee on Committees," presently headed by Alfred Youngwood, appoints the members of all other committees. Paul Weiss has "state-of-the-art" office facilities decorated with an "incredible modern art collection." Every associate is assigned to a private office, and the support staff is excellent. "You can get anything you want done at any hour," marveled one admirer.

academic emphasis in hiring

As for recruitment, Paul Weiss is a selective firm which values high grades and other academic achievements. At the top national law schools, it "looks for an A or two in a real class," and at the other law schools it seeks law review students. It also looks to hire people with an "eclectic or internationally oriented" background. People advised applicants to "emphasize their academic credentials" more than their "desire...to make money." Another counseled applicants to "give the impression that you are a grind and will get the work done."

Paul Weiss associates work long hours and must prove themselves before they are entrusted with significant responsibility. The firm is not terribly stuffy, handles extremely high-profile matters, and has an outstanding reputation for pro bono work, but very few associates have made partner in recent years. It is a large New York law firm with a world-class legal practice and perhaps the best litigation department around.

Pennie & Edmonds

New York Palo Alto Washington

Address: 1155 Avenue of the Americas, New York, NY 10036
Telephone: (212) 790–9090
Hiring Attorney: Frank E. Morris and Thomas E. Friebel
Contact: Patricia Stacey, Recruitment Administrator; (212) 790–2908
Associate Salary: First year $86,000 (1997); second $95,000; third $105,000; fourth $113,000; fifth $125,000; sixth $135,000; seventh $145,000; all figures are base salary figures, additional bonuses are given
Summer Salary: $1650/week (1997)
Average Hours: 2025 worked; 2000 billed; 1900 required
Family Benefits: Health insurance (self-dependents); maternity leave
1996 Summer: Class of 22 students; offers to 21
Partnership: NA
Pro Bono: 1–3% of all work is pro bono

Pennie & Edmonds in 1997
111 Lawyers at the New York Office
1.8 Associates Per Partner

Total Partners 39			Total Associates 72			Practice Areas	
Women	4	10%	Women	26	36%	Patents	81
All Minorities	0	0%	All Minorities	9	13%	Trademarks/Copyright	30
			Afro-Am	1	1%		
			Asian-Am	7	10%		
			Latino	1	1%		

intellectual property practice

One of the nation's most prestigious intellectual property firms, Pennie & Edmonds is flourishing. The firm more than doubled in size during the 1980s, when intellectual property law became "hot," and it opened a Menlo Park office in the heart of Silicon Valley in the early 1990s, which it has since moved into new quarters in Palo Alto. About 70 percent of the firm's work involves patent litigation and prosecution (the drafting and filing of patent applications). The patent department is informally organized in practice groups around areas of expertise such as electrical engineering, mechanical engineering, biotechnology, and chemistry. Pennie & Edmonds also handles other intellectual property work including trademark, copyright, unfair competition, and trade secrets law. The trademark department is less technical than the patent department, and there is little interaction between the two in prosecution matters, though they work together on litigation questions. The firm is also engaged in related licensing and contract litigation issues, and does some general corporate work for smaller companies.

Pennie & Edmonds represents a wide variety of entities and individuals. Its clientele includes large corporations such as Hewlett Packard and Bristol Myers Squibb, a number of pharmaceutical companies, many start-up high-tech companies and universities, and occasionally, small inventors. It is particularly well-regarded for its specialization in intellectual property matters involving biotechnology concerns. The biotech work is handled in all three offices; the largest practice group is in New York. The Palo Alto office has a very large electrical engineering/computer practice, we were told. The firm is famous for defending Hewlett-Packard against a claim brought by Apple alleging theft of a graphic interface. The firm's practice also extends to the international arena; it is affiliated with local counsel in a number of foreign countries, primarily in the European Community and Asia. Pro bono work was described as "virtually non-existent" at the firm. Pennie & Edmonds does, however, give billable hour credit for time spent on pro bono.

businesslike culture

Pennie & Edmonds is a "very busy and work oriented" firm. Its attorneys are "professional and very dedicated to the work that they do." The firm makes clear during the new associate orientation that the male dress code includes a jacket, a tie, and a dress shirt. Attorneys, however, exercise a fair amount of leeway within this code, and the firm recently instituted "casual Fridays" during the summer months firmwide.

professional development

New associates are hired into specific groups, but the group assignment is extremely informal and is based on the associate's educational background and work experience. New associates generally receive work assignments from the senior attorneys in their group and often work with attorneys from other groups as well. Opportunities for responsibility vary by type of work and experience. Those associates engaged in patent prosecution often draft and process patent applications independently, and "there is a great deal of client contact early on," reported one insider. This work almost always requires a strong technical background. Associates in intellectual property litigation, however, receive considerably less responsibility since these cases are unusually large and complex. Responsibility in the larger cases, as in most firms, is "kept pretty close to the partners' chests," revealed one insider. First- and second-year litigation assignments typically involve library research, writing memos, and drafting court papers. Only occasionally do associates take depositions during their first few years. With few exceptions, only senior associates "handle cases with partners."

Pennie & Edmonds "gives its new associates very little formal guidance. It often seems as if we are thrown into the deep end of a pool and are expected to learn to swim on our own," reported one insider. Each practice group does, however, meet regularly to discuss active client matters, and the firm has a continuing legal education program. First-year associates attend a 12 week training course consisting of four two-hour sessions each on litigation, patents, and trademarks/copyrights. The National Institute for Trial Advocacy also conducts a deposition program in-house. People we interviewed were not impressed with the feedback provided on associate work product. Associates have to "really pursue" feedback to get any, disclosed one source, and another labeled the firm's formal reviews a mere "formality."

high turnover

Working at Pennie & Edmonds opens doors to many new career options. We were told that the "headhunters begin to call you once you pass the patent bar." These opportunities, combined with the fact that partnership opportunities are limited, that the firm has a two-tier partnership system, that the work hours are long, and that "salaries are not equal to those at other firms or in-house," have resulted in a fairly high turnover rate among associates.

minimal social life

While Pennie & Edmonds typically sponsors a few social events throughout the year, it is "not a party firm." Associates often go out to lunch together during the day, but socialize infrequently after work. The firm sponsors several sports teams, including co-ed volleyball, basketball, and softball teams, and attorneys often go out for dinner and drinks after games.

homogeneity in attorneys

Like most intellectual property law firms, Pennie & Edmonds is having difficulty increasing the diversity of its attorneys. Those we interviewed claimed that the small number of women and people of color is in part attributable to the "specialized nature" of the firm's practice which traditionally has attracted few people from these groups. Nevertheless, one person commented that though the firm is not discriminatory, it does not actively recruit minority students. Lately, the firm has made some progress with regard to women. Four of the 15 attorneys who became partners since 1993 are women.

conservative management

Pennie & Edmonds is governed by an executive committee. The firm was criticized for being "less structured from a management standpoint than other firms; there are no managing partners or set departments and there are only loosely organized practice groups." Though it does not have a managing partner, a few partners are considered particularly influential at the firm because they generate a lot of clients. S. Leslie Misrock is one of the well-known rainmakers. He greatly contributed to the expansion of the firm's patent practice. As Pennie & Edmonds has thrived economically, it has become increasingly "like a Wall Street law firm." As a part of this process, it has become significantly more leveraged in recent years, with its associate to partner ratio increasing from 1:1 to almost 2:1. With the opening of the Palo Alto office, the firm's biotechnology practice continues to expand. Palo Alto also has a very large and growing computer practice.

The firm's office facilities reflect, according to some people we interviewed, its conservative and "frugal" management style. Despite the additional floor space which the firm has leased in recent years, the office space is still inadequate. We heard complaints about associates sharing crowded offices in their initial years and the cramped library. All associates receive computers that are networked, but according to one person, Pennie & Edmonds is "not on the forefront of computer technology." A firm spokesperson informed us that efforts are underway to address both the office space and computer system inadequacies.

hiring tips

Pennie & Edmonds hires students with a "strong science background" and a willingness to "work hard." Of the 21 summer associates in 1996, 15 had advanced degrees of some sort ranging from the sciences to business management; few attended law school directly from college. The firm also hires a few people with a liberal arts background to work in the trademark department. The firm usually recruits law students who are in the upper-half of their law school class from the top national law schools and New York regional schools. Pennie & Edmonds also recruits at graduate schools in the sciences for Ph.D. candidates. It hires these students as law clerks and covers their night law school expenses. Sources advised applicants to emphasize their technical background, interest in intellectual property, and their competence to handle technical materials. Interviewees should explain why they want to do intellectual property law.

Pennie & Edmonds is one of the premier intellectual property law firms in the country. Young associates have ample opportunity to assume substantial responsibility in patent prosecutions and to be exposed to high-profile, complex litigations. Pennie & Edmonds, moreover, provides a "relaxed working atmosphere," with people who are "generally helpful, friendly, and professional." The drawbacks at Pennie & Edmonds are common to many large New York law firms: its office facilities are somewhat cramped, associates work long hours, "the partners and senior associates are too busy to do much teaching," and as the firm has become larger, it has grown more impersonal. It is, however, a great choice for people who are interested in technology and intellectual property issues.

Proskauer Rose

New York Boca Raton Clifton Los Angeles Washington
Paris

Address: 1585 Broadway, New York, NY 10036
Telephone: (212) 969–3000
Hiring Attorney: Perry A. Cacace
Contact: Kristin J. Williams, Coordinator of Recruiting & Associate Programs; (212) 969–5076
Associate Salary: First year $87,000 (1997); second $103,000; third $121,000; fourth $145,000; fifth $168,000; sixth $190,000; seventh $205,000; salary figures include bonuses
Summer Salary: $1638/week (1997); includes summer bonus
Average Hours: NA worked; NA billed; 2000 required.
Family Benefits: Health & life insurance; paid disability leave; same sex domestic partner benefits; paid childcare leave, followed by unpaid leave; emergency child-care; 4 weeks vacation; 401K plan; flexible spending program
1996 Summer: Class of 41 students; offers to 41
Partnership: NA
Pro Bono: 2% of all work pro bono

Proskauer Rose Goetz & Mendelsohn in 1997
361 Lawyers at the New York Office
1.7 Associates Per Partner

Total Partners 123		
Women	11	9%
All Minorities	2	2%
Afro-Am	2	2%

Total Associates 211		
Women	87	41%
All Minorities	29	14%
Afro-Am	8	4%
Asian-Am	11	5%
Latino	10	5%

Practice Areas	
Litigation/Appellate/Arbitration	80
Labor/Employment	69
Corporate/Securities/Int'l	60
Health/Sports/Intel. Property	29
Real Estate/Environmental	29
Employee Benefits/ERISA	22
Bankruptcy/Creditor's Rights	11
Estates/Trusts/Wills/Probate	8
Tax	8

individualist culture

Although Proskauer Rose was founded over a century ago, the firm is "less traditional" than one might expect. This once largely Jewish firm is characterized by a "culture of individualism," commented a number of insiders. "Women...wear pants and men...have beards because Proskauer emphasizes quality of work rather than appearances," noted one of our contacts. Moreover, with several women in prominent leadership positions, the firm prides itself on welcoming attorneys from traditionally underrepresented groups. It was not until 1993, however, that the first person of color entered the partnership ranks.

The atmosphere at Proskauer is professional, but down-to-earth. A walk through the halls reveals busy attorneys, open doors, and uninhibited exchange. The "stuffiness factor" is rather low, observed one source. Everyone, including the chairman of the firm, is addressed on a first name basis. One contact was quite emphatic that the people at Proskauer are its biggest asset: "I walk down these halls always smiling because the associates and partners alike are not only friendly, but genuinely engaging and interesting people. Everyone can be themselves here, quirks and all." Proskauer attorneys take a well-balanced approach to their work, we were told. One associate noted somewhat tongue-in-cheek that "no matter how busy you are, you are always expected to take calls from your mother." This balanced lifestyle may, however, be changing as the firm increasingly focuses on billable hours. These changes are described below.

Wearing one's jacket around the office is highly uncommon, and attorneys are not bashful in their dress. Double breasted suits are common for men and women don pants without remorse. "Men wear 'funky' ties and women often show off colorful scarves or jewelry," one insider reported. Another contact observed, "No posturing is necessary and you can be yourself as long as you do good work. There is no need to try to fit some pre-conceived mold."

Trashy Movie Club

Litigation associates have a special method of boosting morale in their department. Rather than assembling for another free lunch and inspirational speech, anonymous members of "The Trashy Movie Club" sneak away a couple of times a year during their lunch hour to catch an adventure film; Segal and Stallone are longstanding favorites.

Like a number of its New York counterparts, Proskauer downsized somewhat in the early 1990s but has made a significant recovery since then. The firm now has so much business that associates aren't concerned about job security, we were told. Proskauer added a group of 20 attorneys from the now-defunct firm of Shea & Gould in 1994. The firm continues to hire laterals, including a recent handful of litigators from Anderson Kill and a securities law group from another large New York City firm.

practice areas

Proskauer is a large multi-practice firm with approximately 470 attorneys firmwide. Some of the firm's most high-profile work involves representation of sports-related clients such as the NBA, NHL, Madison Square Garden, and the ATP Tour. With former Proskauer attorneys David Stern and Gary Bettman at the helm of the NBA and NHL respectively, some of our contacts amusedly referred to the firm as "a breeding ground for sports commissioners."

labor

Proskauer is probably best known, however, for its management-side labor and employment law department, which its attorneys consider to be "the best, most diverse practice in New York, and perhaps in the country." The labor department is consistently the busiest in the firm. Its client list includes United Parcel Service, *The New York Times*, NBC, Museum of Modern Art, Columbia University, and the City of New York. Proskauer is involved in all aspects of labor and employment law including collective bargaining, grievance and interest arbitrations, discrimination litigation, employee benefits work, and immigration law.

While labor associates work harder than others at the firm, they are given "a tremendous amount of responsibility." Labor associates reportedly have a "macho," "superior," or "labor-centric" attitude about their hours and responsibilities as compared to other associates in the firm. Cases are routinely staffed with only one partner and one associate, and it is not uncommon for second- and third-year associates to take and defend depositions, conduct arbitrations, and participate in settlement negotiations. One contact informed us that "I have taken or defended at least 50 depositions, managed my own federal litigation, and in several arbitrations presented direct testimony at federal trial." Another labor associate remarked, "I love my job. I just wish I didn't have to do quite so much of it." Labor associates are a "close-knit" group, with "very little competition, rather a spirit of camaraderie, who frequently gather in a conference room for dinner to chat about work, social life, etc." In addition, labor associates hold monthly "union meetings" during which time they discuss issues they would like to bring to the partnership's attention. A result of these efforts was the hiring of an assignment manager "which has greatly improved the work assignment process in the department."

litigation

Proskauer's litigation practice largely developed after Judge Joseph Proskauer joined the firm as its senior member in 1930. Today, it is the biggest department in the firm and handles a number of large complex matters. For instance, over a dozen attorneys recently represented the NBA in various antitrust actions across the country. Like many of their New York counterparts, litigation associates complain about such drawbacks as unpredictable hours and limited responsibility. However, the firm's willingness to take on smaller matters for existing clients provides some opportunities for junior litigators to play a greater role. Proskauer's litigation clients include MCI, AVIS, Met Life, Barney's, ICN Pharmaceuticals, NBA, NHL and the American Association of Publishers.

corporate

The corporate department represents domestic and international enterprises, both for profit and non-profit, in connection with transactional work as well as day-to-day legal counseling. The "non-hierarchical structure" of the department provides associates with frequent one-on-one contact with both partners and clients. Matters are often leanly staffed: a typical associate is involved in everything from corporate minutes and securities work to acquisitions and partnership assignments. Although associates rarely become heavily involved in large securities offerings, they often take charge of small acquisitions. One associate noted that although the responsibility can be daunting, it is eased by the fact that "a lot of people are willing to take an interest in your professional development."

real estate

Proskauer's real estate department expanded with the addition of six attorneys from Shea & Gould, including leasing expert Lawrence Lipson. With that group came a number of high-profile clients. Although the department's practice is broad-ranging, it has a particular expertise in partnership syndications, sale/leaseback transactions, and other forms of complex real estate financings.

pro bono

Proskauer's well-organized pro bono program is coordinated by Special Counsel Will Hellerstein, who is also a professor at Brooklyn Law School and served as Attorney-in-Charge of the Criminal Appeals Bureau of the Legal Aid Society of New York for over 15 years. Our contacts praised Hellerstein for "choosing challenging, cutting-edge cases" for interested attorneys. One third-year associate recently argued a case of first impression before the New York State Court of Appeals. Another commented, "I'm really impressed that the firm allowed three of us to spend a month working almost exclusively on a single prisoner's rights case." While Proskauer is still committed to pro bono work, "it has recently changed its policy of counting all pro bono hours as billable to only counting 125 hours as billable towards the 2000 hours billable requirements," we were told.

Proskauer attorneys maintain a number of leadership positions in New York's legal community. Bettina Plevan, a labor partner and a leading expert on sexual harassment law, serves as Co-Chair of the Second Circuit Committee on Gender Bias in the Law. Litigation partner Steven Krane serves as Chair of the Committee on Professional and Judicial Ethics of the Association of the Bar of the City of New York. Special Counsel Martha Gifford was recently elected President of the New York Women's Bar Association, and Michael Cardozo, president of the Association of the Bar of the City of New York.

professional development

Associates offered mixed reviews about the quality of the training at Proskauer. While labor associates extolled the virtues of learning from some of the best in the country, associates in other departments felt that guidance was "inconsistent" and "sometimes lacking". One remarked, "In litigation, they treat you really nicely, make you feel good and then hand you a terrible assignment on the way out. In labor, they bark and scream, and then give you a fantastic assignment on the way out." In response to associates' concerns regarding training and professional development, the firm created the position of Director of Professional Administration to implement a formal associate development plan. Proskauer also recently initiated a series of communication workshops led by professional consultants and designed to enhance presentation skills.

First-year Proskauer associates may spend up to 30 weeks fielding assignments from a variety of departments before deciding which one to join. Upon joining a department, associates are encouraged to work on a broad range of assignments within that practice area. One associate commented, "At Proskauer, you can be a generalist within your field and not feel pressure to specialize in a particular practice group."

efforts to foster unity

In June 1997, Proskauer will hold its second firm-wide attorney weekend retreat in an effort to foster an atmosphere of teamwork and unity. One associate, commenting on the first retreat held in 1994, stated that "while many associates were reluctant to give up another summer weekend to the firm, most of us were surprised at how much fun it was." This "team building" event included everything from hypothetical discussions about work-related dilemmas to rock climbing and "late night carousing" with members of the Executive Committee.

offices

Proskauer moved to new offices in 1992 at 1585 Broadway, just one block from Times Square. While some of our sources complain about being located in the heart of New York's tourism Mecca, others enjoy the proximity to Penn Station, Port Authority, the major Broadway shows, and "excellent restaurants." The firm recently updated its computer system, converting to Windows 95. The offices are comfortably furnished and most entering associates occupy their own office by the end of their first year. All associate offices are good sized and all have windows. New York Knicks artwork dominates one conference room and provides a welcome diversion for the sports enthusiast. A cafeteria on the 27th floor serves three meals a day, which are described as "surprisingly good, hearty, and cheap."

new focus on the bottom line

While Proskauer may lack some of the name recognition enjoyed by its large Manhattan counterparts, it offers its attorneys an opportunity to do cutting-edge work for high-profile clients, "without having to sacrifice a life outside the office." Some of these attractive features may be changing, however. We were told that the firm is becoming more focused on the bottom line. In January, 1996 Proskauer "specifically announced that it expected its associates to bill a minimum of 2000 billable hours per year," a total which, according to a firm spokesperson, includes up to 125 hours of pro bono work and 75 hours of training experiences. One source informed us that "what made this firm 'unique' and 'the choice' for many of us top law students was that it wasn't like Cravath or Fried Frank or Davis Polk. Now Proskauer is coming in line (both salary-wise and hours-wise) to the other big firms in New York. The 2000 hour minimum requirement itself is not as offensive to me as what it represents: a focus on the bottom-line; a decrease in focus on pro-bono and community service; and a message that says 'all we care about is $$!'"

Rogers & Wells

New York Washington
Frankfurt Hong Kong London Paris

Address: 200 Park Avenue, New York, NY 10166
Telephone: (212) 878–8000
Hiring Attorney: John K. Carroll, Chairperson, Employment Committee
Contact: Kelly R. Murphy, Legal Personnel Manager; (212) 878–8252
Associate Salary: First year $86,000 (1997)
Summer Salary: $1650/week (1997)
Average Hours: NA worked; NA billed; NA required.
Family Benefits: Four weeks vacation; cafeteria plan including medical and dental insurance; 401(K) plan and flexible spending accounts for health and dependent care; life, disability, and malpractice insurance; parental leave; domestic partner benefits; on-site back-up childcare; dependent care referral service
1996 Summer: Class of 49 students; offers to 46
Partnership: 17% of entering associates from 1978–1984 were made partner
Pro Bono: 1–3% of all work is pro bono

Rogers & Wells in 1997
301 Lawyers at the New York Office
2.6 Associates Per Partner

Total Partners 79			Total Associates 206			Practice Areas	
Women	8	10%	Women	77	37%	Litigation	132
All Minorities	1	1%	All Minorities	33	16%	Corporate	127
Latino	1	1%	Afro-Am	8	4%	Real Estate	21
			Asian-Am	19	9%	Tax	17
			Latino	6	3%	Trusts & Estates	4

Reputedly "white shoe" and "deeply traditional," Rogers and Wells has been and is very politically active, particularly in recent Republican administrations. The founder of the firm, William P. Rogers, was Attorney General of the United States under President Eisenhower, Secretary of State under President Nixon, and served as chairman of President Reagan's commission that investigated the explosion of the Challenger space shuttle. James B. Weidner served as Executive Director of President Bush's Commission on Aviation Security and Terrorism. Although the firm has a preponderance of Republicans, it represents a broad range of political views. Anthony P. Essayes, a D.C. partner, is chairman of the National Lawyers Council of the Democratic National Committee. New York partner, Melvin Schweitzer, is currently commissioner of the Port Authority of New Jersey and New York, and counsel to the New York Democratic National Committee.

genteel culture

Rogers & Wells is a "very genteel place" where, "nothing is said out loud." The firm is "nice to your face, but not straightforward," translated one critic, who added that "they wouldn't tell you if you did something wrong. You may end up getting kicked out" before you hear much criticism. Another contact, however, contested this view, commenting that "I know of no one who has ever been fired without extremely bad annual reviews." Rogers & Wells is a relatively formal firm. The nameplates on the doors of each office identify the occupants by their last names. Most attorneys, however, address one another, including partners, by first name, we were told.

practice areas

Rogers & Wells is primarily a corporate law firm that specializes in international financial legal services. Over 40 percent of the firm's work involves international financial transactions. The firm has had offices in London, Paris, and Frankfurt for some time now and established a Hong Kong office in 1995. The German practice group, led by Klaus Jander, "may be unique among large New York firms, with a wide range of German clients," reported one insider. The cross border finance group, slowly recovering from the 1994 Mexican economic crisis, handles a lot of work in Central and South America and Mexico. One person commented that the group "really needs Spanish-speaking associates." Partner Sara Hanks, a former Securities and Exchange Commission (SEC) attorney, is a leading partner in this group. While at the SEC, she wrote SEC Rule 144A and the underlying regulations, which apply to cross border financings. The corporate department has strong practice groups in structured and public finance, and represents large corporations and financial institutions such as Volvo, Hertz Corporation, and Merrill Lynch.

The large litigation department is most famous for representing the *New York Times* in the landmark case, *New York Times v. Sullivan*, which William Rogers argued before the Supreme Court. Rogers & Wells' energetic media practice represents the Associated Press and Hearst Publications, among others, in a number of matters involving First Amendment and intellectual property law. Rogers & Wells' large intellectual property practice, headed by Nicholas Coch and John Kidd, represents such clients as DuPont, Honda, Genentech, Pfizer, Textron, and ITT Corp. The firm also has a healthy securities litigation practice, and its white-collar criminal practice is thriving. Additionally, the firm's government contracts group complements its politically active attorneys.

Warren Feldman is working to expand Rogers & Wells' pro bono program. Currently, a pro bono coordinator is in charge of assigning pro bono work, and the firm is supportive of associates who find their own projects. The firm handles some criminal and family law pro bono matters. Summer associates are encouraged to work for one week with one of a number of public interest organizations in the city while continuing to be paid by the firm.

assignments training feedback

Entering associates join a particular practice area. Each department has different methods for distributing work, ranging from assigning partners to cluster systems. After some time, however, the new associates develop working relationships with certain partners and bypass the formal structures. Much of a junior associate's experience depends upon building working relationships with certain partners. Those who do not develop these relationships can find themselves receiving "scraps" of work, warned one insider. First- and second-year associates typically handle research and "other ministerial work," although they get more responsibility on smaller cases. Third-year associates take depositions and may accompany senior attorneys to court. Junior associates in the transactional practices are often entrusted with more responsibility than their litigation counterparts. Some first-year real estate associates independently negotiate real estate leases. Though summer associates receive fairly good feedback, associate evaluations are often "vague and unhelpful," said one person.

social life varies by group

The social life at Rogers & Wells varies considerably among different groups. Typically the partners get along well together. Overall, however, people noted that the social life isn't exactly active. One person commented that "people work so hard that, given a chance, they go home" after work. The firm does provide a lively summer program, however. Summer associates are taken out to lunch almost every day. The firm also holds an annual bash in the Hamptons, where summer associates and first- and second-year associates are invited to a number of partners' houses for a Saturday at the beach. Rogers & Wells also organizes firm socials once a month in a conference room at the firm.

closed management

Rogers & Wells is governed by an executive committee of "five to seven rainmakers," which does not disclose much information about its management decisions," remarked one source, asserting that there is "no information or input by associates" regarding management issues. To get associates more involved, "associates sit on several key committees at the firm including personnel and employment," a firm spokesperson informed us. A number of people commented that Rogers & Wells has become "more businesslike" since it has sought the assistance of a professional management firm. The firm has taken a number of cost-cutting measures and is reportedly doing well financially. Rogers & Wells has also been expanding its European practice, we were told.

associate salary lags

Associate compensation has been a sore spot between associates and the management. People noted that the compensation lags behind that at other large New York firms, "particularly for the third year and up," claimed one source. Another contact informed us that the firm has recently set its compensation to "match the median level of New York firms for each class of associates." The bonus is, however, a "huge component of the salary—a slow year can lead to an associate's losing $50,000." An additional sore point is that bonuses are not paid until February of the following year; those leaving the firm throughout the year miss out on a possible bonus which, as indicated, constitutes a significant portion of the salary package.

differences not embraced

Rogers & Wells, we were told, "is open to differences, but does not embrace them." The firm has in the past employed relatively small numbers of women and minorities. The summer associate class in 1996 was, however, twenty percent African-American, we were told, and the firm has nearly doubled its percentage of minority associates since our last edition.

Regarding Henry

Rogers & Wells is located on six and a half floors of the Met Life (formerly the Pan Am) building in midtown Manhattan. With its reception area on the 52nd floor, the firm has beautiful views and provided the site for the filming of the movie *Regarding Henry*. Some people complained that the offices are cramped; associates share offices for the first two years at the firm and may be assigned interior offices up to their third year at the firm. All associates receive computers that are networked on a new, modern system. The firm has two cafeterias. The firm's "huge in-house support staff" is "excellent and helpful."

hiring tips

Rogers & Wells fills most of its full-time associate hiring needs from its summer classes. The firm likes "social" people "who can keep a conversation going." The firm looks to hire "well-cultured people." Rogers & Wells also values people with interesting résumés, travel experience, and foreign language skills. The firm hires law students from schools all over the country. The firm is becoming "increasingly selective as it increases its compensation levels and expands its international practice," according to one insider. People advised applicants to be assertive in the interviews. One counseled, "seem enthusiastic...keep the conversation going and don't let it lull."

People we interviewed were somewhat critical of the work atmosphere and compensation structure at Rogers & Wells. Associate morale is not the firm's strong suit. One person qualified the criticisms, noting that the "work is very interesting. Even though associates often don't feel a part of the culture, the firm is deeply respectful. It is trying to shake its image, but that is hard because of its deeply established traditions." Another contact remarked, moreover, that the "firm is friendly and collegial—especially for its size."

Rosenman & Colin

New York *Newark* Washington

Address: 575 Madison Avenue, New York, NY 10022
Telephone: (212) 940–8800
Hiring Attorney: Harry P. Cohen
Contact: Edmar Jane Petterson, Director of Legal Personnel; (212) 940–7009
Associate Salary: First year $87,000 (1996)
Summer Salary: $1673/week (1997)
Average Hours: NA worked; NA billed; NA required
Family Benefits: 12 weeks paid maternity leave (12 unpaid)
1996 Summer: Class of 10 students; offers to 10
Partnership: 15% of entering associates from 1980–1983 were made partner
Pro Bono: 1–3% of all work is pro bono

Rosenman & Colin in 1997
212 Lawyers at the New York Office
1.5 Associates Per Partner

Total Partners 84			Total Associates 128			Practice Areas	
Women	11	13%	Women	48	38%	Corporate	65
All Minorities	2	2%	All Minorities	6	5%	Litigation	60
Afro-Am	2	2%	Afro-Am	2	2%	Insurance/Reinsurance	30
			Latino	4	3%	Real Estate	22
						Tax/Benefits	15
						Trusts & Estates	14
						Creditors Rights	5

You can "look forward to going to work" at Rosenman & Colin. People work hard "but leave at reasonable hours. No one expects your weekend time unless it is necessary." Rosenman & Colin is not particularly hierarchical, and associates are "comfortable with partners." Attorneys address one another by first name, and the dress code is relaxed. Women wear slacks and suits with skirts. The firm instituted "casual dress Fridays" year round in 1996. The firm culture was described as "open and friendly," with a strong emphasis on a team approach to problems.

practice areas

Rosenman & Colin rose to prominence in the 1980s, developing one of the largest real estate practices in the country. The depressed economy and real estate market hurt the firm in the early 1990s and forced it to lay off attorneys in both its real estate and corporate departments at that time. The litigation department, which picked up some of the slack during the real estate slowdown, represents a variety of clients, ranging from large corporations and institutions to individuals, in all aspects of commercial law. The department has, among others, active health care and intellectual property practices. Rosenman & Colin also provides legal services in the area of trusts and estates and tax. It has a bankruptcy practice and a growing corporate and securities department. It is also building securitization and international practices. In recent years, Rosenman & Colin has developed a well-regarded insurance department which covers reinsurance, regulatory, and all areas of insurance coverage and defense.

Rosenman & Colin regularly circulates a list of available pro bono matters and encourages its attorneys to become involved in such activities. In addition, the firm conducts a pro bono seminar on the second day of the summer program to introduce the summer associates to pro bono opportunities at the firm. Summer associates may work for up to two weeks with a public interest organization in the city while the firm pays them their full salary.

professional development

New Rosenman & Colin associates are hired into a particular department and work with partners in that practice. Associates in all departments often work directly with a number of partners on a wide variety of projects. While partners supervise the corporate and litigation associates heavily, bankruptcy and matrimonial associates work more independently than most New York law firm associates. Each department provides a structured training program for associates. The firm also sponsors some full-day training sessions on weekends. Litigation associates reportedly receive a good amount of informal day-to-day feedback because they work closely with the partners on their teams. However, the firm is often late in providing formal feedback, claimed one source, commenting that "internal administration is a big problem" at Rosenman & Colin. Past summer associates have not received their midterm evaluations until the end of the summer. However, the firm is aware of the problem and is focusing on providing better feedback to associates.

fairy-god partners

Rosenman & Colin has a "fairy-god partner" system which has reportedly tremendously improved communication between partners and associates. Under this system, associates nominate seven partners to serve as fairy-god partners. Each associate is then assigned one of the seven fairy-god partners, with whom any concerns may be discussed in complete confidence.

balanced lifestyle

Rosenman & Colin associates "are not worked to death." The average work day is about 10 hours long. Associates are not frequently asked to come in on weekends and are "appreciated if they do." Most lead a "balanced lifestyle" but reportedly pay for it with slightly lower than average salaries, although the salary structure for junior to midlevel associates has "increased substantially," according to one contact. Moreover, the firm has a policy whereby "associates are entitled to up to 20 per cent of fees recovered for a matter which they brought into the firm," one insider informed us.

Rosenman & Colin is a social place, even during the day. The "camaraderie amongst associates" is reflected in "good friendships." There are always people "talking in the library." The firm often dedicates its well-attended cocktail parties to a special event or to an attorney at the firm. Many associates and partners are involved in the firm's sports teams. Softball, volleyball, and basketball are popular. Attorneys often attend the games and then go out for drinks and dinner afterwards.

diversity

Predominantly a Jewish firm when it was founded, Rosenman & Colin has become more diverse over the years. In general, women are treated with respect at the firm. One person did note that "some more traditional men make cracks that would probably offend the PC crowd," but "no one takes it seriously." In recent years, the firm has made an effort to recruit minority associates, but it has not been particularly successful in this task.

Rosenman & Colin, like most firms, is governed by committees. Its management has made an effort to keep associates better informed about its decisions, a task at which it is succeeding, we were told. Economically, the firm has recovered from the slow years of the early 1990s, and is reportedly doing very well at present. Insurance/reinsurance is a significant growth area at the firm; the corporate practice is also doing well.

office facilities

Rosenman & Colin's office facilities are "average: kind of small, neat, and decently decorated." The management committee recently announced a capital improvement plan to refurbish and redecorate the entire office and to purchase new furniture for associates' offices. Every associate is assigned an individual office with a modern computer, which has recently been upgraded to run Windows 95. The support staff is "great," we were told. The cafeteria has a nice view, great prices, and everything you could want to eat except, one contact commented, kosher food. Another contact remarked that the "lines in the cafeteria could move faster." The cafeteria will order dinner from a restaurant for attorneys who work late.

hiring tips

Rosenman & Colin seeks people who "can fit in socially," who "can be fun outside work, and who are not the complaining or crabby" type. Though the firm hires "confident" people, its junior-level associates are definitely not "overwhelming or overbearing," nor are they "arrogant or cocky." Rosenman & Colin's callback interviews often involve discussions about interests outside of the law. People advised interviewees to show that they "can work well with other people," and to display their understanding that the "end product is more important than personal ego." The firm has recently doubled the size of its summer program, and recruits at the top national law schools and New York-area schools.

Rosenman & Colin was most criticized for its administrative problems, particularly in the summer program and in matters related to the extending of full-time employment offers. The new hiring partners are reportedly addressing these problems. People we interviewed praised the firm's high-quality work, pleasant work atmosphere, and high associate morale. One insider highly recommended the firm "to people who are not looking for a formal atmosphere and don't require the nicest facilities. It has a warmer atmosphere and nicer lifestyle" than most other New York firms.

Schulte Roth & Zabel

New York West Palm Beach

Address: 900 Third Avenue, New York, NY 10022
Telephone: (212) 756-2000
Hiring Attorneys: (Ms.) Chaye Zuckerman Shapot and Daniel J. Kramer
Contact: Lisa L. Drew, Recruitment Administrator; (212) 756–2307
Associate Salary: First year $86,000 (1997); second $99,000 plus $3000 bonus; third $113,000 plus $4000; fourth $128,000 plus $6000; fifth $145,000 plus $10,000; sixth $157,000 plus $12,000; seventh $166,000 plus $14,000; eighth $170,000 plus $15,000
Summer Salary: $1654/week (1997)
Average Hours: NA worked; 1900 billed; 1850 required
Family Benefits: 12 weeks paid maternity leave (12 unpaid); 1 week paid paternity leave (cbc unpaid); emergency back-up childcare available; family and medical leave
1996 Summer: Class of 26 2L students; offers to 25
Partnership: 14% of entering associates from 1982–1986 were made partner
Pro Bono: A minimum of 3% of all work is pro bono

Schulte Roth & Zabel in 1997
202 Lawyers at the New York Office
2.8 Associates Per Partner

Total Partners 52		
Women	6	12%
All Minorities	0	0%

Total Associates 144		
Women	55	38%
All Minorities	15	10%
Afro-Am	6	4%
Asian-Am	6	4%
Latino	3	2%

Practice Areas	
Corporate	89
Litigation	53
Real Estate	20
Trusts & Estates	12
Tax	9
Bankruptcy	8
Environmental Law	5
ERISA	5
Prof. Dev./Administrative	1

Founded in 1969, Schulte Roth & Zabel is an aggressive newcomer to the club of prominent New York law firms. Though some may view the firm's client development tactics as "less refined" than those adopted by the old-line firms, Schulte has managed to keep its eye on the bottom line while maintaining a warm and friendly environment for its attorneys. One contact qualified this characterization of the firm's aggressiveness, pointing out that "while the firm has developed an active marketing program, its marketing efforts have been tasteful and in line with other large New York City law firms."

dynamic young culture

Schulte is "young, friendly, and laid-back." Partners are easily accessible. Attorneys address one another by first name and frequently stop to chat with their colleagues in their offices, in the library, and in the hallway. People dress more casually at Schulte than at other New York firms. Men shed their jackets at work and wear "wild ties." Women "get away with wearing anything," said one person. Most Schulte attorneys are Democrats. One partner, John G. McGoldrick, was counsel to former New York Governor Hugh Carey. In addition, as a predominantly Jewish firm, Schulte is sensitive to its attorneys' religious beliefs.

practice area

Schulte grew explosively in the 1980s, primarily in the areas of corporate, litigation, and real estate. The firm now is in the process of restructuring its real estate department to "continue its strong participation in the revitalization of real estate and capital markets," according to a firm spokesperson. The firm represents a number of internationally known lenders, developers, and investors in real estate matters. Further, it has been involved in a number of sophisticated transactions, including the financing of the World Financial Center in downtown Manhattan. Citicorp is one of its largest clients.

Under the leadership of Bill Zabel, Schulte has a nationally renowned "individual client services" practice (trusts and estates). The firm has advised members of such leading American financial dynasties as Armour, Baker, Ford, Lehman, Merck, Ottinger, Rockefeller, Roush, and Schoen.

The litigation department is headed by David Brodsky, a well-known New York litigator and former Assistant U.S. Attorney for the Southern District of New York. Under his leadership, the department has developed a strong and growing white-collar criminal practice and a thriving securities litigation practice. It also has developed expertise in litigation matters that originate in other departments, such as real estate, bankruptcy, trade secrets and unfair competition, ERISA, and trusts and estates.

Schulte's corporate department, the largest at the firm, primarily handles transactional work. It is organized around three groups: mergers and acquisitions, banking, and investment management. Bankruptcy is a rapidly growing area within the corporate practice. It has been involved in a number of high-profile cases, including representations in the Rockefeller Center, and Olympia and York cases. The firm has also developed into a leading player in the private investment fund area, and represents many leading high profile funds.

pro bono

The firm joined the ABA's Law Firm Pro Bono challenge in 1993, and credits pro bono hours towards its billable hour requirement. One first-year associate devoted most of one year to a racial-steering case, representing a housing organization against brokers accused of steering customers based on their race to particular neighborhoods. Summer associates can work with a public interest organization for one week while earning full firm salary.

professional development

First-year associates may elect to join a particular department, or to rotate for nine month periods between two practice areas. An assigning attorney in each department distributes work, but associates may also seek assignments directly. Associate assignments, we were told, are more varied at Schulte than at other large law firms. First- and second-year litigation assignments typically involve researching and writing memos. On smaller or more routine matters, some second-year associates make court appearances by themselves. The pro bono practice offers additional opportunities. Some associates have cross-examined a witness in a pro bono case within their first three months at the firm. Junior corporate associates usually handle the "scut" work surrounding deals. As for formal training, Schulte provides a full range of classes, workshops, seminars, video sessions, and department meetings. Informal feedback is available, but must be pursued. "Partners are not shy about bestowing praise" when it is deserved, commented one insider. Associates are also formally reviewed twice a year.

Partner in Charge of Professional Development

Schulte has one rotating Partner in Charge of Professional Development, currently Chaye Zuckerman Shapot, who is responsible for training, education, evaluations, minority hiring and retention, and pro bono work. The creation of the Partner in Charge of Professional Development position is part of a number of other recent changes implemented by the firm in an effort to improve the work atmosphere for associates at Schulte. The firm significantly increased associate salaries in each of the past several years, and upgraded its computer capability by installing more powerful computers for each attorney and networking the entire firm. The firm has also added another two and a half floors in its building, which increases its space by 40 percent, and is currently contemplating acquiring more space.

family orientation

Most Schulte attorneys are "family people" and "don't hang out much after work." The firm is very supportive of families, praised one admirer, and will "buy you a gift if you have a baby or get married." There is not much firm-sponsored social life at Schulte, but the firm does organize well-attended cocktail parties once a month.

diversity

Schulte accommodates women's concerns, according to the people we interviewed. It has maternity and paternity leave policies and makes emergency back-up child care available to all employees. The firm, which has not had many minority associates in the past, is reportedly actively recruiting minority candidates and "has increased the number of minority associates over the past two years," we were told.

Schulte is run by a five partner executive committee whose members are elected by the partners every other year. The firm has an independent committee which decides partner compensation. As for the future, people we interviewed believed that the litigation and bankruptcy practices will continue to grow and noted that the firm would like to expand its Pacific Rim practice (the firm represents several Japanese banks).

offices

While we were told that Schulte doesn't place a high premium on its office facilities, the firm's recent acquisition of more space may improve its facilities. As things are, the library is cramped, with only three tables and eight carrels. The firm has recently greatly improved its support staff and services, "due in large part to a new, efficient administration department headed by Sylvia Moss." Whereas in the past there were complaints about "atrocious" secretaries available to first-year associates in the firm's secretarial pool, this arrangement has been eliminated and all attorneys now have access to regular secretaries.

hiring

Schulte hires people who are "fun, friendly, outgoing and smart, and who will get along with people at the firm." The firm usually draws its summer class most heavily from Harvard and the New York law schools.

a growing firm

Schulte, Roth & Zabel is a young, aggressive firm that has grown significantly in recent years. The firm presently consists of slightly more than 200 attorneys, up from 185 in 1995. Despite this growth, the firm maintains a "friendly, relaxed" atmosphere where partners are, in general, "very approachable." Schulte responds to "comments, complaints, and suggestions made by associates. From vacation policies to computation of hours, the firm is responsive to associates needs and tries to improve the lifestyles of its employees," we were told. One example of this responsiveness is the recently instituted policy of "attorney dinners." Dinner is served from Monday through Thursday nights "in a conference room so that people from different departments can have dinner together if they are working late. It's certainly more social than eating in your office, and there is also the opportunity for informal partner-associate conversation." A major challenge this growing firm faces, however, concerns the recent trend toward increasing associates' billable hours. "Associates are expected to maintain a high number of billable hours (especially compared with prior years)," according to one contact who added, however, "that said, these expectations are probably in line with the hours expected of associates at other New York city law firms of comparable size."

Shearman & Sterling

New York Los Angeles San Francisco Washington
Abu Dhabi Beijing Dusseldorf Frankfurt Hong Kong London Paris Singapore Tokyo Toronto

Address: 599 Lexington Avenue, New York, NY 10022
Telephone: (212) 848–4000
Hiring Attorney: Stephen T. Giove
Contact: Halle Schargel, Manager, Legal Recruiting; (212) 848–7546
Associate Salary: First year $87,000 (1997) (includes bonuses)
Summer Salary: $1675/week (1997)
Average Hours: NA worked; 2091 billed; NA required
Family Benefits: 12 weeks paid maternity leave; 1 week paid paternity leave; 12 weeks unpaid new child and family leave; offsite emergency childcare facility
1996 Summer: Class of 67 students; offers to 62
Partnership: 14% of entering associates from 1978–1984 were made partner
Pro Bono: 2% of all work is pro bono

Shearman & Sterling in 1997
413 Lawyers at the New York Office
2.9 Associates Per Partner

Total Partners 102		
Women	14	14%
All Minorities	4	4%
Asian-Am	2	2%
Latino	2	2%

Total Associates 298		
Women	121	41%
All Minorities	39	13%
Afro-Am	11	4%
Asian-Am	26	9%
Latino	2	1%

Practice Areas	
Corporate	244
Litigation	66
Real Estate/Environmental	33
Comp. & Ben./Indiv. Clients	25
Tax	24
Antitrust	8

Established in 1873, Shearman & Sterling is one of the oldest mega-firms in the world. It is a full-service law firm which represents large Fortune 500 corporations, financial institutions, governments, state-owned enterprises, and high-net worth individuals. It is expert in virtually all areas of corporate law and is involved in numerous high-profile matters. With approximately 600 attorneys in offices across the world, Shearman has a formidable international practice.

structured mega firm

Shearman & Sterling is highly structured. Each lawyer is assigned to one of the firm's six practice groups. This practice group structure allows lawyers to develop professional relationships within the firm while at the same time allowing them to realize the benefits of practicing law in a large firm environment. At Shearman, "you always know who is responsible," one source remarked. "A partner in each group keeps track of assignments and makes sure that associates work with different partners." Another observed that "everyone knows their place," adding that "the old white shoe partners are in charge, and the associates are employees." One contact noted, with obvious exaggeration, that "everything is divided and people are categorized. I promise you, if there are three people in a room, they will be divided, if by nothing than their height. It's like being a senior in high school." The firm must, we were told, "have a committee for everything, including a committee to decorate and divide office space."

corporate international

Corporate and financial legal services constitute more than half of Shearman's work. This renowned practice is divided into five groups: corporate finance, leasing, project development and finance, mergers and acquisitions (M&A), and specialized finance and bankruptcy. Corporate associates typically work in three of these groups, with rotations generally occurring after the associates' second and fourth years. The most well-regarded of these groups are the mergers and acquisitions, which represented Morgan Stanley in its merger with Dean Witter, and corporate finance, which mainly deals with securities matters, such as LM Ericsson's $11.2 billion global rights offering. A large portion of the firm's expanding corporate practice involves international work. The firm also handles international project development and finance matters, and privatizations, such as the privatization of China Eastern Airlines and of Assurances Generale de France. The burgeoning international practice offers corporate attorneys frequent opportunities for travel. The firm has ten overseas offices, and with the globe as its firm logo, Shearman & Sterling is "bent on becoming" an even bigger "international firm."

other practice areas

The rest of the firm's practice is organized into litigation, real estate/environmental, tax, antitrust, and the compensation and benefits/individual clients departments. The Washington, D.C. office also has international trade and government relations departments. The litigation department handles a wide range of commercial matters, including international arbitrations. Shearman represented one of the largest market makers on the Nasdaq during the antitrust and securities investigations by the U.S. Justice Department and the SEC.

As for pro bono, Shearman credits time spent on these matters when calculating billable hours. The firm represented the female students who challenged The Citadel's male only admissions policy. Shearman is affiliated with a number of public interest organizations, and first- and second-year associates often work on pro bono cases from the Southern District of New York Court.

grueling hours

The work environment at Shearman & Sterling is "frenetic" and "fast-paced." Associates work long and often "grueling" hours. We were told the "office has a pulse, and things are always moving." One person noted, however, that the corporate department work atmosphere is "formal, and it is pretty quiet in the halls."

Associate responsibilities vary by ability. Associate "superstars are treated like superstars," and others "do a lot of grunt work." Typically, first- and second-year assignments involve researching, writing memos, and drafting and organizing documents, all under the supervision of a partner. First-year M&A associates, however, are reportedly entrusted with significant client contact.

spectacular training

Shearman has a "spectacular" training program including in-house seminars and workshops. The library carries an extensive set of videotapes made by people at the firm, and documents for all deals are bound and cataloged for later reference. Shearman & Sterling emphasizes feedback. In the summer, partners critique summer associates' written work line by line. Associates are formally reviewed twice annually. These reviews are "straightforward in the first few years, but in the fifth or sixth year they won't tell you if you won't make partner," claimed one person.

social life

Because Shearman & Sterling is a huge firm, it is common for attorneys not to "know anyone else on any other floors," explained one source. There is, however, frequently a strong camaraderie among attorneys in the same class. Associates often work late and have dinner together. The firm has a huge lawyers' dining room (also open to the senior staff) where associates congregate. It is a very social place. The litigation department, we were told, is more social than the corporate department. The firm organizes a number of cocktail parties throughout the year. Each year the firm holds two conferences, one for all the third-year associates from around the world and another for all the fifth-year associates from around the world.

minority law scholarship

Traditionally known as a "white shoe" firm, Shearman & Sterling has made an effort to increase the diversity of its attorneys. It has, however, had difficulty retaining the minorities that it recruits. Currently, an eighth-year associate is the most senior African-American at the firm. The firm sponsors a Legal Defense Fund scholarship for two to four African-American law students each year. This three-year scholarship funds law school tuition to the tune of $10,000 per year. Recipients of the scholarship are required to clerk during the summer after their second year of law school with both Shearman & Sterling and the Legal Defense Fund.

women's issues

Sensitive to women's concerns, Shearman & Sterling has established a maternity leave policy, an emergency child care plan, and a sexual harassment policy. Attorneys may also work part-time. We were told, however, that attorneys who want to make partner "don't feel comfortable taking leave."

management

Shearman & Sterling is governed by a three partner executive group, and a seven partner policy committee. The membership of the policy committee rotates every year, with each member having a five-year staggered term. A few years ago, the firm moved away from a lockstep seniority based compensation system for its partners to a system designed to reward high achievers. The firm plans to expand and maintain its premier corporate practice. Shearman will also continue to focus on its international work, expanding in its characteristically conservative style.

well-equipped offices

Shearman & Sterling's beautiful and well-maintained offices are spread across two buildings. Associates must share offices for the first few years. The firm has a terrific, well-equipped library, a lawyers' dining room where attorneys and senior staff can purchase a full, sit-down meal for a reasonable price, and a staff cafeteria. The firm also has a "great conference center" of six or seven conference rooms. All employees have access to the Internet from their individual computer terminals and the firm continuously upgrades its computer network.

hiring tips

Shearman & Sterling hires "bright, enthusiastic go-getters" who "will work hard cooperatively." Most students that it hires are people "who are not too aggressive and do not make trouble for the other associates," according to one insider. On the other hand, some people described Shearman & Sterling attorneys as "overachievers," and one person declared that "you will not survive if you are a mouse." The firm hires law students from a wide range of schools all over the country.

Because personality factors heavily into the firm's hiring decisions, people advised applicants to "emphasize what is different" about themselves. "You don't have to talk about how much you like torts," commented one veteran of the process. Another advised interviewees to emphasize that Shearman & Sterling's structure is important to them. Interviewees were also counseled to develop "some notion of how you will focus" and how you will fit into the firm's practice before you interview.

Shearman & Sterling is highly structured, fairly hierarchical, and somewhat of a "sweatshop." Associates react differently to the long hours. "Some are gung ho and others feel like they are sacrificing their lives." Shearman & Sterling has a "great reputation" and offers one of the country's premier international corporate practices. Its associates work on high-profile matters and receive good training and constructive feedback. The firm is a "good stepping stone" for many attorneys who want to go on to work in government, public interest, and business.

Simpson Thacher & Bartlett

New York Columbus
Hong Kong London Singapore Tokyo

Address: 425 Lexington Avenue, New York, NY 10017-3954
Telephone: (212) 455–2000
Hiring Attorney: Mark G. Cunha
Contact: Dee Pifer, Director of Legal Employment; (212) 455–2687
Associate Salary: First year $87,000 (1997)
Summer Salary: $1600/week (1997)
Average Hours: NA worked; NA billed; NA required
Family Benefits: 12 weeks paid maternity leave (12 unpaid); 1 week paid paternity leave (12 unpaid); off-site childcare; emergency childcare program
1996 Summer: Class of 54 students; offers to 54
Partnership: NA
Pro Bono: 3% of all work is pro bono

Simpson Thacher & Bartlett in 1997
463 Lawyers at the New York Office
2.8 Associates Per Partner

Total Partners 118		
Women	8	7%
All Minorities	2	2%
Afro-Am	2	2%

Total Associates 326		
Women	114	35%
All Minorities	59	18%
Afro-Am	17	5%
Asian-Am	33	10%
Latino	9	3%

Practice Areas	
Corp. (incl. Banking & EO)	245
Litigation (incl. Labor & IP)	240
Tax	26
Real Estate	21
Personal Planning	12
Bankruptcy/Restructuring	10
Employee Benefits	9

One of New York's largest and most prestigious law firms, Simpson Thacher & Bartlett combines a diverse practice with an unintimidating atmosphere. Unlike many large firms, Simpson Thacher is relatively unstructured and is committed to the ideal of the "generalist" lawyer. The corporate and litigation departments are not physically separated, and first- and second-year corporate and litigation associates often share offices.

genteel polite culture

Simpson Thacher & Bartlett is "not a super-aggressive law firm." Its attorneys, one person told us, are the "kind of people who like to be friendly, and who like people to be friendly with them." The "emphasis is on people being kind, genteel, and polite." There is "no screaming," and there is "no pressure to be a workaholic" at Simpson Thacher. One insider instructed us that "while all associates understand that nights and weekends are often part of the job, there is never the sense that long hours are a given, and associates are often told not to work on something over a weekend, or that a project can wait until tomorrow. There is absolutely no 'face time' here; associates do not hesitate to leave whenever they are through with their work, even if they will be passing partners on their way out the door." Another contact informed us, relatedly, that "everyone takes their four weeks of vacation, and the firm is reluctant to cancel any vacation time planned in advance." Simpson's attorneys interact informally and usually leave their office doors invitingly open. Some claimed, however, that at times the firm's genteel culture gets carried too far. It "can be cloying," asserted one contact. The dress code at the firm is "pretty conservative," although women frequently wear pantsuits. There are no casual dress Fridays at Simpson Thacher yet; that will change this year, we were informed.. One person praised the generally "stylish" dress at the firm for its contribution to the "feeling of professionalism" in the office.

pre-eminent corporate practice

Simpson Thacher & Bartlett has an excellent corporate practice which represents large banks, financial institutions, and corporations. Notwithstanding the 1992 merger of its longstanding client, Manufacturers Hanover Trust, with Chemical Bank and the 1995 merger of Chemical with Chase, Simpson Thacher has maintained its role as the institution's corporate counsel. It shares this work principally with Cravath, Swaine & Moore and the old Chase's traditional counsel, Milbank Tweed. Some of Simpson Thacher's other prominent clients include American Electric, Travellers Insurance, General Electric, Seagram, Blackstone, Barclays Bank, NBC, Viacom, MCI, Ford, Lehman Brothers, Kohlberg, Kravits & Roberts (KKR), Matsushita, and others. The firm has been involved in many high-profile matters such as representing KKR in its leveraged buyout of RJR Nabisco. Partner Dick Beattie, who is the "unquestioned leader of the firm," rose to prominence as KKR's lawyer. He is a "legendary" rainmaker at the firm.

international orientation

Simpson Thacher's international practice has expanded "dramatically" over the last several years with offices opening in Hong Kong and Singapore, and a tremendous expansion in Latin America. Paul Ford, Rhett Brandon, Walt Looney, David Williams, and Glenn Reiter have been the key movers in this international expansion. The firm's international stature is enhanced by the presence of Cyrus Vance, former Secretary of State under President Carter, and his on-going international public service activities, and by Conrad Harper, who recently returned to Simpson Thacher after four years as the Legal Advisor to the U.S. Department of State. As part of its international strategy, the firm has a strong international associate program and receives attorneys from firms in Latin America, Europe and Asia for six to 12 month stays. One contact informed us that, even with the recent progress in its international practice, Simpson's practice is "not as developed as its competitors"; the upside of this, however, is that "young associates have more opportunities to go abroad, especially to Asia."

litigation

Simpson Thacher & Bartlett has one of the largest and most diverse litigation practices in New York, including securities, antitrust, product liability, white collar crime, insurance coverage, international arbitration and intellectual property. The firm "prides itself on bringing more cases to trial than most of its competitors," and is home to many well-known litigators including Roy Reardon, Chuck Koob, Barry Ostrager, Ken Logan, and Jack Kerr. Several people remarked that the securities practice is "not as strong as it could be" (though a firm spokesperson claimed that this remark is "off-base"). In contrast, the intellectual property practice was recently bolstered with the addition of Hank Gutman and several colleagues from his former office. One insider remarked that "the intellectual property work is a welcome addition to the department, and, because the firm remains committed to developing generalists, it will allow many associates to cut their teeth on this important area of law." Another contact informed us that "the biggest problem in the litigation department is the presence of several enormous litigations. Massive cases are by no means the rule here; however, as the size of the typical case handled by Simpson increases, an individual associate's role becomes smaller and the work is usually less interesting. The firm has tried to avoid this problem where possible by hiring 'project' attorneys; nonetheless it is a genuine concern." The firm has a reputable but small personal planning (trusts and estates) department. The labor department is "negligible," and the environmental practice is in its initial stages.

civic-minded law firm

Simpson Thacher & Bartlett is "self-consciously civic-minded," asserted one source. There is "peer pressure to do pro bono work and be a nice person," declared another. The firm is proud of its pro bono program and "actively encourages" attorneys to become involved. It sends memos to all attorneys listing available matters and does not limit the amount of time that associates devote to pro bono work, "except by otherwise keeping them too busy to take anything else on," quipped one insider. Simpson Thacher handles a wide range of pro bono matters, including work for New York City in its disputes with New York State regarding education funding and for Central American Indians in claims for land rights under international human rights standards. In addition, summer associates may elect to work for one week in a public interest housing law program run by the New York City Bar Association.

departmental rotations

"The idea of teamwork is huge" at Simpson Thacher. The firm expects you "to pool your experience," revealed one source. New associates must select one or more areas of the firm's practice in which to concentrate but can change their area of concentration fairly easily. For departmental assignment purposes, corporate and banking are treated as one department, and associates assigned to this department must rotate through 15 month stints in two of three broad areas—mergers and acquisitions, securities, and financial institutions and banking. Those we spoke with expressed uneasiness over this newly instituted rotation system. One person observed that "the training suffers because the rotations are too long, and many of the partners do not want to take the time to explain things." One or two assigning partners in each department distribute the work. In some areas associates may seek assignments directly from partners. Several commented that, given Simpson Thacher's informal work structure, it is important for junior associates to find "a mentor with whom they work well, otherwise they will get lost in little assignments." One contact labeled it a "sink or swim" environment, but others noted that you are "treated well" and "can always get work." Associate responsibilities vary by department. We were told that associates in banking are much more likely to negotiate a deal, whereas corporate associates do "a lot of grunt work." First- and second-year litigation associates handle mostly research and writing tasks, and by the third year associates begin taking depositions. One contact raved about the variety of opportunities available to young litigation associates: "to date I've had cases involving antitrust, securities, insurance, contract disputes, intellectual property, criminal law and bankruptcy—a wonderful variety for 18 months!"

Simpson Thacher does not emphasize formal training, and associates primarily "learn by doing." The firm provides introductory training to new associates, and the litigation, personal planning, and the corporate departments conduct regular training sessions. Simpson Thacher formally reviews associates annually, but in one contact's opinion, the firm is "sometimes not entirely forthright because of the emphasis on gentility and politeness," or, as another person put it, "maybe self-interest. At the moment, the firm can't afford to lose people," so busy has it been of late. Another source elaborated upon this idea, noting that a "noticeable drawback at Simpson is the lack of information available to associates. Most of my colleagues and I have no idea whether the firm is happy with our work. Of course, the polite atmosphere that prevails prevents brutally honest feedback, but more feedback would be appreciated."

athletic social life

Simpson Thacher is a social place during the day. "People mix and mingle" and "hang out in each others' offices," said one insider, adding that the "only way to get work done is to close your door." Many Simpson Thacher attorneys are drawn together through sports. Squash ladders, baseball pools, and sports-oriented events abound. Although Simpson Thacher attorneys are intelligent, it is "not an intellectual place," praised one admirer. People go white-water rafting and clubbing. At the same time, however, most attorneys work late and many are married. They tend to go home at the end of the day. The firm-sponsored social life is usually family oriented. For example, in the past the firm has organized a trip to the zoo for all attorneys and their families. Other summer events have included the ballet, plays and shows, the firm dinner, and informal departmental dinners and parties.

diversity pioneer

Simpson Thacher is a "nirvana for blacks," asserted one source, despite its relatively low number of minorities. In 1969, it was the first major firm to make an African-American attorney a partner. This partner, the aforementioned Conrad Harper, is an influential litigator and, until June 1992, was President of the New York City Bar Association. John Carr, another prominent African-American corporate partner, actively recruits students on-campus.

Simpson Thacher has made some accommodations for female attorneys. It has a "mommy track" permitting women part-time work arrangements so that they may balance work and family. This track, however, can delay partnership evaluation "considerably," said one person. Another person remarked that the firm "has become increasingly committed to retaining its female associates, adopting flexible schedules and planning a workshop to discuss women's issues. This commitment is appreciated." In conjunction with some other law firms, Simpson Thacher provides emergency day care facilities. In addition, people reported that the firm takes a stern view of sexual harassment.

successful management

Simpson Thacher is managed by Dick Beattie, chair of the firm's executive committee, and a few other powerful partners. The firm is run like a "benevolent dictatorship," commented one person. "People trust the management of the firm." The firm's goals for the future include further development of the international practice and continued growth of existing practice areas. Simpson made eight new partners in 1996, reflecting the firm's success in recent years and "the partnership's optimism regarding the firm's prospects." One contact remarked that one of the drawbacks at Simpson is its absence of other U.S. offices, which causes "associates who want to relocate to leave Simpson Thacher."

beautiful offices

Simpson Thacher's "extraordinarily beautiful" office is decorated primarily with dark wood, white walls and marble, beautiful artwork, and green carpets. Fresh flowers abound. The "top-notch" support staff pampers the firm's attorneys. "You don't have to leave your office for anything," marveled one admirer. The firm is a "well-run machine." The library occupies the top floor of the building. Some people commented, however, that the cafeteria is dingy and feels "like a railroad car" because it is situated in a narrow corridor which runs around the perimeter of the building. Others contested this view, maintaining that the cafeteria is "wonderful," occupying a half-floor and serving "gourmet-prepared meals."

hires relaxed charming applicants

Simpson Thacher hires "highly intelligent and extremely nice people." It "places a big premium on getting along and doesn't want people who will lock themselves in their offices," asserted one insider. It seeks people who are "well-rounded and well-balanced." Simpson Thacher wants "normal people," another declared. The firm primarily hires students from the top national law schools with a B+ or better grade point average, according to the people we interviewed. They advised applicants to "be as personable and engaging as possible" in the interview. The best way to fit into the firm's culture is to be "relaxed and charming," counseled one. "Emphasize other interests besides the law," recommended another. "Don't emphasize money" commented one contact and don't be "anal or pushy." Another insider cautioned: "the easiest way not to get an offer is to appear arrogant," while yet another source remarked that "the firm culture punishes arrogance explicitly." This person further stated that "the firm is proud of its achievement, but unlike certain peer firms (Sullivan & Cromwell, Cravath), not arrogant of its position."

some growing pains

Simpson Thacher & Bartlett is entering a growth spurt "not seen since the 1980s," which in turn is challenging the firm's "vaunted culture." One person reported that "senior associate ranks are stretched, resulting in low morale at certain levels of seniority." Another contact observed that the firm is "very lean with associates at the midyear level and the workload can be heavy and people tend to get impatient because they are stressed." Further, it was remarked that "the firm's ever increasing profitability risks overwhelming the values that distinguish the firm. Commitment to public service does not mean much if lawyers aren't given time to serve." However, another contact assured us that Simpson Thacher is "hiring significantly larger classes in response to the depletion of mid-levels and the continually growing business." The increased volume of work at Simpson is placing strains on both the office space and the support staff, which are having a difficult time staying abreast of the rapid growth.

Most people agreed, however, that Simpson Thacher "has the best combination of good things in a firm." It is one of the five most prestigious firms in New York, has one of the prettiest offices in the city, is not a sweatshop, and is very friendly. Associates receive high quality work and can move on to almost any job of their choice. The firm is also comparatively diverse in terms of minorities. It has not adopted a "macho masculine" attitude and is a good place for women who don't like that attitude. Attorneys at Simpson Thacher are not driven by "intense competition," declared one insider. Another person remarked that the firm is "somewhat competitive, albeit in a healthy way." In short, Simpson Thacher & Bartlett provides "top drawer" quality in an environment with "less angst."

Skadden, Arps, Slate, Meagher & Flom

New York Boston Chicago Houston Los Angeles Newark San Francisco Washington Wilmington
Beijing Brussels Frankfurt Hong Kong London Moscow Paris Singapore Sydney Tokyo Toronto

Address: 919 Third Avenue, New York, NY 10022
Telephone: (212) 735-3000
Hiring Attorney: Wallace L. Schwartz
Contact: Carol Lee Sprague, Director of Legal Hiring; (212) 735-3815
Associate Salary: NA
Summer Salary: NA
Average Hours: NA worked; NA billed; No minimum required
Family Benefits: Primary care; parent leave; emergency childcare and elder care; medical and childcare flexible spending accounts; life, dental and vision
1996 Summer: Class of 60 students; offers to 56
Partnership: 10% of entering associates from 1983–1988 were made partner
Pro Bono: 5% of all work is pro bono

Skadden, Arps, Slate, Meagher & Flom in 1997
585 Lawyers at the New York Office
3.1 Associates Per Partner

Total Partners 137		
Women	24	18%
All Minorities	4	3%
Afro-Am	1	1%
Latino	3	2%
Openly Gay	3	2%

Total Associates 431		
Women	162	38%
All Minorities	56	13%
Afro-Am	18	4%
Asian-Am	22	5%
Latino	16	4%
Openly Gay	9	2%

Practice Areas	
Corporate	279
Litigation	65
Tax	42
Liability	33
Antitrust	27
Real Estate	27
Intellectual Property	21
Bankruptcy & Restructuring	17
Labor	14
EB/EC	10
Trusts & Estates	9
White Collar	5

most frequently consulted law firm

Founded in the late 1940s, Skadden, Arps, Slate, Meagher & Flom "forged its reputation as the pre-eminent mergers and acquisitions firm" in the high-profile takeover battles of the seventies and eighties. The firm has ranked first in 12 of the last 14 *American Lawyer* magazine's "Corporate Scorecards" of firms involved in the 100 biggest merger and acquisition transactions. In the November 1996 *National Law Journal* survey of the nation's 250 largest industrial corporations, Skadden was identified as the most frequently consulted law firm in America. During the early 1980s, under the leadership of Joe Flom, who now has assumed the role of "chairman emeritus" at the firm, Skadden "really exploded" and established offices throughout the country. From 1988 to 1992, the firm developed a substantial international presence and now has offices located across the world. With over 500 lawyers, the New York headquarters is the firm's largest office and the hub of its broad-based practice which includes everything from mergers & acquisitions and finance to products liability, antitrust, and real estate. One contact praised this concentration of talent, noting that "if you need to find an expert in any given field, chances are there is one at Skadden (or someone who can put you in touch with one quickly)." Along with the aforementioned Joe Flom, three Skadden litigation partners, Bob Bennett, Sheila Birnbaum, and Frank Rothman appeared in the most recent *National Law Journal* "Profiles in Power" survey, which lists the 100 most influential lawyers in the country. Some of the cases and lawyers that made this New York powerhouse famous are chronicled in a book simply titled *Skadden*.

work hard play hard

Skadden has a macho "work hard, play hard" reputation, although this picture may be less accurate now that the "wild 1980s" are in the past. We were told that its lawyers now bill 45 to 55 hours per week in contrast to the 50 to 60 hour weeks of the past (although one person remarked that "with the present M&A boom, it's back up to 50 to 60"). In the summer of 1992, Skadden initiated a policy permitting attorneys to dress casually on Fridays, "much to the delight of most attorneys (and all support staff)." This policy was recently extended from summer months only to year-round status.

practice areas

Skadden represents many Fortune 500 corporations and large financial institutions. It also represents President Clinton and two major sports leagues, the NFL and the NHL. The matters it handles are often widely-publicized. Skadden was recently involved in the McDonnell Douglas/Boeing, Norfolk Southern/Conrail and Time-Warner/Turner Broadcasting mergers, and the Dow Corning breast implant products liability case. Sheila Birnbaum, affectionately known as the "Queen of Toxic Torts" and a rainmaker at the firm, is one of many well-regarded Skadden partners; she recently argued in front of the Supreme Court. In addition to its "bread and butter" mergers and acquisitions work, Skadden has come to personify the "full-service" corporate firm, with burgeoning practices in virtually every area, including white-collar crime, real estate, products liability, intellectual property, labor & employment, international trade, energy, corporate finance, structured finance, commodities, restructuring, and privatization. Skadden's Hong Kong office is growing rapidly. The firm has also recently represented the Irish government in telecommunications matters. Banking is "a great department to work in," recommended some people, noting that it has good people and training.

Skadden fellowship

Skadden has a structured pro bono program coordinated by a special counsel and a partner. Once you are identified as willing to do pro bono, one source revealed, they "call you up" with many projects. The firm has also established the Skadden Fellowship which funds 25 Public Interest Fellows every year to do a full year of public interest work.

departmental organization

New associates are assigned to specific practice areas when they join the firm. For the first several months, they are also assigned to a "partner liaison" who monitors their work assignments. Litigation associates are assigned to either litigation general, or to products liability, intellectual property, bankruptcy or antitrust. They do not rotate. Corporate associates, on the other hand, may rotate for six-month periods through two or three corporate practice areas before joining one permanently. Given Skadden's size and structure, some associates feel that the firm is a "compartmentalized" place where it is "easy to feel isolated," unless one makes an effort to socialize; others, however, feel that the numerous smaller practice areas within Skadden offer "many of the benefits of a tight-knit small firm while still enjoying the resources (*e.g.* support staff, library, clout) of a large institution." The firm is, moreover, reportedly "open-minded" about departmental transfers.

Skadden is a firm for "self-starters." First-year litigators typically begin with research assignments, progress to taking a few depositions, and play a "small role" in court by the end of their first year. Junior corporate associates usually do a lot of due diligence and document drafting. However, a large firm like Skadden "offers a wealth of opportunity for individuals up to the challenge," reported one insider. One junior attorney noted that Skadden "calls itself a 'meritocracy,' and for the most part that assessment is correct." As for training, most departments conduct substantive seminars, workshop programs and organize regular lunches at which attorneys discuss their work and new developments in the law, and the firm publishes a brochure which describes its training programs in detail. Skadden was criticized by one contact, nevertheless, for its "lack of formal training for young associates and little time to stop and ask questions." Skadden also maintains a library of videotaped training materials and pays for outside continuing education and seminars. Associates are formally reviewed twice annually.

social life curtailed

Much like other large corporate firms, one of the downsides at Skadden is that the long hours that attorneys work often curtail social life. The firm, however, makes a special effort to ensure that associates have a "good time during the summer." Skadden's summer program is, according to one enthusiast, "the best in the city," offering "choice assignments, matching up with attorney officemates, and entertainment." It picks up the tab for an attorney happy hour every Friday after work at The Old Stand, a bar across the street from the office. The firm also sponsors a well-attended attorney lunch every Thursday.

increased minority hiring

Skadden has a "Jewish culture—it is very vocal and familial," said one person. Overall, Skadden is ethnically diverse, but like most large law firms it has relatively few minority attorneys. The firm has, however, a committee to address issues related to hiring and retaining minority attorneys. The firm also participates in the New York City Bar Association's first-year law student minority clerkship program and in the Tulane minority clerkship program. The 1997 summer associate class is 28% minority and the fall 1997 class is 35% minority. The firm has a number of female partners holding significant positions, such as Irene Sullivan, the head of the New York office and former hiring partner. Skadden has a large number of women partners compared to other New York City firms.

Despite some tough times in the early 1990s, Skadden is economically healthy. To cut costs the firm at that time reduced the salaries of attorneys who work in its branch offices, who were previously paid on the New York scale. A firm spokesperson informed us that "first year associates are paid the same in all offices; the other years are still paid higher than the local law firm salaries in their city." Skadden is governed by a management committee which, we were told, is "somewhat responsive" to associate concerns.

efficient offices with fitness center

Skadden's office facilities are designed to enable attorneys to produce high-quality work. Every attorney is assigned an individual office which is equipped with oak desks, but is not "lavishly furnished." The firm has updated its computer system to a worldwide network that connects all 20 of its offices. Summer associates share offices with third- or fourth-year associates. Many of the first-year associate offices, or "honeycombs" as they are known because of their size, are located together on a few floors, facilitating a lot of interaction among first-year associates. The firm has a cafeteria. Skadden recently announced plans to move into new offices "in a soon-to-be-constructed building overlooking Times Square." The building is reportedly "state-of-the-art" and is the first skyscraper in New York City to be built in the 1990s. The move is presently scheduled to be accomplished prior to December 31, 1999, in order to celebrate the millenium. Skadden's offices also include a fitness center staffed by two full-time trainers. The gym provides attorneys with shirts, shorts, socks, and towels. It is equipped with free weights, Nautilus machines, bikes, rowing machines, and treadmills. It also holds aerobics classes. Attorneys watch the many T.V.s while they exercise and can end the workout with a shower and readily available fruit and juices.

hiring tips

Skadden hires "well-rounded individuals," usually with a B+ or better grade point average at the top national schools. However, the firm draws from a wide range of schools, from prestige campuses to local schools. The firm is most interested in "outgoing," "down-to-earth" people who "take pride in their work and will stay till the work is done." Those we interviewed advised applicants to learn about the firm before they interview and recommended that they emphasize a particular aspect of Skadden that interests them. "Emphasize that you like to work hard and will do whatever it takes," one counseled.

career launch pad

Skadden is one of the premier corporate firms in New York. It demands long hours of associates and can be impersonal and slow to provide feedback. One contact informed us that "the hours are long; opportunities for vacations are few. Working at Skadden requires stamina—at times it can be an endurance contest." Another source commented that "the pace of practice can be supersonic, as business is booming." However, its work is interesting and high-profile. Moreover, the "culture of the firm allows one to handle the intensity of the work much more easily than at other firms," reported one contact. The atmosphere is, one person told us, "informal in comparison to Cravath, and Sullivan." Skadden attorneys "for the most part tend to be real down-to-earth people (at some white shoe firms it seems attorneys display more of an arrogance)," one contact informed us. The firm, moreover, is "first and foremost a meritocracy. Good work results in more interesting and challenging assignments and direct client contact. Junior associates are given many opportunities to shine, and if they do so, soon find themselves interacting with the partners and top client management." Finally, the firm is extremely "well-regarded" and is an excellent place from which to launch one's career. Former Skadden attorneys have gone on to achieve success in many different careers. They have become partners at law firms in New York and throughout the country; they have achieved general counsel and executive status at major Fortune 500 companies and investment and commercial bank; and have been appointed and elected to high-level government positions and judgeships. One contact gave Skadden this high compliment: "If I were to leave Skadden, it would never be to go to another law firm. If I continue practicing law at a private firm, I plan on staying at Skadden."

Stroock & Stroock & Lavan

New York Los Angeles Miami Washington
Budapest

Address:	180 Maiden Lane, New York, New York 10038-4982
Telephone:	(212) 806–5400
Hiring Attorney:	James R. Tanenbaum
Contact:	Diane A. Cohen, Director of Legal Recruiting; (212) 806–5406
Associate Salary:	First year $87,000 (1997)
Summer Salary:	$1600/week (1997)
Average Hours:	2006 worked; 1906 billed; NA required
Family Benefits:	12 weeks paid maternity leave (cbc unpaid); emergency daycare; part-time schedules
1996 Summer:	Class of 18 2L and 2 1L students; offers to all 18 2Ls
Partnership:	10% of entering associates from 1981–1985 were made partner
Pro Bono:	5% of all work is pro bono

Stroock & Stroock & Lavan in 1997
216 Lawyers at the New York Office
1.4 Associates Per Partner

Total Partners 82			Total Associates 115			Practice Areas	
Women	10	12%	Women	55	48%	Litigation	63
All Minorities	0	0%	All Minorities	11	10%	Corporate	57
			Afro Am	3	3%	Real Estate	31
			Asian-Am	4	3%	Insolvency	16
			Latino	4	3%	Intellectual Property	13
						Insurance	9
						Trusts & Estates	9
						Labor/Employment	7
						Tax	7
						ERISA	4

informal atmosphere

Stroock & Stroock & Lavan "is a kinder and gentler place than most other large New York firms, but...you are still going to work very long hours." Stroock offers a "friendly environment." Most people "say hello in the halls" and drop into one another's offices to chat or ask advice about work. Though "the usual partner-associate dichotomy" exists at Stroock, "it is probably less than that at other big New York firms." For example, partners and associates often eat together in the firm's dining room, and the partners "tend to talk to associates in a down-to-earth manner." Overall, Stroock offers a "very informal" atmosphere and gives attorneys "a lot of room to be themselves." We did hear criticisms, however, that "pettiness between partners for control or sharing of business permeates Stroock. While territoriality among partners is to be expected, the level at Stroock tends to cause over-segregation of practice areas that seems counter to working in a 'firm'," one person pointed out.

practice areas

Founded in 1876 as one of the first Wall Street firms, Stroock has grown into a large, full-service law firm. It primarily serves large corporations and financial institutions. It also represents small and midsize companies and wealthy families and individuals. The firm's largest and perhaps most noteworthy practice area is the commercial litigation department, which houses specialty groups in securities, banking, real estate, products liability, environmental and land use, antitrust, and white-collar crime. The litigation attorneys "are more fun and outgoing" than other attorneys at the firm, asserted one contact. Former New York State Attorney General Robert Abrams is a member of this practice group. Stroock also has "one of the best" real estate departments in New York, although it downsized a bit in the early 1990s.

Stroock also has an "excellent" insolvency department which "has been growing in size and importance." Stroock was heavily involved in the widely-publicized LTV bankruptcy. It has also worked on Barney's and other high-profile bankruptcy matters. One person told us that "there is no shortage of work in this practice area." Stroock's insurance and reinsurance department is "one of the most preeminent practices in the country," representing insurers, reinsurers, agents and brokers in both regulatory and transactional matters, including insurer acquisitions. Stroock's "solid" corporate practice includes specialty groups in securities, general corporate/commercial, investment companies, mergers and acquisitions, venture capital, commodities, and structured finance. However, "if one wants to be a corporate attorney this might not be the place as Stroock is rarely involved with cutting-edge deals," counseled one insider. A firm spokesperson pointed out, however, that the corporate department is the firm's largest generator of revenue.

The firm recently added a significant intellectual property practice through its merger with Blum Kaplan, a prestigious intellectual property boutique. Made up of attorneys from various practice groups within the firm, the health care practice has also continued to expand. Although Stroock does not have a large international practice, it established an office in Budapest in 1990 and is "seeking to expand in this area." It anticipates additional expansion into Central Europe.

Stroock encourages junior attorneys "to develop necessary skills" through its pro bono practice. It also permits summer associates to work for one week with a public interest organization while earning the full firm salary.

work assignments

Stroock hires entering associates for a particular department. The larger departments, such as corporate and litigation, have managing attorneys who distribute work assignments and monitor new associate workloads. Associates usually gravitate toward a particular specialty area after a few years. Summer associates choose their assignments through a central assignment system. Hence, "one can avoid areas and partners that he or she does not want to work on or with," praised one contact. Another contact informed us that summer associates receive "real work, which helps them to decide which department to pursue." We were told by some that Stroock does not immediately offer junior associates a lot of responsibility. However, one contact observed that the firm practices "lean staffing, so associates get loads of responsibility." Moreover, a firm spokesperson asserted that new associates take responsibility for appropriate matters as soon as they demonstrate the desire and capacity to do so. Corporate associates often work alone with one partner on transactions and second-year litigation associates defend depositions and make court appearances. As for advancement prospects, according to one person, "office politics are important, but talent rules. It helps to be well-liked, but if you can bring home the bacon, you will thrive."

training feedback

Stroock also "places a real emphasis on continuing legal education." This is particularly true in the litigation department where "several senior attorneys...teach at various law schools." Throughout the year the department conducts, for junior associates, weekly continuing legal education meetings which provide training in specific areas of the law. The firm also pays full tuition for tax and trusts and estates lawyers to attend NYU (at night) for an LLM degree. Each department also has monthly meetings to discuss active clients and other matters. In addition, partners and senior attorneys provide informal feedback to junior associates on their work product. The senior associates are more diligent about this task than the partners, asserted one source.

informal social events

Many Stroock attorneys, particularly those in the litigation department, form close friendships. They throw each other surprise birthday parties and often go out after work. "Although not encouraged, a lot of intra-firm dating occurs," revealed one contact. Aside from the summer program, Stroock does not sponsor many firmwide social events. Summer associate activities have included in recent years a white-water rafting trip on the Lehigh River, a day at the racetrack, a Broadway show, several "mini-cruises" around Manhattan, and other informal events. The firm eliminated its formal firm outing a few years ago.

open to diversity

Though its attorneys come from a range of ethnic backgrounds, people we interviewed commented that Stroock is "a very Jewish firm." One noted that "on Jewish holidays half or more of the office takes off. Accommodations are made for those who keep kosher." This person added that "since Stroock is an ethnic firm, it seems to be more sensitive to making minorities and women feel comfortable." Although the firm has few minority attorneys, it has been "actively and consciously recruiting." The firm provides a comfortable atmosphere for women, agreed most people we interviewed.

"I didn't get any sense that I was treated differently because I am a woman," attested one contact. In one past summer, the firm organized a summer associate luncheon with a female litigation partner to provide a forum to discuss issues involved in balancing a family and a career. Several female attorneys have taken time off from work to have children and have worked part-time. The firm also has a formal sexual harassment policy.

successful management

Stroock is run by an 11 partner executive committee and a managing partner. We heard complaints that associates are not formally involved in the management of the firm. "It seems that the partners just decide things behind closed doors, and the associates just have to accept the decisions," explained one source, noting however that "many associates are friends with the partners and...in such cases the respective partner might be receptive to the associate's ideas." Stroock is economically healthy. Much of the firm's recent success can be attributed to "having strong, varied practices, allowing the firm to weather a downturn in business in any one practice area," explained one source. Another insider believed that Stroock "seems to be taking a measured approach to the future. It wants to expand internationally."

spectacular offices

Stroock is located near Wall Street in downtown Manhattan. The firm recently moved to its new quarters at 180 Maiden Lane, "an impressive building with spectacular views." The office is a "nice, modern, well-lit place with a lot of art work." First- and second-year associates share offices. Every attorney has a new, state-of-the-art personal computer which has E-mail and can access LEXIS and Westlaw. The "phones work well and have every conceivable option," marveled one insider. The large support staff "does good work," and the "outstanding" library staff is "very knowledgeable and extremely helpful," according to one contact. Another person lavishly praised the "invaluable research librarians, who are trained career professionals—not college students (as in some firms)." Not all contacts, however, shared the high appraisal of the firm's support services. One person described them as "poor" and, in particular, complained of difficulties with the secretarial manager.

hiring practices

Stroock hires "people who are highly competent and fit into the firm atmosphere." The "firm likes energetic and fun people." In its hiring, Stroock values grades less than personality for students from "top-tier" schools. For others, it emphasizes grades and law review membership. People advised applicants who interview at Stroock, "Be yourself! There is no real mold...that everyone follows." They also warned that interviewers often ask: "Why should we hire you over all the other people applying?" Stroock draws a significant portion of its summer class from Columbia, Fordham, and New York University. It also hires law students from Boston University, Brooklyn, Duke, Georgetown, Harvard, the University of Chicago, and the University of Pennsylvania.

Stroock requires long work hours and offers "little hands-on experience," we were told. The firm recently "restructured its associate compensation levels to bring associate pay in line with other large New York city firms," one insider informed us. But, another contact pointed out that although compensation for young associates is competitive with other top firms, salaries "tend to lag behind with respect to more senior attorneys." The firm has a merit-based, discretionary bonus system.

Overall, however, "associates feel a real connection to Stroock" and enjoy working at the firm. "There is no party line so people are free to be themselves (within reason). The firm seems very tolerant of younger associates and will give them time to develop into good lawyers. You don't have to look over your shoulder all the time to see who is watching you as it is a relatively informal place." During the past year, according to one firm insider, "the firm has made a significant effort to improve the services it provides, with an eye toward being a market leader in each practice area. The firm has devoted its resources to developing better lawyers." This includes a significant emphasis on training and education of its young attorneys. The one major complaint brought to our attention concerning attorneys' life at Stroock related to the length of the partnership track, which it was observed is "rarely eight years." Indeed, the most recent Stroock partners have been lateral hires or promoted "special counsels." It is "rare for an associate to 'cruise through the ranks' over the traditional eight year period and be elevated to partner," in the words of one insider.

Sullivan & Cromwell

New York Los Angeles Washington
Frankfurt Hong Kong London Melbourne Paris Tokyo

Address: 125 Broad Street, New York, NY 10004
Telephone: (212) 558–4000
Hiring Attorney: (Mr.) Francis J. Aquila
Contact: Maria S. Alkiewicz, Director of Legal Personnel; (212) 558–3733
Associate Salary: First year $85,000 (1997); salary figure includes $2,000 bonus distributed at the end of the first full calendar year
Summer Salary: $3625 semi-monthly (1997)
Average Hours: NA worked; NA billed; NA required
Family Benefits: 12 weeks paid maternity leave (cbc unpaid); 4 weeks paid paternity leave (cbc unpaid); on-site emergency day care center
1996 Summer: Class of 96 students; offers to 95
Partnership: 19% of entering associates from 1978–1984 were made partner
Pro Bono: 3% of all work is pro bono

Sullivan & Cromwell in 1997
451 Lawyers at the New York Office
2.5 Associates Per Partner

Total Partners 115			Total Associates 291			Practice Areas	
Women	9	8%	Women	76	26%	Corporate/General	283
All Minorities	5	4%	All Minorities	38	13%	Litigation	125
Afro-Am	1	1%	Afro-Am	7	2%	Tax	28
Asian-Am	1	1%	Asian-Am	25	9%	Trusts & Estates	15
Latino	3	3%	Latino	6	2%		
Openly Gay	3	3%	Openly Gay	6	2%		

professional
pressured
stuffy

Sullivan & Cromwell is one of the most prestigious corporate law firms in New York. A "very professional" firm, Sullivan places a "huge stress on getting things done professionally, on time, and perfectly." It is an "intense" and "serious" place: this is not a firm where you see "people chatting in the hall." One person commented, "I wouldn't say it's friendly or unfriendly," but there is "little casual chitchat during the day." Attorneys "work really hard and like doing the work—that is, those that don't leave" because of the pressure. One person admitted that the firm is "probably a little stuffy." Another person qualified this remark by noting that it is not so much "stuffiness as intimidation, when faced with lots of smart people working hard. You feel like a lot is expected of you." There is "this feeling that Sullivan & Cromwell attorneys are their own breed." Over the years, many Sullivan partners, such as John Foster Dulles and Arthur Dean, have been famous within and without the legal profession.

corporate finance banking

Founded in 1879 as a litigation firm, Sullivan & Cromwell soon developed the concept of a "business lawyer," as detailed in *A Law Unto Itself*, a history of the firm. Today, 60 percent of the firm's lawyers are engaged in the corporate area, including mergers and acquisitions, project finance, commodities and derivatives, real estate, privatizations, corporate finance, and banking. Securities law is a strong "focus" of Sullivan's practice, and the firm is involved in "every kind of financing vehicle: securitization, project financing, real estate, municipal, and state bonds, etc." Goldman Sachs, a pre-eminent investment banking firm, is Sullivan's largest client. In fact, the firm's main office is located in downtown Manhattan, rather than midtown, in part to be close to Goldman. A former Sullivan partner, Greg Palm, is now Goldman's co-general counsel. In addition, the firm represents large corporations, such as Microsoft, Exxon, British Airways, Pharmacia & Upjohn, Softbank, and Eastman Kodak, and other investment banks. According to one person, Sullivan's Rodgin Cohen "is probably the best banking lawyer" in the country; another contact qualified this a tad, noting "I've never heard this, but he is good." The firm's attorneys reportedly joke that "he's hired just so the other side won't hire him," and "the Fed makes its regulations according to what he says."

With about 50 percent of its clients from outside the U.S., much of Sullivan & Cromwell's corporate and banking work has an international flavor. For example, the firm has handled numerous public offerings in Latin America. Its junior midlevel associates frequently must travel, and lawyers are "often requested to go to a foreign office for a couple of years." Many lawyers volunteer for these two year stints abroad. The firm is expanding its international practice and has offices in London, Paris, Tokyo, Hong Kong, and Melbourne. It also has a "presence" in Frankfurt, and handles an increasing number of matters involving Latin America, Asia, Australia/New Zealand, and Europe. Domestically, Sullivan has Washington, D.C. and L.A. branch offices, which were described as "extensions of New York, doing a lot of securities work." The D.C. and L.A. offices now also do a "significant amount of M&A and litigation work as well," reported one contact.

Litigation occupies about 30 percent of the firm's lawyers. Sullivan & Cromwell mostly handles securities, banking, antitrust, employment, environmental litigation (particularly Superfund matters), and white-collar criminal defense. It also has an intellectual property litigation practice, and represents clients in international arbitrations. Tax and estates constitute the remainder of Sullivan's work. The estates group, though small, has a busy and varied practice and has been involved in the high-profile disputes of the Johnson and Gallo families.

pro bono externship

Sullivan & Cromwell has a well-organized pro bono program, with one firm attorney dedicating her time exclusively to coordinating pro bono work. The firm also has a pro bono externship program, through which every year one associate may spend a year representing pro se clients in federal civil cases, while still maintaining an office and salary at the firm. Sullivan does not limit the time that attorneys may spend on pro bono work, and we were told that a number of people handle these matters. One person explained that the pro bono cases are very appealing to younger associates who "can run them."

truly a meritocracy

Sullivan & Cromwell is premised on a "survival of the strong" mentality. One person suggested that the word "'meritocracy' would describe the firm to a 'T.' They don't care what you do so long as you get your work done;" a second contact remarked that "you are valued for your capabilities and output, not for who you are or whom you know." New associates are assigned an "associate buddy" who assists in orientation to the firm. In theory, senior attorneys call upon the new associates to do their work. In practice, however, we were told that associates often "get assignments" themselves "in order to pursue a particular interest" and to develop working relationships with partners. Associates have "considerable control over obtaining the type of work that they want to do," reported one insider. Another explained that "partners who like you will call" with assignments. This person added that "many people take on more than they can handle and work phenomenal hours." Yet another contact added that "this is almost entirely a personal choice—we all work hard, but quality is much more valued than quantity."

sink or swim

Early responsibility is the norm at Sullivan & Cromwell. One person noted that "you literally learn on the spot...I knew just the basics of securities transactions, but the week I got there, I was put on an equity issue and given an S-1 registration statement to review. I was brought to every meeting with the client and learned from observation and precedents." Without question, Sullivan associates are entrusted with a "very, very high level of responsibility." One contact observed that "nevertheless, associates have a great resource to fall back on, in the fellow associates and partners at the firm, who may be relied on to answer questions or provide support." Though many firms may do likewise, Sullivan is noteworthy because its partners "really trust your judgment...and ask you what the outcome is." First-year litigation associates handle research and draft briefs. By their third or fourth year, litigators argue motions in court. Young corporate associates initially are responsible for drafting documents, but quickly progress to handling negotiations, and may even start "running their own deals if they are good." One contact informed us that "junior associates often negotiate agreements against other firms' senior associates or even their partners. From nearly the first day an attorney starts at S&C, she will be speaking to clients on a daily basis". The responsibility "is great, but it's constant pressure, especially because cases are leanly staffed," noted another contact. Although associates are forced to learn quickly and on-the-job, the firm does have an excellent two-year training program. Associates are reviewed annually, but one contact discerned that you learn more about your performance "in terms of the kind of work you get."

grueling hours

According to one person, "associates are fungible" at Sullivan & Cromwell. Associates are "there to churn out work and start by working 80 hours" per week. Beginning attorneys apparently know what they are getting into. People noticed that "no one talks about billable hours at S&C, because everyone works so hard you just don't count billables." Summer associates quickly learn that it is "not that unusual" for someone to bill 16 hours in a day, and "people routinely bill 12 hour days." "The office is still humming at 9 P.M.," and attorneys frequently work on weekends. People can become unhappy "because they got into this kind of job" but we were told that "it's not the firm; it's the type of and amount of work that's done": "everyone has a lot of pride in the firm...they think it's a good place to be...and are pretty loyal" to it. They believe that if you have to work in a big firm, you "would like it to be S&C." Some people become dejected "because they work so much. Their whole life is the job. They go in to work, go home, go to sleep, and don't stop to think." Not surprisingly, many attorneys leave the firm. "People are generally not there for the long haul," stated one contact. Another remarked that "very few associates make partner," but a third contact pointed out that "approximately 17–18% of entering associates become S&C partners."

minimal social life

Social life at Sullivan & Cromwell is minimal, but not non-existent. One person informed us that "a lot of time is spent at the office, so a big opportunity exists to get to know people. People are considerate, nice to work with, and even be friends with." During the day, "you do your job. You do it well, or people get upset." One person observed that attorneys are "very cooperative and supportive when they work on projects. We have an E-mail system (obviously) and it is used to pose various legal questions in search of precedents, opinions, etc. Lawyers respond actively. There is no backstabbing." Because of their long working hours, attorneys do not have "a huge social life outside the firm." There are "various little groups that hang out—mostly clustered according to class year." The summer program is, however, "great" and attorneys are "thrilled" when summer rolls around. Summer events include the firm outing, held at the Westchester Country Club and the Casino night at the Equitable Tower. Associates "regularly take summer associates out to lunch or dinner," according to one contact. The firm holds monthly cocktail parties and an annual formal dinner/dance.

lacks diversity

The workplace at Sullivan & Cromwell conveys a distinct impression of homogeneity. One person observed that "conventional white shirt and conservative suits dominate." Women "dress meticulously in beautiful clothes" and although dresses or pantsuits are worn often, suits are still common. One contact observed that "women also wear trousers and a jacket or even a sweater." Another source revealed that when she wore a dress to work she "felt like a secretary," to which another source quipped, "it depends on the type of dress she wore. If professional, they're ok." Sullivan attorneys are predominantly white and male. Under the leadership of the firm's one African-American partner, Sullivan actively recruits minority attorneys, but has had "trouble retaining" them. It is to be noted, however, that the new chairman of the firm is Latino, as is the hiring partner of the New York office.

atmosphere for women

In assessing the firm's attitude toward women, one person asserted that Sullivan attorneys "don't care if you are a man or a woman or both as long as you get your job done. You don't get special treatment." Sullivan has made an effort to be sensitive to women's concerns and, according to one person, "does want you to balance your life against the firm's needs." Each summer, the firm organizes a cocktail party for the women at the firm, and there is an annual dinner for the female attorneys as well. Sullivan also has a good maternity leave policy, has an emergency child care center in its building, and permits attorneys to work part-time. A former female partner decided to become of counsel and work out of her Virginia home. The firm has conducted sexual harassment training as part of a larger program in diversity training, but one person remarked that "none of the senior partners thought it was directed to them." A firm spokesperson informed us, however, that "all of our partners take these training sessions seriously and are very interested in any comments and concerns raised by our associates."

Sullivan & Cromwell is run by a management committee, consisting of eight to 10 of the firm's most senior partners. The firm's chairman remains in charge until he elects to step down, unless he reaches the age of 65 first, when he is required to retire. According to one person, "associates are not well-informed" about management decisions. Another person observed that "S&C is managed in a fairly secretive manner—associates are always guessing about how decisions are made." The firm is, according to one insider, "one of the two or three most profitable law firms in the world."

state of the art offices

Sullivan & Cromwell's offices reflect its commitment to do "everything to make a lawyer's life helpful." The offices have "got it all," declared one contact. The firm's main offices are beautiful, occupying 11 floors in a building overlooking the East River and the Statue of Liberty in downtown Manhattan. Sullivan also has a midtown conference center. Only first-year associates share offices. In general, the support services are "well-organized and excellent." Two attorneys are assigned to each secretary. Each attorney is given an IBM Pentium PC, and the firm has a state-of-the-art computer system which is "constantly updated and is absolutely amazing." All of Sullivan's offices are linked by computer for word processing; access to the firm precedent system, online library catalogue, litigation support, and other databases; and for other purposes. One person exclaimed that "the library is the most amazing thing I have ever seen. It's huge with everything you need, and the staff will get you anything in fifteen minutes. There are always people sitting at the desk to help you." The firm has both a lawyers' cafeteria and a staff cafeteria. One person warned that if you eat in the lawyers' cafeteria, you "have to be prepared to have a partner join you." Sullivan & Cromwell recently opened a gym for lawyers in the basement of their building with trainers, full showers, etc., and state-of-the-art equipment.

selective hiring

As might be expected, Sullivan & Cromwell demands virtual perfection from its job applicants. People we interviewed believed that law students need an A- GPA from the top law schools (or need to be at the top of their class at other law schools) to receive a callback interview. Most summer associates are law review members or have similar credentials. The firm wants everything about its attorneys "to be top-notch and the best." A successful candidate must be "well-spoken and well-educated; someone who can converse and is not fatally shy." The firm also values applicants with language skills or investment banking experience. Enthusiasm for mergers and acquisitions, project finance, banking, and securities work is important as well. The firm draws most of its summer associates from the top 10 law schools. However, many also come from other national law schools. In 1996, the summer class contained 96 students from 33 schools and the firm made offers to 95.

résumé grilling interview

A Sullivan & Cromwell interviewer often will engage an applicant in an "in-depth" conversation about his or her accomplishments. One person warned that they "will grill you about stuff on your résumé." But another noted that "you can steer the conversation into an area with which you are comfortable." People also advised candidates to emphasize "how much they want to do securities work. People at S&C are not exciting, vibrant people. They want people who will work, and with whom it will be pleasant to work." Interviewers also "like you to have questions."

Sullivan & Cromwell is a very professional law firm, committed to excellence. It demands a lot of its attorneys and, certainly, is not for everyone. For someone interested in corporate finance, banking, project finance, or mergers and acquisitions, and who is willing to make the commitment to work extraordinarily long hours, Sullivan is a very attractive firm; its "name and stability" may "open a lot of doors for you." One person explained, "I chose it because when I leave I would like to come from the best place I can."

Wachtell, Lipton, Rosen & Katz

New York

Address: 51 West 52nd Street, New York, NY 10019
Telephone: (212) 403–1000
Hiring Attorney: John F. Savarese
Contact: Ruth Ivey, Recruiting Director; (212) 403–1374
Associate Salary: First year $87,500 (1997); second $104,000; third $123,000; fourth $147,000; fifth $173,000
Summer Salary: $1675/week (1997)
Average Hours: NA worked; NA billed; NA required
Family Benefits: 16 weeks paid maternity leave (cbc unpaid); 0 weeks paid paternity leave (cbc unpaid); domestic partner benefits; emergency back-up day care facilities
1996 Summer: Class of 19 students; offers to 18
Partnership: 41% of entering associates from 1980–1986 were made partner
Pro Bono: 1–3% of all work is pro bono

Wachtell, Lipton, Rosen & Katz in 1997
138 Lawyers at the Firm
1.0 Associate Per Partner

Total Partners 65		
Women	7	11%
All Minorities	2	3%
Asian-Am	1	2%
Latino	1	2%

Total Associates 67		
Women	21	31%
All Minorities	9	13%
Afro-Am	4	6%
Asian-Am	4	6%
Latino	1	1%

Practice Areas	
Litigation	50
Corporate	49
Bankruptcy	20
Tax/Trusts & Estates	8
Real Estate	6
Antitrust	5

At a little under 140 lawyers, Wachtell, Lipton, Rosen & Katz is small in size relative to the major New York law firms; yet, no one takes this powerhouse lightly. Its profits per partner are consistently among the highest in the nation. In recent years, it has had the highest revenues per partner in the country. Carrying perhaps more prestige than any other New York firm and producing some of the highest quality work in mergers and acquisitions and bankruptcy law, as well as in civil and regulatory litigation, Wachtell is "busier than any other firm in New York." It handles only the most complex and high-profile matters. Wachtell has been consulted in virtually every major New York deal in the past few decades. Its associates also enjoy an unusual and attractive array of incentives. Wachtell strives to keep its partner to associate ratio close to 1:1. In addition, close working relationships between partners and associates offer junior attorneys great responsibility on the "most interesting work anywhere in the country." As an added incentive, the partners have rewarded associates with large bonuses, "reaching as high as 50% of the top-of-the-market base salaries." First year associates start at $87,500 while third year associates made a base salary of $123,000.

workaholic firm culture

Wachtell's success, however, does not come without "stark" tradeoffs for its attorneys. Wachtell is, to put it mildly, a "workaholic" firm. It is "not abnormal for partners to stay until 2 or 3 A.M." when required by a matter, we were told. An average workday ends around 10 P.M., and attorneys "regularly" bill 2500 hours per year. While there is no minimum work requirement, everybody works long hours, in part because it is difficult for an attorney to work less and still be a "team player."

a true meritocracy

Wachtell was founded in the mid-1960s by four graduates of New York University Law School who worked on the law review together. According to firm legend, they were "excluded" from the large New York firms at the time because they were Jewish. The firm's history continues to shape its "outsider's culture," said one contact. While some New York firms value family connections or lineage, Wachtell "concentrates only on merit," added this person.

cutting-edge M&A practice

Two of the four founding partners are still at the firm, and they continue to "bring in the most business," although this is changing as the next generation of partners increasingly is responsible for bringing in the firm's business. Marty Lipton is the "foremost corporate lawyer in America" and is known as the "God of M&A." Herb Wachtell is one of the firm's most prominent litigators. Wachtell rose to prominence in the 1970s and 1980s as an M&A firm. It is rumored that the firm was involved in so many hostile takeover defenses in the 1980s that arbitrageurs skulked outside its offices to observe the people visiting the firm and determine who "was about to be taken over." Consequently, Wachtell has very tight security and a strict policy which forbids its attorneys from trading or owning any public securities. More recently, it has represented AT&T and W.R. Grace in two of the largest restructurings in history, and has handled the mergers of Pan Energy and Duke Power, CSX and Conrail, and NationsBank and Boatmen. It also handled Raytheon's acquisition of the Hughes defense business, and represents Hilton in its bid to acquire ITT. The firm does not have an extensive international practice but has been involved in a number of international acquisitions, including the largest acquisition by a French company of a U.S. company. Major recent litigation engagements include representing Phillip Morris in its $10 billion defamation case against ABC, representing MCA and Seagram in their month-long trial against Viacom over the fate of USA networks, and several takeover fights.

Wachtell also routinely represents investment banks such as Salomon Brothers, Goldman Sachs, Lazard Freres, Credit Suisse, and First Boston, but does not serve as regular counsel to any of its clients. Instead, Wachtell selects the most complex transactions from all the work it is offered, which according to one person, require "speed and precision, and are always important to the client." Unlike most firms, Wachtell charges its corporate clients a flat rate which typically represents some percentage of the value the "deal" involved.

Wachtell's nationally renowned bankruptcy practice is extremely busy. A bankruptcy partner, Chaim Fortgang, was described as the "foremost guy of the second generation" at the firm. People predict that he will soon become one of the firm's major rainmakers. Another up-and-comer at the firm, we were told, is Ed Herlihy, who heads the financial institutions M&A practice and is nationally recognized as a leading expert in this field. Herb Wachtell and Bernie Nussbaum have built a strong litigation practice that handles securities litigation, contests for corporate control, First Amendment cases, and white-collar crime. Among his many accomplishments, Nussbaum recently served a stint as General Counsel to the White House in the Clinton Administration. Norman Redlich, the former dean of New York University Law School, is well-known for his expertise in First Amendment cases.

When Wachtell attorneys have time, the firm encourages them to work on pro bono matters and counts the time toward billable hours. Attorneys have been involved in death penalty and other precedent setting cases. In recent years, an openly gay partner at the firm litigated *Steffan v. Cheney*, a case which involved the discharge of a gay man from the Naval Academy. Summer associates may elect to work for one week at full summer salary in the New York City Bar's Housing Court Program.

teamwork emphasis

New associates can select the particular department of the firm in which they want to work. Partners always call associates directly when they need work to be done. "Very few matters (no matter what the size) are staffed with more than two associates, and most have just one," one contact informed us. Wachtell is not a firm of individual stars. The "number one priority at Wachtell," according to one insider, "is getting the job done." The firm emphasizes teamwork heavily. "The culture brings people together," asserted one source. Though a "friendly" place where attorneys "work well together," Wachtell is "pretty businesslike." The partners are "very demanding; they expect nothing less than perfection—as they define it." You "work hard and like it because the work is interesting," declared one contact, explaining that "it is a self-selection process. People know what they are getting into." Sometimes, however, "people...feel like they have to be in the office all the time. But that is not the firm, it is the individuals."

immediate opportunities

Junior associates "are thrown out to do deals on their own" soon after joining the firm, according to one person. Another noted that matters are staffed leanly and that "young associates are often the number two guys on multi-billion dollar deals." A Wachtell associate was recently featured as "Dealmaker of the Month" in American Lawyer magazine. The firm provides as much responsibility as its associates can handle. One source declared that Wachtell is a "pure meritocracy...all they care about is your work. You start from ground zero and have to prove yourself every day."

learn by doing

Consistent with its informal structure, Wachtell does not have a structured training program. Associates "learn by doing" and by working closely with partners. Historically, feedback has been a problem, and apparently continues to be a problem. Moreover, as much as Wachtell values its associates, it reportedly does not keep them well informed about their prospects for making partner. Even a successful tenure of six years at the firm is no guarantee that one will become a partner, according to our sources. A firm spokesperson vigorously denied this state of affairs, asserting that the firm believes, "based upon what our associates uniformly tell us, that they feel they get a high degree of feedback and are kept well informed about their partnership chances."

minimal social life

Most Wachtell attorneys do not have much of a social life outside the firm, according to the bulk of people we spoke with, although not all were happy with this "generalization." Within the firm, many attorneys are friends who eat meals and work out at the gym together, but "there is not much hanging out." The firm is, however, a "pretty open" place and in some ways is quite "familial." It is also a firm where "people say what is on their mind." The firm sponsors a well-attended weekly lawyers' lunch "to build cohesion and unity," and "many who work late eat together in the dining room for a catered-in dinner." Wachtell attorneys are predominantly Jewish, and kosher meals are available at all firm functions.

effort to diversify

Roughly twenty percent of all Wachtell attorneys are women. The "lifestyle of the firm is not great for taking time off and having children," explained one contact. Another commented, however, that a higher percentage of women who join the firm are promoted at Wachtell than at any other firm in New York. This person added that the firm has "extremely fair and liberal policies for maternity leave," noting that the firm considers it "important to keep a top performer." The firm has few minority attorneys but, according to one person, is "making Herculean efforts" to recruit them. The firm's summer program for first-year law students focuses on hiring minority law students. The firm also attends minority job fairs and participates in the Sponsors for Educational Opportunity Program.

management

Wachtell's governing authority is concentrated in the hands of a ten-person management committee chaired by Richard Katcher, a "second generation" corporate partner. The management committee requires the approval of the partners before making any major decisions. "Wachtell is one of the best run firms in the city. It makes sure the job gets done," praised one admirer. Associates have little power in the firm's management, but "they are a valued commodity, and people are open about voicing problems." The firm is doing extremely well economically; the firm had an "extraordinarily profitable year" in 1996, according to one insider. It is happy with its present position and is not developing new practice areas. One person observed that it is hard to say "what they will look like in twenty years. The top partners want to keep it small. But there is pressure to become like Skadden," a worldwide mega firm.

excellent support services

Wachtell's offices are located in the CBS Building in Manhattan. The firm has a strong commitment to providing the best facilities and services required to produce excellent legal work. Wachtell even "places a premium on treating the support staff well. They are important and respected." It is the "best support staff in New York," declared one source. Wachtell makes every effort to make its attorneys' lives easier and is "not cheap about the little things. They trust people to be honest and straightforward in expenses." It attends even to the small things; recently a "new free yogurt machine (for a total of two now)" was introduced, "to go along with the free espresso and cappuccino machines" already present.

hires only highest GPAs

Wachtell is an extremely selective law firm. It will "only hire people who meet its standards. It doesn't hire to meet demand," stated one source. The grades it requires of applicants are "reputedly the highest in New York." Most people claimed that applicants must have at least an A- grade point average from the top law schools, though one person believed that the firm may consider B+ students. One contact informed us that the firm has "lots of nerds," which is fine, said this person, "if you like that sort of thing." Other than being "bright, hard-working people," successful applicants need have "no other defining characteristics" to land a job at Wachtell. You "could be from the moon," asserted one contact. The firm values any past business experience or activity that displays initiative. Applicants were advised to emphasize in their interviews with the firm that they are willing to "work hard and dedicate themselves to the practice of law." One insider noted that "attitude is a big thing, and enthusiasm about the firm is important." About 75 percent of the 1996 summer associates attended Columbia, Harvard, New York University, Stanford, and Yale. The remaining 25 percent were from other schools across the country. One contact told us that "the firm only recruits at certain schools, and offers positions to qualified people from other schools only rarely." The firm does not make permanent offers to first-year summer associates.

Wachtell demands an almost single-minded dedication from its attorneys and is not for everyone. For those people willing to commit to this "high-energy" firm, it offers the very real possibility of becoming partner, some of the best legal work in New York under the guidance of some of the country's foremost lawyers, and perhaps the highest salaries in the nation. The firm cannot be beat in terms of the prestige it brings. One person observed, "people really take note of the fact that you work at Wachtell." But be careful, the "Wachtell lifestyle can kill you!"

Weil, Gotshal & Manges

New York Dallas Houston Menlo Park Miami Washington
Brussels Budapest London Prague Warsaw

Address: 767 Fifth Avenue, New York, NY 10153
Telephone: (212) 310–8000
Hiring Attorney: Akiko Mikumo/Steven A. Reiss
Contact: Donna J. Lang, Recruitment Administrator; (212) 735–4553
Associate Salary: First year $88,500 (1997); second $103,000; third $121,250; fourth $145,000; fifth $170,500; sixth $185,000; seventh $196,250; salary figures are the maximum total compensation for each class
Summer Salary: $1650/week (1997)
Average Hours: NA worked; NA billed; none required
Family Benefits: 12 weeks paid maternity leave; emergency childcare program
1996 Summer: Class of 59 students; offers to 56
Partnership: 26% of entering associates from 1979–1985 were made partner
Pro Bono: 2% of all work is pro bono

Weil, Gotshal & Manges in 1997
360 Lawyers at the New York Office
2.0 Associates Per Partner

Total Partners 116			Total Associates 230			Practice Areas	
Women	17	15%	Women	84	37%	Corporate	94
All Minorities	4	3%	All Minorities	33	14%	Trade Practices & Regulatory	64
Afro-Am	2	2%	Afro-Am	10	4%	Litigation	56
Asian-Am	2	2%	Asian-Am	15	7%	Business Fin. & Restructuring	47
			Latino	8	3%	Business & Securities Litigation	34
						Tax	32
						Real Estate	25
						Trusts & Estates	8

no-nonsense intense atmosphere

Founded by a group of Jewish lawyers at a time when they were excluded from the pre-eminent New York law firms, Weil, Gotshal & Manges has a "history of not being clubby, and is good about being open-minded." The firm is now ranked among the top 10 New York law firms in stature, size, and profits per partner. Weil Gotshal's success has, however, not come without costs. Affectionately known as "We'll Get You and Mangle You," Weil Gotshal is a "hard-working, no-nonsense" firm, "but in a good way," one person told us. Weil Gotshal attorneys are "aggressive and hard-working people." You are expected "to be dedicated" and be a "part of the team."

high-energy sweatshop

Weil Gotshal attorneys are "people who decide to come to New York and devote their lives to the law, and are willing to spend all their time at the firm," commented one person. The firm has a reputation for being a "sweatshop." Though it does not have a minimum billable requirement, one person noted that as an associate you "have so much work that you will bill a respectable amount." While associates frequently complain about how hard they have to work, this "high-energy" firm has "a lot of spirit." Weil Gotshal attorneys are "very energetic people who like each other," one person noted. Morale at the firm, which is generally good, reportedly is "down" of late. In part, this may be attributable to the partnership's having "a reputation for being unresponsive to associates," according to one source, who added however that "this seems to be improving." Along with the long hours, Weil Gotshal offers a very informal atmosphere. It is "one of the loosest places" in terms of dress in New York. Many attorneys "wear ugly clothes and whatever tie is handy," declared one contact.

practice areas

As a full-service law firm, which one person labeled a "supermarket" for entering associates, Weil Gotshal's work atmosphere differs in each department. The firm is best known for its bankruptcy department which is "one of the best in the country." The bankruptcy lawyers are a "nice group of attorneys, and the associates are friendly with each other," said one person, but they "take their work really seriously" and "work a lot harder" than attorneys in most other departments. The firm has represented certain Canadian operations of Olympia and York, which is breaking ground as one of the first reorganization cases administered concurrently under the bankruptcy laws of two different jurisdictions.

The corporate department is the largest at the firm, and according to one person, is the "power center of the partnership." The department is organized around five working groups. The firm represents many Fortune 500 and large international corporations, including American Airlines, BMW, Citibank, General Motors, and General Electric. Corporate partners "run the gamut from crazy to laid-back," attested one contact, explaining that associates' experiences "vary considerably" depending on the partners for whom they work. One source informed us that, in the corporate department, "many deals come in through partners outside of the department, which is a disadvantage."

The business and securities litigation department handles a wide range of complex business cases involving contests for corporate control. The group has been involved with successful proxy contests for board representation on or control of companies such as USX, National Intergroup and UJB Financial. This department also handles some of the transactional matters which arise in these disputes. The "business and securities associates don't hang out with other groups," said one person. Another observed that the department is fairly separate from the rest of the firm. "A major rainmaker in the department is a legendary jerk. There are a lot of stories about him throwing tantrums," cautioned one source. The real estate partners, on the other hand, are "really laid-back" and sponsor "ice-cream and beer breaks once a week" during the summer.

Lawyers in the litigation and trade practices and regulatory law departments work closely together to handle virtually all areas of commercial litigation ranging from products liability to intellectual property. These departments have recently been involved in a number of high-profile antitrust suits involving the professional players' associations of baseball, hockey, basketball and football. The trade practices and regulatory department, under the joint leadership of Michael Epstein and Helene Jaffe, has a strong reputation in virtually every aspect of public and private regulation. This department houses a leading regulatory finance practice and an international trade practice, among others. The firm also has significant labor and trusts and estates practices. Many of the firm's matters involve international clients and issues. Weil Gotshal is building an international practice, particularly in Eastern Europe, and now has offices in Budapest, Prague, and Warsaw. More recently, Weil Gotshal has experienced "a huge expansion in its European practice, particularly in the London office, which is now one of the largest for foreign firms in London. Consequently, there are big opportunities for corporate associates to rotate through foreign offices for a deal, a year or two years or more."

Weil Gotshal encourages attorneys to devote at least 30 hours to pro bono work per year, and the firm is a signatory to the ABA Pro Bono Challenge. The firm has been honored with the New York State Bar Association President's Pro Bono Service Award. Ira Millstein, one of the firm's three leading partners and the subject of a recent *Business Week* article describing his role in building and managing the firm, is also

Chairman of the Central Park Conservancy and spearheads the firm's commitment to pro bono and civic activities. Summer associates may work for one week with a public interest organization while earning their full firm salary.

professional development

New associates are hired into a particular department and initially receive work through a formal assignment system, which varies by department. One contact remarked that "Weil is a big place, so often you have to assert yourself to get the type of work you want." Junior corporate associates typically handle drafting, proofreading documents and "going to the printers." One person informed us that the corporate department "is unstructured and there is no specialization until the third or fourth year and even then there is no real specialization." Another contact remarked that "it is important to be aggressive—tell the assigning partner what you like and tell partners whose work you like that you want to work with them." Junior litigators are entrusted with quite a bit of responsibility. First-year associates take depositions. Most appear in court before their third or fourth year. The firm has an organized training program, though most associate training reportedly occurs "on-the-job." In general, Weil Gotshal provides excellent feedback to associates. The firm has an "open culture and partners are up front," explained one admirer.

minimal social life

Because attorneys work long hours and many attorneys are married, social life is minimal at Weil Gotshal. A few groups of associates, however, go out after work, often to Greenwich Village for some "collegiate style fun." The firm organizes a number of social events including an annual dinner for attorneys and staff, a firm outing, annual department get-togethers, numerous summer activities, monthly firmwide cocktail parties, and department happy hours or "study breaks."

diversity workshop

Weil Gotshal is reportedly working hard to make it a comfortable place for women and minorities. Consistent with its open culture, the firm established a committee to promote diversity in its hiring. In addition, the firm hired an independent consultant to provide gender and race sensitivity workshops to attorneys at the firm. Women are encouraged to report any sexual harassment to the diversity committee.

managing triad

Weil Gotshal is run primarily by three main partners, Todd Lang, Harvey Miller, and Ira Millstein, and is very healthy economically. The strong bankruptcy practice, which is "counter-cyclical," has cushioned the firm during downturns in the economy. Weil Gotshal will now probably focus, we were told, on building its corporate department into a top-tier practice comparable to such firms as Sullivan & Cromwell. The firm is also working to increase its presence in Eastern Europe, where it has handled a number of privatizations and other matters.

office renovation underway

Weil Gotshal's office facilities are "not particularly snazzy," but they are presently undergoing a face lift, due to be completed in 1998. Thus far, two floors in the remodeling effort have been completed, along with the installation of a new cafeteria. Weil Gotshal has an in-house catering service which provides the food for all firm events. The firm always has a table with Kosher and vegetarian food available. Attorneys "don't get a lot of space," reported one contact. Associates share offices during their first year at the firm, then progress to a private office with no windows, and are finally assigned an office with a window. The firm has a fully networked Windows-based computer system, and the support staff is very good. Situated in the General Motors building at Central Park South, Weil Gotshal sits above the world-famous, Disney Land-esque toy store FAO Schwarz, which is located on the first floor of the building. "Whenever you get depressed you can run to FAO Schwarz," one person assured those considering working at the firm.

hiring practices

Weil Gotshal seeks to hire "self-motivated, go-getter" law students who have some "spark." The firm generally hires a diverse summer class from the top national law schools and other local schools. Weil Gotshal's summer program is designed for people who want to sample many practice areas. Summer associates typically rotate through three or four of the firm's departments. The firm organizes a weekend orientation in New York for the summer class each April prior to the summer. At this time, the entire summer class meets and is introduced to the firm's different departments. After this meeting, summer associates list their top six choices of departments in which they want to work, and the firm makes every effort to accommodate their choices.

Weil Gotshal is an extremely demanding firm, and its associates must work very hard. The firm's very "open culture," one person noted, "may seem abrasive at times, but candor is well-appreciated." This is a "very live and let live" firm. It is also extremely successful and rewards associates well. One contact informed us that "in terms of business, Weil Gotshal has probably been its busiest in the last five years. The firm has been involved with some of the biggest deals of the century this past year." Alongside this business there is the downside, according to this contact, namely "there is not much downtime."

White & Case

New York Los Angeles Miami Washington

Almaty Ankara Bangkok Bombay Brussels Budapest Hanoi Helsinki Hong Kong Istanbul Jakarta Jeddah Johannesburg London Mexico City Moscow Paris Prague Riyadh Singapore Stockholm Tashkent Tokyo Warsaw

Address: 1155 Avenue of the Americas, New York, NY 10036
Telephone: (212) 819–8200
Hiring Attorney: Eugene W. Goodwillie, Jr.
Contact: Vera P. Murphy, Director of Legal Employment; (212) 819–8785
Associate Salary: First year $85,000 (1997); second $103,500; third $110,000–124,000; fourth $125,000–145,000; fifth $142,000–165,000; sixth $159,000–186,000; seventh $168,000–197,000; eighth $178,000–211,000
Summer Salary: NA
Average Hours: NA worked; NA billed; NA required
Family Benefits: 12 weeks paid maternity leave (integrated with the firm's insurance policy and state and federal law); back-up day care services and caregivers on call
1996 Summer: Class of 45 students; offers to 45
Partnership: 12% of entering associates from 1983–1988 were made partner
Pro Bono: 3% of all work is pro bono

White & Case in 1997
282 Lawyers at the New York Office
2.4 Associates Per Partner

Total Partners 84		
Women	10	12%
All Minorities	3	4%
Afro-Am	1	1%
Asian-Am	2	2%

Total Associates 198		
Women	67	34%
All Minorities	27	14%
Afro-Am	8	4%
Asian-Am	14	7%
Latino	5	3%

Practice Areas	
Corp. & Fin. Services	162
Litigation	71
Tax	28
Trusts & Estates	11
Rotation Program	10

international corporate

White & Case is a pre-eminent New York law firm with an international reputation. Although now located in midtown Manhattan, since its earliest days as a Wall Street firm White & Case has provided financial legal services to banks and other clients. Today, the firm continues to focus on corporate and financial legal services and represents numerous national and international banks and many large multinational corporations.

The firm is most well-known for its unique international practice. The firm's project finance practice is very highly-regarded. With 24 offices in foreign cities, White & Case has an immense international presence. The firm has handled debt restructurings for the Indonesian and Turkish governments, has worked on restructuring the debt of the Polish and Bulgarian governments, has represented the former Czech government in privatizations, and is heavily involved in all types of domestic and international banking, securities, and project finance work. White & Case's unique "philosophy on overseas expansion" distinguishes it from many other well-known international firms. The firm does not permit foreign franchises, as does Baker & McKenzie, nor does it, with a couple of exceptions, enter into joint ventures with foreign law firms as do many other U.S. firms. Instead, a number of White & Case attorneys who have worked in the U.S. office for three or four years have gone on to found offices abroad. This provides an incentive for associates interested in international work to join White & Case for "the long haul." The firm has opened offices in Bombay, Hanoi, Tashkent, and Johannesburg over the past two years.

White & Case also has a significant international arbitration practice and a well-regarded intellectual property group, which has been bolstered by a number of lateral partners and associates over the last few years. There has also been a significant increase in the amount of work for the antitrust practice area recently. The tax group is said to provide a very "nice" work environment and the real estate group reportedly "really needs people." The firm's environmental practice benefits from the expertise of Paul Milmed, formerly Chief of the Environmental Protection Unit at the U.S. Attorney's Office.

White & Case supports attorneys committed to pro bono work. Junior associates are not subject to a strict billable requirement and some spend significant time on pro bono matters. White & Case provides a $10,000 bonus to new associates who join the firm after completing a judicial clerkship. It also pays $10,000 to new associates who work one year for an approved public interest organization before joining the firm. This amount is paid during their public interest employment.

initiative essential

New associates may enter a particular department when they join the firm or rotate through two departments for four months each before selecting an area of specialization. White & Case is not a highly structured firm. Both summer and full-time associates, we were told, are encouraged to obtain their own work. One contact observed that the "unstructured assignment system means in theory you can look for the kind of work you're interested in, but it also means that you will get staffed on projects that do not necessarily interest you." The firm offers junior associates "as much responsibility as you want. It depends on how much work you want to do." A first- or second-year corporate associate often works on "small pieces of big deals and, if lucky, big pieces of small deals." However, like at other large firms, they also mark up documents, handle document distributions, and observe more experienced attorneys. Each department offers a training program which, according to one person, will "teach you everything from start to finish."

long weekend hours

White & Case associates work hard. Because the firm is leanly staffed, the mid- to upper-level associates routinely work to midnight "and beyond," according to one contact. Another contact bemoaned "the long hours and the unpredictable hours—you learn to dread the Friday P.M. call." On the other hand, associates "don't have to stay late if there is no work" and "don't have to work weekends if they have important plans." One insider, upon hearing this, quipped that "they had better be *very* important plans."

Cookie Times

The firm is fairly informal and attorneys interact comfortably. They can wear "all sorts of things" to work provided that their attire is "fairly conservatively cut," and "dress down Fridays" are observed during the summer months. The firm also has a few unusual rules. White & Case is a social firm, and its associates form close friendships. During the day, one person told us that "it is fine to drop by friends' offices and shoot the breeze for 15 minutes." Attorneys jog together in the morning before work, travel together on vacations, and meet for lunch. Many of the social activities involve drinking, noted one person. Another commented that this is certainly a place where you "can have a personality." White & Case encourages firm social life in many ways. It organizes a number of summer events and departmental retreats. The highlight of each day is the 4:30 P.M. "Cookie Time," when the cafeteria, "known in New York for having the best food in town," provides fresh-baked cookies, tea, and coffee. Attorneys literally "run to get it while it's hot." (Well, not literally, if the truth be known). The cafeteria is a social part of the firm, and "unlike some law firm dining facilities, it is open to attorneys and staff alike," reported one contact. At White & Case, "people take sports seriously," and attorneys are even involved in roller-skating and bowling. White & Case has a fully-equipped gym in the basement of its building and a collection of "top movies" which attorneys may view while they work out. "People take full advantage of it, and it's a good place to socialize."

diversity

White & Case has a reputation as a conservative banker's law firm. On the other hand, one of the firm's earliest partners, Colonel Hartfield, was Jewish, and White & Case was one of the first Wall Street firms to promote a woman to partnership. Both Laura Hoguet, a litigator who recently left White & Case to start her own firm, and Maureen Donovan, a tax lawyer, were elected to the firm partnership over 20 years ago. White & Case employs attorneys from a number of foreign countries and targets its recruiting efforts toward increasing its number of minority lawyers.

hiring tips

White & Case hires "people who can deal with an informal atmosphere, know how to get work, and are social people." Many past summer associates had done interesting things before going to law school, disclosed one observer. People counseled students who interview at the firm to "have an agenda for what they are looking for in a firm." One person advised interviewees to emphasize the attractiveness of an international practice. Another added that you should feel free to ask "pointed questions." White & Case hires law students from the top national schools and New York-area law schools.

Whitman Breed Abbott & Morgan

New York Greenwich Los Angeles Newark Palm Beach
London Tokyo

Address: 200 Park Avenue, New York, NY 10166
Telephone: (212) 351-3000
Hiring Attorney: Loran T. Thompson
Contact: Francesca Runge, Legal Personnel Director; (212) 351-3295
Associate Salary: First year $86,000 (1996)
Summer Salary: $1654/week (1997)
Average Hours: 2050 worked; 1900 billed; 1800 required
Family Benefits: 12 weeks paid maternity leave
1996 Summer: Class of 10 students; offers to 10
Partnership: NA
Pro Bono: 1% of all work is pro bono

Whitman Breed Abbott & Morgan in 1997
176 Lawyers at the New York Office
1.0 Associate Per Partner

Total Partners 81		
Women	6	7%
All Minorities	1	1%
Afro-Am	1	1%

Total Associates 85		
Women	36	42%
All Minorities	7	8%
Afro-Am	3	4%
Asian-Am	3	4%
Latino	1	1%

Practice Areas	
Litigation	64
Corporate	43
Real Estate	17
Public Finance	14
Tax	9
Environmental	8
Bankruptcy/Reorganization	7
Labor/Employment	7
Trusts & Estates	7

Whitman Breed Abbott & Morgan is the result of a 1993 combination of Breed Abbott & Morgan with Whitman & Ransom. The merger almost doubled the size of the firm, which now has seven offices located in three countries. Whitman Breed has preserved an easygoing culture in an era of increasing competition. "This place can't be beat in terms of culture," gushed one source. "I give it two thumbs up." As one of the smaller of the large New York firms, Whitman Breed offers a friendly work environment. One insider declared that "doors are always open. Partners are just as interested in teaching me as in getting the work done. It is a real team place." Whitman Breed is not a "sweatshop." One person remarked that "for the most part (with a few notable exceptions), the partners are humane and approachable and have much respect for your personal life." The firm cares about its associates and emphasizes the quality rather than the quantity of the work that they do, asserted one person. Whitman Breed "is very much the type of place where you work hard when it's busy, but when it's slower, the firm encourages you to go out and enjoy life. The firm doesn't demand that you sacrifice life. There is a good balance between work and lifestyle most of the time." However, "quantity is rewarded when it comes to bonuses, which are based completely on reaching 2000 billable hours," one source pointed out.

open culture

Almost every aspect of associate life at Whitman Breed is shaped by the firm's friendly and open culture. Associates dress as informally as the New York lawyer dress code permits. Women wear dresses and pantsuits and men regularly shed their jackets at work. Moreover, with a strong "camaraderie among senior associates, partners, and younger associates, there is no sense of distance or superiority" separating the firm's lawyers. Whitman Breed staffs its cases thinly, usually with a partner, a senior associate, and a younger associate. The associates work closely and develop good professional relationships with partners.

practice areas

Although today Whitman Breed Abbott & Morgan is a full-service law firm, historically it has been particularly recognized for its antitrust practice. Whitman Breed is home to Bob Bicks, a former assistant Attorney General in the antitrust division of the U.S. Department of Justice and "a bigwig in antitrust." In addition, Whitman Breed has a strong commercial litigation practice. The firm's trusts and estates practice draws many clients. Trusts and estates partner Paul Lambert, who served as Ambassador to Ecuador under George Bush, is one of "George Bush's best friends," reported one person. Whitman Breed recently experienced the departure of about ten partners from the corporate department. "They took with them the aircraft finance work and private placement work. The emphasis is now on more traditional securities work, although new partners are being hired and they may change the type of work in the corporate department," one source reported. Whitman Breed has an established international corporate practice. The firm has several major Japanese and European clients. Although Whitman Breed encourages pro bono endeavors, the practice is loosely structured, and individuals must pursue projects on their own initiative. Pro bono hours are credited as billable hours by the firm, however.

opportunities

Entering associates join a particular department, but it is possible to transfer to another department. Though each department assigns work differently, associates usually have some degree of control over the kind of work they get. The firm offers as much responsibility to young associates as they can handle—one person commented, "the quicker the better." Typically, junior litigation associate responsibilities include "plenty of research, writing briefs, second-seating in court, meeting clients, making motions and complaints, and conducting depositions (though usually not alone)."

on-the-job training

Formal training is a weak point at Whitman Breed. One contact noted that "the formal training is minimal and your development as an attorney may depend on the luck of the draw in terms of whom you are assigned to work with." Most training occurs on the job. Each department, however, holds seminars in the fall to introduce new associates to its practice, and also conducts regular meetings where partners (and sometimes associates) make presentations on certain points of the law. The firm also on occasion sends associates to seminars outside the firm, about which they report back to their colleagues. Perhaps because "associates work very closely with partners all the way," partners generally provide extensive feedback to associates. "I walk down the halls and see junior associates in offices with partners all the time. They are intricately involved," attested one contact. Summer associates also receive a lot of attention. "The hiring partner and recruiting coordinator really care," praised one admirer.

active social life

Whitman Breed arranges a lavish summer program, which includes two or three activities every week. Summer events include the Corporate Challenge road race, cocktail parties, a full-day firm outing at a country club, and a trip to the Meadowlands racetrack (some partners own horses). Other events have included A Night at the Palladium (a pro bono benefit at a dance club), a Broadway musical, and the Mostly Mozart Night. Social life outside the summer program is also quite active. Groups of young associates form strong friendships and go out after work for dinner and drinks.

little diversity

Whitman Breed "used to be WASPy, and is still pretty white, but it does not have a WASP culture," said one contact. Another source observed that "certain partners fancy that Whitman Breed is a white-shoe firm, but this is in stark contrast to the reality of the firm culture." The firm, however, does not have many minority attorneys, and the people we interviewed did not notice any active minority recruitment efforts. As for women's issues, one source commented that the firm's "attitude toward maternity leave seemed great." Another noted that "in general, the firm's accommodation of women with young children is determined on a case-by-case basis."

personality driven hiring process

As for recruitment, Whitman Breed Abbott & Morgan carefully considers the personalities of the applicants. One person suggested that "they don't care who you are, whether you are cool or nerdy, as long as you are nice." This firm "wants people who will integrate well." At Whitman Breed, "no one is cutthroat and no one is a jerk," we were told. People we interviewed advised prospective applicants to "be themselves...find something in common with the interviewer and talk about it...have a nice conversation. They can see your accomplishments on your résumé; they want to see if you are a good person and will fit into the firm." Another contact counseled applicants to "emphasize how much they like the atmosphere of a midsize firm and the informal setting in which to do real corporate work." Whitman Breed generally hires from the top national law schools and New York-area schools. While most students the firm recruits from less prestigious law schools are at the top of their class, people noted that Whitman Breed will hire students with average academic records from prestige campuses.

Whitman Breed Abbott & Morgan is not a place for people who want to do the "super-huge, largest takeovers and transactions." It is a place for those who want a friendly, more relaxed environment that will allow them to maintain a balanced lifestyle. Raved one insider, "It is really true at this firm. You can maintain a social life and a private life outside the firm." Others agreed with the sentiments of one insider who observed that "the pay scale is not yet at the level of the major firms in the city" but that "the hours make up for that."

Willkie Farr & Gallagher

New York Washington
London Paris

Address: One Citicorp Center, 153 East 53rd Street, New York, NY 10022-4677
Telephone: (212) 821-8000
Hiring Attorney: Michael J. Kelly/Leslie M. Mazza
Contact: Billie L. Kelly, Director of Legal Personnel & Recruiting; (212) 821-8468
Associate Salary: First year $85,000 plus $2,000 bonus (1997); second $93,000 plus $10,000; third $110,000 plus $12,000; fourth $128,000 plus $17,000; fifth $150,000 plus $20,000; sixth $163,000 plus $20,000; seventh $168,000 plus $25,000; eighth $178,000 plus $25,000
Summer Salary: NA
Average Hours: NA
Family Benefits: Health, life, and disability insurance; 401K Plan; 12 weeks paid maternity leave; 1 week paid paternity leave (24 weeks unpaid); emergency daycare
1996 Summer: Class of 38 students; offers to 36
Partnership: 17% of entering associates from 1982–1988 were made partner
Pro Bono: 3% of all work is pro bono

Willkie Farr & Gallagher in 1997
309 Lawyers at the New York Office
2.4 Associates Per Partner

Total Partners 88		
Women	7	8%
All Minorities	4	5%
Asian-Am	3	3%
Latino	1	1%

Total Associates 207		
Women	79	38%
All Minorities	29	14%
Afro-Am	13	6%
Asian-Am	12	6%
Latino	4	2%

Practice Areas	
Corporate	123
Litigation	87
Real Estate	38
Bankruptcy	16
Tax	15
Trademark	13
Employee Benefits	9
Trusts & Estates	9
General Obligations	5

Founded over 100 years ago, Willkie Farr & Gallagher has a rich history. Many of the firm's partners have been public figures. Perhaps the most well-known is Wendell Willkie, who was commemorated on a U.S. Post Office stamp. He ran for United States President against Roosevelt in 1940. Despite its long history, Willkie attorneys are presently quite young. It is a "relaxed" place where there are "no unwritten rules on the way to act, dress, and handle yourself." Attorneys often return to work after an evening trip to the nearby gym in their work-out clothes. They also typically leave their office doors open all day and share a "camaraderie and friendship." One dissenting voice resisted this description, insisting that the firm has a "non-collegial atmosphere—associates don't seem to socialize" with each other.

practice areas

Like most prominent New York corporate law firms, Willkie was involved in numerous high-profile mergers and acquisitions in the 1980s. Today, the firm has a strong corporate department that represents and advises many large corporations and brokerage houses in matters ranging from mergers and acquisitions to securities issues and regulation. The M&A practice has been busy lately, working on the $10 billion sale of Loral Corporation to Lockheed Martin and the $14 billion sale of MFS Communication to WorldCom. The firm's nationally recognized public finance group has particular expertise in public offerings of the tax-exempt and taxable securities sold by state and local governments to finance such projects as low and moderate income housing, airports, colleges, and hospitals. The firm was retained to act as bond counsel to Orange County, California, in the largest municipal bankruptcy in history. Under the leadership of Myron Trepper, the firm has developed a thriving bankruptcy practice, primarily representing debtors in high profile cases.

Litigation is the firm's second largest department, housing more than 80 attorneys. Benito Romano, former U.S. Attorney for the Southern District of New York, is one of the stars of the litigation department. The department has a growing white-collar criminal practice. It also handles a wide variety of commercial litigation. The firm's practice in securities, mergers and acquisitions, and corporate governance is "extremely active," we were told. In the last five years, the litigation department has handled important cases on behalf of The Trump Corporation, Soros Fund Management, Loral Corporation, Lehman Brothers, and the American Institute of Certified Public Accountants. Willkie recently represented Smith Barney in a securities litigation concerning a real estate "roll-up" transaction. In addition, Willkie has represented Major League Baseball since the 1930s and has been involved in numerous baseball related litigations and arbitrations over the years. Recently the firm joined with American League Counsel in the successful defense of an arbitration claim by the Major League Umpires' Association for more than $1 million of post-season compensation that was withheld because of the cancellation of the 1994 post-season due to the player strike. One contact informed us that, "with the exception of one or two partners, the litigation department is merely a service department for corporate and bankruptcy clients." A firm spokesperson vigorously disputed this judgement, maintaining that Willkie has "one of the pre-eminent litigation practices in the country," further observing that "bluechip clients (such as those listed above) do not select their trial attorneys on who handles their corporate work."

The firm's real estate department is rapidly expanding. Gene Pinover, a former senior real estate partner at Kaye, Scholer, Handler & Fierman, joined the firm five years ago to head its real estate department, which now has 45 attorneys. Willkie also has a strong and well-regarded tax department that includes at least one partner with an expertise in international tax matters. The firm has a small London office and a large and autonomous Paris office whose primarily corporate practice is growing despite the fact that Kristen van Riel, who remains counsel to the firm, has joined Sotheby's France.

As for pro bono, Willkie encourages summer associates to work for one week with a public interest organization in the city while earning full firm salary. Additionally, a number of litigation attorneys are involved in pro bono matters. In fact, one person noted that it is almost "a rite of passage" for young associates to handle a refugee asylum application before their third year at the firm.

opportunities training feedback

Associates typically join a particular department upon entering the firm. Though it is rarely done, associates may elect to rotate through two departments for six months each. First-year corporate associates are usually assigned two or three partner mentors. The work in both the corporate and litigation departments is distributed by designated assigning partners. However, after a few months, "you get a reputation, and people come looking for you" to give you work, said one source. Despite the departure of a number of midlevel associates several years ago, the litigation department "remains bloated with partners, and junior associates obtain responsibility in lockstep," according to one contact. Junior corporate associates occasionally close small deals. Most associate training happens on-the-job, according to people we interviewed. Each department also meets regularly to discuss developments in the law and active client matters. The firm formally reviews associates at least once a year, but as for day-to-day feedback, one person observed, "unless you hear something, you assume you are doing a good job."

social life

Willkie associates enjoy an active social life. Many are involved in the firm's intramural teams and enjoy going out to sporting events and clubbing. Every Friday evening, a group of associates goes out after work to bars in midtown Manhattan. The firm also organizes a well-attended cocktail party once a month called the Informal Gathering or "IG."

diversity

Willkie attorneys have diverse political affiliations. Wendell Willkie ran for President as a Republican candidate, and one source believed that many of the municipal bond attorneys are Republicans. The firm was, however, one of the largest private contributors to Bill Clinton's presidential campaign. Susan Thomases, a former partner at the firm and a "good friend of Hillary Clinton," resigned in 1996. Former New York State Governor, Mario Cuomo, is a partner at the firm.

Although the firm has few minority attorneys, it is ethnically diverse. Among others, people mentioned that many of the firm's attorneys have Italian or Irish backgrounds. Willkie has made an effort to recruit minority attorneys and to improve the quality of life of those at the firm.

management

Willkie is run by an executive committee composed of 10 of the firm's partners who "oversee the direction of the firm." Although the firm accelerated the departures of a number of associates during the recession of the early 1990s, it has since been economically strong. In the future, it expects the litigation, white-collar criminal, real estate, and corporate securities practice areas to grow. While the firm has long had an intellectual property practice (numbering *Bloomberg News* among its clients), it recently established a distinct intellectual property department.

1998 move planned

Willkie's offices occupy the 45th through the 50th floors of the Citicorp building in midtown Manhattan. The firm is scheduled to move to the Equitable Building at 51st Street and 7th Avenue in 1998, which promises to relieve the crowded conditions at the firm at this time. Associates presently share offices for the first three or four years at the firm. Each associate and summer associate receives a private computer. The "information system" is, however, "not exactly cutting-edge," one insider reported. We heard some complaints about the library and support staff, but, in general, the support services are good. In fact, one contact lavishly praised the support services as "outstanding." While the firm does not have its own cafeteria, many attorneys use Citicorp's cafeteria.

melting pot recruiting

Though Willkie employs high academic standards when making hiring decisions, it is not elitist about the schools from which it hires. "Credentials don't mean everything," asserted one source, explaining that "they don't want stuffy people, or people with attitudes. You have to know how to enjoy yourself." Another called the firm a "melting pot" because of the variety of law schools attended by its attorneys. One person noted, however, that the firm allows more leeway in terms of grades for law students from "Tier One" schools like Columbia, Harvard, New York University, and Yale, while hiring primarily "the cream of the crop" from "Tier Two" law schools like Fordham and St. John's. Applicants were advised to display "individuality" and "independence" in the interview. Baseball fans are always welcome, and, in general, the firm prefers people who have "a life outside of work," disclosed one insider.

Willkie Farr & Gallagher is one of New York's top law firms. People we interviewed highly recommended Willkie, particularly "if you are looking to go to a big firm without the associated pressures and formalities." They also praised the firm for its "relaxed atmosphere" and for the fact that "many of the attorneys actually like one another." One person exulted that "the firm has somehow managed to strike a balance between demanding top quality legal work from its associates, and at the same time making it a comfortable and pleasant place to work. I have been amazed at how responsive the firm has been to associates' concerns about 'quality of life' issues." Yet, there were some voices in dissent from this halycon view. One contact asserted that Willkie is "very bureaucratic—you need a partner's approval to cut a $10 check for a client disbursement." Another contact drew our attention to a more serious problem at the firm, namely that "the up or out pyramid structure of the firm has become more pronounced. This is a great launching point for a career, but like many other firms, it is not a place one should expect to spend one's entire career."

Winston & Strawn

New York Chicago Washington
Geneva Paris

Address: 200 Park Avenue, New York, NY 10166
Telephone: (212) 294–6700
Hiring Attorney: Paul H. Hensel
Contact: Lisa Soderberg, Legal Recruiting Coordinator; (212) 294–6815
Associate Salary: First year $85,000 (1997)
Summer Salary: $1635/week (1997)
Average Hours: 2100 worked; 1800 billed; NA required
Family Benefits: Medical, dental, disability, life, vision, and other insurances; maternity/paternity leave; employee assistance program; medical and child-care flexible spending plans; 401(K)
1996 Summer: Class of 15 students; offers to 15
Partnership: NA
Pro Bono: 2% of all work is pro bono

Winston & Strawn in 1997
96 Lawyers at the New York Office
1.2 Associates Per Partner

Total Partners 44			Total Associates 52			Practice Areas	
Women	7	16%	Women	27	52%	Corporate	35
All Minorities	1	2%	All Minorities	5	10%	Litigation	35
Asian-Am	1	2%	Afro-Am	2	4%	Labor	10
			Asian-Am	3	6%	ERISA	5
						Trusts & Estates	4
						Bankruptcy	3
						Tax	2
						Immigration	1
						Real Estate	1

Winston & Strawn is the New York branch office of one of Chicago's most prestigious law firms. Although the New York office is large and fairly independent in practice, much of the firm's administrative work is processed through the Chicago home office, and many of the firm's decisions are made in Chicago. Due to the Chicago influence, this office has less of the "go-go attitude" prevalent in other large New York firms. The office was established in 1989 through a merger with Cole & Dietz, a New York law firm with a significant corporate and banking practice. The office has also picked up lawyers from Milbank Tweed and from Kaye Scholer, and recently several partners and associates joined Winston's employment law department from another Manhattan law firm. These additions have created an eclectic atmosphere within the firm, we were told.

hierarchical atmosphere

Though less "frenetic" than other large New York firms, Winston is very busy. It is, nevertheless, a friendly place with a "laid-back" work atmosphere. People noted that the firm is very hierarchical both within the New York office and firmwide. There is a lot of "space between partners and associates," explained one source. Additionally, like most Chicago firms, Winston & Strawn has a two-tiered partnership. The firm is fairly informal in matters of dress. Winston has casual Fridays all year round and many women wear pant suits. The firm also has an active associates committee, which "has been influential in implementing cocktail parties every other Friday," reported one insider. Although not all associates socialize after work, many do. Also, many associates participate in intramural sports (basketball, soccer, etc.) with other firms, we were told.

banking financial services

Winston's corporate department has a strong bank regulatory group, and also provides general corporate counseling. The firm primarily represents large corporations, such as General Electric and Phillip Morris, and financial institutions. Winston & Strawn has relatively new international offices in Paris and Geneva, and it has been involved in the restructuring of the Brazilian debt through its bank clients. The firm's bankruptcy group has decreased in size, but is known as a "wonderful place to practice; people are more connected to each other" in this group than in others at the firm. In contrast, the litigation department, which is one of the firm's largest practice groups, reportedly has some "notorious type A personalities and screamers."

The firm's commitment to pro bono received mixed reviews. Corporate partner, Susan Berkwitt-Malefakis, sits on the board of the Lawyers Committee for Human Rights and is in charge of pro bono at the firm. Although one person criticized the pro bono program as "disorganized," others feel that the firm encourages attorneys to become involved in pro bono matters. The firm regularly sends around a list of pro bono opportunities, and provides billable hour credit for pro bono work.

opportunities training feedback

New associates are hired into a particular department. First-year litigation associates typically do research and document review. Bankruptcy associates appear in court by their second year at the firm. Winston sponsors some training sessions for corporate and litigation associates. For example, all first- through third-year litigation associates were sent to the Chicago office for a three day NITA deposition training last year, but people we interviewed commented that most of the training occurs "on-the-job." Associates are formally reviewed once a year, at which time first- through third-year associates receive a number grade (1, 2, or 3) for their performance. An associate's base compensation is tied to the evaluation grade, and the bonus is linked to the performance of the firm and to the associate's billable hours. Receiving a 3 is usually a clear indication that the associate should leave the firm.

diversity

Winston & Strawn attorneys are politically diverse. The chairman of the firm is Jim Thompson, the former Republican Governor of Illinois. Walter Mondale, Vice President under Jimmy Carter, used to be a partner at the firm. Winston & Strawn has seven women partners in the New York office. The firm reportedly offers a senior attorney option for "people who want to take things slower," and "a few women have a part-time work arrangement," according to one insider.

management

Winston & Strawn is governed by a firmwide managing committee, but each office also has a managing partner. Although the New York office was affected by a series of events that rocked the firm's Chicago head office in the early 1990s (including the forced resignation of former managing partner Gary Fairchild, after the firm announced its belief that he may have been embezzling significant amounts of money), we were told that that matter is now behind the firm. Winston is financially healthy today. (See the Winston & Strawn, Chicago profile for more.)

Winston & Strawn moved to the Met Life Building in midtown Manhattan in the fall of 1995. The firm typically assigns two or three attorneys to a secretary and provides all attorneys with a computer with E-mail, Internet, LEXIS, and Westlaw access. The firm has a small library.

hiring tips

Winston & Strawn seeks attorneys with strong academic qualifications, but does not place exclusive emphasis on grades. The firm hires "down-to-earth" students who "can work with other people." It is "not looking for super-geeky people." Winston's call-back interviews are "laid-back." One person advised interviewees to "be yourself. Emphasize that you are dedicated and ambitious, a hard worker, and human. The firm truly looks for people they can work with." Another said that the interviewers tend to talk about interesting things on your résumé and want to explore what makes you different. In recent years, Winston has hired a large number of its students from Columbia, Harvard, New York University, and the University of Pennsylvania, but it also recruits at law schools such as Fordham, Hofstra, St. John's, and other New York schools. The firm also hires students from midwest law schools.

Winston & Strawn has been in the New York market only since 1989, and is "continuing to build its practice, market, etc." It is not an extremely high-energy, large New York firm that is in the headlines every day. It does, however, provide a "nice work atmosphere" and in some instances more responsibility than is available at other firms. It provides the "benefits of having the resources of a large firm with several offices, while only being a moderate sized office in New York," according to one insider who added, "I would not move to another firm in New York."

Winthrop, Stimson, Putnam & Roberts

New York Palm Beach Stamford Washington
Brussels Hong Kong London Singapore Tokyo

Address: One Battery Park Plaza, New York, NY 10004-1490
Telephone: (212) 858–1000
Hiring Attorney: Philip Le B. Douglas
Contact: Dorrie Ciavatta, Director of Legal Employment; (212) 858–1526
Associate Salary: First year $86,000 (1997); salary figure includes $3000 bonus
Summer Salary: $1596/week (1997)
Average Hours: 2000 worked; 1850 billed; NA required
Family Benefits: 3 months paid maternity leave (up to 3 months unpaid); 4 weeks vacation; employee assistance program; bonuses; insurance (health, domestic partner, disability, life, malpractice); 401(K); dependent care assistance plan; leaves of absence for public service; subsidized health club
1996 Summer: Class of 26 students; offers to 26
Partnership: 11% of entering associates from 1982-1988 were made partner
Pro Bono: 7% of all work is pro bono

Winthrop, Stimson, Putnam & Roberts in 1997
191 Lawyers at the New York Office
1.6 Associates Per Partner

Total Partners 65			Total Associates 102			Practice Areas	
Women	10	15%	Women	40	39%	Corporate	85
All Minorities	1	2%	All Minorities	25	25%	Litigation	37
Asian-Am	1	2%	Afro-Am	5	5%	Real Estate	13
			Asian-Am	18	18%	Tax	13
			Latino	2	2%	Bankruptcy	11
						Employee Benefits	7
						Trusts & Estates	7

Founded in 1868, Winthrop, Stimson, Putnam & Roberts is a traditional and prominent New York law firm that places a high premium on people treating each other well. The firm emphasizes "teamwork" to summer associates. It reportedly told one summer associate class on their first day of work that "the world outside is a hostile place, but within the firm it should not be like that." Winthrop's consistently successful practice reflects its "cautious, methodical" culture. The firm does not have a "reputation for being go-getters like Skadden," attested one source, noting that as a result it "didn't suffer any losses at the end of the 1980s."

pro bono externship

Founded by Elihu Root, the 19th century lawyer, statesman, and diplomat, Winthrop has a tradition of public service. Name partner Henry L. Stimson served as Secretary of State (1929-33) and twice as Secretary of War (1911-13 and 1940-45). The firm's commitment to public service continues today. Everyone we interviewed uniformly agreed that Winthrop has a well-organized pro bono program, and that a number of partners are committed to pro bono work. Each year, the firm makes presentations to summer associates regarding its pro bono policies and makes opportunities available in matters ranging from the redistricting of Native American reservation land to working with local area high school students. Summer associates may elect to work with a public interest organization for one or two weeks while earning their regular firm salary. Winthrop Stimson has also established a pro bono fellowship program in which one first-year associate works full-time for a public interest organization. During that year, the firm also pays the associate half the regular first-year salary. Winthrop credits time spent on pro bono matters toward its billable hour calculations in a type of "partial credit" system.

practice areas

Winthrop's corporate department is organized into a number of practice groups, including a well-established securities/public utilities group, which has been a leader in utility mergers and takeovers; a transportation and equipment finance group which handles, among other things, large aircraft financing and telecommunications deals; a well-known banking and finance practice group; a strong bankruptcy/workouts group; and, a mergers and acquisitions/business law group. Much of the corporate department's work involves international transactions. Winthrop has offices in London, Brussels, Hong Kong, Singapore and Tokyo. The Tokyo office is "effectively a shell," according to one contact. "No one is there (except maybe a secretary). The firm does not close it so that they don't 'lose face'."

The litigation department primarily handles, along with the traditional array of commercial litigation, large contract actions and securities matters for large corporate clients. It is also prominent for its work in antitrust, banking, and fraud. Mark Hellerer, a former prosecutor in the Helmsley trial, heads up the firm's white-collar criminal practice. The firm also has a small trusts and estates department.

assignments training feedback

Entering associates are not assigned to a practice group during their first six months with the firm. Instead, they receive work from all areas of the firm through an assignment coordinator. The responsibility entrusted to young associates, one person told us, "depends on the trust that the partners have in them." The bulk of the first and second years is typically filled with education, research, writing, and, in the corporate department, a lot of "ground work." Some second-year corporate associates have, however, closed small deals on their own. Young associates usually "work closely with a partner" who "generally" provides good training. There are a few, however, we were told, who "provide virtually none." One person remarked that "there has been more emphasis on training lately, but it is still a department-by department proposition, and this depends on the time and inclination of the department's training partner." The firm provides basic introductory training to first-year associates, and each department is responsible for providing training in specific legal skills to more senior associates. The litigation department provides an intense eight-day trial advocacy workshop which culminates in a mock jury trial.

social traditions

Winthrop "recognizes the fact that you have a personal life" and "believes you shouldn't sacrifice your whole life for the firm." It is "a very social firm." Winthrop attorneys enjoy spending time with each other, and dinner time at the firm is considered "a good time for attorneys to get together." Associates frequently socialize in the firm's cafeteria which is open until 8:30 P.M. In addition, Winthrop is "big in the lawyer's basketball league. Many people go to the firm's basketball and softball games. A partner invariably takes people out after the game." Winthrop also pays for tennis time at the New York Health & Racquet Club. The firm "emphasizes social traditions," declared one source. Winthrop organizes a firm outing to a country club in the early fall and a January/February dinner dance.

diversity

Although Winthrop has a reputation for being a "white shoe" firm, people we interviewed said that it has moved with the times. The firm is open to different points of view, and tries to fashion a comfortable work environment for all types of people. Many female associates and partners have children or take time off to have children. At least one woman attorney at the firm took time off to have two children, worked part-time, and was still promoted to partner. Winthrop is also committed to increasing its minority hiring. The firm informs summer associates of other events held in the city involving minority issues and encourages them to attend these events.

Winthrop is governed by a management committee of partners. The firm is looking to expand its European Community and the Pacific Rim practices. Winthrop represents a few large Korean entities and hopes to boost its practice in this area. It also hopes to increase its presence in Hong Kong and Singapore.

beautiful downtown offices

Located in downtown Manhattan near Battery Park, Winthrop has both beautiful and modern offices with "fantastic views" of the Park, the Statue of Liberty, and the surrounding rivers. The downtown location is, however, considered by some at the firm to be an inconvenient "out of the way" location. The offices are decorated with a "lot of wood paneling, plants, and blue carpet." The library is also beautiful. The support staff and the library staff have recently gone through a complete turnover. One contact remarked that "the new staff is not as good as the old staff. Most charitably one could say the library staff is in transition. We especially feel the loss of long-time head librarian Nancy Haab." First-year associates share offices, and are subsequently assigned to a private office on the floor of the department to which they are assigned. The firm has a brand new computer network system with "all the bells and whistles." All Winthrop offices are connected via computer, and the firm has a document database with a sophisticated search system. A few of those we interviewed complained about the tardiness of the word-processing department.

hiring practices

Winthrop hires all kinds of people from the "extremely intellectual types" to the "more outgoing" kind. The firm doesn't want "obsessively driven" people, stated one insider. It prefers someone "who fits into the friendly atmosphere." Another noted that the firm looks for someone who is "mature and nice," someone who is "not prone to be argumentative for no purpose whatsoever." Winthrop hires students from a wide range of schools, drawing heavily on local schools, such as Brooklyn Law School.

Winthrop is a friendly law firm which attempts to accommodate its associates' concerns. The firm is "gentlemanly" and loyal to its associates. Winthrop is a firm that "recognizes the fact that you have a personal life." The major complaint we heard voiced regarding Winthrop had to do with the "dismal partnership chances." "The firm is not making a lot of partners," according to one contact, and there has been "significant midlevel associate turnover," possibly connected to this blockage. A related concern brought to our attention focused on the salary scale for senior associates who "get an increasing percentage of their compensation in a very complicated bonus system" that does not sit well with those involved. This concern was recently addressed by simplifying the bonus system to increase the guaranteed component of associate compensation, according to a firm spokesperson. At the same time, there has been good news on the compensation front lately, with one source reporting that "the firm seems to be genuinely concerned about the morale of associates. This year was a particularly good year for the firm, and each attorney received a Thanksgiving surprise bonus."

Philadelphia

Law Firms Ranked By Associates Per Partner

1.	COZEN AND O'CONNOR	0.3
2.	SAUL, EWING, REMICK & SAUL	0.7
3.	BLANK, ROME, COMISKY & MCCAULEY	0.8
4.	PEPPER, HAMILTON & SCHEETZ	1.0
5.	SCHNADER, HARRISON, SEGAL & LEWIS	1.0
6.	DUANE, MORRIS & HECKSCHER	1.1
7.	DRINKER BIDDLE & REATH	1.2
8.	MORGAN, LEWIS & BOCKIUS	1.3
9.	REED SMITH SHAW & MCCLAY	1.3
10.	DECHERT PRICE & RHOADS	1.4
11.	BALLARD, SPAHR, ANDREWS & INGERSOLL	1.5
12.	WOLF, BLOCK, SCHORR & SOLIS-COHEN	NA

Law Firms Ranked by Percentage of Associates Who Make Partner
(over varying years)

1.	COZEN AND O'CONNOR	90
2.	DUANE, MORRIS & HECKSCHER	39
3.	SAUL, EWING, REMICK & SAUL	25
4.	DECHERT PRICE & RHOADS	17
5.	BALLARD, SPAHR, ANDREWS & INGERSOLL	16
6.	SCHNADER, HARRISON, SEGAL & LEWIS	16
7.	PEPPER, HAMILTON & SCHEETZ	15
8.	BLANK, ROME, COMISKY & MCCAULEY	NA
9.	DRINKER BIDDLE & REATH	NA
10.	MORGAN, LEWIS & BOCKIUS	NA
11.	REED SMITH SHAW & MCCLAY	NA
12.	WOLF, BLOCK, SCHORR & SOLIS-COHEN	NA

Law Firms Ranked by Percentage of Pro Bono Work

1.	COZEN AND O'CONNOR	5
2.	DUANE, MORRIS & HECKSCHER	3-5
3.	REED SMITH SHAW & MCCLAY	3
4.	SCHNADER, HARRISON, SEGAL & LEWIS	2-3
5.	DRINKER BIDDLE & REATH	2
6.	MORGAN, LEWIS & BOCKIUS	2
7.	BALLARD, SPAHR, ANDREWS & INGERSOLL	1
8.	BLANK, ROME, COMISKY & MCCAULEY	NA
9.	DECHERT PRICE & RHOADS	NA
10.	PEPPER, HAMILTON & SCHEETZ	NA
11.	SAUL, EWING, REMICK & SAUL	NA
12.	WOLF, BLOCK, SCHORR & SOLIS-COHEN	NA

Law Firms Ranked by Percentage of Female Partners

1.	DUANE, MORRIS & HECKSCHER	20
2.	SCHNADER, HARRISON, SEGAL & LEWIS	19
3.	BALLARD, SPAHR, ANDREWS & INGERSOLL	18
4.	PEPPER, HAMILTON & SCHEETZ	16
5.	COZEN AND O'CONNOR	14
6.	DECHERT PRICE & RHOADS	13
7.	DRINKER BIDDLE & REATH	12
8.	SAUL, EWING, REMICK & SAUL	11
9.	BLANK, ROME, COMISKY & MCCAULEY	10
10.	REED SMITH SHAW & MCCLAY	8
11.	MORGAN, LEWIS & BOCKIUS	6
12.	WOLF, BLOCK, SCHORR & SOLIS-COHEN	NA

Law Firms Ranked by Percentage of Female Associates

1.	SCHNADER, HARRISON, SEGAL & LEWIS	52
2.	BALLARD, SPAHR, ANDREWS & INGERSOLL	46
3.	DRINKER BIDDLE & REATH	46
4.	PEPPER, HAMILTON & SCHEETZ	44
5.	COZEN AND O'CONNOR	43
6.	REED SMITH SHAW & MCCLAY	40
7.	SAUL, EWING, REMICK & SAUL	40
8.	MORGAN, LEWIS & BOCKIUS	39
9.	BLANK, ROME, COMISKY & MCCAULEY	38
10.	DECHERT PRICE & RHOADS	38
11.	DUANE, MORRIS & HECKSCHER	32
12.	WOLF, BLOCK, SCHORR & SOLIS-COHEN	NA

Law Firms Ranked by Percentage of Minority Partners

1.	PEPPER, HAMILTON & SCHEETZ	4
2.	DUANE, MORRIS & HECKSCHER	3
3.	MORGAN, LEWIS & BOCKIUS	3
4.	REED SMITH SHAW & MCCLAY	3
5.	BALLARD, SPAHR, ANDREWS & INGERSOLL	2
6.	BLANK, ROME, COMISKY & MCCAULEY	2
7.	COZEN AND O'CONNOR	2
8.	SCHNADER, HARRISON, SEGAL & LEWIS	2
9.	DECHERT PRICE & RHOADS	1
10.	SAUL, EWING, REMICK & SAUL	1
11.	DRINKER BIDDLE & REATH	0
12.	WOLF, BLOCK, SCHORR & SOLIS-COHEN	NA

Law Firms Ranked By Percentage of Minority Associates

1.	DUANE, MORRIS & HECKSCHER	11
2.	SAUL, EWING, REMICK & SAUL	10
3.	SCHNADER, HARRISON, SEGAL & LEWIS	8
4.	MORGAN, LEWIS & BOCKIUS	7
5.	REED SMITH SHAW & MCCLAY	7
6.	BALLARD, SPAHR, ANDREWS & INGERSOLL	6
7.	BLANK, ROME, COMISKY & MCCAULEY	5
8.	COZEN AND O'CONNOR	5
9.	DRINKER BIDDLE & REATH	4
10.	DECHERT PRICE & RHOADS	3
11.	PEPPER, HAMILTON & SCHEETZ	2
12.	WOLF, BLOCK, SCHORR & SOLIS-COHEN	NA

Ballard, Spahr, Andrews & Ingersoll

Philadelphia Baltimore Camden Denver Salt Lake City Washington

Address: 1735 Market Street, 51st Floor, Philadelphia, PA 19103–7599
Telephone: (215) 665–8500
Hiring Attorney: Robert C. Gerlach
Contact: Bonnie Bell, Professional Personnel Administrator; (215) 864–8163
Associate Salary: First year $70,000 plus $5,000 stipend (1997)
Summer Salary: $1250/week (2L); $1200/week (1L) (1997)
Average Hours: 2154 worked; 1900 billed; 1900 required
Family Benefits: 8 weeks paid maternity leave (4 unpaid); 12 weeks unpaid paternity leave; childcare and elder care plans
1996 Summer: Class of 23 students; offers to 20
Partnership: 16% of entering associates from 1977–1978 were made partner
Pro Bono: 1% of all work done is pro bono

Ballard, Spahr, Andrews & Ingersoll in 1997
186 Lawyers at the Philadelphia Office
1.5 Associates Per Partner

Total Partners 115			Total Associates 167			Practice Areas	
Women	21	18%	Women	76	46%	Litigation	90
All Minorities	2	2%	All Minorities	10	6%	Business	81
Afro-Am	2	2%	Afro-Am	3	2%	Real Estate	50
			Asian-Am	4	2%	Public Finance	25
			Latino	3	2%	Trusts & Estates	13
						Employee Benefits	12
						Tax	11

With its strong public finance practice, Ballard Spahr Andrews & Ingersoll is intimately connected to the Philadelphia community. The large municipal bond group works on numerous public financings, both locally and nationally. Not surprisingly, many Ballard Spahr attorneys have strong political ties: Charisse Lillie and Alan Davis have each served as City Solicitor, and David Cohen, who served as Mayor Rendell's chief of staff, recently returned to the firm as managing partner. Although Ballard Spahr's lawyers are politically diverse, one person noted that most of the firm's political bigwigs are Democrats. Ballard Spahr also is known for its strong pro bono practice, under the dynamic leadership of attorney Suzie Turner, and has close relationships with a number of prominent community groups, including the Philadelphia Volunteers for the Indigent Program, Women's Way, the Public Interest Law Center in Philadelphia, the Education Law Center, and Community Legal Services. Significantly, pro bono hours apply toward billable hour requirements.

practice areas

The litigation department, with its environmental and labor subgroups, is the firm's largest. The department has handled a "number of high-profile cases over the past several years," including the largest pending antitrust case in the nation and the merger battle between Norfolk Southern Corporation and CSX Corporation for control of Conrail. The litigation practice includes a number of prominent attorneys such as Arthur Makadon and Alan Davis. The firm's second largest practice, the business and finance department, represents a broad range of clients such as banks, universities, the Phillies, newspapers, hospitals, and biotechnology companies. Representations range from counseling small clients on general business issues to legal management of complex transactions such as mergers, initial public offerings, and project financings.

The firm's real estate group includes veteran real estate lawyer Richard Goldberg who left his vice president and associate general counsel position at Rouse Co. to join Ballard Spahr. This dynamic group has grown from 15 lawyers in 1990 to 50 lawyers in 1997 and has developed a national reputation.

top-notch tax practice

Ballard Spahr's tax department, with 11 attorneys firmwide, is "very highly-regarded." One person observed that some of the most "prominent" tax partners, such as Lou Ricker and Robert McQuiston, are "known all over the country." Ballard Spahr's tax lawyers specialize in diverse areas such as tax-exempt and leveraged lease financing, mergers and acquisitions, mutual fund offerings, real estate syndications, joint ventures with tax-exempt entities, and executive compensation. In addition, the firm has strong complementary practices in pensions and trusts and estates. The atmosphere in the tax department was described as "cerebral." The tax lawyers "have a sense of humor, but it is kind of different," remarked one insider.

flexible department assignments

Ballard Spahr offers a flexible approach for both summer and beginning associates. Summer associates may rotate through the firm's main practice areas. Starting associates are asked for their department preferences before joining the firm in the fall, and "every effort is made to accommodate their first choice," a firm spokesperson informed us.

organized summer

Everyone we interviewed said that the summer program is "well-organized" and noted that the firm goes out of its way to provide training for summer associates. Each summer, Ballard Spahr makes available special writing tutors and schedules a series of mock training exercises, such as conducting depositions, handling negotiations, and assembling documents for a corporate or real estate closing. The summer atmosphere, like that at the firm generally, is very social: "Lots of people go out and have a good time." There are "tons of cocktail parties and other events" during the summer and throughout the year. A highlight of the summer is a softball game played at Veterans Stadium, the home of the Phillies, a client of the firm. Those we interviewed noted, however, that Ballard Spahr is not a "swinging singles" firm, but is rather a very "family oriented" place. Many of the attorneys commonly bring their children with them to firm social events.

opportunity

Although Ballard Spahr provides great formal training, one person cautioned that "you won't get responsibility as fast as at a small firm. You probably won't have your own client in the first two years, and beyond that, you will get responsibility when you prove you can handle it." Another concurred: "In your first year, you spend most of your time getting to know people and how they work. In your second year, the attorneys start to pick the people whose work they like. In your third year, you start getting responsibility."

Ballard Spahr has been stable economically in recent years. Much of the firm's success may be attributable to its "conservative" management, we were told. We did, however, hear complaints that "associate compensation for midlevel associates is not as competitive as other large firms."

diversity

Ballard Spahr generally provides a good atmosphere for women, but one person asserted that the atmosphere varies considerably by department. Litigation tends to be a "male department," whereas much of the work in the business and finance department is "brought in by a female partner." One insider asserted that women have advanced within the firm similarly to men. Over the past half decade, approximately half of the new partners have been women. Women are well-represented on the firm's hiring committee. Ballard Spahr has recently developed formal part-time and maternity leave policies. With respect to ethnic diversity, one person commented that "I never got the impression that the firm was anti-minority," but it "didn't talk much about minorities." One source did note, however, that there are minority attorneys on the hiring committee.

Ballard Spahr is located on the top eight floors of the Mellon Bank Building, one of the newest buildings in Philadelphia, with a "stupendous" view. Each associate and summer associate has an individual office with a computer. One person observed that the computer system is not "state-of-the-art," but it is networked.

hiring tips

Ballard Spahr hires its summer associates from a broad range of law schools. Past summer classes have included students from Georgetown, Harvard, New York University, Penn, Temple, Villanova, and Yale. People commented that Ballard Spahr tends to emphasize law school grades in making its hiring decisions. Most successful candidates from the local schools are in the top 10 percent of their classes. In general, the firm looks for "down-to-earth people." Callbacks at Ballard Spahr usually consist of four or five half-hour interviews. Although most sessions are relaxed and informal, one person warned that some of the interviewers ask very direct and pointed questions. Another emphasized that students should know something about the firm and ask specific questions during the interviews.

With a strong pro bono practice, perhaps the best public finance practice in the city, and close ties to the Philadelphia Phillies, Ballard Spahr is one of the best firms to join if you want to be active in civic affairs.

Blank, Rome, Comisky & McCauley

Philadelphia Allentown Cherry Hill Media New York Trenton Washington West Palm Beach Wilmington

Address: Four Penn Center Plaza, Philadelphia, PA 19103 (As of 9/97 the address will be: One Logan Square, Philadelphia, PA 19103-6998)
Telephone: (215) 569–5500
Hiring Attorney: Henry M. Kuller
Contact: Grace A. Cooke, Attorney Recruiting Coordinator; (215) 569–5751
Associate Salary: First year $70,000 plus $5,000 signing bonus (1997)
Summer Salary: $1200/week (1997)
Average Hours: 2000 worked; 1800 billed; NA required
Family Benefits: Single medical; life; AD&D; long term disability; four weeks vacation; optional benefits available under flex plan include dependent medical; dental; dependent care spending account and life insurance; long term care insurance is also an optional benefit.
1996 Summer: Class of 17 students; offers to 15
Partnership: NA
Pro Bono: NA

Blank, Rome, Comisky & McCauley in 1997
188 Lawyers at the Philadelphia Office
0.8 Associates Per Partner

Total Partners 102			Total Associates 85			Practice Areas	
Women	10	10%	Women	32	38%	Litigation	53
All Minorities	2	2%	All Minorities	4	5%	Corporate	33
Afro-Am	1	1%	Afro-Am	3	4%	Financial Services	24
Latino	1	1%	Asian-Am	1	1%	Real Estate	24
						Tax & Estates/Fiduciary	21
						Labor	17
						Public Finance	5

Founded in 1946, Blank, Rome, Comisky & McCauley has grown to be one of Philadelphia's most prominent law firms. From its inception, Blank Rome has been known as a "Jewish firm" that attracted "the best Jewish lawyers" in the city, although it has become considerably more diverse in the last 15 years. Blank Rome suffered through lean economic times in the late 1980s, but the firm has rebounded and continues to be recognized as one of Philadelphia's best firms.

practice areas

Blank Rome's work atmosphere varies considerably by department. One person commented that "you can tell instantly which department people are in." The litigation group was described as "frantic," a place where "there always appears to be an emergency", the labor group as "casual," and the financial services group as "young." The corporate, financial services, and commercial litigation departments are the "bread and butter" of the firm's business. The corporate department has recently developed a "respectable" intellectual property group which practices copyright, trademark, and computer law, servicing the firm's growing core of software and computer product companies. The financial services group handles a lot of bankruptcy work. Leon Foreman, a prominent partner in the group, is one of the "framers of the Uniform Bankruptcy Code." Summer associates have the opportunity and are encouraged to sample the firm's practices by choosing assignments from a central book.

management

Blank Rome is admittedly cautious in its management, which has served it well in recent years. David Girard-diCarlo, the managing partner, has been given a lot of "credit for turning the firm around." Girard-diCarlo, a Bush appointee to the Amtrak Board of Advisors and a prominent member of current Governor Ridge's election campaign, is considered a "conservative" leader. One summer associate described him as "very friendly to the summer associates but very intimidating." The management and distribution committees make most of the firm's important decisions. One source observed that the associates "are not too crazy" about management's lack of openness and its failure to be receptive to associate ideas. A firm spokesperson informed us, however, that in the last couple of years the managing partner has delivered essentially the same "state of the firm" address to the firm's associates as to the firm's partners, in an effort to keep all abreast of the firm's activities. Another associate remarked that, "overall, the firm is very political—the partners that you work with, the type of assignments you get, and whether you make partner depend on whom you know and who likes whom."

no frills environment

Consistent with its conservative management philosophy, Blank Rome reportedly is downright "cheap" and fails to provide its associates with the amenities "that make you feel good." The offices were described as "no-frills" and "Spartan." Blank Rome is "in the process of updating ineffective technology systems" and will move into new offices in late 1997. According to one contact, "the firm has spent a lot of time, energy, and money surveying the ideas of associates and staff in connection with the move. Associates are optimistic that the firm's new quarters will be more plush, pleasant, and user friendly" than the current offices. The summer program, under the able direction of Grace Cooke, is the "one bright spot in Blank Rome's spending policies on young people," according to one contact. The firm's summer program, having vastly improved in recent years, was rated the best overall in the city in 1995 in *The American Lawyer's* summer associates survey, although one contact remarked that the program "is more like summer camp than reality."

complaints about salary and hours

People were very critical of the firm's compensation schedule. One person informed us that "the bucks stop at your first year salary." Although the first-year compensation is competitive with similar firms in the city, "associates can expect their salaries to lag behind after the first year. There is significant wage compression, with associates who are in their second, third, and fourth year only earning a few thousand more than first-year associates. A yearly bonus is non-existent or a joke, unless associates have large business generation." A second contact elaborated, "salaries are lower across the board, unless you bring in business or you bill a lot. Despite the low salaries, associates are now expected to bill 2000 billable hours per year." The firm, we were told, is "too 'marketing oriented'—young associates feel pressure to bring in business." Another person remarked that Blank Rome is "still a firm where no matter how hard you work, you are only as good as your last deal or case or client!" We were also told that "the vast majority of partners do not bill many hours—there is a *huge* disparity between number of hours partners are expected to work and that of associates." Not surprisingly, there is a "good deal of associate turnover at the firm," according to our contacts.

complaints about training

Blank Rome also does not invest heavily in training programs, such as the trial advocacy and mock transaction programs offered by some large firms. The firm offers a few departmental seminars, departmental training lunches, and a number of all day Saturday training programs, we were told. One insider informed us that the firm did more training in the past, but "the partner who was in charge has recently left the firm and no one else has taken over the role." The firm is developing a mentorship program for associates, but has reportedly not progressed very far. Another contact asserted, however, that "what the firm lacks in formal training, it makes up for in hands-on experience." Although associates do not formally take on their own caseloads until their fifth or sixth years, this person noted that many associates effectively were doing this by their second year. Another person noted that "Blank Rome handles a significant number of small cases which permits young associates to handle a case with little to no supervision." But, another source observed that "training at Blank Rome is inextricably linked to the partner with whom an associate works most. Some are very interested in developing associates and exposing them to legal practice. Other partners actually attempt to insulate associates from client contact. An associate's experience and future at Blank Rome depends on whether you hitch your cart to a stallion or a nag!" One of the biggest "gripes" we heard was the lack of feedback. One person complained that many associates have "no clue" as to where they stand until their reviews. Another remarked that "performance reviews seem to directly correlate to an associate's gross billable hours worked, regardless of quality of work, nature of practice area, or amount of non-billable work assigned." Many people maintained that what counts at Blank Rome is "billables, billables, billables." Summer associates receive mid- and end-of-summer reviews, and associates are reviewed yearly.

diversity

Blank Rome received largely negative reviews for its treatment of women. One person commented that "Blank Rome has few women partners and the few who exist are invisible or have no power." Another reported "that the firm is not a great place for pregnant women. There is a family leave program, but the women are not happy about it." We were also informed that "the firm does not offer a part-time work schedule for women who have children." There are very few minority attorneys at Blank Rome. One person offered that Blank Rome "would love to have more minorities, and it's really looking for this;" a second person, however, observed that "the turnover of minority attorneys is very high."

hiring tips

In recent years, Blank Rome has hired an increasing number of first-year candidates in an effort to attract law students from the top law schools. Blank Rome places special emphasis on stellar grades and law review membership. Almost everyone hired from the local schools was on law review. The callback interviews reportedly are fairly "formal and regimented." Students typically meet with three or four attorneys for 25 to

30 minutes each. Attorneys ask open-ended questions such as: "What are your greatest strengths and weaknesses?" and "What would you do to improve yourself?" The firm often conducts callback interviews on Saturdays when there are fewer distractions. Applicants may elect to interview at the firm during the week if they prefer. One person advised those from national law schools to "play up all your ties to Philadelphia—even if it is just that you like cheese steak." Past summer classes have included students from Boalt Hall, Boston University, Catholic, Chicago, Columbia, Harvard, Penn, Temple, Rutgers, Villanova, and Widener, among others.

Cozen and O'Connor

Philadelphia Atlanta Charlotte Columbia Dallas Los Angeles New York San Diego Seattle Westmont

Address: 1900 Market Street, The Atrium, Philadelphia, PA 19103
Telephone: (215) 665–2000
Hiring Attorney: Elaine M. Rinaldi
Contact: Carla M. Chiaro, Recruitment Coordinator; (215) 665–2100
Associate Salary: First year $60,000 (1996)
Summer Salary: $1154/week (1996)
Average Hours: NA worked; NA billed; NA required
Family Benefits: Cbc paid maternity leave (cbc unpaid); cbc unpaid paternity leave; dependent care reimbursement account
1996 Summer: Class of 7 students; offers to 5
Partnership: 90% of entering associates from 1982-1991 were made partner
Pro Bono: 5% of all work is pro bono

Cozen & O'Connor in 1997
156 Lawyers at the Philadelphia Office
0.3 Associates Per Partner

Total Partners 115		
Women	16	14%
All Minorities	2	2%
Afro-Am	2	2%

Total Associates 40		
Women	17	43%
All Minorities	2	5%
Afro-Am	1	3%
Asian-Am	1	3%

Practice Areas	
Litigation	101
Environmental/Toxic Tort	24
Corporate & Securities	12
Labor/Employment	6
Health Law	5
Tax/Estates & Trusts	5
Construction	4
Creditor's Rts/Bankruptcy	3
Municipal Finance	3
Real Estate	3

a young vigorous firm

Founded in 1968 as a small insurance litigation boutique, Cozen and O'Connor is "younger and hungrier than most firms," we were told. A few years ago, Cozen began its drive to expand the firm's practice areas and is now one of the fastest growing full-service firms in Philadelphia. "It seems like the firm adds an attorney, or a department, or even a new office every other week," exaggerated one contact. From 1995 to 1996, Cozen added 36 lawyers and moved up in *The National Law Journal's* annually published ranking of the nation's 250 largest firms by size from position 142 to 115. Traditionally a trial law firm focused on insurance coverage and subrogation matters, Cozen has vigorously extended its trial practice skills into the commercial and corporate arena. In diversifying its practice, Cozen and O'Connor has acquired practitioners in health law, bankruptcy, taxation, real estate, labor and employment, commercial transactions, securities, municipal finance, estate planning and administration, domestic relations, and white-collar criminal defense. In addition, the firm continues to have a well-reputed insurance litigation practice. It has handled one of the most highly visible cases in Philadelphia involving the One Meridian Plaza fire, one of many disasters in which Cozen and O'Connor represents the insurance industry.

cooperative learning environment

Cozen and O'Connor offers a youthful and energetic environment. Although professional, the work atmosphere at Cozen is "much more laidback than at other large firms," we were told. Cozen attorneys have an "open-door approach" to practicing law said one insider, adding that "senior partners routinely stop in to pick your brain" about various matters in the office. Another added, "the work environment is far from stuffy, and associates and partners interact frequently and learn from each other."

excellent hands-on experience

Cozen received strong reviews for the responsibility that it offers young associates. As opposed to spending years researching and writing briefs, Cozen and O'Connor associates frequently conduct depositions, appear in court for motions and conferences, and handle their own cases. Most associates are actively involved in litigation and transactional matters from their first year of practice. "I have never seen another firm give its associates the hands-on experience given at Cozen. If you do a good job, you will be the one arguing the motion you wrote, handling the case, arbitrating it, or trying it," raved one person. Another associate, speaking only for the firm's insurance and subrogation practice stated, "I believe Cozen associates get better training and more responsibility than our counterparts" working at other firms in subrogation and insurance. "Specifically for this practice area, I believe Cozen to be the best place to be." Yet another contact concurred, "I have complete control of my cases which I have authority to take to trial, if necessary."

summer program

Cozen and O'Connor does not offer a wine and dine summer associate program. Instead, it seeks to provide summer associates with as clear a picture as possible of life as an associate at the firm. Part of the summer experience includes socializing with partners and associates at all levels. Summer associates are taken out to dinners, concerts, and baseball games. The highlight of the summer is the firm's softball event where the firm's attorneys challenge summer associates to a softball game, which is followed by a party at one of the partner's homes. Cozen and O'Connor's goal is to get to know each summer associate on a personal basis. Hiring decisions are based upon personality as much as on academics and performance. The firm extends general offers at the end of the summer and assigns accepting associates to a particular department the following spring.

Cozen and O'Connor "supports pro bono work, but I don't think it encourages it," said one insider, observing that pro bono hours worked by attorneys do not count toward billable hours. About 1% of all work done by the firm is pro bono, and several attorneys have been recognized for their public interest contributions. One of the firm's partners founded the Philadelphia Homeless Advocacy Project, and the firm received a 1995 citation from the Philadelphia City Council for its contributions to this project.

Cozen and O'Connor's modern offices are located in the Philadelphia Stock Exchange Building. The offices are built around a greenery-filled atrium, and all lawyers' offices overlook either the atrium or the streets surrounding the western end of the city.

hiring tips

In its recruiting, Cozen and O'Connor emphasizes personality as much as academics. Although the firm typically looks for those in the top 20 percent of their class, maturity, aggressiveness, and initiative are also traits treasured by Cozen and O'Connor. The firm hires primarily second-year law students and, occasionally, first-year law students. Following on campus recruiting, the firm conducts callback interviews, either during the week or on Saturdays at the convenience of the students. Students usually meet three attorneys, one of whom is a partner and spend time with an associate touring the office.

The firm has eleven offices throughout the country. Its recruiting, although handled regionally, is always geared towards its firmwide needs. For example, although a student may interview in Philadelphia, if an interest is expressed in one of the firm's other offices, the student will be considered for positions in the other offices. Since 1985, Cozen and O'Connor has opened offices in 10 cities across the country. When Cozen and O'Connor opens an office in a new city, it does not merge with an existing firm but starts up with one of its Philadelphia partners. As such, its offices outside of Philadelphia are intimately tied into the Philadelphia system, both personally and technologically.

overall associates are happy

We heard some, though not much, criticism of Cozen and O'Connor. Our contacts noted that "with the recent addition of a large number of attorneys, the firm culture is slightly in a state of flux." We were also told that "associates and partners are underinformed with respect to firm planning and decision-making." But, on the bright side, one person pointed out that "with respect to firm growth and administration, fortunately the past year has been relatively quiet allowing the firm to digest its significant expansion of the previous two years." Finally, many of our contacts agreed with one person who observed that "relative to other firms of our size and prestige, associates are underpaid." Finally, one person believed that Cozen is "not as widely known or respected outside of its traditional practice areas as Morgan, Lewis & Bockius or Dechert."

Overall, however, associates at Cozen reported that they are very happy with the firm's work atmosphere, the interaction with partners, and the tremendous hands-on experience they receive. One person asserted that even "the lower salary does not cause me to leave or be unhappy." If you are interested in a young, "aggressive firm that does not have a long history to rest on," that is vigorously expanding its practice beyond insurance litigation, and that appears to have that rare breed—happy associates—Cozen and O'Connor is worth your consideration.

Dechert Price & Rhoads

Philadelphia Boston Harrisburg Hartford New York Princeton Washington
Brussels London Paris

Address: 4000 Bell Atlantic Tower, 1717 Arch Street, Philadelphia, PA 19103–2793
Telephone: (215) 994–4000
Hiring Attorney: Thomas H. Lee, II
Contact: Carol S. Miller, Director of Professional Recruitment; (215) 994–2147
Associate Salary: First year $72,000 (1997)
Summer Salary: NA
Average Hours: NA worked; 1850 billed; NA required
Family Benefits: 8 weeks paid maternity leave (cbc unpaid); 0 weeks paid paternity leave (cbc unpaid)
1996 Summer: Class of 26 students; offers to 24
Partnership: 17% of entering associates from 1977–1987 were made partner
Pro Bono: NA

Dechert Price & Rhoads in 1997
236 Lawyers at the Philadelphia Office
1.4 Associates Per Partner

Total Partners 84		
Women	11	13%
All Minorities	1	1%
Afro-Am	1	1%

Total Associates 121		
Women	46	38%
All Minorities	4	3%
Afro-Am	2	2%
Asian-Am	1	1%
Latino	1	1%

Practice Areas	
Litigation	110
Business	63
Tax/Emp. Ben./Pvt. Clients	30
Government	9

Dechert Price & Rhoads is one of the 50 largest law firms in the country, and one person commented, one of "the three biggies in Philadelphia." With offices throughout the East Coast, as well as in London, Paris, and Brussels, Dechert is one of the few Philadelphia firms with a strong national and international presence. Bart Winokur took over recently as the firm's chairman. He has a "huge mergers and acquisitions practice with lots of New York and international clients," we were told. The firm is presently "unbelievably busy" and is growing in large part due to his focus on strengthening Dechert's national practice.

reserved atmosphere

"You won't find a bunch of guys cursing at each other at Dechert." The atmosphere is "reserved," "polite," and a bit more "formal than other firms" in Philadelphia. One person remarked that "there is an influential strain of stuffed-shirt partners at the firm who refuse to permit casual days." Dechert's hiring policy heavily emphasizes credentials, with the result, according to one person, that "you get lawyers with a variety of ideas who do their own things." There are very few "packs" or "cliques" at the firm. Dechert's attorneys respect each other and behave professionally. Nor is the firm particularly hierarchical: "There are a lot of brilliant lawyers who are all well-respected in their fields, but the firm is not run in a way to make certain lawyers the stars and the rainmakers. Even the big shots are not held that way by the rest of the firm...people are respected for being good to work with and being smart." One insider remarked that the firm has "multiple personalities." On the one hand, perhaps because of its large size (the firm's attorneys are spread out over eight floors) and labyrinth-like office structure, there will be lawyers on the same floor who, "even after years with the firm, you know less well than the guy at the Wawa next door from whom you buy your daily hoagie for lunch. If you died, these partners would have to have their secretary look you up in the firm face-book." On the other hand, "the partners with whom you work, even the so-called 'top partners,' have you address them by their first names, encourage associate participation in strategy and tactics, and often come by your office to talk about cases, instead of summoning you to theirs."

structured training

Dechert's reserved atmosphere affects many aspects of the firm. Both the summer program and the training programs for young associates were described as "highly organized" and "formal." One person reflected that "the summer program was well-organized in terms of evaluations and projects. I didn't get one dog of a project all summer. I got the kind of work I wanted and a good variety." The firm's hiring coordinator, Carol Miller, is "really on top of things" and does a great job of managing and focusing summer associate workloads. One summer associate reported that she didn't have "much downtime, but was never swamped." Summer associates get assignments both from a general pool and from their work mentors. The feedback system is well-organized and effective. Junior associate training is similarly well-run. The firm offers a range of formal training opportunities, including seminars, retreats, and practice depositions (which are taped).

slow development

One insider asserted that Dechert provides "more training than most places," but commented that there are not many opportunities for responsibility during an associate's early years at the firm. Although one source asserted that some litigators try their own cases by their third year at Dechert, another contended that most do not manage their own caseload until their fifth years. One insider remarked that "Dechert suffers from a problem I imagine is endemic to large firms generally: too much drone work for young associates and not enough high-quality high-discretion work to go around." On the other hand, this person noted, "the firm is very concerned about this and sets a 50% limit on the amount of your work that comes from the mega cases." We also heard some complaints about the feedback system for full-time associates at the firm. One contact informed us that such feedback "consists primarily of your getting additional work from people who liked your last work and waiting for the phone to ring from people who didn't."

practice areas

Dechert's practice is divided into four major departments: business; litigation; tax, employee benefits, and private clients; and government—with numerous subgroups within the departments. Entering associates may choose their department, and most associates work in various subgroups before specializing. Historically, Dechert has been most respected for its business department, spearheaded by the aforementioned Bart Winokur. The firm has a reputation as the premier mergers and acquisitions firm in Philadelphia. The firm's litigation group, described as "laid-back and tight-knit," is also very prominent. Women have leadership roles in this department, we were told. One of its former co-captains, Mary McLaughlin, is a woman, as is its current co-captain, Amy Ginensky. The litigation practice includes a broad range of subgroups, including the rapidly-growing intellectual property and environmental groups. The firm has a small, high-quality First Amendment practice and represents the *Philadelphia Inquirer* and the *Daily News*; "there is always a huge mob of associates trying to get into the action," according to one person. Sam Klein is a well-known First Amendment lawyer at the firm. Dechert has a "good-sized" white-collar crime practice, a number of prominent members of which were "stolen" from another Philadelphia firm; in addition, a number are former federal prosecutors. Dechert also does a lot of appellate litigation work, featuring Steve Feirson. Jeff Weil is a well-known securities litigation lawyer at the firm. Dechert's health care practice is expanding rapidly as well. Recently, the firm has made a big push to expand its European operations, joining forces with a London firm, Titmuss Sainer Dechert, and increasing its presence in Paris and Brussels. The firm now has over 150 lawyers involved in its European practice. In addition, Dechert recently opened an office in Hartford, Connecticut, home to many insurance companies and real estate financial institutions. This move is expected to contribute to the creation of a transatlantic property services group.

pro bono

Dechert's pro bono practice "spans the spectrum. No matter what your political bent or personal interest, you can find something at the firm to do pro bono." You have to get all pro bono approved in advance, we were told, but "the firm encourages creativity here, and hasn't turned down an associate's request yet." Dechert's lawyers have handled cases involving the death penalty, civil rights, and the Lawyers for the Arts. In addition, the firm has done a significant amount of work with the Women's Law Project. Pro bono hours are credited in the firm's evaluation system. Dechert has pledged to meet the ABA's goal of 3% of billable hours and came very close to this in 1995.

Most of the people we interviewed informed us that Dechert provides a good atmosphere for women. There are several prominent women in the firm, including the aforementioned Mary McLaughlin, the former co-chair of the litigation department, and Jan Levine, a health-care partner. One insider stated that the firm is "very reasonable" about maternity leaves and further noted that several women had taken leaves of absence, with the firm being "very flexible in meeting their needs."

controversial decor

Dechert's office decor—"startling" purple and green colors, and "funky" art throughout—is controversial. One person described it as being like a Matisse painting. The interiors have "glass cutouts that give the offices an airy and light feel." Although some praise the decor, others find it "kind of weird." One contact suggested that the offices would be more appropriate for an "ad agency." The offices are located in the Bell Atlantic building, one of Philadelphia's newest, which is set apart from the city and offers great views. The inside of the building is long and narrow with beautiful red marble. Everyone agreed that the library is "really nice" and that the staff is "great." Each associate has an individual office with a computer.

academic emphasis in hiring

In its recruitment, Dechert is "among the most selective in the city." The firm places "a lot of stock in traditional measures of academic intelligence. They put these above a lot of other things. They look for someone with a really sharp mind. There are a lot of really smart people there. They are willing to sacrifice social skills." Most successful candidates from local law schools are in the top of their classes and are members of law reviews. In addition, the firm recruits more students from national law schools than any other firm in the city, we were told. One person noted that, unlike most other firms, Dechert requires summer associates to submit their final second-year grades before it will consider them for permanent associate offers. Dechert's callbacks typically involve meeting with four to six attorneys and having lunch with two or three more. Most of the interviewers are members of the hiring committee and tend to be the more senior attorneys. One person commented, "I met such high-level people, it practically scared me—the chairman of the litigation department, hiring partners, two very senior partners, one midlevel, and one senior associate." He also pointed out that the firm "really makes an effort to match up those interviewing you with your interests." Most of the interviews were described as "pleasant"—the lawyers don't "grill" candidates.

If you thrive in a well-organized, somewhat formal environment, you will do well at Dechert. It provides excellent formal training as well as a professional and somewhat academic atmosphere. It offers, according to one firm enthusiast, "the best clients and interesting complex work. The business and litigation departments are among the best in the city." In addition, Dechert is committed to permitting a life outside the firm. "The hours are great. It's an 8:30 or 9:00 a.m. to 6 p.m. firm. The firm is virtually empty at other hours, including weekends. If you're somewhere around your 1800 hour goal, you don't have to worry and you can take all your vacations," according to one contact. Finally, we were told that, although Dechert is "very cheap on bonuses," the associate salary scale recently was boosted $5,000 per person.

Drinker Biddle & Reath

Philadelphia Berwyn Princeton Washington

Address: 1339 Chestnut Street, Philadelphia, PA 19107
Telephone: (215) 988–2700
Hiring Attorney: Andrew C. Kassner
Contact: Amy E. Feldman, Director of Professional Recruitment; (215) 988–2663
Associate Salary: First year $72,000; second $75,000; third $78,000–$81,000; fourth $81,000–$87,000; fifth $84,500–$94,000; sixth $88,000–$101,000; seventh $92,000–$109,000; eighth $96,500–$118,000 (1997) (salaries based on performance and merit adjustments)
Summer Salary: $1385/week (1997)
Average Hours: NA worked; NA billed; NA required
Family Benefits: Maternity/parental leave; dependent care assistance; health, life, and disability insurance
1996 Summer: Class of 17 students; offers to 17
Partnership: NA
Pro Bono: 2% of all work is pro bono

Drinker Biddle & Reath in 1997
163 Lawyers at the Philadelphia Office
1.2 Associates Per Partner

Total Partners 68		
Women	8	12%
All Minorities	0	0%

Total Associates 83		
Women	38	46%
All Minorities	3	4%
Afro-Am	1	1%
Asian-Am	2	2%

Practice Areas	
Business & Finance	88
Litigation	68
Personal Law	7

Although it is one of Philadelphia's oldest and largest law firms, Drinker Biddle & Reath tends to be more laid-back than many of its competitors. Drinker's friendly atmosphere permeates many aspects of the firm. One source observed that "Drinker is not an extravagant firm....It is much more into low-key social events where people get together informally." This person continued that Drinker "emphasized things like softball games. It's not like some of the other places where people go out on cruises. If you want that kind of lavish atmosphere, this firm is not it. The same is true with the firm's offices. They are not as posh as some I have seen. The firm watches its money more carefully and tries not to bleed associates to get every penny out of them."

practice areas

Drinker is organized into three major departments: litigation; business and finance; and personal and fiduciary law. In turn, each of these departments is further divided into several practice groups. The litigation department, chaired by Jim Sweet, includes the labor and environmental practice groups. The department was described by some as the most "personable group" at the firm and is composed of "very outgoing people with dynamic personalities." In recent years, the department has been particularly prominent in connection with high-profile federal securities and insurance coverage litigation. While the core of the department's work remains traditional business and securities litigation, several of its practice groups have grown significantly in recent years. In 1995, the environmental group added roughly 20 lawyers to become "a formidable presence throughout the eastern United States," according to one contact. Alfred Putnam, a prominent litigator, leads a growing appellate practice. The labor practice represents a diverse range of clients—from individuals and universities to Atlantic City casinos. Kate Levering is a big partner in this area.

The business and finance department, described as "not as outgoing, loud, and rowdy" as the litigators, includes practice groups in investment management, real estate, bankruptcy, mergers and acquisitions, and venture capital among others. Bill Goldstein, a former Assistant Secretary of the Treasury, and Jack Petit, former General Counsel to the Federal Communications Commission, are among the department's more prominent partners. The investment management group is considered "one of the leaders in this industry" across the country. Like most of its Philadelphia counterparts, the real estate group was slow between 1992 and 1995, but has picked up recently. The department's bankruptcy lawyers, considered by one observer to be "a wild group of people," are headed by Andy Kassner, known as a "prominent bankruptcy attorney" across the country, remarked one insider. The mergers and acquisitions and the venture capital practices have reportedly been particularly active in recent years.

The personal and fiduciary lawyers, described as a group who "keep to themselves more," provide advice to charities, for-profit entities, and state agencies in connection with the privatization of previously not-for-profit entities, such as hospitals and insurance companies. One of the department's partners, Pam Schneider, is reportedly among the nation's leading experts in estate planning. Finally, Drinker has a long-standing interest in legal ethics. Henry Drinker, one of the firm's pre-eminent historical figures, was a scholar in the field and three Drinker partners have served as chairman of the American Bar Association's Standing Committee on Ethics and Professional Responsibility.

pro bono

Drinker's pro bono committee is headed by partner David Abernethy, who reportedly has a "huge" commitment to the practice. The firm works closely with a number of national public interest organizations and, in particular, with the American Civil Liberties Union. It also works with local groups such as the Philadelphia Volunteers for the Indigent Program (VIP). Drinker has received the William J. Brennan, Jr. Award as the most outstanding large firm supporter of the Philadelphia VIP on several occasions in recent years.

departmental assignments

Summer associates may work in a variety of Drinker's practice areas by choosing projects from a central assignment book, although at times they must accept rush projects. Each summer associate is responsible for managing his own workload, and most summer associates balance several assignments at the same time. Each assignment is reviewed by the assigning attorney and members of the Summer Committee. Drinker extends general offers for summer associates to join the firm. At the end of the summer, prospective associates specify their preferences and are assigned to a department by the following spring. One contact informed us that "Drinker can and will hire every summer associate if they perform well. This almost eliminates summer associate competition, prevalent in those firms that repeatedly hire 15 summer associates, knowing full well that they will hire only 10."

summer program

Although Drinker does not furnish a lavish summer program, past summer associates have enjoyed a white water rafting trip, firm softball games, and a day trip to the Jersey shore. In addition, partners hosted parties at their homes, and "all attorneys are encouraged to have lunch (on Drinker!) with all of the summer associates." A highlight in recent years has been the clambake at firm partner Ed Posner's house. One commentator advised, however, that a summer at Drinker definitely is not a "wine and dine" experience. In general, Drinker's work atmosphere is social. One contact remarked that "there is a true spirit of congeniality among all attorneys—partners and associates. Associates readily share research and experience, and are not outwardly competitive. People even say 'thank you'!" Many associates form "strong friendships."

One insider stressed, however, that there is "not a big singles group going out. It's not like a big firm in New York City. Most people go home to their families."

training

Drinker provides a wide range of highly-valued formal training opportunities. One person observed that they "throw new associates in and let them do some hunting and pecking until they figure out what's going on, and they provide formal programs throughout the year." The formal programs in the litigation department focus on deposition training, trial advocacy and ethics. The business and finance department provides seminars in each of the first two years covering topics such as mergers and acquisitions, bankruptcy, and real estate fundamentals. In addition, a number of the firm's "rainmakers" offer an ongoing business development training program for all associates.

significant opportunity

By the standards of Philadelphia's largest firms, associates at Drinker reportedly have early opportunities for responsibility. One person commented that "the chance for client contact, responsibility, and close work with partners" flows from the collegial atmosphere at the firm. Another contact informed us that "on smaller matters, partners tell us to 'run with it' and to consult with them as frequently or infrequently as we feel is necessary." While most litigation associates do not handle their own cases until their fourth or fifth years, on occasion some second-year associates conduct depositions and argue motions in court.

morale

Although Drinker avoided large-scale layoffs during the economic downturn in the early 1990s, there was an acceleration of associate departures at that time, making it "hard to say how many departures were voluntary and how much was cutting," according to one source. Another contact informed us that more recently, "there have been many departures, most notably in the business and finance area. Most, if not all, of these departures were for better paying, less hours positions in the same industry (rather than to another law firm). Litigation also recently experienced many defections. They were rather top-heavy in mid-level associates." Morale at the firm is, however, reportedly high. Dick Jones, chairman of the firm, "regularly sends memos or holds formal meetings with all associates to keep them informed of changes" and has put in writing policies on work expectations, partnership, etc., we were told. Also, Drinker now has an Associates Committee, comprised of associates at different levels and from different offices, and it "has been reasonably effective in increasing communications among the ranks." Yet, one source remarked to us, "you sometimes wonder where you stand. As much as Drinker attempts to make reviews constructive, the real partnership vote doesn't happen until your eighth year." Another person confirmed this situation, noting that "the partners don't always keep us informed about where the firm is heading, partnership chances, etc."

diversity

Drinker's traditional image as an "old-boy firm" has been changing over time. One person commented that "the partners I had contact with were all very receptive to seeing females in the work place and they were easy to talk to." Another source remarked, "I wear pant suits, golf at the firm outing, and never feel as if I am treated differently as a woman. Drinker does not require associates to shop at Brooks Brothers!" On the matter of maternity leave policy, however, one insider noted, "I'd like to see Drinker become more progressive in its part-time policy for those returning from maternity. By this, I mean allowing a flat three-day week or allowing work to be completed, in part, at an in-home office." Andy Kassner, the hiring partner, is reportedly committed to hiring more women and minorities, and has "revamped the hiring program" to recruit more aggressively. There are presently few minority attorneys at the firm. In a recent summer class, however, three of the fifteen hires were minorities. There are currently eight female partners at Drinker's Philadelphia office.

Located in one of Philadelphia's older office buildings, Drinker's offices include a cafeteria with "cheap food." The decor is pretty much "what you would expect to find in one of the Main Line estate houses—dark wood and framed pictures of Mrs. Biddle's maps. Lots of old stuff, such as historical pieces about Philadelphia and the firm. It's comfortable, but you have to get used to it." Each attorney has an individual office, "very large compared to those in modern buildings," with a window. The firm has tentative plans to move in the near future to One Logan Square, which is Morgan Lewis' current site. Drinker expects to move to its new quarters in the spring of 1999, following their complete refurbishing.

traditional decor

To serve clients outside of Philadelphia proper, Drinker has established offices in Berwyn, Pennsylvania and Princeton/Lawrenceville, New Jersey with approximately 15 and 45 lawyers, respectively. Since their establishment, each of these offices has developed a substantial practice of its own: principally in securities, underwriting, and venture capital financings in the case of Berwyn; and in estate planning, representation of biotechnology companies, environmental and administrative law, and the representation of regional commercial banks, in the case of Princeton/Lawrenceville. Although the firm does not have any foreign offices and is not well known for international work, two partners spent much of the summer of 1995 developing the firm's business relationships in Western Europe, and several clients have been involved in overseas acquisition programs over the last several years.

new offices

Drinker's management is relatively streamlined. A group of 12 elected and appointed managing partners has oversight authority. Operational authority is vested in a Chief Executive Officer, who is appointed by the managing partners for a four-year term.

In its recruiting, Drinker emphasizes "first and foremost" class rank and law review membership. One person remarked, "I've seen people whom interviewers loved, not get offers, based on grades." Almost all successful candidates from local law schools are in the top 10 percent of their classes. The firm hires primarily second-year students and a limited number of first-year students, usually from top 10 national law schools. The interviews at the firm generally are informal and relaxed. Students usually meet four or five attorneys for a half hour each. Drinker has recently moved toward hiring laterals and also third years who did not participate in their summer program but did participate in another firm's and did receive an offer from that other firm.

hiring

Drinker, one of Philadelphia's oldest and most prestigious firms, offers a friendly atmosphere for work, which according to one person we spoke with "is an advantage relative to other firms in the city. The work is hard, so a good atmosphere makes it a nice place to come to each day." In addition, training and guidance at the firm are strong and "associates are always actively recruited for other jobs. It is a nice sense of security to know how much in demand our services are." Drinker associates "bill less total hours than our counterparts at other firms. We have no 'face time'." On the downside, our contacts mentioned matters of compensation, and also that "technologically, we are always a year or two behind." A firm spokesperson pointed out to us that Drinker's announced salaries for first year associates in 1997 place them in the lead group among Philadelphia firms. Overall, our sources indicated considerable general satisfaction with their work and the ambiance at Drinker.

Duane, Morris & Heckscher

Philadelphia Allentown Harrisburg Newark Cherry Hill New York Washington Wayne Wilmington

Address: One Liberty Place, Suite 4200, Philadelphia, PA 19103
Telephone: (215) 979–1000
Hiring Attorney: Patricia L. Pregmon
Contact: Susan K. Weinreb, Manager of Legal Hiring and Training; (215) 979–1294
Associate Salary: First year $70,000 (1996)
Summer Salary: $1250/week (1997)
Average Hours: 1900–2000 worked; 1712 billed; NA required
Family Benefits: 8 weeks paid maternity leave plus an additional 4 weeks paid leave based on vacation time, otherwise unpaid; unpaid paternity leave (under FMLA)
1996 Summer: Class of 11 students, offers to 10
Partnership: 39% of entering associates from 1980–1987 were made partner
Pro Bono: 3–5% of all work is pro bono

Duane, Morris & Heckscher in 1997
153 Lawyers at the Philadelphia Office
1.1 Associates Per Partner

Total Partners 69			Total Associates 74			Practice Areas	
Women	14	20%	Women	24	32%	Litigation	54
All Minorities	2	3%	All Minorities	8	11%	Corporate	25
Afro-Am	2	3%	Afro-Am	4	5%	Reorganization & Finance	20
			Asian Am	3	4%	Administrative	16
			Latino	1	2%	Tax	10
						Labor	8
						Real Estate	7
						White Collar Crime	7
						Trusts & Estates	6

While many prominent law firms expanded nationally and internationally in the 1980s, Duane, Morris & Heckscher focused on becoming a regional powerhouse. The firm now has offices across the Mid-Atlantic Region, including recently opened offices in New York City, Newark and Washington, D.C. From its formation in 1904, Duane Morris grew quietly. Over the last 20 years, however, the firm has expanded rapidly, growing from 36 to over 150 lawyers. Unlike many of Philadelphia's other large firms, Duane Morris did well through the recession of the early 1990s, and the firm currently "operates with no debt."

top-notch bankruptcy

The firm's recent success is no mystery: Duane Morris has one of the oldest and strongest bankruptcy, or "reorganization," practices in the city, formerly headed by the well-known David Sykes, now the managing partner at the firm but still active in the bankruptcy practice. One insider remarked, "They were doing it before it was in vogue" and noted that the firm "represents almost every bank in the Philadelphia area and, in general, does mostly creditor side bankruptcy work." The reorganization lawyers, who occupy almost an entire floor at the firm, are a very "cohesive" group. Sykes is the immediate past president of the Consumer Bankruptcy Assistance Project, and many group members do pro bono personal bankruptcy cases through this organization. The firm's recently opened Newark office has a focus on bankruptcy.

practice areas

Headed by Reeder Fox, "one of the most respected lawyers in Philadelphia," the litigation department is the largest practice at the firm. The litigators at Duane Morris emphasize commercial and insurance defense work. Although four insurance defense partners left to start their own firm a few years ago, the insurance defense caseload has doubled in recent years. The firm recently attracted national attention in obtaining a $350 million dollar verdict in the Meineke class action suit. Duane Morris also has a "special litigation department" that handles white-collar crime, tax fraud, and divorce cases. This somewhat "exclusive" group occupies the 43rd floor with the tax department. Duane Morris also has a strong tax department, which is a "nice" place to work. The firm's former hiring partner, David Flynn, is a tax lawyer.

summer assignments

Summer associates at Duane Morris split their time equally between "litigation" and "corporate" rotations. Students are assigned projects from every area of the firm and may express preferences about the projects they receive. Duane Morris does not make permanent associate offers by specific departments but does attempt to satisfy individual preferences.

democratic and formal

In many respects, Duane Morris still functions like the mid-sized firm it once was. With very little bureaucracy, the firm is so democratic that one person described it as being run like a "Quaker hall meeting." Duane Morris has largely retained its personal touch, with an "upbeat," "young," and "vibrant" feel to it. The firm reportedly enjoys excellent communications among the attorneys. One contact explained that "it's not a place where you keep quiet." People observed, however, that some aspects of the firm's ambiance are changing, with somewhat less socializing today than in the past. Further, some people found the firm somewhat "formal."

training and feedback

As a "young" and "vibrant" firm, Duane Morris invests heavily in its young associates and "takes training very seriously." For junior associates, the firm offers a wide range of formal programs and workshops in all areas of the practice. There also are opportunities for on-the-job training, although these vary by department. One source noted that the bankruptcy department offers particularly good opportunities for responsibility: "They were even sending people to court in their first year." Others told us of excellent early opportunities and responsibility in the real estate and insurance defense practices. Summer associates may participate in deposition training, complete with a court reporter, so, as one person joked, "we could actually see how stupid we sounded." Duane provides good feedback to its summer associates. There are written evaluations for every project as well as mid- and end-of-summer reviews. By the middle of the summer, most people apparently had a good idea of how they were doing. Each summer associate is assigned three mentors: a junior associate, a mid-level associate, and a partner. "Summer associates have a tremendous amount of support," according to one insider.

golf mecca

Duane Morris is a mecca for golfers, and the firm's golf outing is a major summer event. Although the summer program is not lavish ("Are any, anymore?", quipped one contact.), Duane Morris sponsors trips to the museum, orchestra, a billiards hall and baseball games, among other activities. The firm's softball team adds to the summer fun, and there is a very popular wine and cheese gathering every Thursday. All attorneys at the firm are encouraged to take summer associates to lunch.

excellent for minorities

Duane Morris is one of the best places for African-American lawyers in Philadelphia. In early 1991, the firm added six lawyers from a small, primarily African-American law firm, with Nolan Atkinson and Bob Archie joining as partners. According to one person of color, the firm gives a very "positive impression" through its commitment to diversity. Minorities "feel very comfortable." In addition, everyone we interviewed agreed that the firm provides a supportive environment for women, with the bankruptcy department particularly well-represented. Duane Morris also received high marks on family issues, with one woman commenting that "the maternity leave policy is deliberately flexible." Another contact remarked that "this is one of the best firms for female attorneys. The percentage of female partners is high in comparison with other large Philadelphia firms."

Duane Morris occupies the 37th to 43rd floors in One Liberty Place, the "biggest, newest, nicest office building in Philadelphia," exclaimed one person. The "carpeting and offices are new," with a "light and airy" decor and "stunning" views. Each attorney has an individual office. The computer system has been completely updated recently. It is "state of the art," with internal and external e-mail. "We even have our Internet addresses on our personalized letterhead," gushed one contact. The facilities and management support (marketing, office services, library, etc.) are all "top-notch."

hiring tips

Almost every summer hire at Duane Morris has a strong Philadelphia connection. Most summer associates come from Penn, Temple, or Villanova, but the firm also recruits at the national schools, with Georgetown and Harvard figuring prominently. Although hiring at Duane Morris is as competitive as at other large Philadelphia firms, people emphasized that the firm relies more on personality than academic performance in making its final decisions. At callback interviews, candidates meet about six attorneys over a three-hour period. For example, one person interviewed with a senior partner, the chair of the hiring committee, one junior associate, and three midlevel associates. Hiring committee attorneys are very "gregarious," and the interviews tend to be low-key. One person advised interviewees to "try to be a person and not a law nerd." Another person suggested that the firm looks for "fun-loving, happy people."

While Duane Morris is not the most prestigious firm in the city, it offers some very attractive features. It provides "one of the best places to work from a quality of life standpoint." The hours are "more reasonable" than at other firms in the city and the pay is competitive. There is a lot of "flexibility" in terms of work schedules. "If we get our work done and are available during normal business hours, no one expects us to stay late or work weekends," one source told us. The firm has also shown flexibility in granting leaves of absence. Recently, two litigation associates were granted leave to work full time in political campaigns. The partnership track was recently changed into a two-tier system which, according to one contact, "will provide the opportunity for more associates to make partner." It has one of the best bankruptcy practices in the city and provides an excellent environment for minorities. Though Duane Morris has grown into a large firm, it has maintained the feel of a somewhat smaller firm.

Morgan, Lewis & Bockius

Philadelphia Harrisburg Los Angeles Miami New York Pittsburgh Princeton Washington
Brussels Frankfurt Jakarta London Singapore Tokyo

Address: 2000 One Logan Square, Philadelphia, PA 19103–6993
Telephone: (215) 963–5000
Hiring Attorney: Eric Kraeutler
Contact: Caroline M. Olson, Attorney Recruitment and Development Administrator; (215) 963–5680
Associate Salary: First year $73,000 (1997)
Summer Salary: $1300/week (1997)
Average Hours: 2281 worked; 2060 billed; NA required
Family Benefits: Dependent care reimbursement plan; emergency childcare
1996 Summer: Class of 25 students; offers to 24
Partnership: NA
Pro Bono: 2% of all work is pro bono

Morgan, Lewis & Bockius in 1997
211 Lawyers at the Philadelphia Office
1.3 Associates Per Partner

Total Partners 88			Total Associates 113			Practice Areas	
Women	5	6%	Women	44	39%	Business/Bankruptcy/Securities	68
All Minorities	3	3%	All Minorities	8	7%	Litigation/White Collar	62
Afro-Am	2	2%	Afro-Am	5	4%	Labor/ERISA/Employment	33
Asian-Am	1	1%	Asian-Am	2	2%	Tax/Employee Benefits	21
			Latino	1	1%	Environmental/Insurance	14
						Estates/Trusts/Wills	7
						Antitrust/Intellectual Property	3
						International	3

With its name recognition and national office network, Morgan, Lewis & Bockius is Philadelphia's largest and most prestigious law firm. Its "fairly austere and utilitarian" offices, decorated "much as you would expect," with "dark wood and traditional furniture," might be seen as proof of the firm's longstanding reputation: white shoe, stuffy, and pretentious. Everyone we interviewed, however, asserted that although there remain vestiges of an old-boy atmosphere, this image is far from the reality of Morgan Lewis today. The firm's management is comprised of fairly "progressive-minded," "young and aggressive" lawyers, including a number of prominent attorneys of diverse ethnic and religious backgrounds. Morgan Lewis' attorneys represent a broad range of political views. One Republican contact commented that she felt like a "distinct minority" among her peers because "the most outspoken people are the Democrats." A number of lawyers worked on Lynn Yeakel's campaign for the U.S. Senate, and Marc Sonnenfeld and Gregory Harvey are influential in Democratic circles. But, another person dissented mildly, pointing out that "politics aren't really much discussed" and, in any case, the firm is "more 'conservative' than 'liberal.'"

strong international and corporate

With its strong international practice, as well as its large branch offices in major U.S. cities, Morgan Lewis offers an attractive "alternative to working for a big New York firm," one insider remarked. "If you are interested in doing a big firm practice with an international presence, but don't want to devote your life to it in New York City, and you are willing to be compensated less than in New York City, Morgan Lewis offers a lot of advantages from a corporate law perspective. The quality of the transactions they do is almost as high, although there are some things that only traditional New York corporate firms can do. Because it is a regional firm, you also have the opportunity to work with smaller clients as well as to get involved in the nuts and bolts of business." The business and finance department is the largest practice at Morgan Lewis, handling everything from mergers and acquisitions to initial public offerings. Howard Shecter, who is "well-known in the financial world," is the section vice chair for this area. The Philadelphia office is well-integrated into Morgan Lewis' international practice, particularly its work in London and Frankfurt, as well as in the firm's recently created offices in Singapore and Jakarta. There is a "tremendous amount" of interaction between the Philadelphia office and these two Pacific Rim offices, we were told.

litigation, labor, and IP

Spanning a broad range of areas, the litigation department is the second-largest practice. One person observed that "most of Morgan Lewis' litigation work is in federal court, and there is a significant amount of appellate work." There is also a broad variety of state court matters, and "all litigation runs the gamut of sizes, complexities and subject areas." Ed Dennis, an African-American litigator, was a former Assistant Attorney General for the Criminal Division under President Bush and a former U.S.

Attorney for the Eastern District of Pennsylvania. Accordingly, Morgan Lewis' white-collar criminal defense group is a "significant presence in the legal community." In addition, the firm's litigation section is actively increasing its intellectual property practice. Although Morgan Lewis' labor practice is not the firm's largest, it may be the best-known nationally—and it has been very popular with summer associates as well. The firm's D.C. office also has a substantial labor practice. Both the D.C. and the Philadelphia offices have strong government relations and environmental practices. With very few young associates, the trusts and estates group is noticeably "older" than others at the firm.

pro bono

As for the pro bono practice, one contact remarked that "there is some pro bono work at the firm, but they emphasize that it should not be an all-consuming endeavor. They want you to participate, but not to have it take up too much of your time." A firm spokesperson pointed out that the firm treats pro bono hours as fully billable time, and "has been frequently recognized for its contributions to pro bono services." Moreover, Morgan Lewis participates in the Philadelphia Public Interest Fellowship Program, under which associates have the opportunity to spend their first year of practice paid by the firm but assigned full-time to a legal services organization in Philadelphia. For example, under this program, one of the associates beginning in the fall of 1997 will work at the Philadelphia Health Law Project, we were told.

management

Morgan Lewis has been very solid financially and has not experienced any layoffs, unlike some other large Philadelphia firms. The management does a fair job of communicating with associates. One contact suggested that Morgan Lewis is a prudently managed firm that "doesn't seem interested in making aggressive and unconservative moves." In short, the firm's formula for success has worked for many years, and there are no plans for radical change.

Among the reasons for Morgan Lewis' prosperity is its commitment to minimizing client costs, and the firm recently implemented a new, more detailed billing system toward this end. One person quipped that the firm scrutinizes billing so carefully that "if you take a break to get a Coke, you better not bill it." Alongside the firm's new billing system has come an "increased emphasis on billable hours" which are being emphasized by management more than in the past. One contact pointed out that the pressure for hours is rapidly becoming 'New York like.' This person also noted that Morgan Lewis' compensation is not commensurate with its workload; "while Morgan's starting salary ranks at the top in the city, increases are conservative, leaving many a Morgan associate working New York hours for a salary that lags behind even some Philadelphia firms."

training and opportunities

Morgan Lewis invests heavily in associate training, we were told. The firm provides a variety of seminars and formal training opportunities, including special writing seminars and deposition training for summer associates. In addition, "participation in outside CLE courses and programs is encouraged." The opportunities for on-the-job training and responsibility vary by department, but on the whole appear to be quite good. People noted that first-year associates sometimes conduct their own depositions in the labor department and have client contact in the corporate department. Litigation associates are given "considerable case management responsibility by a variety of partners," according to one contact who further informed us that "in my first two years, I've conducted two small claims trials, taken and defended numerous depositions, argued motions, and handled client contacts."

sports-oriented

Sporting events are a popular activity at Morgan Lewis. The firm's lawyers are "a very athletic group of people" and participate in firm sponsored softball and basketball teams. Morgan Lewis also offers a number of social events throughout the year, with a highlight being a winter dance, affectionately referred to as the "prom." Other opportunities for socializing at the firm include "Friday afternoon cocktail parties, daily lunches in the firm cafeteria, and social gatherings with small groups of fellow colleagues," one contact informed us.

diversity

The female presence at Morgan Lewis is about average for the city. Betsy Fay has headed the hiring committee in the past, and Jami Wintz McKeon, a litigation partner, has for many years been involved in the firm's recruiting program. Judy Harris, an African-American partner in the labor and employment law section, who served from 1992 to 1994 as the City Solicitor for Philadelphia, is a present member of the recruitment committee at Morgan Lewis. During a recent summer, lawyers at the firm met to discuss opportunities for working part-time, a concept that, according to some, "hasn't gone over very well yet." A firm spokesperson informed us that "this concept has moved beyond the discussion stages. We now have a number of part-time associates, one of whom is in the Philadelphia office." As for racial minorities, one of the firm's African-American partners, the aforementioned Ed Dennis, is one of the most politically-connected and high-profile partners.

competitive hiring

Morgan Lewis is one of the most competitive firms in Philadelphia for prospective summer associates. The firm hires from a wide variety of schools with many summer associates from Philadelphia law schools such as Penn, Temple, and Villanova. Morgan Lewis also regularly hires large numbers of summer associates from Harvard, Yale, Georgetown, Cornell, and Virginia. Indeed, Virginia is the third most represented law school in the Philadelphia office. Everyone we interviewed emphasized that Morgan Lewis relies more on personality in its hiring decisions than do many of the other large Philadelphia firms. One person asserted that "to get a job with them, you have to be confident and outgoing," though not necessarily at the top of the class if you are from a national school. Another person remarked that you "must be a team player—prima donnas need not apply. Team spirit and loyalty to fellow colleagues is key." Most people hired from Temple and Villanova, however, are in the top of their classes. During callbacks, most candidates interview with about five attorneys for about one half hour each. The interviews tend to be very informal—one person reported, "I just talked about theater and acting the whole time."

Morgan Lewis offers greater prestige and resources than any firm in Philadelphia. The firm has placed increased emphasis on billable hours of late and is not as "connected to the local and state bar network" as much as some would prefer. It does, however, enjoy "utmost financial stability" and a national reputation. Although it has had a formal and stuffy image in the past, this has been changing. For someone interested in a structured, large firm environment, Morgan Lewis is hard to beat.

Pepper, Hamilton & Scheetz

Philadelphia Berwyn Cherry Hill Detroit Harrisburg New York Pittsburgh Washington Wilmington London Moscow

Address: 3000 Two Logan Square, 18th and Arch Streets, Philadelphia, PA 19103–2799
Telephone: (215) 981–4000
Hiring Attorney: Thomas E. Zemaitis
Contact: Sharon R. Buckingham, Director of Recruitment & Professional Programs; (215) 981–4265
Associate Salary: First year $70,000 (1997); First year $72,000 (effective 1998)
Summer Salary: NA
Average Hours: 1984 worked; 1828 billed; 1940 required
Family Benefits: Short-term disability (including maternity); infant care leave; emergency childcare facility; dependent care reimbursement program; part-time policy
1996 Summer: Class of 7 students; offers to 6
Partnership: 15% of entering associates from 1985–1987 were made partner
Pro Bono: NA

Pepper, Hamilton & Scheetz in 1997
175 Lawyers at the Philadelphia Office
1.0 Associate Per Partner

Total Partners 85		
Women	14	16%
All Minorities	3	4%
Afro-Am	2	2%
Asian-Am	1	1%

Total Associates 82		
Women	36	44%
All Minorities	2	2%
Afro-Am	1	1%
Latino	1	1%

Practice Areas	
Litigation	77
Corporate & Securities	22
Tax, Emp. Benefits & Estates	21
Labor & Employment	19
Construction & Gov't Contracts	13
Corporate Finance	10
Real Estate	7
Bankruptcy	6

Pepper, Hamilton & Scheetz traditionally has been considered one of the top three Philadelphia law firms. It has emerged from a 1992 "shakeup," in which some of Pepper's partners left the firm, "stronger than ever, more stable, more competitive, and more democratic," according to one insider. The leadership baton has been passed and Pepper remains one of Philadelphia's most financially sound law firms. Jim Murray, the current executive partner, is described as "very likeable" with a "good vision for where the firm should be going." The firm strives to be "open and honest with associates." Quarterly meetings are convened by the executive partner with all associates to "update associates on various firm matters and to promote a forum for discussing any questions and concerns associates may have." In addition, Anthony Haller, chairman of the Associates Committee, holds periodic small group meetings with associates to discuss associate issues and concerns. The rebound from the 1992 downslide appears to be complete.

practice areas

Pepper historically has been divided into three departments: litigation, commercial, and labor. There is also a regulatory practice, which is mainly handled out of the firm's D.C. office. In recent years, emphasis has been placed on developing practice groups or sub-specialties within departments. Practice groups in litigation include intellectual property, environmental, commercial litigation and a health effects group (toxic torts, medical devices, radiation). With a "national reputation," Pepper's litigation department is the largest and most well-known at the firm. The commercial department has developed "enormously" in recent years under the guidance of Barry Abelson. The firm does some international work, with offices in Moscow and St.

Petersburg, Russia and in Almaty, Kazakhstan. One person contended, however, that Pepper's international practice is not particularly strong, being less "cosmopolitan" than that of some New York firms.

excellent training

Associates training is described as "excellent." It includes weekly seminar luncheons for first-years and deposition camps and trial training for higher level associates. The firm conducts a multiday deposition workshop together with Dechert, Price & Rhoads, "hiring real actors as witnesses and actual court reporters." In addition, there is a week-long trial practice workshop, culminating in an actual trial, with actors again playing the role of witnesses. One participant described both programs as "extremely useful, underscoring the firm's commitment to training its associates." Associate feedback at Pepper received strong reviews. Associates are reviewed annually under a "good evaluation system," in which "each associate sees what partners and senior associates have written about them."

organized summer

People commented that the summer program is well-organized and "smooth-running." The firm was complimented for being clear about what was expected of summer associates and for providing good feedback. Summer associates choose assignments of interest from a central assignment book. Supervising attorneys complete written evaluations of each project, and summer associates also receive mid- and end-of-summer reviews.

Pepper sponsors "tons" of social events throughout the summer, including a sailing trip, a crab feast, a billiards party, dinners, baseball games, and musical outings. Although people are friendly at work, "they do not tend to socialize with each other outside of work." One person observed that there is "good rapport among the attorneys and good rapport between the attorneys and paralegals;" another noted, however, that "one problem is that there is no system for integrating someone into the firm. How you fit into the firm may depend on the partner for whom you are working."

diversity

People we interviewed praised Pepper's environment for women. There are many women in prominent positions throughout the firm and its management and, in particular, on the executive committee. The reviews on the firm's commitment to racial diversity were mixed. According to one person, "they acknowledge the problem and speak the language," but overall, "they are not committed to diversity." But, another person remarked, from a somewhat different perspective, that "there certainly is a lack of diversity but I do not believe it stems from a lack of commitment on the firm's part. Recent classes of summer and entry-level associates have contained significant numbers of minorities." In fact seven of the fifteen associates joining the Philadelphia office in the fall of 1997 are minorities: four African American, two Latino, one Asian. Moreover, the firm "is continually working on improvements to the mentoring process, which we see as the best way to ensure that minority associates will prosper," we were told. In recent years, two of Pepper's African-American attorneys left the firm for high-profile jobs with the City of Philadelphia. One of these, Michael Pratt, has since rejoined the firm and has recently become a partner at the firm. The second, Judy Harris, who served as the City Solicitor from 1992-1994, now works at Morgan, Lewis & Bockius.

Pepper is located in relatively new offices that include a gym with showers, free weights, and aerobics classes; a cafeteria with "great prices"; and a dining room. Each associate has a private office with a networked computer. The firm is presently implementing an across-the-board computer overhaul which "will bring Windows 95 and the Internet to everyone's desk." The support staff was described as "excellent."

hiring tips Pepper is one of the most competitive firms in Philadelphia regarding summer associate offers. People stressed that Pepper emphasizes personality more than grades in its hiring. One associate stated: "We primarily look for the fit—how the candidate would fit in with the group they want to work in...Most of the candidates are similar academically. There is no academic achievement yardstick that I know of, but there is a basic range." Most successful candidates from the local Philadelphia law schools are in the top 15% of their classes. Callback interviews are "relatively easy" and informal; there is no standard interview format or set list of questions.

Pepper has traditionally been one of the most prestigious Philadelphia firms. It provides some of the best litigation work in the city. It also offers a very social atmosphere and a great working environment for women. It is a firm of "nice people," with "down-to-earth" work groups, "excellent associate feedback" and, in the words of one contact, "there is no such thing as 'face-time' at this firm."

Reed Smith Shaw & McClay

Philadelphia Harrisburg McLean Newark New York Pittsburgh Princeton Washington

Address: 2500 One Liberty Place, Philadelphia, PA 19103
Telephone: (215) 851–8100
Hiring Attorney: Douglas Y. Christian
Contact: Barbara A. Hughes, Manager, Human Resources; (215) 851–1424
Associate Salary: First year $70,000 (1997)
Summer Salary: $1250/week (1997)
Average Hours: 1900 worked; 1800 billed; 1800 required
Family Benefits: NA
1996 Summer: Class of 5 students; offers to 5
Partnership: NA
Pro Bono: 3% of all work is pro bono

Reed Smith Shaw & McClay in 1997
85 Lawyers at the Philadelphia Office
1.3 Associates Per Partner

Total Partners 36		
Women	3	8%
All Minorities	1	3%
Afro-Am	1	3%

Total Associates 45		
Women	18	40%
All Minorities	3	7%
Afro-Am	1	2%
Asian Am	2	4%

Practice Areas	
Business & Finance	25
Litigation	28
Intellectual Property	9
Labor	8
New Associate Group	5
Tax	5
Trusts & Estates	3
Bankruptcy	2
Environmental	2
Consumer Financial Services	NA
Health Care	NA
Real Estate	NA

Reed, Smith, Shaw & McClay's Philadelphia office has grown significantly since its opening in 1978. The Philadelphia branch office—now about 90 lawyers (including those of counsel) and growing "faster than the firm can manage"—has developed its own distinct culture and personality, more informal and tight-knit than that of the home office in Pittsburgh known, to have a more white shoe image. Some summer associates who spent time in both offices reported that, compared to the friendly and laid-back Philadelphia office, the Pittsburgh headquarters had a "drill sergeant" atmosphere. Whereas the Pittsburgh office is highly structured and known for its extensive associate training, the Philadelphia branch office is still adjusting to its recent rapid growth. One person remarked that "the rapid growth and the large proportion of laterals cause the office to experience growing pains." Still, this person was quite happy to be located in the Philadelphia branch office: "It's nice to be part of a large firm but not be located in the main office. Our office is a nice size and doesn't have to deal with a lot of the hassles that would otherwise be associated with practice in a 400 person firm."

Republican firm

Reed Smith reportedly is the most "Republican" firm in Philadelphia, with many of the firm's partners well-known in Republican circles. For example, Ron Castille, a former Philadelphia District Attorney and Reed Smith attorney, was a Republican candidate for Mayor and is now a Pennsylvania Supreme Court Justice. Beyond this, we were told that a number of other partners have conservative leanings. One insider observed that as to politics, most "people with other views kept their opinions to themselves." Another person advised that to be a successful summer associate, it doesn't hurt to "keep out of politics." On the other hand, another source told us that there is now developing at the firm "a large group of Democrats, who were very active in the recent elections."

practice areas

Reed Smith's Philadelphia office is currently organized into three major departments: litigation, business and finance, and specialized services that includes, among others, intellectual property. Both the litigation and the business and finance departments are divided into a number of subgroups. New associates obtain projects from a general pool for their first six months at the firm, after which time they are assigned to a particular group. One contact noted that the intellectual property and business lawyers often work closely with start-up companies to "help get an idea from start to finish—it's a teamwork thing." Although the work atmosphere generally is very pleasant, one source noted that the corporate group has a few partners who are reputedly difficult to work with. The firm's pro bono practice is coordinated by one of the partners and includes representation of organizations for the homeless, battered women's groups, Lawyers for the Arts, and AIDS-related projects. Pro bono hours currently do not count toward billable hour requirements, but there is a non-billable requirement that includes pro bono work.

cohesive atmosphere

Reed Smith has a cohesive work atmosphere. One contact commented that the firm "is definitely not a sweatshop. You have a constant amount of work, and the lawyers are serious about what they do. There is a nice bond among the young associates." Another contact remarked that, "the classes are very tight-knit as they go through. People socialize in the library. They work hard and play hard. On Fridays, many of the young associates go out together for cocktails. Although it's not a big party firm, it's a good place for social life. People put in a long day and work harder than at other places, but they have a good time doing it." Everyone we interviewed said that good relations exist between partners and associates. Moreover, the firm's management, led by managing partner Michael Browne, is very open about its decisions. With weekly department meetings including both partners and associates, there is "good communication, and the partners are open to ideas. They are very down-to-earth. It's a first–name–basis type of place." Not surprisingly, Philadelphia's management was described by people we spoke with as more "receptive" to associates' ideas than the "conservative" Pittsburgh office. One person, with experience in both offices, spiritedly dissented from this view, however.

training feedback

Unlike the home office, the training at Reed Smith Philadelphia is very unstructured, with one associate describing it as "pretty much on-the-job training." Although the firm sponsors some continuing legal education seminars, "there is no real formal training program." Most first- and second-year associates do "a lot of research and memos" and usually are not entrusted with their own matters until their third year. People noted, however, that the bankruptcy and litigation groups are exceptions, with many associates handling their own cases by their second year. One person complained that "there are not a lot of people who are willing to mentor associates." The summer program also is unregimented. One person called it "disorganized," commenting further that "often the summer program was unstructured and even chaotic. However, a second contact informed us that the summer program has made strides to improve this situation. Summer associate assignments are coordinated through one of the firm's associates. The firm provides a written evaluation on each summer associate project assigned and also provides midsummer and end-of-summer reviews. Reed Smith's summer program does have the attraction of making permanent offers to almost all summer hires, according to one contact; in 1996, the firm made offers to all five of its summer associates.

diversity

Although women generally are "respected" at Reed Smith, our contacts commented that there are a few partners whom women may want to avoid. People also observed that Reed Smith is not particularly supportive of part-time and maternity leave issues. One person asserted that the firm has "been dragging its feet on this issue." Another person took exception to this view, pointing out, in addition, that there is an active Women's Associate Group at the firm. There are relatively few minority attorneys at the firm; however, Richard Glanton, an African-American, is one of the firm's most prominent corporate partners.

Reed Smith occupies the 24th through 27th floors at One Liberty Place, the tallest building in Philadelphia. The office decor is "open" and "airy" with "very light colors." Everyone praised the computer system, which fully networks all the firm's offices. Each lawyer has Internet, e-mail, and legal research tools at his or her desk.

hiring tips

Reed Smith's hiring committee is very concerned about hiring individuals with a strong commitment to staying in Philadelphia. Although the committee recruits actively at the top 20 national law schools, it relies heavily on the local Philadelphia schools. One source stressed that Reed Smith pays very close attention to grades. The callback interviews at Reed Smith are relaxed. Students typically meet with about four attorneys for one half hour each and go to lunch. One person said she found "many characters" among her interviewers. Another person advised interviewees, however, to be "pretty serious and direct with the partners, and even though the firm has a flexible system, come in and say you want to work in a specific practice area."

Reed Smith is rapidly becoming a large Philadelphia firm. Although the politics and atmosphere of the office are somewhat conservative, the firm offers an unstructured and flexible working environment. The Philadelphia office carries with it the added prestige of being connected to one of the country's most prestigious law firms, which in recent years expanded considerably beyond its home office in Pittsburgh to offices in a number of East Coast cities. One contact pointed out to us that "the New York office has enabled Reed Smith to expand its growing international practice. The Newark office has allowed the firm to better serve its clients in New Jersey." Moreover, Reed Smith associates form a tight-knit group. Reed Smith is, in the words of one contact, "one of the best big firms to work at while maintaining a sane lifestyle, and there is a lot of room at the firm to find or 'create' your 'niche,' whatever that may be." The one disadvantage of employment at Reed Smith that we heard about concerned compensation; more than one person observed to us that the "pay does not keep pace with other firms at upper associate levels."

Saul, Ewing, Remick & Saul

Philadelphia Berwyn Harrisburg New York Princeton Wilmington

Address: 3800 Centre Square West, Philadelphia, PA 19102
Telephone: (215) 972–7777
Hiring Attorney: Joseph F. O'Dea, Jr.
Contact: Valerie M. Baldi, Recruitment Coordinator; (215) 972–7991
Associate Salary: First year $66,000 (1997)
Summer Salary: $1250/week (1997)
Average Hours: NA worked; 1850 billed; NA required
Family Benefits: Group medical, life, dental and long term disability; 3 month maternity, defined benefits package and four weeks vacation
1996 Summer: Class of 3 2L students; offers to 2
Partnership: 25% of entering associates from 1980–1986 were made partner
Pro Bono: NA

Saul, Ewing, Remick & Saul in 1997
144 Lawyers at the Philadelphia Office
0.7 Associates Per Partner

Total Partners 75			Total Associates 52			Practice Areas	
Women	8	11%	Women	21	40%	Litigation/Labor	41
All Minorities	1	1%	All Minorities	5	10%	Business	27
Latino	1	1%	Afro-Am	1	2%	Real Estate	26
			Asian-Am	2	4%	Bankruptcy	10
			Latino	1	2%	Environmental	9
			Native Am	1	2%	Estates	9
						Public Finance	9
						Health Law	8
						Products Liability	5

During the past few years, Saul Ewing has made significant progress in its plan to grow from a local Philadelphia firm into a truly regional firm. After facing difficult financial times in the early 1990s and flirting with a possible merger with Pittsburgh's Buchanan Ingersoll in 1994, Saul Ewing rejected the merger plan and opted to focus its efforts on becoming a strong regional firm in the Pennsylvania–New Jersey–Delaware region. In the past few years, the firm has seen rapid expansion of its Harrisburg and Berwyn satellite offices in Pennsylvania, its Princeton, New Jersey office and its Wilmington, Delaware office. Saul Ewing's new leadership team, headed by managing partner John F. Stoviak, appears to have refocused the firm's energies. Coming off its 75th anniversary year, the firm reportedly experienced its most profitable year, and associate morale, which had dipped during prior years, has also rebounded, we were told.

practice areas

Spanning a range of subgroups, the litigation department is the largest practice at the firm. It includes a growing white-collar defense practice, comprised of a number of former Justice Department attorneys and headed by former U.S. Attorneys, J. Clayton Undercofler and Robert N. DeLuca, and former Assistant U.S. Attorney for the Eastern District of Pennsylvania, James M. Becker. Undercofler is chairman of the firm and also chair of the litigation department. Another litigation subgroup is the environmental litigation group, which has "carved out a specialty" representing transporters of hazardous waste. This group is headed by the aforementioned John F. Stoviak.

Although the litigation department is the largest at Saul Ewing, "a handful of smaller departments defines the firm," we were told. Among these are the environmental department, headed by Carl B. Everett, which is considered by many to be one of the best large-firm environmental groups in Philadelphia. The real estate department is one of the biggest in the city and is among the few regional real estate groups that can be characterized as "major players." Saul Ewing is "one of the more active firms in real estate right now, and there are uniformly nice people in that department," reported one insider.

The health law department has in recent years established itself as "one of the most respected health law groups in Philadelphia," representing some of the biggest players in this health-care dominated city. Also among the departments that define Saul Ewing is the "very politically connected" public finance group, which consists of a number of lawyers well known for their strong connections to local and state government. Tim Carson, heavily involved in Republican politics, is a prominent partner in this practice.

The firm also has a large business department that includes Saul Ewing's corporate and tax practices. Formerly part of this department, the bankruptcy practice became a department unto itself several years ago. One contact claimed that the "bankruptcy group is one of the more abrasive places to work because of the personality of one of the partners," but noted that "there are people at the firm who have no problem working for him." Responding to one of the hottest segments of American business in the 1990s, Saul Ewing recently created a communications group that has already attracted an impressive list of clients.

pro bono

Everyone we interviewed agreed that Saul Ewing has a strong commitment to pro bono work. David Unkovic is credited with creating a "pro-bono friendly" environment at the firm. Saul Ewing is a regular recipient of the Chancellor's Award from the Philadelphia Bar Association for its ongoing work with the Philadelphia Volunteers for the Indigent program (VIP). Additionally, the firm has established a program for law students from the University of Pennsylvania to work on pro bono cases with Saul Ewing attorneys.

teamwork orientation

Saul Ewing provides a friendly work atmosphere. One summer associate commented: "It's a really pleasant place with a very personalized environment. It's the type of place where people smile at you when you walk by in the hallway. Everyone knew my name by the second or third week I was at the firm, and they went out of their way to get me more involved in the firm events. People there are very down-to-earth and not pretentious at all." Saul Ewing emphasizes "teamwork," and the associates are a tight-knit group. There is a friendly atmosphere at the firm, "especially among associates, who are a very social group. Other firm's lawyers are always calling their law school colleagues at Saul Ewing to find out what's going on for happy hour on Friday," one insider said.

unstructured environment

Despite being one of Philadelphia's largest firms, Saul Ewing offers a fairly unstructured environment. For example, most of the summer program events are casual, such as softball games and a pool party at one partner's home. Saul Ewing also does not provide much formal training for either summer or permanent associates. The firm has, however, recently begun a "structured eleven week" training program for new associates, using a "role playing" format, taught by young partners and senior associates. One person maintained, moreover, that the early opportunities for responsibility at the firm partially compensate for this shortcoming. Although most summer and first-year associate projects involve library research, many of the firm's associates have client contact by their second year. One source told us that "there is a real emphasis in recent times on getting associates 'out there' doing things and 'learning by doing'."

diversity

Saul Ewing provides a comfortable and supportive atmosphere for women. The firm's few female partners are well-respected, and some wield considerable influence. Connie Foster, a partner in the Harrisburg office, was recently elected to the Executive Committee. The Associates Committee has called for "an increased minority hiring effort, but Saul Ewing has a way to go before it achieves its diversity goals," we were told. The firm's Executive Committee has also "charged the Hiring Committee with improving our minority hiring efforts," according to a firm spokesperson. Moreover, of the six students who have been accepted into the firm's upcoming summer program, two are minorities.

renovated beautiful offices

Saul Ewing recently expanded from three to four floors, and completely renovated all four, in its Philadelphia headquarters. The decor is fairly conservative and a bit "formal," with dark wood paneling, 18th Century antiques, and Persian carpets. One contact volunteered that, with the overhaul, Saul Ewing finds itself "among the most beautiful office space in Philadelphia." The firm recently overhauled its computer system. It now has state-of-the-art Pentium PCs on every desk. Saul Ewing was the first firm in Philadelphia to have its own Internet home page on the World Wide Web, and it intends to overhaul its major software programs in the near future, we were told. The firm has "superb library resources" but a support staff (secretaries, legal assistants, paralegals) that is "below average," according to one insider. A representative from the firm pointed out to us that "our 144 attorneys are supported by 143 support staff and paralegals. In terms of 'quality,' our support staff is first rate."

hiring practices

Saul Ewing historically has hired a fair share of first-year students in its summer associate classes. Saul Ewing's hiring committee reportedly believes that the firm has a better chance of recruiting the nation's top students after their first year, and that a summer with Saul Ewing will convince them to join the firm after graduation. Most successful first-year candidates are from top 10 law schools, with Harvard, Michigan, Penn, and Yale figuring prominently. Although the firm apparently emphasizes personality over grades in hiring second-year students, one insider stated that first semester grades are "pretty much the bottom line" for first-year applicants. Many successful second-year candidates come from the top 10 percent of local schools such as Villanova and Temple, as well as the University of Pennsylvania. The interviews at the firm are relaxed and are "more conversational than inquisitive."

Saul Ewing is an unstructured and friendly firm that has made a nice comeback from some troubled times in the early 1990s. The firm is presently "getting tons of business" and is expanding both in Philadelphia and in the regional offices. Morale is high, and there is a strong camaraderie among its attorneys. It has "genuinely nice people and reasonable hours," as well as "some truly excellent departments (e.g. environmental, real estate, healthcare, and public finance)." One insider told us, "it's an exciting time for Saul, Ewing. The firm is just starting to hit its stride."

Schnader, Harrison, Segal & Lewis

Philadelphia Atlanta Cherry Hill Harrisburg New York Norristown Pittsburgh Washington, PA Washington, D.C.

Address: 1600 Market Street, Suite 3600, Philadelphia, PA 19103 (www.shsl.com)
Telephone: (215) 751–2000
Hiring Attorney: Rolin P. Bissell and Mary P. Higgins
Contact: Vivian Funchion, Legal Hiring Coordinator; (215) 751–2049
Associate Salary: First year $70,000 (1997)
Summer Salary: $1200/week (1996)
Average Hours: 2135 worked; 1902 billed; 1900 required
Family Benefits: NA
1996 Summer: Class of 9 students; offers to 8
Partnership: 16% of entering associates from 1979–1984 were made partner
Pro Bono: 2–3% of all work is pro bono

Schnader, Harrison, Segal & Lewis in 1997
136 Lawyers at the Philadelphia Office
1.0 Associate Per Partner

Total Partners 63		
Women	12	19%
All Minorities	1	2%
Afro-Am	1	2%

Total Associates 61		
Women	32	52%
All Minorities	5	8%
Afro-Am	3	5%
Asian Am	2	3%
Latino	1	2%

Practice Areas	
Litigation	59
Business	17
Family/Matrimonial	13
Intellectual Property	10
Real Estate	10
Trusts & Estates	10
Labor (management)	9
Tax	8
Health Care	4

Founded by a Jewish lawyer and a Christian lawyer, Schnader, Harrison, Segal & Lewis takes pride in its diversity and multi-culturalism. One insider commented that Schnader Harrison has always been more "open-minded" than many of the other large Philadelphia firms and has given "more than just lip service" to its commitment to diversity. Bernie Segal, the firm's former name partner who is now of counsel, customarily relates Schnader Harrison's history to summer associates, particularly emphasizing its tradition of inclusiveness. In addition to religious diversity, there is also a broad spectrum of political views at Schnader Harrison. Democratic Senator Harris Wofford is a former partner, but one source observed that "there is no lack of Republicans" at the firm. For example, Arlin Adams, formerly a judge on the Third Circuit Court of Appeals (appointed by Nixon), is "of counsel" and has a very active practice at the firm. Summer associates quickly experience Schnader Harrison's emphasis on multi-culturalism. One person joked that you must "pass the test of being cross-cultural" with Jim Crawford, one of the firm's partners. With a penchant for exotic foreign restaurants, Crawford challenged past summer associates to partake of chicken feet and whole cloves of garlic at his favorite Korean dining place.

practice areas

Schnader Harrison is best-known for its wide-ranging litigation practice, the largest department at the firm. The department includes white-collar crime and First Amendment practices; the latter offers opportunities for junior associates that are rare in this specialized field. United Parcel Service is one of the firm's major litigation clients (and partly the reason for the new Atlanta branch office). The firm recently started an Internet law practice group that is "on the cutting edge of this developing area." The vibrant family law practice is headed by Albert Momjian, a "nationally famous family lawyer." This high-profile group's part of the firm is known as the "floor of stars" because "so many of the stars go there to get divorced." One contact stated,

"If you are very important in Philadelphia and you want to get divorced, you go to Schnader." Another contact assured us that attorneys in this practice do not "fit the stereotype of a divorce lawyer. Rather, I think they are a collection of some of the nicest people I've met. They certainly don't remind me of 'Arnie Becker' of L.A. Law (even if that comparison is rather outdated)."

The business department, which was "slow" in the early 1990s, has picked up considerably of late and "they're looking to hire some more associates," we were told. The labor group is small, with a high proportion of young male associates in the recent past. Our earlier edition described this "bright-young-men-clique" as the "wild bunch" at the firm. This has changed in the intervening years, we were informed. Today, "more or less, the 'clique' members have left. There are many more women in the department. In fact, there are no more male associates. Two of the bright young men were made partners."

Schnader Harrison's pro bono policy, under the direction of attorney Joseph Sullivan, allows associates to spend up to 10 percent of their time on pro bono work. On average, pro bono work constitutes two to three percent of the firm's work. "We are actively encouraged to do pro bono work," one contact informed us, adding that "the firm makes known any pro bono opportunities that come up and alerts you to pro bono organizations in the city."

New associates at Schnader Harrison are hired for a particular department depending on the firm's needs. First-year associates spend most of their time in the library, researching and writing memos. Second-year associates "start doing case management and depositions, and the level of responsibility after that depends on how much you are trusted." One observer recalled that one first-year associate handled a deposition, and another has not done one in four years.

good social life

Overall, people described Schnader Harrison as a "friendly" firm that is "good for social life," particularly among the young associates. There is a happy hour on the first Friday of every month (Thursdays during the summers) for all of the lawyers. Although there is not much pressure to bill hours at Schnader Harrison, "people work very hard" because "there is a lot of work to do." Many regularly work one weekend day. The firm recently increased the billable requirement to a "1900 hour minimum" according to one insider.

hierarchical environment

As one of Philadelphia's largest firms, Schnader Harrison provides a "highly structured" and somewhat hierarchical environment. It is "kind of a pain to deal with the firm," one contact reported. "There is a lot of red tape and paperwork." Even so, Schnader Harrison is quite "democratic." The firm is managed by a number of committees, with broad participation and staggered terms. The executive committee is composed exclusively of partners, and the recruiting committee includes both partners and associates. The associate-partner relationship at the firm is "pretty good—it is fairly open and there is respect up and down," according to one source. However, this person remarked that "occasionally, it seems that management is all thumbs." The firm's recent handling of the debate over potential changes in salaries and billable hours has been conducted "like the game Whisper Down the Lane: partners in the dark about it, rumors flying among the associates, and the firm has done little to achieve the desired effect of any raises, *i.e.* to improve our chances of recruiting the top summer clerks. Any announcement should have been made at a time when it could impact that process—now it's too late."

structured summer

Schnader Harrison's summer program is well-structured. Summer associates choose assignments from a central assignment book. Most work involves litigation, but other projects reportedly are available for the persistent. Perhaps the best aspect of the summer program is its evaluation process. Summer associates are evaluated by the attorneys for whom they work on a project-by-project basis. In addition, after completing projects, summer associates provide copies of their work to a designated "reader" on the summer committee. The reader rates each submission on a one to five scale, with appropriate adjectives linked to each of the five points on the scale. Most people receive threes; a two or a one means you are doing great work and have a strong chance of receiving a permanent offer; a four or a five is cause for concern. The summer program includes one organized social event each week. There are also softball games, and the attorneys are generous about taking summer associates to lunch. One contact notified us that "the firm has tried to increase the number of organized social events, but, let's face it, this isn't the 1980s anymore."

progressive atmosphere

Schnader Harrison is a "very progressive place," and there are "a lot of powerful women at the firm," including partner Sherry Swirsky (prominent in the Clinton campaign), Diana Donaldson, and Mary Higgins. The firm is accommodating to attorneys who want to work on a part time basis while raising children and, "while billable hours are important, the firm does not expect associates to routinely work on weekends just for the sake of billing hours," one contact informed us. There are "only a handful" of minorities at the firm, but Schnader Harrison is committed to diversity and "takes its goal seriously." A firm spokesperson informed us that "in recent years the firm has struggled, like many large firms, to achieve the level of racial diversity it desires. The most recent recruiting effort was successful in this regard but sincere efforts must continue in the future." Partner William Brown, an African-American, is a well-known litigator and former head of the Equal Employment Opportunity Commission.

Schnader Harrison occupies floors 34 to 39 in an approximately fifteen-year-old building in the center of Philadelphia. The "light and airy" decor is complemented by numerous early American and modern paintings. It has recently been refurbished and redecorated to bring the "look" into the 1990s. All attorneys have an individual office and a computer. One source informed us that "technologically, the firm has grown significantly. We are fairly cutting-edge computer wise. All lawyers have Internet access at their desks." Recently Schnader Harrison filed the first ever "cyber brief" in the U.S. Supreme Court. This amicus brief was filed on behalf of the plaintiffs in *ACLU v. Reno*, and it included links to Websites as exhibits.

hiring tips

Although Schnader Harrison undoubtedly emphasizes grades in its hiring, it is "not totally close-minded" about people with other talents. We were told that some of the associates "said they did not do particularly well in law school, but knew they would be good lawyers." Nevertheless, most successful candidates from local schools are in the top 10 to 20 percent of their classes. One person advised, however, that "even if you are in the bottom half of your class, you should still apply." Others cautioned us on this point, noting that this may be true "if you're from an Ivy League law school" but, more generally, "unless your grades are good, you're not going to get a job here." The callback interviews usually involve meeting about four attorneys and going out to lunch. Students should be prepared for an unusual interview with the aforementioned Jim Crawford, who was described as an entertaining and "off-the-wall kind of guy." Most of the interviews are "chatty" and unstructured.

Schnader Harrison's diverse history has shaped the firm into an interesting and open place in which to work. One person praised the "diversity of the people—we have great people to work with." Another exclaimed, "I wouldn't work at any other large firm in Philadelphia." The firm is home to many uncommon lawyers who have carved out unique practices or have unusual personal interests. While some people complained that the firm is somewhat hierarchical and bureaucratic and the management is occasionally "all thumbs," Schnader Harrison offers some flexibility in junior associate career development. If you want to work in a colorful law firm, Schnader Harrison is not a bad choice.

Wolf, Block, Schorr & Solis-Cohen

Philadelphia Blue Bell Camden Harrisburg Malvern Norristown Wilmington

Address: Packard Building, Twelfth Floor, Fifteenth & Chestnut Streets, Philadelphia, PA 19102–2678
Telephone: (215) 977–2000
Hiring Attorney: Mark K. Kessler and Jodi Plavner
Contact: Eileen M. McMahon, Legal Recruitment Administrator; (215) 977–2362
Associate Salary: First year $72,000 (1996)
Summer Salary: $1375/week for 2Ls and 3Ls only (1997)
Average Hours: NA worked; NA billed; NA required
Family Benefits: NA
1996 Summer: NA
Partnership: NA
Pro Bono: NA

Wolf, Block, Schorr & Solis-Cohen in 1997
NA Lawyers at the Philadelphia Office
NA Associates Per Partner

Total Partners NA			Total Associates NA			Practice Areas	
Women	NA	NA%	Women	NA	NA%	Litigation	NA
All Minorities	NA	NA%	All Minorities	NA	NA%	Corp., Bnkrptcy. & Fin. Services	
						Real Estate	
						Tax	
						Rotatees	
						Labor & Employment	
						Estates & Trusts	
						Health	
						Environmental	

significant changes

Wolf Block has undergone significant change in the past few years. In February 1995, seventeen partners left the firm; and many partners and associates have left since then. However, Wolf Block firm acquired three small firms and laterals to replace those that left, so that the firm size is about the same as before. Approximately one third of the firm is new, one of our contacts told us. In addition, Wolf Block has been under new leadership over the past two years, which leadership, we were told by three of our contacts, places an unprecedented emphasis on billable hours, associate performance, and the bottom line. These changes have had a significant impact on firm culture, contributing to a sense of discontent among some associates, according to a few of our contacts.

Although Wolf, Block, Schorr & Solis-Cohen is one of Philadelphia's largest firms, it does not stand on ceremony. One insider declared, "if you are looking for a formal and structured environment with a lot of emphasis on decorum, then Wolf is not the place for you." Wolf Block's lawyers were variously described as very "individualistic," "entrepreneurial," and somewhat "eccentric." They definitely are not the "two dimensional cut-out figures" sometimes associated with big law firms. The atmosphere at the firm is reflected in the way people dress: "as long as you are not dressed like a slob, you can pretty much do what you want." Founded in 1903 as a "haven for Jewish lawyers who were not being hired by the other firms," Wolf Block continues to be known as a "Jewish firm" on law school campuses. Although Wolf Block traditionally has been known as a Republican firm, today the firm is "very Democratic," we were told. Jerry Shestack and Mack Alderman are two well known Wolf Block attorneys who are active in Democratic party politics.

practice areas

Wolf Block historically has been best-known for its real estate practice. When the firm's real estate practice slowed down in the early 1990s, its corporate department became more prominent, representing both large institutions and smaller entrepreneurial clients. Steve Goodman, a former Supreme Court clerk, who had been a driving force in developing Wolf Block's start-up company practice, left the firm, however, for Morgan Lewis and took a number of "top-notch partners and associates with him," according to one contact. Since then the corporate department "has been coming back, with the addition of several excellent partners" and is "bigger and healthier than ever at present," we were told. Currently the department is headed by Jason Shangel, a securities law specialist formerly employed by the SEC, and Herb Hennyson, a merger and acquisitions specialist, formerly a partner at Skadden Arps.

The litigation group was described as a "very hard-working" group. The practice spans a wide variety of areas, and with the addition of Jerry Shestack, is particularly strong in appellate work. Ed Mannino and Jim Griffith have recently joined the firm, and litigation "is now the firm's largest department and may also be its most prominent," one insider informed us. The firm's labor practice represents a number of smaller companies that "don't have a big personnel department but call Wolf Block when a dam is about to break, and they need emergency attention." One of the firm's partners, Jonathan Segal, has developed "cutting-edge" seminars on sexual harassment, AIDS, and substance abuse, which have received national recognition. One person commented that "his reputation is spreading, and he is providing a great service to the client and taking the labor department in a new direction."

Wolf Block's health practice lost most of its attorneys two years ago, but "the partners in the firm are working hard to rebuild it. All in the department are highly regarded. While it may be less well-known now, I believe it is better than ever," attested one contact. The tax group was reported to be a "very scholarly department." One source described the firm's tax lawyers as "the kind of people who can quote from the regulations directly without blinking an eye." The estates department is "conservative, quiet, and scholarly. They have morning meetings at 7:45 a.m., and many people in the department wear bow ties." Starting associates at Wolf Block rotate through three firm departments for four months each before specializing in one particular area. Similarly, summer associates work in three or four departments during their stint at the firm.

pro bono

Although Wolf Block's attorneys handle a range of pro bono matters, there "isn't any centralized effort or promotion" to do pro bono work. Pro bono hours do not count toward billable hour requirements, but one person noted that "there are a surprisingly large number of attorneys doing some kind of pro bono work." Another person remarked that "Wolf Block has historically been at the top of the city in actual pro bono hours worked per lawyer. With the new emphasis on billable hours this is changing, but hopefully the individual attorneys will stay committed."

not for the faint of heart

With its hard-driving lawyers, Wolf Block is "not a place for the faint of heart." The firm staffs its cases thinly, and associates must assume responsibility quickly: "they will throw you into the middle of it. It's not a good place for hand-holding." One source characterized the atmosphere as "sink or swim," while another commented that the "lack of training and guidance makes work very unclear and difficult." One contact pointed out that "actual experience depends on the department: corporate, real estate, and labor have associates doing more; litigation has associates doing less. Overall, with the ratio of partners to associates being 2:1, rather than the other way around like at most firms, junior partners do what senior associates do elsewhere, and senior associates are on a level with midlevel associates at other firms in terms of type of work given."

minimal social life

The social program at Wolf Block is not especially well developed. One contact remarked that "there is no social scene at Wolf; there is a Christmas cocktail party and maybe a summer cookout," while another contact observed that the "new management at Wolf Block is trying to change the lack of firm-sponsored events" but with little success thus far. However, a third contact noted that "a number of departments have scheduled happy hour gatherings a few times a month." On the whole, the summer program is low-key, as the firm is not big on formal social events.

management from the top

Wolf Block's partnership structure is stratified, with five levels of partnership. New partners begin on level five and make their way up the hierarchy over the years. At the top sit the nine members of the firm's executive committee, who make most of the firm's decisions, claimed one source. "The other four levels of partners are assigned to various committees that contribute somewhat, but the final word comes from a small group at the top level." One person claimed that partner compensation varies dramatically, noting that the "huge rainmakers make a huge amount of money." Associate salaries have been a source of dissatisfaction, with a number of mid- and senior-level associates leaving for more remunerative in-house positions or going to other law firms. The associate compensation policy "has been reevaluated recently so that first-years make much more money than previously, but the increments between years are getting smaller and smaller," noted one insider.

aggressive mergers

Overall, as noted above, Wolf Block has stayed about the same size over the past few years. The firm has "aggressively merged with smaller firms to make up for the high number of partner and associate defections," we were told. Wolf Block has opened offices in Wilmington, Delaware and Camden, New Jersey. It has also acquired offices in Blue Bell and Norristown, Pennsylvania. One contact informed us that Wolf Block is "committed to becoming a regional powerhouse."

women and minorities

The people with whom we spoke were generally not complimentary regarding the position of women at Wolf Block. "There are no female partners in corporate and women do not do well in litigation," according to one contact. However, since the firm would not provide us statitistical information, we were unable to confirm the number of female corporate and litigation partners. This contact also stated, "I would venture a guess that most female attorneys feel that they are not given the same respect as men." Another person believed, "women are still second class (if not third) at the firm." A third person instructed us that "there are not many women left at Wolf Block, and more are rumored to be leaving." Although there are not many minorities at the firm, Bernard Lee, an African-American, is prominent in the real estate department.

"seedy" office facilities

Wolf Block's offices got universally bad reviews from our contacts. The offices are located in a "very old building," according to one contact, who complained about the building's "broken elevators" and "bathrooms in firetowers on alternating floors (i.e. women: 7,9,11,13; men: 6,8,10,12)." Another contact remarked that Wolf Block occupies one of the "seediest" office buildings in Philadelphia; the security system is a "sham" and the bathrooms are "horrible." Relief may be on the way, however; one contact informed us that the firm "will be moving to more contemporary space within a year." Another person noted that the firm's computer system, telephone system, and the human resources department are all "pretty good," but the secretarial situation is "really bad."

academic emphasis in hiring

In its recruitment, Wolf Block is not a "grades–don't–matter type of place," stated one insider. The firm makes it very clear that it emphasizes "a good academic record" in its hiring decisions, and one person concluded that "if someone has a mediocre transcript, they don't go any further." This factor, however, is less important for candidates from the country's top law schools. The on-campus interviews ordinarily are conducted by two attorneys, a senior partner and an associate. The callback interviews are "very informal" and "pleasant." Candidates meet with a pair of attorneys for about an hour, followed by lunch with three different attorneys. The attorneys "try to get you into a conversational mode—this is an important element of the process." For Penn, the firm holds an informal party for students with callback offers, providing a chance to meet attorneys.

Wolf Block offers a large firm practice in a relatively unstructured atmosphere. It is a firm for confident self-starters. According to one insider, Wolf Block is "very entrepreneurial" and caters to a wide range of clients, providing opportunities for early responsibility for many associates. At the same time, some of our contacts reported on an undercurrent of tension and unease among associates at the firm, principally arising from the philosophy of the new management team at the firm. A high turnover rate among attorneys, lowered morale, and increased emphasis on billable hours were some of the negatives brought to our attention. One insider poignantly observed that "the new management is moving the firm away from its historic roots…it is no longer much fun," while another contact observed simply, "I would not recommend Wolf."

Pittsburgh

Law Firms Ranked By Associates Per Partner

1.	DICKIE, MCCAMEY & CHILCOTE	0.7
2.	REED SMITH SHAW & MCCLAY	0.7
3.	BABST CALLAND CLEMENTS & ZOMNIR	0.9
4.	KIRKPATRICK & LOCKHART	0.9
5.	BUCHANAN INGERSOLL	1.0
6.	ECKERT SEAMONS CHERIN & MELLOT	1.0

Law Firms Ranked by Percentage of Associates Who Make Partner
(over varying years)

1.	KIRKPATRICK & LOCKHART	32
2.	REED SMITH SHAW & MCCLAY	22
3.	BABST CALLAND CLEMENTS & ZOMNIR	NA
4.	BUCHANAN INGERSOLL	NA
5.	DICKIE, MCCAMEY & CHILCOTE	NA
6.	ECKERT SEAMONS CHERIN & MELLOT	NA

Law Firms Ranked by Percentage of Pro Bono Work

1.	KIRKPATRICK & LOCKHART	3-5
2.	REED SMITH SHAW & MCCLAY	3
3.	ECKERT SEAMONS CHERIN & MELLOT	1-2
4.	DICKIE, MCCAMEY & CHILCOTE	1
5.	BABST CALLAND CLEMENTS & ZOMNIR	NA
6.	BUCHANAN INGERSOLL	NA

Law Firms Ranked by Percentage of Female Partners

1.	BUCHANAN INGERSOLL	17
2.	KIRKPATRICK & LOCKHART	13
3.	BABST CALLAND CLEMENTS & ZOMNIR	12
4.	REED SMITH SHAW & MCCLAY	11
5.	DICKIE, MCCAMEY & CHILCOTE	6
6.	ECKERT SEAMONS CHERIN & MELLOT	NA

Law Firms Ranked by Percentage of Female Associates

1.	REED SMITH SHAW & MCCLAY	52
2.	BUCHANAN INGERSOLL	44
3.	DICKIE, MCCAMEY & CHILCOTE	27
4.	BABST CALLAND CLEMENTS & ZOMNIR	26
5.	KIRKPATRICK & LOCKHART	26
6.	ECKERT SEAMONS CHERIN & MELLOT	NA

Law Firms Ranked by Percentage of Minority Partners

1.	DICKIE, MCCAMEY & CHILCOTE	2
2.	BUCHANAN INGERSOLL	1
3.	KIRKPATRICK & LOCKHART	1
4.	REED SMITH SHAW & MCCLAY	1
5.	BABST CALLAND CLEMENTS & ZOMNIR	NA
6.	ECKERT SEAMONS CHERIN & MELLOT	NA

Law Firms Ranked By Percentage of Minority Associates

1.	REED SMITH SHAW & MCCLAY	9
2.	KIRKPATRICK & LOCKHART	5
3.	BUCHANAN INGERSOLL	4
4.	DICKIE, MCCAMEY & CHILCOTE	4
5.	BABST CALLAND CLEMENTS & ZOMNIR	NA
6.	ECKERT SEAMONS CHERIN & MELLOT	NA

Babst Calland Clements & Zomnir

Pittsburgh

Address: Two Gateway Center, Eighth Floor, Pittsburgh, PA 15222
Telephone: (412) 394–5400
Hiring Attorney: Albert Bates, Jr.
Associate Salary: First year $60,000 (1996) plus recent graduates receive a $4,500 summer stipend while studying for the bar, and reimbursement for bar exam, bar exam review course, and bar admission fees and expenses; annual merit-based increases typically ranging from 6 to 10%
Summer Salary: NA
Average Hours: NA worked; NA billed; NA required
Family Benefits: Family health and dental insurance; attorney life and disability insurance; 401(K) plan with employer matching 50% of attorney's contribution up to 2% of attorney's salary
1996 Summer: NA
Partnership: NA
Pro Bono: NA

Babst Calland Clements & Zomnir in 1997
50 Lawyers at the Firm
0.9 Associates Per Partner

Total Partners 26			Total Associates 23			Practice Areas	
Women	3	12%	Women	6	26%	Litigation	24
All Minorities	NA	NA	All Minorities	NA	NA	Environmental	14
						Corporate	9

Golf enthusiasts feel at home at Babst Calland Clements & Zomnir, which was described as a firm of "real golf addicts." The firm's social activities reflect this penchant. Not only is a golf outing one of the biggest firm outings of the year, but each year at Masters Tournament time, lawyers at the firm convert the twelve wings of its offices into a miniature golf course for the celebrated annual office tournament. Course hazards consist of shredded paper, plants, a spinning windmill and a 4-foot section of PVC pipe. Beer coolers are located in every wing. The trickiest "hole" involves hitting the ball into an elevator and riding it two floors before sinking the shot. This hole is named the Rosalind Sharp Memorial Hole in honor of the *L.A. Law* character who fell to her death in an elevator shaft. The tournament victor enjoys the privilege of wearing a green "Masters" jacket which she keeps until the next year. However, while Babst Calland has a youthful spirit, and its attorneys know how to have fun and work hard at the same time, it is definitely not a young singles firm. Most associates are married, and the people we interviewed said they wouldn't go to Babst Calland to find a social life.

fast-growing

Babst Calland is an informal, high-energy law firm that has been growing by leaps and bounds. It was founded in the mid-1980s by a group of four partners and three associates who split off from Thorp, Reed & Armstrong. The oldest lawyer at the firm just turned fifty. Babst Calland made its name as an environmental boutique firm, but it has expanded to include a growing litigation and corporate practice as well. Both Chester Babst and Dean Calland have national reputations in environmental law, and they, along with the other members of the executive committee, have spearheaded the firm's growth. Much of the environmental practice involves advising corporations to help them comply with regulations. As the environmental practice has grown, it has generated a lot of litigation work, and one insider noted that litigation is now the fastest-growing group and the largest at the firm. Important areas include environmental, construction, and complex commercial litigation. Prominent members of the group include Bob King, Chairman of the Constitution Law Section of the Allegheny County Bar Association, and Jay McKenna, a former president of the Allegheny County Bar Association.

corporate practice

Babst Calland's growing corporate practice primarily represents small and medium-sized companies, but also has represented a number of Fortune 500 companies. Prominent members of the group include Frank Clements, Don Frank and Ted Wesolowski. While there is not much international work currently, Babst Calland has targeted the area of international joint ventures for future development. Lastly, Babst Calland has an established pro bono program, headed by Steve Baicker-McKee.

positive atmosphere

The atmosphere at Babst is "friendly," and people are "very positive and happy" about the firm's success in recent years. People "take pride in doing a good job, and the firm's atmosphere reflects it." One person commented that "people are very pleased with the growth and they want it to continue...It's nice to be on a ship that's rising. It really has to do with the enthusiasm of the partners. The associates and the partners work hand-in-hand and put in similar hours. In some cases, the partners bill more than the associates, and this helps explain why people have such positive responses to the firm." One associate pointed out, however, that a "flipside" of the growth is that there is some "uncertainty about what the firm will become in the future" and noted that Babst has shown signs of taking on big-firm tendencies. The firm, we were told, "saw a relatively large turnover of associates this past year, for the first time. Most of those who left were in the litigation group, and many were looking to become involved in smaller cases with other firms around the city." Moreover, there is a high ratio of shareholders to associates in some of the firm's practice groups, and "the firm's youth means that the existing shareholders won't be going anywhere soon. It will be interesting to see how the firm can respond to this to keep good people," remarked one insider. The positive note in this regard, however, is that the founding partners are "very good at business development, and they work to pass these skills on to the associates."

short honeymoon

Summer associates at Babst have only a short honeymoon before they are treated like permanent associates. After receiving assignments through formal recruiting channels for about two weeks, summer associates are thereafter free to accept assignments from anyone in the firm. Some really like this "open" system. One source commented: "it was up to us to set our priorities, manage our time, and decide when we would say yes and no to projects. I like this a lot, but if someone is looking for a summer position where he is going to be insulated and managed and regulated, this is not the place. They evaluate how well you are able to manage yourself as well as your legal writing skills." Most summer associates usually worked from 8:30 A.M. to 6:30 P.M. on weekdays and worked an occasional weekend.

professional development

Babst Calland has no formal billing requirements for associates. Although the partners insist that they budget for associates to bill about 1800 hours, one associate remarked that most associates aim to bill around 2000 hours. Babst Calland is a firm for people who want to jump into the action right away and have the self-confidence and initiative to do so. Associates at Babst Calland can expect client contact within their first year. One associate we talked to, however, stated that the firm may offer less opportunity in the future as it grows bigger, noting that "someone has to go through the documents" when you are doing "multi-million dollar litigation." Indeed this change appears to be underway. A second contact informed us that although Babst Calland has "a small-firm atmosphere, it has a big-firm caseload. For associates in the litigation group especially, this can mean that a large part of the first year or two might be spent reviewing documents." Nevertheless, our contacts pointed out that one first-year associate has argued a motion in court, and a second-year associate was "second chair on a major commercial litigation trial." Moreover, the firm recently handled several large projects which "combined the talents of the corporate, litigation, and environmental sections in the firm." These projects included purchases of industrial facilities and redevelopment of old industrial sites. Associates at all levels "played a large role in these projects and were often looked to for leadership in client meetings and group decision-making."

inclusive management

Babst Calland is organized as a professional corporation, and the firm's management is conducted by an executive committee (board of directors) of the partners (or shareholders). However, most of the decisions are "made by the shareholder group as a whole." The executive committee holds weekly meetings and was described as very "open and inclusive of associates in the decision process."

comfortable for women

Three of the 26 partners at Babst Calland are women. While there are no women on the firm's executive committee, Michele Gutman and Colleen Donofrio are "influential" in the environmental practice. The firm now has a written maternity/family leave policy. Three women left the firm to have children and have returned to work full-time. People emphasized that "family is very important" at the firm, and that the firm provides a comfortable atmosphere for women. There are no African-American attorneys at Babst Calland.

Although Babst Calland's office facilities are not "extravagant," they are "modern" and each attorney has a private office. The firm has also upgraded its computer system, and each associate has a personal computer.

emphasis on personality hiring

When asked about recruitment, an attorney on the hiring committee at Babst Calland told us that while the firm has informal minimum grade requirements (*e.g.*, a A-/B+ average at the University of Pittsburgh), and a strong preference for law review experience, it "looks more to personality than most firms. If a person looks great on paper and they come in and can't hold a conversation, then they won't be made an offer. We prefer someone who is personable and who can deal with clients." In the past the firm has tended to "hire people who have had some experience before law school since associates at the firm have to take off running. We are small and we don't overstaff cases so there is not much room for people who need to learn how to work," the attorney explained. More recently we were told that "there is about a fifty-fifty percent split between students with experience and students coming straight through undergraduate and law school."

panel interview

While Babst Calland does much of its interviewing at the University of Pittsburgh, West Virginia University, and Duquesne University, it also recruits at many other local and regional schools. On-campus interviews are usually conducted by a team of two Babst Calland attorneys. The firm's callback interviews typically involve six to eight interviews with two attorneys sitting in on each interview. Students meet with a representative from the hiring committee at the beginning of the day. In total, most students meet about 13 to 17 of the firm's attorneys during a callback interview. The attorneys fill out an evaluation form on each student interviewed and "from that point, the decision is made informally within the recruiting committee." One associate on the hiring committee advised that "it doesn't hurt you to come in and say you don't know what you want to do, but it definitely helps you if you are interested in environmental law, or another of Babst Calland's identified practice areas, and have the background to back it up."

In 1996, Babst Calland extended about thirty callback interviews and made seven summer associate offers, three of which were accepted. One associate stressed that the firm never makes more offers than the number it intends to hire permanently. The hiring procedures for laterals are "much less structured" and "focus on the particular section people are interested in." The firm is very "selective" in hiring laterals, and prospective hires usually interview with all of the members of the recruiting committee and all the attorneys in the practice group for which the candidate is being interviewed. Even if only a few of the shareholders do not support a lateral interviewee, one insider claimed, he will not receive an offer to join the firm. On average, Babst Calland receives about twenty résumés per week from attorneys who are interested in interviewing at the firm.

Overall, Babst Calland appears to be one of Pittsburgh's up-and-coming firms. Its success in recent years contrasts with that of many of the city's larger firms and is an attractive feature for prospective summer associates. Perhaps more importantly, the people we interviewed really enjoyed working at the firm which, we were told, "stresses a collegial and professional work environment which differs significantly from other firms in the city." Babst Calland does not "try to be all things to all people. We focus on being the best in certain well-defined and focused practice areas," according to one of our contacts. Another person confirmed this, noting that the type of work at Babst Calland is "very cutting-edge, especially in the environmental and corporate groups." And, this person added, "associates can learn from partners who are nationally known as experts in their fields."

Buchanan Ingersoll

Pittsburgh Buffalo Harrisburg Lexington Miami Philadelphia Princeton Tampa

Address: 301 Grant Street, One Oxford Centre, 20th Floor, Pittsburgh, PA 15219-1410
Telephone: (412) 562–8800
Hiring Attorney: Francis A. Muracca, II
Contact: Laurie S. Lenigan, Recruiting Coordinator; (412) 562–1470
Associate Salary: First year $75,000 (1997)
Summer Salary: $1250/week (1997)
Average Hours: 2175 worked; 1835 billed; none required.
Family Benefits: Comprehensive healthcare plan; paid short and long-term leave; life; 401(K); retirement; flex plan; alternative work schedule policy
1996 Summer: Class of 8 2L students; offers made to 7
Partnership: Since 1993 the firm has promoted 47 shareholders from within
Pro Bono: NA

Buchanan Ingersoll in 1997
260 Lawyers at the Pittsburgh Office
1.0 Associate Per Partner

Total Partners 125		
Women	21	17%
All Minorities	1	1%
Afro-Am	1	1%

Total Associates 135		
Women	59	44%
All Minorities	5	4%
Afro-Am	3	2%
Asian Am	2	2%

Practice Areas	
Corporate/Banking/Business	84
Litigation	54
Labor and Employment	32
Health Care/Family	26
Tax	23
Bankruptcy/Real Estate	22
Environmental	11
Intellectual Property	5
Gov't. Relations	3

As one of the oldest and most established firms in Pittsburgh, Buchanan Ingersoll projects a "white shoe" image to many who have not worked at the firm. Indeed, like many of the large, established firms, Buchanan has certainly had a "white shoe" history, certain elements of which today serve as reminders of the firm's past. For example, the attorneys have an exclusive dining facility called the Moses Hampton room, named after one of the firm's founders. The staff and legal assistants eat in a separate cafeteria. Despite this, everyone we interviewed insisted that Buchanan is anything but "stuffy" or "stodgy." Rather, the atmosphere was described as "casual" and "informal." This is illustrated by a monthly newsletter edited and distributed by attorneys called the "Bugle," which pokes fun at the senior partners. One contact informed us that "the firm doesn't have the feel that would cause you to hesitate before going into anyone's office. The doors are all glass, and no one hides behind them. There is no protection from secretaries." Another person commented that the firm hires an unusually high number of attorneys from working class families and backgrounds: "you won't find many third generation Harvard graduates working at Buchanan." The firm now has casual dress days on Friday which means, we were told, that "attorneys and staff can dress casually but professionally. No suit is required but attorneys must dress appropriately if meeting with clients."

top M&A practice

Buchanan has traditionally been most known for its corporate practice, highlighted by one of the best mergers and acquisitions practices in Pittsburgh. The firm is presently representing Conrail, Inc. in the boardroom and courtroom in the railroad's $9.5 billion merger with CSX Transportation and anti-takeover defense against hostile bidders. Tom Thompson, who heads the firm's corporate practice and also teaches at the University of Pittsburgh, was described as "an incredible individual in terms of expertise, knowledge, and experience. Very impressive." Through affiliations with firms in London and Brussels, Buchanan has, in recent years, developed an international component to its corporate practice. In response to the changing economy, Buchanan is developing practices in such areas as health care, cable, environmental, high technology, and intellectual property. Buchanan's health care practice, in particular, has grown rapidly, and one insider claimed that it is one of the best in the city.

litigation

Buchanan's litigation practice, the second largest group in the firm is also growing. The commercial litigation section, we were told, has developed a "bad reputation (internally)," in terms of work environment. Many associates have left this group to go to labor and employment, which is considered the most "upbeat" section in the firm. There are several partners in the litigation section for whom associates "do not want to work. In particular, one female partner is known to be a nightmare." In contrast, labor and employment offers more responsibility, more client contact, and more interesting work. Mark Hornak, who chairs the labor and employment section, was described as being "universally revered as a great litigator, brilliant, funny, down to earth, and as someone who genuinely cares about associates."

innovative management

Much of the foresight in the recent development and growth of Buchanan Ingersoll is attributable to its chief executive officer, Bill Newlin, who "has been credited with taking Buchanan Ingersoll from a midsized to a large-sized firm...He is very well-respected." Newlin was recently named Chairman of the Board of Kennametal Corporation; he was also recently cited as one of America's 100 most influential lawyers by the *National Law Journal.*

Buchanan is organized as a professional corporation. People gave the firm's management high reviews for being open and for keeping associates informed about the firm's business. "The firm's management usually explains what's going on and is open to input," one insider remarked. Another source claimed, however, that when it comes to the partnership track issue, "the whole thing is rather nebulous for associates." The partnership track, we were told, appears to consist of three levels: voting partners, non-voting partners, and counsel. Some who were designated as counsel have moved to voting or non-voting partners, "but it is not clear how that progression works," reported one insider.

Although Buchanan Ingersoll had a one-time layoff of 10 associates in 1992, the firm has grown considerably since then to its present size of 260 lawyers. Presently, the firm is in "fine shape financially. All associates know this, since we all see the financial statements regularly," said one insider. Four times a year, the associates meet with the CEO (Bill Newlin) and the COO (Tom Van Kirk) to go over the firm's financials.

regimented training and feedback

"Outstanding" is how one person described the professional development for associates. Buchanan provides a "regimented" system of training and feedback for summer associates. Each Friday morning, the firm's summer coordinators collect requests for help on work projects from attorneys and meet with summer associates to distribute projects according to their preferences. Summer associates submit three copies of every assignment they complete. One is given to the assigning attorney, one goes to a special committee of summer coordinators, and the third goes to a "reading committee" whose members complete extensive written evaluations of the summer associate's work, covering "more than 10 different categories." Assigning attorneys often review completed projects in detail with summer associates. One person commented that the firm's attorneys carefully reviewed his work with him on about three-fourths of the assignments he completed. In some cases "it was like sitting down with a writing instructor," he added. The firm also provides a midterm and final review for its summer associates, during which the summer coordinators go over each summer associate's evaluations.

The evaluations for permanent associates are equally thorough. Every shareholder or senior associate for whom more than ten billable hours of work is done reviews the associate's work in writing. These are then summarized by the partner in charge of associate evaluations (Paula Zawadzki). These summaries are then put in a notebook which every shareholder receives and reviews for every associate. In addition, each associate meets with the section chair and the head of personnel to go over the evaluation. That meeting, we were told, "often takes as long as an hour, and you're encouraged to ask questions." The entire process is "*very* thorough," according to one insider.

Buchanan also provides a number of extensive formal training programs for both summer and permanent associates. Responsibility, on the other hand, for new associates varies, we were told. One person commented that most junior associates do mainly "research and writing" assignments, but client contact and first chair experience can come fairly quickly, while a second contact informed us, "I've been doing depositions and arguing motions in court since I got here."

good social life

Buchanan is a "big firm with a lot of young people who do things together," commented one insider. "It's a good firm for social life." Another noted that the older attorneys at the firm live outside the city and tend to go home after work, but said that there is a good cadre of young people to "hang out and have fun with." While the firm has a 2000 billable hour target, there is not an inordinate amount of pressure to meet this target—"as long as you are coming close, it's not an issue," one source commented, noting that "you set your schedule based on the work you have to do and on meeting your goals. There is lots of flexibility." Another contact remarked that "there is so much work that exceeding the 2000 should not be an issue." Still another person observed, in a comparative vein, that "I believe the billable requirement is higher than at Babst Calland and some other firms. But do associates at Babst really bill only 1800?!? Hard to believe."

diversity

Buchanan is a "progressive and forward-thinking" firm regarding women's issues and has been recognized as a leader in employing female attorneys. As an example, one of the firm's women's lawyers was on an alternative work schedule at the time of her election to shareholder, "demonstrating the firm's desire to accommodate needs to balance work and family," reported a firm spokesperson. About half of the hiring committee is composed of women. Although there are few racial minorities at the firm, we were told that the firm has a progressive attitude with respect to minority attorneys. Minority attorneys have held important positions in the firm. In one past year, an African-American headed up the firm's summer program. This person recently made partner at the firm.

modern cluster system offices

The firm is now located at One Oxford Centre. The firm relocated to this new office building in 1995 and the offices reflect a contemporary style. The 20th floor is reserved for conference rooms and is the "showcase" floor. With the move, Buchanan changed to a "cluster" arrangement. Each cluster has, on average, six secretaries and ten to twelve lawyers, as well as its own fax machine, two computer printers, and a Xerox machine. Under this arrangement, according to one insider, "a lot more gets done in one's own cluster. There's little need for attorneys or secretaries to have to go to duplicating or the fax department or word processing. Many attorneys now type all their own documents." Also with the move, all attorneys now have their own Pentium computers, described by one enthusiast as "great," who went on to observe that "we now have Westlaw and Microsoft Word at our fingertips; we also have e-mail and Internet e-mail."

tricky interview

Most interviews on law school campuses are conducted by a team of two interviewers from the firm. In callback interviews, students typically interview with five or six attorneys, two or three of whom are members of the hiring committee. While most interview questions relate to the student's résumé, past work experiences, and personal interests, one person added that "you should be prepared for a think–on–your–feet–type of question." Those we interviewed said that Buchanan, more than other firms, looks for well-rounded people. "There are not many eggheads at the firm," according to one source. Not everyone they hire from a local school is on the law review or in the top 10 percent of their class. However, as with many of the top firms, it is very difficult to get hired as a summer associate at Buchanan. The earlier edition of ***The Insider's Guide*** reported that the firm receives about 3000 résumés a year from which it conducts about 400 first interviews. From these interviews, the firm selects about 100 students for callback interviews. At the University of Pittsburgh, the firm has ordinarily interviewed between 70 and 100 people and extended about 25 callback interview offers. These numbers have, however, been reduced, we were told, as Buchanan presently interviews at "fewer but more prestigious schools and has targeted a summer class size of ten to twelve summer associates."

Dickie, McCamey & Chilcote

Pittsburgh Wheeling

Address: Two PPG Place, Suite 400, Pittsburgh, PA 15222
Telephone: (412) 281–7272
Hiring Attorney: David J. Obermeier, Chair, Employment Committee
Contact: Patricia L. Seward, Human Resources Manager; (412) 281–7272
Associate Salary: NA
Summer Salary: NA
Average Hours: 2150 worked; 1990 billed; NA required
Family Benefits: 13 weeks paid maternity leave (14–26 unpaid)
1996 Summer: Class of 1 student; offer to 1
Partnership: NA
Pro Bono: 1% of all work is pro bono

Dickie, McCamey & Chilcote in 1997
118 Lawyers at the Pittsburgh Office
0.7 Associates Per Partner

Total Partners 68		
Women	4	6%
All Minorities	1	2%
Afro-Am	1	2%

Total Associates 48		
Women	13	27%
All Minorities	2	4%
Asian-Am	1	2%
Latino	1	2%

Practice Areas	
Litigation	65
Health	43
Malpractice	30
Insurance	20
Personal Injury	20
Business	19
Corporate	19
Product Liability	11
Commercial	10
Mergers & Acquisitions	10
Workers' Compensation	10
Toxic Torts	8
Bankruptcy	6
Railroad	6
Environmental	5
Intellectual Property	5
Banking	4
Construction	3
Immigration	2
Labor	2
Trusts & Estates	1

unnerving interviews

For many prospective attorneys, an interview with Dickie, McCamey & Chilcote can be an "intense" and "intimidating" experience. Although on-campus interviews are fairly routine, everyone should be prepared for the firm's unique callback interview format. When interviewees arrive at the firm, they are escorted to and seated at the head of a large conference table. At the table, the interviewee finds six to twelve of the firm's attorneys, often including half the firm's hiring committee, seated and waiting to ask questions. Despite this format, the interview is not meant to be intimidating. Interviewees said that after a few questions about their past work experiences, they felt very much at ease. However, the experience can be "unnerving" and "intimidating" for some. After the conference room interview, students (usually those from out-of-town) are often taken to lunch with an equally large group of the firm's lawyers that includes other members of the hiring committee. Almost immediately after each interview, the interviewers discuss their impressions of the candidate and fill out extensive evaluation forms used for final decision-making. In addition, even after this "intense" day of interviewing, Dickie McCamey has been known to call students (usually those from local schools) to the firm for more interviews before extending a summer associate offer. The firm is very careful about whom it hires.

cohesive atmosphere

This potentially intimidating interview format should not necessarily skew your impression of the firm, however. People described Dickie McCamey as "informal" and cordial, although the firm is not entirely free of rifts among some of its members. The firm is "beyond chatty," one source remarked. "The individuals are very close to each other, and they enjoy working together." The associates are a particularly "cohesive group," reported one contact. Others commented that lawyers at Dickie McCamey genuinely like what they are doing. This is perhaps evidenced by a relatively low turnover rate at the firm, which however has increased in recent years. Dickie McCamey hires its associates with the expectation of their becoming shareholders in the firm. Although its associate salaries are not on par with the other big firms in the city, its lawyers have had the security in the past of knowing that if they do a good job at the firm and are committed to the work, there was a good likelihood they would make partner. Dickie McCamey now has two levels of shareholders, Class A and Class B. The track for Class A shareholders is currently 12 years, and one of the pressing problems currently facing the firm is its "unbalanced" partner to associate ratio.

associates included in management

Part of the firm's cohesiveness stems from the openness of the firm's management. Like other firms, a management committee makes most of Dickie McCamey's business decisions. However, the firm also has an associates committee, headed by Tom Fallert, which meets after every shareholder meeting to inform associates about any decisions that were made and to solicit their input. Even a junior associate at the firm "can be very involved" in shaping some of the firm's decisions, according to one associate at the firm.

practice areas

Traditionally, Dickie McCamey has been best-known for its litigation practice, particularly its insurance defense work. The firm also does a lot of construction, commercial, and medical malpractice litigation. David Armstrong and David Fawcett are two of the firm's biggest rainmakers, and both have excellent reputations in Pittsburgh as top-notch trial lawyers. They have both been named in *Best Lawyers in America.*

While the litigation practice has been the "bread and butter" of the firm, we were told that the corporate practice is growing most rapidly today. One person commented that he was "really impressed and amazed at the number of huge corporations on the firm's client list." Clayton Sweeney, a lawyer at the firm, is a "huge name in the corporate field." In addition to his regional representation, he has also done some international work with a Chinese mine company doing business in Peru. The firm has also done some work in Russia and was asked to help draft some of the country's new commercial statutes.

work assignments

Dickie McCamey provides an unstructured and flexible atmosphere for both summer and permanent associates. Summer associates may take assignments from any of the firm's substantive practice areas. New associates at Dickie McCamey are assigned to a specific practice group, but they can take work from different areas if they choose to do so.

early court exposure

Every new associate who joins the firm is instructed in basic litigation skills. As part of this training, each new associate is assigned to argue a small motion in court within the first year. One associate advised, if you are a young associate, "you hit the ground running or someone will run over you." Dickie McCamey has not in the past provided much formal training, but this is improving in recent years. The firm sponsors a number of informal "lunch 'n learn" sessions during the year to train associates. Early opportunities for responsibility at the firm are considerable, although one contact told us that there is somewhat less opportunity now than in the past since presently there is less insurance work available. Nevertheless, new associates usually get client contact within their first year. One attorney commented, "I know third- or fourth-year associates at other firms that aren't doing the things that our first-year associates do." The firm does not have a good reputation for providing a structured system for feedback. The experience at Dickie McCamey is usually "trial by fire," one contact noted, although another demurred that "if the associate does not want to 'jump into the fire,' they are given the option to move forward at their own pace."

mature social life

The social atmosphere at Dickie McCamey is heavily influenced by the family orientation of its attorneys, and the firm is committed to "quality family life," reported one insider. Most people go home after work and value their private family lives. Another person commented that Dickie McCamey is not a "great firm for social life...There are social events that involve clients, and every once and a while on Friday people go to a bar across the street. But, if you are young and single, and looking to meet a mate at the firm, it's not going to happen." People also noted that much of the firm's social life in the summer revolves around sports. The firm sponsors a golf outing and a law firm league softball team. One source remarked that the attorneys at Dickie McCamey are an athletic group and include some former college basketball and football players.

balanced lifestyle less pay

There is a 2000 billable hour goal in effect at the firm, we were told. The firm tends to pay greater attention to the number of hours worked than those billed, one source noted, because it wants to encourage its associates "to do quality work and to take extra time if it is necessary to do something correctly." Along with this pressure, moreover, comes less pay. One person said that the biggest disadvantage of going to Dickie McCamey is that you won't make "gobs of cash" relative to what you would make at the other big firms in Pittsburgh. Although we did not get precise salary figures, one associate claimed that "the salaries are lower than any other major player in town." Another contact remarked that "compensation is the biggest drawback at Dickie McCamey. Starting salary for new associates is approximately $20,000 less than that of other large firms, and despite representations to the contrary, associates do not catch up to their classmates at other big firms." This person also remarked, however, that Dickie McCamey attorneys have "flexibility and autonomy—they can work extremely hard and be so compensated, or they can choose a less rigorous work schedule and be compensated less. No one breathes down your neck."

diversity

"Pittsburgh is known as an old-boys town," and Dickie McCamey "is an old-boys firm with few minorities and women," we were told. One contact proclaimed that the firm is "more favorable than other big firms in terms of allowing people to take time off to raise a family;" this person also told us that Dickie McCamey has "the best maternity leave policy in the city." Few minority attorneys work at the firm. Gene Berry, a prominent African-American attorney at the firm, is however a member of the hiring committee and is committed to improving the firm's diversity, we were told.

Dickie McCamey's offices occupy three floors in the modern Pittsburgh Plate Glass (PPG) building. The offices are decorated in dark mahogany wood, and each attorney has a private office with a computer linked to the firm's central network.

hires hard workers

Dickie McCamey does not overly emphasize grades in its recruitment. One person commented that the firm tends not to hire the "intellectuals" of the city, but rather more "straitlaced people who work hard." He added that "they look for well-rounded, down-to-earth people." Once you are given a callback interview, "the only thing that matters is how well you perform in the interview. They look to see if you are mature and articulate." One insider noted that Dickie McCamey has had a very high permanent associate offer rate for the summer associates it has hired, adding that "you really have to shoot yourself in the foot not to get an offer."

Dickie McCamey offers an unstructured environment in which associates with initiative can carve out their own career paths. Its attorneys generally like what they are doing and have tended in the past to stay at the firm. However, in the last few years the "firm has experienced growing pains and questions exist as to the future direction of the firm," reported one contact. A new president, Wilbur McCoy Otto, took over this past year, and he intends, we were told, to "address a number of 'problems' facing the firm," including the departure of a number of associates in the last few years. "Otto is making great efforts to stabilize the firm and give it a new direction," according to one contact.

Eckert Seamans Cherin & Mellott

Pittsburgh Allentown Boca Raton Boston Fort Lauderdale Harrisburg Miami Philadelphia Tallahassee Washington

Address: 600 Grant Street; Forty-Second Floor, Pittsburgh, PA 15219
Telephone: (412) 566–6000
Hiring Attorney: Richard K. Dandrea, Chairman, Hiring Committee
Contact: Nancy E. Morrow, Recruiting Coordinator; (412) 566–5986
Associate Salary: First year $60,000 (under review at press time)
Summer Salary: $1150/week (1996)
Average Hours: 1975 worked; 1825 billed; NA required
Family Benefits: Paid maternity leave up to two months
1996 Summer: Class of 7 students; offers to 4
Partnership: NA
Pro Bono: 1–2% of all work is pro bono

Eckert Seamans Cherin & Mellott (firmwide) in 1997
238 Lawyers at the Firm
1.0 Associate Per Partner

Total Partners 112	
Women	NA
All Minorities	NA

Total Associates 101	
Women	NA
All Minorities	NA

Practice Areas	
Corporate & Real Estate	86
Litigation	84
Intellectual Property	17
Labor & Employment Law	13
Municipal Finance	12
Tax	10
Environmental & Energy	9
Trusts & Estates	7

Eckert Seamans Cherin & Mellott is the fourth largest firm in Pittsburgh. In recent years, it has been pushing into the top-tier of the Pittsburgh legal market, along with powerhouses like Reed Smith Shaw & McClay and Kirkpatrick & Lockhart. The firm has expanded aggressively over the past several years. It now has four offices in Florida (Fort Lauderdale, Miami, Boca Raton, and Tallahassee), as well as offices in Harrisburg, Philadelphia, Boston, and Washington, D.C. Eckert presently has as many lawyers outside of Pittsburgh as in the Pittsburgh office. As Eckert has grown, it has taken on a number of characteristics typical of large firm life. People described the atmosphere at the firm as "conservative" and "hierarchical." One person commented that Eckert is not "avant-garde about doing new innovative things. They do things very traditionally." The conservative atmosphere is reflected in the firm's dress code: "men dress very conservatively—gray suits and white and blue shirts...They all look very similar." The firm is changing in this regard, however. One contact pointed out that Eckert "has started 'dress down' days this past year. I believe we have had two or three dress down days in the past six months. The atmosphere is more relaxed."

Although some described the firm as "friendly," it is not exactly "chatty." One insider remarked that most attorneys keep their office doors closed, but officially the firm's partners have an "open-door policy." Another said that two floors of the offices are triangular in design with a "narrow hallway" running around them that cuts down on social interaction. It is "almost isolating in the way it is laid out," said one person. The third floor is "open" and facilitates more interaction. People also commented on a noticeable divide between partners and associates. There are "grumblings" among the associates about the "higher ups" at the firm, although one contact informed us that "the relationship between partners and associates is improving with more communication."

sports law practice

While Eckert is by no stretch a sports law firm, it offers some interesting opportunities for those who are interested in sports. A former managing partner of the firm, Carl Barger, was a president of the Pittsburgh Pirates and part owner of the baseball expansion team, the Florida Marlins. From these connections and others, such as contacts with the Pittsburgh Penguins, the firm has a growing sports law practice that includes contract, commercial lease, and sports management work. Some of the summer associates we interviewed had direct contact with this somewhat unusual practice area.

litigation

Eckert is most known for its litigation practice, which generates almost half of the firm's business. The firm does a lot of work in construction and infrastructure litigation, and was involved in the construction of the new Los Angeles metro system. Eckert has also handled a number of large-scale toxic tort cases, particularly asbestos litigations. The products liability practice continues to grow, so that it is now "the strongest aspect of the litigation group," according to one insider. The litigation group was described as "young" and "friendly." The group is "relatively lean with associates so everybody can succeed without the worry of competition," according to one contact, who further observed that "associates have taken on increasing responsibility due to expanding business."

corporate

The corporate department was described as "laid-back" and more "male-dominated" than the litigation department. There are not many junior associates in the corporate department, and the summer associates we interviewed said it was difficult to get corporate assignments. People also noted that Eckert's intellectual property and health care practices have been growing rapidly. The intellectual property group, many of whose lawyers are former engineers, also was described as "male-dominated." Eckert additionally boasts a strong management-side labor practice.

departmental assignments

Summer associates get exposure to a broad range of the firm's practice areas. All summer projects are kept in a general assignment book, and summer associates may, with some exceptions, choose those on which they would like to work. For one week of the summer, however, each summer associate is placed "on call." During that week, any lawyer in the firm may assign work to that person. The experience is designed to give each summer associate a feel for actual associate life at Eckert. When summer associates join the firm on a permanent basis, the firm matches their department preferences to its needs and assigns each associate to a particular department. People complained that the firm does not let prospective associates know their department assignment until after they have accepted the firm's offer, leaving them uncertain as to whether they will work in their department of choice.

extensive training and feedback

Eckert provides a full range of formal training programs such as trial advocacy workshops and regular departmental training sessions. There are also institutional mechanisms to facilitate informal training. Both summer and permanent associates are assigned to a partner and an associate mentor at the firm who oversee their work and professional development. Further, Eckert has a system that provides "extensive" formal feedback on summer work projects. Each time a summer associate finishes a project, the assigning attorney fills out a detailed evaluation form. The form, often three or four pages long, covers areas such as writing style, analytical ability, oral interaction with attorneys, confidence, and Blue Book skills. It also includes a general assessment as to whether the firm should extend a permanent offer to that summer associate. The attorneys "generally went the extra yard in terms of their comments," one source remarked. The pressure for billable hours is not as great at Eckert as at other large firms in the city, we were told, but the pay also trails behind such leaders as Kirkpatrick and Reed Smith.

red carpet for summer associates

Eckert is not one of the more social firms in Pittsburgh. "There may be some firms in Pittsburgh where people are buddy-buddy and hang out a lot after work," one insider remarked, but "this is not that type of firm. The people at Eckert are mostly married, and they tend to go their separate ways after work." Another contact remarked, "I think the fact that there are not twenty associates in each class contributes to the lack of a buddy-buddy atmosphere. Incoming classes range from four to five per year. I am happy to have a life outside the firm, yet I can go out with fellow associates without obligations when I like. I think it is the best of both worlds." During the summer, however, the firm "rolls out the red carpet" for its summer associates. There are softball games, a golf outing, a picnic, and weekly social gatherings.

diversity

Although there are only a few female partners at Eckert, one person commented that "in the next few years there will be more." This person also claimed that "there is a stronger bond among the female attorneys than among the male attorneys at the firm." Another added, "I didn't get any sense, even in dealing with some of the older partners at the firm, that there were any undertones of discrimination." Women are on the hiring committee, and there are a "good number of female associates relative to other big firms." There are not many racial minorities at the firm, a situation common to most large firms in Pittsburgh, according to one contact, who added that "efforts to improve this are occurring" at Eckert.

Eckert occupies three floors in the USX Tower, the largest office building between New York and Chicago. All attorneys have their own office, but many junior associate offices do not have windows. Some past summer associates complained of being unable to get access to a computer to complete their assignments. More recently, we were assured, this situation has changed. According to one insider, "if you want a computer, you ask. I don't know one person without a computer.'

hiring tips

Eckert hires most of its summer associates from regional schools in the area, but it also recruits some of its students from the top schools across the country. One source noted that most students who are hired from regional schools are in the top 10 to 15 percent of their classes. Callback interviews usually involve meeting with six or seven different attorneys for about half an hour each, typically followed by lunch. One person described the interviews as very "traditional, with most questions pertaining to your résumé." Another described them as "casual" and "laid-back." One contact noted that the firm tries to match interviewees with alumni from their law schools or colleges.'

Eckert is a good choice for someone who does well in a formal, somewhat conservative, hierarchical atmosphere. According to one firm enthusiast, it is a "great choice right now for someone who can hit the ground running and desires increasing responsibility as a young associate." The firm is gaining in status and rapidly rising to be among the city's most prestigious firms.

Kirkpatrick & Lockhart

Pittsburgh Boston Harrisburg Miami New York Washington

Address: 1500 Oliver Building, Pittsburgh, PA 15222 (http://www.kl.com)
Telephone: (412) 355–6500
Hiring Attorney: Michael J. Lynch, Chairman, Hiring Committee
Contact: Amy S. Molinaro, Legal Personnel Director; (412) 355–8979
Associate Salary: First year $75,000 plus $5,000 stipend; fourth year $82,500 to $84,500 (plus 0–$7,000 bonus); seventh year $93,000 to $97,500 (plus 0–$7,000 bonus)
Summer Salary: $1400/week (1997)
Average Hours: 2055 worked; 1870 billed; no requirement
Family Benefits: 13 weeks paid maternity leave, or longer on cbc; emergency childcare arrangements
1996 Summer: Class of 20 students; offers to 16
Partnership: 32% of entering associates from 1979–1988 were made partner
Pro Bono: 3–5% of all work is pro bono

Kirkpatrick & Lockhart in 1997
193 Lawyers at the Pittsburgh Office
0.9 Associates Per Partner

Total Partners 95		
Women	12	13%
All Minorities	1	1%
Asian-Am	1	1%

Total Associates 88		
Women	23	26%
All Minorities	4	5%
Afro-Am	2	2%
Asian Am	1	1%
Latino	1	1%

Practice Areas	
Environmental/Insurance	20%
Litigation	20%
Corporate	15%
Transactional Securities	15%
Banking/Bankruptcy	5%
Healthcare	5%
Intellectual Property	5%
Tax/Estates & Trusts/RE	5%
Labor (management)	5%
Product Liability/Toxic Tort	5%

Founded in 1946 by a group of partners who split off from Reed, Smith, Shaw & McClay, Kirkpatrick & Lockhart has rapidly grown to be Pittsburgh's largest and one of its most prestigious firms. In recent years the firm opened a New York office by laterally hiring a number of partners from New York's now defunct Lord, Day & Lord, Barrett Smith. Unlike many Pittsburgh firms, Kirkpatrick & Lockhart never acquired an "old-boy" reputation. Rather, it is regarded as a firm that places a high premium on "independence" and "free-spiritedness." One person explained that this means Kirkpatrick associates have more freedom to do what they want in their individual practices. On the other hand, the firm provides very little in terms of a "safety net," and, if you "screw up, it comes down on your shoulders."

structured informally

Kirkpatrick's commitment to independence for both summer and permanent associates is reflected in the firm's structure. In contrast to some of the other large Pittsburgh firms, there are few formal channels through which work is assigned. Entering associates have the option of rotating through the litigation and business departments for nine months each before settling in a particular practice area. Although the rotation system has been a big selling point for Kirkpatrick, we heard some complaints regarding how it works in practice. We were told that "certain business partners are reluctant to place a rotating associate on large mergers and acquisitions (and other strung-out projects) because they know that the associate will be rotating from the business practice to the litigation practice during the upcoming months." In addition, it was pointed out to us that "associates who choose to rotate often find themselves in no-man's land. For example, if after nine months in the business department, an associate decides to choose litigation, he may experience difficulty in getting enough work because those associates who either started in the litigation department or elected not to rotate will have already fostered relationships with the litigation partners and/or senior associates doling out litigation work." The firm, aware of these problems, is reportedly re-evaluating the rotation program "to see how to make it function more effectively for young associates and partners alike."

training concerns

Additionally, Kirkpatrick offers very few training programs. One contact informed us that "from a lower level to midlevel associate's standpoint, this is the firm's biggest problem. Not only is there no formal training, but also most partners are reluctant to let younger associates tag along to depositions, hearings, trials, etc. in an effort to save clients' money." The firm set up a Professional Development Committee in early 1996 to address some of these concerns, but to date "this committee has made no substantive progress in the creation and institution of programs designed to assist in the professional development of the firm's young associates," reported one insider. A second contact informed us that the committee has begun offering training programs to associates in a variety of subject matter areas.

problematic organization and structure

Kirkpatrick's weak organizational structure has both its champions and its critics. One contact observed that "there are not many people telling you where to be or when to be there, and the firm's loose structural framework rewards initiative and creative thought." However, this person noted that "the drawback is that some things are not done as efficiently because of a lack of structure, and some attorneys are frustrated by this. For example, there are no hierarchies of partners, very little committee decision-making, and the smaller departments in the firm are not separated. It's amazing that things get done sometimes." A second contact had a very pointed objection to the firm's loose organizational structure: "Because there is no formal system whereby the firm evaluates the associates workload and because every associate is fair game for work from partners via the telephone ('it's open season'), associates are often placed in the unenviable position of having to choose between working for one partner over another. This creates a problem for associates because, like it or not, some partners carry a grudge against associates who choose to work for another at any given point in time. These types of disputes should occur between partners without the involvement of the associate at issue. Unfortunately, however, most of these types of instances result in bad blood between partner and associate rather than between partner and partner." The firm is, however, we were told, attempting to address these organizational matters. One insider instructed us that "presently practice groups are developing along with practice group committees. It indicates a movement of the firm toward a more formal structure. The practice groups are not as well defined as similar groups at other firms, nor is there pressure to join and do work for a particular group. The loosely-defined practice groups indicate an effort to achieve some structure without losing the free-wheeling attitude." A second insider observed, more positively, that "if you are used to being told when, where and what you are to do, then you may initially feel overwhelmed. However, that feeling passes and you come to enjoy your independence and the amount of control you have over the development of your career."

limited opportunity

Most Kirkpatrick associates do not take on their own case load until they have been with the firm for a few years. Much of the work in the early years involves research and writing memos. One contact observed that many of the firm's cases involve complex litigation, and it is difficult for a junior associate to participate at a high level. There are some opportunities for junior associates to handle their own smaller cases and pro bono projects that provide greater client contact and responsibility. Several people noted, however, that there are more opportunities for responsibility on the business side of the firm. One such associate commented that "I spend very little time in the library. On any research I do, I may write a memo for my own personal file, but I usually write a letter to the client. I would say that less than five percent of my time is spent researching and writing memos."

practice areas

The practice at Kirkpatrick is divided into two major departments—litigation and business—each of which is broken into a number of subgroups. The litigation and business departments are approximately the same size, but people commented that the firm is best-known for its litigation work. Peter Kalis, a former Supreme Court clerk, is one of the firm's most prominent litigators and is a member of the firm's management committee. The litigation practice covers a broad range of areas. Kirkpatrick has a particularly good reputation in insurance and asbestos litigation, noted one contact. The construction litigation practice, intellectual property practice, and a developing white-collar crime/medicare fraud practice are all "on the march." The individuals working in the aforementioned areas were described as "young, well-connected, and eager." Many of the attorneys we interviewed noticed a distinct difference in the personalities of the litigation and business departments: "The corporate group is more intense; the litigation group is more laid-back...The corporate group has less of a sense of humor. The litigation people are the ones in the firm who go to parties and make jokes." One contact qualified this contrast, noting that "since corporate associates and junior partners do so much travelling together, and spend so much time together when a transaction is taking place, it is not uncommon for a group to grab a beer or a sandwich after work. When travelling we try to squeeze in some time to enjoy the sights. Some of the older partners are, however, traditionally a bit more reserved."

Kirkpatrick also has a pro bono practice. The firm's attorneys have been involved in matters ranging from representation of an association of developmentally challenged citizens to involvement in "Protection From Abuse" orders. Kirkpatrick received the 1995 Louis Goffman Award from the Pennsylvania Bar Association for its outstanding pro bono contribution.

Kirkpatrick is also known for its connections to politics and the judiciary. Many of its attorneys have gone on to become politicians or judges. Dick Thornburgh, Attorney General under President Bush, was a partner at the firm and is currently of counsel in the firm's Washington, D.C. office, and U.S. Senator Rick Santorum was an associate at the firm.

passion for baseball

It is not accidental that many Kirkpatrick lawyers have a passion for baseball. Until recently, the firm had a special relationship (through partner T.P. Johnson's ownership) with the Pirates. As a result of this connection, Kirkpatrick has enjoyed the opportunity to play its summer softball games in Three River Stadium. The firm organizes its attorneys into different teams to play against each other on such occasions. In addition, there traditionally has been a "competitive" game between the Pittsburgh and D.C. offices which, unlike the other games, the attorneys "take seriously." Kirkpatrick also has "really nice box seats" at Three River Stadium, a nice perk for both the attorneys and many summer associates (but "associates never see those tickets," moaned one insider).

fun-filled summer

In addition to baseball games, summer associates are treated to a full range of summer fun. People we interviewed claimed that Kirkpatrick provides one of the most event-filled summer programs in town. They were quick to note, however, that while Kirkpatrick provides a fun-filled summer, it is not the firm to go to for a vibrant social life. One insider observed that because of an absence of an aggregate of young associates, "it might be difficult to find people to go and unwind with on a Friday night," while a second contact remarked that the fault lies "not so much with the firm as with the city itself." Most attorneys at the firm are married and tend to go home after work.

women's issues

We heard some criticism of Kirkpatrick's handling of women's issues. "Females at the firm generally do not discuss women's issues among themselves or present a united front regarding issues such as part-time policy, harassment on the job, etc.," we were told. One contact informed us that "while in the past, the firm successfully accommodated the need for female associates to work part-time on a case by case basis, recently the firm has encountered difficulty in implementing its ambiguous part-time employment policy." The firm is reportedly aware of this problem and "is working on ways to change." Another contact observed that "the firm is accommodating, but it seems that many associates marry and then leave the Pittsburgh area, so the number of women in the firm is quite low." Even so, a number of women hold key positions at the firm. For example, the chair of the Associates Committee, half the firm's Hiring Committee, and over half of the Associate Liaison Committee are women.

cautious in hiring

In recent years, Kirkpatrick & Lockhart has not extended offers to a high percentage of its summer associates. One insider remarked that the firm is very careful in hiring its summer associates in order to avoid having to fire people later, and noted that Kirkpatrick's permanent associates have safer and more stable jobs than those at other firms. In 1995, of the 24 students eligible for offers, 19 received permanent associate offers. In 1996, the percentage of permanent offers was similar: 16 offers were made to a 20 member summer class. The firm often hires third-year students to make up for any shortfall from its summer program. A strategically placed insider informed us that "the summer program is not, nor is it intended to be, competitive. We offer employment to all or most summer associates if they do good work and we feel they will prosper in the traditional informal work atmosphere at Kirkpatrick."

hiring tips

Kirkpatrick draws many of its summer associates from national law schools across the country, such as Chicago, Duke, Georgetown, Harvard, Penn, UCLA, University of Virginia, and Yale. Generally, three to five summer associates are from the local law schools: University of Pittsburgh and Duquesne University. Kirkpatrick's callback interview ordinarily involves meeting about six attorneys for a half hour each and going to lunch with a couple of associates at the firm. While the interviews are not grilling or intense, they are not as conversational as those at other firms. It is important to demonstrate to the interviewer that "you are a 'self-starter' which is a hiring committee buzzword for persons who demonstrate personal initiative and independent action," one well-placed insider instructed us. Another person remarked that the lawyers at Kirkpatrick are "really down-to-earth" and "it's not a firm that puts on airs." This person continued that "it is best not to come across as a show-off. They look for maturity and commonsense." After people have accepted the firm's summer associate offers, Kirkpatrick flies them back to Pittsburgh for a "glorious three day weekend" of "wining and dining." The event allows the soon-to-be summer associates the opportunity to meet many of the firm's attorneys in a relaxed atmosphere.

overall mixed reviews

Overall, Kirkpatrick received mixed reviews this year. Though it is now the largest firm in Pittsburgh, it has relatively little structure and is best suited for someone who knows what she wants to do and has the confidence to do it. The firm provides an attractive "diversity of practice—the large size and loose structure create an atmosphere in which a lawyer can practice among several practice areas. In fact, such skills are rewarded at Kirkpatrick and Lockhart," reported one firm enthusiast. Another praised the firm for "the ease of moving from department to department. As a junior associate you can work on securities issues, then decide to switch to M&A or banking." In addition, our sources highly praised the people who work at Kirkpatrick: "The attorneys at Kirkpatrick are extremely bright without the pretentiousness that often accompanies intelligence. There is no doubt about it—the biggest advantage at Kirkpatrick is its people."

On the other hand, many of our contacts were critical of the firm's lack of training and its absence of a formally acceptable part-time policy. Moreover, we were informed that the firm is "top heavy" with young partners, "which will push the partnership track back over time." In fact, Kirkpatrick has experienced a very significant departure of attorneys in recent years. A prominent business partner took two other partners and five associates and left to start a Pittsburgh office of a national law firm; in addition four business partners left to either go work for a client or to a competing firm, and approximately 15 associates did the same, we were told. The firm has recently created an Associates Liaison Committee, composed entirely of associates, to discuss issues of associate concern, such as compensation and training. In addition, Kirkpatrick recently increased its starting salary to $75,000, with a "bump" of $10,000 for all other associates.

Reed Smith Shaw & McClay

Pittsburgh Harrisburg Mclean Newark New York Philadelphia Princeton Washington

Address: 435 Sixth Avenue, Pittsburgh, PA 15219–1886
Telephone: (412) 288–3131
Hiring Attorney: (Mr.) Jan A. Marks
Contact: (Ms.) Lonnie Nelson, Recruitment Administrator; (412) 288–4194
Associate Salary: $70,000 plus summer stipend (1996); increases are not lockstep
Summer Salary: $1250/week (1997)
Average Hours: 2125 worked, 1900 billed; NA required
Family Benefits: Paid maternity leave; flex hours; employee assistance program; dependent and healthcare reimbursement accounts
1996 Summer: Class of 10 students, offers to 9
Partnership: 22% of entering associates from 1976–1982 were made partner
Pro Bono: 3% of all work is pro bono

Reed Smith Shaw & McClay in 1997
168 Lawyers at the Pittsburgh Office
0.7 Associates Per Partner

Total Partners 97		
Women	11	11%
All Minorities	1	1%
Afro-Am	1	1%

Total Associates 65		
Women	34	52%
All Minorities	6	9%
Afro-Am	5	8%
Latino	1	1%

Practice Areas	
Litigation	43
Corporate & Finance	27
Labor	22
New Associates	16
Tax/Trusts & Estates	15
Real Estate	13
Benefits	11
Environmental	8
Intellectual Property	8
Bankruptcy	5

Almost every city has a firm that serves as a symbol of the old-boy, white shoe establishment. In most cases, the image far exceeds the reality. This is certainly true of Reed, Smith, Shaw & McClay, but some aspects of the firm have contributed to its reputation. Reed Smith is one of the oldest and traditionally most prestigious firms in Pittsburgh. One contact asserted that after working at Reed Smith, lawyers can "write their ticket in Pittsburgh." Reed Smith has close and longstanding relationships with some of the country's most influential families, including both the Mellons and the Heinzes. In addition, the firm's offices have a formal "feel" about them. The lobby is lined with eight enormous marble pillars stretching two stories high. The office interiors are replete with mahogany, brass, and glass, making them "very impressive when you walk in." Attorneys have their own special lounge at the firm, and there is a separate set of elevators for clients that are nicer than those for attorneys and staff. Some people commented that there is more emphasis on social polish and etiquette at Reed Smith than at the other firms in Pittsburgh. "The atmosphere is formal, and it has a great deal of class to it," one insider remarked. "The people at the firm do things with style...There is a certain amount of refinement among the lawyers at the firm." Another commented that the attorneys dress better at Reed Smith than at other large firms. "It may not be like some of the New York City firms, but it's definitely chic for Pittsburgh."

increasingly progressive

Although Reed Smith has many trappings of establishment, people we interviewed insisted that the atmosphere at the firm is not stuffy. There is now a younger, more progressive group of lawyers managing the firm. Dan Booker, the current managing partner and well-known antitrust litigator, was described as "interested, open, and eager to communicate with everyone at the firm." People claimed that the firm is exploring some innovative management techniques and placing greater emphasis on pro bono work. The "unofficial" minimum for billable hours at Reed Smith is 1850, plus 400 nonbillable hours. Pro bono work goes in the nonbillable category, which according to one insider may explain the low billable requirement.

practice areas

Reed Smith's practice covers a wide range of areas, but the firm has traditionally been best-known for its labor, litigation, and corporate departments. The firm also has an especially strong labor practice, though its size has diminished of late. This group practices both traditional labor law, which involves defending corporations in their disputes with unions, as well as employment law, which involves issues arising from the statutory regulation of the conditions of employment. One insider pointed out that the lawyers in the traditional labor practice tend to be older and "mostly men," whereas the employment law group is "younger and more active." Another commented that there are more opportunities for responsibility in the labor group than in others.

The litigation practice is composed of many subgroups, including an interesting white-collar crime practice, headed by Tom McGough, Jr. The litigation group was described as the "most outgoing group" at the firm. The corporate practice has traditionally been very strong at Reed Smith. Mellon Bank has been its anchor client; additionally, Pittsburgh's largest companies rely on the corporate department at Reed Smith to solve many of their most challenging legal problems. The corporate department has survived the slowdown of the early 1990s, and the firm has made a renewed commitment to expanding it in the areas of initial public offerings and federal transactional work. The firm has also increased its efforts to expand its consumer financial services practice on a national level, with an emphasis on combining consumer financial services expertise with litigation experience in the defense of consumer class actions. People also noted that two of the firm's smaller practices, the intellectual property and health care groups, have been growing, and Reed Smith recently opened small offices in Newark and New York. Entering associates at Reed Smith may rotate through a number of the firm's departments for a year and a half before specializing in any one area.

extensive formal training

Reed Smith provides some of the most extensive formal training in the city, which one person called the "biggest plus at the firm." Another contact praised the "comprehensive" training program at Reed Smith, remarking that "associates at Reed Smith get training before being asked to 'practice law.' This increases efficiency and reduces stress on associates." The firm emphasizes "polishing" its attorneys' skills before letting them do "something that would get them or the firm into trouble." Even summer associates experience Reed Smith's commitment to training. Groups of three summer associates are assigned to a special writing instructor, who reads and critiques every assignment that each summer associate completes. In addition, the firm provides weekly writing seminars in which the writing instructors and other attorneys work with summer associates to help improve their writing skills. Each summer associate is also assigned to a junior and senior associate or partner advisor who oversee the summer associate's development. The firm provides extensive training for associates that includes a full range of formal training programs on all aspects of litigation, and regular departmental seminars in other areas.

Reed Smith has a formal system for providing feedback on each assignment completed by a summer or junior associate. After a project is completed by a summer associate, the assigning attorney fills out a "pink sheet" that evaluates the quality of the work and provides constructive criticism for future projects. Because Reed Smith serves many smaller clients, alongside its large institutional clients, opportunities for early responsibility are plentiful. Although most first- and second-year associate work involves research and writing memos, "it is not unusual to be first chair on a jury trial by the fourth year," reported one contact. The firm's policy seems to be that "they will give an associate as much responsibility as the associate wants and can handle."

businesslike atmosphere

The atmosphere during the day at Reed Smith was described as "quiet" and "businesslike." One contact claimed the loudest people at the firm are the secretaries. New associates can expect to work long hours and weekends from time to time. While there is not exactly a raging social life in the after-hours, those we talked to noted that a number of young associates at the firm like to spend time together after work. The summer is filled with about ten to twelve major social events, including the famed "Hit the Deck Party" held on the firm's outdoor rooftop patio. "They are known for having many parties" during the summer months, one source stated. On the last Friday of every month the firm hosts a happy hour known as "Final Friday." Reed Smith traditionally has had separate annual retreats for partners and associates; however, in 1996 the firm began having a single retreat for all its lawyers. Also, the individual practice groups have summer retreats and get-togethers.

diversity

Reed Smith has one of the higher representations of women attorneys among Pittsburgh law firms. Presently, the firm has an approximately equal number of female and male associates. Women are members of many of the firm's committees. One person noted that a number of women are on the hiring and summer associate committees. Two of the three partners made in Pittsburgh in 1994 were women. Although presently not many minorities work at Reed Smith, the firm has made a special effort to recruit minority attorneys in recent years.

Reed Smith has an ownership interest in the building it occupies, and its extensive renovation of the building has been highly praised. Every associate has a private office, most of which are located in the interior of the building and do not have a window with a view outside. Even those with perimeter offices do not have great views, as Reed Smith's building is located between two other large office buildings. The rooftop patio deck has chairs and tables where people may eat lunch during the warmer months of the year. The support staff and technical facilities are "excellent," and each attorney is provided with his own computer and extensive training on the system.

hiring practices

Reed Smith hires its summer associates primarily from the top ten national and regional law schools. Past summer classes have had students from Cornell, Duke, Duquesne, Harvard, the University of Michigan, New York University, the University of Pittsburgh, Virginia, Yale, and other schools. One person noted that a number of the firm's partners are from the University of Pittsburgh and Duquesne law schools, and the firm has traditionally relied heavily on these schools in its hiring. First-year students are often considered for permanent positions contingent upon their returning to the firm for six weeks during the following summer.

interview tips

On-campus interviews for Reed Smith are usually formal. Interviewers typically ask a series of questions about a student's background and résumé. Before the callback, students from the University of Pittsburgh and Duquesne are invited to a cocktail party held in Reed Smith's lobby. The party provides students the opportunity to meet many of the the firm's lawyers in a more relaxed setting. Callback interviews are laid-back and informal. At the interview, students are first met by the Legal Personnel Manager and then interview with three attorneys from different departments and levels of seniority over the course of two hours. The interviews are followed by lunch or tea with two new associates at a downtown Pittsburgh restaurant. Reed Smith usually requests a writing sample prior to the callback interview, and the firm places special emphasis on writing skills in the hiring process. One person commented that most of the summer associates from the local schools are in the top 10 to 15 percent of their classes, but many of the students that the firm hires from the top schools are not in the top of their classes.

San Francisco/Palo Alto

Law Firms Ranked By Associates Per Partner

1.	BRONSON, BRONSON & MCKINNON	0.6
2.	HOWARD, RICE, NEMEROVSKI, CANADY, ROBERTSON, FALK & RABKIN	0.8
3.	FARELLA, BRAUN & MARTEL	1.0
4.	GRAHAM & JAMES	1.0
5.	HELLER EHRMAN WHITE & MCAULIFFE	1.0
6.	ORRICK, HERRINGTON & SUTCLIFFE	1.1
7.	PILLSBURY MADISON & SUTRO	1.1
8.	MCCUTCHEN, DOYLE, BROWN & ENERSEN	1.3
9.	BROBECK, PHLEGER & HARRISON	1.5
10.	COOLEY GODWARD	1.6
11.	FENWICK & WEST	1.6
12.	MORRISON & FOERSTER	1.6
13.	WILSON, SONSINI, GOODRICH & ROSATI	2.9

Law Firms Ranked by Percentage of Associates Who Make Partner
(over varying years)

1.	FARELLA, BRAUN & MARTEL	59
2.	MORRISON & FOERSTER	31
3.	BROBECK, PHLEGER & HARRISON	26
4.	COOLEY GODWARD	26
5.	WILSON, SONSINI, GOODRICH & ROSATI	25
6.	GRAHAM & JAMES	24
7.	BRONSON, BRONSON & MCKINNON	23
8.	PILLSBURY MADISON & SUTRO	19
9.	MCCUTCHEN, DOYLE, BROWN & ENERSEN	17
10.	ORRICK, HERRINGTON & SUTCLIFFE	17
11.	HELLER EHRMAN WHITE & MCAULIFFE	14
12.	FENWICK & WEST	NA
13.	HOWARD, RICE, NEMEROVSKI, CANADY, ROBERTSON, FALK & RABKIN	NA

Law Firms Ranked by Percentage of Pro Bono Work

1.	HELLER EHRMAN WHITE & MCAULIFFE	5-10
2.	MCCUTCHEN, DOYLE, BROWN & ENERSEN	5
3.	HOWARD, RICE, NEMEROVSKI, CANADY, ROBERTSON, FALK & RABKIN	4-7
4.	MORRISON & FOERSTER	4
5.	PILLSBURY MADISON & SUTRO	4
6.	WILSON, SONSINI, GOODRICH & ROSATI	3-5
7.	FARELLA, BRAUN & MARTEL	3
8.	ORRICK, HERRINGTON & SUTCLIFFE	3
9.	BROBECK, PHLEGER & HARRISON	1.6
10.	COOLEY GODWARD	1-3
11.	BRONSON, BRONSON & MCKINNON	NA
12.	FENWICK & WEST	NA
13.	GRAHAM & JAMES	NA

Law Firms Ranked by Percentage of Female Partners

1.	BRONSON, BRONSON & MCKINNON	29
2.	MCCUTCHEN, DOYLE, BROWN & ENERSEN	23
3.	HELLER EHRMAN WHITE & MCAULIFFE	21
4.	HOWARD, RICE, NEMEROVSKI, CANADY, ROBERTSON, FALK & RABKIN	21
5.	FENWICK & WEST	19
6.	MORRISON & FOERSTER	19
7.	PILLSBURY MADISON & SUTRO	19
8.	BROBECK, PHLEGER & HARRISON	18
9.	FARELLA, BRAUN & MARTEL	15
10.	GRAHAM & JAMES	15
11.	WILSON, SONSINI, GOODRICH & ROSATI	15
12.	COOLEY GODWARD	9
13.	ORRICK, HERRINGTON & SUTCLIFFE	8

Law Firms Ranked by Percentage of Female Associates

1.	COOLEY GODWARD	63
2.	FARELLA, BRAUN & MARTEL	54
3.	BRONSON, BRONSON & MCKINNON	52
4.	MORRISON & FOERSTER	50
5.	HOWARD, RICE, NEMEROVSKI, CANADY, ROBERTSON, FALK & RABKIN	49
6.	MCCUTCHEN, DOYLE, BROWN & ENERSEN	49
7.	PILLSBURY MADISON & SUTRO	48
8.	FENWICK & WEST	46
9.	GRAHAM & JAMES	39
10.	ORRICK, HERRINGTON & SUTCLIFFE	39
11.	BROBECK, PHLEGER & HARRISON	38
12.	HELLER EHRMAN WHITE & MCAULIFFE	35
13.	WILSON, SONSINI, GOODRICH & ROSATI	33

Law Firms Ranked by Percentage of Minority Partners

1.	GRAHAM & JAMES	14
2.	MORRISON & FOERSTER	9
3.	BROBECK, PHLEGER & HARRISON	7
4.	MCCUTCHEN, DOYLE, BROWN & ENERSEN	7
5.	PILLSBURY MADISON & SUTRO	6
6.	BRONSON, BRONSON & MCKINNON	5
7.	FARELLA, BRAUN & MARTEL	5
8.	FENWICK & WEST	4
9.	WILSON, SONSINI, GOODRICH & ROSATI	4
10.	ORRICK, HERRINGTON & SUTCLIFFE	3
11.	HOWARD, RICE, NEMEROVSKI, CANADY, ROBERTSON, FALK & RABKIN	2
12.	HELLER EHRMAN WHITE & MCAULIFFE	1
13.	COOLEY GODWARD	0

Law Firms Ranked By Percentage of Minority Associates

1.	COOLEY GODWARD	33
2.	MCCUTCHEN, DOYLE, BROWN & ENERSEN	29
3.	ORRICK, HERRINGTON & SUTCLIFFE	28
4.	GRAHAM & JAMES	21
5.	HOWARD, RICE, NEMEROVSKI, CANADY, ROBERTSON, FALK & RABKIN	21
6.	MORRISON & FOERSTER	21
7.	WILSON, SONSINI, GOODRICH & ROSATI	21
8.	FARELLA, BRAUN & MARTEL	18
9.	FENWICK & WEST	18
10.	BROBECK, PHLEGER & HARRISON	16
11.	PILLSBURY MADISON & SUTRO	14
12.	BRONSON, BRONSON & MCKINNON	12
13.	HELLER EHRMAN WHITE & MCAULIFFE	12

Brobeck, Phleger & Harrison

San Francisco/Palo Alto Austin Denver Los Angeles Newport Beach New York Palo Alto San Diego
London (joint venture with Hale and Dorr)

Address: SF: One Market Plaza, Spear Street Tower, San Francisco, CA 94105
PA: Two Embarcadero Place, 2200 Geng Road, Palo Alto, CA 94303
Telephone: SF: (415) 442–0900
PA: (415) 424-0160
Hiring Attorney: SF: Douglas E. Van Gessell
PA: Karen N. Ikeda
Contact: SF: Cathy G. Perez, Attorney Recruitment Manager; (415) 979–2557
PA: Tina Gutierrez, Professional Recruiting Manager; (415) 424–0160
Associate Salary: First year $81,000 (1997)
Summer Salary: $1350/week (1997)
Average Hours: SF: 1911 worked; 1856 billed; 1875 required
PA: 2200 worked; 1900 billed; 1900 required
Family Benefits: 401(K); relocation; bar course and bar membership fee expenses; bar stipend; maternity and family leave; life, medical, dental, vision malpractice, and travel insurance; long and short term disability; three weeks vacation; dependent care and childcare assistance; training and MCLE
1996 Summer: Class of 13 students; offers to 12
Partnership: 26% of entering associates from 1979–1984 were made partner
Pro Bono: 1.6% of all work is pro bono

Brobeck, Phleger & Harrison (firmwide) in 1997
427 Lawyers at the Firm
1.5 Associates Per Partner

Total Partners 153		
Women	27	18%
All Minorities	11	7%

Total Associates 237		
Women	91	38%
All Minorities	37	16%

Practice Areas	
Litigation	203
Business & Technology	148
Financial Services/Insolvency	28
Tax/Exec. Comp./Emp. Ben.	26
Real Estate	22

Century-old Brobeck, Phleger & Harrison ranks as one of San Francisco's most profitable and prestigious law firms. About 425 lawyers hang their coats in its San Francisco, Palo Alto, Orange County, Los Angeles, San Diego, Austin, Denver and New York offices. A full-service firm, Brobeck has built a diverse client base ranging from Fortune 500 companies to emerging startups. Brobeck's leadership in representing clients in IPOs, M&A deals, and corporate partnerings has been recognized by *Venture* magazine, which named Brobeck one of the major venture capital law shops in this country. The firm has also made a name for itself with some high-profile litigation cases, especially in the products liability arena.

Brobeck earns its success the old-fashioned way. Its attorneys work hard. Firm management expects attorneys to bill 1875 hours. "People are conscious of their hours, but the key is getting your work done," insisted one insider. Another person told us that "there is no macho game about working weekends or until 11 P.M. But you do work hard."

businesslike atmosphere

Brobeck offers a "serious" and "reserved" atmosphere. "People aren't chatty right away," according to one source. "The place is very businesslike." Contributing to this corporate mood, Brobeck partners maintain a "somewhat hierarchical" attitude toward staffing and associate-partner relations. Nevertheless, one source told us that despite the formal hierarchy, "many partners are approachable, really helpful, and good teachers." Associates also form friendships within their groups. In terms of dress, Brobeck recently adopted a "business casual" dress code in its San Francisco office. The Palo Alto office adopted this dress code some time ago. The Palo Alto office offers a much "looser atmosphere" than the San Francisco office, we were told.

practice areas

Brobeck's San Francisco office is best known for litigation, which accounts for approximately 60 percent of its work. The firm enjoys a "national reputation" in products liability litigation, but it has also earned recognition for its securities litigation practice headed by Tower Snow, one of the country's preeminent securities litigators who joined the firm in January of 1995. The firm also has a strong trust and estates practice, and recently represented the executor of the estate of Jerry Garcia.

The firm's business and technology group represents underwriters, large corporations, and some start-ups. This group is known for its strong contacts in the venture capital community, "a plus for start-ups seeking introductions to financing sources," we were told. Bob Gunderson, reportedly one of the top venture capital attorneys in Palo Alto, recently left the firm.

Brobeck's international group, in which only a few attorneys practice, focuses on financial services. Brobeck and Boston-based Hale and Dorr have a joint venture that maintains an office in London, which serves clients in the U.K., the Middle East, Europe, and former Soviet-bloc countries. Brobeck also helped found the Pacific Rim Advisory Council, a network of law firms with dealings in the Pacific Rim Basin.

pro bono

While Brobeck has set a goal of 50 pro bono hours per lawyer per year, one insider told us that it "does not have the same pro bono atmosphere as Morrison & Foerster," and another remarked that "there does not seem to be much of a commitment to pro bono work" at the firm. Brobeck attorneys staff a free legal clinic once or twice a month, and the firm also does work for a Texas political asylum project.

The San Francisco office asks entering associates to choose one of the firm's practice groups. Partners assign work directly to associates in their group, and with time associates become linked to one or a few partners. One person described this system as a collection of "little fiefdoms" in which "the real path to success is to get a partner to take you under his wing."

varied work experiences

The degree of responsibility an associate may expect varies between offices and among teams and partners. First-year litigation associates in San Francisco can expect to spend a substantial amount of time exploring the library. Junior corporate associates receive more responsibility, perhaps because their department is both busy and small. Not surprisingly, partners entrust junior associates with less responsibility on bigger deals. The Palo Alto office offers corporate associates in their first years exceptional responsibility, assigning each of them emerging growth company clients.

substantial formal training

Brobeck dedicates two full-time administrators to running its substantial training program. The firm offers new associates a two-week venture capital workshop. Each practice group holds weekly meetings for continuing legal education training. The firm puts on a three-day training workshop during its annual summer retreat. In addition, many Brobeck attorneys teach for the National Institute of Trial Advocacy (NITA), and the firm organizes trial advocacy workshops for litigation associates. Less formal training, in the form of direct feedback, is also strongly emphasized, although one insider admitted that "some attorneys are lazy about it." In general, young associates have a good sense of their progress at the firm. The Palo Alto office, in particular, isn't willing "to drag people along," and will let you know if you aren't performing up to par.

social life

Because Brobeck is a large firm, attorneys from different practice groups see little of each other. Within each practice group, however, attorneys can be "really chatty," dropping by to visit, sharing lunch, and going out after work. Summer activities include rollerblading, softball, sailing, water-skiing, and after-work drinks. One source suggested that Brobeck lawyers are a "pretty active group." The firm organizes many summer events and a winter holiday party. The Palo Alto office celebrates weekly "Friday at Five" happy hours.

women and minorities

People we interviewed had generally positive views regarding Brobeck's openness to women. One source described Brobeck as "originally a sexist firm that is making great strides." Another source told us that the firm is very concerned about its reputation, and that there is "no real reason" for women to turn it down. In fact, in the past three years, "incoming associates have averaged about fifty percent female," a firm representative told us, and 18 percent of the firm's partners are female. Female partner, Cecily Waterman, heads the San Francisco office, and female partner, Rebecca Esen, heads the firm's labor and employment group, while Nancy Siegel is the firm's executive director. Women work in every group, take time off to have children, and work from home, we were told.

Brobeck is reportedly "pretty conscious" of issues that minority attorneys must face, and actively recruits attorneys of color. The firm supports and participates in many minority bar associations, including the Asian American Bar Association, the Filipino Bar Association, and the Latino Law Coalition.

management

The firmwide chairman is the "very well respected" partner, Stephen Snyder. Brobeck is governed by a combination of a Policy Committee and an Operations Committee, along with a firmwide managing partner, William Sullivan, who is currently a member of the San Diego office. On a day-to-day basis, each Brobeck office is run by its own managing partner. Brobeck sought the advice of a professional management consultant a few years ago, and today is "run more like a business than a traditional law firm," according to one of our contacts. The San Francisco office is reportedly "retooling for the 1990s;" one source told us that the "San Francisco office is a little stagnant" economically, while the "Palo Alto office is going like gangbusters and driving the rest of the firm." By some estimates, "if the Palo Alto office were freestanding, it would be the most profitable firm in the country."

Brobeck's facilities are comfortable, and are presently in the process of a renovation and enlargement. Every attorney receives an individual office and a computer on a local area network from which one can send E-mail to other Brobeck offices. The firm is in "the final stages of its planned upgrade of the entire computer network." The 24-hour support staff garnered high praise. One secretary supports every two attorneys. The large library is well-stocked.

hiring tips

Brobeck recruits from the top 15 national schools, as well as several others closer to home. It tends to attract students with fairly good grades, but doesn't expect straight As from those at prestige campuses. The firm "looks for people who are well-balanced, and who would be able to work with clients in the future." One insider commented that Brobeck is a "pretty conventional firm" where "people who are different wouldn't fit in."

Brobeck's drawbacks are common to many large firms. The firm is bureaucratic and conventional. It exhibits a "bottom line emphasis" and offers less responsibility on big cases. However, the firm also offers resources and prestige. Brobeck, in particular, is "set up so that you can figure out what you want to do." One person noted that the "work is pretty good, attorneys like their group, you are given time to find your niche, and you don't get stuck with one partner. The offices are nice, and the firm is doing well." Others told us that the firm "has a very good reputation and good training." It "looks good on your résumé," declared one.

Our sources were especially impressed with the Palo Alto office for offering "a lot of opportunities to do things other than law" and giving young attorneys "a feeling that we're doing something productive" by helping emerging growth companies get on their feet. Palo Alto attorneys have in the past often become general counsel for their emerging company clients, or gone on to other business related careers.

Bronson, Bronson & McKinnon

San Francisco Los Angeles

Address: 505 Montgomery Street, San Francisco, CA 94111–2514
Telephone: (415) 986–4200
Hiring Attorney: Patricia H. Cullison
Contact: Sandy C. McCracken, Recruitment Administrator; (415) 986–4200
Associate Salary: Under evaluation at press time
Summer Salary: $4500/month (1997)
Average Hours: 2000 worked; 1850 billed; 1850 required
Family Benefits: NA
1996 Summer: Class of 7 students; offers to 5
Partnership: 23% of entering associates from 1980–1985 were made partner
Pro Bono: NA

Bronson, Bronson & McKinnon (firmwide) in 1997
115 Lawyers at the Firm
0.6 Associates Per Partner

Total Partners 73		
Women	21	29%
All Minorities	4	5%
Asian-Am	1	1%
Latino	3	4%

Total Associates 42		
Women	22	52%
All Minorities	5	12%
Afro-Am	3	7%
Asian-Am	2	5%

Practice Areas	
Commercial Litigation	26
Products Toxic Tort	18
Bankruptcy	15
Real Estate & Constr. Litigation	14
Business	12
Labor & Employment	11
Insurance	10
Defamation	6
Tax	3

Bronson attorneys "balance work with quality of life." In the past two decades, Bronson has grown from primarily an insurance defense firm to a full-service law firm. It has nevertheless maintained its friendly, relaxed, and non-competitive atmosphere. Bronson attorneys are, we were told, "definitely willing to help you with questions," and "everyone is very supportive of everyone else." There is also "no trying to impress people for the sake of impressing" at Bronson. Because most partners are quite young, Bronson is "fairly laid-back" and "not that stiff." Associates are "pretty comfortable around partners."

balanced lifestyle

Despite its laid-back atmosphere, Bronson is a client oriented firm and demands "quality" work from its associates. It can be "intense in terms of time deadlines." Still, Bronson attorneys generally work fewer hours than their counterparts at other large firms, and "partners understand that associates have lives away from the office," reported one insider. Many consciously chose Bronson, despite a slightly lower monetary return, because it offers a more balanced lifestyle and a more pleasant work environment.

practice areas

Bronson's nationally recognized litigation practice constitutes 90 percent of the firm's work. It handles all types of litigation matters including antitrust, banking, bankruptcy, intellectual property, securities, RICO, labor and employment, professional malpractice, defamation, real estate, aviation, construction, products liability, mass toxic torts, environmental, and insurance. Bronson's relatively small business practice involves tax, securities, bankruptcy, banking, labor negotiations, real estate, venture capital, mergers and acquisitions, and general corporate. To give this diverse practice some structure, the firm has organized itself around nine work groups of between three and six attorneys each. The firm's bankruptcy and labor and employment groups are growing, and its intellectual property practice is "extremely" active. Bronson has recently added six new attorneys in Los Angeles, specializing in plaintiff's First Amendment rights and entertainment transactions.

Bronson attorneys take on "a fair amount" of pro bono work. Our sources commented that the "firm seems supportive," and it credits one half the time associates spend on pro bono "up to 50 hours" toward their billable hours. One insider commented that this accounting scheme is "key because we have hours-based bonuses." A designated partner coordinates the firm's pro bono committee, which screens all pro bono matters. The firm is involved in an "Adopt a Business" program, through which a team of law, accounting, and public relations firms adopts and assists female-owned businesses. Many attorneys handle child advocacy cases or volunteer at local legal clinics.

significant opportunities

Though Bronson assigns entering associates to a particular department, partners hand out assignments somewhat informally. As a result, associates often work in more than one practice group. Bronson offers junior associates significant responsibility. "Courtroom and deposition experience is gained at an early stage," according to one insider. First-year associates initially handle library research, but quickly progress to taking depositions and arguing motions. This is particularly true in the products liability group and the bankruptcy group. Perhaps because Bronson takes many of its litigation matters to trial, one person suggested that the firm offers responsibility so "people will be able to do it."

training

A formal training committee organizes firmwide programs, including orientation for entering associates and continuing legal education seminars for the entire firm. Bronson offers a strong litigation skills training program which includes deposition and writing workshops for first-year associates, and a trial advocacy clinic for third- and fourth-year associates. The clinic culminates in a mock trial, which is held at a firmwide weekend retreat. Many Bronson attorneys participate as witnesses and jurors, and two real judges are invited to adjudicate. In addition, many practice groups hold bimonthly meetings to discuss work and new developments in the law. One person noted, "They want you to succeed. If you are not doing well, they help." Bronson associates generally know whether the firm is satisfied with their performance, and partners are happy to sit down and talk with you about your work. The firm provides performance reviews twice a year.

active social life

Bronson associates typically "like the people they work with," often forming close friendships. The younger associates go out on Friday evenings to dinner and bars. The firm sponsors a number of activities such as Friday happy hours held at a local restaurant, a summer picnic, an annual formal dance, two to three firmwide lunches every year, and a number of summer events including river rafting, camping, baseball games, lunches, and a walking tour of the city. One person told us she thought "the women were terrific. They all really like each other. A lot of women went out together."

Overall Bronson associates "feel like they are cared about as people. They are very friendly. There is a family orientation and almost everyone at the firm has family and children." One person commented that, although "your job comes first, families would come in at lunch. You would see kids in the hallway."

high number of female partners

With 15 female partners, Bronson has one of the highest percentages of female members of any San Francisco law firm, and the firm has more female associates than male associates. Michelle Trausch is a member of the management committee, Mary Reilly heads the products liability department and Julia Molander heads the insurance practice group. "My impression was that the movers and shakers below the management committee level were women," one source told us. A number of women at the firm are starting families or have families, and the firm has recently proposed a part-time schedule policy, one insider informed us. Another source commented that "for women, it's the best firm ever. They don't expect you to behave like a man." Although committed to the Bar Association of San Francisco's goals and timetables for minority hiring, Bronson is "not doing as well as it would like to do." The firm recruits at two minority job fairs. One contact informed us that Bronson now has "a women and minority group which is very active."

rooftop garden

Located across from the TransAmerica Pyramid, Bronson offers very comfortable facilities and a "rooftop garden." The firm library, with its big fireplace, easy chairs, and wood paneling, provides a pleasant environment that, according to one source, is the "nicest part of the building." All attorneys receive private offices and personal computers. The support staff is excellent.

management

An elected six partner management committee, including at least one from the Los Angeles office, sets Bronson's policies. Below that, each office has its own managing partner and department heads. The compensation committee determines the point distribution for partners with input from the management committee. Associates offer input on day-to-day operations and exercise significant influence on hiring committee decisions. The firm plans to continue its steady growth, targeted on the employment and intellectual property practices, according to one contact.

hiring tips

Though Bronson hires academic achievers, it "looks beyond" grades (but "not very far beyond," quipped one insider). "It is important to them that the person is nice, has a sense of humor, and is someone they can spend a lot of time with. They are always wisecracking and always telling embarrassing stories about one another," said another person, adding that "grades are fairly important" but a B average from a top school is O.K. "If the interview clicks, they will give you the benefit of doubt," continued this contact. The firm also takes "a lot of pride in the writing ability of its attorneys" and sometimes requests writing samples from applicants. A "good writing sample will help," declared one insider. "They read them." Another advised applicants to "emphasize things that make you different outside law school," perhaps because Bronson is interested in "what kind of person you are."

Bronson is an excellent choice for law students interested in a broad litigation practice who want a friendly work environment and a balanced lifestyle. According to one source, it is not a good choice for someone interested only in corporate work, nor is it a place where you can "make a lot of money." Another source commented that Bronson is a good place to work at "unless all you care about is making the most money." One person advised, with gusto, that "if you are going to work in a law firm, this is the place to be—you make a bit less money, but you have a life!"

Cooley Godward

San Francisco Boulder Denver Palo Alto Menlo Park San Diego

Address: One Maritime Plaza, 20th Floor, San Francisco, CA 94111–3580
Telephone: (415) 693–2010
Hiring Attorney: Julia Davidson and Martin L. Lagod
Contact: Mary J. Ruiz, Recruiting Manager; (415) 693–2074
Associate Salary: First year $81,000 (1997)
Summer Salary: $6000/month (1997)
Average Hours: 2595 worked; 2062 billed; 1900 required
Family Benefits: 10 weeks paid maternity leave; 1 week paid paternity leave
1996 Summer: Class of 30; offers to 26
Partnership: 26% of entering associates from 1980–1988 were made partner
Pro Bono: 1–3% of all work is pro bono

Cooley Godward
88 Lawyers at the San Francisco Office
1.6 Associates Per Partner

Total Partners 32			Total Associates 51			Practice Areas	
Women	3	9%	Women	32	63%	Litigation	33
All Minorities	0	0%	All Minorities	17	33%	Corporate	32
			Afro-Am	5	10%	Tax	8
			Asian-Am	8	16%	Banking	5
			Latino	4	8%	Immigration	5
						Labor	5

When Cooley's founding partners decided to move their offices some years ago from Market Street to the firm's present location, "people thought they were crazy." That new location, once unusual for San Francisco firms, has since become the city's financial district. This story, according to our sources, captures the essence of Cooley Godward—a firm that isn't afraid to be on the cutting edge, and which is "always looking to move into new areas."

Because Cooley represents many small and mid-size entrepreneurial clients, it offers tremendous opportunities to its young associates. Take the example of Alan Mendelson. He was a junior associate at Cooley when Amgen, then a small biotech company, approached the firm for legal services. Amgen needed a lawyer to handle its public offering. Partner Ed Huddleson walked down the halls and picked out young Alan Mendelson to work on the matter. Shortly thereafter, Amgen grew into a huge biotechnology company, and Alan Mendelson became its lead counsel. Today he is a Cooley partner, who specializes in corporate and securities work. According to our source who recounted this story, it "exemplifies the trust Cooley puts in its young associates." The "partners treat associates with a great deal of respect" and try to include associates in firm management. While the "management committee runs things," the firm invites input from young attorneys and entrusts them with significant responsibility. One contact remarked, "I often operate very independently from the partner supposedly in charge. I will run a transaction with only minor input from a partner—with me controlling how much input I feel I want or need."

zest for life

Partners at Cooley are fun to work with and have a zest for life. A highlight of the year is the Christmas brunch, a champagne affair to which all employees (800 plus) are invited. The skits presented on this occasion are "fabulously funny." Recently, the firm's most influential partners did a musical chairs macerena skit, parodying the process for selecting the new managing partners. Despite their ability to enjoy themselves, however, Cooley attorneys do not go overboard. Rather, the firm culture is pleasantly balanced, what one insider called "a very comfortable atmosphere where people work hard without feeling overworked." "It is a very calm firm," one source told us. "Not the kind of place where people constantly go out after work for beers. You come in, do your work, and go home." Cooley is quite informal. It has a firmwide "corporate casual" dress code in effect at all times, with "regular casual" on Fridays.

venture capital pioneer

Cooley has been a "pioneer in venture capital for emerging companies," and is one of the few large San Francisco firms with a significant practice in this area. In fact, venture capital work drives the firm's Palo Alto and Menlo Park offices. Cooley specializes in providing a full range of legal services to emerging high-growth, usually high-tech, companies. While the firm has a particular expertise in biotech, it represents small and medium-sized clients such as Coopervision, venture capital funds, and *Wired* magazine. The firm boasts venture capital partner James Gaither, who one source identified as the "biggest rainmaker in Bay Area venture capital." Gaither is the former president of the Stanford Law School Board of Trustees. The business department also handles public offerings, high profile mergers and acquisitions transactions and other general corporate counseling services for its entrepreneurial clients.

Cooley's litigation department provides litigation services to all the firm's clients in areas including securities, intellectual property, environmental, employment, and white-collar criminal defense. The firm has attracted many well-known litigators including Mike Traynor, a former Deputy Attorney General of the State of California and son of a former California Supreme Court Chief Justice. Traynor is known to some as "a pioneer who is always looking for new growth areas." He is also an "incredible mentor and believes in the power of young people." Other well-known litigators at the firm include Joseph Russoniello and John Young.

commitment to pro bono

Those we interviewed gave the firm positive reviews for its commitment to pro bono. Cooley credits "just like regular hours" any time that an associate spends on pro bono work. The litigators take on the bulk of this pro bono work. Traynor, for example, is a former chairman of the Sierra Club Legal Defense Fund. The firm is very active in the United Way Campaign, and visitors to Cooley's San Francisco office have in the past been greeted by Koko, a stuffed, fake ape awarded for raising the city's largest United Way donation. Cooley also staffs the San Francisco Legal Services clinic quarterly, handling any cases brought to the clinic during that time. The firm also loans interested associates to the District Attorney's office for three-month stints. The Palo Alto office attorneys handle pro bono matters through East Palo Alto Legal Services.

opportunities training

Cooley hires entering associates into either its litigation or business departments. New associates are encouraged to begin in the "general pool," where they can gain a broad range of experience in many areas of the law before deciding on a specialty. Each department appoints an assigning partner to distribute work to the junior attorneys. Over time, associates often develop close working relationships with certain partners, who then assign them work directly. One insider told us that because Cooley has a "small firm kind of mentality toward staffing, transactions are not heavily staffed." Thus, while first- and second-year associates "do most of the back-up paper work," they may at times find themselves as the "only person on a $30 million deal." The firm can be "kind of hectic," noted one contact. Nevertheless, Cooley supports its new hires with an excellent training program. Litigation associates attend workshops in pretrial and trial skills. During their initial weeks at the firm, first-year corporate associates attend "Cooley College," meeting two or more hours each week for seminars at which partners present information on topics ranging from incorporation, the public offering process, and venture capital to corporate governance and legal opinions. Some of our sources suggested that Cooley doesn't always provide much feedback to associates. Still, "people are willing to tell you how you are doing" if you "seek them out." The firm formally reviews associates every six months.

friendly and social firm

Cooley attorneys set the pace of their own social interactions within the firm. Insiders view it as a friendly place where "people lunch together and stop in the halls and chat." Many attorneys have young families and so head on home after work to be with their families, but younger associates may go clubbing, dancing, or to parties. Cooley organizes a number of social activities during the summer and throughout the year. Recent summer events have included a tour of the Anchor brewing company, a group gourmet cooking lesson and gourmet meal, and a trip to a paint-it-yourself ceramics studio. The San Francisco office hosts a well-attended and purely social attorneys lunch every Wednesday. The last Tuesday of every month is designated as associate beer and pizza night. The firm also hosts a holiday party at which attorneys perform skits. In the fall, attorneys and staff hone their knives and their artistic talent for a firmwide Halloween pumpkin carving contest.

supportive of women

Cooley is a "fabulous place for women," asserted one source. Almost two-thirds of the associates at the firm are women. The firm is supportive of those who take a leave of absence to raise children, and women who work part-time have become partners. A woman who had worked part-time for six years made partner just a year or two behind her classmates, according to one insider. Women may continue to work part-time once they become partners. The firm offers both maternity and paternity leaves and is "always willing to try new things." The firm has made "great strides in recent years in recruiting and retaining minority attorneys," we were told. One source told us that Cooley was the "only major San Francisco firm" to send its managing partner to attend the local bar association meeting that set goals for increasing the number of women and minority partners. One insider, however, waved a cautionary flag on these matters, observing that Cooley is not yet "the diversity capital of the U.S. Associates are still about 80% out of the J. Crew catalog."

dynamic management

Cooley is governed by both a managing partner and a management committee that has a rotating membership. An associates committee meets monthly and offers recommendations to the partners. In addition, associates review partners, who reportedly take the grade cards "very seriously;" this program is, however, presently "under review," we were told.

The firm is in excellent economic health and plans to continue its present dynamic growth. One of its newest offices, in San Diego, is experiencing tremendous growth and success, and offers great opportunities for young associates, according to one insider. Cooley has also opened offices in Boulder and Denver, Colorado, to take advantage of the growing biotech industry there. The firm maintains efficient facilities, including a superb computerized central filing system. All associates receive a private office and computer, as well as the assistance of excellent support staff. While one source felt that the library was inadequately stocked, this problem is currently being addressed via high-tech alternatives, such as CD-ROM book titles and Internet access.

values vigor in summer candidates

Years ago, when partner Ed Huddleson wrote Nixon's Executive Order creating the Atomic Energy Commission, the young Huddleson reportedly "made it up as he went along." Years later, the firm still values youthful inspiration and vigor. Cooley seeks out "people with creativity, new ideas, a lot of energy—people who want to take on responsibility and go places." This firm has no use for "blind slaves who will sit in a corner and take orders." Young attorneys should be "confident in their own work," commented one insider, but another warned against appearing "cocky" or "self-interested." You must be a team-player to be successful. Cooley "really cares about who it invites in because it expects you to stay. The firm looks to whether the person would disrupt the fabric, or add to it," said one source, adding that you "need a sense of humor" because Cooley attorneys engage in "a lot of kidding." These are "friendly, warm, smart people." Our sources advised applicants to "emphasize that you are a self-starter. Show instances in which you took responsibility and got things accomplished." It is also important to express an interest in Cooley's unique practice and to have "more reason to be in San Francisco than location." The firm primarily hires law students from the top 25 national law schools.

Those we spoke with leveled few criticisms at Cooley. One person observed that the firm should try to "diversify its practice areas a little." Cooley has experienced "enormous" growth over the past five years with the result that "recently some people have felt overworked" and the support staff has not quite kept pace. These problems have however been recognized by the partnership, we were told. The firm now tries to "take on new clients only if they fit the firm's strategic profile or [will wait] until more excellent people can be hired." The Palo Alto office, in particular, has seen dramatic expansion. The firm's new managing partner, Lee Benton, is from that office, indicative of a "shift in power" to that office. One person commented that despite Cooley's rapid growth (the number of attorneys has more than doubled over the last three years), "the essence of the firm hasn't changed—we are still focused on start-up clients, early responsibility, training (we have a terrific lawyer whose primary responsibility is training), and a supportive, friendly work atmosphere." Overall most of our sources believe that the firm offers a unique "venture capital start-up" practice in San Francisco in a "more relaxed atmosphere." Since Cooley works with many smaller start-up and emerging growth companies, "we're with the client from the beginning and younger attorneys get to work with officers and other key decision-makers," according to one insider. Cooley "still has a small firm mentality which prevents overstaffing and ensures a lot of responsibility" as well as fostering "great communication between partners and associates." Associates feel like they are "part of the firm," said one insider. Another told us that a "lot of people really liked the work and the people they were working for." Cooley has "fresh ideas, a young partnership, a tolerant atmosphere, a steady and secure working environment, and a very congenial atmosphere." One contact summed up nicely the views of many of our sources: "Cooley is a very special place to practice law."

Farella, Braun & Martel

San Francisco

Address: 235 Montgomery Street, Suite 3000, San Francisco, CA 94104
Telephone: (415) 954-4400
Hiring Attorney: Mary E. McCutcheon
Contact: Gail F. Crawford, Human Resources/Recruiting Director; (415) 954-4907
Associate Salary: First year $77,000 (1996); second $81,000; third $85,000; fourth $91,000; fifth $96,000; sixth $101,000; seventh $106,000
Summer Salary: $1350/week (2L); $1300/week (1L) (1996)
Average Hours: NA worked; NA billed; 1850 required
Family Benefits: 8 weeks paid paternity/maternity leave (16 unpaid); domestic partner coverage; emergency childcare assistance
1996 Summer: Class of 3 (2L) students; offers to 3
Partnership: 59% of entering associates from the classes of 1979, 1981, 1982, 1983, 1984, and 1985 were made partner
Pro Bono: 3% of all work is pro bono

Farella, Braun & Martel in 1997
78 Lawyers at the Firm
1.0 Associate Per Partner

Total Partners 39			Total Associates 39			Practice Area	
Women	6	15%	Women	21	54%	Litigation	23
All Minorities	2	5%	All Minorities	7	18%	Corporate	10
Asian-Am	1	3%	Asian-Am	6	15%	Construction	8
Native Am	1	3%	Latino	1	3%	Insurance	8
						Intellectual Property	8
						Real Estate	8
						Employment	3
						Environmental	3
						Tax	3
						Bankruptcy/Insolvency	2
						Criminal	2

Founded in 1962 by three Stanford Law grads, Farella, Braun & Martel has grown into a highly successful, full-service firm that still treats its attorneys like humans. Farella has "always prided itself on being iconoclastic." Its lawyers are "generalists with a sense of perspective on the law." One source told us that "in terms of hours and dress, Farella is probably the most 'liberal' firm I've encountered." But that's about style, not politics. People of all ideological persuasions call Farella home, and they tolerate differences well. Another person observed that the "common bond" among attorneys is that they are "almost uniformly" nice, "very intelligent" and "want to do good work without sacrificing a life outside Farella." This unique firm truthfully claims to have "exacting standards in hiring lawyers who meet the criteria of, among other things...a sense of humor." The founding partners are "really proud of their firm history," we were told. Jerry Braun reportedly still keeps the window pane of the firm's original office near his desk. Perhaps most importantly, while "the partners really love the firm," for that reason they also "care about the people and their lives."

small firm culture

Although Farella has grown, its attorneys still "think of themselves as a firm of only 31 lawyers." Farella attorneys are "very genuine, friendly, and open." One person told us that "the jerk ratio at this firm is the lowest" anywhere. "People don't come to Farella planning to suffer for two to three years and then leave. The firm hires people to be partners. A lot of partners there had been in the summer program," reported one source. Farella is "relatively informal," with "very little pretense" and "no rigid distinction or class gap" between associates and partners. One person remarked that "you can always pop into a partner's office with a question, even if you're not working with that partner on a case.

practice areas

Farella is best known for litigation, which makes up three-fifths of its business. The balance of its practice focuses on general business and real estate work, with a "booming multimedia practice getting off the ground." One contact informed us that the "business department has grown considerably in the last year and is now overflowing with work. The firm has hired a lot of business laterals." Farella represents a variety of small businesses, corporations, financial institutions, vineyards, hotels, real estate developers, and high-tech companies. While many Farella attorneys are generalists, Farella also houses "specialties to sell to particular clients." The firm's construction and development litigators represent a wide range of government entities, developers, and private owners. Other clusters include a highly-regarded insurance coverage group of about nine attorneys; bankruptcy, employment, and environmental teams; and groups that work on class action securities and antitrust litigation, shareholder actions, and lender liability. Farella also engages in an active white-collar criminal practice, and has a recognized expertise in alternative dispute resolution.

Many Farella attorneys enjoy national recognition. Founding partner John Martel is an outstanding trial lawyer. Gary Anderson was recently inducted into the National Organization of Trial Attorneys. John Cooper is well-known for his antitrust practice. Doug Young, is widely respected for his criminal defense work and death penalty appeals.

pro bono

Farella encourages attorneys to participate in pro bono work and to pursue other interests and community activities. Jerry Braun is "very active" in the California Bar Association as the chair of its Committee on Administration of Justice, and other attorneys are actively involved in a variety of legal associations. A significant number of attorneys handle pro bono matters. Summer associates can spend one full day at the Berkeley Community Law Center, and Farella attorneys staff a legal clinic in San Francisco regularly. "Associates are expected to bill 1850 hours with 75 of those hours devoted to pro bono or practice development," reported one insider.

assignments

Entering attorneys elect to work in either business or litigation. First-year business associates are assigned to one partner for the whole year. In the litigation department, the vice-chair of the department, Claudia Lewis, acts as assigning partner. She assigns new associates to cases, monitors associate workloads, and ensures that they receive feedback. With time, associates may seek assignments outside this process; one contact pointed out to us that "generally people start working in groups or with certain people and only get assigned new stuff when not busy." The firm assigns summer associates to work with specific partners for two week rotations.

lean staffing

Farella staffs its cases leanly, offering young associates significant responsibility. During their first or second year, new hires typically take a handful of depositions and often make court appearances. Because there are relatively few business associates, the department often asks junior associates to become the "lead attorney" for smaller clients. One person commented that "if associates make the effort, they can get a good mix of cases and a high level of responsibility on some cases. While true at other firms, this is more consistent at Farella."

on-the-job training

Most associate training occurs on-the-job at Farella, although the firm offers several in-house seminars and workshops to hone writing, speaking, and general litigation skills. Farella also encourages attorneys to attend outside continuing legal education seminars. Summer associates meet once a week with the recruitment coordinator who reportedly "does a great job getting and reporting feedback." Associates have partner mentors who formally review their work twice a year. Day-to-day feedback varies by partner. One person informed us that "there's been a big push lately to get partners to do a better job of this and they're all signed on to the professional development plan."

fun social activities

Though Farella can get "very busy," attorneys generally get along well. One source told us that, despite a "mix of personalities and work styles," the atmosphere is quite relaxed. "People socialize and joke around with partners. The firm carefully hires people who will get along, and it makes a difference." Some partners and associates "hang out" socially, although there is no pressure to do so. Attorneys play golf or basketball on weekends or go out after work for drinks. The firm organizes many social activities during the summer and throughout the year. A summer kickoff dinner at which "[Frank] Farella makes a humorous speech about the summer associates" sets the tone of the summer program. Other summer events have included baseball and basketball games; drinks, dinner, and dancing; a Cirque du Soleil performance; kayaking; white water rafting; and a party at Frank Farella's vineyard. The firm hosts a "purely social" attorney lunch every Friday in its lounge. Farella also hosts an annual Christmas party and other events to mark special occasions.

progressive policies for women

Farella is sensitive to the concerns of women and minority attorneys. Our sources described the firm as "pretty progressive" and "very flexible." Women seem to be doing well at Farella. The executive committee includes one woman, Deborah Ballati, a construction and insurance litigator, and we were told that the firm is "outstanding on leaves. You couldn't expect more." One contact told us that "the firm is flexible in accommodating the needs of lawyers who want to work part-time." Farella has adopted a progressive "Newborn Infant Leave Policy for Associates" and will negotiate part-time schedules, although one source observed that there is "no question that part-time mommying and working makes it harder to become partner." After four years as an associate with the firm, or five years as a partner, attorneys may take a sabbatical.

associate input in management

Farella's executive committee makes most major decisions and supervises the many other committees that address specific issues of management. Associates are members of every committee except the executive committee and "feel like they have a lot of input." For example, "every time it's been raised associates have uniformly defeated any kind of bonus type salary scheme (that the partners have voted for)." The firm takes a conservative approach to growth, and according to one source, although the firm "had a lean year last year, we just settled a huge contingency case and are very busy now." Business and litigation are both reportedly "booming," and we were told to count on the insurance practice to thrive, a development that in fact is now well underway. The firm will continue to develop an intellectual property practice and expects the bankruptcy, employment, and environmental practices to continue to expand.

beautiful offices

Farella's offices are located in the historic Russ Building, built in the 1930s and once the tallest building west of Chicago. This beautiful, all-brick facility offers windows that open to let in the cooling sea breeze, which, according to one fresh air enthusiast, "makes a huge difference," as well as a rooftop sundeck. The firm's offices are on non-contiguous floors. The firm provides private offices and networked personal computers to all attorneys. Attorneys "make a big point to be nice to support staff," who were described as "lifesavers." Farella does not have a cafeteria, but is outfitted with a lounge that serves as a dining area for catered lunches and other events, including the all-attorney lunch every Friday.

hiring practices

Farella hires law students who "have excelled in academics." One insider noted that "everyone at the firm is extremely capable and able to do what she is given." Farella goes beyond grades, however. "If you have excelled and done nothing else, you won't have a chance." Farella wants people "who are vivacious and energetic outside the law." The firm pays close attention to whether an applicant would "fit into the firm on a personal level, whether this is a person people would like to work with," said one insider. Farella conducts interviews only at Boalt, Chicago, Harvard, Hastings, Michigan, Stanford, and Yale, but hires from other top schools as well. Interviews at Farella are informal with "no trick questions or games." Applicants should "be natural and just talk about the things you have done." Applicants from outside the Bay Area should know that they want to live in San Francisco. One person advised, "don't say: 'I want to do a particular thing,'" because the firm has loose practice groups.

Farella offers both the advantages and pitfalls of a mid-sized firm. It is harder to specialize in a narrower field than at a bigger shop. Though its resources are adequate, you should expect fewer facilities and less pay than at many mega firms. One source noted that the smaller compensation at Farella is "only because of no or rare bonuses. The firm tries to keep base salaries competitive. Farella, however, is an excellent choice for someone interested in general litigation, which, among other things, has an "excellent support department, comparable to any big firm." The firm is "in the unique position of having excellent lawyers who do top work but are still interesting." Farella has "great people—the partners are a great group of lawyers: extremely bright, good lawyers and good people to work for." Moreover, alongside an "outstanding reputation," Farella associates believe it is "a humane place, as law firms go." We heard very few criticisms of Farella. One person cautioned, however, that one should avoid Farella if you wish to practice certain types of law, *e.g.* "insurance defense (which we don't do), big M&A work, or a lot of high-tech Silicon Valley type work (although I'm sure we say we do it), or labor law." On a slightly negative note, several people also mentioned that, of late, there has been a rash of associate departures from the firm. One person offered the following perspective on this situation: "although it seems that many left for personal reasons, there is an understandable concern at the firm about the quality of associate life. The partners are very aware of the issue and seem to be making efforts to deal with it." Overall, however, we received a very positive picture of lawyering at Farella. In the words of one of our sources, "having worked here for quite a while, I still believe what I thought when I accepted that original offer—Farella is the best firm to work at in San Francisco."

Fenwick & West

Palo Alto San Francisco Washington

Address: Two Palo Alto Square, Palo Alto, CA 94306
Telephone: (415) 494–0600
Hiring Attorney: Mark S. Ostrau
Contact: Carol N. Ida, Professional Recruiting Manager; (415) 858–7131
Associate Salary: First year $81,000 (1997)
Summer Salary: $5400/month (1996)
Average Hours: 2450 worked; 2046 billed; 1800 required
Family Benefits: Medical, dental, vision coverage (including domestic partners); life, long term disability, and accidental death and dismemberment; employee assistance program; 401(K); flexible spending plan; four weeks vacation; short term disability (illness, injury, and pregnancy); family and medical leave
1996 Summer: Class of 21 students; offers to 19
Partnership NA
Pro Bono: NA

Fenwick & West in 1997
154 Lawyers at the Palo Alto Office
1.6 Associates Per Partner

Total Partners 54		
Women	10	19%
All Minorities	2	4%
Asian-Am	2	4%

Total Associates 85		
Women	39	46%
All Minorities	15	18%
Afro-Am	2	2%
Asian-Am	12	14%
Native Am	1	1%

Practice Areas	
Corporate/Securities	52
Intellectual Property	44
Litigation	31
Patents	17
Tax/Employee Benefits	17
International	12
Trademark	10
Estate Planning	1

Fenwick & West was founded about 25 years ago by four forward-looking associates from New York-based Cleary, Gottlieb, Steen & Hamilton "who thought that Palo Alto would be a good place to start a law firm." They were right. Fenwick & West tripled in size during the 1980s, continues to grow in the 1990s, and today is a successful full-service law firm serving high-growth, high-tech businesses in Silicon Valley.

cooperative atmosphere

This Northern California law firm, which retains a touch of Cleary's intellectually liberal atmosphere, is a pleasant place to work. While Fenwick is a "professional" firm that "really emphasizes quality," it also offers a "friendly and cooperative atmosphere" where "everyone helps each other out in a group effort." The firm tries to avoid a big-firm mentality by sponsoring various "teambuilding" retreats for the firm and individual practice groups.

Fenwick is casual rather than hierarchical. "I never had qualms talking to people or knocking on doors and asking questions," one source reported. In general, both the attorneys and their clients are young. Many Fenwick attorneys are athletic, and most enjoy active lives outside the firm, though this is "declining lately" as the work load has increased in recent years. Fenwick comes across as an open firm that allows young attorneys to be "whoever you want to be."

practice areas

Fenwick practices in loosely organized corporate, litigation, intellectual property, and tax groups. The first three clusters represent many Silicon Valley-based clients, primarily in the computer and secondarily in life science industries. Fenwick handles corporate matters in areas such as venture capital and securities, and litigates employment, intellectual property, and other cases. Gordon Davidson, known by many as "the best lawyer in the valley," has developed a strong nationwide reputation in the technology area. According to those we interviewed, the firm's intellectual property practice is much "further along than any other Silicon Valley firm." About two dozen Fenwick lawyers are admitted to the Patent Bar. The firm offers a thriving patent prosecution group, in addition to plenty of trademark and copyright work.

international tax expertise

Fenwick's nationally recognized tax department has earned special acclaim for its international tax expertise. Partner Jim Fuller is widely recognized as one of the country's top international tax practitioners. Due to its strength and comparatively large size, the tax department draws larger clients with international operations, including Levi's, CISCO Systems, Sun Microsystems, Hewlett-Packard, The Gap, The Limited, Advanced Micro Devices, Intel, Apple Computer, and several Japanese corporations. Through its corporate department, Fenwick also handles international mergers and acquisitions and joint ventures. Most of this work centers on the Pacific Rim.

case-by-case pro bono

Pro bono activity is mostly left to "individual attorney choice." The firm only recently in 1996 adopted a pro bono policy, which "recognizes pro bono as an important part of the firm's and each attorney's professional responsibility," a firm spokesperson informed us. Our sources agreed that there are "not really a lot of people doing it." One person commented that the attorneys are "really busy and people don't have the time for it." Another person stated that the firm sends a "mixed message," explaining that while "some partners are active, it is not clear how pro bono billing is really handled." The firm regularly staffs the East Palo Alto Legal Services clinic, and has handled some capital punishment criminal defense cases, but attorneys generally must "find their own pro bono work."

flexible professional development

Entering associates are asked to select a particular practice area when they join the firm, but there is a lot of flexibility regarding this choice. The firm sometimes allows associates to "split" their time between two different fields. For example, a young attorney might spend three-quarters of her time on patent issues and the balance on licensing matters. Intellectual property associates typically specialize in either patent, trademark, or copyright work. The tax department hires its associates separately. The work assignment system was described as "very unstructured"; it is essentially a "free market" system for obtaining work. Assignment coordinators distribute work to summer hires.

professional development varies by practice

Fenwick tailors responsibility to the talents and interests of each junior associate. Nevertheless, experiences vary among practice areas. Intellectual property and patent associates are given "a lot right away," sources said. Litigation associates receive smaller cases "immediately," but work with more experienced attorneys on larger cases. Young corporate associates handle incorporations for their own entrepreneurial clients, but only seasoned veterans get to solo on international, M&A, and securities work; however, "even junior associates who have demonstrated an ability to take on large amounts of responsibility get it," we were told.

Fenwick trains associates "on-the-job" and formally. It pays Patent Bar expenses for intellectual property associates. Corporate and litigation associates have at least one hour per week of continuing legal education. The tax and intellectual property groups organize lectures every two weeks. Day-to-day feedback varies among supervisors. The firm formally reviews associates twice a year. We got mixed reviews on the firm's attentiveness to these formal evaluations, ranging from "anal" to "it's hard to get the firm to do them." Attorneys do, however, complete detailed evaluations of work done by summer associates which they "take very seriously."

condos in Hawaii and Park City

Fenwick attorneys generally "like the work they are doing and the people they work with." It undoubtedly helps that Fenwick's "overriding criterion" in selecting new work is the project's inherent interest. Combine that with the firm's informality, and it is no surprise that "a lot of people go to work at Fenwick because it is livable. You are not working for the clock." Fenwick shows its concern for its associates by maintaining condos in Hawaii and Park City, Utah that they may book on a rotating basis for one week vacations. The condos are free and the firm pays the airfare. The firm encourages associates to take their vacations because, according to one source, partners believe that "a well-rested attorney is a more efficient attorney."

Thursday Teas and more

Fenwick organizes numerous social events throughout the year, starting with a "Tea" held about once a month on Thursday afternoons for all attorneys and staff. Tea is no longer offered, but "pies, cookies, and make-your-own tacos" are the order of the day. The event's popularity means that you must arrive at 4 P.M. sharp if you want to eat. Each month, the firm springs for a joint birthday cake for each floor's celebrants, often with a different flavor on each floor. Every other year, the firm also hosts a retreat for partners, associates and paralegals. It also organizes an annual summer picnic for attorneys, staff, and their families. Once each year, lawyers new to the firm produce and perform a play or series of skits parodying the partners. This tradition purportedly "unbelievably breaks barriers and creates camaraderie." One source told us that the skits "often go to extremes in how they make fun of partners—beyond the boundaries of taste according to some (but not me)."

Fenwick tries to make its summer program "a blast." The program includes lunches, dinners, movies, comedy shows, small parties for summer associates to get to know a few people at a time, and a two-day river rafting and camping trip. Summer hires also socialize informally and go out after work to movies, the theater, or dinner.

diversity

Interviewees generally agreed that the firm maintains a "professional, respectful attitude" toward women. There are "some powerful women partners who didn't have to act like men" to be successful, one source attested. The head of the trademark group is a woman. Another source commented that the firm has a "good attitude" toward leaves. Several associates, male and female, work part-time. Fenwick employs a number of openly gay attorneys.

management

An elected, four partner management committee governs Fenwick, but separate committees address specific areas of firm management. The firm appears to be economically healthy and has grown dramatically in the past few years. It recently acquired additional floors in its building and has remodeled other floors.

facilities

Fenwick's offices are located in a complex of buildings that house several other Palo Alto firms. The offices look out across the street onto a recently built office complex that "looks like a high-tech prison." The firm provides every attorney an individual office and a laptop computer, Macintosh for litigation and PC for others. The support staff receives mixed reviews. Each practice area has a separate library and every floor is equipped with a kitchen.

academic orientation in hiring

Fenwick places a premium on academic achievement when making hiring decisions, emphasizing school name and GPA. One source suggested that Fenwick seeks "people who have demonstrated a lot of ambition, energy, and creativity." The firm seeks out individuals "who are excited about taking on responsibility and developing their own practice area." Sources advised applicants to indicate why they are interested in a particular area, as well as the firm. One person advised applicants with technical backgrounds to mention it. The firm typically hires law students from Boalt, Davis, Harvard, Hastings, Michigan, Santa Clara, Stanford, UCLA, Virginia, and Yale.

People we interviewed gave Fenwick rave reviews. The only criticism we heard was that "Palo Alto is not as nice as San Francisco." Many people live in San Francisco while working in Palo Alto which, according to one insider, is "the most exciting place to practice law in the country." For someone who is interested in a firm with a strong high-tech client base and a "livable," flexible atmosphere, Fenwick would make an excellent choice. This prestigious firm appears to be "going places," and offers a "good balance between work and play." Despite its rapid growth, "it still retains some of its small-firm feel." It is, as one insider put it, "the kind of place where you look forward to going to work each morning."

Graham & James

San Francisco Los Angeles New York Orange County Palo Alto Sacramento Seattle Washington
Bangkok Beijing Dusseldorf Hong Kong Jakarta Kuwait London Milan Taipei Tokyo

Address: 1 Maritime Plaza, Suite 300, San Francisco, CA 94111
Telephone: (415) 954–0200
Hiring Attorney: NA
Contact: Edie Dykstra, Human Resources Manager; (415) 954–0326
Associate Salary: First year $81,000 (1996)
Summer Salary: $1350/week (1997)
Average Hours: NA worked; NA billed; NA required.
Family Benefits: Family care and medical leave; 90 days paid maternity leave; flexible spending; dependent care account; 14 day paid leave for primary care provider; 56 day paid leave for adoption or foster care placement.
1996 Summer: Class of 4 students; offers to 4
Partnership: 24% of entering associates from 1980–1986 were made partner
Pro Bono: NA

Graham & James (firmwide) in 1997
391 Lawyers at the Firm
1.0 Associate Per Partner

Total Partners 184		
Women	27	15%
All Minorities	26	14%
Asian-Am	24	13%
Latino	2	1%

Total Associates 183		
Women	71	39%
All Minorities	38	21%
Afro-Am	4	2%
Asian-Am	31	17%
Latino	3	2%

Practice Areas	
Business	118
Litigation	76
Intellectual Property	60
Real Estate	25
Labor (management)	16
Banking	15
Public Utilities	10
Tax	10
Environmental	10
Immigration	10
Admiralty/Maritime	8
Bankruptcy	5

A prestigious San Francisco firm Graham & James is "refreshingly casual" and makes a "distinct effort to avoid hierarchical structures and patronizing attitudes." Graham & James' informal atmosphere informs many aspects of life at the firm. "I was expecting something stuffier," one person commented. "Women wear pants whenever they want. The firm is not uptight about that sort of thing. It is a comfortable place."

changing culture

Although the firm is still known for placing a high premium on quality of life, Graham & James has undergone some changes. There is now "more a sense of the bottom line," one person commented. "There is more tension, more pressure to put out hours, more hierarchy. But compared to other large firms, Graham is better. These are tougher times now, but my overall impression is good."

international law firm

Founded in 1934 as a maritime law firm, Graham & James is a "great place for international law." Many of its original clients were Japanese shipping companies or had dealings with Japan. One of the early partners practiced in Japan after World War II, making connections that helped the firm develop its strong Pacific Rim practice. Today, Alexander Calhoun, one of thc few American lawyers to be admitted to the Japanese bar still works at the firm as "of counsel." Graham has been "aggressive" in client development, particularly on the "international side." In the years 1994 through 1996, the firm "dramatically changed shape," adding to its offices in the U.S. and abroad. It formed an international network with the Asian powerhouse, Deacons, which included a 100-person Hong Kong office, and the leading Australian firm of Sly & Weigall. It also merged with the Seattle-based Riddell, Williams. In addition, it added affiliates to the network, including the 200-member London-based Taylor Joynson Garrett and firms in the Middle East and in Europe. Graham & James is now one of the largest U.S.-based international firms and has an extensive presence throughout Asia, including Japan, Hong Kong, China, Vietnam, and Taiwan.

practice areas

Graham & James' practice is organized around seven departments: business and finance, labor and employment, intellectual property, maritime, regulatory, immigration, and litigation. The business and finance department includes a real estate group, a tax group, and a banking group. The firm primarily represents corporations and financial institutions in all types of matters including litigation, labor, intellectual property, aviation, bankruptcy, maritime, and tax.

The corporate practice represents the American subsidiaries of foreign corporations and also represents a significant number of banks, many of which are foreign. The firm's intellectual property group is growing rapidly and its maritime practice continues to represent many shipping industry clients. Graham & James recently added a nationally recognized real estate partner to head the real estate practice. The firm's environmental group left a few years ago, and the regulatory practice has "decreased significantly" of late, we were told.

unstructured pro bono

Like other aspects of the firm, Graham's pro bono program is somewhat unstructured. "Opportunities don't knock on your door, but you can do it if you want," stated one insider. Attorneys are free to participate in projects that interest them. For example, the firm's attorneys advised and helped form a non-profit dedicated to educating kids about the protection of endangered species. But we were told that because of a lack of coordination, it is "hard to get someone to supervise you as a young attorney" working on pro bono matters.

professional development

Graham assigns entering associates to particular departments. Each group distributes its work slightly differently, though all do it fairly informally. The firm's mentoring system "has been very poor," according to one insider, but efforts are underway to make improvements. "The litigation department recently implemented a formal training program which may or may not work. Corporate associates must still struggle to find a mentor on their own. In the smaller departments, such as labor and real estate, the mentoring relationships are very solid and associates tend to be more satisfied," reported one insider.

Each department offers its associates varying degrees of responsibility and training. Associates in smaller and busier groups such as employment, real estate, and intellectual property, are entrusted with "a good deal of responsibility." The litigation department offers a trial advocacy workshop through the National Institute of Trial Advocacy (NITA). It also shows films on deposition tactics and other topics and meets regularly to discuss new developments in the law. Apart from the litigation training, those we interviewed criticized the firm's formal training. "All my training has been on the job," commented one source. "Graham & James falls down on this area," another concurred. One contact informed us that "the firm has left training to the individual departments, resulting in varied levels of training (from none to lots)" However, Graham & James has recently instituted a junior associate training program and a marketing (client development) program which it hopes will rectify these shortcomings, we were told. Graham formally evaluates associates in an extremely "straightforward, fair process," permitting permanent and summer associates to see written evaluations of their work.

limited social life

Graham is a "friendly place," but according to one source, "not on a deep personal level...People have their own lives and there is not much going out unless you coordinate it." Occasionally, people within the same class or the same department go out to lunch or go out after work together. Graham organizes a few social events such as associates-only get-togethers and monthly happy hours. The firm hosts annual Halloween and Christmas parties. One source commented that "Graham & James is definitely not a 'rah-rah' type place, which has its advantages."

Summer associate events include a cruise on the San Francisco Bay, a cooking class at Tante Marie's where "everyone is responsible for a different part of the dinner" and there is "good wine to drink while you cook," and numerous lunches and fancy meals.

culturally sensitive

Graham & James is a "San Francisco liberal" firm, said one person. Its attorneys "describe themselves as being plaid," reported another. Graham & James "wants to encourage different viewpoints," this person added, noting that because the firm does "a lot of international work, it is culturally sensitive."

Graham "would very much like to attract more minority associates." It presently does very well with respect to Asian-Americans; it reportedly has the highest number of Asian-American partners of the top 250 U.S. law firms. The firm also has a "very active gay/lesbian group which has a voice at the firm." The firm recently implemented a domestic benefits policy for gay partners.

makes women comfortable

Graham has also "made a lot of strides" in "making women comfortable" at the firm. It recently had an outside consultant organize a series of programs at the firm on the topic of gender in the workplace. "I consider myself a pretty strong feminist," one person told us, "and I have no feeling that they are sexist." Some women are active in the firm's management, and the firm "really values family." Graham is "very conscious of allowing part-time parents" and has sponsored quality of life seminars to discuss parenting. One person remarked that "several women have made partner despite taking time to have kids. There is *no* sense that an associate will not make partner if she has a family." The firm is very clear about its sexual harassment policy. "We have a very strong labor department which is on the forefront of developing these policies," one person commented.

management

Graham & James is governed by a Board of Directors and a firmwide managing partner who, subject to a confirming vote, appoints the managing partner of each of the domestic offices—San Francisco/Sacramento, Palo Alto, Los Angeles, New York, Seattle, and Washington D.C. In San Francisco, the firm headquarters, associate representatives meet regularly with the managing partner and have a voice in developing office policies. According to one contact, "the system works well; not a lot of time is wasted by other attorneys, yet management seems committed to soliciting input and being sensitive to that input."

Tom Woofter, an attorney with a busy Japan practice, has recently been appointed the new San Francisco managing partner, and plans to bring a hands-off style to management, while relying on his administrative staff for much of the day-to-day office operation. The former managing partner, Michael Levin, who in April 1997 was appointed firmwide managing partner, "implemented a lot of changes immediately. The result has been a general increase in morale and profitability, and 1996 saw a dramatic increase in revenue for the San Francisco office," we were told.

office remodeling due

Graham & James' offices are "in desperate need of remodeling and updating (which is due to happen soon), but overall the facilities get the job done." The firm assigns each attorney a fairly large private office with windows and views of either the San Francisco Bay or the city. Every associate has a computer hooked into an open system so that attorneys can access one another's documents. The firm is currently replacing the present computer system, described as "hopelessly outdated," with state-of-the-art equipment and software. The support staff is "excellent," and the firm has specialized libraries for each department.

hiring tips

Graham & James hires people "who can do high quality work" but is emphatically "not looking for standard nerds." The firm is "sincerely looking for personality and for tolerant people." It hires applicants with "wide-ranging experiences," including international backgrounds or volunteer experiences. Applicants who interview with the firm should "emphasize your differences and what makes you special." One insider advised that "if there is you have done and really cared about, bring it up. The firm is interested in people that are dedicated to something that demonstrates character. They are impressed with it." Graham hires law students from all over the country but draws heavily from schools in the Bay Area.

Graham & James, though a friendly firm, is not particularly cohesive or organized. It is a firm for people with "a lot of independence." It "is not corporate America" and is "not the place that stuffed shirts fit in." One person commented that "a lot of people want structure and formality. It is not here." Graham & James is, however, an excellent place if you are "self-motivated" and entrepreneurial and prefer to seek and define your own work. It is a place that allows you to be your own person and exposes you to many interesting people. "You can do your work and then do your own thing outside the office." The firm has growing and interesting practices in international and intellectual property law. If you do decide to work at the firm, remember to pat the stone walrus, rescued from the firm's previous office building, which sits on the third floor. One person told us that "a lot of attorneys pat it for good luck when they start at the firm."

Heller Ehrman White & McAuliffe

San Francisco Anchorage Los Angeles Palo Alto Portland Seattle Tacoma Washington
Hong Kong Singapore

Address: 333 Bush Street, San Francisco, CA 94104–2878
Telephone: (415) 772–6000
Hiring Attorney: Michael K. Plimack
Contact: Janet L. Sikirica, Professional Recruitment Manager; (415) 772–6047
Associate Salary: First year $82,000 (1997); second $82,000; third $88,000; fourth $95,000; fifth $101,000; sixth $108,000; seventh $114,000; eighth $122,000
Summer Salary: $1350/week (1997)
Average Hours: 2358 worked; 1877 billed; 1850 required.
Family Benefits: Parental leave; family leave; cafeteria reimbursement plan
1996 Summer: Class of 32 students; offers to 31
Partnership: 14% of entering associates from 1985–1989 were made partner
Pro Bono: 5–10% of all work is pro bono

Heller Ehrman White & McAuliffe in 1997
166 Lawyers at the San Francisco Office
1.0 Associate Per Partner

Total Partners 67		
Women	14	21%
All Minorities	1	1%
Afro-Am	1	1%

Total Associates 69		
Women	24	35%
All Minorities	8	12%
Afro-Am	2	3%
Asian-Am	5	7%
Native Am	1	1%

Practice Areas	
Litigation	84
Corporate	23
Environmental	18
Real Estate	16
Tax	11
Labor	8
Bankruptcy	5
Probate	1

established and progressive

Founded over a century ago, Heller Ehrman in some ways is a very traditional firm. At the same time, however, having been founded by a Protestant, a Catholic, and a Jew, Heller Ehrman has never been considered an old-line, blue-blood firm. While it is one of San Francisco's most prestigious establishment firms and many of its partners are "pillars of the legal community," it is also a very progressive place, with a noteworthy commitment to diversity. One contact asserted that "no one cares about your personal life and diversity is encouraged. The firm does not have a cookie-cutter image of a successful attorney."

recent changes

Since the last edition of *The Insider's Guide*, Heller Ehrman has experienced significant changes. Peter Weiner, former head of the environmental practice, left to join Paul

Hastings, and prominent litigator, Peter Wald, joined Latham & Watkins. One source informed us that "turnover has been high, although probably not much different from that at other large firms." This person further observed that "Heller seems to attract young associates who might be happier doing public interest work. Associates seem to leave more frequently to go to public interest/public sector work than to go to other firms." Another person pointed out that whereas "in the past, Heller has touted itself as a 'quality of life' firm with a lower emphasis on billable hours than other large Bay Area firms, this is changing." Along with recent increases in salary at the firm has come a greater emphasis on billable hours.

intense atmosphere

With respect to work atmosphere, some sources described Heller Ehrman as a "happy place," but others claimed that the work atmosphere is "pretty quiet and intense." One even labeled it "stiff and antisocial." Another explained that, in part because the offices are located on many separate corridors, you "could go days without seeing people, even those on your own floor." A major office renovation will begin in the fall of 1997 which should address this problem, we were told. The firm is also said to be "somewhat" hierarchical. "People are concerned about making a mistake in front of partners," one reviewer commented. "It is a place that touts itself as doing perfect work and associates are very aware of that." This source added that most Heller Ehrman associates don't "shoot the breeze with partners."

large litigation practice

Heller Ehrman is best known for its large litigation practice, which keeps about half the firm busy. Larry Popofsky, widely regarded as one of San Francisco's best litigators, and according to one person, "one of the top rainmakers in the country," provides leadership in the group that handles antitrust and trade regulations, securities, financial services, and accountant liability litigation for corporations and financial institutions such as Bank of America and Wells Fargo. The firm also specializes in insurance coverage, intellectual property litigation, and labor and employment matters. One critic asserted that in the 1980s, "litigation got way too big." The department has since shrunk from 98 attorneys in 1993 to its present size of 84 attorneys.

growing business practice

In recent years, Heller Ehrman's business practice has greatly expanded, driven by its participation in a number of high visibility corporate transactions and its active role in the continuing Silicon Valley high-tech expansion. Under the leadership of firmwide business practice chair, August Moretti, based in the firm's Palo Alto office, the corporate/securities department has represented clients ranging from individual entrepreneurs to multinational corporations in matters including mergers and acquisitions, intellectual property, securities, and joint ventures and partnerships. The business law group includes corporate, real estate, finance, tax, bankruptcy, and estates and trusts practice areas. The firm's activity within its business law practice extends beyond its northern California base to include offices throughout the West Coast and the Pacific Rim. However, one insider volunteered that the business practice "is not what it should be; we are not strong enough in high tech/intellectual property (except biotech); and there is too much insurance coverage litigation!" It was further noted, "if you are interested in high-tech, the firm is somewhat less tied to Silicon Valley than some others."

Heller Ehrman has a large environmental practice that used to be led by the aforementioned Peter Weiner. The firm's Palo Alto office has recently added several lawyers practicing environmental law for life science companies. One person told us that Heller "often represents public interest environmental groups in pro bono cases, which is rare for firms with large environmental practices." The firm recently represented Phillip Morris in a suit "brought by several California counties to recover increased Medicaid payments allegedly caused by smoking-related illness," according to one insider, who added that "the firm has been great about this; no one has to work on this if they don't want to."

pro bono expected

Heller Ehrman "prides itself on being liberal and Democratic…and on doing a lot of pro bono work." The firm "encourages young associates to have a pro bono project at all times," one source commented. Its attorneys "feel like they are expected to do pro bono," even though the firm does not credit pro bono hours toward the 1850 annual billable hours target. Pro bono hours do count, however, towards the "combat pay" bonus system, "which pays a bonus of $3,000 to $10,000 to associates who bill 2200 hours or more." Heller Ehrman attorneys handle "a huge range" of pro bono matters, from staffing a legal clinic to representing a number of larger foundations such as Equal Rights Advocates. The firm frequently "takes on high profile pro bono cases, especially immigration and prisoner cases." Attorneys are also active in many bar association committees.

professional development varies by person

Heller Ehrman hires entering associates for a particular department in which they are interested. Each department assigns work differently. In some departments, associates are randomly assigned to two attorneys, at least one of whom is a partner. New associates typically work directly for one year for these two attorneys, who are responsible for their development. Associates may also accept assignments from others in the department. Other departments have different systems.

Heller Ehrman offers a "very slow road" to responsibility, according to one person. In the first two years, associate assignments involve mainly research and writing. Litigators take depositions if they "get lucky," although here the "experience of different people varies widely," according to one contact, who further informed us that "I have gotten a lot of responsibility in my first two years with the firm. I've done depositions, argued motions, etc." Heller Ehrman provides some formal training. The environmental group offers new associates a "mini-class on certain provisions" of the law, and the litigation department has an initial "structured training" program and an annual trial advocacy workshop. Feedback and direction are generally hard to come by. One contact informed us that "partners are generally nice people but they are very busy. It's often hard to get direction or feedback. Sometimes I feel that I'm expected to know what to do, and to do it perfectly, without ever having done it before!"

Heller Ehrman is a "fun place to be if you are young," said one contributor. "Because it is seen as a progressive place, it attracts those kind of young people." Some claimed, however, that "most people do work and leave." The firm organizes white water rafting and hiking trips for summer associates and gives them symphony and theater tickets. It also hosts bi-weekly Friday evening cocktail parties.

management

Heller Ehrman is governed by a single chairman, Robert A. Rosenfeld. In addition, each office has a managing partner and the two firmwide practice groups, business and litigation/environmental, each has a chairperson. There is also a seven member compensation committee which determines partner compensation. The chairman, appointed for a three-year term, is responsible for the development of the firm's practice areas and works with the managing partners in each of the firm's offices. Heller has nine firmwide committees and a number of specific committees for each office.

Heller Ehrman has comfortable offices, which are to be renovated later this year, located in San Francisco's financial district. Each attorney has an individual office equipped with a computer on a local network system. Many attorneys are given laptop computers. The firm is equipped with a nice library. The lunchroom offers vending machines and, on weeknights, a hot dinner is brought in from outside for those working late.

academic emphasis in hiring

According to people we interviewed, Heller Ehrman emphasizes traditional academic qualifications such as "good grades...good law schools, and law review" in its hiring. One person commented that the lawyers "put forward" by the firm to recruit "are young women, minority, and gay and lesbian attorneys," but this person warned that they are not entirely representative of the firm.

People criticized Heller Ehrman for its inability to retain traditionally under represented groups of attorneys, despite its professed commitment to diversity. However, people recommended the firm as a "great place for openly gay and lesbian attorneys" and pointed out that it has a "reputation as a good firm." Overall, Heller Ehrman is a large firm with strong corporate and litigation practices, it offers a "lot of diversity of people," and it provides colleagues who are "nice, decent people."

Howard, Rice, Nemerovski, Canady, Falk & Rabkin

San Francisco Newport Beach Palo Alto

Address: Three Embarcadero Center, 7th Floor, San Francisco, CA 94111-4065
Telephone: (415) 434–1600
Hiring Attorney: Pamela T. Johann
Contact: Evelyn Cruz, Recruiting Coordinator; (415) 434–1600
Associate Salary: First year $81,000 (1997); second $85,000; third $92,000; fourth $97,000; fifth $102,000; sixth $107,000; seventh $116,000
Summer Salary: $1442/week (1997)
Average Hours: NA worked; 1841 billed; 1850 goal
Family Benefits Twelve weeks parental leave
1996 Summer: Class of 8 students; offers to 5
Partnership: NA
Pro Bono: 4–7% of all work is pro bono

Howard, Rice, Nemerovski, Canady, Falk & Rabkin in 1997
99 Lawyers at the San Francisco Office
0.8 Associates Per Partner

Total Partners 56			Total Associates 43			Practice Areas	
Women	12	21%	Women	21	49%	Litigation	56
All Minorities	1	2%	All Minorities	9	21%	Corporate	47
			Afro-Am	2	5%		
			Asian-Am	7	16%		

Howard, Rice, Nemerovski, Canady, Robertson, Falk & Rabkin is an "intense place" which sets a "very high quality standard" for its work. The firm's philosophy—"learn by doing"—and the "enormous amount of client contact and responsibility" given to young associates can "breed anxiety." One person told us that "it is trial by fire," and added that the firm's attitude is: "We expect you can do the job...so you always feel scared. Maybe that is why people work so hard."

brilliant well-rounded attorneys

According to the people we interviewed, a typical Howard Rice attorney is "brilliant" and well-rounded. "It's really intimidating when you look at *Martindale-Hubbell*," remarked one contact. Another commented that "overall, I was really impressed by the quality of people at the firm. Everyone was a really interesting, well-rounded personality." Another observer noted that "everybody had one neat thing in their background." For example, one attorney has managed a rock group, one is a concert cellist, and three are former philosophy professors. Howard Rice reportedly is "tolerant of people with diverse backgrounds and of people who have done things before becoming lawyers. The firm likes people who can plunge in."

hard-driving

Howard Rice attorneys work "very hard" and are "very driven about work." However, "most of the drive you feel at the firm is self-driven," suggested one source. The Howard Rice attorney "is the type of person who is self-motivated." These are, one person conjectured, the "type of people who worked hard in every law school class." The lawyers "are so energized by their work, they feel privileged to be at the firm." In fact, "they fancy themselves as intellectuals and like to put themselves out as fairly elite." One person admitted that "other firms see it as egotistical."

democratic governance

Howard Rice is a young firm with almost all its name partners still practicing. Not long ago, all major decisions were made at meetings of the entire firm. Today, some major decisions such as those involving lateral hires continue to be made at full firm meetings. Although the firm has become somewhat less democratic as it has grown, Howard Rice "encourages young associates to be very vocal" and "stresses a lot of involvement in committees." Associates are full voting members of almost all committees, including those for administration, strategic planning, practice development, and recruiting. The firm, which is not heavily departmentalized, also provides associates with "extensive financial information about firm operations." One person affirmed that it "helps morale when people have an opportunity to voice concerns." Not surprisingly, this successful, democratic firm does not have a morale problem.

litigation

Though it was founded primarily as a business firm, Howard Rice is now best known for its outstanding litigation practice. Approximately one-tenth of this practice involves public law and the representation of universities (including the University of California) and various cities. The remainder covers high-profile commercial matters involving intellectual property, employment, constitutional law, securities, secured transactions, antitrust, banking, professional malpractice, products liability, and other disputes. For example, the firm has represented K-Mart in several consumer class actions and is representing the Raiders in litigation against the NFL. Name partner Jerry Falk is a pre-eminent litigator and a rainmaker for the firm. A constitutional law expert, he has also taught at Boalt. Under the leadership of Marty Glick, the firm's "blossoming intellectual property practice" successfully represented Lewis Galoob Toys, Inc. in a significant copyright lawsuit against Nintendo of America. The firm also represented American Express in major trademark litigation, represents the Gap in various intellectual property matters, and is defending Major League Baseball Properties in several cases brought by former players concerning their publicity rights. The firm's five year old Orange County office, under the leadership of Bob Gooding, has eight litigators handling intellectual property, professional responsibility, and other commercial litigation matters for such clients as Callaway Golf and the Scripps Institute.

corporate

The transactional lawyers at Howard Rice represent a variety of domestic and foreign corporations, financial institutions, real estate developers, city governments, and public entities in a wide assortment of matters: real estate, land use and environmental, general corporate planning, mergers and acquisitions, finance and securities, bankruptcy, and tax. Corporate lawyer Larry Rabkin is one of the big players in town and primarily handles securities matters. He serves as the firm's lead counsel to Charles Schwab & Co., a significant client. Under the leadership of Howard Nemerovski and Ron Star, the firm also has a start-up company and venture capital practice. The firm also has one of the West Coast's leading financial services practices advising a number of hedge funds, investment managers, and other financial institutions. Howard Rice handles international corporate transactions, mainly involving Pacific Rim countries and recently opened an office in Palo Alto to service the firm's substantial Silicon Valley client base.

committed to pro bono

People complimented Howard Rice for its commitment to pro bono work. Partner Steve Mayer is in charge and "puts together an extensive list" of matters. The firm is currently representing Andy Holmes in his lawsuit challenging the U.S. Military's "Don't Ask, Don't Tell" policy regarding sexual orientation. Last summer, the firm flew all its summer associates to Seattle to see one of the firm's associates argue before the Ninth Circuit in this case. Attorneys can develop their own pro bono projects as well. Attorneys take on pro bono matters at their discretion, however, and are "aware they must also carry a fair share of remunerative matters."

sink or swim assignment distribution

Howard Rice hires new associates into a particular department. In the litigation department, initially work is assigned from a central source. Work distribution is more *ad hoc* in the corporate area. In both areas, associates are expected to develop working relationships with partners: "at some point your work should be coming to you." This system evidences the firm's "sink or swim mentality," remarked one person, attesting that a "high level of stress is associated with that, but it is also rewarding." Specifically, the rewards come from Howard Rice's lean staffing of matters: "you are not buried on a huge team." A partner and an associate usually work together, and "a big team might be four people." Without question, the firm offers junior associates significant responsibility. In their first year, litigation associates may draft or argue motions, sit second chair at trials, take depositions, and even write briefs on major matters. Similarly, business associates will work on two or three lawyer teams to complete securities offerings and significant transactions.

supportive on-the-job training

Most associate training occurs "on-the-job" at Howard Rice. Training is "less formal than at bigger firms," remarked one source. Another agreed that the firm is "not big on training, you can plunge in." Despite the aforementioned "sink or swim" work distribution method, Howard Rice offers a supportive work environment. Training manuals are readily available reported one contact, and "people openly ask for advice over e-mail." There is a "tremendous amount of contact and sharing." Each new associate is assigned an associate "buddy," who serves as a "legal resource, mentor, confidante, and social secretary," we were told. In its formal training efforts, the firm sends associates to National Institute of Trial Advocacy (NITA) training programs, and sponsors in-house continuing legal education seminars. Day-to-day feedback is, according to one person, hard to come by "because people are busy." This person added, however, that "if you catch them, they are willing to talk." The firm formally reviews associates every six months.

long work hours and social life

Howard Rice attorneys work long hours. The office atmosphere is "quiet, friendly, and intense with people rushing around." Overall, Howard Rice is a "very tight-knit place where associates are well-respected." The firm consciously strives for cohesiveness. Associates have a six month "welcome window" after first starting during which they are taken for lunch by various groups of lawyers to introduce them to the firm. Associates working late can order dinner from the "Waiters on Wheels" program. The firm also organizes annual Halloween and holiday parties, as well as a retreat to Pebble Beach and an annual picnic.

Howard Rice is, according to one person, a place where you "do your work, go home, get some sleep, and come back." Those desiring a more active social life can find it at the firm, however. Associates sometimes go out together after work for dinner and drinks, or biking on weekends. "You are supposed to keep jeans in the office," explained one person. Perhaps the highlight of the summer associate calendar is a Wednesday daytrip by ferry to Angel Island—for summer associates only. This allows summer associates to get to know each other outside the firm and to compare notes. Howard Rice is a nurturing firm where people "get along very well, are very supportive of each other...and develop good friendships."

Howard Rice actively recruits women and minority attorneys and works hard to address their issues of concern. The firm has a remarkable representation of women and minorities, and is very "gay friendly," reported one contact. The firm has a generous parental leave policy, we were told, but "some complain about the lack of a clear policy on part-time work."

new focus on bottom line

Howard Rice is governed by committees. The managing director and the administrative committee, which includes two associates, handle the day-to-day administration. The firm reportedly is economically sound, with both the litigation and corporate departments contributing to its success. A recent move away from lock-step compensation in the partnership has caused some tension, we were told, but the "greater rewards for rainmaking have contributed to the firm's bottom line. Associates have continued to insist on lock-step bonuses to avoid competition and pressure to bill more hours. However, the perception among some associates is that the firm has become much more focused on hours than it was in the past."

egalitarian office assignments

Howard Rice's offices are "fairly modern and light" and contain a "nice collection of modern art." The firm assigns every attorney a private office and holds periodic "office shuffles" that allow all attorneys an opportunity to select an office with a Bay view. The firm provides every attorney a personal computer and has a firmwide computer network. The secretaries are good, and the librarians reportedly are "fantastic" and very responsive.

selective hiring

Howard Rice is "very selective" in its hiring decisions. The firm has "pretty high standards in terms of credentials" and looks for people who "are real bright and can take responsibility and work a lot." Howard Rice prefers "people with a high energy level" as well as "well-rounded" applicants. People advised candidates to "not appear nervous," to "emphasize your individuality," and to "ask questions...that are thoughtful." The interviews are "chatty"—the firm is trying to get to know the applicants personally. Howard Rice hires law students from Bay Area law schools and the top national schools.

Howard Rice is a "pretty serious and hard-working" place, and the "intensity can translate into stress." It is not a firm for those who want a balanced lifestyle, or for those who need some "hand-holding." Further, complained one insider, "the rather ad hoc nature of firm politics leaves some feeling excluded—especially associates without strong relationships with powerful partners." However, "if you really want to become a lawyer," Howard Rice provides the "chance to be a lawyer right off the bat." Everyone agreed that Howard Rice attorneys "really enjoyed practicing law there." There is "a lot of opportunity to define your practice area," asserted one insider. This firm offers "a great opportunity to work with a lot of interesting people" and to "learn from good people." Howard Rice has an "excellent reputation in San Francisco," and you "can go anywhere from it in San Francisco."

McCutchen, Doyle, Brown & Enersen

San Francisco Los Angeles Palo Alto San Jose Walnut Creek Washington
Taipei

Address: Three Embarcadero Center, San Francisco, CA 94111
Telephone: (415) 393–2000
Hiring Attorney: John C. Morrissey
Contact: Wendy R. Broderick, Director of Attorney Recruitment; (415) 393–2289
Associate Salary: First year $81,000 (1997)
Summer Salary: $5800/month (1996)
Average Hours: 1983 worked; 1881 billed; 1850 billable and 50 pro bono required
Family Benefits: Health; dental; vision; maternity; paternity
1996 Summer: Class of 31 students; offers to 29
Partnership: 17% of entering associates from 1979–1985 were made partner
Pro Bono: 5% of all work is pro bono

McCutchen, Doyle, Brown & Enersen in 1997
165 Lawyers at the San Francisco Office
1.3 Associates Per Partner

Total Partners 61		
Women	14	23%
All Minorities	4	7%
Afro-Am	2	3%
Asian-Am	2	3%

Total Associates 82		
Women	40	49%
All Minorities	24	29%
Afro-Am	6	7%
Asian-Am	14	17%
Latino	2	2%
Native Am	2	2%

Practice Areas	
Litigation	104
Corporate	15
Environmental	15
Tax/Probate	8
Health	7
Patent	6
Bankruptcy	5
Real Estate/Land Use	3
Labor	2

a liberal firm

One of San Francisco's top five most prestigious law firms, McCutchen, Doyle, Brown & Enersen provides a "very open, respectful, introspective environment," raved one reviewer. The firm is "very liberal even for San Francisco, and people are very comfortable voicing liberal opinions." This well-established firm actively recruits women and minorities and has a remarkably high number of women, gay and lesbian, and minority associates.

large and established

Though it is "a very young, friendly place" that "treats the staff very well," McCutchen nevertheless exhibits the character of a "big firm." Attorneys "dress up" in business attire for work, though women may wear pants. There is a "definitely a divide" between partners and associates, one contact told us. Others did note, however, that the firm has an "open-door policy," that "partners are pretty accessible," and that "associates have input into the firm's decisions."

primarily litigation practice

Two-thirds of McCutchen's attorneys are involved in the firm's well-regarded litigation practice, which is organized around a number of groups ranging from securities and intellectual property to maritime and torts. One of McCutchen's better known "rain-making" commercial litigation partners is David Balabanian who, one reviewer exaggerated, has "never tried a case before a jury and yet brings in $5 million a day." McCutchen's environmental department, which handles both litigation and counseling, boasts "big environmental stud" David Andrews, the chair of the firm and former Legal Counsel and Special Assistant for Policy at the Environmental Protection Agency under President Carter.

small corporate

McCutchen's corporate practice is not large, although the recent addition of several new corporate partners on the peninsula (San Jose, Palo Alto) may revitalize business in this area. McCutchen recently absorbed a banking group from another firm. Also, the firm's intellectual property practice is expanding. McCutchen represents a wide range of clients, mostly corporations, but also financial institutions, firms, hospitals, and government entities. Some well-known clients include Exxon (maritime), the City of Honolulu (environmental), Toyota, General Motors, Intel, and Microsoft (litigation). More recently, AT&T has become a huge client of McCutchen.

active pro bono

McCutchen's pro bono practice is "a very big deal" at the firm. Each lawyer is expected to contribute at least 50 hours per year to pro bono legal services, and in past years the per-lawyer average contribution to pro bono was much higher. The firm is affiliated with a wide variety of public interest organizations and makes pro bono projects readily available. Along with other San Francisco firms, McCutchen attorneys staff a legal clinic sponsored by the Lawyers Committee of Urban Affairs. The firm has also established a program with the San Francisco City Attorney's Office under which associates try small cases in juvenile court. One intellectual property partner, Beth Parker, serves as counsel to Planned Parenthood. Litigation partner, Warren George, is involved in prisoners' rights cases. The firm also handles death penalty cases and has an active environmental pro bono practice.

family system organization

Entering associates are hired to work for a particular practice group within the litigation and business departments. The firm has organized the litigation partners into four "families." Each family is meant to include partners with compatible practices, but at the same time to offer a wide variety of work to junior associates. Each new associate is assigned to a particular family. A new associate is assigned to work half the time with one partner in the family, and may obtain the remaining work from the other dozen or so partners in the family. Summer associates choose their own work from a wide variety of available assignments, and work with a number of attorneys.

opportunities

McCutchen "suffers the big firm problem of too many attorneys on big cases," one critic complained. Although some "swamped" areas such as environmental litigation entrust associates with significant early responsibility, most first- and second-year associates handle research and document production. Associates in their third and fourth year at the firm routinely argue motions. Junior associates may independently handle smaller pro bono cases. There are significant opportunities for early development in the branch offices, we were told.

training feedback

The litigation, environmental, corporate, and health practices each offer training programs which include a series of in-house seminars, workshops, and videos on a variety of specific topics. The training program got very good grades from those contacted. The firm formally reviews associates twice annually, and the associates are permitted to see the written evaluations of their performance completed by the firm's partners. Summer associates receive "a lot" of day-to-day informal feedback and are reviewed formally twice during the summer. Although summer associates may review their written evaluations, one remarked that they are "sort of wimpy over the summer."

low-key social life

McCutchen attorneys do not exhibit "a total neuroticism about work," perhaps because many "were not born wanting to be lawyers," speculated one source. The social life at McCutchen is also low-key. Though the attorneys are "very friendly," said one contact, "people are into their own thing." The summer program includes softball games followed by jaunts to bars, a beer bash every other Thursday, and a gay and lesbian picnic.

tolerant and progressive

Though McCutchen's partnership is predominantly white and male, this firm boasts more women and minority associates than most of the nation's large law shops. McCutchen is "generally a tolerant firm for women." It offers a generous maternity leave policy, belongs to an emergency childcare consortium, and partially subsidizes the cost of the care. The firm's commitment to minority recruitment is evident in the number of minority attorneys that it hires, although its commitment to retention has been questioned. McCutchen is "studying the problem" of retaining minority attorneys and has solicited attorney input on the issue. During the summer, McCutchen organizes a diversity luncheon for minority partners and summer associates.

management

McCutchen is run by a seven partner executive committee that oversees all other committees. The members of the executive committee are elected by the partnership for three-year terms. The executive committee in turn appoints the partner members of all other committees. Associates annually elect their colleagues to become members of all committees other than the executive committee.

offices

Located on the Embarcadero, McCutchen's offices offer beautiful views of the San Francisco Bay and the Golden Gate Bridge. The firm occupies four floors that are equipped with one large kitchen area and many small coffee stations. Each attorney has a private office and personal computer. The computer system was described as "less than stellar—it regularly freezes and you sometimes can't work on your computer for one to two hours." The support staff is "very good and competent," and the library is well-stocked.

hiring tips

McCutchen hires bright and interesting people. One person commented that they "don't dwell on grades, but they do look at them." This firm wants "interesting people...whose life is not all studying." People advised applicants interviewing at McCutchen to emphasize "that you are a responsible person who has no problem working on your own." The interviewers want to see if you are "someone whom they would want to work with and have dinner with," said one insider. McCutchen hires law students from the top national schools and Bay Area law schools.

McCutchen, one of San Francisco's elite firms, has a strong commitment to pro bono and provides a good training program for its associates. The people are "outgoing and friendly and have outside interests," said one contact. The firm "really accommodates your lifestyle and interests," although "a better bonus program at the firm could help this even more," asserted one insider. Lastly, McCutchen offers "really interesting work in litigation" and allows for a great deal of professional development, declared one contact.

Morrison & Foerster

San Francisco Denver Los Angeles New York Orange County Palo Alto Sacramento Walnut Creek Washington
Brussels Hong Kong London Singapore Tokyo

Address: 425 Market Street, San Francisco, CA 94105–2482
Telephone: (415) 268–7000
Hiring Attorney: Craig B. Etlin
Contact: Sara A. Williams, Recruiting Coordinator; (415) 268–7409
Associate Salary: First year $81,000 (1997)
Summer Salary: $1300/week (1996)
Average Hours: NA worked; NA billed; 1850 required.
Family Benefits: 12 weeks paid maternity leave; family care leave; medical, dental, vision; 401(K); health and dependent care reimbursement accounts; domestic partner coverage; liability, accident and life insurance; relocation, child and eldercare referral
1996 Summer: Class of 43 students; offers to 43
Partnership: 31% of entering associates from 1979–1985 were made partner
Pro Bono: 4% of all work is pro bono (firmwide)

Morrison & Foerster in 1997
210 Lawyers at the San Francisco Office
1.6 Associates Per Partner

Total Partners 70		
Women	13	19%
All Minorities	6	9%
Afro-Am	3	4%
Asian-Am	2	3%
Latino	1	1%

Total Associates 110		
Women	55	50%
All Minorities	23	21%
Afro-Am	5	5%
Asian-Am	12	11%
Latino	6	6%

Practice Areas	
Litigation	106
Tax & Estate	16
Land Use/Envir./Energy	12
Corporate Finance	10
Labor & Employment Law	10
Real Estate	10
International	8
Intellectual Property & Patents	7
Finance	6
Bankruptcy	1

With over 500 lawyers, nine domestic, and five international offices, Morrison & Foerster has a national and international reputation that perhaps no other prestigious San Francisco firm can match. Affectionately referred to as MoFo, this is a "San Francisco liberal" firm which made a strong commitment to pro bono and diversity early in its history, asserted one admirer. The firm "is definitely out there as far as taking initiatives in the work place," attested another. "It is often the first to do things." The firm takes pride in its selection as the only law firm represented in *The 100 Best Companies to Work for in America.*

comfortable environment

Morrison & Foerster is "hard-working, but not obsessive." One source commented that "people put in full days and are serious, but it's not a bunch of miserable drones." Another concurred that there are "a fair number of young attorneys" who are "pretty outgoing" and "relaxed." This firm is "not prohibitively hierarchical," and "a lot of associates have fairly good relationships with partners" who are "on the whole, approachable." Those who like to dress casually will appreciate Morrison & Foerster. Even summer associates feel comfortable biking to work in shorts and changing at the office. Women freely wear pants, and there is at least one female associate at the firm who wears "jeans every other day with a nice jacket."

practice areas

Morrison & Foerster is organized around four firmwide departments: litigation, business, tax, and labor and employment. Each of the four departments is further divided into practice groups which together handle virtually all areas of law pertinent to the firm's wide range of business and institutional clients, many of whom are Fortune 500 companies. Morrison & Foerster also has many interdisciplinary and international practice groups, ranging from intellectual property to European Community. The firm is "so big, it does a little of everything," said one source.

The "well-regarded" tax department is said to be "a real fun group" and "very social." Litigation attorneys were described as "nice." Many of the firm's attorneys are well-known in San Francisco and nationally. James Brosnahan, a litigation partner at the firm, is a former Assistant U.S. Attorney and president of the San Francisco Bar Association. He enjoys a national reputation as a litigator and, among other accomplishments, was retained by Special Prosecutor Walsh to prosecute Caspar Weinberger in the Iran-Contra matter.

commitment to pro bono

Morrison & Foerster professes to be more committed to pro bono than virtually any other large law firm. It has "one of the best pro bono programs in the country," claimed one source. In recent years, its lawyers on average have devoted approximately 110 hours per attorney to pro bono matters, a contribution that the firm valued at more than $20 million. The pro bono practice includes a pilot program that provides legal services for poor children. Morrison & Foerster attorneys also staff, on a rotating basis, a public defender's office, district and city attorneys' offices, and a number of legal services clinics. The firm and some of its attorneys have received public awards and recognition from the NAACP Legal Defense Fund and the American Bar Association.

work assignments

Entering associates join one of the firm's four major departments. New litigation associates are initially assigned to one of several litigation teams. Litigation associates receive most assignments from the attorneys in their teams, but may seek additional work from other teams. The other departments distribute work more informally. Overall, MoFo would appear to offer its associates a fair amount of early responsibility. In particular, junior associates in the litigation and business departments report ample opportunities for early engagement. A litigation associate informed us that, as a second-year, "I had sole responsibility for prepping witnesses and defending depositions in a securities class action case. I've also written lots of briefs with minimal partner involvement and had a very active role drafting an amicus brief for the Supreme Court." Junior tax associates also receive considerable responsibility, particularly on smaller projects. Some first-year tax attorneys have written briefs with minimal supervision from partners.

extensive formal training

Morrison & Foerster offers an extensive formal training program which it believes is "among the most comprehensive in the country." The firm provides an orientation for new attorneys and offers training sessions in legal writing and negotiation to all lawyers. Each department separately conducts a series of clinics, seminars, and departmental and practice group meetings. The firm encourages attorneys to attend outside continuing legal education programs, including the National Institute for Trial Advocacy (NITA) training program. Morrison & Foerster evaluates first- and second-year associates twice a year, and evaluates other associates annually. The firm formally evaluates summer associates twice during the summer. Associates annually evaluate the training abilities of partners on a confidential basis. These evaluations are considered by the partner compensation committee in its decisions. People disagreed as to the effectiveness of the formal feedback. One commented that "people seemed to know where they stood," but another stated that associates were "walking on eggshells."

Social life at Morrison & Foerster "can be what you want it to be." Groups of associates are close friends and go out after work. Morrison & Foerster organizes weekly social dinners. It also throws parties when an attorney wins a big case, or on other special occasions. The firm arranges "a very active summer program" which includes baseball games, picnics, and outings.

tolerant and supportive of diversity

Morrison & Foerster employs a high number of female and minority attorneys relative to other major national law firms. Some "very impressive" female partners work at the firm. Partners Linda Shostak, Annette Carnegie and Lori Schechter tried and won a case challenging a parental consent law as unconstitutional under the California State Constitution. Morrison & Foerster has been named by *Working Mother* magazine as one of the 10 best places for mothers to work. The firm offers flex-time arrangements, and two female partners work part-time. MoFo also provides free access to the Dependent Care Connection, a resource agency providing names of care providers nationwide. Morrison & Foerster has made clear to all attorneys that harassment will not be tolerated. It has mandatory training sessions and a broad harassment policy which reads in part: "Harassing conduct can take many forms and includes, but is not limited to, slurs, jokes, statements, gestures, pictures, or cartoons regarding an employee's race, color, religion, national origin, ancestry, sex, age, disability, marital status, or sexual orientation."

Morrison & Foerster goes "out of its way to" to be tolerant and supportive of alternative lifestyles. You "don't have to separate your social life from work," praised one contact. The firm has adopted many progressive social and employment policies including a policy on AIDS and AIDS-related Conditions in the Workplace, which provides attorneys with the disease "reasonable accommodation as long as they are medically able to perform the duties of their position." Morrison & Foerster participates in San Francisco's Gay Pride Parade.

management

Morrison & Foerster is governed by committees. The partnership elects a chairperson and two managing partners for operations, who in conjunction with the chairs of the litigation and business departments, monitor day-to-day matters and long range planning. A Board of Directors, which is headed by the chairman of the firm, represents the interests of the partners. Associates serve on other committees. According to people we interviewed, the firm is planning to expand into new legal areas and new markets, particularly in Asia, where the firm opened an office in Singapore this year.

new offices

Morrison & Foerster recently moved to a new building in downtown San Francisco, a few blocks away from the firm's former location. Although the views are not as spectacular, "the firm is saving a lot of money on the rent," and overall the offices are "functional and pleasant." Every attorney has a private office and a computer. The firm has a "great" library, lunchrooms, and men's and women's locker rooms.

hiring tips

Morrison & Foerster hires people who are smart, but it also "wants someone who will add to their diverse environment—someone who is committed to being a good lawyer and doing good things." Another source added that they "don't want people who are dull or drones." Morrison & Foerster interviews are "very chatty." Many of the firm's lawyers have a "liberal bent," claimed one insider, who advised applicants to "emphasize commitment to the liberal public interest type thing" The "farther to the left you are, the better," continued this source. Interviewers are likely to ask "about what you want to do with life and your values," mentioned past successful applicants, explaining that "a lot of people there originally wanted to go into public interest." Morrison & Foerster hires law students from the top national schools, Howard, and a few Bay Area schools.

Morrison & Foerster is a unique and pleasant place to work. The people we interviewed highly recommended this firm. Some commented, however, that the firm's large size makes it somewhat impersonal. You "can walk through the halls and not know people," warned one. Others cautioned that "they work hard and long hours." In fact, one person believed that the associates are "incredibly overworked." Despite these drawbacks, Morrison & Foerster has "progressive employment and social policies," a "wonderful pro bono program," an "interesting variety of people," and "better diversity than most other firms in the country." Morrison & Foerster allows "real lifestyle permissiveness and is even sort of encouraging of people to be different." It is a place for someone looking for the stability of a large, prestigious law firm with little stuffiness.

Orrick, Herrington & Sutcliffe

San Francisco Los Angeles New York Sacramento Silicon Valley Washington Singapore

Address: Old Federal Reserve Bank Building, 400 Sansome Street, San Francisco, CA 94111
Telephone: (415) 392–1122
Hiring Attorney: John H. Kanberg
Contact: Kari A. Blair, Recruiting Administrator; (415) 773–5414
Associate Salary: First year $81,000 (1997); second $85,000; third $92,000; fourth $97,000; fifth $102,000; sixth $107,000; seventh $112,000; eighth $115,000
Summer Salary: NA
Average Hours: 2100 worked; 1900 billed; 1900 required
Family Benefits: Maternity leave/paternity leave; on site day care
1996 Summer: Class of 17 students; offers to 15
Partnership: 17% of entering associates from 1980–1985 were made partner
Pro Bono: 3% of all work is pro bono

Orrick, Herrington & Sutcliffe in 1997
130 Lawyers at the San Francisco Office
1.1 Associates Per Partner

Total Partners 59		
Women	5	8%
All Minorities	2	3%
Asian-Am	1	2%
Latino	1	2%

Total Associates 64		
Women	25	39%
All Minorities	18	28%
Afro-Am	4	6%
Asian-Am	10	16%
Latino	4	6%

Practice Areas	
Corporate	46
Litigation	23
Public Finance	23
Tax	20
Unclassified	11
Employment Law	7

a San Francisco institution

For over 125 years, Orrick has been "a San Francisco institution." The firm contributed to the formation of what became the Pacific Gas & Electric Company and worked on the financings of the Golden Gate Bridge, Candlestick Park, and BART. In recent years, the firm's New York office has grown considerably, so that today it has more attorneys than does the San Francisco office. Unlike many other well-known San Francisco firms, Orrick is not particularly politically active. One reason for this is that the firm "regularly represents scores of state and local governments as part of its huge public finance practice, and accordingly can't 'take sides' in political contests." Its attorneys "are apolitical" by and large, commented one contact. Another contact remarked that Orrick is "not a liberal firm" like Morrison & Foerster and some other large, well-established San Francisco firms. Orrick's "legal philosophy is conservative," asserted one source. "They are risk averse and work hard in areas they know well." The dress code at the firm is, however, becoming more relaxed, we were told. "Casual day on Friday often slips into other days in the week as well," reported one insider.

impersonal atmosphere

The atmosphere at the firm was described as "friendly, but not necessarily warm." The attorneys "are interested in what each other is doing, but only to a point," said one source. "People seemed congenial...but boring," remarked another. "Some people are very friendly, really reach out, and are very supportive," qualified one source, who nevertheless cautioned that "it's a large firm. I'm not sure whether it's that or the personality of lawyers which makes the environment somewhat cold."

nationally recognized public finance

Orrick offers a full-service practice which covers litigation, corporate, tax, environmental, labor, and real estate. It also represents a range of large and midsize corporate and institutional clients including Safeway, Lucky's, Comtel of California, and Montgomery Securities. Orrick's nationally recognized public finance practice is one of the largest in the country. For the past several years, it has handled a greater volume of public finance work than any other law firm in the country. This department regularly represents the state of California, the city of San Francisco, and other municipalities nationwide. Orrick offers a developing international practice and has represented Japanese clients in a variety of cases, including patent infringement cases. The firm opened an office in Singapore in 1996. In addition, several of the firm's intellectual property attorneys opened an office in Silicon Valley in 1995, which has since been joined by a number of non-Orrick partners.

Orrick is run by an executive committee including a chief executive officer and four other partners. They serve staggered three-year terms, at the end of which they are replaced by a new member voted on by the partnership. The firm has lately cut back on some frills, but its profits per partner remain among the top five in San Francisco. In recent years the firm has added a number of new partners and practice groups. A former Graham & James partner with expertise in project finance joined the firm's San Francisco office. A large group (8) of real estate partners left Morrison & Foerster to join Orrick in San Francisco. In addition, nationally prominent trial lawyer and former federal judge Barbara Caulfield recently resigned her partnership at Latham & Watkins to join Orrick as head of the San Francisco litigation department..

pro bono

Orrick's pro bono practice received good reviews. The firm credits pro bono hours to its annual 1900 hour billable requirement and does not set a maximum on pro bono time. The firm has been engaged in a number of substantial pro bono projects and has received a number of awards honoring the extent of its commitment. Many of the firm's attorneys voluntarily work for (and three partners are on the Board of) the San Francisco Lawyer's Committee for Civil Rights (which has sponsored the most significant litigation challenging California Propositions 186 and 211). Orrick was the first major San Francisco law firm to handle automatic death penalty appeals and habeas corpus proceedings through the California Appellate Project. The firm's lawyers have won major victories on behalf of the disabled (through A.D.A. claims against Amtrak) and the environment (Orrick attorneys created the League to Save Lake Tahoe).

professional development

Associates at Orrick are not hired for a particular department. Instead, the firm has a smorgasbord program, and associates typically "float" for their first year at the firm. However, associates are permitted to concentrate in one particular area from the beginning of their employment if they so desire. Each practice area assigns work differently, and each offers junior associates varying responsibilities. The lean labor department entrusts its junior associates with more than average responsibility, said one observer. Similarly, junior public finance associates handle "more than drafting." Litigation and corporate associates, however, typically do not handle their own matters until they have been at the firm for a few years.

Each department sponsors a formal training program which includes seminars, workshops, and regular departmental meetings. The firm's 40-session litigation training program includes participation in the National Institute of Trial Advocacy (NITA) workshop and a three-month rotation in a District Attorney's office. Orrick formally reviews associates twice a year during their first two years. One admirer praised the "excellent" recruitment coordinator for being highly organized and for ensuring that summer associates receive written evaluations on their work.

limited social life

Because many Orrick attorneys are older and married, the firm does not offer an especially active after-work social life. People agreed that most attorneys "come in, do their work, and leave." In the past year or so, however, Orrick's mid-level associates "have developed a real social network including a well-attended 'happy hour' at a different venue each week," stated one contact. The summer social program has considerably improved, we were told. One person lauded the summer program as a "great balance of real work and fun events." Summer functions begin with an informal dinner at the home of the partner in charge of attorney development, and include a firm retreat at Lake Tahoe, evenings at Tante Marie's cooking school, a golf outing, trips to Angel Island, baseball games, brewery tours "and much more," according to one enthusiast.

The Trough

Orrick offers some unusual perks. Both breakfast and lunch are available to attorneys every day, free of charge, in a room affectionately referred to as The Trough. Orrick's breakfast, featuring a spread of coffee, tea, fruits, pastries, and bagels is available to all personnel every morning. The attorney lunch includes sandwiches, salads, soups, and drinks every afternoon. Any left over food is donated to local food banks. Orrick's offices are also equipped with "a workout room with stairmasters, weights, and showers."

diversity

Orrick makes a "strong effort to recruit minorities." The firm long ago surpassed its goal of 15 percent minority associate representation in its attorney population. In addition, the firm has institutionalized its commitment to minority attorneys by establishing the Diversity Committee to promote the employment, retention and advancement of minority and gay and lesbian attorneys. Orrick recently hired many openly gay attorneys and offers a welcoming environment. "Some of the firm's most influential partners went out of their way to attend and send wedding gifts," on the occasion of a church wedding of one of the firm's gay attorneys, we were told. To make the firm more desirable for parents, Orrick now offers four months unpaid childcare leave in addition to eight weeks paid maternity leave. The childcare leave policy is reportedly widely used by the firm's attorneys, both men and women. Alternative work schedules are available for attorneys with two years experience and in good standing at the firm. Orrick also has an on-site back-up emergency childcare center.

beautiful traditional offices

Orrick's offices occupy almost the entire beautiful Old Federal Reserve Bank Building. The neo-classical building opens into a marble banking hall showcasing chandeliers. The offices feature lots of dark wood and beautiful artwork. The library with its carrels, comfortable couches, and periodical reading room, was described as "great." Attorneys all receive individual offices with 14 to 20 foot high ceilings and windows that open to admit fresh San Francisco Bay air. Each attorney has a personal computer which is "seriously behind technologically," according to one source. A firm spokesperson informed us that "Orrick is currently undergoing a major computer conversion to a Windows 95 based operating system, the latest Novell network, and document management systems." The support staff was described as "really good."

hiring practices

As for recruitment, Orrick hires good students with strong research and writing skills, preferably with connections to the Bay Area. Past successful applicants advised interviewees to display "a lot of energy" in the interviews. The firm hires law students primarily from the top national schools, particularly Boalt, Stanford, and Harvard. One half of a recent summer class was comprised of Harvard law students, we were told.

Pillsbury Madison & Sutro

San Francisco Los Angeles New York Orange County Sacramento San Diego Silicon Valley Washington Hong Kong Tokyo

Address: 235 Montgomery Street, San Francisco, CA 94104
Telephone: (415) 983–1000
Hiring Attorney: Shawn Hanson
Contact: Suzanne Close, Professional Recruitment Manager; (415) 983–1320
Associate Salary: First year $81,000 (1997)
Summer Salary: $1300/week (1996)
Average Hours: NA worked; NA billed; 1900 required (including pro bono & internal legal)
Family Benefits: Up to 13 weeks paid maternity leave; up to 4 months unpaid leave for care of a newborn or child, parent, spouse or domestic partner with serious health condition
1996 Summer: Class of 28 students; offers to 28
Partnership: 19% of associates made partner 1980–1986
Pro Bono: 4% of all work is pro bono

Pillsbury Madison & Sutro in 1997
230 Lawyers at the San Francisco Office
1.1 Associates Per Partner

Total Partners 112		
Women	21	19%
All Minorities	7	6%
Afro-Am	2	2%
Asian-Am	4	4%
Native Am	1	1%

Total Associates 118		
Women	57	48%
All Minorities	17	14%
Afro-Am	5	4%
Asian-Am	6	5%
Latino	5	4%
Native Am	1	1%

Practice Areas	
Litigation	78
Corporate Securities	29
Tax/Estate/International	23
Labor/Employee Benefits	21
Banking/Finance	20
Environmental	19
Commercial/Energy	12
Intellectual Property	10
Real Estate	10
Bankruptcy/Creditor's Rights	5

Founded in 1874, Pillsbury Madison & Sutro has grown to be one of the largest law firms in California. The firm now has approximately 550 lawyers in its California, New York, Washington, D.C., Hong Kong, and Tokyo offices. As a prestigious and well-established firm, Pillsbury has the reputation of being "really stuffy and conservative," but people we interviewed considered this view outdated. One person "didn't think it was very liberal or conservative," and another said that "people should give it a chance…it really is progressive."

militaristic culture

Without question, however, Pillsbury is a structured, well-organized firm. One person characterized it as "almost militaristic. You definitely knew where you were in the pecking order. The support staff were your non-commissioned officers, entering associates were lieutenants, and on up to your Brigadier General." Another suggested that "people are just a little scared around the senior managing partner because of who he is," but asserted that there is "generally no discomfort between partners and associates," who often work closely together.

professional atmosphere

Pillsbury has a "down-to-business, professional…and hard-working atmosphere." This firm is not "intensely formal" and the attorneys are "really friendly." Referring to the initial days on the job, one contact reported that "attorneys made a point of coming by and stopping in to see how I was doing. I always felt like I was working with very professional people. Attorneys took the time to stop and explain things to me, but not condescendingly." Pillsbury has a "very relaxed and helpful environment," concurred another. Fridays are designated casual days but, overall, Pillsbury attorneys dress relatively conservatively. Men and women usually wear suits to work, although some younger female attorneys in the environmental and employment groups reportedly wear "conservative pantsuits" on occasion.

changes in practice and management

Pillsbury has recently experienced significant changes in its practice and management. In 1991, the firm merged with the former Los Angeles-based Lillick & McHose, thereby tripling the size of its Los Angeles office. In 1996, Pillsbury merged with Cushman, Darby & Cushman of Washington, D.C., adding almost 100 attorneys thereby to its intellectual property practice, including some "heavy hitters in the patent and trademark areas." In the spring of 1997, there were some "pretty serious defections and resignations," we were told. Fred Alvarez, a member of the firm's executive committee and head of the labor group, left to practice at Wilson Sonsini. In addition, one partner and one senior associate left the corporate securities and technologies group from the Silicon Valley office. According to one insider, "Alvarez's defection probably caused more of a morale problem than the CS&T defections." In the last edition of *The Insider's Guide* we reported that Pillsbury is very concerned that it "has one of the highest revenues before cost and one of the lowest rates of profit in the nation." This appears to still be the state of affairs at Pillsbury.

practice areas

Pillsbury is a large, full-service law firm. One insider remarked that "the firm does just about everything and has experts in almost all fields. Pillsbury has a strong and diverse practice in San Francisco, owing partly to its ability to keep several large clients." The firm's practice is broadly divided into business and litigation departments, each of which includes a number of firmwide practice groups. Some of the more unusual practice groups include alternative dispute resolution, libel/media, and white collar crime. Major clients include Chevron, Bank of America, Pacific Telesis, Air Touch Communications, Wells Fargo and a growing number of Silicon Valley companies.

Pillsbury, we were told, "got in early on environmental and intellectual property" work. Its big antitrust practice enjoys a fine reputation. The firm has an extensive tax department which engages in state, federal, and international tax planning, as well as handling tax litigation. One admirer complimented the tax attorneys as being "personable and professional." After the Lillick merger, Pillsbury targeted the Pacific Rim practice and, according to one source, is "looking for people who speak foreign languages."

pro bono

Pillsbury expects its attorneys to participate in a variety of pro bono and bar association activities. According to firm policy, pro bono hours "are counted for purposes of the associate bonus program and compliance with the firm's billable and non-billable hours for associates." Pillsbury assigns third- and fourth-year litigation associates to four-month rotations with the San Francisco Public Defender's Office. Attorneys also staff local legal clinics and counsel many public interest organizations. The firm has been one of the "biggest providers of pro bono services" to the ACLU in California.

work assigned on a need basis

Summer associates generally are assigned to one of the litigation or business departments, but may seek assignments in the other as well. Two coordinators (one in each department) maintain lists of potential projects. The firm hires entering associates into specific practice groups, but according to one contact, it is "not guaranteed that you will get your preference"—a lot depends on the firm's need at the time. The firm usually does not assign new associates to specific partners within a group. Instead, new associates work with a number of attorneys on a "need basis."

Associate responsibility varies by practice group. First-year associates typically handle research and writing assignments, except in the bankruptcy group where they find themselves in court almost immediately. Litigation associates also reportedly "do not sit in the library a lot;" they get into court early on, though in part this "depends on which group you are in." Labor and antitrust associates, on the other hand, are likely to still be exploring the library in their third year. Of course, young associates can assume more responsibility on pro bono matters.

extensive formal training

Each practice group at Pillsbury holds regular training sessions, and has a coordinator to facilitate associate training. The firm offers "an extensive litigation training program." First-year litigators attend sessions in everything from the filing of a lawsuit to post-trial procedures, and conclude with a full day of mock trial practice conducted in a local courtroom over a weekend. For more senior associates, Pillsbury offers an advanced trial advocacy workshop, based on the National Institute of Trial Advocacy (NITA) program, which includes a full jury trial. The trial "occurs during the summer and summer associates take part in it. It's lots of fun," reported one source. Another source reported that the "training in litigation is good; there is not a lot of hand holding there, but there is a lot of good teaching about how to litigate."

formal feedback

Pillsbury "is not a place for one who needs constant positive reinforcement." Associates generally hear quickly if their work is below Pillsbury's standards. Otherwise, they must wait for their annual evaluations. Summer associates, by contrast, receive more feedback. The firm assigns a "Partner Responsible For (PRF)" to each summer associate. The PRF periodically discusses written performance evaluations with the summer associate. Summer associates also are assigned two "Associates Responsible For (ARFs)". Not part of the evaluation process, the ARFs respond to summer associate concerns and organize informal summer social events.

social life

Pillsbury organizes many social activities, particularly during the summer. These include a party at the zoo, a walking tour of San Francisco, Thursday night cocktail parties, and informal events organized by ARFs. The firm also takes a weekend trip to Lake Tahoe, and hosts a barbecue for attorneys, staff, and their family members. The firm hosts an annual picnic in its beautiful library, when it also holds the yearly chocolate chip cookie baking contest. One person appreciated that the firm "seemed to treat their staff really nicely." Pillsbury displays its employees' art throughout the firm, and often has showings. For example, one summer a stained glass window created by an employee was hung in the library.

many female role models

In comparison to other large San Francisco firms, Pillsbury is above average in its number of minority attorneys. Nevertheless, the firm has fewer minority attorneys than it would like and continues to actively recruit minority law students and participate in minority recruitment fairs. There will be several openly gay summer associates in 1997. We were told, however, that "there is little by way of a support network at the firm for either minorities or gays and lesbians, as exists at other firms in the city." Women are quite successful at Pillsbury. There are several women in management positions at the firm: Debra Zumwalt is on the Executive Committee, and women are office management committee chairs for the San Francisco, Silicon Valley, and San Diego offices. One insider informed us that "while I cannot speak as to benefits, I think the firm is a decent place for women to work. In some groups, at least at the associate levels, women seem to be represented at parity with men." In the recent past, the firm has promoted two part-time female attorneys to part-time partners. Pillsbury also has a broad harassment policy that protects workers from "sexual propositions, foul language, offensive jokes or remarks, obscene gestures or the display of pictures, cartoons, or other materials" that may be considered offensive based on an "individual's sex, race, religion, color, national origin, ancestry, physical or mental disability, medical condition, marital status, age, veteran status, sexual preference or any other legally protected characteristics."

An executive committee, whose members are elected by the partnership for two-year terms, manages the firm. The executive committee makes firm financial information available to both partners and associates. Pillsbury is economically stable, although the San Francisco office has downsized considerably in the last few years. People speculated that, in the future, the firm will focus on developing its international practice, and will continue to work on its efficiency.

painful PC conversion

Pillsbury's offices were described as "perfectly comfortable, functional, and clean," but not "ostentatious or glamorous." The main firm library is "gorgeous," with a "very open feeling," huge windows, graceful spiral staircases, red carpet, comfortable couches, and office supplies everywhere. One person commented that the "library services are like no other I've ever seen." Attorneys have private offices with windows (which open). Pillsbury "still has not joined the PC revolution"—for various reasons, most offices are still using dummy terminals tied to a central VAX mainframe, which are, as we reported in our earlier edition, "slow as molasses." The Silicon Valley office has "migrated" to desktop PCs running Windows, but "there have been so many problems with the conversion" that many in the San Francisco office, which will be the last to convert, are "despairing of getting PCs before 1998. (We had been scheduled to get them by 1996)," reported one contact. A firm spokesperson informed us that the "roll out of PCs in San Francisco is due to commence in June 1997."

personality interviews

Pillsbury hires law students who "tend to excel" and are "likable." The firm also seeks people who are genuinely interested in living in San Francisco. The interview is primarily designed for Pillsbury to "get a feel for your personality." Pillsbury interviews on 22 law school campuses, and hires from many national and California law schools. The firm draws a significant portion of its summer class from Boalt Hall.

Many of the drawbacks of working at Pillsbury, cited by people we interviewed, are typical of large firms, such as "less individualized attention" and a heavy workload. The firm certainly is not the place for a shy person: "you have to be able to motivate yourself." One person remarked, "I did sense a morale problem. A lot of it had to do with administrative control" on billing and cost-cutting. Pillsbury is, however, one of San Francisco's top law firms and has "a national, solid reputation." According to people we interviewed, it "handles a lot of interesting work" and has "more flexibility than other firms in terms of breadth of practice areas." One person commented that it had a "warm atmosphere overall," and another concluded, "I would recommend Pillsbury as large firms go."

Wilson, Sonsini, Goodrich & Rosati

Palo Alto

Address: 650 Page Mill Road, Palo Alto, CA 94304-1050
Telephone: (415) 493–9300
Hiring Attorney: Aileen Arrieta and Mark Bonham (law school); Gail Husick and Ron Shulman (lateral)
Contact: Kelly McHaffie, Esq., Director of Attorney Recruiting; (415) 493–9300
Associate Salary: First year $85,000 (including guaranteed $4,000 bonus) (1997)
Summer Salary: NA
Average Hours: 2277 worked; 2118 billed; NA required
Family Benefits: 10 weeks paid pregnancy leave (16 unpaid); family leave (unpaid)
1996 Summer: Class of 54 students; offers to 54
Partnership: 25% of entering associates from 1979–1985 were made partner
Pro Bono: 3–5% of all work is pro bono

Wilson, Sonsini, Goodrich & Rosati in 1997
374 Lawyers at the Firm
2.9 Associates Per Partner

Total Partners 97		
Women	15	15%
All Minorities	4	4%
Afro-Am	1	1%
Asian-Am	2	2%
Latino	1	1%

Total Associates 277		
Women	92	33%
All Minorities	58	21%
Afro-Am	12	4%
Asian-Am	36	13%
Latino	10	4%

Practice Areas	
Securities	129*
Corporate	72*
Intellectual Property	80
Litigation	64
Employ., Ben., Wills & Trusts	13
Real Estate	9
Tax	7

Wilson, Sonsini, Goodrich & Rosati is the legal powerhouse of Silicon Valley. As one of the first firms to set up shop in this high-tech mecca with the intention of capitalizing on a burgeoning start-up company practice, it has grown from under 30 lawyers in 1980 to around 380 today. Wilson Sonsini attorneys, like many others in Silicon Valley, work long and hard hours, but they "work with relish." They are energized by their exciting high-technology clients and the dreams of entrepreneurs with whom they work. With profits per partner now over $450,000, it is the only Palo Alto-based firm to be among the 30 most profitable law firms in the country.

associates must perform at high levels

Because of the high volume of small clients, junior Wilson Sonsini lawyers have "much more responsibility in terms of business and legal advice" than attorneys at other large firms. One source commented that this is a "culture where people are very independent." The "pace is frenetic." "You get tons of responsibility, deal with clients yourself, meet a lot of different entrepreneurs, and are their counsel. If that energizes you, Wilson is the place. If it scares you, then go elsewhere." It was also observed that "there is a lot of money in Silicon Valley right now. Everyone has a lot of work and partners fight over 'resources' (*i.e.* associates with a heart beat). Everyone here is very self-interested."

egalitarian culture

At Wilson Sonsini, the "emphasis is on getting deals done and on making money for the firm." This is "not the kind of place where you have to be of a certain type" or have to fit into a narrow mold. Though the most well-known partners and rainmakers are "treated very respectfully," Wilson Sonsini is an "easygoing place" and is "pretty egalitarian." The partners are young and friendly, and often "make jokes." Attorneys change into shorts and T-shirts at about 5 or 6 P.M. and usually dress casually on Fridays, or when they don't have client meetings. "Dress casual" attire is becoming very popular year round.

venture capital dynamo firm

As for practice, Wilson Sonsini primarily incorporates high-growth companies, protects their intellectual property, and handles their venture capital financings, their strategic investments, their initial public offerings, and mergers and acquisitions. The firm has grown rapidly as Silicon Valley has matured. It now represents established corporations such as Apple, Hewlett-Packard, Netscape, Sun Microsystems, and Seagate, as well as many investment banks. The corporate practice is organized around practice groups headed by the partners who developed their client bases. Each group provides the full range of corporate services. Larry Sonsini and his group represent many of the larger clients. Known for, among other things, helping Apple become a public company, he is particularly well-regarded for his securities expertise and is a member of the Legal Advisory Committee to the Board of Governors of the New York Stock Exchange.

diversifying litigation practice

The litigation department focuses on commercial, securities, and intellectual property litigation. Although the litigation department includes some very highly regarded lawyers, one contact warned that it is also home to some "abrasive partners," noting that associates in the department "are not as pleased with their work environment as other associates" at the firm. One contact informed us that the passage of the Securities Reform Act "threatens to make life better for Wilson Sonsini clients but worse for its litigators by cutting back on their work. The firm has thus sought to grow other areas of its litigation practice, including intellectual property and employment litigation, acquiring added strength in these areas through lateral hires, including partner Fred Alvarez from Pillsbury, Madison & Sutro."

One of the fastest-growing practices at Wilson Sonsini is the licensing and technology department, according to our sources. Representative clients include Netscape, Disney Interactive, and Pixar. Attorneys in this department negotiate and draft complex licensing agreements. Wilson Sonsini also provides real estate, tax and employment (compensation) and estate planning services to its clients. The firm offers a budding international practice which handles joint ventures and other aspects of international business primarily involving the Pacific Rim and Europe.

pro bono

Although in the past Wilson Sonsini has been "focused on the bottom line," it has recently "reached out to the community." The firm has handled some high-visibility pro bono litigation including prisoners' rights and other civil rights cases. Attorneys also volunteer at a legal aid clinic and the firm makes charitable contributions. The firm has received pro bono awards from the bar associations of San Francisco and the State of California.

free market distribution of work

Wilson Sonsini assigns entering associates to a particular department or group. Though associates work primarily with the attorneys in their group, the firm is "more entrepreneurial than most" and associates "are encouraged to go work with lots of different people." The distribution of work is "not very centralized or coordinated," said one contact. Another source noted that "staffing tends to be chaotic. Partners will walk through the halls looking for 'bodies' to put on deals." Most summer associates choose assignments from a book maintained by the recruiting coordinator, "but summer people are also encouraged to meet people and get their own assignments." The program for summer associates at Wilson Sonsini was described as "a *great* program: wine tasting, a Yosemite trip, rafting, and great high-tech deals. Summer associates do *real* work."

sink or swim professional development

Because Wilson Sonsini represents a range of entrepreneurial clients, first- and second-year corporate associates often serve as the lead attorney for small start-up companies. They have "day-to-day contact with the clients, deal with client questions, and are responsible for figuring out how to do what the start-ups want," one person commented. They also negotiate with venture capital companies, draft licensing agreements, and work on small public offerings. The intellectual property and litigation practices also entrust young associates with a lot of responsibility, asserted one insider. Another person commented that the environment at Wilson Sonsini is "somewhat sink or swim and you have to have an appetite for risk."

Most junior associates must be "aggressive about having questions answered," claimed one person. Another person opined that "junior associates often find themselves unable to get answers for days at a time from the partners responsible for their clients. Especially in the past two years, with Silicon Valley booming, partners have taken on more than they and their associates can properly handle but no one considers limiting their practice." Wilson Sonsini has in place 13-week clinical training programs in both the corporate and litigation departments. In addition, practice groups meet regularly for lunch or departmental meetings. Feedback is also downplayed. "You have to go after it," remarked one contact.

long work hours

Wilson Sonsini associates work long hours. In the last edition of *The Insider's Guide*, we reported that although the associates "love the work" and the clients, some are "not that happy with compensation." We further reported that "there is a feeling among some associates that they work New York hours and get paid San Francisco salaries." It appears that Wilson Sonsini has made efforts to rectify the compensation situation. The firm has raised first-year associate salaries to $85,000, which is comparable to New York law firm starting salaries. It also recently "implemented a bonus structure based on firm profits that is expected to increase associate bonuses 15%," we were told.

limited social life

Wilson Sonsini is "not a particularly social place." Many attorneys have families and "a lot of people go home" after work. The firm does, however, organize a number of social events during the summer and throughout the year. These include a three-day retreat to Pebble Beach, cocktail parties every few weeks during the summer months, and informal events organized by department at the firm. The firm also hosts a Christmas Party, as well as activities to mark the Fourth of July and Halloween.

diversity

Wilson Sonsini is very tolerant and accepting of its attorneys if they are "doing a good job," said one source. The firm employs a substantial number of minority associates and, according to one person, is "very interested in recruiting" more. It also attends minority student job fairs.

an opaque glass ceiling

Though women are "not shut out" at Wilson Sonsini, one contact remarked that the "general attitude is that work is most important. Other things like pro bono or probaby take a back seat." Another insider informed us that "women know that to attempt having a family in their first seven years at the firm is to endanger their partnership chances, their marriages and family, or both." Still another contact remarked that "the glass ceiling is turning more and more opaque at Wilson Sonsini. One partner doles out basketball and hockey tickets solely to male associates and rarely staffs women on his deals. Women are routinely excluded from golfing and drinking events." When asked about harassment, one source stated that Wilson Sonsini is "not a place for someone who is on guard about this sort of thing. It is a very informal atmosphere with joking around. It is a tolerant place. People are themselves."

management struggling with high growth

Wilson Sonsini is governed by a nine partner executive committee chaired by Larry Sonsini, who exercises a lot of influence at the firm. The day-to-day matters are handled by managing partner, Alan Austin, and three professional administrators, an executive director, a chief information officer, and a chief financial officer. One contact observed critically that "the firm would be much more enjoyable if the administrators were more experienced." The major challenge facing the management, according to one person, is to safely shepherd the firm through its "period of change." Another source remarked that presently "management is exhibiting signs of growing pains, including poor planning for space and lack of consistent firm policies. Much of the management seems very ad hoc and shoots from the hip." Wilson Sonsini anticipates growing to about 500 lawyers by the end of 1998, mostly in the corporate and technology transactions departments. Because it is drawing an increasing number of national clients, the firm has been considering opening offices in other cities. In the midst of digesting its past growth and preparing for more in the future, the firm is "having a bit of an identity crisis," asserted one insider, speaking for a large bloc of voices. "They have questions about how they will govern themselves and who their clients are."

hiring tips

As for recruitment, Wilson Sonsini is "drawn to aggressive people" who "are personable and like to deal with other people." The firm seeks "people who aren't afraid of going out and not having their hands held." The "most important characteristics are independence and general amicability," declared one person. People advised applicants who interview with the firm to emphasize their interest in entrepreneurial companies or in the firm's corporate or intellectual property practice, and to demonstrate some knowledge of and commitment to the firm's practice. Callback interviews are generally friendly and informal. One source advised that "they don't like geeks there." The firm draws a significant portion of its summer class from Harvard and Stanford, and the remainder from other top national schools and some local California law schools. In past years, the firm has recruited heavily from Boalt, the University of Chicago, and the University of Virginia.

Wilson Sonsini has been experiencing growth pains, according to those we interviewed. The firm is facing an "enormous space crunch" and first-years are temporarily sharing offices. In response, the firm is presently renovating one building to house fifty attorneys and building another to hold over one hundred attorneys, we were told. People also mentioned that the firm demands a "singularity of focus on work," which can be intimidating, and which causes some, who are "in search of a life outside their work," to choose to go in-house with a client, according to one insider. Most, however, noted that Wilson Sonsini's "breadth of practice in high technology is unparalleled" and observed that the firm offers "exciting business opportunities." Others praised the significant responsibility given to junior associates, including daily client contact with top management including CEO, CFO, and General Counsel level officers. Another insider praised Wilson Sonsini as "the clear market leader in Silicon Valley. We have the most clients, the largest facilities, and the largest summer class. The experience is unbeatable." Another contact declared, "I wouldn't go elsewhere in California for corporate" work."

Washington, D.C.

Law Firms Ranked By Associates Per Partner

1.	CAPLIN & DRYSDALE	0.3
2.	SPIEGEL & MCDIARMID	0.4
3.	FULBRIGHT & JAWORSKI	0.5
4.	BRYAN CAVE	0.6
5.	PATTON & BOGGS	0.7
6.	MILLER & CHEVALIER	0.8
7.	SHEA & GARDNER	0.8
8.	VERNER, LIIPFERT, BERNHARD, MCPHERSON AND HAND	0.8
9.	ARENT, FOX, KINTNER, PLOTKIN & KAHN	0.9
10.	BRACEWELL & PATTERSON	0.9
11.	POWELL, GOLDSTEIN, FRAZER & MURPHY	0.9
12.	SHAW, PITTMAN, POTTS & TROWBRIDGE	0.9
13.	STEPTOE & JOHNSON	0.9
14.	VENABLE, BAETJER, HOWARD & CIVILETTI	0.9
15.	ARNOLD & PORTER	1.0
16.	BAKER & MCKENZIE	1.0
17.	DOW, LOHNES & ALBERTSON	1.0
18.	HOGAN & HARTSON	1.0
19.	KIRKLAND & ELLIS	1.0
20.	PIPER & MARBURY	1.0
21.	SIDLEY & AUSTIN	1.1
22.	WILLIAMS & CONNOLLY	1.1
23.	HUNTON & WILLIAMS	1.2
24.	JENNER & BLOCK	1.2
25.	DICKSTEIN, SHAPIRO, MORIN & OSHINSKY	1.3
26.	AKIN, GUMP, STRAUSS, HAUER & FELD	1.4
27.	COLLIER, SHANNON, RILL & SCOTT	1.4
28.	COVINGTON & BURLING	1.4
29.	FOLEY & LARDNER	1.4
30.	VINSON & ELKINS	1.4
31.	WILMER, CUTLER & PICKERING	1.4
32.	CROWELL & MORING	1.5
33.	GIBSON, DUNN & CRUTCHER	1.5
34.	HOWREY & SIMON	1.5
35.	MORRISON & FOERSTER	1.6
36.	WEIL, GOTSHAL & MANGES	1.6
37.	FRIED, FRANK, HARRIS, SHRIVER & JACOBSON	1.8
38.	JONES, DAY, REAVIS & POGUE	1.8
39.	WINTHROP, STIMSON, PUTNAM & ROBERTS	2.0
40.	PAUL, HASTINGS, JANOFSKY & WALKER	2.1
41.	CHADBOURNE & PARKE	2.2
42.	SWIDLER & BERLIN	2.2
43.	SKADDEN, ARPS, SLATE, MEAGHER & FLOM	2.3

Law Firms Ranked by Percentage of Associates Who Make Partner
(over varying years)

1.	BAKER & MCKENZIE	60
2.	ARENT, FOX, KINTNER, PLOTKIN & KAHN	39
3.	HUNTON & WILLIAMS	39
4.	BRYAN CAVE	38
5.	WILLIAMS & CONNOLLY	38
6.	BRACEWELL & PATTERSON	36
7.	KIRKLAND & ELLIS	36
8.	POWELL, GOLDSTEIN, FRAZER & MURPHY	35
9.	FULBRIGHT & JAWORSKI	33
10.	MORRISON & FOERSTER	31
11.	VINSON & ELKINS	31
12.	PATTON & BOGGS	27
13.	SHAW, PITTMAN, POTTS & TROWBRIDGE	25
14.	SHEA & GARDNER	25
15.	VENABLE, BAETJER, HOWARD & CIVILETTI	25
16.	HOWREY & SIMON	24
17.	MILLER & CHEVALIER	23
18.	AKIN, GUMP, STRAUSS, HAUER & FELD	22
19.	FRIED, FRANK, HARRIS, SHRIVER & JACOBSON	20
20.	HOGAN & HARTSON	20
21.	WILMER, CUTLER & PICKERING	17
22.	ARNOLD & PORTER	16
23.	GIBSON, DUNN & CRUTCHER	15
24.	STEPTOE & JOHNSON	14
25.	COVINGTON & BURLING	12
26.	CROWELL & MORING	9.3
27.	CAPLIN & DRYSDALE	NA
28.	CHADBOURNE & PARKE	NA
29.	COLLIER, SHANNON, RILL & SCOTT	NA
30.	DICKSTEIN, SHAPIRO, MORIN & OSHINSKY	NA
31.	DOW, LOHNES & ALBERTSON	NA
32.	FOLEY & LARDNER	NA
33.	JENNER & BLOCK	NA
34.	JONES, DAY, REAVIS & POGUE	NA
35.	PAUL, HASTINGS, JANOFSKY & WALKER	NA
36.	PIPER & MARBURY	NA
37.	SIDLEY & AUSTIN	NA
38.	SKADDEN, ARPS, SLATE, MEAGHER & FLOM	NA
39.	SPIEGEL & MCDIARMID	NA
40.	SWIDLER & BERLIN	NA
41.	VERNER, LIIPFERT, BERNHARD, MCPHERSON AND HAND	NA
42.	WEIL, GOTSHAL & MANGES	NA
43.	WINTHROP, STIMSON, PUTNAM & ROBERTS	NA

Law Firms Ranked by Percentage of Pro Bono Work

1.	ARENT, FOX, KINTNER, PLOTKIN & KAHN	10
2.	WINTHROP, STIMSON, PUTNAM & ROBERTS	8-10
3.	JENNER & BLOCK	8
4.	COVINGTON & BURLING	7-9
5.	SHAW, PITTMAN, POTTS & TROWBRIDGE	7-8
6.	WILMER, CUTLER & PICKERING	6.5
7.	ARNOLD & PORTER	5-7
8.	SHEA & GARDNER	5-10
9.	HOWREY & SIMON	5
10.	STEPTOE & JOHNSON	5
11.	PATTON & BOGGS	4.6
12.	CROWELL & MORING	4
13.	AKIN, GUMP, STRAUSS, HAUER & FELD	3-5
14.	PIPER & MARBURY	3-5
15.	POWELL, GOLDSTEIN, FRAZER & MURPHY	3-5
16.	VENABLE, BAETJER, HOWARD & CIVILETTI	3-5
17.	VERNER, LIIPFERT, BERNHARD, MCPHERSON AND HAND	3-5
18.	WEIL, GOTSHAL & MANGES	3-5
19.	SPIEGEL & MCDIARMID	3-4
20.	FRIED, FRANK, HARRIS, SHRIVER & JACOBSON	3
21.	GIBSON, DUNN & CRUTCHER	3
22.	JONES, DAY, REAVIS & POGUE	3
23.	PAUL, HASTINGS, JANOFSKY & WALKER	3
24.	KIRKLAND & ELLIS	2-4
25.	DICKSTEIN, SHAPIRO, MORIN & OSHINSKY	2
26.	DOW, LOHNES & ALBERTSON	2
27.	MILLER & CHEVALIER	2
28.	SWIDLER & BERLIN	1.5
29.	CHADBOURNE & PARKE	1.3
30.	FULBRIGHT & JAWORSKI	1-3
31.	SIDLEY & AUSTIN	1-3
32.	VINSON & ELKINS	0.8
33.	BAKER & MCKENZIE	NA
34.	BRACEWELL & PATTERSON	NA
35.	BRYAN CAVE	NA
36.	CAPLIN & DRYSDALE	NA
37.	COLLIER, SHANNON, RILL & SCOTT	NA
38.	FOLEY & LARDNER	NA
39.	HOGAN & HARTSON	NA
40.	HUNTON & WILLIAMS	NA
41.	MORRISON & FOERSTER	NA
42.	SKADDEN, ARPS, SLATE, MEAGHER & FLOM	NA
43.	WILLIAMS & CONNOLLY	NA

Law Firms Ranked by Percentage of Female Partners

1.	SPIEGEL & MCDIARMID	29
2.	MORRISON & FOERSTER	27
3.	MILLER & CHEVALIER	22
4.	BRACEWELL & PATTERSON	21
5.	POWELL, GOLDSTEIN, FRAZER & MURPHY	20
6.	SKADDEN, ARPS, SLATE, MEAGHER & FLOM	20
7.	JONES, DAY, REAVIS & POGUE	19
8.	ARNOLD & PORTER	18
9.	SHAW, PITTMAN, POTTS & TROWBRIDGE	18
10.	SHEA & GARDNER	18
11.	DOW, LOHNES & ALBERTSON	16
12.	FOLEY & LARDNER	16
13.	SWIDLER & BERLIN	16
14.	ARENT, FOX, KINTNER, PLOTKIN & KAHN	15
15.	BRYAN CAVE	15
16.	CHADBOURNE & PARKE	15
17.	HOWREY & SIMON	15
18.	COLLIER, SHANNON, RILL & SCOTT	14
19.	KIRKLAND & ELLIS	14
20.	PIPER & MARBURY	14
21.	STEPTOE & JOHNSON	14
22.	WEIL, GOTSHAL & MANGES	14
23.	WINTHROP, STIMSON, PUTNAM & ROBERTS	14
24.	AKIN, GUMP, STRAUSS, HAUER & FELD	13
25.	CROWELL & MORING	13
26.	FRIED, FRANK, HARRIS, SHRIVER & JACOBSON	13
27.	VERNER, LIIPFERT, BERNHARD, MCPHERSON AND HAND	13
28.	WILMER, CUTLER & PICKERING	13
29.	COVINGTON & BURLING	12
30.	JENNER & BLOCK	12
31.	WILLIAMS & CONNOLLY	12
32.	DICKSTEIN, SHAPIRO, MORIN & OSHINSKY	11
33.	HUNTON & WILLIAMS	11
34.	VINSON & ELKINS	11
35.	VENABLE, BAETJER, HOWARD & CIVILETTI	10
36.	CAPLIN & DRYSDALE	9
37.	SIDLEY & AUSTIN	9
38.	BAKER & MCKENZIE	8
39.	PATTON & BOGGS	8
40.	GIBSON, DUNN & CRUTCHER	6
41.	PAUL, HASTINGS, JANOFSKY & WALKER	6
42.	FULBRIGHT & JAWORSKI	5
43.	HOGAN & HARTSON	NA

Law Firms Ranked by Percentage of Female Associates

1.	PIPER & MARBURY	58
2.	CHADBOURNE & PARKE	52
3.	VERNER, LIIPFERT, BERNHARD, MCPHERSON AND HAND	50
4.	MILLER & CHEVALIER	47
5.	BAKER & MCKENZIE	46
6.	HUNTON & WILLIAMS	46
7.	POWELL, GOLDSTEIN, FRAZER & MURPHY	46
8.	DOW, LOHNES & ALBERTSON	44
9.	ARENT, FOX, KINTNER, PLOTKIN & KAHN	43
10.	CROWELL & MORING	42
11.	SHEA & GARDNER	42
12.	STEPTOE & JOHNSON	42
13.	AKIN, GUMP, STRAUSS, HAUER & FELD	41
14.	BRYAN CAVE	40
15.	COVINGTON & BURLING	40
16.	SIDLEY & AUSTIN	40
17.	FRIED, FRANK, HARRIS, SHRIVER & JACOBSON	39
18.	JONES, DAY, REAVIS & POGUE	39
19.	SWIDLER & BERLIN	39
20.	WEIL, GOTSHAL & MANGES	39
21.	BRACEWELL & PATTERSON	38
22.	COLLIER, SHANNON, RILL & SCOTT	38
23.	DICKSTEIN, SHAPIRO, MORIN & OSHINSKY	38
24.	FULBRIGHT & JAWORSKI	38
25.	MORRISON & FOERSTER	38
26.	WILMER, CUTLER & PICKERING	38
27.	ARNOLD & PORTER	37
28.	GIBSON, DUNN & CRUTCHER	37
29.	JENNER & BLOCK	37
30.	SHAW, PITTMAN, POTTS & TROWBRIDGE	37
31.	VENABLE, BAETJER, HOWARD & CIVILETTI	36
32.	PATTON & BOGGS	33
33.	PAUL, HASTINGS, JANOFSKY & WALKER	33
34.	WILLIAMS & CONNOLLY	33
35.	FOLEY & LARDNER	32
36.	CAPLIN & DRYSDALE	30
37.	HOWREY & SIMON	30
38.	VINSON & ELKINS	29
39.	SPIEGEL & MCDIARMID	28
40.	KIRKLAND & ELLIS	27
41.	WINTHROP, STIMSON, PUTNAM & ROBERTS	7
42.	HOGAN & HARTSON	NA
43.	SKADDEN, ARPS, SLATE, MEAGHER & FLOM	NA

Law Firms Ranked by Percentage of Minority Partners

1.	BRACEWELL & PATTERSON	7
2.	AKIN, GUMP, STRAUSS, HAUER & FELD	6
3.	COVINGTON & BURLING	6
4.	PAUL, HASTINGS, JANOFSKY & WALKER	6
5.	SPIEGEL & MCDIARMID	6
6.	VERNER, LIIPFERT, BERNHARD, MCPHERSON AND HAND	6
7.	HOWREY & SIMON	5
8.	HUNTON & WILLIAMS	5
9.	PIPER & MARBURY	5
10.	SIDLEY & AUSTIN	5
11.	WILMER, CUTLER & PICKERING	5
12.	ARNOLD & PORTER	4
13.	DOW, LOHNES & ALBERTSON	4
14.	SHAW, PITTMAN, POTTS & TROWBRIDGE	4
15.	SWIDLER & BERLIN	4
16.	CAPLIN & DRYSDALE	3
17.	CROWELL & MORING	3
18.	FOLEY & LARDNER	3
19.	GIBSON, DUNN & CRUTCHER	3
20.	POWELL, GOLDSTEIN, FRAZER & MURPHY	3
21.	SKADDEN, ARPS, SLATE, MEAGHER & FLOM	3
22.	WILLIAMS & CONNOLLY	3
23.	ARENT, FOX, KINTNER, PLOTKIN & KAHN	2
24.	FULBRIGHT & JAWORSKI	2
25.	JONES, DAY, REAVIS & POGUE	2
26.	KIRKLAND & ELLIS	2
27.	PATTON & BOGGS	2
28.	STEPTOE & JOHNSON	2
29.	VENABLE, BAETJER, HOWARD & CIVILETTI	2
30.	DICKSTEIN, SHAPIRO, MORIN & OSHINSKY	1
31.	BAKER & MCKENZIE	0
32.	BRYAN CAVE	0
33.	CHADBOURNE & PARKE	0
34.	COLLIER, SHANNON, RILL & SCOTT	0
35.	FRIED, FRANK, HARRIS, SHRIVER & JACOBSON	0
36.	JENNER & BLOCK	0
37.	MILLER & CHEVALIER	0
38.	MORRISON & FOERSTER	0
39.	SHEA & GARDNER	0
40.	VINSON & ELKINS	0
41.	WEIL, GOTSHAL & MANGES	0
42.	WINTHROP, STIMSON, PUTNAM & ROBERTS	0
43.	HOGAN & HARTSON	NA

Law Firms Ranked By Percentage of Minority Associates

1.	PATTON & BOGGS	23
2.	BAKER & MCKENZIE	21
3.	DOW, LOHNES & ALBERTSON	21
4.	MORRISON & FOERSTER	21
5.	SHAW, PITTMAN, POTTS & TROWBRIDGE	20
6.	SKADDEN, ARPS, SLATE, MEAGHER & FLOM	20
7.	FULBRIGHT & JAWORSKI	19
8.	MILLER & CHEVALIER	16
9.	WILMER, CUTLER & PICKERING	16
10.	FOLEY & LARDNER	15
11.	CHADBOURNE & PARKE	14
12.	PAUL, HASTINGS, JANOFSKY & WALKER	14
13.	WILLIAMS & CONNOLLY	14
14.	WINTHROP, STIMSON, PUTNAM & ROBERTS	14
15.	AKIN, GUMP, STRAUSS, HAUER & FELD	13
16.	GIBSON, DUNN & CRUTCHER	13
17.	CROWELL & MORING	12
18.	STEPTOE & JOHNSON	12
19.	VERNER, LIIPFERT, BERNHARD, MCPHERSON AND HAND	12
20.	ARENT, FOX, KINTNER, PLOTKIN & KAHN	11
21.	HOWREY & SIMON	11
22.	JONES, DAY, REAVIS & POGUE	11
23.	SIDLEY & AUSTIN	11
24.	VINSON & ELKINS	11
25.	BRYAN CAVE	10
26.	CAPLIN & DRYSDALE	10
27.	JENNER & BLOCK	10
28.	KIRKLAND & ELLIS	10
29.	SHEA & GARDNER	10
30.	COVINGTON & BURLING	9
31.	DICKSTEIN, SHAPIRO, MORIN & OSHINSKY	9
32.	HUNTON & WILLIAMS	9
33.	SWIDLER & BERLIN	9
34.	BRACEWELL & PATTERSON	8
35.	COLLIER, SHANNON, RILL & SCOTT	8
36.	PIPER & MARBURY	8
37.	VENABLE, BAETJER, HOWARD & CIVILETTI	8
38.	FRIED, FRANK, HARRIS, SHRIVER & JACOBSON	7
39.	ARNOLD & PORTER	6
40.	POWELL, GOLDSTEIN, FRAZER & MURPHY	4
41.	WEIL, GOTSHAL & MANGES	4
42.	HOGAN & HARTSON	NA
43.	SPIEGEL & MCDIARMID	NA

Akin, Gump, Strauss, Hauer & Feld

Washington Austin Dallas Houston New York Philadelphia San Antonio
Brussels Moscow

Address: 1333 New Hampshire Avenue, N.W., Suite 400, Washington, D.C. 20036
Telephone: (202) 887–4000
Hiring Attorney: Dennis M. Race
Contact: Mary G. Beal, Recruitment Administrator; (202) 887–4181
Associate Salary: First year $74,000 (1997); second $79,000; third $84,000; fourth $90,000
Summer Salary: $1300/week (1997)
Average Hours: 2050 worked; 1875 billed; NA required
Family Benefits: Health, dental, life insurance; disability plan; 401(k) plan; emergency child-care; flexible benefits; maternity leave; D.C. bar dues and license fee; vacation; employee assistance program
1996 Summer: Class of 38 students; offers to 34
Partnership: 22% of entering associates from 1981–1984 were made partner
Pro Bono: 3–5% of all work is pro bono

Akin, Gump, Strauss, Hauer & Feld in 1997
254 Lawyers at the Washington D.C. Office
1.4 Associates Per Partner

Total Partners 106		
Women	14	13%
All Minorities	6	6%
Afro-Am	3	3%
Asian-Am	1	1%
Latino	2	2%

Total Associates 148		
Women	61	41%
All Minorities	19	13%
Afro-Am	6	4%
Asian-Am	8	6%
Latino	5	3%

Practice Areas	
Litigation	74
Labor (management)	44
Public Law & Politics	26
International	22
Corporate	15
Energy	11
Food & Drug	10
General	9
Real Estate	9
Tax	9
Environmental	8
Health	8
Communications	5
Bankruptcy	4

Akin, Gump, Strauss, Hauer & Feld was founded in Dallas, Texas in 1945, and some aspects of the firm's southern culture influence the Washington D.C. office. One source said that the D.C. office is like a "big, happy family." Others also described the work atmosphere as friendly and comfortable. Most partners have an open door policy and are good mentors to junior associates. It is a casual and laid-back place: one partner takes a break by playing one-on-one nerf basketball with associates while another challenges applicants to putting contests. With over 250 lawyers, the Washington office is the largest of the firm's nine offices. All the offices have been strategically integrated over the past several years to create the 12th largest firm in the nation. New offices in London and Los Angeles will open in 1997.

well-connected legislative practice

Akin Gump's lawyers are well-connected in both major political parties, and many of them previously worked in the government. The firm's big name partners include the firm's founder Robert Strauss, former chair of the Democratic National Committee and Ambassador to Russia; Vernon Jordan, former President of the National Urban League, and "a major player in Democratic politics;" Tom Foley, former Speaker of the House of Representatives; Dan Spiegel, former Ambassador to the European Office of the United Nations; Don Alexander, former Commissioner of the Internal Revenue Service; Jim Cicconi, former special assistant to both Reagan and Bush; and Joel Jankowsky, who heads the legislative practice.

The firm's legislative group is one of the largest in the country, handling a full range of legislative and lobbying matters. Since the firm makes offers for specific departments, one person cautioned that it is very difficult to be hired into the legislative group. This caution is important to note since a firm spokesperson stated that the legislative section hires only one first-year associate per year. However, many other sections of the firm work with the legislative group on projects, so there is an opportunity to work on legislative matters.

other practice areas

Although Akin Gump D.C. may be most famous for its legislative work, it is a "full-service" firm and has large litigation, labor and international practices as well as other specialty groups. Litigation, the firm's largest department, includes a broad range of subgroups from toxic tort to antitrust. The white-collar defense practice has been of particular interest since its recent high profile settlement for Volkswagen. The firm's labor practice group primarily represents management interests and recently won a landmark case for Food Lion against ABC's *Primetime Live* show. The corporate section handles some international transactional work. For example, the firm represented LuKOil, a Russian oil company, in the first transaction in which a Russian company raised funds in Western capital markets.

The international trade group has won a number of well-published cases, and, according to one person, it is "gaining in prestige." The group represents mostly foreign clients, particularly those from Central Asia and the Pacific Rim, and represents some prominent Korean clients. It also does work in Europe, Mexico, and other parts of Latin America. While the transactional side of the international work is growing the most quickly, much of the group's work involves anti-dumping and countervailing duty cases as well as other trade regulatory work; trade policy is also an important part of the practice.

training program

Akin Gump considers its formal training program to be among the best in the country. The firm received high marks for its "outstanding" six-week summer associate training program on discovery, service of motions, depositions, trial preparation, and client negotiations. The program culminates in a mock trial using partners as judges. Akin Gump also provides in-house continuing legal education programs for lawyers and hires outside consultants for further training.

pro bono

Akin Gump's pro bono practice is coordinated by one of the firm's senior litigators and a Pro Bono Committee comprised of partners and associates. The firm's pro bono matters are listed in a weekly memo, and attorneys also may pursue their own interests. Pro bono hours are credited toward billable hours. In 1996, 22 out of 38 summer associates worked on a total of 32 pro bono projects.

Akin Gump provides a vibrant social atmosphere. A large number of young associates lead active social lives. Although the firm sponsors social events such as a holiday party, a formal attorney dinner-dance, section dinners, monthly associate breakfasts, monthly happy hours, and a family picnic, the social life is generally unstructured. The firm sponsors co-ed softball and touch football teams each year, and many people participate in an annual golf tournament as well as in an area lawyer's 10K run.

increased emphasis on billables

The workload is not considered overly demanding, "although there does seem to be a trend toward increased billable hours," reported one insider. The firm recently amended its business plan to "include a target of 2100 billable/pro bono hours per associate," one insider reported. A firm spokesperson informed us that "while there is no minimum or billable hours requirement, associates who bill 2000 or more (including pro bono hours) receive a year-end bonus. Those associates who bill over 2100 hours are eligible for an additional merit bonus." Additionally, we were told that the associate salary structure was recently reformulated, ensuring that the lock-step compensation system is "competitive with other D.C. firms."

progressive on diversity

Akin Gump D.C. is progressive in its treatment of women and minorities. One person commented that Akin Gump is as "racially and gender diverse" as any firm he had been to in D.C. Vernon Jordan, one of the firm's most influential partners and a prominent African-American, has made major contributions towards promoting racial diversity both at Akin Gump and in Washington, D.C. In 1997, nine of the firm's 37 summer associates are African American. In addition, the 1996 and 1997 summer associates classes had more women than men. Thirteen percent of the partners and 41 percent of the associates are women. The firm is fairly flexible in allowing attorneys to schedule their own working hours. For example, the firm reportedly has been very accommodating to several attorneys, both male and female who desired part-time schedules.

management

Akin Gump's management received mixed reviews. Although one person commented that the firm's management committee was "pretty open" about its decisions and receptive to new ideas, another felt that it was "a bit disingenuous" in dealing with issues of advancement at the firm and noted that feedback on individual advancement is not very good. In addition, one insider noted that "mid- and upper-level associate salaries significantly lag behind other prominent D.C. firms." The firm formally evaluates all associates in the fall and conducts an additional spring evaluation for senior associates to discuss partnership potential. An elected firmwide management committee makes firmwide decisions, while each office has its own operating committee made up of partners. An associates committee, elected by the associates, provides a formal vehicle for communication with the partners. In addition, the firm's chairman regularly meets with the associates to keep them apprised of the firm's strategic plans and progress.

unsightly offices

Akin Gump's offices are conveniently located in Dupont Circle, easily accessible by public transportation and offering many shops, restaurants and museums. Many attorneys jog at lunch on the paths through nearby Rock Creek Park. Parking is available in the building. By the standards of most large firms, Akin Gump's offices "leave something to be desired," we were told. "The elevators do not always function properly, wall paper is peeling off the walls, and the firm has been known to repair carpeting with a strip of unsightly duct tape," according to one insider. The firm's lease expires in 1999; until then, "significant capital expenditures are unlikely." The firm informed us that it is "currently addressing options for its future space requirements...should the firm remain in the current building, massive renovations (including a takeover of the entire building) are planned." The firm's support staff was also subject to criticism, and the library is said to "lack certain key texts" crucial for research purposes. The library does, however, contain a separate legislative history section with specially trained research assistants "which is greatly appreciated." The office contains a small gym available to attorneys, "though it is rarely used due to the outdated nature of its equipment."

interview tips

Callback interviews at Akin Gump are casual and relaxed. Most interviewers ask candidates why they want to practice in D.C., which practice area they are interested in, and whether they have any background in that area. In its hiring decisions, Akin Gump reportedly emphasizes personality almost as much as grades and writing skills. Although the firm hires most of its associates from the top ranked national law schools, it also hires students from many other qualified law schools across the country. Akin Gump places a premium on writing skills. It requests and carefully evaluates a writing sample before making a hiring decision.

Arent, Fox, Kintner, Plotkin & Kahn

Washington New York
Budapest Jeddah

Address: 1050 Connecticut Avenue, N.W., Washington, D.C. 20036-5339; (www.arentfox.com)
Telephone: (202) 857–6000
Hiring Attorney: Richard L. Brand
Contact: Colleen Mattingly, Recruitment Coordinator; (202) 857–6443
Associate Salary: First year $75,000 (1997)
Summer Salary: $1300/week (1997)
Average Hours: 1700–2200 worked; 1600–2100 billed; 1900 required
Family Benefits: Family and medical leave of absence; emergency day care
1996 Summer: Class of 12 students; offers to 11
Partnership: 39% of entering associates from 1980–1985 were made partner
Pro Bono: 10% of all work is pro bono

Arent, Fox, Kintner, Plotkin & Kahn in 1997
191 Lawyers at the Washington D.C. Office
0.9 Associates Per Partner

Total Partners 98			Total Associates 90			Practice Areas	
Women	15	15%	Women	39	43%	General Business	56
All Minorities	2	2%	All Minorities	10	11%	Federal Practice	46
Afro-Am	2	2%	Afro-Am	4	4%	Litigation	41
			Asian-Am	3	3%	Employment/ERISA/Health	32
			Latino	3	3%	International	28

Arent, Fox, Kinter, Plotkin & Kahn cares about its image. The firm's main office is located in a "super modern" building, which also houses Morton's Steak House, which attracts "a lot of big names." The offices are set in "dusty rose and sea foam green;" one person suggested that they project a "Miami Vice-like atmosphere." Arent Fox boasts an impressive art collection, including a Warhol signed print series and an original Rodin sculpture. Summer associates are given a special guided tour of the collection, followed by a wine and cheese reception.

diverse practice

Arent Fox's practice is quite diverse. Originally a local firm, Arent Fox now maintains a mix of local and national clients but continues to have a high profile in the D.C. community. One source estimated that about half of the firm's practice involves the representation of local D.C. clients. The largest practices are corporate, litigation, and international. Arent Fox also has a broad federal regulatory practice, which houses a number of specialties such as communications, intellectual property, environmental, products safety, and food and drug, among others. Many of its attorneys formerly worked in the government, where they helped write the regulations about which they now advise their clients. The firm's government contracts department handles many defense contract matters and "local construction matters." The international practice involves both regulatory and transactional work for foreign clients; the transactional attorneys travel frequently. The litigation department, which handles a lot of tort cases among other matters, offers a unique plaintiff's practice, which one person estimated to constitute about one-quarter of the firm's litigation work. The litigation department reportedly is the hardest-working group at the firm, but one person said that the quality of its lawyers is "spotty." Other sources indicated that the litigators evince a distinct "attitude," describing them as "cool and distant" but with "esprit de corps." Finally, like many D.C. firms, Arent Fox's real estate practice has picked up after having been slow in the early 1990s. One contact informed us that Arent Fox is "growing rapidly in a number of 'hot' areas, such as healthcare and intellectual property," as well as in international project finance.

award-winning pro bono

Arent Fox's pro bono activities are organized by a pro bono committee, which is coordinated by partners. People stated that the practice is "excellent." Associates may do a rotation on the four-attorney pro bono committee, during which time they spend about one-third of their time doing pro bono work. The firm annually recognizes the lawyer who has done the most significant pro bono work for the year. Arent Fox handles human rights matters, both in D.C. and internationally. Attorneys at the firm work closely with the Washington Lawyers Committee for Civil Rights and the Legal Aid Society, as well as with the Holocaust Museum and the Whitman Walker Clinic, from all of whom the firm has received awards for its activities.

top-notch training program

The level of responsibility given to associates at Arent Fox is "tremendous," reported one insider. "Second- and third-year associates negotiate deals directly with opposing counsel, and even first-year associates have significant client contact. Almost every transaction is staffed with just one partner and one associate. This gives associates more substantive experience." Additionally, the firm reportedly places a "strong emphasis on training." There are numerous in-house CLE programs and "there is a 'training number' whereby partners can write off time if they wish to take an associate to a meeting, deposition, etc. for which the client is unwilling to pay." Arent Fox recently won an award for the top training program among D.C.-based firms, we were told.

lack of organization

People we interviewed had mixed views regarding the firm's organizational structure and management style. Although Arent Fox's executive committee is reportedly open to associate ideas and up-front about its decisions, some people complained that the firm's lack of organization is a major drawback. At times, the firm reportedly borders on being "anarchical," with little communication among departments and "some interdepartmental rivalry, fired by bitter rivalries among certain partners." The lack of communication has been a source of tension at the firm. One contact reported, however, that "communication and organization have improved" under Bill Charyk as managing partner. An additional source of fragmentation at Arent Fox relates to the high turnover the firm has experienced in recent years. One contact pointed out that "with the rapid turnover I now know only two or three people in my 'associate row;' everyone else is new or visiting."

salary partnership complaints

Associate compensation and partnership prospects also got mixed reviews from our sources. One insider claimed that, after a few years, Arent Fox's salaries lag behind those of other large D.C. firms. Another contact informed us, however, that "associate salaries were given a 'market adjustment' in 1996 to ensure that they were in line with other large firms." Although people commented that the firm is very up-front about each attorney's partnership prospects, some noted that the firm has been delaying "most partnership decisions beyond the seventh year and many beyond the eighth year." One person informed us that "the firm is top-heavy. There are many partners who are not bringing in business but are allowed to remain in the partnership. This is making it increasingly harder for associates to be promoted to partner."

diversity

Arent Fox reportedly is "politically correct" and received generally positive reviews for its treatment of women in the workplace. One person pointed out that because many of the firm's lawyers draft sexual harassment policies for corporate clients, Arent Fox is very aware of and responsive to these issues. The firm has a part-time work policy, although one person commented that it is better "in theory than in practice." Another observed that many female associates who had children were on the "of counsel track." The firm is also "well known in Washington as a friendly atmosphere for gay attorneys," we were told. Even though the firm employs a number of minority attorneys, Arent Fox reputedly "does better" with respect to "women than minorities." The firm states that it has a strong commitment to diversity, and its 1997 summer class of 17 contains three minority members.

hiring tips Arent Fox is not traditionally among the most prestigious D.C. firms, but it still is very difficult to land a summer associate position at the firm. People we interviewed noted that although the firm requires a high minimum standard of academic performance, it emphasizes personality over grades in making its hiring decisions. In past summers, Arent Fox has hired approximately half of its summer classes from the top 10 national law schools and the remainder from a variety of D.C. and other schools. The firm hires many people with interesting backgrounds and unusual talents. One person noted that the firm's lawyers also look for "commitment" and advised applicants that "any way you can demonstrate your commitment to the law or to the firm would be in your favor." The callback interviews are informal and unstructured.

Arnold & Porter

Washington Denver Los Angeles New York
Budapest Istanbul London

Address: 555 12th Street, N.W., Washington, D.C. 20004
Telephone: (202) 942-5000
Hiring Attorney: Claire E. Reade
Contact: (Ms.) Taylor C. Kell, Attorney Recruitment Manager; (202) 942-5059
Associate Salary: First year $74,000 (1997)
Summer Salary: $1300/week (1997)
Average Hours: 2300 worked; 1850 billed; NA required
Family Benefits: 12 weeks paid maternity leave (12 unpaid); 6 weeks paid paternity leave (12 unpaid); full-time, on-site childcare center and free backup childcare
1996 Summer: Class of 42 students; offers to 42
Partnership: 16% of entering associates from 1983–1988 were made partner
Pro Bono: 5–7% of all work is pro bono

Arnold & Porter in 1997
274 Lawyers at the Washington D.C. Office
1.0 Associate Per Partner

Total Partners 140		
Women	25	18%
All Minorities	5	4%
Afro-Am	3	2%
Asian Am	2	1%

Total Associates 134		
Women	49	37%
All Minorities	8	6%
Afro-Am	2	1%
Asian-Am	5	4%
Latino	1	1%

Practice Areas	
Litigation/Product Liability	85
Corporate	37
Antitrust	31
Tax/Employee Benefits	22
Government Contracts	17
Real Estate	15
Banking	13
Environmental	11
Communications	10
Legislative	10
Food & Drug	9
International	9
Intellectual Property	8
Bankruptcy	4
Public Policy	2

makes history

With a virtually unparalleled history of involvement in some of the most important cases of our time, Arnold & Porter is one of the most prestigious firms in Washington, D.C. It was founded shortly after World War II by Thurman Arnold, Abe Fortas, who later became a Supreme Court Justice, and Paul Porter, all of whom served in President Roosevelt's Administration where they played significant roles in drafting New Deal legislation. Many of Arnold & Porter's attorneys believe that "at any moment the firm could make history again." Throughout its history, Arnold & Porter has handled high-profile constitutional cases. It argued *Gideon v. Wainwright* before the Supreme Court. During the McCarthy period of the 1950s, it was on the forefront of defending academics and government officials. More recently, it defended Roger Coleman against the death penalty.

practice areas

Arnold & Porter is a full-service law firm with a broad range of practice areas. Its most noteworthy departments include antitrust, banking, corporate and securities, international, litigation, and legislative law. Litigation, the firm's largest practice area, reportedly rose to prominence by handling "groundbreaking, cutting-edge litigation." Most of the firm's litigation involves representing large institutional clients such as the Red Cross and Xerox. The firm also represents Phillip Morris in tobacco-related cases, but attorneys may elect to refuse these matters. Major corporate and securities matters are an important part of the firm's practice. Arnold & Porter obtained a court decision for The Business Roundtable invalidating the SEC "one share, one vote" rule and finding that the SEC had no authority to regulate corporate governance. Arnold & Porter also "made its name" in the field of antitrust and has been counsel in many landmark antitrust cases throughout its history. Arnold & Porter's international practice includes an office in London and a sister office in Istanbul. This practice consists of international trade work, countervailing duties litigation, and international arbitration. In addition, many of its lawyers handle international pro bono matters, such as election supervision in Nicaragua and elsewhere. Arnold & Porter also has an active "foreign attorney program" through which the firm "takes on foreign attorneys for one-half to three-quarter year stints."

model pro bono

Arnold & Porter's pro bono program has served as a "model" for law firms across the country. One insider asserted that the firm has "one of the top five pro bono practices in the country" and commented that pro bono work is a "real matter of pride" for Arnold & Porter attorneys. Another said that they believe that "no one has an excuse for not doing it." The firm handles a wide variety of pro bono cases, many of which it receives from the Lawyers Committee for Civil Rights. People also described Arnold & Porter as a big "anti-death penalty" firm.

not a firm for everyone

The prestige of working at one of Washington's acclaimed law firms does not come without tradeoffs. Although people we interviewed enjoyed working at Arnold & Porter, they confirmed that the firm is not for everyone. You "can't be a shy person at this firm," said one person. "You have to assert what you want to do." Because Arnold & Porter is large and unstructured, you "have to take initiative to get what you want." One source said that some of the associates, who had been assigned to large litigation projects for a couple of years, felt "bitter." You "have to take care of yourself" at Arnold & Porter because "no one is there to take care of you and this can be a very negative experience." Another noted that "some partners do run roughshod over associates." You cannot "go into Arnold & Porter expecting to have your hand held." Sometimes associates can "fall through the cracks."

steps to address low morale

The long work hours may also contribute to the associates' somewhat low morale. One insider observed that "quite a bit is expected of you" and commented that attorneys "have to work very hard and put in a lot of time." Some of the attorneys can become "disgruntled" as a result of "a hard work week." Another contact pointed out, however, that "although Arnold & Porter may work long hours, we're no different in this area from any other big D.C. law firm." Finally, a third source commented that, presently, the firm is "so concerned about associate morale that it is very responsive to associate concerns," especially since the senior management of the firm has changed, "with Jim Sandman, a favorite of associates, taking over as managing partner." A firm spokesperson informed us that management efforts designed to address morale problems include "a re-invigorated partner evaluation program by associates, management training for partners, an ombudsperson program, and the addition of an associate member to the management committee."

assignments

Associates are generally assigned to one practice area initially. The firm tries to accommodate associates' interests in making assignments, and some associates are members of more than one practice group. Even after an associate is assigned to a particular group, some room for flexibility remains. One source, however, pointed out that "several of the most recent first year classes have found that some of their members are not given any leeway in selecting a particular group but, rather, are locked into a certain group that is short-staffed at the time." A firm spokesperson pointed out that "in every instance where this has occurred, the firm has, over time, been able to accommodate a move to the desired practice group."

Opportunities for responsibility at Arnold & Porter vary by department, with more opportunity in the transactional and specialized departments than in the litigation department. One source remarked that the "attitude among the transactional partners with whom I do the majority of my work is that I will get as much work as I can handle. This is a great experience that I likely wouldn't get somewhere else." Litigation associates are "expected to do their fair share of document discovery and research before getting into court," which can take some years. One contact had "serious concern" about the lack of opportunity for experience in the litigation department, but noted that if one must "write memos" at a law firm, at least at Arnold & Porter one could work on "cutting-edge memos." Litigators may, however, obtain early responsibility by accepting one of the readily available pro bono cases.

training program

Associates at Arnold & Porter have access to some of the best formal training in the city. The firm provides a year-long formal orientation program for new associates, which varies by practice group. It also offers a series of seminars and lectures. The "opportunities for feedback exist but only if you seek them out," stated one source. Some partners give "extraordinary amounts of time" in training, and others "would just call briefly and say bye." One source noted that "unfortunately, this (the latter) seems to be more of the rule now than the exception. Many partners claim they are too busy to give feedback and so it's up to the associate to actively seek it." Another contact remarked, in a similar vein, that "because partners are always so busy, they often don't have the time or interest in establishing good mentoring relationships with associates." The firm formally evaluates associates annually. Associates also receive comprehensive reviews from their fifth year on.

businesslike atmosphere

Arnold & Porter is hard-working and serious. It has a businesslike atmosphere. At the same time, it is "informal" and "everyone is on a first name basis—even with senior partners." There is no formal dress code. The firm has "casual Fridays" year round and an (unwritten) "first snowflake" rule that says, "when the weather may be bad, dress casually." Though clear divisions exist between associates and partners, the firm does not have much hierarchical structure. The work atmosphere varies somewhat by practice group. One person said that smaller groups such as bankruptcy, tax, and trusts and estates are particularly "chummy," "close-knit, and friendly," whereas the litigation group, the firm's largest, is not as "warm and tight."

Garden Room

Though Arnold & Porter provides excellent opportunities for social life, it does not place a premium on socializing in order to advance in the firm. Because Arnold & Porter is such a large firm, not everyone knows each other. However, "networks" of people socialize together and get along well. In addition, with large incoming associate classes each year, many people form "close friendships" with members of their class. "If you are looking for a social network and friends, the opportunity is there...there is a good esprit de corps among the new attorneys" at the firm. One person noted that there is "tons" of intra-firm dating, and there have been a number of intra-firm marriages. Throughout the year, Arnold and Porter provides a wide array of firm-sponsored social events such as picnics and parties. Every evening after work, in a long-standing tradition, attorneys gather in the "Garden Room" for refreshments. On Friday evenings, the firm also serves pizza. The Garden Room provides a "good opportunity to meet people." Each practice group also hosts regular lunches.

steps to promote diversity

Arnold & Porter has taken some path-breaking steps with respect to issues of diversity and is reportedly one of the more "progressive" firms in the city. It is, we were told, "more sensitive to women than most other firms." One insider did comment, however, that some of the older partners are "old-school" and "of the darling crowd." The firm "takes child care very seriously" and provides emergency day care services to all its employees. Arnold & Porter also has a full-time child-care center in the building for all firm personnel which is run on an at-cost basis. Its maternity and paternity leave policies are "very flexible."

Arnold & Porter is one of the few firms in the country to sponsor forums to discuss women's issues and the concerns of minority attorneys. In addition, one person commented that Arnold & Porter "was one of the first firms in D.C. to have a written policy not to discriminate against people with AIDS." There are both openly gay and physically challenged lawyers in the firm, and the firm "prides itself" on its diversity. A majority of the associates at Arnold & Porter are Democrats, but a wide range of political views are represented at the firm.

new offices

Everyone we interviewed said that the firm is doing well economically. One person said that Arnold & Porter has been the "number one money maker in D.C." in recent years. The firm recently moved into a new office building, an indicator of its success, thus consolidating its two D.C. offices in one location. The new building is located downtown, near the Justice Department and the Metro Center metro stop. The facilities include an expanded cafeteria that is subsidized by the firm, an upgraded computer system, a gym, a childcare center, and conference rooms, one of which was was featured in the movie, *Contact*, starring Jodie Foster.

hiring tips

It is no surprise that Arnold & Porter is one of the most competitive firms at which to obtain a summer associate position. One insider pointed out, however, that once you are hired as a summer associate, "you are set" because the firm does most of its screening at the interview level and makes full-time associate offers to almost everyone in the summer class. In the past few years, we were told, Arnold & Porter "has extended offers to *all* of its summer associates." Summer associates "typically only have one project to work on at any given time (and usually only have four or five for an entire summer)," according to one contact. Arnold & Porter makes a strong effort to hire students from all over the country and has no particular geographical preference. Recent summer classes have included students from Duke, Emory, Minnesota, Stanford, UCLA, and Vanderbilt, as well as the Ivy League. One person noted that Arnold & Porter's summer class is "not a shy group" and tends to include more "go-getter" types than is usual at law firms.

Arnold & Porter is different from its competition in many ways. One person explained: Wilmer, Cutler & Pickering is a "lot less friendly and much more uptight." At Covington & Burling, the people are really nice but it is "more formal and conservative than Arnold & Porter." Covington is of the "dark wood, Persian rug variety. Arnold & Porter has very light wood...and...avoids the formal, hushed attitude." Another contact highlighted the recent significant developments at the firm by noting that Arnold & Porter has just concluded "its most profitable year; merged with a small firm in L.A.; increased its hiring; laid off 10% of its administrative staff; and adjusted to its new building." If working for a firm that is steeped in tradition and getting comfortable in its new location appeals to you, then you should give A&P a whirl.

Baker & McKenzie

Washington Chicago Dallas Los Angeles Miami New York Palo Alto San Diego San Francisco
41 Foreign Locations

Address: 815 Connecticut Avenue, N.W., Suite 900, Washington, D.C. 20006-4078
Telephone: (202) 452–7000
Hiring Attorney: Mary C. Bennett
Contact: Lisa O. Waniel, Director of Recruiting and Professional Development; (202) 452–7024
Associate Salary: First year $76,000 (1997)
Summer Salary: $1300/week (1997)
Average Hours: 2000 worked; 1700 billed; NA required
Family Benefits: Life, health, travel, dental, and disability insurance; 401(K) plan; vacation and parental leave
1996 Summer: Class of 9 students; offers made to 7
Partnership: 60% of entering associates from 1981–1983 were made partner
Pro Bono: NA

Baker & McKenzie in 1997
51 Lawyers at the Washington D.C. Office
1.0 Associate Per Partner

Total Partners 24		
Women	2	8%
All Minorities	0	0%

Total Associates 24		
Women	11	46%
All Minorities	5	21%
Afro-Am	1	4%
Asian-Am	2	8%
Latino	2	8%

Practice Areas	
Tax	23
Trade Regulation	11
Corporate and Banking	10
Antitrust	3
Immigration	2
Legislation	1
Litigation	1

an international firm

With 55 locations in 34 countries, Baker & McKenzie is one of the country's premier international law firms. The D.C. office is fully integrated into the firm's international network and, in particular, has extensive contact with China, Europe, the Pacific Rim, and the Soviet Union. On occasion, the D.C. associates have the opportunity to work in the firm's international offices. The firm sponsors a special program in which it occasionally sends an associate to a foreign office for a year or two. "Almost every assignment I got my hands on involved some international aspect," one person marveled. Another contact remarked, "hands down, it's the absolute best place to do international law. If an associate somewhere else wants to give advice about doing business in, say Germany, he or she has to rely on secondary sources. I can call my friends in the Frankfurt office. It's a quantum leap in the quality of your experience." Among other things, the D.C. office has handled the legal work for joint ventures in Russia, helped advise China in developing a stock market, and has provided U.S. representation to a number of foreign governments. One person summed up the firm by stating that, Baker D.C. "is unique in some very qualitative ways. Its network is unmatched in the world in international terms. On my third day there, I sat in on a conference on the stock market in China. The kind of things coming into the firm are very interesting. It's pretty flexible, and you can do what you want."

international tax and trade

Baker's D.C. practice centers around tax, international trade, and corporate work, which together generate a large majority of the firm's clients. The office was founded in 1957 by Walter Slowinski, a prominent tax lawyer. The D.C. office continues to be recognized for its tax practice. Both Leonard Terr and Philip Morison, well-known tax attorneys, formerly served as International Tax Counsel to the Treasury Department. The firm also boasts two Deputy Counsels and one Associate Counsel. Most of the firm's tax work involves corporate and "cutting-edge" international work. One source noted that, unlike in the past, the firm does about half controversy and half transactional work, and commented that it is a "myth that the firm does only transfer pricing work." One of the major reasons for this new emphasis on transactional work is the "transfer" of a financial products group to this office from the Chicago office. The international trade practice handles the full array of trade issues, including antidumping, countervailing duties, and customs and export controls. The firm helped draft the North American Free Trade Agreement (NAFTA). One person noted that the international trade practice offers great "opportunities" to travel and to represent foreign governments. Kevin O'Brien is well-known in the area. Eugene Theroux and Tom Peele have done high-profile work involving Russia, Mongolia, and China. Theroux has represented the Chinese government for many years and, according to one person, was one of the first attorneys to establish an American law office in China (Beijing 1980). The firm also has offices in Shanghai and Moscow, and is currently opening an office in India.

other practice areas

Baker also has a corporate group that, according to one insider, is "the fastest growing practice group in the office." Dan Goelzer, former General Counsel of the Securities and Exchange Commission, is one of the firm's best known corporate partners. The corporate group does transactional, securities, and corporate governance work. Some industries in which the firm specializes are telecommunications, cable television and computer software. The firm also has an immigration practice and one intellectual property partner, Brad Kile, but these areas are considerably smaller than the other departments at the firm. Baker & McKenzie also has a three-attorney antitrust practice, including Howard Adler. Edward Dyson (international) and Adler were recently mentioned in the *Washington Magazine* as two of the top lawyers in D.C.

Pro bono work is "becoming more prominent" at Baker & McKenzie, commented one insider. Although Baker & McKenzie still does not have a formalized pro bono department, there was a recent partner initiative to increase pro bono activities, *e.g.* by getting involved on a department-wide basis in a pro bono clinic with the U.S. Tax Court and the D.C. Bar Association. One associate observed that if you have a pro bono project, and you can "sell" it to the partners, then you are welcome to do it.

self-starters thrive

Baker & McKenzie hires associates for a specialized practice, and if all goes well, a partner "who likes you will take you under his wing." Baker & McKenzie provides formal training programs, but these are mostly associate-initiated efforts. One contact informed us that the partners have "responded to widespread criticism of the training here. Now, in addition to department lunches every two weeks, tax associates attend a technical training session every Tuesday morning (focusing on aspects of transactional planning) and a multi-session brown bag training program." The firm recently hired a professional development liaison for the North American offices; he visits the D.C. office every couple of months to conduct training seminars.

individualist work atmosphere

Baker & McKenzie is "ideal for the entrepreneurial type. The firm wants you to get yourself going and steer yourself through different things." "No one here is big on hand holding," commented one insider. Another insider observed that "the best and worst thing about the firm is that you make your own way. This is a place where people who know what they want and how to fit in can thrive, but that describes only a small percentage of law students." Feedback depends on the partner with whom an associate works. An associate development committee was formed recently to review associate progress and provide feedback. General feedback is provided annually during the formal evaluation process, which recently has been expanded to include a personal professional development plan to be written by the associate. A number of summer associates we interviewed complained in the past about feedback in the summer program and, in particular, the lack of constructive criticism or indication of individual summer associate performance. This situation may be in the process of change, however, as a new recruiting director and hiring partner are focusing on improving the summer program, we were told.

The work atmosphere and work load varies considerably by department. The tax lawyers are considered a "breed apart from the firm" and are known as particularly "hard-driven," "intense," and hard-working. One source claimed that it was "generally accepted that the tax group had to stay in the office for much longer hours. It seemed like no big deal for them to stay until midnight. But everyone seemed to like it." However, the new emphasis on transactional work in the tax department may see their work hours come down somewhat, one insider informed us.

Overall, the work atmosphere at Baker & McKenzie is entrepreneurial, individualistic, and heavily impacted by the firm's compensation system, known to some as the "eat–what–you–kill" system. Partnership compensation at Baker is determined by a four-point formula, which essentially allocates the firm's profits to a partner based upon the amount of the firm's business attributed to the partner and the portion of overall firm revenue earned by the D.C. office. Factors such as seniority, which do not necessarily impact the firm's revenues, account for only a small part of the overall formula. The figures for how much each partner is paid are available to any of the partners firmwide. One insider claimed that the system provides an incentive for each partner to keep as many of the firm's clients and associates under his control as possible, resulting in small "partner fiefdoms." For some, this system creates an atmosphere that can be "isolating for associates." One associate at the firm, however, emphasized that it provides much more individual freedom than is usually found in law firms. The atmosphere also helps the associates. For example, if an associate can persuade the partners that an idea will increase profits or productivity, it will be immediately implemented. "It's a tough system sometimes, but it's good to know that you can get what you want if you push all the right buttons," said one contact.

salary

The D.C. associates compensation system, which was recently restructured, "incorporates a non-lockstep base salary and potential target and performance bonuses." This change addressed historical disparities between the compensation progression at Baker and other D.C. firms. Baker has a two-tier partner system. The "local" partners are paid a salary plus a share of their profits, and the "international" partners have an equity share in the firm on a global basis. There are four local partners in the D.C. office. One of the associates noted that the firm is "top-heavy" and expressed concern regarding the number of new partners the firm will be able to accommodate in future years. However, some of that concern is mitigated by the "eat–what–you–kill" system.

Baker & McKenzie's management is loosely structured. One person noted that because "everyone is responsible for his own clients," there is no real "directing bureaucracy."

The D.C. office committee coordinates with the firmwide executive committee, but it has primarily administrative functions. Baker's lawyers value individuality and entrepreneurialism and many see little need for bureaucratic committees to interfere in the practice of law.

spotty record on diversity

Firmwide, Baker & McKenzie does not have a good reputation for its treatment of women and minorities. The firm received considerable negative publicity for its handling of sexual harassment complaints made by a woman who sued one of the firm's former partners. A female partner is suing the Chicago office for breach of contract. At one time a number of law schools prevented the firm from interviewing on their campuses because of alleged racist remarks by one of the firm's attorneys while interviewing at Michigan in 1989 (the firm is now allowed to interview at those campus locations again); and the estate of a deceased employee of the New York office is suing the firm, alleging that the office discharged the employee because he exhibited the symptoms of the HIV virus. Although none of these incidents involved D.C. partners or associates, people we interviewed nevertheless criticized the firm's general attitude towards women and minorities.

continuing complaints on gender issues

"One partner was shocked that any woman or minority could ever feel uncomfortable in Baker's old-boy atmosphere. The partners here are extremely clueless about modern cultural attitudes. On the other hand, they tend to run things like a pure meritocracy, so there's the feeling that race and gender are truly non-issues (good or bad) with them," according to one source. The D.C. office recently actively started diversifying its associate pool, and now has about 50% women associates. This year, Baker promoted to partnership its first woman who joined the firm as a first-year associate. One person we interviewed insisted that Baker is in reality a good place for women to work, explaining that, although the male partners may not be "sensitive" to women's concerns on an external level, they are responsive as a practical matter if the women can tie "their issues" to the firm's bottom line. However, several associates we interviewed said that the firm is not a comfortable place for women to work. They described the atmosphere at the firm as "stodgy," "conservative," and "old-boy." One commented that it's "a place where you have to be tough and have thick skin. You have to be able to take a joke." Although the firm has a formal parental leave policy, it has very little track record to judge on thus far. To date, only two associates have requested leave, although several more requests are expected soon, by both associates and partners. One contact expressed a sense of frustration on these matters at Baker & McKenzie, observing that the firm "will never be on the cutting edge of social progress, unless it can get some demonstrable business advantage from it. I suppose it's the same everywhere, but it gets really frustrating, especially with the U.S. offices' checkered history."

minority recruiting efforts

Although we did not receive many comments regarding the way the firm treats minorities, those we interviewed noted that there are no minority partners in the D.C. office. One insider commented that the "outlook and ideology" of the partners at the firm dissuade minorities from going to Baker. One of the associates, however, said there is "no problem" with respect to minority issues at the firm and claimed that the firm is "actively seeking more minority candidates." The firm has participated in a minority clerkship program at Georgetown University Law School for the past several years, and actively recruits at the regional BLSA Job Fairs. Firmwide, Baker & McKenzie is very aware of its reputation among women and minorities and has made concerted efforts to improve the situation (see profile of the Baker & McKenzie Chicago office).

Baker's offices are located near the Farragut West metro stop. Decorated in cherry wood, hardwood floors, and antiques, these offices have an "old-time," "gentlemen's club" law firm feel and the "Washington establishment" look. One contact described them as "conservative." The firm rents one of its individual offices to John Sununu, Chief of Staff under President Bush.

hiring tips Because Baker & McKenzie has many highly specialized practice areas, it places a premium on hiring students who have a specific interest in an area. In addition, Baker & McKenzie seeks "uncommon" people with international backgrounds. Many past summer associates have had international experiences. A few had backgrounds in China, several spoke fluent Russian, and one of the summer associates was from Great Britain. One source emphasized that the firm will take "risks" on people who might not be traditional law firm candidates, such as people pursuing joint degree programs, or those who have interesting work backgrounds. Another person said the firm really looks for people with a "commitment to the firm." One associate advised applicants to "tell them how much you love international work and be able to articulate exactly why." Another insider informed us that "hiring targets people who are absolutely intent on doing international legal work." Baker reportedly prefers students from top tier schools, although they will look at great work experience and good grades before they'll look at the name of your law school.

During the callback interview, an applicant meets individually with four attorneys at the firm and then lunches with two more. The recruiting director is present at every on-campus interview and provides an overview perspective on all the candidates when the firm assesses them. One associate who interviews many applicants always asks students: "Why do you want to go to Baker & McKenzie over all other firms in D.C.?"; "Why do you want to be in Washington, D.C.?"; "Which one of Baker's practice areas are you interested in?"; and "What in your background demonstrates an interest in this area?" In addition, this person usually asks the interviewee to describe a previous work experience in detail.

Bracewell & Patterson

Washington Austin Dallas Houston
London

Address: 2000 K Street, N.W., Suite 500, Washington, D.C. 20006
Telephone: (202) 828–5800
Hiring Attorney: Scott H. Segal
Contact: Delores A. Horvath, Office Manager; (202) 828–5800
Associate Salary: First year $75,000 (1997) (includes bonus)
Summer Salary: $1300/week (1997)
Average Hours: 1800 worked; 1800 billed; 1800 required.
Family Benefits: 3 months paid maternity leave; paternity leave; flexible spending plan
1996 Summer: Class of 8; offers to 6
Partnership: 36% of entering associates from 1979–1983 were made partner
Pro Bono: NA

Bracewell & Patterson in 1997
27 Lawyers at the Washington D.C. Office
0.9 Associates Per Partner

Total Partners 14		
Women	3	21%
All Minorities	1	7%
Latino	1	7%

Total Associates 13		
Women	5	38%
All Minorities	1	8%
Asian-Am	1	8%

Practice Areas	
Energy	6
Legislative	5
Litigation	5
Real Estate	5
Environmental	4
Finance	2

Bracewell & Patterson was described as a "good old-boy" firm with a strong Texas influence. The firm's home office is located in Houston, and for those who like Texas culture, it is "one of the nicest places to work" in D.C. Its attorneys are young and know how to have a good time. One contact commented that—from playing softball to painting the town red—"Bracewell is good about doing stuff after work." Bracewell's D.C. office, however, is not entirely like a Texas firm; one person drawled with some regret that in D.C., you just can't "tear it up" on the town like you can with Texas attorneys.

Bracewell D.C. was founded in the mid 1970s, principally to represent the firm's clients in energy regulatory matters. Everyone we interviewed thought the firm was doing well economically. Growth has been fairly conservative throughout the 1990s.

practice areas

Although the office is small by Washington standards, Bracewell boasts six major practice groups—banking (finance), corporate/transactional, regulated industries (energy), environmental, legislation, and litigation—with the legislative and regulated industries practices being the largest and most high-profile. The legislative practice group includes Gene Godley, who has served as Assistant Secretary of the Treasury for Legislative Affairs, and Mike Pate, who served as Lloyd Bentsen's legislative director. The regulated industries section has an active energy practice representing clients before the Federal Energy Regulatory Commission, state public service commissions, and other federal agencies. One of the mainstays of the firm, Bracewell's energy practice is one of the most active in the Washington office. Recently the firm developed a high-profile electric practice with the addition of Jeffrey D. Watkiss, who has been prominent in representing clients pushing for deregulation of the electric utility industry. The group works closely with the firm's Austin office, which has a burgeoning telecommunications practice.

The firm's strong financial institutions practice is headed by Bob Clarke, the former Comptroller of the Currency, who splits his time between the D.C. and the Houston offices. Clarke has developed Bracewell's international banking practice, particularly through his work on restructuring a number of Polish banks. Bracewell's environmental group maintains close contact with the Houston office and represents a variety of municipalities and corporations. Litigation is not one of the firm's strongest sections. One contact described the practice as "weak" compared to other areas in the firm and claimed that some of the litigators are difficult to work with. Another complained that the department does not provide many opportunities for courtroom experience. One midlevel litigation associate "hadn't seen the light of a courtroom" yet, we were told.

pro bono

Bracewell is not known for its pro bono practice. Although the firm offers occasional pro bono opportunities, such work is neither emphasized nor encouraged. One person said it was "never mentioned"; a second declared that it is not the "focal point" of the firm, and a third "knew of no pro bono initiative whatsoever."

work assignments

Associates are hired to work for a specific practice group according to the firm's needs, but they frequently have the opportunity to work in other practice areas. Although summer associates work in all sections of the firm, by the end of the summer they are asked to choose a specific section for permanent employment. This aspect of the program has been criticized as unfair to summer associates who are not always aware of which sections are hiring and which are not. A majority of associates at the firm now are laterals, due in part to a string of summer programs that produced few incoming associates, but associates report that the last two years have attracted several outstanding students, most of whom have accepted permanent offers.

For a small office, the summer program is on the whole well managed. In addition to being taken to lunch two or three times a week, summer associates attend a number of organized excursions to professional baseball and soccer games, dinners, softball league games, and parties at the houses of the firm's senior partners. As is the case with most Texas-based firms, Bracewell encourages clerks to split the summer and only recently has permitted summer clerks to spend more than eight weeks working there during a single summer.

salary and partnership

Most people we interviewed said that Bracewell provides a very pleasant working environment. The atmosphere is informal and laid-back, although not as much as at some Texas firms. On average, attorneys work from 9:00 A.M. to 7:00 P.M. on weekdays and rarely come to the office on weekends. Bracewell recently raised its starting salary to $75,000 to stay competitive with other large Texas firms with Washington offices. Bonuses are fixed for junior and mid-level associates, whereas senior associates and partners are eligible for higher bonuses based on merit for hours worked or client development. Bracewell is considered a very "up front and honest" place, and one in which good lawyers who work hard make partner. The partnership track officially is seven years, although some associates have waited eight or nine years to make partner. The firm recently announced a two-track partnership system for non-equity and equity partners. New partners now are automatically made "stage one" non-equity partners for a period of two years, at which time the firm decides whether to elevate the partner to equity status.

buoyant social life

There is no shortage of social life at Bracewell. The social highlight of the year is the Annual Founders Day Dinner, a black-tie affair held in Houston to which all Bracewell attorneys and their spouse or guest are invited. In addition, summer associates are flown to Houston for a weekend retreat and, although no details were provided, one source joked that "substantial debauchery at all levels" has been known to occur. Bracewell attorneys are remarkably "athletic," and it is a good firm for sports enthusiasts.

diversity

Bracewell has eight female attorneys, three of whom are partners. The firm has a formal three month maternity leave policy and is good about permitting part-time arrangements, we were told. Bracewell has one minority partner who is Puerto Rican, and one minority associate who is an Asian-American. One person said the firm is not a "supportive place for minorities." Another commented that the firm's "good old-boy" atmosphere is not very accepting or supportive of homosexuals, but a firm spokesperson sharply denied that this was the case.

hiring tips

Bracewell traditionally hires most of its summer associates from D.C.-area and southern law schools such as the University of Texas, the University of Virginia, and Vanderbilt. Like other aspects of the firm, the interview process is informal and "*ad hoc*." Bracewell provides an alternative to the standard D.C. law firm, with a touch of Texas culture and the camaraderie of a small 30 person office. These qualities, plus the good social life at the firm, make Bracewell, D.C. an attractive prospect for those in search of something different on the D.C. scene.

Bryan Cave

Washington Irvine Kansas City Los Angeles New York Overland Park Phoenix St. Louis Santa Monica
Abu Dhabi Dubai Hong Kong Kuwait London Riyadh Shanghai

Address: 700 Thirteenth Street, N.W., Washington, D.C. 20005–3960
Telephone: (202) 508–6000
Hiring Attorney: Samuel G. Rubenstein
Contact: Lacey S. Wingard, Recruitment and Marketing Coordinator; (202) 508–6053
Associate Salary: First year $74,000 (1997)
Summer Salary: $1200/week (1996)
Average Hours: 2148 worked; 1836 billed; NA required
Family Benefits: Comprehensive insurance program; 3 weeks vacation; 3 months maternity leave; savings plan; bar association dues; EAP; dependent care; associate year-end bonus
1996 Summer: Class of 5 students; offers to 4
Partnership: 38% of entering associates from the classes of 1980, 1983, and 1984 were made partner
Pro Bono: NA

Bryan Cave in 1997
56 Lawyers at the Washington D.C. Office
0.6 Associates Per Partner

Total Partners 34		
Women	5	15%
All Minorities	0	0%

Total Associates 20		
Women	8	40%
All Minorities	2	10%
Afro-Am	1	5%
Asian-Am	1	5%

Practice Areas	
Regulatory & Tax	26
Litigation & Dispute Resolution	17
Business & Transactional	13
Private Clients	3

Until recently, Bryan Cave reputedly provided an oasis of midwestern culture in the hustle and bustle of Washington, D.C. Like the firm's founding office in St. Louis, Missouri, the D.C. office was relaxed, informal, and polite. However, these qualities have come under attack of late: "An increased emphasis on billable hours and a high level of attorney attrition—16 attorneys have left or announced their departure" are changing the office's dynamics, we were told. Still, "a majority of the people are extremely nice and friendly," reported one contact, who went on to remark that "the hours are not terrible."

St. Louis influence

The strong St. Louis influence on the D.C. office was the main source of criticism we received about the firm. Some were critical of the firm's homogeneous culture and the lack of ethnic and cultural diversity among its attorneys. Others expressed frustration that the D.C. office has little autonomy because some of its key clients and firm policies come from outside the D.C. office. For example, when the D.C. office introduced a casual dress day, the policy was rescinded by the St. Louis office. However, a firm representative stated that the D.C. office is not overly dependent on St. Louis for work. In fact, just under 30 percent of the work managed by the D.C. office lawyers is performed by lawyers resident elsewhere within Bryan Cave, we were told.

changing practice areas

Formerly most well-known for its communications practice, Bryan Cave's major practice areas are now litigation, corporate, banking, and environmental. The litigation department is well-known for its work in aviation-related cases. This work was praised as "very interesting litigation" by our contacts. McDonnell Douglas is one of the firm's anchor clients. Much of its work, however, originates in the St. Louis office. The firm has a growing white-collar crime practice and has expanded its practice with new partners in other areas, such as antitrust, and trusts and estates work. Jim Cole leads the white-collar crime group with his investigation of the ethics violations alleged against Newt Gingrich. These growing areas are augmenting the diminution of the office's healthcare, food and drug, and communications practices. A large portion of the communications group left Bryan Cave for another firm last year; however, the firm has brought in a partner, Kevin Curtin, from Capitol Hill who helped draft the Telecom Act of 1996 and who is rebuilding a communications practice, we were told.

Most of the firm's international practice involves "helping foreign clients negotiate through the D.C. regulatory maze." The firm has offices in London, Riyadh, Dubai, Kuwait, Abu Dhabi, and Hong Kong, and is affiliated with a firm in Shanghai. Supreme Court Justice O'Connor's husband is a partner at Bryan Cave, but he spends much of his time at the firm's Phoenix office. In past years Justice O'Connor has invited summer associates to meet with her at the Supreme Court. Visits to the Supreme Court have expanded to include Justice Thomas, a close friend of St. Louis partner, Senator Jack Danforth.

Bryan Cave has a pro bono practice, coordinated by a pro bono committee that presents opportunities to lawyers in the office. The firm's work with the Whitman Walker clinic serves as the cornerstone of its pro bono practice. One insider reported, however, that "there is some question as to the firm's real commitment to pro bono work due to the fact that pro bono hours do no count toward billable hours and that pro bono work should not come before billable work." A firm spokesperson informed us, however, that the counting of pro bono as separate from billable hours "does not diminish the importance that we attribute to pro bono commitment by our attorneys."

Beer Tasting

Consistent with the firm's midwestern culture, most lawyers are married and value their family lives. Nevertheless, one can find a social life at the firm. For example, two partners and an associate frequently host an informal gathering called the "Environmental Section Beer Tasting." All attendees contribute a rare beer for tasting; the person introducing a beer not previously sampled takes home the leftovers.

training

Our contacts praised the training opportunities for associates in the litigation group. The firm has a strong commitment to the National Institute of Trial Advocacy (NITA) training programs, and it emphasizes writing skills as well. Partner Doug Winter, also a horror fiction novelist, conducts writing seminars for Bryan Cave lawyers. Formal training in the other departments exists as well, and is supplemented by outside CLE courses. Senior attorneys usually provide good feedback and are supportive of associates in their work. Firmwide, associates are formally reviewed once a year.

offices

The office environment is modern and comfortable, but not flashy. All associates have a private office with a window and a personal computer at their desks which provides access to the Internet for E-mails, LEXIS, and Westlaw. The computer system was recently upgraded to a Windows 95 based system, and the firm has introduced on-site video conferencing facilities as well. The building that houses the firm contains a small gym that is outfitted with an exercise bike, a stairmaster, and a Universal weight system. Parking is available in the building at no cost.

salary and partnership

With an admittedly conservative growth strategy, the firm's management committee does not spend money rashly. Bryan Cave is proud of its economic stability and the fact that it did not overextend itself in the booming 1980s. Bryan Cave salaries are competitive with other comparable D.C. firms. The first-year salary is $74,000 plus a signing bonus. The firm gives performance bonuses after the first year, based in part on billable hours. In addition, associates receive a portion of the profits from any new business they bring in. One contact pointed out that there is "not enough billable work in the office but there is constant pressure to bill (as if associates ought to be generating business)." The firm recently changed its criteria for partnership to include proven business development skills. This change has been a major source of concern for Bryan Cave associates who, according to one insider, now experience increasing pressure to lure new clients to the firm. Bryan Cave has, however, sponsored seminars and other training to help improve associate business development skills.

diversity

Although the firm is ethnically homogeneous, it employs a significant number of female attorneys. People noted that most Bryan Cave attorneys have progressive views on women in the workplace and commented that the firm takes women's issues very seriously. One contact informed us that the firm is presently conducting a firmwide diversity study through an outside consultant "to aid in the hiring, development, and advancement of women and minorities." While a few people commented that one of the senior partners is condescending and patronizing toward women (actually, "towards basically everyone," one insider noted), they added that he can generally be avoided.

hiring tips

Interviews—both on-campus and at the firm—are unusually informal, friendly, and relaxed. Most students commented that a high GPA is the threshold requirement, but personality still counts. The current hiring criteria at Bryan Cave include some demonstrated interest in practicing law (beyond going to law school) and a commitment to Washington, D.C., we were told.

Caplin & Drysdale

Washington New York

Address: One Thomas Circle, N.W., Washington, D.C. 20005
Telephone: (202) 862–5000
Hiring Attorney: Scott D. Michel
Contact: Patty A. Oldham, Recruiting Coordinator; (202) 862–7837
Associate Salary: First year $75,000 (1997)
Summer Salary: $1300/week (1L); $1350/week (2L); $1400/week (post-3L) (1997)
Average Hours: 1850 worked; NA billed; NA required
Family Benefits: NA
1996 Summer: Class of 3; offers to 2
Partnership: NA
Pro Bono: NA

Caplin & Drysdale in 1997
49 Lawyers at the Washington D.C. Office
0.3 Associates Per Partner

Total Partners 33			Total Associates 10			Practice Areas	
Women	3	9%	Women	3	30%	Tax	31
All Minorities	1	3%	All Minorities	1	10%	Litigation	23
Latino	1	3%	Asian-Am	1	10%		

As one of the premier tax firms in the country, Caplin & Drysdale attracts the "superstars" of tax law. The environment at the firm was described as "very intellectual" and "very academic." People we interviewed, who themselves had very impressive backgrounds, admitted to being intimidated by the firm's high-powered atmosphere. One person commented that a high percentage of the firm's lawyers are former Circuit of Appeals or Supreme Court clerks.

Mortimer Caplin

Not all Caplin lawyers, however, are exclusively intellectual. A visit with Mortimer Caplin, the founder of the firm, who at one time was an amateur boxer, will dispel that notion. Caplin went from boxing to a law professorship at the University of Virginia, where he became acquainted with the Kennedy family. He then served as Commissioner of Internal Revenue under Presidents Kennedy and Johnson. In 1964, he founded Caplin & Drysdale, which today is best-known for its tax practice, but also has a large litigation department.

politically liberal

Caplin continues to practice at the firm and often interviews prospective associates. He is reportedly "very nice to summer associates" and works side by side with everyone in the firm. It is, one person marveled, "amazing to have a guy of that stature researching next to you in the library." Because Caplin brought many lawyers to the firm from the Kennedy and Johnson Administrations, the firm traditionally has been politically liberal—"almost every partner is a Democrat." The firm has strong connections to government, particularly the U.S. Treasury Department. Many Caplin lawyers go from the firm to work in the upper echelons of the Senate Finance Committee or the Joint Committee on Taxation, or to take senior positions in the Internal Revenue Service and in the Department of Treasury and Justice. One person pointed out, however, that, unlike many other D.C. lawyers, Caplin attorneys are not "hung up on the political process." Instead, they are lawyers who are "looking for solutions to tax problems." They do not exude the same "political feel" as some lawyers at other firms. A number of the firm's attorneys have also gone on to assume prominent teaching positions at such universities as Harvard, Michigan, and Virginia.

old-time law firm

One person described Caplin & Drysdale as more like an "old-time law firm" in that it is a "collection of very able talented partners doing their own unrelated work. Each has his own shingle and his own clients. While there is a firm culture, it is not a cultivated culture." The tax practice does not depend upon a few "institutional clients." Instead, the tax lawyers tend to be "single issue problem solvers" for big, "superstar" clients, including both wealthy individuals and corporations. Caplin's tax practice also tends to be less litigation oriented than that of another well-known D.C. tax firm, Miller & Chevalier. Its international tax practice, headed by H. David Rosenbloom, one of the country's top international tax lawyers, is a "big feature and large part of the firm's practice." A "young associate might spend lots of time" working in this area, which is "growing quickly."

Other noteworthy areas of the tax practice include exempt organizations, headed by Tom Troyer, described as the "dean of the field," and criminal tax, chaired by Cono Namorato, who is very well-known in the area. In addition to the firm's criminal tax practice, Caplin & Drysdale has recently been involved in a series of high-profile white-collar matters arising under Independent Counsel investigations, major criminal antitrust matters, and similar cases. The tax department also houses an employee benefits practice that handles a full range of corporate, regulatory, and legislative work.

litigation practice

The litigation department—considered quite "different" from the tax department—handles some tax litigation, particularly criminal tax matters, but it also covers a broad range of civil litigation, including constitutional and commercial litigation. The department does a substantial amount of plaintiff's work, such as representing the group of lawyers who handle asbestos-related claims on behalf of injured workers in complex civil class-action litigation, and handling significant "toxic tort" and related cases. David Webster is one of the firm's most prominent litigators. Finally, Caplin has an informally organized pro bono practice.

Caplin & Drysdale associates "work directly with very accomplished people." The attorneys "sit down and really show you how to do things—people really take the time." Because the firm employs so few associates, it offers "meaningful work" and responsibility more quickly than larger firms. One source said that it is the general practice to be "the only associate working with one partner on huge issues." You "will just be given the assignment and told to go do it." The firm's "best strength" is that an associate is "treated as a colleague by impressive partners." One contact pointed out, however, that the firm does not "spend much time formally training young associates." It does, however, encourage and fund training through outside resources. The firm typically hires "seasoned" attorneys with clerkship experience and provides them with the opportunities to develop practical experience working side by side with the firm's veteran attorneys.

heretical associates

Caplin associates work "shorter and more intense" hours than associates at other D.C. firms. One insider remarked that "for a D.C. firm, the demands are pretty light for billable hours," but heavy for high quality work. Performance expectations are high even for young attorneys. Caplin may be high-powered, but it also is informal and friendly—a mid-sized firm that has successfully preserved a small firm atmosphere. "Not everyone wears ties at the firm, and the kitchen is full of free food," one contact noted. Another commented that as a result of their close working relationships with partners, the associates are somewhat "heretical" and tend to show "a little less deference" to partners than associates at other firms. "If you do good work, then just about everything else is forgiven," one contact noted. The associates who do advance are those who produce "good work," but "the standard is very high."

minimal social life

Moreover, Caplin & Drysdale is not a place where office politics and social appearances are particularly important. The firm doesn't emphasize "face time" or "going to parties." One source remarked that Caplin does not take "affirmative steps to encourage" socializing, noting that the firm's associates do not see each other much outside work. Another concurred that the firm tends to "keep formal socialization to a minimum." This statement applies to the summer program as well; Caplin is not known for sponsoring a lot of fancy dinners and social events.

diversity

Overall, Caplin & Drysdale received positive reviews for its treatment of women in the workplace. The firm is very "flexible" about permitting women with children to work part-time, and a number do. One source claimed that, although Caplin employs few female partners, they strongly influence the firm. Patricia Lewis, for example, is the firm's president for calendar year 1997. There are not many minority attorneys at Caplin, and the firm has not made tremendous efforts at minority recruitment. Caplin "does not look upon itself as a structured law firm," claimed one insider. It is "foreign for them to say as a firm, 'We should hire a minority.'" This appears to be changing, however. One contact indicated to us that, more recently, the firm has stepped up the pace in the quest for minority attorneys.

management

Like other aspects of the firm, Caplin's management is personal and informal. The firm is governed by a three member management committee, with each member serving a three year term. The partners "hash out" decisions in an "unstructured" fashion. There is relatively little openness about management decisions: "associates merely speculate on what's going on. They don't even know what their salary jump will be when they make partner...and they have no idea about the firm's financial books."

links to government agencies

Although the perception exists that partnership prospects at Caplin & Drysdale are limited, those at the firm deny this. There has historically been a close link between employment at the firm and government service. "A large percentage of attorneys migrate to and from government organizations such as DOJ, IRS, Treasury, and the SEC," one insider told us, adding that "there is no set career path at Caplin & Drysdale, however, and more than a few have ridden the associate track all the way to partner." A second contact confirmed this observation, emphasizing that the firm "strongly encourages talented associates to come through the ranks. Government experience is valued but is by no means required for partnership." For the past several years, all associates who have come up for partnership have been made partners.

Caplin's offices are "clean and modern." The countertops are black marble, and there is a lot of stainless steel and gray. One contact advanced the untutored opinion that the office ambiance has a "sort of conservative, techy look." Some of the firm's offices face the center of the building, so the associates do not have an outside view. The offices are located at Thomas Circle, attached to the Westin hotel, in an area that is "not exactly Park Avenue," as one insider felicitously phrased it.

hiring tips

Caplin & Drysdale hires most of its summer associates from the top 10 law schools, with Harvard, Yale, and the University of Virginia figuring most prominently. One source claimed that the firm does not have a specific grade cutoff, but noted that the attorneys value superior academic achievement. As indicated above, many of the partners were former Supreme Court clerks, presidents of their law reviews, or law school valedictorians. One person observed, however, that a "good number of people don't have these credentials." Caplin tends to be less concerned about personality in making its hiring decisions than other firms. One person commented: "I guess they care about personality, but it is less important." Before the callback interview, students generally specify an interest in either tax or litigation, but not always. If they do indicate a preference, they are primarily interviewed by attorneys in that area.

Chadbourne & Parke

Washington Los Angeles New York
Hong Kong London Moscow Singapore

Address: 1200 New Hampshire Avenue, N.W., Washington, D.C. 20036
Telephone: (202) 974-5600
Hiring Attorney: Andrew A. Giaccia
Contact: Andrew A. Giaccia; (202) 974-5600
Associate Salary: First year $89,000 (1997) plus bar review course, moving allowance, bar ass'n dues for 1 year; second $94,000 plus potential merit bonus $10,000; third $108,000 plus pmb $14,000; fourth $127,000 plus pmb $18,000; fifth $145,000 plus pmb $25,000; sixth $160,000 plus pmb $25,000; seventh $165,000 plus pmb $30,000; eighth $170,000 plus pmb $30,000
Summer Salary: $1700/week (1997)
Average Hours: 2189 worked; 1746 billed; NA required
Family Benefits: Paid maternity and paternity leave; medical insurance; same sex domestic partner benefits; flexible spending account for medical and childcare; emergency day care program, employee assistance program (addendum to medical insurance)
1996 Summer: No summer program in 1996
Partnership: NA
Pro Bono: 1.3% of all work is pro bono

Chadbourne & Parke in 1997
47 Lawyers at the Washington D.C. Office
2.2 Associates Per Partner

Total Partners 13			Total Associates 29			Practice Areas	
Women	2	15%	Women	15	52%	Project Finance	17
All Minorities	0	0%	All Minorities	4	14%	Insurance/Reinsurance	16
			Afro-Am	1	3%	Environmental	6
			Asian-Am	1	3%	Tax	4
			Latino	2	7%	Litigation	2
						Bankruptcy	1
						Corporate	1

Chadbourne & Parke, a mid-sized branch of a large and well-known New York law firm, offers its associates New York salaries in D.C. New associates start at $89,000 a year. The base salary increases significantly in subsequent years and is supplemented by potentially large merit bonuses starting in the second year. Including bonuses, fourth-year associates can earn up to about $145,000, seventh-years up to $195,000, and ninth-years up to about $205,000, more than many partners in D.C.-based firms. Chadbourne recently restructured its bonus system. The firm no longer insists on a minimum of 1800 billable hours as a requisite for a bonus. Instead, it "includes billable hours among the several criteria for awarding bonuses," according to one insider, who added that "associates are uncertain about how this change will work out in practice." Because the merit bonuses figure heavily into associate compensation, some sources claimed that the system encourages a serious and hard-working atmosphere. Unlike Chadbourne, which has maintained a uniform scale for its New York and D.C. offices, a number of other New York-based D.C. firms, such as Skadden Arps, Weil Gotshal, and Fried Frank have separate and lower salary scales for their D.C. offices.

serious atmosphere

The work atmosphere at Chadbourne is "businesslike," "professional," and "a little more serious than at other firms," we were told. "Many attorneys have lunch at their desks, and third- and fourth-year associates never leave before 6:30 P.M," reported one contact. Chadbourne is not the best firm for young associates who are looking to find a social life at their firm, claimed another, stating that "although people work well together, they look elsewhere for their social life." The very small size of recent summer programs (the firm did not have a summer program in 1996) is not likely to positively impact this situation. The firm has, however, "recently been having more Happy Hours and outings, such as plays and a rafting trip," reported one contact.

energy and reinsurance practices

Chadbourne & Parke has a distinguished reputation for its project finance and insurance/reinsurance practices. The project finance group is the firm's "most dynamic," commented one observer; however, its lawyers work more demanding hours than those in other groups at the firm, noted people we interviewed. The "length and intensity of the hours gets to people," claimed one insider. The project finance practice is divided into a regulatory practice, which primarily handles work involving the Federal Energy Regulatory Commission (FERC), and a corporate practice, which structures large power and cogeneration power plant operations, as well as other infrastructure projects, such as roads, telecom, and stadiums. The firm handles relatively little regulatory work, focusing instead on the corporate transactional part of the practice. The project finance group also does substantial international work involving the firm's foreign offices. The firm's international energy practice has "taken off" recently as the firm was involved in and closed deals in India and China, "making it a leader in the field," exclaimed one insider. The firm recently opened an office in Singapore.

other practice areas

Chadbourne also proudly houses the "largest reinsurance group in the nation." Much of the practice involves the legal aspects of global risk spreading of large corporate liabilities. The reinsurance practice is the primary group at the firm that does litigation, but a greater share of its work involves arbitration proceedings. "If you're interested in high stakes arbitration, then this is your deal," advised one insider, noting that "it's a different side of the legal practice" that is not common in other law firms. One contact cautioned, however, that "there is a very high turnover rate in this department lately, probably due to the *boring* work."

The environmental practice group is less focused than either energy or reinsurance. It is "sort of a generalized practice to service the firm's big clients." One contact asserted that the group offers the "best working atmosphere at the firm," and its "people are great." The firm also has a small corporate and tax practice, which mainly services the firm's project finance clients. Chadbourne primarily represents large corporations, conglomerates and trade associations such as American Brands, American Forest Products Association, the AES corporation, Newell, Westinghouse, and Republic Insurance Company, as well as many financial institutions such as the International Finance Corporation, and Citibank, N.A. Chadbourne does not have a highly developed pro bono practice, though recently a few attorneys have been involved with Whitman Walker Legal Services for AIDs advocacy.

assignments

Entering associates typically do not join a particular department or specialize in any one area. Instead, they spend about one year "on call," receiving assignments from any of the firm's practice groups. These are likely to be rather limited, we were informed, due to the "small number of practice groups" in the D.C. office. Entering associates with focused interests may specialize in certain areas, however. We heard some complaints that associates do not have much control over their permanent departmental assignments, but one contact believed that the firm "will not place an associate in a group that she does not want to work in on a permanent basis." On the other hand, we were told that two of the five 1995 summer associates hired to enter the D.C. office in 1996 were instead unilaterally "sent to the New York office on their first day of work. Their stay was supposed to last six months. One is still up there." A firm spokesperson informed us that "both of those associates were invited to stay in New York and one chose to do so."

training

Chadbourne offers very few formal training programs, writing seminars, or mock trials. The project finance group, however, runs a year-long training program: "there are about two luncheon sessions per month, led by a partner," reported one insider. Individual training varies by department. In tax, the training is "extraordinarily good—one partner is a very patient teacher; he really views training as a good investment," we were told. There was some disagreement regarding the training provided by the environmental and reinsurance groups. One source praised the "great training" of these groups, commenting that the partners "take lots of time with young attorneys and let them know what is going on." In contrast, a second contact described the experience in reinsurance as "sink or swim," and a third expressed concern about the training and feedback provided in the group. Chadbourne's summer program has in past years been unstructured, and at times, its lack of organization can be "frustrating," according to one interviewee; another person, however, opined that it was "very well organized."

diversity

Chadbourne treats women "really well" and is taking "affirmative steps to get more women," said one source. Ellen Woodbury is a partner in the D.C. office, as was Nancy Percechino, who however recently moved to the firm's London office. A couple of women are counsel. The firm's attitude toward women is "very refreshing," said another. On the other hand, we were informed that firmwide Chadbourne did very "poorly in a survey done by a women's group at Harvard Law School," and consequently, since then, every employee has been required to attend diversity training. Chadbourne does less well in general with racial diversity, although its numbers at the associate level have improved in recent years.

management

Although Chadbourne is the branch office of a major New York firm, it enjoys considerable autonomy from the New York home office, perhaps because three or four of the firm's top 10 clients are primarily the D.C. office's clients. Chadbourne has also made a "big push on marketing," said one source. Its practice groups meet regularly to discuss marketing strategies and to review the results of past marketing efforts. In addition, the tax group has developed and marketed some innovative software, which addresses issues of partnership allocation. The D.C. office is economically successful and busy and transfers some of its work to the New York office, claimed one reviewer. However, one contact remarked that the D.C. office has recently suffered "some loss of autonomy to the New York office; and many larger decisions concerning the D.C. branch are made in the New York office, including decisions regarding advancement of attorneys." Consequently, you "have to get known" by the partners in New York, commented some people we interviewed. The firm outing and Christmas parties are less social occasions and more a "chance to schmooze the New York people," according to one source.

new office facilities

Chadbourne's old office facilities were described as "sparse," "plain, and bare." The firm has recently moved into new larger offices, located near Dupont Circle, which "are much nicer than the old facility," we were told. Every associate has a private office and a laptop computer that slides into a desktop docking station when in the office. The state-of the art computers have interchangeable floppy disk and CD-ROM drives and access to Westlaw, Lexis, and Internet e-mail. Those who want access to the World Wide Web receive it immediately. Firmwide, Chadbourne attorneys can communicate by e-mail and share computer documents with each other through the firm's document management system. Finally, when on the road all attorneys can use their laptops to remote dial-in to the firm's computer system. The secretarial staff at the firm was described as "excellent," as was the extremely capable office manager, Suze Sheehan, who runs the office "like a well-oiled machine."

hiring tips

Chadbourne hires "very driven people" and does not place a "high premium on name schools," one source told us. The firm is "more interested in hiring people who will get along well and don't have big ego problems than in hiring exclusively from the top schools," agreed another. In past years, Chadbourne has drawn most of its summer class from D.C.-area schools, although this has been changing. The firm also emphasizes practical experience "much more than educational background." Many Chadbourne attorneys have worked in the government, and until recently the reinsurance group hired most of its attorneys laterally.

The interview at Chadbourne usually involves meeting about six associates and partners. Some have been asked to identify a hardship in their lives and to explain how they worked to overcome it. This year, for the first time, an interview may also involve lunch with two associates.

For Washington, D.C., Chadbourne is a fast-paced and serious law firm that compensates its attorneys with New York salaries; the "money is great," our contacts reported. One contact remarked, however, that the firm is "undergoing lots of changes, with resulting uncertainty." For those who want to maintain contact with a New York practice while working in D.C., Chadbourne may be the place for you.

Collier, Shannon, Rill & Scott

Washington
Sydney

Address: 3050 K Street, N.W., Suite 400, Washington, D.C. 20007
Telephone: (202) 342–8400
Hiring Attorney: (Ms.) Robin H. Gilbert
Contact: Suzanne K. Gralow, Director of Recruiting; (202) 342–8585
Associate Salary: First year $74,000 (1997)
Summer Salary: $1350/week (1997)
Average Hours: 2050 worked; 1900 billed; 1950 required
Family Benefits: Dependent care flex plan
1996 Summer: Class of 10 students; offers to 9
Partnership: NA
Pro Bono: NA

Collier, Shannon, Rill & Scott in 1997
94 Lawyers at the Firm
1.4 Associates Per Partner

Total Partners 35		
Women	5	14%
All Minorities	0	0%

Total Associates 50		
Women	19	38%
All Minorities	4	8%
Afro-Am	3	6%
Latino	1	2%

Practice Areas	
Antitrust	26
International	21
Litigation	16
Patents/Intellectual Property	11
Environmental	9
Energy	8
Labor	3

The last line of Collier, Shannon, Rill & Scott's recruitment letter to summer associates, which announces that associates' golf scores are expected to be in the low 80s, "epitomized the whole place," one person told us. Collier Shannon is an athletic firm. The managing partner is an avid jogger and biker; he recently rode his bike from Washington, D.C. to Nantucket, Massachusetts for charity. Another partner ran a five-minute mile on his fiftieth birthday and claims that he will only slow to six-minute miles on his sixtieth. A third partner races cars professionally.

quality of life

Collier Shannon is distinguished by its commitment to quality of life, and the "biggest plus of the firm," according to one source, is the way in which the attorneys interact. Partners rarely disagree seriously, everyone gets along well, and communication among attorneys is excellent. There is great camaraderie at the firm, and many of the young attorneys "hang out" together socially. Collier Shannon has a "relaxed," "friendly," "young," and vibrant work atmosphere. Most of the firm's partners are young, and the ones who are not seem like they are. Almost all Collier Shannon attorneys pursue interests outside the firm. Many are parents of young children. One insider claimed that Collier Shannon has no "pinheads," and its attorneys are "ungeeky." Everyone we interviewed enjoyed working at the firm. Junior associate salaries at Collier Shannon are comparable to other large D.C. firms, but senior associate salaries tend to be less competitive. However, many associates seem to have made a lifestyle choice, trading a lower salary for a higher quality of life.

international antitrust

Collier Shannon is best known for its antitrust practices and international trade, but the most rapid growth is taking place in the environmental, litigation and intellectual property practice areas. The antitrust section is led by such partners as Jim Rill, the Assistant Attorney General for the Antitrust Division of the Department of Justice in the Bush Administration; Jim Loftis, who heads the ABA Antitrust Section; and Bill

MacLeod, formerly the director of the Bureau of Consumer Protection at the Federal Trade Commission. The antitrust practice is particularly proud of its high-tech document management system. All of the firm's documents have been placed on-line in the firm's computer system, which is interfaced with every attorney's computer.

international trade

A core practice for the international trade section is representing U.S. companies as petitioners in countervailing duty and antidumping cases. For example, the firm recently won a major case on behalf of the U.S. pasta industries involving pasta from Italy and Turkey. This case was handled by Paul Rosenthal, who also conducts many of the firm's interviews and is widely regarded as having "a great personality and being fun to interview and work with." The section also deals with a wide range of matters involving customs law and export controls.

litigation

Litigation is a "growing" practice area, which represents a number of interesting clients including G. Gordon Liddy. Several attorneys in the litigation section are involved in major litigation on behalf of GTE over the 1996 Telecom Act, including arbitration in over 20 states. The firm's intellectual property practice has grown substantially in the past few years. The intellectual property and litigation groups have successfully handled several large patent infringement suits in recent years. The firm as a whole has a broad client base. Some of the largest clients, whose work spans several sections of the firm, included the Specialty Steel Industry of North America and Petroleos de Venezuela, the Venezuelan national oil company. Collier Shannon leaves pro bono work to an individual's initiative. One person remarked that "you are encouraged to do pro bono work as long as you put in the regular hours."

early client contact

Associates work closely with partners at Collier Shannon. The firm represents both large and small clients and consequently offers many opportunities for responsibility on "interesting, realistic, tangible projects." One person commented that junior associates are not limited to small pieces of larger cases, but often see the broad picture behind their work project. Collier Shannon also offers good opportunities for client contact. One summer associate reportedly worked directly for a client. Collier Shannon does not emphasize formal training programs, but it does sponsor seminars in specific practice areas. Certain partners are "more willing than others to send associates to outside seminars and training programs,"we were told.

training

On an individual level, however, most partners exhibit a strong commitment to training young associates. The partners "really take you under their wings and teach you," said one source. People gave equally strong reviews regarding the feedback at the firm. The firm is "very up front," remarked one person, adding that "everyone feels comfortable with the partners." Associates receive written evaluations twice a year. In general, one source said, there are "not many surprises." If you are "not doing well, you know about it." A special associates committee acts as a channel of communication to the partners, and people praised the management for its open communication with associates.

growth

Collier Shannon has planned its growth carefully and the firm is financially very sound. There have not been any economic layoffs in recent years. Several of the firm's practices are expanding. Recently, the antitrust group has taken on more international matters. One person noted that Collier Shannon has made a focused effort to attract international business. The intellectual property practice works with a network of foreign attorneys to handle its substantial international practice.

management

Collier Shannon's success has come at a cost, however. The firm's rapid growth has been accompanied by growing pains as the firm strives to develop "smooth" administrative systems necessary for its larger size. Administrative issues "can get irritating at times." In addition, one insider complained that Collier Shannon is somewhat inflexible with associates wishing to switch practice areas. In certain cases, however, associates are permitted to "split" their time between sections.

Georgetown offices

Collier Shannon's office is located in the heart of Georgetown, on the Potomac River, overlooking the Kennedy Center in "one of the most unique buildings" in D.C. Every attorney's office has windows and some have balconies. The office is outfitted with an "incredible round conference room that looks like King Arthur's table." One person especially praised the office's concierge service that, among other things, handles dry cleaning, plane reservations, car rentals, and flower deliveries. Moreover, attorneys and support staff may use, free of charge, the gym located in the building, although during the summer you are more likely to see attorneys jogging along the Potomac River. The one drawback of the office is that it is difficult to reach. There is no metro stop nearby (although there is a shuttle that runs between Georgetown and the nearest metro stop) and traffic can be a problem. Parking is available in the building and in nearby locations but, as in other parts of the city, it is very expensive. One person remarked positively on the firm's location that "some people might prefer to be more 'downtown,' although I think our office location is a positive factor."

great for women

The women at Collier Shannon receive "incredibly fair treatment," according to people we interviewed. Because many Collier Shannon attorneys have worked in government, they evince more progressive views of women in the workplace, according to one source we interviewed. A female attorney claims that she lateralled from another D.C. firm because Collier Shannon provides better opportunities for women. There are "big hitter" female partners at the firm. The firm has "great" parental leave and part-time work policies. Although there are not many minority attorneys at the firm, Collier appears to have begun more aggressively recruiting minorities in recent years and to "have been successful in its efforts," added a firm spokesperson.

hiring tips

"Personality figures most prominently" in the hiring process at Collier Shannon. The firm is "looking for down-to-earth people," claimed one insider. "If you are a workaholic, you would not like it here and you would be an anomaly." One source commented that the firm hires a "hipper crowd" than other Washington law firms. Collier Shannon hires most of its summer associates from Harvard, Georgetown, and the University of Virginia, but also has made an effort to recruit at law schools in the D.C. region. Callback interviews are "energetic" and pleasant. It doesn't hurt to mention your golf score.

Collier Shannon is a firm with lots of positives. The firm has enjoyed continued steady growth and record revenues recently due to some "big wins in high profile cases." It provides its associates "extensive client contact and interesting, substantial work" early in their careers. Most of all, Collier Shannon "prides itself on its quality of life." Associates don't necessarily work fewer hours than at other firms, but the interaction between partners and associates is excellent. The location of the firm's offices on the Potomac River in Georgetown also "adds to a more relaxed working environment." In the words of one contact, "all in all, Collier Shannon is a great place to work."

Covington & Burling

Washington
Brussels London

Address:	1201 Pennsylvania Avenue, N.W., P.O. Box 7566, Washington, D.C. 20044
Telephone:	(202) 662–6000
Hiring Attorney:	Timothy C. Hester and Neil K. Roman
Contact:	Lorraine Brown, Director, Legal Personnel Recruiting; (202) 662–6200
Associate Salary:	First year $74,000 (1997); annual increases of approx. $6,000
Summer Salary:	$1300/week (2Ls); $1420/week (3Ls) (1996)
Average Hours:	2250 worked; 1950 billed; NA required
Family Benefits:	12 weeks paid maternity leave (cbc unpaid); 2 weeks paid paternity leave; flexible working arrangements; emergency childcare; flexible spending account for childcare and elder care expenses
1996 Summer:	Class of 36 students; offers to 32
Partnership:	12% of associates from law school classes of 1982–1988 were made partner
Pro Bono:	7–9% of all work is pro bono

Covington & Burling in 1997
327 Lawyers at the Firm
1.4 Associates Per Partner

Total Partners 121			Total Associates 169			Practice Areas
Women	15	12%	Women	67	40%	NA
All Minorities	7	6%	All Minorities	16	9%	
Afro-Am	4	3%	Afro-Am	13	8%	
Asian Am	1	1%	Asian-Am	2	1%	
Latino	2	2%	Latino	1	1%	

Perhaps the most well-known firm in Washington, D.C., Covington & Burling carries a powerful and prestigious image. Covington's "prestigious mystique comes from its high standards—the firm produces excellent work, and its reputation is well deserved," one source remarked. Others noted that famous statesmen such as Dean Acheson have passed through its halls and that lawyers at the firm have taken high-profile constitutional cases such as *Korematsu* (the World War II Japanese-American detention camp case) to the Supreme Court.

stuffy feel

When asked about the firm, most who have worked there immediately begin dispelling rumors that it is "stuffy." One insider claimed that this reputation was "very undeserved" and believed that the "stuffy feel" of the firm's offices may explain this image. The office decor consists of hardwood floor hallways, Persian rugs, and Colonial furniture. In addition, most of the offices are arranged in suites and do not open directly onto hallways. While these offices provide greater privacy, they reduce social interaction among lawyers. One floor of the firm is designed with hallway offices for those who dislike the suite system, but the suites are in high demand. The art displayed at the firm is selected by a special committee. One contact singled out the art committee for praise and described it as a "metaphor for how the firm takes details seriously and puts people who are interested in a subject on a committee to do something about it." Though the interior office design may create a stuffy image, those interviewed insisted that the firm itself is not "stuffy." One observer described the atmosphere at the firm as "professional; people treat each other with courtesy, candor, and fairness." Another said the atmosphere is not "formal," but the lawyers take their work very seriously.

practice areas

Founded in 1919, Covington & Burling has grown into a full-service firm with a broad practice. The firm's international, communications, and food and drug practice areas are its most well-known. The FDA practice, led by the nationally recognized Peter Hutt, is reputedly one of the best in the country. The firm also handles some high-profile antitrust work and has represented both the National Football League and the National Hockey League in this capacity. Covington's clients are primarily major corporations. It represents some tobacco industry clients, but according to one commentator, the firm is "very up front about it," and attorneys may elect not to work on a tobacco case. With offices in London and Brussels and affiliations with firms in Tokyo and Paris, Covington & Burling's international practice is considerable. In addition to general litigation, the firm's constitutional litigation practice has done innovative work involving national security and civil rights issues. According to people interviewed, the litigators tend to "work harder" than attorneys in other practice areas. Those in litigation have to travel frequently.

top-notch pro bono

Everyone we interviewed praised the firm's pro bono practice. One said the firm "does tons of pro bono work;" another said that the "pro bono opportunities are tremendous!" The pro bono section is not formally structured—in fact, there are no formal departments in the firm. One person coordinates the firm's pro bono work, and attorneys may request work from her. Covington's pro bono practice includes a range of matters, from death penalty cases to representation of political prisoners in Malawi. Some noted that the firm has a special commitment to international human rights. Two special pro bono programs provide hands-on litigation training. The firm permits some attorneys to do a six-month rotation with Neighborhood Legal Services, working on landlord-tenant matters, employment discrimination cases, etc., while earning full firm salary. More recently, the firm has begun a similar program with the D.C. Corporation's Counsel on child welfare cases. Covington sponsors a criminal justice program that provides training and the opportunity to try misdemeanor and felony cases. It also does a lot of work on behalf of the homeless in D.C.

extensive training and feedback

Covington's series of formal training programs for associates, and the partners' commitment to individual training, are "really good." The feedback is also excellent. "Evaluation sessions are very detailed, comprehensive and fair." "The firm takes this very seriously, and if there is any problem, they let you know as soon as possible." One person emphasized that there is a "very structured feedback system." Attorneys complete written evaluations of associates who work for them, and partners have a strong commitment to informing associates about their progress (or lack thereof). Covington has as much turnover as any other firm, but those interviewed said that people who leave Covington go into academic positions to a greater degree than at other firms. The firm is also very proud of its history of having lost very few of its partners to other D.C. firms. We received mixed reviews on the matter of responsibility accorded junior associates at Covington. One source commented that few attorneys are fully entrusted with paying client matters until their fourth or fifth year; another person, however, contested this, asserting that "relatively speaking, I think junior associates get a lot of responsibility and tons of client contact."

summer program

Most of those interviewed commented that, particularly in the summer, Covington organizes many social activities. The firm sponsors a "good" summer associate program, which includes a special-theme happy hour on numerous Fridays throughout the summer, sailing, bike trips, amusement park trips, and other events. Every few years, Covington sponsors an associate and partner retreat at the Homestead resort in Virginia. Much of the social activity, however, is carried on outside of the firm. Inside the firm, the atmosphere is serious. One person commented that, "people come in, do their work and leave." Covington has no specified number of required billable hours—it is "unique and outstanding on this," one source remarked. People feel pressure to produce high-quality work rather than a high number of billable hours.

diversity

Covington has traditionally been regarded as a "WASP" firm, but this image is changing. The firm received good reviews regarding its treatment of women and minorities. Women are members of the management and hiring committees. Many attorneys take advantage of the firm's accommodating maternity leave and part-time work policies and emergency day care center. Covington actively recruits minority attorneys. Wes Williams, who recently served as the president of the Harvard Law School Alumni Association, is a prominent and highly-respected African-American partner at the firm. He attends many of the firm's social events and is easily accessible. Many Harvard and Yale alumni are at the firm, and one student heard a joke that if you are a "double-barreled" Harvard person (*i.e.*, undergraduate and law school), "they'll make you partner as soon as you walk through the door!"

pay

Associate compensation at Covington starts at $74,000 and increases in lockstep increments by approximately six thousand dollars annually during the initial four or five years. Additionally, after the second year, the firm contributes an amount equal to 10 percent of the annual salary into a pension fund. Other amenities at Covington include a small workout room with a stairmaster, exercise bikes, treadmills, weights, aerobics, sauna, and hot tub available to all employees.

unique hiring process

Covington's hiring process is unique. When interviewing with the firm, students must submit a writing sample and references, both of which the firm relies upon heavily. One insider strongly recommended that applicants choose their references very carefully and alert them that Covington representatives will probably call them. A bad or even neutral recommendation can minimize the prospect of being hired at this selective firm. In addition, one person commented that "interviewers do not restrict their calls to people the applicant names. If an interviewer knows someone else with whom you have worked or has any other kind of connection, she will contact those people, too. In other words, you can't guarantee your own references." One successful applicant commented that grades and other indicators of success are important, but that references are the single most important criterion used in evaluating students. Another student commented that the firm places a premium on writing experience and on people who have "a sense of what their own interests are and have a wide range of interests that they take seriously and with which they do things." While it is not necessary to be first in your class or on law review to be offered a job at Covington, one must be outstanding in some way.

Some students commented that Covington's on-campus interview is more intense than others because the firm extends summer associate offers after the initial on-campus interview and before the callback. One contact said that the interview was more like a "deposition" than any other interview he had. Two students reported that their interviewers engaged them in an in-depth discussion of one item on their résumés. According to one, the interviewer wants to see if you can "articulate and talk passionately" about something that interests you. Another said that the interview was "more substantial and sophisticated" than those at other firms. The callback, on the other hand, is much more relaxed. It provides students the opportunity to learn about the firm in a low pressure environment and enables the firm's attorneys to sell the firm to those with summer associate offers.

Covington recruits from a broad range of schools, primarily the top 10 national schools, but also a number of other schools including William & Mary, Northwestern and Boston University. In 1996, the firm hired 36 summer associates and 32 received offers for full-time employment.

When asked why they chose Covington over other firms in the city, students responded in various ways: One said that Covington "has a track record of doing great work and training great lawyers, and no matter whether you want to stay there or not, the experience there will serve you tremendously." Another said that it has "less of a sweatshop feel than Arnold & Porter," and the training is better at Covington than at the other large D.C. firms. A third source said the reputation of other firms is not quite at the "caliber of Covington."

Crowell & Moring

Washington Irvine
London

Address: 1001 Pennsylvania Avenue, N.W., Washington, D.C. 20004–2595
Telephone: (202) 624–2500
Hiring Attorney: John A. Macleod, Chair, Recruiting Committee
Contact: Susan R. Sedlock, Recruiting Administrator; (202) 624–2729
Associate Salary: First year $74,000 (1997)
Summer Salary: $1300/week (1997)
Average Hours: NA worked; NA billed; 1800 required.
Family Benefits: 10 weeks paid maternity and 2 weeks paid paternity leave; family and medical leave according to applicable federal and state law; dependent care flexible spending account
1996 Summer: Class of 37 students; offers to 32
Partnership: 9.3% of entering associates from 1979–1989 were made partner
Pro Bono: 4% of all work is pro bono

Crowell & Moring in 1997
203 Lawyers at the Washington D.C. Office
1.5 Associates Per Partner

Total Partners 80		
Women	10	13%
All Minorities	2	3%
Afro-Am	2	3%

Total Associates 123		
Women	51	42%
All Minorities	15	12%
Afro-Am	6	5%
Asian-Am	4	3%
Latino	5	4%

Practice Areas	
General Litigation	74
Government Contracts	60
Natural Resources & Environ.	19
Antitrust	18
Labor & Employment	14
Business Crimes	12
Communications	11
Health	11
Energy	9
Tax	7
Corporate	6
Aviation	5
Products Liability & Insurance	4
International	3

On their first day of work, summer associates attended a welcoming reception in a Crowell & Moring conference room. After half an hour they began to notice a senior partner with his back turned to everyone at the reception. When people started to leave, he let out a sudden roar, "I can't believe it's 9:30 A.M., and none of the summer associates are in the library yet!!!"

firm culture

This is how one class of summer associates first met name partner, now counsel, Mr. "Took" Crowell, who was only joking about being in the library, and is affectionately described as "quite a character." Both name partners still practice at Crowell & Moring, and their unique and well-liked personalities strongly influence the tone of the office. Though the firm was nicknamed "Cruel & Boring," it is now anything but that. Twice a year, Crowell lawyers gather for a big dinner outing that is frequently followed by a "crazy" night on the town. The bill for the evening is footed by Moring, who has been known to stay late into the night on these occasions. The firm also has a Christmas party, which however, one person criticized for not permitting attorneys' spouses to attend. People described the firm as exhibiting a social and "chit chatty" atmosphere. Every Friday afternoon, the attorneys enjoy a cocktail party known as "Cheap Booze." Crowell recently created a firm committee dedicated to improving "firm life" and building a better sense of community; relatedly, the firm holds a firmwide retreat directed at building "firm community."

Founded in 1979 as a small government contracts firm that split from the D.C. office of Jones, Day, Reavis & Pogue, Crowell & Moring was, in its early days, known as a "maverick" or "renegade" firm. Crowell's founding attorneys left Jones Day because they wanted greater autonomy from the Jones Day Cleveland headquarters. Consequently, as Crowell has grown, its founders have emphasized a democratic management and decision-making process. One contact remarked that there is "less distinction between partners and associates" at Crowell than at other D.C. firms.

practice areas

Today the firm employs almost 230 lawyers and offers a first-rate litigation practice that encompasses a broad range of areas including antitrust, business crimes, energy, environmental, insurance, labor, and products liability. Crowell & Moring primarily represents large corporations, particularly major insurance and manufacturing companies, defense contractors, utilities, telecommunications companies, and airlines. The firm handles environmental litigation for large corporations, and Greyhound is a major client of the firm's labor practice. Crowell also represents the American Psychiatric Association, and the firm has established a hotline to provide legal services for psychiatrists.

A number of Crowell's litigators are well-known in the city. Victor Schwartz, the firm's "products liability guru," has written textbooks and has been actively involved with tort reform issues. Rick Beizer and Pete Romatowski, both former federal prosecutors, are prominent white-collar criminal lawyers. William Randolf Smith came to the firm from the Federal Trade Commission, and Don Flexner held a high position in the Antitrust Division of the Department of Justice.

Though it is no longer a rapidly-growing practice area, the government contracts department is still an important part of the firm. Crowell also offers a small corporate practice which, unlike most D.C. firms, handles transactional work such as secured financing deals and initial public offerings, in addition to the characteristically D.C. corporate work involving regulatory matters that relate to the Securities and Exchange Commission (SEC). One contact stated that the head of the corporate department, formerly a partner in a large midwest firm, played a large role in building this unusual corporate practice. A few people commented that attorneys in the corporate group work particularly hard in comparison to other attorneys at the firm and one person remarked that the corporate practice is "not the best place to be at the firm."

international practice

Crowell's international practice enjoys a special affiliation with an international economics consulting group. Among other things, this group represented a Mexican client in the North American Free Trade Agreement (NAFTA) treaty negotiations, and does consulting work for numerous foreign governments. Lastly, Crowell's health care practice is headed by Joe Onek, former Deputy Counsel to President Carter, and an active participant in health care public policy issues.

pro bono

Crowell's pro bono practice is reportedly one of its most attractive features. One person raved that the firm devotes "serious time and resources" to pro bono work. The practice is managed by a partner and a full-time lawyer pro bono coordinator. In recent years, lawyers at the firm represented Tracy Thorne, the homosexual naval aviator who was discharged from the Navy on the basis of his sexual preference, at an administrative hearing and beyond into federal court. Crowell attorneys "take pride in" the pro bono practice, and the partners are "very committed" to pro bono work. A number have received awards for their pro bono service. As long as Crowell associates bill 1800 hours to paying clients, up to 200 hours of pro bono work is fully credited. The firm also offers its summer associates a unique pro bono opportunity. Every summer, the firm sends eight or nine summer associates to work for a public interest group for four to six weeks, while continuing to pay them their regular firm salary. People who took advantage of this program in past summers worked at such locations as the D.C. Public Defender Service, NAACP Legal Defense Fund, and the Children's Defense Fund.

expansion

The *Washingtonian* has ranked Crowell & Moring among the top performing D.C. firms. Many of its practice areas are growing—insurance, antitrust, products liability, labor, and intellectual property are doing particularly well. The firm has an office in London, which is staffed by three attorneys, as well as an office in Southern California. Partnership prospects are perceived as better at Crowell & Moring than at many other D.C. firms (but see above stats). The firm does not formally require associates to bring in business to be promoted to partner. People also commented that Crowell is very flexible in accommodating individual careers—many at the firm have gone back and forth between the firm and the government. Additionally, the firm has a strong "of counsel" program, which provides for a "balancing of work and outside life as associates reach higher levels of seniority, as an alternative to partnership and its demands," reported one insider.

training feedback

Everyone we interviewed commented that the training and feedback at Crowell could be improved. One person said that getting feedback was like "pulling teeth;" another said that "feedback is virtually non-existent." "The partners are very busy and don't have time to go over your work." One summer associate said his midsummer review and exit lunch didn't tell him anything about the quality of his work, and he was never shown any of the forms with which the attorneys evaluated his work.

diversity

Although one person commented that Crowell & Moring is no "Shangri-La" for women, the firm provides a more comfortable work atmosphere for women than many other D.C. firms. Karen Hastie Williams, a female African-American partner, is a "bigwig" at the firm. She makes herself accessible by attending many summer social events. One source observed that both men and women felt comfortable participating in all the summer events, and added that they were not the kind of activities at which some women feel "disenfranchised." One woman commented that there was "no organized women's group at the firm, but there was never a time when I felt that I couldn't ask a question." People also claimed that Crowell has good maternity leave and part-time work policies. Lastly, a "considerate" security guard, who is on duty at the firm's building until 2:00 A.M. each weeknight, will escort people to the metro or a cab.

For a big firm, Crowell offers a very accommodating environment for racial minorities, we were told. Minority recruitment and retention is a priority at the firm. It's partnership includes two African-American women. Some of the firm's partners teach a special class in legal reasoning for minority students who are interested in going to law school that helps improve their academic performance.

Crowell's offices are comfortable and slightly out of the ordinary. Eldon Crowell, a world traveler, has decorated the firm's offices with interesting items which he collected from remote parts of the world. A number of junior associate offices are located on the fifth floor, and some of these offices do not have windows. The firm's library is open in the center of the main floors, thus providing an area that is "conducive to socializing and team work," remarked one contact.

hiring tips

Crowell hires most summer associates from Ivy League and D.C.-area schools. New York University, Stanford, the University of Michigan, and Vanderbilt are also strongly represented in the summer classes. One successful applicant claimed that Crowell & Moring tends to hire "public interest minded" people and described the firm as a "magnet" for those who have public interest leanings. Another observed that the firm likes to hire people with interesting and unusual backgrounds.

Those who interview at the firm are assigned a "shepherd" (a first-year associate) who escorts interviewees around the firm and often takes them out to lunch. Ordinarily, interviews involve meeting four to six attorneys and going out to lunch with two. One person noted that the hiring committee is particularly concerned about each person's commitment to Washington D.C. Many attorneys ask students to explain their interest in practicing in Washington, D.C. and question their long-term commitment to the city.

Dickstein, Shapiro, Morin & Oshinsky

Washington New York
St. Petersburg

Address: 2101 L Street, N.W., Washington, D.C. 20037
Telephone: (202) 785–9700
Hiring Attorney: Emanuel Faust, Jr., Chairman, Hiring Committee
Contact: Lisa Gasiewicz, Director of Human Resources; (202) 828–2230; Caroline Gasser, Recruitment Coordinator; (202) 828-4251
Associate Salary: First year $76,000 (1997); second $80,000; third $85,000; fourth $91,000; fifth $98,000; sixth $105,000; seventh $111,000; eighth $119,000
Summer Salary: $1300/week (1997)
Average Hours: 1828 worked; 1610 billed; NA required
Family Benefits: 14 weeks paid maternity leave (16 unpaid); 12 weeks paid paternity leave (16 unpaid)
1996 Summer: Class of 23 students; offers to 21
Partnership: NA
Pro Bono: 2% of all work is pro bono

Dickstein, Shapiro, Morin & Oshinsky in 1997
210 Lawyers at the Washington D.C. Office
1.3 Associates Per Partner

Total Partners 92			Total Associates 122			Practice Areas	
Women	10	11%	Women	46	38%	Insurance Litigation	35
All Minorities	1	1%	All Minorities	11	9%	Energy/Natural Resources	22
Afro-Am	1	1%	Afro-Am	3	2%	Intellectual Property	22
			Asian Am	4	3%	Civil Litigation	20
			Latino	3	2%	Labor/General Litigation	15
			Native Am	1	1%	Corporate	14
						Government Contracts	12
						Public Sector Litigation	12
						Trade - International	10
						Business Crimes/Reg. Enforce.	9
						Fin. Institutions/Real Estate	9
						Securities Litigation	9
						Government Affairs	8
						Communications	7
						Tax	7
						Bankruptcy/Creditor's Rights	6
						Environmental	1

Founded in 1956, Dickstein, Shapiro, Morin & Oshinsky has grown rapidly to become a prominent D.C. law firm. Dickstein Shapiro originally specialized in union-side litigation and plaintiff's antitrust actions. Although the firm's practice has expanded considerably, it has remained strong in these areas and offers attorneys the unusual opportunity to represent unions in their disputes with management while working at a large law firm. Formerly Dickstein, Shapiro & Morin, the firm added the Oshinsky part of its name as a result of a 1996 merger with an insurance practice group from the D.C. office of Anderson Kill. The merger added approximately 45 lawyers to the firm, bringing the total number of attorneys to more than 200. One of the new partners is former Senator Joseph D. Tydings.

personal initiative required

"Entrepreneurial" may be the word most applicable to Dickstein Shapiro, a firm best suited to people with a lot of personal initiative. Unlike many other firms which formally assign work to summer associates, Dickstein Shapiro's summer associates are encouraged to pursue their own interests and to solicit their own work from the firm's attorneys. Those who are not shy about asking for work in their areas of interest are happy with the results. One person who has worked at four law firms said the "most exciting things I did at my other three firms were not as exciting as the least exciting thing I did at Dickstein."

significant opportunity

Dickstein Shapiro offers significant responsibility early, which according to one person, accounts for the consistently high attorney morale. Client contact occurs as early as the first year. In fact, one summer associate even had her "own" clients. It is not uncommon for first-year associates to represent clients in court. The firm "holds you close for about nine months," one insider noted. "After that, you have the potential to do whatever you want."

high pressure

Not surprisingly, the resulting work atmosphere is "high-pressure." One source stated, however, that "the pressure is worth it. It comes from the fact that you can do things at Dickstein that you don't get to do at other places." The associates may be "stressed out, but are learning a lot." We were told that "junior associates feel rewarded" by these opportunities.

not for the timid

Though most people praised the firm's unstructured and entrepreneurial environment, one contact cautioned that it is "not a firm to go to if you are timid." Dickstein Shapiro lawyers are a "very verbal group" and provide frank feedback. Associates rarely have "doubts about where they stand" with the firm. One summer associate was "yelled at" after handing in her first assignment. She said that this treatment does not happen on a "regular basis," but it "does happen." No one from the summer class voiced any complaints about being left in the dark with respect to their evaluations. One person said, "I can't imagine someone not knowing where they stood in the summer."

represents unions

Dickstein Shapiro has grown uninterruptedly since 1956, and it has maintained a somewhat informal working structure. In 1992, Dickstein Shapiro reorganized into fourteen separate practice groups, each with a designated department head. It remains well-known for its union-side labor litigation and antitrust work. The labor group was described as the most "cooperative group" at the firm, and its lawyers are reportedly "great to work with." The managing partner of the firm, Angelo Arcadipane, is a prominent labor attorney.

white-collar practice

Now a full-service law firm, Dickstein Shapiro also offers a high-profile white-collar criminal defense practice, which was described as a "high-pressure group." People cautioned that it is particularly difficult to get hired into this group. Among the prominent white-collar criminal lawyers are Barry Levine and Seymour Glanzer, who has handled high-profile Securities and Exchange Commission (SEC) enforcement work.

other practices

Dickstein Shapiro's general litigation practice represents a wide spectrum of plaintiffs and defendants that include the government and individuals, as well as small and large companies. The practice includes an appellate and Supreme Court litigation group. Described as "small and cozy," the firm's environmental practice is headed by John Agar. Dickstein Shapiro's intellectual property practice is one of the "fastest-growing" at the firm. Partner Gary Hoffman is renowned in the field, and has successfully built one of the biggest intellectual property groups in any of the D.C. general practice firms.

Dickstein Shapiro also has an international trade practice, and the firm has recently aggressively pursued international markets. Name partner David Shapiro was an organizer of the food drop into St. Petersburg, and the firm has since opened an office there. In addition, the firm maintains an office in New York City and handles considerable work involving Japan.

Recently, Dickstein Shapiro has been involved in a number of high-profile matters, including the Iran-Contra proceedings, Mike Tyson's representation, and the Exxon Valdez case. Dickstein Shapiro also has well-developed energy, environmental, and natural resource practices, led by Ken Simon and Fred Lowther. The expansive practice includes electric, gas, waste matter, and all facets of environmental law. Dickstein Shapiro attorneys are involved in transactional and regulatory aspects in these fields.

pro bono

People praised Dickstein Shapiro's pro bono practice. One source raved that it is "one of the best practices in D.C." The firm's pro bono committee assigns and screens projects, and a coordinator keeps track of individual attorney interests and contacts them when there is work available in those areas. In addition, many pro bono cases available through the firm are listed in a daily newsletter. The firm does work for the Zaccharus Legal Clinic. It has also worked on abortion and gender discrimination matters. All pro bono hours count toward billable hours.

loyalty

Dickstein Shapiro was described as "open," "chatty," and "friendly." A special associates committee serves as a formal channel through which associates express their views to the partners, who are typically receptive to associates' ideas. One source commented that "the new associate training program was revolutionized...as a direct result of this committee." Another person remarked that the firm sees itself as a "family" and places great emphasis on "loyalty once you are there." The firm is like a collection of "brothers and sisters. They do things for each other and look out for each other. The whole trick to success in the firm is finding your allies. They are incredibly loyal and will stick with you."

social life

Dickstein Shapiro offers a good social life. Indeed it is common to "see the entire intellectual property associate section commandeering a conference room to gather during their daily lunch routine." Many lawyers go out to lunch and socialize together after work. Dickstein Shapiro is not, however, a "wine and dine" firm and organizes few formal social events. One person noted that many attorneys are married and tend to go home to their families rather than socialize after work. Another person cited this as an especially attractive aspect of the firm—it offers "alternative arrangements for attorneys who desire to spend more time with their family."

diversity efforts

A controversial event in one past summer raised concerns about the atmosphere for women at Dickstein Shapiro. While making a presentation about the firm's history, a name partner made some comments which implied that, in general, women do not make great attorneys. These remarks "caused a furor at the firm," claimed one insider. "Everyone at the firm apologized" to the summer associates and "went out of their way to make clear that his statements didn't represent" the firm's views. Although this event had a big impact on summer associates, many people insisted that the incident was an aberration. People defended the firm and noted that many influential women practice at Dickstein Shapiro. One source told us that "in fact, the firm is very responsive to the concerns of women who practice at the firm. The female partners (10 in total) have in the past year taken an active role in communicating with each other, with women associates, and with other partners at the firm in an effort to ensure that Dickstein Shapiro maintains an environment in which women feel comfortable practicing law."

Although Dickstein Shapiro employs few racial minorities, the people we interviewed said there was no indication that the firm is any better or worse than other firms in its treatment of minority groups. More than one insider observed that the firm is known as being open-minded to homosexual attorneys and noted that openly gay and lesbian attorneys practice at the firm.

office facilities

Dickstein Shapiro's offices are "nice and comfortable" but "not snooty." The firm's networked, state-of-the-art computer system is "one of the finest among law firms in the city." The library staff at Dickstein Shapiro is so "helpful and knowledgeable" that some summer associates continued to rely on them for help even after they left to work at other firms. One contact remarked that "the library staff is able to get almost any resource you might need and has done an incredible job of staying on top of what's new." A group of people jog together during the lunch hour, while others gather for a game of basketball, and the offices are equipped with showers.

hiring tips

Dickstein Shapiro primarily hires summer associates from the top 15 national law schools. One insider emphasized, however, that it is possible to get a job at Dickstein Shapiro from any law school in the country. Although Dickstein Shapiro is one of D.C.'s most prestigious firms, it is less competitive than top tier firms like Covington & Burling and Arnold & Porter. The firm looks for "unusual backgrounds" and values individual initiative over "great grades." Many members of the summer class had journal experience or had participated in their school's moot court competition. People also noted that Dickstein Shapiro emphasizes writing skills in its hiring and requests a writing sample from each third-year and lateral applicant. It frequently requests them from second-year students as well. Students who are invited to the firm for callback interviews usually interview with four to five attorneys and go to lunch with two. Most callback interviews are casual, relaxed, and conversational. Attorney's often ask students to explain their interest in practicing in D.C. and, in particular, at Dickstein Shapiro and ask whether they have a long-term commitment to the city.

Dickstein Shapiro is a large, growing and attractive firm. It faces a challenge of handling its recent rapid expansion. One source commented that "the increase in size will eventually lead to the unfortunate situation where partners do not even recognize their own fellow partners." But that has not happened yet. Indeed the firm is praised for having "the most collegial group of attorneys of any firm, big or small," according to one contact. Several of the people we spoke with mentioned that salaries "need to be adjusted to compete with other upper tier firms." The firm is, however, attempting to respond to associates' concerns in this area, we were told. People broadly praised the summer associate program, described by one contact as "the best in the city because it emphasizes the integration of students into the firm." If all this sounds attractive, Dickstein Shapiro is your place.

Dow, Lohnes & Albertson

Washington Atlanta

Address: 1200 New Hampshire Avenue, N.W., Washington, D.C. 20036–6802
Telephone: (202) 776–2000
Hiring Attorney: David E. Mills
Contact: Judith D. Busch, Director, Legal Personnel; (202) 776–2605
Associate Salary: First year $85,000 (1997); second $90,000; third $95,000; fourth $100,000; fifth $105,000; sixth $110,000; seventh $117,000; eighth $125,000
Summer Salary: $1500/week (1997)
Average Hours: 2100 worked; 2000 billed; no minimum required
Family Benefits: 12 weeks paid maternity leave (cbc unpaid); cbc weeks paid paternity leave (cbc unpaid); emergency day care
1996 Summer: Class of 14 students; offers to 13
Partnership: NA
Pro Bono: 2% of all work is pro bono

Dow, Lohnes & Albertson in 1997
116 Lawyers at the Washington D.C. Office
1.0 Associate Per Partner

Total Partners 54		
Women	9	16%
All Minorities	2	4%
Afro-Am	1	2%
Latino	1	2%

Total Associates 57		
Women	25	44%
All Minorities	12	21%
Afro-Am	4	7%
Asian-Am	4	7%
Latino	4	7%

Practice Areas	
Communications	26
Corporate	21
Tax	14
Higher Education	11
Litigation	11
Media & Inform. Technologies	11
Compensation & Benefits	7
Labor	3

telecommunications practice

Dow, Lohnes & Albertson offers one of the nation's premier communications practices that handles "cutting-edge work" in a wide variety of areas including telecommunications, broadcast, cable, and satellite work. It represents a number of companies that develop emerging technologies relating to telecommunications and the Internet. Dow Lohnes also offers a "growing" complementary First Amendment practice which, among other things, represents a number of newspaper, radio, and television clients in libel litigation. Much of the firm's communications practice has been built around its representation of the Cox umbrella of communications companies, and the family that runs this media giant. Dow Lohnes also does work for several other big players in the communications industry, including American Radio Systems and Paxson Communications. Anyone interested in pursuing a career in communications law in D.C. should seriously consider Dow, Lohnes & Albertson.

other practice areas

Although largely considered a communication firm, Dow Lohnes has developed a number of top-rate practice groups in other areas. Dow Lohnes' corporate department boasts one of the firm's biggest rainmakers, Dick Braunstein, who (along with several other of the firm's members) is a personal friend of the Cox family and is its lead lawyer in D.C. Chip Allen, prominent in the firm's Atlanta office, is the Cox family's lead lawyer in that city. The corporate group tends to be "territorial and selective about whom they allow in the group," noted one source. Another claimed that the corporate lawyers exhibit "inflated egos" and stated that "you have to handle them with gloves on."

The firm has a well-known tax department that handles a lot of large-scale tax litigation. In fact, a former Dow Lohnes tax litigator was reportedly "responsible for the largest tax case in the history of the IRS." The tax group also includes an employee benefits practice, with attorneys who are "genuine and easy to work" with. Dow Lohnes is also one of the few firms in D.C. that has a large education practice group which represents large universities in a variety of matters from private litigation to representation before school boards. Finally, Dow Lohnes has a small, but dynamic, general litigation practice and an even smaller labor practice.

media and information technology group

A recent development in the Dow Lohnes structure has been the creation of the MIT (Media and Information Technology) group. A conglomerate of the former intellectual property group and the public broadcasting group, MIT was formed to deal with emerging Internet issues as well as the standard intellectual property fare. This new and dynamic group has been extremely busy and has been involved in the drafting of numerous online contracts.

pro bono

Dow Lohnes' anti-pro bono mentality perpetuated by the attitude of the firm's management is one of its drawbacks, we were told. Although associates are told that pro bono hours count toward "billable" hours, they do not count as "client-chargeable" hours, generally deemed a more important indicator of an associate's worth to the firm. Nevertheless, associates who desire to engage in pro bono work can find opportunities to work with the Associated Catholic Charities and the Washington Lawyers Committee for Civil Rights under the Law, as well as other public interest law groups. Presently, each member of the litigation group is involved in the representation of claimants in a sexual harassment class action suit filed by District of Columbia corrections employees against the D.C. Department of Corrections.

Overall, Dow Lohnes provides a "laid-back environment." The firm does not subject its attorneys to "huge amounts of stress" (although one contact observed the "the firm isn't always as 'low stress' as it would like to believe"), and its attorneys reportedly "enjoy working together." Lawyers at the firm are generally friendly and "there is really no sense of competition." Many pursue a variety of interests outside of the law. Although Dow Lohnes is structured in practice groups, many practice groups service the same communications clients; they share a "symbiotic relationship" and enjoy close working relationships. As a result, Dow Lohnes provides a smaller firm feel.

social firm

Dow Lohnes is a social firm. Its large incoming classes include young lawyers of all types, from "sports enthusiasts to theater buffs." These friendly attorneys are "always looking to recruit people to do social things." The summer social calendar includes events ranging from formal concerts to informal barbecues and night golf games. To encourage interaction among attorneys, the firm sponsors monthly "lawyers lunches"—where a catered lunch is served for all attorneys in the firm's largest conference room—as well as firmwide Friday social hours. A number of contacts indicated, however, that the firm is "stubbornly resistant" to adopting a regular "casual day;" casual days are "kept to a strict minimum (four or five per year) and are *always* preceded by a memo from the managing member reminding associates of what is and is not appropriate attire."

good experience; weak training

Entering associates rotate through two of the firm's departments for about six to eight months before specializing in one area in the second half of their first year. Each department offers junior associates different responsibilities. Attorneys have greater responsibility in the communications group, where "you live or die by your contacts with the Federal Communications Commission (FCC)." One person added that, "if you can make good connections with staff members of the FCC, the clients will contact you directly." It is also not uncommon for first- and second-year associates in the education group to represent their own clients. In contrast, the litigation, corporate, and tax departments are more structured and hierarchical. In general, however, people praised the firm for the early responsibility and opportunity for client contact provided. One insider pointed out that "the firm's clients (generally media-based) provide a variety of cutting-edge projects in all practice groups and foster a creative and interesting environment. The firm encourages direct client contact for all associates, at even junior levels—no lawyer ends up buried in the library, never speaking with the outside world." Another contact concurred that there is a "good degree of responsibility for young associates—second-year associates often have primary responsibility for drafting pleadings to be filed at FCC, with the partner responsible for the project merely serving as an 'editor' of the associate's work." In contrast, we were told that "compared to other firms, the training at Dow Lohnes isn't the greatest. There is no formal mentorship or writing program." Perhaps because of such criticisms, the firm has expanded its in-house seminars and "reinvigorated" its mentoring program. Feedback, however, may still be hard to obtain. One source claimed that associates only get feedback if someone has a problem with their work.

diversity

Dow Lohnes reportedly provides a work environment that is "very hospitable for women." The firm has adopted a formal paid parental leave program. Currently, the management evaluates requests for unpaid parental leave and for part-time on a "case-by-case" basis. The firm will accommodate you if you are "vital" to the department, claimed one insider, but you can't count on having unpaid parental leave. Dow Lohnes employs relatively few minority attorneys, though it has increased its numbers in recent years, especially of Asian-Americans and Latinos.

management focus on the bottom line

Dow Lohnes recently transformed from a partnership to a limited liability company. Currently, it is managed by a board of members and a managing member, Bill Perry. The forceful managing member was described by one source as a "native of Oklahoma who shoots from the hip," who added that he exhibits "an offbeat sense of humor" and is readily "approachable for a confident associate." In recent years, Dow Lohnes has required strong management to shepherd the firm through its ups and downs. It grew explosively in the 1980s from a relatively small firm to about 200 attorneys firmwide. In the early 1990s, it contracted rapidly, however. The international group left the firm and the New York office closed in December 1992. Despite the tough times, most people we interviewed said the firm has stabilized. The firm provided significant salary increases to all associates in 1996, and "salaries are now comparable to New York-based firms," according to one source. On the other hand, we were told that the firm is increasingly attentive to the bottom line and to billable hours: "if you are in corporate or communications, the hours can be very high—rumor has it that the average billables for 1996 were *well* over 2200. If you are in one of the 'lower' groups such as education or litigation, there is a general sense that the group is expendable and that, if the firm does not make a profit from the group, then the group is essentially useless or a second class citizen," one insider reported.

new offices

The Dow Lohnes office facilities were described in our earlier edition as "minimalist," with no "overpowering architecture and no expensive artwork," to which a firm spokesperson responded at that time as follows: "Stung by the criticism of our office facilities, the firm instituted a search for new space, the prime goal being to locate the most overpowering architecture. This search was successful, and our offices will be moved to swankier digs in late 1995–early 1996. We have also acquired some excellent new (but admittedly inexpensive) artwork by a rising new artist, who just happens to be married to one of our associates." We are delighted to inform our readers that the firm has lived up to all (well, almost all) of its earlier promises. In February 1996, Dow Lohnes moved its office facilities to part of the space formerly occupied by Arnold & Porter (the remaining space was taken over by Chadbourne & Parke's D.C. office). The newly refurbished space is an "immense aesthetic improvement" in terms of furniture and other amenities, we were told. Further, one contact informed us that the present facilities "have some good art and some works that try hard to be 'art'" The offices are not far from DuPont Circle and a short walk from Georgetown. Every attorney has a private office, and all but a few have external windows. Dow Lohnes has also "renewed its commitment" to providing its attorneys with updated technology, upgrading its computer system to a Windows operating system and providing telephones with caller identification to each attorney.

hiring tips

Although described as "somewhat grade-obsessed " by one contact, Dow Lohnes seeks summer associates "who are outgoing team players." We were told that the people it hires "tend to be mainstream types who have normal lives outside of their work. Almost everyone had other interests." In addition, "experience before law school is very important." One person commented that the firm looks for "how well one understands the Washington legal climate and practice." Dow Lohnes consciously attempts to hire only as many summer associates as it can offer permanent positions, and, in past years, all or nearly all summer associates have been extended offers of permanent employment at the conclusion of their summer.

Traditionally, Dow Lohnes has not enjoyed the prestige of D.C.'s top firms, but in recent years, its management has made a strong effort to have the firm known as more than "one of the best kept secrets in D.C." It has actively recruited the nation's top law students for its summer program. Dow Lohnes hires its summer associates from across the country, but primarily from the top 15 national schools.

The callback interview at Dow Lohnes is relaxed and low-key. Students usually meet with a "good sampling of attorneys" and often with one "bigwig" at the firm. One person advised people to emphasize that they have "something to offer as a lawyer outside of the law." Another said the firm looks for well-rounded people with a good sense of humor. People who are invited for callback interviews have a very strong chance of receiving a summer associate offer.

Foley & Lardner

Washington Chicago Jacksonville Los Angeles Madison Milwaukee Orlando Sacrament San Diego San Francisco Tallahassee Tampa West Palm Beach

Address: 3000 K Street, N.W., Washington Harbour, Suite 500, Washington, D.C. 20007–5109
Telephone: (202) 672–5300
Hiring Attorney: Patrick A. Doody, Allison George Newbold
Contact: Brenda M. Marconi, Recruiting Coordinator; (202) 672–5469
Associate Salary: Salary contingent upon background and experience
Summer Salary: $1250/week (1997)
Average Hours: 2000 worked; 1800 billed; 1800 required
Family Benefits: 3 weeks paid vacation; 26 weeks paid disability; 4 weeks paid childcare leave (2 unpaid); dependent care; medical spending accounts; 401(K) plan
1996 Summer: Class of 10 students
Partnership: NA
Pro Bono: NA

Foley & Lardner in 1997
93 Lawyers at the Washington D.C. Office
1.4 Associates Per Partner

Total Partners 38		
Women	6	16%
All Minorities	1	3%
Asian-Am	1	3%

Total Associates 54		
Women	17	32%
All Minorities	8	15%
Afro-Am	1	2%
Asian-Am	6	11%
Latino	1	2%

Practice Areas	
Intellectual Property	46
Litigation	21
Corporate	17
Health	4
Tax	3
Real Estate	2
Finance/Public Finance	na
Regulatory	na
Securities	na

Foley & Lardner is "the firm you can bring home to mom," remarked one source. Based in Milwaukee, Foley reflects the Midwest in its solid and hardworking culture. This "low key" firm hires "decent people," rather than the "glossy" lawyers that some might associate with Washington D.C. You don't see too many double-breasted suits at Foley, but "most attorneys dress fairly conservatively." The lawyers in this fairly small, somewhat staid branch office are "cooperative" and "down-to-earth." They place a premium on quality of life and are committed to traditional family values. Foley reportedly "treats the associates well." One contact reported that it is not a "sweatshop"—the firm cares a great deal "about the associates," while another contact remarked upon the "approachability" of the firm's partners.

family orientation

However, Foley is "not the place to turn for the center of your social life." A few young attorneys spend a lot of time socializing with summer associates, but one commented that, "I wouldn't say the social life is swinging." The firm is very family oriented, and one source observed that Foley associates' favorite topic of conversation is buying a house. The firm does sponsor a number of summer social activities, such as concerts at Wolf Trap and baseball games. In addition, summer associates take a trip to Milwaukee for a weekend to visit the firm's headquarters. Foley's "housekeepers," Maria and Doris, who have been with the firm for years, "take care of everything" at the firm, including preparing food for the monthly happy hours.

practice areas

Founded in 1971 to handle the firm's regulatory matters, Foley D.C. merged in 1974 with an existing antitrust boutique firm to begin broadening its practice. Over the years the D.C. office has expanded considerably. Foley is not organized in structured departments. Instead, the work of the firm is organized informally around partners who practice in certain specialty areas. One of the most noteworthy and rapidly growing areas at the firm is the health law practice, which handles a lot of antitrust work and has a developing legislative and lobbying component. The firm recently merged with a West Coast healthcare law firm, Weissberg & Aronson, to augment this practice even further.

A significant number of attorneys are involved in Foley's "booming" litigation practice, which represents a broad range of clients, including a number of Pacific Rim companies. As the result of a merger between Foley D.C. and the firm's Alexandria office (which exclusively handled patent work), patent law is one of the firm's largest practice areas. All of the patent lawyers have technical backgrounds. One contact informed us that Foley is "probably the only firm in the D.C. area that is about 50% patent attorneys and 50% non-patent attorneys. Other firms are either 'patent boutique' firms, or have a small patent group; our 50/50 mix gives us a solid footing for handling patent litigation and patent prosecution matters."

A number of people expressed disappointment in Foley's pro bono practice. One person commented that "firmwide" there is not much "commitment" to pro bono. Some people at the firm are "frustrated" with the firm's pro bono policy. Pro bono hours are not counted toward billable hours, but the firm claims they are considered in annual associate reviews. Foley receives most of its pro bono work through the Washington Lawyers Committee for Civil Rights under the Law.

significant opportunity

Foley is a good firm for those seeking early responsibility. The litigation partners try to "get people into court right off the bat," we were told. Foley D.C. recently inaugurated extensive training programs for all new associates, especially those practicing in the area of intellectual property. Feedback is "available" but must be "actively sought out."

management

Although Foley is a branch office and can draw upon the resources of a large firm, it enjoys an independent client base and maintains a fair degree of autonomy from the Milwaukee headquarters. The firm prides itself on its diverse clientele and the fact that no single client represents more than two percent of its total business. Over the years, the firm has grown steadily and conservatively. Everyone we interviewed said the firm has been doing very well in recent years, with growth more marked than in earlier years.

Firmwide, Foley is run by a management committee, of which the D.C. office's managing partner, Jim Bierman, is a member. The "managing partner has a lot of power" in the D.C. office, and those we interviewed had good things to say about him. He is accessible, has an open door policy, and one source reported "his heart is in a good place." One contact noted that the managing partner does not exactly fit into the midwestern mold. One described him as an "intense" person who would probably feel more comfortable in New York than in Wisconsin.

morale

Morale at Foley is "good, positive, and upbeat, but not ecstatic." One source described the firm as the type of place where "if you do your work well, you'll make partner," although this is reportedly less true today than in the past. Work pressures have been increasing in recent years.

Foley's offices are located in Washington Harbor, near Georgetown. The offices have balconies overlooking the Potomac River and the facilities are "spacious," although "associate offices may be on the small side." People praised the location as being one of the "most beautiful in Washington;" however, it is not within easy walking distance of any of D.C.'s metro rail stops, which makes it inconvenient for the public transportation commuter. All attorneys receive personal computers. There is also a small exercise room in the basement which is outfitted with a Universal weight system and a shower.

hiring tips

Foley has traditionally hired a number of students from George Washington, Georgetown, and the University of Virginia. People emphasized that in its hiring, Foley looks more for people who are down-to-earth, and who fit in well with the firm's midwestern culture, rather than for people with high grades. Interviews involve "candid" discussions with about three to four partners and associates and lunch with two to three. The attorneys "are both anxious to elicit information regarding your interests and to sell the firm," noted one insider. "You don't need a particular focus to get hired."

Fried, Frank, Harris, Shriver & Jacobson

Washington Los Angeles New York
London Paris

Address: 1001 Pennsylvania Avenue, N.W., Suite 800, Washington, D.C. 20004–2505
Telephone: (202) 639–7000
Hiring Attorney: Stephen I. Glover
Contact: Sandra M. Lucian, Recruitment Coordinator; (202) 639–7118
Associate Salary: First year $77,000 (1997)
Summer Salary: $1300/week (1997)
Average Hours: 2103 worked; 1605 billed; NA required
Family Benefits: 12 weeks paid maternity leave; 4 weeks paid paternity leave; childcare
1996 Summer: Class of 20 students; offers to 17
Partnership: 20% of entering associates from 1979–1984 were made partner
Pro Bono: 3% of all work is pro bono

Fried, Frank, Harris, Shriver & Jacobson in 1997
95 Lawyers at the Washington D.C. Office
1.8 Associates Per Partner

Total Partners 32			Total Associates 56			Practice Areas	
Women	4	13%	Women	22	39%	Corporate	45
All Minorities	0	0%	All Minorities	4	7%	Litigation	39
			Afro-Am	1	2%	Tax	5
			Asian-Am	2	4%		
			Latino	1	2%		

As the branch office of a pre-eminent New York firm, Fried, Frank, Harris, Shriver & Jacobson offers a national practice which involves some of the country's most complex legal work. The firm was founded by Jewish lawyers during a time when Jews were excluded from the established firms of the day. In its early days, Fried Frank was regarded as a "progressive" and "with it" firm because it hired lawyers that were overlooked by other large law firms. To this day, consistent with its tradition of drawing attorneys from outside elitist circles, Fried Frank D.C. recruits less than other old-line firms at the 10 most elite law schools. "The big thing they care about is getting people who can do the work," one insider noted. "They don't care if you went to a fancy school or not. They see themselves as less elitist." Still, "only about one quarter of new hires come from schools outside the top ten to fifteen schools," cautioned one insider.

diversity

Fried Frank's "progressive" image has waned in recent years because, though the firm is religiously and ethnically diverse, it has no minority partners and only one African-American associate. One source stated that though minority attorneys receive "no overt adverse treatment," the firm exhibits "not much apparent effort or consciousness to increase the numbers." Fried Frank has reportedly made less of an effort to be inclusive of minority groups and to provide a comfortable environment than other D.C. firms, although Fried Frank recently did host a firmwide reception for minority attorneys. One associate at the firm commented that most minority issues are "not even a consideration."A firm spokesperson informed us that "the firm does make an effort to recruit minorities," and was selected by the Northeast Black Law Students Association as their "Sponsor of the Year." People did comment that the firm provides a good atmosphere for women, particularly with respect to family issues. One associate remarked that the firm has adopted "a fairly liberal maternity and paternity leave policy," and it has recently instituted an emergency day care program.

long hours

The work atmosphere at Fried Frank is "informal" and "busy." The firm does not have a strict dress code and attorneys occasionally work in casual clothes when they are not scheduled to meet with clients. Fridays are now casual dress days at the firm. Overall, Fried Frank "is not a chatty firm. People get down to work and get out of there." Perhaps reflecting its New York roots, long work hours are not uncommon, and attorneys often work until 10 P.M. While the firm has no minimum billable hours requirement, "it expects associates to put in long hours. Twelve hour days and working on weekends is common." Moreover, while the firm has a generous four-week vacation policy which all associates are "encouraged" to take, one source told us that "many associates, particularly senior associates, have had to cancel or reschedule vacations because of work. The partners like to give associates the impression that they're indispensable on projects, and cannot be spared for a vacation. Most of it depends on who you work for—some partners are better than others."

social life

Fried Frank is not the place to go if you are looking to find a social life. Though some associates are "willing to go out," many are married and value their home lives. However, one contact noted that "associates as a whole are very friendly. There is always someone to have lunch with or order dinner with. Many associates do socialize with each other outside the office." Another source remarked that "associates are more than willing to help each other out." Aside from hosting a number of well-attended cocktail parties and an annual Holiday Party at the Four Seasons, Fried Frank does not go out of its way to sponsor lavish social occasions.

strong securities practice

Fried Frank rose to prominence most recently in New York during the 1980s as a fast-paced mergers and acquisitions law firm. Not surprisingly, in the D.C. office the corporate department is the strongest and largest practice area. However, unlike the corporate practice of the New York head office, the branch office's corporate practice handles a large volume of securities regulatory, enforcement, and compliance work, in addition to transactional work. This department has handled some of the most high-profile securities litigation matters, including representation of Ivan Boesky and Lloyd's of London, and offers one of the best practices of its kind in the city. Harvey Pitt, former General Counsel to the Securities and Exchange Commission (SEC), is a pre-eminent securities lawyer, an expert on insider trading issues, and a driving force behind the firm's enforcement practice.

other practice areas

Fried Frank also offers litigation, government contracts, and international trade departments. The international trade department was recently re-established with the return of David Birenbaum from serving as Representative of the United Nations for U.N. Management and Reform. Fried Frank's small tax practice is under the leadership of the nationally reputed Martin Ginsburg, a professor at Georgetown University Law School and husband of Supreme Court Justice Ruth Bader Ginsburg. Martin Ginsburg, known as a merger and acquisitions expert, also provides services to some high-profile individuals, including H. Ross Perot, who endowed the Ginsburg chair at Georgetown after Ginsburg solved some of Perot's tax problems. The firm's environmental practice in D.C. recently collapsed when its environmental lawyers migrated to another D.C. firm. However, according to one source, "the department was sort of isolated and off to themselves, so I'm not sure anyone else at the firm noticed or was particularly affected by it."

pro bono commitment

Fried Frank has an organized commitment to public service. One of the firm's partners is in charge of the pro bono practice and a pro bono committee screens all projects. The firm recently appointed an associate who is now responsible for coordinating pro bono activities, along with the partner in charge and the committee. "She devotes a significant amount of time recruiting attorneys for projects and seeking out lots of pro bono opportunities to choose from," we were told. Fried Frank attorneys handle a broad variety of criminal and civil pro bono work which has included work for the Children's Defense Fund, work for the National Law Center for Homelessness and Poverty, and assistance to veterans who have been denied benefits. As is evident by the careers of Fried Frank partners, who have served with the SEC, the EPA, the U.S. Attorney's Office, and others, they are also committed to government service. Perhaps the most famous is now retired name partner and President Kennedy's brother-in-law Sargent Shriver. A former Democratic Vice Presidential nominee who served as U.S. Ambassador to France and Director of the Peace Corps, he still maintains an office in D.C.

morale somewhat problematic

Associate morale is somewhat of a problem at Fried Frank, according to some of our contacts. Although the D.C. associates earn salaries that are above average for D.C., "there is grumbling" because their New York counterparts earn more. All associates were given across-the-board raises in 1996, and most "were pleased by the amount of the raise. However, no one in the D.C. office made partner this past year, so many senior associates were unhappy," reported one insider. Indeed, this person further remarked that "the firm has gotten into the trend of naming some senior associates, particularly in New York, as 'special counsel.' None of the younger associates suffer any delusions that they'll stick around long enough and make partner."

professional development

In addition, many associates are unhappy with the degree of responsibility and training that Fried Frank offers. Because most of Fried Frank's work involves large complex matters for huge corporations, it offers less significant early responsibility than some other D.C. firms, and much of the work at the firm is very "memorandum" oriented, observed one insider. But, another contact softened this observation somewhat, pointing out that "partners and senior associates have an open door policy for pointing you in the right direction, thus allowing associates to take on high levels of responsibility." Moreover, a firm spokesperson noted that "many corporate associates, even in their first and second year, get a significant amount of client contact." Although the firm offers a few formal training sessions in particular substantive areas, most training occurs informally on-the-job. Relying on informal training is a problem, according to one source, because the partners "don't have a strong commitment to training. They think they do, but there are complaints." One contact stated, however, that the corporate department provides a detailed formal training program for new associates which covers a broad range of areas and is conducted over the course of several months. Corporate associates are expected, in addition, to attend PLI or other conferences to keep up to date on developments. Another contact pointed out that the litigation department is also now making an effort to provide some formal training sessions.

management

Firmwide, Fried Frank is managed by committee. The D.C. office is run on a daily basis by a separate coordinating committee composed of attorneys from the D.C. office. This coordinating committee can offer a "fair amount of input" into the firmwide management structure. An associates committee also meets regularly to discuss associate concerns and to serve as a formal channel to the partners. However, people claimed that this committee does not have much impact and noted that associate input into the firm's management is minimal. The associates committee went to a great deal of effort recently, however, to convince partners to give associates the aforementioned raise. The prevailing attitude at the firm appears to be that "the partners call the main shots." One person commented that the associates are "seen as functional people. They are there to do the work." The firm does not communicate especially well with associates. For example, one person told us that "two of counsels left the firm this year, and the partners never even acknowledged, such as in a memo, that the of counsels were leaving. Associates must depend on firm gossip to find out firm news. Also, the partners are very secretive about how much the firm and partners make each year."

Fried Frank's offices are not out of the ordinary, except that they are adorned with an unusual avant-garde art collection on which the attorneys reportedly "pride themselves." The office cafeteria serves breakfast and lunch, and the food is "good and cheap." The firm has a "good library" and "phenomenal" support services. One contact marvelled that the "fantastic support services allows attorneys to focus on their practice, while everything that needs to be done gets done." Another contact had reservations about the library, however. This person pointed out that "although the library staff is wonderful, I often find the research sources and books in our library to be inadequate. We can borrow books from other libraries, but it is not the same as being able to browse through an area filled with books on the subject you are researching." There are no workout facilities in the office, but the firm subsidizes a membership at a local gym.

hiring tips

Although Fried Frank has traditionally relied less on the most prestigious law schools to meet its hiring needs, as the market for summer associate jobs has become more competitive, the firm has drawn an increasing portion of its summer class from the top 10 law schools. The firm is reportedly not as "grade conscious" as others in D.C. Fried Frank's attorneys are more concerned about an individual's commitment to working hard and an ability to do a thorough job. Interviews usually involve meeting four or five attorneys for a half-hour to an hour each and lunching with two.

Fried Frank interviews are not formally structured. One person observed that the people at the firm are, "by far, more frank than people at other firms. There was no cheerleading going on. The big thing they told people was that Fried Frank is not a firm where people stay or stick around. So it you are looking to stay, don't come." One successful applicant advised that interviewees should "express an interest in being available to move between projects." "You won't always get the work you want," and it is important to demonstrate flexibility. One person commented that the firm "rarely recruits more than it needs."

Fried Frank is a fast-paced, down-to-business firm. It services national clients and has one of the best corporate securities practices in the country. The firm's associates work harder and are paid more than most in D.C., but there are continuing complaints that you "don't get the New York pay scale and other firms that work just as hard pay a little more at some levels." The work at Fried Frank is challenging. "It's exciting to work on the big cases that are in the paper all the time. Associates who have left the firm often complain that the work at their new firms can be boring in comparison. The work is complex and intellectually stimulating at Fried Frank." In short, Fried Frank is a no-nonsense, no-frills, hard-working firm that offers its lawyers challenging high-profile work on a regular basis.

Fulbright & Jaworski

Washington Austin Dallas Houston Los Angeles New York San Antonio
Hong Kong London

Address: 801 Pennsylvania Avenue, N.W., Washington, D.C. 20004
Telephone: (202) 662–0200
Hiring Attorney: Richard L. Jacobson
Contact: Marilynn J. Fuller, Recruiting Coordinator; (202) 662–4614
Associate Salary: First year $75,000 including bonus (1997)
Summer Salary: $1250/week (1993)
Average Hours: 2375 worked; 1950 billed; NA required
Family Benefits: Maternity leave
1996 Summer: Class of 17 students; offers to 14
Partnership: 33% of entering associates from 1979–1986 were made partner
Pro Bono: 1–3% of all work is pro bono

Fulbright & Jaworski in 1997
67 Lawyers at the Washington D.C. Office
0.5 Associates Per Partner

Total Partners 41		
Women	2	5%
All Minorities	1	2%
Asian-Am	1	2%

Total Associates 21		
Women	8	38%
All Minorities	4	19%
Afro-Am	1	5%
Asian-Am	3	14%

Practice Areas	
Litig./Antitrust, Sec, Civ., Crim.	17
Banking, Bus., Corp., Securities	13
International, Gen. Commercial	12
Energy	6
Health	6
Intellectual Property	6
Real Estate	3
Tax	3
Transportation	1

Fulbright & Jaworski brings a very "southern flavor" to the heart of the D.C. legal community. Based in Houston, many of its attorneys are from the South. This Texas-based firm is not stuffy and offers an "informal" and "laid-back" work atmosphere and social life. Firm sponsored activities include a Thursday office lunch for all attorneys, and in the summer, softball and other sporting events. Although most Fulbright attorneys are married and do not share a cohesive and active social life, they are "friendly" and "relaxed," several people told us.

increased emphasis on billable hours

Fulbright does not impose a formal billable hour requirement. It does, however, generally expect attorneys to bill eight or more hours per day. Hours worked have increased in recent years. Several departments have been extremely busy of late and "attorneys in these departments work long hours." Fulbright offers associates who have been at the firm for four or five years an incentive to contribute to the firm by permitting them to share in the firm's equity as "Participating Associates." This option does not exist, however, according to one contact, for attorneys in offices outside of Texas.

controlled from Houston

This increased emphasis on billable hours and a long work day in part reflects a change in managing partner which occurred in the early 1990s. After the economically troubled years of the late 1980s, the firm headquarters sent a Houston partner to manage the D.C. office and, in part, to "buckle down" on its operations, claimed one insider. This new managing partner is described as "bottom line" oriented. He has cut costs by subjecting billable hours to careful scrutiny, "micro managing," and reducing the firm's social activities. The new managing partner represents greater control by the Houston home office over the D.C. branch, said several people who also noted that this control is a source of frustration to some at the firm, especially in the context of partnership decisions. One source informed us that "there is the sense that, despite the D.C. office's profitability, the cards are dealt from the Houston office, where many large issues, such as partnership decisions are rendered."

practice areas

Fulbright's practice is divided into a number of sections, producing an "eclectic atmosphere in the workplace," said one person. The firm's most prominent practice areas are white-collar criminal defense, securities, and litigation. The white-collar practice has been involved in a number of high-profile cases, including representation of Admiral Poindexter. The white-collar lawyers are very pleasant to work with, we were told. Fulbright's strong securities group primarily handles shareholder suits and securities fraud cases. Partner Alan Levenson, previously Director of the Division of Corporate Finance at the Securities and Exchange Commission (SEC), is well-known in the field. The litigation practice "cuts across all areas" at the firm. Recently, the antitrust, civil, and criminal practices all merged into one "general" litigation section, which provides "a good opportunity to work on a wide variety of issues but makes it difficult to specialize in any one thing." Many of the firm's litigation clients are also represented by other practice areas of the firm. For example, Fulbright represents Duke University, a prominent litigation client, in a broad range of issues ranging from the medical malpractice cases of its medical school to legal issues involving new research techniques. The litigation practice is an excellent place to work because its lawyers are "great people," raved one person.

Fulbright also offers a health care group which is reportedly "very overworked." This group has been subject to some "turmoil" involving a few of its rainmaking partners, said one person. Fulbright also has a strong intellectual property practice. In addition, the international department is fast becoming a prominent group at the firm. The international practice is head-quartered at the D.C. office and is headed by Steve Pfeiffer, a highly regarded "star" partner. The D.C. office does a lot of work with the London and Hong Kong offices of the firm. The firm's pro bono practice is the "worst part of Fulbright," remarked one source. You "have to take a lot of initiative" to do pro bono work and it is "not credited" toward billable hours. The firm has, however, been developing a new pro bono policy, which we were told makes pro bono cases easier to get but they still do not earn billable hours credit.

development and training

Fulbright is not a "memo" firm. Although it represents a number of large corporations, such as Bacardi, and oil and gas companies, such as Exxon, its client base includes many small to medium-sized clients. The smaller clients, coupled with the fact that associates typically work directly with partners, permit Fulbright to offer new associates first-hand legal experience soon after they join the firm. One contact elaborated upon this by noting that associates "do get to work directly with partners but it is very difficult to get experience outside the office." Formal training at Fulbright is not a strong point of the firm. Indeed, one source pointed out to us that "we've had a lot of associate attrition in the past year which alarmed partners into trying to correct problems such as training and experience."

family issues

Fulbright & Jaworski is reported not to be one of the more "progressive" firms regarding women's issues. "None of the top partners are women" and the firm "doesn't have any policies for time off and part-time status," noted one person. Another told us that the firm makes "no effort to permit women to work and have a family. The only women who succeed are those who do not marry and have children." Fulbright has significantly increased its minority population since our last edition, to a point where now roughly 20 percent of its associates are minorities.

lavish offices

Fulbright's beautiful offices at Market Square are situated in a crescent around the Navy Memorial and have a view down Pennsylvania Avenue. Many attorney offices have outdoor balconies. The office is decorated with marble that Fulbright specially imported from Italy. The office is so nice, it is almost "embarrassingly lavish," commented one person, though others cautioned that this may be a bit of an overstatement. The firm's office building also houses a sauna and a gym with a stairmaster, exercise bikes, and showers, which attorneys and staff may use at no cost.

hiring tips

Fulbright recruits a number of its lawyers from southern schools such as the University of Texas, Vanderbilt, and the University of Virginia. The firm also does on-campus interviews at, among others, Harvard, Georgetown, Catholic, Howard, Duke, Stanford, South Carolina, NYU, Columbia, and Cornell, as well as at the BLSA Conference. The firm's callback interviews are relaxed and casual. Fulbright prefers "nice" people and doesn't go for "strong personalities," commented one source. A second contact informed us, however, that this is changing: "with the new hiring partner, a former U.S. Supreme Court Clerk, there is now more emphasis on high grades and top school than on 'personality'."

Fulbright is a fiscally conservative firm and reportedly did not take on any debt in the booming 1980s. Moreover, the firm's new emphasis on the bottom line has resulted in high profits in the D.C. office over the past few years. However, the control exerted by the home office in Houston rankles some and Fulbright's less than sterling record on women's issues troubles others. Still, according to people we interviewed, Fulbright is an attractive firm to be at. It is poised to take advantage of a number of international markets such as Britain, Hong Kong, and Eastern Europe. Additionally, the firm has experienced rapid growth in the corporate, international, and securities departments in recent years. For those who would like to experience a touch of the South, but still want to live in D.C., Fulbright may be the place to be.

Gibson, Dunn & Crutcher

Washington Century City Dallas Denver Los Angeles Menlo Park New York Orange County San Diego San Francisco Seattle Hong Kong London Riyadh Tokyo

Address: 1050 Connecticut Avenue, N.W., Suite 900, Washington, D.C. 20036
Telephone: (202) 955–8500
Hiring Attorney: Peter Wallison
Contact: Jill Sterner, Recruiting Coordinator; (202) 955–8546
Associate Salary: First year $83,000 (1997)
Summer Salary: $1300/week (1996)
Average Hours: NA worked; 1967 billed; NA required
Family Benefits: Disability leave as needed
1996 Summer: Class of 12 students; offers to 12
Partnership: 15%
Pro Bono: 3% of all work is pro bono

Gibson, Dunn & Crutcher in 1997
87 Lawyers at the Washington D.C. Office
1.5 Associate Per Partner

Total Partners 35		
Women	2	6%
All Minorities	1	3%
Native Am	1	3%

Total Associates 52		
Women	19	37%
All Minorities	7	13%
Afro-Am	2	4%
Asian Am	5	10%

Practice Areas	
Litigation	43
Corporate	35
Unassigned	22
Labor	10
Tax	5
Real Estate	2

With offices across the world, including foreign offices in Europe, the Middle East, and the Pacific Rim, L.A.-based Gibson, Dunn & Crutcher is one of the country's largest mega firms. Many attorneys in the D.C. office work closely with lawyers in other firm offices, and the firm is flexible about allowing transfers among its offices, provided a need for one's services exists at the desired end point. Summer associates acquire first-hand experience with Gibson's worldwide management, as they must be approved by the firm's overall hiring committee before permanent offers are extended.

free market system

Despite its size, Gibson Dunn is loosely structured. Work projects for permanent associates are assigned through the firm's unique "free market" system. The firm usually assigns the first project, but thereafter junior associates must solicit their own work. One person confirmed that this system can be somewhat "alarming and unnerving in the first few months." It also can lead to competitive pressure. Over time, the system "can be either a boon or a bust. If things don't work out and you don't find your niche, there can be big problems. It's important to make connections with people from work. After your first and second years things settle down." One contact informed us that "when work is plentiful, as it has been at Gibson Dunn for the past several years, the free market system is at its best, giving associates their choice of projects, practice areas, and partners to work for." During such times, the system is a buyer's market with associates in the driver's seat. Under this system, a junior associate's success at Gibson depends in part on having good working relationships with partners and senior associates, many of which are established during the summer program. One insider observed that junior associates who did not spend a summer with the firm have a more difficult time adapting. The summer program is more structured. Work is assigned through work coordinators to assure that summer clerks get broad exposure to the various practice groups.

practice areas

Firmwide, Gibson Dunn is divided into litigation, corporate, tax, labor, and real estate departments. Certain subgroups, however, are particularly important in the D.C. office, where a large amount of the work involves legislative and regulatory matters. The litigation practice, considered particularly selective in its hiring, is highly regarded for its appellate work. Ted Olson is a prominent Supreme Court litigator, and many lawyers in this group are former Supreme Court clerks. Gibson also is renowned for its fast-growing labor practice, which primarily represents management. Bill Killberg, formerly the Solicitor of the Labor Department, is highly regarded in this practice area. One contact informed us that recently "several liberal labor lawyers left, leaving a very conservative group in the D.C. office." Gibson does a lot of corporate and securities work as well, although one person noted that this practice has been slow in recent years. The corporate practice boasts Chuck Muckenfuss, who previously worked at the Federal Insurance Deposit Corporation and in the Office of the Comptroller. Gibson has a strong international trade practice, which services a number of clients in the Pacific Rim. The group includes Don Harrison, who does a lot of work for Honda.

The firm also has a small but growing environmental practice. In 1993, Ray Ludwiszewski, former General Counsel at the EPA, joined the firm and has raised considerably the profile of Gibson Dunn in the environmental field.

Gibson Dunn has targeted a number of practice areas in its strategic plan. It recently added Mike Denger, formerly head of the ABA's antitrust section, to continue growing the firm's antitrust practice, and Joe Warin to lead a white-collar crime group. In addition, Gibson Dunn is focusing on its overseas offices to achieve its goal of becoming a "totally complete full-service law firm" around the globe.

pro bono

Gibson Dunn attorneys may pursue their own pro bono matters. Pro bono hours count towards the firm's billable hour requirement. The pro bono practice is "structured informally," and one person alleged that it is "not particularly emphasized." The firm's attorneys have, however, done a wide range of pro bono work, from helping the local Whitman Walker clinic to doing legal work for the former Republics of the Soviet Union. The firm also has made a $10,000 contribution to Howard Law School to fund fellowships for Howard students to provide legal services to indigent clients in D.C.

professional development

Most associates at Gibson Dunn spend a few years "in the library, cranking out memos," before taking charge of their own clients. This is not universally the case, however. One source informed us that "I never spent time 'in the library' and I had substantial client interaction in my first and second years." The firm apparently does not provide as much formal training as many of its competitors. One person informed us that "no training was provided in 1994–1996, though such training is scheduled to begin in 1997." We also heard criticisms regarding associate performance feedback. Although associates are supposed to meet regularly with a partner mentor for this purpose, we were told that "in practice, the mentor system does not exist." A firm spokesperson informed us, however, that "associates are given comprehensive feedback during a formalized year end review process." Gibson received high marks, however, for its timely and complete evaluations of summer associate work. One source remarked that the attorneys provided feedback throughout the summer and are "good about letting you know how things are going and where you stand."

Gibson Dunn provides good opportunities for social life. There is a "solid group of younger associates who go out regularly." One summer highlight is the "summer associate academy" when the firm flies all its summer associates to Los Angeles for four fun-filled days of firm events and socializing.

diversity complaints

Gibson Dunn received caustic reviews about its work atmosphere for women and minorities. There are only two women partners in the D.C. office. One person lamented that there is a "feeling that women at Gibson have a more difficult time making bonds with some of the older partners to get work," which is crucial to success in the free market system. Another contact observed that, "in general, the D.C. office and perhaps the whole firm has shifted to the right and become more purely business oriented and less friendly to women, minorities, and homosexuals," A firm spokesperson adamantly denied that this is the case, insisting that "it is absolutely not true that the D.C. office has become less friendly to women, minorities, and homosexuals."

offices

All of the firm's associates have their own offices with networked computers. The offices have a small gym with a Universal weight machine and exercise bikes. Located four blocks from the White House, the offices are right above the Farragut North metro stop so that metro commuters "don't have to get wet when it's raining." The previously impressive support services and staff "have been cut severely," according to one insider.

hiring tips

Gibson Dunn is "heavily credential-oriented" in its hiring. One successful applicant advised that they "look for people of caliber and with a lot of involvement in law school. They are pretty grade conscious and have specific grade cutoffs for different schools." Most successful candidates are from the top 20 national or D.C.-area law schools. Unlike most D.C. firms, the callback interview at Gibson lasts all day. It is "long, but not grueling," remarked one source. Typically, an associate from the applicant's law school supervises the visit. Interviews usually begin around 10 A.M., and students meet with three or four people before going to lunch with a couple of associates. After lunch, the interviews continue until about 3:30 P.M. Applicants then have a break before going to dinner with more firm attorneys. The interview process is considered "more comprehensive" than those at other firms, although the individual interviews are fairly laid-back. One person explained that the firm is "extraordinarily conscientious about personality and personality fits," and noted that the full day interview is an opportunity for the firm's attorneys to observe a student's personality in many different contexts. Since Gibson Dunn gives virtually all of the summer associates offers of full-time employment, the summer associate interview process is particularly emphasized.

Hogan & Hartson

Washington Baltimore Bethesda Colorado Springs Denver Los Angeles Mclean
Brussels Budapest London Moscow Prague Warsaw

Address: Columbia Square, 555 Thirteenth Street, N.W., Washington, D.C. 20004
Telephone: (202) 637–5600
Hiring Attorney: Stephen J. Immelt
Contact: Ellen M. Swank, Associate Recruitment & Professional Development Administrator; (202) 637–8601
Associate Salary: First year $74,000 (1996)
Summer Salary: $1350/week (1997)
Average Hours: NA worked; NA billed; 1800 target
Family Benefits: Medical/family leave; emergency daycare
1996 Summer: Class of 30 students; offers to 30
Partnership: 20% of entering associates from 1980–1985 were made partner
Pro Bono: NA

Hogan & Hartson in 1997
346 Lawyers at the Washington D.C. Office
1.0 Associate Per Partner

Total Partners 169			Total Associates 177			Practice Areas	
Women	NA	NA%	Women	NA	NA%	Commercial	NA
All Minorities	NA	NA%	All Minorities	NA	NA%	Litigation	
						Health	
						Food & Drug	
						Trade Regulation	
						Communications	
						Education	
						Antitrust	
						Labor	
						Environmental	
						Government Contracts	
						Legislative	
						Energy	
						Transportation	
						Administrative	
						Community Services	

top-notch pro bono

Founded in 1904, Hogan & Hartson is the largest and one of the most prestigious D.C. law firms. Like its competitors, the firm has a broad-ranging practice and is particularly known for its pro bono work. Hogan's pro bono department, referred to as the Community Services Department, has received numerous honors, such as the 1995 Pro Bono Law Firm of the Year Award from the D.C. Bar and is "constantly being recognized as the best pro bono department" in D.C. The group is staffed by one partner and one senior associate who work in the department for 18 months at a time and by other junior associates who do four month rotations. This department, which is treated like any other at the firm, "farms out" the pro bono work to interested attorneys and "almost everyone does it." Hogan's attorneys have worked on death penalty appeals, Medicaid issues, racial discrimination cases, mental institution litigation, and the preservation of the Grand Canyon. They have also represented a Central American Savings Cooperative, Amnesty International, Greenpeace, and migrant workers in Baltimore. Although pro bono hours do not count as billable hours, except in the case of the several associates assigned to the Community Services Department, people noted that the firm's billable hour target (1800 hours) is lower than that at some other firms. Many also commented that the pro bono department provides junior associates with excellent opportunities for responsibility, which are much more limited on paying matters.

practice areas

Hogan & Hartson's practice is divided into three areas: commercial, government regulation, and litigation. Each of these areas is further split into practice groups, giving Hogan the feel of a smaller firm. Summer associates can sample many aspects of the firm's practice, but one person observed that it was difficult to get corporate assignments (though this may be true for summer associates, it is not true for regular associates: "there's *plenty* of corporate work for the latter right now," reported one insider). Starting associates have an opportunity to rotate for four month stints among different practice groups over the course of a year (or more) before deciding which group to join; the firm is also very flexible in permitting transfers.

local client base

Hogan & Hartson's practice can be distinguished from those of its D.C. counterparts in a number of ways. Unlike many other prestigious D.C. firms, Hogan has a strong local client base, allowing its attorneys to get involved in the D.C. community. In addition, Hogan has a number of interesting and somewhat unusual practice groups. For instance, it has one of D.C.'s best education law groups, which represents high schools, universities, and educational associations on a broad range of issues from taxation to civil rights. The firm also has an aviation law group and a food, drug, medical device and agriculture practice. In addition, Hogan is "poised" to take advantage of developments throughout Europe; the firm has offices in Brussels, Budapest, London, Moscow, Prague, and Warsaw. It also has an affiliate in Paris. Among Hogan's interesting litigation subgroups is a strong appellate and Supreme Court litigation section, headed by John Roberts, former Deputy Solicitor-General, and a white-collar criminal defense practice, headed by the "heavy hitter," Ty Cobb. The firm also is home to a number of high-profile partners, including two former Chairmen of the Republican National Committee, a former outside General Counsel to the Democratic National Committee, the former Deputy Ambassador of the Russian Federation in Washington, D.C., a former Secretary of Agriculture, and three former Congressmen.

training and development criticized

Hogan & Hartson received generally critical reviews for its associate training. One person reported that associates generally "want more structured programs and professional development." Another person described the training and development at the firm as "very poor. There are fifth- and sixth-year litigation associates who still have never attended NITA. The firm is so busy that it has all but eliminated its in-house training." However, we were told by the firm that "in fact all fifth- and sixth-year litigation associates are offered the opportunity to attend NITA. If associates at this level have not attended it is because of scheduling difficulties or because they have chosen not to attend." A firm representative further informed us that Hogan & Hartson also conducts a two-part workshop for its younger associates that focuses on critical litigation skills and provides an advanced oral advocacy program for its senior litigation associates. Finally, we were told that the firm is in "the process of restructuring its commercial training programs for the fall." In general, summer associates were happy with the amount of feedback they received. One commented that there were "regular reviews" and that people were "always warned in advance if there was a problem." Another observed that "people got evaluations from everyone they worked for which were very specific." The firm's associate evaluation committee is very "serious" about its work, and keeps detailed files on each individual's progress.

women

Hogan & Hartson was one of the first D.C. firms to hire women, and today there are almost as many women as men among the associates. Influential female attorneys at the firm include Jan McDavid, Jean Moore, Sally Determan, a past President of the District of Columbia Bar, and Executive Committee member Ann Morgan Vickery. The firm sponsors on-site emergency day care for all of its employees.

high turnover name tags necessary

Hogan & Hartson is managed by a five member executive committee. In addition, the firm has an associates committee to provide a means for formal communication between associates and partners. Everyone agreed that Hogan was doing well economically. One contact quipped, "it must be doing well because it keeps growing and growing." The firm has hired a number of laterals in recent years and continues to have large summer classes. Hogan has been very busy over the past several years. Indeed, one contact informed us that "the firm is so busy and associates keep leaving so fast, that the ones that remain experience an incredible amount of work and pressure. Turn-over at the firm is so high that attorneys are asked to wear name tags at 'good-bye' parties—Hogan's most frequent (and pretty much sole) social events." A firm representative responded that Hogan & Hartson sponsors a number of social events, including a dinner dance, a holiday party, and a summer picnic.

mystery bonus

First-year associate salaries include an automatic bonus, but past the first year bonuses are merit-based. "Although the firm vigorously insists that bonuses are tied to quality rather than quantity of work," one insider believed that bonuses are given to those who bill above the 1800 hour threshold. Another contact informed us that "the bonus system is very much a mystery to associates." Yet another source complained that "associate bonuses are not competitive with those given at other firms." In general, Hogan offers the traditional tradeoff: it is less high-pressured—and less financially rewarding—than other prestigious firms such as Williams & Connolly and Covington & Burling. Partnership prospects, however, are reputedly comparatively good at Hogan. One contact reported that "it appears that nearly every associate who sticks around long enough makes partner," while another informed us that "Hogan does have a good partnership record. However, after eight years of hard work, one is only qualified to be a non-equity 'special' partner. When the transition to equity partner actually occurs is yet another firm mystery." Many of the firm's partners have worked their way up through the firm. There is no requirement for associates to develop business to make partner.

office facilities

In 1987 Hogan & Hartson moved into new "light and airy" offices in a "beautiful building right at Metro Center," a few blocks from the White House. People told us, however, that associates have interior, windowless offices "well into their third year" at the firm. The office building features a gym with a weight room and aerobics classes. Associates must pay for their own memberships, however. Many associates work out or run in the middle of the day. Another group plays volleyball once a week in the summer. The firm has two softball teams, and participates in less formal football and basketball leagues.

hiring tips

Hogan & Hartson is a top-tier D.C. firm, and summer associate hiring is very competitive. Most summer associates are from top 10 law schools and on law review. Some discerned that Hogan has a slight preference for students from both Harvard and the University of Virginia, although the firm recruits its associates from a broad array of schools. Others observed that it places special emphasis on law school extracurricular activities, such as the Board of Student Advisors at Harvard. The 1996 summer class had 30 summer associates, all of whom received permanent associate offers. People noted that Hogan is strongly committed to making a high percentage of permanent offers, even in years with unexpectedly large summer classes. Callback interviews usually involve meeting four or five attorneys, and it is not uncommon to encounter three or more "big" partners. The on-campus interviewer serves as the candidate's escort, providing a "friendly connection" and acting as an "advocate" for the person in the firm. More than at most D.C. firms, Hogan makes its hiring decisions (both for summer associate and permanent positions) based on personalities and seeks "friendly," outgoing types, "to the point of rejecting ultra-top-notch applicants who come off as arrogant or obnoxious in their interviews." People reported that past summer classes have had some "characters" and that the hiring committee values a "sense of humor."

Howrey & Simon

Washington Los Angeles Menlo Park

Address: 1299 Pennsylvania Avenue, N.W., Washington, D.C. 20004–2402
Telephone: (202) 783–0800
Hiring Attorney: Margaret M. Zwisler, Chairman, Hiring Committee
Contact: Ellen P. Dougherty, Director of Recruiting; (202) 383–7167
Associate Salary: First year $74,000 (1997)
Summer Salary: $1400/week (1997)
Average Hours: 1950 worked; 1850 billed; NA required
Family Benefits: 8 weeks paid family leave plus 4 weeks paid vacation leave upon the birth or adoption of a child (4 unpaid)
1996 Summer: Class of 23 (2L) students; offers to 23
Partnership: 24% of entering associates from 1978–1984 were made partner
Pro Bono: 5% of all work is pro bono

Howrey & Simon in 1997
249 Lawyers at the Washington D.C. Office
1.5 Associates Per Partner

Total Partners 100		
Women	15	15%
All Minorities	5	5%
Afro-Am	3	3%
Asian-Am	1	1%
Latino	1	1%

Total Associates 149		
Women	45	30%
All Minorities	16	11%
Afro-Am	9	6%
Asian-Am	7	5%

Practice Areas	
Antitrust	20%
Commercial	20%
Intellectual Property	20%
Government Contracts	10%
International	10%
Insurance	10%
Environmental	5%
White Collar Crime	5%

Howrey & Simon is a high-energy D.C. litigation firm. It has grown by more than 120 lawyers since 1991. The firm is "aggressive" both in the courtroom and in developing business. Its "hard core litigators" are "go-getters" with "outgoing personalities," we were told. A "brash, young firm," Howrey exhibits "no stuffiness," remarked one source.

growing pains

Howrey's recent rapid growth has created some problems at the firm, according to our contacts. Some partners were recently laid off or demoted to partial-equity status. This new partial-equity level added before partnership "extends the partner track three years," reported one contact. Another person told us that "a large number of associates have left the firm over the last couple of years (an average number for most big firms but a higher percentage than Howrey has had in the past)." In fact, despite its overall growth since 1991, Howrey is smaller by 21 lawyers today than in 1994. The growth has also resulted in problems of disorganization and impersonalization. One person observed that "the increased size has resulted in more bureaucratic procedures." Another person commented that the firm has grown "so large many people do not know each other, even by sight sometimes," and "unless a person is in one of the smaller practice groups, it can be very impersonal" at the firm. Finally, the firm, according to our contacts, is "not a leader in salaries" and "patent associates are leaving for more money elsewhere, despite the recent pay hike." However, we were also informed that the firm is making efforts to "cure that situation" ("intellectual property salaries were increased to well above market again in February, 1997," reported a firm spokesperson). Further "numerous associates serve on the associate affairs committee which has input into associate development, evaluation, training, and recruitment programs."

practice areas

Founded in 1956 as an antitrust litigation boutique firm, Howrey & Simon's antitrust practice has "declined" somewhat, reported one person, as the firm has expanded to handle all types of litigation. Despite its increasing size, Howrey has not become highly departmentalized and movement among practice areas remains relatively easy. The largest share of the firm's work involves general commercial litigation for large Fortune 100 corporations such as the Exxon Corporation and the H.J. Heinz Company. Other practice areas include administrative, environmental, government contracts, intellectual property, insurance coverage, international trade, and white-collar defense. The firm's environmental practice has slowed somewhat of late, but the firm has "recently added a new group of environmental lawyers to assist with its environmental practice," according to a firm representative. In contrast, the firm's intellectual property practice is "growing most rapidly," we were told. Howrey also offers a "high-profile" white-collar crime practice, which includes prominent partners John Nields and Neil Eggleston. Nields was Chief Counsel for the Select Committee to Investigate Covert Arms Transactions with Iran. He is "very well-connected and gets amazing clients," raved one insider. Howrey's international trade group is also noteworthy, and international trade partner, Paul Plaia, is well-known for his treatise on anti-dumping issues. A number of the group's lawyers frequently travel to Korea and Japan. Paul Warnke, former Deputy Secretary of Defense for International Security Affairs and "a high profile" figure in D.C., practices at the firm.

pro bono

Howrey & Simon's pro bono practice is headed by partner Lois Williams and Libby Saypol, a full-time non-lawyer pro bono coordinator. We were told that Williams and Saypol have "been around the business" and are well "connected to the ACLU and the Washington Lawyers Committee for Civil Rights under the Law." Lois Williams was named the D.C. Bar's Pro Bono Lawyer of the Year in 1996. Howrey has handled a lot of pro bono work for Mitch Snyder's organization for the homeless. Howrey participates in the ABA program in which firms pledge to devote 5% of their hours to pro bono work. Pro bono hours do not, however, count toward billable hours.

intensive formal training

Because Howrey is not highly departmentalized, it offers a "broader experience" than many other firms, we were told. Although most summer and junior associates must work on commercial litigation matters, they are exposed to a variety of litigation projects. After the initial weeks of the summer, when they work with a supervising partner, summer associates may select their projects from a loose-leaf book of assignments. Summer and starting associates primarily research and write memos, with one source stating that "most cases have many associates, though exceptions exist, of course." Despite its loose structure in other areas, Howrey places heavy "emphasis" on its "intensive" formal training programs, claimed one person. It provides a "complete training program" for litigators, including mock trial and deposition training, oral advocacy training, and other seminars. Howrey also organizes a trial exercise and training programs for summer associates. One source observed, caustically, that Howrey's focus on the formal litigation training is "an effort to make up for the lack of actual courtroom experience" available at the firm. It was also pointed out to us that Howrey's "focus on large cases makes for extremely dull, document-intensive work for most (not all) associates in the commercial litigation/antitrust group." More positively, we were told that Howrey emphasizes the use of technology "in court and in its practice. There's a technology committee and the firm devotes a lot of resources to the purchase and development of such equipment and devices."

feedback

Permanent associates must "ask for feedback, but the partners are pretty receptive," reported one contact. None of the summer associates we interviewed complained about the firm's review procedures. The firm "makes a special effort" to provide feedback on each assignment completed by a summer associate, said one. Howrey is "not the type of place where you would get lost" or where people "don't know where they stand," said another.

informal social life

Howrey's "Underground Social Committee," which organized many fun social events in the past, is now defunct, we were told. Associates, however, continue to go out after work, and on Thursday nights in the summer, a number socialize at a local bar. Past summer programs included "three or four big events and the rest was informal," we were told. "No one was penalized for not being a big happy hour beer drinking person," noted one observer. The firm also hosts a firm lunch once a month for all attorneys and organizes an annual Christmas party. The firm's "prom" has recently been "abolished as an economy measure," according to one contact.

diversity

"Women feel very comfortable" at Howrey & Simon. Groups of female attorneys get together socially; one group jogs regularly. Women are "influential in all management committees," and one of the top partners in the international trade group, Cecilia Gonzalez, is a woman. Three women partners are members of the firm's policy committee and the chair of the firm's hiring committee. Although Howrey has acknowledged the need to hire more minorities, one person questioned its recruitment policies, claiming that the firm tends to hire minority law students only from top schools like Harvard and Yale, rather than from a broad range of law schools. A firm spokesperson informed us, however, that "Howrey hires from four minority job fairs in addition to recruiting a diverse class of new and summer associates from all law school campuses."

offices

In response to its rapid expansion, Howrey moved its offices to the famous Warner building in 1992, next to the original Warner vaudeville theater. A John Harvard's brewhouse is located in the building, and the offices are located in the "new place to be," according to one contact. I.M. Pei's architectural firm designed the atrium of the building, and the offices include a gym in the basement, equipped with Lifecycles with T.V.s, and an aerobics room. The MCI Arena, home of the Washington Capitals and the Bullets, is being built near the firm's offices; it is scheduled to open in a year or so.

hiring tips

Howrey hires "outgoing" candidates with a "go-getter attitude." The firm's callback interviews usually involve meeting with six attorneys and the recruiting director and having lunch. Howrey hires a good number of its students from D.C.-area schools such as Georgetown and George Washington University, but its associates come from a large number of law schools across the country. The hiring committee does not emphasize high grade point averages more than other D.C. firms, but most summer associates have been members of a law review or had significant journal experience.

Howrey offers broad exposure to a high-energy, fast-growing litigation practice, while simultaneously providing excellent formal training in litigation skills. Revenues at the firm continue to increase, we were told, and the firm recently opened an office in Silicon Valley. This young firm is a place for someone who does not mind working hard and can cope with the firm's growing pains.

Hunton & Williams

Washington Atlanta Charlotte Fairfax Greenville Knoxville New York Norfolk Raleigh Richmond Brussels Warsaw Hong Kong

Address: 1900 K Street, N.W., Suite 1200, Washington, D.C. 20006
Telephone: (202) 955–1500
Hiring Attorney: Pauline A. Schneider
Contact: Cynthia W. Kolbe, Legal Recruiting Administrator; (202) 955–1560
Associate Salary: First year $72,000 plus $2,000 settling-in allowance (1997)
Summer Salary: $1250/week (1997)
Average Hours: NA worked; NA billed; NA required
Family Benefits: 12 weeks maternity leave; emergency corporate childcare; dependent and health spending accounts
1996 Summer: Class of 8 students; offers to 4
Partnership: 39% of entering associates from 1979–1984 were made partner
Pro Bono: NA

Hunton & Williams in 1997
84 Lawyers at the Washington D.C. Office
1.2 Associates Per Partner

Total Partners 38		
Women	4	11%
All Minorities	2	5%
Afro-Am	2	5%

Total Associates 46		
Women	21	46%
All Minorities	4	9%
Afro-Am	2	4%
Asian-Am	1	2%
Latino	1	2%

Practice Areas	
Administrative	35
Litigation	25
Corporate	24
Patent	3
Telecommunications	3

Hunton & Williams, one of Virginia's two leading firms, has grown rapidly over the last two decades, and has established itself as a regional power. Hunton's D.C. office is fairly independent of the firm's Richmond headquarters, both in terms of culture and practice. The D.C. office atmosphere is much less conservative than the Richmond office, without an old-boy feel. While the D.C. office leans to the Republican side (Phillip Morris is one of the firm's largest clients, and many Hunton lawyers regularly support conservative politicians), there are prominent ties in the other direction as well. A partner, Gerald Baliles, is a former Democratic Governor of

Virginia; another former Governor, and now Senator, Charles Robb was a Hunton & William's partner. In addition, the D.C. office, particularly its public finance practice, works closely with the D.C. government. In general, the office is friendly and fairly relaxed. Fridays are "casual attire" days.

practice areas

"The strength of the D.C. office" is its environmental practice, which, one person explained, involves "everything from air to water to Superfund. It's a cradle to grave approach. They are involved in making legislation. They are also involved in compliance counseling and litigation." The practice is largely regulatory, however, which also includes challenging final EPA rules in the D.C. circuit. The strength of this department is their Clean Air Act practice. Hunton has been involved in "almost every major Clean Air Act proceeding affecting stationary sources since 1970." One source described the department as a "very varied group of people. It has young partners and a good mix of conservative and liberal attorneys. It's a relaxed place, and you can be yourself there." Hunton's well-known public utilities practice includes a municipal finance group with close ties to the local D.C. government.

Prominent partners in the office include Henry Nickel on the environmental team; Andrew Strenio, former Commissioner of the Federal Trade Commission; and Pauline Schneider, a recent D. C. Bar President. The telecommunications, antitrust and international project finance groups are "hot" and rapidly growing. Other noteworthy groups include the labor practice, "one of the most cohesive groups—like a firm within a firm," and a small tax practice. Firmwide, Hunton has focused on developing its international practice, with offices in Hong Kong, Brussels and Warsaw. It recently worked on the privatization of power projects in Pakistan, Thailand, Tanzania, Jordan, and South America. Not surprisingly, Hunton is home to a number of well-known Virginians, such as retired Supreme Court Justice Lewis Powell, who maintains an office there. Lewis Powell, Jr., the Justice's son, is also at the firm. The firm reportedly has a "strong commitment" to pro bono. The firm "expects 40 hours annually per lawyer," according to a firm spokesperson. Hunton publishes a monthly newsletter describing pro bono activities at all its offices.

professional development

The D.C. office has a "great, informal personality." There is "a lot of variety" in the types of people at the office and "the associates are particularly cohesive and supportive of one another." Everyone is on a first name basis, "except for a few old curmudgeons," we were told. Associates often work closely with partners or handle matters on their own. For example, junior associates sometimes conduct depositions and argue motions in court; other associates travel abroad as part of the international practice. The opportunities for responsibility vary by department, however. One contact observed that associates in the labor, litigation, and bankruptcy groups have particularly good prospects, whereas there is more "research and memo writing" and less client contact in the environmental practice.

Most training at Hunton occurs informally "through frequent interactions with partners." Although there are some seminars and mock trial programs, it is mostly "on-the-job training." Each practice group has held summer associate "show and tell" sessions that highlight new developments in its practice.

summer program

Summer associate projects are assigned by two attorneys based on individual preferences and firm needs. One person, however, characterized the system as "first come, first serve" in practice. Another emphasized that summer associates do not always get the projects they want and must work in a number of areas: "If you are sure you want to do tax, for example, and that's all you want to do, then Hunton is not a good place for the summer." One firm apologist pointed out that the philosophy behind the summer program is to "allow summer associates wide exposure to the firm and vice versa. The firm considers itself one organic whole rather than a composite of independent fiefdoms. Therefore, everyone has an interest in hiring decisions, even of someone who will not be in his practice area." Written evaluations are completed on each project, and there are mid- and end-of-summer reviews. Feedback was described as "good" for both summer and permanent associates. Permanent associates are given yearly evaluations that are reportedly taken very "seriously."

social life

Individual practice groups usually have a firmwide retreat once a year or every other year. Apart from this, one insider suggested that "poker and golf are the firm's big things." One important summer event is a "huge poker game, which is really wild. Attorneys at the firm are always joking about its legality." Other summer activities have included a dinner cruise on the Potomac, a beach party at Chesapeake Bay, and Shakespeare Theatre performances at Carter Barron, an outdoor amphitheater in D.C.'s Rock Creek Park. Hunton also has a firm softball team; the lawyers are really "big on this."

diversity

Hunton was described as an "up-and-coming" place for women, with numerous female associates. Prominent women partners include the previously mentioned Pauline Schneider, current hiring partner and an African-American woman, and Andy Bear Field, who is "very senior in the environmental department and wields a lot of influence." Hunton reportedly has had a difficult time attracting minority attorneys because of its "southern, old-boy" image. To remedy these shortcomings, Hunton has established a firmwide minority hiring committee, and the firm participates in a number of minority job fairs each fall. Firmwide, Hunton includes three very prominent African-American partners among its rainmakers: John Thomas in Richmond, Kevin Ross in Atlanta, and Pauline Schneider in Washington, who was recently the subject of an article in the *Washington Post* on "Women Rainmakers."

office facilities

Hunton & Williams moved into new offices in July 1996. The new space, which occupies the top three floors of a new building on K Street, "sheds the former Virginia decor for a moderate, sleek design emphasizing clean lines, glass and chrome, cherry wood and penetration of natural light." Every attorney has an individual window office. Computer facilities are now state-of-the-art, and the library facility is described as good. Its collection is "excellent," according to one source, and "the librarian is among the best there are; she is able to track down the hardest-to-find documents and publications."

hiring tips

Although Hunton hires from the "big name schools," it also makes numerous offers to those from Virginia and D.C.-area law schools. One person discerned that the firm looks for people who are "not afraid to speak their minds." Another noted that about half of the summer associates were on their school's law review and most were very outgoing. Some of those with whom we talked suggested that, although Hunton D.C. frequently permits summer associates from other offices to spend a few weeks there, it sometimes does not consider them for permanent offers. Callback interviews at Hunton customarily involve meeting five attorneys and going to lunch with a few more. The interviews are relaxed and the attorneys usually do not ask "probing questions." One person advised that what really "broke the ice" in the interview was being "able to speak the language of the practice" and to discuss developments in a particular area of interest.

Hunton & Williams is a firm that is continuing to grow, especially in the Southeast, where its new Charlotte, N.C. office has added several new attorneys. In the D.C. office, Hunton has added several partners in its "booming" telecommunications practice. The firm's project finance and leasing group is handling numerous international power projects. The environmental practice is "among the fore" in representing industrial clients in Clean Air Act proceedings. The firm offers significant early responsibility and "substantial and meaningful mentoring." The only sustained negative comments that we heard concerned hours and compensation. These misgivings were aptly summarized by one contact who observed that "we probably have higher billable and non-billable hour requirements than other D.C.firms that pay comparable salaries. Required (or strongly encouraged) non-billable work (like pro bono) is not counted toward your billable requirement. Our salaries are probably at market, but bonuses are very difficult to qualify for because of numerous criteria that are hard to meet." Another insider added, simply, that "bonuses are few and far between."

Jenner & Block

Washington Chicago Lake Forest Miami

Address: 12th Floor, 601 Thirteenth Street, N.W., Washington, D.C. 20005
Telephone: (202) 639–6000
Hiring Attorney: Donald B. Verrilli, Jr.
Contact: Chandanie Botejue, Recruiting Manager; (202) 639–6088
Associate Salary: First year $73,000 (1997); second $78,000; third $84,000; fourth $90,000; fifth $98,000; sixth $106,000; seventh $115,000
Summer Salary: $1400/week (1997)
Average Hours: 2429 worked; 2030 billed; 1900 required
Family Benefits: Maternity leave (9 weeks)
1996 Summer: Class of 9 students; offers to 9
Partnership: NA
Pro Bono: 8% of all work is pro bono

Jenner & Block in 1997
57 Lawyers at the Washington D.C. Office
1.2 Associates Per Partner

Total Partners 26		
Women	3	12%
All Minorities	0	0%

Total Associates 30		
Women	11	37%
All Minorities	3	10%
Afro-Am	2	7%
Asian-Am	1	3%

Practice Areas	
Litigation	33
Government Contracts	7
First Amendment & Apellate	5
Communications & Antitrust	4
Associations & Govt. Affairs	3
Regulatory	3
Environmental	1

"If there is a perfect firm, this is it!!" gushed one insider. The D.C. office of prominent Chicago-based Jenner & Block received rave reviews from those we interviewed. Perhaps the only catch is getting hired at this competitive firm. Known as the firm of "Supreme Court clerks" because eleven of the firm's 57 attorneys have held these prestigious clerkships, Jenner hires almost exclusively at the nation's top law schools. Most successful candidates, with the exception of a number of first-year students, are members of a law review. In a recent year, seven of the nine summer associates who received offers attended Harvard or Yale Law Schools. Most Jenner & Block lawyers currently at the firm graduated from Harvard, Yale, and a few other top law schools.

liberal law firm

Jenner & Block is not a "stuffed-shirt type of place." The "very relaxed" and "very liberal" Jenner attorneys form a "live and let live crowd," said one contact. "People of all stripes" work at this cohesive firm and "get along well," marveled some people. One source noted that "the people who make up the firm remain extraordinarily decent; I'd doubt there is any firm of comparable size with so many genuinely good folks and so few jerks." Jenner is also "informal" and "aggressively non-hierarchical," making it difficult to distinguish partners and associates. One past summer associate recalled that, at times, the summer associates would speculate on whether a particular attorney was a partner or an associate. However, "don't be deceived by the laid-back atmosphere—people work very hard here," warned one source. Jenner attorneys are "very hard-working" and can sometimes set a "hectic" pace, yet office morale is high. These lawyers are very interested in their work, which one contact informed us is "the best part of the firm." Most "feel they're doing good and important work and are happy to be with the other lawyers" in the firm.

appellate litigation

Jenner's top-rate constitutional and appellate litigation practice is one of its most attractive features. This area is spearheaded by Bruce Ennis, a former National Legal Director of the American Civil Liberties Union and a prominent Supreme Court litigator who joined Jenner in 1988, when the firm absorbed his Supreme Court litigation boutique firm. The attorneys in this group have argued a number of prominent Supreme Court cases, including *Barnes v. Glen Theater* (the nude dancing case), *Romer v. Evans* (opposing discrimination on the basis of sexual orientation), and *Turner Broadcasting v. FCC*, a First Amendment case. They also submitted an *amicus* brief in the Alcee Hastings appeal and have done a substantial amount of voting rights work at the trial court and Supreme Court levels.

other practice areas

Although Jenner's D.C. office is best known for its Supreme Court work, it was established as an antitrust firm. Former managing partner Mike Salsbury, well-known in the communications field, left recently to become general counsel at MCI. MCI, Jenner's original anchor client, continues to provide the firm with a substantial amount of work. Other prominent Jenner attorneys include Jerry Jacobs, author of a book on lobbying and association law practice, Brent Rushforth, a SALT I treaty negotiator, Don Verrilli, considered "quite the star" by those at the firm, and Paul Smith, who recently argued several cases before the Supreme Court.

strong pro bono

Jenner received strong reviews for its pro bono practice, which is taken "very seriously" at the firm. Partners David DeBruin and David Handzo oversee the practice, which has handled a wide range of matters including death penalty cases, prison issues, and other civil rights matters. One source noted that the firm has received a number of awards for its commitment in this area. In recent years, the firm has taken on a number of asylum cases for the Lawyers' Committee for Human Rights, including cases from Somalia, China, Ethiopia, Latin America and South Africa.

on-the-job training

One person characterized Jenner as a "very informal" place where you don't receive any assignments by memo. Similarly, Jenner does not emphasize formal training. As the firm only hires the country's top law students, it expects new associates to arrive at the firm with a basic level of training and to learn quickly on their own. Most of the training occurs "on-the-job." Attorneys do not work on discrete issues of major cases at Jenner, explained one contact. Rather, associates are frequently given an entire case and asked to do what they can with it, an experience that can be "bewildering at first." Associates are also frequently assigned to work on a "think piece," in which they are confronted with a case and must find analogies to it in other areas of legal doctrine and explore new arguments and approaches. As at most firms, junior associates still do the "nuts and bolts" work, but they also draft the documents and write briefs. Like the training, most feedback at Jenner is informal and must be pursued on an individual basis.

branch office syndrome

Though it is a branch office, Jenner D.C. is fairly autonomous in its culture and client base. We heard some complaints, however, about the Chicago office's influence on administrative matters. One person complained that most administrative policies, the "big decisions" affecting attorneys, and staff salaries, are all decided in the Chicago office. There is some "grumbling among the attorneys because they want more freedom" on these matters. One contact, with detached understatement, observed that "all things being equal, it's better not to be in a branch office." Another source reported that Chicago recently "forced" the layoffs of several D.C. office support staff personnel and that this news was received in the Washington office with anger and disbelief. The same source further reported that partners and associates were all of the opinion that the layoffs were simply unnecessary because the Washington office is doing so well, and "if a reduction in support staff was what Chicago was looking for, it could have been achieved through attrition and prevented morale problems in the D.C. office."

family orientation

Jenner is a "family oriented" place and does not offer a lavish social life. Although one source noted that in recent years the firm "has seen a fairly large influx of new associates and a welcome dose of singlehood for the firm," most Jenner attorneys are married and try to do their work and leave as early as possible. Very few attorneys socialize after work. Jenner organizes an annual outing to Johnson Island in the Chesapeake Bay, but it is not a "high frills law firm." Summer associates are treated to "little wining and dining" and in the past, we were told, have had to pay their own way to the firm's annual golf outing. One firm contact responded that this situation is "not true today; we don't play much golf around here." Other sports, however, are very popular among the attorneys. Many play on the firm's softball and basketball teams.

diversity

The partnership in the D.C. office includes three women, but no minorities. No one we interviewed offered any complaints about the treatment of women or minority attorneys at Jenner. Most agreed that the firm "is very aware of and sensitive to deficiencies in the numbers of women and minorities." A number of the women at the firm have had babies, and some of the men in the office have taken paternal leaves. Everyone interviewed attested that the firm is supportive in these matters.

selective hiring

The hiring process at Jenner is among the most selective in the city. In addition to placing a premium on high grades, law review membership, and other journal experience, Jenner tends to hire people who are active in political and social causes, according to one source. Jenner usually hires a few first-year students each year.

Jenner & Block has grown rapidly in recent years. It is expanding its communications practice, and recently added two government relations partners. Reportedly thriving economically, Jenner's D.C. office pays Chicago salaries, which are above the average for D.C.-based firms. Attorneys also get free use of a gym located in the firm's building. Jenner is "too busy" and greatly needs more lawyers, asserted one source; the firm grew in size by about 10% in 1996 alone. It continues to hire a steady stream of summer associates. One contact noted that the firm's steadily increasing size has become "more noticeable as we have had to expand to another floor in our building. Down the road, one might expect this growth to bear some not wholly favorable consequences for firm culture." But, at present, the firm's size is fairly ideal—"large enough to ensure an interesting variety of work; small enough to know everyone." Jenner & Block's combination of "very interesting work" and "very decent people" makes the firm an attractive place to be working at, a consensus view among all those we spoke with.

Jones, Day, Reavis & Pogue

Washington Atlanta Chicago Cleveland Columbus Dallas Irvine Los Angeles New York Pittsburgh
Brussels Frankfurt Geneva Hong Kong London New Delhi Paris Riyadh Taipei Tokyo

Address: Metropolitan Square, 1450 G Street, N.W., Suite 700, Washington, D.C. 20005–2088
Telephone: (202) 879–3939
Hiring Attorney: Barbara McDowell
Contact: Charlotte John Siegler, Recruiting Coordinator; (202) 879–4692
Associate Salary: First year $84,000 (1997)
Summer Salary: $1312.50/week (1997)
Average Hours: 2100 worked; 1900 billed; NA required
Family Benefits: Family & maternity leave (6–8 weeks paid disability, 4 weeks paid family leave, plus 12 weeks unpaid leave); emergency childcare facility in building
1996 Summer: Class of 23 students; offers to 20
Partnership: NA
Pro Bono: 3% of all legal work is pro bono

Jones, Day, Reavis & Pogue in 1997
180 Lawyers at the Washington D.C. Office
1.8 Associates Per Partner

Total Partners 64		
Women	12	19%
All Minorities	1	2%
Afro-Am	1	2%

Total Associates 116		
Women	45	39%
All Minorities	13	11%
Afro-Am	9	8%
Asian-Am	4	3%

Practice Areas	
Litigation	53
Corporate	20
Antitrust	17
Appellate Litigation	15
Labor	11
Environmental	9
Energy	8
Tax	8
Government Regulations	6
Health	6

For those seeking a national firm with first-rate litigation training and state-of-the-art technology, Jones Day Reavis & Pogue may be the place. Its D.C. office has one of the best large-scale litigation practices in the country and is committed to maintaining this excellence. The firm takes pride in its special litigation center, one of several throughout the firm, housed in a separate building in downtown D.C., from which many of its large cases are managed. These cases are assigned their own exclusive conference room and document production facilities in the center. Moreover, Jones Day uses the latest technology to help its lawyers manage large cases. All the documents on file at the litigation center are coded and computerized, so that any of the firm's lawyers working on the case "can access each detail in a large case at the press of a button." In addition, many documents produced by lawyers at the firm are networked on a central computer, making them available to Jones Day attorneys worldwide. For example, the firm maintains a "brief" bank, which attorneys can access and do word searches to find and use relevant briefs as models. A past criticism levelled against the computer system was that, since it is a firmwide and Cleveland-based system, "logging into the system is very slow." However, according to a firm spokesperson, "each lawyer has received upgraded PC hardware with greater memory capacity and the network has been upgraded so that the log-on process is much faster." In addition, a variety of word processing softwares are available on the Jones Day Network so that lawyers can use the software of their choice.

all-American law firm

With 20 offices in 11 countries, Jones Day is one of the world's largest law firms. Jones' Day's operations throughout the world and its one-firm structure "brings the talents of the entire firm to bear on matters originating in any office, promotes the exchange of information, and allows for efficient project management within and among various practices," reported one firm enthusiast. Based in Cleveland, Ohio, Jones Day was described as "an all-American firm—most of its clients are older, established American companies," including tobacco companies such as RJR Nabisco and approximately half the Fortune 500 corporations. The firm's fast-growing and renowned large litigation practice includes a small "issues and appeals" practice, headed by Tim Dyk, a former Supreme Court clerk and a well-known appellate litigator. Many of its lawyers are former Supreme Court clerks; people suggested that it is very difficult to be hired by this group. Our contacts described these attorneys as "other worldly," "professorial," and distinct from the rest of the litigation department. Another person opined, "okay, some of them are odd, but most are just regular people."

practice areas

Jones Day's firmwide tax practice is centered in the D.C. office, with much of its work arising from other firm offices. The practice includes a number of well-known corporate tax and employee benefits lawyers. Jones Day rarely hires its tax lawyers directly from law school, preferring to hire laterals with several years of experience. One contact informed us that the "D.C. tax group is still fairly small and very partner-heavy." One of the firm's growing practices, Jones Day's employment and labor practice represents the managements of large corporations in employment and labor disputes. "Everyone in this group really likes it," commented one person. Another noted that the labor practice offers the opportunity to litigate smaller cases. Jones Day's business practice and government regulation groups handle both "pure corporate" transactions and regulatory matters. The business lawyers also do substantial international work, often involving the firm's foreign offices.

In contrast to other aspects of Jones Day, its pro bono practice was described as "decentralized." Attorneys "have to take initiative" to do pro bono work; there is "no clear policy about how pro bono hours are treated." One person remarked that "the firm didn't overwhelm me with its pro bono program." Another person commented that "there are terrific pro bono opportunities but there is still pressure to bill hours." Jones Day attorneys, however, are involved in a broad range of pro bono matters, from death penalty appeals to international human rights issues. The firm also staffs a monthly free legal clinic sponsored by the D.C. Bar.

New Associates Group training

Entering Jones Day associates are assigned to the New Associates Group (NAG) for their first year with the firm. The NAG program is designed to develop associate skills in a broad range of areas. An assigning partner distributes work from all areas and oversees the development of the associates. The firm also makes an effort to provide each associate with a high proportion of assignments in his particular area of interest. After an associate joins a practice area, he receives assignments from the assignment coordinator in that group and sometimes directly from the partners in that group.

litigation experience comes late

Not surprisingly, since Jones Day handles mostly large, complex cases, litigation associates usually are not entrusted with their own matters for a number of years. Litigators assume responsibility "pretty late in the game. You have to be close to partnership to sit first chair in a major case. Most of the associates help out on bigger cases run by partners." By contrast, there is "a lot more scope for people to get involved" in the transactional work. Midlevel associates often have primary responsibility for business transactions, and there are many opportunities to take charge of smaller deals.

conservative atmosphere

Most people described Jones Day as somewhat conservative, both politically and socially. The dress code also is "fairly conservative"; attorneys do "not wear flashy ties" and the attire is "pretty much cut and dried." A lot of women do, however, "wear pantsuits (yes, that is a big deal)," reported one contact. The firm is "split on casual Fridays, which means you are free to be casual if you'd like." People we contacted agreed that generally "the atmosphere at the firm is "somewhat relaxed and supportive," and there is a "lot of casual joking around." One insider observed that "the NAG class of this year jokes around, plays pranks, socializes together outside the firm, and meets for lunches, etc. during the week. We have a lot of spirit and tons of fun together."

social life

Although the majority of Jones Day attorneys have families, there still are plenty of opportunities for young, single attorneys to socialize. There reportedly is a "big core group of associates" who go out together. The firm has an array of activities, including golf and tennis tournaments, and a winter formal. Many Jones Day attorneys are interested in sports and the firm sponsors softball, soccer, and basketball teams. The firm also sponsored a race this past year. Every Friday the new associates circulate a humorous memo, reminding everyone to come to the weekly happy hour held in the conference room.

billable hours and partnership

Although some people dismissed the firm's annual billable hour requirement (2000) as not "a big deal" and noted that some associates do not meet the target, others insisted that the billing pressure has increased in recent years and "is an issue." One person opined that those desiring to make partner at Jones Day must bill substantially more than 2000 hours a year. Compared with other firms, however, making partner apparently is "not exceedingly hard." In part because Jones Day makes more partners, the average profits per partner are lower than some other large, prestigious firms.

diversity

With a large number of female associates, Jones Day received high reviews regarding its atmosphere for women. Many "key players" at the firm are women, including the firmwide administrative partner (Mary Ellen Powers), the current hiring partner (Barbara McDowell), and the current head of the summer associate program (Denise Fee). A number of women have worked part-time. Although one person observed, critically, that the firm has no "on-site childcare," the firm has recently begun to participate in an emergency childcare facility located in the building, we were told. While there are few racial minorities at Jones Day, people commented that the firm is "making progress," and has a proactive recruiting program headed by Washington-based antitrust practice chair, Charles A. James. Additionally, the new classes "reflect greater diversity," reported one insider.

centralized management

Jones Day operates as one firm throughout the world and is managed by a sole managing partner, Patrick F. McCartan, who functions much like a CEO. Jones Day's Cleveland headquarters wields considerable power over the D.C. office, we were told. The Washington office's managing partner, Steve Brogan, was described as a "big litigator" and "accessible." The son of a New York City police officer, Brogan frequently attends the Friday cocktail party and reportedly is very "easy to talk to." Even so, many expressed frustration with the D.C. office's overall management. Associates "don't have much say," criticized one person. "Things like salary and hiring are pretty much dictated," and the firm is "not open about its decisions." The D.C. office contracted somewhat in the early 1990s and cut back on its summer hiring at that time. More recently, the office is in a "growth mode" and the hiring numbers for summer associates are again very strong, averaging about 25 over the past several years. Firmwide, with 1,175 lawyers, Jones Day has grown by almost 150 lawyers in the past two years. The firm enjoyed record profits this past year and "raised the starting salary for starting associates from $70,000 to $84,000," reported one insider.

spacious offices

Jones Day's offices are located in "prime downtown space" in the Metropolitan Square Building, across from the Treasury Department and a few blocks from the White House. In 1999, the Washington office will relocate to its own building near Capitol Hill. The firm has a "really nice art collection" put together by Ray Wiacek who, in addition to being a prominent tax lawyer, is an art historian. Associates all have individual offices, though not all have outside windows, and the support staff is "excellent." The library is "really big" for a law firm; one person reported that it is "one of the biggest in town." The library staff is very helpful; associates can leave a list of cases, which the staff will locate, photocopy, and deliver. One firm enthusiast exclaimed, "Yes! The case pull is awesome." By contrast, the offices have only a small workout room which "isn't even worth mentioning; there is very little equipment which often does not work," reported one insider who decried the fact that the firm has "no real workout facility."

hiring tips

Jones Day hires people from varied and interesting backgrounds. Many of its summer associates are "older" and have prior work experience. One person reported that "almost everyone was on a law review" in the summer class, and "all had done well academically" at their law schools. Of those not on a law review, many had worked on journals. People had different impressions of the firm's callback interviews. Most had a standard interviewing experience, meeting about four attorneys and going to lunch with a few more. Some, however, had "very extensive" interviews. One candidate met seven attorneys and had lunch at the firm. The process took "all day—from 9 A.M. to 3 P.M." Some partners ask casual questions, but others "make you argue" with them.

Kirkland & Ellis

Washington Chicago Los Angeles New York
London

Address: 655 Fifteenth Street, N.W., Suite 1200, Washington, D.C. 20005
Telephone: (202) 879–5000
Hiring Attorney: Mark D. Young
Contact: Julie M. Mulhern, Attorney Recruiting and Training Manager; (202) 879–5124
Associate Salary: First year $73,000 (1997)
Summer Salary: $1400/week (averaged weekly salary based on annualized salary of $73,000)
Average Hours: 2200 worked; 2000 billed; NA required
Family Benefits: Moving expenses; house hunting trip; 3 weeks vacation; health, life and dental insurance; employee assistance; long and short term disability
1996 Summer: Class of 18 students; offers to 17
Partnership: 36% of entering associates from 1980–1986 were made partner
Pro Bono: 2–4% of all work is pro bono

Kirkland & Ellis in 1997
98 Lawyers at the Washington D.C.
1.0 Associate Per Partner

Total Partners 50			Total Associates 48			Practice Areas	
Women	7	14%	Women	13	27%	Litigation	47
All Minorities	1	2%	All Minorities	5	10%	Environmental	16
Afro-Am	1	2%	Afro-Am	2	4%	Corporate	10
			Asian-Am	3	6%	Finance/Commodities	5
						Government Contracts	5
						Intellectual Property	5
						International Trade	5
						Communications	2
						Employment	2

"Litigation dominates" at Kirkland & Ellis D.C. "If you want to go into complex courtroom litigation, this is the firm," exclaimed one insider. With its largest office located in Chicago, Kirkland D.C. has represented a number of large corporate clients such as GM, Brown & Williamson Tobacco, Dow, GTE, Amoco, Siemens, and Hitachi. The firm's litigators are considered to be "hard-nosed," with somewhat of a "macho image." Kirkland is best known for its trial work, although it has a growing appellate practice. Additionally, the litigation group has recently added former Acting Deputy Assistant Attorney General, Criminal Division, Laurence A. Urgenson. Mr. Urgenson, who was lead counsel on the investigation of BCCI, heads up the white collar crime section of the litigation practice.

serious litigation training

As might be expected, Kirkland & Ellis takes its litigation training "very seriously." Each winter, Kirkland associates may participate in an "intense," three-day Kirkland Institute of Trial Advocacy (KITA) program, where they are videotaped as they present oral arguments and conduct trials. Professional actors play the parts of the witnesses and "honest-to-goodness" civilians sit as juries. Many senior partners attend and provide feedback throughout the training. Summer associates participate in a slightly scaled-down version as part of the summer program. While there are great opportunities for formal litigation training, one source felt that the prospects for associate responsibility are not as great as at some other firms because Kirkland represents mostly large, institutional clients. This viewpoint was, however, vigorously contested by others we spoke with, one of whom assured us that "one of Kirkland's true strengths is that young lawyers get great experience." For most litigation associates, extensive travel usually accompanies increasing responsibility. With its national practice, Kirkland has a geographically diverse clientele.

practice areas

Kirkland & Ellis D.C. has a number of other practice areas, although litigation remains the focus. One person pointed out to us that "some would say it is hard being a non-litigator at Kirkland. Non-litigators feel like they don't get as much respect as they deserve within the firm by the powers-that-be." Kirkland's corporate practice is relatively good-sized for D.C., which is not a corporate town. This practice area has been "incredibly busy, which may contribute to associate burn-out in this area," one person informed us. There are "mid-sized deals" and "discrete issues" in corporate work, offering significant opportunities for associate responsibility. Kirkland also has an antitrust (or "competition") practice group, which includes both general antitrust issues and a more specialized telecommunication/antitrust practice. The energy practice involves extensive work with Federal Energy Regulatory Commission matters. The government contracts practice, which is not growing, is focused on a developing health care practice. Kirkland's labor practice includes John Irving, former General

Counsel to the National Labor Relations Board. The firm also has an international trade practice group, which consists of two partners and three associates.

pro bono

Kirkland's pro bono practice is coordinated by two of the firm's partners, and much of its pro bono work is done for public interest organizations such as the Washington Lawyers' Committee for Civil Rights, the American Civil Liberties Union, and the Legal Counsel for the Elderly. In addition, many attorneys pursue projects of their own, subject to firm approval. People discerned that, although Kirkland formally encourages associates to give five percent of their working time to pro bono activities, in practice there is not a strong "pro bono ethos" at the firm. One person we spoke with observed that "Kirkland has a more practical view of pro bono than other firms: if the pro bono helps you develop skills useful to Kirkland, it will back you 110%." Many associates view pro bono as an excellent way to get courtroom experience. One person noted that the firm "wants people to feel comfortable in the courtroom, and the pro bono practice is a good way to combine interests." Pro bono hours count as billable hours for purposes of associate evaluations.

hard working and conservative

Firmwide, Kirkland & Ellis is managed by a committee with representatives from all of its offices. Locally, one associate stated that the D.C. office is managed fairly "loosely" by a committee, the members of which are "open and accessible." Everyone considered the D.C. office to be distinctly different from the Chicago office, in both practice and culture. One person described the Chicago office as having a real "shark mentality"; another characterized it as "competitive," whereas the D.C. office is comparatively "friendly" and "supportive." In some respects, however, the cultures are quite similar, particularly with respect to the firm's "midwestern work ethic." Kirkland is a "down-to-business" firm, and one associate cautioned, "Don't come if you don't like hard work." Politically, the partners tend to be conservative. Robert Bork was once a partner in the D.C. office, and many of the senior partners align themselves "with the Bork crowd and tend to be conservative," although the younger attorneys are more liberal. Kirkland also is conservative in dress. One person quipped that the attorneys look like they are right out of a "Catholic school": "this means gray suits for men with maroon ties and white shirts, and women wear gray, navy, and black. There are very few flashy ties." Another person instructed us, however, that things are changing on the dress front: "There is some room for style and fashion. Men wear more than gray suits and women have even been known to wear red." Moreover, Fridays are now casual dress days at the firm.

management

Kirkland's management is very businesslike and has been responsive to competition. The firm has taken a number of steps, including reducing certain legal fees, to remain competitive in the 1990s. One person pointed out that the firm is very concerned with cost effectiveness and is "meticulous in its records."

minimal social life

Kirkland & Ellis is better known for its hard work than its social life. The firm sponsors occasional wine and cheese social gatherings, as well as attorney lunches. One person opined that "if you want to do black tie dinners and have retreats in mountains, it is not the firm for you." Some young associates manage to lead active social lives, but one person observed that most attorneys at the firm are either old or young; there are very few middle-aged attorneys.

free-form development

Associate development is not highly structured, and new associates are given considerable flexibility for "free-form development." One person asserted that "the best thing about Kirkland is that it doesn't require you to specialize. It allows you to work with whomever you want. Your first few assignments are assigned, but after that you are on your own. As your reputation grows, then people start to call on you." This person continued that "by the time someone is in his fourth year, he is specializing in litigation or corporate, but it is not unusual to have corporate persons involved in litigation and vice versa." Without question, the free-form system caters to self-starters. One source cautioned that "there is no fairy-godmother" to guide fledgling attorneys at Kirkland. This also means, observed a second source, that "associates have a lot of responsibility to manage their own schedules and dockets. No one is going to check to see if you are in the office by 9:30 a.m., but no one is going to take you aside to tell you that you have been working too hard."

partnership

Kirkland & Ellis has a two-tier partnership system. After six years with the firm, associates are considered for non-share partnership; after nine years, non-share partners are considered for share partnership. Although the firm has had a good track record in making income partners, one associate lamented that it is very difficult to make equity partner and pointed out that there is a large differential in compensation between the two tiers. Another contact pointed out, somewhat more positively, that "Kirkland only hires those individuals that have the ability to make non-equity partner. Thus, when you get your offer, you know that the firm believes that you at least have the potential for a seven year future with the firm. This is different from other firms in which associates are made to feel as if they are dispensable robots that can be easily replaced in two years." Kirkland is very good about letting associates know where they stand on the partnership track: "If you make it past your third or fourth year, you have a serious prospect of making partner. The review process makes it clear early on." There is a "very rigorous review system which provides extensive feedback. The firm is very open with you and, as a result, there is less politicking." Attorneys annually receive evaluations from each partner with whom they work, containing extensive information about performance and future expectations. Everyone takes the evaluations very seriously—"partnership prospects and bonuses follow directly from the reviews." Associate compensation starts at $73,000, and thereafter depends to a large extent on merit bonuses, which can vary considerably. There are "large gaps in what people make" after the second year. Benefits at Kirkland are "not a strong point (paltry contributions to health insurance, no 401(K) matching, and no free parking)," observed one insider. Further, trials are work-intensive and unpredictable and "tend not to conform to your vacation schedule," one source reminded us.

"big boys club"

One associate considered Kirkland & Ellis to be a "tough firm for women," describing it as a "big boys club." Another person noted that "the difficult thing for me is the lack of female role models in partnership positions." The firm is a real "meritocracy, and if you're not pulling your weight, then you won't advance." Many women have had to choose between the firm and having children. One person observed that, invariably, the "baby wins." A firm spokesperson, however, countered this opinion by noting that Kirkland "has several women partners with children—full-time and part-time partners." Many of the challenges women face at Kirkland may be inherent in the nature of trial practice and not Kirkland-specific, one contact observed for us. People noted, however, that Kirkland is very "sensitive to the problems" and has hired outside consultants to review this situation, among other things. Additionally, there are not many racial minorities at the firm; another person reiterated that Kirkland is a "meritocracy—it doesn't have an affirmative action program."

beautiful offices

Kirkland's "beautiful" offices feature a conference table made from African bubinga wood. The interiors, lined with dark wood paneling, complement the central showpiece. Each associate has an individual office with a window, and laptop computers are available to any associate who wants one. "Laptops rather than desktops are part of the Kirkland mentality; ready to bring the show on the road and set up a trial office" is how one source described this preference. The excellent support staff includes a special group of computer technicians who specialize in data analysis and computer graphics. The firm provides a light breakfast every morning, with fresh fruit, pastries, bagels, and coffee available.

hiring tips

Kirkland's callback interviews typically involve meeting a number of the firm's attorneys for about thirty minutes each and usually going to lunch with two associates. The interviews, which were described as "sell jobs" in earlier editions, have become more competitive in recent years. Now, "a call-back does not necessarily guarantee an offer," one contact informed us. Each interviewer completes a written evaluation of a candidate, often including assessments of areas such as "intellectual firepower, specific interest in the office, interest in D.C., sense of professional goals, and work ethic." The applicant's dining companions also complete an evaluation form.

Kirkland & Ellis hires most of its attorneys from the top 10 national and D.C.-area law schools. People commented that its lawyers value work ethic as much as academic achievement. One person ventured that many Kirkland attorneys "believe law school is a joke," and are looking for someone who is willing to work hard, rather than a mere academic type. Unlike many D.C. firms, Kirkland has hired first-year students into its summer program. In the past, Kirkland has conducted first-year interviews very early in the hiring season, usually before the winter holidays, and soon thereafter makes offers with a short acceptance deadline. Kirkland also hires summer associates who have completed law school for the summer before a clerkship. The firm, moreover, increasingly hires associates who have clerked and has been successful recently in recruiting Supreme Court clerks (five in the past year).

Kirkland reports that approximately 85% of its summer associates in recent years have received permanent associate offers. Apparently, short of spilling a beer all over a senior partner, as one student did a few years ago, it is difficult to avoid receiving a permanent associate offer. "And actually, this person did receive an offer and is still with the firm," one spirited insider informed us. Another contact cautioned, however, against becoming too blase in these matters: "Kirkland & Ellis is very selective these days. Especially for summer positions, the majority of candidates still need to sell themselves once they get to Kirkland."

Miller & Chevalier

Washington

Address: 655 Fifteenth Street, N.W., Suite 900, Washington, D.C. 20005-5701
Telephone: (202) 626–5800
Hiring Attorney: Grant D. Aldonas, Hiring Attorney
Contact: Holly S. Hand, Director of Attorney Recruiting and Development; (202) 626–5820
Associate Salary: First year $74,000 (1997)
Summer Salary: NA
Average Hours: 2289 worked; 1858 billed; 1900 required
Family Benefits: 12 weeks paid maternity leave to primary caregiver; 8 weeks paid leave to primary caregiver in adoption; 6 weeks paid paternity leave to primary caregiver; 2 weeks paid to secondary caregiver
1996 Summer: Class of 12 students; offers to 10
Partnership 23% of entering associates from 1946 to present have made partner
Pro Bono: 2% of all work is pro bono

Miller & Chevalier in 1997
98 Lawyers at the Washington D.C. Office
0.8 Associates Per Partner

Total Partners 55			Total Associates 43			Practice Areas	
Women	12	22%	Women	20	47%	Tax	50
All Minorities	0	0%	All Minorities	7	16%	Litigation	20
			Afro-Am	6	14%	International	17
			Latino	1	2%	Government Contracts	11

Founded as one of the country's first tax boutique firms, Miller & Chevalier today is best known for its premier tax litigation practice. Over the years, Miller's leading attorneys have included Robert Miller, the first Chief Counsel of the Internal Revenue Service, and Jack Nolan, a former Deputy Assistant Secretary of the Treasury for Tax Policy, who still practices at the firm and traditionally has been one of its most influential partners. These men viewed the firm as more than just a "group of lawyers making a living," but rather as an "association of very gifted practitioners, many of whom have an academic bent, where young lawyers can come and receive training and work their way up through the firm, be partners and stay for 30 years, with a possible government service hiatus." This view has produced Miller's strong sense of "camaraderie." Many attorneys there are long-time close friends. One insider remarked that "the people at Miller & Chevalier are generally happy; I find it is a rare day that does not contain at least one humorous interlude."

friendly culture

The atmosphere at Miller & Chevalier is "friendly." "People work intensely" but relate well to each other. Attorneys work with their doors open, and it is not uncommon to find them chatting up a storm about non-legal issues. Despite the informality, one source observed that the lawyers at Miller "are very interested in their work." Miller attorneys currently have a significant role in ABA leadership positions. Philip Mann is chair-elect of the Tax Section, Marcia Madsen is chair-elect of the Public Contracts Law Section, and Cindy Low is chair of the International Section. The firm's attorneys are "concerned with producing the finest cutting-edge work and have a good reputation for being high-quality." There are not many "huge egos" at the firm. One insider observed that "the firm culture does not abide prima donnas. Instead, everyone is an important part of the team.

practice areas

Miller's tax practice includes legislative and planning work, but tax litigation is the "bread and butter" of the practice. The group includes Bob Moore, a "highly-respected" tax litigator, Larry Gibbs, a former Commissioner of Internal Revenue, and the aforementioned Phillip Mann. Most of the firm's tax clients are Fortune 100 companies, with oil and defense industry clients figuring prominently. Some clients, such as Exxon, retain Miller from time to time for highly specialized controversy work. The tax group recently engineered a "strategic alliance" with the accounting firm of Price Waterhouse, which is expected to be "mutually beneficial" to both firms. The firm also has developed strong practices in general litigation, government contracts, and does some international work. The government contracts group has traditionally handled defense contract work, but has recently branched out into more computer and technology-oriented and non-defense work, particularly health care procurement. The practice has expanded "exponentially" with the addition of several lateral attorneys from other D.C. firms. The aforementioned Marcia Madsen, joined this group in mid-1996, "infusing it with new energy and with a new way of doing business," according to one insider. The international group handles unfair trade litigation, export controls and trade sanctions, and a variety of other international legal and policy issues, including the representation of Canada in some high-profile trade matters. People noted that this practice has not been "very busy recently." The general litigation practice, in contrast, has been "very busy of late," supporting other practices in litigating tax and false claims act cases, as well as with its own health care work, primarily for various Blue Cross plans. Pro bono work at Miller is credited as billable hours, but is a low-key item at the firm. Miller attorneys work primarily for the D.C. Bar's Law Firms Pro Bono Clinic on family law, public benefits, and landlord-tenant matters.

social life

Our earlier edition described a "vibrant social atmosphere" for the young associates at Miller & Chevalier. More recently, we have been told, "many of the junior and mid-level associates are married or seriously involved, " and so the extra-firm socializing has slowed down somewhat. There are firm happy hours every Friday afternoon, which are "well attended and very enjoyable; but firm socializing generally stops at the building's door," reported one insider.

training and feedback

Miller received strong reviews for its training and evaluation programs for both summer and permanent associates. During the summer, the firm holds weekly sessions to help summer associates improve their research skills. One summer associate enthused that the training "was really good. You have an associate work coordinator whose job is to get you work and feedback. The coordinator made a big effort to get feedback from each partner. I received really honest feedback, not a pat on the back." The partners are "really big on feedback. It's part of their way of doing things—to sit down and talk to you," reported another contact. Similarly, the evaluation system for permanent associates is very detailed. Associates are given "full-scale evaluations every six months on everything, including partnership prospects." One person commented that there is an expectation that those attorneys who are with the firm for seven and a half years will be made partner. Partners and associates work closely together at Miller. One person explained that Miller "is not a 'leveraged' firm. The result is that cases have equal numbers of partners and associates, or more often than not, more partners than associates. The bottom line is that associates learn their trade directly from the people that brought the client in the door." However, one person warned that although most associates have client contact in their first year, "the nature of the firm's clients, viz. large Fortune 50 companies, means that there are less opportunities for on-your-feet experience for associates. The firm has, however, established a Lawyers Development Committee to look at this and other associates training issues." We were also told that partners sometimes are reluctant to "push down" work to associates, and will sometimes "micro-manage"cases.

diversity

Miller was described as "progressive" on women's issues. "There are a number of women who are active partners," and "there is a strongly articulated anti-sexual harassment policy." Moreover, one person remarked that "pregnant women are treated very well. There are quite a few younger women who have taken time off. One woman didn't work a whole summer because she had a baby. The firm doesn't look upon this badly." Miller subsidizes the use of a day care program that is offered in the building. People also commented that Miller is "very interested in hiring minorities and considers it a very important thing." The firm presently has a strong representation of minorities in its associate ranks.

management

Miller is managed by an executive committee of its members, who hold bi-monthly meetings. Much of the firm's administrative business is conducted by committees, some of which have a good representation of associates. In addition, associates hold regular meetings and report their concerns to the partners. The firm, we were told, values associate input. It has, for example, at the instigation of past associates committees, "re-instituted a yearly firm retreat and raised associate salaries." Each practice group holds a regularly scheduled status meeting, whose frequency varies from group to group.

finances and pay

Miller has done "very well financially over the past two years" and has been "extremely" busy in all the practice groups (with the possible exception of the international group). The firm is "looking to hire many new lateral associates" because of the volume of work it now has. The firm has an executive director who is emphasizing strategic planning and aggressive marketing. One contact observed that the executive director has done "very well in assisting the executive committee in managing the firm. While no one in his position is completely loved by everyone all the time, his contributions to the firm cannot go unmentioned." Miller has developed a five-year strategic marketing plan, and each practice group must develop a mission statement and set of goals. One insider remarked that the firm's "long-term planning is very stable," and that Miller is "less susceptible to swings in the market than many full-service law firms are."

Miller has a lockstep compensation system for associates, which "helps prevent the back-stabbing and competitiveness that occurs at many other firms and helps enforce camaraderie." Another contact elaborated that "while associate salaries at Miller & Chevalier remain competitive with the largest, most prestigious firms in the city, partner salaries lag behind. This is due in large part to the high partner to associate ratio, which—despite its good points—leads to comparably lower firm profits. Any associate planning on 'gunning' for partner has to realize that the rewards of working at Miller & Chevalier cannot be measured solely in money."

office facilities

Miller's offices, which have recently been renovated, are located across from the White House and the Treasury Department. The offices have a "tremendous terrace for parties and lunch," causing one insider to exult: "Miller & Chevalier's 10th floor terrace is one of the finest locations in the city." Almost all the offices have windows, although some offices are internal with atrium windows. One person claimed that they are some "of the nicest offices I have seen." Miller has "great library facilities" and its support services are "top of the line." One contact especially praised the firm's library staff, headed by Carol Gruenburg, for making the library "one of the best run in town." Another source commented that "everything was done to allow me to maximize my performance."

hiring

Miller & Chevalier places a premium on hiring "smart people." Put simply, tax work is intellectually challenging, and Miller looks to hire individuals who can handle its demands. The firm recruits most actively from the top 15 to 20 law schools. Because the firm's practice emphasizes litigation, writing skills are highly valued. The interviews at Miller are relaxed and casual—no one reported any grilling about substantive law. One person described the encounter as a "nice–to–get–to–know–you type conversation." Interviews usually involve meeting five to six attorneys at the firm. In the summer of 1996, the firm hired twelve summer associates, ten of whom received permanent offers.

Miller & Chevalier is a "specialty firm—tax, government contracts, litigation, and international trade. It does not seek to be all things to all people, but focuses sharply on providing highly effective assistance to clients in these specialized areas," reported one contact. One insider pointed out that "the nature of federal regulatory type litigation that Miller specializes in is such that there is less pettiness and scorched-earth type tactics that occur in commercial litigation." One contact summarized nicely the attractions and challenges of working at Miller & Chevalier, observing that "the firm usually gets client problems that have already been refined, massaged, and pondered by others: corporate counsel, frequently tax specialists. No problem comes in that doesn't have challenging and unique aspects. Working well in this environment requires a lot of energy."

Morrison & Foerster

Washington Denver Los Angeles New York Orange County Palo Alto Sacramento San Francisco Walnut Creek Brussels Hong Kong London Singapore Tokyo

Address: 2000 Pennsylvania Avenue, N.W., Suite 5500, Washington, D.C. 20006–1812
Telephone: (202) 887–1500
Hiring Attorney: Jonathan Band/Richard Morris
Contact: Joyce W. Burgwyn, Recruiting Coordinator; (202) 887–1535
Associate Salary: First year $74,000 (1997); second $74,000; third $79,000; fourth $84,000; fifth $90,000; sixth $95,000; seventh $102,000; eighth $107,000
Summer Salary: NA
Average Hours: NA worked; NA billed; NA required
Family Benefits: Flexible benefits: medical, dental, vision, LTD, 401(K); maternity, adoption, family care leaves; EAP; flexible work schedule; health and dependent care reimbursement accounts; domestic partner coverage; liability accident and life insurance; relocation; child and eldercare referral; professional dues; other benefits
1996 Summer: Class of 6 students, offers to 6
Partnership: 31% of entering associates from 1979–1985 were made partner
Pro Bono: NA

Morrison & Foerster in 1997
54 Lawyers at the Washington D.C. Office
1.6 Associates Per Partner

Total Partners 18		
Women	5	27%
All Minorities	0	0%

Total Associates 29		
Women	11	38%
All Minorities	6	21%
Afro-Am	1	3%
Asian-Am	4	14%
Native Am	1	3%

Practice Areas	
Litigation	25
Business	20
Patent	8
Tax	1

A branch office of one of San Francisco's most prominent firms, Morrison & Foerster (affectionately known as MoFo) is regarded as a firm that promotes "humane values." Firmwide, its partnership includes among the highest percentage of women of any firm. MoFo has also gone to great lengths to accommodate working mothers and parents in general, providing comparatively generous flex-time, part-time, and parental leave policies. MoFo was listed as one of the 10 best places for women to work in the country by *Working Mother* magazine. The firm also provides a comfortable atmosphere for racial minorities, although like many other D.C. firms, it has had a difficult time retaining minority attorneys. "The attorneys go out of their way to recruit and hire qualified minority and female associates," reported one contact. The D.C. office has a "distinctly liberal Democratic bent," we were told.

excellent pro bono

MoFo's humanity extends to its "outstanding" pro bono practice. The firm's "walls are covered with pro bono plaques" from awards it has won, admired one source. MoFo has one of the best pro bono practices in a city where firms are noted for their pro bono work, claimed others. A MoFo attorney oversees the practice, and the firm's daily newsletter updates attorneys about availability of pro bono cases. All pro bono hours count toward billable hours. MoFo receives a variety of pro bono cases from organizations such as the Washington Lawyer's Committee for Civil Rights Under the Law involving human, civil, and gay rights, the death penalty, and employment discrimination. It also handles a lot of immigration and education matters.

practice areas

Founded in 1883, Morrison & Foerster is one of the nation's older law firms. The D.C. office opened in 1979 and has since grown by "leaps and bounds," although it has not grown in the past few years. Its strongest practice areas are banking, communications, international trade, energy, intellectual property, and investment management. Firmwide, MoFo has a nationally pre-eminent banking law practice, and not surprisingly, banking constitutes a substantial portion of the D.C. practice. The communications practice group is also solid under the leadership of Diane Hinson, former Chief Counsel to the FCC in the Bush Administration. Cheryl Tritt is also well known in this practice. The department represents a number of large telephone users and mass media clients before the Federal Communications Commission (FCC). It also represents "glamour clients" such as Paramount and other studios and has done work for some T.V. shows and the Disney Corporation. The international trade practice is "booming." Some stated that it is the busiest practice at the firm. Prominent partner, Don Cameron, is a "big name in antidumping and countervailing duties" matters. The investment management practice group led by Bob Kurucza and Marco Adelfio, was recently "ranked number four nationally by the *American Lawyer* Corporate Scorecard as Mutual Fund Counsel with the most new issues," according to one contact. Their biggest clients include the fund families of NationsBank and Wells Fargo Bank. The D.C. patent practice was broadened when partner, Kate Murashige, one of the firm's big "rainmakers," moved her biotech patent practice from Palo Alto to the D.C. office. The firm's real estate practice, which had been described as "slow" in the last edition of *The Insider's Guide*, recently left the firm to join Mayer, Brown & Platt.

supportive atmosphere

The atmosphere at MoFo was described as "supportive," "cooperative," "friendly," and "much less hierarchical" than at many other D.C. firms. One contact observed that MoFo Washington has a "more relaxed corporate culture than is typical in D.C., probably stemming from the fact that the firm is California-based." The dress code is also less formal. Women frequently wear dresses and pantsuits in the office. Fridays are casual dress days at the firm. The casual day is "like getting an extra day off. It has a very positive effect on people," noted one observer. Apparently so, as the D.C. office recently declared the entire month of August as "casual month." MoFo attorneys get along "really well." Despite its informal atmosphere, however, MoFo can be a "high-pressure firm," we were told. You hear "yelling every now and then," but it is the "exception and not the rule," reported one contact. From time to time, the attorneys are a little "nutty and anal," agreed another. "Many of the attorneys socialize together," but MoFo is "not a partying firm," summarized one commentator. Morrison & Foerster recently eliminated its summer associate program.

training professional development

We heard mostly positive reviews of the firm's formal training. One person commented that MoFo provides "tons of formal training." Another observed that the "investment management practice group provides monthly training sessions by senior associates." The feedback to associates provided by the firm, however, was criticized, with some of our contacts complaining about the "lack of feedback and positive reinforcement." You "have to ask specifically" for a critique of your work, complained one. On the other hand, people praised the firm for offering early responsibility. Though some groups are better than others, you have to "hit the ground running" at

MoFo, advised one contributor. Associates may "work on briefs for appellate cases almost immediately." The communications group is "more memo oriented. But, if you have experience in a particular area, you can get responsibility early." One person commented that, "at least by their third year, most people function autonomously."

associates review partners

Morrison & Foerster is one of the few firms in the country where associates not only review partners' performance as supervisors, but where these reviews can affect partner compensation. This practice originated in the D.C. office and has since been adopted by other MoFo offices. The D.C. office managing partner, G. Brian Busey, was described as "approachable;" he replaces the "outstanding" Nicholas Spiliotes, who was recently elevated to the position of managing partner for operations for the entire firm. Partners and associates enjoy good communication, and the management is open and receptive to associates' ideas. Although the management has been "very cost conscious" in recent years, people claimed the firm is economically very healthy. One contact noted that the firm is becoming "more efficient administratively and more business-oriented" of late.

Located in the Tower Records building on Pennsylvania Avenue, MoFo has "nicely decorated" offices, which were recently remodeled. All associates have private offices with windows. The firm's library, which had been criticized as "lacking" in resources, recently underwent expansion and is presently complaint-free, according to our sources.

hiring tips

As noted above, MoFo eliminated its summer associate program, but it does hire first-year associates. A large percentage of the lawyers that the firm hires are members of a law review, but this is not a prerequisite to being hired. The firm also hires people with "interesting backgrounds" who have done interesting things. A knowledge of politics is helpful in getting hired because a number of the interviews involve political discussions, asserted this person, an observation, however, with which not all our contacts agreed. Callback interviews involve meeting three or four different attorneys at the firm. The hiring process, we were told, "can be long and drawn out."

Our contacts described MoFo as "socially progressive," a place where an "individual can retain his or her individuality," but also as demanding "incredibly long hours (though this may be peculiar to only a few practice groups)." The biggest downside to working at the firm, we were told, is that there is "no assurance of making partner (more specifically, senior associates are being made of counsel instead—for an undefined term)." This situation has reportedly had a "demoralizing effect on associates." The elimination of the summer associate program will also not be good news for our readers. On the other hand, those we interviewed agreed that the firm displays an unusual commitment to pro bono work and to promoting and accommodating diversity. Morrison & Foerster provides an especially good work environment for women, and, more generally, people praised the firm's "sense of teamwork among partners, associates, legal assistants, and staff."

Patton & Boggs

Washington Baltimore Boulder Dallas Denver Greensboro Raleigh Seattle

Address:	2550 M Street, N.W., Washington, D.C. 20037
Telephone:	(202) 457–6000
Hiring Attorney:	John Fithian
Contact:	Kara P. Reidy, Recruitment Administrator; (202) 457–6342
Associate Salary:	First year $74,000 (1996)
Summer Salary:	$1225/week (1997)
Average Hours:	2007 worked; 1794 billed; 1800 required
Family Benefits:	10 weeks paid maternity leave; 2 weeks paid paternity leave
1996 Summer:	Class of 11 students; offers to 9
Partnership:	27% of entering associates from 1985–1988 were made partner
Pro Bono:	4.6% of all work is pro bono

Patton & Boggs in 1997
161 Lawyers at the Washington D.C. Office
0.7 Associates Per Partner

Total Partners 89			Total Associates 64			Practice Areas	
Women	7	8%	Women	21	33%	Litigation	NA
All Minorities	2	2%	All Minorities	15	23%	Legislative	
Afro-Am	2	2%	Afro-Am	12	19%	Unassigned (1st & 2nd year)	
			Asian-Am	2	3%	Corporate	
			Latino	1	1%	Administrative	
						International	
						Environmental	
						Government Contracts	
						Antitrust	
						Food & Drug	
						Health	
						Intellectual Property	
						Native American	
						Occupational Health & Safety	
						Real Estate	
						Tax	
						Telecommunications	

a prominent lobbying firm

Patton & Boggs is perhaps the most well-known and successful lobbying firm in Washington, D.C. The firm has been home to two of the most high-profile political insiders in the city: the late Ron Brown, former head of the Democratic National Committee and Secretary of Commerce, and Tom Boggs, son of the former House Majority Leader and one of the premier lobbyists in D.C. Although Patton Boggs principally represents clients in administrative and judicial proceedings, its lawyers also directly lobby members of Congress. One person claimed that Patton Boggs' powerful lobbying practice provides "more options" for clients: instead of spending years in protracted litigation, it is "often cheaper to go directly to Congress and lobby" for a legislative solution. Patton Boggs is a quintessential "Democratic" insider firm, although it also has ties to the Republican Party. Since 1992, it has increased its Republican profile, including making a partner of Ben Ginsburg, former general counsel to the Republican National Committee, and hiring former Congressman Greg Laughlin, Republican of Texas. One source observed that "a lot of partners and associates are active in the Democratic party and in campaigns. They raise a lot of money. Some of it has to do with the firm's connection to Congress. Many of the lawyers are very politically committed." Indeed, many young associates see Patton Boggs as a springboard to government and would not work for any other firm. In short, many go to Patton Boggs to "pay back bills and have one foot in government."

stresses social abilities

As might be expected, Patton Boggs places great emphasis on political contacts and networking. One person opined that it is "not a place for introverted people" and noted that "there is a premium placed on social abilities and the ability to communicate with clients." This person continued that "there is a threshold of work quality that everyone has to make, but because the firm has an impressive list of D.C. clients, there is a social quotient—they want people who will reassure clients that they get quality representation. How you handle yourself in a room may be important."

For those who are not "introverted," Patton Boggs provides a "very social atmosphere." Described as "nice," "informal," and "friendly," the work atmosphere received uniformly high reviews, although one person noted that "there are a lot of egos to appease" at the firm. One contact explained that the lawyers are not a "high-pressure, nervous bunch of people. Associates and summer associates do a lot of things together after work. It's a very social group of people, and they become friends in the course of practice." The firm encourages a healthy social life by sponsoring social events such as "Third Thursday," held, not surprisingly, on the third Thursday of every month. On these occasions, everyone at the firm gets together for drinks and hors d'oeuvres at the end of the day.

practice areas

Although Patton Boggs unquestionably is best-known for its lobbying practice, it has expanded into many other areas. As the fastest-growing practice at the firm, litigation "carried Patton Boggs through" the early 1990s, one source asserted. The litigation group, which includes a white-collar crime practice, handles a broad variety of matters; Bluebonnet Savings Bank is one of its large clients. Ron Liebman, a "big name in the litigation community," headed the firm's representation of Abu Dhabi in its BCCI litigation. Patton Boggs also has growing practices in environmental and administrative law; its food and drug practice is doing particularly well. The firm's international group handles corporate, trade, and litigation work. This practice, with its strong connections in the Arab world, has represented a few Saudi princes. Although hurt by the oil market decline in the late 1980s, international work reportedly has been "picking up again." The firm recently acquired a telecommunications practice and a health and safety practice, both of which are "thriving." New associates at Patton Boggs may explore a number of different practice areas for two years before concentrating in a specialty.

pro bono

Patton Boggs has a "very strong" pro bono practice, run by partner Steve Schneebaum. In 1995, the firm hired a full-time Public Service Counsel to direct the firm's pro bono work. One person asserted that this practice is in the "top five" in the city. Patton Boggs lawyers have worked on death penalty cases, children's rights issues, Burmese election law and human rights issues, and Social Security benefit disputes. Pro bono hours are considered non-billable hours by the firm, but count toward billable hours after a threshold of 100 hours. Also, an associate who fails to bill 100 pro bono hours two years in a row is ineligible for a performance bonus.

training and feedback

Described as a very "entrepreneurial" law firm, Patton Boggs rewards individual initiative and achievement. The firm is organized more like a loose collection of sole practitioners than a traditional partnership. One insider praised the "free nature of relationships—not bound by excessive hierarchies or practice groups" at the firm. Firm profits are divided according to the amount of work each partner generates, as well as the amount of an associate's billings. In addition, training and opportunities for responsibility depend greatly on personal initiative and motivation. One source commented that "there is very little formal training, if any." Another person remarked that "because the partners are concerned with being entrepreneurs, they are not as concerned with training or morale." After a basic training program, entering associates are "on their own." A firm spokesperson informed us that the firm has reassessed "its commitment to the training of its associates. The assignment of a 'training partner' for each practice group and the implementation of a formal mentor program are two elements of that commitment." One contact noted that "Patton Boggs greatest advantage is its flexibility. You will never be pigeon-holed into a single practice field here. Patton Boggs is full of entrepreneurs and attorneys are free to shape their own careers." If associates want "good assignments, they have to seek them out." We were told that for permanent associates, feedback generally follows this catch–as–catch–can principle, but a firm spokesperson stated that the firm provides permanent associates with annual reviews based on detailed evaluations completed by partners and senior associates. The firm also makes a concerted effort to formally evaluate its summer associates. Each supervising partner completes a detailed evaluation form, and summer associates receive mid- and end-of-summer reviews.

diversity

Patton Boggs received plaudits for its treatment of minorities. One person observed that the firm is "sensitive to minority issues, and minorities in the firm are very helpful and encouraging" to each other. Another person reported a strong effort by the firm to recruit minorities, noting that many of the summer associates in past classes have been minorities. The reviews were not uniformly positive, however, regarding the atmosphere for women. People commented that the firm is "trying to recruit women and encourages women to apply" and that there is good "solidarity" among women at the firm. In one summer the firm sponsored a couple of special women's events, including a brunch at a partner's house. However, one person mentioned that there "have been some complaints about a couple of partners and associates at the firm who have behaved inappropriately." In particular, one source noted that there is a group of partners who are "old-fashioned" and there "have been some problems," but added that these are "being corrected." One contact told us that "the firm has taken these problems very seriously and has obviously addressed the few partners involved." On the other hand, another source informed us that "the firm has recently experienced the departure of a large number of midlevel and senior women associates."

management addressing associate concerns

Patton Boggs is run by a management committee which, our earlier edition reported, had "encountered some associate criticism." One item at issue was the matter of the associate bonus system. The current management committee, headed by Tom Boggs as managing partner and Stuart Pape as deputy managing partner, "appears to be more involved with associate concerns and is making an effort to be accessible," one insider reported. The firm is, moreover, making a focused effort "to communicate more clearly the scope and intent" of the bonus system, we were informed. In addition, the new management committee has attempted to address the disparity in representation by female and minority attorneys at the firm. They are also considering proposals from the women attorneys on topics such as family leave, part-time work policy, training and mentoring, etc. Indeed, effective January 1, 1997 the firm instituted a newly expanded paid Family Medical and Short-Term Disability Leave policy, and is developing new policies in "alternative" work arrangements, such as part-time attorney schedules, a firm spokesperson informed us.

associate salaries

Patton Boggs recently restructured associate salaries in order to become more competitive. The base salary for the class of 1996 was $74,000. Salaries increase by block amounts thereafter, ranging from $4,000 to $7,000 each year. Associate compensation apparently continues to be an issue, however, in part because Patton Boggs partners are among the highest paid in D.C. One contact mentioned "the relatively poor associate pay scale and bonus structure" as a major drawback in working at Patton Boggs.

On the positive side, the firm does subsidize memberships for associates at the West End Fitness Center, which is located a block away from the firm and is "probably the nicest gym in the city," according to one person. Further, a representative of the firm remarked that, "overlooked in compensation computation, significant monetary advantages are provided in our contribution and profit-sharing retirement plans. Of all the law firm retirement plans of which we are aware, Patton Boggs clearly has one of the most generous."

office facilities

Patton Boggs' "open and airy" offices are located near Georgetown. Each associate has an individual office and computer. Patton Boggs has a strikingly beautiful art collection, including an original work by Robert Rauschenberg; one former partner, also an artist, displays some of his own works. The library, which had not been a major selling point of the firm in the past, has been remodeled and expanded considerably.

hiring tips

In its hiring, Patton Boggs focuses on candidates with a "mature and sophisticated personality." The hiring attorneys are "not sticklers for grades." "They figure everyone will be a good lawyer," but what they want is "someone who can handle the social environment in D.C." Another contact explained that the firm does not necessarily seek the "cream of the crop," "law review" type, but often hires "people in the second quartile of their class." One source disagreed slightly, however, claiming that a fair number of the firm's lawyers "were members of their school's law review or were Phi Beta Kappa in college, but they don't wear their academic laurels on their sleeves." Callback interviews usually consist of meeting six attorneys, who primarily are looking to assess the applicant's "personality." The interviews are free-form and vary considerably. For example, one person refrained from discussing any political subjects, but another person sensed very strong "political overtones," commenting that if "you are not politically wired," you do not feel like you are "one of them." It is "not a packaged interview. It is very subjective." One person suspected that candidates are rated on whether the interviewers "think you would be fun to work with."

Paul, Hastings, Janofsky & Walker

Washington Atlanta Los Angeles New York Orange County San Francisco Santa Monica Stamford London Tokyo

Address: 1299 Pennsylvania Ave., N.W., 10th Floor, Washington, D.C. 20004
Telephone: (202) 508–9500
Hiring Attorney: Scott M. Flicker
Contact: Sheryl Manning, Recruitment Coordinator; (202) 508–9867
Associate Salary: First year $74,000 (1997); second $78,000; third $85,000; fourth $90,000; fifth $98,000; sixth $111,000; seventh $125,000; eighth $131,000
Summer Salary: $1300/week (1997)
Average Hours: NA worked; NA billed; 1960 budget
Family Benefits: 6 weeks paid maternity leave (cbc unpaid); 6 weeks paid paternity leave
1996 Summer: Class of 3 students; offers to 3
Partnership: NA
Pro Bono: 3% of all work is pro bono

Paul, Hastings, Janofsky & Walker in 1997
53 Lawyers at the Washington D.C. Office
2.1 Associates Per Partner

Total Partners 17			Total Associates 36			Practice Areas	
Women	1	6%	Women	12	33%	Litigation	19
All Minorities	1	6%	All Minorities	5	14%	Employment/Benefits	19
Afro-Am	1	6%	Afro-Am	3	8%	Business	16
			Asian-Am	2	6%	Communications	5
						Real Estate	3

politically connected

Paul Hastings enjoys many close ties to government and politics. "Big in the Republican party," one of its lawyers, Judy Hope was nominated for the D.C. Circuit Court by President Reagan. Another Paul Hastings attorney, Ralph Everett served as parliamentarian of the Democratic National Convention and counsel to the Senate Commerce Committee. The firm has a small legislative practice which is headed by Ralph Everett. It is, however, very hard to be hired into this group unless you have previous experience working on Capitol Hill, one person told us.

practice areas

Paul Hastings is best known, however, for its litigation, particularly its employment and white-collar crime litigation practices. Both Barbara Brown, the former chair of the D.C. office, and Zach Fasman are well-known in the employment and labor law fields. Jack Gallagher is nationally known as a labor and employment lawyer, particularly with respect to the airline industry. The white-collar crime practice is headed by Larry Barcella and Paul Perito. Both Barcella and the aforementioned Barbara Brown were cited in a February 1997 *Washingtonian* magazine story on the city's 50 best lawyers; Perito has handled a number of high-profile cases, including representing the Hunt brothers and William Casey, former director of the CIA.

international practice

Paul Hastings also offers a small international practice. Under the leadership of Hamilton Loeb, the chair of the D.C. office, this practice is expanding into Eastern Europe, as well as the Far East and Latin America. The group handles a wide variety of trade and export issues, as well as providing "monitorings and advice in the context of multilateral trade negotiations to both private and governmental clients." The former President of U.S. Air is of counsel at the firm and is prominent in the firm's aviation employment and regulatory practice. The firm has a small energy practice. In addition, Paul Hastings recently "dramatically" expanded its capabilities in the telecommunications and environmental regulatory areas with the addition of eight new attorneys in these areas. Don Elliott, former EPA General Counsel, joined the environmental group, and a number of lawyers from Bryan Cave, including Carl Northrup and W.G. ("Grif") Johnson, joined the telecom practice. Both the environmental and telecommunications groups are part of larger inter-office and cross-departmental practice groups and interact with lawyers from the firm's eight offices.

pro bono

Although Paul Hastings has a formal pro bono practice, one source remarked that you won't find the firm "knocking on your door with pro bono work." Though attorneys may pursue independent pro bono projects as long as they are approved by the pro bono committee, Paul Hastings is more likely to take on "broader impact" litigation than narrow individual-related matters and has shied away from approving "divisive" pro bono projects, an insider remarked. In fact, we were told that an attorney had to take a leave of absence from the firm to work on a pro bono abortion matter which involved a pro-life position. This year, associates at the firm handled several smaller cases assigned from the D.C. Bar's Public Service Activities Corp. Although pro bono hours count toward billable hours, one person pointed out that the firm only "budgets a certain number of pro bono hours firmwide. You have to get any proposed pro bono approved out of the budget and if the budget is already used up, then you are out of luck." The firm has, however, been somewhat flexible with its pro bono budget.

team structure

Everyone at Paul Hastings is assigned to work on a "team," usually consisting of three to 10 lawyers. People stressed, however, that due to the firm's small size, junior associates must be prepared to work at any time in the area in which the firm has the greatest demand. New associates are, however, "asked for a department assignment preference, which is usually followed," a firm spokesperson instructed us.

training

Paul Hastings provides a "full-scale" litigation workshop for its summer associates, which involves mock depositions, negotiations, settlements, and more. In addition, partners regularly lecture about different practice areas at the firm. Paul Hastings is organized as a "shallow hierarchy" and does not staff cases "heavily"; hence, its associates work closely with the partners. Nevertheless, most attorneys do not progress to independently handle "big paying cases" until their seventh or eighth year. They typically take depositions by their second and third years, and some fourth- and fifth-year employment associates "run their own cases, going to partners with questions" only.

youthful culture

Paul Hastings was described as "laid-back," "relaxed," and "informal." The attorneys are "friendly," and one contact remarked that the "partners and associates still like to consider themselves young people who like to have fun...The office has a youthful feel." Though most associates are married, "there is a small core of young attorneys who go out a lot," one source said. Paul Hastings is not, however, the firm to go to if you want to be wined and dined for the summer. Recent summer associates were, however, treated to an overnight trip with white water rafting, a U2 rock concert, the annual jazz/blues and Cajun/Zydeco music festivals at Wolf Trap, an outing to an Orioles game in Baltimore, and informal dinners and parties at lawyers' homes.

Paul Hastings provides a comfortable atmosphere for women, we were told. The aforementioned Judy Hope was a significant player in the founding of the D.C. office, and Barbara Brown is a former chair of the D.C. office. Among many other accomplishments, Brown founded the Women's Law Project in Philadelphia. In addition, as a discrimination lawyer, she is sensitive to issues involving women and minorities in the workplace. One person noted that "there are three new moms and two new dads among the associate ranks, and the firm seems to be handling this well." Nevertheless, the current number of women at the office is not very impressive. In particular, only one of the office's 17 partners is a woman.

management

The practice of the Paul Hastings, D.C. office is fairly independent of the L.A. home office, but "everything is processed from L.A. and the rules emanate from there," one contact told us. The D.C. management is part of a larger group that sets firmwide policy. Although Paul Hastings went through some difficult economic times in the early 1990s, which included laying off a number of attorneys around the country, in recent years "both the firm as a whole and the D.C. office have grown steadily, reaching historically high levels," we were told.

office facilities

Paul Hastings moved its Washington offices in late 1993 to a custom-designed space in the historic Warner Theater building, overlooking Freedom Plaza and Pennsylvania Avenue. The firm occupies all of the 10th floor. All attorneys have their own offices and personal computers. The main atrium of the building was featured in the film "Pelican Brief," based on John Grisham's best-seller novel. The offices boast a unique design feature—a conference room constructed inside a second atrium that extends from the 10th floor to the penthouse level.

hiring tips

Recent Paul Hastings summer associates have come from a variety of schools around the country, including Harvard, George Washington, Howard, Loyola, the University of Chicago, Michigan, Vanderbilt, the University of Virginia, and California law schools, such as Boalt. Paul Hastings callback interviews are laid-back and friendly and are conducted over the course of a half day. The interview begins with meeting a member of the hiring committee who will inform the interviewee about other attorneys on the interview schedule. Most callback interviews involve meeting four attorneys and going to lunch with two.

Piper & Marbury

Washington Annapolis Baltimore Cherry Hill Easton New York Philadelphia Vienna

Address: 1200 Nineteenth Street, N.W., Washington, D.C. 20036
Telephone: (202) 861–3900
Hiring Attorney: Larry D. Harris
Contact: Jane Pontone, Recruitment Coordinator; (202) 861–3856
Associate Salary: First year $75,000 (1997); second $77,000; third $80,000; varies from fourth year to eighth year—up to $116,000
Summer Salary: $1300/week (1997)
Average Hours: 2482 worked; 1785 billed; 1875 required for bonus eligibility
Family Benefits: 12 weeks paid maternity leave (cbc unpaid); cbc weeks paid paternity leave (cbc unpaid)
1996 Summer: Class of 9 students; offers to 5
Partnership: NA
Pro Bono: 3–5% of all work is pro bono

Piper & Marbury in 1997
91 Lawyers at the Washington D.C. Office
1.0 Associate Per Partner

Total Partners 42		
Women	6	14%
All Minorities	2	5%
Afro-Am	1	2%
Latino	1	2%

Total Associates 40		
Women	23	58%
All Minorities	3	8%
Afro-Am	2	5%
Asian-Am	1	3%

Practice Areas	
Government Contracts	21
Corporate/Venture Capital	18
Environmental	17
Communications	11
Litigation	11
Comm. Lending/Bankruptcy	6
Antitrust & Trade	5
White Collar Crime	5

The D.C. branch office of a Baltimore-based firm, Piper & Marbury provides advantages that stem from its connection to one of the largest and best regional firms in the Baltimore-D.C. area and offers the added benefit of a midsize firm atmosphere. Piper is closely affiliated with the Baltimore home office. Its associates have access to the training and other resources of the headquarters, yet the D.C. office maintains a distinct firm culture. Whereas people described the Baltimore office as a "blue-blood" firm, the D.C. office evinces an eclectic atmosphere that reflects its growth as a collection of practice groups which Piper absorbed from other firms. The firm's departments are self-contained, and "there is not a lot of cross-over in work areas," we were told.

practice areas

Founded in 1981, the D.C. office has a strong environmental practice group, which joined Piper in its entirety from another D.C. firm after that firm's dissolution. The environmental work primarily involves advising large corporations regarding their rights, duties, and liabilities under CERCLA and RICRA. Partner Tom Truitt has handled "precedent-setting" cases in environmental law and is well-known in the field. Many of the environmental partners have worked with and known each other for years and enjoy relationships that are reportedly "a lot deeper" than the relationships among the other Piper D.C. partners. The environmental practice is notably "partner heavy," which reportedly lengthens its partnership track.

Piper's litigation practice primarily handles litigation matters for clients of its other practice areas, particularly environmental clients. A number of litigators from the Baltimore office joined the branch, which strengthened the practice and also enhanced the stature of the D.C. office firmwide. Piper's bankruptcy practice has done a lot of work for the Resolution Trust Corporation (RTC). The bankruptcy attorneys often engage in discovery-related travel.

Piper's government contracts group was recently increased sizably by the addition of a group from Pettit & Martin, and the practice now enjoys a pre-eminent national reputation, we were told. It is presently the largest practice in the firm. The firm also offers a corporate venture capital practice which has grown rapidly in the past few years. The venture capital practice represents venture capital funds in both fund formation and portfolio investments, in a wide range of industries, from life sciences and high technology to manufacturing, distribution, and retail. Piper's expanding communications group represents cable television companies and long distance communications carriers in property rights disputes and other matters. Piper has added a food and drug lawyer and has a small but growing intellectual property practice.

pro bono

Piper has a special connection to pro bono work. Administrative partner Jeffrey Liss serves on the board of the Washington Lawyers' Committee for Civil Rights Under the Law. One person expressed surprise "that the partners paid as much attention to pro bono as they did. The issue came up in departmental meetings and the partners were enthusiastic." The office instituted a "Pro Bono Lawyer of the Year" award in the D.C. office for the associate whose contributions are the most outstanding for the year involved. All pro bono cases must be screened by a firm committee. In addition to issues involving civil rights, lawyers at the firm do work for the Boy Scout Explorers Program, RICO cases, and other matters. The firm has won pro bono awards in recognition of its service in past years, and it is fairly flexible in allowing attorneys to handle the projects of their choice as long as it doesn't "eat up all their time," one person said.

training

First–year Piper associates select a department to work for upon joining the firm; one contact complained that there is "less opportunity to have a broad experience" at Piper than at other similar D.C. firms. Though Piper does not provide a highly structured work atmosphere, it has recently strived to develop its formal training programs. The firm provides a mock trial exercise for summer associates and offers a "strong" mentor program for associates. Summer associates are assigned to both a midlevel and a partner mentor. People noted, however, that the feedback varies greatly among the partners. We also heard complaints regarding the limited responsibility and distinct "lack of small manageable cases." The "clients are huge institutions and the second- and third-year associates do not do a lot," related one contact, noting that associates typically must wait seven years to try a case. A firm spokesperson noted, however, that a number of junior and midlevel associates in Washington and Baltimore have tried cases and have very substantial trial experience. Most associates argue pre-trial motions by their fourth year.

social life

Most Piper associates are married and the firm is not exactly a hopping social place, though matters have improved somewhat of late with the injection of "a lot of new young blood," according to one contact. There is "a lot of joshing between partners and associates," we were told. Not known for its lavish summer program, Piper has cut back on its activities in recent years. The firm has a softball team and regular happy hours. One of the highlights of the summer program is a sailing trip.

diversity

Piper is "really progressive about getting a lot of women into the firm and having them rise as quickly as men. There are six female partners." Past summer classes have included a high number of women, and the firm presently has more female than male associates. Two female partners have children, we were told.

Piper, however, was described as "not very diverse" with respect to racial minorities. We were told that "statistically they don't look impressive but they are trying to correct the problem. The Baltimore office is much better in this respect. There are many African–American attorneys at the junior associate level there."

management

Firmwide, Piper is run by a management committee whose members include some D.C. partners. The D.C. office is gaining influence in the overall firm management because it is increasing in size, having grown by roughly fifty percent since our last edition, to its present size of 91 attorneys. The branch office has a separate management structure, which is headed by an administrative partner who makes the firm's "day-to-day decisions." Most of the big decisions, however, are made in conjunction with the Baltimore office. The D.C. hiring committee functions independently of the Baltimore office. In addition, one source claimed that the D.C. branch exercises "a lot of authority in making partners in the D.C. office." But another source indicated that the "partnership track is very uncertain" at Piper at present. The firm did not make available to us its partnership data. The D.C. management was said to communicate well with its associates. The firm also has an associates committee, which holds a monthly luncheon attended by a liaison from the management committee.

Piper's offices are "not extremely luxurious, but comfortable with a nice atmosphere." The decor is "plain with subtle colors. There is nothing wild going on." Piper's library is well developed for a firm its size and owns specialized materials for the environmental, bankruptcy, tax, and government contracts practices.

hiring tips

Piper hires students from all over the country, from the top law schools and others. Many past summer associates were members of a law review, but people commented that the firm does not necessarily place much weight on law review membership in its hiring. Callback interviews at Piper typically involve meeting four to five attorneys and going out to lunch with a couple more. At these laid-back and pleasant interviews, "no one tries to scare you or pose hypos or do anything to shock you," one person reassuringly said. Another reported that she just "chatted" about non-legal topics in her interview. Piper "looks for a certain type of person. They don't like the aggressive loud types. They like the laid-back types. Everyone they hired was like that—not timid, but not the go–out–and–get'em–New–York–City–types."

Powell, Goldstein, Frazer & Murphy

Washington Atlanta

Address: 1001 Pennsylvania Avenue, N.W., 6th Floor, Washington, D.C. 20004
Telephone: (202) 347–0066
Hiring Attorney: Robert Torresen
Contact: Meegan Tracy, Assistant Human Resources Manager; (202) 624–7293
Associate Salary: First year $72,000 (1997); second $76,000; third $79,000; fourth $85,000; fifth $91,000; sixth $97,000; seventh $103,000; eighth $108,000
Summer Salary: $1250/week (1997)
Average Hours: NA worked; NA required; 1850 targeted
Family Benefits: Maternity/parental leave; comprehensive benefits package
1996 Summer: Class of 6 students; offers to 6
Partnership: 35% of entering associates from 1982–1989 were made partner
Pro Bono: 3–5% of all work is pro bono

Powell, Goldstein, Frazer & Murphy in 1997
56 Lawyers at the Washington D.C. Office
0.9 Associate Per Partner

Total Partners 30		
Women	6	20%
All Minorities	1	3%
Afro-Am	1	3%

Total Associates 26		
Women	12	46%
All Minorities	1	4%
Afro-Am	1	4%

Practice Areas	
International Trade/Customs	12
Housing/Real Estate	11
Health Care	10
Litigation	8
Corporate	6
International Business	6
Government Relations	3

Though its home office is located in Atlanta, Powell Goldstein D.C. is a fairly independent branch office in terms of clients and practice. It was founded in 1977 as a small housing and lobbying firm by a number of attorneys who had served in government. The most prominent of the group was Stuart Eizenstat, formerly the Domestic Policy Advisor for President Carter, and most recently, nominated by President Clinton as the Under Secretary for Economics, Business and Agricultural Affairs at the State Department. Twenty years ago, Powell Goldstein was primarily a legislative firm. Over the years, the office has evolved to become more of a full-service law firm, though "we still have a very strong Washington public policy focus," according to one insider.

recovering from turnover

Recently, most of the firm's prominent lobbyists entered the Clinton Administration, which has caused the legislative lobbying group to struggle. The group, led by Simon Lazarus, continues however to represent some high-profile clients, such as British Airways, IBM, and America Online. The firm's health care practice has also experienced some difficult times recently with "significant turnover at both the associate and partner levels," according to one insider, who added however that "these problems seem to be behind us and the health care practice is as busy as ever." Another contact observed that "the healthcare practice was so busy for awhile that they couldn't see straight. Three associates have been hired in the last year."

unique housing practice survives

Powell Goldstein's housing practice has seen the departure or retirement of key partners since our last edition, but is reportedly doing well today. According to one contact, the practice does "significant cutting-edge work re-engineering the federally-subsidized portion of the nation's housing stock, both on the transactional and the policy level." John Knapp, a former general counsel at HUD, and Jerry Breed, one of the nation's recognized experts on tax credit policy matters, along with the recent addition of a real estate practice, "have kept Powell Goldstein the cornerstone of housing policy work in D.C.," claimed one insider. Another contact observed that the firm "is doing as much affordable housing lending-related work as it has ever done."

other practice areas

Powell Goldstein also has litigation (including white-collar crime), government contracts, and corporate governance practices which have experienced "significant growth" in recent years. In particular, we were told that the addition of Harry Huge, "a phenomenal generator of interesting litigation work," has lent a considerable boost to the litigation and white-collar practice, which was described as "booming at present." Similarly, the international trade and customs practice, the largest group at the firm, is reportedly doing very well. This practice first joined the office in 1989 and "has consistently been one of the premier trade practices in the city ever since." It is "deeply involved in pioneering efforts to represent client interests in multilateral dispute resolution forums. This is cutting-edge stuff, and it is the sort of thing I never dreamed I would be able to do in the private sector," enthused one contact. Another insider remarked, "we joke about this group being ideal: we have great communication between partners and associates, lots of business, and are well managed (and we get discounts on rollerblades)." Yet another person in this group remarked: "Like the two guys in the commercial said: 'It doesn't get any better than this'."

Powell Goldstein is by no means a utopia, however. Its evolution over the past several years has forced it to cope with significant departures of partners and associates, which reportedly led to serious tensions and morale problems at the firm. Some of our contacts mentioned a past rift at the firm between "home grown" attorneys who had come through the firm's summer associate program and laterals from other law firms. Other strains were also brought to our attention, but most of our contacts spoke of a strong esprit de corps at the firm today. In particular, we were told that the firm's partners "go to great efforts" to maintain a friendly and cooperative atmosphere at the firm.

pro bono

Powell's pro bono practice was described by one person as "decentralized" and "*ad hoc*." Another insider informed us, however, that "pro bono is alive and well here; it represents the publicly minded nature of the people that work here and is not a top-down dictated practice." We were told that "numerous folks, both partners and associates, devote significant time to pro bono work because it is the right thing to do." The firm has done work on Title IX issues, non-profit assistance and formation, AIDS law, asylum work, homeless issues, and family issues.

progressive on diversity issues

People gave Powell Goldstein strong reviews for its treatment of women in the workplace. One insider described the firm as "very progressive" on family leave issues. "Both men and women can take substantial amounts of time off (six weeks for men, six months for women) for the birth of a child," reported one contact. Powell Goldstein also strives to promote discussions of women's issues at the firm. For the past several summers, the firm has organized a "women's barbecue" to provide an informal setting for women at the firm to socialize. There are not, however, many racial minorities at the D.C. branch, but one person observed that a number of influential minority attorneys work in the home office. People we interviewed believed the firm is progressive on minority issues and actively recruits minority attorneys.

management partnership prospects

Firmwide, Powell Goldstein is organized in three management units. Two of the units—litigation and business—are located in the Atlanta office. The Washington office is the third unit. The entire firm is managed by a management committee which includes partners from the D.C. office. The partnership system is structured in 10 different tiers with partners increasing their draw of the equity as they move up through the tiers. Powell Goldstein has a partnership track lasting "a minimum of seven and a maximum of ten years;" and, we were told, "all of the ten associates elevated to partner in the D.C. office since 1992 had just completed their seventh year as associates." The partnership prospects at the firm have, however, decreased in recent years; the rate of partnership dropped from 49% for associates who joined the firm during the 1979–1985 period to 35% for those who joined during the 1982–1989 period. One insider remarked that "in the past two years, the firm has seen a significant number of senior associates leave the firm because their partnership chances are so bleak." The firm's associate evaluation process was, however, lauded by one contact as the "most open and fair that I have seen. Associates read reviews submitted prior to the evaluation conference; this occurs in only a handful of firms," according to this person. Associates are paid a fixed salary according to their class year, which is raised in lockstep increments with no merit bonuses. However, one contact informed us that "the firm is currently implementing a salary adjustment program that will provide for some increase in salary based on merit." Presently, associate compensation in D.C. is slightly lower than at many other D.C. firms.

office facilities

Powell Goldstein's offices are located in a new Oliver Carr building, near the White House and Capitol and "uniquely situated" within two blocks of every metro line. A special art committee is charged with decorating the office, which displays, among other things, architectural pieces such as an elevator grate from the old Chicago Stock Exchange. The firm is in the process of upgrading its computer and phone equipment. The firm's library is not as extensive as those in other D.C. firms, but the firm's Director of Human Resources is beloved by the associates. "I have heard her described as the firm's 'ombudsman' and 'Mother Superior,'" observed one insider.

hiring tips

Seeking a summer associate position at Powell Goldstein can be a "hit or miss" experience. The firm emphasizes grades and similar law school achievements less than other firms. Instead, the firm places a premium on special work or other experiences which are relevant to its practice areas. Powell Goldstein hires most of its summer associate class from the top 10 law schools and draws heavily from Harvard, Yale, the University of Virginia, and Georgetown. Its hiring process is somewhat unique and very consensus oriented. The entire hiring committee meets to discuss each candidate, and usually arrives at consensus on an applicant before extending an offer. The committee rarely takes a majority vote on an offer—a few people can sink your ship. This system underscores the importance of getting along well with every person with whom you interview. One person commented that an applicant's ability to fit into the firm culture is the committee's most important consideration. Important also is the ability to "hit the ground running," since typically "significant responsibility comes early" in one's career at Powell Goldstein.

rumors of a merger

Powell Goldstein has experienced a significant amount of change and a shift in orientation over the past several years, and 1996 saw a sizeable number of departures of partners and associates from the firm. Most, but not all, of our contacts were upbeat regarding the firm's future prospects. One contact spoke of the firm's "traumatic transition" from a public policy-oriented lobbying firm to a much more traditional corporate/litigation/real estate firm. This insider observed, "it remains to be seen whether Powell Goldstein can survive as a general corporate law firm in the highly competitive Washington, D.C. market." As we go to press, there are reports that the firm is considering a merger with McGuire, Woods, Battle & Boothe of Richmond,Virginia.

Shaw, Pittman, Potts & Trowbridge

Washington Alexandria Leesburg McLean New York

Address: 2300 N Street, N.W., Washington, D.C. 20037
Telephone: (202) 663–8000
Hiring Attorney: Christine N. Kearns, Esq.
Contact: Kathleen A. Kelly, Director, Legal Personnel & Recruitment; (202) 663–8394
Associate Salary: First year $74,000 (1997)
Summer Salary: $1250/week (1997)
Average Hours: 2100 worked; 1825 billed; NA required.
Family Benefits: NA
1996 Summer: Class of 26 students; offers to 25
Partnership: 25% of entering associates from 1978–1984 were made partner
Pro Bono: 7–8% of all work is pro bono

Shaw, Pittman, Potts & Trowbridge in 1997
237 Lawyers at the Washington D.C. Office
0.9 Associates Per Partner

Total Partners 105		
Women	19	18%
All Minorities	4	4%
Afro-Am	2	2%
Latino	2	2%

Total Associates 97		
Women	36	37%
All Minorities	19	20%
Afro-Am	12	12%
Asian-Am	3	3%
Latino	4	4%

Practice Areas	
Corporate	72
Litigation	42
Real Estate	33
Energy	20
Financial Institutions	18
Environmental	13
Tax	11
Employment/Benefits	8
Bankruptcy	5
Legislative	2

Founded in 1955, Shaw, Pittman, Potts & Trowbridge has grown to become one of D.C.'s most prominent firms. Unlike attorneys at many of the city's other large law firms, Shaw Pittman lawyers enjoy "great unity." The firm's cohesive atmosphere was attributed, in part, to its "state-of-the-art" fitness center, which is perhaps D.C.'s finest law firm gym. It offers aerobics classes and is equipped with squash courts, a full range of weightlifting equipment, showers, and more. The gym serves as an "important social center" at this "very athletic" firm. It is not uncommon, we were told, for a partner and an associate to take a break at mid-day for a quick game of squash. Shaw Pittman fitness enthusiasts organize teams, which include partners, associates, and support staff, to compete in fitness competitions where the team which attains the most overall improvement in certain exercises wins. The firm has also formed basketball and softball teams. Shaw Pittman's fitness center and sporting activities draw the lawyers together, creating an integrated atmosphere despite the firm's large size. The only criticism we heard about the firm's offices concerned their location: "there are few affordable restaurants nearby or places to shop during lunch," reported one contact.

social unity

Shaw Pittman encourages social unity among its attorneys in other ways. Before the summer associates arrive, the firm distributes "a sheet of information on each new summer associate" to the entire firm, thus ensuring that they are properly welcomed. One person marveled that "everyone came up and welcomed people to the firm." Another raved that Shaw Pittman is "excellent about making you feel that you have a place in the firm." During summers, the firm organizes many social activities which enable associates to meet the attorneys. It arranges a wine and cheese reception in its main conference room on Fridays, weekly during the summer period and monthly otherwise, and partners generally take summer associates out to lunch once a week. Past summer events have included barbecues, white water rafting trips, bowling nights, baseball games, and theatre nights. The informal social life at Shaw Pittman is also active. A group of young associates rents a beach house each summer, and many of the firm's attorneys vacation together. Intra-firm dates abound, and several marriages have resulted.

long hard work hours

The harmonious work atmosphere has developed in part because Shaw Pittman associates work "long hard hours" together, in what one source described as a "grind atmosphere." The firm, we were told, exerts "lots of pressure to put in hours and to do a quality job with every assignment." It is not uncommon for junior associates to work significantly longer than the standard working hours, often until 9 or 10 P.M. Most associates also work one or two weekend days a month. However, one contact demurred that associates' hours are "usually reasonable."

practice areas

Shaw Pittman offers a broad-ranging practice, but it has reportedly "tried to resist" creating the formal practice area distinctions that so often accompany large law firms. Three of its major practice areas are litigation, corporate, and real estate. Most of the firm's litigation involves large commercial cases, much of it linked to the corporate, real estate, and banking practices. The department also handles white-collar criminal cases, and houses appellate and Supreme Court practices as well. Litigation partner Chuck Cooper, described to us as one of the city's "foremost conservative litigators," recently left the firm together with Mike Carvin to form their own boutique. The litigation group is considerably smaller today than at the time of our last edition. By contrast, the corporate group has grown significantly.

Shaw Pittman's real estate practice is one of the most "significant" in the city, according to one insider. Shaw Pittman also offers a "pre-eminent" energy practice, which primarily advises nuclear energy clients on federal regulatory matters. John Rhinelander, an arms control expert who assisted in the SALT treaty negotiations, has a high profile in this area. Shaw Pittman also offers a strong banking department which represents both domestic and foreign banks.

Much of the firm's work is being done internationally today, we were told. Four attorneys have been working in Australia for the past six months on a set of privatizations for both the Australian Federal government and for the government of South Australia in Adelaide. Shaw Pittman also handles matters for clients in the Netherlands (joint venture), Paris (licensing agreements), Japan (service agreement), as well as several other locations.

Shaw Pittman closed its Alexandria, Virginia office this year and expanded its McLean, Virginia office to accommodate what has been a "gradual, but dramatic, shift to a technology-focused practice," reported one contact. The McLean office services what are called "beltway bandits"—high technology start-up companies "that are growing by leaps and bounds and require all sorts of hands-on corporate, litigation, and licensing legal advice." This complements the growing number of matters handled by the D.C. office, involving a very broad base of Fortune 500 companies' large-scale service contracts of data processing, telephone services, and high-technology issues.

pro bono

Shaw Pittman's pro bono program has recently "been augmented and is now one of the top ten in the city," one insider reported. The firm credits pro bono hours toward billable hours. Partner Tom Hill oversees the pro bono program. However, attorneys must display "personal initiative" to become involved, one source indicated. Shaw Pittman participates in events such as monthly intake nights conducted by the D.C.

Bar and by the Whitman-Walker Aids Clinic. The firm recently won a major pro bono class action lawsuit against Circuit City for racially discriminating employment practices.

professional development

We received generally positive comments regarding the amount of responsibility available to associates at Shaw Pittman. Although one insider described Shaw Pittman as "more of a memo firm," this person went on to note that some small practice areas such as banking permit junior associates greater client contact. Another person noted that "litigation cases are often thinly staffed, so junior associates work directly with partners and have extensive client contacts." Additionally, one source praised the firm for "encouraging entrepreneurial initiatives on behalf of associates," while another described the firm as being "incredibly entrepreneurial, constantly growing new areas, and happy to see associates develop expertise in emerging areas."

tendency to compete

To assist in the transition to the firm, Shaw Pittman assigns starting and summer associates to advisors who oversee their work and show them around. One contact informed us that Shaw Pittman has a "drawer-system" for work, which means that "partners receive assignments from their clients and then staff those assignments with associates with whom they are familiar or who come recommended by others or by reputation." This person pointed out that this system "can have negative implications. Although salary structures are lock-stepped for the first two years, young associates have a natural tendency to compete with each other to achieve the higher levels of recognition and demand among the partners. This can result in overwork if associates are not properly 'mentored'."

poor feedback

Shaw Pittman was criticized for the feedback it provides to summer and permanent associates, which one source described as virtually "nonexistent," and another said "can be sparse." Attorneys complete forms to evaluate the work of each summer associate. However, the firm provides only oral feedback to the summer associates. One person complained: "Shaw was secretive about their evaluation process. It wasn't their policy to give open evaluations to summer associates...The official policy is to have the assigning attorneys give you oral feedback, but this is kind of silly if only the written evaluation is real." The permanent associates, on the other hand, receive a formal evaluation twice a year for their first two years, after which they receive an annual review.

mystery management

People also expressed frustration regarding access to the firm's management, which one insider described as "impersonal and shrouded in a mystery process." Another commented that "the management committee isn't receptive to new ideas. Associates are there to work and partners manage things and set the tone." In particular, one person reported, "summer associates are not informed" about the firm's decisions and do not know much about firm management.

great for women

Shaw Pittman is committed to assisting attorneys balance their work and family obligations and, we were told, is a "great" firm for women. The firm offers a "good maternity leave policy." It also maintains a "connection" with a day care facility across the street, which provides emergency day care services. The firm has established a lengthened partnership track for attorneys who choose to work part-time. The partnership includes 19 women, some of whom are members of the management committee, run the summer associate program, and occupy other "positions of influence," including that of the hiring partner. Several are active in the Women's Legal Defense Fund, and a number work on pro bono cases related to women's issues.

hiring tips

Shaw Pittman draws most of its students from the top 20 east coast law schools. One person noted that the firm has special connections with George Washington

University, the University of Georgia, and the University of Miami, as some Shaw Pittman partners are alumni of these institutions. Although Shaw Pittman had traditionally hired a large number of first-year students, this is "no longer true," we were told.

Shaw Pittman seeks someone with an "ambitious personality who is willing to put in the time to get a great job done," according to one contact. The firm is "also very interested in outgoing people." Shaw Pittman "places some emphasis on grades but there is not an excessive fixation on it." Its callback interviews involve meeting with three to four attorneys and going to lunch with a couple more. The lawyers reportedly "only talk a little about classes and law school" and, instead, "ask about everything in the interviews and try to get to know you and your personal interests."

Shaw Pittman attorneys are a hard-working, cohesive group. If you want the prestige of one of D.C.'s prominent firms, and easy access to one of the best firm gyms in town, Shaw Pittman may be the place for you.

Shea & Gardner

Washington

Address:	1800 Massachusetts Avenue, N.W., Washington, D.C. 20036
Telephone:	(202) 828–2000
Hiring Attorney:	William R. Hanlon
Contact:	Nancy Clark, Recruitment Coordinator, (202) 828–2039
Associate Salary:	First year $76,000 (1996)
Summer Salary:	$1300/week for 3Ls (1996)
Average Hours:	1830 worked; 1600 billed; NA required
Family Benefits:	12 weeks paid maternity leave (cbc unpaid); 4 weeks paid paternity leave (cbc unpaid)
1996 Summer:	Class of 9 students; offers to 8
Partnership:	25% of entering associates from 1980–1988 were made partner
Pro Bono:	5–10% of all work is pro bono

Shea & Gardner in 1997
74 Lawyers at the Firm
0.8 Associates Per Partner

Total Partners 38			Total Associates 31			Practice Areas	
Women	7	18%	Women	13	42%	Litigation	NA
All Minorities	0	0%	All Minorities	3	10%	Appellate	
			Afro-Am	3	10%	Corporate/Transactions	
						Labor	
						Environmental	
						Products Liability/Toxic Torts	
						Professional Malpractice	
						Maritime	
						Railroad	
						Administrative	
						Banking	
						Civil Rights/Constitutional	
						Government Contracts	
						Project Finance/M&A	
						Employment/Benefits	
						Transportation	
						White Collar Crime	
						Securities	
						International	
						Intellectual Property	
						Bankruptcy	

Every Friday afternoon at Shea & Gardner, the entire firm hovers around the kitchen waiting for the end-of-week snacks and candy to arrive. One person joked that "you need to wear a shin guard" to get at the kitchen table when the food appears. According to another, this social tradition epitomizes the firm's laid-back atmosphere and culture. Shea is also an egalitarian firm, so much so that it is difficult to distinguish between the partners and the associates, we were told. One insider elaborated on this point by noting that there's no question as to who's in charge but "associates never need to grovel, put in face time or brown-nose—just do good work."

premier litigation

One of Washington, D.C.'s most high-powered litigation firms, Shea & Gardner offers the rare combination of a premier litigation practice and an unstructured, humane environment. Shea is not organized in formal departments, nor does it assign associates to any one practice area. Rather, it expects attorneys to handle anything "from labor work to shipping regulation to general litigation matters." One person raved that the firm offers an "extremely diverse practice—everyone is exposed to a huge range of things."

Shea's litigation practice handles a broad variety of matters, from mass tort class actions to representing the D.C. Council. Its active appellate practice is primarily involved in appellate cases at, what one person termed, the "strategic" level. The department boasts the well-known Warner Gardner who attracts a number of high-profile cases to the firm. He helped Anita Hill prepare for her testimony before Congress and represented her at the hearings. Other prominent partners include Steve Pollak, a former Assistant Attorney General, who has extensive contacts in the civil rights community; John Aldock, the firm's chairman, who represents major corporations in toxic tort litigation; Tony Lapham, former General Counsel to the CIA; and Jim Woolsey, Director of the CIA under President Clinton. Shea also practices in general administrative law and environmental litigation. Other specialty areas include products liability, mining, professional malpractice, government contracts, corporate, and pensions.

extensive pro bono

Although Shea's pro bono practice is administered by a rotating committee of partners and associates, pro bono work is a "very big" aspect of the firm's practice. In 1996, the firm was honored as Pro Bono Firm of the Year by the D.C. Bar, and in 1997, Shea was one of two firms selected for the ABA's Pro Bono Publico Award. One person said that many Shea associates contribute 10 percent of their time to pro bono work and "some do much more." Much of the firm's pro bono work is litigation-oriented, with particular emphasis on filing *amicus* briefs, or handling cases at the trial level through the D.C. Bar's Pro Bono Clinic, but the firm also handles the work of some nonprofit organizations. Additionally, Shea is associated with the Washington Lawyers' Committee for Civil Rights and other public interest groups from which it receives many of its pro bono cases. In recent years, the firm has argued a number of cases in the Supreme Court, including *City of Edmonds*, *Denver Area Educational*, and *Alliance for Community Media*. Shea lawyers have also represented prisoners, schools, AIDS organizations, and churches in the area.

loose structure

Shea is a loosely organized firm. One contact said the firm trades "democracy" for "efficiency." Another said the firm is "so unbureaucratic that it can be tough to get things done." Shea provides very little formal training, and feedback on assignments is difficult to come by. We understand, however, that the firm has recently instituted a "new, more formalized assignment and review system for associates" to address these problems. Although the firm is reportedly "very receptive" to associates' assignment preferences, "because Shea is a small firm, it is not always possible to immediately assign associates the project of their dreams," one person told us. Shea, despite representing a number of small and diverse clients, assigns most junior associates "mainly memo work," according to some we spoke with. Others clarified or rebutted this observation. One person informed us that "memo work is taken very seriously; all associates do it and it is used, discussed and relied upon." Another person told us that "in my years as a junior associate, I have written numerous briefs, motions, and opinion letters, prepared partners for oral argument, worked extensively with expert witnesses, and had extensive client contact." This person further assured us that "my experience has not been in the least unusual." It does, however, appear to be the case that "it takes longer to get significant on-your-feet litigation experience in the form of depositions or oral arguments at Shea than it does at other firms. For someone who only plans to work at this firm for a few years (3-4 at most), that might be a significant drawback."

quality of life

Although Shea's practice is similar to that at other pre-eminent Washington, D.C. litigation firms such as Jenner & Block and Mayer, Brown & Platt, people commented that one of Shea's "biggest selling points" is that its attorneys place greater emphasis on quality of life. Shea attorneys, it was pointed out to us, are "very intense about the quality and type of work they do but they also have lives outside the law—most are parents—that they value and attend to and they are less into the status game." One person remarked that the firm "attracts married people" because it "lets you take time off for the kids" and is "very supportive of families." Shea also offers one of "the most casual places" to work in the city. It is not uncommon to see attorneys at work in jeans. Recently, the new managing partner "has begun a subtle campaign to change this habit—so far, without success," one insider informed us.

diversity

People praised the work environment that Shea offers women. One woman noted that the firm has a "very liberal leave policy" and many attorneys "work part-time." Another person said that "women command substantial authority." One person described the firm as "very accommodating to lifestyles." Another person remarked that "the firm is very homogeneous in terms of the 'lifestyles' led, but permits personal idiosyncrasies. However, I would not think it would be terribly comfortable for gay attorneys (unfortunately)." Though Shea employs few minority attorneys, it is said to be "actively looking." One insider stated that the firm "prides itself on being sensitive" to such issues.

academic atmosphere

Shea's work atmosphere was said to be "very academic," and many of those attorneys who do leave the firm go into academia and government. These "very bright" attorneys treat each other with respect. One source commented that the firm practices law "the way it was done 30 years ago. The firm is seen as a family of dignified, interesting people who practice law." It is not uncommon to find Shea lawyers debating the merits of recent Supreme Court opinions while sitting around the big table in the firm library. The library, according to one contact, is "excellent for a firm of its size," but another claimed that it is so chatty that it can be hard to get work done there.

Shea's offices occupy three floors and are very "discreet" and not "ostentatious." One person said they exude a "funky feel;" another commented that "actually, they are a bit shabby, but we're working on it." All attorneys have private offices and personal computers, but the facilities are "not incredibly high tech."

hiring tips

Shea is extremely competitive in terms of hiring. The firm seeks people with extremely high academic credentials, particularly "the law review type." Many Shea attorneys are former judicial clerks, and a number have clerked for Supreme Court justices. The firm recruits from a good cross section of the top national law schools.

People stressed, however, that though the hiring process is extremely competitive, the atmosphere at the firm is not. Shea is the type of place where, "if you stay and do the work, you will make partner," although making partner is reportedly more difficult now than in past years. We were also told that there has recently been a larger exodus than usual among young associates at the firm, perhaps because the firm is "moving too slowly," speculated one insider. Shea does not exert pressure to bring in clients, and there is a "genuine lack of emphasis on billable hours and a commitment to allowing attorneys to have lives outside the firm." One insider disclosed that Shea doesn't make as much money as the highest grossing firms in D.C., but it makes "conscious decisions" about which cases it accepts so that its attorneys can do the type of work they like. If you are seeking a law firm where you can pursue the law in both the practical and the academic arena, while avoiding a competitive environment and maintaining a balanced lifestyle, Shea & Gardner may well be the place for you.

Sidley & Austin

Washington Chicago Dallas Los Angeles New York
London Singapore Tokyo

Address: 1722 Eye Street, N.W., Washington, D.C. 20006
Telephone: (202) 736–8000
Hiring Attorney: Peter D. Keisler
Contact: Kimberley Stalker Jacob, Recruitment Administrator; (202) 736–8086
Associate Salary: First year $73,000 (1997)
Summer Salary: $1,400/week (1997)
Average Hours: 2000 worked; 1900 billed; no minimum required
Family Benefits: 12 weeks paid maternity leave
1996 Summer: Class of 14 students; offers to 13
Partnership: NA
Pro Bono: 1–3% of all work is pro bono

Sidley & Austin in 1997
127 Lawyers at the Washington D.C. Office
1.1 Associates Per Partner

Total Partners 56		
Women	5	9%
All Minorities	3	5%
Afro-Am	3	5%

Total Associates 62		
Women	25	40%
All Minorities	7	11%
Afro-Am	3	5%
Asian-Am	2	3%
Latino	2	3%

Practice Areas	
Litigation	47
Environmental	16
Appellate	16
Government Contracts	11
Banking	10
Energy	8
Transportation	7
Communications	5
Criminal	4
Corporate/Tax	3

Sidley & Austin is one of Chicago's largest and most prestigious firms. Though its D.C. branch office maintains considerable autonomy from the Chicago home office, its work atmosphere reflects some aspects of the headquarters' Chicago culture. Many summer and permanent associates in the D.C. office are from the Midwest or went to school there. Consistent with its midwestern culture, Sidley lawyers place a "big emphasis on family." People commented that the firm has a very good maternity leave policy. Most Sidley attorneys are married and there are very few young, single people. The associates are "very involved with their families" and "lots of people have young kids." "It's not a great place for a young person who wants a social life based at the office," remarked one person. But, although there is little socializing after work, relationships at the firm are "friendly and very non-competitive."

midwestern work ethic

Firmwide, Sidley & Austin is also known for its strong "midwestern work ethic." Though the Chicago office is reputed to be an extremely hard-working firm, we were told that work does not consume the D.C. lawyers. One person explained, "this means that they don't expect you to bill your life away...They have realistic expectations for how much work you need to do and they are tolerant of families in the process." Though some claimed that the attorneys "lacked passion," others praised the lawyers for leading balanced life styles. One person clarified the lack of passion remark by noting that "most attorneys are passionate about law, but many are not broadly involved in other things (except family which is typically very important)."

practice areas

Sidley's most noteworthy practice areas are litigation, environmental, telecommunications, transportation and government contracts. The litigation practice handles a variety of civil and regulatory matters, but is also known for some of its smaller subgroups. Thomas Green, a nationally known criminal trial lawyer, heads the white-collar crime practice group. Green has a defense role in the Whitewater Independent Counsel investigations. In addition, Sidley offers a "highly respected" appellate and Supreme Court litigation practice. The practice is led by Carter Phillips, a prominent appellate litigator, and presently managing partner of the D.C. office. Generally, this work is highly sought after by many associates (including summer associates) at the firm and "Carter does a good job of spreading the work around," one insider informed us. Recent successes include the controversial Supreme Court cases striking down term limits legislation and the Federal Act barring guns from local schools.

Sidley's environmental practice group enjoys a national reach and clients. Much of its work involves representing clients before the Environmental Protection Agency (EPA). The firm also handles a lot of Superfund litigation in federal court. Many of the lawyers in this group formerly worked at the Department of Justice or the EPA. Sidley also has a significant telecommunications regulatory and litigation practice, primarily for AT&T, but also for Tribune and other telecom companies. The firm's relationship with AT&T dates back to the very early days of the firm, and Sidley is well-regarded at AT&T. Several Sidley partners in the last 10 to 15 years have moved into top in-house positions at AT&T. Sidley also offers a top-rate transportation practice, which was established to represent railroad clients in regulatory matters, but now handles a broad range of transportation issues. Sidley has a prominent government contracts practice representing the government of Israel as well as top contractors. Unlike other litigation subgroups (*e.g.* white collar), this group retains a distinct identity; its attorneys practice exclusively in this group.

pro bono

Sidley & Austin is "very supportive" of pro bono work. It established a pro bono committee and credits pro bono hours toward billable hours. The firm receives many of its cases from the Washington Lawyers Committee for Civil Rights Under the Law and provides opportunities to do a "good variety of pro bono," including asylum cases, matters involving the rights of the elderly, and death penalty cases. The firm also offers appellate pro bono, and in the past has handled some high-profile cases in the Supreme Court, such as the Lopez case, in which the court struck down a law for violating the Commerce Clause for the first time in over 50 years. We were told that the pro bono practice is "loosely organized." It is supervised by one partner, and "you don't have to go through lots of bureaucracy to do things." Though only about one to three percent of the firm's overall work is devoted to pro bono, individual attorneys "can do as little or as much as they want" within certain limits.

unstructured work atmosphere

Although Sidley is one of the nation's larger firms, its work environment in Washington is relatively unstructured. Summer associates choose their projects from a central notebook of work assignments. One person noted, however, that the "notebook's contents were frequently skimpy. Work tended to come from people stopping by [and directly requesting assistance on a matter]." Like summer associates, the permanent associates also enjoy flexibility in selecting their work. Though the firm frequently assigns associates to work with a particular group, one person stated that "the lines are not clearly drawn. Junior associates can usually do work in any area they want. If you don't like the practice group you chose, you can do other types of work. Early on there is lots of mobility." Sidley's unstructured environment is ideal for "self-starters." One insider explained that, though there is "not much blatant sucking up to people...you have to make yourself known to the right people."

Each practice group offers its junior associates differing levels of responsibility. The first-year litigation associates, we were told, "do a lot of document production, research, and interrogatories," whereas the environmental practice area's "junior associates do a greater variety of projects." One person complained that summer associates must spend "too much time in the library," to which another contact retorted, "summer associates typically want to do appellate work—which involves the library!"

training feedback

Sidley's work environment is also influenced by its unstructured training and feedback. New associates are sent to Chicago for a full orientation to the firm, and the D.C. office provides a short formal litigation training program, of approximately one session per month throughout the associate's first year. Summer associates receive mid- and end-of-summer reviews, but one person commented that there is little written feedback. Associates are reviewed twice a year, although the reviews were reported to be "somewhat vague," leaving some people (but apparently not all) without a clear understanding of their partnership prospects. The firm has recently "made efforts to improve in this area but results are not yet clear," one contact informed us. Sidley's partnership track is seven to nine years. It can be lengthened when attorneys work part-time. Partnership decisions are made firmwide.

centralized management

Many people we interviewed asserted that Sidley's firmwide management is not very accessible to the junior members of the firm. One source asserted that "decisions are often postponed or are not on the ball. There is a...freewheeling atmosphere, and an almost amazing lack of coherent guidelines." Some people pointed to differences "between the way the attorneys in the D.C. office and the Chicago office are treated. Chicago gets preferential treatment in terms of the quality of the office building and in fringe benefits. This provides a point of tension." Carter Phillips took over as managing partner of the D.C. office in 1995. He got rave reviews from all of our contacts. "He is popular among the attorneys and is considered to be very accessible to the associates. He explains firm decisions to associates in quarterly lunch meetings" elaborated one insider. Another described him as "low-key, pragmatic, and despite his numerous accomplishments, very accessible and down to earth."

hours

Sidley does not impose a formal minimum billable hour requirement, but most attorneys aim for 1900 billable hours. In general, the firm is laid-back about hours for young associates, but one contact remarked that "if a second- or third-year associate is not billing 1800 hours, then they may be concerned." The pressures on summer associates are similarly modest. One contact informed us that, during his summer in the program, "I was encouraged to do good work, but not to work too hard."

diversity

"Women are very supportive of each other" at Sidley. The partnership includes five women. Women partners have arranged an annual women's dinner for female associates and summer associates. In addition, the firm sponsors a number of seminars which address women's issues. When it comes to racial diversity, we were told that Sidley is "WASPy in the old name tradition, but not in practice." George Jones, an influential litigation partner who sits on the Associates Committee, is a minority. He was described as a "mover and shaker," both inside and outside the firm.

weak office facilities

Do not join Sidley expecting lavish office facilities. Its office building, located one-half block from the Farragut West metro stop, is "wedged in between two buildings." Primarily, the front and back faces of the building have windows. In addition, while, "the East side has windows—it gets minimal light on lower floors," stated one contact. The front windows offer a view of a building under construction and the back of an alley. The firm is reportedly making plans to move "when its lease expires around the year 2000." One person described the office decor as "almost government issue type stuff." Some floors have, however, been renovated and are reportedly "really nice." One source summed up the Sidley feelings on this matter by noting that the office facilities are "unquestionably a very weak spot with the firm, even with some significant renovations. They're functional and conveniently located, but that's about all." Every attorney has a private office with a computer at his desk with access to Westlaw and LEXIS. The support staff is "generally very good," and the paralegals are "outstanding." The word processing center was recently outsourced, and "there have been some problems in transition," reported one contact. The firm subsidizes memberships to a private gym located in its office building.

hiring tips

Sidley recruits most of its summer associates from top national law schools. As mentioned, it hires many applicants with midwestern backgrounds. The firm also strongly favors students who will clerk for judges before joining the firm. One person commented that "half of the summer class were third-year law students with clerkships." Another source noted that the firm closely examines law school grades. The "laid-back and very friendly" callback interviews usually involve meeting with five attorneys and going out to lunch. Traditionally, Sidley has made a very high percentage of permanent offers to its summer associates. One person declared that, if you go to Sidley for the summer, you are virtually "guaranteed" of receiving a permanent job offer.

With the exception of the office complex and, perhaps, compensation ("Sidley usually tries to stay at the market, and *never* above it, but there are sometimes lags where it falls behind"), we heard very positive accounts about Sidley & Austin. It is a firm that is growing—it recently opened a new office in Dallas and added a banking group from another D.C. firm. It offers interesting work, reasonable hours, flexible work groups, "stunning associates and partners as colleagues and a managing partner who has the respect and admiration of the attorneys at the firm." If this combination of positives appeals to you, then Sidley & Austin may be your place.

Skadden, Arps, Slate, Meagher & Flom

Washington Boston Chicago Houston Los Angeles Newark New York San Francisco Wilmington
Beijing Brussels Frankfurt Hong Kong London Moscow Paris Singapore Sydney Tokyo Toronto

Address: 1440 New York Avenue, N.W., Washington, D.C. 20005
Telephone: (202) 371–7000
Hiring Attorney: C. Benjamin Crisman, Jr., Antoinette Cook Bush, Pamela F. Olson
Contact: Patricia Spencer Favreau, Professional Personnel Administrator; (202) 371–7730; (202) 371-7787 (fax)
Associate Salary: First year $87,500 (1997)
Summer Salary: $1500/week (1996)
Average Hours: 2285 worked; 1990 billed; no requirements
Family Benefits: 12 weeks paid maternity leave; 4 weeks paid paternity leave; emergency childcare; 4 weeks vacation
1996 Summer: Class of 23 students; offers to 23
Partnership: NA
Pro Bono: NA

Skadden, Arps, Slate, Meagher & Flom in 1997
153 Lawyers at the Washington D.C. Office
2.3 Associates Per Partner

Total Partners 39		
Women	8	20%
All Minorities	1	3%
Afro-Am	1	3%

Total Associates 88		
Women		NA
All Minorities	18	20%
Afro-Am	7	8%
Asian-Am	7	8%
Latino	4	5%

Practice Areas	
Energy	30
Litigation	19
Corporate	12
Tax	12
Communications	8
International Trade	8
Antitrust	7
Banking	6
Environmental	4
Legislation	1
White Collar Crime	NA

Numbers above exclude partners

Skadden, Arps, Slate, Meagher & Flom is reputed to be one of New York's hardest working and aggressive law firms. Everyone we interviewed from its D.C. office, however, claimed that the branch "didn't fit the sweatshop stereotype of Skadden's New York office." Though Skadden D.C. exhorts its attorneys to produce extremely high-quality work and the lawyers work hard, the firm does not pressure associates to bill the high New York hours. In fact, although associates are expected to bill at least seven hours a day, the firm is, according to one person, more concerned about minimizing costs to its clients. In addition, one source noted that because it is so difficult to make partner at Skadden, many join the firm intending to move on after a few years and are not overly concerned with partnership competition.

young attorneys

People were "surprised" by the "friendly" atmosphere at Skadden. One person remarked that Skadden's "very friendly and capable people are the firm's strongest asset; I enjoy spending time with the people with whom I work." Fridays are casual days and, unless attorneys have meetings with clients, they come to work in very relaxed attire. In the summer, the firm sponsors an "all-about-the-town" outing where associates take summer associates to a restaurant in a different section of town each week for socializing, dinner, and drinks. Skadden attorneys, both partners and management, are relatively young. People praised the firm's managing partner, Neal McCoy, who was described as a friendly and very accessible person. One person commented that "Neal," as he insists everyone call him, frequently takes summer associates out to lunch.

salaries de-linked from NY

Skadden D.C., along with many other large law firms, experienced economic troubles in the early 1990s. As a result, there was a wave of associate layoffs and morale plummeted. The economic picture is decidedly improved today. Skadden is in a strong "growth mode" presently. Moreover, as a result of the earlier layoffs, "certain groups in the firm are thin in the mid-level area, so that junior associates often work directly with partners." Also as a result of the early 1990s economic experience, Skadden set a separate salary scale for the D.C. office, "de-linked" from the New York office salary system. Our interviews revealed that the new salaries are considerably ahead of average D.C. firm salaries, but are less than Skadden's New York salaries, a source of resentment among some D.C. associates.

practice areas

Although Skadden's practice is broad-ranging, a number of particularly strong areas stand out. People commented that Skadden's rapidly growing white-collar crime department is one of the most prominent in the city, and Bob Bennett is one of the city's most well-known white-collar crime lawyers. The white-collar crime department has represented former Defense Secretary Caspar Weinberger, and relatively recently represented Clark Clifford and Robert Altman against allegations relating to their involvement in the BCCI scandal. Bob Bennett was special counsel to the U.S. Senate Select Committee on Ethics during the investigation of Charles Keating. He currently represents President Clinton in connection with the sexual harassment suit filed in the District Court of Arkansas by a former state employee.

Skadden also offers an international trade department. Bob Lighthizer, a former staffer for Senator Bob Dole, is prominent in the department. Skadden is also well known for its tax department, which handles international and domestic corporate tax matters as well as leasing and tax lobbying work. Paul Oosterhuis is highly-regarded in the field, and Fred Goldberg rejoined the firm after completing his tenure as Commissioner of the Internal Revenue Service. Several people commented that the tax group is a particularly nice group of people with whom to work. Energy is the firm's largest practice area. The energy group does everything from regulatory work to project finance "some of which, like the financing of the MCI arena and the new Redskins Stadium in Washington, have nothing to do with energy. Martin Klepper is the project finance partner of note, and Lynn Coleman, the former Secretary of Energy, is the head of the whole group." The litigation, banking, and antitrust practices were reported to be doing well. Skadden's communications practice is growing and is a department "lacking in mid-levels." Prominent in this practice is partner Toni Cook Bush, former senior counsel to the Senate Commerce Committee for Telecommunications where she was one of the prime authors of the Cable Act of 1992. Recently the firm has represented Bell Atlantic in its proposed merger with TCI, and telecom privatizations in Thailand, Indonesia, Hungary, Greece, and several South American countries among others. Skadden recently hired partner John Quale to add to their expertise in this practice area.

Skadden's corporate department is one of its largest; one person commented that "sometimes the corporate practice, based in New York, dominates priorities and the atmosphere of the D.C. office." Though many practice areas are independent of the New York office, the home office decides most major policy issues. Perhaps because the firm is so large, those we interviewed felt that associates did not have much or any say in the firm's management.

pro bono

Although Skadden is not known for its pro bono practice, people we interviewed gave it high reviews. One person commented that "pro bono is very big; we have one of the highest percentages of time spent on pro bono in D.C." Skadden participates in the ABA pro bono challenge. Firmwide, Skadden annually awards 25 Skadden Fellowships which enable attorneys to work full-time for one year for the public interest. In addition, the D.C. office recently instituted a program under which an associate who has been at the firm for at least one year will have an opportunity to work six months with the Legal Aid Society of Washington to provide legal services to the poor. During this six month separation from the firm, the associate continues to receive a Skadden salary. Pro bono hours are counted as billable hours, although one contact observed that "there is a strong feeling among some associates that they are silently, mentally subtracted at evaluation time."

assignments Both summer and junior permanent associates enjoy some flexibility in their career development at Skadden. Before joining the firm, summer associates complete a form on which they indicate their practice area preferences. The summer assignment committee matches each summer associate's preferences with the work that is available. Although Skadden works with incoming associates to match their departmental preferences with the needs of the firm, each associate is assigned to a specific department upon joining the firm.

opportunity feedback Skadden reportedly offers limited client contact and early responsibility to both summer and permanent associates. This varies, however, by practice area, depending on the number of mid-level associates in that area. One source noted that many associates do not independently represent clients until their fourth year at the firm. Another remarked that six to seven people work on certain cases, and observed that a "command structure" is in place for each case. This again varies by practice area; it is not true in "smaller, more thinly staffed departments." One person remarked that "I've had a lot of client contact; in fact, early on clients were encouraged to contact me directly." People praised the feedback that the firm provides to summer associates. Attorneys complete extensive evaluation forms on each assignment which are used to formally review summer associates at mid- and end-of-summer.

social life Despite its relatively "long hard hours," Skadden encourages attorney social life. The attorney offices are located randomly throughout the office and are not organized by practice area which, one person commented, offers the advantage of helping associates meet people outside their practice area, even though it results in the inconvenience of "many trips to the elevator (or stairs!)" to work with attorneys in one's own department. It is also possible to "get inter-department contact through pro bono." After work, social life can be quite active because many lawyers, including partners, are relatively young, and form a group that enjoys going out socially. The firm also treats summer associates to a variety of social events which have included sailing on the managing partner's yacht, whitewater rafting, concerts, and a Skaddenger Hunt (*i.e.*, a D.C. scavenger hunt, Skadden style). One person was especially enthusiastic about the Skadden summer program, informing us that "the summer program, I can tell you, kicked a_ _. From my conversation with other summer associates, Skadden's program was far and away the best in Washington. Literally extravagance on a New York scale. During my summer they paid for us to go to a race track and race old cop cars." A firm spokesperson responded with, "One of our summer events is a trip to a defensive driving school. While this school uses old police cars for their driver training program, we do not make this trip to enable our summer associates to 'race old cop cars'."

diversity Twenty percent of the Skadden partners are women. The firm was described as "open and progressive on women's issues." One person commented that a number of women have children and work part-time. One discordant note was raised in this context by an insider who observed that "single associates without children often feel that they are asked to work longer; they don't have the 'my spouse and kids' card to play." Skadden has a solid group of minorities in the D.C. office. Linda Rickman, the recruitment coordinator, is African-American. She is reportedly known for her commitment to improving the firm's diversity. She has worked to organize culturally diverse summer events which draw the participation of a wide range of summer associates and attorneys.

office with gym

Skadden's offices offer two particularly attractive features: a pleasant rooftop patio, which overlooks the White House and which is a popular place to have a drink after work; and a gym with a personal trainer, which is equipped with free weights, a stair-climber, a stairmaster, rowing machines, and other equipment. Every associate has a private office with a window. The library holdings were described as "not very extensive." There is, we were told, "nothing lacking" at the firm in terms of support services. One contact pointed out, however, that some "Skadden secretaries are not as skilled or as content" as you would hope.

hiring tips

Skadden draws the bulk of its summer class from the top 10 national and D.C.-area schools; however, it recruits students from a diverse range of law schools, including the Universities of Illinois, Minnesota, and Wisconsin. The firm does not necessarily seek to hire "law review students," according to one source, although, according to another insider, in fact "most of us were law review." Most noted that the firm "places a premium on people with balance." Skadden's callback interviews last about half a day. They are low-key and involve meeting three or four attorneys and lunching with two associates. Some candidates were asked about particular projects they had worked on in past jobs; others were asked about their interests outside the law. One person was surprised at how many high-level partners conduct interviews. It is not uncommon to be interviewed by Neal McCoy, the managing partner.

While Skadden has a lot in common with its New York headquarters, namely long work hours and high turnover, it provides associates a fast-paced New York practice in a more relaxed environment, with very attractive compensation. Skadden faced some very tough times in the early 1990s but has adjusted robustly, creating opportunities for newcomers. One person summarized well the attractions at Skadden, remarking that "if you are going to work at a big firm in D.C., you might as well work at Skadden. The pay is much better, the cases are cooler (especially deal stuff but a lot of other areas as well), the people are laid-back, and there's not a lot of office b.s. like how to dress or what time you need to be there."

Spiegel & McDiarmid

Washington

Address: 1350 New York Avenue, N.W., Washington, D.C. 20005–4798
Telephone: (202) 879–4000
Hiring Attorney: Mark S. Hegedus
Contact: Sabrina Palmer, Recruitment Coordinator; (202) 879–4000
Associate Salary: First year $60,000 plus $2,000 starting bonus (1997)
Summer Salary: NA
Average Hours: 2130 worked; 1600 billed; 1800 required
Family Benefits: Maternity leave; maternity disability; flexible spending; health, dental, vision insurance; employee assistance program; 401(K); profit sharing
1996 Summer: Class of 1 student; offers to 0
Partnership: NA
Pro Bono: 3–4% of all work is pro bono

Spiegel & McDiarmid in 1997
29 Lawyers at the Firm
0.4 Associates Per Partner

Total Partners 17			Total Associates 7			Practice Areas	
Women	5	29%	Women	2	28%	Energy	11
All Minorities	1	6%	All Minorities		NA	Antitrust	3
Asian-Am	1	6%	Openly Gay	2	28%	Communications	3
						Litigation	3
						Transportation	3
						Environmental	2
						Government Contracts	2
						Intellectual Property	1
						Legislative	1

Spiegel & McDiarmid is not a typical private law firm. Unique in its clients, ideology, work atmosphere, and goals, it was founded by George Spiegel. He was described to us as "sort of an idealistic, rebellious type who wanted to start a different kind of law firm where people could work and do what they believe in, and still make money." Spiegel does not accept "just any client that comes through the door." Its lawyers scrutinize clients carefully and, unlike many other firms, accept only those "whose causes they believe in." One insider declared, "the firm would never take a client who didn't in good faith try to comply with federal and state environmental regulations. The violator type client just wouldn't last at the firm...and if anyone has any strong objections, they won't accept that client." Many Spiegel partners have developed "real strong ties to the clients and a commitment between the firm and the client." We were told that clients appreciate Spiegel for "being a firm that sticks up for the little guy."

free atmosphere

Spiegel & McDiarmid offers an "extremely laid-back" work atmosphere. While the attorneys work very hard to put out first rate work, it was said that "people can work in any room they please, including the lobby if they like, and in any position they want—sitting, standing up, and occasionally lying down." A few attorneys don't wear ties in the office. One woman said that when she wore suits, many attorneys asked her why she didn't wear something more comfortable. One person asserted that "more than most firms, Spiegel tries to avoid making people fit into any kind of mold. People have freedom to be whoever they want to be there."

hands-off management

Even the management style is laid-back and almost freewheeling. One insider asserted, "it's a good place if you really like hands-off management. Basically, there isn't any—no planning, goals, or objectives for the future. You just do your work and take things as they come." Another insider remarked that "the lack of planning can make Spiegel a very frustrating place." Spiegel is less hierarchical than most other firms and places "fewer divisions between the lowest levels of staff and the highest level of partners than you find at most traditional law firms." One person commented that "money is not the bottom line there. They do as well as they need to, in order to keep going. It's not a place that's swimming in the dough and never will be. That is not what it's about. The kind of work they do is more important to them than how much money they make." One contact observed, however, that this attitude is changing. "The firm is becoming more interested in the bottom line. It has had no choice. But being interested in the bottom line has not meant that the firm has found a way to become more profitable. Attracting new clients has not been Spiegel's forte. While the partners have the most to gain or lose based on the performance of the firm, the associates and support staff have also become more concerned about the firm's finances."

unique practices

Spiegel is primarily an energy litigation firm. The energy practice also handles lobbying and policy work. According to one contact, Spiegel rose to prominence in the energy field by applying antitrust theories to the regulation of utilities and using novel methods to apply them; Spiegel has "a lot to do with the way we talk about utilities today." Most of the energy clients are small towns, municipal governments, and cooperatives which own utility systems. Spiegel's environmental practice, which was quite prominent in the past, is less so today. Its former head, Rena Steinzor, has left for a professorship at the University of Maryland, and the size of the practice has shrunk in recent years. The focus of the practice today ranges from Clean Air Act counseling and advocacy to promoting alternative environmental technologies and environmental compliance strategies. The other practice areas of the firm (*e.g.* transportation, publishing, telecommunications), "tend to provide more interesting assignments than the energy practice does," reported one insider. In these areas, "associates are given a substantial level of responsibility."

Overall, opportunities for responsibility at Spiegel are constrained by the "top heavy structure of the firm: 17 partners and 7 associates." This is especially so in the energy practice, which suffers additional liabilities according to people we spoke with. The "problem with the practice," according to one person, "is that it is Federal Energy Regulatory Commission (FERC) work. If you read through a FERC decision and don't fall asleep, this is the place for you." Another source concurred that, while some of the work is challenging and exciting, a large portion of it is "boring." This person advised that if you are not interested in Spiegel's particular practice areas, "think hard before taking a position at the firm." A firm spokesperson informed us that the nature of the energy industry and, therefore, of Spiegel's energy practice is changing. "The firm is very much involved in the restructuring of the industry from one that is largely cost-based and regulated to one that is market-driven. Our activities in this area include legislative advocacy concerning restructuring issues. In addition, the work we do for our energy clients increasingly involves agencies other than FERC or involves greater emphasis on policy issues." One interesting, but smaller practice area involves Spiegel's representation of *qui tam* plaintiffs, usually employees of government contractors who have blown the whistle on the fraudulent practices of their employers. Spiegel handles these plaintiffs' actions, which involve the potential for treble damages, on a contingency fee basis. One partner specializes in this practice and the firm is trying to build up this area. "Most people find these cases more exciting than the run-of-the-mill litigation and, in particular, the energy litigation," noted one source.

pro bono

Spiegel does not offer a formally structured pro bono department, but there are some opportunities to do pro bono work. One source claimed that "there was a little less opportunity to do pro bono work than at other firms in D.C. There is less time to do pro bono work of your choice than at other firms because Spiegel is already doing the work that it believes in, and its clients are paying less than traditional firms' clients. There is a greater need for people to spend somewhat more time on the firm's main practice than at other places." Nevertheless, Spiegel adopted a formal pro bono policy statement in 1994, and in recent years the firm's work has included litigation on behalf of the deaf and individuals discriminated against on the basis of sexual orientation or HIV status. The firm also does significant First Amendment work on behalf of public access channels across the country.

firm for self-starters

Some people reported difficulty integrating into Spiegel's practice. Most of the firm's work is "highly technical," and one summer associate felt "confused the whole summer." One person explained, "it's a place where you do well if you are self-motivated. If you need structure, then you are lost." The firm has not arranged a formal method of assigning work to either summer associates or permanent associates, although a summer coordinator attempts to play "matchmaker" for summer associate work assignments. One source remarked that you "just do things on a priority basis, but you can target things on your own, and work with the people you want to work with. You will do a good amount of FERC work. There is no escaping it and associates usually work directly with partners."

The training at the firm is relatively "informal." Most training occurs in the individual working relationships between the partners and associates. One person declared it is a "sink or swim" (on your own) type of place.

social life

Spiegel is a "good place for social life." More than at other firms, "the attorneys there are friends. People go out after work together." According to one source, Spiegel attorneys "really like each other and were more friendly with each other than those at other firms. Because of the firm's small size and close-knit atmosphere, it tends to attract people looking for the kind of environment that it has. People like to socialize in the library to the point where it is occasionally difficult to get work done in common areas." Another commented, however, that though associates form a "tight-knit group," there exists a "big age gap between partners and associates." Spiegel does not organize many formal social events. The firm is, we were told, "relatively poor compared to other firms and does not have money to spend on lavish meals." It does sponsor a well-attended happy hour every Friday at 5:30 P.M.

diversity

Two of the six members of the management committee are women, and the firm is "flexible" regarding issues that involve parental leave and part-time work, according to some, but not all, of our contacts. One contact noted that "there are more than a few openly gay attorneys at Spiegel, and it's a very comfortable and open place on that score." Politically, we were told, the firm leans "left."

sparse office facilities

Spiegel's offices are located near the White House, one block from Metro Center. "By private firm standards," the office facilities are "pretty sparse." Spiegel offers all the "necessities," but not top-of-the-line facilities. People reported that "the desks weren't quite as spacious, the drawers would stick, and the chairs weren't as comfortable" as those at other firms. The firm has a state-of-the-art computer system that "works very well." There is a "gym" in the office basement outfitted with a couple of "broken down bike machines and some old rusty weights." The firm has a lunchroom where everyone from junior staff to senior partners eat their lunches. Many of Spiegel's attorneys "don't go out and eat fancy meals," one insider observed. "They eat at the firm in a less lavish, more comfortable environment." The firm also provides free sodas and juice.

hiring tips

Spiegel "hires people who are motivated and a little quirky," remarked one successful applicant. "They attract people who are off the beaten track—more of the public service, than the corporate types." Callback interviews involve meeting three or four attorneys, each for about a half hour. One student remarked that Spiegel interviews are a bit more informal than those at other firms, but some partners ask challenging questions. One person was asked, what would you do with your life if money were not a concern? And, where is your life, existentially speaking? Another person said that the attorneys try "to ask you one hard question, see how well you argue your point or stand your ground. They try to pick something you can talk about, wind you up, and let you go."

If you have public interest inclinations and are interested in energy work, then Spiegel & McDiarmid may provide an interesting career choice. People we spoke with, however, expressed some serious reservations about the firm. The partner-associate ratio is "probably unworkable in the long run," according to one contact. Another observed that the firm is "far less sociable than it used to be. It's also become more money-oriented, more like other firms." Finally, one insider, while observing that the people at the firm are still "largely proud of the work Spiegel does," pointed out that "nothing changes—that needs to be changed. The firm reinvents the wheel every year on the same administrative and promotional issues."

Steptoe & Johnson

Washington Phoenix
Moscow and Almaty Affiliates

Address: 1330 Connecticut Avenue, N.W., Washington, D.C. 20036–1795
Telephone: (202) 429–3000
Hiring Attorney: F. Michael Kail
Contact: Rosemary K. Morgan, Director of Recruiting; (202) 429–8036
Associate Salary: First year $74,000 (1997); second $79,000; third $84,000; fourth $89,000; fifth $94,000; sixth $99,000; seventh $104,000; eighth $109,000
Summer Salary: NA
Average Hours: NA worked; NA billed; 1900 required
Family Benefits: Maternity/paternity; childcare emergency center
1996 Summer: Class of 34 students
Partnership: 14% of entering associates from 1978–1984 were made partner
Pro Bono: 5% of all work is pro bono

Steptoe & Johnson in 1997
210 Lawyers at the Washington D.C. Office
0.9 Associates Per Partner

Total Partners 95		
Women	13	14%
All Minorities	2	2%
Afro Am	1	1%
Latino	1	1%

Total Associates 89		
Women	37	42%
All Minorities	11	12%
Afro-Am	9	10%
Asian-Am	1	1%
Latino	1	1%

Practice Areas	
Administrative Law	NA
Alternative Dispute Resolution	
Antitrust	
Appellate & Supreme Ct. Litigation	
Business Transaction	
Civil Litigation	
Communications	
Debtor/Creditor Rel. & Workout	
Electric Power	
Emp. Benefits & Exec. Comp.	
Employment, Labor Relations & Labor Standards	
Energy & Energy Transportation	
Environmental, Health & Safety	
Ethics & Prof. Responsibility	
Financial Services	
Government Contracts	
Information Technology	
Insurance	
Intellectual Property	
Int'l Law, Trade & Investment	
Media & Communications	
Natural Resources & Native American Issues	
Professional Liability	
Securities Financing, Reg. & Enf.	
Taxation	
Transactions in Russia & C. Asia	
Transportation	
Trusts & Estates	
White Collar Criminal Defense	

Steptoe & Johnson offers one of the largest and most well-known international practices in D.C. In addition to its unique international work, Steptoe is reportedly distinguished by its lack of the self-promotional "arrogance" which often accompanies the top firms in the city. Steptoe's work atmosphere reflects its reserved nature. The firm was described as "intellectual," if somewhat "fragmented." One source said there is "not much sense of humor or spunk." Another commented that it is hard to get to know people at the firm. The attorneys "really leave you alone. You do your own work and they don't look over your shoulder." People disputed, however, Steptoe's reputation as a "white shoe" firm. One person commented that this is no longer true as the firm is currently "20 to 30 percent Jewish," and there are currently nine African-American associates at Steptoe.

international practice

Perhaps the most attractive and distinguishing feature of Steptoe's international practice is that the firm permits its D.C. lawyers to actually practice international law rather than farming out the international matters to foreign law firms. Unlike many other American firms with large international practices, Steptoe maintains only two foreign affiliate offices—in Moscow and Almaty, Kazakhstan—ensuring that its D.C lawyers remain integral participants in the international practice.

Steptoe offers the additional attraction of an unusually broad-ranging international practice that covers both public and private international law. Monroe Leigh, former Legal Adviser to the State Department, is a prominent Steptoe partner and draws more public international work to the firm "than just about anyone else in D.C.," raved one person. The public international practice routinely works on trade relation agreements between countries. It also handles many matters such as trade sanction issues for a consortium of multinational companies known as the Rule of Law Committee.

Steptoe's international practice also includes an extensive international trade group, led by Richard Cunningham, whose lawyers frequently represent clients before the International Trade Commission and Department of Commerce in matters relating to import and export regulations. One of the hottest and most "demanding" of the firm's international areas is the Russian and Eastern European practice, which involves both trade matters and issues arising from the privatization of formerly state-owned economies.

Steptoe offers an exciting array of international practice areas, as well as numerous other specialty areas. People reported that the practice areas are fairly independent of one another. However, Steptoe does represent a few larger clients whose needs span different practice areas and allow some practice group interaction. For example, the Transactions Group handles international transactions that involve the expertise of the firm's international trade, antitrust, and tax attorneys, among others.

other practices

Steptoe is organized into nine main departments: energy; transportation and telecommunications; transactions; tax and ERISA; international; antitrust; insurance, litigation, professional liability, and white collar crime; commercial litigation and employment; and technology, government contracts, intellectual property, and natural resources. The firm usually encourages entering associates to choose a primary and secondary practice group, and associates may split their time between the two; the firm offers no formal rotation system. People remarked that Steptoe is flexible in allowing associates to transfer between departments.

Steptoe offers many highly regarded practice areas in addition to its renowned international practice. The firm's telecommunications practice has grown into a global telecommunications practice specializing in international satellite and foreign carrier matters. Steptoe has long had premier practices in railroad regulation (particularly recent mergers) and oil pipeline regulation (representing the Trans-Alaska pipeline system, among others). The tax, tax lobbying, and government contracts departments are extremely strong. Steptoe is also well-known for its significant insurance defense litigation practice, as well as for its electric power practice. Within the last few years, the firm's intellectual property group has grown and developed expertise in all phases of intellectual property representation.

prominent attorneys

Not surprisingly, the partnership of this prestigious firm includes prominent attorneys, such as Richard Willard, a "superstar" appellate litigator, and Bob Jordan, who has served as the hiring partner and chairman of the firm as well as the chair of the D.C. Bar Special Committee on Model Rules of Professional Conduct and the president of the D.C. Bar. Additionally, partner Reid Weingarten, formerly head of the Public Integrity Section of the U.S. Justice Department, handles a lot of high-profile white-collar crime and ethics matters, including representations of former Agriculture Secretary Mike Espy and the late Commerce Secretary Ron Brown.

public service fellowships

Since 1990, Steptoe has sponsored an "incredibly generous" public interest program under which as many as nine summer associates may work eight weeks at the firm and three or four weeks with a public interest organization in D.C. Steptoe also established a six-month public service fellowship in honor of the firm's 50th anniversary. Associates who have been with the firm for at least two years are eligible. The firm additionally offers a formally structured pro bono practice, but does not credit pro bono hours toward billable hours. These hours do count, however, toward associate bonus calculations. Steptoe lawyers, nevertheless, have been involved in a wide variety of pro bono matters. They have represented human rights prisoners in Nigeria and Syria, worked for Amnesty International and Human Rights Watch, handled death penalty matters on both sides of the issue, and litigated employment discrimination cases.

feedback

Steptoe offers junior associates a number of formal training programs, including mock trials and oral advocacy training programs. The firm also provides an "overly formal" feedback system on an annual basis, with only very general comments, we were told. Many associates complained about the lack of feedback regarding day-to-day work and their long-term partnership prospects. The firm has career development meetings, however, with each associate every six months to monitor whether the associate is getting the experience desired by that associate. Summer associates receive mid- and end-of-summer reviews, but most people stated that these were not particularly helpful. Every attorney for whom a summer associate works completes an evaluation form on that summer associate's assignment, but all these written evaluations are kept confidential.

overworked and undervalued

Steptoe does not offer much early responsibility. Most summer projects are "research and writing" assignments. Junior associates also reportedly do a lot of research work, although many in the international trade group spend some time traveling overseas, even in their first year with the firm. The firm assigns a "deputy" in each practice group who oversees projects and assigns work. One person commented that the main function of the deputy is to "protect" associates from being overworked. In addition, we were told that although Steptoe does not impose a significantly higher billable hour requirement than other firms, associates were reported to often "feel overworked" because of the volume of the firm's work. One person remarked that you "don't get the feeling that many associates are skipping along in the air" contented in their work. Instead, we were told that "it seemed like associates between years three and seven worked very hard. They didn't have much personal time. They only talked about work." Some of the senior associates, on the other hand, are said to be happier than the junior associates because "they can see the end." Steptoe is also reportedly not aggressive with merit or bonus pay, even for those who work very long hours. "The firm's legendary cheapness contributes to a feeling of being undervalued as an associate with respect to social events and even expense reimbursement," one insider told us.

minimal social life

Steptoe is "not as social as other firms." According to one person, the Steptoe associates are "not very outgoing." Reportedly, most associates at the firm are married and "people don't socialize in large groups after work." One source commented that "there are some groups, but it is not the go-out-for-brewskies type of place." The summer program is filled with fun events. It has included a sailing trip on the Chesapeake Bay, summer softball, and occasional happy hours.

diversity

Steptoe's partnership includes a number of women. Sarah Carey is the leader of the Eastern European international practice group, and Betty Jo Christian was said to be a "big shot" appellate litigator, particularly with Commerce Clause issues involving railroads and garbage. One person commented that Steptoe is "one of the best firms for part-time work. They are really open to those arrangements."

democratic management

Steptoe is run by an 11 partner committee whose members are elected out of the entire partnership (including junior partners) for three-year staggered periods. Almost all decisions are handled by committees, and one person commented that "the system is democratic to the point of paralysis. They did everything by vote and it was a very slow-moving decision making process."

office facilities

Steptoe & Johnson takes great pride in its office decor, reminiscent of Mount Vernon, particularly in its "prize collection" Remington Horse statue. For security reasons, the statue was bolted to a table, which ironically, was later discovered to be a fine table itself (folklore has it that it was worth more than the statue). Steptoe's office facilities include a gym equipped with dumbbells, Universal weights, stairmasters, treadmills, and locker rooms. The offices are located at Dupont Circle, near the metro and close to many restaurants and shops. Each associate has a private office with a window and a computer. In addition, one person commented that Steptoe has one of the largest private law firm libraries in D.C.

extremely selective hiring

Steptoe is among D.C.'s five most selective firms with respect to recruiting attorneys. "If you don't go to a top school," remarked one insider, "you have to be on law review" to be offered a summer associate position by this firm. Although Steptoe hires people with "high grades," it also looks for people with "interesting" backgrounds. One person observed that many past summer associates were older or had previous work experience. The firm hires from a broad range of schools, "but most people who get offers are from Harvard, Yale, Chicago, Columbia, etc." Past summer classes included students from Boston College, the University of Arizona, and the University of Vermont. Callback interviews at the firm are laid-back and are conducted by a mixture of both partners and associates.

Swidler & Berlin

Washington

Address:	3000 K Street, N.W., Suite 300, Washington, D.C. 20007
Telephone:	(202) 424–7500
Hiring Attorney:	J. Phillip Jordan
Contact:	Linda L. Rickman, Director of Recruiting; (202) 424–7739
Associate Salary:	First year $74,000 (1997)
Summer Salary:	$1300/week (1997)
Average Hours:	2000 worked; 1900 billed; 1900 required
Family Benefits:	Benefits package which includes medical, life, dental, and long term disability
1996 Summer:	Class of 12 students; offers to 11
Partnership:	NA
Pro Bono:	1.5% of all work is pro bono

Swidler & Berlin in 1997
174 Lawyers at the Firm
2.2 Associates Per Partner

Total Partners 55			Total Associates 119			Practice Areas	
Women	9	16%	Women	47	39%	Litigation/Insurance Litigation	54
All Minorities	2	4%	All Minorities	11	9%	Telecommunications	42
Afro-Am	1	2%	Afro-Am	4	3%	Bnkrptcy/Bnkng./Corp./Tax	26
Asian-Am	1	2%	Asian-Am	3	3%	Environmental	23
			Latino	3	3%	Energy/Utilities	11
			Native Am	1	1%	Government Affairs	9
						Structured Finance	8
						Pro Bono (Partner Coordinator)	1

A dynamic newcomer to Washington, D.C., Swidler & Berlin "is aggressive in everything." Described "as a young, entrepreneurial firm," its partners, we were told, are "slash and burn lawyers. They take no prisoners." One source reported that the firm "doesn't have a lot of institutional clients. The partners are really out there trying to break into new areas of law." The firm has grown considerably in recent years, by more than fifty percent since our last edition, and is reportedly the fastest growing firm in D.C. Not all at the firm are thrilled with this development, however. One contact remarked that: "Swidler's magical recipe for success is to bring or steal the younger rainmakers from other firms and cut dead wood whenever possible. This has worked well recently because the partners have the foresight to determine what will be the hot areas of the law, *i.e.* telecommunications and environmental insurance recovery."

highly profitable

We were told that Swidler & Berlin "is the most profitable firm in D.C. for partners." The associates, on the other hand, with starting salaries of $74,000, earn only slightly above the D.C. market rate. However, the firm recently raised associate salaries and initiated a profit sharing plan for associates. Swidler rewards attorneys according to their contribution to the firm. One source remarked that "the people who advance are the ones who bring in the business. You must do this to become partner at Swidler. You can't just hang out and make partner."

practice areas

Founded in 1982, Swidler rapidly rose to prominence as a top-notch energy, electric, and natural gas/utility law firm. Its unique energy practice was built largely under the leadership of the firm's founders, Edward Berlin and Joe Swidler, former chairman of the old Federal Power Commission. However, this signature practice is, according to one insider, "getting less important." Recently, Swidler's environmental, telecommunications, and litigation practices have generated much of the firm's business. Swidler represents a number of "small clients" in these practice areas and the partners "hustle hard to get them." The environmental practice involves both litigation and lobbying. One source raved that the firm does "some of the best Clean Air Act work in the city." An environmental partner, Len Miller, helped pioneer the National Pollution Discharge Elimination System. The telecommunications practice has been doing extremely well in recent years, but one person commented that some "tough" personalities work in the group. The litigation department boasts Alexia Morrison, a party in the landmark Supreme Court Case, *Olson v. Morrison,* which involved the question of whether a special prosecutor could be terminated by a member of the Executive Branch. Swidler has recently added several significant practice groups, including a structured finance group headed by Ken Lore, and an insurance litigation group, led by Rick Fields. In addition, Swidler has the fifth largest government affairs/legislative practice in Washington, we were told.

hot bankruptcy practice

Swidler's bankruptcy practice is also one of the firm's "hot" areas. The group includes Roger Frankel, a highly regarded bankruptcy lawyer, who formerly worked at Arent Fox. Other well-known Swidler partners include H.P. Goldfield, former Assistant Counsel to President Reagan and prominent in Republican circles, and Jim Hamilton, who was very active in President Clinton's Transition Team. One person commented that the firm "leans Democratic but not strongly." Swidler's pro bono efforts are coordinated by partner Andrew Lipps, and the firm has been "extremely active" in pro bono work of late. It has won several significant cases on behalf of children's rights in the past year. In addition, Swidler is a sponsor of Project Excellence, which provides financial support for prospective minority college students. Additionally, the firm has committed $60,000 to construct a home for a disadvantaged family through the Habitat for Humanity Program; several attorneys will assist in the construction of the home. Pro bono hours are credited as billable.

associate partner conflict

Swidler has grown rapidly into a large firm. As a result, some people noted that the firm has suffered "growing pains." One insider commented that "with growth comes growing pains and Swidler has some serious stretch marks, [such as] low associate morale and a high attrition rate." The firm is reportedly "poorly run from a human resources perspective." We were told, however, that the firm has "restructured its management organization to help better manage the growing size of the firm." The firm now has a board and a number of committees which permit a "degree of associate participation," according to one contact. Others, however, are skeptical of this. We were told, for example, that, for various reasons, the associates formed an associate committee with elected representatives "who would go to the partnership with associate issues. After all but ignoring this group for a few months, the partnership *sua sponte* formed an associate task force comprised of partners and associates, none of whom were on the associate committee elected by the associates. Rather, the associates appointed to the task force were those obviously close to the partners."

Swidler provides a small formal training program, but most training and feedback depends on the partner with whom "you get hooked up." Though people asserted that the formal training and feedback need improvement, the firm offers significant early responsibility. Client contact can reportedly be had as early as the first year, especially in the busy telecommunications group.

The lack of structure at Swidler is accompanied by a casual work and social atmosphere. "It's a great place for young people," remarked one observer. Most young associates enjoy "active social lives" and even the "older partners try to wear funky ties and think they are cool."

office facilities

Swidler's office facilities overlook the Potomac River and the Kennedy Center from the Washington Harbour, which one person declared is "the nicest place to work in Washington D.C. and no one can dispute that." Incidentally, Swidler's office building was filmed in an Eddie Murphy movie, *Boomerang*. The offices were described as "light and airy with lots of modern art," and provide enough room for each attorney to have a private office. Many of the private offices open onto balconies that overlook the Potomac River, and the building offers a terrace where the firm holds monthly parties in the summer. Starbucks coffee and free soda are readily available, and the workroom staff was described as "nice and competent." A fitness center, located in the building, is available for all Swidler attorneys and staff to use. Though the offices are beautiful, they are not perfect: "The chairs for visitors don't match the desks—everyone comments on that."

diversity

People described Swidler as "progressive" on diversity issues. One insider remarked that "the firm as a whole treats women very well, but there are one or two problem individuals." Another commented that the firm is "flexible" in dealing with attorneys who want to work part-time. Swidler employs very few minority attorneys, but those we interviewed believe that it provides a comfortable environment for minorities. One person pointed out that Swidler recently made a minority partner and "has hired more minorities in the last year." Another person added that Swidler is very "open" to gays.

hiring tips

It is "increasingly" competitive to receive a summer associate offer from Swidler. The firm primarily draws its summer class from the top 10 national and D.C.-area law schools. People commented that Swidler places less emphasis in its hiring decisions on high grades than on an entrepreneurial personality and other related character traits. One person commented that Swidler tends to favor "assertive and aggressive" personalities. He also advised that the most important thing to understand when interviewing with Swidler is that the practice is "less broad-based. You must express a particular interest in the type of work" done at the firm.

Venable, Baetjer, Howard & Civiletti

Washington Baltimore Rockville Towson

Address:	1201 New York Avenue, N.W., Suite 1000, Washington, D.C. 20005
Telephone:	(202) 962–4800
Hiring Attorney:	Gary M. Hnath
Contact:	Grace Cunningham, Director of Legal Personnel; (410) 962–4875
Associate Salary:	First year $70,000 (1996)
Summer Salary:	$1100/week (1997)
Average Hours:	2000 worked; 1750 billed; 2200 required (billable and nonbillable)
Family Benefits:	Medical, dental, vision, life insurance; long and short term disability; maternity/paternity leave; 401(K); employee assistance program; moving allowance
1996 Summer:	Class of 8 students; offers to 6
Partnership:	25% of entering associates from 1983–1985 were made partner
Pro Bono:	3–5% of all work is pro bono (firmwide)

Venable, Baetjer, Howard & Civiletti in 1997
81 Lawyers at the Washington D.C. Office
0.9 Associate Per Partner

Total Partners 42			Total Associates 39			Practice Areas	
Women	4	10%	Women	14	36%	Intellectual Property	16
All Minorities	1	2%	All Minorities	3	8%	Regulatory & Legislative	15
Afro-Am	1	2%	Afro-Am	2	5%	Business	13
			Asian-Am	1	3%	Environmental	10
						Government Contracts	8
						Litigation	8
						Labor and Employment	7
						International	4

government oriented firm

Venable, Baetjer, Howard & Civiletti is one of Baltimore's largest and most prestigious firms. This successful regional firm offers an extensive network of offices in Maryland, Virginia, and Washington, D.C. The D.C. office is developing its own identity separate from the home office, with a practice focused on government and regulatory work, and power between the D.C. and Baltimore offices is more shared now than in the past, we were told. Venable made a strategic decision in 1994 to focus its D.C. office on government-oriented work. Since that time, the D.C. office has increased from 60 to 81 lawyers; much of this expansion has come via lateral hires.

A number of Venable attorneys came to the firm from the government. Perhaps the most well-known is Ben Civiletti, who served as Attorney General under President Carter. The firm's chairman, Civiletti maintains an office in D.C. and also works out of the Baltimore office. We were told that, though a broad spectrum of political views are represented at the firm, most high-profile Venable partners are Democrats.

practice areas

In addition to its expanding government and regulatory practice, Venable boasts strong environmental and litigation practices. Judson Starr and Jerry Block, who were both prominent in the Environmental Crimes Section of the Department of Justice, have built Venable's high-profile criminal environmental practice. Ron Glancz, prominent in the banking practice, came to the firm from the Federal Deposit Insurance Corporation. This practice represents some of Maryland's largest banks and has been heavily involved in savings and loan litigation.

Venable's busy government contracts practice, headed by Thomas Madden, represents well-known corporations, such as the Martin Marietta Corporation. The firm also has a management-side labor group whose lawyers, according to one person, are known as being particularly "demanding." Venable's intellectual property practice has grown considerably since our last edition, and is now the largest group in the office. This group represents Thigh Master, which people reported resulted in the proliferation of these exercise devices "all over the firm." Venable's business group is "now growing again" after a slowdown period, and although the firm's international practice is not well-developed, Venable recently added a new associate and made a new partner in the international group. In addition, Venable does work in the areas of telecommunications and media, and health care, which are "growth areas" at the firm, we were told.

pro bono

Venable exhibits a strong commitment to pro bono work. A number of Venable attorneys work with Greater D.C. Cares, through which, once a month, the staff participates in a group event, such as making meals for shut-ins or sorting food at a food bank. In addition, some of the firm's attorneys helped found the Zacchaeus legal services clinic in D.C. which addresses housing law matters. Many Venable attorneys staff the clinic, and a Venable associate is chairman of the Executive Committee. The firm has also created the Venable Foundation which provides assistance to children and the homeless, both in D.C. and Baltimore. The Foundation contributes money to over 300 agencies which provide human and legal services to indigents. Each Venable partner contributes two percent of his annual earnings to the Foundation.

Unlike most large, national D.C. firms, Venable represents small companies in addition to serving large institutional clients. Consequently, it offers its associates early work experiences with smaller clients. People noted that the firm's litigation practice, in particular, provides junior associates significant responsibility. Most second-year associates get courtroom experience handling "minor" issues. By their third year, associates independently handle cases.

training and career development

In the fall of 1996, Venable introduced a new training program for first- and second-year associates, in which associates are assigned a "preceptor" who is responsible for their training and career development. "Preceptors are encouraged to bring junior associates along to meet clients, sit in on depositions or trials, etc. Correspondingly, the billing requirement for junior associates has been reduced by several hundred hours," reported one contact. While most D.C. firms expect between 1800 and 2000 billable hours, Venable requires only 1750 hours of billable time; associates are expected, however, to devote at least 300 hours to training time each year and 100 hours to pro bono time. As part of its formal training program, the firm offers a monthly, in-house CLE program for business and litigation attorneys. People praised the firm for its flexibility in dealing with individual associate careers. One source noted that the firm has a policy of "recommending" an associate to a government or public interest job for a few years, from which the attorney may return to the firm and rejoin the same partnership class. Venable places a high premium on government service. Summer associates receive mid- and end-of-summer reviews, and associates are formally evaluated every six months.

Venable's summer program has reportedly been considerably improved in recent years. Assignments are handed out by a central coordinator who monitors interests and workload. "There is a big emphasis on giving the summer associates substantive work, and since the office has been busy there has been plenty of such work to go around," according to a strategically placed insider. Socially, the D.C. office sponsors a number of events, including a comedy club night, a wine tasting session, and outings to Orioles baseball games.

informal atmosphere

The work atmosphere at Venable was described as informal and the firm has adopted "casual dress" day on select Fridays. Partners and associates "tend to work together very closely and socialize as well. There is also a good deal of joking at the office, much of which finds its source in D.C. office managing partner, Bill Coston," reported one insider. Young attorneys often get together for informal happy hours, etc., and "the women attorneys at the firm try to get together quarterly for informal pot-luck dinners." There is also a strong emphasis on a team approach in the office, we were told. Matters are staffed cross-divisionally (*e.g.* lawyers from litigation and the government groups work together regularly), which "positively influences the office atmosphere."

diversity

Venable was described as "progressive" on minority hiring issues. One of Venable's most prominent African-American partners, William Quarles, left the firm recently to serve on the bench. Although not many women are partners at the firm, people said that Venable provides a comfortable work environment for women. Partner Kathy Cox is head of the legal personnel committee, and a number of women are on the management committee for the firm. Venable is reportedly very good about parental leave and flexible about part-time work. The firm recently made two women working part-time partners, including D.C. lawyer Lindsay Meyer. Venable received the first President's Award from the National Association of Women Lawyers in recognition of the firm's commitment to advancing women within the firm, we were told.

office facilities Venable's offices, built around a central atrium, were described as "open and light." A gym located in the building offers aerobics classes, weights, and a stairmaster. People complained in the past that the firm is located at the border of the red light district, but we were informed that the area is now well-developed and the red-light district has moved. Each associate occupies a private office. The technology at the firm, which was severely criticized in our earlier edition, has "improved dramatically" in the last few years. It is now state-of-the-art consisting of an "excellent and useful master document management system, file sharing between offices, and e-mail which is inter- and intra-office with the capability to mail documents." All attorneys have either a 486- or a Pentium-chip computer running Microsoft Office. A firmwide upgrade is in progress so that all computers will be Pentium-chip computers. There is also desktop access to LEXIS and Westlaw, and there are Internet research kiosks throughout the firm. In addition, the firm's system permits remote dial-in for those working at home or on the road. Finally, attorneys have access to multimedia laptops and multimedia presentation rooms.

Like a number of other Baltimore-based firms, Venable struggled through the economic slowdown of the early 1990s but is reportedly financially healthy today. The firm had "one of its best years ever in 1996" and the D.C. office is "actively growing." First-year and mid-to-senior-level associate salaries were raised in the fall of 1996.

hiring tips Venable hires its summer associates from a variety of schools. It recruits particularly heavily at Georgetown, Harvard, and the University of Virginia, but has also drawn summer associates from law schools across the country, such as the University of Maryland, the University of Texas, and Vanderbilt. The firm emphasizes "credentials" in its hiring decisions. Callback interviews usually involve meeting with four attorneys. The firm assigns each interviewee a "host" to take him around the firm. One contact said the firm "really made an effort to place you with people whom you had things in common, such as similar interests and school background. It was a tailored interview—very easy and comfortable." Others advised that it is important to "indicate that you understand the concept of the D.C. and Baltimore offices interacting closely. The firm is very proud of this."

Verner, Liipfert, Bernhard, McPherson and Hand

Washington Austin Honolulu Houston

Address: 901 15th Street, N.W., Suite 700, Washington, D.C. 20005-2301
Telephone: (202) 371–6000
Hiring Attorney: John H. Zentay, Hiring Chairperson
Contact: Diane F. Ross, Recruitment Administrator; (202) 371–6077
Associate Salary: First year $75,000 (1997)
Summer Salary: $1,325/week (1997)
Average Hours: 2000 worked; 1800 billed; 2000 required (goal)
Family Benefits: Maternity leave; cafeteria plan (pre-tax deductible for day care/healthcare)
1996 Summer: Class of 7 students; offers to 6
Partnership: NA
Pro Bono: 3–5% of all work is pro bono

Verner, Liipfert, Bernhard, McPherson and Hand in 1997
150 Lawyers at the Firm
0.8 Associates Per Partner

Total Partners 64		
Women	8	13%
All Minorities	4	6%
Afro-Am	1	2%
Asian-Am	3	5%

Total Associates 52		
Women	26	50%
All Minorities	6	12%
Afro-Am	1	2%
Asian-Am	3	6%
Latino	2	4%

Practice Areas	
Legislative	23
Litigation	19
Corporate/Transactional/Int'l.	17
Energy	17
Bankruptcy	13
Labor	12
Communications	10
Tax	9
Government Contracts	5
Transportation	5

changing management

Verner, Liipfert, Bernhard, McPherson and Hand is reputed to be one of the nation's foremost Democratic political-insider firms. Two influential partners, Harry McPherson and Lloyd Hand, were prominent in President Lyndon Johnson's Administration and are mainstays of the firm's legislative practice. They were described as "good old-boy liberals" who lend a southern feel to the firm's culture. Berl Bernhard, long recognized as a major D.C. political insider, contributes additional luster to the political work at Verner Liipfert. The firm is currently undergoing a significant change from management by one—chairman Berl Bernhard, who was for years the "life blood of the firm, both in terms of culture and business development"—to management by a newly appointed executive committee led by Clint Vince and Joe Manson. The change has resulted in a more "bottom-line" atmosphere at the firm, especially in terms of billable hour expectations for associates, as well as a "sense of short-term instability as new leaders become comfortable with their roles and agree on the firm's future needs," we were told.

top lobbying firm

Originally founded as a transportation firm, Verner Liipfert is best known today for its legislative practice. One person placed it among the top five lobbying firms in D.C. In addition to high-profile lobbyists such as the aforementioned McPherson, Hand and Bernhard, the firm's partnership includes Jim Blanchard, the former Governor of Michigan, John Waihee, the former Governor of Hawaii, Ann Richards, the former Governor of Texas, George Mitchell, the former Senate Majority Leader, and Lloyd Bentsen, the former Secretary of the Treasury and Chairman of the Senate Finance Committee. Bob Dole recently joined the firm as special counsel, "indicating that the firm wishes (and will) enhance its presence within the Republican Party and continue to grow the size of its legislative practice," one insider informed us. Everyone we interviewed said that the legislative practice is a "terrific" place to work, although one person cautioned that the group is extremely selective in its hiring decisions.

Verner Liipfert's other noteworthy practice areas include communications and energy. The firm's communication practice, which primarily handles lobbying for telecommunications companies, has also been involved in satellite projects and other space law matters. The energy group is headed by Clint Vince, who sets the tone of its "group-oriented" work environment. However, this group is "very insulated, and associates in this group seldom work with, or even are acquainted with, others at the firm," according to one insider. They have had a high turnover rate in recent years and hire mostly "lateral and contract attorneys," we were told. Though the corporate group traditionally has been one of the firm's largest, it has been slow of late.

pro bono

Verner Liipfert does not provide a highly structured pro bono practice comparable to those at some other large D.C. firms. We were told that those who want to pursue pro bono "have to take their own initiative" to do it. Pro bono hours count toward billable hours up to a certain limit. One source commented that the "liberal Democrat attitude" at the firm creates a comfortable atmosphere for pro bono work, although the recent emphasis on billable hours at the firm has detracted somewhat from the firm's commitment to pro bono work. Many associates, nevertheless, work in a special pro bono project to help homeless clients, and others provide legal counsel for the elderly. Verner Liipfert also offers a number of pro bono criminal law opportunities.

flexible associate development

Verner Liipfert does a good job in the area of associate development. The firm assigns to each associate a mentor who is a more senior associate, and who purposely is chosen from a practice area different from that of the associate. Though each associate's training depends on the partners with whom he works, people noted that the firm's "coddling" culture generally promotes close "teacher-student relationships." Our contacts described the overall communication between partners and associates as "wonderful." Verner Liipfert provides associates with a great deal of flexibility in developing their careers. Verner Liipfert is reportedly flexible about allowing lawyers to take time off to work on political campaigns, and to do stints in the government.

The close partner-associate relationships have generally enabled partners to entrust junior associates with significant responsibility. However, in recent years, as the number of partners has grown to exceed the number of associates, "many associates reach a 'plateau' of responsibility where the partners do most of the high profile work such as court appearances, depositions, hearings, etc.," reported one insider. In any event, third- and fourth-year associates often independently manage cases. Verner Liipfert's legislative and communications practices are known for offering early responsibility. Though Verner Liipfert does not provide extensive formal training, one source commented that the "training is good because the feedback is generally good." Attorneys provide detailed written evaluations of both summer and permanent associate work. People commented that, in general, Verner Liipfert does a good job of informing both summer and permanent associates about their status at the firm.

fragmented firm culture

Verner Liipfert, despite its size, is a firm "run according to each group leader's preference," resulting in much more of a "small-firm" feel than one would expect. The atmosphere at the firm was described as "laid-back," especially in litigation and labor, though this differs by group. While some viewed the firm's culture as "friendly" and hospitable, one source felt the firm tended to be "paternalistic" in supporting the people it considers "special." Another person concurred that the firm has many attorneys "who play favorites with certain people." However, there is virtually no "face time" required, we were told. "This is a place where if you keep busy enough and do good work, they let you do pretty much what you want," remarked one insider. The chances for partnership at Verner Liipfert are not strong, however, since there is a high ratio of partners to associates at the firm. Because the firm has recently almost doubled in size, only a small "core" of its associates have known each other for more than a few years. Moreover, Verner Liipfert has a relatively high turnover rate, perhaps because many associates join the firm as a springboard to careers in government and politics; this is "more true than ever" now, with Clinton in the White House, we were told. Consequently, the social atmosphere is somewhat fragmented.

diversity

People gave Verner Liipfert's work environment for women mixed reviews. Though a large number of women work at the firm, many of whom hold influential positions, one person said that some aspects of the firm's culture may make some women feel uncomfortable. She said that it was "not surprising to hear older partners refer to female associates as girls," and that on some occasions she felt uncomfortable as a woman at the firm. However, another person we interviewed said, "I actually felt more comfortable with women's issues at this firm than at any other." The firm recently appointed a sensitivity ombudsman to ensure that complaints and issues regarding sensitivity training, sexual harassment, and racial sensitivity are addressed.

The firm received positive reviews for its commitment to racial diversity. One person noted that many Verner Liipfert lawyers have been involved in civil rights issues and are sensitive to minority concerns. Another person remarked that "though Verner Liipfert has few African-American attorneys, the firm has a fair number of Latino and Asian American attorneys, probably due to our active Puerto Rico practice and the recent opening of a Honolulu office." Also, Verner Liipfert has several openly gay attorneys, "including an associate who co-authored *The Unofficial Gay Manual* and took leave on firm time to do a book tour," reported one contact.

Verner Liipfert's offices are located near the White House. People complained that the firm's library is small; summer associates frequently had to use the Georgetown library facilities. We were also told that the firm's support services are not ideal—two or three attorneys share a secretary, and that the firm is "relatively slow to adapt and take advantage of new technologies."

hiring

Verner Liipfert hires many of its summer associates from southern law schools. One insider commented that they don't want just the "straight A law review types" and noted that the firm makes "an effort to get interesting people with interesting political ideas or goals." In addition, "Verner Liipfert likes people who have strong ideas or an interest in politics." The callback interviews usually involve meeting with about four attorneys at the firm.

Vinson & Elkins

Washington Austin Dallas Houston
London Moscow Singapore

Address: 1455 Pennsylvania Avenue, N.W., Suite 700, Washington, D.C. 20004–1008
Telephone: (202) 639–6500
Hiring Attorney: Alden L. Atkins
Contact: Cynthia S. Dollahite, Administrative and Recruitment Coordinator; (202) 639–6719
Associate Salary: First year $72,000 (plus bonuses)
Summer Salary: $1,300/week (1997)
Average Hours: 1977 worked; 1942 billed; NA required
Family Benefits: NA
1996 Summer: Class of 6 2L students; offers to 6
Partnership: 31% of entering associates from 1981–1982 were made partner
Pro Bono: 0.8% of all work is pro bono

Vinson & Elkins in 1997
65 Lawyers at the Washington D.C. Office
1.4 Associates Per Partner

Total Partners 27		
Women	3	11%
All Minorities	0	0%

Total Associates 38		
Women	11	29%
All Minorities	4	11%
Afro-Am	2	5%
Latino	2	5%

Practice Areas	
Litigation/Antitrust	21
Business	15
Tax	9
Health	7
Energy	5
Environmental	4
Intellectual Property	2
Public Policy	2

The branch office of a prominent Texas firm, Vinson & Elkins exhibits, we were told, "very much of a branch mentality." V&E D.C. is closely integrated with the Houston home office in both culture and practice. The office is characterized by a "southern atmosphere." Friendliness and hospitality are important to the lawyers at the firm. One contact declared it is one of the "friendliest" firms in D.C. When he first started working at the firm, this person explained, "I would get six visits a day, and I got nothing done for the whole first week."

buoyant social life

Throughout the year, Vinson & Elkins organizes "all sorts of social activities," in true Texas-style. The famous Vinson & Elkins "Prom," held in Houston, is perhaps the social highlight of the year. The firm frequently rents a "humongous hotel" for the occasion and flies its attorneys and their guests to Houston for the event. One person remarked, "the wives all buy dresses specifically for the Ball—it's one of the major events." V&E's hospitality extends to wining and dining summer associates, many of whom are treated to lunch a few times a week during the summer. The firm also flies all the summer associates to Houston for one of two training programs.

energy practices

V&E's D.C. practice is closely linked to Houston, although it does not primarily represent the home office's clients. Energy clients represent a large part of the firm's revenues. The firm represents clients such as large pipeline exploration and production companies, and oil field service companies on a variety of matters. This practice boasts a number of partners who are well-known and distinguished in their fields. We were informed that the energy regulation group is extremely busy.

strong tax practice

The tax practice involves litigation, some transactional work, some lobbying on Capitol Hill, and work with the IRS. Buck Chapoton is one of the firm's most well-known tax lawyers. Chapoton, formerly a member of the Reagan Administration, heads the firm's tax practice, and is the managing partner of the office. We were told that he has a personal friendship with former President Bush and was involved in the 1992 presidential campaign.

international practice growth

V&E also offers a rapidly expanding business group which handles a variety of domestic and international corporate transactions. The business group has become increasingly involved in matters relating to Mexico and to Eastern Europe since the opening of its Moscow office in 1991. V&E's small but "growing" international trade practice has also been forging "new links with Europe." The firm's project finance group represents clients with energy and development projects in South America, Central America, Asia, Africa, Europe, and the Caribbean. V&E has opened a Singapore office, and is expanding into Beijing.

other practice areas

V&E offers a variety of other practice areas. It has an established health care practice, and its environmental group, headed by the well-respected Kevin Gaynor, is expanding. It has an antitrust practice which boasts the nationally known Ky Ewing, and an intellectual property practice that includes nationally known Robert Armitage. The firm recently added a communications practice that is "generating a substantial amount of work." The telecommunications practice performs both licensing and corporate work for clients in emerging technologies of satellite and broadcast communication. V&E also made a significant addition to its white-collar crime litigation practice by bringing in Mark Touhey, former Special Assistant to Kenneth Starr in the Whitewater investigation. The firm now represents one of the prominent clients in the Whitewater investigation. The firm's growing legislative and public policy practice is anchored around Chris Vaughn and Mike Andrews, former Congressman from Texas. V&E offers a structured pro bono practice, headed by partner Mike Henke, and many attorneys are involved in pro bono projects ranging from death penalty matters to landlord-tenant disputes. As of 1996, pro bono hours have been credited toward billable hours.

summer program

V&E's summer program is well-organized. Summer associates receive assignments either through a summer coordinator, from attorney work coordinators (who collect projects from each section of the office), or often directly from attorneys with whom they are working. Every week summer associates complete assignment forms where they indicate the matters on which they have worked and the projects in which they are interested. The firm ensures that summer associates receive broad exposure to different areas of the firm by rotating them informally through specific departments throughout the summer. V&E does not extend offers of employment for particular departments; rather, once the student accepts, the firm makes its decision on practice area based on the student's preferences and the office's needs.

V&E gradually eases new associates into the demanding life of a big firm lawyer. Junior associates do not face much billable hour pressure, but it mounts considerably in the years prior to partnership consideration. A partner reportedly told one person that to make partner, you should bill "200 hours a month" and come in "every Saturday and most Sundays."

Houston training center

Vinson & Elkins takes associate training very seriously. The firm reportedly "invested a fortune" in building a huge training facility at the Houston office which is utilized by all the lawyers firmwide. Each department devises its own highly structured and formal training program schedule, much of which is conducted at the Houston center. Summer associates participate each summer in a mock deposition training session and a negotiation skills workshop in Houston. The firm frequently hires distinguished professors to conduct the training sessions, many of which are videotaped and critiqued extensively by the firm's partners.

feedback and partnership

In addition to the formal training, V&E also offers junior associates significant early responsibility. One junior associate, who made connections at the World Bank, was encouraged to start his own practice "niche" at the firm. Because V&E represents a number of medium- and small-sized clients, one contact claimed that junior associates are almost "guaranteed first-hand exposure" to clients. The feedback, like the training at the firm, is "very structured and organized." In general, the firm informally reviews junior associates from time to time. At the end of the year, "associates are told their hours compared with the rest of their class and how partners and senior associates they work with view them and their work." One person said there is "not much controversy surrounding this process. Associates get advance notice early and there are not many surprises on the partnership track." The feedback in the summer program, described as not very extensive in our earlier edition, has been revised. Summer associates are evaluated upon completion of each project by the assigning attorney. In addition, there is a mid-summer evaluation, and, at the end of the summer, the hiring partner meets with each clerk to discuss the clerk's summer experience and the evaluations that have been completed for that clerk.

management

A firmwide committee is responsible for V&E's management. The D.C. office, however, makes its own hiring decisions for summer associates and entry-level lawyers, and has its own managing partner, administrative partner, and administrative staff. Buck Chapoton, the managing partner of the D.C. office, is a member of the firmwide committee and was said to be well-liked, open, and approachable. Those we talked to said that in general, the management is very open about its decisions and the financial condition of the firm. In fact, the firm circulates a daily statement which contains financial information that indicates the daily firm revenues.

diversity

V&E provides a comfortable atmosphere for women. One person commented that "because there are a few women in particularly important positions, it is rare that you encounter insensitive attitudes." Several women serve on important committees within the firm. One person commented that the firm is very committed to hiring more women and minorities.

expensive offices

Located in the Willard building, V&E's offices reportedly occupy some of the most expensive commercial real estate in the city. Decorated in contemporary dark wood, the firm's beautiful offices have a spacious interior design. The library, partially surrounded by glass, offers people a view into it from two sides. The terrace overlooks the Washington Monument and the Treasury Department and is the site for many firm parties. The Willard complex houses a nice, but small, gym which V&E attorneys and staff may use for free. Whereas in the past every associate had an individual office with a window, this is no longer the case; lateral hires have made office space tighter. The firm also has a small kitchen.

hiring tips

"If you are a Northern type-A stress person, you wouldn't be a good match for Vinson & Elkins," cautioned one insider. Still, V&E recruits heavily at the Ivy League schools, as well as other prominent law schools across the country. The firm "places a lot of emphasis on the interview" in making hiring decisions. Callback interviews are very "relaxed" and slightly more structured than interviews at other firms. Each interviewee is taken out for dinner the night before or after the interview. One person noted that the firm hires summer associates according to the needs of its departments and advised students to be "strategic" in selecting the departments in which they express interest.

Vincent & Elkins is a pleasant, hospitable firm in our nation's capital. It provides a friendly work environment with very informal relationships between partners and associates. As one contact told us, "our Texas roots show." Associates are "not pushed to bill outrageous amounts of hours" and, since many partners have young children, "they understand the importance of life outside the office." The single negative we encountered was the criticism that Houston dominates the D.C. operation. "This office needs to get more of its own clients," said one person, while another remarked that the "litigation practice is heavily dependent on the Houston office." This aside, for those who enjoy whistling Dixie, V&E is an attractive target.

Weil, Gotshal & Manges

Washington Dallas Houston Miami New York Silicon Valley
Brussels Budapest London Prague Warsaw

Address: 1615 L Street, N.W., Washington, D.C. 20036
Telephone: (202) 682–7000
Hiring Attorney: Peter D. Isakoff and W. Michael Bond, Co-Chairpersons, Hiring Committee
Contact: Beth M. Hopkins, Recruitment Coordinator; (202) 682–7044
Associate Salary: First year $78,000 (1997); second $92,750; third $108,000; fourth $125,000; fifth $140,750
Summer Salary: $1369/week (1996)
Average Hours: NA worked; 2000 billed; NA required
Family Benefits: 12 weeks paid maternity leave
1996 Summer: Class of 4 students; offers to 4
Partnership: NA
Pro Bono: 3-5% of all work is pro bono

Weil, Gotshal & Manges in 1997
39 Lawyers at the Washington D.C. Office
1.6 Associates Per Partner

Total Partners 14			Total Associates 23			Practice Areas	
Women	2	14%	Women	9	39%	Litigation	8
All Minorities	0	0%	All Minorities	1	4%	Tax	8
			Afro-Am	1	4%	Environmental	7
						International	6
						Administrative	4
						Real Estate	4
						Corporate	2

The only concession to the nation's capital that New York-based Weil, Gotshal & Manges made when it opened its D.C. office was the establishment of a predominantly regulatory practice. Other than that, Weil Gotshal attorneys may as well be working in New York, "although the atmosphere in a 40-lawyer office is naturally much different from a 400-lawyer office." Like the New York head office, this is a high-energy, businesslike firm, where "people come in and do the work until it's done." Weil, Gotshal & Manges was founded in the 1930s in New York by Jewish lawyers who were excluded from the established firms of the time. The firm's history has produced a culture that is committed to creating "an open attitude." This is apparent in the colorful D.C. office, which despite its small size, employs a diverse collection of attorneys. One person amusedly informed us that "if you met a dozen Weil Gotshal attorneys in the same room, you wouldn't know they worked in the same firm. They work well together, but the firm does not bring in a crew of people who think alike or look alike. In fact, to some they may seem like legal misfits...They are all different—a strange little group in which no one looks like an attorney." The common thread is that they are all highly intelligent, extremely hard-working, and competent attorneys who are committed to the law.

environmental practice

Weil Gotshal's environmental department is very well-reputed. Traditionally, the department has counseled many corporations on a variety of complex environmental issues and represented many of them in state and federal proceedings. In the past few years, Weil Gotshal has expanded its broad based practice to represent corporations with claims against their insurers for the costs associated with environmental cleanups. Under the leadership of managing partner David Berz, the department has a stable of regular clients and also supports other departments of the firm. For example, in recent years lawyers in the environmental group have worked closely with the bankruptcy department, negotiating with state and federal agencies to resolve environmental claims in chapter 11 reorganization proceedings.

demanding international trade

Weil Gotshal also has an international trade department which at one point included former U.S. Trade Representative Carla Hills. This department, led by female partner Jean Anderson, is known as being loud and boisterous. One source exaggerated that she "is there all day and night and expects that of associates." This department represents both corporations and public clients such as the Government of Canada.

premier international tax practice

The firm also has a strong international tax practice under the leadership of Kevin Dolan, former Associate Chief Counsel, Technical and International to the Internal Revenue Service and a "big time tax stud." One contact remarked that "you can't say enough about Kevin Dolan—most transactional partners in the firm will not do an international deal without him." This department is reported to be "more quiet and thoughtful" than the rest of the firm. In 1995, Mary ("Handy") Hevener joined Weil

Gotshal, bringing with her a thriving employee benefits tax practice. Although no less "thoughtful" than their international tax colleagues, the benefits group is far from "quiet."

litigation

Weil Gotshal's litigation department is headed by Richard Ben-Veniste who was a Watergate prosecutor "as a young maverick lawyer" and counsel to the U.S. Senate Democrats on the Whitewater hearings in more recent times. One contact informed us that the "brains" of the D.C. litigation department is Peter Isakoff, a former Supreme Court clerk. "This is a department on the rise within the firm; it now sports at least five senior and midlevel associates in addition to three partners." Weil Gotshal represents primarily large Fortune 500 and international corporations, and handles cases in federal courts across the country as well as in local courts. While civil litigation is the majority of the work, the group also does white-collar and environmental criminal defense work, and provides litigation support to various practice groups throughout the office.

Weil Gotshal has a fledgling public policy group under the direction of two partners (one Democrat, one Republican), both experienced governmental affairs practitioners. The Republican, Robert C. Odle, Jr., is a veteran of the Nixon and Reagan administrations, and is a former Deputy Assistant Secretary of Energy. The public policy group does not engage in "lobbying" in the street sense, but rather develops comprehensive legal strategies to assist clients through the legislative and regulatory processes in addition to the courts. Attorneys in the public policy group work with members of Congress and their staffs, the White House, Cabinet departments, and independent agencies, as well as think-tanks, trade associations, the news media, and the trade press.

pro bono

Pro bono work is "not the firm's strongest suit," said one person. Individual attorneys are free to use the firm's resources to pursue pro bono activities provided they are properly supervised, but there is no organized program. Several years ago, the firm adopted a pro bono policy that strongly encourages attorneys to provide at least 50 hours annually in pro bono services. Further, the office has an open-membership pro bono committee, consisting of both lawyers and support staff, that coordinates public service activities such as participation in food and clothing drives, tutoring at a local elementary school, and other projects. One associate noted that "at Weil Gotshal, pro bono work really is left up to each lawyer. Some lawyers who seek out pro bono clients do quite a bit, and the firm supports it whole-heartedly, but pro bono matters won't be dropped into your lap on a regular basis."

training feedback

Weil Gotshal is a very informal firm that offers easy interaction between partners and associates and an almost "lax" dress code. It is not a "stuffy," old-fashioned firm with a "quiet, bow tie atmosphere." Nor is it a highly structured firm. New associates often pick one or two practice areas in which they would most like to work and develop relationships with the partners in those groups. Associate responsibilities vary by department and depend, one person told us, on whether "you prove yourself." Another contact informed us that "there are virtually limitless possibilities to take on responsibility for a project, and if you show you can handle it, you will be given more. This can be both exciting and stress-inducing, as you may find yourself being relied on for many things at the same time, some of which are slightly over your head." Junior associates typically handle "a huge amount of research and writing." One source claimed that the international trade department offers new associates very little responsibility, whereas the litigation group gives its new members responsibility somewhat earlier. Aside from a few formal seminars and workshops, Weil Gotshal does not offer extensive formal training. Instead, associates develop close working relationships with partners who provide on-the-job training. Feedback for summer associates at the firm received mixed reviews. As for associates, people generally felt that if you are "not working out as an associate, the firm will communicate with you early."

minimal social life

Perhaps because they work long, hard hours, most Weil Gotshal attorneys have time for only a minimal social life. During the day, everyone is busy. "People don't hang around the watercooler much," elaborated one source. There is a group of attorneys who go out after work, but the "married with children" crew (most of the office) generally goes straight home. The firm organizes monthly happy hours on Fridays throughout the year. And each summer, attorneys and summer hires fly to New York for the firm outing at a scenic country club. Other activities include playing softball on the firm's team, followed by a meal of pizza and beer, a boat trip, baseball games, and plays.

diversity

Weil Gotshal has a progressive, open culture. Many of its partners have been involved in the government. However, the firm has not had much success in attracting minority attorneys. To address issues involved in hiring both women and minorities, the firm has formed a diversity committee. Though Weil Gotshal generally is very open to different types of people, the firm is reportedly "not very tolerant generally of people's lives." One insider noted that people are often called back to work from vacations and that vacations are canceled regularly. Another contact challenged this statement, noting that "the outright cancelling of vacation is very rare, although you are asked to call in regularly, and may be required to participate in a conference call or spend an afternoon working here or there." In general, "the whole climate of the firm is that work comes first." In recent years, the Washington office has hired a couple of associates on "alternative" career tracks. These lawyers generally accept reduced pay in exchange for reduced hours.

management partnership

The D.C. office is fairly independent from the New York home office and is run by its own managing partner. Most partners in the D.C. office were hired laterally, and the firm only rarely confers partnership on associates from the Washington office. One mid-level associate reported that he was "decidedly pessimistic" about the chances for partnership, but saw the recent promotion of a senior litigation associate to partner as a "step in the right direction." Another insider informed us that "this office is now well-established and rumor has it that some associates might make partner this year or next in the growing departments. The firm overall has shown an increasing willingness to make partners in the 'satellite' offices." The D.C. office is managed conservatively and has been very successful economically. Committed to slow growth, it is working towards the goal of developing a full-service, independent litigation department.

Weil Gotshal's D.C. office is well-administered. Every attorney has a private office and computer with LEXIS and Westlaw. The library is excellent and can obtain books from the New York office overnight. The support staff is helpful and efficient. The firm has no cafeteria, but does have coffee rooms.

hiring tips

As for recruitment, Weil Gotshal seeks people from top schools with high grades. It also looks for people with "distinctive personalities," who are interesting. The firm usually hires from the top national law schools, but on occasion will hire exceptional students from "second-tier schools." People commented that it is not necessary "to be totally somber and serious" in the interviews for Weil Gotshal. The firm views itself as an "innovator," declared one insider, who advised that "if you do have any far-reaching aspirations, don't be afraid to offer them. The firm likes to see people that are reaching out and willing to explore new areas of the law and new ideas." Weil Gotshal was described as an "entrepreneurial" firm which still considers itself a "maverick." There are a lot of strong characters at this firm, and they are not looking for "fragile personalities," disclosed another source. One contact instructed us that Weil Gotshal has "an openly expressed preference for strong, independent, well-balanced people who can roll with the punches, take criticism, and stand up for what they think even if a partner disagrees (sometimes loudly)."

Working at Weil, Gotshal & Manges is in many ways "a two-edged sword." If you decide to work at the firm you "may have to sacrifice the rest of your life." Yet the firm has a lot to offer people. One contact noted that "we have the opportunity to work for the major Fortune-500 clients of the firm, while working out of a smaller, less bureaucratic office with a comparatively friendly atmosphere." Another insider confirmed this judgement, pointing out that Weil Gotshal is "the best of both worlds—challenging work of an international powerhouse firm, but the atmosphere of a small office." It has an open and colorful, even entertaining, work atmosphere. It is also stable, has an interesting practice, and has an excellent reputation. Although associate turnover is high because partnership prospects are fairly limited, one insider asserted that "attorneys who work at the firm for its name value and money reasons are happy." And, in the bargain, "associates get to do everything, and good ones are treated as members of the team, not as cogs in the machinery."

Williams & Connolly

Washington

Address: The Edward Bennett Williams Building, 725 12th Street, N.W., Washington, D.C. 20005
Telephone: (202) 434–5000
Hiring Attorney: Carolyn H. Williams
Contact: Donna M. Downing, Recruitment Coordinator; (202) 434–5605
Associate Salary: First year $81,000 (1996); second $86,000; third $94,000; fourth $100,000; fifth $107,000; sixth $115,000; seventh $123,000; eighth $131,000
Summer Salary: $1350/week (1997)
Average Hours: NA worked; NA billed; minimum requirement is seven hours/day
Family Benefits: Health, dental, life; LTD; vision; unlimited vacation; 12 weeks maternity; unlimited sick leave; moving and bar expenses paid
1996 Summer: Class of 24 students
Partnership: 38% of entering associates from 1978–1984 were made partner
Pro Bono: NA

Williams & Connolly in 1997
147 Lawyers at the Firm
1.1 Associates Per Partner

Total Partners 69			Total Associates 78			Practice Areas	
Women	8	12%	Women	26	33%	Litigation	133
All Minorities	2	3%	All Minorities	11	14%	Corporate	7
Afro-Am	1	1%	Afro-Am	7	9%	Tax	7
Latino	1	1%	Asian-Am	3	4%		
			Latino	1	1%		

Housed in the Edward Bennett Williams office building, Williams & Connolly is steeped in traditions set by its founder whose "spirit and legacy" continues to shape the firm culture. "They worship Edward Bennett Williams at the firm," remarked one source. "Half of the partners have pictures of him in their offices, and his name is invoked on a daily basis." An Irish Catholic of modest beginnings, Williams, who passed away in 1988, rose to wield enormous political and business influence as a prominent defense attorney, a major Washington political insider, and for some time, a part owner of the Washington Redskins and owner of the Baltimore Orioles. One insider quipped that "upon joining Williams & Connolly, one feels as though one has entered the 'Cult of Ed.'" Today, although the firm reportedly still exudes an Irish Catholic "feel," Williams & Connolly attorneys represent diverse backgrounds and a broad spectrum of interests in politics, sport, and community activities.

high-powered atmosphere

Williams & Connolly lawyers are devoted to their work and the firm is reputedly "intense." One explained, however, that this reputation stems from the fact that Williams & Connolly lawyers are "very excited about what they are doing. There is a real energy about the place." The firm's high-powered attorneys, many of whom have clerked for Supreme Court Justices, exhibit a drive to succeed and achieve excellence in the law. One insider highly recommended the firm to people "who will enjoy being a lawyer and trying cases," but cautioned that it is "not the kind of place to go if you want a good balance in your life. Not that you couldn't have it if you went there, but if this is what you are looking for, it's not the place to go."

premier white-collar practice

Williams & Connolly offers one of the nation's most high-powered defense litigation practices. The firm handles both civil and criminal matters. While one source raved that the firm has the "best white-collar crime practice in the country," another contact informed us that "recently there has been a decline in the number of white-collar cases." The firm vigorously disputes this judgment, noting that recently the firm represented Archer-Daniels Midland in a celebrated white-collar case involving an FBI "mole." Moreover, partner David Kendall represents the President and First Lady in Whitewater matters. Williams & Connolly is also renowned for its First Amendment practice and represents the *Washington Post, Newsweek, The National Enquirer,* and other media. In addition, the firm has developed banking, tax, and corporate practices, but about 80 percent of the firm's practice involves litigation.

anarchic management

Williams & Connolly is managed by a committee composed of five partners, prominent among whom are Brendan Sullivan and Jack Vandaniam, who reportedly exert great influence at the firm. Perhaps because Williams & Connolly recently grew so rapidly, it has not yet organized itself as a large law firm and has very few formal firm policies or structures. People described the firm as being almost "anarchic," but, according to a representative of the firm, "those who thrive on freedom and the lack of a lot of bureaucracy love the laissez faire atmosphere."

free market system

The lack of structure and formal systems affects many aspects of associate life. For example, both summer and permanent associates obtain their work through the firm's "free market" system, under which each person "floats around" and solicits work according to interest. One contact told us that the "free market" approach "gives associates unusual latitude in deciding what types of cases to work on and which partners to work for. A nice consequence of this system is that partners have an incentive to treat associates well—otherwise, they'll have problems staffing their cases (only a handful of partners fall into this category)." We were told that sometimes "people fight over the real choice cases, but, by and large, there is plenty of interesting work for people to do."

"training by fire"

Perhaps because Williams & Connolly lacks significant formal training programs, preferring to rely on mentoring and informal lunchtime seminars, "'training by fire' is the firm's motto," reported one insider. Associates "get lots of responsibility early. There is no tracking system where you do memos and then depositions. People do depositions and get full responsibility for writing briefs in their first year." Williams & Connolly, one person raved, also encourages "everyone to get into court and be part of a trial within the first few years. In terms of hands-on experience, it is amazing what young associates are doing." Another contact informed us that "one associate played an active role, including examination of witnesses, in a federal civil trial within his first 15 months at the firm." Associates at the firm are formally evaluated each fall after the associate evaluation committee interviews each partner about each associate, but one ought not to expect much from this effort. One insider informed us that "the evaluation process during the first few years is perfunctory." In later years, however, the evaluation process is quite thorough, we were informed.

driven attorneys

Williams & Connolly also does not impose a formal billable hour requirement and the firm permits attorneys a great deal of flexibility in scheduling their work hours. However, because Williams & Connolly attorneys are "driven and ambitious," they work long and hard hours. One person reported that many attorneys seek "a lot of responsibility and do a lot of work. Many people work ten or eleven hours each day and...come in one weekend day each week." Another person remarked that "although the firm has its share of run-of-the-mill, pay-the-bills civil cases that are just plain boring, there is plenty of interesting work to go around. Indeed, many associates—especially newer ones—end up taking on more work than they probably should (there go the weekends) because they find it difficult to say 'no' to interesting cases or partners who are good to work for." Perhaps for this reason, Williams & Connolly suffers an undeserved reputation for being a "sweatshop."

unstructured summer

Nor does Williams & Connolly provide a highly-organized, lavish summer program. In past summers, the firm has arranged a few events which were held at partners' homes, but one source told us that the firm "takes pride in...not being big into wining and dining." The goal is to make the summer program as much like real associates' experience as possible; "as a result, the focus is on the work, not the parties," we were told. According to a firm spokesperson, "we give real assignments, incorporate summer associates in our trial teams, and make sure summer associates participate in meetings with clients, witnesses, and adversaries."

formal pro bono practice

Williams & Connolly has belatedly fashioned a formal pro bono practice, under the leadership of one of the firm's senior partners, the engaging Jerry Collins. Pro bono work at the firm ranges from death penalty appeals to mental health issues. One person believed that the firm is so "unstructured" that no "one would complain about your doing pro bono work." Another person remarked that "you can spend as much time as you like on pro bono work without receiving flak from others (everyone is too involved with their own practices to fret about what you're doing). And, significantly, you receive full billable credit for pro bono work."

increasing diversity

Williams & Connolly used to have a reputation for "not being a good place for women to work." It was known "as a hardball litigation place with a bunch of guys trying cases," and as being "somewhat men's clubby." However, the firm has successfully recruited many women in recent years, increasing the percentage of associates who are women from 25% in 1994 to 33% in 1997. Furthermore, its partnership includes some influential women such as Carolyn Williams, who chairs the hiring committee, and litigators Nancy Lesser, Nicole Seligman, and Heidi Hubbard. One insider informed us that "perhaps the most significant development at Williams & Connolly during the last year or so is the increased diversity among the associate ranks. The last two in-coming associate classes have seen a dramatic rise in the number of women and minority associates. Indeed, the most recent crop of new associates includes more women than men. Also, in just two years, the aggregate number of African-American and Latino associates has jumped from one to eight."

social attorney dining room

Williams & Connolly's office building, located directly above the Metro Center metro stop, features a private rooftop terrace and a street-level park. The firm library is located in the basement; one person complained that it does not have any windows. Another contact pointed out that "although associates are paid very well, quality-of-associate-life items such as copiers, fax machines, and the library are markedly inferior to other major D.C. firms. If you stay after hours, don't expect secretarial or word-processing help." The firm is also outfitted with a small gym which is available for attorneys and staff to use. The firm provides attorneys with private offices that are "bigger than those in most firms;" all have windows and are equipped with state-of-the-art computers. The firm dining room, which serves a free lunch every work day, was described as the firm's "biggest bonanza." The attorney dining room provides a social center at the firm where, because you "can just sit down with anyone, you quickly get to know everyone" at the firm. Whether it is due to the dining facilities or, as one person commented, the fact that the lawyers "spend all their time at the firm," there is a real "closeness" among the attorneys at Williams & Connolly. They enjoy a surprising number of "good friendships."

hiring: the Dulles to LAX test

Williams & Connolly's interesting and high-profile practice attracts the nation's most talented law students, which results in one of the most competitive summer associate selection processes in the city. The firm has hired a "remarkable" number of former Supreme Court clerks in recent years. Membership on the law review of a prestigious law school is almost an application prerequisite, and the firm scrutinizes grades and credentials. The firm "looks for people on law review who have strong recommendations from faculty and other jobs." Even top students are surprised to get offers from the firm. One person we interviewed, who was a member of the law review at one of the nation's most prestigious schools, exclaimed: "I couldn't believe I got the job." One insider wryly noted that "the key test in the recruiting process is the Dulles to LAX test; that is, would you want to sit next to this person on a plane for five hours."

Though many Williams & Connolly attorneys become law professors later in their careers, and the firm displays an academic bent in its hiring, one source remarked that they are not looking for the "wretched academic" type. Another noted that the firm is not averse to taking "chances" on some applicants who, though they may lack fancy credentials, exhibit Edward Bennett William's example of success by hard work and sheer force of character.

hiring practices

Past summer classes have included students from Columbia, Chicago, Georgetown, Harvard, Stanford, the University of Michigan, the University of Texas, the University of Virginia, and Yale. Many Williams & Connolly partners are alumni of Georgetown, and not coincidentally, Georgetown's law library is named after Edward Bennett Williams. The firm has experimented with extending summer associate offers after the brief on-campus interview. The firm varies this practice from year to year and from school to school. It is employed more commonly at law schools on the West Coast.

Williams & Connolly offers one of the best litigation practices in the city. Though lawyers at this firm work very hard, they are genuinely enthusiastic about their work and exhibit a strong camaraderie. The firm offers associates lots of individual clients and "a real commitment to lean staffing." One insider, in affirming the above, nevertheless pointed out that Williams & Connolly "like every other major law firm in the known universe, has a number of disgruntled associates. Several associates have recently left the law entirely." But this does not detract from the appeal that Williams & Connolly holds for its attorneys. We were told by one insider that "the partnership has kept its word in making partnership merit-dependent and has made five or six partners this year." All things considered, it is no surprise that we heard this sentiment expressed by one of our contacts: "the firm lives up to its reputation—there is no better place to practice in D.C."

Wilmer, Cutler & Pickering

Washington Baltimore
Berlin Brussels London

Address: 2445 M Street, N.W., Washington, D.C. 20037–1420
Telephone: (202) 663–6000
Hiring Attorney: David P. Donovan
Contact: Cheryl B. Shigo, Lawyer Recruitment Coordinator; (202) 663–6368
Associate Salary: First year $74,000 (1997); second $80,000; third $86,000; fourth $94,000; fifth $100,000
Summer Salary: $1300/week (2L) (1997); $1400/week (3L)
Average Hours: 2246 worked; 1854 billed (including pro bono); NA required
Family Benefits: Health, domestic partner, dental options, life, disability, and malpractice insurance; maternity/paternity leave; 401(K) plan employer contribution, optional pre-tax employee contribution; bar dues; 4 weeks vacation; dependent care reimbursement plan; emergency childcare
1996 Summer: Class of 25 students; offers to 24
Partnership: 17% of entering associates from 1979–1985 were made partner
Pro Bono: 6.5% of all work is pro bono

Wilmer, Cutler & Pickering in 1997
220 Lawyers at the Washington D.C. Office
1.4 Associates Per Partner

Total Partners 80			Total Associates 112		
Women	10	13%	Women	42	38%
All Minorities	4	5%	All Minorities	18	16%
Afro-Am	1	1%	Afro-Am	7	6%
Asian-Am	1	1%	Asian-Am	7	6%
Latino	2	3%	Latino	4	4%

Practice Areas	
Litigation	66
Corporate	50
Securities	48
International	28
Antitrust	21
Communications	16
Environmental	13
Bankruptcy	12
Financial Institution	12
Project Finance	12
Tax	11
Insurance	8

Founded in 1962, Wilmer, Cutler & Pickering is among the most prestigious, top-tier D.C. law firms. The firm prides itself on attracting "interesting work that raises interesting issues" and reportedly seeks "cases that are of first impression" and broad impact. Wilmer attorneys think of themselves as "lawyers' lawyers," to whom other lawyers turn for help on the most cutting-edge work. Not surprisingly, Wilmer draws the "best and the brightest" law students in the country, an ability about which, one person told us, the firm "prides itself...just a little too much." Another person remarked that "a few people know they're very smart, and always let you know it as well."

intellectual atmosphere

Almost everyone we interviewed described Wilmer as an "intellectual" law firm. These attorneys are very serious about their work. "They are less lighthearted during the day and it comes off as a coolness," remarked one source. "It takes a while to get to know people before this fades away." Others pointed out, however, that although people are "hard working and care deeply about their work," Wilmer is "extremely informal socially. Everybody talks to and socializes with everyone else, so that there is no need for a formal 'open door' policy." Moreover, one contact remarked that Wilmer is the "least formal and bureaucratic of the leading D.C. firms."

practice areas

Wilmer's broad-ranging practice includes one of the largest international practices in D.C. This section houses both private and public international law practice groups. The private international law group represents a number of large foreign and U.S. entities in international corporate transactions. The group also includes a strong aviation practice which represents, among others, Lufthansa airlines and Virgin Atlantic Airways. With offices in London, Brussels, and Berlin, Wilmer has focused on developing its practice in the European Community. The firm also sponsors an international lawyer program under which a number of lawyers from other countries work in the D.C. office. Wilmer's public international practice group has worked on NAFTA, the General Agreement on Tariffs and Trade (GATT), the Business Roundtable negotiations, and on numerous trade agreements between countries. One person commented that the group is very selective in hiring new permanent associates. The practice was recently further expanded with the addition of nine lawyers from Rogers & Wells with a strong Latin American and public finance practice.

The litigation department, the firm's largest practice area, houses an attractive and strong constitutional litigation section. Wilmer lawyers have handled a number of high-profile constitutional matters involving, among others, term-limit cases and the challenge to the line-item veto statute, as well as "lots of free speech stuff." Wilmer also offers a strong securities enforcement practice ("lots of cops-and-robbers work"), which one person described as heavily "male" and a bit "macho," and other strong regulatory and transactional practices, notably antitrust, communications and banking. The firm recently significantly increased the size and depth of its corporate practice by adding two partners formerly with Piper & Marbury, and opening a Baltimore office which, along with the D.C. office, supports this new practice. Additionally, Wilmer has an environmental law practice, and the securities regulatory work is also growing, "thanks to the lateral addition of several partners from the S.E.C."

pro bono practice

Wilmer also "prides itself on its active and well-organized pro bono program." A full-time pro bono coordinator, Christopher Herrling, was recently hired to run the program, with the assistance of a partner and an associate. They regularly circulate a list of all available pro bono projects to all attorneys. Wilmer partners exhibit "a strong commitment to pro bono work." One contact informed us that "this place *expects* people to do lots of pro bono; it counts just as much as your paying work (and often more, if you're on one of the high profile cases)." At Wilmer, "you're a freak if you don't do pro bono," we were informed. Many Wilmer lawyers have handled pro bono constitutional cases, and associates frequently get to argue cases in local and federal court.

political connections

Wilmer attorneys pursue other interests and activities related to and even completely outside the law. Like many D.C. attorneys, Wilmer lawyers are politically well-connected. Name partner Lloyd Cutler (now counsel at the firm) was described as a "Washington insider extraordinare." Both Cutler and partner C. Boyden Gray have served as White House Counsel. In addition to providing legal services, some Wilmer partners have developed and marketed computer software products that are designed to assist lawyers in managing their caseloads.

fluid assignments Wilmer provides a fluid work environment. Most practice groups are "very loose" and the firm's structure is "much less rigid than at other firms," one insider reported. The firm initially assigns each summer associate to a specific practice area according to the summer associate's expressed preferences, but summer associates may work in a variety of practice areas throughout the summer. Wilmer also assigns entering associates to one practice area when they join the firm, and the majority, although not all, of their assignments are likely to come from that practice area. Associates may rotate into a second practice area for their second year and may rotate again thereafter. Wilmer "encourages its associates to work in more than one practice area," according to one contact. Another person informed us that "assignments are completely fluid, and you can get anything you want by speaking up, regardless of the practice group you are formally assigned to. Lots of people split between groups, whether formally or informally. In general, this place rewards the 'squeaky wheel,' although the flip side of that is that you can find yourself with less interesting work (or experience) if you aren't willing to speak up and take active control of your assignments and training."

experience Each practice area offers junior associates varying responsibilities. Some areas, such as banking, entrust their junior associates with significant responsibility, according to one source. The litigation practice area, on the other hand, reportedly offers less early responsibility, and we were told that "a lot of people get stuck on big cases in litigation." However, one insider informed us that responsibility opportunities depend on the "mix of cases" the firm happens to be handling, and that "right now, small cases are much more common than big ones. Also, there's a lot of non-traditional work in the litigation group: sports arbitrations, international aid, mediation, etc." Many junior litigators rely as well on the pro bono practice and the firm's extensive formal training programs for their professional development.

training feedback Wilmer's training and feedback systems are highly structured for litigation and corporate associates. With respect to the other practice areas, one person noted: "outside litigation and corporate, the practice groups are smaller and tight enough that you get feedback and training constantly." Junior associates' work is closely monitored for the first six months by the recently instituted New Associates Working Group ("NAWG"), and they receive frequent feedback during this period. In addition, they receive formal reviews every six months for the first year and once a year thereafter. The firm also assigns each associate to a mentor, but, "unlike other firms, only after you have developed working relations with other attorneys, so that the choice of a mentor is meaningful," asserted one contact. Two and one-third years before they are considered for partnership, associates receive the first of three partnership evaluations at which time they are placed in general categories of performance which are designed to give them an idea of their partnership prospects. Summer associates receive oral evaluations of their written work and other aspects of their performance. The firm does not, however, permit them to see the written evaluations completed by the assigning attorneys, and some people complained that the oral evaluations are "not detailed," and "do not always give fully honest appraisals of the associate's progress."

social life A hardworking firm, Wilmer, we were told, is not a "big chummy place where everyone goes out after work." The firm, however, arranges a number of social activities for both summer and permanent associates. It organizes a park picnic annually and a "big firm bash" every year. Every Friday the firm hosts a cocktail hour. The summer program includes a sailing outing, numerous dinners, and plays.

diversity Most people we interviewed praised Wilmer's commitment to diversity and its efforts to address its problems in retaining minority attorneys. The firm has a mentoring system for minority attorneys that is designed to create a more comfortable work atmosphere.

People raved about Wilmer's treatment of female attorneys. A number of women at the firm are involved in the summer associate recruitment and evaluation process. As part of its effort to provide women a supportive environment, a "women's forum" committee at the firm regularly organizes lunches, dinners, and other events for women attorneys. Wilmer also strives to address family issues. It provides on-site emergency day care. There is also an active attorney mothers group for women associates with young children. Some women work part-time, although those we interviewed said that such arrangements are made on a "case-by-case basis." One source commented that if you accept "part-time status, then you don't get as much power in the firm and it is doubtful that you will make partner," although another contact pointed out to us that precisely this has happened in recent years. In general, most people believe that "if you work hard and do good work, they will make allowances for families. They think families are important."

supportive to women

Wilmer's office facilities are located near Georgetown, a 10 minute shuttle bus ride away from the Foggy Bottom and Dupont Circle metro stops, which, however, one person described as "an inconvenient location." The offices are comfortable, but not extravagant. Everyone has a private office with a window and a personal computer that can access Westlaw, LEXIS, the Internet, and a host of other research materials. Some private offices offer outdoor balconies. The firm offices are outfitted with an outdoor deck, a gym, and a cafeteria.

Wilmer's summer associate hiring process is one of the most competitive in Washington, D.C. This selective firm is inundated with applications and hires primarily, but not exclusively, from the top 10 national schools. One insider observed that "most people in the summer program are pretty academically oriented," and many Wilmer attorneys clerked for judges before joining the firm. Another pointed out that Wilmer is very "open to people who don't have any corporate experience or a corporate attitude. They try to get interesting people." The interviews at the firm are "very relaxed." One successful applicant believed that most hiring decisions are based primarily on "grades and credentials."

hiring tips

Wilmer, Cutler & Pickering has experienced significant expansion in the past several years, solidifying its reputation as one of Washington's most prestigious law firms. It offers very interesting legal work: "because of its reputation of being able to handle difficult issues, much of the work is far more interesting than that at other firms." The firm has excellent colleagues: "Wilmer attracts and hires some of the brightest lawyers in the country, the vast majority of whom are also extremely nice people." Wilmer also provides a good work atmosphere: "in general, Wilmer lawyers are happy with what they are doing and who they are doing it with." The praise for and the satisfaction with the firm that we heard from those we spoke with are significant testimony to its illustrious reputation.

significant expansion

However, a few points of concern were brought to our attention. In recent years "the firm has been increasingly focused on the bottom line. This has reduced collegiality somewhat and has also noticeably diminished the quality and availability of support services," reported one contact. Another person remarked that "although there are currently no billing targets or minimums, several partners in management have let it be known that they want the low-hour culture to change. Luckily, there's a lot of resistance within the partnership to tightening the screws, but if the bottom-line focused partners succeed, the tenor of this place will change for the worse." A related concern involves the large number of lateral attorneys that have recently joined the firm. One contact, exasperated at this pollution of the firm's culture, remarked: "Hopefully this trend will stop. It's a little hard for the laterals to become socialized into the (low-hour, very heavy pro bono) Wilmer culture when there are so many of them reinforcing their old bad habits (*i.e.* billing a lot)." These matters aside, work at Wilmer, Cutler & Pickering is exciting, fast-paced, and challenging—performed, moreover, in an atmosphere where "if you speak up, you can do whatever you want to," according to one voice which aptly expressed the tenor at the firm.

Winthrop, Stimson, Putnam & Roberts

Washington New York Palm Beach Stamford
Brussels Hong Kong London Tokyo

Address: 1133 Connecticut Ave., N.W., Washington, D.C. 20036
Telephone: (202) 775–9800
Hiring Attorney: Aileen (Chuca) Meyer
Contact: NA
Associate Salary: First year $83,000 plus $3,000 starting bonus (1997)
Summer Salary: $1596/week (1997)
Average Hours: 2100 worked; 1800 billed; 2000 targeted
Family Benefits: 12 weeks paid maternity leave; emergency childcare arrangements
1996 Summer: Class of 1 student; offers to 1
Partnership: NA
Pro Bono: 8–10% of all work is pro bono

Winthrop, Stimson, Putnam & Roberts in 1997
27 Lawyers at the Washington D.C. Office
2.0 Associates Per Partner

Total Partners 7		
Women	1	14%
All Minorities	0	0%

Total Associates 14		
Women	1	7%
All Minorities	2	14%
Afro-Am	1	7%
Asian-Am	1	7%

Practice Areas	
International	8
Energy	5
Aviation	4
Environmental	4
Contracting & Bus. Trans.	2
Litigation	2
Finance	1
Space Law	1

Winthrop, Stimson, Putnam & Roberts offers the prestige, resources, and salary of a prominent New York law firm. The D.C. office was established in 1985, and provides a comfortable working environment with a "small firm feel." Although the associates still "contribute to certain aspects of policy-making" in the D.C. office, the office recently has become more structured and management decisions now are not nearly as "amorphous" as was reported in our earlier edition. The firm, however, reportedly remains "a very open place" where lawyers can "feel free to criticize."

humane atmosphere

The D.C. office is closely tied to the New York home office in terms of management. Its "beautiful offices with a marble floor and stairs" are also reminiscent of New York. However, everyone we interviewed claimed the D.C. office is more "humane," and less "stuffy" than traditional New York law firms. It is not uncommon for a lawyer to "come in to the office in khakis on Fridays." Though Winthrop retains a high-quality practice, it is not accompanied by all of the characteristics of a stereotypical high-pressure, top-flight New York law firm.

Nevertheless, Winthrop recently imposed a firmwide a billable target of 2000 hours per year. One source believed that "with the continued development of the firm, it is expected that the workload will be such that the 2000 hour target will be met easily." The D.C. associates are well-compensated for their long work hours because the D.C. office's associate salaries are close to the firm's New York salaries, which are well above the average large D.C. firm salaries. In fact, senior Winthrop associates earn more than junior partners in some D.C. law firms.

minimal partnership prospects

Unfortunately, however, Winthrop D.C. suffers a disadvantage that affects many branch offices. One person commented that "because it is a branch office, and small, we are almost completely removed from management decisions. If one experiences problems or has issues within one's small circle, one is virtually on one's own in attempting to work these out." Because the D.C. office exercises less influence firmwide, it experiences difficulty in promoting its associates to partnership. It was explained to us that "D.C. doesn't call the shots on partnership...Even if you know New York partners, it's very hard to make partner." Of the three tenth-year plus associates discussed in our last edition, "one was forced to leave, one left on her own, and the other, now a thirteenth-year (class of 1984), has yet to be made partner. It's a big issue for D.C. associates," reported one insider.

D.C. office politically oriented

Many Winthrop lawyers have backgrounds in government or politics. This is not true of the firm's New York-based partners and substantially distinguishes the two offices. Although, like the firm's founders, many Winthrop partners are "Democrats and liberal," many Republicans also work at the firm. Not surprisingly, we were told that Winthrop lawyers "love talking politics" and "people don't hold back" in their discussions. The lawyers were described as "very opinionated, but respectful of different views."

practice areas

Because Winthrop is small and not highly-structured, both summer and permanent associates work "in a variety of areas." One person commented that "by the second or third year, most associates have an established area of practice. However, attorneys must be prepared to handle any of the work of the office." Winthrop's D.C. office is most known for its expertise in legislative and regulatory matters involving, among others, international trade, environmental, energy, space law, government contracts, and financing, and aviation. A somewhat unique practice, the aviation work involves everything from monitoring regulatory policy to advising municipalities on aviation matters appearing before regulatory boards. The D.C. office does not have an independent litigation practice. Therefore, according to one contact, "the litigation associates are tied to New York for work and partnership prospects. In fact, one senior litigation associate is actually relocating to New York soon." In general, the attorneys travel a great deal within the U.S.; the international trade lawyers frequently make trips to Europe and Asia.

pro bono

For an office of its size, Winthrop D.C. offers a strong pro bono practice. Though the practice is not formally structured, the attorneys exhibit a strong commitment to pro bono work, which has constituted eight to 10 percent of the firm's total work. They have represented the World Wildlife Fund, the Chesapeake Bay Foundation, the National Audubon Society, and the National Trust for Historic Preservation.

Though most people praised Winthrop's less-structured organization, some cautioned that attorneys need a lot of personal initiative to succeed at the firm. One person observed that "you can't just sit there and have work come to you. You have to be pro-active" about obtaining work. Though the New York office provides a range of training programs which the D.C. associates can attend, the D.C. office offers no formal training. Moreover, the office only recently developed a formal evaluation system for summer and full-time associates. Most people we interviewed believed that the feedback needs improvement. One person declared that the feedback is "terrible. You never know where you stand. The associates are so nice they don't know how to tell you anything...The communication is very poor." Overall, Winthrop's unstructured summer program offers few of the "wine and dine" events that are often associated with New York firms.

Though it fails to provide formal training, Winthrop was said to offer unusually good opportunities for early responsibility. One person advised prospective attorneys to "expect a lot of responsibility from the start." Junior associates enjoy significant client contact and often participate in administrative hearings. People we interviewed observed that the D.C. office is top-heavy, in part because three to four years ago a number of junior associates were asked to leave or left on their own, and the firm has not replaced them. Although this means that incoming junior associates may get excellent work, it also means that staffing matters properly is often difficult and senior attorneys commonly perform work more appropriate for junior associates.

diversity

The D.C. office's partnership includes one woman, but no people of color. Although the firm says it is committed to recruiting minority attorneys, few have advanced through the ranks; the firm as a whole has no African-American partners. Those we interviewed believe that the firm provides a comfortable environment for both female and minority attorneys despite their few numbers. In particular, we were told, that firmwide there is a "good community" for women and the firm exhibits a pro-woman atmosphere.

Winthrop's offices are located two blocks from Dupont Circle, near many restaurants and shops. Each associate has a private office outfitted with a computer that can access LEXIS and Westlaw. The only criticism of the offices that we heard involved the library which, we were told, was originally "made for four people and they haven't upgraded it since the firm began."

hiring tips

One successful applicant remarked that the firm seeks an "interesting mix of people—individuals who can show their personalities and contribute." The firm fills most of its summer class with students from the top eastern law schools but also recruits at some western schools such as Boalt and Stanford. Winthrop's callback interviews can be interesting and dynamic. According to one person, the firm really "wants to know that you can back up your arguments." This person talked about "religion, politics, and abortion" in his interviews. He said, "it didn't matter what you talked about, they just wanted to see that you can get along and work with them." In essence, the firm seeks individuals that will be "enjoyable to work with."

Law Firms Ranked by Associates Per Partner

1.	**CAPLIN & DRYSDALE** WASHINGTON, D.C.	0.3
2.	**COZEN AND O'CONNOR** PHILADELPHIA	0.3
3.	**SACHNOFF & WEAVER** CHICAGO	0.4
4.	**SPIEGEL & MCDIARMID** WASHINGTON, D.C.	0.4
5.	**WEINBERG AND GREEN** BALTIMORE	0.4
6.	**BROWN, RUDNICK, FREED & GESMER** BOSTON	0.5
7.	**FULBRIGHT & JAWORSKI** WASHINGTON, D.C.	0.5
8.	**GARDERE & WYNNE** DALLAS	0.5
9.	**HOPKINS & SUTTER** CHICAGO	0.5
10.	**MCDERMOTT, WILL & EMERY** CHICAGO	0.5
11.	**SMITH, GAMBRELL & RUSSELL** ATLANTA	0.5
12.	**BRONSON, BRONSON & MCKINNON** SAN FRANCISCO	0.6
13.	**BRYAN CAVE** WASHINGTON, D.C.	0.6
14.	**MANATT, PHELPS, PHILLIPS & KANTOR** LOS ANGELES	0.6
15.	**PEABODY & ARNOLD** BOSTON	0.6
16.	**ROSS & HARDIES** CHICAGO	0.6
17.	**RUDNICK & WOLFE** CHICAGO	0.6
18.	**SHERBURNE, POWERS & NEEDHAM** BOSTON	0.6
19.	**THOMPSON & KNIGHT** DALLAS	0.6
20.	**ANDREWS & KURTH** HOUSTON	0.7
21.	**CHAPMAN AND CUTLER** CHICAGO	0.7
22.	**DICKIE, MCCAMEY & CHILCOTE** PITTSBURGH	0.7
23.	**PATTON & BOGGS** WASHINGTON, D.C.	0.7
24.	**REED SMITH SHAW & MCCLAY** PITTSBURGH	0.7
25.	**SAUL, EWING, REMICK & SAUL** PHILADELPHIA	0.7
26.	**STRASBURGER & PRICE** DALLAS	0.7
27.	**SUTHERLAND, ASBILL & BRENNAN** ATLANTA	0.7
28.	**WHITEFORD, TAYLOR & PRESTON** BALTIMORE	0.7
29.	**BLANK, ROME, COMISKY & MCCAULEY** PHILADELPHIA	0.8
30.	**GOULSTON & STORRS** BOSTON	0.8
31.	**GREENBERG, GLUSKER, FIELDS, CLAMAN & MACHTINGER** LOS ANGELES	0.8
32.	**HILL & BARLOW** BOSTON	0.8
33.	**HOWARD, RICE, NEMEROVSKI ET. AL.** SAN FRANCISCO	0.8
34.	**JEFFER, MANGELS, BUTLER & MARMARO** LOS ANGELES	0.8
35.	**JENNER & BLOCK** CHICAGO	0.8
36.	**KILPATRICK STOCKTON** ATLANTA	0.8
37.	**MILES & STOCKBRIDGE** BALTIMORE	0.8
38.	**MILLER & CHEVALIER** WASHINGTON, D.C.	0.8
39.	**MITCHELL, SILBERBERG & KNUPP** LOS ANGELES	0.8
40.	**MUNGER, TOLLES & OLSON** LOS ANGELES	0.8
41.	**POWELL, GOLDSTEIN, FRAZER & MURPHY** ATLANTA	0.8
42.	**SHEA & GARDNER** WASHINGTON, D.C.	0.8
43.	**SIDLEY & AUSTIN** CHICAGO	0.8
44.	**SONNENSCHEIN NATH & ROSENTHAL** CHICAGO	0.8
45.	**SULLIVAN & WORCESTER** BOSTON	0.8
46.	**VERNER, LIIPFERT, BERNHARD, MCPHERSON AND HAND** WASHINGTON, D.C.	0.8
47.	**ARENT, FOX, KINTNER, PLOTKIN & KAHN** WASHINGTON, D.C.	0.9
48.	**BABST CALLAND CLEMENTS & ZOMNIR** PITTSBURGH	0.9
49.	**BAKER & MCKENZIE** CHICAGO	0.9
50.	**BRACEWELL & PATTERSON** WASHINGTON, D.C.	0.9
51.	**BURNS & LEVINSON** BOSTON	0.9
52.	**IRELL & MANELLA** LOS ANGELES	0.9
53.	**KATTEN MUCHIN & ZAVIS** CHICAGO	0.9
54.	**KECK, MAHIN & CATE** CHICAGO	0.9
55.	**KIRKPATRICK & LOCKHART** PITTSBURGH	0.9
56.	**POWELL, GOLDSTEIN, FRAZER & MURPHY** WASHINGTON, D.C.	0.9
57.	**SEMMES, BOWEN & SEMMES** BALTIMORE	0.9
58.	**SHAW, PITTMAN, POTTS & TROWBRIDGE** WASHINGTON, D.C.	0.9
59.	**STEPTOE & JOHNSON** WASHINGTON, D.C.	0.9
60.	**VENABLE, BAETJER, HOWARD & CIVILETTI** WASHINGTON, D.C.	0.9
61.	**ALSTON & BIRD** ATLANTA	1.0
62.	**ARNOLD & PORTER** WASHINGTON, D.C.	1.0
63.	**BAKER & MCKENZIE** WASHINGTON, D.C.	1.0
64.	**BUCHANAN INGERSOLL** PITTSBURGH	1.0
65.	**DOW, LOHNES & ALBERTSON** WASHINGTON, D.C.	1.0
66.	**ECKERT SEAMONS CHERIN & MELLOT** PITTSBURGH	1.0
67.	**FARELLA, BRAUN & MARTEL** SAN FRANCISCO	1.0

68.	**FULBRIGHT & JAWORSKI** Houston	1.0
69.	**GARDNER, CARTON & DOUGLAS** Chicago	1.0
70.	**GRAHAM & JAMES** San Francisco	1.0
71.	**HELLER EHRMAN WHITE & MCAULIFFE** San Francisco	1.0
72.	**HOGAN & HARTSON** Washington, D.C.	1.0
73.	**HOLLEB & COFF** Chicago	1.0
74.	**HUGHES & LUCE** Dallas	1.0
75.	**KIRKLAND & ELLIS** Washington, D.C.	1.0
76.	**LIDDELL, SAPP, ZIVLEY, HILL & LABOON** Houston	1.0
77.	**MORGAN, LEWIS & BOCKIUS** Los Angeles	1.0
78.	**PEPPER, HAMILTON & SCHEETZ** Philadelphia	1.0
79.	**PIPER & MARBURY** Washington, D.C.	1.0
80.	**SCHNADER, HARRISON, SEGAL & LEWIS** Philadelphia	1.0
81.	**SHEPPARD, MULLIN, RICHTER & HAMPTON** Los Angeles	1.0
82.	**VENABLE, BAETJER AND HOWARD** Baltimore	1.0
83.	**VINSON & ELKINS** Houston	1.0
84.	**WACHTELL, LIPTON, ROSEN & KATZ** New York	1.0
85.	**WHITMAN BREED ABBOTT & MORGAN** New York	1.0
86.	**WINSTEAD, SECHREST & MINICK** Dallas	1.0
87.	**COUDERT BROTHERS** New York	1.1
88.	**DUANE, MORRIS & HECKSCHER** Philadelphia	1.1
89.	**FISH & RICHARDSON** Boston	1.1
90.	**HAIGHT, GARDNER, POOR & HAVENS** New York	1.1
91.	**NUTTER, MCCLENNEN & FISH** Boston	1.1
92.	**ORRICK, HERRINGTON & SUTCLIFFE** San Francisco	1.1
93.	**PILLSBURY MADISON & SUTRO** San Francisco	1.1
94.	**SIDLEY & AUSTIN** Washington, D.C.	1.1
95.	**TROUTMAN SANDERS** Atlanta	1.1
96.	**WILLIAMS & CONNOLLY** Washington, D.C.	1.1
97.	**DRINKER BIDDLE & REATH** Philadelphia	1.2
98.	**FOLEY, HOAG & ELIOT** Boston	1.2
99.	**GIBSON, DUNN & CRUTCHER** Los Angeles	1.2
100.	**HALE AND DORR** Boston	1.2
101.	**HUNTON & WILLIAMS** Washington, D.C.	1.2
102.	**JENNER & BLOCK** Washington, D.C.	1.2
103.	**KING & SPALDING** Atlanta	1.2
104.	**LORD, BISSELL & BROOK** Chicago	1.2
105.	**MAYER, BROWN & PLATT** Chicago	1.2
106.	**MINTZ, LEVIN, COHN, FERRIS, GLOVSKY AND POPEO** Boston	1.2
107.	**PALMER & DODGE** Boston	1.2
108.	**PIPER & MARBURY** Baltimore	1.2
109.	**WINSTON & STRAWN** New York	1.2
110.	**BINGHAM, DANA & GOULD** Boston	1.3
111.	**BRACEWELL & PATTERSON** Houston	1.3
112.	**CHOATE, HALL & STEWART** Boston	1.3
113.	**DICKSTEIN, SHAPIRO, MORIN & OSHINSKY** Washington, D.C.	1.3
114.	**HUGHES HUBBARD & REED** New York	1.3
115.	**KELLEY DRYE & WARREN** New York	1.3
116.	**KIRKLAND & ELLIS** Chicago	1.3
117.	**LEBOEUF, LAMB, LEIBY & MACRAE** New York	1.3
118.	**LONG, ALDRIDGE & NORMAN** Atlanta	1.3
119.	**MAYOR, DAY, CALDWELL & KEETON** Houston	1.3
120.	**MCCUTCHEN, DOYLE, BROWN & ENERSEN** San Francisco	1.3
121.	**MORGAN, LEWIS & BOCKIUS** Philadelphia	1.3
122.	**REED SMITH SHAW & MCCLAY** Philadelphia	1.3
123.	**ROPES & GRAY** Boston	1.3
124.	**SIDLEY & AUSTIN** Los Angeles	1.3
125.	**AKIN, GUMP, STRAUSS, HAUER & FELD** Dallas	1.4
126.	**AKIN, GUMP, STRAUSS, HAUER & FELD** Washington, D.C.	1.4
127.	**BAKER & BOTTS** Houston	1.4
128.	**COLLIER, SHANNON, RILL & SCOTT** Washington, D.C.	1.4
129.	**COVINGTON & BURLING** Washington, D.C.	1.4
130.	**DECHERT PRICE & RHOADS** Philadelphia	1.4
131.	**DONOVAN LEISURE NEWTON & IRVINE** New York	1.4
132.	**FOLEY & LARDNER** Washington, D.C.	1.4
133.	**LATHAM & WATKINS** Los Angeles	1.4
134.	**MORRISON & FOERSTER** Los Angeles	1.4
135.	**STROOCK & STROOCK & LAVAN** New York	1.4
136.	**VINSON & ELKINS** Washington, D.C.	1.4
137.	**WILMER, CUTLER & PICKERING** Washington, D.C.	1.4
138.	**BALLARD, SPAHR, ANDREWS & INGERSOLL** Philadelphia	1.5

139.	**BROBECK, PHLEGER & HARRISON** Los Angeles	**1.5**
140.	**BROBECK, PHLEGER & HARRISON** San Francisco	**1.5**
141.	**CROWELL & MORING** Washington, D.C.	**1.5**
142.	**GIBSON, DUNN & CRUTCHER** Washington, D.C.	**1.5**
143.	**HOWREY & SIMON** Washington, D.C.	**1.5**
144.	**JONES, DAY, REAVIS & POGUE** Chicago	**1.5**
145.	**KAYE, SCHOLER, FIERMAN, HAYS & HANDLER** New York	**1.5**
146.	**PAUL, HASTINGS, JANOFSKY & WALKER** Los Angeles	**1.5**
147.	**ROSENMAN & COLIN** New York	**1.5**
148.	**BAKER & MCKENZIE** New York	**1.6**
149.	**COOLEY GODWARD** San Francisco	**1.6**
150.	**FENWICK & WEST** Palo Alto	**1.6**
151.	**MORRISON & FOERSTER** San Francisco	**1.6**
152.	**MORRISON & FOERSTER** Washington, D.C.	**1.6**
153.	**O'MELVENY & MYERS** Los Angeles	**1.6**
154.	**WEIL, GOTSHAL & MANGES** Washington, D.C.	**1.6**
155.	**WINSTON & STRAWN** Chicago	**1.6**
156.	**WINTHROP, STIMSON, PUTNAM & ROBERTS** New York	**1.6**
157.	**GOODWIN, PROCTER & HOAR** Boston	**1.7**
158.	**JONES, DAY, REAVIS & POGUE** New York	**1.7**
159.	**MILBANK, TWEED, HADLEY & MCCLOY** New York	**1.7**
160.	**PROSKAUER ROSE** New York	**1.7**
161.	**CHADBOURNE & PARKE** New York	**1.8**
162.	**FRIED, FRANK, HARRIS, SHRIVER & JACOBSON** Washington, D.C.	**1.8**
163.	**JONES, DAY, REAVIS & POGUE** Washington, D.C.	**1.8**
164.	**PATTERSON, BELKNAP, WEBB & TYLER** New York	**1.8**
165.	**PENNIE & EDMONDS** New York	**1.8**
166.	**CAHILL GORDON & REINDEL** New York	**2.0**
167.	**MORGAN, LEWIS & BOCKIUS** New York	**2.0**
168.	**WEIL, GOTSHAL & MANGES** New York	**2.0**
169.	**WINTHROP, STIMSON, PUTNAM & ROBERTS** Washington, D.C.	**2.0**
170.	**BROWN & WOOD** New York	**2.1**
171.	**DEWEY BALLANTINE** New York	**2.1**
172.	**PAUL, HASTINGS, JANOFSKY & WALKER** Washington, D.C.	**2.1**
173.	**CHADBOURNE & PARKE** Washington, D.C.	**2.2**
174.	**SWIDLER & BERLIN** Washington, D.C.	**2.2**
175.	**PAUL, WEISS, RIFKIND, WHARTON & GARRISON** New York	**2.3**
176.	**SKADDEN, ARPS, SLATE, MEAGHER & FLOM** Washington, D.C.	**2.3**
177.	**WHITE & CASE** New York	**2.4**
178.	**WILLKIE FARR & GALLAGHER** New York	**2.4**
179.	**KENYON & KENYON** New York	**2.5**
180.	**SULLIVAN & CROMWELL** New York	**2.5**
181.	**DAVIS POLK & WARDWELL** New York	**2.6**
182.	**ROGERS & WELLS** New York	**2.6**
183.	**TESTA, HURWITZ & THIBEAULT** Boston	**2.6**
184.	**DEBEVOISE & PLIMPTON** New York	**2.7**
185.	**FRIED, FRANK, HARRIS, SHRIVER & JACOBSON** New York	**2.7**
186.	**SKADDEN, ARPS, SLATE, MEAGHER & FLOM** Los Angeles	**2.7**
187.	**SCHULTE ROTH & ZABEL** New York	**2.8**
188.	**SIMPSON THACHER & BARTLETT** New York	**2.8**
189.	**FISH & NEAVE** New York	**2.9**
190.	**SHEARMAN & STERLING** New York	**2.9**
191.	**WILSON, SONSINI, GOODRICH & ROSATI** Palo Alto	**2.9**
192.	**CLEARY, GOTTLIEB, STEEN & HAMILTON** New York	**3.0**
193.	**SKADDEN, ARPS, SLATE, MEAGHER & FLOM** New York	**3.1**
194.	**CRAVATH, SWAINE & MOORE** New York	**3.9**
195.	**ANDERSON KILL & OLICK** New York	**NA**
196.	**WOLF, BLOCK, SCHORR & SOLIS-COHEN** Philadelphia	**NA**

Law Firms Ranked by Percentage of Associates Who Make Partner (over varying years)

1.	**ANDERSON KILL & OLICK** New York	**100**
2.	**JENNER & BLOCK** Chicago	**91**
3.	**COZEN AND O'CONNOR** Philadelphia	**90**
4.	**HOPKINS & SUTTER CHICAGO**	**90**
5.	**SHERBURNE, POWERS & NEEDHAM** Boston	**90**
6.	**AKIN, GUMP, STRAUSS, HAUER & FELD** Dallas	**86**
7.	**SMITH, GAMBRELL & RUSSELL** Atlanta	**77**

8.	**ANDREWS & KURTH** HOUSTON	**70**
9.	**LIDDELL, SAPP, ZIVLEY, HILL & LABOON** HOUSTON	**67**
10.	**GARDERE & WYNNE** DALLAS	**65**
11.	**SACHNOFF & WEAVER** CHICAGO	**64**
12.	**STRASBURGER & PRICE** DALLAS	**63**
13.	**BAKER & MCKENZIE** WASHINGTON, D.C.	**60**
14.	**GARDNER, CARTON & DOUGLAS** CHICAGO	**60**
15.	**FARELLA, BRAUN & MARTEL** SAN FRANCISCO	**59**
16.	**HUGHES & LUCE** DALLAS	**56**
17.	**SWIDLER & BERLIN** WASHINGTON, D.C.	**54**
18.	**MITCHELL, SILBERBERG & KNUPP** LOS ANGELES	**46**
19.	**PIPER & MARBURY** BALTIMORE	**46**
20.	**MORGAN, LEWIS & BOCKIUS** LOS ANGELES	**43**
21.	**WEINBERG AND GREEN** BALTIMORE	**43**
22.	**BROWN, RUDNICK, FREED & GESMER** BOSTON	**42**
23.	**SEMMES, BOWEN & SEMMES** BALTIMORE	**42**
24.	**WACHTELL, LIPTON, ROSEN & KATZ** NEW YORK	**41**
25.	**ARENT, FOX, KINTNER, PLOTKIN & KAHN** WASHINGTON, D.C.	**39**
26.	**DUANE, MORRIS & HECKSCHER** PHILADELPHIA	**39**
27.	**HUNTON & WILLIAMS** WASHINGTON, D.C.	**39**
28.	**BRYAN CAVE** WASHINGTON, D.C.	**38**
29.	**WILLIAMS & CONNOLLY** WASHINGTON, D.C.	**38**
30.	**BRACEWELL & PATTERSON** WASHINGTON, D.C.	**36**
31.	**FULBRIGHT & JAWORSKI** HOUSTON	**36**
32.	**KIRKLAND & ELLIS** WASHINGTON, D.C.	**36**
33.	**LATHAM & WATKINS** LOS ANGELES	**36**
34.	**POWELL, GOLDSTEIN, FRAZER & MURPHY** WASHINGTON, D.C.	**35**
35.	**BRACEWELL & PATTERSON** HOUSTON	**33**
36.	**FULBRIGHT & JAWORSKI** WASHINGTON, D.C.	**33**
37.	**MAYOR, DAY, CALDWELL & KEETON** HOUSTON	**33**
38.	**KIRKPATRICK & LOCKHART** PITTSBURGH	**32**
39.	**BAKER & BOTTS** HOUSTON	**31**
40.	**MORRISON & FOERSTER** LOS ANGELES	**31**
41.	**MORRISON & FOERSTER** SAN FRANCISCO	**31**
42.	**MORRISON & FOERSTER** WASHINGTON, D.C.	**31**
43.	**SULLIVAN & WORCESTER** BOSTON	**31**
44.	**VINSON & ELKINS** WASHINGTON, D.C.	**31**
45.	**BAKER & MCKENZIE** CHICAGO	**30**
46.	**CHAPMAN AND CUTLER** CHICAGO	**30**
47.	**WINSTEAD, SECHREST & MINICK** DALLAS	**30**
48.	**MINTZ, LEVIN, COHN, FERRIS, GLOVSKY AND POPEO** BOSTON	**29**
49.	**MUNGER, TOLLES & OLSON** LOS ANGELES	**29**
50.	**BROBECK, PHLEGER & HARRISON** LOS ANGELES	**28**
51.	**GOODWIN, PROCTER & HOAR** BOSTON	**28**
52.	**KECK, MAHIN & CATE** CHICAGO	**28**
53.	**NUTTER, MCCLENNEN & FISH** BOSTON	**27**
54.	**PATTON & BOGGS** WASHINGTON, D.C.	**27**
55.	**BROBECK, PHLEGER & HARRISON** SAN FRANCISCO	**26**
56.	**COOLEY GODWARD** SAN FRANCISCO	**26**
57.	**ROPES & GRAY** BOSTON	**26**
58.	**SIDLEY & AUSTIN** CHICAGO	**26**
59.	**WEIL, GOTSHAL & MANGES** NEW YORK	**26**
60.	**KATTEN MUCHIN & ZAVIS** CHICAGO	**25**
61.	**SAUL, EWING, REMICK & SAUL** PHILADELPHIA	**25**
62.	**SHAW, PITTMAN, POTTS & TROWBRIDGE** WASHINGTON, D.C.	**25**
63.	**SHEA & GARDNER** WASHINGTON, D.C.	**25**
64.	**SHEPPARD, MULLIN, RICHTER & HAMPTON** LOS ANGELES	**25**
65.	**SONNENSCHEIN NATH & ROSENTHAL** CHICAGO	**25**
66.	**VENABLE, BAETJER, HOWARD & CIVILETTI** WASHINGTON, D.C.	**25**
67.	**WILSON, SONSINI, GOODRICH & ROSATI** PALO ALTO	**25**
68.	**CHOATE, HALL & STEWART** BOSTON	**24**
69.	**GRAHAM & JAMES** SAN FRANCISCO	**24**
70.	**GREENBERG, GLUSKER, FIELDS, CLAMAN & MACHTINGER** LOS ANGELES	**24**
71.	**HOWREY & SIMON** WASHINGTON, D.C.	**24**
72.	**BRONSON, BRONSON & MCKINNON** SAN FRANCISCO	**23**
73.	**KILPATRICK STOCKTON** ATLANTA	**23**
74.	**MILLER & CHEVALIER** WASHINGTON, D.C.	**23**
75.	**AKIN, GUMP, STRAUSS, HAUER & FELD** WASHINGTON, D.C.	**22**
76.	**REED SMITH SHAW & MCCLAY** PITTSBURGH	**22**
77.	**PAUL, HASTINGS, JANOFSKY & WALKER** LOS ANGELES	**21**
78.	**FRIED, FRANK, HARRIS, SHRIVER & JACOBSON** WASHINGTON, D.C.	**20**

79.	**HOGAN & HARTSON** Washington, D.C.	20
80.	**TESTA, HURWITZ & THIBEAULT** Boston	20
81.	**PILLSBURY MADISON & SUTRO** San Francisco	19
82.	**SULLIVAN & CROMWELL** New York	19
83.	**MILBANK, TWEED, HADLEY & MCCLOY** New York	18
84.	**PALMER & DODGE** Boston	18
85.	**BINGHAM, DANA & GOULD** Boston	17
86.	**BROWN & WOOD** New York	17
87.	**DECHERT PRICE & RHOADS** Philadelphia	17
88.	**MCCUTCHEN, DOYLE, BROWN & ENERSEN** San Francisco	17
89.	**O'MELVENY & MYERS** Los Angeles	17
90.	**ORRICK, HERRINGTON & SUTCLIFFE** San Francisco	17
91.	**ROGERS & WELLS** New York	17
92.	**WILLKIE FARR & GALLAGHER** New York	17
93.	**WILMER, CUTLER & PICKERING** Washington, D.C.	17
94.	**ARNOLD & PORTER** Washington, D.C.	16
95.	**BALLARD, SPAHR, ANDREWS & INGERSOLL** Philadelphia	16
96.	**FRIED, FRANK, HARRIS, SHRIVER & JACOBSON** New York	16
97.	**LEBOEUF, LAMB, LEIBY & MACRAE** New York	16
98.	**SCHNADER, HARRISON, SEGAL & LEWIS** Philadelphia	16
99.	**FISH & NEAVE** New York	15-20
100.	**CLEARY, GOTTLIEB, STEEN & HAMILTON** New York	15
101.	**GIBSON, DUNN & CRUTCHER** Washington, D.C.	15
102.	**KENYON & KENYON** New York	15
103.	**PEPPER, HAMILTON & SCHEETZ** Philadelphia	15
104.	**ROSENMAN & COLIN** New York	15
105.	**HALE AND DORR** Boston	14
106.	**HELLER EHRMAN WHITE & MCAULIFFE** San Francisco	14
107.	**SCHULTE ROTH & ZABEL** New York	14
108.	**SHEARMAN & STERLING** New York	14
109.	**STEPTOE & JOHNSON** Washington, D.C.	14
110.	**CHADBOURNE & PARKE** New York	13
111.	**COUDERT BROTHERS** New York	12
112.	**COVINGTON & BURLING** Washington, D.C.	12
113.	**DONOVAN LEISURE NEWTON & IRVINE** New York	12
114.	**WHITE & CASE** New York	12
115.	**WINTHROP, STIMSON, PUTNAM & ROBERTS** New York	11
116.	**KELLEY DRYE & WARREN** New York	10
117.	**SKADDEN, ARPS, SLATE, MEAGHER & FLOM** New York	10
118.	**STROOCK & STROOCK & LAVAN** New York	10
119.	**CROWELL & MORING** Washington, D.C.	9.3
120.	**CAHILL GORDON & REINDEL** New York	9
121.	**DEWEY BALLANTINE** New York	9
122.	**PEABODY & ARNOLD** Boston	9
123.	**DAVIS POLK & WARDWELL** New York	8
124.	**HUGHES HUBBARD & REED** New York	8
125.	**KAYE, SCHOLER, FIERMAN, HAYS & HANDLER** New York	7
126.	**CRAVATH, SWAINE & MOORE** New York	6
127.	**PAUL, WEISS, RIFKIND, WHARTON & GARRISON** New York	5
128.	**ALSTON & BIRD** Atlanta	NA
129.	**BABST CALLAND CLEMENTS & ZOMNIR** Pittsburgh	NA
130.	**BAKER & MCKENZIE** New York	NA
131.	**BLANK, ROME, COMISKY & MCCAULEY** Philadelphia	NA
132.	**BUCHANAN INGERSOLL** Pittsburgh	NA
133.	**BURNS & LEVINSON** Boston	NA
134.	**CAPLIN & DRYSDALE** Washington, D.C.	NA
135.	**CHADBOURNE & PARKE** Washington, D.C.	NA
136.	**COLLIER, SHANNON, RILL & SCOTT** Washington, D.C.	NA
137.	**DEBEVOISE & PLIMPTON** New York	NA
138.	**DICKIE, MCCAMEY & CHILCOTE** Pittsburgh	NA
139.	**DICKSTEIN, SHAPIRO, MORIN & OSHINSKY** Washington, D.C.	NA
140.	**DOW, LOHNES & ALBERTSON** Washington, D.C.	NA
141.	**DRINKER BIDDLE & REATH** Philadelphia	NA
142.	**ECKERT SEAMONS CHERIN & MELLOT** Pittsburgh	NA
143.	**FENWICK & WEST** Palo Alto	NA
144.	**FISH & RICHARDSON** Boston	NA
145.	**FOLEY, HOAG & ELIOT** Boston	NA
146.	**FOLEY & LARDNER** Washington, D.C.	NA
147.	**GIBSON, DUNN & CRUTCHER** Los Angeles	NA
148.	**GOULSTON & STORRS** Boston	NA
149.	**HAIGHT, GARDNER, POOR & HAVENS** New York	NA

150.	**HILL & BARLOW** BOSTON	NA
151.	**HOLLEB & COFF** CHICAGO	NA
152.	**HOWARD, RICE, NEMEROVSKI, ET. AL.** SAN FRANCISCO	NA
153.	**IRELL & MANELLA** LOS ANGELES	NA
154.	**JEFFER, MANGELS, BUTLER & MARMARO** LOS ANGELES	NA
155.	**JENNER & BLOCK** WASHINGTON, D.C.	NA
156.	**JONES, DAY, REAVIS & POGUE** CHICAGO	NA
157.	**JONES, DAY, REAVIS & POGUE** NEW YORK	NA
158.	**JONES, DAY, REAVIS & POGUE** WASHINGTON, D.C.	NA
159.	**KING & SPALDING** ATLANTA	NA
160.	**KIRKLAND & ELLIS** CHICAGO	NA
161.	**LONG, ALDRIDGE & NORMAN** ATLANTA	NA
162.	**LORD, BISSELL & BROOK** CHICAGO	NA
163.	**MANATT, PHELPS, PHILLIPS & KANTOR** LOS ANGELES	NA
164.	**MAYER, BROWN & PLATT** CHICAGO	NA
165.	**MCDERMOTT, WILL & EMERY** CHICAGO	NA
166.	**MILES & STOCKBRIDGE** BALTIMORE	NA
167.	**MORGAN, LEWIS & BOCKIUS** NEW YORK	NA
168.	**MORGAN, LEWIS & BOCKIUS** PHILADELPHIA	NA
169.	**PATTERSON, BELKNAP, WEBB & TYLER** NEW YORK	NA
170.	**PAUL, HASTINGS, JANOFSKY & WALKER** WASHINGTON, D.C.	NA
171.	**PENNIE & EDMONDS** NEW YORK	NA
172.	**PIPER & MARBURY** WASHINGTON, D.C.	NA
173.	**POWELL, GOLDSTEIN, FRAZER & MURPHY** ATLANTA	NA
174.	**PROSKAUER ROSE** NEW YORK	NA
175.	**REED SMITH SHAW & MCCLAY** PHILADELPHIA	NA
176.	**ROSS & HARDIES** CHICAGO	NA
177.	**RUDNICK & WOLFE** CHICAGO	NA
178.	**SIDLEY & AUSTIN** LOS ANGELES	NA
179.	**SIDLEY & AUSTIN** WASHINGTON, D.C.	NA
180.	**SIMPSON THACHER & BARTLETT** NEW YORK	NA
181.	**SKADDEN, ARPS, SLATE, MEAGHER & FLOM** LOS ANGELES	NA
182.	**SKADDEN, ARPS, SLATE, MEAGHER & FLOM** WASHINGTON, D.C.	NA
183.	**SPIEGEL & MCDIARMID** WASHINGTON, D.C.	NA
184.	**SUTHERLAND, ASBILL & BRENNAN** ATLANTA	NA
185.	**THOMPSON & KNIGHT** DALLAS	NA
186.	**TROUTMAN SANDERS** ATLANTA	NA
187.	**VENABLE, BAETJER AND HOWARD** BALTIMORE	NA
188.	**VERNER, LIIPFERT, BERNHARD, MCPHERSON AND HAND** WASHINGTON, D.C.	NA
189.	**VINSON & ELKINS** HOUSTON	NA
190.	**WEIL, GOTSHAL & MANGES** WASHINGTON, D.C.	NA
191.	**WHITEFORD, TAYLOR & PRESTON** BALTIMORE	NA
192.	**WHITMAN BREED ABBOTT & MORGAN** NEW YORK	NA
193.	**WINSTON & STRAWN** CHICAGO	NA
194.	**WINSTON & STRAWN** NEW YORK	NA
195.	**WINTHROP, STIMSON, PUTNAM & ROBERTS** WASHINGTON, D.C.	NA
196.	**WOLF, BLOCK, SCHORR & SOLIS-COHEN** PHILADELPHIA	NA

Law Firms Ranked by Pro Bono Work as a Percentage of Total Work

1.	**ARENT, FOX, KINTNER, PLOTKIN & KAHN** WASHINGTON, D.C.	10
2.	**SMITH, GAMBRELL & RUSSELL** ATLANTA	8-10
3.	**WHITEFORD, TAYLOR & PRESTON** BALTIMORE	8-10
4.	**WINTHROP, STIMSON, PUTNAM & ROBERTS** WASHINGTON, D.C.	8-10
5.	**GOULSTON & STORRS** BOSTON	8
6.	**JENNER & BLOCK** WASHINGTON, D.C.	8
7.	**COVINGTON & BURLING** WASHINGTON, D.C.	7-9
8.	**SHAW, PITTMAN, POTTS & TROWBRIDGE** WASHINGTON, D.C.	7-8
9.	**WINTHROP, STIMSON, PUTNAM & ROBERTS** NEW YORK	7
10.	**WILMER, CUTLER & PICKERING** WASHINGTON, D.C.	6.5
11.	**DEBEVOISE & PLIMPTON** NEW YORK	6
12.	**FISH & NEAVE** NEW YORK	5-10
13.	**HELLER EHRMAN WHITE & MCAULIFFE** SAN FRANCISCO	5-10
14.	**SEMMES, BOWEN & SEMMES** BALTIMORE	5-10
15.	**SHEA & GARDNER** WASHINGTON, D.C.	5-10
16.	**ARNOLD & PORTER** WASHINGTON, D.C.	5-7
17.	**CHOATE, HALL & STEWART** BOSTON	5-7
18.	**COZEN AND O'CONNOR** PHILADELPHIA	5
19.	**FOLEY, HOAG & ELIOT** BOSTON	5
20.	**HOWREY & SIMON** WASHINGTON, D.C.	5

21.	**JENNER & BLOCK** Chicago	5
22.	**MCCUTCHEN, DOYLE, BROWN & ENERSEN** San Francisco	5
23.	**NUTTER, MCCLENNEN & FISH** Boston	5
24.	**PAUL, WEISS, RIFKIND, WHARTON & GARRISON** New York	5
25.	**SHERBURNE, POWERS & NEEDHAM** Boston	5
26.	**SKADDEN, ARPS, SLATE, MEAGHER & FLOM** Los Angeles	5
27.	**SKADDEN, ARPS, SLATE, MEAGHER & FLOM** New York	5
28.	**STEPTOE & JOHNSON** Washington, D.C.	5
29.	**STROOCK & STROOCK & LAVAN** New York	5
30.	**SUTHERLAND, ASBILL & BRENNAN** Atlanta	5
31.	**PATTON & BOGGS** Washington, D.C.	4.6
32.	**HILL & BARLOW** Boston	4.5
33.	**GARDNER, CARTON & DOUGLAS** Chicago	4-7
34.	**HOWARD, RICE, NEMEROVSKI ET. AL.** San Francisco	4-7
35.	**O'MELVENY & MYERS** Los Angeles	4-7
36.	**BAKER & BOTTS** Houston	4-6
37.	**BINGHAM, DANA & GOULD** Boston	4-5
38.	**CLEARY, GOTTLIEB, STEEN & HAMILTON** New York	4
39.	**CROWELL & MORING** Washington, D.C.	4
40.	**HOLLEB & COFF** Chicago	4
41.	**KILPATRICK STOCKTON** Atlanta	4
42.	**MORRISON & FOERSTER** Los Angeles	4
43.	**MORRISON & FOERSTER** San Francisco	4
44.	**PILLSBURY MADISON & SUTRO** San Francisco	4
45.	**ROPES & GRAY** Boston	4
46.	**SONNENSCHEIN NATH & ROSENTHAL** Chicago	4
47.	**HUGHES HUBBARD & REED** New York	3.3
48.	**AKIN, GUMP, STRAUSS, HAUER & FELD** Washington, D.C.	3-5
49.	**DUANE, MORRIS & HECKSCHER** Philadelphia	3-5
50.	**FRIED, FRANK, HARRIS, SHRIVER & JACOBSON** New York	3-5
51.	**KIRKPATRICK & LOCKHART** Pittsburgh	3-5
52.	**PALMER & DODGE** Boston	3-5
53.	**PIPER & MARBURY** Washington, D.C.	3-5
54.	**POWELL, GOLDSTEIN, FRAZER & MURPHY** Washington, D.C.	3-5
55.	**VENABLE, BAETJER, HOWARD & CIVILETTI** Washington, D.C.	3-5
56.	**VERNER, LIIPFERT, BERNHARD, MCPHERSON AND HAND** Washington, D.C.	3-5
57.	**WEIL, GOTSHAL & MANGES** Washington, D.C.	3-5
58.	**WILSON, SONSINI, GOODRICH & ROSATI** Palo Alto	3-5
59.	**SPIEGEL & MCDIARMID** Washington, D.C.	3-4
60.	**CRAVATH, SWAINE & MOORE** New York	3
61.	**DAVIS POLK & WARDWELL** New York	3
62.	**DONOVAN LEISURE NEWTON & IRVINE** New York	3
63.	**FARELLA, BRAUN & MARTEL** San Francisco	3
64.	**FRIED, FRANK, HARRIS, SHRIVER & JACOBSON** Washington, D.C.	3
65.	**GIBSON, DUNN & CRUTCHER** Los Angeles	3
66.	**GIBSON, DUNN & CRUTCHER** Washington, D.C.	3
67.	**HAIGHT, GARDNER, POOR & HAVENS** New York	3
68.	**HOPKINS & SUTTER** Chicago	3
69.	**JONES, DAY, REAVIS & POGUE** Washington, D.C.	3
70.	**KENYON & KENYON** New York	3
71.	**KIRKLAND & ELLIS** Chicago	3
72.	**LEBOEUF, LAMB, LEIBY & MACRAE** New York	3
73.	**MILBANK, TWEED, HADLEY & MCCLOY** New York	3
74.	**ORRICK, HERRINGTON & SUTCLIFFE** San Francisco	3
75.	**PAUL, HASTINGS, JANOFSKY & WALKER** Los Angeles	3
76.	**PAUL, HASTINGS, JANOFSKY & WALKER** Washington, D.C.	3
77.	**PIPER & MARBURY** Baltimore	3
78.	**REED SMITH SHAW & MCCLAY** Philadelphia	3
79.	**REED SMITH SHAW & MCCLAY** Pittsburgh	3
80.	**SACHNOFF & WEAVER** Chicago	3
81.	**SCHULTE ROTH & ZABEL** New York	3
82.	**SIDLEY & AUSTIN** Chicago	3
83.	**SIMPSON THACHER & BARTLETT** New York	3
84.	**SULLIVAN & CROMWELL** New York	3
85.	**SULLIVAN & WORCESTER** Boston	3
86.	**WEINBERG AND GREEN** Baltimore	3
87.	**WHITE & CASE** New York	3
88.	**WILLKIE FARR & GALLAGHER** New York	3
89.	**HALE AND DORR** Boston	2.7
90.	**MUNGER, TOLLES & OLSON** Los Angeles	2-5
91.	**KIRKLAND & ELLIS** Washington, D.C.	2-4

92. **LONG, ALDRIDGE & NORMAN** Atlanta 2-4
93. **BROWN, RUDNICK, FREED & GESMER** Boston 2-3
94. **SCHNADER, HARRISON, SEGAL & LEWIS** Philadelphia 2-3
95. **DICKSTEIN, SHAPIRO, MORIN & OSHINSKY** Washington, D.C. 2
96. **DOW, LOHNES & ALBERTSON** Washington, D.C. 2
97. **DRINKER BIDDLE & REATH** Philadelphia 2
98. **GARDERE & WYNNE** Dallas 2
99. **GOODWIN, PROCTER & HOAR** Boston 2
100. **KAYE, SCHOLER, FIERMAN, HAYS & HANDLER** New York 2
101. **MILLER & CHEVALIER** Washington, D.C. 2
102. **MINTZ, LEVIN, COHN, FERRIS, GLOVSKY AND POPEO** Boston 2
103. **MORGAN, LEWIS & BOCKIUS** Los Angeles 2
104. **MORGAN, LEWIS & BOCKIUS** Philadelphia 2
105. **PROSKAUER ROSE** New York 2
106. **ROSS & HARDIES** Chicago 2
107. **SHEARMAN & STERLING** New York 2
108. **WEIL, GOTSHAL & MANGES** New York 2
109. **WINSTON & STRAWN** Chicago 2
110. **WINSTON & STRAWN** New York 2
111. **BROBECK, PHLEGER & HARRISON** San Francisco 1.6
112. **CHADBOURNE & PARKE** New York 1.6
113. **TESTA, HURWITZ & THIBEAULT** Boston 1.6
114. **SWIDLER & BERLIN** Washington, D.C. 1.5
115. **CHADBOURNE & PARKE** Washington, D.C. 1.3
116. **HUGHES & LUCE** Dallas 1-5
117. **IRELL & MANELLA** Los Angeles 1-5
118. **CHAPMAN AND CUTLER** Chicago 1-3
119. **COOLEY GODWARD** San Francisco 1-3
120. **COUDERT BROTHERS** New York 1-3
121. **FULBRIGHT & JAWORSKI** Houston 1-3
122. **FULBRIGHT & JAWORSKI** Washington, D.C. 1-3
123. **GREENBERG, GLUSKER, FIELDS, CLAMAN & MACHTINGER** Los Angeles 1-3
124. **KATTEN MUCHIN & ZAVIS** Chicago 1-3
125. **LIDDELL, SAPP, ZIVLEY, HILL & LABOON** Houston 1-3
126. **MANATT, PHELPS, PHILLIPS & KANTOR** Los Angeles 1-3
127. **MCDERMOTT, WILL & EMERY** Chicago 1-3
128. **PENNIE & EDMONDS** New York 1-3
129. **ROGERS & WELLS** New York 1-3
130. **ROSENMAN & COLIN** New York 1-3
131. **SIDLEY & AUSTIN** Los Angeles 1-3
132. **SIDLEY & AUSTIN** Washington, D.C. 1-3
133. **STRASBURGER & PRICE** Dallas 1-3
134. **WACHTELL, LIPTON, ROSEN & KATZ** New York 1-3
135. **ANDREWS & KURTH** Houston 1-2
136. **ECKERT SEAMONS CHERIN & MELLOT** Pittsburgh 1-2
137. **AKIN, GUMP, STRAUSS, HAUER & FELD** Dallas 1
138. **ANDERSON KILL & OLICK** New York 1
139. **BALLARD, SPAHR, ANDREWS & INGERSOLL** Philadelphia 1
140. **DICKIE, MCCAMEY & CHILCOTE** Pittsburgh 1
141. **KELLEY DRYE & WARREN** New York 1
142. **MORGAN, LEWIS & BOCKIUS** New York 1
143. **SHEPPARD, MULLIN, RICHTER & HAMPTON** Los Angeles 1
144. **WHITMAN BREED ABBOTT & MORGAN** New York 1
145. **VINSON & ELKINS** Washington, D.C. 0.8
146. **WINSTEAD, SECHREST & MINICK** Dallas 0.5
147. **ALSTON & BIRD** Atlanta NA
148. **BABST CALLAND CLEMENTS & ZOMNIR** Pittsburgh NA
149. **BAKER & MCKENZIE** Chicago NA
150. **BAKER & MCKENZIE** New York NA
151. **BAKER & MCKENZIE** Washington, D.C. NA
152. **BLANK, ROME, COMISKY & MCCAULEY** Philadelphia NA
153. **BRACEWELL & PATTERSON** Houston NA
154. **BRACEWELL & PATTERSON** Washington, D.C. NA
155. **BROBECK, PHLEGER & HARRISON** Los Angeles NA
156. **BRONSON, BRONSON & MCKINNON** San Francisco NA
157. **BROWN & WOOD** New York NA
158. **BRYAN CAVE** Washington, D.C. NA
159. **BUCHANAN INGERSOLL** Pittsburgh NA
160. **BURNS & LEVINSON** Boston NA
161. **CAHILL GORDON & REINDEL** New York NA
162. **CAPLIN & DRYSDALE** Washington, D.C. NA

163.	**COLLIER, SHANNON, RILL & SCOTT** WASHINGTON, D.C.	NA
164.	**DECHERT PRICE & RHOADS** PHILADELPHIA	NA
165.	**DEWEY BALLANTINE** NEW YORK	NA
166.	**FENWICK & WEST** PALO ALTO	NA
167.	**FISH & RICHARDSON** BOSTON	NA
168.	**FOLEY & LARDNER** WASHINGTON, D.C.	NA
169.	**GRAHAM & JAMES** SAN FRANCISCO	NA
170.	**HOGAN & HARTSON** WASHINGTON, D.C.	NA
171.	**HUNTON & WILLIAMS** WASHINGTON, D.C.	NA
172.	**JEFFER, MANGELS, BUTLER & MARMARO** LOS ANGELES	NA
173.	**JONES, DAY, REAVIS & POGUE** CHICAGO	NA
174.	**JONES, DAY, REAVIS & POGUE** NEW YORK	NA
175.	**KECK, MAHIN & CATE** CHICAGO	NA
176.	**KING & SPALDING** ATLANTA	NA
177.	**LATHAM & WATKINS** LOS ANGELES	NA
178.	**LORD, BISSELL & BROOK** CHICAGO	NA
179.	**MAYER, BROWN & PLATT** CHICAGO	NA
180.	**MAYOR, DAY, CALDWELL & KEETON** HOUSTON	NA
181.	**MILES & STOCKBRIDGE** BALTIMORE	NA
182.	**MITCHELL, SILBERBERG & KNUPP** LOS ANGELES	NA
183.	**MORRISON & FOERSTER** WASHINGTON, D.C.	NA
184.	**PATTERSON, BELKNAP, WEBB & TYLER** NEW YORK	NA
185.	**PEABODY & ARNOLD** BOSTON	NA
186.	**PEPPER, HAMILTON & SCHEETZ** PHILADELPHIA	NA
187.	**POWELL, GOLDSTEIN, FRAZER & MURPHY** ATLANTA	NA
188.	**RUDNICK & WOLFE** CHICAGO	NA
189.	**SAUL, EWING, REMICK & SAUL** PHILADELPHIA	NA
190.	**SKADDEN, ARPS, SLATE, MEAGHER & FLOM** WASHINGTON, D.C.	NA
191.	**THOMPSON & KNIGHT** DALLAS	NA
192.	**TROUTMAN SANDERS** ATLANTA	NA
193.	**VENABLE, BAETJER AND HOWARD** BALTIMORE	NA
194.	**VINSON & ELKINS** HOUSTON	NA
195.	**WILLIAMS & CONNOLLY** WASHINGTON, D.C.	NA
196.	**WOLF, BLOCK, SCHORR & SOLIS-COHEN** PHILADELPHIA	NA

Law Firms Ranked by Percentage of Female Partners

1.	**JEFFER, MANGELS, BUTLER & MARMARO** LOS ANGELES	42
2.	**ANDERSON KILL & OLICK** NEW YORK	35
3.	**BRONSON, BRONSON & MCKINNON** SAN FRANCISCO	29
4.	**SPIEGEL & MCDIARMID** WASHINGTON, D.C.	29
5.	**MORRISON & FOERSTER** LOS ANGELES	27
6.	**MORRISON & FOERSTER** WASHINGTON, D.C.	27
7.	**HUGHES HUBBARD & REED** NEW YORK	25
8.	**MCDERMOTT, WILL & EMERY** CHICAGO	24
9.	**MCCUTCHEN, DOYLE, BROWN & ENERSEN** SAN FRANCISCO	23
10.	**THOMPSON & KNIGHT** DALLAS	23
11.	**MILLER & CHEVALIER** WASHINGTON, D.C.	22
12.	**PAUL, HASTINGS, JANOFSKY & WALKER** LOS ANGELES	22
13.	**AKIN, GUMP, STRAUSS, HAUER & FELD** DALLAS	21
14.	**BRACEWELL & PATTERSON** WASHINGTON, D.C.	21
15.	**HELLER EHRMAN WHITE & MCAULIFFE** SAN FRANCISCO	21
16.	**HOWARD, RICE, NEMEROVSKI ET. AL.** SAN FRANCISCO	21
17.	**JONES, DAY, REAVIS & POGUE** CHICAGO	21
18.	**LATHAM & WATKINS** LOS ANGELES	21
19.	**SULLIVAN & WORCESTER** BOSTON	21
20.	**DUANE, MORRIS & HECKSCHER** PHILADELPHIA	20
21.	**KATTEN MUCHIN & ZAVIS** CHICAGO	20
22.	**POWELL, GOLDSTEIN, FRAZER & MURPHY** WASHINGTON, D.C.	20
23.	**SKADDEN, ARPS, SLATE, MEAGHER & FLOM** WASHINGTON, D.C.	20
24.	**FENWICK & WEST** PALO ALTO	19
25.	**GOULSTON & STORRS** BOSTON	19
26.	**JONES, DAY, REAVIS & POGUE** WASHINGTON, D.C.	19
27.	**MANATT, PHELPS, PHILLIPS & KANTOR** LOS ANGELES	19
28.	**MORRISON & FOERSTER** SAN FRANCISCO	19
29.	**PILLSBURY MADISON & SUTRO** SAN FRANCISCO	19
30.	**SCHNADER, HARRISON, SEGAL & LEWIS** PHILADELPHIA	19
31.	**SEMMES, BOWEN & SEMMES** BALTIMORE	19
32.	**SONNENSCHEIN NATH & ROSENTHAL** CHICAGO	19

33. **ARNOLD & PORTER** Washington, D.C. 18
34. **BALLARD, SPAHR, ANDREWS & INGERSOLL** Philadelphia 18
35. **BRACEWELL & PATTERSON** Houston 18
36. **BROBECK, PHLEGER & HARRISON** San Francisco 18
37. **FOLEY, HOAG & ELIOT** Boston 18
38. **HILL & BARLOW** Boston 18
39. **JONES, DAY, REAVIS & POGUE** New York 18
40. **KILPATRICK STOCKTON** Atlanta 18
41. **MINTZ, LEVIN, COHN, FERRIS, GLOVSKY AND POPEO** Boston 18
42. **NUTTER, MCCLENNEN & FISH** Boston 18
43. **ROSS & HARDIES** Chicago 18
44. **SHAW, PITTMAN, POTTS & TROWBRIDGE** Washington, D.C. 18
45. **SHEA & GARDNER** Washington, D.C. 18
46. **SKADDEN, ARPS, SLATE, MEAGHER & FLOM** New York 18
47. **BUCHANAN INGERSOLL** Pittsburgh 17
48. **DAVIS POLK & WARDWELL** New York 17
49. **GARDNER, CARTON & DOUGLAS** Chicago 17
50. **HOPKINS & SUTTER** Chicago 17
51. **MAYER, BROWN & PLATT** Chicago 17
52. **MAYOR, DAY, CALDWELL & KEETON** Houston 17
53. **MORGAN, LEWIS & BOCKIUS** Los Angeles 17
54. **PATTERSON, BELKNAP, WEBB & TYLER** New York 17
55. **PEABODY & ARNOLD** Boston 17
56. **SIDLEY & AUSTIN** Los Angeles 17
57. **VINSON & ELKINS** Houston 17
58. **WEINBERG AND GREEN** Baltimore 17
59. **CHOATE, HALL & STEWART** Boston 16
60. **DOW, LOHNES & ALBERTSON** Washington, D.C. 16
61. **FOLEY & LARDNER** Washington, D.C. 16
62. **FRIED, FRANK, HARRIS, SHRIVER & JACOBSON** New York 16
63. **GOODWIN, PROCTER & HOAR** Boston 16
64. **GREENBERG, GLUSKER, FIELDS, CLAMAN & MACHTINGER** Los Angeles 16
65. **LORD, BISSELL & BROOK** Chicago 16
66. **PEPPER, HAMILTON & SCHEETZ** Philadelphia 16
67. **SHERBURNE, POWERS & NEEDHAM** Boston 16
68. **SWIDLER & BERLIN** Washington, D.C. 16
69. **WINSTON & STRAWN** New York 16
70. **ANDREWS & KURTH** Houston 15
71. **ARENT, FOX, KINTNER, PLOTKIN & KAHN** Washington, D.C. 15
72. **BROBECK, PHLEGER & HARRISON** Los Angeles 15
73. **BROWN, RUDNICK, FREED & GESMER** Boston 15
74. **BRYAN CAVE** Washington, D.C. 15
75. **CHADBOURNE & PARKE** Washington, D.C. 15
76. **FARELLA, BRAUN & MARTEL** San Francisco 15
77. **GARDERE & WYNNE** Dallas 15
78. **GIBSON, DUNN & CRUTCHER** Los Angeles 15
79. **GRAHAM & JAMES** San Francisco 15
80. **HOWREY & SIMON** Washington, D.C. 15
81. **KAYE, SCHOLER, FIERMAN, HAYS & HANDLER** New York 15
82. **LIDDELL, SAPP, ZIVLEY, HILL & LABOON** Houston 15
83. **MUNGER, TOLLES & OLSON** Los Angeles 15
84. **ROPES & GRAY** Boston 15
85. **WEIL, GOTSHAL & MANGES** New York 15
86. **WILSON, SONSINI, GOODRICH & ROSATI** Palo Alto 15
87. **WINSTEAD, SECHREST & MINICK** Dallas 15
88. **WINTHROP, STIMSON, PUTNAM & ROBERTS** New York 15
89. **ALSTON & BIRD** Atlanta 14
90. **COLLIER, SHANNON, RILL & SCOTT** Washington, D.C. 14
91. **COZEN AND O'CONNOR** Philadelphia 14
92. **KIRKLAND & ELLIS** Chicago 14
93. **KIRKLAND & ELLIS** Washington, D.C. 14
94. **LONG, ALDRIDGE & NORMAN** Atlanta 14
95. **PIPER & MARBURY** Washington, D.C. 14
96. **POWELL, GOLDSTEIN, FRAZER & MURPHY** Atlanta 14
97. **SHEARMAN & STERLING** New York 14
98. **SIDLEY & AUSTIN** Chicago 14
99. **STEPTOE & JOHNSON** Washington, D.C. 14
100. **WEIL, GOTSHAL & MANGES** Washington, D.C. 14
101. **WHITEFORD, TAYLOR & PRESTON** Baltimore 14
102. **WINTHROP, STIMSON, PUTNAM & ROBERTS** Washington, D.C. 14
103. **AKIN, GUMP, STRAUSS, HAUER & FELD** Washington, D.C. 13

104. **CHADBOURNE & PARKE** New York 13
105. **CROWELL & MORING** Washington, D.C. 13
106. **DECHERT PRICE & RHOADS** Philadelphia 13
107. **FISH & NEAVE** New York 13
108. **FRIED, FRANK, HARRIS, SHRIVER & JACOBSON** Washington, D.C. 13
109. **HALE AND DORR** Boston 13
110. **IRELL & MANELLA** Los Angeles 13
111. **KELLEY DRYE & WARREN** New York 13
112. **KIRKPATRICK & LOCKHART** Pittsburgh 13
113. **PALMER & DODGE** Boston 13
114. **PIPER & MARBURY** Baltimore 13
115. **ROSENMAN & COLIN** New York 13
116. **RUDNICK & WOLFE** Chicago 13
117. **TESTA, HURWITZ & THIBEAULT** Boston 13
118. **TROUTMAN SANDERS** Atlanta 13
119. **VENABLE, BAETJER AND HOWARD** Baltimore 13
120. **VERNER, LIIPFERT, BERNHARD, MCPHERSON AND HAND** Washington, D.C. 13
121. **WILMER, CUTLER & PICKERING** Washington, D.C. 13
122. **WINSTON & STRAWN** Chicago 13
123. **BABST CALLAND CLEMENTS & ZOMNIR** Pittsburgh 12
124. **COVINGTON & BURLING** Washington, D.C. 12
125. **DEWEY BALLANTINE** New York 12
126. **DRINKER BIDDLE & REATH** Philadelphia 12
127. **FULBRIGHT & JAWORSKI** Houston 12
128. **JENNER & BLOCK** Washington, D.C. 12
129. **KECK, MAHIN & CATE** Chicago 12
130. **MITCHELL, SILBERBERG & KNUPP** Los Angeles 12
131. **SACHNOFF & WEAVER** Chicago 12
132. **SCHULTE ROTH & ZABEL** New York 12
133. **STRASBURGER & PRICE** Dallas 12
134. **STROOCK & STROOCK & LAVAN** New York 12
135. **SUTHERLAND, ASBILL & BRENNAN** Atlanta 12
136. **WHITE & CASE** New York 12
137. **WILLIAMS & CONNOLLY** Washington, D.C. 12
138. **BINGHAM, DANA & GOULD** Boston 11
139. **BROWN & WOOD** New York 11
140. **BURNS & LEVINSON** Boston 11
141. **DICKSTEIN, SHAPIRO, MORIN & OSHINSKY** Washington, D.C. 11
142. **DONOVAN LEISURE NEWTON & IRVINE** New York 11
143. **HAIGHT, GARDNER, POOR & HAVENS** New York 11
144. **HUNTON & WILLIAMS** Washington, D.C. 11
145. **LEBOEUF, LAMB, LEIBY & MACRAE** New York 11
146. **MILES & STOCKBRIDGE** Baltimore 11
147. **O'MELVENY & MYERS** Los Angeles 11
148. **REED SMITH SHAW & MCCLAY** Pittsburgh 11
149. **SAUL, EWING, REMICK & SAUL** Philadelphia 11
150. **VINSON & ELKINS** Washington, D.C. 11
151. **WACHTELL, LIPTON, ROSEN & KATZ** New York 11
152. **BAKER & BOTTS** Houston 10
153. **BLANK, ROME, COMISKY & MCCAULEY** Philadelphia 10
154. **CHAPMAN AND CUTLER** Chicago 10
155. **CLEARY, GOTTLIEB, STEEN & HAMILTON** New York 10
156. **HUGHES & LUCE** Dallas 10
157. **KING & SPALDING** Atlanta 10
158. **PAUL, WEISS, RIFKIND, WHARTON & GARRISON** New York 10
159. **PENNIE & EDMONDS** New York 10
160. **ROGERS & WELLS** New York 10
161. **SHEPPARD, MULLIN, RICHTER & HAMPTON** Los Angeles 10
162. **VENABLE, BAETJER, HOWARD & CIVILETTI** Washington, D.C. 10
163. **BAKER & MCKENZIE** Chicago 9
164. **CAPLIN & DRYSDALE** Washington, D.C. 9
165. **COOLEY GODWARD** San Francisco 9
166. **COUDERT BROTHERS** New York 9
167. **CRAVATH, SWAINE & MOORE** New York 9
168. **DEBEVOISE & PLIMPTON** New York 9
169. **PROSKAUER ROSE** New York 9
170. **SIDLEY & AUSTIN** Washington, D.C. 9
171. **BAKER & MCKENZIE** Washington, D.C. 8
172. **FISH & RICHARDSON** Boston 8
173. **HOLLEB & COFF** Chicago 8
174. **MILBANK, TWEED, HADLEY & MCCLOY** New York 8

175.	**MORGAN, LEWIS & BOCKIUS** New York	8
176.	**ORRICK, HERRINGTON & SUTCLIFFE** San Francisco	8
177.	**PATTON & BOGGS** Washington, D.C.	8
178.	**REED SMITH SHAW & MCCLAY** Philadelphia	8
179.	**SULLIVAN & CROMWELL** New York	8
180.	**WILLKIE FARR & GALLAGHER** New York	8
181.	**BAKER & MCKENZIE** New York	7
182.	**CAHILL GORDON & REINDEL** New York	7
183.	**SIMPSON THACHER & BARTLETT** New York	7
184.	**SKADDEN, ARPS, SLATE, MEAGHER & FLOM** Los Angeles	7
185.	**SMITH, GAMBRELL & RUSSELL** Atlanta	7
186.	**WHITMAN BREED ABBOTT & MORGAN** New York	7
187.	**DICKIE, MCCAMEY & CHILCOTE** Pittsburgh	6
188.	**GIBSON, DUNN & CRUTCHER** Washington, D.C.	6
189.	**MORGAN, LEWIS & BOCKIUS** Philadelphia	6
190.	**PAUL, HASTINGS, JANOFSKY & WALKER** Washington, D.C.	6
191.	**FULBRIGHT & JAWORSKI** Washington, D.C.	5
192.	**KENYON & KENYON** New York	3
193.	**ECKERT SEAMONS CHERIN & MELLOT** Pittsburgh	NA
194.	**HOGAN & HARTSON** Washington, D.C.	NA
195.	**JENNER & BLOCK** Chicago	NA
196.	**WOLF, BLOCK, SCHORR & SOLIS-COHEN** Philadelphia	NA

Law Firms Ranked by Percentage of Female Associates

1.	**COOLEY GODWARD** San Francisco	63
2.	**KECK, MAHIN & CATE** Chicago	58
3.	**PIPER & MARBURY** Washington, D.C.	58
4.	**SACHNOFF & WEAVER** Chicago	57
5.	**MCDERMOTT, WILL & EMERY** Chicago	56
6.	**FARELLA, BRAUN & MARTEL** San Francisco	54
7.	**PALMER & DODGE** Boston	54
8.	**SMITH, GAMBRELL & RUSSELL** Atlanta	53
9.	**SONNENSCHEIN NATH & ROSENTHAL** Chicago	53
10.	**WHITEFORD, TAYLOR & PRESTON** Baltimore	53
11.	**BRONSON, BRONSON & MCKINNON** San Francisco	52
12.	**CHADBOURNE & PARKE** Washington, D.C.	52
13.	**JONES, DAY, REAVIS & POGUE** New York	52
14.	**REED SMITH SHAW & MCCLAY** Pittsburgh	52
15.	**SCHNADER, HARRISON, SEGAL & LEWIS** Philadelphia	52
16.	**WINSTON & STRAWN** New York	52
17.	**HOPKINS & SUTTER** Chicago	51
18.	**RUDNICK & WOLFE** Chicago	51
19.	**GARDERE & WYNNE** Dallas	50
20.	**GOULSTON & STORRS** Boston	50
21.	**MORRISON & FOERSTER** San Francisco	50
22.	**POWELL, GOLDSTEIN, FRAZER & MURPHY** Atlanta	50
23.	**VERNER, LIIPFERT, BERNHARD, MCPHERSON AND HAND** Washington, D.C.	50
24.	**CHAPMAN AND CUTLER** Chicago	49
25.	**HOWARD, RICE, NEMEROVSKI ET. AL.** San Francisco	49
26.	**HUGHES HUBBARD & REED** New York	49
27.	**MCCUTCHEN, DOYLE, BROWN & ENERSEN** San Francisco	49
28.	**MANATT, PHELPS, PHILLIPS & KANTOR** Los Angeles	48
29.	**PILLSBURY MADISON & SUTRO** San Francisco	48
30.	**ROSS & HARDIES** Chicago	48
31.	**SHERBURNE, POWERS & NEEDHAM** Boston	48
32.	**STROOCK & STROOCK & LAVAN** New York	48
33.	**BAKER & BOTTS** Houston	47
34.	**BURNS & LEVINSON** Boston	47
35.	**MILLER & CHEVALIER** Washington, D.C.	47
36.	**NUTTER, MCCLENNEN & FISH** Boston	47
37.	**TESTA, HURWITZ & THIBEAULT** Boston	47
38.	**TROUTMAN SANDERS** Atlanta	47
39.	**BAKER & MCKENZIE** Washington, D.C.	46
40.	**BALLARD, SPAHR, ANDREWS & INGERSOLL** Philadelphia	46
41.	**DAVIS POLK & WARDWELL** New York	46
42.	**DRINKER BIDDLE & REATH** Philadelphia	46
43.	**FENWICK & WEST** Palo Alto	46

44.	**HUNTON & WILLIAMS** WASHINGTON, D.C.	46
45.	**PATTERSON, BELKNAP, WEBB & TYLER** NEW YORK	46
46.	**PAUL, HASTINGS, JANOFSKY & WALKER** LOS ANGELES	46
47.	**POWELL, GOLDSTEIN, FRAZER & MURPHY** WASHINGTON, D.C.	46
48.	**SIDLEY & AUSTIN** LOS ANGELES	46
49.	**ALSTON & BIRD** ATLANTA	45
50.	**DEWEY BALLANTINE** NEW YORK	45
51.	**HAIGHT, GARDNER, POOR & HAVENS** NEW YORK	45
52.	**MINTZ, LEVIN, COHN, FERRIS, GLOVSKY AND POPEO** BOSTON	45
53.	**PIPER & MARBURY** BALTIMORE	45
54.	**VENABLE, BAETJER AND HOWARD** BALTIMORE	45
55.	**BUCHANAN INGERSOLL** PITTSBURGH	44
56.	**COUDERT BROTHERS** NEW YORK	44
57.	**DOW, LOHNES & ALBERTSON** WASHINGTON, D.C.	44
58.	**GARDNER, CARTON & DOUGLAS** CHICAGO	44
59.	**GREENBERG, GLUSKER, FIELDS, CLAMAN & MACHTINGER** LOS ANGELES	44
60.	**LEBOEUF, LAMB, LEIBY & MACRAE** NEW YORK	44
61.	**PEPPER, HAMILTON & SCHEETZ** PHILADELPHIA	44
62.	**ARENT, FOX, KINTNER, PLOTKIN & KAHN** WASHINGTON, D.C.	43
63.	**BINGHAM, DANA & GOULD** BOSTON	43
64.	**COZEN AND O'CONNOR** PHILADELPHIA	43
65.	**DEBEVOISE & PLIMPTON** NEW YORK	43
66.	**DONOVAN LEISURE NEWTON & IRVINE** NEW YORK	43
67.	**GIBSON, DUNN & CRUTCHER** LOS ANGELES	43
68.	**STRASBURGER & PRICE** DALLAS	43
69.	**CHADBOURNE & PARKE** NEW YORK	42
70.	**CROWELL & MORING** WASHINGTON, D.C.	42
71.	**MORGAN, LEWIS & BOCKIUS** NEW YORK	42
72.	**SHEA & GARDNER** WASHINGTON, D.C.	42
73.	**STEPTOE & JOHNSON** WASHINGTON, D.C.	42
74.	**SUTHERLAND, ASBILL & BRENNAN** ATLANTA	42
75.	**WHITMAN BREED ABBOTT & MORGAN** NEW YORK	42
76.	**AKIN, GUMP, STRAUSS, HAUER & FELD** WASHINGTON, D.C.	41
77.	**CLEARY, GOTTLIEB, STEEN & HAMILTON** NEW YORK	41
78.	**GOODWIN, PROCTER & HOAR** BOSTON	41
79.	**HILL & BARLOW** BOSTON	41
80.	**LORD, BISSELL & BROOK** CHICAGO	41
81.	**PAUL, WEISS, RIFKIND, WHARTON & GARRISON** NEW YORK	41
82.	**PROSKAUER ROSE** NEW YORK	41
83.	**SHEARMAN & STERLING** NEW YORK	41
84.	**THOMPSON & KNIGHT** DALLAS	41
85.	**BROWN, RUDNICK, FREED & GESMER** BOSTON	40
86.	**BRYAN CAVE** WASHINGTON, D.C.	40
87.	**CHOATE, HALL & STEWART** BOSTON	40
88.	**COVINGTON & BURLING** WASHINGTON, D.C.	40
89.	**REED SMITH SHAW & MCCLAY** PHILADELPHIA	40
90.	**ROPES & GRAY** BOSTON	40
91.	**SAUL, EWING, REMICK & SAUL** PHILADELPHIA	40
92.	**SIDLEY & AUSTIN** WASHINGTON, D.C.	40
93.	**WEINBERG AND GREEN** BALTIMORE	40
94.	**FRIED, FRANK, HARRIS, SHRIVER & JACOBSON** NEW YORK	39
95.	**FRIED, FRANK, HARRIS, SHRIVER & JACOBSON** WASHINGTON, D.C.	39
96.	**GRAHAM & JAMES SAN FRANCISCO**	39
97.	**HOLLEB & COFF** CHICAGO	39
98.	**JONES, DAY, REAVIS & POGUE** CHICAGO	39
99.	**JONES, DAY, REAVIS & POGUE** WASHINGTON, D.C.	39
100.	**KATTEN MUCHIN & ZAVIS** CHICAGO	39
101.	**KAYE, SCHOLER, FIERMAN, HAYS & HANDLER** NEW YORK	39
102.	**MAYOR, DAY, CALDWELL & KEETON** HOUSTON	39
103.	**MORGAN, LEWIS & BOCKIUS** PHILADELPHIA	39
104.	**MORRISON & FOERSTER** LOS ANGELES	39
105.	**ORRICK, HERRINGTON & SUTCLIFFE SAN FRANCISCO**	39
106.	**SWIDLER & BERLIN** WASHINGTON, D.C.	39
107.	**WEIL, GOTSHAL & MANGES** WASHINGTON, D.C.	39
108.	**WINTHROP, STIMSON, PUTNAM & ROBERTS** NEW YORK	39
109.	**BLANK, ROME, COMISKY & MCCAULEY** PHILADELPHIA	38
110.	**BRACEWELL & PATTERSON** WASHINGTON, D.C.	38
111.	**BROBECK, PHLEGER & HARRISON SAN FRANCISCO**	38
112.	**BROWN & WOOD** NEW YORK	38
113.	**COLLIER, SHANNON, RILL & SCOTT** WASHINGTON, D.C.	38

114.	**DECHERT PRICE & RHOADS** Philadelphia	38
115.	**DICKSTEIN, SHAPIRO, MORIN & OSHINSKY** Washington, D.C.	38
116.	**FULBRIGHT & JAWORSKI** Washington, D.C.	38
117.	**KELLEY DRYE & WARREN** New York	38
118.	**KING & SPALDING** Atlanta	38
119.	**LONG, ALDRIDGE & NORMAN** Atlanta	38
120.	**MITCHELL, SILBERBERG & KNUPP** Los Angeles	38
121.	**MORRISON & FOERSTER** Washington, D.C.	38
122.	**ROSENMAN & COLIN** New York	38
123.	**SCHULTE ROTH & ZABEL** New York	38
124.	**SKADDEN, ARPS, SLATE, MEAGHER & FLOM** Los Angeles	38
125.	**SKADDEN, ARPS, SLATE, MEAGHER & FLOM** New York	38
126.	**WILLKIE FARR & GALLAGHER** New York	38
127.	**WILMER, CUTLER & PICKERING** Washington, D.C.	38
128.	**AKIN, GUMP, STRAUSS, HAUER & FELD** Dallas	37
129.	**ARNOLD & PORTER** Washington, D.C.	37
130.	**FOLEY, HOAG & ELIOT** Boston	37
131.	**GIBSON, DUNN & CRUTCHER** Washington, D.C.	37
132.	**JENNER & BLOCK** Washington, D.C.	37
133.	**LATHAM & WATKINS** Los Angeles	37
134.	**ROGERS & WELLS** New York	37
135.	**SHAW, PITTMAN, POTTS & TROWBRIDGE** Washington, D.C.	37
136.	**SIDLEY & AUSTIN** Chicago	37
137.	**WEIL, GOTSHAL & MANGES** New York	37
138.	**MILES & STOCKBRIDGE** Baltimore	36
139.	**PENNIE & EDMONDS** New York	36
140.	**VENABLE, BAETJER, HOWARD & CIVILETTI** Washington, D.C.	36
141.	**ANDREWS & KURTH** Houston	35
142.	**FISH & RICHARDSON** Boston	35
143.	**HELLER EHRMAN WHITE & MCAULIFFE SAN FRANCISCO**	35
144.	**LIDDELL, SAPP, ZIVLEY, HILL & LABOON** Houston	35
145.	**MILBANK, TWEED, HADLEY & MCCLOY** New York	35
146.	**MORGAN, LEWIS & BOCKIUS** Los Angeles	35
147.	**PEABODY & ARNOLD** Boston	35
148.	**SHEPPARD, MULLIN, RICHTER & HAMPTON** Los Angeles	35
149.	**SIMPSON THACHER & BARTLETT** New York	35
150.	**BRACEWELL & PATTERSON** Houston	34
151.	**HALE AND DORR** Boston	34
152.	**KIRKLAND & ELLIS** Chicago	34
153.	**SULLIVAN & WORCESTER** Boston	34
154.	**WHITE & CASE** New York	34
155.	**WINSTON & STRAWN** Chicago	34
156.	**BAKER & MCKENZIE** Chicago	33
157.	**CAHILL GORDON & REINDEL** New York	33
158.	**FULBRIGHT & JAWORSKI** Houston	33
159.	**HUGHES & LUCE** Dallas	33
160.	**JEFFER, MANGELS, BUTLER & MARMARO** Los Angeles	33
161.	**PATTON & BOGGS** Washington, D.C.	33
162.	**PAUL, HASTINGS, JANOFSKY & WALKER** Washington, D.C.	33
163.	**VINSON & ELKINS** Houston	33
164.	**WILLIAMS & CONNOLLY** Washington, D.C.	33
165.	**WILSON, SONSINI, GOODRICH & ROSATI** Palo Alto	33
166.	**DUANE, MORRIS & HECKSCHER** Philadelphia	32
167.	**FOLEY & LARDNER** Washington, D.C.	32
168.	**O'MELVENY & MYERS** Los Angeles	32
169.	**SEMMES, BOWEN & SEMMES** Baltimore	32
170.	**MAYER, BROWN & PLATT** Chicago	31
171.	**MUNGER, TOLLES & OLSON** Los Angeles	31
172.	**WACHTELL, LIPTON, ROSEN & KATZ** New York	31
173.	**CAPLIN & DRYSDALE** Washington, D.C.	30
174.	**HOWREY & SIMON** Washington, D.C.	30
175.	**KILPATRICK STOCKTON** Atlanta	29
176.	**VINSON & ELKINS** Washington, D.C.	29
177.	**WINSTEAD, SECHREST & MINICK** Dallas	29
178.	**FISH & NEAVE** New York	28
179.	**IRELL & MANELLA** Los Angeles	28
180.	**SPIEGEL & MCDIARMID** Washington, D.C.	28
181.	**CRAVATH, SWAINE & MOORE** New York	27
182.	**DICKIE, MCCAMEY & CHILCOTE** Pittsburgh	27
183.	**KIRKLAND & ELLIS** Washington, D.C.	27
184.	**BABST CALLAND CLEMENTS & ZOMNIR** Pittsburgh	26

185. **KIRKPATRICK & LOCKHART** Pittsburgh 26
186. **SULLIVAN & CROMWELL** New York 26
187. **BAKER & MCKENZIE** New York 22
188. **KENYON & KENYON** New York 22
189. **BROBECK, PHLEGER & HARRISON** Los Angeles 21
190. **WINTHROP, STIMSON, PUTNAM & ROBERTS** Washington, D.C. 7
191. **ANDERSON KILL & OLICK** New York NA
192. **ECKERT SEAMONS CHERIN & MELLOT** Pittsburgh NA
193. **HOGAN & HARTSON** Washington, D.C. NA
194. **JENNER & BLOCK** Chicago NA
195. **SKADDEN, ARPS, SLATE, MEAGHER & FLOM** Washington, D.C. NA
196. **WOLF, BLOCK, SCHORR & SOLIS-COHEN** Philadelphia NA

Law Firms Ranked by Percentage of Minority Partners

1. **GRAHAM & JAMES** San Francisco 14
2. **BAKER & MCKENZIE** Chicago 11
3. **IRELL & MANELLA** Los Angeles 10
4. **SKADDEN, ARPS, SLATE, MEAGHER & FLOM** Los Angeles 10
5. **ANDERSON KILL & OLICK** New York 9
6. **MORRISON & FOERSTER** San Francisco 9
7. **MUNGER, TOLLES & OLSON** Los Angeles 8
8. **PAUL, HASTINGS, JANOFSKY & WALKER** Los Angeles 8
9. **BRACEWELL & PATTERSON** Washington, D.C. 7
10. **BROBECK, PHLEGER & HARRISON** San Francisco 7
11. **KELLEY DRYE & WARREN** New York 7
12. **MCCUTCHEN, DOYLE, BROWN & ENERSEN** San Francisco 7
13. **AKIN, GUMP, STRAUSS, HAUER & FELD** Washington, D.C. 6
14. **BRACEWELL & PATTERSON** Houston 6
15. **CLEARY, GOTTLIEB, STEEN & HAMILTON** New York 6
16. **COVINGTON & BURLING** Washington, D.C. 6
17. **HAIGHT, GARDNER, POOR & HAVENS** New York 6
18. **JEFFER, MANGELS, BUTLER & MARMARO** Los Angeles 6
19. **LATHAM & WATKINS** Los Angeles 6
20. **PAUL, HASTINGS, JANOFSKY & WALKER** Washington, D.C. 6
21. **PILLSBURY MADISON & SUTRO** San Francisco 6
22. **PIPER & MARBURY** Baltimore 6
23. **SPIEGEL & MCDIARMID** Washington, D.C. 6
24. **VERNER, LIIPFERT, BERNHARD, MCPHERSON AND HAND** Washington, D.C. 6
25. **ANDREWS & KURTH** Houston 5
26. **BRONSON, BRONSON & MCKINNON** San Francisco 5
27. **DAVIS POLK & WARDWELL** New York 5
28. **FARELLA, BRAUN & MARTEL** San Francisco 5
29. **HOWREY & SIMON** Washington, D.C. 5
30. **HUNTON & WILLIAMS** Washington, D.C. 5
31. **KILPATRICK STOCKTON** Atlanta 5
32. **MANATT, PHELPS, PHILLIPS & KANTOR** Los Angeles 5
33. **O'MELVENY & MYERS** Los Angeles 5
34. **PEABODY & ARNOLD** Boston 5
35. **PIPER & MARBURY** Washington, D.C. 5
36. **SIDLEY & AUSTIN** Washington, D.C. 5
37. **WEINBERG AND GREEN** Baltimore 5
38. **WILLKIE FARR & GALLAGHER** New York 5
39. **WILMER, CUTLER & PICKERING** Washington, D.C. 5
40. **WINSTON & STRAWN** Chicago 5
41. **ARNOLD & PORTER** Washington, D.C. 4
42. **BROBECK, PHLEGER & HARRISON** Los Angeles 4
43. **BROWN & WOOD** New York 4
44. **DOW, LOHNES & ALBERTSON** Washington, D.C. 4
45. **FENWICK & WEST** Palo Alto 4
46. **FISH & RICHARDSON** Boston 4
47. **FOLEY, HOAG & ELIOT** Boston 4
48. **GOODWIN, PROCTER & HOAR** Boston 4
49. **HUGHES HUBBARD & REED** New York 4
50. **MORGAN, LEWIS & BOCKIUS** New York 4
51. **PAUL, WEISS, RIFKIND, WHARTON & GARRISON** New York 4
52. **PEPPER, HAMILTON & SCHEETZ** Philadelphia 4
53. **SHAW, PITTMAN, POTTS & TROWBRIDGE** Washington, D.C. 4
54. **SHEARMAN & STERLING** New York 4

55.	**SHEPPARD, MULLIN, RICHTER & HAMPTON** Los Angeles	4
56.	**SULLIVAN & CROMWELL** New York	4
57.	**SWIDLER & BERLIN** Washington, D.C.	4
58.	**WHITE & CASE** New York	4
59.	**WHITEFORD, TAYLOR & PRESTON** Baltimore	4
60.	**WILSON, SONSINI, GOODRICH & ROSATI** Palo Alto	4
61.	**BURNS & LEVINSON** Boston	3
62.	**CAPLIN & DRYSDALE** Washington, D.C.	3
63.	**CHOATE, HALL & STEWART** Boston	3
64.	**CROWELL & MORING** Washington, D.C.	3
65.	**DEBEVOISE & PLIMPTON** New York	3
66.	**DUANE, MORRIS & HECKSCHER** Philadelphia	3
67.	**FOLEY & LARDNER** Washington, D.C.	3
68.	**GARDERE & WYNNE** Dallas	3
69.	**GARDNER, CARTON & DOUGLAS** Chicago	3
70.	**GIBSON, DUNN & CRUTCHER** Washington, D.C.	3
71.	**HALE AND DORR** Boston	3
72.	**HOLLEB & COFF** Chicago	3
73.	**HUGHES & LUCE** Dallas	3
74.	**JONES, DAY, REAVIS & POGUE** New York	3
75.	**KENYON & KENYON** New York	3
76.	**LONG, ALDRIDGE & NORMAN** Atlanta	3
77.	**MITCHELL, SILBERBERG & KNUPP** Los Angeles	3
78.	**MORGAN, LEWIS & BOCKIUS** Los Angeles	3
79.	**MORGAN, LEWIS & BOCKIUS** Philadelphia	3
80.	**ORRICK, HERRINGTON & SUTCLIFFE** San Francisco	3
81.	**PALMER & DODGE** Boston	3
82.	**POWELL, GOLDSTEIN, FRAZER & MURPHY** Atlanta	3
83.	**POWELL, GOLDSTEIN, FRAZER & MURPHY** Washington, D.C.	3
84.	**REED SMITH SHAW & MCCLAY** Philadelphia	3
85.	**RUDNICK & WOLFE** Chicago	3
86.	**SKADDEN, ARPS, SLATE, MEAGHER & FLOM** New York	3
87.	**SKADDEN, ARPS, SLATE, MEAGHER & FLOM** Washington, D.C.	3
88.	**SUTHERLAND, ASBILL & BRENNAN** Atlanta	3
89.	**WACHTELL, LIPTON, ROSEN & KATZ** New York	3
90.	**WEIL, GOTSHAL & MANGES** New York	3
91.	**WILLIAMS & CONNOLLY** Washington, D.C.	3
92.	**ARENT, FOX, KINTNER, PLOTKIN & KAHN** Washington, D.C.	2
93.	**BAKER & BOTTS** Houston	2
94.	**BALLARD, SPAHR, ANDREWS & INGERSOLL** Philadelphia	2
95.	**BLANK, ROME, COMISKY & MCCAULEY** Philadelphia	2
96.	**BROWN, RUDNICK, FREED & GESMER** Boston	2
97.	**CHAPMAN AND CUTLER** Chicago	2
98.	**COUDERT BROTHERS** New York	2
99.	**COZEN AND O'CONNOR** Philadelphia	2
100.	**DICKIE, MCCAMEY & CHILCOTE** Pittsburgh	2
101.	**FULBRIGHT & JAWORSKI** Washington, D.C.	2
102.	**GIBSON, DUNN & CRUTCHER** Los Angeles	2
103.	**HILL & BARLOW** Boston	2
104.	**HOPKINS & SUTTER** Chicago	2
105.	**HOWARD, RICE, NEMEROVSKI ET. AL.** San Francisco	2
106.	**JONES, DAY, REAVIS & POGUE** Washington, D.C.	2
107.	**KATTEN MUCHIN & ZAVIS** Chicago	2
108.	**KING & SPALDING** Atlanta	2
109.	**KIRKLAND & ELLIS** Washington, D.C.	2
110.	**LEBOEUF, LAMB, LEIBY & MACRAE** New York	2
111.	**LIDDELL, SAPP, ZIVLEY, HILL & LABOON** Houston	2
112.	**MAYOR, DAY, CALDWELL & KEETON** Houston	2
113.	**MCDERMOTT, WILL & EMERY** Chicago	2
114.	**MILBANK, TWEED, HADLEY & MCCLOY** New York	2
115.	**MILES & STOCKBRIDGE** Baltimore	2
116.	**PATTON & BOGGS** Washington, D.C.	2
117.	**PROSKAUER ROSE** New York	2
118.	**ROPES & GRAY** Boston	2
119.	**ROSENMAN & COLIN** New York	2
120.	**SACHNOFF & WEAVER** Chicago	2
121.	**SCHNADER, HARRISON, SEGAL & LEWIS** Philadelphia	2
122.	**SIDLEY & AUSTIN** Los Angeles	2
123.	**SIMPSON THACHER & BARTLETT** New York	2
124.	**SONNENSCHEIN NATH & ROSENTHAL** Chicago	2
125.	**STEPTOE & JOHNSON** Washington, D.C.	2

126.	**STRASBURGER & PRICE** DALLAS	**2**
127.	**SULLIVAN & WORCESTER** BOSTON	**2**
128.	**TESTA, HURWITZ & THIBEAULT** BOSTON	**2**
129.	**TROUTMAN SANDERS** ATLANTA	**2**
130.	**VENABLE, BAETJER, HOWARD & CIVILETTI** WASHINGTON, D.C.	**2**
131.	**VINSON & ELKINS** HOUSTON	**2**
132.	**WINSTON & STRAWN** NEW YORK	**2**
133.	**WINTHROP, STIMSON, PUTNAM & ROBERTS** NEW YORK	**2**
134.	**ALSTON & BIRD** ATLANTA	**1**
135.	**BINGHAM, DANA & GOULD** BOSTON	**1**
136.	**BUCHANAN INGERSOLL** PITTSBURGH	**1**
137.	**CHADBOURNE & PARKE** NEW YORK	**1**
138.	**CRAVATH, SWAINE & MOORE** NEW YORK	**1**
139.	**DECHERT PRICE & RHOADS** PHILADELPHIA	**1**
140.	**DEWEY BALLANTINE** NEW YORK	**1**
141.	**DICKSTEIN, SHAPIRO, MORIN & OSHINSKY** WASHINGTON, D.C.	**1**
142.	**FRIED, FRANK, HARRIS, SHRIVER & JACOBSON** NEW YORK	**1**
143.	**FULBRIGHT & JAWORSKI** HOUSTON	**1**
144.	**GOULSTON & STORRS** BOSTON	**1**
145.	**HELLER EHRMAN WHITE & MCAULIFFE** SAN FRANCISCO	**1**
146.	**KAYE, SCHOLER, FIERMAN, HAYS & HANDLER** NEW YORK	**1**
147.	**KIRKLAND & ELLIS** CHICAGO	**1**
148.	**KIRKPATRICK & LOCKHART** PITTSBURGH	**1**
149.	**LORD, BISSELL & BROOK** CHICAGO	**1**
150.	**MAYER, BROWN & PLATT** CHICAGO	**1**
151.	**MINTZ, LEVIN, COHN, FERRIS, GLOVSKY AND POPEO** BOSTON	**1**
152.	**REED SMITH SHAW & MCCLAY** PITTSBURGH	**1**
153.	**ROGERS & WELLS** NEW YORK	**1**
154.	**SAUL, EWING, REMICK & SAUL** PHILADELPHIA	**1**
155.	**SIDLEY & AUSTIN** CHICAGO	**1**
156.	**SMITH, GAMBRELL & RUSSELL** ATLANTA	**1**
157.	**THOMPSON & KNIGHT** DALLAS	**1**
158.	**VENABLE, BAETJER AND HOWARD** BALTIMORE	**1**
159.	**WHITMAN BREED ABBOTT & MORGAN** NEW YORK	**1**
160.	**WINSTEAD, SECHREST & MINICK** DALLAS	**1**
161.	**AKIN, GUMP, STRAUSS, HAUER & FELD** DALLAS	**0**
162.	**BAKER & MCKENZIE** NEW YORK	**0**
163.	**BAKER & MCKENZIE** WASHINGTON, D.C.	**0**
164.	**BRYAN CAVE** WASHINGTON, D.C.	**0**
165.	**CAHILL GORDON & REINDEL** NEW YORK	**0**
166.	**CHADBOURNE & PARKE** WASHINGTON, D.C.	**0**
167.	**COLLIER, SHANNON, RILL & SCOTT** WASHINGTON, D.C.	**0**
168.	**COOLEY GODWARD** SAN FRANCISCO	**0**
169.	**DONOVAN LEISURE NEWTON & IRVINE** NEW YORK	**0**
170.	**DRINKER BIDDLE & REATH** PHILADELPHIA	**0**
171.	**FISH & NEAVE** NEW YORK	**0**
172.	**FRIED, FRANK, HARRIS, SHRIVER & JACOBSON** WASHINGTON, D.C.	**0**
173.	**GREENBERG, GLUSKER, FIELDS, CLAMAN & MACHTINGER** LOS ANGELES	**0**
174.	**JENNER & BLOCK** WASHINGTON, D.C.	**0**
175.	**JONES, DAY, REAVIS & POGUE** CHICAGO	**0**
176.	**MILLER & CHEVALIER** WASHINGTON, D.C.	**0**
177.	**MORRISON & FOERSTER** LOS ANGELES	**0**
178.	**MORRISON & FOERSTER** WASHINGTON, D.C.	**0**
179.	**NUTTER, MCCLENNEN & FISH** BOSTON	**0**
180.	**PATTERSON, BELKNAP, WEBB & TYLER** NEW YORK	**0**
181.	**PENNIE & EDMONDS** NEW YORK	**0**
182.	**ROSS & HARDIES** CHICAGO	**0**
183.	**SCHULTE ROTH & ZABEL** NEW YORK	**0**
184.	**SEMMES, BOWEN & SEMMES** BALTIMORE	**0**
185.	**SHEA & GARDNER** WASHINGTON, D.C.	**0**
186.	**SHERBURNE, POWERS & NEEDHAM** BOSTON	**0**
187.	**STROOCK & STROOCK & LAVAN** NEW YORK	**0**
188.	**VINSON & ELKINS** WASHINGTON, D.C.	**0**
189.	**WEIL, GOTSHAL & MANGES** WASHINGTON, D.C.	**0**
190.	**WINTHROP, STIMSON, PUTNAM & ROBERTS** WASHINGTON, D.C.	**0**
191.	**BABST CALLAND CLEMENTS & ZOMNIR** PITTSBURGH	**NA**
192.	**ECKERT SEAMONS CHERIN & MELLOT** PITTSBURGH	**NA**
193.	**HOGAN & HARTSON** WASHINGTON, D.C.	**NA**
194.	**JENNER & BLOCK** CHICAGO	**NA**
195.	**KECK, MAHIN & CATE** CHICAGO	**NA**
196.	**WOLF, BLOCK, SCHORR & SOLIS-COHEN** PHILADELPHIA	**NA**

Law Firms Ranked by Percentage of Minority Associates

1.	**DAVIS POLK & WARDWELL** New York	34
2.	**COOLEY GODWARD** San Francisco	33
3.	**MCCUTCHEN, DOYLE, BROWN & ENERSEN** San Francisco	29
4.	**ORRICK, HERRINGTON & SUTCLIFFE** San Francisco	28
5.	**CLEARY, GOTTLIEB, STEEN & HAMILTON** New York	26
6.	**WINTHROP, STIMSON, PUTNAM & ROBERTS** New York	25
7.	**MORGAN, LEWIS & BOCKIUS** Los Angeles	24
8.	**MORRISON & FOERSTER** Los Angeles	24
9.	**GIBSON, DUNN & CRUTCHER** Los Angeles	23
10.	**MITCHELL, SILBERBERG & KNUPP** Los Angeles	23
11.	**PATTON & BOGGS** Washington, D.C.	23
12.	**LATHAM & WATKINS** Los Angeles	22
13.	**PAUL, WEISS, RIFKIND, WHARTON & GARRISON** New York	22
14.	**BAKER & MCKENZIE** Washington, D.C.	21
15.	**BROBECK, PHLEGER & HARRISON** Los Angeles	21
16.	**DOW, LOHNES & ALBERTSON** Washington, D.C.	21
17.	**GRAHAM & JAMES** San Francisco	21
18.	**GREENBERG, GLUSKER, FIELDS, CLAMAN & MACHTINGER** Los Angeles	21
19.	**HOWARD, RICE, NEMEROVSKI, ET. AL.** San Francisco	21
20.	**MORRISON & FOERSTER** San Francisco	21
21.	**MORRISON & FOERSTER** Washington, D.C.	21
22.	**WILSON, SONSINI, GOODRICH & ROSATI** Palo Alto	21
23.	**HAIGHT, GARDNER, POOR & HAVENS** New York	20
24.	**SHAW, PITTMAN, POTTS & TROWBRIDGE** Washington, D.C.	20
25.	**SKADDEN, ARPS, SLATE, MEAGHER & FLOM** Washington, D.C.	20
26.	**FULBRIGHT & JAWORSKI** Washington, D.C.	19
27.	**O'MELVENY & MYERS** Los Angeles	19
28.	**PAUL, HASTINGS, JANOFSKY & WALKER** Los Angeles	19
29.	**DEWEY BALLANTINE** New York	18
30.	**FARELLA, BRAUN & MARTEL** San Francisco	18
31.	**FENWICK & WEST** Palo Alto	18
32.	**MUNGER, TOLLES & OLSON** Los Angeles	18
33.	**SIMPSON THACHER & BARTLETT** New York	18
34.	**FISH & NEAVE** New York	17
35.	**LEBOEUF, LAMB, LEIBY & MACRAE** New York	17
36.	**SHEPPARD, MULLIN, RICHTER & HAMPTON** Los Angeles	17
37.	**SIDLEY & AUSTIN** Los Angeles	17
38.	**BAKER & MCKENZIE** Chicago	16
39.	**BROBECK, PHLEGER & HARRISON** San Francisco	16
40.	**BROWN & WOOD** New York	16
41.	**MILLER & CHEVALIER** Washington, D.C.	16
42.	**ROGERS & WELLS** New York	16
43.	**VENABLE, BAETJER AND HOWARD** Baltimore	16
44.	**WILMER, CUTLER & PICKERING** Washington, D.C.	16
45.	**COUDERT BROTHERS** New York	15
46.	**FOLEY & LARDNER** Washington, D.C.	15
47.	**GARDERE & WYNNE** Dallas	15
48.	**HUGHES & LUCE** Dallas	15
49.	**KAYE, SCHOLER, FIERMAN, HAYS & HANDLER** New York	15
50.	**ANDREWS & KURTH** Houston	14
51.	**CHADBOURNE & PARKE** New York	14
52.	**CHADBOURNE & PARKE** Washington, D.C.	14
53.	**HUGHES HUBBARD & REED** New York	14
54.	**JEFFER, MANGELS, BUTLER & MARMARO** Los Angeles	14
55.	**PAUL, HASTINGS, JANOFSKY & WALKER** Washington, D.C.	14
56.	**PILLSBURY MADISON & SUTRO** San Francisco	14
57.	**PROSKAUER ROSE** New York	14
58.	**SACHNOFF & WEAVER** Chicago	14
59.	**SIDLEY & AUSTIN** Chicago	14
60.	**SKADDEN, ARPS, SLATE, MEAGHER & FLOM** Los Angeles	14
61.	**WEIL, GOTSHAL & MANGES** New York	14
62.	**WHITE & CASE** New York	14
63.	**WILLIAMS & CONNOLLY** Washington, D.C.	14
64.	**WILLKIE FARR & GALLAGHER** New York	14
65.	**WINTHROP, STIMSON, PUTNAM & ROBERTS** Washington, D.C.	14
66.	**AKIN, GUMP, STRAUSS, HAUER & FELD** Washington, D.C.	13

67.	**BAKER & MCKENZIE** New York	13
68.	**BROWN, RUDNICK, FREED & GESMER** Boston	13
69.	**GIBSON, DUNN & CRUTCHER** Washington, D.C.	13
70.	**HOLLEB & COFF** Chicago	13
71.	**IRELL & MANELLA** Los Angeles	13
72.	**MAYOR, DAY, CALDWELL & KEETON** Houston	13
73.	**MILBANK, TWEED, HADLEY & MCCLOY** New York	13
74.	**PENNIE & EDMONDS** New York	13
75.	**POWELL, GOLDSTEIN, FRAZER & MURPHY** Atlanta	13
76.	**SHEARMAN & STERLING** New York	13
77.	**SKADDEN, ARPS, SLATE, MEAGHER & FLOM** New York	13
78.	**SMITH, GAMBRELL & RUSSELL** Atlanta	13
79.	**SULLIVAN & CROMWELL** New York	13
80.	**TROUTMAN SANDERS** Atlanta	13
81.	**WACHTELL, LIPTON, ROSEN & KATZ** New York	13
82.	**WINSTON & STRAWN** Chicago	13
83.	**BRONSON, BRONSON & MCKINNON** San Francisco	12
84.	**CAHILL GORDON & REINDEL** New York	12
85.	**CROWELL & MORING** Washington, D.C.	12
86.	**DEBEVOISE & PLIMPTON** New York	12
87.	**FISH & RICHARDSON** Boston	12
88.	**FRIED, FRANK, HARRIS, SHRIVER & JACOBSON** New York	12
89.	**HELLER EHRMAN WHITE & MCAULIFFE** San Francisco	12
90.	**KELLEY DRYE & WARREN** New York	12
91.	**PIPER & MARBURY** Baltimore	12
92.	**STEPTOE & JOHNSON** Washington, D.C.	12
93.	**VERNER, LIIPFERT, BERNHARD, MCPHERSON AND HAND** Washington, D.C.	12
94.	**VINSON & ELKINS** Houston	12
95.	**ALSTON & BIRD** Atlanta	11
96.	**ARENT, FOX, KINTNER, PLOTKIN & KAHN** Washington, D.C.	11
97.	**DUANE, MORRIS & HECKSCHER** Philadelphia	11
98.	**HOWREY & SIMON** Washington, D.C.	11
99.	**JONES, DAY, REAVIS & POGUE** Washington, D.C.	11
100.	**RUDNICK & WOLFE** Chicago	11
101.	**SIDLEY & AUSTIN** Washington, D.C.	11
102.	**VINSON & ELKINS** Washington, D.C.	11
103.	**BRYAN CAVE** Washington, D.C.	10
104.	**CAPLIN & DRYSDALE** Washington, D.C.	10
105.	**FOLEY, HOAG & ELIOT** Boston	10
106.	**JENNER & BLOCK** Washington, D.C.	10
107.	**KATTEN MUCHIN & ZAVIS** Chicago	10
108.	**KIRKLAND & ELLIS** Washington, D.C.	10
109.	**LIDDELL, SAPP, ZIVLEY, HILL & LABOON** Houston	10
110.	**MANATT, PHELPS, PHILLIPS & KANTOR** Los Angeles	10
111.	**MINTZ, LEVIN, COHN, FERRIS, GLOVSKY AND POPEO** Boston	10
112.	**PEABODY & ARNOLD** Boston	10
113.	**ROPES & GRAY** Boston	10
114.	**SAUL, EWING, REMICK & SAUL** Philadelphia	10
115.	**SCHULTE ROTH & ZABEL** New York	10
116.	**SHEA & GARDNER** Washington, D.C.	10
117.	**STROOCK & STROOCK & LAVAN** New York	10
118.	**WINSTON & STRAWN** New York	10
119.	**BAKER & BOTTS** Houston	9
120.	**CHAPMAN AND CUTLER** Chicago	9
121.	**COVINGTON & BURLING** Washington, D.C.	9
122.	**DICKSTEIN, SHAPIRO, MORIN & OSHINSKY** Washington, D.C.	9
123.	**GOODWIN, PROCTER & HOAR** Boston	9
124.	**GOULSTON & STORRS** Boston	9
125.	**HUNTON & WILLIAMS** Washington, D.C.	9
126.	**KING & SPALDING** Atlanta	9
127.	**MAYER, BROWN & PLATT** Chicago	9
128.	**PATTERSON, BELKNAP, WEBB & TYLER** New York	9
129.	**REED SMITH SHAW & MCCLAY** Pittsburgh	9
130.	**SONNENSCHEIN NATH & ROSENTHAL** Chicago	9
131.	**SWIDLER & BERLIN** Washington, D.C.	9
132.	**THOMPSON & KNIGHT** Dallas	9
133.	**BINGHAM, DANA & GOULD** Boston	8
134.	**BRACEWELL & PATTERSON** Houston	8
135.	**BRACEWELL & PATTERSON** Washington, D.C.	8
136.	**COLLIER, SHANNON, RILL & SCOTT** Washington, D.C.	8

137. **GARDNER, CARTON & DOUGLAS** CHICAGO 8
138. **MORGAN, LEWIS & BOCKIUS** NEW YORK 8
139. **PIPER & MARBURY** WASHINGTON, D.C. 8
140. **SCHNADER, HARRISON, SEGAL & LEWIS** PHILADELPHIA 8
141. **VENABLE, BAETJER, HOWARD & CIVILETTI** WASHINGTON, D.C. 8
142. **WHITEFORD, TAYLOR & PRESTON** BALTIMORE 8
143. **WHITMAN BREED ABBOTT & MORGAN** NEW YORK 8
144. **CRAVATH, SWAINE & MOORE** NEW YORK 7
145. **FRIED, FRANK, HARRIS, SHRIVER & JACOBSON** WASHINGTON, D.C. 7
146. **HILL & BARLOW** BOSTON 7
147. **JONES, DAY, REAVIS & POGUE** CHICAGO 7
148. **KENYON & KENYON** NEW YORK 7
149. **KILPATRICK STOCKTON** ATLANTA 7
150. **MORGAN, LEWIS & BOCKIUS** PHILADELPHIA 7
151. **NUTTER, MCCLENNEN & FISH** BOSTON 7
152. **REED SMITH SHAW & MCCLAY** PHILADELPHIA 7
153. **WEINBERG AND GREEN** BALTIMORE 7
154. **WINSTEAD, SECHREST & MINICK** DALLAS 7
155. **ARNOLD & PORTER** WASHINGTON, D.C. 6
156. **BALLARD, SPAHR, ANDREWS & INGERSOLL** PHILADELPHIA 6
157. **BURNS & LEVINSON** BOSTON 6
158. **DONOVAN LEISURE NEWTON & IRVINE** NEW YORK 6
159. **HALE AND DORR** BOSTON 6
160. **JONES, DAY, REAVIS & POGUE** NEW YORK 6
161. **KIRKLAND & ELLIS** CHICAGO 6
162. **ROSS & HARDIES** CHICAGO 6
163. **SULLIVAN & WORCESTER** BOSTON 6
164. **BLANK, ROME, COMISKY & MCCAULEY** PHILADELPHIA 5
165. **COZEN AND O'CONNOR** PHILADELPHIA 5
166. **FULBRIGHT & JAWORSKI** HOUSTON 5
167. **HOPKINS & SUTTER** CHICAGO 5
168. **KIRKPATRICK & LOCKHART** PITTSBURGH 5
169. **LORD, BISSELL & BROOK** CHICAGO 5
170. **PALMER & DODGE** BOSTON 5
171. **ROSENMAN & COLIN** NEW YORK 5
172. **BUCHANAN INGERSOLL** PITTSBURGH 4
173. **DICKIE, MCCAMEY & CHILCOTE** PITTSBURGH 4
174. **DRINKER BIDDLE & REATH** PHILADELPHIA 4
175. **MCDERMOTT, WILL & EMERY** CHICAGO 4
176. **MILES & STOCKBRIDGE** BALTIMORE 4
177. **POWELL, GOLDSTEIN, FRAZER & MURPHY** WASHINGTON, D.C. 4
178. **SHERBURNE, POWERS & NEEDHAM** BOSTON 4
179. **SUTHERLAND, ASBILL & BRENNAN** ATLANTA 4
180. **TESTA, HURWITZ & THIBEAULT** BOSTON 4
181. **WEIL, GOTSHAL & MANGES** WASHINGTON, D.C. 4
182. **CHOATE, HALL & STEWART** BOSTON 3
183. **DECHERT PRICE & RHOADS** PHILADELPHIA 3
184. **LONG, ALDRIDGE & NORMAN** ATLANTA 3
185. **STRASBURGER & PRICE** DALLAS 3
186. **PEPPER, HAMILTON & SCHEETZ** PHILADELPHIA 2
187. **AKIN, GUMP, STRAUSS, HAUER & FELD** DALLAS 0
188. **SEMMES, BOWEN & SEMMES** BALTIMORE 0
189. **ANDERSON KILL & OLICK** NEW YORK NA
190. **BABST CALLAND CLEMENTS & ZOMNIR** PITTSBURGH NA
191. **ECKERT SEAMONS CHERIN & MELLOT** PITTSBURGH NA
192. **HOGAN & HARTSON** WASHINGTON, D.C. NA
193. **JENNER & BLOCK** CHICAGO NA
194. **KECK, MAHIN & CATE** CHICAGO NA
195. **SPIEGEL & MCDIARMID** WASHINGTON, D.C. NA
196. **WOLF, BLOCK, SCHORR & SOLIS-COHEN** PHILADELPHIA NA